Informatik aktuell

Herausgeber: W. Brauer
im Auftrag der Gesellschaft für Informatik (GI)

Peter Paul Spies (Hrsg.)

Europäischer Informatik Kongreß Architektur von Rechensystemen Euro-ARCH '93

München, 18.-19.Oktober 1993

Springer-Verlag
Berlin Heidelberg New York
London Paris Tokyo
Hong Kong Barcelona
Budapest

Herausgeber

Peter Paul Spies
Technische Universität München, Institut für Informatik
Arcisstraße 21, D-80290 München

Kongreßleitung
Prof. Dr. P. P. Spies, Technische Universität München

Lenkungs- und Programmausschuß

Prof. Dr. A. Bode	Technische Universität München
Dr. K. H. Brenner	Universität Erlangen-Nürnberg
Prof. Dr. H. Burkhart	Universität Basel
Prof. Dr. M. Dal Cin	Universität Erlangen-Nürnberg
Dipl.-Inform. C. Eckert	Technische Universität München
Prof. Dr. W. Görke	Universität Karlsruhe
Prof. Dr. W. Grass	Universität Passau
Prof. Dr. H. Grünbacher	Technische Universität Wien
Prof. Dr. W. Hahn	Universität Passau
Dipl.-Ing. Ralf Hillemann	Siemens-Nixdorf AG München
Dr. E. Holler	Kernforschungszentrum Karlsruhe
Prof. Dr. A. Jammel	Universität Kiel
Prof. Dr. P. Müller-Stoy	Siemens AG München
Prof. Dr. J. Nehmer	Universität Kaiserslautern
Prof. Dr. P. P. Spies	Technische Universität München
Prof. Dr. K. Waldschmidt	Universität Frankfurt
Prof. Dr. B. Walke	Technische Hochschule Aachen
Prof. Dr. W. Wilhelmi	Technische Universität Berlin
Dipl.-Inform. H.-M. Windisch	Technische Universität München
Prof. Dr. H. Ch. Zeidler	Universität der Bundeswehr Hamburg

CR Subject Classification (1993): C.1.2, C.1.3, C.2.1, C.2.4, D.2.2, D.4.6, D.4.7

ISBN-13:978-3-540-57315-9 e-ISBN-13:978-3-642-78565-8
DOI: 10.1007/978-3-642-78565-8

Satz: Reproduktionsfertige Vorlage vom Autor/Herausgeber

33/3140-543210 – Gedruckt auf säurefreiem Papier

Vorwort

Der Kongreß **Euro–ARCH'93** setzt die Tradition der GI–Kongresse im Rahmen der SYSTEMS und die Tradition der gemeinsamen Fachtagungen des Fachbereichs 3 der GI und des Fachbereichs 4 der ITG mit einer neuen, den aktuellen Entwicklungen entsprechenden Konzeption fort. Er lenkt mit dem Thema *Architektur von Rechensystemen* in seiner gewandelten Bedeutung die Aufmerksamkeit auf die dringend notwendige Integration von Rechensystemen zu Gesamtsystemen und in Gesamtsysteme. Er fördert mit der Gestaltung seines Programms und mit seinen Veranstaltern das Zusammenwirken aller an der Entwicklung zukünftiger Rechensysteme Beteiligten. Euro–ARCH'93 findet erstmalig als **Europäischer Informatik Kongreß** unter dem Dach des Council of European Informatics Societies (CEPIS) im Rahmen der SYSTEMS statt.

Das Thema **Architektur von Rechensystemen** ist von zentraler Bedeutung für die Rolle, die Rechensysteme als unverzichtbare Hilfsmittel für den Umgang mit Information heute und in Zukunft bei der Lösung der immer komplexer werdenden Probleme in allen Bereichen unserer Gesellschaft spielen. Die Rechensysteme, die benötigt werden, sind eingebettet in sozio–technische Systeme, die in der Industrie, in der Wirtschaft und in den Verwaltungen eingesetzt werden. Sie bilden die Informatik–Kerne dieser Systeme und sind die Grundlage dafür, die vielfältigen Zusammenhänge in komplexen Abläufen zu erfassen, zu ordnen und auszuwerten.

Rechensysteme sind **Anwendungssysteme**; bei ihren Entwicklungen sollen entsprechend die spezifischen Anforderungen der Anwendungsbereiche, für die sie eingesetzt werden, im Vordergrund stehen. Rechensysteme sind **vernetzte und verteilte Systeme**, die ihre Fähigkeiten jeweils dort zur Verfügung stellen sollen, wo diese benötigt werden; sie bestehen aus vielen Komponenten und Subsystemen, die untereinander Nachrichten austauschen und über institutionelle und räumliche Grenzen hinweg miteinander kooperieren können.

Die Fortschritte der Hardware– und Software–Techniken in den letzten Jahren haben die Voraussetzungen für die Entwicklung von Rechensystemen mit diesen Eigenschaften wesentlich verbessert. Die erste Phase der Entwicklungsgeschichte von Rechensystemen hat einige zentrale, monolithische Systeme gebracht. In der zweiten Phase ist es gelungen, Rechensysteme als allgegenwärtige Hilfsmittel für vielfältige Anwendungsbereiche verfügbar zu machen und sie durch Nachrichtennetze miteinander zu verbinden. Jetzt, in der dritten Phase, ist die Aufgabe gestellt, dieses **Po-**

tential zu Gesamtsystemen zu integrieren: zu den Aufgaben, Komponenten und Subsysteme zu entwickeln, kommt die Aufgabe, die Subsysteme zu einem Gesamtsystem zusammenzufassen und die Voraussetzungen für systemweite, kooperative Problemlösungen zu schaffen. Diesen gewandelten Anforderungen an Rechensysteme entspricht die erweiterte Bedeutung des Themas Architektur von Rechensystemen: erforderlich sind **Prinzipien und Konzepte für die Gestaltung von Gesamtsystemen**, die dabei helfen, die zunehmende Komplexität zu meistern, und Richtlinien für die Konstruktion leistungsfähiger und beherrschbarer Systeme liefern. Der Kongreß behandelt das Thema Architektur von Rechensystemen in dieser erweiterten Sicht; es erfaßt die Schichten der Systeme von den Hardware–Komponenten und –Konfigurationen über die Betriebssoftware bis zu den Anwendungsschnittstellen und schließt innovative Anwendungsgebiete mit ihren charakteristischen Anforderungen ein.

Die Konstruktion der leistungsfähigen und beherrschbaren Gesamtsysteme, die benötigt werden, erfordert das Zusammenwirken von Anwendern und Herstellern, von Forschern und Entwicklern.

Diesen thematischen Zielen des Kongresses entsprechend gibt das **Programm** einen Überblick über die laufenden Arbeiten der Institutionen, die maßgebliche Beiträge zur Entwicklung zukünftiger Rechensysteme leisten. Im Programm sind Berichte über aktuelle Forschungs– und Entwicklungsarbeiten der Industrie, der Hochschulen und weiterer Institutionen zusammengefaßt, die in Hauptvorträgen, in Projektberichten und Einzelbeiträgen präsentiert werden. Sie zeigen den erreichten Kenntnis– und Entwicklungsstand sowie die Probleme, die noch zu lösen sind; sie zeigen Perspektiven und Trends für die Architektur und für die Anwendungsgebiete von Rechensystemen.

Euro–ARCH'93 wird vom Fachbereich 3 der GI und vom Fachbereich 4 der ITG veranstaltet und findet erstmals unter dem Dach der CEPIS statt; er versucht die **Zusammenarbeit der Europäischen Informatik Gesellschaften** zu intensivieren. Diese Entwicklung befindet sich noch in den Anfängen und wird in Zukunft verstärkt weitergeführt werden. Förderung der Zusammenarbeit sowie Intensivierung des Gedankenaustauschs mit allen an der Entwicklung von Rechensystemen Beteiligten und allen an dieser Entwicklung Interessierten ist auch das Motiv für die Durchführung von Euro–ARCH'93 im Rahmen der SYSTEMS und die Fortsetzung der bewährten Zusammenarbeit mit der Münchener Messe– und Ausstellungsgesellschaft.

An den Vorbereitungen und an der Durchführung des Kongresses waren und sind viele Institutionen und viele Personen beteiligt, die durch ihre Förderung und durch ihre tatkräftige Mitwirkung den Kongreß ermöglicht haben. Ihnen allen möchte ich an dieser Stelle für ihre Unterstützung herzlich danken. Mein besonderer Dank gilt

- den Mitgliedern des Lenkungs- und des Programmausschusses, insbesondere Herrn Kollegen W. Grass, für ihre Hilfe bei der Gestaltung des Programms,
- den Vortragenden, Autoren und Sitzungsleitern für ihre Bereitschaft, aktiv zum Gelingen des Kongresses beizutragen,
- den Mitgliedern des Organisationsausschusses, insbesondere Herrn H. Benesch, und Frau R. Kohlbecher von der MMG für ihren tatkräftigen Einsatz und
- meinen hiesigen Mitarbeiterinnen und Mitarbeitern für ihre allseitige Unterstützung, vor allem Frau C. Eckert, die mir bei allen Arbeiten für den Kongreß einschließlich der Vorbereitungen dieses Kongreßberichts sehr geholfen hat.

Die Herausforderung, die leistungsfähigen und beherrschbaren Rechensysteme, die in unserer Gesellschaft benötigt werden, zu entwickeln, erfordert Beiträge von allen Beteiligten. Euro-ARCH'93 soll für Anwender und Hersteller, für Forscher und Entwickler, welche die kommenden Rechensysteme und ihre Einsatzbereiche mitgestalten, ein Forum zur Präsentation und zur Diskussion ihrer Ideen und Arbeiten sein.

Allen Kongreßteilnehmern wünsche ich, daß ihre und unsere Erwartungen erfüllt werden.

München, im August 1993 — Peter Paul Spies

An den Vorbereitungen und an der Durchführung des Kongresses waren und sind viele Institutionen und viele Personen beteiligt, die durch ihre Förderung und durch ihre tatkräftige Mitwirkung den Kongreß erst ermöglicht haben. Ihnen allen möchte ich an dieser Stelle für ihre Unterstützung herzlich danken. Mein besonderer Dank gilt

- den Mitgliedern des Lenkungs- und des Programmausschusses, insbesondere Herrn Kollegen A. Strass, für ihre Hilfe bei der Gestaltung des Programms,
- den Vortragenden, Autoren und Sitzungsleitern für ihre Bereitschaft, aktiv zum Gelingen des Kongresses beizutragen,
- den Mitgliedern des Organisationsausschusses, insbesondere Herrn H. Bauersch, und Herrn K. Kallweit von der MMG für ihren tatkräftigen Einsatz und
- meinen beiden Mitarbeiterinnen und Mitarbeitern für ihre allseitige Unterstützung, vor allem Frau [illegible]. Eckert, die mir bei allen Arbeiten für den Kongreß und namentlich bei der Vorbereitung dieses Konferenzbandes sehr geholfen hat.

Die Herausforderung, die Fertigungsanlagen und Dienste moderner Rechensysteme, die in unserer Gesellschaft benötigt werden, zu entwickeln, erfordert Beiträge von allen Beteiligten. Euro-ARCH'93 soll für Anwender und Hersteller, für Forscher und Entwickler, welche die Innovationen in Rechensystemen und ihre Einsatzbereiche mitgestalten, ein Forum der Präsentation und zur Diskussion ihrer Ideen und Arbeiten sein.

Allen Kongreßteilnehmern wünsche ich, daß ihre und unsere Erwartungen erfüllt werden.

München, im August 1993 — Peter Paul Spies

1. Hoch– und Höchstleistungs–Rechensysteme / High and Very High Performance Computing

2. Neuronale Netze / Neural Networks

6. Verteilte und parallele Systeme / Distributed and Parallel Systems

7. Werkzeuge und Methoden / Tools and Methods

Werkzeuge und Methoden / Tools and Methods

Strukturen zukünftiger kommerzieller Hochleistungsrechensysteme

Ulrich Lang

IBM Deutschland Entwicklungs GmbH
Abt. 0444
Hans Klemm Straße 45
71034 Böblingen

Abstract. Ausgehend von einer Diskussion der elementaren Wechselwirkung von Anwendungen, Architekturen und Technologie wird die Zukunft von großen Systemen zur kommerziellen Transaktionsverarbeitung untersucht. Grundlegende Aspekte von Kosten und Leistung der Technologie von Großsystemen werden betrachtet, und Trends werden verglichen mit denen von Preis/Leistungsoptimierten Mikrosystemtechnologien. Die Implikationen dieses Vergleichs führen zu parallelen Systemarchitekturen und -Strukturen.
Die grundlegenden Aspekte der Parallelverarbeitung und die Pro's und Con's verfügbarer Kopplungsmechanismen werden verglichen, was zu der gewählten Synthese zwischen den Schemata führt.

1 Anwendungen, Architekturen und Technologie

Große kommerzielle Systeme zur Transaktionsverarbeitung waren über zwanzig Jahre lang prinzipiell in allen drei Bereichen stabil. Der Fortschritt war eher quantitativer Natur. Mit der stetig wachsenden Nachfrage nach Durchsatz von Transaktionen durch die Systeme wurden Architektur und Struktur der Systeme kontinuierlich aufgebohrt, ohne daß eine grundlegende Neuorientierung erfolgte. Der Adreßraum der IBM Systeme 360, 370, 390 wuchs von 16Mbyte auf 16Tbyte, die Hauptspeichergröße von 16Mbyte auf 2Gbyte, die Anzahl der Kanäle von 16 auf mehrere hundert, die Anzahl der CPUs pro Hauptspeicher von 1 auf 8. Fortschritte im CPU design senkten die Anzahl der nötigen Rechnerzyklen bis unter 2 pro 360 Instruktionen im Standard CISC mix, und Fortschritte in der bipolaren Halbleitertechnologie senkten die Gatterlaufzeit in den Picosekundenbereich. Die damit notwendig werdende hohe Packungsdichte der CPUs wurde mit wassergekühlten Mehrschichtkeramikträgern ermöglicht. Die obere Asymptote der erreichbaren Uniprozessorleistung, RISC oder CISC, ist immer gegeben durch die Anzahl der Schaltkreise, die in einer Nanosekunde erreichbar sind. In einer Nanosekunde legt das Licht im Vacuum 30 cm zurück, ein elektrisches Feld auf einer Leitung deutlich weniger.

Am Anfang der Evolution waren die Economies of Scale auf der Seite der Großmaschinen, d.h. die Einheit Rechnerleistung war auf der größten Maschine am billigsten herzustellen. Heute ist es bei der ES9000 Linie umgekehrt. Der Nulldurchgang war ca. 1979.

Diese Umkehrung erzeugte ein Nachfragepotential nach anderen Lösungen für Architekturen und Strukturen von Großsystemen ganz allgemein. Die ersten erfolgreichen Lösungen wurden von DEC mit den VAX Clusters zur Verfügung gestellt, die allerdings nicht wesentlich in der kommerziellen Transaktionsverarbeitung eingesetzt wurden.

Das Problem hier ist nämlich die Integrität des Zugriffs auf einzelne Records einer sehr großen Datenbank, und das bei hunderten bis tausenden von Transaktionen pro Sekunde. Integrität ist zwar immer herstellbar, es fragt sich nur, mit welcher Performance, wenn mehrere bis viele CPUs gleichzeitig am Werk sind.

Da die Nachfrage nach Transaktionsdurchsatz über viele Jahre hinweg mit 40% pro Jahr stieg und steigt, mindestens bei innovativen Großkunden, entstand intensiver Handlungsbedarf.

Innerhalb der 370 Produktlinie wurde der Softwaresupport für festgekoppeltes symmetrisches Multiprocessing bis auf 8 CPUs an einem Hauptspeicher erhöht. Der eine Hauptspeicher ermöglichte vergleichsweise einfaches locking.

Hinzu kam die Sysplexarchitektur zur Kopplung von mehreren Großsystemen bei shared Plattenzugriff.

Diese beiden Maßnahmen kompensierten das sich verlangsamende Wachstum der schnellsten bipolaren Uniprozessoren. Sie änderten aber nichts an der hohen Kostenplattform der bipolaren Systeme, und sie waren nur in der Lage, eine verhältnismäßig kleine Anzahl von CPUs effizient zur Transaktionsverarbeitung einzusetzen. Mehr als 8 festgekoppelte CPUs können heute noch nicht effizient genutzt werden, der Speicherzugang wird zum Flaschenhals, und die Workloadverteilung im SYSPLEX kann nur sehr wenig granular erfolgen, da das Resource Management zwischen den System Images nicht sehr effizient ist.

Die CMOS Technologie, die Logikschaltkreise mit einem drastisch besseren Preis/Leistungsverhältnis zur Verfügung stellt, macht nun einen völlig neuen Ansatz möglich.

2 CMOS Mikroprozessoren

Metall–Oxyd–Halbleiter lassen aufgrund ihres Fertigungsprozesses eine sehr viel höhere Packungsdichte von Logikschaltkreisen auf einem Chip zu, sind also die ideale Basis für Mikroprozessoren. Complementary Metal Oxide Semiconductors, CMOS Halbleiter, haben noch einen weiteren Vorteil: Aufgrund der Komplementärtechnologie ihrer Gatter, mit N– und P–dotierten Gates, fließt in den Gattern nur bei logischer Zustandsänderung Strom. Dies reduziert drastisch die Verlustleistung und erlaubt sehr hohe Packungsdichten auf dem Chip ohne aufwendige Kühlungsmaßnahmen. Außerdem mildert die Push Pull Technolgie der Drivers die wesentliche Schwäche von MOS Technologie, das nur langsame Umladen von Netzen mit hoher Kapazität, die man immer dann antrifft, wenn Off Chip Netze getrieben werden müssen.

Diese Eigenschaften, zusammen mit den rasanten Fortschritten bei der Fertigung und bei den Designsystemen, sind für das explosionsartige Wachstum der Mikroprozessorleistungsfähigkeit verantwortlich, ebenso wie für den dramatischen Preisverfall von Rechnerleistung.

Es gelingt heute auch im CISC Bereich CPUs mit 5 tiefer Pipeline auf einem einzigen Chip unterzubringen und dadurch Taktzeiten von deutlich unter 20ns zu erreichen.

3 Rückwirkung Technologie–Systemstruktur

Diese Mikroprozessor Leistung, verfügbar auch im 390 Bereich, macht es möglich, eine Randbedingung für Großsystemdesign auch mit diesen kostengünstigen Chips zu erfüllen: Die nötige Pfadlänge für eine einzige komplexe Transaktion in der Datenbank muß auf einer einzigen CPU im Subsekundenbereich abgearbeitet werden können.

Damit wird es möglich, die letzte große Idiosynkrasie im Großsystembereich zu eliminieren. Bisher wurden in Großsystemen logisch unabhängige, von Natur aus parallele Arbeitseinheiten, nämlich die einzelnen Transaktionen, per Betriebssystem serialisiert und auf wenigen sehr schnellen CPUs abgearbeitet.

Die Aufgabe besteht nun darin, Systemstrukturen und Rechnerkopplungsarchitekturen so zu definieren, daß sehr viele von diesen vergleichsweise langsamen Mikroprozessoren eine sehr hohe Anzahl von Transaktionen (> 1000) pro Sekunde abarbeiten können. Wenn es gelingt, auf dieser Systemstruktur und mit diesen Kopplungsarchitekturen die Datenintegrität herzustellen, die auf klassischen Großsystemstrukturen vergleichsweise einfach über shared memory erreicht wurde, dann steht das Preisleistungsverhältnis von Mikrosystemen prinzipiell auch bei sehr großen 390 Systemen (Mainframes) zur Verfügung. Falls die Kopplungsmechanismen genügend effizient sind.

Wenn man sich ansieht, wie rapide die verschiedenen Mikroprozessor–basierenden Lösungen großer OLTP Probleme sich weiterentwickeln, so wird klar, daß es für IBM Zeit wird, mit einer Mikro–390 Großsystemplattform auf den Markt zu kommen.

Der Hauptvorteil von Downsizing, nämlich kostengünstige Hardware, wäre dann auch mit allen Vorteilen von MVS erreichbar: Verfügbarkeit, inkrementelle Skalierbarkeit und hohe Verfügbarkeit.

4 Kopplungsstrategie

Nachdem feste Kopplung an einem gemeinsamen Hauptspeicher für Hunderte von CPUs ausscheidet, muß man sich überlegen, wie ein Strom zufälliger unabhängiger durch ein Netz von CPUs mit vielen Hauptspeichern, vielen Timern und vielen Magnetplatten mit vielen Zugriffspfaden geführt werden kann, ohne daß man die Übersicht verliert, und ohne daß bei einem Fehler zu beliebiger Zeit an beliebiger Stelle das System zum Stillstand kommt oder gar die Integrität der Datenbank verlorengeht. Und ohne daß die beliebigen Transaktionen sich gegenseitig ins Gehege kommen.

Weder logisch mit widersprüchlichen Datenzugriffen noch durchsatzmäßig über Engstellen bei CPU–Power oder Datenpfaden.

Die favorisierte Lösung besteht aus einer Parallelschaltung von 6–way CPU-Memory Komplexen, die zum Austausch von Nachrichten und Kontrollinformationen einen gemeinsamen externen Hauptspeicher besitzen, der an jeden Komplex mit ultraschnellen Glasfiberverbindungen in Punkt–zu–Punkt Topologie angeschlossen ist.

Die Datenbank ist shared angelegt und über eine sternförmige Topologie angeschlossen, so daß jede Platte von jedem Systemkomplex aus über eine geschaltete Punkt zu Punkt Glasfiber–Verbindung erreichbar ist. Dies erlaubt optimale Nutzung der Zugriffspfade unter allen Betriebsbedingungen und vergleichsweise einfaches Balancieren der Workload über die beteiligten Systemkomplexe.

Eine globale Zeitbasis sorgt für eine genaue Zeitreferenz und Zeitsynchronisation in einem Systemkomplex.

5 Zusammenfassung

Mit dieser Parallelrechnerstruktur wird es gelingen, die klassischen Stärken des Mainframes, nämlich Verfügbarkeit, Skalierbarkeit, robuste Performance und evolutionäre Weiterentwicklung mit Investitionsschutz für bestehende Software auf einer neuen, drastisch wettbewerbsfähigeren Technologie–Grundlage zur Verfügung zu stellen, und dazu noch in völlig neue Größenordnungen der Systemleistungsfähigkeit vorzudringen.

Der Mainframe lebt. Schneller und agiler denn je.

MMK/X — Using a Network of Workstations as a Supercomputer

Georg Stellner

Technische Universität München
Institut für Informatik
80290 München
stellner@informatik.tu-muenchen.de

Abstract. Today expensive supercomputer and multiprocessor systems are available which offer computational power that can be used to solve Grand Challenge Problems. But these systems are often very expensive and difficult to maintain. Typical environments in companies and universities offer the programmer a local area network of dozens of workstations. Together they offer a computational power which is comparable to currently available supercomputer and multiprocessor systems. To exploit this computational resource a programming environment is needed which enables the user to distribute his application among the workstations. Using MMK/X and TOPSYS/X is one way to achieve this goal. MMK/X offers a programming model that allows the programmer to use a net of workstations similar to a conventional multiprocessor system. Apart from the user interface the paper also describes the implementation of the programming environment and the adaptation of the tool environment for workstation based message-passing systems.

1 Motivation

In the wake of the need for more powerful machines todays supercomputers have been developed. The computational power these machines can achieve is sufficient to solve some of the so called *Grand Challenges Problems*. Typically, these machines are very expensive and difficult to maintain, e.g. they need a water-cooling system. To reduce the costs for such powerful machines a different approach has been made. Assembling cheap and simple standard components such as processors and memory chips into a single machine saves purchase as well as maintenance costs. These machines are the classical distributed memory multiprocessor systems where standard microprocessor nodes are interconnected with a high performance interconnection network. Most of these machines offer only a proprietary programming environment which makes it difficult to port application codes from one architecture to another.

Today, typical environments in universities and companies offer several workstations all interconnected via standard Ethernet. Most of these machines are running some kind of UNIX operating system which makes it possible to port application codes from one architecture to another with minor efforts. In addition the accumulated power offered by those coupled workstations comes close to that of todays supercomputer or multiprocessor systems. As most of the workstations are idle during the night anyway a new approach would be to run computation intensive application during these periods.

Two restrictions apply for the above mentioned approach. First, the computational power offered by a number of workstations in a local area network does not reach todays supercomputers or multiprocessor systems. And second the communication speed of the interconnection network is magnitudes less than of conventional multiprocessor systems. Thus, not all *Grand Challenge Problems* are suitable to be solved on a network of workstations. Suitable applications should have limited demands concerning computational power and the granularity of parallelism should be medium or even better coarse. Running those applications on the workstations takes away workload from the number crunchers and frees them for very computation intensive problems.

A further usage of coupled workstations is as a development and debugging platform for conventional multiprocessor systems. Neglecting the reduced power which is not necessary to implement a correct algorithm the workstation can be used to get a running version of the application. So conventional programming errors are detected on machines where computation time is not too precious and the parallel computer has only to be used to do the performance tuning of the application. Again the advantage is that workload is withdrawn from the number cruncher which can then be used to run production code.

Finally, writing parallel applications is a difficult task for the programmer. In addition to conventional programming errors he is confronted with new error classes which are due to the parallel programming model. Examples for such errors are deadlocks or synchronization errors. A pivotal point is therefore the availability of a tool set which enables the user to efficiently detect these errors.

2 Design Goals of MMK/X

As outlined above it is very desirable to have a programming environment which treats a network of workstations as a single computational resource. The discussion above also emerged some important design goals which have to be considered in the design of such an environment.

If some coupled workstations should be used as a development platform for multiprocessor systems a prerequisite is a common programming model for the multiprocessor and the workstations. After having tested the application on the network of workstations there should be no need for the programmer to modify the source code to move the application to the multiprocessor system. A simple re-compilation of the sources should be the only thing that has to be done to run the application on the multiprocessor system.

In our approach we have decided to use the MMK[9][12] user interface which is available for Intel iPSC multiprocessor systems. The version which can be used for coupled workstations has been called MMK/X. In concert with the tool environment TOPSYS[1] the programming environment of MMK provides the user with a message-passing interface based on objects and a tool set which is suitable to assist the user to efficiently implement parallel applications. The next section will give a short overview over both the basic message-passing interface and the tool set.

Due to the transparency of the underlying message-passing interface developing applications with MMK/X can serve two different aspects. First of all the workstation environment can be used to test and implement applications which should finally run on an multiprocessor system. Consequently, during the implementation phase of an application no computational power from the multiprocessor system is necessary. Already a single workstation can be used to substitute a whole multiprocessor system with for example 64 nodes. Of course the computational power of a 64 node multiprocessor system can not be replaced by a single workstation. After having compiled the code for the multiprocessor system the user may find it necessary to improve the performance of the application. Therefore the same tool set as for the workstation environment can be used.

In difference to the first approach where the workstations were only used as a development platform there is also a second possibility. The computational power of several workstations can be used as a multiprocessor substitute. Especially during times of low user activity this approach seems to be quite promising. Suitable applications also achieve good speed-ups on a larger number of workstations. For those applications which are suited for coupled workstation environments this approach has the advantage that a user can add as many workstations as necessary until the desired computational power is reached. Thus the computational power of workstations which would otherwise be lost during idle times can be efficiently used to run production versions of computation intensive problems.

A pivotal point for programming environments for workstations is multithreading. Conventional UNIX processes are characterized through a large process context which causes long context switching times. Especially RISC based workstations suffer from long context switching times. The new process requires a new address space which makes it usually necessary to invalidate the caches. In contrast to that lightweight processes (threads) share a common address space within a conventional UNIX process. Therefore, the need for invalidating caches is not given and caches can keep their original contents. In addition the context of lightweight processes mostly consists only of the CPU register set and an execution stack. Thus, switching from one lightweight process to another can simply be done by pushing the registers on the stack, exchanging the stack pointer and then restoring the registers with the values from the new stack.

A further important design goal emerges from the heterogeneity of todays workstation market. The programming environment must be easily portable to different hardware platforms to install the environment on a wide range of workstations with as little effort as possible. So not only source code portability from the workstation to the multiprocessor is highly desirable but also portability of the underlying programming environment from one hardware to another.

Following the guidelines that were introduced in this section the subsequent sections will show that MMK/X matches these requirements for a message-passing environment. The next section introduces the user interface and the tool set. The discussion there will show, that MMK/X offers a programming environment which can be used to write parallel applications which can run on both multiprocessor systems and networks of workstations. Thus a network of workstations can serve as a development platform or as far as computational power is concerned as a supercomputer substitute. Although the underlying process model uses lightweight processes the environment can be easily ported to different workstation platforms which will be shown in the section about the implementation of MMK/X. Finally a performance comparison between the communication speeds of MMK and MMK/X will be given and some future work will be presented.

3 The Environment of MMK, MMK/X and TOPSYS

This section introduces the programming model of MMK/X. At the end there will also be a brief introduction of the TOPSYS/X environment. For a more detailed discussion see [4].

A programmer writing a parallel application is mainly confronted with three basic units. First of all he needs some kind of execution units like in the sequential case. Then the execution units have to synchronize from time to time to achieve a correct behavior of the algorithm. Finally the execution units must exchange some information to insure the cooperation of all workers. In the MMK/X programming environment these basic requirements are modelled through three different object-types: tasks, mailboxes and semaphores.

The execution unit in the MMK/X programming model is called a task. Tasks are lightweight processes, thus sharing a common address space. The context of the tasks is limited to the contents of the CPU registers and some additional information which is used in the scheduling process. However, in contrast to many other implementations of lightweight processes it is possible to introduce a simple protection mechanism for the address spaces of the different tasks. The protection scheme implemented makes use of the page protection mechanism of the underlying operation system. Pages that should be protected are marked read only, hence triggering an exception if a write access occurs. Only the currently running task may write on its own stack pages and it is only possible to modify internal data structures within MMK/X system calls. Possible programming errors lead to an exception which can be caught and dealt with. The default action is to stop the task which triggered the exception whereas all other tasks remain uninfluenced. Especially during the implementation phase of an application this is very useful as pointer garbage can be easily detected. For the production version of the code the user may switch to a version of the library without the memory protection mechanism to achieve the best possible performance.

The task objects are the only active objects within an MMK/X application. The remaining two objects are passive. Mailboxes can be used to exchange messages between tasks and semaphores can be used to synchronize tasks.

All objects can be dynamically created and destroyed within an application. The creation of an object returns an identifier by which the object can be referenced. The identifiers have a global character, i. e. each object in the application has an unique identifier regardless on which node it has been created.

To establish an initial distribution of objects a special mapping table is used. Within that table it is possible to specify which tasks, mailboxes and semaphores should be automatically created on which node during the startup of the application. Symbolic names of the objects can be used to supply tasks declared in the mapping table with identifiers of other objects, which have been declared before those tasks in the mapping table. The mapping table therefore represents a static process graph of the application at startup time.

Due to the global character of the identifiers of the objects, the tasks can access each object transparently without knowing on which node the object resides. The only thing which is necessary to deal with an object is its identifier. Apart from creation and destruction operations mentioned above, MMK offers several other object manipulation functions. Tasks can be started and stopped or simply wait some time. Messages can be sent to or received from a mailbox. Semaphore units can be requested from or returned to a semaphore. All objects can be transparently accessed from any node. To achieve transparency the function calls can distinguish between local and remote operations on objects. If an object resides on the local node a corresponding local function is invoked to perform the operation. If the object is remote the function performs an remote procedure call to the node where the object resides. A remote handler on that node then performs a call to the corresponding local function and returns the result of that call to the initiator of the remote procedure call.

Although the underlying operating system is different on both systems the same user interface has been provided. How this common interface has been achieved will be intensively discussed in the next section.

Closely related to the basic message-passing interface MMK/X is the tool environment TOPSYS. It provides the programmer with a tool set reflecting the special issues needed to handle parallel applications. The tool set TOPSYS includes a visualization tool (VISTOP), a performance measurement tool (PATOP) and a debugger (DETOP). All tools are based on a common monitoring interface[3]. The monitor used may either be a software or hardware monitor. The difference of both systems concerns the degree of intrusion. The hardware solution adds additional hardware to the system which gathers the necessary monitoring information via bus-snooping. Consequently hardly any additional software causes any change in the computation of an application. In difference to that the software monitor uses an additional software layer and source code instrumentation to monitor an application. Of course this changes the characteristics of a running application. The overhead introduced is about 1%. The implementation of the hardware monitor has only been done for our iPSC/2 system, whereas both MMK for the iPSC/860 and MMK/X for the workstations can only use a software monitor. All tools send their requests and commands to the monitor which in turn processes the requests and sends answers back to the connected tools. As the tools communicate via a defined interface the implementation of the tools must not pay any regard to whether an application is running on the iPSC/860 or on a network of workstations. The only prerequisite is that a suitable monitoring interface exists.

The visualization tool VISTOP[5] gives a graphical animation of a running MMK/X application. The user can gain an on-line view of the program flow and the communication relations of a running application, i. e. deadlock situations can be easily detected. At that point the debugger can be used to examine in detail why the deadlock situation has occurred. DETOP[6] offers the functionality of a conventional debugger enhanced with several features that are useful for debugging parallel applications like specifying a breakpoint for several tasks which is only triggered if all tasks reach the breakpoint condition. Apart from correct programs it is important for applications on supercomputers to achieve the best possible performance. PATOP[2] can be applied to do performance debugging, i. e. to determine those parts of the application that are currently inefficient.

4 The Implementation of MMK/X

As outlined in the section above MMK/X offers the same programming model for workstations as MMK does the for iPSC systems. Apart from source code compatibility of the applications being developed with MMK/X a further major design goal was the portability of message-passing library itself as stated in section 2.

On the iPSC systems MMK is based on the native NX/2[8] message-passing interface offered by those machines. To minimize the changes that were necessary to the source code of MMK to implement MMK/X on a network of workstations an additional software layer was implemented. This additional layer offers a set of calls which is equivalent to Intel' s NX/2 system calls. Figure 1 shows the layers of MMK and MMK/X. Due to the decision to implement the necessary calls of the NX/2 message-passing system for workstations and to put on top of that the MMK source code only minor changes were necessary. Modifications only had to be made to highly machine dependent parts of the MMK message-passing library such as the scheduler and the interrupt service routines.

A further important aspect, that enforces the portability of MMK/X, is the usage of standard UNIX communication calls. As a network of workstations is usually connected via Ethernet running TCP/IP protocols, the usage of UNIX socket communication [10] proposes best portability properties. Therefore, NX/2 message-passing calls are transformed into corresponding socket-communication calls. Two major problems that had to be solved during the implementation of MMK/X are the naming of the nodes and the missing hardware routing mechanism between these nodes.

On the iPSC systems the communication partners address each other via the node number of the node they are running on. Thus, a message which is sent from one process to another is first directed to the node of the receiver and then

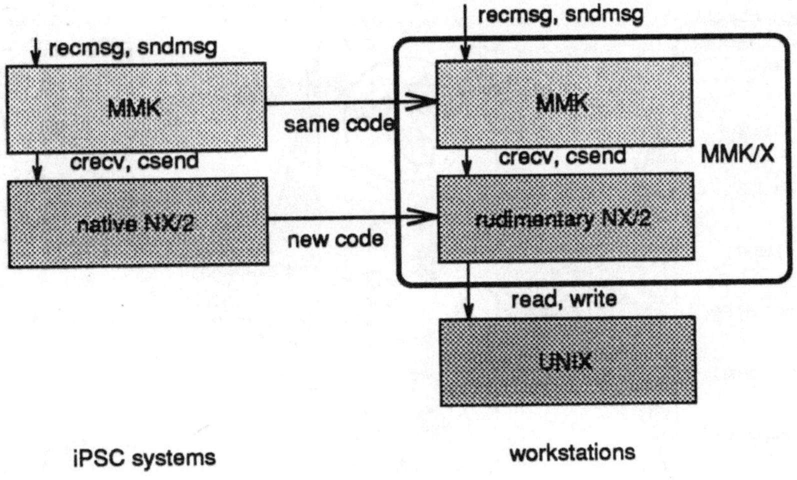

Fig. 1. Layers of MMK and MMK/X

directed to the process which matches the process type argument of the send call. The nodes which take part in the computation of an application are contiguously numbered from 0 to $n-1$, where n is the number of nodes. In contrast, workstations use a different addressing scheme, which is based on the definitions of the Internet Protocol. Every workstation has a unique network address which is segmented into four integers each with a range from 0 to 255. The Internet addresses of the workstations are not necessarily contiguous, consequently they cannot directly be used as a replacement for the node numbers.

To overcome this problem a second level mapping has been introduced. In contrast to the first level mapping (see section 3), where MMK/X objects are mapped onto a certain node, the second level mapping maps Internet addresses to node numbers. As these node numbers do not represent a physical node, they are called virtual node numbers. Similarly each node defined in the second level mapping is called a virtual node. Each virtual node resembles exactly one physical node in an iPSC system. On the other hand on a workstation each virtual node represents exactly one UNIX process. UNIX systems allow the user to run several processes concurrently. In addition to that the communication of two processes via TCP sockets is transparent in regard to the location of the communication partners, i.e. there is no difference between a local or a remote communication over the network. As a consequence, it is possible to have more than one virtual node on a single workstation. Thus a workstation may represent either a single node of an iPSC system (only one virtual node is mapped on the workstation in the second level mapping) or may represent a whole iPSC system for instance with 64 nodes (all 64 virtual nodes are mapped on the workstation). Figure 2 illustrates both mapping stages.

A consequence of the above is, that already a single workstation can be

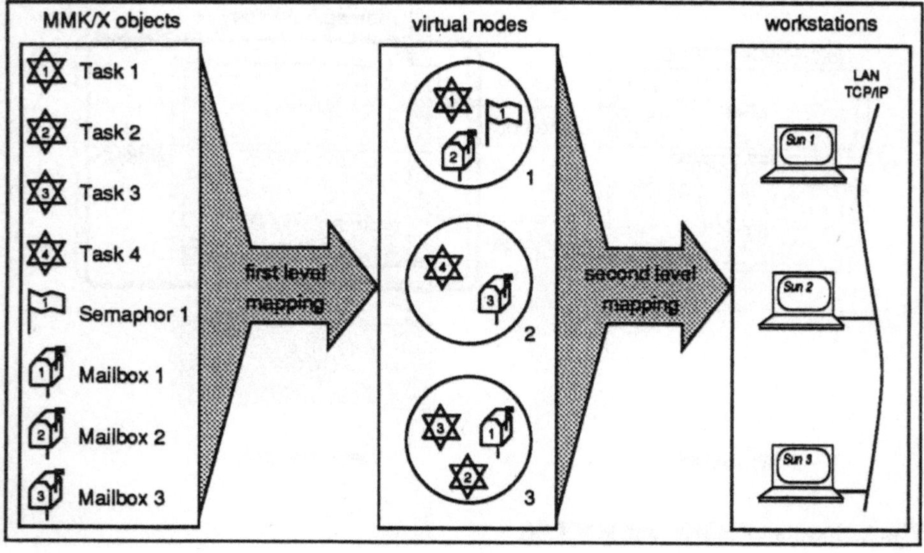

Fig. 2. First Level and Second Level Mapping

used to develop parallel MMK/X applications. To achieve this, the secondary mapping must simply be modified so that all virtual nodes are mapped onto the same workstation. Engineers can therefore debug their application using their own workstation without interfering with the other users in the network. If the user wants to test his application with the virtual nodes distributed among several workstations this can be done at any time through a simple modification of the secondary mapping. No re-compilation of the application will be necessary and the next time the application will be started the new secondary mapping will be used. A further advantage of the second level mapping is that within that mapping table the user is not restricted to the Internet addresses of the machines. Moreover, the symbolic names of the machines can be used within that mapping table, which makes the table more userfriendly.

To get a better understanding of how the second major problem, namely the missing hardware routing units, has been solved in the implementation of MMK/X, it is necessary to understand how the virtual nodes of an application are started. This will be explained in the following paragraphs.

Consider again the application with the mapping of figure 2. In contrast to the situation there, where the objects were mapped to three different virtual nodes in the first level mapping, the user now wants to have four virtual nodes. A reason for this could be, that Task 2 of figure 2 needs that much computation time that its virtual node is overloaded. The mapping of the remaining objects of figure 2 is unchanged. So the situation is exactly the same like in figure 2 with the difference that Task 2 is mapped onto an additional virtual node.

Similar to figure 2 the user still can only use three workstations Sun 1, Sun 2 and Sun 3. In regard to the modified first level mapping where an additional virtual node was introduced the user has to adapt the second level mapping to that situation. As Sun 2 is the most powerful machine the user decides to have two virtual nodes on that machine and one of the remaining virtual nodes on Sun 1 and and the other one on Sun 3. Figure 3 shows the distribution of the virtual nodes among the workstations and the objects after the application has been started[1].

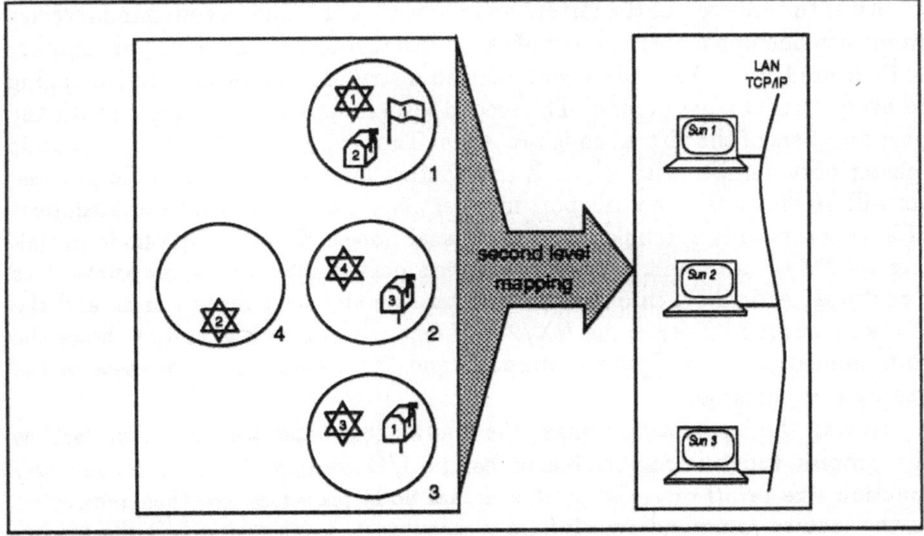

Fig. 3. Modified second level mapping with one additional virtual node

A process representing a virtual node is called a virtual node process. On Sun 1 there is the virtual node process 1, on Sun 2 there are the virtual node processes 2 and 4. Finally virtual node process 3 is located on Sun 3. All machines which should execute a virtual node process need to have a daemon running, the so called MMK/X daemon *mmkd*. To start an application the user specifies a MMK/X specific command called *loadws* which contacts the daemons on all machines which were specified in the second level mapping table. During that phase the loadws command distributes the binary of the virtual node processes

[1] The same effect could have been reached without changing the second level mapping. Therefore, Task 2 would have been mapped onto node 2 in the first level mapping resulting in a similar distribution of the single objects. But then Task 2 and Task 4 always would reside on the same machine whereas in the approach above Task 2 and its corresponding virtual node can be mapped to an additional workstation

to the mmkd on every machine[2]. Figure 4.a) shows this for the above example mapping. The daemons on Sun 1, Sun 2 and Sun 3 get a copy of the MMK_{any} binary.

In the next step the daemon processes on every machine create the virtual node processes. The daemon forks as many child processes as have been mapped onto that workstation in the second level mapping. Each child process then executes the binary which the daemon has received during the distribution phase. In figure 4.b) the daemon on Sun 2 forks two children which in turn execute the virtual node binary MMK_{any} and become virtual node 2 and 4. The daemons on Sun 1 and Sun 3 fork one child which then becomes node 1 and 3 respectively.

After the creation of the virtual node processes the loadws command receives from each daemon a port number of each virtual node process. This port number is then used from the loadws command to distribute the second level mapping to every virtual node process. The second level mapping is augmented with the port numbers of the virtual node processes. Thus every virtual node has a public master-port number with which it can contact any other virtual node process. As will be shown later on this port number plays a key-role in the establishment of new communication links between virtual nodes. Every virtual node initializes its NX/2 layer and stores the received port numbers in appropriate data structures. A final synchronization between the virtual node processes and the loadws command finishes the NX/2 initialization phase. Figure 4.c) shows the communication of the loadws command and the virtual node processes of the example application.

During the initialization phase the loadws command also identifies itself as the process which is responsible to handle I/O commands. Calls to any I/O function like *printf* or *scanf* on the virtual node processes are then redirected to the loadws command, which finally executes it. Considering I/O the loadws command to some extent resembles the host task of MMK applications. Also in a second sense the loadws command is similar to the host task. The loadws command reads the first level mapping table and sends it to every virtual node process. Each process in turn examines the first level mapping for objects which should reside on that particular node and creates them. In the example above virtual node process 1, for instance, creates Task 1, Semaphore 1 and Mailbox 2. The functions which are used to evaluate and establish the first level mapping are unchanged to those used by MMK for the iPSC systems.

After having completed the initialization of the NX/2 layer and the creation of the objects, the state of the application is as follows. Each virtual node process has a communication link to the loadws command via a socket. Amongst each other the virtual node processes are not yet connected. The connections are dynamically created when the application issues an MMK/X call which needs to communicate with a virtual node to which it is not yet connected. This is done transparently without the notion of the MMK layer. Figure 4.d) shows a scenario of communication links of the example application after it has been executing for a while.

---

[2] The executable for all virtual node processes is the same, so that only one binary must be distributed.

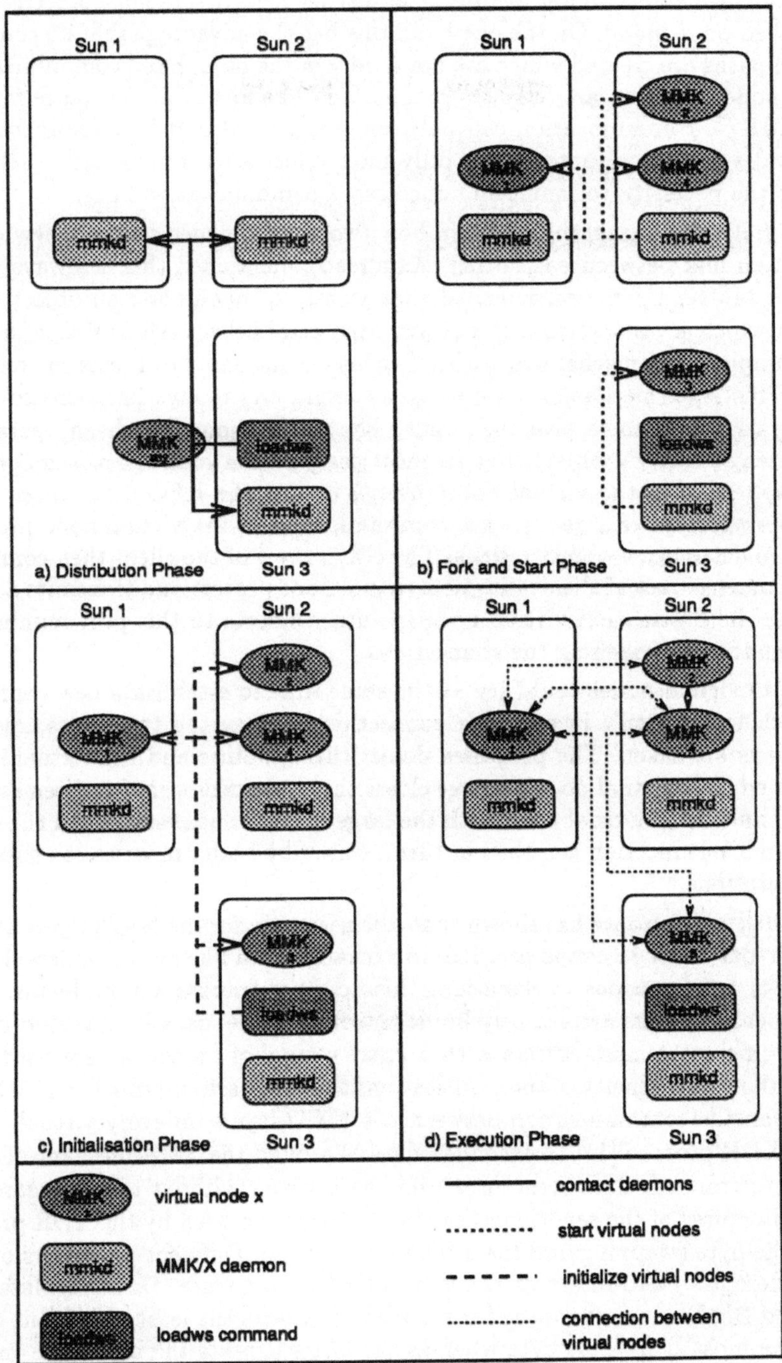

Fig. 4. Start up of an MMK/X Application

As outlined above, socket communications between virtual node processes are established on demand. On the one hand this has the advantage that no communication paths are created which are not used. On the other hand communicating virtual node processes are fully interconnected. The loss of performance for the first MMK/X communication call between two virtual nodes is dominated by magnitudes by the advantage of a fully interconnected communication scheme without the necessity to maintain unnecessary communication links.

The following paragraphs explain how two virtual nodes set up a new communication link between each other. As already mentioned this is always done when an MMK/X function is called that wants to manipulate an object on a node to which a connection has not yet been established. All MMK functions use a simple RPC mechanism to implement operations on objects on remote nodes. This RPC mechanism uses the NX/2 send and receive functions to send the operation and to receive the result. The destination of such an operation may be any MMK/X object, but in most cases it is a mailbox or semaphore. The NX/2 layer of the virtual node (client) issuing the RPC determines, that there exists not yet a direct socket communication to the virtual node process where the destination object resides. The NX/2 layer of the client then connects to the master-socket of the destination virtual node process and transmits a port number. The destination virtual node in turn connects to this port number of the client thus establishing the connection.

As two virtual nodes could try at the same time to establish a new connecting which would result in a double connection between the two nodes, special precautions are taken. The processes detect this situation and the virtual node with the smaller virtual node number closes the connection that has been set up and waits until the virtual node with the larger number has established the connection. This connection can then in turn be used by both processes to complete their operations.

The discussion above has shown that it is necessary for the NX/2 layers of the single virtual nodes to cooperate, i. e. to exchange data like port numbers. For a network of homogeneous workstations this does not impose any problems. But todays local networks are scarcely homogeneous. In fact, usually many workstations of different manufacturers with a great variety of processors are used. To manage the heterogeneity of the workstations that are participating in a MMK/X application the communication between the NX/2 layers on every virtual node use the XDR protocol[11] to exchange data. Through the XDR mechanism it is possible to transmit data structures over the network without taking regard to the architectures of the sender and receiver. Caveats covered by the XDR protocol are the byte swapping and the alignment problem. Different processors often use a different way to interpret the value of a byte sequence. Usual formats are Little and Big Endian where the former format expects the least significant byte before the most significant byte whereas the latter expects the bytes vice versa. Another point the XDR protocol takes care of is the data alignment. Processors often expect integers or floating point numbers to start at an address that fulfills a certain condition, e.g. that the address is a multiply of four or eight. In complex data structures where different data types are mixed this leads to so called alignment gaps which are bytes that are left unused to satisfy the alignment requirements of the processor. Also these alignment gaps are transformed to the appropriate size for the receiver. Thus the XDR protocol is a comfortable way for the user to convert data which is transmitted over the net. On the other hand, due to its great flexibility, the XDR mechanism introduces a lot of overhead.

Hence, the MMK layer of MMK/X uses a less complex protocol. As the transport of data structures within the that layer is simpler and more uniform the XDR protocol is not used there. Instead, every data structure which has to be exchanged is converted to an array of integer values. Before its transmittal the array is converted to network byte order. As only simple data structures have to be transmitted this approach is sufficient for the needs of the MMK layer and has the advantage of being faster than the XDR protocol. The exchange of data structures is only necessary to perform remote procedure calls. The data structure used for a RPC consists only of integer values. Consequently it is sufficient to convert the RPC data structure to network byte order. User specified data which is often part of a RPC is left unchanged. The application programmer has to take responsibility for choosing a method in his application to insure correct exchange of data. Thus the overhead of the MMK/X communication functions is reasonable and matches well the lightweight process character of the MMK/X tasks.

A final issue that had to be dealt with during the implementation of MMK/X on a network of workstations is the context switch mechanism. In the MMK for the iPSC supercomputer systems a machine language routine is used to implement a coroutine like context switch, which works as follows. First the current register set is saved on the stack of the running task and the current stack pointer is saved in the task description block in the system data structures. Then the stack pointer of the next running task is loaded into the appropriate register of the processor and the other registers are restored from the new stack into the processor. Finally the routine issues a return and the new task continues its execution[3].

For MMK/X the decision has been made to use a similar scheme. Implementations have been done for Sparc and i860 based systems. For i860 based systems the routines from the iPSC/860 could be used without any changes. For the Sparc based version some changes with regard to the Sparc architecture were necessary [7]. The initial Sparc stack frame depends on the number and kind of parameters, the number of local variables and the optimization level used to compile the code. Consequently the scheduler has to distinguish between tasks which were already running and tasks which have not yet been scheduled. For the latter the scheduler has therefore to determine the stack layout during the

[3] If a task is scheduled for the first time, it must be guaranteed that a correct stack has been set up, i.e. the registers are at the appropriate places and the return address which is poped from the stack by the return instruction points to the starting address of the tasks code.

first attempt to schedule the task. The second change concerns the register architecture of the Sparc processor which uses the technique of register windows to implement fast calls to subroutines. During these register windows are written to the stack signals are allowed. Thus an incoming signal during context switch may lead to inconsistencies: parts of the register windows are written to the old stack and parts to the new one. To overcome this problem, a simple coherency protocol has been included in the context switching routine. This protocol uses an additional magic save area for the current register window. This save area serves as a small system stack. The saving and reloading of the registers is not done via direct push and pop operations, but is simulated via corresponding processor instructions. So an incoming interrupt saves the registers completely on the magic save area and not partly on the old and the new stack as it would be the case in an implementation without the magic save area.

5 Performance Figures

To give an impression on the performance that can be achieved a simple comparison between MMK/860 and MMK/X has been done. The measurements of the MMK/860 were done on an Intel iPSC/860 with 16 nodes and 16MB memory on each node. For the MMK/X the measurements were carried out on two Sun Sparc 10 each with 32MB main memory. The workstations were connected via Ethernet with other users working on the net. Figure 5 summarizes the results. Each line shows the duration of a send-receive pair with increasing message length.

For the local communication, where two tasks on one (virtual) node send and receive the MMK/860 and MMK/X nearly the same times have been measured. Concerning local communication a virtual node on a Sparc 10 is comparable to a node of an iPSC/860.

For remote communication the situation is totally different. Here the communication speed of the iPSC/860 version is one order of magnitude faster. The reason for this behavior is on the one hand the communication protocol which is used for the communication. On the iPSC there are highly optimized communication calls of the NX/x operating system whereas for the workstations the general purpose TCP protocol with unnecessary overhead is used. A second reason for this is of course the difference in the communication hardware. The iPSC/860 uses a dedicated communication network with a maximum throughput of 2.7MB/s and an exclusive access of the application. In contrast to that the workstations are interconnected via a standard Ethernet with 1.25MB/s maximum throughput. In addition to that the network is shared with many other users which are currently working.

The above performance figure underlines again that Ethernet coupled workstations can only be used for applications with only limited communication needs. Fine grain parallelism is not well suited to achieve speed-ups on coupled workstations.

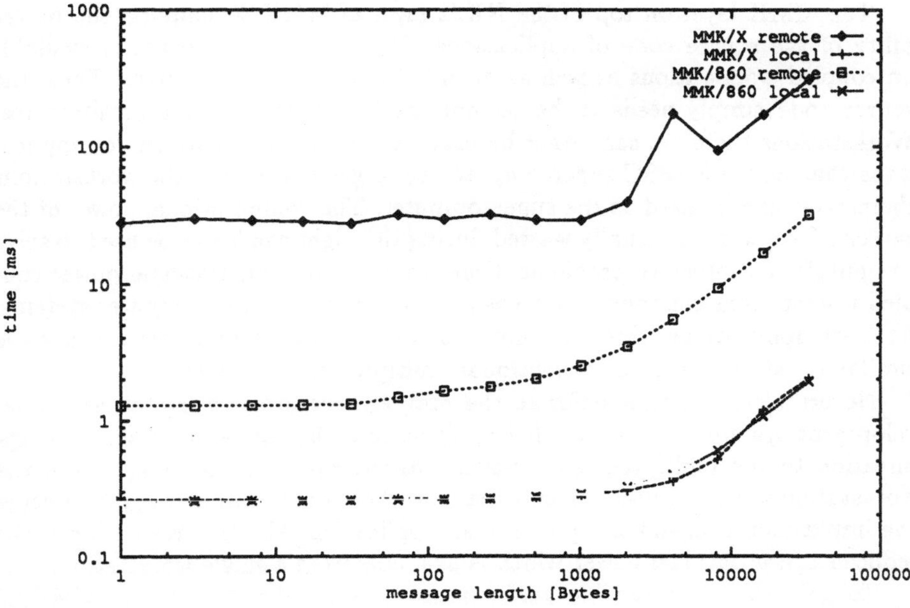

Fig. 5. Communication speed of MMK/860 and MMK/X with different message lengths

6 Conclusion

The discussion above has shown that MMK/X fulfills all goals stated in section 2. Easy portability of the message-passing library has been achieved through the implementation of the additional NX/2 communication layer which uses standard UNIX TCP socket communication. Ports to different hardware platforms are therefore possible with minor effort. Using the XDR protocol to transmit data between the virtual nodes further enhances the portability of the system. Also the implementation of the MMK layer on top of the NX/2 layer is easily portable to different architectures. Only small parts of the code are operating system or machine dependent. As long as the machine offers a standard UNIX interface no modifications concerning operating system dependencies are necessary. Due to the implementation in assembly language the context switch mechanism is the only part which has to be rewritten when the message-passing interface should be ported to another system. But also this is not too difficult as the basic scheme is rather simple and straight forward: push the current register set on the stack, save the stack pointer in the task description block and load a the new stack pointer into the processor register. Then restore the register set from the new stack and continue execution of the tasks code.

The MMK layer on top of the NX/2 layer of MMK/X supports the portability of the source code of applications. The same user interface is available on coupled workstations as well as on iPSC multiprocessor systems. Thus, the source code simply needs to be recompiled to run on different architectures. Workstations therefore can either be used as development platform for applications that have the iPSC supercomputer as target machine or the workstations themselves can be used as the supercomputer. The computational power of the workstations which is usually wasted during the night can hence be used to solve computational intensive problems. Concerning their computational power coupled workstations can indeed serve as a replacement for supercomputer systems. At least applications which are not too communication intensive can achieve similar speed-ups than on conventional multiprocessor systems.

Nevertheless MMK/X enforces the programmer to use workstations as development systems for any parallel application as he can later on shift the application to the multiprocessor system without changing anything. Thus, the workstation of an engineer can substitute a whole supercomputer system during the implementation and test phase of an application. The only restriction is the reduced computational power which is available from a single workstation.

To gain the best possible performance of a parallel application MMK/X uses a lightweight process model which makes it very well suited for client server communication. The context of the tasks consist only of the CPU registers. Thus, fast context switches between the single tasks are possible. The implementation in assembly language further improves the performance of the context switch.

Finally, a tool set, which has been designed to assist the programmer to develop parallel applications, can also be used for MMK/X applications. The TOPSYS tool environment not only supports applications on iPSC supercomputers but also applications on a network of workstations. Therefore the user can use the same tool set with the same functionality without taking regard to the current hardware platform.

7 Future Work

The next step to be undertaken is to achieve the interoperability between MMK on the iPSC systems and MMK/X on the workstations. For this purpose the physical nodes of the iPSC systems have to be included into the virtual node concept of MMK/X. The second level mapping must hence allow to specify nodes of an iPSC system as virtual nodes. The mixed operation of nodes from the iPSC system and (virtual) nodes from the workstation network enables the user to split his application among the multiprocessor system and the coupled workstations. Each part can so do a dedicated job which is best suited for the underlying hardware. The supercomputer part for instance can mainly be used to do high performance number crunching whereas the part on the workstation can be used to implement the graphics output via corresponding graphic libraries. So each hardware can be used for that part of the application which it is best suited for, with the advantage of sharing a common programming and tool interface.

8 Acknowledgments

For their contributions to this paper I would like to thank Christian Kasperbauer who did most of the implementation work and Bernhard Ries for interesting discussions.

References

1. H.J. Beier, T. Bemmerl, A. Bode, et al. TOPSYS — Tools for Parallel Systems. SFB-Bericht 342/9/90 A, Technische Universität München, München, January 1990.
2. T. Bemmerl, O. Hansen, and T. Ludwig. PATOP for Performance Tuning of Parallel Programs. In H. Burkhart, editor, *Proceedings of CONPAR90 VAPP IV*, volume 457 of *LNCS*, pages 840–751, Zürich, Schweiz, 1990. Springer-Verlag.
3. T. Bemmerl, R. Lindhof, and T. Treml. The Distributed Monitor System of TOPSYS. In H. Burkhart, editor, *Proceedings of CONPAR90 VAPP IV*, volume 457 of *LNCS*, pages 756–765, Zürich, Schweiz, 1990. Springer-Verlag.
4. Thomas Bemmerl, Christian Kasperbauer, Martin Mairandres, and Bernhard Ries. Programming Tools for Distributed Multiprocessor Computing Environments. SFB-Bericht 342/31/91 A 342/31/91 A, Technische Universität München, München, October 1991.
5. Arndt Bode and Peter Braun. Monitoring and Visualization in TOPSYS. In Günter Haring and Gabriele Kotsis, editors, *Performance Measurement and Visualization of Parallel Systems: Proceedings of the Workshop on Performance Measurment and Visuzlization*, pages 97–118, Moravany, October 1992. Elsevier Science Publishers.
6. Marcus Clemente and Stephan Gillich. DETOP — Ein graphischer Debugger für den iPSC/2 Hypercube. Fortgeschrittenenpraktikum. Technische Universität München, Institut für Informatik, Lehrstuhl für Rechnertechnik und Rechnerorganisation, 1990.
7. David Keppel. Register windows and user-space threads on the SPARC. Technical Report 91-08-01, Department of Computer Science and Engeneering, University of Washington, Seattle, Washington 98195, 1. August 1991.
8. Paul Pierce. The NX/2 Operating System. In *Proceedings of the 3rd Conference on Hypercube Concurrent Computers and Applications*, pages 384–391. ACM, 1988.
9. Georg Stellner. Weiterentwicklung und Portierung eines verteilten Betriebssystems für Multiprozessoren. Master's thesis, Technische Universität München, Institut für Informatik, Lehrstuhl für Rechnertechnik und Rechnerorganisation, 1991.
10. Richard W. Stevens. *UNIX Network Programming*. Software Series. Prentice Hall, Englewood Cliffs, 1. edition, 1990.
11. Sun Microsystems Inc., California. *SunOS 4.1.1b Network Programming Guide*, 1991.
12. Technische Universität München, Institut für Informatik, Lehrstuhl für Rechnertechnik und Rechnerorganisation. *MMK User's Reference Manual*, 1.1 edition, December 1990.

Technology for TeraFLOPS Architectures

Thomas Bemmerl
Intel Corporation
European Supercomputer Development Center (ESDC)
Dornacherstr. 1, D-85622 Feldkirchen b. München
E-mail: thomas@esdc.intel.com

Abstract

The solutions of today's foremost scientific challenges require order-of-magnitude increases in computing power (3). The route to TeraFLOPS computing lies in parallel multi-computers that exploit advances in microprocessor technology. The *Touchstone program*, a joint effort by Intel and the U.S. Advanced Research Projects Agency (ARPA), has led already to the development of one of the world's fastest supercomputers - a mesh-interconnected distributed memory machine in the performance range of 100 GFLOPS. The fourth and final Touchstone prototype Sigma has been the base for Intel's latest supercomputer product - the Paragon XP/S capable of performing up to 300 GFLOPS. Based on the Touchstone experiences, a new research and development program at Intel is on the way for approx. one year now to develop parallel supercomputer technologies required for TeraFLOPS computers. This paper gives an overview of the goals and the research activities of the *TeraFLOPS program*.

1 The TeraFLOPS Technology Goal

The TeraFLOPS technology program is a collaborative effort between Intel Corporation, the Advanced Research Project Agency ARPA and other funding agencies in the context of the High Performance Computing and Communications (HPCC) initiative (10). This collaborative effort is a research, development and demonstration (RD&D) program to develop the technology crucial for the design and use of massively parallel high performance supercomputers. The research for this technology program will involve multiple collaborations between academia, government and industry. The overall and joint investment for this RD&D program will be in the order of $ 80 to $ 140 Million.

The key goal of this technology program is to develop early in the second half of this decade the technology that will enable the delivery of sustained one TeraFLOPS machines at the price of today's vector supercomputers. There are two important points to be noted here:

* The goal of the TeraFLOP program is to reach the performance level of sustained one trillion floating point operations per second (double precision), not just peak performance. This means that the machines to be developed should be general purpose parallel supercomputers delivering *sustained TeraFLOPS* performance over a wide range of applications (from Computational Fluid Dynamics to Computational Electromagnetics) primarily defined by the so called *Grand Challenges* of Science and Industry (10).

* Secondly the goal of the program is defined on the basis of the *costs and prices of todays vector supercomputers* (which equals approx. § 30 Mio.). This is very important, because it would already be possible to build TeraFLOPS machines with todays technology, but at a price which is far beyond what potential users can afford. So, the price/performance ratio of TeraFLOPS supercomputers will be much improved within this program.

2 TeraFLOPS as an Extension of Touchstone

The TeraFLOPS RD&D program will produce subsequent generations of system architectures demonstrated in prototype systems between *now and 1996*. The basis for the new TeraFLOPS program are the results of the Touchstone (6) program, Intel's previous RD&D program in collaboration with ARPA. The Touchstone program has delivered the technology for massively parallel supercomputers capable of performing up to hundreds of GFLOPS peak. The final prototype of the Touchstone program, the Sigma prototype has formed the basis for Intel's new supercomputer product line, the Paragon XP/S which has a peak performance of 300 GFLOPS.

The system prototypes defined in the new TeraFLOPS program, will perform approx. at a *peak level of 600 and 1.600 Billion Floating Point Operations per second.* As in Touchstone, Intel will decide later on during this technology program which one of the prototypes it may turn into a product. Figure 1 shows the high performance system development methodology of the Touchstone and the TeraFLOPS program with the associated prototypes.

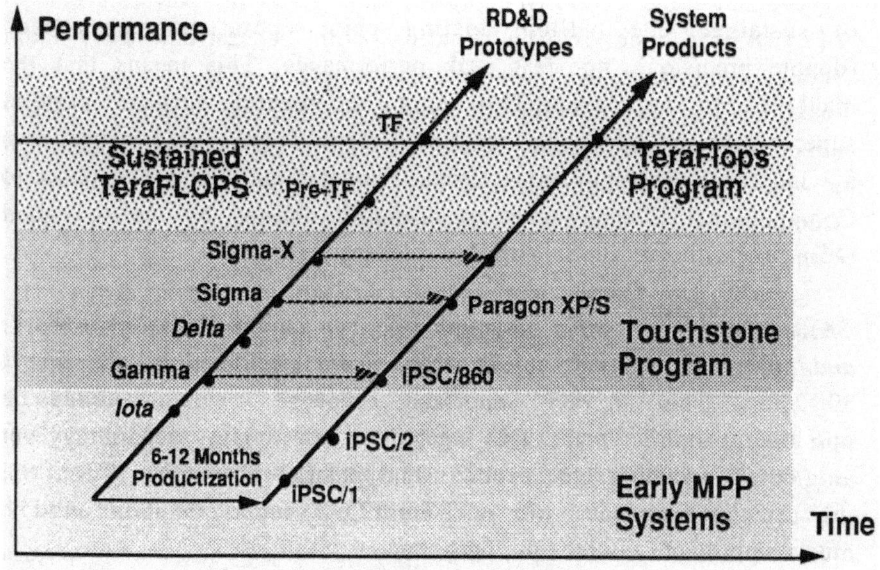

Figure 1 High Performance System Engineering

3 Design Ideas and Research Activities

A few governing design ideas drive Intel's technology development toward TeraFLOPS machines. Before focusing on the R&D activities of the new TeraFLOPS program the most important design ideas are highlighted:

Governing Design Ideas

The central concept of all Intel supercomputers has been and will continue to be the *Multiple Instruction Multiple Data MIMD* concept with physically *distributed memory*. Only this type of parallel architecture makes it possible to build flexible massively parallel systems with up to thousands of processing elements without running into resource bottlenecks (4), (5). The interconnection networks of these machines is based on the philosophy of the *"flat" interconnect*. Flat in this context does not just indicate, that the interconnect relies on low dimensional grids as topology. More importantly flat expresses that the design of interconnection networks hides the topology from the application programmer through *wormhole routing*. The user of this type of machines does not need to know the topology of the underlying hardware, he can rely on a virtually fully connected architecture (4), (5). The processing elements of these massively parallel systems are based on the fastest microprocessors available (and suitable), rather than slower but less complex processing elements (*"fat nodes"*). With this design concept, we combine the improvements in todays microprocessor architectures (RISC, CISC). and silicon technology with the improvement of parallel supercomputer technology.

As important as the design ideas on the hardware side are the appropriate concepts in the software architecture. As the use of todays massively parallel systems is limited by software constraints, improvements in this area become much more important in the new TeraFLOPS program. The software architecture of Intel's parallel supercomputers is based on *open, scalable and standard software concepts*. The operating system is based on the *Mach microkernel* technology and on scalable UNIX services provided by the *OSF/1 UNIX* servers. Both technologies are the basis for the transparent services provided and the fact, that the machines look like one single computer which is able to handle multiple user requests simultaneously (8). For programming these type of machines, we rely on the use of standard programming languages like *Fortran and C* (including the extensions for high performance systems; message passing, HPF; shared virtual memory) as well as on integrated programming tools with graphical user interfaces based on *Motif and X-Windows* graphics primitives.

Overview on Research Activities

According to these basic design ideas, the following R&D activities with their corresponding technology focus goals have been defined for the TeraFLOPS program:

Improvements in silicon technology will lead to new generations of microprocessors based on 0.4 and 0.6 submicron CMOS semiconductor processes. Intel will develop and/or use two new generations of high performance floating point microprocessors, performing at approx. *150 to 400 MFLOPS* double precision peak, which is an improvement of the processor performance by approx. a factor of 4. At least the second generation of microprocessors to be used/developed will offer a *64-bit architecture*. The performance of the interconnection network will be improved nearly by the same factor in terms of communication bandwidth, which is a prerequsite to keeping the balance of the system architecture. New generations of *2- or 2.5 dimensional routing units* will provide part of the system performance increase.

The Mach and OSF based open operating system (8) and the integrated tool set (1), (2), (7) will continue to be extended and enhanced with further functionality for process management and resource scheduling as well as dynamic loadbalancing (9). The system and component development can not make sufficient progress, without major input from the user and application community. Therefore Intel will conduct collaborative projects to solve grand challenge problems like global climate modelling, human genome mapping and high speed civil transportation. The experiences of these grand challenge science projects will be constantly fed back into the development of the system prototypes, capable of performing in the 600 and 1.600 GFLOPS range.

4 The TeraFLOPS Research Agenda

In the rest of the paper, a selected set of issues of the TeraFLOPS research agenda is presented and discussed in more detail. However, this description does not give a complete list of all the research activities necessary for this program.

System Architecture Research

Intel's architecture for TeraFLOPS technology is based on the concept of scalable heterogeneous multicomputers. In this architecture a varying number of processing elements, the "nodes", with different functionality are integrated into a scalable interconnection network to provide all the functionality of a complete high performance computing system. The core of the system is formed by the *computational array*, consisting of processing elements with high floating point performance, the numeric nodes. These numeric nodes are interconnected in the flat topology via the 2- or 2.5-dimensional grid. This core partition can be enhanced with scalable parallel *Input/Output nodes* to provide a massive amount of secondary storage. The disk nodes are interconnected by the same interconnection network as the numeric nodes, to provide not just fast parallel (32- and/or 64-bit) floating point computations but also fast parallel I/O operations. The system is interfaced to the user via a *scalable service partition* consisting of a varying number of service nodes. The scalable service partition supports a large number of users simultaneously on the machine and makes the massively parallel system look like one single computer. The service partition is interfaced to slow I/O devices via standard interfaces. It is very important to note that the borders between the various partitions are not fixed, they are rather a parameter of configuration. This makes the architecture very flexible and allows the system to be configured according to the users' needs dynamically during operation. Figure 2 gives a block diagram of the base TeraFLOPS system architecture.

The microprocessor RD&D within the new program will demonstrate *prototypes* with two new generations of high performance floating-point microprocessors in *late 1995 and late 1996*. At least the second prototype will be based on a 64-bit architecture. The designs of these microprocessors will extend the capabilities of the processing elements used in Touchstone beyond the current floating point performance and addressing capabilities. The two implementations will provide a peak floating point performance of approx. *150 to 400 double precision MFLOPS* within a transistor budget of 3 to 7 million transistors.

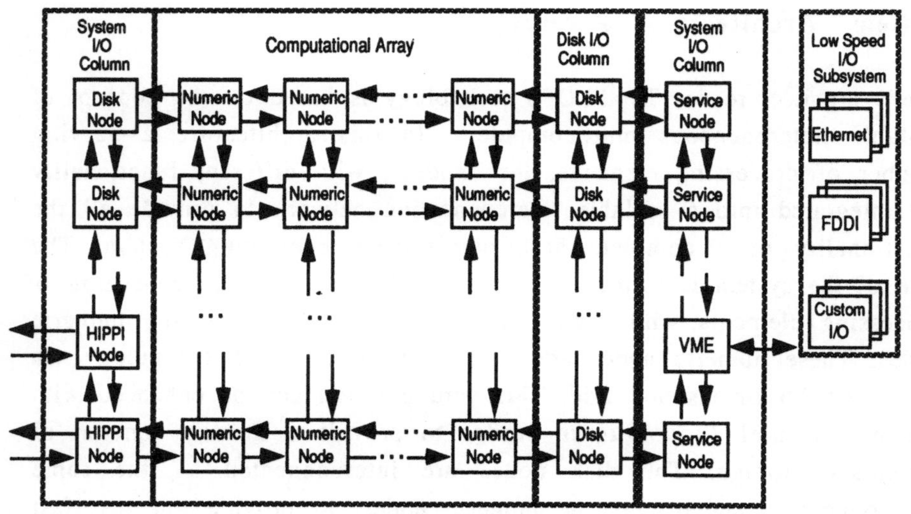

Figure 2 Versatile TeraFLOPS System Architecture

The implementation of these new microprocessors will be inherently parallel and will cover extensive fine-grain parallelism internally. Superscalar and superpipelined concepts will be used to execute multiple instructions per clock cycle and to increase on-chip operating speed. Out-of-order execution calculates operands when they become available and moves the implementation toward data-flow machines. It is already claimed, that microprocessor designs of this type are not limited by the available transistor budget, they are rather more limited by the architectural concepts discovered so far by computer scientists.

Interconnect Research

Interconnect RD&D is based on the results of the Touchstone Sigma prototype (6) and the iWarp technology. Improvements are planned in multiple steps. The basic goal of all these improvements is to increase the overall communication bandwidth by the same factor as the processor performance, while keeping the communication latency as low as possible. This will lead to a communication *bandwidth of 400 to 600+ MBytes/s* for each channel of the routing network by late 1996 with a targeted *latency of 1 microsecond.* The technology of express routing will be used to reduce the communication delay and latency in large interconnection networks when building systems with large numbers of processing elements. In all stages the medium to coarse grain routing technology of the Touchstone prototypes and the fine grain routing technology of the iWarp program will be combined. Traditional *send/receive functionality* will be available for message passing programming as well as *read/write functionality* for shared memory programming. Major efforts will be made to optimize the hardware/software interface in the interconnection network to reduce the software overhead needed for communication. Figure 3 shows the combination of the Touchstone and iWarp technology for the TeraFLOPS routers.

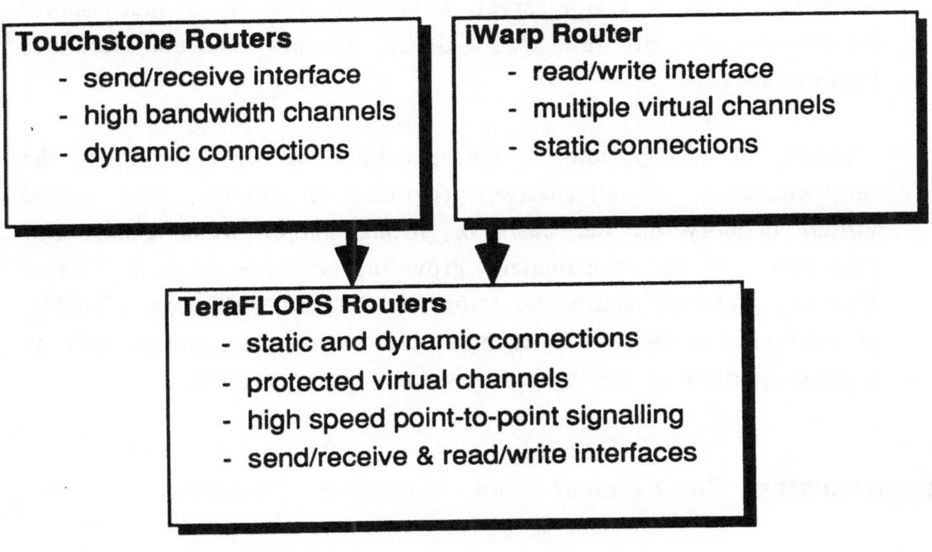

Firgure 3 Mixed Grain Interconnect

Operating System Research

As important as improvements in the hardware architecture are the improvements in the software technology for TeraFLOPS class machines. Within the new program Intel has defined three basic areas for research and development, which are the OS technology, the compiler and tools area and the concepts for the parallelization of applications. The Mach and OSF based scalable OS technology developed within Touchstone (6), (8), will be enhanced in various ways. Three areas of improvement should be highlighted here:

* Increased *scalability, reliability and availability* are key features of systems capable to perform at sustained one TeraFLOPS. Appropriate resource management and scheduling policies need to be integrated into the Mach microkernel, the OSF/1 AD servers and the whole design of the operating system including a port to 64-bit microprocessor architectures.

* Realizing, that *multi-user operation* of scalable high performance systems will be the norm rather than the exception, the scalable UNIX services have to be further enhanced to deliver better efficiency and modularity. Activities in this direction are a transition from a single-server implementation to a multi-server implementation of the OSF UNIX servers or emulator-less kernels/servers.

* Finally, the integration of concepts into the OS to support the implementation of alternative programming models, like global virtual memory on the basis of strong and/or weak consistency protocols will be investigated. Providing scalable *Shared Virtual Memory (SVM)* and/or *Distributed Shared Memory (DSM)* programming models with sophisticated caching algorithms will be a major portion of the operating system research track.

Programming Environment and Compiler Research

Very critical to the success of TeraFLOPS class machines in the future will be their richness of programming languages and tools and their ease of use (1). We will therefore make major efforts in the new program to address these issues. Intel is already in cooperation with other major supercomputer software vendors contributing to the *High Performance Fortran* Forum (HPFF). Two pieces of this work are addressed in the new program: The early establishment of a language standard based on F77, F90 and Fortran D. as well as the optimization of the run-time system of the new parallel HPF compilers for our class of machines on the basis of the fat node MIMD architecture with flat interconnect.

In addition to the optimization of the parallel compiler technology, we will work on improvements of the sequential compilers for *better utilization of the hardware resources* of the single processing element.

One area of improvement will be compiler optimizations to support the superscalar and superpiplined architecture of new processors. The other important issue to be addressed is compiler-controlled memory hierarchy management.

Finally, in the language and tools area, we will develop environments to *support specific application fields*, like the real-time based image processing applications and numerically intensive quantum chromo dynamics applications. Also, integrated *tool support for alternative programming models* (shared virtual memory) and mixed model programming will be addressed (message passing, high performance fortran and shared virtual memory) (7).

Applications Research to guide the System Development

Last but not least, the systems and components development work needs significant input from the user community. Experiences from collaborative grand challenge science projects with selected users will guide the system and components design process. Three activities will be undertaken in the TeraFLOPS program to support this strategy. The establishment of a *grand challenge knowledge base* will deliver important information how to solve grand challenge problems on massively parallel supercomputers. Based on this knowledge, the development of *scalable, parallel numerical libraries* will form the computational core of the applications to be addressed. Finally, we will demonstrate and evaluate the various grand challenge applications on the system prototypes and will feed back these experiences into the system and components development.

5 Conclusion

The paper has given a technical overview on Intel's research, development and demonstration program to develop early in the second half of the decade technology for parallel supercomputers capable of performing at sustained one TeraFLOPS. The motivation, goals and the research agenda of this technology program has been outlined. A good summarizing, non-technical statement is a quote of Craig Barrett, Chief

Operating Officer of Intel, which expresses Intel's committment to this program: *"Intel is committed to making this fundamental advance in supercomputing happen on schedule. We have aligned our organization and resources to focus on every aspect of supercomputing from systems and software to components and semiconductor processes".*

Bibliography

(1) T. Bemmerl
Programming Tools for Massively Parallel Supercomputers.
Proceedings of Workshop on Environments and Tools for Parallel Scientific Computing, St. Hilaire du Touvet, France, Sept. 1992

(2) D. Breazeal, R. Anderson, W.D. Smith, W. Auld, K. Callaghan
A Software Monitor for Parallel Debugging and Performance Tools.
Supercomputer Debugging Workshop '92, Dallas, Nov. 1992.

(3) Computer Technology Research Corp.
Supercomputer Technology.
Computer Technology Research Corp., ISBN 0-927695-25-1, April 1990.

(4) W.J. Dally, C.L. Seitz
Deadlock-free message routing in multiprocessor connection networks.
IEEE Transactions on Computers, Vol. C-36, No. 5, pp. 547 - 553, 1987.

(5) D. May
The Next Generation Transputers and Beyond.
In: A. Bode (Editor): Distributed Memory Computing, Lecture Notes in Computer Science, Vol. 487, Springer-Verlag, Berlin, Heidelberg, New York, pp. 7 - 22, April 1991

(6) J. Rattner
The New Age of supercomputing.
In: A. Bode (Editor): Distributed Memory Computing, Lecture Notes in Computer Science, Vol. 487, Springer-Verlag, April 1991

(7) B. Ries, W. Auld, W.D. Smith, D. Breazeal, K. Callaghan, E. Richards
The Paragon Performance Monitoring Environment.
Accepted for publication at ACPC'93, Salzburg, Austria, Oct. 1993.

(8) R. Zajcew, P. Roy, D. Black, C. Peak, P. Guedes, B. Kemp
An OSF/1 UNIX for Massively Parallel Multicomputers.
1993 Winter USENIX, January 1993, San Diego, CA

(9) R. Zajecew, S. Tritscher, M. Barnett
Load Leveling Using Process Migration On Massively Parallel Multicomputers.
Submitted for publication.

(10) Committee on Physical, Mathematical, and Engineering Sciences; Federal Coordinating Council for Science, Engineering, and Technology
Grand Challenges 1993: High Performance Computing and Communications.
The FY 1993 U.S. Research and Development Program

Der Einfluß der Kommunikationszeiten auf die Effizienz von Parallelrechnern

Jochen Gries, Axel Kern[1], Hans–Otto Leilich

Institut für Datenverarbeitungsanlagen
Technische Universität Braunschweig
Hans–Sommer–Str. 66, 38106 Braunschweig

Zusammenfassung

Das Problem der Effizienzminderung aufgrund von notwendigen Kommunikationsprozessen bei Parallelrechnern wird auf der Basis von Messungen am Prototyp des PIPELINEBUS als Verbindungssystem des SUPRENUM–Rechners dargestellt. Die effektiven „Startzeiten" der einzelnen Übertragungsoperationen erwiesen sich als sehr hoch. Verbesserungen an verschiedenen Ebenen des Übertragungsprotokolls wurden vorgeschlagen und durch Simulationen sowie Analysen bewertet. Eine Modellanalyse für ein vereinfachtes Mehrgitterverfahren zeigt, daß die Startzeit um etwa zwei Größenordnungen reduziert werden muß, um in einem weiten Parameterbereich die Prozessorleistung gut ausnutzen zu können. Dazu wird ein PIPELINEBUS–System mit einer an die Rechenprozesse gekoppelten Transportsteuerung vorgeschlagen.

1 Einleitung

In weiten Bereichen von Wissenschaft und Technik lassen sich zahlreiche Probleme nur über die sehr rechenintensive Lösung großer Differentialgleichungssysteme bearbeiten, wobei zunehmend massiv parallele Rechner eingesetzt werden. Ein Hauptproblem bei deren Anwendung ist, daß der Beschleunigungsfaktor (*Speedup* S) oft sehr viel geringer als die Anzahl P der Prozessoren steigt und damit die Effizienz E in der Nutzungsfähigkeit der Rechenleistung sehr klein ist. Die Gründe hierfür liegen zu einem großen Teil an der Parallelisierbarkeit der Programme sowie an den verfügbaren Sprachen. Einen großen Einfluß hat auch die Architektur des Multiprozessorsystems, wobei insbesondere die Struktur und der Aufbau des Kommunikationssystems sowie dessen Zeitverhalten eine große Rolle spielen.

Dieser Beitrag basiert auf den Arbeiten am „PIPELINEBUS", der an unserem Institut als oberes Verbindungssystem für den SUPRENUM–Rechner unter besonderer Berücksichtigung der Mehrgitterverfahren geplant und als funktionsfähiger Prototyp realisiert wurde [GHH+90a]. Nach einer kurzen Einführung wollen wir hier einige wichtige Ergebnisse darstellen, die auf umfangreichen Messungen sowie Simulationen und Analysen beruhen, und dabei inbesondere den Einfluß der Kommunikationszeit T_{Kom} auf die Effizienz behandeln. Damit unsere Ergebnisse auf ähnliche und künftige Systeme übertragbar sind, stellen

[1] jetzt Schumann Unternehmensberatung AG, Köln

wir außerdem Varianten zu der Verbindungsstruktur und den Protokollen des realisierten Systems vor.

Um ein quantitatives Beispiel zu geben, werden wir in Abschnitt 4 den Einfluß der Kommunikation bei den Mehrgitteralgorithmen darstellen. Dabei werden die regulären Zyklen einer vielverwendeten, kommunikationsintensiven Aufgabenklasse, der iterativen diskreten Lösung der Poisson-Gleichung nach [MFL+91], zugrunde gelegt. Im Gegensatz zu den lose gekoppelten Multiprozessorsystemen von heterogenen Rechnern (z. B. Workstations und „Servern") untersuchen wir hier die Klasse von Parallelrechnern, die jeweils nur eine einzige Aufgabe bearbeiten und in der die Prozesse in den einzelnen Rechnern weitgehend synchron ablaufen. Die funktionellen Anforderungen an das Kommunikationsnetz sind für diesen Betriebsmodus ziemlich primitiv, die Zeitanforderungen aber sehr hoch. Real muß das Netz natürlich auch allgemeinere Kommunikationsaufgaben ausführen können. Neben den dafür notwendigen Diensten darf man jedoch bei der Implementierung die Effizienz im synchronen Betriebsmodus nicht vernachlässigen.

Die diesem Beitrag zugrunde liegenden Vorhaben wurden vom Bundesminister für Forschung und Technologie unter den Förderkennzeichen ITR8502L sowie IR201B gefördert. An den Projekten waren auch die Herren Prof. Dr. H. Ch. Zeidler, Dr. B. Franke, Dipl.-Ing. A. Hahlweg und Dipl.-Ing. R. Harneit beteiligt, denen wir an dieser Stelle danken.

2 SUPRENUM und PIPELINEBUS

Als Grundlage unserer Arbeiten dienen der SUPRENUM-Rechner [Gil88] und das PIPELINEBUS-Kommunikationssystem [FHKZ88] [GHH+91], die daher im folgenden kurz vorgestellt werden. SUPRENUM (SUPerREchner für NUMerische Anwendungen) war ein vom BMFT gefördertes Gemeinschaftsprojekt von Industrie, Hochschulen und Großforschungseinrichtungen zur Entwicklung eines Höchstleistungsrechners für numerische Applikationen mit folgenden Zielvorstellungen [Tro85]:

1) Massive Parallelrechnung (MIMD-Multiprozessorsystem),

2) Ausnutzung der regulären, lokalen Gitterstruktur einer sehr großen und wichtigen Klasse numerischer Anwendungen,

3) Unterstützung von Verfahren nach dem Mehrgitterprinzip.

Das Ergebnis war ein MIMD/SIMD-Parallelrechner, der aus bis zu 256 Rechenknoten mit je einer Vektoreinheit besteht und über eine maximale Rechenleistung von 5000 MFLOPS verfügt [Gil88]. Jeder Rechenknoten enthält einen Mikroprozessor Motorola M68020, lokalen Hauptspeicher (8 MByte), eine Vektorarithmetikeinheit (20 MFLOPS) und spezielle Kommunikationshardware. Sechzehn dieser Rechenknoten werden zusammen mit einigen Spezialknoten in einem Cluster zusammengefaßt und über zwei parallele, 64 Bit breite Clusterbusse verbunden, deren Datenrate zusammen 320 MByte/s beträgt. Die Verbindung der Cluster untereinander und mit den Steuerrechnern erfolgt über das sogenannte obere Verbindungssystem, dessen Topologie der bidirektionale Torus ist. Der linke Teil von

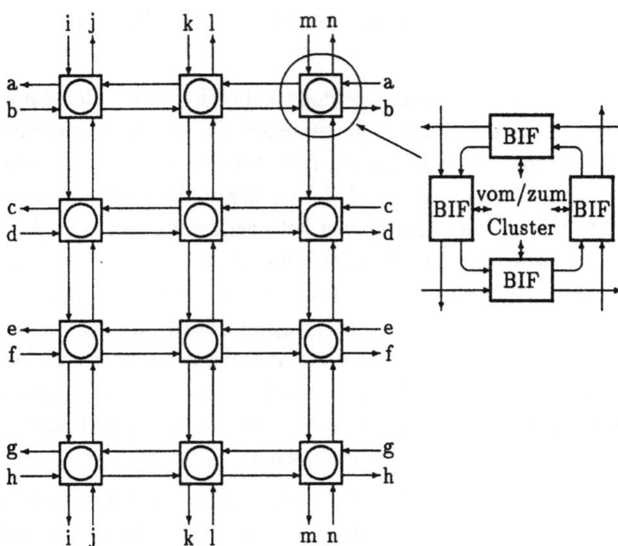

Bild 1: SUPRENUM-Struktur mit bidirektionalem Torus und Clusteranschluß mit vier Businterfaces für die PIPELINEBUS-Realisierung (nach [GHH+90a])

Bild 1 zeigt allgemein die Torus-Struktur, die mit Hilfe von gekoppelten bidirektionalen Tokenringen realisiert wurde.

Am Institut wurde im Rahmen des SUPRENUM-Projektes der PIPELINEBUS als Alternative für das obere Verbindungssystem entwickelt und realisiert (siehe [GHH+90b]). Aufbauend auf einer Abschätzung der erforderlichen Datenraten in [FL85] wurde dabei zunächst ein Konzept entwickelt, das die Kommunikation der erwähnten Gitterverfahren optimal unterstützt. Der PIPELINEBUS basiert auf Register-Insertion-Ringen mit fester Registerlänge [Liu78], auf denen Datenpakete[2] byteseriell übertragen werden – im Gegensatz zu der Tokenring-Lösung allerdings auf allen Teilverbindungen gleichzeitig. Die Ringe des PIPELINEBUS werden über Kreuzschalter miteinander verkoppelt. Ringzugriff und Kreuzschalter werden zu einem sogenannten Businterface (BIF) zusammengefaßt, das als Gatearray gefertigt wurde und die Grundeinheit des PIPELINEBUS bildet [Fra92]. Jedes Cluster wird über vier Businterfaces an das Netzwerk angeschlossen, das aus Ringen besteht, die einen bidirektionalen Torus bilden (siehe Bild 1).

Zum Anschluß der Cluster an das Netzwerk wurden „PIPELINEBUS-Knoten" aufgebaut, die das Übertragungsprotokoll über den PIPELINEBUS bearbeiten und als Gateway zum Clusterbus dienen. Eine entsprechende Hardwarekomponente wurde auch zum Anschluß der Steuerrechner an das Netz realisiert. Vervollständigt wird das Kommunikationssystem durch Software zum Betrieb des PIPELINEBUS und Treiberprogramme im SUPRENUM-Betriebssystem.

Nach dem Ablauf der Hauptentwicklungsphase des SUPRENUM-Projekts von 1986 bis 1989 erfolgte die Auslieferung der Cluster, so daß im Jahre 1990 am Institut ein kleines 4-Cluster-System mit vier Rechenknoten in Betrieb genommen werden konnte, in das der PIPELINEBUS integriert wurde. Nach der erfolgreichen Inbetriebnahme wurden zahl-

[2]Jedes Datenpaket enthält ein 64-Bit-Datenwort.

reiche Messungen durchgeführt, deren wesentliche Ergebnisse hier kurz zusammengefaßt werden [Ker93].

Für die Dauer der Übertragung einer kurzen Betriebssystem–Nachricht fester Länge wurden etwa 500 μs und für die Übertragung von 128 Bytes Daten etwa 2 ms gemessen. Diese erstaunlich hohen Werte werden unten näher erläutert. Die Datenrate auf dem PIPELINEBUS ergab sich zu 7,2 MByte/s und entsprach damit ungefähr dem theoretischen Wert. Für einzelne Übertragungen stimmen diese Meßergebnisse mit den am 16–Cluster-System der GMD gemessenen überein (siehe [MT92b] und [MT92a]). Im Gegensatz zu diesem Tokenring–Netzwerk erhöhen sich die Werte unter Belastung für den PIPELINEBUS jedoch nicht wesentlich, da hier auf jeder einzelnen Strecke parallel gesendet werden kann.

Eine Analyse ergab, daß der größte Teil der Übertragungszeiten auf Startzeiten (*startup-times*, vergl. Kapitel 4) bei der Bearbeitung im Betriebssystem und zum Verbindungsauf- und -abbau im Kommunikationssystem entfällt; die Datenrate spielt dagegen nur eine geringe Rolle. Im folgenden Kapitel werden daher Möglichkeiten zur Beschleunigung durch eine Optimierung der Kommunikationsprotokolle verschiedener Ebenen sowie der Verbindungsstruktur diskutiert.

3 Optimierung der Kommunikationsprotokolle

Als wichtigste Maßnahme muß eine starke Verkürzung der Startzeit gefordert werden, die den größten Teil der Kommunikationszeit bildet. Dazu ist es notwendig, ein Betriebssystem mit einem effizienten Kommunikationskern einzusetzen. Es gibt hier gegensätzliche Anforderungen: die hohe Effizienz für die angestrebten Anwendungen und die Universalität des Systems. Im Gegensatz beispielsweise zu LAN–gekoppelten verteilten Systemen ist ein Parallelrechner gewöhnlich ein räumlich konzentriert aufgebautes, homogenes Multiprozessorsystem, in dem die Teilprozesse — wie bei den angesprochenen Gitterverfahren — zumeist stark gekoppelt sind.

Es erscheint also sinnvoll, die Funktionalität der *Kommunikationsprimitiven* auf das notwendige Maß zu reduzieren und sie auf kurze Übertragungszeiten zu optimieren. Außerdem sollten Prozeßumschaltzeiten durch spezielle Maßnahmen reduziert [Mul89] oder durch das Umschalten in den Ein–Prozeß–Betrieb während der Bearbeitung des Kernteils der Algorithmen vermieden werden. Durch ein spezielles Transportprotokoll konnte im betrachteten Fall des SUPRENUM–Rechners zudem die Anzahl der zu versendenden Nachrichten pro Datenübertragung halbiert und damit die Kommunikationszeit deutlich verringert werden [Ker93].

In einem hierarchisch aufgebauten Kommunikationssystem ist eine Verbindung der Netze untereinander erforderlich, die hier durch die auf den PIPELINEBUS–Knoten realisierten Gateways hergestellt wird. Die Auswertung der Meßergebnisse zeigte, daß diese Gateways zu lange belegt und damit die Möglichkeiten für parallele Übertragungen stark eingeschränkt werden. Es wurden daher neue Varianten für das Gateway–Protokoll entworfen, die durch eine effizientere Verwendung der vorhandenen Ressourcen eine bessere Auslastung des PIPELINEBUS ermöglichen und damit zu einer höheren Leistungsfähigkeit des Gesamtsystems führen [Ker93].

Die erste, dem Prinzip der Leitungsvermittlung folgende Variante **B1** wurde für den PIPELINEBUS im Rahmen des SUPRENUM-Projekts entwickelt und berücksichtigt die dort vorgegebenen Randbedingungen. Nachdem zunächst eine Verbindung über sämtliche Teilstrecken hinweg aufgebaut und damit die Protokollsteuerwerke der beteiligten Kanäle auf den PIPELINEBUS-Knoten (PBK) belegt wurden, erfolgt die Übertragung der Daten. Abschließend wird die Verbindung wieder abgebaut, wobei mit der Rückmeldung gleichzeitig eine Quittierung der empfangenen Daten erfolgt.

Die wesentliche Motivation für den „Ende–Ende–Verbindungsaufbau" ist die Sicherstellung der Empfangsbereitschaft des Ziel–Rechenknotens. Da jedoch in einem Parallelrechner die Prozesse auf den verschiedenen Prozessoren stark gekoppelt sind, so daß Daten auf der Empfängerseite normalerweise „erwartet" werden, ist es möglich, den Verbindungsaufbau auf den einzelnen Strecken getrennt und teilweise parallel durchzuführen. In der Variante **B2** kann die Übertragung der Daten schon dann beginnen, wenn die Verbindung auf der ersten Teilstrecke aufgebaut ist. Die Daten werden in den Gateways zwischengespeichert und weitergeleitet, sobald die Verbindung auf der nachfolgenden Teilstrecke hergestellt ist.

Da die Verbindungen auf den Teilstrecken einzeln aufgebaut werden, können negative Quittungen den Verbindungsaufbau auf einer davorliegenden Teilstrecke nicht mehr abbrechen. Der sendende Rechenknoten wird demnach auch dann beginnen, die Daten zu senden, wenn die Verbindung zum Ziel nicht vollständig aufgebaut werden konnte. In diesem Fall empfängt der Gateway, bis zu dem die Verbindung hergestellt wurde, die gesendeten Daten, ignoriert sie und reagiert beim Verbindungsabbau mit einer negativen Quittung, so daß die Übertragung wiederholt werden muß. Die Vorteile dieser Protokollvariante sind kürzere Übertragungs- und Belegungszeiten der Gateways unter der meist erfüllten Voraussetzung, daß keine Fehler auftreten und der Ziel–Rechenknoten empfangsbereit ist. Der andernfalls auftretende Verlust an Bandbreite fällt demgegenüber nicht so sehr ins Gewicht, da der Einfluß der Datenrate auf die Kommunikationszeit gering ist.

Eine konsequente Weiterentwicklung ist das Protokoll **B3**, das der Durchschaltevermittlung entspricht. Analog zum Verbindungsaufbau in Variante B2 wird hier auch der Abbau der Verbindung auf jeder Teilstrecke getrennt ausgeführt. Übertragungsfehler auf den hinteren Übertragungsstrecken werden allerdings nicht mehr sofort dem Sender mitgeteilt. Der fehlerhafte Empfang oder das Ausbleiben einer Sendung wird vom Betriebssystem oder der Applikation erkannt[3] und muß dort zur Wiederholung der Übertragung oder zur Meldung an eine Fehlerüberwachung des Systems führen. Der Vorteil der Protokollvariante B3 liegt in den weiter verkürzten Übertragungszeiten für einen Datenblock auf den vorderen Strecken. Der Gateway auf der Senderseite wird damit durch eine Übertragung nicht mehr so lange belegt, so daß die Kommunikationsbandbreite eines Clusters erhöht wird.

In den beiden Verbindungsnetzen PIPELINEBUS und Clusterbus werden die einzelnen Datenpakete getrennt übertragen. Bei den bisher beschriebenen Protokollvarianten B1 bis B3, die in der aufgebauten Kommunikationshardware implementiert wurden, erfolgt in jedem Netz eine blockorientierte Übertragung. Eine grundsätzlich andere Möglichkeit

---

[3] Nach [SRC84] ist ohnehin ein Ende–Ende–Protokoll auf höchster Ebene erforderlich.

besteht nun darin, die Pakete entsprechend dem Prinzip der Paketvermittlung transparent über beide Netze und die Gateways zu übertragen. Das Blockübertragungsprotokoll wird dann zwischen dem sendenden und dem empfangenden Rechenknoten abgewickelt. Um eine eindeutige Zuordnung der einzelnen Pakete zu einem Block zu erreichen, ist aber das Paketformat zumindest des PIPELINEBUS um zusätzliche Steuerinformationen zu erweitern. Durch die verringerte Komplexität der Gateways, die dann kein aufwendiges Protokoll mehr verwalten, sondern die Pakete nur puffern und transparent weiterleiten müssen, dürfte dieser Mehraufwand jedoch ausgeglichen werden.

Der Vorteil dieses **P1** genannten Protokolls besteht darin, daß die Kanäle des Gateway nicht für die Übertragung ganzer Datenblöcke belegt werden. Dadurch können mehrere Rechenknoten eines Clusters gleichzeitig über einen Gateway mit anderen Clustern kommunizieren. Nachteilig kann sich auswirken, daß Verbindungsauf- und -abbau des Blockübertragungsprotokolls zwischen den kommunizierenden Rechenknoten genauso lange dauern wie in der Variante B1.

Die Verwendung eines hierarchischen Kommunikationssystems führt neben dem generell erhöhten Aufwand zur Abhängigkeit der Übertragungszeiten von der Position der Prozessoren im Netz. Da nach den bisherigen Betrachtungen die Datenrate nur eine geringe Rolle spielt, wurde der ausschließliche Einsatz eines PIPELINEBUS-Netzes zur Verbindung der Prozessoren untersucht. Der dafür benötigte direkte Prozessoranschluß an den PIPELINEBUS, der auch prototypisch realisiert wurde, besitzt etwa die gleiche Komplexität wie das Interface zum Clusterbus; außerdem entfallen natürlich die Gateways. Da hier jeder Prozessor einen direkten Zugang zum globalen Verbindungsnetz besitzt, ist die Anzahl der Blockierungen sehr gering.

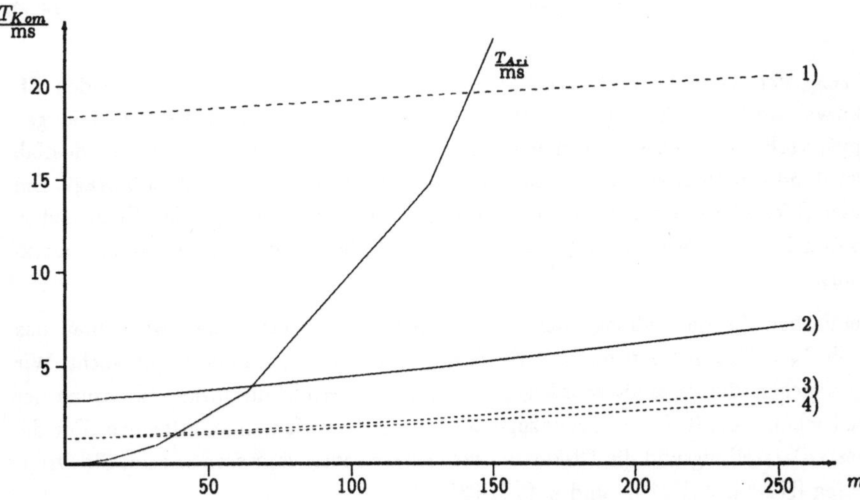

Bild 2: Rechen- und Kommunikationsaufwand für einen Mehrgitter-Algorithmus in Abhängigkeit von der Kantenlänge m

Eine detaillierte Bewertung der genannten Maßnahmen konnte nicht durch Messungen erfolgen, da nur ein kleines SUPRENUM-System mit vier Rechenknoten zur Verfügung stand. Das realisierte System und seine Alternativen wurden daher modelliert und auf einer SUN-Workstation simuliert [Ker93]. In Bild 2 sind die Ergebnisse für die Simulation des in Abschnitt 4 beschriebenen Mehrgitterverfahrens wiedergegeben. Dargestellt ist für ein zweidimensionales Gitter jeweils die Dauer einer Kommunikationsphase T_{Kom} auf einer Gitterebene in Abhängigkeit von der Kantenlänge m, wobei zum Vergleich die Rechenzeit T_{Ari} für die korrespondierende Gitterebene wiedergegeben wird. Kurve 1) zeigt die Werte für den SUPRENUM-Rechner mit dem PIPELINEBUS als oberem Kommunikationssystem. Durch die aufgrund der beschriebenen Maßnahmen mögliche Reduzierung der Startzeiten für jede Nachricht auf 50 μs kann T_{Kom} um drei Viertel reduziert werden (Kurve 2). Eine weitere Verbesserung um den Faktor 2 ergibt sich beim Einsatz der verbesserten Protokolle: Kurve 3) zeigt das Ergebnis für das transparente Protokoll P1, Kurve 4) für das nicht-hierarchische Netzwerk. In den beiden letztgenannten Fällen ist das System zudem gut skalierbar [Ker93].

4 Effizienz bei Mehrgitterverfahren

An einem idealisierten Mehrgitteralgorithmus auf der Basis einer mit dem PIPELINEBUS gekoppelten Gitterstruktur von Prozessoren soll im folgenden der Einfluß der Kommunikationsparameter und der Gittergröße dargestellt werden. Unter der Annahme einer regelmäßigen Folge von *Rechenoperationen* mit der Rechenzeit T_{Ari} und *Kommunikationsoperationen* mit der Kommunikationszeit T_{Kom} in allen Prozessoren, kann man als grundsätzlichen Wirkungsgrad des Parallelrechners die Effizienz E in bezug auf den Einfluß der Kommunikationszeit berechnen:

$$E = \frac{T_{Ari}}{T_{Ari} + T_{Kom}} = \frac{1}{1 + \frac{T_{Kom}}{T_{Ari}}}. \tag{4.1}$$

Bild 3 zeigt den Verlauf von E über T_{Kom}/T_{Ari} zum Vergleich mit den folgenden Effizienzkurven im logarithmischen Maßstab. Falls die Kommunikation die Berechnungen überlappt, verbessert sich der Wirkungsgrad (schraffierter Bereich), bis er im Idealfall einer vollständigen Überlappung bis zur Gleichheit der beiden Zeiten 100% beträgt. Ein markanter Eckwert ist sicher der Grenzwert $T_{Kom} = T_{Ari}$. In den folgenden Effizienzdarstellungen gehen wir aber von *nicht-überlappenden* Rechen- und Kommunikationsoperationen aus.

Diese einfachen Zusammenhänge werden für unser Thema interessant, wenn man das Verhältnis T_{Kom}/T_{Ari} für bestimmte Aufgaben- und Prozessorparameter untersucht. Wir wollen versuchen, die Parameterabhängigkeiten für das Beispiel der diskreten Lösung der Poissongleichung mit Hilfe der Grundzüge der Mehrgitterverfahren zu erläutern. Für die detaillierte Darstellung und die Diskussion von Alternativen verweisen wir auf die Originalarbeiten [HT82], [MFL+91] und auf [Gri93].

Als gesamtes Aufgabengebiet betrachten wir ein quadratisches zweidimensionales Feld mit einem diskreten orthogonalen Gitter von $N = n^2$ Punkten (siehe Bild 4). Die Gitterwerte seien auf dem Rand vorgegeben und im Inneren unbekannt. Die Lösung des durch die Diskretisierung erhaltenen Gleichungssystems erfolgt mit Hilfe eines sogenannten *Relaxationsverfahrens* (z. B. Jacobi, Gauß-Seidel), dessen Arbeitsweise darauf beruht, daß

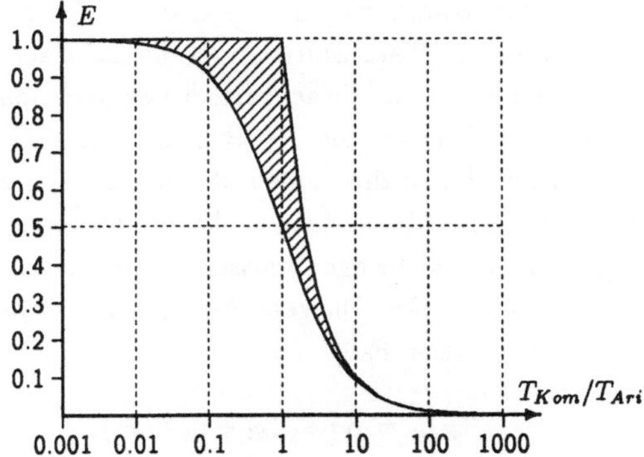

Bild 3: Wirkungsgrad in Abhängigkeit des Verhältnisses von Kommunikationszeit zu Rechenzeit

ein neuer Wert für jeden inneren Punkt durch gewichtete Mittelung des alten Werts und der vier Nachbarwerte errechnet wird. Man nähert sich der Lösung iterativ, indem die Relaxation des gesamten Feldes wiederholt wird.

Wenn diese Prozedur auf P gleiche Prozessoren verteilt wird und jeder Prozessor nur ein Teilfeld von $M = N/P$ Punkten zu bearbeiten hat, müßte die Aufgabe P–mal schneller zu lösen sein, da sie ideal parallelisierbar ist. Die Zahl der pro Gitterpunkt auszuführenden Gleitkommaoperationen nennen wir hier A_D; der Wert ist den in [MFL+91] angegebenen Verfahren entnommen und beträgt für zwei Dimensionen $A_2 = 9$ und für dreidimensionale Felder $A_3 = 13$. Kennzeichnet man die mittlere Dauer einer Gleitkommaoperation mit T_{Fl}, dann beträgt die Rechenzeit für eine Iteration über alle Punkte eines Prozessors

$$T_{Ari} = M \cdot A_D \cdot T_{Fl}. \tag{4.2}$$

Zur Bestimmung der Kommunikationszeit T_{Kom} für den Austausch der Randpunkte der Prozessorteilfelder, die durch offene Kreise in Bild 4 gekennzeichnet wurden, nehmen wir an [MFL+91], daß eine *Transportoperation* immer alle $m = \sqrt{N/P}$ Randpunkte einer Seite umfaßt (bei drei Dimensionen $m^2 = \sqrt[3]{N/P^2}$). Mit T_{Tr} als *Transportzeit* für

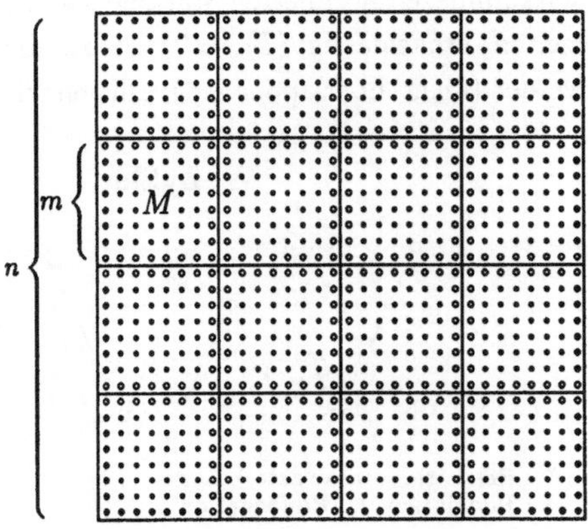

Bild 4: Beispiel für die Aufteilung eines zweidimensionalen Gitters auf Prozessoren

einen Gitterwert dauert eine Transportoperation also $m \cdot T_{Tr}$. Für jede Transportoperation kommt noch eine unvermeidbare *Startzeit* T_{St} hinzu. Nach jeder Iteration für ein Prozessor–Gitterfeld setzen wir für jede Nachbarrichtung nacheinander je eine Transportoperation an, also für zwei Dimensionen $K_2 = 4$ und für drei Dimensionen $K_3 = 6$. Aufgrund des PIPELINEBUS–Prinzips laufen alle Randwerttransporte einer Richtung in allen Prozessoren *gleichzeitig* ab, so daß wir keinen weiteren Zuschlag aufgrund der Anzahl der Prozessoren in Ansatz bringen müssen, wie es beispielsweise bei Tokenring–Kommunikationssystemen nötig wäre. Die gesamte Kommunikationszeit für eine Iteration beträgt dann im zweidimensionalen Fall

$$T_{Kom} = K_D \cdot (T_{St} + m \cdot T_{Tr}). \tag{4.3}$$

Eine Komplizierung dieser relativ einfachen Abhängigkeitsverhältnisse ergibt sich aus der Tatsache, daß das oben skizzierte einstufige Gitterverfahren bei großen Punktzahlen sehr schlecht konvergiert. Man setzt deshalb *Mehrgitterverfahren* [HT82] ein und „relaxiert" nicht nur auf der *feinsten* Gitterebene, sondern auch auf *gröberen* Gitterebenen, die im hier angenommenen Falle aus der Verdoppelung der Rasterweite der jeweils feineren Ebene entstehen. Dazu benötigt man allerdings zusätzliche Operationen für jeden Gitterpunkt, die *Interpolation* und die *Prolongation*. Die Gitterebenen werden unterschiedlich oft und in verschiedenen Reihenfolgen durchlaufen. Bild 5 zeigt den V–Zyklus und den W–Zyklus als Beispiele für Iterationszyklen. Auf der gröbsten Ebene $l = 0$ gibt es theoretisch nur noch einen Gitterpunkt pro Prozessor, so daß dann andere Verfahren angewandt werden, die in Bild 5 mit *exakte Lösung* gekennzeichnet sind. Wir berechnen daher nur die Rechen- und Transportzeiten bis zur Ebene $l = 1$.

Die gröberen Ebenen enthalten erheblich weniger zu berechnende Gitterpunkte, so daß in den Formeln für T_{Ari} und T_{Kom} (Gleichungen 4.2 und 4.3) für M und m sehr viel kleinere Werte einzusetzen sind. Da sich die Rechenzeit T_{Ari} linear mit der Zahl der Gitterpunkte $M = m^2$ verringert, die Kommunikationszeit T_{Kom} aber in erster Näherung konstant ist, wird der Anteil der Kommunikation bei den gröberen Ebenen immer stärker und damit die Effizienz immer schlechter.

Bild 6a zeigt die Effizienz für die Bearbeitung von *einzelnen Gittern* verschiedener Größe M als Funktion der auf die Gleitkommazeit normierten Startzeit T_{St}. Im oberen Diagramm werden zunächst die Transferzeiten vernachlässigt ($T_{Tr} = 0$). Bis auf die Maßstabskonstante entspricht dann jede Kurve der (nicht–überlappenden) Effizienzkurve von Bild 3 mit

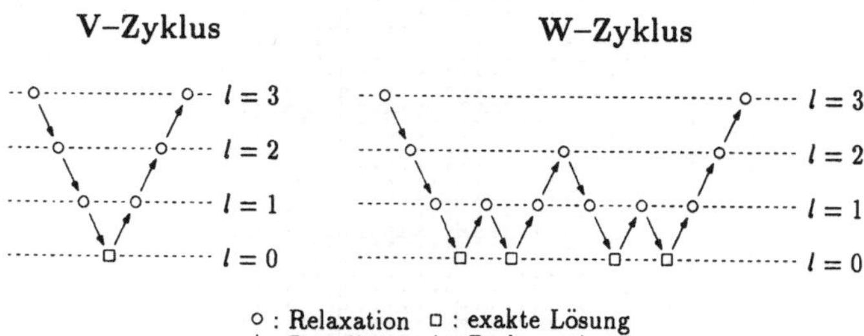

Bild 5: Struktur von Mehrgitterzyklen

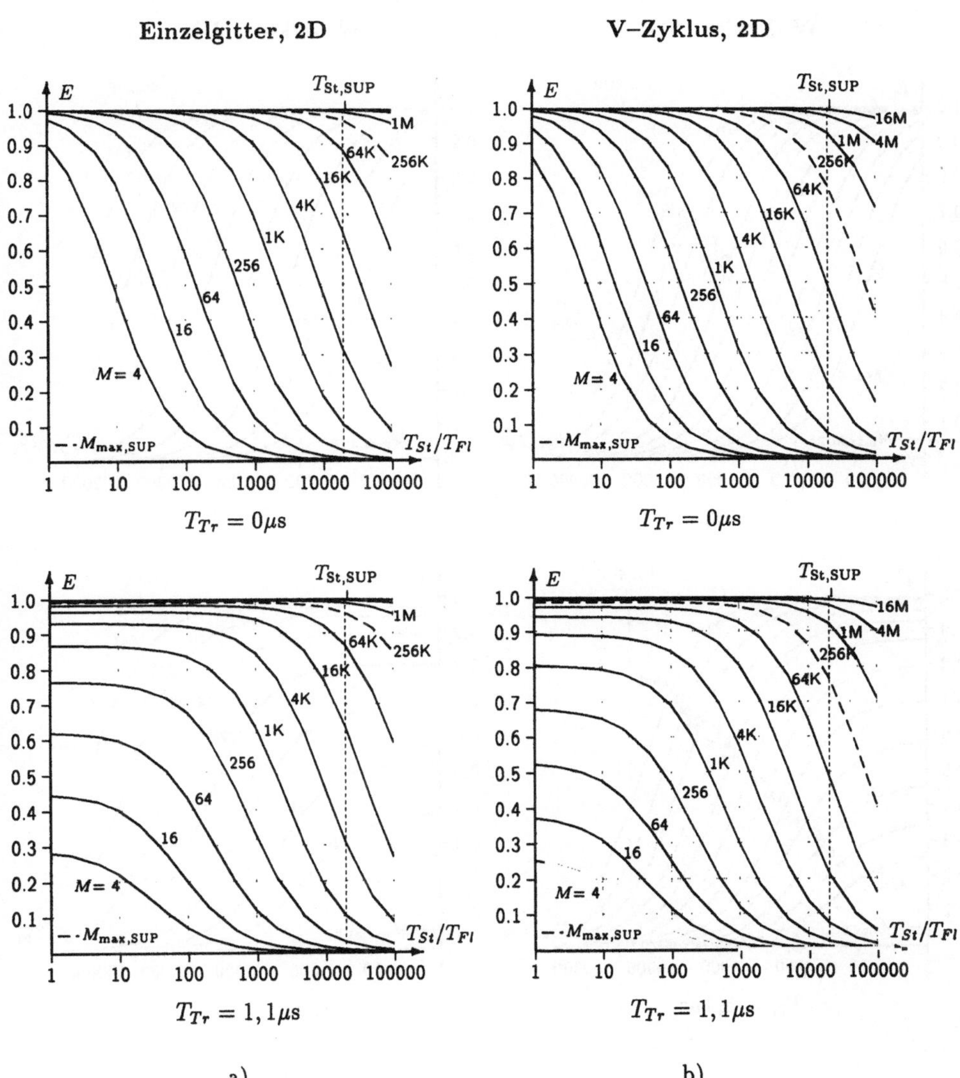

Bild 6: Effizienz in Abhängigkeit der normierten Startzeit für die Bearbeitung von Einzelgittern und V–Zyklen (Gittergröße M als Kurvenparameter)

einer gleichen Horizontalverschiebung für jeden Schritt (Faktor 4) des Gitterparameters M. Das untere Diagramm von Bild 6a zeigt zusätzlich den Einfluß der Transferzeit T_{Tr} für einen Wert von 1,1 μs, der von dem realisierten PIPELINEBUS übernommen wurde. Die typische Startzeit von SUPRENUM T_{St} = 2000 μs, normiert auf die entsprechende Gleitkommazeit T_{Fl} = 0,1 μs, wurde in diesen Diagrammen besonders markiert; ebenso die maximale Zahl der Gitterpunkte $M_{max,SUP}$, die auf der feinsten Ebene im SUPRENUM–Knoten gespeichert werden können. Wir sehen also, daß der Wirkungsgrad auf der feinsten Ebene für diese beiden Parameterwerte sehr gut ist, bei den gröberen Ebenen, deren

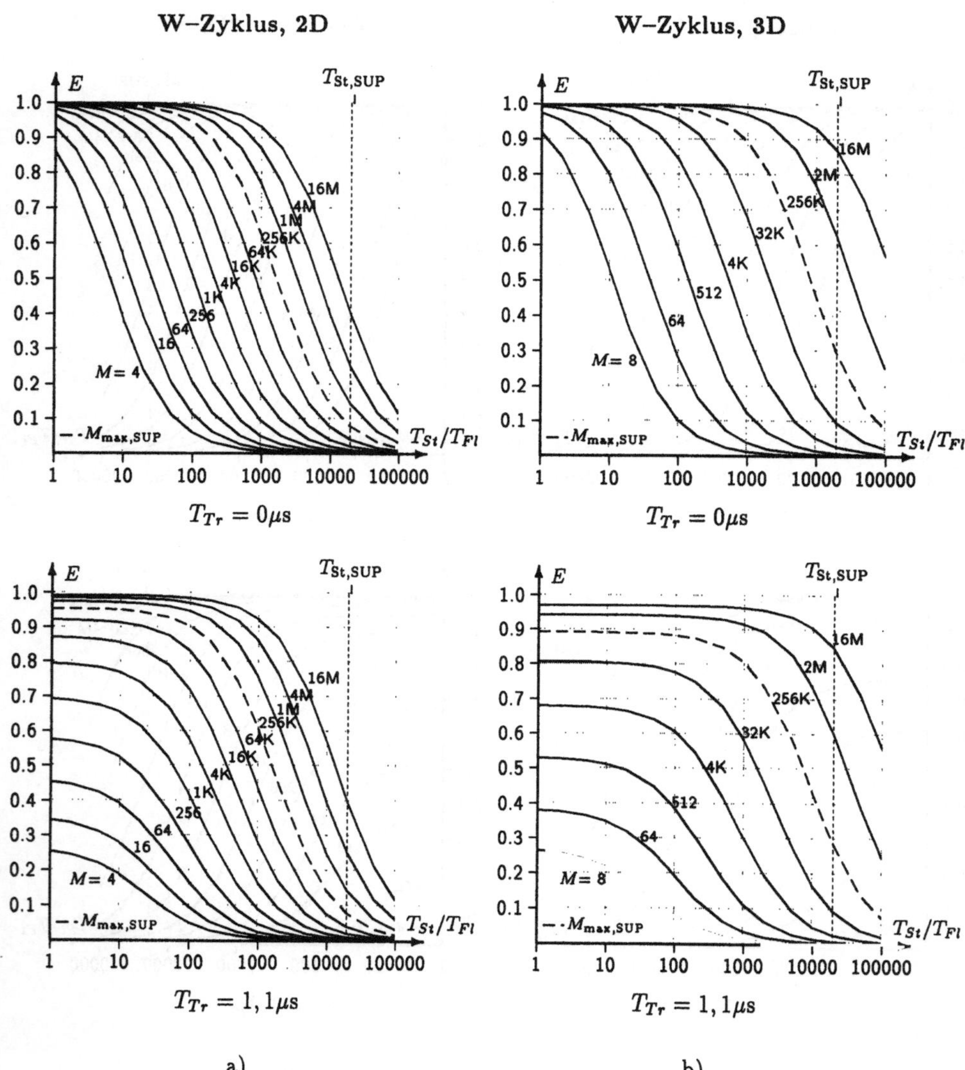

Bild 7: Effizienz in Abhängigkeit der normierten Startzeit für die Bearbeitung von W–Zyklen (Gittergröße M als Kurvenparameter)

Effizienz hier jeweils einzeln dargestellt ist, jedoch sehr schnell und sehr stark abnimmt.

Wenn nun *Mehrgitterverfahren* mit der zyklischen Benutzung verschiedener Gitterebenen angewandt werden, müssen die entsprechend gewichteten Zeitanteile aus diesen Gitterebenen berücksichtigt werden. Bild 6b und 7a zeigen die Ergebnisse für die beiden als Beispiel genannten V– und W–Zyklen im zweidimensionalen Fall. Hier kennzeichnet allerdings der Parameter M die Gitterpunktzahl der feinsten Ebene. Man kann durch Vergleich mit den Einzelgittereffizienzen in Bild 6a erkennen, daß der Verlangsamungseinfluß der gröberen Ebenen (mit der kleineren Rechenzeit für jede Kommunikation) für den Gesamtzyklus sehr stark ist, insbesondere bei den W–Zyklen, die relativ oft auf den gröberen Ebenen arbeiten.

Die Effizienzkurven für den W–Zyklus im zwei- und dreidimensionalen Fall (Bild 7a und 7b) unterscheiden sich nicht grundsätzlich: die Stufung der Punktezahlen zwischen den Gitterebenen ist im dreidimensionalen Fall 8 statt 4. Daher gibt es für die gleiche Problemgröße weniger Ebenen und Transportoperationen (die Effizienzwerte für das obere Diagramm in Bild 7b sind besser als die entsprechenden Werte in Bild 7a), jedoch ist die Anzahl der zu transportierenden Daten größer.

Man möchte daraus den Schluß ziehen, daß möglichst große Teilgebiete in jedem Prozessor *sequentiell* bearbeitet werden sollten, wozu sehr große Speicher nötig wären. Das erhöht sicher die Effizienz, widerspricht allerdings dem Grundgedanken der Parallelisierung. Wenn man jedoch nicht den Wirkungsgrad jedes einzelnen Prozessors, sondern die Beschleunigung der Gesamtarbeit (*Speedup*)

$$S(P) = E \cdot P \tag{4.4}$$

durch Parallelarbeit im Auge hat, so sollte man bei einem Problem fester Größe möglichst viele Prozessoren einsetzen, obwohl die Effizienz im oben gebrauchten Sinne abnimmt, weil ja in jedem Prozessor bei wachsender Anzahl weniger Gitterpunkte zu bearbeiten sind. In Bild 8 ist der Beschleunigungsfaktor $S(P)$ mit T_{St} als Parameter für den Fall des W–

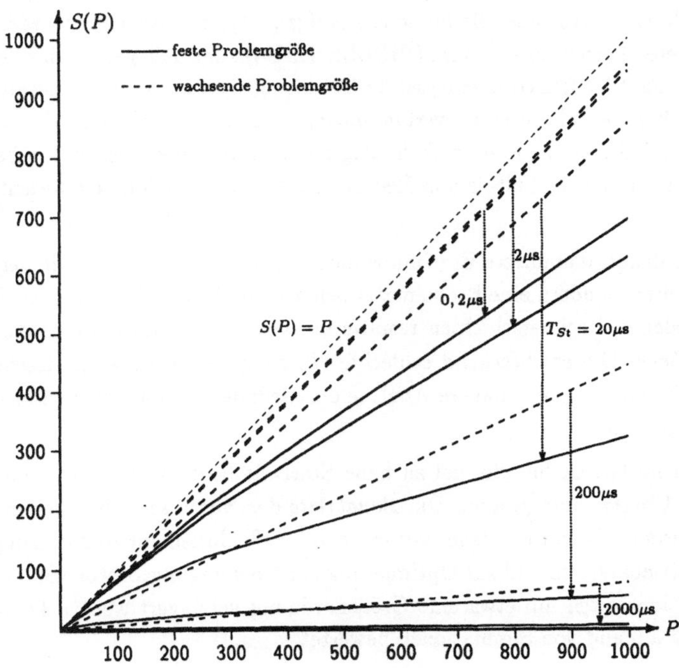

Bild 8: Beschleunigungsfaktor in Abhängigkeit der Prozessorzahl bei fester und wachsender Problemgröße

Zyklus mit endlichem T_{Tr} dargestellt. Zum Vergleich werden auch die berechneten Werte für eine mit der Prozessorzahl wachsenden Problemgröße (gestrichelte gerade Linien in Bild 8) dargestellt.

Hier kommt besonders stark zum Ausdruck, daß die Startzeiten gegenüber den bei universellen Kommunikationssystemen üblichen Werten um etwa zwei Größenordnungen kleiner sein müßten. Die Effizienzreduktion durch die endliche Transportzeit, ausgedrückt durch T_{Tr}, ist für den Wertebereich aus dem SUPRENUM-Projekt längst nicht so kritisch.

Die Zahl der genannten Einflußparameter (T_{St}, T_{Tr}, M, D, Zyklustyp) ist selbst bei den starken Idealisierungen bereits so groß, daß man in diesem Rahmen nicht alle Kombinationen darstellen und diskutieren kann. In [Gri93] erfolgt eine ausführliche Diskussion dieser Problematik.

5 Schlußfolgerungen

Der Einfluß der Kommunikationszeit - vorwiegend der *Startzeit* T_{St} - auf die Effizienz von Parallelrechnern erwies sich als unerwartet hoch. Abhängig von der Punkteanzahl des in jedem Prozessor bearbeiteten Gitters liegt der Wirkungsgrad teilweise unter 10%.

Zur Qualifikation dieses Befundes müssen wir sagen, daß wir zwar eine Aufgabe (Lösung der Poisson-Gleichung) betrachtet haben, die eine sehr starke Kommunikation zwischen benachbarten Prozessoren erfordert, die aber repräsentativ ist für eine große und wichtige Klasse von Algorithmen. Andererseits gingen wir von einer gitterförmig verbundenen MIMD-Rechnerstruktur aus, die für solche Aufgabentypen entwickelt wurde. Wir haben sogar ein oberes Verbindungssystem (PIPELINEBUS) zugrunde gelegt, das besser als das gegenwärtig bei SUPRENUM eingesetzte Tokenring-System an die Mehrgitteralgorithmen angepaßt ist — alle Nachbarverbindungen arbeiten echt parallel. Es ist auch nicht anzunehmen, daß eine modernere Technologie mit noch schnelleren und höher integrierten Schaltkreisen das Verhältnis von Rechen- zu Kommunikationszeit wesentlich ändern könnte.

Wir glauben daher, daß unsere Ergebnisse nicht nur für das hier zugrunde liegende Rechnersystem gelten, sondern eine Problematik beleuchten, die aus der isolierten Betrachtung der verschiedenen Rechnerschichten resultiert - von der *Anwenderebene* bis zur *Physikalischen Ebene*. Die erschreckend schlechte Nutzung der investierten Rechenkapazität rechtfertigt demnach eine genauere Analyse der Gründe und die Diskussion von Verbesserungsvorschlägen.

Der wesentliche Grund für die viel zu hohe Startzeit liegt in dem aufwendigen und zu universellen Übertragungssystem. Die *Bandbreite* der Busse kann bei weitem nicht ausgeschöpft werden. Es wurden daher verschiedene Maßnahmen zur Reduzierung des Overheads im Betriebssystem und zur Optimierung der Übertragungsprotokolle, mit denen die Kommunikationszeiten um etwa eine Größenordnung verringert werden konnten, vorgeschlagen und anhand von Simulationen bewertet.

In Abschnitt 4 wurde abgeschätzt, inwieweit sich quantitativ die Reduktion der Startzeit lohnt. Es zeigt sich (siehe Bild 7), daß das Verhältnis T_{St}/T_{Fl} gegenüber den SUPRENUM-Werten um etwa zwei Größenordnungen reduziert werden müßte, um auch bei mittleren Gitterpunktzahlen auf etwa 50% Wirkungsgrad (oder theoretisch vollkommene Überlappung der Transportzeiten) zu kommen. Das bedeutet, daß Feinarbeit am Betriebssystem oder an den Protokollen keine grundsätzliche Lösung des Problems bringen kann, sondern daß bis in die Hardware reichende Strukturänderungen nötig sind.

Als mögliche Kommunikationsarchitektur sehen wir ein PIPELINEBUS-System, das über unabhängig arbeitende Kommunikationsprozessoren direkt an die Rechenprozessoren angeschlossen ist. In [Gri93] wird ausgeführt, wie die Anschlußknoten strukturiert sein könnten, um die Transporte an allen Schnittstellen gleichzeitig abwickeln zu können. Dazu wird ein Betriebsmodus vorgeschlagen, in dem alle nötigen Teiltransporte für einen ganzen Mehrgitterzyklus mit den Rechenprozessen automatisch verknüpft werden. Das setzt natürlich eine hardwareunterstützte Ablaufsteuerung voraus, die – möglichst transparent für den Anwender – die Algorithmenparameter umsetzt. Sicher ist dann auch eine teilweise Überlappung von Berechnung und Kommunikation möglich.

Auf der Seite der Mehrgitteralgorithmen sind dann auch Folgerungen zu erwarten. Insbesondere könnte die intensivere Benutzung gröberer Ebenen und kleinerer Felder ermutigt werden, wenn man davon ausgehen kann, nicht durch starke Ineffizienz bestraft zu werden.

6 Literaturverzeichnis

[FHKZ88] Bernd Franke, Ralf Harneit, Axel Kern und Hans Christoph Zeidler: „The Pipeline Bus: An interconnection network for multiprocessor systems“. *Parallel Computing*, 7(3): S. 403–412, September 1988.

[FL85] Bernd Franke und Hans-Otto Leilich: „Berechnungsgrundlagen für das Datenkommunikationssystem in einem Multiprozessor für Mehrgitterverfahren“. In Ulrich Trottenberg und Peter Wypior [Hrsg.]: *Rechnerarchitekturen für die numerische Simulation auf der Basis superschneller Lösungsverfahren II*, S. 17–119. GMD, Sankt Augustin, September 1985. GMD-Studien Nr. 102.

[Fra92] Bernd Franke: *Gekoppelte Register Insertion-Ringe in Mehrrechner-Verbindungsnetzen.* Dissertation, Institut für Datenverarbeitungsanlagen der Technischen Universität Braunschweig, November 1992.

[GHH+90a] Jochen Gries, Axel Hahlweg, Ralf Harneit, Axel Kern und Hans Christoph Zeidler: „Ein leistungsfähiges Kommunikationssystem für Multiprozessorsysteme“. In *Architektur von Rechensystemen, Tagungsband der 11. ITG/GI-Fachtagung, München*, S. 159–167, März 1990.

[GHH+90b] Jochen Gries, Axel Hahlweg, Ralf Harneit, Axel Kern und Hans Christoph Zeidler: „Superrechner für numerische Anwendungen (SUPRENUM), Teilvorhaben: Pipelinebus“. Schlußbericht, Institut für Datenverarbeitungsanlagen der Technischen Universität Braunschweig, April 1990.

[GHH+91] Jochen Gries, Axel Hahlweg, Ralf Harneit, Axel Kern und Hans Christoph Zeidler: „High Performance Communication for MIMD Supercomputers“.

In *Proceedings of the 1991 International Conference on Supercomputing (ICS'91), Köln*, S. 20–27, Juni 1991.

[Gil88] Wolfgang K. Giloi: „SUPRENUM: A trendsetter in modern supercomputer development". *Parallel Computing*, 7(3): S. 283–296, September 1988.

[Gri93] Jochen Gries: *Ein Parallelrechner–Verbindungssystem für die hocheffiziente Bearbeitung von Gitterverfahren.* Dissertation, Institut für Datenverarbeitungsanlagen der Technischen Universität Braunschweig, Juni 1993.

[HT82] Wolfgang Hackbusch und Ulrich Trottenberg [Hrsg.]: *Multigrid Methods.* Springer–Verlag, Berlin, 1982. Lecture Notes in Mathematics 960.

[Ker93] Axel Kern: *Entwurf, Bewertung und Optimierung eines Kommunikationssystems für Parallelrechner.* Dissertation, Institut für Datenverarbeitungsanlagen der Technischen Universität Braunschweig, Januar 1993.

[Liu78] Ming T. Liu: „Distributed Loop Computer Networks". *Advances in Computers*, 17: S. 163–221, 1978.

[MFL+91] Oliver A. McBryan, Paul O. Frederickson, Johannes Linden, Anton Schüller, Karl Solchenbach, Klaus Stüben, Clemens–August Thole und Ulrich Trottenberg: „Multigrid Methods on Parallel Computers — A Survey of Recent Developments". *IMPACT of Computing in Science and Engineering*, 3: S. 1–75, 1991.

[MT92a] Hermann Mierendorff und Ulrich Trottenberg [Hrsg.]: *Ergänzende Leistungsmessungen für technisch–wissenschaftliche Anwendungen auf dem SUPRENUM–System.* GMD, St. Augustin, Juli 1992. Arbeitspapiere der GMD 669.

[MT92b] Hermann Mierendorff und Ulrich Trottenberg [Hrsg.]: *Leistungsmessungen für technisch–wissenschaftliche Anwendungen auf dem SUPRENUM–System.* GMD, St. Augustin, März 1992. Arbeitspapiere der GMD 624.

[Mul89] Sape J. Mullender [Hrsg.]: *Distributed Systems*, Kapitel 3: Interprocess Communication, S. 37–64. Addison–Wesley, Wokingham (England), 1989.

[SRC84] J. H. Saltzer, D. P. Reed und D. D. Clark: „End–To–End Arguments in System Design". *ACM Transactions on Computer Systems*, 2(4): S. 277–288, November 1984.

[Tro85] Ulrich Trottenberg: „Zur SUPRENUM–Konzeption". In Ulrich Trottenberg und Peter Wypior [Hrsg.]: *Rechnerarchitekturen für die numerische Simulation auf der Basis superschneller Lösungsverfahren II*, S. 315–328. GMD, Sankt Augustin, September 1985. GMD–Studien Nr. 102.

Analysis and application of local/global multistage interconnection architectures

Josef Giglmayr
Heinrich-Hertz-Institut für Nachrichtentechnik Berlin GmbH
Einsteinufer 37, D-1000 Berlin 10

Abstract

Multistage interconnection networks (MINs) with nearest-neighbour interconnects are the simplest interconnection scheme within the class of local interconnects. (Local means the distance of communication is bounded by a constant.) The global interconnection scheme is generated by shuffling the switches and is thus isomorphic to the local interconnects. The generation of local/global interconnects by holographic elements allows to utilize the large space-bandwidth product of optics. In the frequency domain, tuning a laser to regularly spaced frequency channels and interchanging data of nearest-neighbour channels represents the simplest organization of laser tuning. The local/global interconnection schemes are extended to any dimension of the interconnected data set and the multistage architectures (=interconnects+switches) are analysed and compared with shuffle nets.

1. Introduction

The local interconnection of data is a challenge in many fields of communication and computation. The nearest-neighbour interconnection of data, processes and processors is the simplest local interconnection scheme. The generation of local interconnects by holographic elements allows to apply the massive parallelism of optics by means of a large space-bandwidth product.[1,2] But for some algorithms a global interconnection scheme which offer similar advantages is needed. Therefore, the global interconnection scheme has been introduced by shuffling the switches.[3]

In the frequency domain data/subscribers may be interconnected by links composed of tunable lasers, detecting diodes, tunable filters and buffers, respectively. Then tuning the laser to the regularly spaced frequency channels and interchanging data of nearest-neighbour channels allows the simplest organization of laser tuning.[4] The prize one has to pay for this simplicity is a large number of stages. However the number of stages may be reduced considerably by increasing the dimension of the interstage pattern and switches.[5]

2. Basic Elements

The generation of regular interconnects is based on an appropriate number system. For example, shuffle interconnects are based on the mixed radix number (MRN) system and its binary representation may be applied to implement the selfrouting principle. For switches of size $k \times k$ ($k \geq 4$) we may leave the binary system and ap-

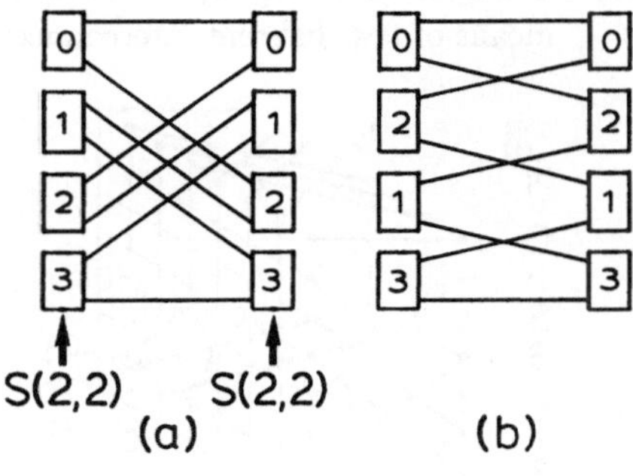

Fig. 1. Shuflling the switches of global and local interstage pattern.

ply a k-ary number system for the generation of interconnects and for the control.[3] In contrast, the topology of local interconnects is simple and for their generation no number system is needed except for selfrouting which operates with regard to the state of the most significant bit (MSB).

For the sake of completeness the generation of interconnects is briefly described. Let us number the paths of the 1-D local pattern $L(N)$ where $N \geq 6$ by the n-tuple ($n \geq 1$) of a k-ary number $(x_{n-1}, x_{n-2}, ..., x_j, ..., x_0)$ where $k = 2^d$ and d is the dimension of the interconnected data, respectively. Then the local interconnects are described by:

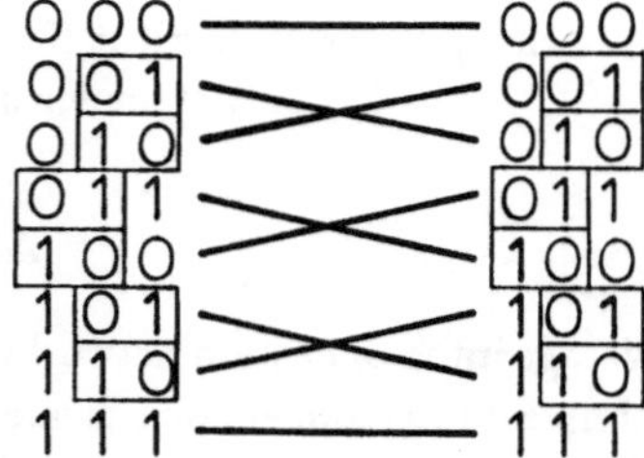

Fig. 2. Exchange operation.

$$(x_{n-1}, x_{n-2}, ..., x_j, ..., x_0) \longrightarrow (x_{n-1}, x_{n-2}, ..., x_j, ..., x_0 \oplus x_j) \tag{1}$$

where $\oplus$ means the exclusive or operation. For d-dimensional local interconnects Eq.(1) may be applied to any of the d coordinates or we may apply Eq.(1) to the transformed local interconnects.

There exist several advantages for 2-D local/global interconnects (numbered in the sequence of our interest):

(1) Reduction of the number of stages for the rearrangeable nonblocking interconnection (Section 3)

(2) Reduction of the number of different (nonzero) deflection angles:

$$\alpha_i = arctan(d_i/d_h) \tag{2}$$

where d_i is the index displacement (skew) of the ith path and d_h is the horizontal distance between arrays (Fig. 3)

(3) Reduction of the interconnection length (packaging) of the ith path according to:

$$l_i = d_h\sqrt{1 + (d_i/d_h)^2} \tag{3}$$

(4) Utilization of a large space-bandwidth (SBW) product of an optical system by means of few different interconnects.[1,2,3]

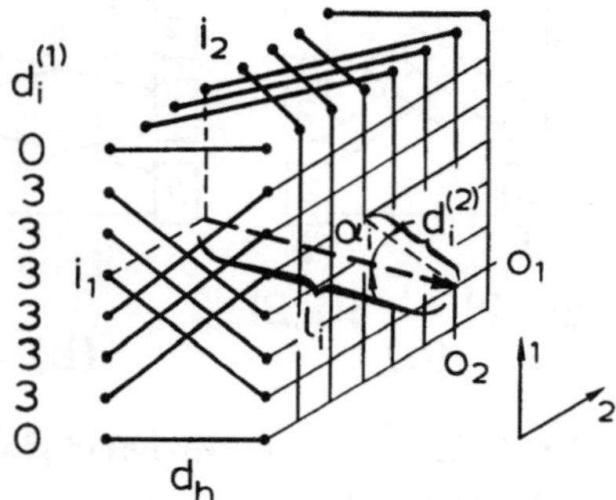

Fig. 3. 2-D global interconnection pattern $G_{2-D}(8,8)$. $d_i^{(2)} = \sqrt{(i_1 - o_i)^2 + (i_2 - o_2)^2}$ where (2) means 2-D and $i_{1,2}$ and $o_{1,2}$ are the input/output coordinates. For shuffles (i, o) has to be chosen according to the MRN system.

Local/global interstage (=link stage+switch stage) patterns may be extended into two directions:

- Neighbourhood classes[3] and
- Higher dimensions.[5,6]

For example, neighbourhood classes of local interconnects means the interconnection of modules/switches with its 1st neighbour, 2nd neighbour etc. The corresponding results for global interconnects are described by shuffling the modules (Fig. 1). This interconnection scheme is of interest for signal processing and allows to cover a broad range of algorithms. Neighbourhood classes of local interconnects are of general interest for photonics (overlay structure in Fig. 4).

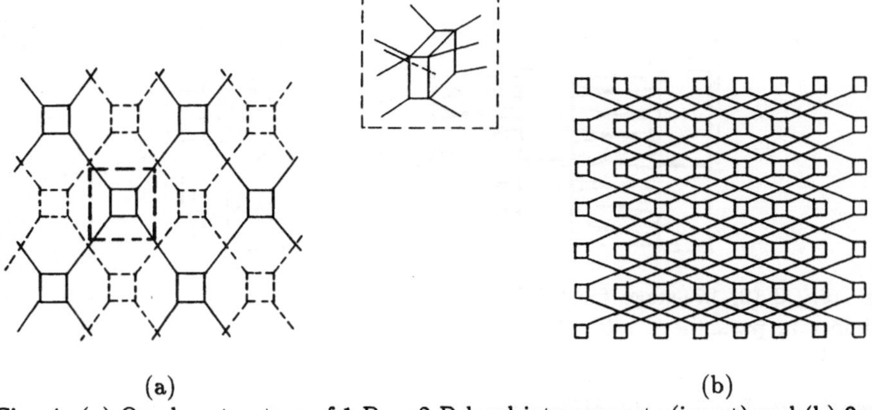

(a) (b)

Fig. 4. (a) Overlay structure of 1-D or 2-D local interconnects (insert) and (b) 2nd neighbour local interconnects.

Higher dimensional local/global interconnects exist similar to shuffles.[5,6] They may be applied to signal processing (2-D lay-out of d-dimensional interconnects)[3] as well as to the multiplexing of data described by space-frequency interconnects.[5]

3. Local Multistage Interconnection Networks

Local interstage patterns may be composed to a local MIN which provides the desired permutations.

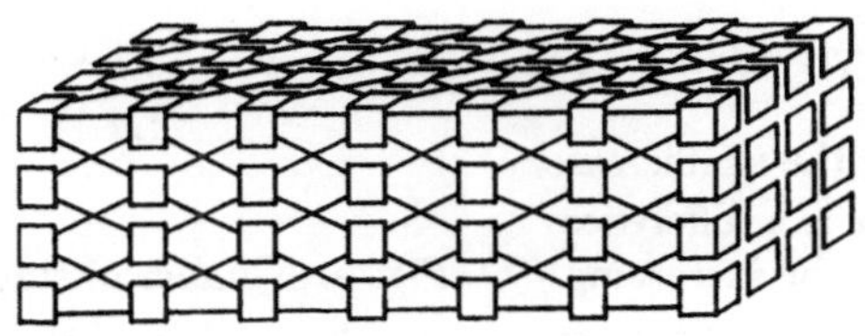

Fig. 5. Local multistage interconnection network for the interconnection of 8×8-data arrays [$L_{2-D}(8,8)$ interstage pattern, 4×4-switches].

A 1-D local MIN is rearrangeable nonblocking if and only if (iff) the number of stages (NS) is:

$$NS \geq 2N/k - 1 \qquad (4)$$

where N is the number of input/output lines and k is the size of the switches. Eq.(4) also applies for a 2-D local MIN with N^2 inputs and 4×4-switches.

Result 1: The switch algorithm for a $k \times k$-switch applies sorting.

This is well known for shuffle nets. For data sets of size 4^d the shuffle and the local/global interconnects are equal and thus sorting is the algorithm for the $2^d \times 2^d$-switches ($d \geq 1$). The 3-stage MIN in Fig. 6 is in accordance with Eq.(4). For 2×2-switches the switch setting is 0 for the bar state and 1 for the cross state. Thus an algorithm has to be found which routes data through the MIN in Fig. 6. This MIN may be redrawn by applying Eq.(4) to the 8 × 8-switches, then to the 4×4-switches etc. (see the inserts in Fig. 6).

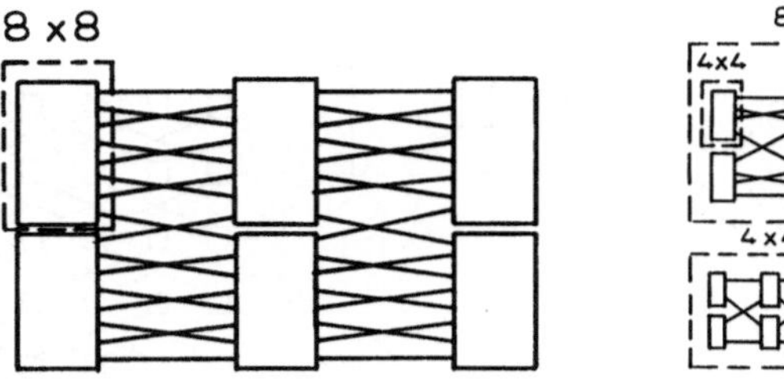

Fig. 6. 3 (9, 27)-stage local MIN (number in paranthesis refers to the inserts).

Result 2: Local/global MINs are competitive to the shuffle nets for the interconnection of data cubes of size $\leq 8^d$ for $d \geq 3$ (assuming an efficient routing algorithm exists).

Proof: Throughout Fig. 7 the number of stages (NS) is presented for both cases. For the interconnection of cubes of size 4^d both cases equals topologically and thus the extension of Eq.(4):

$$NS \geq 2\sqrt[d]{N^2/k} - 1. \qquad (5)$$

gives results equal to the shuffle case. For larger cubes there is a difference which may be reduced by increasing the dimension and the size of the switches, respectively.

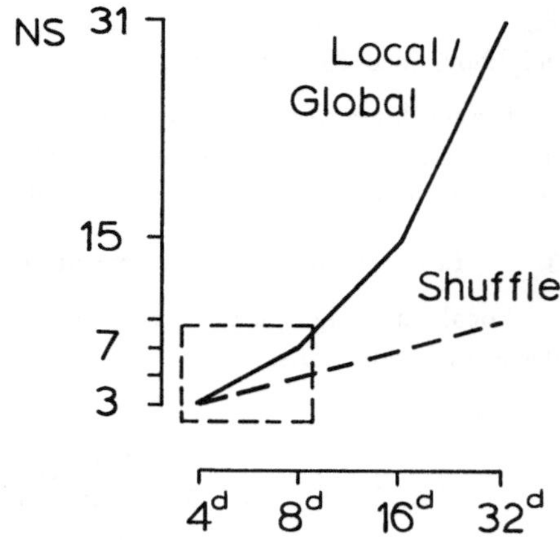

Fig. 7. Number of stages (NS) for shuffle and local/global MINs.

4. Architectural properties

In the following, MINs are assumed to be implemented in the frequency domain where arbitrary dimensional architectures are obtained by reorganizing the 3rd coordinate (frequency scale). In the following, the location and geometry of the subdivided switches is described.

Throughout the paper the d-dimensional local/global architecture is described by the following quantities (k refers to switches of size $k \times k$):

(1) Switch spacing (d_k)

(2) Total number ($d_{total\,\sum|k}$)

(3) Average number ($\overline{d}_k$)

(4) Maximum number ($d_{max|k}$) and

(5) Effective number of crossed channels ($d_{\sum|k}$).

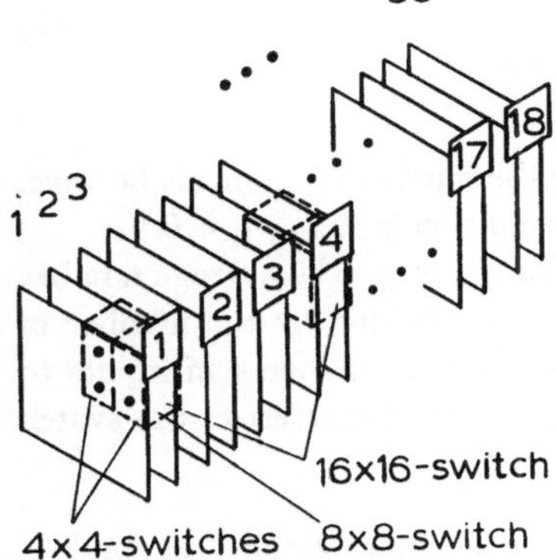

Fig. 8. Spatial arrangement of subdivided switches (4-D switching cube for the interconnection of 6^4 data).

The organization of local interconnects in the frequency domain is simple which is shown in Fig. 9. Subdivided switches are distributed at the frequency domain (Fig. 8) and each subdivided switch is located in different 3-D, 4-D etc. cubes. The 1st 3-D cube contains 8×8- switches and in the case of a 4-D space-frequency pattern the 2nd 8×8-switch is located at another 3-D cube and both are composed to a 16×16-switch (Fig. 8).

The subdivided switches have to be interconnected in order to avoid blocking. For establishing interconnections in the frequency domain one has to cross several channels de-

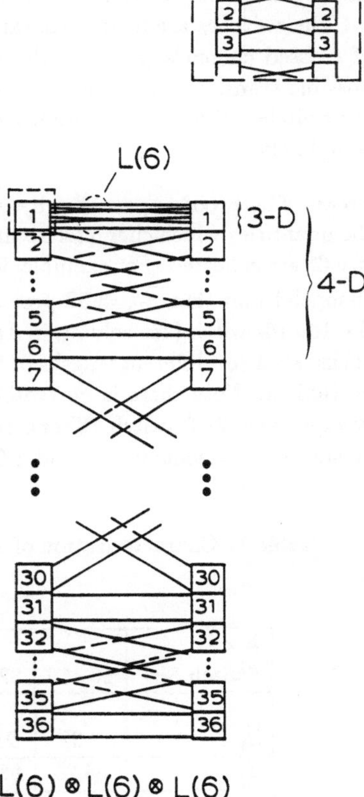

Fig. 9. Organization of 5-D space-frequency interconnects.

pendent on the size of the switches and on the size of the interconnected data arrays.

Result 3: Let us assume the interconnection of cubes of size N^d where $N \geq 6$ and $d \geq 3$. Let us further denote the number of channels between the two $k/2 \times k/2$-switches by the switch spacing (Fig. 8). Then, assuming the number of N channels on each link the switch spacing is:

$$d_k = N \times d_{k/2} + N - 2 \tag{6}$$

with the initial conditions $d_8=0$ (multiplexing on arrays), $d_4 = 0$ (vectors) and $d_2=0$ (fibers), respectively.

The total number of crossed channels arising during the operation of a $k \times k$-switch is described by:

$$d_{total \sum|k} = 2 \times d_{total \sum|k/2} + \sum_{i,j=1}^{2^{d-3}} \alpha_{ij} \tag{7}$$

where $d \geq 6$, $k = 2^d$ and α_{ij} are integers representing the number of channels between the subdivided switches (Appendix C). The initial condition is $d_{total \sum|8} = 0$.

The switches are further characterized in the following way. The average number of crossed channels per link ($\bar{d}_k$) is computed ($d_{total \sum|k}$ divided by the number of possible transitions N_k) and this quantity multiplied by the number k of inputs to the switch is the effective number of crossings ($d_{\sum|k}$) which characterizes the switch completely.

Proof: The proof is provided by verifying the equations. In particular, in Table 1 the quantities which characterize the switches for the interconnection of data cubes of size 6^d are collected. For example, for the 16×16-switch $d_{total \sum|16}$=20 units (=crossed channels) und thus $\bar{d}_{16}$=3.33 providing $d_{\sum|16}$=53.28 which completely characterizes the 16×16-switch (1st column in Table 1). The spacing between subdivided switches of size $k \times k$ for different lengths of the frequency coordinate $N^{(3)}$ ($=6^{d-2}$) is presented in Table 2. Note there is no switch spacing for the 8×8-switch (array), 4×4-switch (vector) and 2×2-switch (fiber), respectively. All results have been computed by means of the scheme in Appendix C.

Table 1: Characterization of switches for the interconnection of 6^d cubes.

$k \times k$-Switch Size	16×16	32×32	64×64	128×128	256×256
$\bar{d}_k$	3.33	21.42	124.66	970.64	7777.24
$d_{\sum\|k}$	53.28	685.44	7978.24	124241.92	1990973.4
$d_{max\|k}$	6	42	258	1554	9730
N_k	6	28	120	496	2016
d_k	4	28	172	1036	6620

Table 2: Switch spacing which verifies Eq.(6) (6^d data cubes).

Switch	Dimension	Switch Spacing														
16×16	4-D								4							
32×32	5-D							4	28	4						
64×64	6-D					4	28	4	172	4	28	4				
128×128	7-D	4	28	4	172	4	28	4	1036	4	28	4	172	4	28	4

The subdivided switches have to be interconnected in order to avoid blocking. The subdivision of the switches into sub-switches of size 4×4 (multiplexing on arrays) and 2×2 (vectors), respectively, is illustrated in Fig. 8. Two 4×4 (2×2)-switches are located at subsequently arranged frequency channels and thus in this case no crossing occurs (Fig. 10). The spacing (=number of channels) between the subdivided switches for various lengths of the frequency scale has been presented in Table 2.

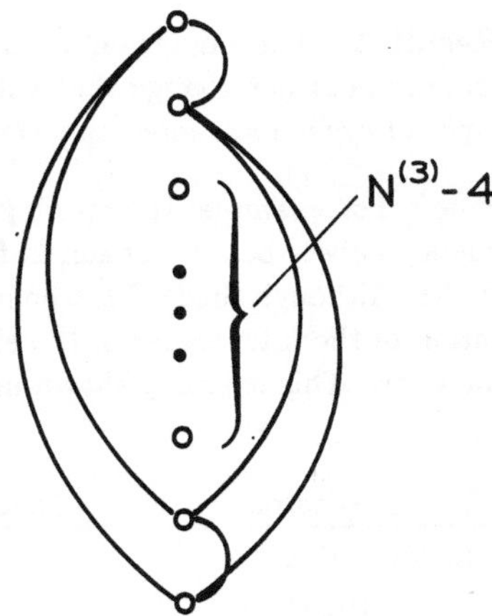

Fig. 10. 16×16-switch.

5. Application

The application discussed in the following is the interconnection of data in the space-frequency domain by laser tuning. The number of $N^{(1)} \times N^{(2)}$ links and each link carrying $N^{(3)}$ frequency channels is assumed. For each link and each stage a tunable laser, a detecting diode, a tunable filter and buffers are assumed. However for a more complete design study a buffer management has to be established and analysed.[7]

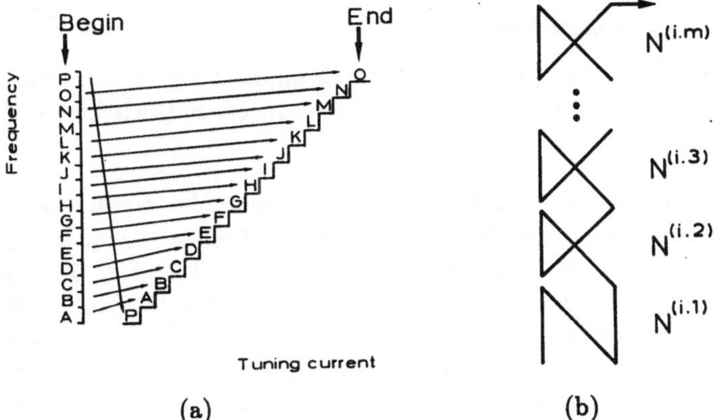

Fig. 11. (a) Scheme of laser tuning and (b) number of crossed channels $\sum_k N^{(i,k)}, i \geq 3$.

The laser is tuned to a channel, the signal (represented by the modulation of the carrier) is transmitted to the next stage and stored in buffers. This procedure is applied to any channel of a link until all signals are forwarded to the next stage.

Result 4: For a fixed data set, by increasing the dimension of the architecture the number of crossed channels decreases during the generation of space-frequency interconnects.

Proof: This result is simply caused by the reduction of the number of stages because of dimension-dependent switches of size $k \times k$ where $k = 2^d$.

Result 5: The implementation of local (L) interconnects in a cyclic-local (C-L) manner does not change the switch spacing. However by the generation of parallel pipes of cyclic-local interconnects (P-C-L) the spacing increases.

Proof: For example, the spacing between subdivided switches on a 4-D space frequency cube - being 4 channels for L and C-L - changes to 10 and 16 channels for P-C-L. Although the P-C-L scheme is the best from the point of view of the implementation of the interconnects, the effort for the interconnection of subdivided switches increases. This is briefly shown in the following Fig. 12 and verified in Table 3.

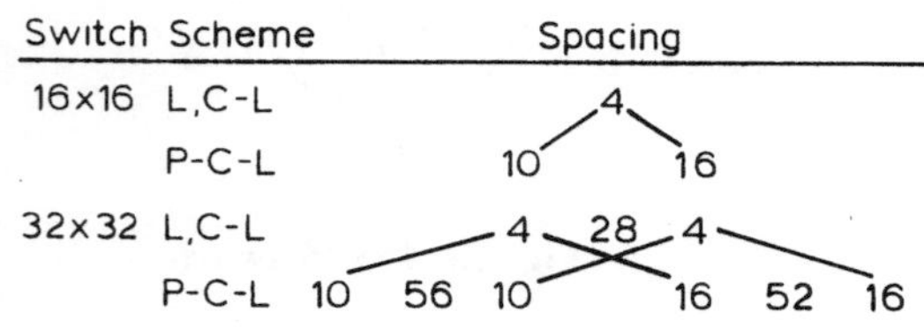

(a)

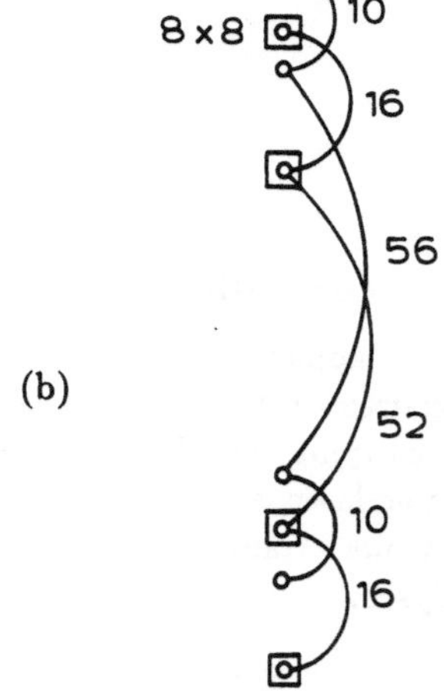

(b)

Fig. 12 (a) Switch spacing for local (L), cyclic- local (C-L) and parallel cyclic-local (P-C-L). (b) 32×32-switch for P-C-L.

Result 6: There exists no balance for the total number of crossed channels with regard to the dimension of the interconnected data set.

Proof: The proof is provided by means of the Examples 1 and 2. In particular, the superposition of the number of crossings for interconnects and switching in Tables 3 and 4 verifies this result.

Example 1: The number of 6^4=1296 data are interconnected in a rearrangeable non-blocking manner. Selfrouting works proper if and only if (iff) a 4-D lay-out is chosen. Then the switch size is 16×16 and the number of stages is 5 (Fig. 13). We have 24 crossing per link, 24×36=864 crossings per stage and a totality of 4×864=3456 crossings for the generation of local (L) interconnects in the frequency domain. For frequency switching (L and C-L) the total number of crossings is 5×81×53.28≈21578. All the other results are in Table 3. The P-C-L switching result is a weighted superposition of d_{16}=10 and d_{16}=16, respectively (Fig. 13).

Table 3 (F for frequency):

Data Set: 6^4=1296			
Scheme	Presentation	F-Interconnects	F-Switching
L	Figs. 1, 4, 5, 9	3456	21578.4
C-L	Fig. 11 (a)	4320	21578.4
P-C-L	Fig. 13 (b)	4320	55821.7

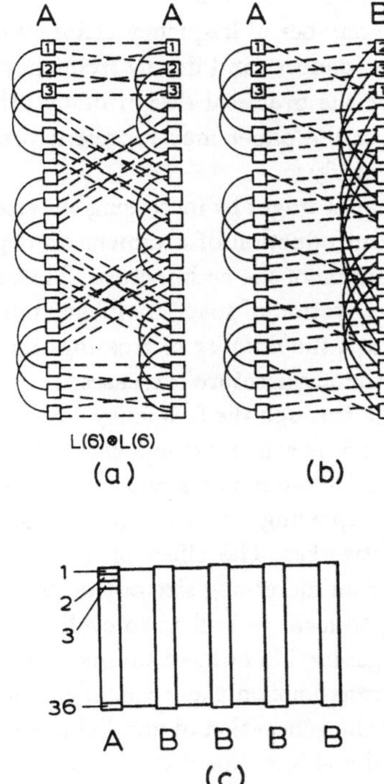

Fig. 13. (a), (b) Top view of space-frequency cubes (2 stages) for L in (a) and P-C-L in (b) , (c) Top view of a 5-stage MIN.

The framework presented is finally applied throughout Example 2 where the interconnection of data cubes of size 6^d ensures the proper operation of selfrouting.[5]

Example 2: The number of 6^6=46656 data are interconnected by local space-frequency patterns. Then 2-D, 3-D and 6-D lay-outs are possible. Quantities of interest are collected in the following.

Table 4:

Data Set	6^6=46656		
Dimension	2-D	3-D	6-D
Switch Size	4×4	8×8	64×64
Stages	215	18	5
Crossings:			
Interconnects	-	110160	25920
Switches	-	0	29×10^6

6. Conclusions

Our aim was to leave the shuffle environment but arrive at well defined interconnection topologies for arbitrary large systems. The organization of laser tuning is simplest if data are exchanged between nearest-neigbour channels. Also the components may be simple and uniform in this case. The arising interconnection topology is within the class of local interconnects. (Local means the distance of communication is bounded by a constant.) The prize for this simple organization is the large number of stages for the nonblocking interconnection.

Throughout the paper the number of frequency channels crossed during the generation of space-frequency interconnects and during frequency switching is the chosen design objective. However for the practical design many other quantities are of interest. Therefore the results of the paper may represent properties of the proposed systems rather than a design study.

The reduction of the number of stages by increasing the size of the switches is a well established strategy. By the introduction of a dimension-dependent switch size this strategy is related to the dimension of the architecture. Thus the number of frequency channels crossed during the generation of space-frequency interconnects reduces if the dimension increases. In contrast, the number of crossings during frequency switching increases if the dimension of the architecture increases.

Tuning the laser by running through the frequency scale in one direction generates a variant of local networks which is called cyclic-local. Cyclic-local interconnects are topologically equivalent to local interconnects and the performance of the proposed optical frequency division multiplexing system may be evaluated by means of local multistage interconnection networks. The effect of an increase of crossed channels during frequency switching for an increasing size of the switches is recognized if laser tuning is organized according to local as well as to cyclic-local interconnects. Unfortunately, in both cases the organization of laser tuning is complicated because of the numerous back and forward transtions on the frequency scale. The most appropriate organization of laser tuning is the generation of parallel pipes of cyclic-local networks. Although in this case an additional increase of the number of crossed channels occurs during frequency switching. However efficient selfrouting algorithms have still to be developed.

Appendix

The sum of skews and the maximum sum of skews of the Kronecker product (KP) of local interconnects and the computation scheme of switch interconnects is presented in the following. Throughout the Appendix for the reason of a simplification N means the length of the 3rd (multiplexing on arrays), 2nd (vectors) and 1st coordinate (fibers).

(A)

Given the KP of 2nd order the sum of skews is:

$$d_{\sum}^{(2)} = (N-2)(2+N^2) \tag{8}$$

and similar for $m = 3$:

$$d_{\sum}^{(3)} = (N-2)(2\times(2+N^2)+N^4). \tag{9}$$

The general equation is transparent from m=4:

$$d_{\Sigma}^{(4)} = (N-2)(2 \times (2 \times (2 + N^2) + N^4) + N^6). \tag{10}$$

providing:

$$d_{\Sigma}^{(m)} = (N-2)(2 \times (2 \times (2 \times \cdots (2 + N^2) + N^4) + N^6) + \cdots + N^{m+2}). \tag{11}$$

Results which verify Eqs.(8) to (13) are presented in Table 5.

(B)

The maximum of the sum of skews of the KP of local/global interconnects of mth order is described by a simple recurrence equation (KP of mth order means the KP of m permutation matrices):

$$d_{max}^{(m)} = N \times d_{max}^{(m-1)} + 1 \tag{12}$$

with the initial condition $d_{max}^{(1)}$=0. But we may also obtain $d_{max}^{(m)}$ from a geometric progression:

$$d_{max}^{(m)}(N) = (N^{m+1} - 1)/(N-1). \tag{13}$$

Note the results for global interconnects are twice the results for local interconnects.

Table 5: Verification of Eqs.(8) to (13).

N	$d_{\Sigma}^{(2)}$	max $d^{(2)}$	$d_{\Sigma}^{(3)}$	max $d^{(3)}$
6	152	7	5488	43
8	396	9	25368	73
10	824	11	81632	111
12	1460	13	210280	157

(C)

The computation scheme is presented for a 32×32-switch interconnected by local (L) or cyclic-local (C-L) patterns. The scheme of the switch characteristics starts with the switch spacing d_k=28 (=number of channels between the subdivided pairs) and ends up with the maximum switch spacing (42):

	1	5	1	
	28	29	34	35
1				
	29	30	35	36
5				
	34	35	40	41
1				
	35	36	41	42

The numbers in the forgoeing computation scheme increase with regard to $d_k + 1$, i.e. d_8+1=1 and d_{16}+1=5.

References:

1. N. Davidson, A. Friesem and E. Hasman, 'On the limits of optical interconnects,' Appl. Opt. **31**, 123-134 (1992).

2. G. E. Lohman and K.-H. Brenner, 'Space-variance in optical computing systems,' Optik **89**, 123-134 (1992).

3. J. Giglmayr, 'Comparison of regular 3-D interconnections,' Topical Meeting on Optical Computing, June 29 - July 1, Minsk, 1992, Proc. SPIE **1806**, pp.109-120.

4. J. Giglmayr, 'Translation of laser tuning experiments into networks,' Topical Meeting on Photonics in Switching, Optical Society of America, Palm Springs, March 15-17, 1993, OSA Technical Digest, paper PTuD3, pp.136-139.

5. J. Giglmayr, 'Selfrouting in multistage interconnection networks based on nearest-neighbour interconnects,' Multigigabit Fiber Communication Conference, 11-16 July, 1993, San Diego, Proc. SPIE **2404**, paper 15.

6. J. Giglmayr, 'd-dimensional (d $\geq$3) shuffle interconnections,' Appl. Opt. **31**, 1695-1708 (1992).

7. M. J. Karol, 'Queueing in optical packet switches,' in *Proceedings of Multigigabit Fiber Communications Conference*, September 8-9, 1992, Boston, Proc. SPIE **1787**, pp.192-199.

Eine neue HW-Architektur für BS2000-Systeme

M. Köhler
Siemens Nixdorf Informationssysteme AG
System Unit BS2000
Otto-Hahn-Ring 6, 81730 München

Abstract

Die Bürocomputer C70 sind leistungsfähige Rechner für kommerzielle und technisch-wissenschaftliche Anwendungen. Sie werden vom Betriebssystem BS2000 unterstützt. Die Modellreihe C70 ist lieferbar als Uni-, Dyadic- und Tripleprozessorsystem. Die Ein/Ausgabebusse nehmen bis zu 15 Ein/Ausgabe-Module auf. Die integrierten 3,5" Festplatten haben im Vollausbau eine Kapazität von 95 GByte. Durch modernste CMOS-Technologie kann die BS2000-CPU in 3 ASIC's realisiert werden (Hauptprozessor + 2 Coprozessoren). Im Detail werden erläutert:

o Die CPU-Architektur: Hauptprozessor und Coprozessoren.

o Die 4-stufige Zweistrom-Befehlspipeline.

o Die Arbeitsweise des 3-stufigen Cache im Multiprozessorsystem.

1 Einleitung

BS2000-Computer wurden lange Zeit ausschließlich in ECL-Technik entwickelt. Mit steigender Gatterdichte in den ECL-Schaltkreisen mußte sogar die Wasserkühlung eingeführt werden. Nach und nach, zuerst bei den Ein/Ausgabe-Prozessoren und Kanälen, hielt die CMOS-Technik Einzug in die BS2000-Rechner. Die hohe Integration der CMOS-Technik erlaubt seit einigen Jahren auch die Realisierung der BS2000-CPU in 3-5 ASIC's und damit inkl. Cache auf einer Baugruppe. Da inzwischen mehrere Ein/Ausgabekanäle und Gerätesteuerungen jeweils auf einer Baugruppe untergebracht werden können, lassen sich heute auch im mittleren BS2000-Leistungsbereich sehr kompakte Bürocomputer mit Pipeline- und Multiprozessor-Architektur bei sehr gutem Preis/Leistungsverhältnis realisieren.

Aufgrund von immer feineren ASIC-Strukturen (1996/97: 0,25 µm) und damit weiter steigenden Gatter- und embedded RAM-Dichten, werden CMOS-Prozessoren in wenigen Jahren die ECL-Prozessoren auch im oberen Leistungsbereich verdrängen.

2 Technischer Aufbau des Systems C70

Die Bürocomputer C70 des Systems 7.500 sind leistungsfähige Rechner für kommerzielle und technisch-wissenschaftliche Anwendungen. Sie werden vom universellen Betriebssystem BS2000/OSD unterstützt. OSD steht für Offenes System und bedeutet, daß Betriebssystem und die C70 unter Beachtung von weltweiten Standards entwickelt wurden bzw. weiterentwickelt werden, die die Zusammenarbeit in herstellerunabhängigen Client/Server-Architekturen erlauben.

Durch die Verwendung von hochintegrierten CMOS-Halbleiterbausteinen, durch kompakte Einbautechnik und integrierte Peripheriegeräte sind die Bürocomputer C70 besonders raum- und energiesparend sowie geräuscharm. Kleine Anlagenkonfigurationen können in normaler Büroumgebung eingesetzt werden.

Mit der CMOS-basierten Modellreihe C70 beginnt der mittlere BS2000-Leistungsbereich. Die Modellreihe C70 übernimmt, mit wesentlich kleineren Abmessungen und mit deutlich verbessertem Preis/Leistungsverhältnis, die Nachfolge der bisherigen ECL-Reihe H60.

Die C70 ist lieferbar als Uni-, Dyadic- und Tripleprozessorsystem. Der Hauptspeicher kann durch 1-3 Module von 32 MByte bis auf 384 MByte ausgebaut werden. Dabei werden 16 MBit Bausteine verwendet.

Bild 1 zeigt die Maximalkonfiguration des Systems C70. Die Modellreihe C70 verfügt über die für BS2000-Bürocomputer charakteristische Busarchitektur mit einem internen Systembus und je nach Konfiguration 1-4 Ein-/Ausgabebussen. Am internen 8 Byte breiten Systembus mit einer Datenrate von 60 MByte/s arbeiten 1-3 Verarbeitungsprozessoren (CPU), 1-3 Speichermodule (MU) und 1-2 BUS-Steuerungen (BCU). Die BUS-Steuerungen treiben die Ein-/Ausgabebusse.

Die Ein-/Ausgabebusse vom Typ A erlauben eine Datenrate von 30 MByte/s und es können jeweils bis zu 6 Kanalmodule mit je 2 Kanalschnittstellen eingebaut werden. Es sind Blockmultiplex-Kanäle und IPI-Kanäle verfügbar. Über die Blockmultiplex-Kanäle wird die Hochleistungsperipherie aus dem Mainframe-Bereich, wie Systemdrucker, Plattenspeicher- und Magnetbandkassetten-Subsysteme angeschlossen. Über diese Kanalschnittstelle erfolgt auch eine LAN-Vernetzung oder - mittels Vorrechner - die Anbindung an das TRANSDATA-Netz.

An die IPI-Kanäle sind Strangsteuerungen des integrierten Plattenspeichersystems ein- oder zweipfadig anschließbar. Pro Pfad wird eine maximale Datenrate von 10 MByte/s erreicht. Die integrierten Festplatten in 3,5 Zoll Technologie haben eine Kapazität von 1,7 GByte je Laufwerk. Im Vollausbau werden 95 GByte erreicht.

Der Ein-/Ausgabebus vom Typ B ist Bestandteil des Service- und Konsolprozessors SKP und bietet maximal 9 E/A-Module für den Anschluß von kostengünstigen Peripheriegeräten, die teilweise in den C70-Schrank integriert wurden. Der SKP ist ein autonomes Prozessor-Subsystem, das aus einem Serviceprozessor und einem Konsol- und Ein-/Ausgabeprozessor besteht.

Der Serviceprozessor dient zum Ein- und Ausschalten von Systemkomponenten, zur Initialisierung, zur Überwachung und Fehlerdiagnose sowie zur Wartung des Systems. Der Konsol- und Ein-/Ausgabeprozessor enthält einen leistungsstarken SINIX-Mikroprozessor und den Ein-/Ausgabebus vom Typ B. In seiner Funktion als Konsolprozessor steuert er die Kommunikation zwischen Betriebssystem und der Bedienperipherie bzw. dem Teleservice. In seiner Funktion als Ein-/Ausgabeprozessor führt er die über den Ein-/Ausgabebus B laufenden EA-Aufträge der Verarbeitungsprozessoren und des Serviceprozessors aus.

Bis zu 9 Ein-/Ausgabesteuerungen sind am E/A-Bus Typ B betreibbar und können direkt im Schrank des Systems C70 untergebracht werden. Dabei handelt es sich um:

- o Mehrfachperipherie-Adapter zum Anschluß der integrierten Geräte des SKP: Magnetband-Kassettengerät (0,25 Zoll), Diskettenlaufwerk (3,5 Zoll), Plattenspeicher (648 MByte).
- o Kassetten-Adapter zum Betrieb des integrierten Magnetbandkassettengerätes.
- o Terminaladapter für Datenstationen und Drucker.
- o Magnetband-Adapter für Magnetbandgeräte.
- o TAK- bzw. AKA-Adapter zum Anschluß von Terminal-Anschlußkonzentratoren.
- o LAN-Prozessoren zur Anbindung der C70 an ein Ethernet-Netz.
- o WAN-Prozessoren zur Kopplung der C70 mit anderen Rechnern über öffentliche oder private Netze.

3 Technologie

Das System C70 wurde in moderner CMOS-Technologie realisiert. Im Verarbeitungsprozessor (CPU) kommen hochintegrierte Anwender-Spezifische Integrierte Schaltkreise (ASIC) mit bis zu 118.000 Gattern zum Einsatz. In den Speichermodulen (MU) werden DRAM-

Bausteine mit 16 MBit Kapazität verwendet. Die Baugruppen haben das Multibus I- bzw. Multibus II-Format.

Die höchsten Ansprüche an die Technologie stellt der Verarbeitungsprozessor. Deshalb wurden, stellvertretend für die C70, die Technologie-Parameter der BS2000-CPU aufgeführt:

Technologie des BS2000-Prozessors:

Single Board CPU: Format 22 x 23 cm

9 Signallagen, 80 µm Leiterbahn-Breite

6 CMOS-ASIC's (0,7 µ) im CPGA-Gehäuse, max. Die Size: $[17,5\ mm]^2$

480 000 Gatterfunktionen plus 165 kBit embedded RAM

CPU-Zyklus: 40 ns, Verlustleistung Board: ca. 60 Watt.

Übersicht: CPU-ASIC's				
Name	Funktion	Gatter	RAMs [kb]	Signalpins
PLU	Hauptprozessor	118000	43	329
EXU	Coprozessor 1	92000	25	347
FPU	Coprozessor 2	92000	---	158
CFC	Cache Function Controller	50000	95	332
CDT	Cache Data Controller	85000	---	332
TCU	Timing Control Unit	45000	2,5	196

4 Architektur des Prozessorkomplexes

Die Baugruppe des Verarbeitungsprozessors trägt die BS2000-CPU und das 3-stufige Cache-System (Bild 2). Die BS2000-CPU besteht aus 3 ASIC's; es sind dies der Hauptprozessor (PLU), der Coprozessor für Dezimal- und Privilegierte Befehle (EXU) sowie der Gleitpunkt-Coprozessor (FPU). Der Coprozessor (EXU) besitzt einen Mikroprogrammspeicher (CM), der in 9 diskreten SRAM-Bausteinen realisiert wurde.

Das 3-stufige Cache-System besteht aus dem First Level Cache (FLC), aus dem Second Level Cache (SLC) und aus dem Befehls-Cache (IC). Die Steuerung für FLC und SLC wurde in zwei weiteren ASIC's (CDT, CFC) untergebracht, über die auch der Anschluß zum Systembus hergestellt wird. Das Befehls-Cache, samt Steuerung, befindet sich im Hauptprozessor (PLU). In diskreten SRAM-Bausteinen wurden realisiert: die Datenbuffer für First Level Cache (FLC) und Second Level Cache (SLC) sowie Original und Kopie des SLC-Tag/Flag-Feldes. Ein sechster, nicht dargestellter ASIC enthält die Timer, die Taktversorgung und stellt die Verbindung zum Serviceprozessor her.

Die Verbindung der ASIC's untereinander erfolgt im wesentlichen über ein BUS-System, bestehend aus dem Registerbus (REGBUS), dem Datenbus (DBUS) und aus dem Adressenbus (ABUS). Über den ABUS laufen i.w. die reellen Speicheradressen zum Second Level Cache und über den Systembus zum Hauptspeicher. Über den 8 Byte breiten DBUS werden i.w. die Lese- und Schreibdaten für das Second Level Cache und via CDT-ASIC und Systembus für den Hauptspeicher transferiert. Der REGBUS ermöglicht den Austausch von Registerinhalten zwischen den 3 Prozessoren. Der Mikroprogrammspeicher und die RAM-Felder der Caches sind über bidirektionale Leitungsbündel mit den zugehörigen ASIC's verbunden.

Das BS2000 ist ein Mainframe-Betriebssystem und basiert auf einem Befehlssatz von ca. 200 Assemblerbefehlen. Beim Entwurf der CPU bestand die wesentliche Aufgabe darin, den CISC-Befehlssatz, unter Einhaltung der vorgegebenen Performance-Ziele, auf weitgehend unabhängige Prozessoren zu verteilen. Dies bedeutet, bei ebenfalls vorgegebenen Technologie-Parametern, wie Die-Size und Pinzahl, einen möglichst kurzen Maschinenzyklus und möglichst wenig Zyklen pro Befehl zu erreichen.

4.1 BS2000-CPU

Die BS2000-CPU besteht, ähnlich wie bei Mikroprozessor-Architekturen, aus einem Hauptprozessor und aus zwei Coprozessoren, die unabhängig bzw. im Verbund den BS2000-Befehlssatz verarbeiten.
Der Hauptprozessor (PLU) ist eine RISC-Maschine, komplett Hardware-gesteuert und besitzt eine 4-stufige Befehls-Pipeline. Die Aufgabe des Hauptprozessors besteht in der Ausführung von 53 logischen und arithmetischen Festpunktbefehlen im RR- und RX-Format. Zum zweiten arbeiten Pipeline-Stufe 1 und 2 auch für die Coprozessoren, d.h.: der Hauptprozessor führt die Befehlsbereitstellung, die Befehlsdecodierung, die Speicheroperanden-Adreßberechnung inkl. Adreßübersetzung für alle BS2000-Befehle aus. Aus diesem Grund wurden folgende HW-Resourcen im Hauptprozessor implementiert: das 4 KByte große Befehls-Cache, die 16 Mehrzweckregister, ein kleiner assoziativer Adreßübersetzungsspeicher mit 16 Einträgen, das 3-Operanden-Adreßrechenwerk, eine schnelle Einheit zur Verknüpfung von RR- und RX-Operanden sowie ein Schreibpuffer zum Zwischenspeichern von Ergebnissen, die in das Speichersystem zu schreiben sind.
Pipeline-Stufe 1 und 2 wurden zweifach ausgelegt, was die parallele Verarbeitung von zwei Befehlsströmen nach bedingten Sprungbefehlen erlaubt. Die Doppelbefehlsverarbeitung, die das Verarbeiten einiger wichtiger Befehle in effektiv null Zyklen ermöglicht, wird in Kap. 6 erläutert. Im Ergebnis benötigt der Hauptprozessor PLU für "seine" Befehle jeweils nur einen bzw. null Maschinenzyklen.
Die Aufgabe des Coprozessors (FPU) besteht in der Ausführung der 52 Gleitpunktbefehle mit einfacher, doppelter und erweiterter Genauigkeit; zusätzlich führt er die 20 SAF-Befehle aus. (Die Scientific Arithmetic Facility SAF ist die Verifikationsnumerik für Berechnungen mit gesicherter Genauigkeit).

Der Gleitpunkt-Coprozessor ist ebenfalls vollständig Hardware-gesteuert und enthält den Gleitpunktregistersatz sowie 4 spezialisierte Rechenwerke. Das Addierwerk übernimmt die Ausführung der Addier-, Subtrahier-, Compare- und Rundungsbefehle im kurzen und langen Format sowie das Normalisieren der Operanden bei Gleitpunkt-Multiplikation und Division. Das Multiplizierwerk enthält eine Multipliziermatrix für 28x56 Bit. Das Dividierwerk liefert bei Operanden im kurzen und langen Format 5 Bit Ergebnis pro Zyklus. Das Extended-Werk führt für erweiterte Operanden und für SAF-Operanden die Multiplikation und Division aus. Bei der Multiplikation werden pro Zyklus 4x116 Bit verarbeitet, bei der Division entstehen 3 Ergebnisbit pro Zyklus. Bei HW-Störungen kann das Extended-Werk die Aufgaben der drei anderen Gleitpunktwerke übernehmen. Die Verarbeitung der Gleitpunktbefehle ist relativ performant: Ladebefehle benötigen einen Zyklus, Addieren/Subtrahieren/Vergleichen/Multiplizieren werden in 2-3 Zyklen ausgeführt und für die Division sind je nach Operandenlänge 8-16 Zyklen erforderlich.

Die Aufgabe des Coprozessors (EXU) ist es, die restlichen BS2000-Assemblerbefehle und die Sonderroutinen auszuführen. Es sind dies i.w. die logischen und die dezimalen SS-Befehle sowie die ausschließlich dem Betriebssystem vorbehaltenen privilegierten Befehle, zu denen beispielsweise die Ein-/Ausgabebefehle gehören. Sonder-Routinen sind Abläufe wie die Interrupt-Routine, das Urladen, die ESA-Adreßübersetzung, der Betrieb der Virtuellen Maschine oder die Maschinenfehlerbehandlung. Da es sich hierbei um teilweise sehr komplexe Befehle bzw. Abläufe handelt, wurde der Coprozessor (EXU) mit einer komfortablen Mikroprogrammsteuerung ausgerüstet. Der aus 9 diskreten SRAM's bestehende Mikroprogrammspeicher hat 32 K Mikrobefehle zu je 64 Bit. 8 Stackebenen erleichtern Verzweigungen und Unterprogrammaufrufe in den Mikroprogrammen. Das Verarbeitungswerk des Coprozessors (EXU) hat eine Verarbeitungsbreite von 64 Bit und verfügt über folgende Hardware-Einrichtungen:

- o 64 Bit ALU (Arithmetisch/Logische Einheit)
- o 64 Bit Shifter
- o Multiplizierwerk 32x16 Bit
- o 6 schnelle Arbeitsregister
- o Registerspeicher mit 64 Einträgen à 64 Bit
- o Spezial-HW zur Beschleunigung komplexer Befehle.

Das Lesen von Speicheroperanden bzw. das Schreiben von Ergebnissen in das Speichersystem erfolgt über den FLCADR-BUS und den DBUS. Die Verarbeitung der Befehle innerhalb des Coprozessors (EXU) erfolgt im 2-stufigen Pipeline-Betrieb.

Die Architektur der Modellreihe C70 ist gegenüber der XS-Architektur, die Funktionen wie die 31 Bit-Adressierung bietet, um die ESA-Adressierung erweitert. Diese ermöglicht je Task außer einem 2 GByte-Adreßraum für Programme und Daten zusätzlich eine Vielzahl von 2 GByte-Adreßräumen für Daten. Auch diese neuen Funktionen wurden im Coprozessor (EXU) realisiert.

4.2 Cache-System

Der Verarbeitungsprozessor der C70 hat ein 3-stufiges Cache-System bestehend aus dem Befehls-Cache, dem First Level Cache und dem Second Level Cache (Bild 3). Der Hauptspeicher (MU) stellt die 4. Speicherhierarchiestufe dar. Bezüglich der Speicherdaten ist das Cache-System jedoch nur 2-stufig, da im Befehls-Cache nur Befehlscode eingetragen wird. Das 4 KByte große Befehls-Cache (IC) wurde über embedded RAM's im Hauptprozessor-ASIC realisiert. Das IC besteht aus einer einzigen Cache-Bank und hat eine Blockbreite von 8 Byte. Die Tag/Flag-Felder samt Steuerung wurden ebenfalls im Hauptprozessor untergebracht.

Das 256 KByte große First Level Cache (FLC) wurde in diskreten SRAM's realisiert. Wie das Befehls-Cache besteht auch das FLC aus einer einzigen Cache-Bank und hat eine Blockbreite von 8 Byte. Die Flag-Bits und die FLC-Steuerung sind im CFC-ASIC, die Tag-Felder sind in diskreten SRAM's untergebracht.

Das Second Level Cache (SLC) hat eine Kapazität von 1 MByte. Sowohl der Cache-Buffer als auch die Tag/Flag-Felder wurden per SRAM's realisiert, während die Steuerung im CFC-ASIC untergebracht wurde. Das Second Level Cache ist in 4 Bänke gegliedert. Da beim Laden des SLC aus dem Hauptspeicher 8x8 Byte über den Systembus transferiert werden, beträgt die Blockbreite 64 Byte. Zusätzlich gibt es noch eine SLC-Tag-Kopie, deren Bedeutung in Kapitel 5 erläutert wird.

Für die Realisierung eines 3-stufigen Cache-Systems beim Verarbeitungsprozessor der C70 sprachen mehrere Gründe:

- o Das Second Level Cache führt zu einer Verbesserung der effektiven Lesezugriffszeit, da bei Miss im First Level Cache, jedoch Hit im SLC, die CPU nur für 5 Zyklen den Wait-Zustand einnimmt, während für Lesen aus dem Hauptspeicher mindestens 20 Wait-Zyklen erforderlich sind.
- o Zum zweiten wird durch das SLC der Systembus entlastet. Dies gilt in besonderem Maße bei Schreibvorgängen, da das SLC nach dem Store In-Verfahren arbeitet. Dies ist speziell bei Multiprozessor-Konfigurationen wichtig.
- o Zum dritten ermöglicht das Second Level Cache der CPU, daß sie auch bei belegtem Systembus, in der Mehrzahl der Fälle autark weiterarbeiten kann. Aus Sicht der Ein-/Ausgabekanäle führen die Second Level Caches der CPU'en zu einer Verbesserung der mittleren Datenrate.
- o Die Einführung des relativ kleinen, aber sehr schnellen Befehls-Caches in den Hauptprozessor, erlaubte einen relativ

kurzen Maschinenzyklus bzw. die Einsparung einer 5. Pipeline-Stufe.

- o Ein separates Befehls-Cache führt darüberhinaus zu einer Entkopplung von Haupt- und Coprozessoren, da parallele Lesezugriffe auf Befehle und Daten ermöglicht werden.
- o Die Realisierung eines einbänkigen First Level Caches wirkt sich auch hier positiv auf den Maschinenzyklus bzw. die Pipeline-Stufenzahl aus. Der negative Effekt auf die Cache-Trefferrate, ist bei der relativ großen Kapazität von 256 KByte recht gering.

5 Arbeitsweise des Cache-Systems

5.1 Ablauf der Lesezugriffe

Lesezugriffe zum Speichersystem werden direkt aus derjenigen Cache-Stufe bedient, die die verlangten Daten enthält (Bild 3). In der Hierarchie niedriger angeordnete Stufen werden hierbei jeweils parallel zum eigentlichen Speicherzugriff, d.h. zum Laden des Befehls-Caches oder des Lesedatenregisters in den Coprozessoren beschrieben. Um schnelle Zugriffe zum First Level Cache (FLC) zu ermöglichen, werden bei jedem Zugriff bereits Daten aus dem FLC übernommen, bevor das Ergebnis der Hit/Miss-Erkennung vorliegt. Die Hit-Miss-Prüfung erfolgt erst parallel zur Verarbeitung der Lesedaten. Ergibt die Prüfung, daß kein Hit vorliegt, versetzt die Cache-Steuerung die BS2000-CPU in den Wait-Zustand und bewirkt damit, daß die Weiterverarbeitung der fälschlich übernommenen Lesedaten abgebrochen wird. Liegt nun wenigstens im Second Level Cache (SLC) oder im Last Miss Buffer (LMB) ein Hit vor, so werden die Daten direkt aus dieser Cache-Stufe zum jeweiligen Empfänger übermittelt und zusätzlich in das FLC eingetragen. Danach wird die vorher abgebrochene

Verarbeitung der Lesedaten bzw. die Befehlsbereitstellung erneut gestartet.

Liegt in keiner Cache-Stufe ein Hit vor, müssen die gewünschten Daten über den Systembus aus dem nachgeordneten Hauptspeicher angefordert werden. Während der Wartezeit auf die Lesedaten werden zunächst die im LMB gespeicherten Daten, die dem letzten Cache-Miss zuzuordnen sind, in das SLC übertragen. Anschließend werden die über den Systembus eintreffenden Lesedaten in den LMB übernommen und an die anfordernde Einheit übermittelt.

Das Second Level Cache ist ein Store In-Cache. Da bei einem Store In-Cache ein Block, auf den ein Schreibzugriff erfolgte, nur jeweils in dem betreffenden Cache vorhanden und gültig ist, müssen bei der Substitution eines solchen "written into" -Blocks die ausgelagerten Daten in den Hauptspeicher zurückgeschrieben werden. Hierzu werden vor der Übernahme der LMB-Daten in das SLC, die im SLC ursprünglich gespeicherten Daten in den Swap-Buffer (SWB) übernommen. Von dort werden sie dann, sobald der Systembus nach dem Transfer der Lesedaten frei ist, in einem gesonderten Schreibzyklus (Swapping) in den Hauptspeicher übertragen.

5.2 Ablauf der Schreibzugriffe

Bei Schreibzugriffen seitens der CPU werden die Schreibdaten grundsätzlich in das FLC eingetragen, ohne daß das Ergebnis der Hit-Miss-Prüfung abgewartet wird. Stellt sich heraus, daß ein Hit nicht vorlag, so wird von der Cache-Steuerung durch Modifikation der Tag/Flag -Einträge die Datenkonsistenz wieder hergestellt. Bei einem SLC-Hit werden die Schreibdaten zusätzlich zum Eintrag in das FLC in das SLC übernommen und der betreffende Block wird als "written into" gekennzeichnet. Bei der Mehrzahl der Schreibzugriffe ergibt sich ein Hit im SLC und der Schreibvorgang ist nach dem Eintragen der Schreibdaten in das SLC abgeschlossen, d.h. Systembus und Hauptspeicher bleiben unbehelligt. (Analog wird bei Hit im LMB verfahren).

Nur wenn in relativ seltenen Fällen der adressierte Block im SLC nicht vorhanden ist, wird die Anforderung als "Lesen Block" an den Hauptspeicher weitergeleitet. Beim Eintreffen der Lesedaten werden diese mit den zu schreibenden Bytes gemischt und sowohl in den LMB als auch in das FLC eingetragen.

Beim Schreiben auf einen Eintrag, für den ein Hit im Befehls-Cache vorliegt, wird der Konflikt von der Cache-Steuerung erkannt und durch Ungültigsetzen des betreffenden Eintrages im Befehls-Cache bereinigt. Bei einem erneuten Befehlslesen auf die betroffene Adresse werden dann die modifizierten Daten aus einer höheren Cache-Stufe in das Befehls-Cache geladen und es wird der modifizierte Befehl ausgeführt.

5.3 Anforderungen externer Prozessoren (Multiprozessor-Betrieb)

Da bei einem Speicherzugriff einer beliebigen, an den gemeinsamen Systembus angeschlossenen Komponente nicht vorausgesetzt werden kann, daß die zu lesenden bzw. zu überschreibenden Daten im bzw. nur im Hauptspeicher resident sind, muß jedes SLC den Systembus laufend überwachen und prüfen, ob er von einer Anforderung betroffen ist (snooping). Hierzu ist zunächst festzustellen, ob ein Hit vorliegt. Anschließend ist allen beteiligten Komponenten der jeweilige Cache-Status anzuzeigen. Diese notwendige Hit-Miss-Prüfung erfolgt an einer eigenen TAG-Kopie, ist daher unabhängig von parallel laufenden CPU-Anforderungen an das SLC möglich und führt folglich nicht zu einer Behinderung der CPU. Im Hit-Fall wird die Beeinträchtigung der CPU dadurch minimiert, daß im Normalfall die Daten vom Speicher gesendet bzw. in den Speicher geschrieben werden und das Aufrechterhalten der Datenkonsistenz durch Ungültigsetzen von Cache-Einträgen erreicht wird. Lediglich bei Zugriffen auf von einer CPU modifizierte Blöcke muß der zugeordnete Cache-Speicher die Daten auf den Systembus schalten.

Um die Anzahl der Zugriffe, die über den Systembus abgewickelt werden, gering zu halten und damit sowohl die Busauslastung als auch die CPU-Leistung zu optimieren, wurde ein Datenkonsistenzschema gewählt, bei dem Daten und Befehle in mehreren Caches gleichzeitig gültig sein können. Lediglich bei einem Schreibzugriff auf solche als "shared" markierte Blöcke muß in den anderen Caches der Eintrag für ungültig erklärt werden, was die CPU durch das Einholen der Schreibberechtigung über den Systembus veranlaßt.

6 Zweistrom-Befehlspipeline

6.1 Prinzipieller Ablauf eines Maschinenbefehls

Im Hauptprozessor der BS2000-CPU wurde eine Zweistrom-Befehlspipeline realisiert. Die Zweistrom-Pipeline der C70 bedeutet Mehraufwand an Hardware und komplexere Abläufe, sie hat jedoch gegenüber konventionellen Pipelines zwei Vorteile, die zu einer Steigerung der CPU-Leistung führen:

- o Die in üblichen Befehls-Mixen sehr häufigen bedingten und unbedingten Sprungbefehle (Anteil: ca. 33 %) können sehr performant abgearbeitet werden.
- o Definierte Paare von aufeinander folgenden Befehlen können parallel durch die Pipeline laufen und damit effektiv in einem Zyklus verarbeitet werden. Anteil solcher Befehlspaare in typischen Programmen 15-20 %.

Die Befehlspipeline der C70 besteht aus 4 Pipeline-Stufen. Der prinzipielle Ablauf eines Maschinenbefehls, z.B.: Addieren Festpunkt (im RX-Format) ist wie folgt:

Pipeline-Stufe 1 (Prefetch PF):

o	Befehlsblock aus IC lesen || Befehlsadresse übersetzen	15 ns
o	Befehl extrahieren || IC-Hit/Miss-Check	8 ns
o	Prefetch-Befehlszähler erhöhen	12 ns

Pipeline-Stufe 2 (Adreßrechnung AC):

o	Befehl decodieren || Lesen Basis-/Index-Register	10 ns
o	Speicheroperandenadresse berechnen	14 ns
o	Speicheroperandenadresse übersetzen	15 ns

Pipeline-Stufe 3 (Lesen Speicheroperand RM):

o	Speicheroperand aus First Level Cache lesen	40 ns

Pipeline-Stufe 4 (Execute EX):

o	Rechenoperation (z.B.: ALU)	31 ns
o	Ergebnis in Register schreiben || Condition Code bilden	8 ns

Obiger Ablauf zeigt eindeutig, daß der Vorgang "Lesen Speicheroperand aus dem First Level Cache" in PL-Stufe 3 den Maschinenzyklus bestimmt. Der relativ hohe Zeitaufwand ergibt sich aus der Zugriffszeit der externen SRAM's, aus der im Vergleich zur ECL-Technik geringen Treiberleistung von CMOS, aus der Leitungslaufzeit auf der Baugruppe und aus den Laufzeitstreuungen in den Adreß- und Datenwegen.

Zum zweiten zeigt obige Herleitung, daß die Verarbeitung eines typischen RX-Befehls in insgesamt 160 ns möglich ist. Hierbei wirkt sich positiv aus, daß außer Lesen FLC, alle anderen Abläufe der Befehlsverarbeitung Hauptprozessor-intern durchzuführen sind. Beide Kriterien stützen die Realisierung einer 4-stufigen-Fließband-Architektur mit einem Maschinenzyklus von

40 ns (4x40 ns = 160 ns).

Im folgenden soll die Befehlsverarbeitung unter Einschluß der beiden Coprozessoren beschrieben werden. Als Beispiel dient der Ablauf des Befehls "Addieren Gleitpunkt" (im RX-Format), der im Coprozessor (FPU) abläuft. Wie bereits erwähnt, beginnt die Verarbeitung aller Befehle im Hauptprozessor, d.h.: der Ablauf in Pipeline-Stufe 1 und 2 ist für alle Befehle nahezu gleich. In Pipeline-Stufe 3 wird, wie bei "Addieren Festpunkt", das Lesen des Speicheroperanden aus dem FL-Cache veranlaßt und parallel dazu werden die Befehlsparameter (Operationscode + Registeradresse) an den Gleitpunktprozessor (FPU) übergeben. Der Hauptprozessor geht nach dem 3. Zyklus in den Wartezustand. Der Ablauf im Gleitpunkt-Coprozessor ist dann wie folgt:

Pipeline-Stufe 4 (Execute EX1):

o Start Coprozessor FPU

o Übernahme Speicheroperand vom DBUS

Execute EX2:

o Lesen Registeroperand aus Gleitpunktregister

o Gleitpunkt-Charakteristik angleichen

o Gleitpunkt-Addition (Teil 1)

Execute EX3:

o Gleitpunkt-Addition (Teil 2)

o Ergebnis normalisieren

o Abspeichern Ergebnis im Gleitpunktregister

o Condition Code bilden und Übergabe an den Hauptprozessor

o Start Hauptprozessor

Der Aufruf des Coprozessors (EXU) und die Rückmeldung beim

Hauptprozessor geschieht nach dem gleichen Verfahren. Der Coprozessor (EXU) kann mit Hilfe einer komfortablen Mikroprogrammsteuerung umfangreiche Mikroprogramme inkl. Speicherverkehr ausführen und ist damit in der Lage auch komplexe Maschinenbefehle und Funktionsabläufe abzuwickeln.

6.2 Zweistrom-Befehlspipeline

Die Implementierung der Zweistrom-Pipeline führte zur Verdoppelung von einigen HW-Einheiten im Hauptprozessor. An einigen Stellen mußte der HW-Aufwand sogar vervierfacht werden.
Für die parallele Verarbeitung von zwei Befehlsströmen, die nach bedingten Sprungbefehlen erforderlich ist, mußten die Pipeline-Stufen 1 und 2 verdoppelt werden (Bild 4). Dies bedeutet jeweils zwei Prefetch-Befehlszähler, zwei Befehlspuffer, zwei Befehlsregister, zwei Satz Adreßrechenwerke sowie die Verdoppelung der Ports am Registersatz und am Adreßübersetzungsspeicher.
Zusätzlich zur parallelen Verarbeitung von zwei Befehlsströmen im Hauptprozessor, ist in jedem Befehlsstrom auch noch das gleichzeitige Verarbeiten von zwei aufeinanderfolgenden Befehlen möglich (Bild 4), aus Aufwandsgründen allerdings nicht in Pipeline-Stufe 3, und in PL-Stufe 4 nur mit Einschränkungen. Dies führte insgesamt zur Vervierfachung der Adreßrechenwerke und zu einer nochmaligen Verdoppelung der Schreib- und Lese-Ports am Registersatz. In Summe wurde eine ökonomische Lösung gefunden, die Hauptprozessor-intern zu realisieren war, die andererseits jedoch zu einer Steigerung der CPU-Leistung um ca. 30 % führte.

Bild 4 zeigt die Verarbeitung von 9 konsekutiven Befehlen in der Zweistrom-Pipeline der C70. Die Befehlsfolge ist: Laden-Festpunkt (L), Addieren-Festpunkt (A), Springen Bedingt (BC), Subtrahieren-FP (S), Laden Adresse (LA), Schieben Rechts Arithmetisch (SRA), Springen Bedingt (BCR), Store-FP (ST) und Addieren Register-FP (AR).

Nach Verarbeitung des Befehls L, läuft das Befehlspaar A und BC völlig parallel durch alle Pipeline-Stufen. Dies ist möglich, da der Befehl BC in PL-Stufe 3 und 4 keine wichtigen HW-Resourcen belegt. Die in der AC-Stufe berechnete Sprungzieladresse startet die Pipeline B und ab hier arbeiten beide Pipelines parallel, da erst am Ende des zweiten Zyklusses in der EX-Stufe entschieden wird, daß der Sprungbefehl erfüllt ist. Die Ausführung des 4. Befehls (C) aus Befehlsstrom A wird abgebrochen. Im 3. Zyklus (bezogen auf die EX-Stufe) kommt das erste Befehlspaar (S und LA) aus Befehlsstrom B in der Pipeline-Stufe 3 an. Da der Befehl "Laden Adresse (LA)" weder das FLC (PL-ST3) noch das Rechenwerk ALU (PL-ST4) benötigt, ist die parallele Verarbeitung von S und LA bis zum Ende möglich. Auch die beiden folgenden Befehlspaare SRA/BCR und ST/AR können parallel durch alle 4 PL-Stufen laufen, da sie sich in PL-Stufe 3 und 4 nicht behindern und in PL-Stufe 1 und 2 die HW-Resourcen doppelt vorhanden sind. Im 4. Zyklus (bezogen auf die EX-Stufe) wird durch den bedingten Sprungbefehl BCR wieder die Pipeline A gestartet (Befehle L und S). Nach Ausführung des Befehls SRA in der EX-Stufe wird erkannt, daß der Sprung nicht erfüllt ist und die Pipeline A wird wieder gestoppt.

Der Ablauf des aus 9 Befehlen bestehenden Programmbeispieles, das allerdings nicht repräsentativ ist, zeigt folgendes:

- o Die Ausführungszeit der Sprungbefehle (bedingt und unbedingt) beträgt bei Sprung bzw. Nichtsprung 1 bzw. 0 Zyklen. Dies gilt immer, da die Sprungbefehle in PL-Stufe 3 und 4 keine wichtigen HW-Resourcen benötigen.
- o Auch einige Ladebefehle sind immer 0-Zyklus-Befehle.
- o Es wurden 7 kurze 1-Zyklus-Befehle und 2 bedingte Sprungbe-

fehle in effektiv 6 Zyklen ausgeführt. Bei einer konventionellen Befehlspipeline wären ca. 11 Zyklen angefallen (Annahme: 1 Zyklus pro Befehl plus 2 Wait-Zyklen für den erfüllten Sprungbefehl BC).
Um das Prinzip der bei C70 realisierten Fließband-Architektur zu verdeutlichen, wurden die aufeinanderfolgenden Befehle so gewählt, daß sie sich nicht gegenseitig behindern.
Ein Verbesserungsfaktor von 1,8, wie im Beispiel, läßt sich in realistischen Programmen nicht erreichen und hängt stark von der zufälligen Paarung aufeinanderfolgender Befehle ab.

Allgemein läßt sich jedoch feststellen:
Die Fließband-Architektur der C70 steigert den Befehlsdurchsatz über zwei Maßnahmen: Das Zweistrom-Prinzip (Pipeline A und B) verbessert die Verarbeitung von Sprungbefehlen. Die Doppelbefehlsverarbeitung innerhalb des einzelnen Befehlsstromes kommt ebenfalls den Sprungbefehlen zugute, beschleunigt den Pipeline-Ablauf aber auch allgemein bei geeigneten Befehlspaaren. Beide Effekte zusammengenommen, erbrachten bei der Zykluszahl pro Durchschnittsbefehl eine Verbesserung von ca. 30 % gegenüber dem Vorgängermodell.

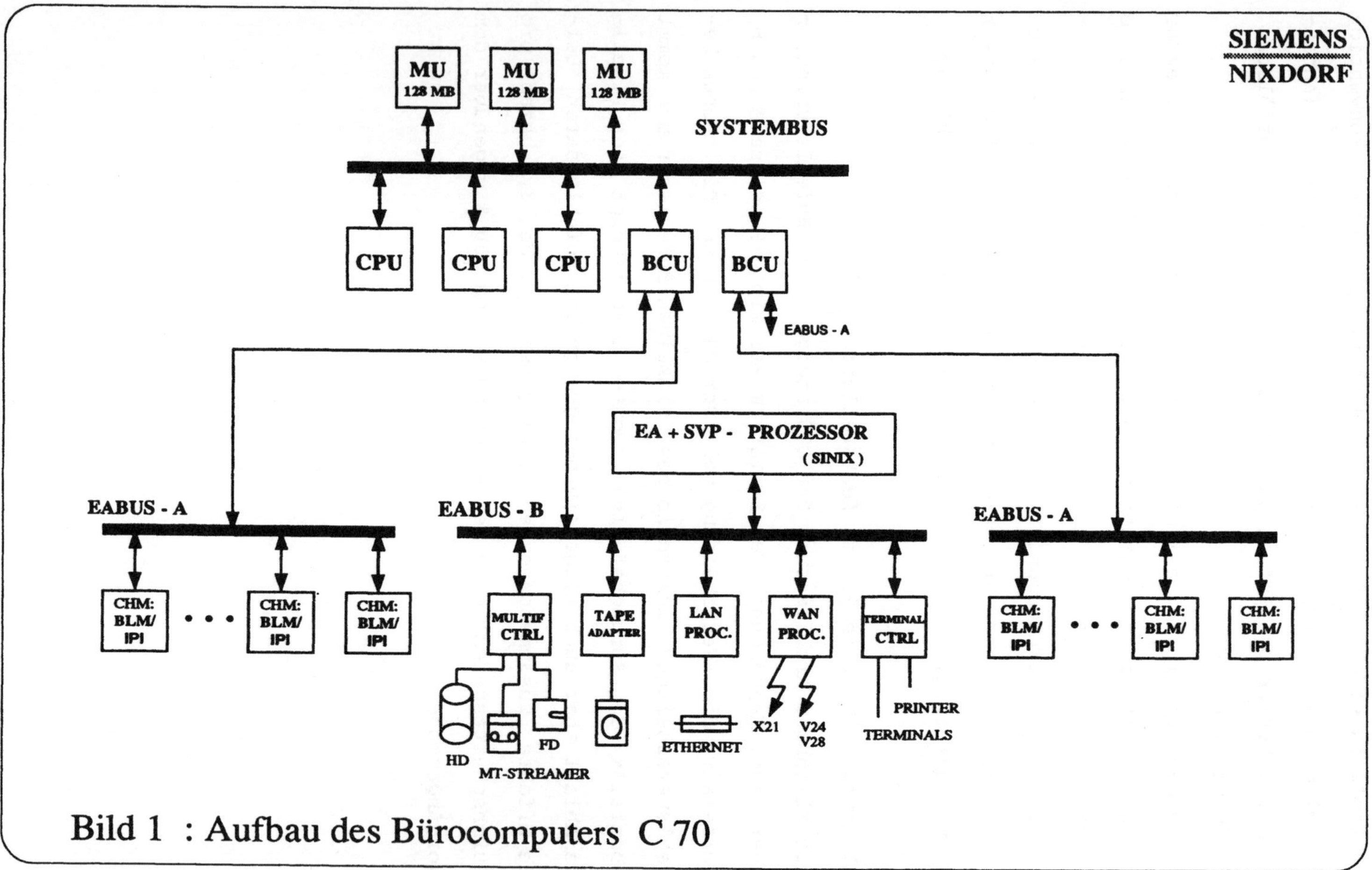

Bild 1 : Aufbau des Bürocomputers C 70

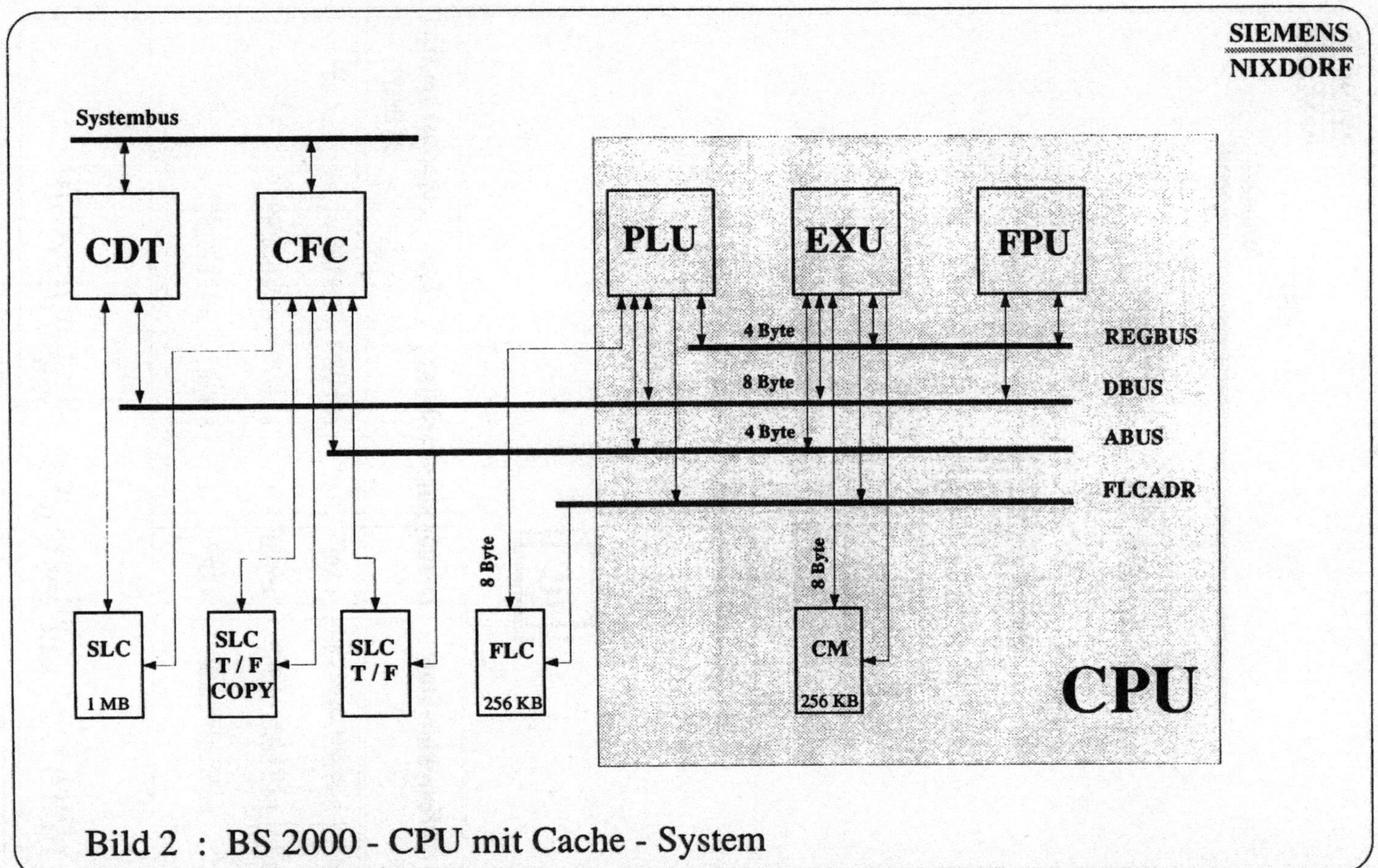

Bild 2 : BS 2000 - CPU mit Cache - System

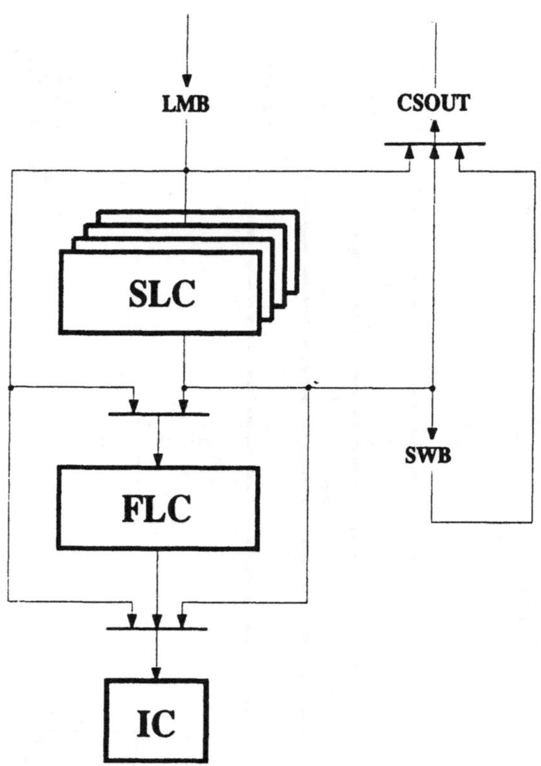

Hierarchie-Stufe		Größe	Bänke	Block	Typ	Verlust bei Miss (Zyklen)
SLC	Second Level Cache	1 MB	4	64 Byte	store in	>= 20
FLC	First Level Cache	256 kB	1	8 Byte	store trough	3
IC	Instruction Cache	4 kB	1	8 Byte	store trough	2

Bild 3 : 3 - stufiges Cache - System der C 70

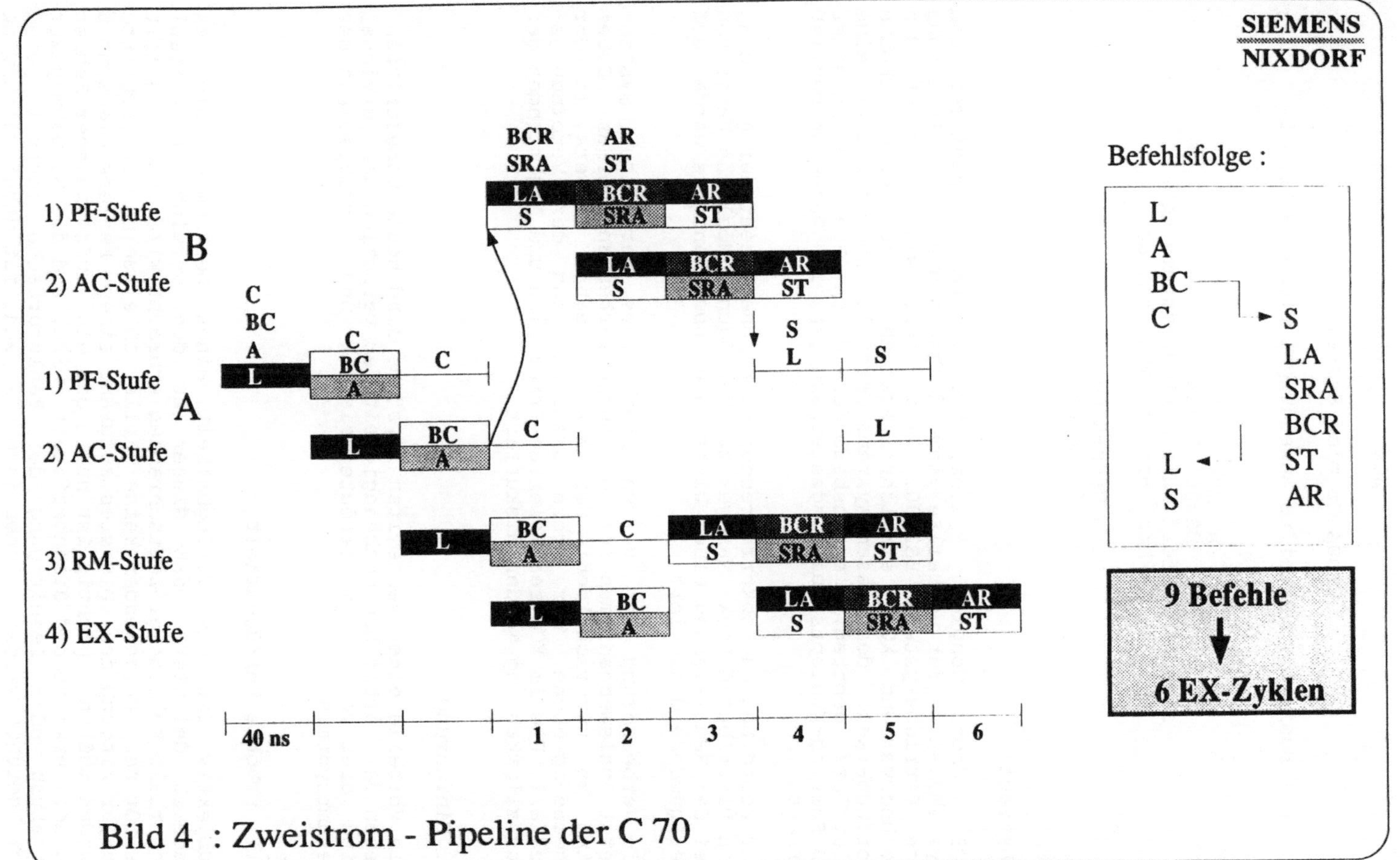

Bild 4 : Zweistrom - Pipeline der C 70

XCS

Cross Coupled System

Die Basis für verteilte Anwendungssysteme im BS2000

H. Boellner
BS2000 OS225
Siemens Nixdorf Informationssysteme AG
E-mail: Herbert.Boellner@mch.sni.de

Otto-Hahn-Ring 6
81730 München

Abstract

XCS (Cross Coupled System) bietet Basismechanismen und Systemdienste für verteilte Anwendungssysteme unter Steuerung des Betriebssystems BS2000. Zwei Ziele werden durch den Rechnerverbund XCS erreicht: erstens wird eine erhöhte Verfügbarkeit des Gesamtsystems erzielt und zweitens eine Plattform geboten, die insbesondere durch Realisierung eines DB-Sharing-Konzepts Leistungssteigerungen im Datenbankbetrieb erlaubt.

Zur Koordination konkurrierender Funktionen steht der Anwendung ein Distributed Lock Manager zur Verfügung. Mögliche Varianten bei der Realisierung eines Distributed Lock Managers werden auf Designebene diskutiert.

Die Verbesserung der Verfügbarkeit eines verteilten Systems setzt Basismechanismen für die Ausfallerkennung voraus. Dabei sind zu unterscheiden: der Ausfall eines Servers in der Anwendungsebene, der Prozessorausfall und der Verbindungsausfall. Die im XCS realisierten Prinzipien und Algorithmen der Ausfallerkennung werden diskutiert.

1. Einführung

Die Vorteile eines verteilten Systems sind heute unbestritten. Neben der örtlichen Unabhängigkeit der verschiedenen Services, sind dies vor allem erhöhte Leistung und Verfügbarkeit des Gesamtsystems.

1.1. Erhöhte Verfügbarkeit

Subjektiv ist die Verfügbarkeit eines bestimmten Dienstes dadurch definiert, daß dieser (zu den vereinbarten Zeiten) innerhalb tolerabler Zeitschranken erbracht wird. Dabei spielt es für den Endanwender keine Rolle, ob einzelne Teilschritte zur Erbringung des Dienstes aufgrund eines Fehlers wiederholt werden mußten. Wichtig ist nur, daß ein aufgetretener Fehler schnell erkannt und diagnostiziert wird, und die Maßnahmen zur Umgehung oder Beseitigung der Fehlerursache schnell genug durchgeführt werden können (schnell genug ist dabei relativ zu den subjektiv vorgegebenen Zeitschranken zu sehen).

Der entscheidende Vorteil eines verteilten Systems gegenüber einem zentralen System ist, daß durch geeignete Maßnahmen (gegenseitige Überwachung, automatische Rekonfiguration, redundante Ressourcen,...) sowohl die Fehlererkennung und Diagnose, wie auch die Maßnahmen zur Fehlerumgehung sich automatisieren und damit beschleunigen lassen.

Eine verbesserte Verfügbarkeit in verteilten Systemen kann insbesondere durch redundante Datenhaltung erreicht werden. Ist der Datenbestand jedoch starken Änderungen unterworfen, erfordert eine redundante Datenführung nicht nur komplexe Algorithmen, sondern kostet - auch im Normalbetrieb - einen erheblichen Teil an Rechnerleistung, verringert den Durchsatz und erhöht die Antwortzeiten. Ein grundsätzliches Problem verteilter Datenbanksysteme.

DB-Sharing-Konzepte erlauben es, diese Komplexität aus der Applikationsebene zu nehmen (Redundanz kann z.B. auch durch Spiegelplatten im I/O-System erzeugt werden).

1.2. Erhöhte Leistung

Durch den Einsatz von mehreren Prozessoren kann, die Unabhängigkeit der Prozesse bezüglich aller Ressourcen vorausgesetzt , die Verarbeitung vollständig parallelisiert werden, und die Leistungssteigerung korreliert linear mit der Anzahl der Prozessoren -- best case.

Leistungseinbußen sind jedoch immer dann hinzunehmen, wenn die Prozesse bezüglich einer oder mehrerer Ressourcen konkurrieren; der Gebrauch der Ressourcen also serialisiert werden muß. Der zusätzliche Prozessor bringt keine zusätzliche Leistung, sondern im Gegenteil: es muß zusätzlich noch Rechnerleistung für die Serialisierung spendiert werden -- worst case.

Die Realität bewegt sich zwischen diesen Extremen.

Durch ein verteiltes System besteht die Option einer Verbesserung von Verfügbarkeit und Leistung. Die Kunst besteht nun darin, geeignete Verteilungsebenen auszuwählen und die geeigneten Ressourcen zu verteilen, um für ein möglichst breites Anwendungsspektrum diese Option tatsächlich nutzen zu können.

2. Die angestrebte Konfiguration

Bevor die einzelnen Schwerpunkte, der im BS2000 ® (BS2000 ® ist ein eingetragenes Warenzeichen der Siemens Nixdorf Informationssysteme AG) gewählten Lösung zur Verbesserung von Verfügbarkeit und Leistung näher betrachtet werden, zunächst eine Schilderung des allgemeinen Szenario.

Erläuterungen zur Abbildung 1 (Konfiguration):
Über ein Kommunikationsnetz sind Front-Ends, Hosts und Terminals miteinander verbunden. Jeder dieser Knoten hat seine spezifischen Aufgaben im Netz. Der mit XCS (= Cross Coupled System) gekennzeichnete große Kasten nimmt im Netz die Stellung eines Hosts mit Knotennamen ABZ ein. Aus Leistungs- und/oder Verfügbarkeitsaspekten wird der Service, den der Knoten ABZ bietet, jedoch nicht durch einen Host

sondern durch mehrere Hosts, die zu einem XCS zusammengeschlossen sind, erbracht.

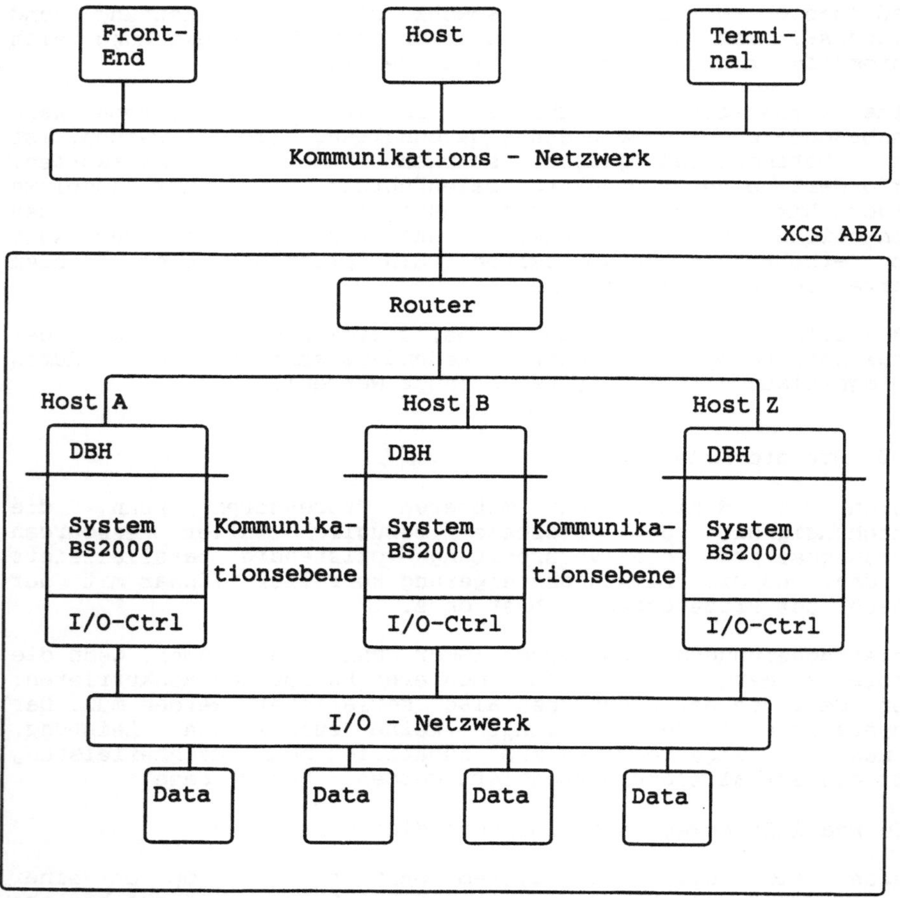

Abb. 1 Konfiguration

Betrachten wir das XCS näher. Es setzt sich aus mehreren Hosts zusammen, wobei jeder Host zu jedem eine virtuelle Punkt-zu-Punkt Verbindung besitzt. Theoretisch lassen sich in einem XCS beliebig viele Hosts zusammenschließen. Für die derzeitige Realisierung des Projekts im Rahmen der BS2000-Entwicklung gehen wir allerdings von maximal 8 Hosts in einem XCS aus. Die Leistung des einzelnen Rechners soll im Mid-Range- bis Mainframebereich liegen und innerhalb eines XCS homogen sein.

Schließlich hat jeder Host über einen Hardware-Pfad direkten Zugriff auf den gesamten Datenbestand. Die Modifikation eines Datums auf den permanenten Datenbehältern kann also von jedem Host autark erfolgen und der aktuelle Datenbestand ist damit sofort für alle XCS-Hosts verfügbar. Auf jedem Knoten ist mindestens ein DBH (Data Base Handler) aktiv. Zur Synchronisation und zur Koordination konkurrierender Transaktionen stellt das Betriebssystem einen XCS-weiten

Lockmechanismus zur Verfügung - den DLM (Distributed Lock Manager) auf den im folgenden näher eingegangen wird. Die logische Zugreifbarkeit auf den Datenbestand wird durch ein Shared File System, das ebenfalls im Betriebssystem angesiedelt ist, sichergestellt.

Die zur Unterstützung eines Shared-DB-Betriebs nötige Kommunikation wird in der Betriebssystemebene realisiert. Die DBH selbst benötigen keine Kommunikation, sie teilen dem Betriebssystem über geeignete Schnittstellen lokal mit, daß die Dateien einem XCS-weiten Sharing unterliegen sollen und daß der Synchronisationsmechanismus XCS-weit wirken soll.

Das Shared File System ist bereits realisiert und steht mit BS2000/OSD zur Verfügung. Der XCS-weite Synchronisationsmechanismus befindet sich derzeit in seiner Design-Phase.

3. Das Design

Um der Anwendung einen Synchronistationsmechanismus bieten zu können, muß das Betriebssystem die nötige Infrastruktur aufbauen und eine Abstimmung zwischen den beteiligten Prozessen ermöglichen. Auf 3 Systemebenen (vgl. Abb 2. Schichtenmodell) soll im folgenden näher eingegangen werden.

Erbrachter Dienst	Instanz im XCS
Prozeß-Synchronisation	Distributed Lock Manager
Knoten-Synchronisation	Node Synchronisation Manager
Basis-Mechanismen	XCS-Manager

Abb 2. Schichtenmodell

3.1 Der DLM (Distributed Lock Manger)

Die Aufgabe des DLM ist es, eine Anwendung in ihrer verbundweiten Koordination und Synchronisation zu unterstützen. Dazu bietet der DLM die Möglichkeit Ressourcen zu definieren, die er über einen frei gewählten Namen anspricht. Um diese Ressourcen, im weiteren Locks genannt, kann sich nun jeder Prozeß bewerben. Bei dieser Bewerbung kann der Prozeß unter 6 verschiedenen Lockmodi wählen. Er kann z.B. ein exklusives Schreiblock anfordern oder einen sharable Leselock. Die Verträglichkeit der einzelnen Modi ist in einer Matrix festgelegt. Bewirbt sich also ein Prozeß um einen bestimmten Lock, so wird vom DLM geprüft, ob diese Anforderung XCS-weit verträglich ist. Wenn ja, wird der Lock zugeteilt, wenn nein, kann sich der Prozeß in eine Warteschlange einreihen. Der Prozeß kann synchron auf die Lockzuteilung warten oder sich die Zuteilung asynchron über einen Eventingmechanismus zustellen lassen.

Weiter kann sich ein Lockhalter, ebenfalls über einen Eventingmechanismus benachrichtigen lassen, wenn von einem anderen Prozeß eine inkompatible Lockanforderung erzeugt wird. Diese Funktion kann für konfliktarme Locks von der Anwendung genutzt werden, um die Anzahl der Lockanforderungen zu senken.

Dazu gibt die Anwendung einen Lock nicht sofort bei Beendigung der zugehörigen Aktion frei, sondern hält den Lock weiter. Der Lock muß also bei neuen Aktionen, die wieder diesen Lock benötigen, nicht erneut angefordert werden. Die Freigabe des Locks erfolgt erst nach Aufforderung (d.h. inkompatible Lockanforderung durch anderen Prozeß) oder aber nach anwendungsspezifischen Algorithmen (z.B. LRU-Prinzip). Je höher die Lokalität der Lockanforderungen, desto höher ist der Wirkungsgrad dieser Strategie.

Für das Leistungsverhalten ist es von entscheidender Bedeutung, daß eine konfliktfreie Lockanforderung möglichst schnell, d.h. ohne Kommunikation und auch ohne lokale IPK (Interprozesskommunikation), zugeteilt werden kann. Dazu soll folgender Weg beschritten werden:

Der DLM hält seine Daten in einer hostlokalen Common Memory Area, also einem Arbeitsspeicherbereich, der von jedem lokalen Prozeß aus zugreifbar ist. Dort werden alle lokalen (=von diesem Host) Locks verwaltet, sowohl die zugeteilten Locks wie auch die Warteschlangen vor den Locks. Der DLM verwaltet also nur die lokalen Lockanforderungen und entscheidet bei seiner Verträglichkeitsprüfung nur aufgrund seiner lokalen Daten. Diese Prüfung erfolgt im lock-anfordernden Prozeß.

Um die verbundweite Verträglichkeit sicherzustellen, bedient sich der DLM der Dienste einer weiteren Instanz: des NSM (= Node Serialization Manager). Bei der lokalen Erstanforderung eines Locks bewirbt sich der DLM beim NSM um einen verbundweiten Lock. Der NSM ist ein eigenständiger Server-Prozeß. An dieser Stelle ist also eine lokale IPK nötig. Der NSM ist an jedem Knoten im XCS etabliert. Bei der lokalen Initialisierung des NSM wurde zu jedem aktiven Partner-NSM eine Verbindung aufgebaut. Nun erwirbt der lokale NSM (in Abstimmung mit seinen Partnern) einen verbundweit verträglichen Lock für seinen Knoten. Die Zuteilung gibt der NSM (wieder über lokale IPK) dem DLM bekannt. Damit kann der Lock dem anfordernden Prozeß zugeteilt werden.

Mit dieser Teilung der Lockverwaltung in eine nur lokal, d.h. prozeßspezifisch agierende Instanz (DLM) und eine nur global, d.h. knotenspezifisch agierende Instanz (NSM) ist es gelungen das komplexe Problem in zwei - immer noch anspruchsvolle - Teilbereiche zu trennen. Die Vereinfachung ist beim Design von erheblichem Wert.

3.2. Der NSM (Node Serialization Manager)

Ein Ziel, das mit der Einführung des XCS angestrebt wird, ist ein verbessertes Verhalten bezüglich Durchsatz und Antwortzeit. Ein wesentlicher Faktor ist dabei die Frage, wie schnell es gelingt, eine Lockanforderung im Verbund abzustimmen. Hier sind verschiedene Strategien zu diskutieren. Im Rahmen des OSMOD'92-Forschungsprojekts (einer Kooperation der Universität Dortmund und der Siemens Nixdorf Informationssysteme AG) wurden die verschiedenen Strategien modelliert und bewertet [Z92]. Hier eine kurze Zusammenfassung der für das NSM-Design relevanten Ergebnisse. Die verschiedenen Strategien lassen sich klassifizieren nach:

- der Art der Datenhaltung:

  - zentrale Datenhaltung (genau ein Rechner hat Kenntnis über alle Locks im Verbund)
  - vollständige Replikation (jeder Rechner hat Kenntnis über alle Locks im Verbund)
  - partitionierte Datenhaltung (kein Rechner hat Kenntnis über alle Locks im Verbund)

- der Art der Kommunikation:

  - virtueller Token Ring
  - Punkt-zu-Punkt

Zur Illustration zwei Ansätze:

Ansatz I: Virtueller Token Ring mit vollständiger Replikation ([I90])

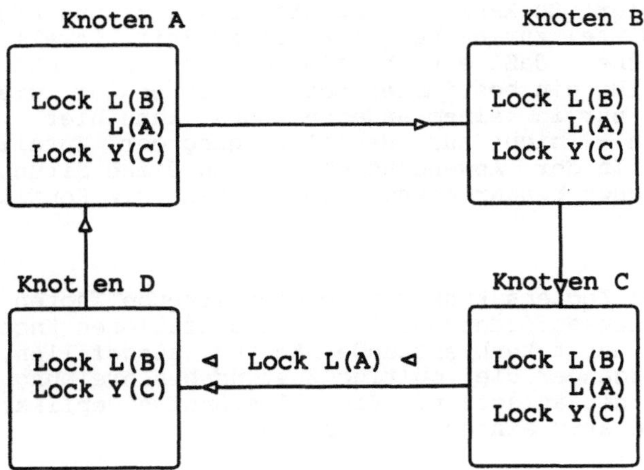

Abb. 3 Token Ring mit vollständiger Replikation
Der Lock L wird vom Knoten B, der Lock Y wird vom Knoten C gehalten. Die Lockanforderung des Knoten A für Lock L ist am Knoten B und Knoten C bereits eingearbeitet und kommt nun zu Knoten D.

Erläuterung zum Ansatz I:
Der NSM des Knoten A bewirbt sich um ein Lock L. Dazu wartet er, bis er in Tokenbesitz kommt und arbeitet dann alle Locks, die sich im Token befinden, in seine lokalen Daten ein (dabei entfernt er all jene Daten, die er selbst beim vormaligen Tokenbesitz in das Token gesetzt hat). Jetzt kann am Knoten A entschieden werden, ob das Lock L konfliktfrei ist und damit zugeteilt werden kann. Wenn ja, setzt er die Information, daß der Knoten A den Lock L hält, im Token ab, wenn nein, setzt er die Lockanforderung in das Token. Sind alle Anforderungen des Knoten A auf diese Weise bearbeitet, wird das Token an den nächsten Knoten im Ring weitergeleitet. Dieser verfährt analog. Damit ist sichergestellt, daß jeder Knoten (bei Tokenbesitz) alle im Verbund gehaltenen und angeforderten Locks kennt.

Bewertung des virtuellen Token Ring mit vollständiger Replikation:

- Durchsatz
  Durch die tokengesteuerten Kommunikationszeitpunkte ergibt sich automatisch eine Bündelung der Lockaufträge bezüglich der Kommunikation. Damit verringert sich der Kommunikationsoverhead pro Lockauftrag. Die Tokenverweilzeit je Knoten ist ein einfaches, lastunabhängiges Mittel, um den CPU-Bedarf für die Kommunikation je Knoten zu steuern. Eine obere Grenze ist erst gegeben, wenn ein Knoten in einer Tokenumlaufzeit mehr Lockaufträge stellt, als (bei Tokenbesitz) in das Token eingearbeitet werden können (Tokenverweilzeit, Tokenlänge).

- Antwortzeit
  Die vollständige Replikation erlaubt es, bei Tokenbesitz sofort feststellen zu können, ob eine Lockanforderung im Verbund kompatibel ist. Die Eigenschaft Lockverwalterknoten zu sein, wandert für alle Locks mit dem Token. Die Wartezeit von (konfliktfreier) Lockanforderung bis Lockzuteilung ergibt sich damit im Mittel zur halben Tokenumlaufzeit. Lokalität, also die Tatsache, daß ein bestimmter Knoten nach der Erstanforderung für ein bestimmtes Lock diesen gehäuft wieder anfordert, ggfs. nur in einem anderen Modus, kann hier - in der Basisfunktion - nicht zur Beschleunigung der Zuteilung genutzt werden. (In der Anwendungsebene kann diese Situation durch das eingangs beschriebene "Lockhalten bis Konflikt" behandelt werden.)

- Recovery
  Bei Ausfall eines Knotens kann der tokenbesitzende Knoten die Locks (und die Lockanforderungen) des ausgefallenen Knotens freigeben. Ist der tokenbesitzende Knoten ausgefallen, so besitzt sein Vorgänger die gültige Zustandsbeschreibung und kann das Token neu aufsetzen. Die vollständige Replikation erlaubt dieses relativ einfache Verfahren.

- Skalierbarkeit
  Das Anwortzeitverhalten nimmt mindestens linear mit der Anzahl der Knoten ab. Durch einen zusätzlichen Knoten verlängert sich die Umlaufzeit nicht nur durch die Ringverlängerung, es muß auch ein größeres Datenvolumen im Ring transportiert werden. Also: Ansatz nicht skalierbar.

- Modifikationen
  Die unter Punkt "Durchsatz" genannte Grenze kann z.B. erhöht werden, indem man mehrere Tokens (nicht mehr als Knoten), jedes zuständig für eine bestimmte Teilmenge des Lock-Namensraums, schafft.

Ansatz II: Punkt-zu-Punkt mit partionierter Datenhaltung ([S87])

Zu Abb. 4:
Der Knoten B ist Lockhalter und Lockverwalter
des Locks L. Der Knoten D ist Lockverwalter des Locks Y, der vom Knoten C gehalten wird.

Knoten A schickt seine Lockanforderung für Lock L an den

Lockverwalter B. Weil L(B) und L(A) kompatibel, kann Knoten B das Lock L direkt zuteilen.

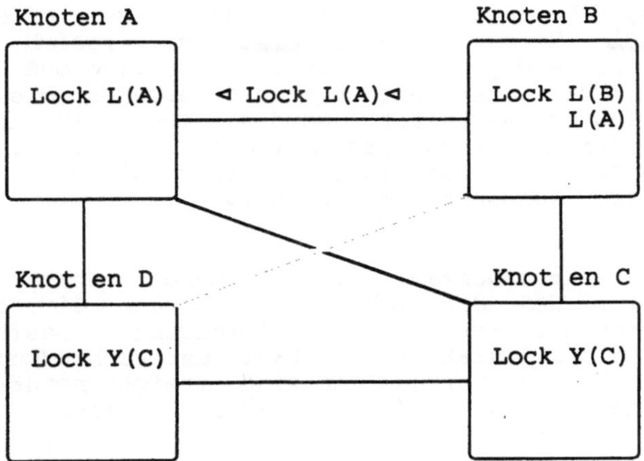

Abb. 4 Punkt-zu-Punkt-Kommunikation mit partitionierter Datenhaltung.

Erläuterung zum Ansatz II:
Durch eine Hashfunktion hash wird der Namensraum der Locks in n Klassen aufgeteilt (n = Anzahl der aktiven Knoten im XCS). Jedem Knoten wird nun der Directory Service für genau eine Klasse zugeteilt. Die Aufteilung ist an jedem Knoten bekannt.

Bewirbt sich Knoten A erstmalig für den Lock L, so wird zuerst der zuständige Directory Service Knoten bestimmt: hash(L). Nun wendet sich der NSM des Knotens A an den Directory Service des Knoten hash(L). Von dort kommt die Information, ob es sich um eine globale Erstanforderung handelt. Wenn ja, wird Knoten A Lock-Verwalter für den Lock L. Wenn nein, teilt der Directory Service den aktuellen Lockverwalter-Knoten mit. Der NSM des Knotens A wendet sich jetzt (und für weitere Anforderungen direkt) an den Lockverwalter-Knoten und bekommt, ggfs. nachdem er eine gewisse Zeit in der Warteschlange verbracht hat, den Lock L zugeteilt.

Bewertung der Punkt-zu-Punkt-Kommunikation mit partionierter Datenhaltung:

- Durchsatz
  Der Kommunikationsoverhead ist bei dieser Variante stark lastabhängig. Jede Lockanforderung impliziert eine Kommunikation (falls der Lockverwalter-Knoten nicht der lokale Knoten ist). Für eine lokale Erstanforderung kommt gegebenenfalls noch die Kommunikation mit dem Directory Service hinzu. Die CPU-Auslastung durch Kommunikation bildet eine obere Schranke für den erreichbaren Durchsatz.

- Antwortzeit
  Sie setzt sich nur aus der Bearbeitungszeit und der Zeit für eine direkte Punkt-zu-Punkt-Kommunikation zusammen. Durch einen hohen Lokalitätsfaktor (Lockanforderung am Lockverwalter-Knoten) verkürzt sich diese weiter.

- Recovery
  Um bei Ausfall eines Rechners Recovery bieten zu können, muß jede Message solange wiederholbar bleiben, bis die Ausführung durch den Empfänger bestätigt ist (-> Verwaltung der offenen Messagebuffer). Die Recovery selbst ist (im Vergeich zum Ansatz I) sehr aufwendig. (Der Directory Service muß neu verteilt werden. Für Locks und Lockanforderungen, die am ausgefallenen Knoten verwaltet wurden, muß ein neuer Lockverwalter bestimmt werden; dazu ist eine lockspezifische Abstimmung zwischen den beteiligten Knoten nötig.) Die Recovery ist äußerst kommunikationsintensiv.

- Skalierbarkeit
  Mit zunehmender Knotenanzahl im Verbund sinkt die Wahrscheinlichkeit, daß der lokale Knoten den Directory Service - relevant bei lokaler Érstanforderung - besitzt. Auch sinkt der Lokalitätsfaktor. Die Zahl der Verbindungen, die am lokalen Knoten vorzuhalten sind steigt natürlich linear. Trotzdem zeigt dieser Ansatz eine gute Skalierbarkeit.

- Modifikationen
  Um die unter dem Punkt "Durchsatz" genannten Nachteile auszugleichen, kann man auch bei diesem Ansatz Bündelung der Lockanforderungen, z.B. durch einen lokalen Taktgeber, vorsehen. Mit derartigen Maßnahmen, geht allerdings die Skalierbarkeit verloren.

3.3. Die vorgeschlagene Lockzuteilungsstrategie

Die Idee ist nun, wie in ([Z93], [S92]) zusammengefaßt, eine Lösung zu realisieren, die die Vorteile der beiden Beispiele vereint.

Ansatz III: Virtueller Token Ring mit partitionierter Datenhaltung:

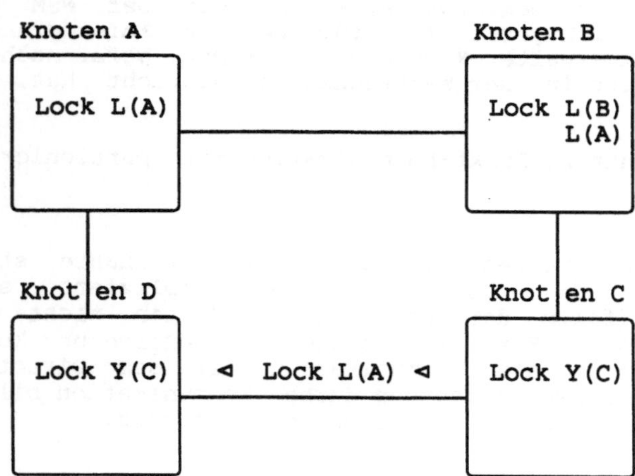

Abb. 5 Token Ring mit partitionierter Datenhaltung

Der Knoten B ist Lockhalter und Lockverwalter des Locks L.

Der Knoten C ist Lockverwalter des Locks Y, der vom Knoten C gehalten wird.

Knoten B hat die Anforderung von Knoten A für Lock L aufgenommen, bearbeitet und die Zuteilung (L(B) und L(A) seien kompatibel) wieder in das Token gesetzt. Knoten A wartet derzeit auf das Token.

Erläuterung zum Ansatz III:
Entsteht auf Knoten A eine knotenlokale Erstanforderung für den Lock L, so wartet A bis zum Erhalt des Tokens und gibt mit diesem seine Anforderung für den Lock L weiter.

Ist diese Anforderung auch verbundglobal eine Erstanforderung, so kommt die Anforderung unverändert nach einem Ringumlauf bei A an. A erhält damit die Lock-Verwaltung für den Lock L, und alle weiteren Lockanforderungen des Knotens A bezüglich des Locks L können nun lokal (ohne weitere Kommunikation) bearbeitet werden.

Gibt es aber für den Lock L bereits einen Lock-Verwalter z.B. Knoten B, so bearbeitet dieser (bei Erhalt des Tokens) die Lockanforderung von A bezüglich des Locks L: Ist die Lockanforderung verträglich, wird die Lockzuteilung gegeben; sonst wird sie in die Warteschlange eingereiht.

Bewertung des virtuellen Token Ringes mit partionierter Datenhaltung

- Durchsatz
  Der geringe Kommunikationsoverhead bleibt erhalten. Hoher Durchsatz erreichbar (aus Ansatz I).

- Antwortzeit
  Für eine lokale Erstanforderung bleibt es bei dem unter Ansatz I beschriebenen Verhalten (Ringumlaufzeit geht in die Antwortzeit ein). Der große Vorteil aus Ansatz II - Berücksichtigung der Lokalität einer Lockanforderung - findet sich auch in dieser Lösung wieder.

- Recovery
  Bei Knotenausfall muß für die Locks, die vom ausgefallenen Knoten verwaltet wurden, ein neuer Verwaltungsknoten bestimmt werden, d.h. die Information über die Lockhalter und die wartenden Lockanforderungen der verschiedenen Knoten muß (pro Lock) wieder auf einem Knoten gesammelt werden. Dies kann im Prinzip in zwei Ringumläufen geschehen. Ausgehend von einem ausgezeichneten Knoten (z.B. der Vorgänger im Ring) wird die Recovery gestartet. Im ersten Umlauf werden von allen Knoten die Lockzustände (für Locks, die am ausgefallenen Knoten verwaltet wurde) gesammelt. Neuer Lockverwalter für einen bestimmten Lock wird der Knoten, der (in Ringfolge) als erster Information zu diesem Lock besitzt. Im zweiten Umlauf erhalten die Lockverwalter, die für ihre neue Zuständigkeit nötige Information.

- Skalierbarkeit
  Die Lösung ist in dieser Grundform nicht skalierbar. Mit zunehmender Knotenzahl sinkt das Antwortzeitverhalten ins Unerträgliche ab. Die Simulationsergebnisse [Z92] lassen die

Schranke bei ca. 8 Knoten vermuten; wobei die Werte stark vom angenommenen Lokalitätsfaktor (also der Frage danach, wieviele Lockanforderungen werden lokal am Lock-Verwalterknoten gestellt und wieviele remote) beeinflußt werden.

- Modifikationen
  Um mit diesem Ansatz mehr als 8 Knoten unterstützen zu können, kann man wie folgt vorgehen: Statt daß jeder Knoten an genau einem Ring der Länge n (n ist Anzahl der Knoten) teilnimmt, kann jeder Knoten an mehreren kürzeren Ringen teilnehmen. Die Bedingung ist dabei, daß jedes Knotenpaar in mindestens einem Ring liegen muß. Als Extremfall ergibt sich hierbei: Jeder Knoten nimmt an n-1 Ringen der Länge 2 teil. Damit ist (fast) das Verhalten, wie in Ansatz II geschildert, erreicht (der Unterschied besteht in den Kommunikationszeitpunkten: hier tokengesteuert; Ansatz II ist timer- oder eventgesteuert).

Für das Betriebssystem BS2000 hat man sich entschlossen, den unter Ansatz III geschilderten Mechanismus zu verwenden. Er scheint für hohen Durchsatz und akzeptabler Antwortzeit (bei geringer Knotenzahl) gut geeignet. Durch Modifikation der Tokenverweilzeit ist eine Anpassung an gegebene Lastprofile flexibel möglich.

3.4. Der XCS - Manager [A92]

Die erhöhte Leistungsfähigkeit z.B. durch ein DB-Sharing-Konzept war bisher der Ausgangspunkt, relevante Betriebssystem-Funktionen zu verteilen. Ein zweiter Aspekt ist, wie in der Einführung bereits erwähnt, die erhöhte Verfügbarkeit des Gesamtsystems. Um dieses Ziel erreichen zu können, müssen folgende zwei Grundvoraussetzungen gegeben sein:

- Dynamische Rekonfiguration
  D.h. ohne wesentliche Beeinträchtigung des laufenden Betriebs müssen Knoten zugeschaltet und auch wieder weggeschaltet werden können.

- Fehlererkennung und Behandlung
  D.h. es muß auf jedem Knoten eine Instanz existieren, die die Funktionsfähigkeit der Partnerknoten und der Verbindungen überwacht und bei einer Störung geeignete Recoverymaßnahmen einleitet.

Die Realisierung dieser beiden Voraussetzungen wird sinnvollerweise nicht durch jede verteilte Funktion selbst erbracht, sondern als Dienst an jedem Knoten durch eine Basisfunktion - dem XCS-Manager - zur Verfügung gestellt.

3.4.1 Konsistenz

Die wichtigste Aufgabe des XCS-Managers ist es, jeder (verteilten) Funktion auf jedem Knoten im XCS die konsistente Sicht über die aktiven Verbundteilnehmer zu vermitteln. Der Begriff der Konsistenz ist hierbei von zentraler Bedeutung. Je schärfer er gefaßt werden kann, desto geringer wird der Aufwand in den darüberliegenden verteilten Funktionen, eine funktionsspezifische Recovery zu betreiben. Zur Präzisierung folgende zwei Definitionen:

Die Menge der aktiven Verbundteilnehmer soll hier mit XCS(K) bezeichnet werden.

Eine Auskunftsfunktion heißt **konsistent**, wenn gilt: Zu einem beliebig gewählten Zeitpunkt t, liefert die Auskunftsfunktion an jedem Knoten aus XCS(K) die Menge XCS(K) oder aber den Hinweis, daß derzeit keine abgestimmte Information zur Verfügung steht.

Dieser Konsistenzbegriff kann in einem XCS-Verbund durch ein 2-Phasen-Ring-Protokoll realisiert werden.

Ein XCS-Verbund heißt **global konsistent** zum Zeitpunkt t, wenn eine konsistente Auskunftsfunktion zu t an jedem Knoten aus XCS(K) die Menge XCS(K) liefert.

Globale Konsistenz steht im Widerspruch zur Forderung nach einer dynamischen Rekonfiguration. Nehmen wir an, ein XCS-Verbund ist im Zeitpunkt t global konsistent. So tritt eine Störung dieser globalen Konsistenz genau dann auf, wenn ein Knoten hinzu- oder herausgenommen werden muß.

Damit sind die Aufgaben des XCS-Managers klar umrissen:

- Er überwacht das Hinzu- und Wegschalten eines Knotens, wobei das Wegschalten gezielt durch einen Eingriff des Systemverwalters erfolgen oder aber durch einen Knotenausfall provoziert werden kann.

- Er bietet eine konsistente Auskunftsfunktion und bringt den XCS-Verbund (nach einer Störung) in einen global konsistenten Zustand.

- Nach einer Störung leitet er die funktionsspezifische Recovery für die Systemfunktionen ein. Anwendungen können sich an der DLM-Schnittstelle über eine Störung informieren lassen.

3.4.2 Fehlererkennung und Behandlung

Der XCS-Manager erkennt und unterscheidet folgende Fehlersituationen:

- Ausfall eines Partnerknotens,
- Ausfall einer Verbindung.

Die Differenzierung dieser beiden Fehlersituation ist kein Selbstzweck. Betrachten wir nochmals kurz das in Abschnitt 2. vorgestellte Einsatzszenario. Um atomare und isolierte Transaktionen realisieren zu können, nutzt jeder DBH die DLM-Schnittstelle. Die fundamentale Eigenschaft, die der DLM an dieser Schnittstelle erbringt, ist kompatible Locks (und nur solche) zuzuteilen.

Wird durch den XCS-Manager ein Partnerausfall diagnostiziert, so impliziert dies die Terminierung aller Lockhalter auf dem ausgefallenen Knoten. D.h. der NSM kann alle durch den ausgefallenen Knoten gehaltenen Locks freigeben und ggfs. einem anderen Knoten zuteilen.

Wird durch den XCS-Manager nur ein Verbindungsausfall diagnostiziert, dürfen aus dieser Tatsache heraus keine Locks freigegeben werden (der Zugriff auf die shared Daten erfolgt direkt und ist vom Verbindungsausfall nicht betroffen).

Ein fehlerhafterweise diagnostizierter Partnerausfall würde zu einer (unerkannten) Netzpartition führen, die Konsistenzeigenschaft der Auskunftsfunktion wäre (unerkannt) nicht mehr gewährleistet, die Folgen würden bis zu Datenverlust und Datenzerstörung reichen.

Bei der Diagnose stützt sich der XCS-Manager auf zwei (bereits mit BS2000/OSD) freigegebene Überwachungsfunktionen:

1) Jeder Knoten überwacht seine Verbindungen zu jedem Verbundteilnehmer (dazu wird, falls eine Verbindung in einem bestimmten Toleranzintervall nicht genutzt wurde, eine Control-Message erzeugt). Bei Ausfall einer Verbindung wird versucht über alternative Pfade die Verbindung wieder zu etablieren.

2) Jeder Knoten schreibt auf die shared Datenträger sog. Lebendmeldungen, versehen mit einem inkrementierenden Zähler. Diese Lebendmeldungen werden von allen Partnern in konstanten Zeitabständen gelesen und es wird geprüft, ob sich der Zähler erhöht hat.

Der XCM diagnostiziert nun lokal für einen bestimmten Partner das Ereignis "Partnerausfall", wenn sowohl das Platten- (auf allen Platten) wie auch das Verbindungsprotokoll ausfällt. Dieses Ereignis wird mit den verbleibenden XCS-Knoten abgestimmt. Sind alle zu demselben Ergebnis gekommen, so wird die Rekonfiguration eingeleitet.

Dieses Verfahren basiert, wie alle bekannten Verfahren, auf zeitlichen Annahmen, bietet aber durch das Zwei-Wege-Prinzip (Kommunikation und Platte) eine genügende Robustheit.

Auf Grund des bereits erwähnten hohen Schadens, den ein irrtümlich angenommener Partnerausfall verursachen kann, ist nach dem Prinzip der sich selbst erfüllenden Prophezeihung noch folgender Algorithmus implementiert: Kann ein Knoten, wieder innerhalb eines bestimmten Zeitintervalls, weder mit einem Partner kommunizieren noch seine Lebendmeldung schreiben, so leitet er für sich selbst einen Zwangsshutdown ein.

4. Zusammenfassung

XCS - Cross Coupled System - bietet Systemdienste und Basismechanismen für verteilte Anwendungen im BS2000. Das sind im einzelnen:

Sollen Prozesse, die auch auf unterschiedlichen Knoten ablaufen, auf gemeinsamen permanenten Daten operieren (und werden die Daten dabei modifiziert), so müssen sich diese Prozesse untereinander koordinieren und synchronisieren.

Diese Synchronisation kann durch Kommunikation in der Applikationsebene oder aber, wie hier aufgezeigt, in der Betriebssystemebene erfolgen. Die Applikation erhält so eine Programmieroberfläche, die die Tatsache, ob und wenn ja, wieviele weitere Prozesse auf anderen Knoten existieren vollständig verbirgt. Die Schnittstelle zur Koordination bietet der Distributed Lock Manager.

Um von unterschiedlichen Knoten aus, auf gemeinsame Daten zugreifen zu können, müssen die Metadaten, wie z.B. physischer Ort eines Datums oder Zugriffsrechte für bestimmte Daten, an allen beteiligten Knoten bekannt sein. Dieser Dienst wird durch die Schnittstellen des Shared File Systems im BS2000 bereitgestellt.

Die Verfügbarkeit eines Services kann durch Verteilung erhöht werden. Dazu sind jedoch Basismechanismen, wie Überwachung, Fehleranalyse und Recovery bereitzustellen (und zu nutzen). Ohne diese Gegenmaßnahmen sinkt durch die Verteilung einer Funktion ihre Verfügbarkeit.

Die Schwierigkeiten, die sich hinter einer transaktionsgesicherten Modifikation eines verteilten Datenbestands verbergen, wurden im vorgestellten Szenario durch die Voraussetzung eines gemeinsam zugreifbaren Datenbestandes umgangen. Damit ist die örtliche Unabhängigkeit der einzelnen Knoten zueinander nur noch sehr eingeschränkt gegeben. Die angestrebten Ziele "erhöhte Leistung" und "verbesserte Verfügbarkeit" insbesondere im DB-Sharing-Betrieb - aber auch für andere verteilte Server - können jedoch gerade dadurch in hohem Maß erfüllt werden.

References

[A92] J.Anselment
XCS Konfigurationsverwaltung/Überwachung
SNI, internal November 1992

[B92] P. Bergmaier
Distributed Task Lock Manager
SNI, internal November 1992

[I90] MVS/ESA SP Version
Sysplex Technical Presentation Guide, September 90
IBM International Technical Support Center

[S87] W.E. Snaman, D.W. Thiel
Digital Technical Journal
No. 5, September 87

[S92] B. Speckmann
Node Synchronisation Management (NSM)
SNI, internal, November 1992

[Z92] S. Zäske
Different Implementations of a Distributed Lock Manager (DLM) and their Performance Evaluation, Modeling Results

Universität Dortmund, LS Informatik IV,
Project OSMOD '92, internal report

[Z93] S. Zäske
Different Implementations of a Distributed Lock Manager (DLM) and their Performance Evaluation, The Proposed Strategy
Universität Dortmund, LS Informatik IV,
Project OSMOD '92, internal report

MANTRA I:
An SIMD Processor Array for Neural Computation

Marc A. Viredaz
Swiss Federal Institute of Technology
EPFL - LAMI, IN-F Ecublens, CH - 1015 Lausanne
E-mail: viredaz@di.epfl.ch

Abstract

This paper presents an SIMD processor array dedicated to the implementation of neural networks. The heart of this machine is a systolic array of simple processing elements (PEs). *A VLSI custom chip containing 2×2 PEs was built. The machine is designed to sustain sufficient instruction and data flows to keep a utilization rate close to 100 %. Finally, this computer is intended to be inserted in a network of heterogeneous nodes.*

1 Introduction

Artificial neural networks have experienced, in the past ten years, a very rapidly growing interest. A large part of the researches and applications in this domain however still relies on simulations. Many researchers and a few commercial companies have proposed specialized hardware implementations. The majority of these are however dedicated to a single neural-network model or algorithm. At the present day, there is no platform which is, at the same time, versatile enough to implement any model, and fast enough to be used on large problems. In this paper a dedicated SIMD processor array is proposed as a *multi-model neural computer*.

This machine is based on a 2-D systolic array of VLSI custom chips. The whole machine is designed to sustain a utilization rate of the array close to 100 %. Several features were added for this purpose. A large part of the hardware is dedicated to an efficient internal storage and to input/output. Finally, provision has been made to integrate this machine in a heterogeneous-node network.

The MANTRA I machine has been designed with the following models in mind:

- Mono-layer networks: Perceptron [1], ADALINE [2], and delta rule.
- Multi-layer feed-forward networks: back-propagation rule [3].
- Fully-connected recurrent networks: Hopfield model [4].
- Self-organizing feature maps: Kohonen model [5].

For most of these algorithms, different versions can be run. It should however be stressed that the machine does not hard-wire these algorithms, but provides a set of basic operations. Any model making use of only these operations, can therefore be implemented.

A description of these algorithms is beyond the scope of this paper. However, to appreciate the proposed architecture from the computer architect point-of-view, it is sufficient

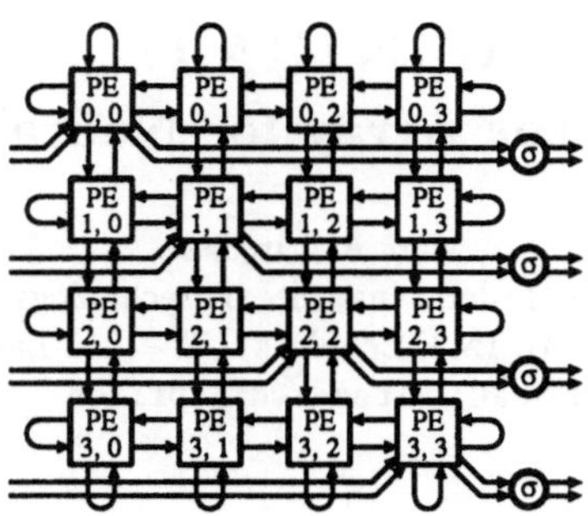

Figure 1 : Square systolic array of GENES IV processing elements.

to know what kind of computation should be performed. For this purpose, appendix A.1 describes the back-propagation rule, and appendix A.2 a version of the Kohonen model. The delta rule can be viewed as a single-layer back-propagation.

In collaboration with other laboratories, this experimental machine will be applied to static security assessment in power distribution networks [6] and to meteorology.

2 The GENES IV systolic array

In his Ph.D. thesis [7], F. Blayo observed that four basic scalar and matrix operations are sufficient to implement most widely-used neural-network models. He showed that these operations can be efficiently implemented on a 2-D systolic array. The same analysis was then extended to a larger set of models in a paper by C. Lehmann *et al.* [8], resulting in nine operations.[1] The computer architect should however observe that some operations can always be combined, hence allowing a smaller set of "composed operations."

Based on these considerations, a few VLSI digital circuits called *Generic Element for Neuro-Emulator Systolic arrays* or *GENES* were implemented. The first prototype, referred to as *GENES HN8* [9], was used to show that a such array can be effective. The latest version, called *GENES IV*, forms the heart of the MANTRA I machine. Since this chip has already been described elsewhere [10] only a short overview is provided here.

A GENES IV array is a square mesh of simple *processing elements (PEs)*. Each PE is connected by serial lines to its four neighbors as shown in figure 1. All input and output operations are performed by the PEs located on the north-west to south-east diagonal.

The GENES IV structure implements six different operations, grouped in three categories. The first operation is the *matrix-vector product*:

$$\vec{\mathbf{p}} = \mathbf{W} \cdot \vec{\mathbf{x}} \tag{1}$$

This operation can also be viewed as the *scalar* or *dot product* between the input vector $\vec{\mathbf{x}}$ and each row $\mathbf{W}_i$ of the synaptic weight matrix $\mathbf{W}$. The second operation is the computation of the *squared Euclidean distance* between a vector and each row of a matrix:

$$p_i = \sum_{j=1}^{N} (x_j - W_{i,j})^2 \tag{2}$$

The systolic flow of data for these two operations is shown in figure 2 (a). Each cell

[1]It should be noticed that some of the original operations proposed in [7] were divided or decomposed into several operations in [8], in an attempt to provided a more rigorous analysis.

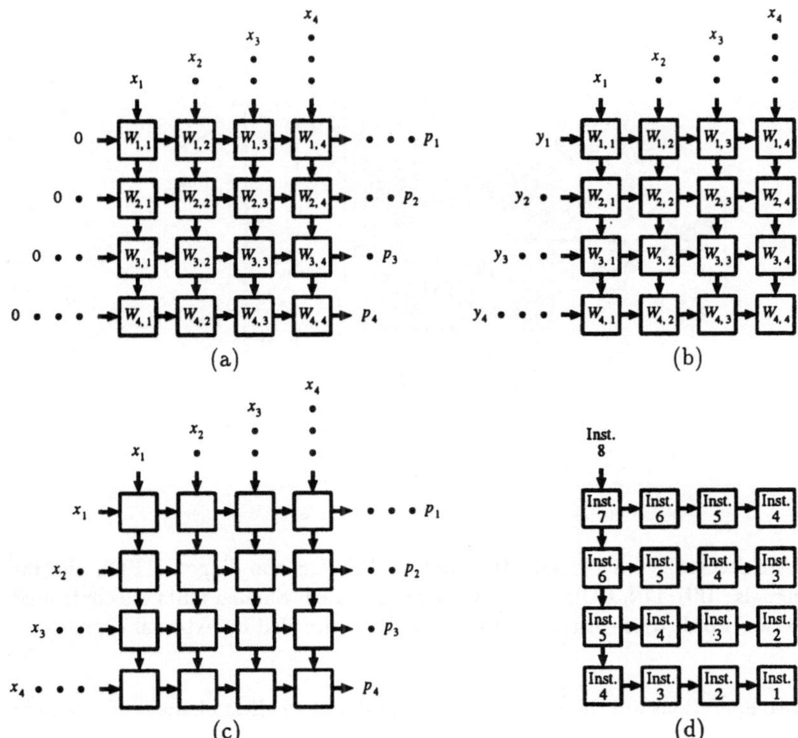

Figure 2 : Systolic flows in the GENES IV array. (a) Matrix-vector product or Euclidean distance computation. (b) Synaptic weight updating using the Hebbian or Kohonen learning rules. (c) Search for the smallest/largest element of a vector. (d) Instruction flow.

contains an element $W_{i,j}$ of the matrix $\mathbf{W}$. The input vector $\vec{\mathbf{x}}$ arrives from the north. Each PE computes either the product $x_j \cdot W_{i,j}$ of its north input and the stored weight or the squared difference $(x_j - W_{i,j})^2$ of the same two values. This result is then added to the partial sum received from the west, and sent to the east. The partial sums are initially set to zero. For the sake of clarity, figure 2 shows the input values "diagonally" entered from the north and west sides, and the output vector retrieved from the east one. In the actual operation, all inputs are entered on the diagonal, and initially flow in the reverse direction until they are reflected. In the same way, the outputs are reflected on the east side and then extracted from the diagonal. This feature allows to enter and retrieve all the elements of a vector at the same time.

The second category groups the synaptic weight updating by the *Hebbian learning rule* and the *Kohonen learning rule*, described by equation (3) and (4) respectively:

$$W_{i,j} := W_{i,j} + y_i \cdot x_j \tag{3}$$

$$W_{i,j} := W_{i,j} + y_i \cdot (x_j - W_{i,j}) \tag{4}$$

Equation (3) can be written in a matrix form as $\mathbf{W} := \mathbf{W} + \vec{\mathbf{y}} \cdot \vec{\mathbf{x}}^{\mathrm{T}}$. The data flow for both operations is shown in figure 2(b). Two vectors $\vec{\mathbf{x}}$ and $\vec{\mathbf{y}}$ flow from the north and west. On each PE, the stored synaptic weight is updated according to equation (3) or (4).

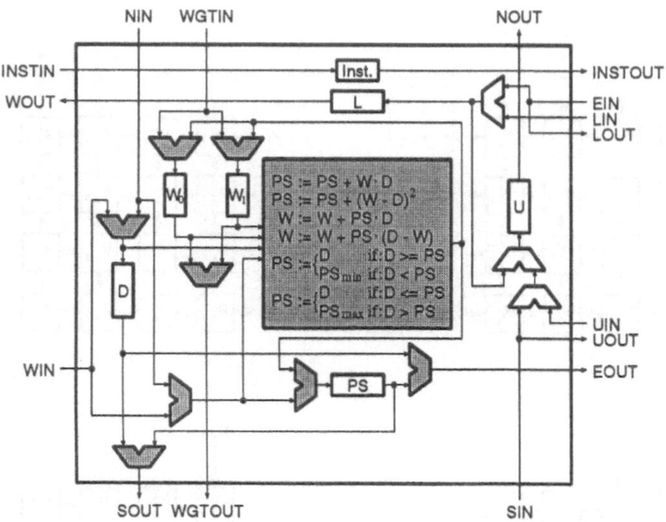

Figure 3: Architecture of a GENES IV diagonal PE. On non-diagonal PEs, the input/output signals: UIN, LIN, UOUT, and LOUT are disabled. Shaded units are controlled by the instruction word, while other units are globally controlled by external signals.

The last two operations are the search for the largest and smallest element of a vector:

$$y_i = \begin{cases} x_i & \text{if: } x_i = \max_j(x_j) \\ N_{\min} & \text{if: } x_i < \max_j(x_j) \end{cases} \tag{5}$$

$$y_i = \begin{cases} x_i & \text{if: } x_i = \min_j(x_j) \\ N_{\max} & \text{if: } x_i > \min_j(x_j) \end{cases} \tag{6}$$

Where $N_{\min}$ is the smallest representable number, and $N_{\max}$ the largest one. Figure 2 (c) shows the flow of data for these operations. The vector $\vec{x}$ is injected from the north and west. Each PE forwards the data received from the west if it is larger (smaller) than that received form the north, otherwise it replaces it with $N_{\min}$ ($N_{\max}$).

Like any systolic array, a GENES IV system behaves as a pipeline. The performance, may therefore dramatically decrease if it is not kept full. When the operations have to be changed often,[2] as it is the case with neural algorithms, it would be disastrous to have every PE executing the same instruction at the same time (conventional SIMD paradigm), because the pipeline would have to be emptied and refilled for each change. To avoid this inefficiency, instructions flow as shown by figure 2 (d), accompanying the corresponding data. This feature ensures that the pipeline is kept full during any possible computation.

Figure 3 shows the resulting PE. An important feature is that two registers W_0 and W_1 can hold the synaptic weights. This characteristic gives to the GENES IV architecture the ability to deal with virtual matrixes larger than the physical array. The virtual matrix is divided into sub-matrixes that fit on the array, which is then time-shared between them. A sub-matrix can therefore be used for computation while the previous one is saved to memory and the next one simultaneously loaded, maintaining a 100 % utilization rate.

[2]In the present context, "often" means: after a number of operations that is smaller or of the same order of magnitude than twice the number of PEs per side (pipeline depth).

Model	Evaluation phase	Learning phase
Perceptron, ADALINE, Delta rule	$400 \cdot 10^6$ CPS	$200 \cdot 10^6$ CUPS
Back-propagation rule	$400 \cdot 10^6$ CPS	$133 \cdot 10^6$ CUPS
Kohonen with minimum/maximum	$200 \cdot 10^6$ CPS	$100 \cdot 10^6$ CUPS

Table 1 : Peak performance of a 40 × 40 PE GENES IV array (MANTRA I machine).

Another particularity is the use of multiplexers to exchange the functionality of the rows and columns. The transpose matrix $\mathbf{W}^T$ can therefore be used for the matrix-vector multiplication (or any other operation) as required by the back-propagation rule.

A VLSI chip, containing 2 × 2 PEs, was designed with standard cells in a CMOS 1 μm technology. It is composed of 71690 transistors (3179 standard cells) on a die of $6.3 \times 6.1\,\text{mm}^2$. The registers W_0 and W_1 are 33 bits wide (including an overflow bit), but only the most significant 16 bits are used for non-learning operations. The other registers D, PS, U, and L are all 40 bits wide. Only 16 bits of the register D are however used for other operations than the search for the largest/smallest element of a vector. Similarly, the register PS is used as a 17-bit value for the two learning operations. Finally, since the computation is serial, a PE requires 40 clock cycles to complete an instruction. This period is referred to as a *macro-cycle*.

The heart of the MANTRA I machine, shown in figure 4, is a GENES IV array of 40 × 40 PEs running at 10 MHz. Like any SIMD computer, this machine is composed of a parallel or SIMD part, described in section 3, and of a controller, discussed in section 4. The peak performance of a such array is given in table 1

3 The SIMD part

3.1 The input/output units

Neural networks require different types of data: (1) the synaptic weights $\mathbf{W}$, (2) the inputs $\vec{\mathbf{x}}$, (3) the outputs $\vec{\mathbf{y}}$, and (4) the desired outputs $\vec{\mathbf{d}}$. Since the outputs $\vec{\mathbf{y}}$ of an iteration is often the inputs $\vec{\mathbf{x}}$ of the next one, both should be stored in the same memory. Furthermore, during weight updating phases, two such values must be simultaneously input to the array. This imposes the use of two memory banks, referred to as *XY memory* and *auxiliary Y memory*. Other data can be stored in separate memories, namely the *weight memory* and *desired output memory*.

The weight, XY, and auxiliary Y memories must support a read and a write access every clock cycle. At the same time, the controller should be able to store or retrieve data without disturbing the SIMD part. These two requirements make multi-port memories good candidates. However, only two types of these devices can be found as conventional off-the-shelf chips: dual-port static RAMs and Video RAMs. The first type was discarded because of its small capacity and large package, and the second one because there is no way to remove one of the serial/parallel conversion units by using their serial port.[3]

FIFOs were instead used to let the controller store and retrieve data. Inputs can be read from a FIFO or from memory. In the former case they can also be simultaneously written into the corresponding memory for a later use. Similarly outputs can be written into a FIFO, into memory, or into both at the same time.

[3]This is due to the parallel nature of the sigma and function of Y units described in section 3.2.

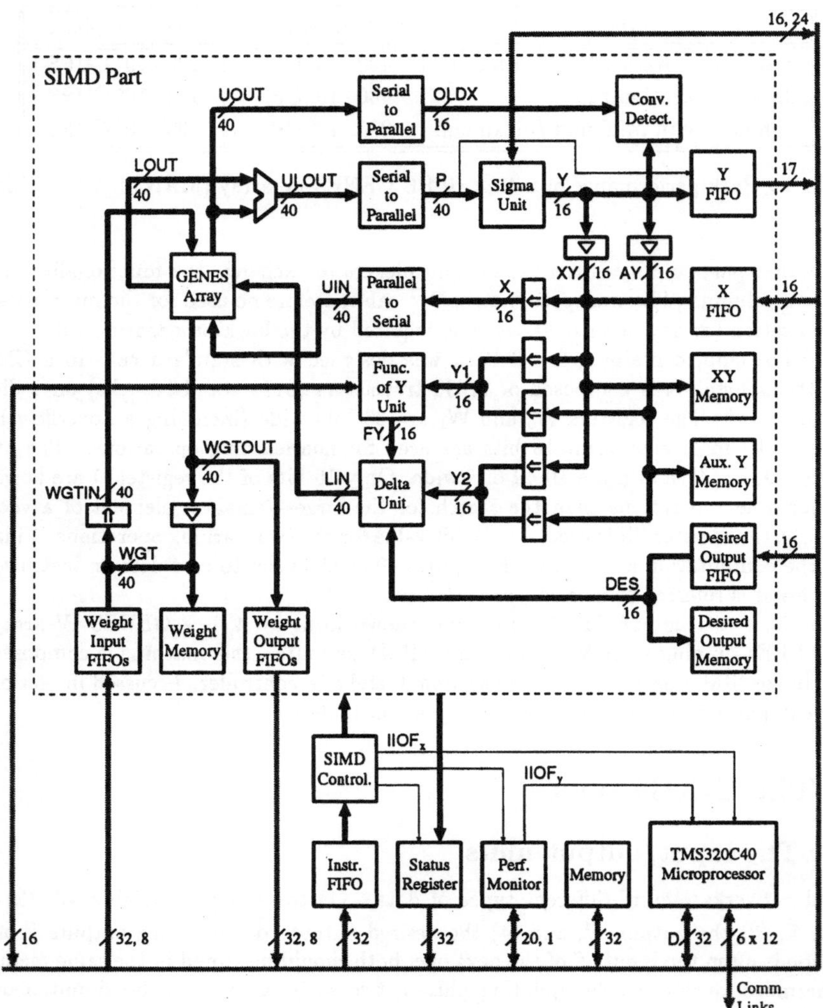

Figure 4 : Architecture of the MANTRA I machine.

3.2 The non-linear function units

The *sigma unit* and the *function of Y unit* are used to implement arbitrary, usually non-linear, functions. In order to keep the hardware simple, they were implemented as look-up tables. Since the inputs and outputs of the function of Y unit are 16 bits wide, there was no problem to implement a full table. Four such tables can actually be prepared in memory and selected at run-time without stopping the SIMD part.

The design of the sigma unit was less simple, because it converts a 40-bit value into a 16-bit one. Since a table of 2^{40} entries (2 Tbyte) is obviously unrealistic, and since the truncation of the input bits would not yield an accurate enough result — at least for some parts of the function — another solution had to be found. The chosen implementation is

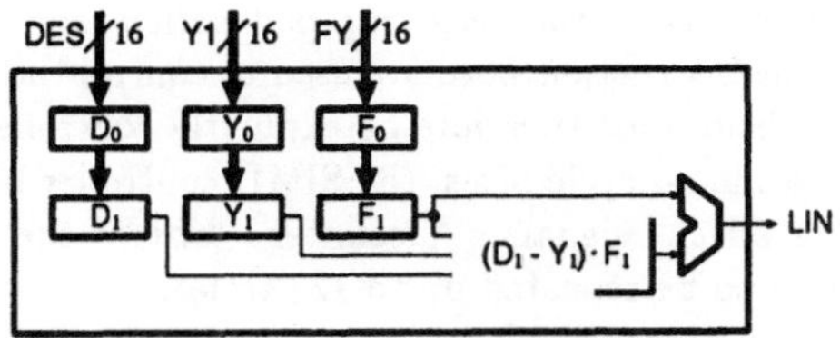

Figure 5 : Architecture of a delta unit's cell.

a double look-up table, consisting in a *coarse-grain table* mapping the whole input space at reduced precision, and a *fine-grain table* mapping a small window at high precision. A comparator allows to place this window anywhere in the input space (aligned on multiples of half of its size). A mechanism allows to zoom from full precision (one entry per input) to one entry for 128 inputs, hence trading the table's size with its precision.

3.3 The delta unit

Algorithms such as the delta or back-propagation rules, require the multiplication of the corresponding elements of two vectors, one of them being the difference of two vectors:

$$\delta_i \;=\; \varepsilon_i \cdot \sigma'(p_i) \;=\; (d_i - y_i) \cdot \sigma'(p_i) \tag{7}$$

This operation can not be efficiently performed by the 2-D GENES IV array, but can be carried out by the *delta unit*, an extra column of specialized cells. The inputs of these cells, shown in figure 5, are parallel while their outputs are serial. The cell's arithmetic unit can be bypassed when the computation of equation (7) is not required, the delta unit acts then as a parallel-to-serial converter. Three such cells are integrated on a VLSI chip, called *GACD1*, containing 16896 transistors (769 standard cells) on a die of $3.2 \times 3.2\,\mathrm{mm}^2$.

4 The control part

The control part of the MANTRA I machine, groups all the units shown outside the dashed box of figure 4. Its tasks are to configure the SIMD part, to dispatch instructions, and to manage the inputs and outputs. This part is a complete SISD system based on the TMS320C40 microprocessor from Texas Instruments running at 20 MHz. It should also handle the communications with a host computer and between different interconnected MANTRA I computers.

The main feature, that led to the choice of the TMS320C40 microprocessor, is the availability of six built-in communication channels (8 bits wide, 20 Mbyte/s). These links allow to connect multiple MANTRA I machines together and to a host computer. Other characteristics of the TMS320C40 taken into account are its two busses, its six built-in general-purpose DMA channels, and its 8 Kbyte of internal RAM.

4.1 The SIMD interface

As discussed in section 3.1, FIFOs are used to transfer data from the microprocessor to the SIMD part and vice-versa. Instructions are also written into the *instruction FIFO* by the microprocessor before being interpreted by the *SIMD controller*. If this FIFO becomes empty, the whole SIMD part is frozen until a new instruction is available.

The MANTRA I system follows the *very long instruction word (VLIW)* philosophy, that is, different fields of the instruction word are used to control the different units of the machine. Resource parallelism must therefore be explicitly controlled by the instruction flow. Instructions act on a macro-cycle basis, the SIMD controller being in charge, every clock cycle, of generating all the signals. A counter — one of the instruction's field — allows the same instruction to be repeated up to 128 times.

Besides the actual instructions, *auxiliary instructions* can also be sent through the instruction FIFO. They are either configuration information — such as which table should be used in the sigma or function of Y units — or initial addresses for the different memories. Except for the desired output memory, two addresses are attached to each memory, one being used for the data transmitted to the GENES IV array, and the other for the data received from it. These addresses are incremented after each access.

Since the interface between the SIMD and control parts consist only of asynchronous FIFOs and of a few double-synchronized status signals,[4] these two parts can run on two separate clocks.

4.2 The performance monitor

Performance degradation in the MANTRA I machine can be of two types: static and dynamic. The former type occurs when only a subset of the PEs is used during all or part of the computation. This is the case when the synaptic weight matrix — or sub-matrix if virtual networks are used, as described in section 2 — is smaller than the GENES IV array. Though, the penalty of filling and emptying the pipeline at the beginning and end of the computation belongs to this category, it is usually neglectable. Dynamic performance degradation, on the other hand, is due to stall cycles when instructions are lacking.

Given an algorithm and a set of parameters, the static performance of the MANTRA I computer can be calculated with simple formulas. There is therefore no need for a special hardware. The dynamic performance is however not deterministic, since it can be caused by delays in the communication between the MANTRA I system and a host computer, or any other systems providing inputs or requiring outputs. A dedicated unit, the *performance monitor*, was therefore implemented to compute the percentage of clock cycles when the SIMD part is active.

5 Heterogeneous-node network

As explained in section 4, a key feature of the TMS320C40 microprocessor is the availability of built-in communication channels, which allow the MANTRA I machine to be connected to a network of heterogeneous nodes, as shown in figure 6.

The first type of nodes a MANTRA I system can be connected to, is a host computer. An SBus board containing a TMS320C40 was developed to connect the system to any SUN 4 or SUN SPARCstation. It implements *direct virtual memory access (DVMA)*.

Another important element of this network, is a TMS320C40-based parallel processor, that can be used for any type of non-neural pre- or post-processing. Such a machine was developed at our laboratory [11]. In this system, individual processors are interconnected through cables. Though figure 6 shows a torus, any topology can be hard-wired: 1-D rings (or linear arrays) to 3-D hyper-tori (meshes), hypercubes up to six dimensions, etc. If the six communication links are used by the parallel processor (3-D hyper-tori or 6-D

[4]Figure 4 shows that the sigma and function of Y units are also directly interfaced to the microprocessor. However, these units are accessed (initialized) only when the SIMD part is inactive (frozen).

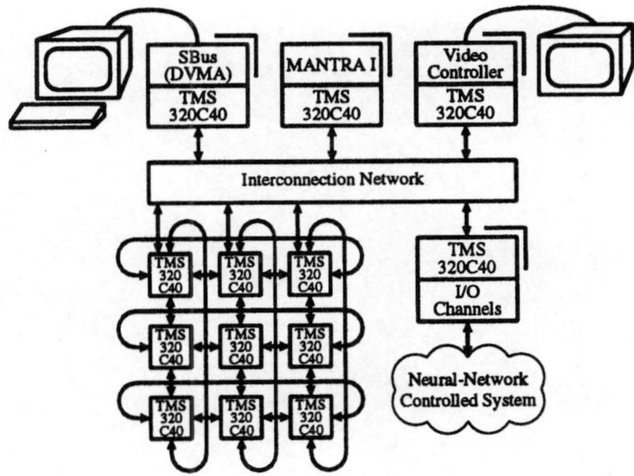

Figure 6 : Possible heterogeneous network hosting MANTRA I machines.

hypercubes), than the topology must be slightly altered to implement a connection to other nodes of the heterogeneous-node network.

Any other dedicated node, such as a video-controller or an interface to a real-time system to be controlled, can easily be implemented as an extension to the TMS320C40 processor board of the presented system.[5]

6 Project status

The MANTRA I machine is built of four different boards: a general-purpose processor board and three dedicated boards shown in figure 7:

1. **Processor board:** This board was designed by C. Marguerat [11] as a building block for a parallel processor. It contains 33 chips.
2. **Control board:** This board groups all the control logic and the storage units of figure 4 (138 chips).
3. **Input/output board:** This board contains the delta, parallel-to-serial, and serial-to-parallel units of figure 4. It is made of 465 chips including 14 GACD1 chips.
4. **GENES IV array board:** This board houses a matrix of 100 GENES IV chips. One such board is required for small configurations (up to $20 \times 20 = 400$ PEs), and four boards for larger ones (up to $40 \times 40 = 1600$ PEs),

As of June 1993, a first prototype of the machine has been designed, manufactured, and successfully debugged. It is running on a scaled-down clock of 8 MHz (instead of 10 MHz). A second revision of the control board is currently under manufacturing. It should eliminate the electrical problems (ground bounce and reflections) encountered on the first version and allow the machine to run at its nominal clock.

A first algorithm, the delta rule, has already been ported. It showed that dynamic utilization rates of 97 % to 99 % can easily be achieved when the data are present in

[5]The MANTRA I computer is actually implemented as such an extension.

(a)

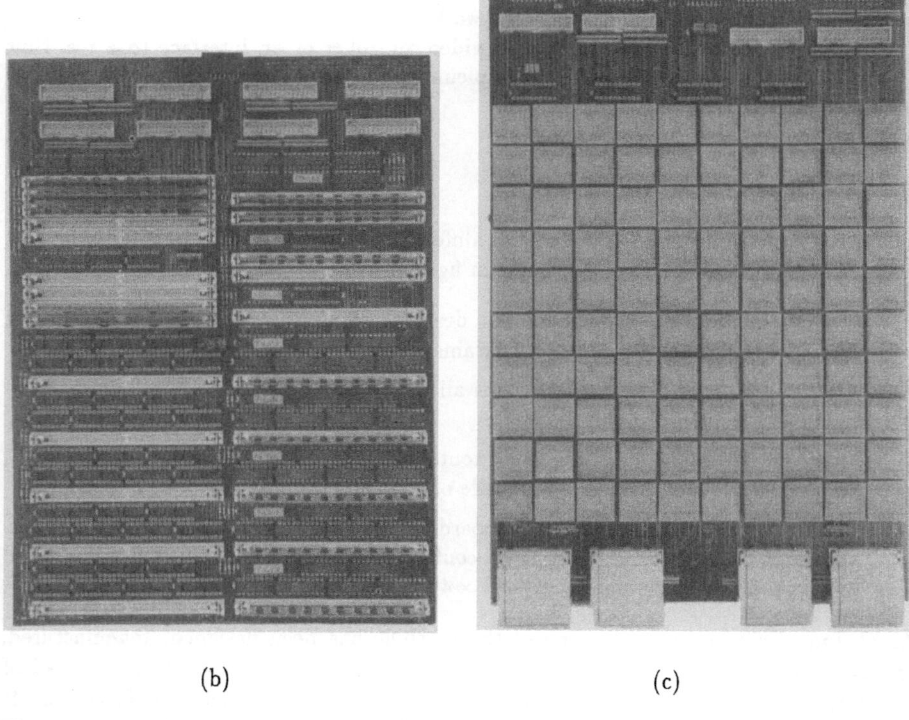

(b) (c)

Figure 7 : MANTRA I printed circuit boards. (a) Control board. (b) Input/output board. (c) GENES IV array board. (Photographs: Heidi Viredaz-Bader.)

the microprocessor's memory. Other algorithms (back-propagation rule, Kohonen model, etc.) as well as a communication library are currently under development.

7 Conclusion

The GENES IV architecture, presented here, is a good candidate for an SIMD processor array dedicated to neural computation. Its strength comes from its large number of simple PEs that can sustain a utilization rate close to 100 %. Its good scalability, makes it well suited for WSI.

This systolic array has been integrated in the MANTRA I neural computer. Its design was mainly focussed on sustaining the instruction flow and input/output data flows required to keep the GENES IV array busy.

Due to its heavily pipelined nature, the MANTRA I machine suffers from the typical restrictions of large pipelines. That is, the targeted applications must present an intrinsic parallelism, that is large enough to hide the pipeline latency — which has, in the framework of neural computation, for consequence that applications should be insensitive to the use of large epochs — and the problems must be sufficiently large.

Acknowledgements

The author would like to thank Prof. Jean-Daniel Nicoud, the laboratory director, without whom this project would not have been possible. The work of François Blayo and Christian Lehmann provided the bases of the present project. The author deeply acknowledges the help of Paolo Ienne who co-designed the architecture of the GENES IV and GACD1 chips, and whose careful work at implementing and simulating these chips led to a first working silicon in both cases. Special thanks go to Christophe Marguerat for his advise with the TMS320C40, and whose processor board proved to be of great help in testing the MANTRA I machine. Finally, Georges Vaucher and Peter Brühlmeier should be thanked for their outstanding work at placing and routing the different printed circuit boards, and André Guignard for his help in packaging the VLSI circuits.

A Summary of neural algorithms

A.1 The back-propagation rule

The following equations describe the back-propagation rule using epoch updating for an L-layer feed-forward network. Equations 8 to 10 are evaluated for each layer q and for each vector $\vec{\mathbf{x}}(s)$ of the current epoch: $s_1 \leq s \leq s_2$. The synaptic weights $\mathbf{W}^{[q]}$ are then updated according to equation 11. This process is repeated for each epoch.

$$\vec{\mathbf{y}}^{[q]}(s) = \sigma(\vec{\mathbf{p}}^{[q]}(s)) = \sigma(\mathbf{W}^{[q]} \cdot \vec{\mathbf{y}}^{[q-1]}(s)) \quad \text{for}: q = 1, 2, \ldots, L \tag{8}$$

$$\delta_i^{[L]}(s) = \left(d_i(s) - y_i^{[L]}(s)\right) \cdot \sigma'(p_i^{[L]}(s)) \tag{9}$$

$$\delta_i^{[q]}(s) = \vec{\mathbf{W}}_i^{[q+1]\mathrm{T}} \cdot \vec{\boldsymbol{\delta}}^{[q+1]}(s) \cdot \sigma'(p_i^{[q]}(s)) \quad \text{for}: q = 1, 2, \ldots, L-1 \tag{10}$$

$$\mathbf{W}^{[q]} := \mathbf{W}^{[q]} + \alpha \cdot \sum_{s=s_1}^{s_2} \vec{\boldsymbol{\delta}}^{[q]}(s) \cdot \vec{\mathbf{y}}^{[q-1]\mathrm{T}}(s) \quad \text{for}: q = 1, 2, \ldots, L \tag{11}$$

Where the vector $\vec{\mathbf{W}}_i^{[q]}$ is the ith column of the matrix $\mathbf{W}^{[q]}$, and $\vec{\mathbf{y}}^{[0]}(s) = \vec{\mathbf{x}}(s)$.

A.2 The Kohonen model

The following equations describe the Kohonen model, using the Euclidean distance, winner take-all, and epoch updating.

$$y_i(s) = \sqrt{\sum_{j=1}^{N} (x_j(s) - W_{i,j})^2} \tag{12}$$

$$y_{I(s)}(s) = \min_i (y_i(s)) \tag{13}$$

$$\mathbf{W}_i := \mathbf{W}_i + \alpha \cdot \sum_{\substack{s=s_1 \\ \forall s:\, i \in N(I(s))}}^{s_2} \left(\vec{\mathbf{x}}^{\mathrm{T}}(s) - \mathbf{W}_i\right) \tag{14}$$

Where the vector $\mathbf{W}_i$ is the ith row of the matrix $\mathbf{W}$, and $N(i)$ is the set of neighbors of i. Neuron $I(s)$ is usually called the winner (for the input s).

References

[1] F. Rosenblatt. *The Perceptron: A Probabilistic Model for Information Storage and Organization in the Brain. Psychological Review*, 65:386-408, 1958.

[2] Bernard Widrow and Marcian E. Hoff. *Adaptive Switching Circuits.* In *IRE-WESCON Convention Record*, pages 96-104, New-York, USA, 1960.

[3] Yann Le Cun. *A Learning Scheme for Asymmetric Threshold Network.* In *Proceedings of Cognitiva 85*, Paris, France, June 1985.

[4] John J. Hopfield. *Neural Networks and Physical Systems with Emergent Collective Computational Abilities. Proceedings of the National Academy of Sciences*, 79:2254-2258, April 1982.

[5] Teuvo Kohonen. *Analysis of a Simple Self-Organizing Process. Biological cybernetics*, 44:135-140, 1982.

[6] Dagmar Niebur and Alain J. Germond. *Unsupervised Neural Net Classification of Power System Static Security States. International Journal on Electrical Power and Energy Systems*, 114(2 & 3):233-242, April & June 1992.

[7] François Blayo. *Une Implantation Systolique des Algorithmes Connexionnistes.* Ph.D. thesis N° 904, EPFL, Lausanne, Switzerland, 1990.

[8] Christian Lehmann, Marc Viredaz, and François Blayo. *A Generic Systolic Array Building Block for Neural Networks with On-Chip Learning. IEEE Transactions on Neural Networks*, 4(3), May 1993. To appear.

[9] Christian Lehmann and François Blayo. *A VLSI Implementation of a Generic Systolic Synaptic Building Block for Neural Networks.* In José G. Delgado-Frias and William R. Moore, editors, *VLSI for Artificial Intelligence and Neural Networks*, chapter 4.8, pages 325-334. Plenum Press, 1991.

[10] Marc A. Viredaz, Christian Lehmann, François Blayo, and Paolo Ienne. *MANTRA: A Multi-Model Neural-Network Computer.* In *Proceedings of the 3rd International Workshop on VLSI for Neural Networks and Artificial Intelligence*, Oxford, UK, September 1992.

[11] Christophe Marguerat. *Artificial Neural Network Algorithms on a Parallel DSP System.* Internal Report no. R93.23C, LAMI, EPFL, Lausanne, Switzerland, 1993.

Simulation Neuronaler Netze auf SIMD- und MIMD-Parallelrechnern

Andreas Zell, Günter Mamier, Niels Mache, Michael Vogt

Universität Stuttgart,
Institut für Parallele und Verteilte Höchstleistungsrechner (IPVR),
Abt. Prakt. Informatik - Bildverstehen
Breitwiesenstr. 20-22, D-70565 Stuttgart

E-mail: zell@informatik.uni-stuttgart.de

Abstract

Wir beschreiben hier Erfahrungen mit verschiedenen Implementierungen neuronaler Netze auf einem massiv parallelen SIMD-Rechner und einem MIMD-Supercomputer. Bei dem SIMD-Rechner handelt es sich um eine MasPar MP-1216 mit 16384 Prozessoren, der MIMD-Rechner ist eine Intel Paragon mit 72 Prozessoren. Zwei der Implementierungen wurden als knoten- und trainingsmusterparallele Simulatorkerne des Stuttgarter Neuronale Netze Simulators (SNNS) entwickelt, die MIMD-Implementierung auf der Intel Paragon verwendet nur Trainingsmusterparallelität. Die parallelen Implementierungen liefern bei optimaler Netztopologie sehr hohe Leistungsdaten: unsere Höchstwerte liegen bei 348 MCPS und 129 MCUPS für Backpropagation auf der MasPar MP-1. Auf einer MasPar MP-2 mit ebenfalls 16384 Prozessoren konnten 972 MCPS und 360 MCUPS gemessen werden.

1 Einführung und Motivation

Neuronale Netze eignen sich nach verbreiteter Ansicht ideal für eine Implementierung auf Parallelrechnern. Da neuronale Netze aus einer großen Zahl einfacher Einheiten (Zellen, künstlichen Neuronen) bestehen, die parallel arbeiten und Information über ein Netzwerk gerichteter, gewichteter Verbindungen (links, connections) austauschen, erscheint es naheliegend, diese auf Parallelrechner mit sehr vielen (tausenden) Prozessoren abzubilden, die über ein Kommunikationsnetzwerk miteinander kommunizieren. Kommerziell verfügbare Parallelrechner dieses Typs, die mit tausenden einfacher Prozessoren arbeiten, besitzen meist eine SIMD-Architektur, d.h. alle Prozessoren führen zu einem Zeitpunkt synchron die gleichen Instruktionen auf den verteilten Daten durch. Zu diesen SIMD-Parallelrechnern zählen z.B. die Connection Machine CM-2, die MasPar MP-1 und MP-2. Ihre größte Konkurrenz sind die in letzter Zeit verfügbar gewordenen skalierbaren MIMD-Rechner wie die Connection Machine CM-5, die Intel Paragon oder Parsytec Gigacluster-Transputersysteme. Diese sind allerdings derzeit noch durch praktische Grenzen (Preis, Kühlung, Verfügbarkeit der Prozessoren etc.) auf vergleichsweise kleine Konfigurationen (30-1000 Prozessoren) beschränkt. Wir beschreiben hier verschiedene parallele Implementierungen neuronaler Netze auf einem SIMD-Parallelrechner MasPar MP-1216 unseres Instituts und einem MIMD-Parallelrechner Intel Paragon. Die hier vorgestellten parallelen Simulatoren wurden alle als parallele Simulatorkerne für den Stuttgarter Neuronale Netze Simulator (SNNS) [Zell et al. 90, 91a, 91b, 92, 93a, 93b] entwickelt.

2 Der Stuttgarter Neuronale Netze Simulator

Der Stuttgarter Neuronale Netze Simulator ist ein Simulator für Unix Workstations (Sun, DEC, HP, IBM), der am Institut für Parallele und Verteilte Höchstleistungsrechner (IPVR) an der Universität Stuttgart seit mehreren Jahren entwickelt wird. Er hat sich für die Forschung über Lernalgorithmen und ihre Effizienz, zur Visualisierung neuronaler Netze und zu Fragen der Eignung für eine massiv parallele Implementierung als gut geeignet erwiesen.

2.1 Struktur von SNNS

Die parallele Version von SNNS besteht aus zur Zeit aus dem sequentiellen Simulatorkern auf Unix Workstations, einem parallelen Simulatorkern für die MasPar MP-1 bzw für die Intel Paragon und der graphischen Oberfläche unter X-Windows. Jeder Simulatorkern operiert auf seiner internen Repräsentation der neuronalen Netze und führt alle Aktionen der Lern- und Arbeitsphase durch. Er ist eng gekoppelt mit der graphischen Benutzeroberfläche über eine Funktions-schnittstelle. Die Simulatorkerne sind aus Effizienz- und Portabilitätsgründen in ANSI C bzw. AMPL, einem parallelen ANSI-C-Derivat für den Parallelrechner geschrieben.

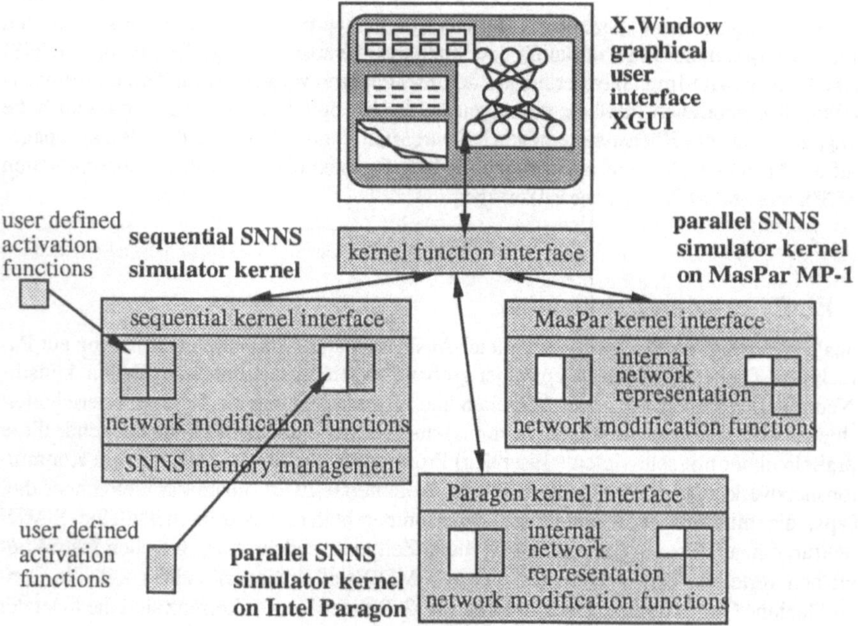

Abb. 1 Struktur des Stuttgarter Neuronale Netze Simulators bestehend aus sequentiellem Simulatorkern, parallelem Simulatorkern und graphischer Oberfläche.

Die graphische Benutzeroberfläche [Hübner 92], basierend auf X-Windows, ist ein Werkzeug zur Konstruktion und zur Visualisierung und interaktiven Modifikation von Netzen. Netze können durch die Benutzeroberfläche während der Simulation modifiziert werden, Zellen können eingefügt, entfernt oder verändert werden, Verbindungen zwischen den Zellen können eingefügt, gelöscht oder verändert werden. Die meisten Modifikationen können auf eine einfache Art direkt auf der visuellen Repräsentation der Netzwerktopologie durchgeführt werden.

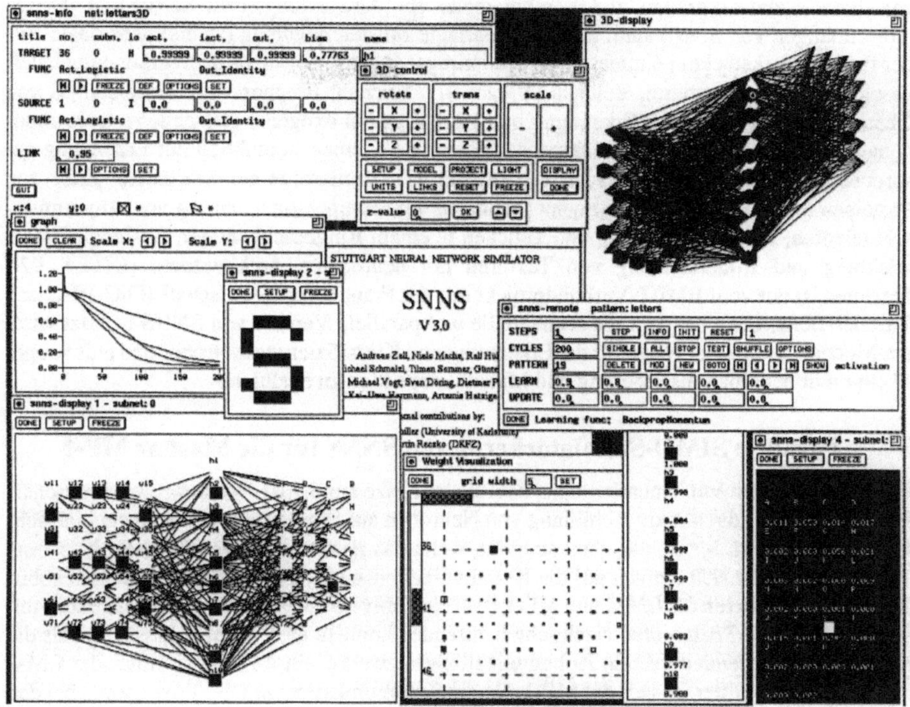

Abb. 2 Graphische Benutzeroberfläche von SNNS mit einem einfachen Netz zur Buchstabenerkennung: *info panel* (oben links), *3D control panel* (oben Mitte) und *3D-display* (oben rechts), *error graph* (Mitte links), *SNNS banner* (Mitte), *remote panel* (Mitte rechts), *2D-display* (unten links), *Hinton diagram* (unten Mitte), *2D-display* (unten rechts)

2.2 Von SNNS unterstützte konnektionistische Modelle

Vom Konzept her unterstützt SNNS eine große Zahl neuronaler Modelle. Jedes Netzwerk, das als gerichteter, gewichteter Graph dargestellt werden kann, kann simuliert werden. Die meisten Benutzer von SNNS benutzen jedoch einfache feedforward-Netze mit einer oder zwei Ebenen verdeckter Neuronen mit sigmoiden Aktivierungsfunktionen, obwohl die SNNS-Datenstrukturen auch rekurrente Netze unterstützen. Folgende Lernverfahren sind derzeit in SNNS implementiert: Backpropagation [Rumelhart, McClelland 86], Backpropagation mit Momentum und "flat spot elimination", Batch-Backpropagation, Quickprop [Fahlman 88], Backpercolation1 [Jurik 89], Rprop [Riedmiller, Braun 91], Cascade Correlation, Recurrent Cascade Correlation [Fahlman 90], Dynamic LVQ, Counterpropagation [Hecht-Nielsen 90], Radial Basis Functions [Poggio, Girosi 89] [Vogt 92], ART-1, ARTMAP und ART-2 [Carpenter, Grossberg 88], Backpropagation Through Time (BPTT), Quickprop Through Time (QPTT), Time-Delay Netze [Waibel 89] und selbstorganisierende Karten.

2.3 Anwendungen von SNNS

SNNS wird derzeit in über 300 Installationen weltweit verwendet, davon ca. je ein Drittel in Deutschland, dem übrigen Europa und den USA. Sein Hauptanwendungsbereich ist die universitäre Forschung, aber auch Firmen nutzen verstärkt SNNS als Werkzeug, um optimale Lernverfahren, Netzwerkgrößen und Lernparameter für Anwendungen zu bestimmen. Einige Anwendungen von SNNS sind: rotationsinvariante Mustererkennung (zweidimensionale Bilder flacher Werkstücke) [Zimmerer91], skalierungs- und positionsinvariante Erkennung handgeschriebener segmentierter Zeichen [Veigel 91], Kurzzeit-Prognose des Aktienkurses von Chemieaktien [Kubiak 91], Erkennung und Klassifikation exogener und endogener Komponenten ereigniskorrelierter hirnelektrischer Potentiale, Geräuschreduktion zur Erkennung gesprochener Sprache in Telefonsystemen [Sienel 91], Vorhersage der Sekundärstruktur von Proteinen aus der Aminosäuresequenz [Schnabel 92], Temperatursteuerung von Aluminiumschmelzöfen, Bahnstabilisierung von Teilchen in einem Ringbeschleuniger, Stoßdämpferentwicklung und Bilderkennung von Texturen mit neuronalen Architekturen [BITEX 92]. Letzteres ist ein vom BMFT-Verbundprojekt mit der Fraunhofer Gesellschaft (FhG-IPA) und Daimler-Benz, Ulm, bei dem die sequentielle und parallele Version von SNNS benutzt wird, um Modelle neuronaler Netze für die Erkennung und Klassifizierung isotroper und anisotroper Texturen in der Qualitätssicherung und Materialinspektion zu evaluieren.

3 Parallele SIMD-Simulatorkerne von SNNS für die MasPar MP-1

Wer sich näher mit Implementierungen neuronaler Netze auf SIMD-Parallelrechnern beschäftigt hat weiß, daß die direkte Abbildung von Neuronen auf Prozessoren in der Regel eine sehr schlechte Wahl ist. Sie ist nur dann sinnvoll, wenn das zu simulierende neuronale Netz eine Topologie hat, die sich einfach auf die Kommunikationstopologie des Parallelrechners abbilden läßt. Nun besitzen die CM-2 und MP-1 zwar eine universelle Kommunikationsstruktur, mit der sich beliebige Prozessoren Nachrichten zusenden können, diese ist aber langsamer als die zusätzlich existierenden lokalen Kommunikationsnetzwerke, ein 4-Nachbar-Gitter der CM-2 bzw. 8-Nachbar-Gitter (X-net) der MP-1. Da die Kommunikationszeit der Prozessoren bei den sehr einfachen Operationen der künstlichen Neuronen ein entscheidender Zeitfaktor ist versuchen die effizientesten Implementierungen neuronaler Netze auf SIMD-Rechnern eine Abbildung von Neuronen auf Prozessoren zu finden, die nur das Nachbar-Gitter benötigt.

Für die häufig verwendeten mehrstufigen feedforward-Netze mit Lernverfahren wie Backpropagation, Quickprop, Counterpropagation, Rprop, Backpercolation etc. ist eine 1:1-Abbildung von Neuronen auf Prozessoren sehr ineffizient, weil bei vollständig verbundenen Netzen jedes Neuron von allen Neuronen der Vorgängerschicht Eingaben erhält. Dies führt zu einem Kommunikationsmuster, das mit den Strukturen der Parallelrechner nicht mehr harmoniert. Glücklicherweise gibt es eine Reihe von Methoden, derartige vorwärtsgerichtete Netze doch sehr effizient auf Parallelrechner abzubilden. Einige davon sind in [Singer 90] beschrieben, wir stellen hier unsere Implementierungen vor, die momentan mit zu den effizientesten gehören.

3.1 Architektur der MasPar MP-1 und MP-2

Die MasPar MP-1216 ist ein SIMD-Parallelrechner mit bis zu 16384 Vier-Bit-Prozessoren. 32 Prozessoren sind auf einem einzigen Chip integriert, 32 Chips passen auf ein Board. Unser Modell soll eine Höchstleistung von 26000 MIPS (32 Bit Addition) und 1.5 bzw. 0.6 GFLOPS (32 Bit bzw. 64 Bit) besitzen.

Das Nachfolgermodell MasPar MP-2 besitzt die gleiche Anzahl von Prozessoren, jedoch sind dies 32-Bit-Prozessoren, und hat auch die gleiche interne Struktur und Kommunikationsarchitektur. Die Höchstleistung der MP-2216 wird mit 68000 MIPS und 6.3 bzw. 2.4 GFLOPS (32 Bit bzw. 64 Bit) angegeben.

Es gibt zwei getrennte Kommunikationssysteme auf der MasPar: eines ist ein dreistufiger Kreuzschienenverteiler (router) der bis zu 1024 simultane Verbindungen zwischen je zwei Prozessoren zuläßt, das andere ein torroidales 8-Nachbar-Gitter (X-Net). Die Kommunikationsbandbreite ist im ersten Fall (router) max. 1.5 GB/s, im zweiten Fall (X-Net) bis zu 24 GB/s. Dies macht deutlich, daß es vorteilhaft ist, das lokale Gitter so viel wie möglich zu nutzen, da hierbei die Kommunikationsbandbreite viel größer ist.

Die MasPar kann mit parallelen Versionen von C (AMPL) und Fortran programmiert werden MPPE (MasPar parallel programming environment), ein integriertes, auf X-Windows basierendes Entwicklungssystem, erleichtert die Programmentwicklung und Fehlersuche.

Von unserer Gruppe wurden mehrere massiv parallele Simulatorkerne für mehrstufige feedforward-Netzwerke für den Parallelrechner MasPar MP-1216 entwickelt. Ziel war die Simulation großer neuronaler Netze, speziell für Aufgaben der Bildverarbeitung, und Mustererkennung. Die parallelen Simulatorkerne wurden als Alternative zu dem sequentiellen Kern konzipiert. Aus der Graphikoberfläche heraus ist es möglich, zwischen beiden Kernen zur Laufzeit umzuschalten, vorausgesetzt, der Benutzer beschränkt sich auf mehrstufige feedforward-Netze.

Nach Vergleich einiger in der Literatur vorgeschlagener Ansätze zur Parallelisierung neuronaler Netze ([Singer 90], [Grajski et al. 90], [Chinn et al. 90] und [Zhang et al. 89]) entschieden wir uns zuerst für eine Kombination von Zellen-Parallelität und Trainingsmuster-Parallelität.

3.2 Erster SIMD-Simulatorkern für die MasPar MP-1

Die Implementierung des ersten parallelen Simulatorkerns [Mache 92] wurde in MPL durchgeführt, einem datenparallelen C-Derivat. Sie benutzt folgende Technik (Abb. 3):

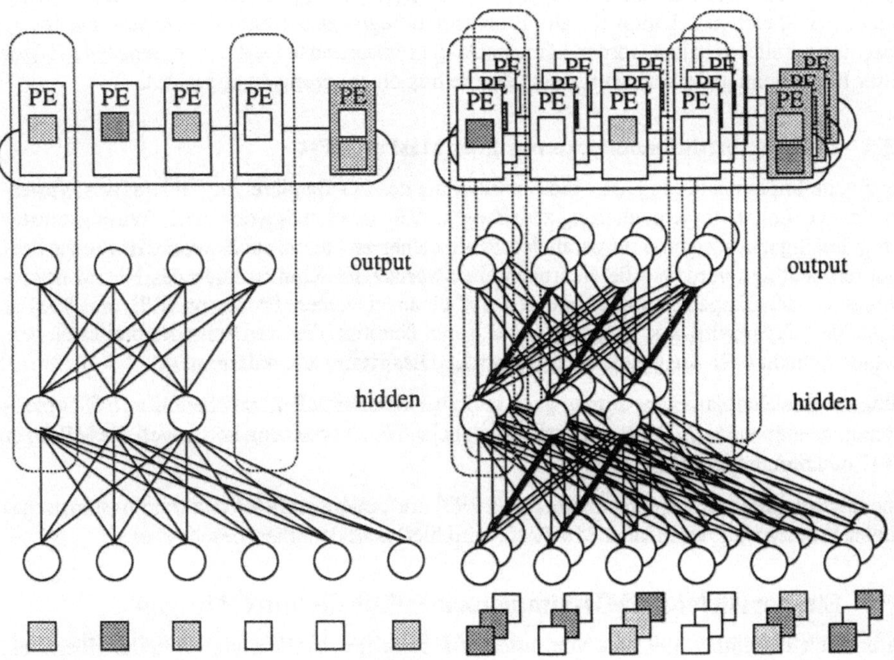

Abb. 3 Erster paralleler MasPar SNNS Kern mit einem 6-3-4 feedforward-Netz: alle verdeckten Neuronen und Ausgabeneuronen eines senkrechten Schnitts durch das Netz werden auf einen Prozessor abgebildet, alle Neuronen einer Ebene werden parallel trainiert (Knotenparallelität). Mehrere Netzwerkkopien mit gleichen Gewichten werden mit verschiedenen Trainingsmustern parallel trainiert (Trainingsmusterparallelität).

Alle verdeckten Neuronen und Ausgabeneuronen eines vertikalen Schnitts durch das Netzwerk werden auf einen einzelnen Prozessor (PE) der MasPar abgebildet. Jeder Prozessor speichert die Gewichte seiner Eingabeverbindungen. Die Aktivierung wird für alle Zellen einer Ebene parallel berechnet. Dafür wird eine Zahl von Prozessoren benötigt, die der Breite der breitesten verdeckten Schicht oder Ausgabeschicht entspricht. Ist die Eingabeschicht größer als die anderen Schichten, so speichert ein zusätzlicher Prozessor die übrigen Komponenten der Eingabemuster und sendet sie bei Bedarf an seinen linken Nachbarn. Die Prozessoren sind in einer logischen Ringarchitektur angeordnet, die mit dem X-Net sehr einfach realisiert werden kann (evtl. mit Kopieren an den Rändern). Während der Vorwärts- oder Rückpropagierung werden die Zwischenwerte für die Netzeingabe bzw. das akkumulierte Fehlersignal zyklisch nach links geschoben. Die Gewichte werden mit einem Verschiebefaktor von 1 in jedem Prozessor gespeichert. Dies erlaubt es, daß alle Zellen einer Ebene die Summe aller gewichteten Ausgaben der Vorgängerzellen in n Schritten berechnen, wenn n die Größe der Vorgängerschicht ist. Da die Breite eines feedforward-Netzes oft viel kleiner ist als die Zahl der Prozessoren der MasPar werden viele Kopien des gleichen Netzwerks mit verschiedenen Eingabemustern parallel auf der Maschine trainiert. Dadurch müssen Gewichtsänderungen für jedes Netzwerk einzeln berechnet werden, aber nur die Summe der Änderungen wird auf alle entsprechenden Gewichte der Netzwerkkopien angewandt. Dies ergibt einen "batch"-Lernalgorithmus, bei dem die "batch"-Größe ein Vielfaches der Zahl der gleichzeitig trainierten Netze ist.

Ein Vorteil dieses Ansatzes ist, daß die Zahl der benötigten Prozessoren unabhängig von der Größe der Eingabeschicht ist, die meist viel größer ist als die anderen Schichten. Somit kann eine größere Zahl von Netzen parallel trainiert werden. Ein Nachteil ist die Tatsache, daß ein PE viel mehr Musterkomponenten als die anderen speichern muß. In einer SIMD-Maschine mit identischer Speicherallokation für alle Prozessoren begrenzt die Zahl der Muster, die in der Maschine parallel gehalten werden können. Da die Mustertransferzeit der begrenzende Faktor dieser Implementierung war, wurde eine zweite Implementierung durchgeführt.

3.3 Zweiter SIMD-Simulatorkern auf der MasPar MP-1

Die zweite Implementierung hatte die Eliminierung des I/O-Bandbreitenproblems des Mustertransfers der ersten Implementierung zum Zweck. Ziel war es, möglichst viele Trainingsmuster in regelmäßiger Anordnung im parallelen PE-Speicher zu halten, auch wenn dafür mehr Prozessoren benötigt werden. Alle Neuronen eines vertikalen Schnitts durch das Netzwerk einschließlich der Eingabeneuronen werden auf einen einzelnen Prozessor (PE) der MasPar abgebildet. Dafür wird eine Zahl von Prozessoren benötigt, die der Breite der breitesten verdeckten Schicht oder Ausgabeschicht entspricht. Dies ist in Abb. 4 dargestellt.

Dieser zweite Simulatorkern konnte auch auf einer MasPar MP-2 mit ebenfalls 16 K Prozessoren gemessen werden. Dazu war nicht einmal eine Neuübersetzung nötig, weil die MP-2 zur MP-1 binärkompatibel ist.

Eine dritte parallele Implementierung [Hüttel 92] ein kantenparalleler und trainingsmusterparalleler Prototyp auf der MasPar MP-1216, wird hier nicht detailliert beschrieben.

4 Ein paralleler MIMD-Simulatorkern für die Intel Paragon

Da uns seit Dezember 1992 ein von unserem Institut für Parallele und Verteilte Höchstleistungsrechner (IPVR) gemeinsam mit dem Rechenzentrum der Universität Stuttgart (RUS) beschaffter Paralleler Supercomputer Intel Paragon mit 72 Prozessorknoten zur Verfügung steht, wird derzeit intensiv an einer Implementierung von SNNS für diesen MIMD-Rechner gearbeitet. Da es sich bei dieser Maschine um eine der ersten Installationen in Europa handelt und die Software noch im Beta-Test ist, sind unsere Ergebnisse mit Vorsicht zu bewerten.

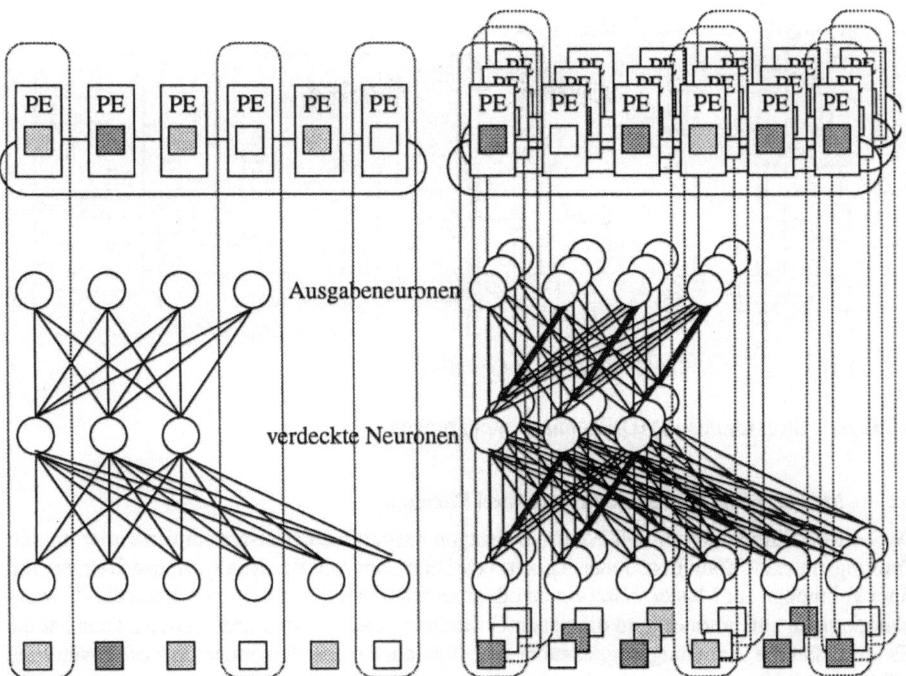

Abb. 4 Zweiter paralleler SNNS-Kern mit einem 6-3-4 feedforward-Netz: alle Neuronen einer Spalte und ihre Eingangsverbindungen werden auf einen Prozessor abgebildet, alle Neuronen einer Ebene werden parallel trainiert (Knoten-Parallelität). Viele Kopien des Netzwerks werden mit versch. Eingabemustern parallel trainiert (Trainingsmusterparallelität).

4.1 Architektur der Intel Paragon

Die an der Universität Stuttgart installierte Intel Paragon ist ein MIMD-Rechner mit physisch verteiltem Speicher und sehr leistungsfähigen Prozessorknoten. Die Installation besteht derzeit aus 72 Prozessorknoten, die in einer 2D-Gitterstruktur angeordnet sind. 66 Prozessoren davon sind Rechenknoten (compute nodes), die anderen sind Service-Knoten, Netzwerk- oder Disk I/O Knoten. Jeder Knoten besteht aus 2 Intel i860XP Prozessoren. Davon ist einer für die Anwendung zuständig (application processor), der andere nur für die Kommunikation mit den anderen Prozessoren (message processor). Jeder i860XP Prozessor besitzt einen Daten- und Codecache von je 16 KB und liefert 75 MFLOPS und 42 MIPS bei 50 MHz.Die Bus-Bandbreite beträgt 400 MB/s. Ein Knoten besitzt zwischen 16 und 128 MB Speicher (Abb. 5).

Als Betriebssystem läuft OSF/1. Neben einem datenparallelen Programmiermodell (date parallel model) und einem Modell mit virtuellem gemeinsamen Speicher (shared memory model), die beide als Optionen angeboten werden, wird in erster Linie das Modell der Prozeßkommunikation mit Nachrichten (message passing model) als flexibelstes, leistungsfähigstes und ausgereiftestes Programmiermodell für diese Hardware angeboten. Als Programmiersprachen stehen Fortran-77 und ANSI C zur Verfügung. Leider steht momentan noch keine leistungsfähige Programmierumgebung (X-Windows, Motif, emacs, etc.) auf unserer Paragon zur Verfügung, auch die Stabilität des Betriebssystems läßt noch einiges zu wünschen übrig.

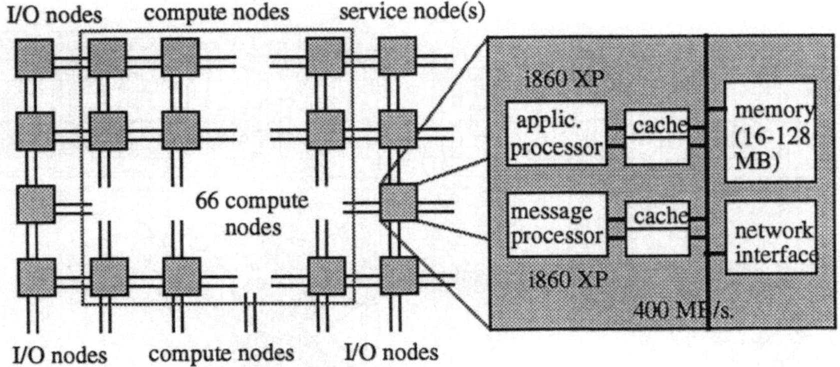

Abb. 5 Struktur des SIMD-Rechners Intel Paragon

4.2 MIMD-Simulatorkern auf der Intel Paragon

Der MIMD-Simulator von SNNS für die Paragon besitzt in einer ersten Implementierung nur Trainingsmuster-Parallelität. Jeder Knoten bearbeitet ein vollständiges Netz und trainiert mit einer Teilmenge der Muster. Nach einem oder mehreren parallelen Zyklen werden die Gewichtsänderungen aufsummiert und die neuen Gewichte auf alle Prozessoren verteilt. Dies hat die Vorteile, daß die Änderungen gegenüber der sequentiellen Implementierung gering sind und daß beliebige Netze trainiert werden können und nicht nur feedforward-Netze.

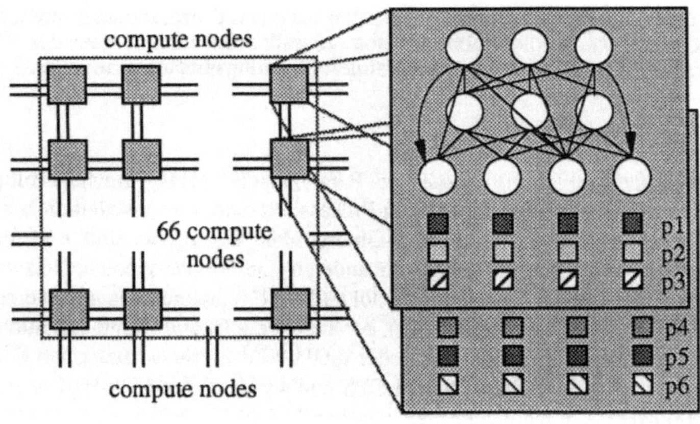

Abb. 6 Trainingsmuster-parallele Simulation neuronaler Netze auf der Intel Paragon. Jeder Knoten hält das vollständige Netz und einen Teil der Trainingsmuster. Das Netz kann dabei unregelmäßige Topologien und sogar rekurrente Verbindungen besitzen.

Eine Portierung des sequentiellen Simulatorkerns von SNNS auf die Intel Paragon ist bereits erfolgt. Erste Messungen von SNNS auf einem Prozessor lieferten bisher eher durchschnittliche Leistungswerte von 1,216 MCPS bzw. 0,532 MCUPS für Backpropagation. Nach unserer Meinung hängt das aber wohl auch damit zusammen, daß der C-Compiler beim Optimieren auf der Paragon noch nicht effizient arbeitet. An der parallelen Implementierung wird derzeit noch gearbeitet, sodaß hierzu derzeit noch keine Meßwerte vorliegen. Basierend auf einer Extrapolation der Meßergebnisse eines Prozessors kann man aber jetzt schon sagen, daß diese wohl nicht leistungsfähiger werden kann als die MasPar-Implementierung.

5 Leistungsvergleich der parallelen Implementierungen

Die parallelen SNNS-Kerne auf der MasPar liefern beeindruckende Leistungswerte. Die erste Implementierung des parallelen Simulatorkerns liefert für ein optimales 128-128-128-Netzwerk, das kein Kopieren am Ende eines Zyklus benötigt, 176 MCPS (million connections per second) beim Recall und 67 MCUPS (million connection updates per second) für Backpropagation beim Lernen, während NETtalk [Sejnowski, Rosenberg 86] mit 98 MCPS und 41 MCUPS trainiert wurde. Diese Meßwerte beinhalteten allerdings nicht die Zeit für den Mustertransfer, die um Größenordnungen höher lag. Die zweite, optimierte Implementierung erreicht für das 128-128-128-Netz 348 MCPS und 129 MCUPS für Backpropagation in der Lernphase. Das NETtalk-Netzwerk liefert 47 MCPS und 17.6 MCUPS. Diese gemessenen Zeiten beinhalten jetzt die Zeit für den Mustertransfer. Diese Werte sind in Tabelle 1 den Werten für Workstations gegenübergestellt. Diese Leistungen wurden erst nach einer längeren Optimierung erreicht. Die größte Hürde war dabei der langsame Transfer der Trainingsmuster zwischen dem Unix-Workstation-Frontend und dem parallelen Backend, der in der ersten Implementierung Minuten benötigte, während das eigentliche Training Millisekunden dauerte. Viel Arbeit wurde daher darin investiert, die Trainingsmuster in großen Blöcken zu laden und so viele wie möglich im verteilten PE-Speicher zu halten.

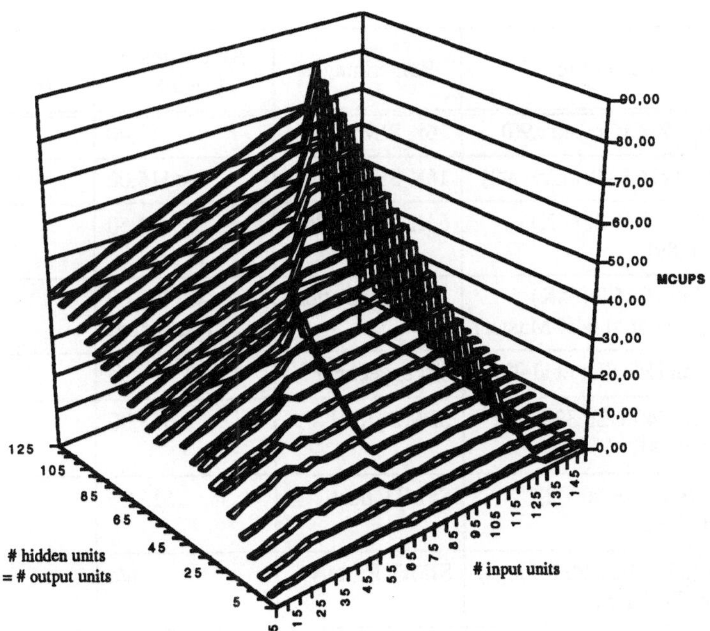

Abb. 7 Leistungsdaten des parallelen SNNS-Simulatorkerns auf der MasPar MP-1216 für nicht-optimale Topologien (Messungen von M. Vogt). Man sieht gut den Leistungsknick bei mehr als 128 Eingabeneuronen. Ein kleinerer Knick existiert bei 64 Eingabeneuronen. Ein ähnlicher Leistungsabfall existiert bei über 128 verdeckten Neuronen bzw. Ausgabeneuronen.

Maschinentyp, Implementierung	Betriebssystem	Arbeitsphase (MCPS)	Training (MCUPS)
DECstation 5000/200, SNNSv3.0	Ultrix V4.2	0,73	0,24
Sun SPARCStation 2, SNNSv3.0	Sun-OS 4.1.1	0,95	0,42
Intel Paragon 1 Prozessor	OSF/1	1,22	0,53
IBM RS 6000/320, SNNSv3.0	AIX V.3.1	1,75	0,66
HP 9000/730, SNNSv3.0	HP-UX 8.0.7	2,14	1,09
MasPar MP-1216, Implem. 1	MPPE 3.0	176,00	98,00
MasPar MP-1216, Implem. 2	MPPE 3.0	348,70	129,00
MasPar MP-1216, Prototyp	MPPE 3.0	n/a	150,00
MasPar MP-2216, Implem. 2	MPPE 3.1b	972,00	360,00
MasPar MP-2216, Prototyp	MPPE 3.1b	n/a	432,00
Intel Paragon 66 Proz. (geschätzt)	OSF/1	< 60,00	< 30,00

Tabelle 1: Benchmark-Ergebnisse der sequentiellen und parallelen Simulatorkerne von SNNS (Backpropagation), maximale Werte für ein 128-128-128-Netz.

Implementierung	Bemerkungen	Arbeitsphase (MCPS)	Training (MCUPS)
MasPar MP-1216 [Grajski ..90]	16K SIMD, float	18,40	9,80
MasPar MP-1216 [Allen,Sch..92]	16K SIMD, float	< 116,00	< 32,00
Conn. Machine CM-2 (64K) [Zhang et al. 89]	64K SIMD, float	182,50	40,10
Conn. Machine CM-2 (64K) [Singer 90] (benötigt 64K Muster)	64K SIMD, float	< 1300,00 (geschätzt)	n/a
NEC SX-3 (in [Mueller et al 92])	Vektorrechner	n/a	130,00
ICSI RAP-10, (40 DSP 320C30) [Morgan et al. 90]	SPMD, float	558,00	102,00
MUSIC-20 (60 DSP 96002) [Mueller et al. 92]	SPMD, float	515,00	246,00
IBM GF11 (356 PEs a 20 MFlops) [Whitbrock, Zagha 90]	SIMD, Prototyp	n/a	901,00
Adaptive Solutions CNAPS-512	Neurocomputer	7600,00	1400,00

Tabelle 2: Vergleich mit anderen Implementierungen neuronaler Netze auf Parallelrechnern bzw. Neurocomputern. Hier sind nur die Werte bei optimaler Netztopologie angegeben.

6 Literatur

[Allen, Schimmel 92] J. D. Allen, D. E. Schimmel: Efficient Neural Networks on SIMD Machines, School of EE., Georgie Inst. of Technology, Atlanta, Georgia 30332-0250, MasPar Challenge Competition Paper, MasPar Corp., Sunnyvale, CA, 1992.

[Carpenter, Grossberg 88] Carpenter, G.A., Grossberg, S.: The ART of Adaptive Pattern Recognition by a Self-Organizing Neural Network, IEEE Computer, March 1988, 77-88

[Chinn et al. 90] G. Chinn, K.A. Grajski, C. Chen, C. Kuszmaul, S. Tomboulian: Systolic Array Implementations of Neural Nets on the MasPar MP-1 Massively Parallel Processor, MasPar Corp. Int. Report

[Fahlman 88] Fahlman, S.E.: Faster Learning Variations on Backpropagation: An Empirical Study, in [Touretzky et al. 88]

[Fahlman 90] S. E. Fahlman, C. Lebiere: The Cascade Correlation Learning Architecture, Report CMU-CS-90-100, Computer Science, CMU, Pittsburgh, PA 15213, August 1991

[Goddard et al. 89] Goddard, N.H., Lynne, K.J., Mintz, T., Bukys, L.: The Rochester Connectionist Simulator: User Manual, Tech Report 233 (revised), Univ. Rochester, NY, 1989

[Grajski et al. 90] K.A. Grajski, G. Chinn, C. Chen, C. Kuszmaul, S. Tomboulian: Neural Network Simulation on the MasPar MP-1 Massively Parallel Processor, INNC, Paris, 1990

[Hecht-Nielsen 90] Hecht-Nielsen, R.: Neurocomputing, Addison-Wesley, 1990

[Hübner 92] R. Hübner: 3D-Visualisierung der Topologie und der Aktivität neuronaler Netze, Diplomarbeit Nr. 846, Univ. Stuttgart, Fakultät Informatik, Jan. 92

[Hüttel 92] M. Hüttel: Parallele Implementierungen mehrstufiger feedforward-Netze auf einem SIMD-Parallelrechner, Studienarbeit Nr. 1124, Univ. Stuttgart, Fak. Informatik, Juli 92

[Jurik 89] M. Jurik: Backpercolation, (probably unpublished) paper distributed by Jurik Research and Consulting, PO 2379, Aptos, CA 95001 USA

[Mache 92] N. Mache: Entwicklung eines massiv parallelen Simulatorkerns für neuronale Netze auf der MasPar MP- 1216, Diplomarbeit Nr. 845, Univ. Stuttgart, Fakultät Informatik, Feb. 92

[Morgan et al. 90] N. Morgan, J. Beck, P. Kohn, J. Bilmes, E. Allman, J. Beer: The Ring Array Procesor (RAP): A Multiprocessing Peripheral for Connectionist Applications, Journal of Parallel and Distributed Computing, Special Issue on Neural Networks, XIV: 248-259, 1992

[Mueller et al 92] U. Mueller, B. Baumle, P. Kohler, A. Gunzinger, W. Guggenbuhl: Achieving Supercomputer Performance for Neural Network Simulation with an Array of Digital Signal Processors, IEEE Micro, Oct. 1992, pp 55-65

[Poggio, Girosi 89] T. Poggio, F. Girosi: A Theory of Networks for Approximation and Learning, A.I. Memo No. 1140, A.I. Lab., M.I.T., 1989

[Riedmiller, Braun 91] RPROP - A Fast Adaptive Learning Algorithm, Proc. of the Int. Symp. on Computer and Information Science VII, 1992

[Rumelhart, McClelland 86] Rumelhart, D.E., McClelland, J.A., the PDP Research Group: Parallel Distributed Processing, Vol. 1, 2, MIT Press, Cambridge MA, 1986

[Schmalzl 91] M. Schmalzl: Rotations- und translationsinvariante Erkennung maschinengeschriebener Zeichen mit neuronalen Netzen, Studienarbeit Nr. 1011, Univ. Stuttgart, Fakultät Informatik, Juli 91

[Schnabel 92] O. Schnabel: Sekundärstrukturvorhersage von Proteinen mit Time-Delay-Netzwerken, Studienarbeit Nr. 1097, Univ. Stuttgart, Fak. Informatik, Mai 92

[Sejnowski, Rosenberg 86] T. J. Sejnowski, C.R. Rosenberg: NETtalk: a parallel network that learns to read aloud, The John Hopkins Univ. EE and Comp. Science Technical Report

JHU/EECS-86/01, 32 pp., also in: Anderson, Rosenfeld: Neurocomputing: Foundations of Research, ch. 40, pp. 661-672, MIT Press, 1988

[Sienel 91] J. Sienel: Kompensation von Störgeräuschen in Spracherkennungssystemen mittels Neuronaler Netze, Studienarbeit 1037, Univ. Stuttgart, Fakultät Informatik, Okt. 1991

[Singer 90] A. Singer: Implementations of Artificial Neural Networks on the Connection Machine, Thinking Machines Corp. Tech. Rep. RL 90-2, Jan. 1990, auch in: Parallel Computing 14 (1990) pp. 305-315, North Holland

[Touretzky 89] Touretzky, D.: Advances in Neural Information Processing Systems 1, Morgan Kaufmann, 1989

[Touretzky et al. 88] Touretzky, D., Hinton, G., Sejnowski, T.: Proc. of the 1988 Connectonist Models Summer School, June 17-26, Carnegie Mellon Univ., Morgan Kaufmann, 1988

[Veigel 91] A. Veigel: Rotations- und translationsinvariante Erkennung handgeschriebener Zeichen mit neuronalen Netzwerken, Diplomarbeit Nr. 811, Univ. Stuttgart, Fakultät Informatik, Sept. 91

[Vogt 92] M. Vogt: Implementierung und Anwendung von "Generalized Radial Basis Functions" in einem Simulator neuronaler Netze, Diplomarbeit Nr. 875, Univ. Stuttgart, Fakultät Informatik, Jan. 92

[Waibel 89] A. Waibel: Consonant Recognition by Modular Construction of Large Phonemic Time-Delay Neural Networks, in [Touretzky 89] pp. 215-223

[Whitbrock, Zagha 90] M. Witbrock, M. Zagha: An Implementation of backpropagation learning on GF11, a large SIMD parallel computer, Parallel Computing 14 (1990) pp. 329-346, North Holland

[Zhang et al. 89] X. Zhang, M. Mckenna, J.P. Mesirov, D. L. Waltz: An efficient implementation of Backpropagation on the Connection Machine CM-2, TMC TR, auch in: Parallel Computing 14 (1990) pp. 317-327, North Holland

[Zell et al. 90] A. Zell, Th. Korb, T. Sommer, R. Bayer: A Neural Network Simulation Environment, Proc. Applications of Neural Networks Conf., SPIE Vol. 1294, pp. 535-544

[Zell et al. 91a] A. Zell, Th. Korb, N. Mache, T. Sommer: SNNS, Stuttgarter Neuronale Netze Simulator, Nessus-Handbuch, Univ. Stuttgart, Fakultät Informatik, Bericht 3/91

[Zell et al. 91b] A. Zell, N. Mache, T. Sommer. T. Korb: The SNNS Neural Network Simulator, Mustererkennung 1991, 13. DAGM Symposium Mustererkennung, Okt. 1991, München, Informatik-Fachberichte 290, Springer, pp. 454-461

[Zell et al. 92] A. Zell (Ed.): Workshop: Simulation Neuronaler Netze mit SNNS, Universität Stuttgart, Fakultät Informatik, Report No. 10/92, Sept. 1992

[Zell et al. 93a] A. Zell, N. Mache, M. Vogt, M. Hüttel: Problems of Massive Parallelism in Neural Network Simulation, IEEE Int. Conf. on Neural Networks ICNN-93, San Francisco, pp 1890-1895, CA, March 28-April 1, 1993

[Zell et al. 93b] A. Zell, N. Mache, R. Hübner, G. Mamier, M. Vogt, K.-U. Hermann, M. Schmalzl, T. Sommer, A. Hatzigeorgiou, S. Döring, D. Posselt, M. Reczko, M. Riedmiller: SNNS User Manual, Vers. 3.0, Univ. Stuttgart, Fakultät Informatik, Report 3/93

[Zimmerer, Zell 91] P. Zimmerer, A. Zell:Translations- und rotationsinvariante Erkennung von Werkstücken mit neuronalen Netzen, Mustererkennung 1991, 13. DAGM Symposium, Okt. 1991, München, Informatik-Fachberichte 290, Springer, pp. 51-58

Simulation und Visualisierung künstlicher neuronaler Netze unter Verwendung paralleler Hardware mit NeuroGraph

Peter Wilke und Ralf Scholz
Lehrstuhl für Programmiersprachen der Universität Erlangen- Nürnberg
Martensstraße 3, 91058 Erlangen, BR Deutschland
Tel. +49+9131 85-7624 Fax +49+9131 39388
E-mail: wilke@informatik.uni-erlangen.de

Zusammenfassung

NeuroGraph ist ein Programm zur Simulation künstlicher neuronaler Netze unter Verwendung paralleler Hardware. Über eine grafische Bedienoberfläche wird die Topologie eines Netzes spezifiziert, das dann sequentiell oder parallel ausgeführt werden kann. Bei der Verteilung der Last auf die verfügbare Hardware werden Restriktionen berücksichtigt, die sich aus der Rechnerarchtektur und dem zugrundeliegenden neuronalen Netzwerkmodell ergeben. Es wird beschrieben, wie die in NeuroGraph implementierte Parallelisierung des Netzes vorgenommen wird und welche Leistungssteigerungen bei einer Implementierung auf MIMD-Rechnern und Workstation-Clustern erreicht wurden. Abschließend werden die für die Berechnung von künstlichen neuronalen Netzen in Frage kommenden Methoden zur Parallelisierung bewertet und die Konsequenzen für die Hard- und Software-Architekturen diskutiert. Von den vorgestellten Verfahren sind die Musterverteilung auf einer lose gekoppelten und die Netzverteilung auf einer eng gekoppelten Rechnerstruktur am besten für paralleles Verarbeiten und Lernen auf einem Workstation-Cluster geeignet.

1 Überblick

Auf neuronalen Strukturen basierende Problemlösungsverfahren werden erfolgreich in den Bereichen Musterklassifikation, Bildverarbeitung, Spracherkennung, Robotersteuerung, Optimierung und assoziativer Wissensrepräsentation eingesetzt. Bei einem sich ständig erweiternden Anwendungsspektrum neuronaler Ansätze stößt man jedoch auf die Schwierigkeit, neuronale Lösungsverfahren an konkrete, in der Praxis relevante Problemstellungen anzupassen und in eine Anwendungsumgebung zu integrieren.

NeuroGraph [5][13][14] ist eine grafikorientierte, interaktive Entwicklungsumgebung zur Unterstützung der Konstruktion, der Simulation und des Trainings künstlicher neu-

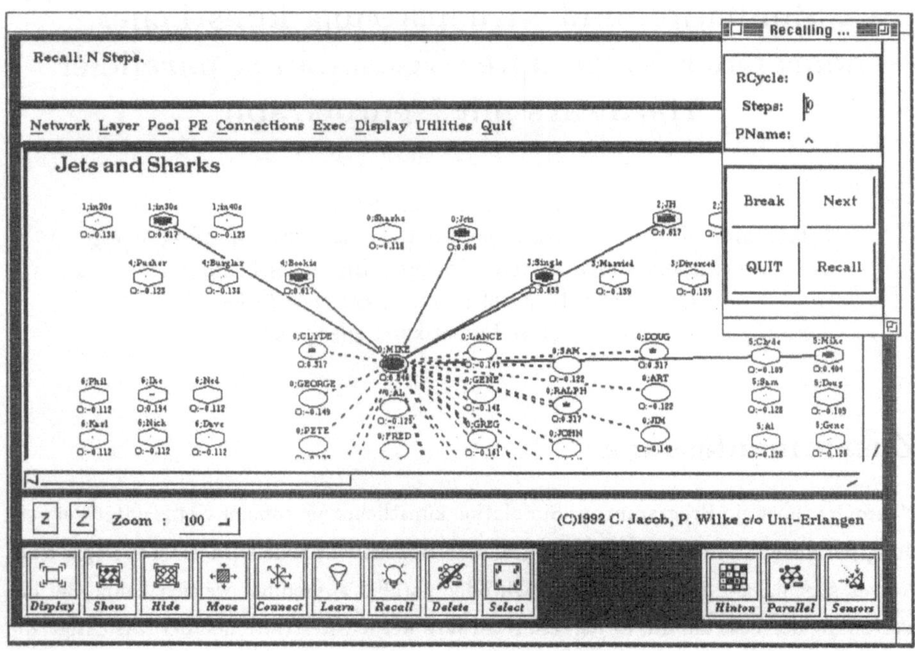

Abbildung 1: Jets&Sharks Netz: Darstellung der Eigenschaften der Person "Mike"

ronaler Netze. Als Beispiel dient die als Jets&Sharks [10][9] bekannte Datenbank, die das Netzmodell "Interaktive Hemmung und Aktivierung" (Interactive Activation and Competition) für inhaltsadressiertes und assoziatives Erinnern verwendet. Das IAC Modell ist ein einschichtiges Modell mit synchroner Verarbeitung. Die Neuronen werden in Pools eingeteilt; zwischen Neuronen eines Pools bestehen inhibitorische, zwischen Neuronen verschiedener Pools exzitatorische Verbindungen. Das Jets&Sharks Netz ist unter anderem in der Lage, die unvollständige Beschreibung eines oder mehrerer Individuen zu komplettieren, z.B. alle unverheirateten Mitglieder der Sharks zu ermitteln, die über 40 Jahre alt sind oder alle Eigenschaften einer Person zu ermitteln (siehe Abb. 1).

Besonderer Wert wurde auf standardisierte Schnittstellen (X, Motif, Unix, C++, ASCII) gelegt, die eine einfache Integration trainierter Netze in eine Anwendung gestatten. Als weitere Besonderheit ist die Einbindung von Multi-Prozessorsystemen in den Simulationsprozeß möglich.

Die grafische Bedienoberfläche von NeuroGraph erlaubt sowohl die Konstruktion neuronaler Standardarchitekturen und -modelle, als auch die interaktive Entwicklung eigener Netztopologien und Kontrollstrategien. Insbesondere zur Definition der Signalverarbeitung der neuronalen Berechnungselemente stehen eine Reihe von Standardfunktionen zur Auswahl. Während der Trainings- und Testphasen der Netzwerke stehen verschiedene

Visualisierungsmöglichkeiten der Netzdynamik zur Verfügung, die eine Analyse des Verhaltens der Netzwerke ermöglichen, und damit eine interaktive Anpassung von Netzparametern an konkrete Problemstellungen vereinfachen.

Zur Reduktion der Rechenzeiten bei zeitaufwendigen Trainings- oder Testphasen bietet Neuro Graph eine Reihe von Parallelisierungsmethoden für Kontrollstrategien neuronaler Netze und entsprechend konfigurierte Schnittstellen (X-Protocol) zur Kommunikation mit einem Multi- Prozessorsystem an (zur Zeit: Sequent Symmetry System, in Vorbereitung: MasPar, Workstation-Cluster) [14].

2 Kommunikation und parallele Simulation

Im Zusammenhang mit neuronalen Netzen ist Parallelität unter zwei Aspekten besonders interessant:

- Natürliche neuronale Netze sind selbst massiv parallele Systeme, die ihnen zugrunde liegenden Prinzipien stellen ein Paradigma für die Programmierung von Parallelrechnern dar.

- Künstliche neuronale Netze können auf Mono-Prozessoren wegen fehlender asynchroner Verarbeitung und nicht ausreichender Rechenleistung nur schwer simuliert werden.

In beiden Fällen ist also die Verwendung von Multi-Prozessoren angeraten. Bei unseren Untersuchungen haben wir uns mit verschiedenen Parallel- Rechner-Konzepten beschäftigt. Dabei haben Workstation-Cluster gegenüber speziellen Parallelrechnern den Vorteil der größeren Verbreitung und geringeren Rechenzeitkosten pro Instruktion.

Sind die Trainingszeiten für ein Netz sehr lang, so erscheint es nicht sinnvoll, das Training ständig zu beobachten, d.h. die Grafikkomponente von NeuroGraph ist nur zeitweilig erforderlich. In diesen Fällen kann die Verbindung zum Parallelrechner jederzeit unterbrochen und wieder aufgebaut werden, ohne daß die Berechnung des Netzes unterbrochen wird, die als eigenständiger Prozeß auf dem Parallelrechner läuft.

Ein allgemeines Konzept für die Parallelisierung neuronaler Netze erfordert eine Trennung zwischen der Berechnungsstrategie und den Neuronenfunktionen, da diese Ebenen verschiedene Arten der Parallelität darstellen. Unser Ansatz sieht daher eine Verteilung der Last auf die verfügbare Hardware vor, wobei die folgenden Restriktionen zu berücksichtigen sind: die Eigenschaften des zu simulierenden Modells, die Architektur des zu verwendenden Parallelrechners und vom Benutzer des Simulators einstellbare Optionen. Dabei wird zwischen eng (d.h. mit gemeinsamen Speicher) und lose (d.h. über ein Verbindungssystem, z.B. Bus) gekoppelten Multi-Prozessor-Systemen unterschieden.

Ziel der Parallelisierung ist es, für eine möglichst große Klasse von neuronalen Netzen eine günstige Verteilung auf die verfügbaren Resourcen zu finden, wobei der Schwerpunkt auf dem zeitaufwendigen Lernen von Mustern liegen soll. Als Bewertung dient dabei die voraussichtliche Rechenzeit T_R pro Muster auf R Rechnern oder Prozessoren, die es zu minimieren gilt:

$$T_R = T_{Communication/Recall} + T_{Communication/Learn} + T_{Recall} + T_{Learn} + T_{Overhead}$$

Wird z.B. von der seriellen Rechenzeit für NETtalk [12], einem neuronalen Netz mit 203 Neuronen und 18320 Gewichten, das englischen Text laut vorlesen kann, ausgegangen, können in der Zeit eines Learn/Recall-Zyklus entweder ca. zwanzigmal die Aktivierungen aller Neuronen oder aber ca. $\frac{1}{3}$ aller Gewichte übertragen werden, wenn für das Netzwerk eine Datenübertragungsrate von unter 5200 adressierten Werten pro Sekunde angenommen wird.

Im folgenden werden verschiedene Aufteilungen vorgestellt und bewertet. Dabei beschreibt N die Anzahl der Neuronen, W die Gesamtzahl aller Gewichte, R die Anzahl der verwendeten Rechner minus eins, P die Anzahl der zu lernenden Muster und t_{Comm} die Zeit, die ein Datum benötigt, um über den Bus übertragen zu werden. Es wird zur Vereinfachung von einem Netz aus Workstations gleicher Leistung ausgegangen und für die Kommunikation jede andere Aktivität auf dem Bus vernachlässigt.

<table>
<tr><th>Bewertung überwiegend
positiv (+) oder negativ (−)</th><th colspan="2">(a) Enge Kopplung
(Shared Memory)</th><th colspan="2">(b) Lose Kopplung
(Bus)</th></tr>
<tr><td>(1) Netz verteilen</td><td colspan="2">+</td><td colspan="2">− . . . +</td></tr>
<tr><td>(2) Muster verteilen</td><td colspan="2">−</td><td colspan="2">+</td></tr>
<tr><td>(3) Netz & Muster verteilen</td><td>−</td><td colspan="2">+</td><td>−</td></tr>
</table>

3 Parallelisierung für eng gekoppelte Systeme

3.1 Bestimmung der Parallelität

Die von uns verwendeten Algorithmen sind in der Lage neuronale Netze mit synchroner Verarbeitung, Vorwärtsvermittlung, Rückwärtsvermittlung und asynchrone Verarbeitung zu parallelisieren.

Die asynchrone Verarbeitung ist für die Modellierung biologischer Neuronennetze von besonderer Bedeutung, da sie der natürlichen Arbeitsweise am nächsten kommt. Die Bestimmung der Parallelität erfolgt in folgenden Schritten:

1. Erzeugung von maximal parallelen Mengen.

2. Ermittlung der minimalen Anzahl von Unterzyklen bei unbeschränkten Ressourcen.

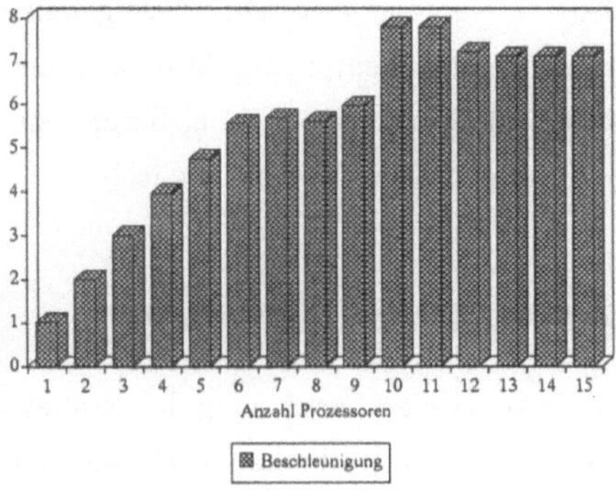

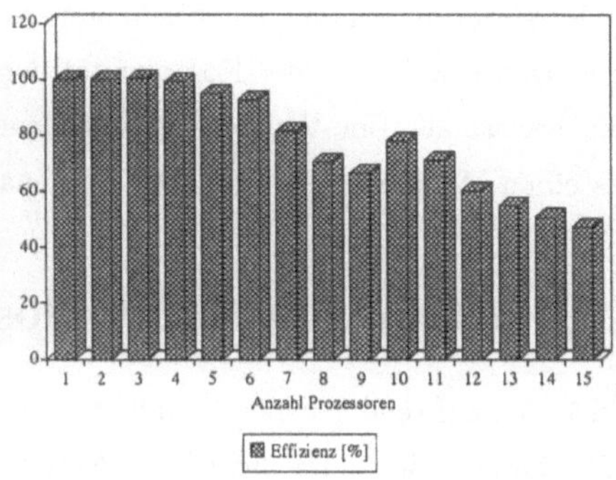

Abbildung 2: Ergebnisse der Leistungsmessung an der parallelen Implementierung des Jets&Sharks Netzes

3. Bestimmung der minimalen Ressourcen, die möglicherweise noch das Auffinden von optimalen Lösungen gestatten.

4. Erzeugung ressourcenkonformer parallel bearbeitbarer Mengen.

5. Suche nach einer Lösung, die bei beschränkten Ressourcen dennoch zu der oben bestimmten minimalen Anzahl von Unterzyklen führt.

6. Wiederholung der Schritte 4. und 5. mit vergrößerten Ressourcen, solange noch keine optimale Lösung gefunden wurde.

3.2 Leistungsmessung

Für den von uns implementierten Ansatz zur Parallelisierung wurden Leistungsmessungen (siehe Abb. 2) auf einer Sequent S81 unter dem Betriebssystem DYNIX durchgeführt. Es handelt sich dabei um ein Multiprozessorsystem mit 15 speichergekoppelten Prozessoren.Wir geben hier die für das Jets&Sharks Netz (vgl. Abbildung 1) ermittelten Werte wieder. Das Netz besteht aus 68 Neuronen und 1394 Verbindungen. Gemessen wurde die Zeit, die für 1000 Abrufzyklen an das nicht verteilte Netz benötigt wurde.

Die Optimierungskomponente erkennt, daß für eine synchrone Parallelisierung der Einsatz von 11 (bzw. 15) Prozessoren nicht sinnvoll ist, da zur synchronen Berechnung von 68 Neuronen durch 11 (15) Prozessoren 7 (5) Zyklen notwendig sind. Mit 10 (14) Prozessoren können die Neuronen jedoch in der gleichen Anzahl von Zyklen effizienter aktualisiert werden[1]. In der Abb. 2 ist dies an den Plateaus in den Kurven erkennbar.

[1]Eine noch geringere Anzahl von Zyklen ist nicht möglich, da bei 6 Zyklen und 10 Prozessoren nur 60 Neuronen aktualisiert werden können. Gleiches gilt für die anderen Kombinationen.

Es ergibt sich damit ein Höchstwert von 10967.42 Neuronen/sec. Die Meßergebnisse hängen sowohl von der Komplexität der zu berechnenden Neuronenfunktion und der Rechnerlast ab. Ein Vergleich verschiedener Implementierungen ist nur bei Simulation desselben Modells auf der gleichen Rechenanlage unter denselben Lasten möglich.

4 Parallelisierung für lose gekoppelte Systeme

Bei vielen aufwendigen Lernverfahren neuronaler Netze ist eine Verkürzung der Rechenzeit wünschenswert. Da nicht jeder Anwender massiv parallele Rechnerarchitekturen zur Verfügung hat, bietet sich eine Parallelisierung auf einem Workstation-Cluster an, einer Konfiguration die häufig am Einsatzort von NeuroGraph zu finden ist.

4.1 Modell für die Messungen

Unabhängig von der Art des neuronalen Netzes ergeben sich für die synchrone Musterverteilung mit zentraler Mittelwertbildung (MW) im eingeschwungenen System die Zeitverteilungen, dargestellt in den Abb. 3 bis 5, wobei der Backpropagation Algorithmus [3] oder zufallsgesteuerte Optimierungsverfahren (siehe [2], [8]) zu Einsatz kommen.

Für die Messungen wurden vorausgesetzt:

- Jeder Rechner erhält das vollständige neuronale Netz und einen Teil der zu erlernenden Muster (Patterns P) zur Berechnung.
- Alle Daten werden zur Mittelwertbildung auf einem zusätzlichen Rechner gesammelt und anschließend wieder zu jedem einzelnen verschickt.
- Es erfolgt ein synchroner Datenabgleich, der im Gegensatz zum asynchronen (vgl. [11]) einen Vergleich mit seriellen Verfahren ermöglicht.
- Auf dem Bussystem können keine zwei Datenpakete zur gleichen Zeit verschickt werden.

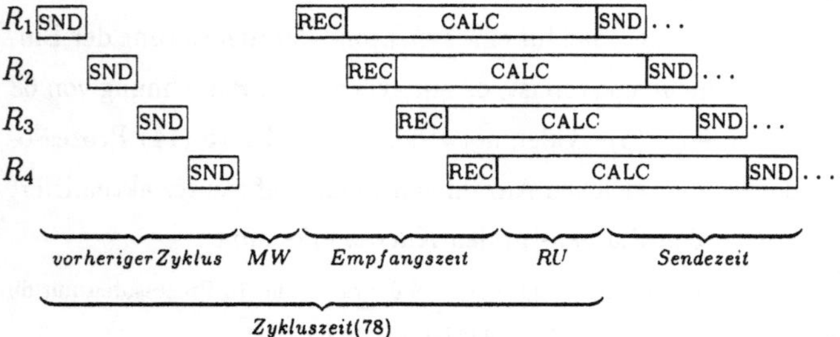

Abbildung 3: Beispiel für eine Konfiguration mit Rechenzeitüberhang (RU)

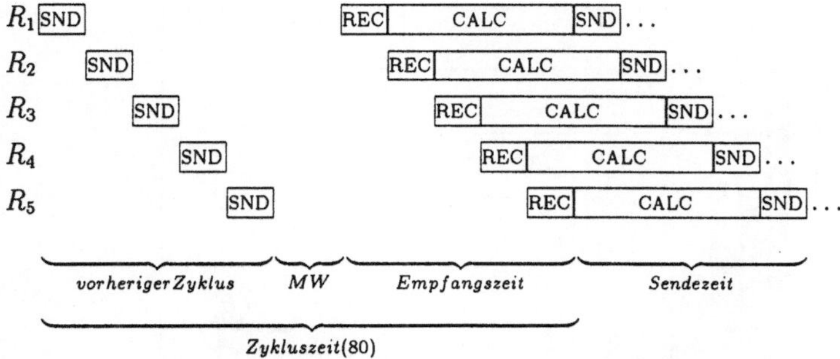

Abbildung 4: Beispiel für eine Konfiguration ohne Überhänge

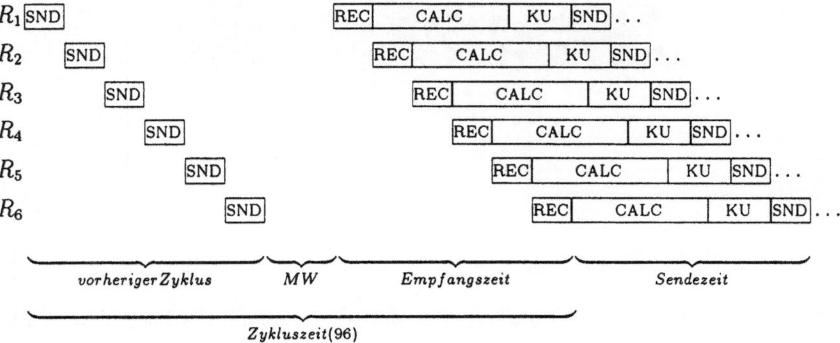

Abbildung 5: Beispiel für eine Konfiguration mit Kommunikationsüberhang (KU)

- Der zusätzliche Rechner ist nicht an der Berechnung beteiligt.

Die Zahlen für die Zykluszeiten geben lediglich eine Vergleichsgröße an. Für die folgenden Auswertungen wurde NETtalk [12] verwendet, ein neuronales Netz aus 203 Neuronen mit zusammen 18320 Gewichten, die mittels Backpropagation 800 Muster "lernen". Der Bus erlaubt eine Datenübertragungsrate von 5200 Gewichten pro Sekunde (inclusive Verwaltung).

Das Beispiel zeigt mit den gemessenen Zeiten eine Verteilung für die relativ kleine Zahl von 58 Trainingsmustern. Die Abb. 3 bis 5 zeigen die Laufzeiten in Sekunden.

Für die Zykluszeit ergibt sich bei R Rechnern (plus Server), W Gewichten, einer Buskapazität von K Gewichten pro Sekunde und einer seriellen Lernzeit T_{Ser} für eines der P

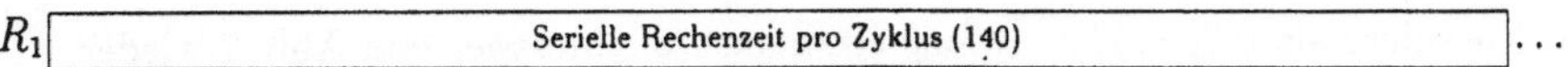

Abbildung 6: Die aufgewendete serielle Zeit

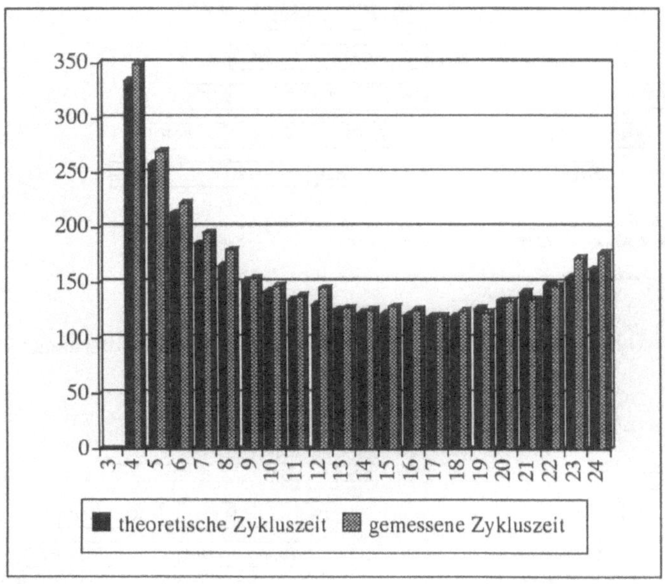

Abbildung 7: Rechenzeit in Abhängigkeit von der Rechnerzahl (P=800, W=18320, K=5200)

Lernmuster theoretisch:

$$T_{Zyklus,1} = \underbrace{R\frac{W}{K}}_{Senden} + \underbrace{\frac{W}{K}}_{1.Empfangen} + \underbrace{max\{ \underbrace{\frac{P}{R}T_{Ser}}_{X_1=Rechenzeit}, \underbrace{(R-1)\frac{W}{K}}_{X_2=restlichesEmpfangen} \}}_{Rechenzeit-oder Kommunikationsueberhang} \qquad (*)$$

Der Zusammenhang ist leicht anhand der obigen Abbildungen zu erkennen. Da für wachsendes R der Werte von X_1 monoton fallen sowie von X_2 monoton wachsen, nimmt (*) sein Minimum im Schnittpunkt beider Funktionen an. Nach R aufgelöst, ergibt sich als theoretisch günstigste Anzahl von Rechnern:

$$R = \frac{1}{2}\sqrt{\frac{PT_{Ser}K}{W} + \frac{1}{2}}$$

Mit den Zahlenwerten ist R ungefähr 17, allerdings ist die Zeit auch bei nur 11 Rechnern noch weniger als 10% größer. Das spiegeln auch die Messwerte in Abb. 7 wieder.

4.2 Effizienz und Speedup

Zur Ermittlung des Speedup und der Effizienz müssen die Ladezeiten berücksichtigt werden, die hier etwa 5 Sekunden zur Übertragung des Netzes je Rechner und zusammen etwa 80 Sekunden zur Übertragung aller Gewichte betragen. Bei 100 Lernzyklen bleiben auf 17+1 Rechnern 1.6 und auf 11+1 Rechnern 1.3 Sekunden pro Zyklus. Wird davon ausgegangen, daß die steuernden Prozesse der anderen Rechner schon zusammen mit NeuroGraph hochgefahren wurden, beträgt die gemessene Zykluszeit bei 17+1 (11+1) Rechnern 126 (133) Sekunden, statt 960 Sekunden auf einem einzelnen Rechner. Es ergibt sich ein Speedup von 7.6 (7.2) und eine Effizienz von 42% (60%).

Die Zeiten wurden während des normalen Betriebes ermittelt, wobei besonders belastete Rechner ausgelassen wurden.

5 Verbesserte Nutzung des Busses

Die Kapazität des Busses wurde über mehrere Wochen von einen Testprogramm ermittelt. Da sich kaum lastabhängige Schwankungen in dieser Kapazität finden, liegt nahe. daß sie durch die implementierten Kommunikationsroutinen gar nicht erreicht wird. Ein Test mit starkem Kommunikationsüberhang, bei dem praktisch nur kommuniziert wurde. bestätigte, daß zumindest zwei Übertragungen zur gleichen Zeit ohne sichtbaren Zeitverlust stattfinden können (auch auf demselben Subnetz).

5.1 Reduktion der Ausführungszeit

Sind zwei Übertragungen gleichzeitig möglich, könnten die Gewichte auf zwei Rechnern gesammelt und erst dann, nach einem weiteren Kommunikationsschritt, verrechnet werden. Diese beiden Rechner sollten sich nicht an der Berechnung beteiligen, um eine minimale Rechenzeit zu erhalten.

Beide Teile (der Einfachheit halber sei die Zahl der beteiligten Rechner gerade) können getrennt nach (*) betracht werden, dazu kommt ein Schritt um die Daten auf einem Rechner zu sammeln, zu verrechnen und wieder zurück zu übertragen.

Für R+2 Rechner ergibt sich trivialerweise:

$$T_{Zyklus,2} = \underbrace{R/2\frac{W}{K}}_{Senden} + \underbrace{\frac{W}{K}}_{Empfangen} + \underbrace{max\{ \underbrace{\frac{P}{R}T_{Ser}}_{Y_1=Rechenzeit} , \underbrace{(R/2-1)\frac{W}{K}}_{Y_2=restl.Empfangen} \}}_{Rechenzeit-oder Kommunikationsueberhang} + \underbrace{2\frac{W}{K}}_{Zus.Komm.} \qquad (**)$$

Die Zykluszeit wird schon für gleichbleibendes R verkürzt, es ist jedoch sinnvoll noch weitere Rechner hinzuzunehmen um sie weiter zu reduzieren. Die Abb. 8 verdeutlicht den Zusammenhang noch einmal für obiges Beispiel (NETtalk).

5.2 Best-case Reduktion

Im Idealfall werden die Daten binär gesammelt, d.h. jeweils zwei Rechner mitteln ihren Gewichte arithmetisch (eine Übertragung), um diesen Mittelwert an anderer Stelle mit ebenso vorbereiteten Werten zu verknüpfen. Dabei entstehen insgesamt $2log_2(R)$ (aufgerundet) Kommunikationsschritte, die jedoch nicht verzahnt mit dem Berechnungszyklus

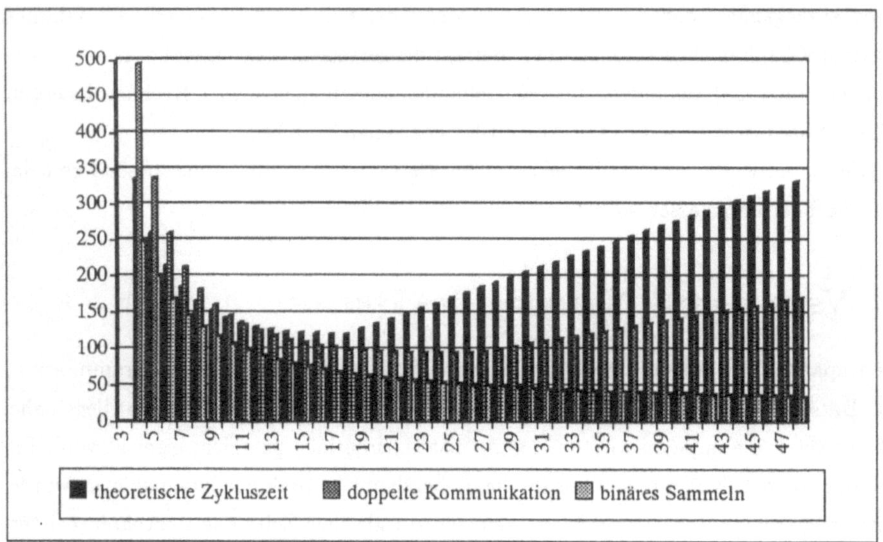

Abbildung 8: Verbesserung durch binäres Sammeln und doppelte Kommunikation

arbeiten können. Erst nach Abschluß aller Schritte wird die Berechnung auf den letzten Maschinen starten.

Das Verfahren ist die letzte Stufe einer rekursiven Anwendung des oben vorgestellten Verfahrens der doppelten Kommunikation.

Das System kann so nur funktionieren, wenn sich R/2 Übertragungen auf dem Bus nicht gegenseitig beeinflussen. Sollte der maximale Wert im installierten System groß genug sein, so ergibt sich als Rechenzeit pro Zyklus (log_2 zur nächsten ganzen Zahl aufgerundet, vgl. Abb. 8):

$$T_{Zyklus,b} = \underbrace{2log_2 R\frac{W}{K}}_{Senden/Empfang} + \underbrace{\frac{P}{R}T_{Ser}}_{Z_1=Rechenzeit} \qquad (***)$$

In der Regel wird nicht genügend Buskapazität zur Verfügung stehen, um für beliebig viele Rechner binär zu sammeln. Durch Reduzierung der Anzahl der rekursiven Anwendungen der doppelten Kommunikation wird jedoch auch für weniger Rechner ein, wenn auch geringerer, Speedup erreicht.

5.3 Weitere Verbesserungen

Das alles kann nicht darüber hinwegtäuschen, daß eine Verdoppelung der Übertragungskapazität eines einzelnen Prozesses besser ist, als eine zweifache gleichzeitige Kommunikation. Da die Parallelisierungskomponente jedoch portabel sein muß, ist es unumgänglich, daß solche Schwächen der Betriebssysteme berücksichtigt werden.

6 Schlußbemerkung

Die Simulation künstlicher neuronaler Netze stellt hohe Anforderungen an die verwendete Soft- und Hardware. Neben den notwendigen Softwarewerkzeugen zur Konstruktion und der Visualisierung muß die zur Verfügung stehende Hardware effizient genutzt werden. um den Anforderungen der Benutzer gerecht zu werden.

Wie die Leistungsmessungen ergeben, ist die effiziente Implementierung von neuronalen Netzen auf paralleler Hardware möglich. Von den vorgestellten Verfahren sind die Musterverteilung auf einer lose gekoppelten und die Netzverteilung auf einer eng gekoppelten Rechnerstruktur am besten für paralleles Verarbeiten und Lernen auf einem Workstation-Cluster geeignet. Eine Kombination aus beiden ist vorteilhaft. Feed-Back-Netze erzeugen zusätzlichen Rechenaufwand, aber keine zusätzliche Kommunikation und verbessern dadurch den Speedup. Das System läßt sich mit wenig Aufwand fehlertolerant ausbauen (zusätzlicher Verteiler, Ersatzrechner), da sämtliche Daten ohnehin mehrfach vorhanden sind.

Literatur

[1] N.Baba: A New Approach for Finding the Global Minimum of Error Function of Neural Networks, Neural Networks, Vol 2, 1989, 367-373.

[2] G.M.Baudet: Asynchronous Iterative Methods for Multiprocessors, Journal of the ACM 1978, 226-244

[3] L.Ceci, P.Lynn, P.Gardner: Efficient Distribution of Back- Propagation Models on Parallel Architecture, Computer Science Technical Report #CU-CS-409-88, University of Colorado, Sept. 1988

[4] Hertz, J., Krogh, A., Palmer, R.G. (1991): Introduction to the Theory of Neural Computation, Addison-Wesley

[5] Jacob, C., Wilke, P. (1991): A Dristributed Network Simulation Environment For Multi-Processing Systems, IJCANN Singapore 1991

[6] Khanna, T. (1990): Foundations of Neural Networks, Addison- Wesley

[7] E.J.Kerckhoffs: Speeding up Backpropagation on hypercubes, Neurocomputing Vol 4, No 1-2,Feb 1992, 43ff.

[8] J.Matyas: Random Optimization, Automation and Remote Control Vol 26, No 2, 1965, Übersetzung aus Avtomatika i Telemekhanika, Vol 26, No 2.

[9] J.L. McClelland, D.E. Rumelhart: Explorations in Parallel Distributed Processing, MIT Press, Cambridge, 1988.

[10] Rumelhart, D., McClelland, J. (1986): Parallel Distributed Processing, Vol. 1&2, MIT Press

[11] G.Sawitzki, StatLab Heidelberg: The Network Project: Distributed Computing on the Macintosh, Develop, August 1992

[12] Sejnowski, T., Rosenberg, C. (1986): NETtalk, a Parallel Network That Learns to Read Aloud, Tech. Rep. JHU/EECS-86/01 John Hopkins University

[13] P. Wilke, C. Jacob,: The NeuroGraph Neural Network Simulator, Proceedings Int. Workshop on Modelling, Analysis and Simulation of Computer and Telecommunication Systems MASCOTS93, Simulation Series Vol.25,1, San Diego, 1993, p. 341pp

[14] P. Wilke, C. Jacob,: Simulating Neural Networks in a Distributed Computing Environment Using NeuroGraph, Proceedings Int. Workshop on Modelling, Analysis and Simulation of Computer and Telecommunication Systems MASCOTS93, Simulation Series Vol.25,1, San Diego, 1993, p. 382pp

[15] P. Wilke: Simulation of Neural Networks and Genetic Algorithms in a Distributed Computing Environment Using NeuroGraph, Proc. WCNN World Congress On Neural Networks, Portland, Oregon

[16] P. Wilke: Simulation of Neural Networks and Genetic Algorithms in a Distributed Computing Environment Using NeuroGraph, Proc. ICANN Int. Conf. on Artificial Neural Networks, Amsterdam, Netherlands

Multiprozessor– und Speicher–Architektur des Neurocomputer SYNAPSE–1

U. Ramacher, W. Raab, J. Anlauf, U. Hachmann, J. Beichter, N. Brüls, M. Weßeling, E. Sicheneder[1] und R. Männer, J. Gläß, A. Wurz[2]

[1] Siemens AG, ZFE ST SN 43, Otto–Hahn–Ring 6, München
[2] Universität Mannheim, A5, Mannheim

Extended abstract

Um den Zeitaufwand für die Entwicklung neuronaler Applikationen verringern und die Anwendungsforschung weiter vorantreiben zu können, hat ZFE den Neurocomputer SYNAPSE–1 gebaut. SYNAPSE–1 bezieht seine Leistungsfähigkeit (peak performance $5,1 \cdot 10^9$ Verbindungen bzw. Multiplikationen und Additionen pro Sekunde) aus einer skalierbaren Multi–Prozessor– und –Speicherarchitektur und aus dem selbst entwickelten Neuro–Signalprozessor MA16 (full custom VLSI, $1\mu m$ CMOS, 610 000 Transistoren), welcher die rechenintensiven Operationen der neuronalen Algorithmen ausführt. SYNAPSE–1 besteht hardwareseitig aus 4 Boards: einem mit 8 MA16 bestückten Board, einem 'Data Unit'–Board, welches die restlichen, nicht–rechenintensiven neuronalen Operationen ausführt, einer Speicherplatine hoher Bandbreite für die Gewichte und einer Controller–Platine für Steuerung und Koordination der anderen Boards. Die Kommunikation mit Host–Workstation und spezialisierten Ein–/Ausgabeeinheiten (z.B. frame grabber) wird von Controller und Data Unit über den VME–Bus abgewickelt (Data und Control Unit wurden in Kooperation mit Prof. Männer, Universität Mannheim, entwickelt).

SYNAPSE1-1 wird vervollständigt durch mehrere Firmware/Software–Schichten. Beginnend bei den Mikroprogrammen des Sequencers auf der Control Unit reichen sie über die Betriebssoftware für die 68040–CPUs auf Control und Data Unit bis hin zu der auf der Host–Workstation zur Verfügung stehenden neural Algorithms Programming Language, die den Anwender bei der Synthese seiner Algorithmen aus rechenintensiven und nicht–rechenintensiven Operationen unterstützt. nAPL ist eingebettet in C++ und im wesentlichen realisiert als Klassenbibliothek. Dieser objekt–orientierte Ansatz gewährleistet eine enge Anbindung an SENN++, der bei ZFE entwickelten Software–Simulationsumgebung für neuronale Netze.

Der Neurocomputer SYNAPSE–1 vereint ein hohes Maß an Flexibilität mit bisher unerreichter Rechengeschwindigkeit. Bei Benchmark–Tests wurde im Vergleich mit einer SUN SparcStation 2 ein Beschleunigungsfaktor von 8000 ermittelt. Neben neuronalen Algorithmen (einschließlich Lernphase) können auch Operationen der klassischen Bild– und Signalverarbeitung sehr schnell ausgeführt werden.

The MANTRA Center for Neuro-Mimetic Systems

of the Swiss Federal Institute of Technology of Lausanne

Prof. J.D. Nicoud

LAMI-EPFL
CH-1015 Lausanne
Tel 0041 21 693-2642, Fax 0041 21 693-5263
nicoud@di.epfl.ch

Abstract

The MANTRA Center for Neuro-Mimetic Systems is coordinated by 6 professors and consists now of 12 researchers working on theoretical approaches, hardware implementations and applications of neural networks. It is subdivided in three groups (theory, technology and applications), each of them led by a scientific director. Projects are handled in an orthogonal manner: people are supported by specific projects, the planning of the work is optimized according to the overall research and contract objectives.

Theory efforts are concentrated on self-organizing feature maps and multilayer perceptrons. The Kohonen model has already found many applications, but many interesting theoretical questions are still open, e.g. convergence criteria and best distance measure.

As neural network accelerators, preprocessing analog neural nets, DPS's arrays (based on the 320C40) and a systolic architecture based on VLSI dedicated chips are developped. The MANTRA systolic machine will peak 200 MCPs (Mega Connections per Second) and will be used for running a Kohonen network for the security analysis of electric power systems.

Several applications are under way (bank notes recognition, financial applications, autonomous robotic agents and voice recognition). The group is also sollicited to help neurobiologists to modelize their observations.

1 Introduction

Several institutes of the EPFL (Ecole Polytechnique Fédérale de Lausanne, same as above) have been working on neural networks since 1988. They have been actively involved in national and international programs supported by research and educational projects financed by Swiss funding as well as European Esprit and Comett projects. Since 1988, the CARNAC group hosted an extensive exchange of ideas, followed by a cooperation within the MANTRA project, which led to the newly created MANTRA Center for Neuro-Mimetic Systems. At the moment, 12 researchers are attached to the center and are working on theoretical approaches, hardware implementations and applications of neural networks.

The six following professors are supporting the Center by their expertise and by providing temporary resources. In parallel, all of them are undertaking additional researches in this field:

- Prof. D. de Werra, Laboratory for Operations Research: Supervised training of feedforward networks with continuous or discrete outputs and/or weights, complexity and constructive algorithms.
- Prof. M. Hasler, Circuit and Systems Laboratory: Theoretical study of electrical non-linear networks and learning algorithms.
- Prof. J.D. Nicoud, Microprocessors and Interfaces Laboratory: Systolic VLSI architectures, incremental algorithms, application of neural networks to robotic.
- Prof. M. Declercq, Electronics laboratory: Mixed analog and digital VLSI circuits for Kohonen networks.
- Prof. E. Vittoz, Electronics Lab and Swiss Center for Electronics and Micromechanics (CSEM): VLSI analogue circuits for perceptive processing.
- Prof. A. Germond, Electric Power Systems Laboratory: Security and diagnosis problems in large non-linear systems (electric power systems).

2 Directions of research

The Center deals with neural network theory, hardware accelerators and applications. It is subdivided in three groups (theory, technology and applications), each of them led by a scientific director. Projects are handled in an orthogonal manner: people are supported by specific projects, the planning of the work is optimized according to the overall research and contract objectives.

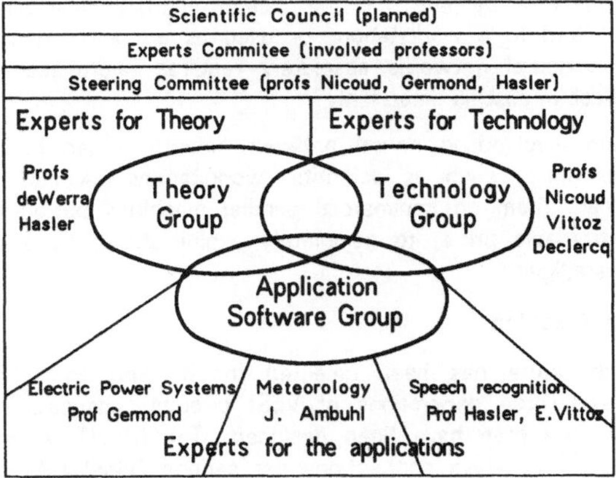

2.1. Neural Network Algorithms

Good neural network algorithms are not easy to design. Backpropagation and self-organization algorithms were significant steps, but living creatures show much faster learning procedures. One can hope an increase in the number of neurons for future artificial neural network implementations, but the number and the arrangement of interconnections will never look like real neurons. International cross-fertilization is important in the process of selecting and studying new types of algorithms, better suited for given applications, more robust, converging faster, easier to implement. Two directions of research have been selected: self-organizing feature maps and multilayer perceptrons. The Kohonen model has already found many applications, but many interesting theoretical questions are still open, e.g. convergence criteria and best distance measure [Demartines92] [Zrehen92]. The effect of weights discretization has been studied [Thiran93a] [Thiran93b]. Multilayer networks with discrete parameters are investigated using tools from discrete mathematics. In particular, the computational power of such models has been analysed and new combinational optimization algorithms have been proposed [Amaldi91], [Mayoraz91], [Mayoraz92].

New methods for constructing and training multilayer networks with continuous weights have also been developed [Amaldi92]. They are better suited for large size problems because they involve a local computation and convergence is faster than standard techniques like back propagation.

Other research directions are supported by Swiss and European projects. Esprit "Himarnnet" is concerned about speech recognition using a combination of neural network algorithms and hidden Markov models. Esprit-BRA "ELENA" (Enhanced Learning of Evolutive Neural Architectures) is mostly concerned with learning in neural networks, both by adding or removing neurons, and by synaptic adaptation. Theoretical work, simulations, benchmarks on realistic industrial data (classification tasks), and VLSI hardware implementation have to be performed. A previous Esprit project "NERVES" allowed intensive work on connectionist algorithms, simulators, neurocomputing machines, modular interfaces and ASINC's (Application Specified Integrated Neuro Circuits).

2.2. Neural Network Accelerators

Neural network algorithms do not map efficiently on Von Neumann processor architectures. DPS's are faster, but dedicated hardware can perform much more efficiently, especially if analog features are used. Preprocessing analog neural nets are studied at the EPFL and at the CSEM.

Digital neural network systems can be named neuro-accelerators since they will always be directly linked to a workstation, or used as a computation server on a local network. Progress in neural networks absolutely requires neuro-accelerators, especially if real time or affordable cost is important.

The computation involved in neural network algorithms can be performed serially on conventional computers, such as scientific workstations. A more efficient solution would be to implement them on commercial parallel machines but in many cases these would fail, at an affordable price, to completely exploit the massive parallelism present in neural network paradigms.

2.3. The MANTRA Machine

A systolic architecture has been selected for building an accelerator based on VLSI dedicated chips. Three generations of VLSI circuits, adequate for Hopfield, then Kohonen and finally back-prop have been designed. The MANTRA machine now under construction will peak 200 Mega connections per second [Viredaz92] [Lehmann93].

Testing, characterizing and using the MANTRA machine will be an important step. Developing new machines is a race in time against the commercial processor stream, proposing machines with performance doubling each coming year. For the MANTRA architecture to remain competitive, a Genes circuit including at least one million transistors has to be developed within the next 3 years. This will open the door to a fascinating research and development effort. Keeping-up with the VLSI evolution trend toward Wafer Scale Integration will be a key-need for a project of this size and in such a technology driven field. Nevertheless, it is equally important to develop a versatile algorithmic framework, easily portable to technology advances and expandable to future theoric developments. Thus, the optimal architecture should be "scalable", to easily take advantage of higher density integration, "modular", to allow creation of compatible new elements compensating the high specificity of the hardware and devoted to novel algorithms or learning rules, and "programmable", in the sense of allowing the users to make the most at software level of existing hardware without requiring a complete understanding of the machine structure.

Systolic Arrays are synchronous regular 1D or 2D meshes where each elementary operation (e.g. a multiplication followed by a sum) is allocated to one particular processing element: each processor gets its data from the previous one, performs its operation and passes the results over to the next one. Input data has to pass through all the N processors to produce the result after N cycles. The advantage is evident when the same computation has to be repeated on several input data (as it is often the case in neural networks): when a processor has performed its operation on a set of inputs and has sent the result to the next one, it may start processing the next input data set. This produces an optimal parallelism of N processors concurrently performing the elementary operation on N input data sets. The mesh regularity allows to improve the data throughput with minimal connections and it is well adapted to VLSI integration.

The regularity of computation is broken only at the beginning and at the end of the data sets, or when a new operation has to be performed. Introducing a dynamic reconfiguration of the array via a systolic instruction flow, as done in GENES IV, allows to change the operating mode "on-the-run": thus, the added complexity is compensated by an improved performance.

The set of add/multiply operations required by all neural network algorithms can be performed serially, as on a workstation microprocessor, or in parallel with a lot of hardware and problems to access a common memory. An elegant compromize combines both architecture: the data flow through harware adders and multipliers, being progressively processed.

2.4. DSP based architectures

Digital signal processors (DSP) have adequate primitives for neural computation. The TMS320C40 is a fast DSP floating point processor with six high speed communication channels. It performs as a controller in the MANTRA machine. The developed C40 board is to be used as a component to design quickly, according to the application, the hardware and software modules for real time architectures including sensors, analog and digital dedicated neural network circuits, activators and human interfaces.

3. Applications

Several applications are under way and are listed below. Due to the hardware and software evolution, and to the new neural network algorithms, it is considered important that the implementation of an application does not take more than two years.

3.1. Security of electric power systems

The application of a Kohonen network for the security of electric power systems is powerful for defining limits of safe operations [Niebur92]. This will be the first application of the MANTRA machine, which will be able to meet the real time requirements. A project with the research laboratory of the EDF (Electricité de France) strengthens this study. Swiss electric utilities are also interested in the application of artificial neural networks to electric load forecasting [Macabrey92].

3.2. Meteorological prediction

The Swiss Institute of Meteorology is concerned by recognizing specific meteorological situations next to airports. The Ametisl system is partly manual; a neural network updated with 30 values every 10 seconds is planned to help the expert system to take the best decisions.

3.3. Recognition

A feasibility study for a special pattern recognition problem is funded by the Swiss company Landis & Gyr. The first results show that the neural network approach is superior to the present implementation that uses conventional signal processing techniques.

3.4. Motion sensors

Research for a neuromimetic VLSI implementation of a pattern mouvement measure, developped at CSEM and supported by the Swiss Government and Logitech.

4. Related activities

Research projects should never be isolated. Cultural, scientific and educational pluridisciplinary activities are importants to build-up a tissue of exchanges in which ideas can grow and competence of individuals can develop. This has been rather successful in the french part of Switzerland.

4.1. Carnac

The CARNAC group (Concertation Avancée en Réseaux de Neurones et Automates Cellulaires) was founded in 1988, after a successful one-day seminar on neural networks and cellular automata. The group is indeed a pluridisciplinary group which meets every month for a conference and publishes yearly proceedings made of the contributions of the speakers. The fifty regular members come from the EPFL, the Universities of Geneva, Neuchâtel and Fribourg, research labs and companies of the French part of Switzerland. Topics of conferences cover neurobiology, mathematics, modeling and VLSI. Speakers are both local researchers and international guests visiting Switzerland. The proceedings of the presentations (mostly written in French) have been published since 1988 and can be ordered for at CARNAC Group, LAMI-EPFL, CH-1015 Lausanne.

4.2 Neuroscience

Software simulation is essential for the neurobiologist to understand real neurons. A better understanding of the processing steps between our sophisticated sensors and efficient actuators will help in structuring neural network models. Perhaps, some day, biotechnologies will provide the 3-D technology required to master neural networks of large complexity. Modelization of the sensori-motor cortex, with the hope of finding applications for smart robots, is one direction of work, studied in a national project on Robotics and Artificial intelligence. The other is the development of software tools for the modelization of the axon tree of neural cells, as found in particular in the lateral connections of the cortex (Research project in cooperation with the University of Lausanne).

4.3 Education

In 1991, a Comett set of courses named "Neural" was organised by five European partners. Five 2-day courses were organized in 6 cities. Given in 1992 and repeated in 1993, the Postgraduate course on Natural and Artificial Neural Networks addresses itself to engineers in industry and to researchers. One of the results of the Nerves Esprit project and the Comett course was the Soma simulators [Blayo92] that run on SUN workstations and include the following modules: Kohonen network, Hopfield network, Herault-Jutten network, Backpropagation network, Inverted pendulum experiment, Cooperation-competition network. These simulators are very effective for education. They can also be easily modified for any model and completed with dedicated graphical representations, e.g. moving robots.

References

[Amaldi91] E. Amaldi, "On the complexity of Training Perceptrons", ICANN'91, Helsinki, Elsvier 1991, pp 55-60

[Amaldi92] E.Amaldi, B.Guenin, "Constructive Methods for Designing Compact Feedforward Networks of Threshold Units", OR Working paper, EPFL, 1992

[Blayo92] F. Blayo, P. Demartines, "Simulation de réseaux de neurones artificiels", Bulletin ASE, 1992, 13 mars, pp 31-36

[Demartines92] P. Demartines, F. Blayo, "Kohonen Self-organizing Maps: is the Normalisation necessary?", Complex Systems, No 6, 1992, pp 105-123

[Lehmann93] C. Lehmann, M.Viredaz, F.Blayo, "A Generic Systolic Array Building Block for Neural Networks with On-Chip Learning", IEEE Transaction on Neural Networks, Special Issue on VLSI for NN, March 1993, to be publisned

[Macabrey92] N.Macabrey, Th.Baumann, A.J.Germond, "Prévision de charge dans un réseau électrique à l'aide du réseau de neurones de Kohonen", Bulletin ASE, 1992, 13 mars, pp 13-19

[Mayoraz91] E. Mayoraz, "On the Power of Networks of Majority Functions", IWANN'91, Springer Verlag, 1991, pp 78-85

[Mayoraz92] E. Mayoraz, "Maximizing the Stability of a Majority Perceptron using Tabu Search", IJCNN'92 Baltimore, 1992, pp 254-259

[Niebur92] D.Niebur, A.Germond, "Unsupervised Neural Net Classification of Power System Static Security States", Intl Journal on Electrical Power and Energy Systems, Vol 114, No2&3, April&June 1992, pp 233-242

[Thiran93a] P.Thiran et al., "Quantization Effects in VLSI Digital Circuit Implementations of Kohonen Networks" Submitted to the IEEE Trans. on Neural Networks

[Thiran93b] P.Thiran, M.Hasler, "Study of the Kohonen Network with a Discrete State Space", to be presented at the Conference on Probability and Numerical Methods, Paris, March 1993.

[Viredaz92] M. Viredaz, C. Lehmann, F. Blayo, P. Ienne, "MANTRA: A Multi-Model Neural-Network Computer", VLSI for Neural Networks and Artificial Intelligence,Oxford, September 1992

[Zrehen92] S. Zrehen, F.Blayo, "A Geometric Organization Measure for Kohonen's Map", Neuro-Nîmes, 1992, Novembre

The PAN System and the WINA Project

G. Palm
Abt. Neuroinformatik
Universität Ulm
D-89069 Ulm

e-mail: palm@neuro.informatik.uni-ulm.de

Abstract

The PAN system is a parallel computer architecture implementing a large associative memory, which is realized as a large network of simple artificial neurons. PAN IV realizes a 256Kx4K binary memory matrix and contains 4K parallel processors. The WINA project, sponsored by the BMFT, investigates the integration of neural networks and knowledge-based systems. The elementary neural components in the hybrid WINA architecture are a neural associative memory (e.g. the PAN system) and a Kohonen map or a similar neural clustering algorithm. Our main research objectives are: (i) studying the interaction of neural and rule-based components in a prototypical hybrid system, (ii) developing new designs for special hardware for parallel processing in all components of the system, (iii) building an application-oriented information retrieval system based on the PAN architecture.

1 Introduction

Neural Networks are the structural basis for the impressive information processing capabilities of real brains. It is therefore no surprise, that also in the science and technology of artificial intelligence there is recently a growing interest in neural networks. Artificial neural networks can be used in computer science both as a software concept and as a hardware concept. There are essentially two reasons why one should consider artifical neural networks:

- their adaptability makes it possible (within limits) to replace reprogramming by learning
- their massive parallel processing capability allows the conception and hardware implementation of parallel processing strategies.

There is one area where both these aspects of information processing in neural networks are already elaborated, namely associative memory ([7], [9]). Associative memories are used for two types of tasks: fault tolerant pattern mapping and pattern completion. As a typical example, consider the search for some data by means of a key. If the key points directly to the data, this is called pattern mapping; if this also works for incomplete or distorted keys, the pattern mapping is called fault tolerant; if the key is itself a part of the data, we are dealing with pattern completion. Thus, pattern completion can be regarded as a special case of fault tolerant pattern matching, where the data are the keys. For this reason we have developed a parallel computing system for the more general case of pattern mapping. The basic task of pattern mapping consists in producing the proper responses Y^i to a number of stimuli X^i (for i=1,2,...,M). The proper responses are learned during a learning phase, during which the input-output pairs (X^i,Y^i) are presented to the memory. After learning the memory should not only respond with Y^i to the input X^i, but also to inputs similar to X^i. The components of the input and output vectors X and Y can take continuous or discrete values. In our first implementations of the PAN system we have restricted ourselves to the case of binary values, i.e. we assume that the components X^i_j and Y^i_j of input and output vectors are in {0,1}.

2 Sparse Coding

In most neural network models for associative memory the problem of coding of the input and output information into neural activity vectors is not explicitly discussed. In many practical cases a straightforward coding procedure comes to mind. In theoretical investigations, usually one assumes randomly generated activity vectors with a certain probability p for a component to be active (1), and a corresponding probability 1-p for a component to be inactive (0). Many models only consider p=1/2. In this case, the information content of each vector is maximal (n bits). Therefore the number M of storable patterns is limited to $M=E \cdot n$, where E is the storage efficiency, i.e. the number of bits per synapse that can effectively be stored. The value for E is estimated as 0.14 for the Hopfield model with p=1/2 ([1]). For sparse activity vectors (i.e., small p) this limit to M is much larger because the information content of each pattern is much smaller.

Furthermore, also the storage efficiency E is much higher for sparse vectors ([9], [12], [10], [11]). For very large networks and very small p an efficiency E up to 72% can be reached. Even with binary synapses a limiting value of E=ln 2=69% can be obtained. In this case the optimal asymptotic formula for the sparseness is p=(ld n)/n. Although this limit can only be reached for very large n, one can achieve efficiencies E>50% already for n=1000. For p=1/1000 this yields an information content of about 70 bit per pattern and thus $M=E\cdot 10^6/70=7000$. For auto-association the theoretical limit with binary synapses is ln2/4=17.33%, but this limit is actually exceeded for iterative pattern retrieval with reasonable finite values of n (see Fig. 1).

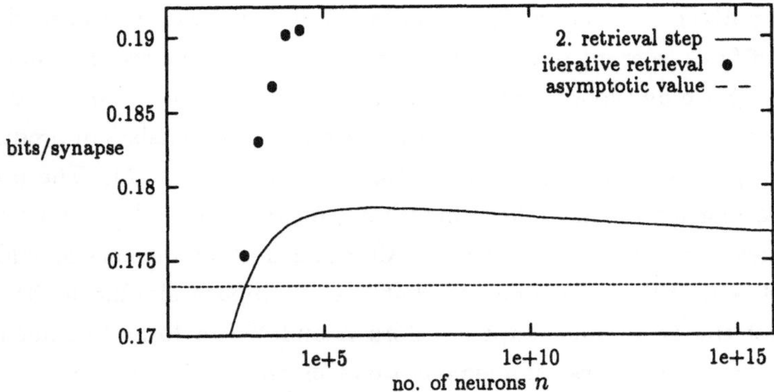

Figure 1: Storage efficiency

Thus one has to use sparse patterns if one wants to use a neural associative memory efficiently. Furthermore, the problem of sparse coding of the data is one of the basic problems that has to be considered for each prospective application of a neural associative memory.

3 Computational Complexity and Data Flow

An important aspect of our system design for the PAN system is the balance between parallel computing power and the maximal possible data flow through the system. For this purpose we consider one retrieval step, i.e. one pattern mapping step, which is the most frequent basic operation of the system (besides the learning of an additional association from X to Y) and also produces the highest flow of input and output data. This operation X⟶Y requires a vector-matrix multiplication XxC between the input vector X and the storage (or connectivity) matrix C. This operation requires about n^2 multiplications (m) and additions (a): $XxC \sim n^2 \cdot m + n^2 \cdot a$. In addition the retrieval step R requires n comparisons (c) with a preset threshold value, thus a complete retrieval step needs: $R \sim n^2 \cdot m + n^2 \cdot a + n \cdot c$ operations. For binary neurons, binary synapses and sparse activity vectors ($k \sim \log n$ neurons active per vector), the multiplications can be replaced by ANDs and the additions by counting. More precisely, both operations can be replaced by conditional decrements (d), if one uses addressing techniques where only the positions of the ones are addressed. For this we need to encode (e) k addresses. Thus we have for the binary sparse case $R_{bs} \sim k \cdot n \cdot d + n \cdot c + k \cdot e$, which only grows slightly larger than n.

The communication in the mapping operation consists of presenting the input vector X to the system and receiving the output vector Y from the system. This produces a data flow of at least n bit (for 1-bit neurons) input and output. Fortunately, one can encode just the positions of the k ones in the sparse case. Thus the total data flow is reduced to $k \cdot (\log n)$ bit for input and output. Typically one will use log n bit wide data buses, so the time for communication increases as $k \cdot \log n$. The time for computation increases as $k \cdot n$ and so the maximal useful parallelism is of order n: in principle one can use one processor per neuron. Then the time required for one mapping step increases as $k \sim \log n$. This is the degree of parallelism employed in the later versions of the PAN system. A first description of the PAN concept and the PAN I system is given in ([12]).

4 The PAN System

Our considerations on complexity have led to a data format for the activity vectors (positions of active neuron), which strongly resembles the addressing of RAMs. All our realizations of the PAN system (PAN I to IV) use this data format. The second essential idea is the organization of the memory for the synaptic connectivity matrix C in such a way that the position address of an input can be used directly to address in parallel the RAMs holding the synaptic values of all neurons (or as many neurons as possible). This leads to a memory architecture where the input synapses of one neuron are realized in one column of the memory and each processor has access to the memory columns corresponding to its neurons (only one neuron per processor in the extreme). The processor should finally encode the addresses of the activated neurons in the output vector, to yield the same data format in the output and by that also simplify iterative applications of the retrieval step besides reducing the data flow as shown above.

In PAN I and PAN II we used a small number (9 or 22) of 8-bit microprocessors (Z80) in parallel; each of them worked on a fixed number of neurons and the corresponding columns of the storage matrix. The input and output vectors were communicated on a common data bus. This approach could be further pursued by taking more and faster 16-bit or 32-bit processors off the shelf. There are two major drawbacks with this approach:

- The processors are too complex: they can also perform operations that are not needed and they may have to use several instructions to perform only one of the required operations.
- They are usually not designed for independent parallel addressing of their RAMs through a common external address bus.

A good alternative to this approach is the development of special purpose ICs, which perform exactly the necessary operations and support parallel addressing of the whole storage matrix via a common bus. For the realization of our system concept several VLSI-designs (BACCHUS I to III) were made in a joint project sponsored by the BMFT at the Institute for Microelectronics in Darmstadt by the group of Prof. Dr. M. Glesner ([4], [6], [17]). The PAN III and PAN IV were built using two of these designs. All BACCHUS chips contain 32 8-bit counters, which perform the neural operations summing and threshold comparison (Fig. 2). Furthermore all of them provide a priority-encoding read logic. By way of a read access, this logic puts the address of the first of the activated neurons onto the data bus, switching this neuron to inactive afterwards. This logic is cascadable with all BACCHUS chips, for each in a slightly different way, allowing the priority encoding reading of the whole output vector in the neuron address format. In addition the BACCHUS II and BACCHUS III provide a special write logic, which performs a read-OR-write access to the synaptical memory, according to the simplified Hebb rule.

The PAN III was built in Darmstadt, based on our PAN concept using 16 BACCHUS I chips. These are controlled by a specially designed circuit board mounted in a PC. This configuration is used as a demonstrator runnig an image recognition application.

With BACCHUS III we achieved a cost reduction compared to the use of BACCHUS I by leaving the memory chip control logic off the chip. By that the number of pins could be reduced from 108 to 68 with BACCHUS III. Furthermore, it is possible to use BACCHUS II and BACCHUS III with arbitrary RAM types. For mass production a third design was necessary. By this redesign it was also possible to increase the speed and the flexibility of application with BACCHUS III. It may be run with a clock rate of 10 MHz, at which speed one address per cycle can be processed. Since the counter logic is independent of the address read logic, pipelining is possible: while processing one input vector by conditional counting it is possible to process the previous output vector at the same time by reading the addresses of its activated neurons.

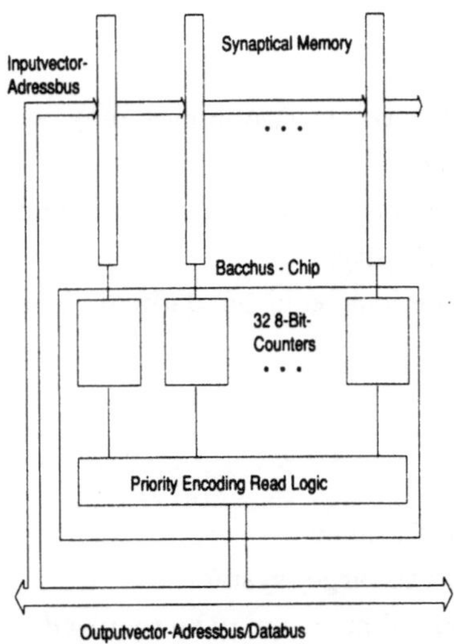

Figure 2: BACCHUS chip with memory and busses

With PAN IV we intended to design a system particularly applicable to large networks and easily extensible by using more BACCHUS ICs and more RAMs. Furthermore it should be possible to use it with widely varying hardware environments. Therefore its data processing rate should be compatible with that of standard bus systems, i.e. with transfer rates ranging from 1 MBaud to 200 MBaud (microprocessor, microcomputer, mainframe, and network buses). With a 16-bit bidirectional data bus (and an additional 32-bit address bus) the PAN IV fits in this range, allowing a maximal square matrix of 64K neurons. With a 32-bit data bus it would still be in this range and would be nearly infinitely extensible, i.e. up to 4G neurons.

5 Applications and Software

Applications of neural networks as associative memory are still a matter of research and development, especially where problems of finding or developing proper sparse codings for different applications are concerned. Therefore it must be expected that further requirements may be specified later, when PAN systems are already in use. On the other hand, applications still have to be developed and implemented; considering the high speed performance of PAN systems, real-time applications will be an interesting field. This leads to quite contrary requirements:

Development systems:

- Multiuser capability, several programmers may work at one or several projects at the same time;
- User friendly environment, debugging tools, high level programming language interfaces, portability;
- Expandability, new functions can be defined in some kind of "macro" language.

Real time systems:

- Minimization of communications;
- Minimal hardware with the target system;
- Certain quality or security features may be required, e.g.:
- Guaranteed response times;
- Well defined error handling;
- Reduction and optimization of the required software, e.g.:
- Only direct acces by the corresponding host/program/system;
- Reduced instruction set;
- Adaptation and optimization of interfaces should be possible.

These requirements cannot be satisfied with a hard-wired controller like that of PAN III. Therefore, our concept for the PAN IV relies on the flexibility and multi-purpose capability provided by the use of a microprocessor. On that hardware platform our software concept of "virtual networks" represents the fundamental base for multiuser/multitasking operation. With one particular hardware configuration, arbitrary "virtual" memory matrices may be placed anywhere into the hardware supported "physical" memory matrix. The "physical" addresses will be computed with each access, using the given "virtual" addresses plus the physical addresses of the "virtual" matrix. This is analog to the treatment of linear memory spaces of several users/processes in computer systems with virtual memory management (e.g. VMS). Therefore we called the hardware unit which realizes this concept "Associative Memory Management Unit" (AMMU). It provides communication with the connected computer system via a 16-bit bidirectional interface buffered with fast FIFOs. Its operating system PANOS accepts and computes requests transferred by the connected host. Several "virtual networks" may be defined and placed arbitrarily into the "physical network" provided by the PAN IV hardware.

The AMMU of our PAN IV prototype system uses a Motorola 68030 CPU. For communication with network memory and BACCHUS chips it controls the PAN bus, through which it is able to drive up to 19 memory boards (Fig. 3). Each of the memory boards of our prototype system contains 2 Mbytes of memory and 8 BACCHUS III ICs. The PAN IV concept allows for a wide range of configurations according to different needs since the use of arbitrary RAMs is supported. Our software system for the prototype limits neuron addresses to 16-bit values according to the height of the physical network of our prototypes hardware, but this limit may be increased easily by adding height to the hardware matrix and some lines to the PAN bus. With our concept the width of virtual networks is not restricted in the same way as the height; it may increase the width of the physical network. Such wider networks have to be "sliced" and the slices placed above each other. Therefore the computation time will be multiplied by the number of slices for the sliced network.

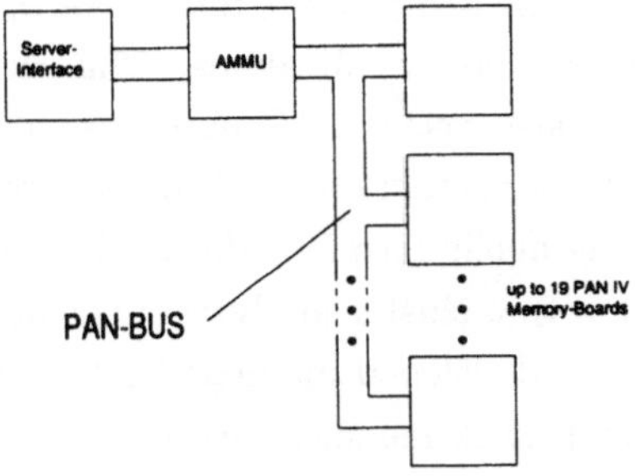

Figure 3: The PAN IV system

For multiuser operation the PAN IV has to be connected to a PAN server with multitasking features. This server has to dispatch and deliver requests and responses of several users related to several virtual networks on one or several PANs, and of course it also has to place virtual networks properly into physical networks (mapping). We are designing and implementing such a multi-user-multi-PAN server for use as a development system. With our server the user (-programs) have access to the connected PAN IV systems by function calls collected in a C-library. The basic functions in this library are:

- login, logout (user),
- create, load, save, open, close, clear (nets),
- learn, quest (patterns),
- getresult, cancel (tasks).

The communication between user programs and the PAN server relies on the TCP/IP interface, supporting multiuser operation with a server-client model. In this way, the PAN server is accessible as an Internet service in our local area network.

6 Information Retrieval with the PAN System

Since the most straightforward applications of the PAN system are in the area of information retrieval, we developed a general information retrieval system based on the PAN hardware. The first problem encountered in the conception of such a system is the development of flexible sparse coding techniques that are appropriate for a large range of typical applications. If the data are already expressed on a relatively high symbolic level they can often be reasonably regarded as sequences of discrete symbols. Such sequences can be coded for example by long sparse binary vectors, where each component stands for a triplet of symbols and a 1 indicates the occurence of the triplet in the string. Such a code has already been used in some applications. The situation is much more complicated if the data are vectors of numbers obtained from different measurements, or if they are combinations of measurements and comments or observations provided in symbolic form. In the case of measurement vectors it seems reasonable to start with a cluster analysis of the data and sparse coding of the cluster centers. We have developed methods for this, which are based either on Kohonen maps or on adaptive k-means clustering ([14], [15]).

In the most common case of a combination of one or several types of measurement data and one or several types of symbolic data one can concatenate the sparse representations of the different types of data to form the input vector to the associative memory. Depending on the application the output vector can be the same (auto-association) or - in addition - an expert output, such as a diagnosis or an advice or pointer to a large data set.

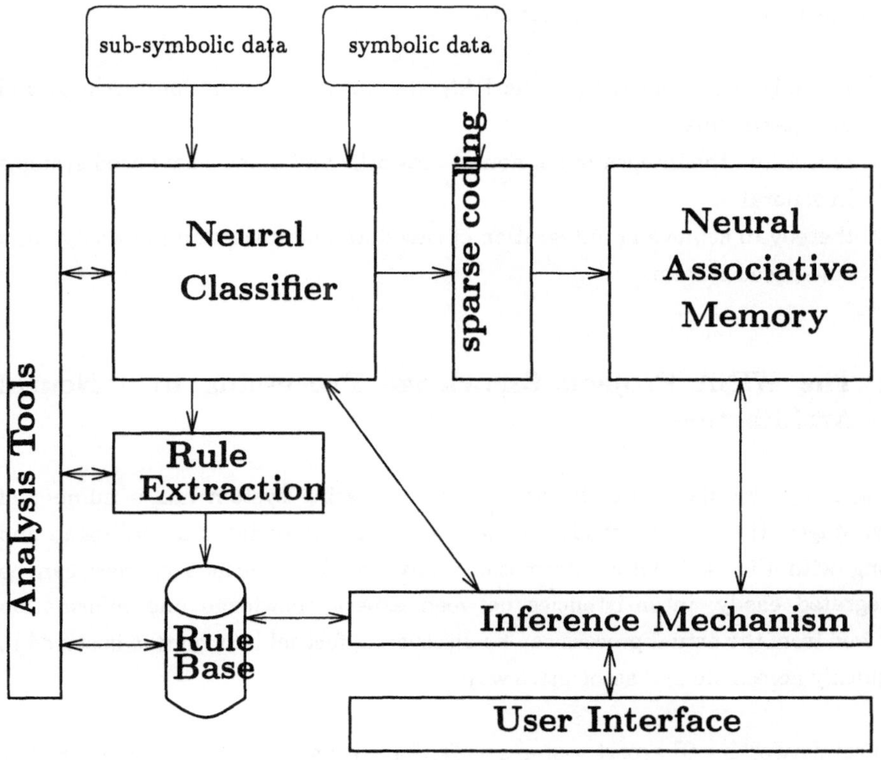

Figure 4: WINA Architecture

At this stage it seemed appropriate to provide an interface from the information retrieval system to a high-level expert system or a data-base management system (see Fig. 4). This was the initial idea that started the WINA project. The aim of the project was to provide an integrated system that contains neural network components and rule-based components ([14]). The rule based system could use the associative memory in essentially two different ways:

- when there is no rule that matches with the input data, the associative memory can be used to create the set of familiar data that best matches the input.
- when there are too many rules matching the input data, the association memory can be used to select a rule that has led to a succesful answer in a similar situation during a previous query. To this end one needs a separate associative memory that stores the relation between previous query situations and the rules chosen for evaluation ([18]).

Thus the aims of the WINA project are:

(i) to study the integration of the PAN system into information retrieval and expert-systems
(ii) to work on the integration of neural networks and knowledge based systems in general
(iii) thereby to achieve an integration of raw data and uncertain knowledge in a rule-based system.

7 The WINA Project: Knowledge Processing in a Neural Architecture

Integrating raw data into the knowledge processing system has a number of advantages: the internal model of the data source is updated according to and along with the real data; information delivered from various sources can be integrated easily; inconsistencies between expert knowledge and information derived from the actual process can be discovered; factual information is stored in a quickly accessible and associative way.

Neural networks and expert systems so far have largely been used for two rather different purposes: the former for the processing of data where the essential information often is hidden in large quantities of raw data, the latter in cases where problems and their solutions can be stated in a relatively formal way, e.g. as rules and facts. Many real-world problems, however, share aspects of both cases, and may require components based on different paradigms for the solution of subtasks. The WINA project investigates the architecture of a system comprising neural network and artificial intelligence approaches ([14]).

An overview of the hybrid knowledge processing system developed in the WINA project is given in Figure 4. It uses data in symbolic as well as sub-symbolic form, possibly from different sources, and integrates these with the rule base of an inference system. Some of these rules might express problem-specific knowlegde, e.g. from an expert in the field, whereas others are used to describe more general information. Thus one important path in the system, with the neural classifier as central element, is fed with raw data (e.g. from a process to be controlled) some additional data, possibly in symbolic form (e.g. from the operator of the process), extracts the essential information from these data, transforms them into rules, and adds these rules to the rule base of the inference mechanism. Since there is still a lack of understanding and experience in all these steps, analysis tools for a further investigation of the transformations are an important part of this part of the system.

The other path, which goes through the neural associative memory, uses also data in symbolic or sub-symbolic form, possibly pre-processed by the neural classifier, stores them in an appropriate way in the associative memory, and from there the data are accessible to the inference mechanism. This memory is not used to store rules as in the first path, but rather serves as a repository for factual information extracted from the raw input data (e.g. process parameters like the temperature, status of devices, actions of the operator). An important aspect here is that access to stored information is based on similarity: if an object with exactly the features specified is not available, another one with similar features is provided.

As an inference mechanism, Prolog is used in WINA. This choice is not critical, an expert system shell or knowlege representation system could be used as well. The inference mechanism is the component mostly visible to the user. It answers queries from the user by accessing the relevant rules in the rule base, and the relevant facts from the neural associative memory. The interaction between inference mechanism and associative memory can be either data- or demand-driven. In the first case, an incoming pattern to the classifier would be classified, and if considered dangerous or questionable, would associate some features through the associative memory, which in turn would initiate further investigation via the inference mechanism. In the demand-driven case, the inference would apply a partially instantiated fact to the associative memory, and the asociative memory would return the best match from its stored patterns for completion of the instantiation. Such a method can be used on one hand to initiate action or further investigations when necessary, e.g. if input values are out of the normal range; on the other hand, it can be used to avoid the storage of a prohibitive number of facts in the knowledge base, and generate appropriate facts from raw or preprocessed data in an abductive way only when needed in the inference process.

The inference mechanism also has access to the neural classifier; either to obtain detailed information on the input data, or to provide additional input for the classification of those data. This can be important if there already exists knowledge about regularities in the input data, which might be used to find a good starting point, or during the classification process itself.

Understanding the processes and results of neural-network based systems can be quite difficult at times, in particular for large networks. For our task to integrate several components into one architecture it was obvious that statistical evaluations of the single components are not sufficient. Instruments and methods to visualize dynamical aspects of the components were developed ([19], [16]) and turned out to be important not only to investigate the behavior of existing modules but also gave a lot of insight for the development of new algorithms and methods. Of particular importance is the display of the interaction between and among weights, units, and subnetworks; it is not sufficient to show the values of weights and units only.

The general application area for the WINA system is characterized by the need to process knowledge from different sources, such as human expertise, data bases, data from sensors, or of other origin. The core part of the system alone - neural classifier, sparse coding, and neural associative memory - can be used for associative information retrieval.

Currently the prototype system is being tested with data sets from the areas of speech processing and analysis, medical diagnostics, quality assurance, process control, and environmental assessment. It is also used as a testbed for the evaluation of methods and ideas in other projects, e.g. the protection of computer networks from intrusions and viruses ([3]), or the development of a model for the interaction between cognitive and sensory processes ([2]).

8 Conclusions and Perspectives

The goal of the WINA system described here is to provide a framework for processing knowledge provided both in symbolic and sub-symbolic form. It is composed of modules based on neural networks and artificial intelligence techniques. Single modules within the system can be exchanged easily; thus, a program implementing the neural associative memory can be replaced by dedicated hardware such as the Parallel Associative Network (PAN IV) ([13]). The Prolog inference engine also can be replaced by a connectionist inference mechanism like CHCL ([5]), which leads towards the exploitation of massive parallelism in the inference process ([8]). To the user it looks like an inference mechanism with the additional capability to integrate raw data into existing rule bases, and to access large amounts of factual information in an associative way.

By using this hybrid system on real data and expert knowledge we hope to obtain a better insight into the handling of uncertainties of various kinds in a knowlege based system and eventually also a better practical and theoretical understanding of the relation between neural networks and fuzzy logics.

9 Acknowledgement

This work is supported by the German Ministery for Research and Technology under project number 413-4001-01 IN 103 E/9 (WINA).

10 References

[1] Amit, D.J., Gutfreund, H., Sompolinsky, H.: Scientific American. 1989

[2] Beringer, A., Hölldobler, S., Kurfeß, F.: Spatial reasoning and connectionist inference. Technical report, Universität Ulm, Abteilung Neuroinformatik (accepted for presentation at IJCAI 93), 1992

[3] Denault, M., Karagiannis, D., Kurfeß, F.: Securenet technical report. Technical report, FAW Ulm, 1992

[4] Glesner, M., Huch, M., Pöchmüller, W.: Hardware Implementation for Neural Network. IFIP Workshop on Parallel Architectures on Silicon. Grenoble, 1989

[5] Hölldobler, S., Kurfeß, F.: CHCL - A Connectionist Inference System, in: Fronhöfer, B., Wrightson, G. (eds.): Parallelization in Inference Systems. Lecture Notes in Computer Science. Springer, 1991

[6] Huch, M., Pöchmüller, W., Glesner, M.: Bacchus: a VLSI Architecture for a Large Binary Associative Memory. International Neural Network Conference INNC. Paris, 1990

[7] Kohonen, T.: Associative Memory. Springer Verlag, 1977

[8] Kurfeß, F.: Massive Parallelism in Inference Systems, in: Kanal, L., Kumar, V., Modovan, D., Suttner C. (eds.): Parallel Processing for Machine Intelligence. Elsevier, 1993

[9] Palm, G.: On Associative Memory. Biol. Cybern. 31, 19-31, 1980

[10] Palm, G.: Assoziatives Gedächtnis und Gehirntheorie, in: Spektrum der Wissenschaft, 1988

[11] Palm, G.: Local Learning Rules and Sparse Coding in Neural Networks, in: Eckmiller, R. (ed.): Advanced Neural Computers. 1990

[12] Palm, G., Bonhoeffer, T.: Parallel Processing for Associative and Neuronal Networks, in: Biol. Cybern., 201-204, 1984

[13] Palm, G. and Palm, M.: Parallel associative networks: The PAN System and the BACCHUS-Chip, in: Ramacher, U., Rückert, U. Nossek, J.A. (eds.): Microelectronics for Neural Networks. Kyrill & Method Verlag, München, 411-416, 1991

[14] Palm, G., Rückert, U., Ultsch, A.: Wissensverarbeitung in neuronaler Architektur, in: Brauer, W., Hernández, D. (eds.): Verteilte Künstliche Intelligenz und kooperatives Arbeiten. Informatik-Fachberichte. Springer Verlag, Berlin, Heidelberg, New York, 1991

[15] Palm, G., Stellmann, U., Schwenker, F.: Analyse, Darstellung und ähnlichkeitserhaltende Codierung von Daten. Submitted for publication, 1993

[16] Pietrek, G.: Neuronaler Klassifikatior. WINA Technical Report, Informatik, Universität Dortmund, 1992

[17] Pöchmüller, W., Glesner, M.: A Cascadable VLSI Architecture for the Realization of Large Binary Associative Networks. International Workshop on VLSI for Artificial Intelligence and Neural Networks. Oxford, 1990

[18] Ultsch, A., et al.: Optimizing Logical Proofs with Connectionist Networks. Int. Conf. Artificial Neural Networks. Helsinki, 1991

[19] Ultsch, A. Siemon, H.P.: Kohonen's self organizing feature map for exploratory data analysis, in: International Neural Network Conference. 305-308, 1990

NERVES and ELENA : the Basic Research on Artificial Neural Networks in Europe

M. Verleysen
Université Catholique de Louvain
Microelectronics Laboratory
REGARDS
pl. du Levant 3, 1348 Louvain-la-Neuve (Belgium)
E-mail: verleysen@dice.ucl.ac.be

Abstract
Research on artificial neural networks goes beyond classical models and learning algorithms, and their application to adaptive tasks. The need for basic research exists, i.e. for research on learning algorithms, possibilities for specialized hardware, for interfaces between the world of conventional computers and neural networks, and especially for objective comparative studies between neural and classical methods.

These are roughly the aims of the Nerves project (July 1989 - June 1991), and of the Elena project (July 1992 - June 1995). The purpose of the Nerves project was to develop theoretical tools and technical means in order to design algorithms, machines and VLSI circuits for neurocomputing. The Elena project aims to investigate the relations between statistical methods of data classification (estimation of Bayes boundaries between classes,...), and the neural methods. It concerns theoretical studies on evolutive algorithms and relations with statistics, development of a graphical software environment and of test databases, and definition of VLSI architecture and analog/digital chips for evolutive neural networks. Conclusions of the NERVES project and preliminary results of the ELENA project are presented here.

1 Introduction

"Artificial neural networks": what does it mean? Since the pioneering works of MacCullogh and Pitts, a lot of literature was published in the various domains covered by neural networks. In fact, neural networks are not really a field. It is a collection of ideas, more or less related to the biological networks of neurons, and based on the same principles which will be detailed later. What concerns artificial neural networks, the study of models of course occupies the first place. Models are based on biological background, at least in the description of the behavior of neurons; some models also mimic biology at the structural level, i.e. in the way of how neurons are connected and organize themselves. Models can also be a way to study parallel structures, realizing simple, fast, and mostly non-linear operations, and whose only the global behavior is of importance. Models can also be a pretext to characterize a process, which needs to be described in simple terms to be efficiently analyzed. Finally, neural networks models can also be a means to describe methods already known in signal processing, in classification, in statistics, ..., but to describe them in terms more accessible to non-specialists, also providing tools which are most of the time not available in the original domain of the method.

By enumerating a non-exhaustive list of different types of models, we pointed out two important concepts which will govern the field. First, some properties make the definition of artificial neural networks: parallelism, simple computations, global behavior, asynchronism, fault-tolerance, learning, non-explanatory models,... The link between biology and neural systems is often not obvious, except that some properties are shared by the two domains. This fuzzy description of artificial neural networks, which is not, and does not have to be, a definition, leads to the second important concept: neural networks include a lot of very various fields, so much that it is impossible to find scientists aware of all developments in all branches of this research. The problem is even more complex: specialists of one of the application fields of neural networks, who want to introduce such new methods of computation and to compare them to results obtained with more "classical" methods, hardly find their way in the huge amount of papers, books, conference proceedings and lecture notes that are available. This is perhaps the point where most criticisms can be done against the neural networks field: too few studies compare the results obtained with neural networks to those obtained with classical methods of information or data processing, statistics, classification, signal processing,... The whole field has obviously much to win by setting links with other fields; we will come again later to this aspect.

But models are not alone in the different aspects of the field. There is also an abundance of application fields, and many researchers prefer to use top-down approaches from the application to the system than the opposite. Applications go from image compression to prediction of temporal series, through classification, OCR, speech processing, process control,... Again, the diversity of applications makes it difficult to have common views, common goals and common tools.

Finally, the way how to use neural networks are also varied: software simulation, parallel implementations on transputers or other specialized machines, dedicated stand-alone VLSI, dedicated accelerators, ..., all solutions providing of course advantages and drawbacks in various applications.

Considering these aspects, it should be more appropriate to speak about neural networks fields than field. Covering the whole domain is impossible, but interactions between the various aspects are beneficial for everybody. Sharing of knowledge between neural networks researchers and scientists from more classical fields is also necessary, and the domain of ANN can thus be viewed as a huge scientific field where differences and lack of understanding is the key for a healthy and beneficial future.

2 Research funded by the CEC

2.1 ESPRIT projects

The interest from the Commission of the European Communities towards artificial neural networks is not new. Specific problems and issues have already been addressed in the BRAIN program, in the 80s. Phases II and III of the ESPRIT program in Information Technology went however a step further in the interest towards artificial neural networks.

Industrial projects have been lead in the domain: to mention only one of the most important, let us cite PYGMALION, and its second phase GALATEA. As stated in its synopsis [1], "the aim of PYGMALION was to create an independent European technological base for the applications, algorithms and software aspects of neurocomputing. The project led to the coordination of research on connectionist computing techniques and provided the means for developing the necessary software tools for productive research".

Aims of PYGMALION, besides the dissemination of information in the European research community, were to develop tools to stand as interface between applications and emulation architectures, both software and hardware, and to prove the usefulness and the potential of neural network approaches through chosen industrial applications (software and hardware). What concerns the results, the PYGMALION project led to the developments of specification languages for neural network programming, to first VLSI demonstrators which may be used for several neural models, and to positive results in some applications domains: low-level imaging (image compression, segmentation and texture analysis), high-level imaging, speech recognition and acoustic signal classification.

The objective of GALATEA obviously is to finalize the first results obtained in PYGMALION, and "to construct a general-purpose neural computing system for Europe" [1]. This system will encompass general-purpose neurocomputer hardware build to support a large class of neural networks, a programming environment for this hardware, for domain-specific processors and for ASICs, and a silicon compiler for the production of ASICs. The usefulness of the hardware and software developed will be demonstrated through three industrial applications: an Optical Character Recognition (OCR) system based on neural techniques, and an industrial vision package used in Surface Mounted Devices (SMD) techniques and in fruit video-grading systems.

PYGMALION and GALATEA are two industrial ESPRIT projects. Many industrial partners are involved in it, and a company MIMETICS was created to exploit the results of the two projects. Encouraging results obtained in these projects concern not only the development of hardware and software, but also the dissemination of information in industrial domains, by showing working demonstrators in specific applications. The coordinator of these two projects is THOMSON-CSF (France).

2.2 NERVES

The aims of the NERVES project, proposed to the Commission in 1988, were quite different from those of industrial projects PYGMALION and GALATEA. At the beginning, NERVES was intended to include 6 partners, with various experiences in the field of neural networks. The purpose of this proposal was clearly to coordinate the actions undertaken in some recognized European laboratories in this field, to avoid too important overlappings between the different works, and to exchange ideas necessary for the continuation of projects already started. The project was mainly oriented towards VLSI and machines, while some other aspects were included too.

In the 1989 call for proposals for ESPRIT projects, another proposal from Edinburgh, with 4 partners, had roughly the same objectives of sharing of knowledge. Moreover, some aspects on VLSI implementations of neural networks overlapped with the NERVES proposal. The EEC asked thus to merge the two proposals, even adding one supplementary laboratory. After a 3-months definition phase, financially supported by the Commission, a new proposal was sent to the Commission and accepted. This proposal included 11 partners from 7 countries :

Institution	Team coordinators
INPG Grenoble /LTIRF(coordinator) (F)	J. Hérault
EPFL Lausanne (CH)	J.D. Nicoud, F. Blayo
IMAG Grenobla (F)	T. Muntean, P. Bessière
IMS Stuttgart (D)	L. Spaanenburg
Politecnico di Torino (I)	D. Del Corso
St-Patrick's College Dublin (IR)	R. Reilly
UCL Louvain-la-Neuve (B)	P. Jespers, M. Verleysen
Universität Dortmund (D)	K. Goser, V. Tryba
University of Edinburgh (GB)	A. Murray
University of Oxford (GB)	L. Tarassenko
CSEM Neuchâtel (CH)	E. Vittoz

table 1: partners of the NERVES project

The purpose of the NERVES project was clearly more to create a network of abilities, to share knowledge and to benefit from the experience of some to conduct projects of others than to really work towards a common objective. A lot of aspects of the neural network field were covered by NERVES; the main results are explained here [2].

1) task B1: visual processing of text

The aim of this task was ambitious, and could obviously not be reached in the lifetime of the project. It consisted in the design and the implementation of a connectionnist software system for the visual processing of text that would take as input a pixel-based text image and produce as output a semantic-level representation. Optical text recognition techniques are generally not based on cognitive modeling; the purpose here was to model as much as possible the retinal architecture and eye-movement control mechanism of human readers, and to build a vertical connectionnist model with different levels of representation (from the visual to the linguistic). Having several representation levels in the same model is of most importance to have the possibility to include contextual information, like limited number of possible characters in the lowest levels and linguistic context in the highest levels [3].

2) task B2: silicon implementation constraints and implications
While implementing neural algorithms on VLSI, several supplementary parameters have to be taken into consideration. The main one is the accuracy that is needed to efficiently perform the operations in VLSI neural networks. By using analog techniques, accuracy in circuits is limited to the matching of components (transistors, capacitors,...), which generally does not exceed 6-7 bits unless special area-consuming design is used. Digital networks can reach any accuracy provided all cells (memory points, multipliers, adders,...) cope with this accuracy; increasing the number of necessary bits automatically increases either the silicon area, either the computation times, either a compromise between the two. Specific techniques, like pulse-stream circuits developed by some partners of the NERVES project [4], are an interesting compromise between the accuracy reached, the silicon area used and the performances of the circuit.

Investigations of task B2 showed that Hamming networks are the most insensitive to reduction of accuracy. Binary-valued networks are ideal for implementation, even if simple analog cells are used. Nearest-neighbor classifiers show almost the same insensitivity. It was also proved that the pulse-stream technique and others developed in the project could lead to accuracies around 6-7 bits, which is sufficient for such types of networks, but not for Multi-Layer Perceptrons (MLP) learning. It was however shown on the text-to-speech problem that the use of a MLP network after learning can be achieved with such accuracy.

3) task B3: high-level specification language
Implementing neural algorithms either on standard computers either on specialized hardware can be done in various ways, going from standard C programming with adequate interfaces to design of hardware implementing a particular model. In this task, it was chosen to develop several layers of software between the description of artificial neural networks models and their implementation on standard or specialized computers [5]. A high-level description language (MENTAL) was specified, together with a virtual machine layer aimed to describe the execution of the algorithms. This constitutes a top-down approach, where the compilers between these two layers and between the virtual machines and the hardware were also considered.

A bottom-up axis was also developed, starting from the target machines considered in the project (SMART and SuperNode), and adding several software layers around their kernel language. The last of these layers consisted in Vectorial-C, an extension of the C language with abilities to manipulate matrices and vectors for the SMART machine, and NEURAL, an extension of OCCAM, for SuperNode. Both Vectorial-C and NEURAL are linked to the virtual machine layer through a compiler.

Finally, several applications were implemented, mostly in low-level languages, to prove the feasibility of this task. Specifications of languages were finalized before the end of the project, but not all the implementations.

4) task D1: architectures for neurocomputers
To implement neural networks on hardware, three main issues must be considered: the flexibility for implementing diverse ANN models, the huge number of interconnected cells, and the interfacing with existing machines. During the NERVES project, several partners studied several possibilities to consider these three issues. The problem of interfacing was studied both between two "intelligent" systems (a workstation and a neural architecture based accelerator board for example), and for a master-slave configuration (a workstation and a chip), leading to two definitions of interfaces.

Three architectures were also studied and developed. GENES [6], developed at EPFL, is based on systolic computations and is very efficient if the algorithms are adequately transformed in a systolic representation; this work has been done for single-layer and Hopfield networks, implementing Hebb, perceptron and Kohonen rules. Secondly, an architecture specially adapted to sparse matrix computations, SMART [7], was developed at INPG. It consists in a loose pipe-line with FIFO buffering, connected to a SparcStation. Finally, IMAG focused on the possibility to run concurrent processes on different processors to accelerate the computations; the main problems which have been addressed concern the communications between chips.

5) tasks E1/E2: design of associative memories
Associative memories may be used in many classification problems (speech and image recognition,...). Many techniques are however grouped under the term "associative memories": single-layer networks (Hamming nets in the case of binary weights), Hopfield and related nets, Kohonen maps, vector quantizers,... The purpose of these tasks were to investigate different possibilities to implement either analog or digital associative memories. Digital Kohonen maps [8] and analog single-layer networks (Hopfield nets) [9] were realized to prove the feasibility of the architectures and to evaluate the performances in what concerns accuracy and speed. The use of analog, digital, stochastic and pulse-stream computations was considered.

6) task E3: design of source separation circuits
Independent sources separation certainly is one of the most impressive examples of applications of neural networks. Considering two independent sources which are not observable, and two different observable linear mixings of these two sources, the problem is to retrieve the two original signals, the mixing matrix being of course unknown. The solution of this problem has many applications in signal processing, data transmission,... INPG has shown how to solve the independent sources separation problem for linear instantaneous mixings [10]; the work is still under progress for convolutive mixings. During the NERVES project, the problem has been addressed both theoretically by the analyses of convergence and stability of the proposed neural network solution, and on the implementation level by proposing a fully analog realization of the algorithm [11].

6) task F1: design of pulse-stream synapses
Several VLSI architectures for neural network implementations were developed during the NERVES project. These architectures need of course, to be implemented, the design of VLSI cells, paying special attention to some parameters such as accuracy and size. Tasks F1 to F3 concern the design of analog and mixed analog-digital building blocks for these implementations.

In task F1, cells for pulse-stream architectures were developed [4]. Two cells have been implemented, one based on time division of pulses, the other one on pseudo-switched-capacitor techniques, and test chips were realized. Coupled to digital weight memory and pulse-width input-weight multiplication, a complete chip with 4 blocks of 16 neurons with 16 synapses each has been designed. Four-transistors transconductance multiplier-based synapses with weight leakage compensation, new neuron oscillators, and several cells aimed to reduce the area needed for pulse-stream computations were also designed.

7) task F2: design of building blocks for analog implementations
This task is more or less the equivalent to task F1 but this time for analog realizations instead of pulse-stream techniques. The problem of analog sum-of-products has been examined through the realization of test chips and through theoretical studies about matching. Reconfigurable neurons and cascadable matrices of synapses were also studied. The storage of analog weights is also of great importance in the analog realizations of neural networks; this problem has been studied by CSEM and UCL, who propose two solutions [12]: the first one relies on local refreshment of weights through the comparison of the stored value to an external ramp, the second one on a global sequential refreshment of all weights stored on the chip by comparing each stored value to a set of predefined levels. In both cases, once the comparison is realized, the weight is refreshed to the next upper discretized level, allowing thus a subsequent decrease during a defined period because of the leakage currents. By these methods, weights will be kept into the range between two defined levels, corresponding to the accuracy achieved in the memory.

8) task F3: design of technology for analog synapse memory
The same problem of analog synapse memories has been addressed in task F3, but here by proposing new VLSI technologies or the use of specialized ones to realize the memory points. Several solutions have been proposed: analog EEPROMs where the floating gate is accurately controlled by special programming techniques [12], use of UV-light to modify the conductance of a special technological layer used to connect the storage capacitor with the rest of the circuit, use of non-volatile 2-terminal α-SI (amorphous silicon) metal/p^+ junctions, and use of special technological layers to reduce the programming voltages of EEPROMs. Some studies have also been carried out on circuitry for the compensation of leakage currents.

As it can be seen in this description, many ways have been explored under the NERVES project. The expertise areas of the different partners were very different one from another, and this project had the merit to open new perspectives to all researchers who contributed in it by the sharing of their knowledge and their new results. The good results obtained in the NERVES project are not only due to common works, but also to the frequent meetings (three per year), to the participation of members of the consortium to various international conferences, to the dissemination of information realized by many of them through courses and lectures in their institutions and abroad, to the participation in exhibits (Neuro-Nîmes),... The state-of-the-art in the neural network field, between 1989 and 1991, period during which the NERVES contract was running, certainly needed such opening of new perspectives and dissemination of information.

The situation is now different. While sharing of knowledge and dissemination of information is still needed in the neural network field, as in any scientific domain, people now begin to be more aware of the progress in their domain of interest, and, which is very important, begin to make the difference between real innovations and rediscoveries of known methods. The projects proposed to the Commission in 1991 reflected such tendency: they were more specialized, gathered less partners, and generally not concerned only neural networks but more often relations between neural networks and other fields.

2.3 ELENA

ELENA may be considered as a continuation of the NERVES project, as it gathers several of its partners (through some of the researchers moved from one institution to another; this is also a result of the European collaboration...). ELENA is a project focused on classification and evolutive neural algorithms.

Classification concerns a lot of applications where data (often high-dimensional) must be associated to a finite number of classes. Most often however, neural networks are used in classification tasks without any study of comparisons with more classical statistical methods. In particular, the Bayes theory shows where to fix limits between classes when their distributions are overlapping; most neural networks even don't try to approximate the Bayes boundaries, and give thus results much worst than statistical methods...

Neural networks however can find advantages in the evolutive character of some structures; many statistical methods indeed only give asymptotic proves of convergence, with no indication on the sizes (learning set, number of kernels in case of kernel estimators,...) needed to obtain a defined accuracy in the estimation of classes boundaries.

The ELENA project tries to make the link between evolutive architectures for neural networks, i.e. networks whose size evolves with the number, the nature and the complexity of the data to handle, and statistical methods of classification, based on kernel estimators of probability densities. The project includes three axes, detailed below: theory, software and benchmarks, and hardware. Six partners are involved in the ELENA project, which runs since July 1992.

Institution	Team coordinators
INPG Grenoble /LTIRF (coordinator) (F)	C. Jutten
EPFL Lausanne (CH)	J.D. Nicoud, Y. Cheneval
UCL Louvain-la-Neuve (B)	M. Verleysen
EERIE Nîmes (France)	F. Blayo
Universidad Politecnica de Catalunya (SP)	J. Cabestany
Thomson-Sintra Sophia-Antipolis (F)	P. Comon

table 2: partners of the ELENA project

1) Axis A: theory

Axis A basically covers the theory of kernel estimators of probability densities and radial-basis functions. Once probability densities of classes are known, the Bayes criterion gives the best limits between classes to use to decrease the number of misclassifications, a priori probabilities of classes being given. The first results of this axis [13] concern the estimation of probability densities by kernel estimators, including their choice and the number of samples required in large dimensions, the probability of errors and the computation of the confusion matrix, the relations between these methods and radial-basis functions (RBF), and practical issues concerning the use of RCE and LVQ procedures to approximated Bayes boundaries [14-15-16].

2) Axis B: simulations and benchmarks

Studies about classification cannot be performed without comparisons between different techniques. For objective comparisons, it was decided to collect two types of databases to use as standards, at least inside the project: artificially-generated databases for preliminary tests on algorithms, and real databases collected in the literature of this field and among often tested problems of classification (Fisher's Iris database, ATT Bell labs characters database,...).

Testing new algorithms is also fastidious to implement in low-level programming languages such as C, especially when graphical input-outputs are needed. Based on the experience of the NERVES project where some graphical simulators were developed, it was decided to create a graphical environment for neural networks simulation, called PACKLIB, which includes abilities for easy visualization of neural networks, graphical description of neural algorithms based on modules developed in C,... Many algorithms have already been implemented in this environment; its main advantage is that changes in the use of basic functional blocks to describe an algorithm may be achieved without any programming, giving thus an incredible flexibility to test new models. Finally, since the development of basic modules must be done in C, matrix computations and graphical libraries were develop to help the programmer in his task.

3) Axis C: VLSI implementations

Different problems are encountered when implementing evolutive neural algorithms on VLSI chips rather than other neural networks. Problems of precision must be reconsidered, and the cascadability is of course important too. The first work achieved in this axis concerns the influence of the limitations of accuracy in evolutive algorithms, and investigations to evaluate the attainable accuracy in analog VLSI chips. In particular, it is studied how the SOI (Silicon-On-Insulator) technology could be used to exploit the reduced leakage currents obtained with such process.

A second task in this axis concerns the definition of VLSI architectures aimed to implement PLS (Piecewise Linear Separation) and ROI (Region-Of-Influence) algorithms; two digital architectures have been up to now proposed [17].

Finally, a last task will include the realization of VLSI building blocks for analog and digital chips.

The work of the ELENA project is currently under progress. The aim for the remaining of the project is to clearly set methods and evaluate their condition of use and their limitations for the classification of data, and to set up both software and hardware tools which could be used for classification applications. Evolutive neural algorithms with be mainly studied, but without forgetting their links with the statistical Bayesian methods.

Acknowledgments

This paper (too) briefly summarizes the work realized by more than 70 researchers during several years. It would be too long to cite them here, but I would like to thank them for the wonderful job they did and they are still doing. My special thanks go to Jeanny Hérault and Christian Jutten, respectively coordinators of the NERVES and ELENA project, who make the European collaboration described here possible.

References

[1] Esprit Synopses: Information processing Systems and Software. Commission of the European Communities, Publication office, Luxemburg, 1992.

[2] NERVES, an ESPRIT Basic Research Action : final Report. J. Hérault, INPG Grenoble, 1991.

[3] Connectionist approaches to sentence processing. R. Reilly, C. Doherty, proceedings of Neuro-Nîmes 1990 (Nîmes, France, November 1990), EC2, Paris.

[4] Pulse Stream VLSI neural networks - mixing analog and digital techniques. A. Murray, D. Del Corso, L. Tarassenko, IEEE Transactions on Neural Networks, 1991, pp. 193-204.

[5] A virtual machine model for artificial neural networks programming. P. Bessière, A. Chams, T. Muntean, proceedings of INNC90, Paris, 1990.

[6] Digital VLSI generic elements for neuro-emulators using systolization. C. Lehmann, F. Blayo, proceedings of the International Workshop on Algorithm and Parallel VLSI Architectures, Pont-à-Mousson (France), June 1990.

[7] SMART: how to simulate huge networks. J.C. Lawson, A. Chams, J. Hérault, ITG-IEEE Workshop on Microelectronics for Neural Networks, Dortmund (Germany), June 1990.

[8] VLSI implementation of an associative memory based on distributed storage of information. U. Rückert, K. Goser, ITG-IEEE Workshop on Microelectronics for Neural Networks, Dortmund (Germany), June 1990.

[9] Analog VLSI implementations of Hopfield's neural network. M. Verleysen, P. Jespers, IEEE Micro, December 1989.

[10] Separation of sources, part 1: an adaptive algorithm based on neuromimetic architecture. C. Jutten, J. Hérault, Signal Processing, July 1991.

[11] CMOS integration of Hérault-Jutten cells for separation of sources. E. Vittoz, X. Arreguit, in: "Analog Implementations of Neural Systems", C. Mead and M. Ismail eds., Kluwer Academic Publishers, Norwell (MA), 1990.

[12] Analog storage of adjustable synaptic weights. E. Vittoz et al., ITG-IEEE Workshop on Microelectronics for Neural Networks, Dortmund (Germany), June 1990.

[13] Neural Bayesian Classifier. C. Jutten, P. Comon, proceedings of the International Workshop on Artificial Neural Networks, Sitges (Barcelona, Spain), June 1993.

[14] Setting initial conditions for the RCE model. F. Blayo, M. Verleysen, proceedings of the First IFIP Working Group 10.6 Workshop, Grenoble (France), March 1992.

[15] Optimal decision surfaces in LVQ1 classification of patterns. M. Verleysen, P. Thissen, J.D. Legat, proceedings of the European Symposium on Artificial Neural Networks 1993, Brussels (Belgium), May 1993.

[16] Learning Vector Classification: an improvement on LVQ algorithms to create classes of patterns. M. Verleysen, P. Thissen, J.D. Legat, proceedings of the International Workshop on Artificial Neural Networks, Sitges (Barcelona, Spain), June 1993.

[17] Hardware implementation of piecewise linear separation incremental algorithms, J.M. Moreno, F. Castillo, J. Cabestany, proceedings of Neuro-Nîmes93 (Nîmes, France, October 1993), EC2, Paris.

RACE BANK –
a Multimedia Broadband Cooperation Project in the Banking Business Sector[1]

Norbert Luttenberger[1]
Rainer Oechsle[1]
Wolfgang Johannsen[2]
Matthias Kloidt[2]
Andreas Henrich[2]
Thomas Humer-Hager[3]
Diethelm Bauer[3]

1. IBM Germany
Europ. Netw. Center
Vangerowstr. 18
D-69115 Heidelberg
Fed. Rep. of Germany

2. Deutsche Bank AG
Organisation and
Operations Dept.
Alfred-Herrhausen-Allee 16-24
D-65760 Eschborn
Fed. Rep. of Germany

3. Siemens AG
Public Communication
Networks Group
Hofmannstr. 51
D-81359 München
Fed. Rep. of Germany

Abstract. In the framework of the European programme RACE ("Research and Development in Advanced Communications Technologies in Europe"), a project called BANK has been established. In this project, two major European banks work together with three software houses, a telecom supplier and an IT supplier with the goal to investigate and prototype a multimedia banking terminal. This terminal will allow the banks to offer to their customers both high-quality, eye-catching information on banking services and the opportunity to enter a desktop conference with a remote bank expert. The conference includes audio, face-to-face video and shared text/graphics applications that support the expert in promoting certain banking services to the customer. The paper gives the project scenario background and then discusses some networking and multimedia related questions in the given environment. It closes with some conclusions on system evaluation and system acceptance.

1. Introduction

The commercial availability of powerful workstations and high-speed networks both in the WAN and the LAN domain, e.g. Broadband-ISDN and FDDI, enables the design of various new types of applications among which multimedia applications

---

1 The work described in this paper is sponsored by the Commission of the European Community in the RACE-II programme as project R2027.

play a predominant role. Multimedia application systems can be characterized by the integrated use of text, graphics, audio and video (or a subset thereof) as presentation media, by which they aim at the implementation of a user interface that is closer to human perception, thus transforming the computer effectively into a communication instrument.

While the use of high-speed networks for multimedia applications makes much sense especially because of the high data rate and low latency requirements of video and audio, it still has to be found out in which respect individual businesses will profit from high-speed networking and multimedia technology and what the relevant application scenarios in these businesses are.

In the framework of the second phase of the European RACE programme ("Research and Development in Advanced Communications Technologies in Europe"), a three-year project called BANK has been established in early 1992. BANK tries to give an answer to the above question with regard to the financial business sector. BANK is the abbreviation for "**B**anking **A**pplications using IBC **N**etwor**K**", and in the RACE context denotes a consortium, in which the following bodies cooperate:

- Users: Deutsche Bank (D), Générale de Banque (B)
- Telecom/IT: Siemens (D), IBM (F/D)
- Software: GSI (F), Norcontel (IRL), Financial Courseware (IRL)

Five further banks and the subsidiary of a network operator act as sponsoring partners, which means that they help in application definition and prototype evaluation, but do not participate in the actual development activities.

After its requirements analysis phase, the BANK project decided to prototype a multimedia-based "Advanced Self-Service Terminal". This terminal will allow the bank customer to receive complex financial services either in "full self-service" mode or in "assisted" mode. Assisted mode implies that the bank customer can get the help of a remote banking expert with whom he/she can interact from the self-service terminal via a multimedia desktop conference.

In the following chapter, we describe the application scenario and its background. Technical aspects for multimedia integration and for the banking application design are analyzed in sections 3 and 4. In section 5, we present the networking testbeds which have been chosen in the project. Some conclusions are drawn in the final section.

2. Banking Application Scenario

Self-service in Retail Banking allows customer access to banking services independent of office hours and location. However, up to now only a limited set of services have been made available via Automated Teller Machines and kiosk systems. In the following we describe the Retail Banking application scenario which has been selected by Deutsche Bank for investigation of the potential of the combined application of multimedia and high-speed networking technologies for advanced self-service facilities. The advanced kiosk system mentioned in this context (we call it the "BANKstation" in the remainder of this paper) is intended to be used within the premises of bank branches, at places with limited public access (e.g. large office buildings), and at home. The system comprises features of advanced self-service and the assistance of a remote expert who is made available on customer request.

2.1 Retail Banking Scenario

The application scenario for the BANK project was chosen with respect to the fact that both self-service and consultation of a branch office clerk both have their own special advantages. Furthermore it is based on the understanding that it is impossible to have an expert for each bank product in every branch. Hence, the selected scenario is designed to combine the advantages of self-service, branch office support and remote expertise. It is made up of the following components:

- a multimedia self-service terminal which allows the customer to gather product information and to set up a multimedia desktop conference with a remote expert for further information and/or contract preparation,
- a branch office support workstation which allows the branch office clerk to set up a multimedia desktop conference with a remote expert when his personal expertise is not sufficient,
- a remote expert located e.g. in the head office of the bank who can support the customer at the self-service terminal and the branch office clerk by the means of a multimedia desktop conference with features for joint editing, joint form filling, etc., and
- a remote multimedia document server containing multimedia product information offered to the customer at the self-service terminal.

The operation of the BANKstation can be subdivided in five process steps. These will be described first for the case of a customer interacting with the multimedia self-service terminal solely in full self-service mode, i.e. without interaction with a remote expert. The possibility to enrich the dialog by an interpersonal communication ("assisted mode") is treated separately in chapter 2.3. Thereafter we will refer to the branch office support part of our scenario.

2.2 The Self-Service Process

It is assumed that a typical self-service process comprises the following steps (Figure 1):

Attraction: A multimedia document (video, graphics, animation) is presented at the BANKstation while no customer is using it. The aim of this presentation is to attract customers to use the BANKstation.

General Product Information: The general product information is presented to the customer by means of a highly interactive dialog using multimedia techniques. The media used will be text, structured data and graphics (e.g. for technical chart analysis). Video and graphics animation may be used for illustration. The use of audio is debatable. The presentation of the information has to be adaptable to the customer's information needs and to his/her skill in using the self-service terminal. Generally spoken: The user should neither be bored nor confused by information overload. There must be a "walk-through mode" for the naive user in order to give an overview over the information available. Additionally there should be a quick search possibility for the skilled user who wants to look up a specific information and an intelligent means to navigate through the information (hypermedia functions).

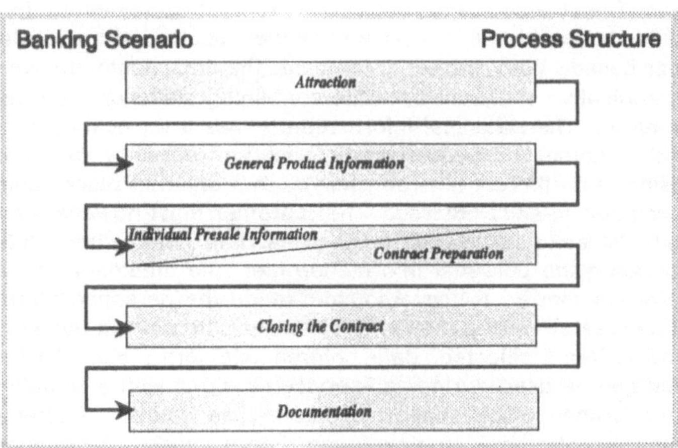

Figure 1. Self Service Process Structure

Individual Presale Information/Contract Preparation: After the General Product Information step, the incorporation of customer specific data leads to the phase of presale information and contract preparation. Therefore the customer is asked to insert his eurocheque card and to key in his Personal Identification Number (PIN). Then some customer specific data are extracted from the bank's central data base. The customer will type in further information (e.g. on his/her income and age) which is necessary for offering e.g. an optimal investment plan. Although the user interface should enable the customer to perform the individual information process without external help, it is likely that the customer calls a remote expert for support. In this case, the customer can show paper documents to the expert during the communication whenever necessary. The input device may be a scanner or a document camera.

Closing the Contract: The customer actually closes the contract at the self-service terminal. Security issues and the legal situation for this way of closing contracts have to be examined. There will be different levels of security requirements for different contract types: Some deals require from the customer only the eurocheque card plus PIN legitimation and/or an electronic signature via a smart card. An example for this type of deal is submitting a securities purchase order. In this case the customer simply gets a printout of the order he submitted. After-sale documentation and billing will be handled by mail. If for legal reasons a paper contract with the customer's signature is needed, two copies of the contract will be printed. One copy for the customer and, if needed, one for the bank. The customer will sign the copy for the bank. We see two alternatives for further processing the paper document: Either, the customer can drop the signed contract in a mailbox located nearby the self-service terminal, or he will insert the signed contract in a scanning device.

Documentation: The closing of the contract has to be documented to the customer and to the bank. For the customer the documentation will have to be paper-based. With respect to the bank, the documentation can be stored electronically. It should be a file containing statistical and personal information. The statistical information is meant for evaluating the usage of the terminal. The personal information is meant for reopening the session at a different time and maybe at a different place without losing information already entered. The customer must however have the option to refuse to storing his/her personal data. We distinguish two modes of creating the personal information file: the automatic mode and the interactive mode. In the automatic mode the personal information file will be created during the self-service session and will include customer number, items selected, data entered into forms etc. The interactive mode can be used during self-service sessions with a remote expert or in the branch office support scenario (see below). Interactive mode means that the bank employee can record specific informations during the session, edit the information later and store it.

Obviously, the self-service option is best suited for the early phases in this process and the use of remote expertise will usually occur in the later phases. This leads to the following figure which shows the expected preferred mode of communication (expressed in percent) for the different phases of the described process (Figure 2).

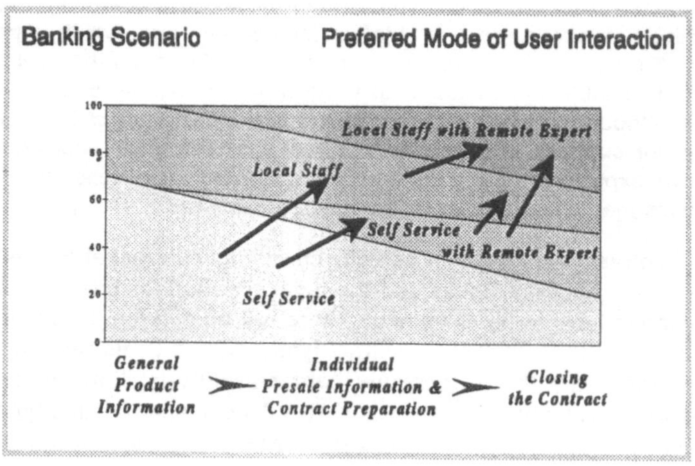

Figure 2. User Interaction Modes

For the general product information phase, full self-service is the interaction mode of the choice. Nevertheless, some bank customers will continue to prefer consulting a branch office clerk. During the information process the need for support by a remote expert may arise. In this case, a connection to an expert at a bank office can be established from the self-service terminal as well as from the branch office support station. In addition there should be a possibility for the customer at a self-service terminal to stop the self-service session at any time and continue the consultation with a branch office clerk immediately or even with a delay of a few days. To this end, the state of the self-service session and the already input personal information should be stored for the later continuation of the consultation.

2.3 Remote Expert Support

The conferencing option enlarges the scope of self-service banking: The customer has access to personal consultation via self-service terminal. The customer can call a remote expert at any time during one of the aforementioned steps. After opening of a conference the expert takes over the selection of the information that he needs for advising the customer. The remote expert support incorporates the following features:

Video and Audio Streams: The expert is visible for the customer. It is debatable and should be explored during the project, whether the customer should be seen by the expert as well. The use of voice is required for the conference with the remote expert. Privacy issues and ergonomic aspects have to be considered in deciding on the adequate I/O devices.

Documents from Multimedia Server: During the conference the expert will make use of documents containing general product information. He will also use forms and application routines from the Individual Presale Information phase.

Paper Documents: During the communication between customer and expert there may arise the need for showing paper documents to each other. Therefore, a scanner or a document camera will be needed at both stations.

Joint Editing: Although the typing actions of the customer during the conference should be kept at a minimum, some typing may nevertheless be advisable. For instance there may be secret information (e.g. PIN) that the customer has to type in by himself. Possibly the customer also prefers typing in private information (e.g. personal income) so that nobody in the self-service area can listen.

Private Workspace for the Expert: The expert should be able to use his private application programs and databases during the conference. He may decide to transfer some of his private information to the common workspace (e.g. by cut-and-paste).

2.4 Branch Office Support

The BANKstation usage mode in the branch office support scenario will be different from the self-service scenario. Nevertheless, the general application process structure of the self-service scenario also holds for the branch office support scenario. The following minor adaptions in the process structure are required.

1. The first phase (Attraction) is not necessarily included in the branch office support scenario.
2. During the conference the control of the session is passed between the calling and the answering 'expert' station. This contrasts to the self-service scenario where the remote expert chooses which information the customer should see. Therefore, a mechanism for passing the session control has to be implemented in the branch office support scenario.
3. Some of the I/O devices that are appropriate for the self-service scenario are not appropriate for the branch office support scenario. The input devices touch screen and button should be substituted by a mouse. Loudspeakers can be used for audio output in the branch office support scenario whereas their usage in the self-service scenario conflicts with privacy issues.
4. More than two stations can be involved in a conference within the branch office scenario (e.g. the calling station and two experts for different subjects).

3. Multimedia Integration

The integration of audio and video in a computerized environment has been in various aspects one of the major technical work items for the BANKstation design. From the BANK application context, audio and video come as both conversational and (for the sake of symmetrical wording) "presentational" audio and video. **Conversational** audio/video is in support of the conference between the bank customer and the bank expert, and provides to the conference participants a voice connection accompanied by a head-and-shoulder video of the remote participant. **Presentational** audio/video is included in multimedia documents (the term document been used here in a very general sense) which are e.g. displayed for product promotion in the attraction phase of the BANKstation operation.

In the next chapter, we will discuss some basic issues and choices concerning audio and video integration, and after that present our technical solutions concerning protocol and OS support for audio/video stream transfer in data networks.

3.1 Basic Issues

For selecting among the many technical choices for the integration of audio and video into a computerized environment a list of criteria has been developed by the project which is given in the following.

1. For presentational audio/video no additional storage devices, e.g. VCRs or video disc players, beyond the workstation disc storage should be used.

2. Though the BANK project clearly aims at using upcoming or experimental broadband networks for wide area connectivity (e.g. ATM and DQDB pilot networks), the solution should be compatible with existing local area networks.

3. The equipment for audio/video integration should be commercially available at a reasonable price (no professional studio equipment).

Requirement 1 proposes a fully digital solution, i.e. a solution where audio and video data are stored digitally. Solutions where e.g. an analog video stream is retrieved from a VCR and displayed in a window via a video overlay adapter are thus excluded.

Requirement 2 has a number of different implications:

1. To be compatible with existing LANs, video compression is a must. Uncompressed video would require a bandwidth that exceeds the capacity of today's LANs like Ethernet or Token Ring or, on higher bandwidth networks like FDDI B-ISDN, would leave virtually no capacity for additional data communication. Additionally, in wide area networks, bandwidth will not be "for free". As the described application context obviously requires a cost-effective solution, video compression is highly recommendable to decrease transmission costs to an acceptable degree.

2. Continuous media like audio and video are normally transmitted as *continuous bit streams*, according e.g. to the CCITT G.703 standard. Local area networks like Ethernet and Token Ring on the contrary have been designed for *packetized* data transfer. In order to be compatible with existing LAN technology, packetized audio/video has to be used. This means that audio/video data units (commonly denoted as "samples" or "frames" respectively) must be assembled into packets and sent at regular intervals (see below). The audio/video playback device has to recuperate a continuous stream from these packets.

As it is not in the scope of an application project like BANK to develop basic technologies like e.g. audio/video compression, requirement 3 is the most important requirement. It was predominant for the selection of the powerful Digital Video Interactive (DVI) technology [Luth91] for audio/video integration, because this technology is incorporated in the commercially available ActionMedia-2 (AM-2) adapter. This adapter integrates audio/video compression and packetization, video decompression and windowed video overlay, and audio output to active loudspeakers. DVI and the AM-2 adapter were jointly developed by IBM and Intel.

The AM-2 adapter supports two video modes, namely Real-Time Video (RTV) and Production Level Video (PLV). In the RTV mode, video is compressed and decompressed in real-time which makes this mode appropriate for conversational video. At the CD data rate (1.4 Mbit/s), RTV delivers a good video quality. For high quality presentational video, the PLV mode is appropriate. PLV employs an asymmetric compression/decompression scheme: Video is compressed off-line on a powerful computer and decompressed in real-time on the AM-2 adapter. For DVI a number of tools for multimedia conferencing and authoring exist.

Core processing component of the BANKstation hosting the AM-2 adapter is the IBM PS/2 under the OS/2 operating system. Operation of the AM-2 adapter is supported by the Audio/Video Kernel (AVK) and an AM-2 toolkit.

3.2 Protocol Support for Audio/Video

The transfer of packetized audio/video streams over data networks reverses some of the paradigms being used for the design of data communication systems. While data communication is not bound e.g. to tight timing constraints, timely delivery of audio/video frames is absolutely required; frames arriving "too late" are of no worth for the presentation of the audio/video sequence.

The requirements for correct audio/video delivery can be comprehended in the term **continuity**. The required continuous flow of frames from the capture to the playback system is disrupted whenever frames are corrupted, lost or delayed beyond their frame time, i.e. the time interval where a given frame must logically be displayed in the sequence of frames. The frame time is the inverse of the frame rate (e.g. 33 ms for a frame rate of 30 frames/s). In data communication, packet corruption and loss are normally handled by retransmissions; but audio/video frame retransmissions are not allowable as they would offend the given real-time constraints.

Discontinuities decrease the audio/video quality, whereby the allowable rate of discontinuities thus is highly user dependent. If compression is applied, a single discontinuity can be become very severe if the compression algorithm comprises inter-frame compression. In this case the loss of a "reference" frame invalidates all following "delta" frames. On the other hand, the loss of a delta frame is in most cases hardly noticeable.

In order to guarantee a sufficient quality of the application as a whole the system must provide a certain "Quality-of-Service" (QoS) to the audio/video stream. The most important QoS parameters are:

Bit Rate: For audio/video streams with DVI compression a bit rate of approx. 2 Mbit/s is required. To have capacity for accompanying data streams, e.g. in a conferencing application, the bit rate should be beyond this value.

Error Rate: An error rate is normally specified for bit errors and for packet errors. While bit errors can often be handled by error correcting codes, packet errors would require the retransmission of the errored packet. In ATM networks (see section 5) packet errors can occur when, because of congestion, one or more cells from a packet are discarded in an ATM switch or multiplexer.

Delay: Time elapsing between capturing and playback of an audio/video frame. This parameter is important especially for conferencing applications. Here, the delay must not exceed a value of approx. 200 ms [Russ93].

Delay Jitter: Variation of the delay. Delay jitter will reduce the quality of the presentation. Acceptable limits are below frame times.

To obtain a given QoS especially with regard to timing parameters, certain resources both in the endsystem and in the network must be reserved for exclusive use by an audio/video stream before the stream can actually be started. Typically, network bandwidth, processing time, and code and buffer space are among these resources. Resource reservation has a number of implications among which the most important are the following:

1. **Resource negotiation**: Before starting a stream it has to be found out in a resource negotiation process if all required resources are actually available. From a protocol design point of view, this implies a connection-oriented approach where the negotiation process is conducted during connection setup. To provide resource negotiation on a per-link basis, especially a connection-oriented network layer protocol is required.

2. **Resource management**: All resources contributing to the transfer of streams must be managed by related resource managers which keep book of their momentarily available capacities. These resource managers are involved in the resource negotiation process.

3. **Resource scheduling**: Resources must be allocated to the streams requiring them. In shared medium LANs this means that a higher access priority must be assigned to audio/video streams to give them priority over data streams. For processor usage this means that the operating system scheduling policy, which in a normal workstation environment aims at a fair sharing of the processor resource between all active processes, has to be extended by a real-time component that gives real-time processes priority over non-real-time processes and schedules them according to their relative urgency (deadline scheduling).

In the BANKstation, support for audio/video streams is provided by HeiTS, the Heidelberg Transport System ([HeHS91]), an experimental multimedia communication system currently under development at IBM's European Networking Center in Heidelberg. HeiTS is at the same time a protocol stack and an environment augmenting the standard workstation OS environment with components for stream handling, resource management and scheduling.

Key component of the HeiTS protocol stack is the STreams Protocol II (ST-2, [Topo90]). ST-2 is a connection-oriented network layer protocol from the Internet family comprising mechanisms for resource negotiation and multicast. Streams in the ST-2 context are unidirectional and flow from one origin to a number of targets.

ST-2 actually consists of two protocols, namely the Stream Control Message Protocol (SCMP) and the Stream Protocol. SCMP is responsible for connection setup and release and uses the standard IP Address Resolution Protocol (ARP) for routing. Borrowing a term from the telecommunications world, SCMP could be called a signalling protocol concerning connection setup/release. At connection setup, an SCMP CONNECT message flows upstream hop-by-hop to each target carrying a so-called flow specification specifying the stream parameters and the minimum required QoS values. At each hop an ST-2 agent (located e.g. inside a router) negotiates the availability of the hop-related resources with the responsible resource managers, reserves the required resources, and passes the so-far achievable QoS to the next hop ST-2 agent. Finally the target nodes and the origin together decide on accepting the connection based on the resulting QoS values. SCMP is a reliable request/response protocol using acknowledgements, timers and retransmissions.

After successful connection setup the Stream Protocol forwards packets from the origin to the targets along the path that has been established by the SCMP CONNECT operation; it is unidirectional, and it is unreliable. Its very simple protocol header and operation facilitate quick data delivery.

On top of ST-2, HeiTS employs a lightweight transport protocol called HeiTP. HeiTP provides segmentation/reassembly for packets being bigger as the maximum allowed MAC layer PDU sizes, and beyond segmentation/reassembly HeiTP offers a selectable degree of reliability.

Major components of the HeiTS environment are a Stream Handler System, a Resource Management System, and a Buffer Management System (a specialized resource manager). For further information on these sub-systems the reader is referred to [Herr92].

4. Banking Application Design

A key component of the BANKstation software system is the so-called banking application. It is active from the General Product Information phase until the Contract Closing phase and allows the bank customer to collect more information on the financial services being offered via the BANKstation and to close a related contract. The contents of the banking application are obviously specific for each bank participating in the project.

The design of the banking application is complicated by the requirement that it must be able to run in both "self-service" mode and in "assisted" mode, i.e. inside a conference between the bank customer and the bank expert. In self-service mode, the banking application follows the paradigm of a dialogue system, and the related design issues are well understood. The main focus is on the design of a graphically attractive, consistent and self-explanatory user interface.

But once the customer opens a conference with the bank expert, the "simple" dialogue system is metamorphosed into a so-called Computer Supported Cooperative Work application, or for short: into a shared application. Behind this term, a new cooperation model for distributed systems becomes visible [Geih93]. Cooperation models for distributed systems so far mostly follow the client/server paradigm or, to a lesser extent, the producer/consumer paradigm. Both are very successful models because they easily allow the distribution of tasks or data in a distributed system. The cooperation model behind shared applications is the **group model** modelling the situation where a group works jointly on a common object. The group cooperatively and iteratively transforms its object, while all group members see all changes, and the object consistency is maintained by appropriate synchronisation protocols. At least two components are required by this approach:

1. Between the application code and the IO and/or window system a "wedge" is inserted which intercepts the IO stream generated locally and distributes them to all conference participants.

2. To maintain consistency of common objects a "floor manager" is introduced which distributes the right to change the object state. This floor manager can be fully automatic or, on the other extreme, it can be based only on an informal agreement by the conference participants.

For the design of shared applications following this cooperation model, two different approaches exist: the distribution-unaware and the distribution-aware approach. It is the goal of the **distribution-unaware** approach to turn existing non-shared applications into shared applications without touching the existing code. In **distribution-aware** applications, different instances of the application code exist which still lets the conference participants work together as a group, but allows to assign different roles to them accompanied by different capabilities.

In the context of BANK, the role of the conference participants is very unequal: a very experienced bank expert opposed to a customer with little or no computer knowledge. The unequal role of the conference participants seems to give favour to distribution-aware applications. This will allow e.g. the bank expert to perform some intermediate calculations before he/she will present the result to the customer without leaving the application.

In addition to the banking application, the BANKstation will have a remote kiosk control application which allows the expert to control the customer terminal remotely.

The conference between bank customer and bank expert is controlled by a so-called call manager. In the case of multimedia desktop conferences, a call is no longer a monolithic object as in the olden days of telephony, but a complex interacting assembly of various multipoint connections, among them at least the mentioned shared banking application and an audio/video connection. We call this a **composite multipoint call** (cf. [ArWi92]). It will be identified by the call control software as single entity consisting of several one-to-many connections, but it must be possible to add or remove single participants in the course of the conference. The call manager thus has to accomplish call control, connection control, and media control.

5. BANK Networking Testbeds

The networking environment for the BANK project will be developed in two testbeds. The first testbed will use a Token Ring LAN. The focus of this stage is both on multimedia networking over LANs and on an early evaluation of the application system. The second stage will include the use of wide-area networks. One prototype testbed will be located in Belgium and use the Brussels MAN field trial. The other prototype testbed will be located in Germany and use the German ATM field trial network. In both cases, the end-systems on both ends will remain LAN-attached, and the LANs will be connected to the wide-area networks via experimental bridges/routers.

In the following, we will cover all three mentioned networks and show the feasibility of multimedia integration in these networks.

5.1 Token Ring LAN

As outlined in section 3, the real-time transport of audio/video data requires the reservation of network resources for exclusive use by the audio/video stream. In the following, we will cover how Token Ring bandwidth is managed and how access to a Token Ring is scheduled so that for audio/video streams a given Quality-of-Service can be guaranteed.

Bandwidth management implies that each station willing to send a stream with a given QoS involves a chain of bandwidth managers along the stream route before starting to send. A network bandwidth manager keeps book of the actually reserved amount of bandwidth. If it finds out that the required bandwidth is available, it is reserved for the requesting stream; otherwise the bandwidth manager gives a negative response.

For **dynamic** distribution of Token Ring bandwidth between attached stations, there must one bandwidth manager per Token Ring segment. The protocol between a station and the bandwidth manager is the network management protocol CMIP (Common Management Interface Protocol) which is intended to be replaced by CMOL (CMIP over LLC). In the first testbed, bandwidths will be **statically** assigned to the attached stations, i.e. a bandwidth manager resides in each station and manages the assigned bandwidth.

To enable the calculation of available bandwidth and the resulting delay a regulator within each multimedia workstation shapes the traffic generated by a source from an irregular to a regular traffic pattern according to the LBAP (linear bounded arrival process) model. In this model the amount of data N(t) sent in time t is bounded by the equation $N(t) \leq R \cdot t + W$ with R being the data rate and W being a certain workahead.

For guaranteed connections a pessimistic approach with worst-case assumptions is followed. Because this approach tends to under-utilization of the medium, best-effort connections following an optimistic approach with weaker assumptions can also be used. Packets belonging to pure data, best-effort or guaranteed connections are put into different queues with different priorities, with guaranteed connections having the highest priority and pure data connections having the lowest priority. Within the best-effort and guaranteed traffic queues internal priorities according to the rate monotonic scheduling scheme are used. The packets are then forwarded to the adapter based on their priorities.

Conflicts between real-time streams and "standard" discrete data traffic are resolved by assigning a high priority to audio and video data and a low-priority to all other traffic which will be delayed in tolerable limits. Priority assignment is part of the Token Ring standard. For further information on Token Ring stream handling the reader is referred to [NaVo92] and [VoHN92].

Token Ring segments may be interconnected by bridges at the MAC layer, or by IP and ST-2 routers at the network layer. Both alternatives are also possible for the interconnection of Token Ring segments over a wide area network (WAN).

They may even coexist. So one may think of routing the IP and ST-2 traffic, and bridging the rest (e.g. SNA, NetBIOS). This is possible because each Token Ring MAC frame contains fields for the identification of the protocol.

5.2 Token Ring/Metropolitan Area Network Testbed

For the second prototype of the BANK project a public broadband connection between two sites of Générale de Banque in Brussels is required. The Belgian PTT (RTT-Belgacom) operates a Metropolitan Area Network (MAN) in the Brussels area as a first step towards the introduction of public broadband networks.

The MAN offers two types of services: a service providing transparent isochronous 2 Mbit/s connections and a connectionless service supporting asynchronous communication. The isochronous MAN facility is normally employed for permanent or reserved connections e.g. between two PABXs. In order to guarantee the isochronous delivery of a 2 Mbit/s data stream so-called pre-abitrated slots are allocated by network management procedures to the isochronous connection. Asynchronous communication is handled using so-called queue-arbitrated slots that are dynamically assigned by the DQDB access protocol. Depending on the load on the MAN the delay experienced by data packets may vary and thus delay and delay jitter are not predictable. The advantage is that the customer can transmit data on demand with a variable bit rate.

The Brussels MAN is configured as a fibre optic ring covering an area of approx. 6 km in diameter. Four nodes will be operated on the MAN. Two of them are Edge Gateways (EGWs) intended for connecting customer access networks (CANs) to the MAN via a 34 Mbit/s DQDB line. Since they are directly attached to the MAN ring they stay under the responsibility of the network provider. Two important functions specific for the subscriber/network boundary are performed by the EGW: address screening and generation of charging information. The other two are Customer Network Interface Units (CNIUs) where special routers provide a 2 Mbit/s customer access to the MAN. However, CNIUs will not be considered in detail because they will not be used for the BANK prototype.

Figure 3 shows two possible customer premises configurations for the attachment of a Token Ring to the public MAN. In the upper configuration the Token Ring is connected to a customer gateway (CGW). The CGW acts as bridge operating at the medium access control (MAC) level and provides users with the ability to link their Token Rings over the MAN transparently.

The other configuration in Figure 3 is possible if the public MAN provides the so-called Switched Multi-megabit Data Service (SMDS). This service was specified by Bellcore in 1991 and is currently being deployed in the U.S. In Europe a similar service is in the standardization process. It is named Connectionless Broadband Data Service (CBDS). Already available customer premises equipment supports both services.

SMDS offers LAN interconnection of user LANs via a router. This router has to support a special SMDS protocol (SMDS interface protocol level 3 or SIP-L3) which is based on the DQDB protocol IEEE 802.6. It is assumed that the router in Figure 3 provides this protocol with an SMDS interface board. The Digital Service

Unit (DSU) located next to the router supports the SMDS protocol stack and delivers the connectivity to the MAN. The interface between router and DSU is a DXI interface. The interface between DSU and the specially equipped EGW-S at the MAN side is called Subscriber Network Interface (SNI) and supports data rates of 1.5, 2, 34 and 45 Mbit/s, depending on the country and type of interface. The EGW-S provides the access to the MAN and is responsible for the billing information of the customer.

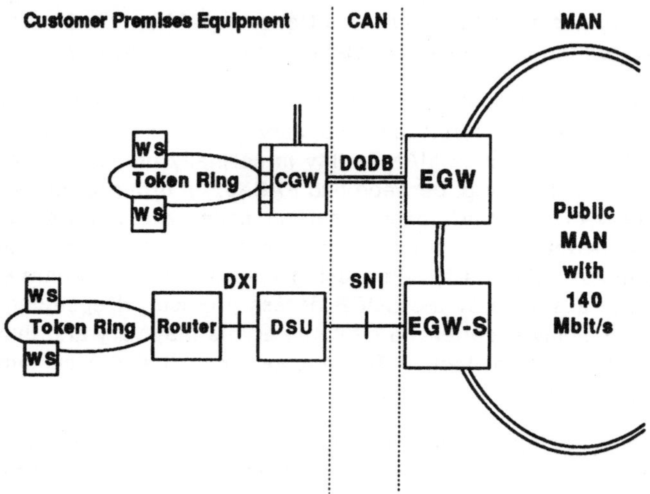

Figure 3. MAN Access via DSU and Router

Note that the MAN does not grant access to any resource managers for a resource negotiation process as depicted for Token Ring. Thus using a combined IP/ST-2 router only allows to propagate the ST-2 primitives from the sending LAN to the receiving LAN in order to provide the required resources at least in the attached LANs (which are the bottlenecks anyway). The ST-2 router between the source Token Ring segment and the MAN would have to skip the network resource reservation during the stream set-up phase. We rely on the MAN offering enough resources to fulfil all the needs for the prototype.

5.3 Token Ring/ATM Pilot Network Testbed

In Germany, the second prototype of the BANK project will have to be operated between two sites of Deutsche Bank. Since it is the aim of the project to exploit advanced technology as far as possible a decision was made to use the German ATM pilot network. This provides the project partners with a competitive advantage since they will be prepared early for the fully functional Broadband-ISDN (B-ISDN) that will become operational after the pilot phase.

The German pilot network is realized in five distinct stages. During the first phase starting at the beginning of 1994 only national permanent B-ISDN connections will be offered by the network. This facility will be extended step by step to include direct subscriber dialling on a national and international basis as well as interworking between B-ISDN on the one hand and Narrowband-ISDN and packet-oriented data networks on the other hand. This final phase is planned to start in September 1995.

Due to the time constraints of the project — the final prototype has to be operational in March 1994 — only phase 1 of the ATM pilot network is of relevance for the prototype. The configuration and components described in the subsequent paragraphs are therefore to be seen in the context of the restricted functionality of the first phase.

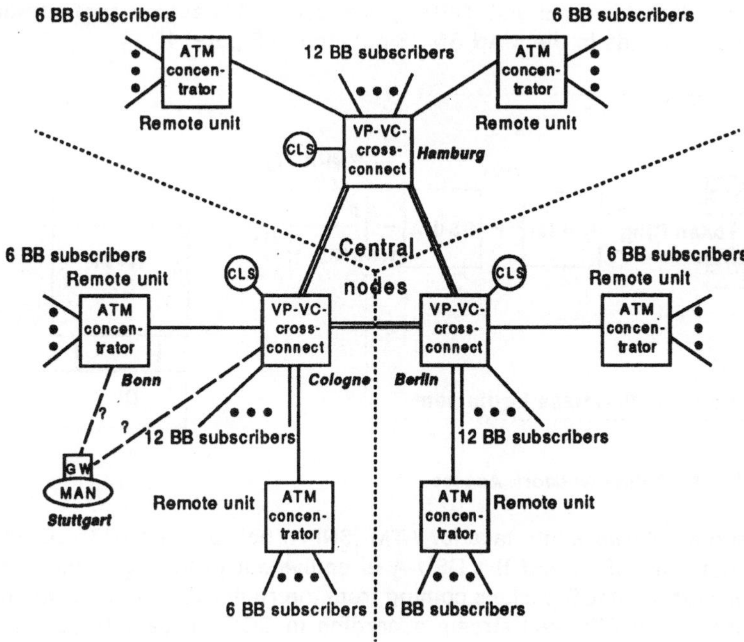

Figure 4. Confiuration of the German ATM Pilot Network

The topology of the pilot network (phase 1) is shown in Figure 4. Central elements are the three virtual channel/virtual path cross-connects (CCs) to which broadband subscriber lines as well as remote units are connected. The cross-connects will be installed in Hamburg, Cologne and Berlin. It is intended to have two remote units per cross-connect. These remote units act as ATM concentrators. Up to now the location of only one remote unit was mentioned: there will be one in Bonn which is connected to the cross-connect in Cologne. Other remote units will be deployed at places where a sufficient telecommunications demand has to be met. Connectionless servers (CLSs) will be connected to the three cross-connects. Broadband subscriber access is accomplished either by a direct connection between subscriber and ATM cross-connect or via a remote ATM concentrator. A DQDB/ATM gateway will permit interworking between the MAN in Stuttgart and the ATM pilot network.

One of the most conspicuous properties of the pilot network in phase 1 is the lack of any subscriber signalling procedures. As a consequence, all traffic has to use permanent or semi-permanent virtual connections. These connections are installed via operation and maintenance procedures by the network management. Corresponding sets of virtual path and virtual channel identifiers (VPIs and VCIs) are allocated once and are entered into switching tables resident in the cross-connects. The ATM cells are then switched exclusively by their VPI/VCI according to the entries made in the switching tables.

In Figure 5 the attachment of a TR to the public ATM network via a conventional router and a digital service unit (DSU-A) is shown. This access configuration essentially corresponds to the MAN SMDS solution of Figure 4.

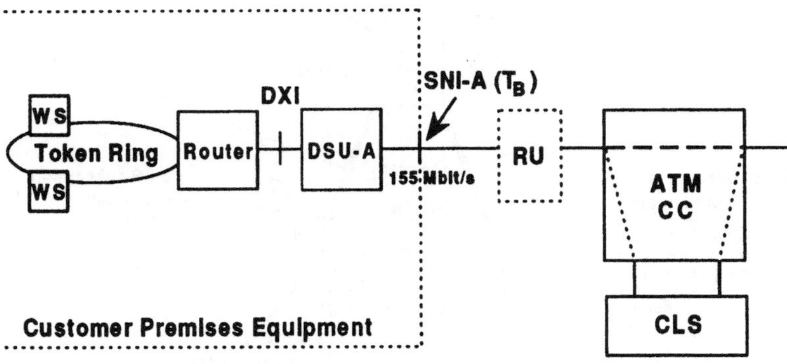

Figure 5. ATM Pilot Network Access

The Subscriber Network Interface for ATM (SNI-A) between the ATM-CC or possibly a Remote Unit (RU) and the DSU-A is equivalent to the T_B interface. The DSU-A transforms SMDS packets coming from the router to a signal compatible to G.703, carrying an ATM cell stream according to CCITT I.432 with segmentation and reassembly according to AAL type 3/4. It also converts E.164 addresses to preassigned VPI/VCI values to establish a point-to-point virtual connection. Since the DSU-A belongs to the network provider's domain, the creation of the corresponding table entries will be done by the network provider himself. Router and DSU-A are interconnected via the DXI interface which has the same functionality as in the MAN case. The protocol stack at the DXI side of the DSU-A contains the SMDS interface protocol level-3 (corresponding to ISO/OSI layer 2a). Higher level protocol data units are transmitted transparently through the DSU-A.

In the first step, it will not be possible to use the ST-2 primitives for the reservation ATM network resources. These resources have to be reserved by network management procedures instead when the ATM permanent virtual circuits are established. But the ST-2 primitives will be propagated from the sending LAN to the receiving LAN in order to provide the required resources at least in the attached LANs (which are the bottlenecks anyway).

6. Conclusions

We presented a banking kiosk system that goes beyond the scope of todays self-service systems by introducing an enriched interactive mode, the assistance of a remote expert via integrated desktop videoconference and the ability of closing contracts.

We have based our assumptions so far on extended self-service support of complex although still retail banking standard products. However the basic components of the system presented may also be used for custodian services and for support of internal business processes. In fact these components form the basic set for new types of kiosk systems which are typically interconnected to an information support center via high-speed links to keep the product parameters up to date and allow for assistance of remote human expertise.

Legal questions have to be examined and user acceptance has to be tested before the kiosk system might be applied to a greater extend in branch offices.

From a technical point of view, we presented solutions for multimedia integration and shared application design, and discussed the envisaged networking testbeds. With respect to networking, the acceptance of the described approach will depend to a great extent on competitive tariffs for high-speed lines. Therefore in the BANK project, a detailed business evaluation will be performed after availability of the mentioned prototypes.

References

[ArWi92] **Armbrüster, H., Wimmer, K.:** *Broadband Multimedia Applications Using ATM Networks: High-Performance Computing, High-Capacity Storage, and High-Speed Communication.* IEEE Journal on Selected Areas in Communications, vol. 10, no. 9 (Dec. 1992), pp. 1382-1396.

[Geih93] **Geihs, K.:** *Infrastrukturen für heterogene verteilte Systeme.* Informatik Spektrum, vol. 16, no. 1 (2/93), pp. 11-23.

[HeHS91] **Hehmann, D., Herrtwich, R.G., Steinmetz, R.:** *Creating HeiTS: Objectives of the Heidelberg High-Speed Transport System.* IBM ENC Technical Report TR43.9102, Heidelberg, 1991.

[Herr92] **Herrtwich, R.G.:** *The HeiProjects: Support for Distributed Multimedia Applications.* IBM ENC Technical Report TR43.9206, Heidelberg, 1992.

[Luth91] **Luther, A.C.:** *Digital Video in the PC Environment.* McGraw-Hill, 1991.

[NaVo92] **Nagarajan, R., Vogt, C.:** *Guaranteed-Performance Transport of Multimedia Traffic over the Token Ring.* IBM ENC Technical Report No. 43.9201, Heidelberg, 1992.

[Russ93] **Russell, J.:** *Multimedia Networking Performance Requirements.* in: Proceedings of TriComm'93, pp.187-197, Plenum Press, New York.

[Topo90] **Topolcic, C. (Ed.):** *Experimental Internet Stream Protocol, Version 2 (ST-2).* Internet Networking Working Group, RFC 1190, October 1990.

[VoHN92] **Vogt, C., Herrtwich, R.G., Nagarajan, R.:** *HeiRAT: The Heidelberg Resource Adminstration Technique — Design Philosophy and Goals.* IBM ENC Technical Report No. 43.9213, Heidelberg, 1992.

Architecture of Distributed Multimedia Systems

Dr. Lothar Mackert

IBM European Networking Center
Vangerowstraße 18
69115 Heidelberg

Extended abstract

In the coming years multimedia will significantly change the way, in which we use computers. Some multimedia applications already exist today (e.g. multimedia kiosks, computer based training), however, most of them are restricted to local use. A full exploitation of the excellent capabilities multimedia offers for communication and cooperation will depend on the availability of efficient and integrated methods for exchanging multimedia information between computers.

The evolution to distributed multimedia systems will require substantial extensions and modifications to the architectures of communication systems, operating systems and applications. The strong constraints multimedia puts on bandwidth and transmission delays require new communication mechanisms and protocols. Operating systems will have to process and handle realtime streams. Finally, distributed applications require generic mechanisms for integrating new information elements and for supporting new paradigms, like cooperative work. The presentation will discuss recent developments and trends and sketch ongoing research efforts.

AN OBJECT-ORIENTED CHARACTER RECOGNITION ENGINE

B. Klauer K. Waldschmidt
J.W.Goethe - Universität Frankfurt, Professur für Technische Informatik
Robert Mayer Straße 11 - 15D - 6000 Frankfurt am Main
R. Heinrich
INFOS GmbH
Ludwigstr. 78, D - 6050 Offenbach

Abstract

This paper introduces the object-oriented character recognition engine AQUIRE which was originally designed as a general pattern-classifier under the academic aspects of object-orientation and parallelism together with low space and time complexity. When industry expressed interest in using AQUIRE to provide pen-based computers with a powerful character-recognition engine, AQUIRE was revised to meet the commercial requirements. Together with a brief discussion of some special pen-related problems, this paper contains the theoretical background for the recognition mechanism and a description of the methods used to perform a high quality and high speed recognition-process with a minimum of executable code. The proposed method has been implemented on an INFOS NotePad 386-SX pen-computer and on the associative processor AM^3 developed within the PROMETHEUS project at the Department for Technical Computer Sciences at J.W.Goethe-University. The acceleration of the recognition mechanism by using the associative type of parallelism will be shown.

1. Pen computing

Pen-computer environments offer a lot of opportunities to their users but also a lot of restrictions to hardware and software designers. The first and most obvious opportunity of pen computers on one hand and restriction on the other hand is their physical size and the fact that they are intentionally used with a pen instead of a keyboard as user-input device. From a user's point of view nothing is more familiar than processing data using pen and paper. Pen-based knowledge- and data-aquisition can help to lower the barrier between non-experienced users and computers and terminals. It can help experienced users to enter commands and data in a more natuaral way.
From a programmer's point of view the replacement of the keyboard by a pen requires pen-based user interfaces, providing a complete control mechanism for a pen as central input device. The User-Interface has to provide comfortable methods to handle the control and data streams to an application. The control stream can easily be handled using window and menu techniques which are the state-of-the-art in modern applications even in non pen-related environments. The data entry is more complex. Menu techniques, like so-called virtual keyboards are usable for data entry but less comfortable than data input via handprinted characters or digits.
This feature requires a highly sophisticated character recognition engine to be embedded into pen-based applications. The recognizer can be used to transform drawings like characters or gestures into their semantics. The semantics can then be used to trigger functions in case of gestures or as character or digit in case of character like entries.

The physical and logical restrictions and requirements as mentioned above raised academic and commercial interest in the developement of a powerful recognition engine for handwriten symbols with the following outlines:

- Small executable code
- Small database size
- High accuracy
- Directness (speed)

"Directness" means that users should have the feeling of controlling the system directly with the tip of the pen. Actions of the application should follow immediatly after a handprinted symbol has been completed. [RHY86] contains proposals how the completeness of handprinted symbols can be decided.

1.1 Design-decisions

Due to the above mentioned restrictions and requirements the following design decisions concerning the archtitecture of the recognizer and it's implementation have been made:

1.1.1 Online-Recognition vs. Offline-recognition

In comparison to off-line recognition, on-line recognition performs recognition while the pattern is beeing drawn on any kind of digitizing device. Directness, which means that user actions like gestures are immediately translated into machine action is an ergonimic requirement for pen-related applications. The directness usually implies online-recognition systems in pen-based applications.

1.1.2 Static recognition vs. dynamic recognition

Static character recognition evaluates patterns without looking on how the pattern has been created. Dynamic recognition is focussed on strokes, edges in strokes, drawing speeds and accelerations in the drawing history. AQUIRE is a heterogeneous recognition engine combining a static (PATTMA) and a dynamic (MAGIC) module.

1.1.3 Source Language

Due to the portability of the source-code the recognizer has been programmed in C++. This decision seems to be contradictory to the size and speed requirement but is actually not. Analyzing the code produced by the Borland C++ compiler used for the MS-DOS version, it can be observed that it generates efficient machine-code. The runtime-libraries and the startup-code are the most space-expensive modules due to their generality. Special startup and runtime routines have been designed to gain efficiency in size and speed.

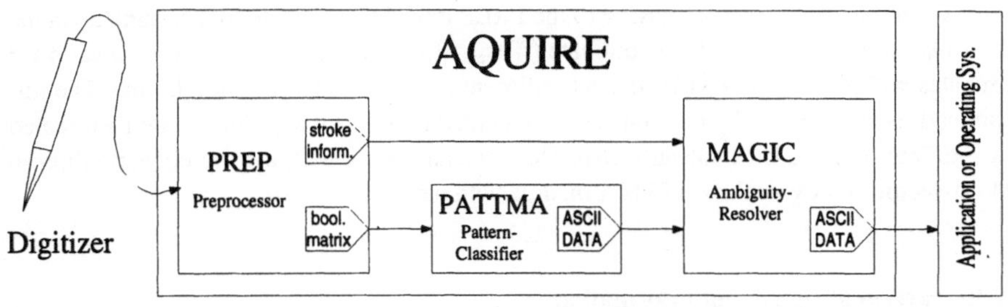

figure 1

1.1.4 Software architecture

The recognizer consists of three modules a preprocessor (PREP), a pattern-matcher (PATTMA) and an ambiguity resolver (MAGIC: **MA**nual **G**esture **I**nconsistancy **C**learance) as shown in figure 1. The PREP module contains an Application Programming Interface (API) and an extractor providing the PATTMA and MAGIC modules with significant information on the symbol to be recognized. PREP works "on-line" during the drawing phase. It passes a boolean pattern to the PATTMA pattern matcher and stroke-information to the MAGIC module. PATTMA is a very fast pre-classifier but is in case of optically similar characters such as "B" and "8" or "b" and "6" insufficient in recognition accuracy. MAGIC detects - and resolves ambiguities. The resolving mechanism is activated only in case that an ambiguous pattern has been detected.

2. Methods

2.1 The PREP module

PREP provides the Application Programming Interface (API) and an extractor to retrieve significant information from the input data. The API for the Intel 80x86 processors consists of an interrupt-service routine supporting one of the 80x86 processors software interrupts. The API for the AM^3 processor consists of a set of C++ functions to control the recognizer. It provides the following functions:

1. Setup-functions for the recognition engine
2. Aquisition and storage of handdrawn symbols as defined below
3. Functions to control the recognition of patterns

2.1.1 Recording and Scaling

The following expressions be informally defined:

Def 1.0 Handdrawn Symbols
Let a handdrawn symbol be defiened as a sequence of strokes

Def 1.1 Strokes
Let a stroke be defined as a sequence of coordinates

The strokes as defined above are passed to the PREP module coordinate by coordinate via the API. Strokes are separated by the coordinate ($ffff_{hex}$,$ffff_{hex}$) which is defined to be invalid for coordinates within a stroke. PREP connects adjacent coordinates whit a straight line. The minimum and maximum x and y coordinates are recorded online. All coordinates are then scaled to fit into into a 32*32-bit boolean matrix.The boolean matrix will later be converted into a 1024-bit vector to provide the PATTMA module with data.

2.1.2 Extraction of significant information

A mask and a search argument are computed by the extractor and sent to the PATTMA module. The Pattern matcher computes the semantics by retrieving the most similar pattern in it's database. The ambiguity resolver is also provided with data from the extractor. If envoked, MAGIC consumes the total of strokes, start- and end-coordinates, as well as the start- and end-directions of the strokes, to examine ambiguous characters.

2.2 Methods used in PATTMA

The description of the basic classification mechanism of PATTMA requires formal definitions of some important expressions:

Def 2.0 Patterns
Let a pattern be a boolean vector

$P = [p_i];\ 1 \le i \le L;$
L : length of the pattern

An element p_i of a vector P is called a pixel. The value of the pixel corresponds to it's color (e.g. black and white in case of boolean patterns). All pattern-data used in PATTMA is derived from the handprinted input symbols by the extractor of the PREP module. PREP converts handdrawn symbols (Def 1.0) into images (Def 2.1) with unknown semantics.

Def 2.1 Images
Let an image be a tupel I consisting of a pattern P and the symbol s indicating the semantics of the pattern P.

$I = (P,s);\ s \in S$

s is a member of the set S of all symbols. S must contain a symbol ϕ indicating that the semantics of a symbol is unknown. All well known images have the semantics $s \neq \phi$. The database used by PATTMA contains images with semantics $s \neq \phi$. Unknown images as derived from the PREP module from handprinted symbols have a semantic $s = \phi$.

Def 2.2 Hamming Distance
The Hamming Distance HD(A,B) of two patterns is the total of all pixels a_i,b_i with $a_i \neq b_i$.

$HD(A,B) = \Sigma (a_i, \oplus b_i)$
$\oplus$: boolean XOR

Def 2.3 The Masked Hamming Distance
The Masked Hamming Distance MHD of two patterns A,B and a mask M is defined as follows:

$MHD(A,B,M) = \Sigma ((a_i \oplus b_i) \bullet \neg m_i)$
$\bullet$: boolean AND
$\neg$: boolean NOT

MHD behaves as HD if $M = \underline{0}$. In this case MHD computes the total of all different elements a_i,b_i with $a_i \neq b_i$ which are not hidden by m_i. HD as well as MHD can be used as similarity indicators in recognition systems. The following method can be used to find the semantics of an unknown image $U = (X,\phi)$:

Let $W = \{(P_1,s_1),(P_2,s_2), \ldots\}$ be a set of well known images.

1. Compute the mask argument M
(A method to compute the mask will be shown in the following paragraph)
2. Compute $MHD(X,P_i,M)$ for all i
3. Replace ϕ with s_i if $MHD(X,P_i,M)$ is minimal for all i

2.2.1 The mask-argument of MHD

As one might expect the computation of the mask-argument is the key to obtain good recognition results using the MHD function.To classify handprinted characters using the MHD classifier the following informal method can be used to compute the mask:

Let X be the pattern of an unknown image
Let M be the mask argument to be computed

A function BOLD(PATTERN A, INTEGER N) returning a boolean pattern, be defined as follows:

```
1.   if N>0 set R:=A else R:=0
2.   repeat N times
     for all a_ij with a_ij = 0 do
       if an adjacent element of a_ij = 1 then
                    set r_ij:=1
3.   return(R)
```

The Mask M can then be computed as follows:

1. set Bold_X :=BOLD(X,ntimes)
2. set Bold2_X := BOLD(BX,mtimes)
3. set M := Bold2_X-Bold_X

The result of the computation is shown in figure 2. The mask has been derived from pattern A with the parameters ntimes=1 and mtimes=0.

2.2.2 Hamming-Distance vs. Masked Hamming- Distance

The Hamming-Distance classifier is very popular to compute a similarity indicator for boolean patterns [KOH87]. The Masked Hamming-Distance distinguishes from the pure Hamming-Distance in the simple fact that specific areas of the patterns to be compared can be hidden. The MHD classifier computes the Hamming-Distance of all bits which are not masked. This special feature can be used for fault-tolerant classification.
Example:

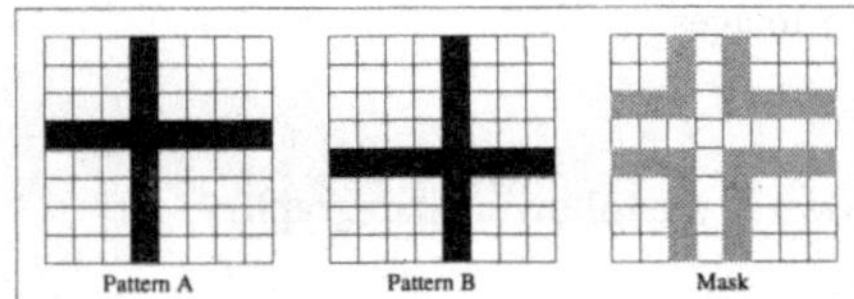

figure 2

figure 3

Figure 2 shows two "+ " symbols which are similar but not equal. A recognition system holding one of both symbols in it's database should classify them to be similar.The Hamming-Distance of pattern A and B is 28, indicating that both patterns are different even if they are not from a human point of view. The masked Hamming-Distance of A and B and a mask argument as shown in figure 2 is 13, indicating that both patterns are similar. This result is more adequate to the human impression. The next example (figure 3) shows that the MHD classifier works also in case that both symbols are different. In this case MHD(A,C,Mask) = 24, indicating that both symbols are much more different. Figure 4 shows a statistical evaluation of 135 handdrawn symbols to find optimal values for the parameters "ntimes" and "mtimes" for 1024-bit patterns (32*32-bit). It shows that the pure Hamming-Distance

parameter ntimes →

parameter mtimes ↓	0														
0	12	12	13	16	22	25	25	31	29	26	28	24	20	19	19
	18	18	58	100	110	121	118	116	110	107	106	104	102	99	95
	13	13	18	68	117	121	124	126	126	123	116	112	109	108	105
	14	14	14	27	93	118	124	126	122	120	117	113	109	105	104
	10	10	10	16	54	94	120	127	124	120	117	112	109	103	98
	10	10	10	12	35	52	87	117	113	107	104	96	89	83	77
	10	10	10	12	21	32	54	87	94	93	87	82	73	69	63
	5	5	5	12	16	25	32	58	66	81	80	71	63	59	55
	5	5	5	10	15	17	20	39	48	62	72	66	53	53	46
	5	5	5	10	16	15	17	24	33	45	54	64	52	47	44
	5	5	5	10	9	13	18	21	32	43	46	52	54	48	42
	5	5	5	8	11	11	14	16	19	22	28	36	45	46	42
	5	5	5	8	13	15	14	16	16	17	20	24	28	36	35
	5	5	5	8	13	15	15	15	16	17	19	21	22	25	28
	5	5	5	8	11	11	10	11	11	11	13	14	15	19	23

figure 4

(ntimes=mtimes=0) is not optimal for the pattern-classification of human handprinted characters. It shows an optimum at ntimes=7 and mtimes=4. The parameters depend on the database-size, the type of symbols, the cardinality of the alphabet and on the dimension of the boolean matrix used to store the patterns.

2.3 Methods used for MAGIC

The ambiguity resolver MAGIC consists of a set of routines to detect and resolve ambiguities. Handprinted characters from 102 Persons from different countries on different continents have therefore been statistically evaluated to find ambiguities in the human style of handwriting. Ambiguities will be denoted as follows:

$(A_1, A_2, \ldots A_n)$

The intended meaning of the above expression is that symbol $A_1, A_2, \ldots A_n$ cannot properly be distinguished by their optical image as represented by the 32*32 bit matrix.

Example:

(Z,2)

(O,0)

figure 5

All ambiguities detected within the evaluation have been classified to be *hard* or *soft*. Soft ambiguities can in most cases be resolved by counting and tracing the strokes as in the (B,8) ambiguity. Hard ambiguities cannot be resolved by stroke-evaluation as in the (Z,2) ambiguity. Figure 5 shows two symbols of a 2 and a Z and two examples of an O and a 0 recorded from different writers. Even a human can not classify them correctly without any context. To solve the above mentionened problems rules have been stated for the writers to gain proper recognition. E.g. a Z must always be drawn with a horizontal stroke at it's center. MAGIC contains a subroutine for each ambiguity which has been statistically detected. The routines to resolve the hard ambiguities require that specific rules be obeyed by writers.

3. Implementations

The first version of AQUIRE has been programmed in C++. The three major modules PREP, PATTMA and MAGIC have been programmed as separate C++ classes. The PATTMA module has been derived from a module called CAM (s. figure 6). CAM performes a retrieval of the best matching database item using the MHD classifier.

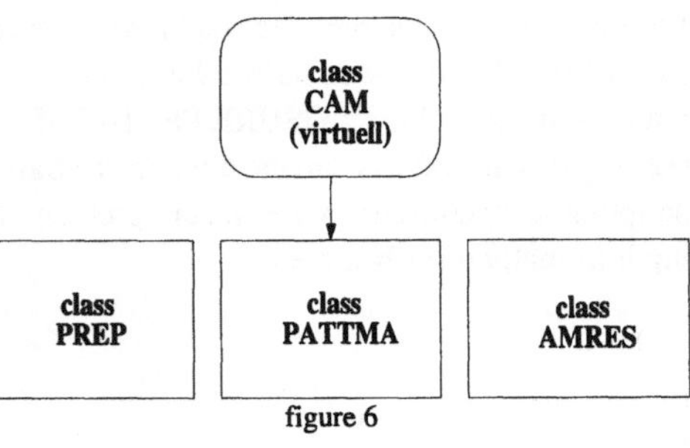

figure 6

3.1 The MS-DOS implementation

The MS-DOS implementation uses a CAM module which computes the MHD classifier for all database items sequentially. It provides functions to handle the database containing the set of known images.The runtime-behaviour has then been analyzed and some critical routines have been reprogrammed in assembly language. Portability has been lost in the optimized assembly language version but speed was significantly increased. The size of the executable program was reduced. Application programmers have access to the recognizer via the software interrupts of the Intel 80x86 processors. This provides an interface which is completely independent of languages and developement environments. The Application Programming Interface (API) provides the following functions:

INITIALIZE
This function presets all global variables with proper initial values

INSERT COORDINATE
This function is used to pass a coordinate of a stroke to the PREP module for preprocessing.

INSERT STROKE SEPARATOR
This function is used to declare a stroke consisting of previously entered coordinates to be complete. It is envoked by inserting the coordinate ($ffff_{hex}$,$ffff_{hex}$) with the INSERT COORDINATE function. ($ffff_{hex}$,$ffff_{hex}$) is defined to be invalid within a stroke.

ENABLE/DISABLE MAGIC
The MAGIC module has been designed to resolve ambiguities in the recognition process of handprinted latin characters. It can not optimize the recognition process for arbitrary symbolsets. To recognize arbitrary non-latin character sets MAGIC should be turned off.

SELECT DRAWING AREA
A drawing area is an invisible ribbon specified by it's upper and lower bounds. It is used by MAGIC to distinguish ambiguous characters like (Ww). AQUIRE also supports a so called free-drawing mode. In this mode the screen is divided into two halfes. Characters drawn into the lower half of the screen are always converted into lower-case. Characters drawn into the upper half are recognized as they are in upper- or lower-case with upper-case preference in case of (Ww)-like ambiguities.

RECOGNIZE
This function starts the recognition process for previously inserted and preprocessed data. It returns an integer value representing the semantics of the unknown symbol as result. It has been derived from the most-similar database-item. An important problem to be mentioned in this context is the so called CLOSURE PROBLEM. It discribes the decision of the question *Is the symbol complete now?* occurring after an arbitrary stroke has been drawn. [RHY86] contains a discription and solutions to the closure problem. Good results have been made with the following informally discribed methods.

1. Time method
A symbol be complete if a pen-up condition for more than 500ms has been detected.

2. Space method
A visible grid be defined on the screen. Characters are assumed to be drawn into the grid spaces. A symbol be complete if the user starts a stroke in a new grid space.

3.2 The AM^3 implementation

The AM^3 processor [SCH89,SCH92, DAR90] is an associative 32-bit processor with a modified Harvard-architecture. It has one bus to handle the data and instruction streams and a separate addressless associative bus-system to provide a link to a varity of associative memory components. One basic function which is supported by all memory components within the AM^3 is the masked search function. The masked search function has been described by Kohonen [KOH87] as one of the basic associative functions.The above mentioned character recognition method was mapped onto the AM^3 processor by replacing the CAM module implemented as virtual base class in C++ by a compatible module which uses directly the associative functions of the AM^3 processor.

3.3 Performance parameters

The most important performance parameters of a character recognizer for pen-computers are code-size, database-size, speed and accuracy. The recognition speed and the size of the executable code are machine and operating-system dependent while database-size and accuracy are pure method-related parameters.

3.3.1 MS-DOS implementation

executable code size: ~18KB
recognition speed: ~ 80 µs per character in the database on a 486 machine running at 33MHz

3.3.2 AM^3 implementation

One goal of the AM^3 implementation was to show that the method as proposed is suitable to be computed and to be accelerated by associative hardware. The academic intention was to show a sub-linear run-time behaviour with a growing database-size. Due to the memories used within the AM^3, a logarithmic run-time behaviour could be measured. Due to the low system clock of the machine (4 MHz) the AM^3 is much slower for reasonable database-sizes than the MS-DOS implementation.

3.3.3 Machine independent parameters

Database-size and accuracy are tighly related parameters. They depend on each other and on the cardinality of the alphabet to be recognized. The parameters as presented below require some comments on how they have been measured since recognition accuracy of recognizers can in general be very good with cooperative users and very bad with users intentionally trying to fool the system. The following reasonable experiment has been performed to measure the recognition quality: The handprinted character sets (upper-case, lower-case and numeric) of 102 people have been evaluated. A character set of 600 characters has then been extracted from the complete set as database. The other characters have been used as test-patterns. The recognition rate has been measured under 2 conditions. In the first test only rule consistant characters (see Methods used for MAGIC) have been used. In the second test all characters have been exposed to the recognizer. The following recognition rates under the above mentioned conditions could be measured:

97% Recognition-rate with rule consistant characters
92% With an arbitrary character set

4. Applications

4.1 Commercial application

In tight cooperation with INFOS GmbH AQUIRE has been optimized for the INFOS NotePad 386-SX computer. It is commercially available with the INFOS Notepad computer.

4.1.1 The INFOS NotePad 386-SX computer

The INFOS NotePad computer is standard 386-SX machine running at 20MHz under the operating system MS-DOS. It has a backlit LCD screen with a pen-digitizer and two PCMCIA slots. It is provided with 4MB RAM and serial and parallel interfaces. Via it's keyboard interface it can be connected with an optional physical keyboard. The complete machine fits into a 28mm(H)*335mm(L)*270mm(W) package.

4.1.2 The pure recognition engine

The recognition-engine can be loaded as TSR (terminate and stay resident) module into the standard DOS memory area or into the high-memory area. Applications can then access the recognizer via it's API. The recognition engine comes together with a training-program to improve the recognition-rate for individual styles of handwriting or to create customized symbol sets.

```
C:\PENSTAR>DIR

 Datenträger in Laufwerk C ist MS-DOS_5
 Datenträgernummer: 1963-046C
 Verzeichnis von C:\PENSTAR

.             <DIR>        11.02.93   10:57
..            <DIR>        11.02.93   10:57
PENSTAR  EXE       18016 26.01.93   16:56
PENSTAR  PAT      111123 17.11.92   16:29
DIR      PCX       23610 11.02.93   12:20
PRINT    POS       42383 11.02.93   12:20
        6 Datei(en)      195132 Byte
                       83795968 Byte frei

C:\PENSTAR>
```

figure 7

4.1.3 The PEN-COMMANDER for DOS

The PEN-COMMANDER is a special application for the INFOS 386-SX notepad computer. It has been designed to replace the keyboard in standard keyboard-oriented DOS applications by a pen. All handprinted data is converted into keyboard-like data. Therefore the PEN-COMMANDER emulates the standard keyboard by recognizing and converting handprinted pen input data into keyboard data. The operating-system can not distinguish input data provided by the real hardware keyboard or by the emulation. Standard DOS applications can be used with the notepad computer even if they are not provided with a pen-based user interface. Figure 7 shows a handprinted DOS DIR command. It has been converted into ASCII and sent to the operating-system. The operating system shows the command at the DOS-prompt. The "┘" symbol is a guesture used as RETURN key. After drawing the "┘" the command is executed and the directory shows up. The PEN-COMMANDER is restricted to applications getting keyboard data via DOS interrupt 21hex. Applications using their own keyboard driver are not suitable since they are observing the physical keyboard hardware directly. The PEN-COMMANDER cannot be used with mouse oriented applications since it behaves logically like a keyboard and not like a digitizing device. Therefore the PEN-COMMANDER shuts down and passes control to the mouse-driver if an application request mouse specific functions.

4.1.4 Scientific application

A scientific application is the implementation on the AM^3 Processor. The recognizer is used to evaluate guestures of a car-driver, drawn on a touch-panel with a fingertip to control certain functions of a car and a car-co-pilot. An important scientific result was that the CAM module of AQUIRE can be accelerated using the associative type of parallelism. The linear run-time behaviour on a sequential processor of the module became approximately logarithmic on the associative processor. The logarithmic runtime-behaviour is due to the logarithmic access-time of the emulated memories of the AM^3 processor.

5. Future work

We expect that the base-method of PATTMA is suitable to support a speech-recognizer. The opportunity of associative parallelism supports this investigation since online-speech-recognition requires fast retrieval mechanisms for large databases. A special associative memory derived from the experiances with associatively supported pattern recognition is currently under developement to compute the MHD classificator in constant time.

References

[DAR90] M. Darianian, Ch. Schönfeld, K. Waldschmidt, Ein Assoziativspeicherfeld hoher Kapazizät im Bit-Slice-Prozessor AM^3, Tagungsband der 11. GI/ITG-Fachtagung: Architektur von Rechensystemen, VDE 1990

[KOH87] T. Kohonen, Content Addressable Memories, Springer, 1987

[RHY86] J.R.Rhyne, Dialogue Management for gestural interfaces. Computer Graphics, 21 (2), Workshop on User Interface Software, April 1987

[SCH89] M. Schulz et al. An Associative Microprogrammable Bit-Slice-Processor for Sensor Control, Proceedings of the 3rd CompEuro, Hamburg 1989

[SCH92] M.Schulz, An Object-Oriented interface in C++ to an associative processor, Proceedings of the 6th CompEuro, The Hague 1992

[WAL92] K. Waldschmidt, M. Schulz, Der assoziative Universalprozessor AM3: Architektur, Befehlssatz und objektorientiertes Programmierinterface, Tagungsband der 12. GI/ITG-Fachtagung: Architektur von Rechensystemen, Kiel 1992

Special thanks to Fred Schuchard who collected some MBs of handprinted data for testing and verification, to Reiner Heinrich who provided us with the INFOS 386SX Notepad Computer and to Ronald Moore.

Spool & Print: Service and Management in Distributed Environment

Jean-Marc BODART

Siemens Nixdorf Software S.A.

Rue de Néverlée,11, B-5020 Namur, Belgium

E-mail: jmb@swn.sni.be

Abstract

This paper presents an attempt to approach in a new way the problem of spool & print service and management in distributed environments. Thanks to an object-oriented model, high consistency is brought between the user and administrator functions. New concepts are introduced, such as the Printer Capability List object, describing in a flexible and affordable fashion the characteristics of a printer type. Filters customising the functionality can be inserted at different places in the data flow. Features such as the location transparency and the single point administration capability make the administrator's life easier. The resulted SPOOL V4/Xprint system is running successfully on multiple UNIX platforms, supporting all usual types of printers, emulations and attachments. Further advanced extensions are under the way.

1. INTRODUCTION

Printing is an essential activity associated with computing and information processing. With the generalisation of networked environments, the necessity emerges for a transparent and controlled access to distributed and shared print resources.

Printing has the distinctive characteristic that it is a user oriented task (print job submission), which requires substantial administration activity. The Spool & Print System described in this document, addresses both aspects of print service (*the submission of jobs and the associated activities that ultimately result in a form of output*), and print management (*the activities that ensure the tuning and availability of the print system: configuration, monitoring, start/stop, security, etc.*) in a perspective of consistent and integrated sharing of involved software and hardware resources.

Nowadays, most print spoolers delivered with open systems offer some kind of distributed functionality. They are mainly derived from the SVR4 *lp* utility, or the BSD *lpd* daemon. These spoolers are merely evolutions of local printing systems, and have not been designed initially with the distributed functionality as primary requirement. They lack a global and consistent approach of the print system management in distributed environments; configuration still requires the manual update of cryptic files on several hosts: the scope of the handled objects (such as the logical forms) is essentially local; there is no possibility to manage all the jobs of the distributed system transparently, from a single point. With such characteristics, these products should be seen as interoperating local spoolers rather than as one global distributed print system.

Requirements for a networked print system are the following [1]:

- Ease of use and administration
- Distributed functionality
- Fast support of new printer types
- Customisation
- Robustness
- Security
- Interoperability and openness
- Portability.

This paper presents Siemens Nixdorf's SPOOL V4/Xprint. It discusses the various concepts, capabilities and properties of this distributed print spooler, with respect to the listed requirements.

2. CONCEPTS AND FACILITIES

2.1. Client-Server Architecture

The architecture of SPOOL V4/Xprint is based on the Client-Server paradigm. Its architectural entities are depicted on Figure 1.

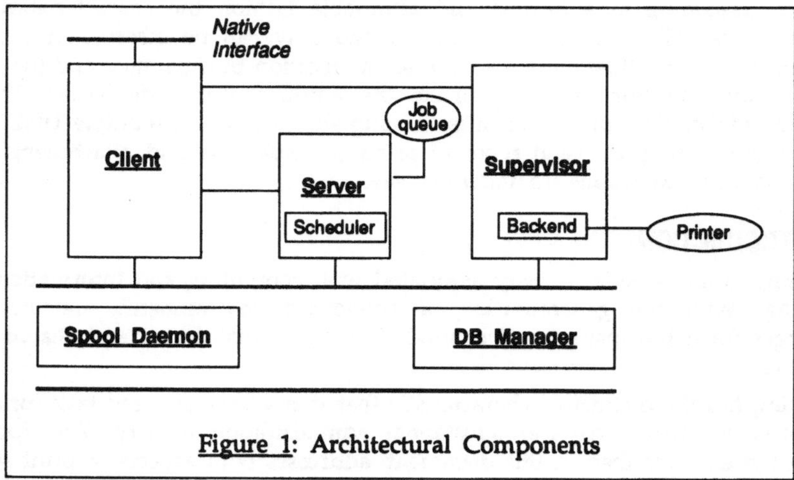

Figure 1: Architectural Components

Client

All requests to the print system are channelled via the Client. The Client semantically validates the requests issued to the print system, including access privileges. It provides the parameter default values, formats the requests, and transmits the requests to the other entities involved in the execution process. The Client also unformats the responses from the other entities and passes them to the caller. The Client selects and applies slow filters on the user data if needed or requested. The execution of the slow filters on the Client rather than on the Server alleviates the latter, to the benefit of the global throughput. The Client is also responsible for the print server selection.

Server

The server administers print job queues. It schedules the jobs on devices and transmits the jobs to the supervisors for printing. The Server also manages the job states. It accepts and performs requests for job modification, including redirection and deletion.

Supervisor

The Supervisor handles the activation and deactivation of the attached printers and provides the Backend, a subcomponent, with the user data to be printed. The Supervisor requests print jobs from the Server to keep devices as busy as possible. The Supervisor also executes the requests for deletion or interruption of active jobs. The Backend manages the connection with the physical device. It initialises the printer and sends the data according to the job options and the device type. The Backend controls the data flow to the device and performs the printer error recovery.

The Server and Supervisor entities enforce the concepts of queue manager and device manager. The splitting in two separate entities improves the configuration modularity and enable a more refined tuning of the load distribution among the hosts (at the cost of a higher network traffic).

Database Manager

The Database Manager stores static (i.e. configuration-related) and dynamic (i.e. state-related) information about the objects, and enables the addition, deletion, modification and copying of object instances. The Database Manager makes the object information available to the other entities independently of their location, and ensures its permanent availability in case of failure or shutdown of hosts in the configuration. It frees the administrator from the tedious task of replicating manually configuration information on several hosts.

Spool Daemon

The Spool Daemon runs on each host of the environment and provides remote services to the other entities (file transfer, login account check, notification, etc.). The Spool Daemon is the ancestor of the other entities. This enables him to take the appropriate recovery measures in the eventuality an entity would unexpectedly stop.

The Database Manager and the Spool Daemon are present on each involved host. The other entities (Client, Server, Supervisor) can be distributed on different machines for customisation purpose. The entities interact with each other, regardless of their location in order to provide the spool & print service and management. Those interactions reside on a proprietary implementation of remote procedure calls, named *Entity Calls*. The use of a proprietary implementation ensures the maximal independence and portability of the product.

2.2. Network Configuration and Communication Path

The print system described in this document is well suited to a Local Area Network configuration. It extends over a set of cooperating machines whose local administrators accept to share the print management functions on their host with a central, coordinating authority.

The communications between the print system entities use the TCP or the ISO protocols, and require the bandwidth of a Local Area Network to offer acceptable response times.

2.3. Printer Virtualisation and Backends

A spooler system must manage information on the capabilities of each printer type its supports: indeed, printer selection at job submission depends on the capabilities offered by the printers. Moreover, the process responsible for printing a job must be able to activate specific functions of a printer and be able to respond to special circumstances such as paper end, open cover or an empty toner cartridge.

The data which describe these functions may be included in the code of the spooler system, or may be located externally, where the spooler can retrieve the needed information. The latter, decoupling the executable code from the data, makes the support of new printers faster and easier as only data is affected and not the code.

SPOOL V4/Xprint is based on the second solution. The data related to a given printer type is registered in the Database as attributes of an object called PCL (Printer Capability List) and describes most of the capabilities offered by a particular printer type.

The support of a new printer by SPOOL V4/Xprint only involves the provision of information about the capabilities of the printer and how they may be selected. This is simply achieved by defining a new PCL object.

Both Client and Backend use PCL objects; the Client uses attributes of the PCL to check whether requested printing functionalities are available on a given printer type; the Backend needs the PCL for selecting requested capabilities on the printer, obtaining the status of the printer and understanding printer feedback.

The main features provided by the PCL mechanism are, among others:

Support of standard control characters
All spoolers support simple files as input. They are made of printable data and some standard control characters such as line feed, form feed and son one. Capabilities are registered for those control characters. They identify the sequence of characters to be sent to the printer to obtain the desired result.

Translation of job options
As the user is allowed to select job options when submitting a job, the spooler system must be able to select the corresponding feature on the printer. One or several capabilities are associated to each job option (such as character pitch, page orientation, ...).

Data analysis
Data to be printed is not limited to simple files but may include specific codes which may influence the motion of the printer head on the page. As SPOOL V4/Xprint checks for page overflow (length and/or width), it should be able to trap and decode those specific sequences of characters.

Dialogue with the printer
Spooler systems should be able to trap printer faults. This means they should be able to obtain the status of the printer and analyse it so that a specific action can be taken. This goal is achieved thanks to appropriate capabilities of the PCL object which specify the printer protocol.

2.4. Filters Technology

Allowing users to integrate their own filters in the print system improves its flexibility, and enables an actual tailoring of the system. In SPOOL V4/Xprint, filters can be inserted in the data flow at two different places: slow filters at job submission (on the user's data), and fast filters before the physical printing (on the data formatted by the Backend). Figure 2 illustrates the global data flow in the spooler, when filters are involved.

Slow Filters
The *slow* filters are applied asynchronously by the Client, at job submission, be-

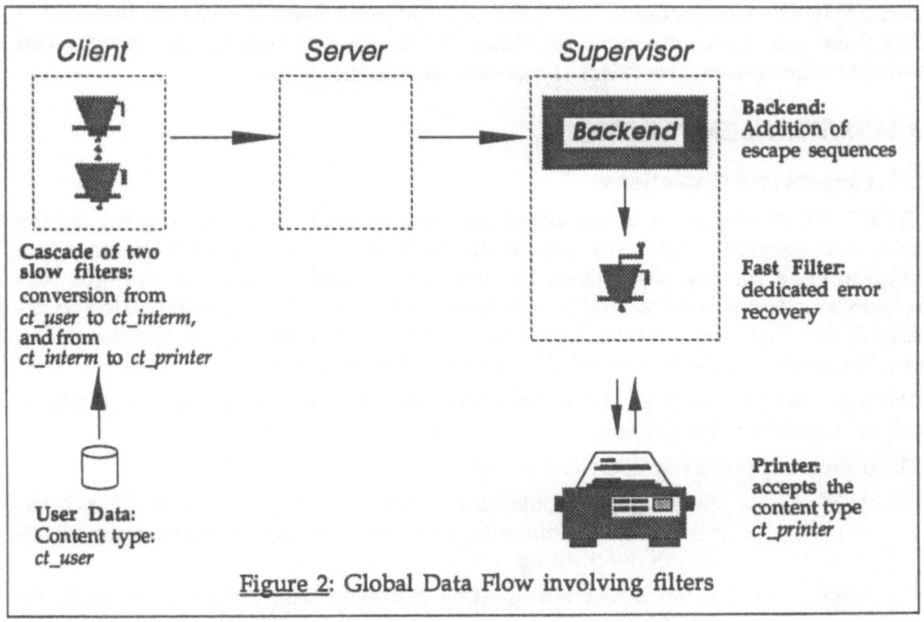

Figure 2: Global Data Flow involving filters

fore the job is effectively passed to the Server. Each printer model is characterised by one or several data content types it can accept in input, corresponding generally to the native language of the printer: a PostScript printer can usually not print directly plain ascii text, and accepts only PostScript data. Similarly, the contents of a file to be printed can also be identified by a type in the job description. This type may vary according to the application that has generated the file. The filter mechanism ensures the automatic selection of one or several filters (in cascade) to convert the job content type into a content type accepted by the device. Figure 2 illustrates the selection of two slow filters to convert the job content type *ct_user* into a printer compatible content type *ct_printer*. The first filter converts from *ct_user* to *ct_interm*, and the second filter from *ct_interm* to *ct_printer*.

Moreover, a job may require special printing modes, such as the presentation of two logical pages on a sheet, side by side. The selection mechanism chooses a filter supporting the requested modes.

So, the two functions of a slow filter are to convert data from an input content type into an output content type (for example from simple ascii to PostScript), and to support special printing modes (for example to magnify a PostScript picture by a given factor). These characteristics are used as criteria for the automatic selection of the filters at job submission.

Fast Filters

The *fast* filters are inserted between the output of the Backend and the input of the printer, under control of the Supervisor. They are executed synchronously with the printing and are able to write to and read from the printer. Fast filters perform generally a printer dedicated processing: specific error recovery after reading of the status returned by the printer, or particular connection management. A fast filter can interpret the status codes returned by the printer to select and apply adequate actions. By means of a defined interface with the Backend, a fast filter can reflect the error condition to the print system which, in turn, can warn administrators. Fast filters are never executed in cascade.

3. FUNCTIONAL CAPABILITIES

3.1. Objects and Operations

SPOOL V4/Xprint provides an object-oriented view of the spool & print service and management. Each user interaction with the system consists in an operation applied on one object class. So, removing a printer from the configuration is seen as *deleting a printer*, while submitting a file for printing is translated to *adding a job*. This object-oriented approach induces orthogonality in the interfaces, and increases user friendliness and management consistency.

There are seven possible actions on fifteen manageable object types. All actions can be applied on most objects.

The objects supported by SPOOL V4/Xprint are:

- **job** — an object containing references to the data to be printed and to various attributes and processing instructions affecting the printing
- **user** — an object representing a user; a user needs to be explicitly defined only if granted special privileges or if accounting is required; any user has access to the print system (see Section 4.1)
- **device** — an object corresponding to the physical printer
- **device group** — an object corresponding to a set of devices grouped for convenience and accessible as a unique destination
- **server** — an object representing the logical entity controlling job queues
- **supervisor** — an object representing the logical entity controlling devices
- **font** — an object describing characteristics of the print output such as character set and print densities
- **form** — an object describing the physical characteristics of the print medium, such as page length and width
- **permission** — an object holding an access and a deny list, controlling access to other objects
- **PCL** — an object for the Printer Capability List describing a printer type capabilities and the way to activate them
- **recovery rule** — an object describing actions to be taken when device errors occur
- **filter** — an object representing standard or user-defined utilities converting data at job submission or providing customised device control
- **job template** — an object that contains re-defined parameter default values for job submission
- **host** — an object representing a computer system taking part in the networked print environment

system a unique object containing the print administrator's identity

Seven operations apply to most objects: *add, show, modify, copy, status, change* and *delete.* The operation names are self-explanatory, with the following refinements: *show* retrieves the static attributes (such as a device's connection type), while *status* retrieves the dynamic attributes (such as a job's position in the queue). The same distinction applies to *modify* (static attributes) versus *change* (dynamic attributes). Table 1 presents the allowed object/operation pairs.

	add	show	modify	copy	status	change	delete
job	✓	✓	✓	.	✓	✓	✓
user	✓	✓	✓	✓	✓	✓	✓
device	✓	✓	✓	✓	✓	✓	✓
dev. group	✓	✓	✓	✓	✓	✓	✓
server	✓	✓	✓	✓	✓	✓	✓
supervisor	✓	✓	✓	✓	✓	✓	✓
font	✓	✓	✓	✓	.	.	✓
form	✓	✓	✓	✓	.	.	✓
permission	✓	✓	✓	✓	.	.	✓
PCL	✓	✓	✓	.	.	.	✓
recovery rule	✓	✓	✓	.	.	.	✓
filter	✓	✓	✓	✓	.	.	✓
job template	✓	✓	✓	✓	.	.	✓
host	✓	✓	✓	.	✓	.	✓
system	.	✓	✓	.	.	.	.

Table 1: Objects and Operations

3.2. User Interfaces

The Spool & Print Client is accessible through four different interfaces: the C function library Application Programme Interface (API), the Command Line Interface (CLI), the character-based screen-oriented interfaces for user and administrator (CUI/CAI), and the Graphical User Interface (GUI), illustrated on Figure 3. Each interface reflects the above object-oriented approach of the model.

The C library API offers a set of functions enabling the development of new applications on the print system. This interface is also used as building block for the other standard interfaces.

The command line interface is twofold. On one side, it presents specific commands reflecting directly the operations defined above (*xpadd, xpshow, xpmod,* ...). These commands are used for both service and management of the print system. On the other side, it presents the X/Open XPG3 compliant commands *lp,*

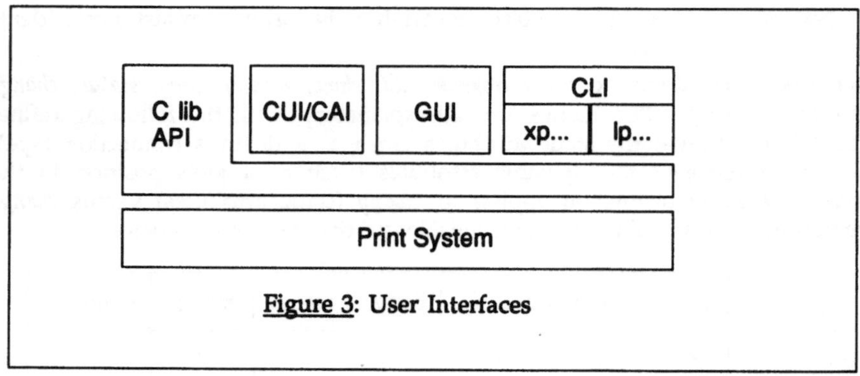

Figure 3: User Interfaces

lpstat and *cancel* [2], used for print service only.

The character-based user and administrator interfaces are built on the Form and Menu Language Interpreter (FMLI). They provide guided interfaces on dumb terminals.

The Graphical User Interface is limited to the service functions. It is based on OSF/Motif™ and offers a state-of-the-art, user friendly interface to the print functions.

4. ADMINISTRATION AND MANAGEMENT

4.1. Usage and Administration levels

In order to cope with the high delegation degree often required in networked environments, five nested print management levels are supported:

Print Administrator
omnipotent master on the whole spool & print configuration; he can see and act on the entire print environment

Local System Administrator
administrator of one host; as manager of one computer in the print environment, he may also administer the spool & print system, with a scope restricted to his host

Local Print Sub-administrator
print administrator of one host; he has roughly the same privileges as the Local System Administrator, restricted to the spool & print administration

Privileged User plain user granted with specific privileges: authorisation to print on any device and/or ability to submit jobs for immediate printing (without waiting in the job queues); he has no access to the administration functions

Plain user print service user, without access to the management functions

Those management levels are generally recorded by the Database Manager Entity, as attributes of objects.

4.2. Initialisation

Thanks to the Database Manager Entity, the configuration information is available on all participating hosts, without the need to manually replicate data. The initialisation process is straightforward. It differs between the first host of the configuration and the following ones.

On the first host, an initialisation program is executed, which defines locally the basic objects (system, local host, Print Administrator), and the permanent objects, which cannot be deleted (generic form, generic font, generic PCL). It also defines various functional objects delivered with the print system, such as standard filters and PCLs for the most common printer types.

To add a new host in the configuration, it is merely necessary to define it in the existing configuration (by means of the corresponding *xpadd host* command), and run an initialisation utility which imports a copy of the database contents. The print system can then be started normally on the new host.

4.3. Single System Image and Single Point Administration Capability

SPOOL V4/Xprint hides the physical boundaries between the hosts, and gives the vision of one, consistent print system. The various objects are named in a flat convention, without reference to their physical location (*single system image*). Similarly, the Print Administrator can manage the entire networked system from whichever host: he sees the remote objects as if they were local.

If desired for security purpose, the Print Administrator can restrict the access to global management services to a few selected hosts, or even one single host (*single point administration*). The Print Administrator can then administer the entirety of the print system from the selected hosts exclusively. There is no constraint about the choice of the administration points, which can be changed at any moment.

All parameters of the configuration can be modified dynamically, while the system is in operation. Without affecting the services, it is possible for example to enable/disable the print service and management functions on some nodes, define and configure new printers and servers, or add/delete hosts in the configuration.

5. SUPPORTED PRINTERS

Thanks to the mechanisms of printer virtualisation, backends and filters presented in Section 2, new printer types can be supported in a simple and fast fashion. Printer Capability List objects can normally be developed by administrators. A standard set of PCLs is however delivered, with the freedom left to the administrators to install them or not. The following list enumerates those industry standard printer types and/or emulations:

- HP Laserjet
- PostScript
- Proprinter
- EPSON-FX
- EPSON-LQ
- Diablo 630
- Reno

All usual types of attachment are supported (RS232, Centronics, Dataproduct, SCSI). Furthermore, connectivity is provided with printers connected to DOS PCs or terminal servers.

6. SYSTEM PROPERTIES

6.1. Customisation

Customisation has been a major issue in the design of the SPOOL V4/Xprint. The tailoring possibility appears at different levels.

Filters

Administrators can add virtually unlimited functionality in the job processing by means of filters, as outlined in Section 2.4. Slow filters process the user data and can compute, format, strip, generate statistics, etc. Fast filters run close to the printer and can manage exotic connections, or perform dedicated error recovery.

Backends

Instead of using the standard Backend of the print system, administrators can substitute their own ones for a given printer type. As described in Section 2.3, the standard Backend interprets the printer type descriptions contained in the Printer Capability List objects. Though the writing of a new PCL is normally sufficient to support a new printer type, the replacement by a customised backend may be preferred in some cases (f.i. reuse of older scripts/programmes).

Job Templates

The spool & print system provides default values to most object attributes. In the case of the job submission, the default values of the system may be replaced by default values defined in job templates. Job templates can be either global, or private. The global job templates are defined by the administrators and are stored in the Database. The private job templates are defined by the plain users in a file for their own usage. Both types are referred in the same way in the print operation.

6.2. Robustness and Reliability

The spool & print system does not present any single point of failure. The Database Manager, built on a Master/Slave role model, enables various levels of automatic transfer of the master role when the master host is stopped or crashes. Additionally, if a host becomes unavailable, most objects that are defined on it can be moved to another host dynamically.

If an architectural entity of the print system disappears unexpectedly, it is automatically relaunched in a specific recovery mode. This guarantees the continuity of the service.

The Backend is prepared to the various problems likely to occur during the printing. The support of the ETX/ACK protocol and the possibility of device polling ensure that no data is lost.

6.3. Security

As described in Section 4.1, the concept of Print Administrator obeys the principle of task delegation and role attribution. The Print Administrator is able to manage the print system on all nodes from a subset of machines, but only the print system. He does not need the superuser privilege on the managed hosts.

The spool & print system supports security levels on the objects *job, device* and *user*. A job can only be scheduled on a device with a higher security level. Moreover, a job cannot be scheduled on a device whose security level is higher than the one of the job submitter.

Permission lists can be attached to several objects, among which the devices. Those lists can be either access lists enumerating the allowed users, or deny lists forbidding the use to the mentioned subjects. The users can be identified by host and/or by name criteria.

6.4. Interoperability and Openness

The print functionality of the system complies with the one described in ISO DPA 10175.1 [3]. This is the base for an easy interoperability with other compliant print services, as well as for portability of print applications.

Moreover, SPOOL V4/Xprint offers among others an X/Open XPG3 compliant interface.

6.5. Portability

The implementation, developed in C language, uses exclusively X/Open compliant system calls and library functions. It does not rely on a specific hardware architecture. There is no need for specific device drivers, nor for kernal reconfiguration at installation. SPOOL V4/Xprint does not demand that a distributed file system is installed.

At network communication level, the interface can be chosen between BSD sockets, XTI or TLI.

These characteristics guarantee a fast and easy portability to a wide range of systems.

7. SUPPORTED PLATFORMS

The print system is currently available as SPOOL V4 on the Siemens Nixdorf Informationsystems' SINIX platforms, and as Xprint on the OEM market. Both products are perfectly interoperable in heterogeneous environments.

The list of supported platforms is regularly extended. At the time of writing, it covers:

- UNIX V.4 on i386
- SunOS 4.1 on Sparc
- SCO ODT 5.3 on i386
- SINIX 5.24 on NSC 32000
- SINIX 5.40 and 5.41 on i386 and RISC
- IRIX 5.0 on RISC

8. ON-GOING EXTENSIONS AND PERSPECTIVES

SPOOL V4/Xprint has been selected by UNIX System Laboratories as "*its general purpose distributed print management reference technology for UNIX System Laboratories' Distributed System Management Framework*".

The support of a new generation of SNI high quality fast printers, working with the HP-PCL language, and attached via a Small Computer System Interface (SCSI) is in development. The porting to Solaris 2.1 on Sparc, and Unisys V.3 on i386 is in process. Functional enhancements for the management of print resources, and for an increased comfort of administration are in study. The extension of the Model to enable the interoperability between distinct, independently managed print systems (identified as *clusters*) is in process. This extension will also support communications in a Wide Area Network environment. The interoperability with mainframes (starting with the SNI BS2000 Spool & Print) is also in development. It gives access to heavy duty, very fast printers for mass production from small computers.

Foreseen extensions and perspectives include: porting to new platforms (AIX, HP UIX, ...), light PCs as clients, and the compliance with POSIX 1003.7a [4].

9. SUMMARY

Feed-back from real usage shows that SPOOL V4/Xprint addresses in a satisfactory way all requirements of print service and management in distributed environments. The object-oriented model, reflected in the various interfaces, provides a better consistency between the user and management functions. The concept of Printer Capability List object, describing the characteristics of a printer type, enables the flexible support of new device types without the need to substitute software components. Customisation is made possible by the powerful filter mechanism. Single system image, location transparency and single point administration improve the management efficiency and comfort.

10. REFERENCES

[1] *Requirements for Distributed Print Service and Management*, UNIX International System Management Work Group, Revision 3. November 1991

[2] *X/Open Portability Guide, XSI Commands and Utilities*, X/Open Company Limited, 1989

[3] *ISO/IEC DIS 10175-1, Information Technology - Text and Office Systems - Document Printing Application - Part 1: Abstract Service Definition and Procedures*

[4] *POSIX 1003.7a - System Administration Interface/Printing*

11. ACKNOWLEDGEMENTS

The design and development of SPOOL V4/Xprint is the result of a team work, in which many people have brought their ideas. The members of the SWN17 team should be specially thanked for their deep involvement and their permanent availability, as well as P. Seghin, project leader, for his pertinent suggestions during the preparation of this paper.

Replication Algorithms for Highly-Available Systems

Barbara Liskov*

MIT Laboratory for Computer Science
Cambridge, MA 02139

Abstract. Some replication algorithms guarantee that all updates are performed in the same order at all replicas. Others only guarantee that updates are executed in causal order; updates that are not causally related may be performed in different orders at different replicas. This paper discusses the conditions under which the two schemes are applicable and describes an algorithm from each class. It also compares the performance of the algorithms and identifies the situations in which one is superior to the other.

1 Introduction

Distributed systems offer the promise that applications can behave better than in a centralized system because they can be more fault tolerant. An application that runs on just one node becomes inaccessible if that node crashes. If the application runs on a collection of nodes connected by a network, however, it can be implemented in a way that allows it to continue to run even when some nodes are crashed, or when network problems make some nodes inaccessible.

The key to fault tolerance is replication. If the data and code for an application reside at several places, loss of some copies can be tolerated: The application can continue to provide service by using the copies at other sites. This paper is concerned with the algorithms that manage the replicated data. Such replication algorithms can ensure both that information is *highly reliable*, i.e., very likely to persist in spite of failures, and *highly available*, i.e., very likely to be accessible when needed.

When information is replicated, care must be taken to ensure that the replication itself does not cause problems. Users of the information interact with it by reading and modifying the objects of which it is composed. These interactions occur as invocations of operations provided by the object; some of the operations are *updates* that modify the object, and others are *queries* that observe the current value of the object. For example, a location service that keeps track of the current locations of mobile entities in a distributed system provides operations to move and locate an entity; move is an update operation and locate is

* Supported in part by the Advanced Research Projects Agency of the Department of Defense, monitored by the Office of Naval Research under contract N00014-91-J-4136 and in part by the National Science Foundation under Grant CCR-8822158

a query. As a second example, a mail system provides operations to send and receive mail; send is an update and receive is a query.

When updates are executed, they may cause different copies of the modified object to differ from one another. This in turn might cause queries to return different results depending on which copy is read. As a result, the behavior of the application using the object may be ill-defined.

Replication algorithms have been developed to avoid such problems. These algorithms carry out protocols that ensure that even though there are multiple copies of objects, and even though there are multiple processes that may call operations concurrently, the operations calls are always performed correctly.

There are two main kinds of replication algorithms:

1. *Universal order* algorithms ensure that all updates to the replicated data appear to occur in the same order at all sites.
2. *Causal order* algorithms ensure that updates that are causally ordered appear to occur in the same order at all sites, but updates that are not causally ordered may occur in different orders at different sites.

One operation execution is causally related to another if a single process performs the calls sequentially or if the second call is done by a different process after a communication from the first process that occurred after the first call completed[14].

This paper describes a universal order algorithm and a causal order algorithm; the algorithm selected in each case is a good one that provides as good or better performance as others in its class. The paper also provides an analysis of algorithm performance and identifies the situations under which each is superior to the other. The discussion is limited to operations that are individually atomic, i.e., each query and update appears to occur indivisibly with respect to all other operations. The alternative to atomic operations is to run atomic transactions, in which groups of operations appear to occur indivisibly with respect to one another. Universal order algorithms can be easily extended to atomic transactions; how to extend causal order algorithms to handle this case is an open research question.

The remainder of the paper is organized as follows. Section 2 describes the distributed environment. Section 3 describes a universal order algorithm (the primary copy algorithm) while Section 4 describes a causal order algorithm (lazy replication). Section 5 compares the performance of the two algorithms and draws some conclusions about when to use them.

2 The Environment

We assume an environment in which individual computers, or *nodes*, are connected by a communication network. Both the nodes and the network may fail, but the failures are not Byzantine. The nodes are fail-stop processors[20]. The network can partition, and messages can be lost, delayed, duplicated, and delivered out of order. The configuration of the system can change; nodes can leave and join the network at any time.

Applications do not provide replication themselves. Instead they make use of a *replication service* that provides highly available and reliable storage for objects. The service stores many different types of objects, for use by many applications. Applications (or their users) are *clients* of the service; they interact with it by invoking operations on the objects it stores.

Some of the nodes are *servers* that store (replicas of) the objects. The replication service stores all of its objects at the servers; each object is stored at a *replica group* consisting of several servers. The number of replicas in the group and the algorithm in use determine the reliability and availability of the storage provided by the service. Some number of simultaneous failures can be accomodated; if more than this number occur simultaneously, there is a "catastrophe" in which information is lost or service is not provided.

Client code runs on other, *client machines.* Each client machine also runs some *front end* code that hides replication from client and carries out the details of the replication protocol. To call an operation, the client code makes a local call to the front end; the front end then communicates with the servers to carry out that operation. The operation is actually executed at the servers.

The goal of a replication algorithm is to provide *one-copy consistency*[3]: even though there are multiple copies of an object, as far as clients can observe by calling operations there is just one copy. This requirement has two consequences:

1. All updates must appear to occur in the same order at all copies. E.g., if a client reads an object and observes the effects of update executions u_1 and u_2 in that order, it should not be the case that a later read observes the opposite order.
2. Once a modification is observed to occur, it cannot disappear. E.g., if a client reads an object and observes the effects of the execution of update u, it should not be the case that a later read that is causally related to the first can observe a state in which u has not yet happened.

One-copy consistency does not imply that the copies are identical; copies need only *appear* to be identical as far as users can tell by calling operations. For example, suppose the specification of a mail system states that when a user receives mail, what is returned is a subset of the mail that has been sent to the user. This specification allows an implementation in which send operations are carried out in different orders at the replicas. Since the receive operation is nondeterministic, the user cannot deduce that a particular send has not occurred just because its message is not returned by the receive operation.

A universal order algorithm will always ensure one-copy consistency because all operation calls are performed in the same order at all copies of the object, and furthermore because an operation does not complete until its effects are visible to all future calls. However, such stringent guarantees are not always needed. This was the case for the mail service discussed above. In this case, a different kind of replication algorithm can be used. Such an algorithm would be desirable if it provided better performance than a universal algorithm.

3 Primary Copy: a Universal Order Algorithm

There are two main universal order algorithms, voting[2, 9, 10] and primary copy[1, 7, 16, 17, 18]. This section contains a brief description of the primary copy algorithm. Primary copy is simpler than voting and also has better performance both in terms of delay as observed by clients and in terms of overall system throughput.

Recall that each object is stored by a group of servers. In the primary copy method, one of these servers acts as the *primary*. All client operation calls (coming from front ends) are directed to the primary. The primary decides what to do and communicates with the other servers in the group as needed; the other servers are the *backups*. All servers maintain copies of the replicated objects on disk.

As with any universal replication scheme that tolerates network partition, primary copy requires 2N + 1 servers in order to survive N simultaneous server failures[3]; more than N failures is a catastrophe.[2] For example, to continue to provide access to objects when there is just one failure, there must be three servers. Having three servers is the usual case.

Operations require a two-phase protocol. Both the primary and the backup have logs in which they record information about recent operations. In phase 1, the primary records information about the operation in the log, and then informs the backups about the operation by sending the new log record to them. The backups store the new record in their logs and send acknowledgments to the primary. When acknowledgments from N backups arrive, the primary commits the operation and returns any results to the front end; if there are no results (as is the case for an update), an acknowledgement message is sent to the front end. The second phase is done in the background. The primary installs the operation by changing the disk copies of modified objects to reflect its changes, and also notifies the backup about the commit by piggybacking information on subsequent messages sent on behalf of other operations. The log record for an operation can be removed after the operation is installed at all replicas.

With this scheme, the primary determines the universal order for the operations; this is the order they are performed at the primary and also the order of their entries in the log. The primary informs the backups of the ordering as part of telling them about the operations.

When a failure or recovery occurs (such as the loss of the primary, or the recovery of a member of the replica group), the group runs a failover protocol called a *view change*[5, 6, 8]. The result of a view change is a reorganization of the replica group in which a failed node is removed from service, or a recovered node is put back in to service. The result of such a reorganization is called a *view*. One of the nodes in a view is the primary of that view; the others are

[2] Actually, the situation is a bit more complicated. For example, in a three replica service informationn may survive even if all replicas crash simultaneously provided their disks are intact, although clearly the replicated information is not accessible at this point.

backups. The primary of the new view may be a different node than the primary of the old view. The front ends at client machines track the primary, so that if the primary changes they can direct requests to the new primary.

N + 1 members of the replica group must agree to a view change in order for one to occur. Since every operation that commits is also known to N + 1 group members (the old primary and N backups), the protocol guarantees that every operation that committed in the old view is known to at least one member of the new view. This fact ensures that the new view can start up in a state that contains all committed operations. Furthermore, since the backups know about the operation order, the committed operations can be ordered in the new view in the same order they occurred in the old one.

Three important optimizations have been developed for this scheme. These optimizations are incorporated in the Harp replicated file system[16]; the first two are also present in the Echo replicated file system[11].

1. If the clocks at the replicas are loosely synchronized (or have loosely synchronized rates), it is not necessary for the primary to notify the backups about queries. Each message sent by a backup contains a time that is a lower bound on when the next view might start. As long as the current time at the primary is less than the times sent to it by all backups, there cannot be a new view. Therefore this replica is still the primary and can safely perform the query without communicating with the backups. Without the synchronized clocks, the only way a replica can be sure it is still the primary is to communicate with the backups.[3]
2. Only N + 1 nodes store copies of the objects. The other N nodes are called *witnesses*. (Witnesses were originally proposed in [19] for use with a voting algorithm.) Furthermore, a view contains just N + 1 active members (one primary and N backups); only the active members exchange messages during normal operation. Witnesses are active view members only when some of the non-witnesses are crashed or inaccessible; while a witness is active it stores information about recent updates. Witnesses also participate in view changes.
3. To provide reliability, recent updates must be recorded on a stable storage medium before they commit. Since the information is known at more than one replica, it cannot be lost unless a single failure might cause all replicas that store the information to fail. This situation is possible if a power failure can bring down all the replicas. One way to avoid loss of information in this case is to write an update's log record to disk at all the replicas before replying to the client. However disk access is expensive, and since the write must occur in the foreground, it would add delay to processing updates. Disk access can be avoided if each replica has a small uninterruptible power supply (UPS) sufficient to allow its log to be copied to disk in case of a power failure. This approach ensures that updates require just two message round trips (front end to primary, primary to backups) to complete.

[3] An analysis of the use of synchronized clocks to avoid communication can be found in [15].

The third optimization is not possible in a non-replicated system because if the node crashed all information about recent updates would be lost; in the replicated system, a copy of the information exists at the other replicas.

The primary copy technique is quite efficient in a system that contains these optimizations. For example, performance studies for Harp indicate that it outperforms a non-replicated system; the increase in performance is due primarily to the fact that the UPS's allow disk writes to be done in the background. Figure 1 shows the cost of primary copy for a system with 2N + 1 replicas. Thus for the case of a three-server group, an update requires four messages.

Delay:

update	2 message round trips
query	1 message round trip

Number of Messages:

update	2 + 2N
query	2

Fig. 1. Performance of Primary Copy.

However, there is one big problem: the primary can easily become a bottleneck since it must handle all requests. It's possible to work around this problem by having many replica groups within the service and assigning different objects to different groups. The groups can share the servers; for example, each server could run a primary from one group, a backup from another, and a witness from a third. In this way system load can be spread among the servers.[4]

This section has only sketched how primary copy works. More information, including details of the failover code, details about when records can be removed from the log, and performance data can be found in[16].

4 Lazy Replication: a Causal Order Algorithm

As was discussed earlier, sometimes a universal order isn't needed. Whether this is true or not depends on the specification of the replicated objects. Users are

[4] Voting schemes allow any replica to be used for queries. The replica can handle the query locally by relying on synchronized clocks to ensure the replica is still a member of the current view. However, the overhead for updates is higher than with primary copy. Also, it's worth noting that in the primary copy scheme, if the replica group has three members of which two are active, either the primary or the backup can handle read requests, because once an update is known at the backup, it is certain to commit.

only permitted to observe and modify objects by calling their operations. If the specifications of these operations are weak enough, users will be unable to observe deviations from universal order. This was the case in the example of the mail system; the receive operation had a weak, nondeterministic specification that kept a user from deducing the order in which two concurrent send operations actually occurred.

However, some ordering constraints are still required. Normally, the delivery order of mail messages sent by different senders to different recipients, or even to the same recipient, is unimportant, as is the delivery order of messages sent by a single sender to different recipients. However suppose user X sends a message *m1* to user Y and then a later message *m2* to Z that refers to information in the earlier message. If, as a result of reading *m2*, Z sends an inquiry message *m3* to Y, Z would expect *m3* to be delivered to Y after *m1*. The problem here is that there is a causal relationship between the messages that needs to be preserved by the replication method.

This section provides a sketch of the lazy replication technique[13], which preserves causal order. (Another, similar technique is the one provided by Isis[4].) The scheme works as follows. As before the replicated service is implemented as a replica group that stores copies of the objects, but now a front end can communicate with any convenient replica. The front end informs the service about the causal order of operations. Every reply message for an update operation contains a unique identifier, *uid*, that names that invocation. In addition, every (query and update) operation *o* contains a *label*, which is a set of uids; the label contains the uids of all updates whose execution must precede the execution of *o*. In the mail service, for example, the front end can indicate that one send_mail must precede another by including the uid of the first send_mail in the label passed to the second. Finally, a query operation returns a value and also a label that identifies the updates reflected in the value; this label is a superset of the argument label, ensuring that every update that must have preceded the query is reflected in the result.

The front end preserves causality by making sure that each operation call message sent to a replica contains the right uids in its label. The front end maintains a label that contains all uids returned to it in replies from replicas. In addition, this label is sent on any message from the front end's client C1 to another client C2; when the message arrives, C2's front end picks up the label and adds all its uids to its own label. Thus the label contains all the uids needed to preserve causal order. The front end sends its label in each message sent to a replica.

Replicas maintain a database and a log. The database is stored on disk and contains a copy of each object. It reflects the effects of executing updates on objects; it has an associated label that contains the uids of all these updates.

When a replica receives an update, it assigns it a uid, records the update with its label and uid in the log, and returns the uid to the front end. Other replicas are not informed about the update until later. Replicas exchange *gossip* messages, containing information about the updates in their logs, in the background. (The technique is called lazy replication because the information about updates propagates lazily.)

Updates are also performed in the background. An update cannot be executed until it is *ready*, i.e., all updates identified by its label have been performed and their effects are reflected in the database. At this point, the replica modifies the disk copy of the modified object to reflect the update's changes and also adds the update's uid to the database's label.

When a replica receives a query, it waits until all updates identified by the query's label have been reflected in the database, i.e., until their uids are all contained in the database's label. Then it evaluates the query and returns its result to the front end. It does not log any information about the query and replicas do not gossip about queries.

If a front end does not get a timely response from a replica, it can send a request to another replica. This means that the same update might be sent to two different replicas, and therefore receive two distinct uids. Nevertheless, it is important that the update be performed only once at each replica. This is accomplished by having the front end assign its own unique identifier, a *cid*, to each update operation. Each message sent by the front end on behalf of the update contains this cid. Cids are recorded in the log along with the other information about an update; in addition, there is a set maintained for the database that records the cids of all updates reflected in it. When an update is ready to be performed, the replica checks whether it is a duplicate of an update that has already been performed. If so the replica does not perform the update. However it adds the update's uid to the database's label. This is necessary because an operation that is causally dependent on the update might indicate this by having the uid of the duplicate in its label.

The key to making this technique work well is finding a cheap way to implement uids and label. This is accomplished by implementing them as multipart timestamps. A timestamp $< t1, \ldots, tn >$ contains a part for each replica; each part is just a counter. Adding a uid to a label is done by merging the two timestamps; the merge retains the larger counter for each part. Each replica has a label that records the uids of all updates it has ever seen; whenever it learns about a new update (in a gossip message) it adds the update's uid to this label (by merging the uid timestamp with the label timestamp). To create a new uid, the replica simply advances its part of its label timestamp. Since it is the only one that changes this part, we can be sure that the resulting timestamp truly is unique. Determining whether an operation is ready is easy to do; its label must be less than or equal to that of the database, where (for an N-part timestamp)

$$L1 \leq L2 \textit{ iff } L1_1 \leq L2_1 \ \& \ \ldots \ \& \ L1_N \leq L2_N$$

Lazy replication has very good performance. The cost of performing an operation is:

2 messages for queries
2 + (N-1)/K messages for updates

The calculation about messages is done as follows: all other replicas must be informed about the update, but this is done in gossip messages that on average contain information about K updates. The delay for performing an operation is:

1 round trip for queries
1 round trip for updates

However, this analysis ignores the problem of reliability. In the scheme discussed so far, if a replica crashes, any updates that exist only in its log are lost forever. Therefore, the scheme needs to be changed to provide better reliability. One possibility is for the replica to write each log record to disk before replying to the front end. Not only is this expensive, but it has availability problems: if the server crashes, the update isn't lost, but its effects cannot be observed until after the replica recovers. This can delay subsequent queries, since they may contain the update's uid in their labels.

Therefore, a better way is to have the replica send the log record for the update to other replicas before replying. Then the logs need not be stored on disk provided replicas have UPS's or are far enough apart that they are not all affected by a single power failure. It isn't necessary for a majority of replicas to know about the new update, however. For example, if there were seven replicas in the group, we might choose to communicate with just one other replica, since this would take care of the most likely case of a single crash. Using this scheme increases both the number of messages sent and the delay for updates.

The performance information is given in Figure 2, where R is the number of nodes that can fail without danger of losing information about an update. For example, if $R = 1$ (so that information can survive one failure) and there are three replicas, each update requires $4 + 1/K$ messages.

Delay:

update	2 message round trips
query	1 message round trip

Number of Messages:

update	$2 + 2R + (N - (R + 1))/K$
query	2

Fig. 2. Performance of Lazy Replication.

The choice of R affects not just the reliability of updates but also their availability. An update can be performed only if $R + 1$ replicas are up and communicating. By contrast, a query can usually be performed provided the front end can reach just one replica, since usually the updates a query depend on are known at a replica by the time a query arrives there. This is true for the following reason: Front ends have a preferred replica with which they communicate, and therefore almost always the replica knows about earlier updates by the front end sending a message. In addition it almost always knows about earlier updates done by another client that are causally related to the current request because replicas are fairly prompt about sending gossip and can use the same communication paths that allow the clients to communicate.

One final point: The discussion above has not mentioned what to do when a node fails or recovers. The reason is that nothing needs to be done. When a node fails, the other nodes just continue as they were; when a node recovers, it picks up the log records that are missing from its log (by gossiping with the other replicas), and then continues processing client requests. Therefore no view change algorithm is needed. (A related algorithm is needed if the system is reconfigured, however[12].)

The above discussion has omitted many details of the lazy replication scheme. More information can be found in [13], including details of when entries can be removed from the log, when cids can be removed from the set of cids associated with the database, and performance data.

5 Discussion

The previous sections have described two replication algorithms. Primary copy guarantees that updates are performed in the same order at all replicas, while lazy replication only ensures that updates are performed in a way that preserves causal order.

Figure 3 compares the performance of the two schemes. It shows the message cost and delay, assuming a system with three replicas, and assuming a replica communicates with one other replica when performing an update in the lazy replication scheme. From the figure we can see both schemes delay updates by the same amount, and they delay queries by the same amount provide primary copy makes use of synchronized clocks or synchronized clock rates to avoid having the primary communicate with the backup when processing queries. Synchronized clocks or clock rates are not absolutely guaranteed to remain in synch, however. If synchronization fails, the primary copy scheme can suffer from a loss of causality. For example, a client may find out about an update via a communication from another client, but then send a query to an obsolete primary that is not aware of the fact that it is obsolete and thus observe a state in which the update hasn't happened. Probably it is reasonable to accept this risk since the chance of a problem arising is very small. However, lazy replication achieves the better performance without running any such risk (the situation above might cause it to delay the response to the query but it won't return the wrong answer).

Lazy replication uses the same number of messages for queries as primary copy (again assuming primary copy depends on clock synchronization), but more messages for updates. The additional cost for updates depends on how many replicas there are and how big gossip messages are, i.e., how many updates are sent at once. The lazy replication system has to balance the size of gossip

	lazy replication	primary copy
Delay:		
update	2 round trips	2 round trips
query	1 round trip	1 round trip
Number of Messages:		
update	4 + 1/K	4
query	2	2

Fig. 3. Comparison for a three-replica system.

messages against the speed of propagation: if messages are not sent very often, queries may have to wait, but there will be more updates per message and therefore fewer messages will be sent.

The number of messages is an indication of system throughput. Sending and receiving messages takes time. Acting on the received message also takes time: All replicas that hear about an update must record it in their log and later install its results. One point to note here is that with primary copy, a log record might describe the effects of an update (e.g., by containing the new state of the modified object), which might reduce the cost of processing the update at the backup (but might also increase the size of messages, which could increase the processing cost). Such an approach is more difficult with lazy replication because different replicas are in different states when updates are performed. Therefore, most likely all replicas in a lazy replication scheme actually execute the update.

Given that the differences in performance are relatively small, we must consider whether it is worthwhile to use a causal scheme. Since a universal scheme works for all objects, no matter what their specifications, is it really a good idea to use a more specialized causal scheme? The answer is that sometimes the causal scheme is worthwhile, because it outperforms the universal schemes in three ways:

1. It scales better.
2. It provides better support for load balancing.
3. It provides better availability.

It's easy to see that lazy replication scales better than primary copy. When a replica group in a universal scheme is enlarged so that it can handle one more failure, the cost of updates increases by two messages; this also increases delay because of the extra cost at the primary of sending the extra message to the new backup (assuming a scheme with witnesses) and handling the extra reply. By contrast, adding another replica in the lazy replication scheme increases the cost of updates by 1/K. For example, if there are five replicas in the group, primary copy requires six messages to do an update; lazy replication requires only 4 + 3/K. Thus lazy replication now requires fewer messages even if K is as small as two updates per gossip message. There are two reasons for the gain. First, the log records sent to the backups in the primary copy scheme must be acknowledged, but gossip messages are not; instead later gossip messages in the other direction act as acknowledgments. Second, one gossip message serves to convey information about many updates. A similar technique could be used in primary copy. The primary could delay communicating with the backups until K updates had been requested. But unlike in lazy replication, this delay would also delay the response to the client.

In fact, because enlarging the replica group increases the cost so dramatically, it is unlikely that a universal scheme will be run with more than three replicas. By contrast, lazy replication can run with lots of replicas. Having more replicas increases the size of the timestamps used as labels, however. Since these timestamps must be sent in all messages (recall that they were sent in client-to-client messages as well as in client-to-server messages), it's not desirable for them to be huge. But this does not rule out quite large replica groups.

Having lots of replicas means that they can be placed in a network in such a way that every client is geographically close to at least one of them, thus reducing the delay in processing client calls. Furthermore, the replicas can spread the load of running operations. It is true that all replicas must run each update, but a query only runs at one replica, and in most applications, the majority of operation calls are to queries. Primary copy can also spread the load, by assigning different objects to different groups; this scheme was discussed in Section 3. However, such a scheme cannot do load balancing as well as a dynamic scheme like lazy replication. Also, it doesn't help at all for the case where a single object is a hot spot; lazy replication works fine in this case provided a reasonable proportion of the operation calls are to queries.

Another point is that with lazy replication it is easy to add read-only replicas. In such a system, read/write replicas handle both updates and queries and the timestamp contains an entry for each of them. They send gossip to the read-only replicas as well as to one another. Read-only replicas just handle queries and do not have entries in the timestamp. Queries still run in the proper causal order at them because their label indicates when they are ready. It isn't as easy to add read-only replicas to a universal scheme because there isn't anything like a label to indicate when a query should run.

Finally, lazy replication has better availability than a universal scheme. It can handle updates if two nodes are up and can communicate (in a system in which R = 1), and it can handle queries if just one node is up (although occasionally a query might be delayed). Thus in a three-replica system lazy replication can continue to service queries when a universal scheme cannot. In a system with five or more replicas, lazy replica can continue to service both updates and queries when a universal scheme cannot. Furthermore, the availability of lazy replication can be increased by adding a single replica; in a universal scheme, replicas must always be added in pairs (because a majority of replicas must accept a new view or know about an update), although one of the new nodes can be a witness.

In conclusion, some kinds of objects must be replicated using a universal ordering scheme, because deviations from a universal order would be visible to users. Primary copy is a good technique for implementing universal order. Like all universal order schemes, however, it doesn't work well unless there is a small number of replicas. This means it won't perform well for objects that are heavily and widely used, because many requests will need to travel a long way to reach a replica, and because the small number of replicas means replicas will be bottlenecks.

Lazy replication is desirable for applications with heavily used objects. The number of replicas can be chosen to fit the expected load and geographical constraints. Of course applications can use the scheme only if their specifications allow it. There are important applications that require the performance provided by lazy replication and have the necessary weak semantics. Examples are a location service (which maps mobile objects to their current location) and a name service (which maps high level names to entities, e.g., a yellow pages mechanism).

Acknowledgments
Thanks to Liuba Shrira who read an earlier version of this paper and provided perspective and insight about the comparative analysis of the two replication schemes.

References

1. P. Alsberg and J. Day. A principle for resilient sharing of distributed resources. In *Proc. of the 2nd International Conference on Software Engineering*, pages 627–644, October 1976.
2. P. A. Bernstein and N. Goodman. An algorithm for concurrency control and recovery in replicated distributed databases. *ACM Trans. on Database Systems*, 9(4):596–615, December 1984.
3. P. A. Bernstein, V. Hadzilacos, and N. Goodman. *Concurrency Control and Recovery in Database Systems*. Addison Wesley, 1987.
4. K. Birman, A. Schiper, and P. Stephenson. Lightweight causal and atomic group multicast. *ACM Trans. on Computer Systems*, 9(3), August 1991.
5. A. El-Abbadi, D. Skeen, and F. Cristian. An efficient fault-tolerant protocol for replicated data management. In *Proc. of the Fourth Symposium on Principles of Database Systems*, pages 215–229, ACM, 1985.
6. A. El-Abbadi and S. Toueg. Maintaining availability in partitioned replicated databases. In *Proc. of the Fifth Symposium on Principles of Database Systems*, pages 240–251, ACM, 1986.
7. S. Ghemawat. *Automatic Replication for Highly Available Services*. Technical Report MIT/LCS/TR-473, MIT Laboratory for Computer Science, Cambridge, MA, 1990.
8. D. Gifford. *Information Storage in a Decentralized Computer System*. Technical Report CSL-81-8, Xerox Corporation, March 1983.

9. D. K. Gifford. Weighted voting for replicated data. In *Proc. of the Seventh Symposium on Operating Systems Principles*, pages 150–162, ACM SIGOPS, Pacific Grove, CA, December 1979.
10. M. Herlihy. A quorum-consensus replication method for abstract data types. *ACM Trans. on Computer Systems*, 4(1):32–53, February 1986.
11. A. Hisgen, A. Birrell, C. Jerian, T. Mann, M. Schroeder, and G. Swart. Granularity and semantic level of replication in the Echo distributed file system. In *Proc. of the Workshop on Management of Replicated Data*, IEEE, Houston, TX, November 1990.
12. D. J. Hwang. *Constructing a Highly-Available Location Service for a Distributed Environment.* Technical Report MIT/LCS/TR-410, M.I.T. Laboratory for Computer Science, Cambridge, MA, November 1987.
13. R. Ladin, B. Liskov, L. Shrira, and S. Ghemawat. Providing high availability using lazy replication. *ACM Trans. on Computer Systems*, 10(4):360–391, November 1992.
14. L. Lamport. Time, clocks, and the ordering of events in a distributed system. *Comm. of the ACM*, 21(7):558–565, July 1978.
15. B. Liskov. Practical uses of synchronized clocks in distributed systems. To appear in *Distributed Computing.*
16. B. Liskov, S. Ghemawat, R. Gruber, P. Johnson, L. Shrira, and M. Williams. Replication in the Harp file system. In *Proc. of the Thirteenth ACM Symposium on Operating Systems Principles*, October 1991.
17. B. M. Oki. *Viewstamped Replication for Highly Available Distributed Systems.* Technical Report MIT/LCS/TR-423, MIT Laboratory for Computer Science, Cambridge, MA, 1988.
18. B. M. Oki and B. Liskov. Viewstamped replication: a new primary copy method to support highly-available distributed systems. In *Proc. of the 7th ACM Symposium on Principles of Distributed Computing*, ACM, August 1988.
19. J. Paris. Voting with witnesses: a consistency scheme for replicated files. In *Proc. of the 6th International Conference on Distributed Computer Systems*, pages 606–612, IEEE, 1986.
20. R. D. Schlichting and F. B. Schneider. Fail-stop processors: an approach to designing fault-tolerant computing systems. *ACM Trans. on Computing Systems*, 1(3):222–238, 1983.

REMO
Referenzmodell für sichere IT-Systeme
- Zusammenfassung -

Das vom deutschen Bundesministerium für Forschung und Technologie (BMFT) geförderte Verbundvorhaben REMO (Referenzmodell für sichere IT-Systeme) bringt industrielle und wissenschaftliche Partner zusammen, um notwendige Grundlagen für den Bau neuer, sicherer informationstechnischer (IT) Systeme zu erarbeiten. Die fünf Partner in REMO sind: Europäisches Institut für Systemsicherheit (E.I.S.S.) an der Universität Karlsruhe, Gesellschaft für Mathematik und Datenverarbeitung (GMD), Industrieanlagen–Betriebsgesellschaft (IABG), Siemens AG und Telematic Services (TELES) GmbH. Die Koordinierung der Arbeiten in REMO obliegt der IABG.

Sicherheit ist eine integrative Gesamtsystemeigenschaft mit Beiträgen vieler Systemkomponenten. Deshalb verfolgt REMO einen konstruktiven Ansatz (REMO-K), der die Gestaltung neuer IT-Systeme mit integrierter Sicherheitsfunktionalität zum Ziel hat. Andererseits werden bestehende IT-Systeme in einem komplementären ergänzenden Ansatz (REMO-E) berücksichtigt, um zu zeigen, wie durch Integration von Sicherheitsmoduln die Sicherheitseigenschaft verbessert werden kann. Beide Ansätze konzentrieren sich auf die technischen Aspekte der Systemsicherheit. Organisatorische, bauliche oder personelle Maßnahmen werden als Rahmenbedingungen betrachtet.

Konstruktiver Ansatz

REMO betont den Bezug von Sicherheit zum Anwender und seinen eigenen Maßstäben. Das schließt nicht aus, Bausteine, Anleitungen, Architekturen allgemein gültig so zu entwickeln, daß damit individuell passende IT-Systeme zu bauen sind. Die speziellen Sicherheitsbedürfnisse der Anwender müssen geeignet ermittelt und dargestellt werden. Sicherheitsmodelle sind anwendungsorientiert zu entwickeln. Für die Realisierung der Sicherheitsanforderungen werden Sicherheitsmechanismen benötigt, aus denen ausgewählt werden kann. Als Leitfaden wird eine Methodik entworfen, die zeigt, welche besonderen Schritte und Aufgaben zu erledigen sind, um Sicherheit zu integrieren. An realitätsnahen Szenarien soll die Einsatzfähigkeit der Vorgehensweise gezeigt werden.

Ergänzender Ansatz

Bestehende IT-Systeme sollen kurzfristig so ergänzt werden, daß auch sie bestimmten Sicherheitsanforderungen gerecht werden. Dafür sind Sicherheitsmodule und eine Technik nötig, wie diese Sicherheitsmodule in Anwendungen integriert werden können. Um einen breiten und schnellen Einsatz der Sicherheitsmodule zu ermöglichen, dürfen die originären Systeme nicht oder nur unwesentlich verändert werden.

REMO
Referenzmodell für sichere IT-Systeme
- Überblick -

Dr. H. Atzmüller
IABG
Einsteinstraße 20, 85521 Ottobrunn
E-mail: atz@ite.iabg.de

Abstract

Sicherheit in informationstechnischen (IT) Systemen muß schon bei deren Konzeption berücksichtigt werden. Um eine Basis für praktikable Lösungen zur Integration von Sicherheit und Zuverlässigkeit in IT-Systemen zu schaffen, fördert der Bundesminister für Forschung und Entwicklung (BMFT) das Projekt „Referenzmodell für sichere IT-Systeme (REMO)" als Verbundprojekt zwischen Forschungsinstituten und Industriefirmen.

Das Projekt REMO soll einen Leitfaden für die Entwicklung sicherer IT-Systeme entwickeln. Es umfaßt zwei Ansätze, mit unterschiedlicher Zielsetzung:

- Der konstruktive Ansatz (REMO-K) verfolgt das Ziel bei der Realisierung neuer IT-Systeme zu helfen, bei denen die Sicherheit Entwurfskriterium ist.
- Der ergänzende Ansatz (REMO-E) will den Umgang mit und die externe Kommunikation zwischen bestehenden IT-Systemen sichern.

1 REMO - Aufgaben und Ziele

Unsere Gesellschaft wandelt sich mehr und mehr zu einer Informationsgesellschaft. Wir werden in allen Bereichen zunehmend abhängig von der Informationstechnik. IT-Sicherheit wird damit ebenso wichtig wie IT-Funktionalität. Garantierte Sicherheit ist Triebfeder für die Nutzung der IT-Fähigkeiten und gleichzeitig wichtiger Wettbewerbsfaktor.

Sicherheit zu ermöglichen, ist zunächst eine Aufgabe für Hersteller von IT-Systemen – aber nur insoweit, daß sie eine entsprechende Funktionalität zur Verfügung stellen und die Unumgehbarkeit der Sicherheitsvorkehrungen garantieren. Sicherheit anwendungs- und einsatzspezifisch zu definieren und im Systembetrieb zu gewährleisten, ist ureigene Aufgabe der Anwender bzw. der Betreiber von IT-Systemen. Die Realisierung von Sicherheit ist nicht völlig an Experten delegierbar, weil sie erst im täglichen Umgang mit IT-Systemen verwirklicht werden kann.

1.1 REMO im Überblick

Das Projekt REMO baut auf den früher vom BMFT geförderten Projekten „Sichere und zuverlässige Software (SECURE/E)" und „Software-Manipulationssicherheit

(SOMASI)" auf. Die SOMASI-Ergebnisse wurden in dem Buch „Manipulation in Rechnern und Netzen" [GGHI89] veröffentlicht.

Das Vorhaben REMO lief von Anfang 1991 bis Mitte 1993 in seiner ersten Phase (REMO-I). Vorgelagert war eine Definitionsphase mit Partnerauswahl und einer Expertenbewertung der geplanten Arbeiten. In REMO-I wurden nicht Systeme gebaut, sondern Grundlagen geschaffen als Voraussetzung für die Entwicklung von IT-Systemen mit integrierter Sicherheit. Ergebnisse sind veröffentlicht. REMO sucht die externe Diskussion über die Projektgrenzen hinaus, um den Bedürfnissen der Praxis gerecht zu werden.

Die fünf Partner in REMO sind: Europäisches Institut für Systemsicherheit (E.I.S.S.) an der Universität Karlsruhe, Gesellschaft für Mathematik und Datenverarbeitung (GMD), Industrieanlagen–Betriebsgesellschaft (IABG), Siemens AG und Telematic Services (TELES) GmbH. Die Koordinationsrolle hat die IABG übernommen.

Das Umfeld von REMO wird charakterisiert durch Standards wie z.B. die Kriteriendokumente der Rainbow Series, IT-Sicherheitskriterien ITSK, harmonisierte europäische Kriterien ITSEC, die Evaluationsanleitungen (ITSEM) und das Sicherheitshandbuch sowie durch andere Forschungsprojekte wie z.B. das Parallelprojekt KORSO, das die Entwicklung neuer Hilfsmittel für formale Spezifikation und Verifikation zum Ziel hat.

1.2 REMO-Leitsätze, Ergebnisse, Erkenntnisse, Wünsche

Folgende Aussagen umreißen die Leitsätze, unter denen in REMO gearbeitet wurde:

- Sicherheit ist anwendergesteuert und einsatzabhängig. Sie muß entsprechend verstanden und definiert werden.
- Die Orientierung an und die Fortentwicklung von neuen Forschungsansätzen im Bereich Sicherheit ist unverzichtbar für neuartige IT-Systeme.
- Anleitungen zur Konstruktion sicherer Systeme (neue methodische Schritte in bewährten Software-Engineering-Verfahren) fehlen weitgehend und müssen erst entwickelt werden. Sie ergänzen Entwicklungsverfahren, ersetzen sie nicht.
- Die Sicherheit des Gesamtsystems umfaßt neben der Sicherheit einzelner Komponenten immer auch Verteilungs-, Kommunikations- und Kooperationsaspekte.
- Eine offene und flexible System-Architektur mit Basisdiensten für Sicherheit ist notwendig und daher ein wesentliches Ziel.
- Bausteine und „Handwerkszeug" (Mechanismen, Modelle) sind Voraussetzung für den Bau sicherer IT-Systeme und somit zuerst aufzubereiten.
- Die Reduzierung der Sicherheitsrisiken ist auch bei existenten Systemen sinnvoll möglich und dringend geboten.

Zwei Ansätze wurden verfolgt: Der konstruktive Zweig (REMO-K) konzentriert sich auf neue Systeme: was kann mit dem jetzigen Wissensstand erreicht werden und wo sind Wissenslücken zu füllen? Der ergänzende Zweig (REMO-E) will bestehende Systeme ohne große Änderungen in den Systemen selbst so nachrüsten, daß sie dort sicherer werden, wo die größten Bedrohungen bestehen (Sicherheitsschale und-module).

Die wichtigsten REMO-K Resultate lassen sich in folgende Themenbereiche gliedern:

- Anwenderorientiertes Verständnis von Sicherheit (Terminologie) [AmAt92], d. h. Sicherheit als vom Anwender bewertete Eigenschaft.
- Erschließung des Wissensstands für die Anwendung, d.h. Zusammenstellung, Wertung und Einsatzaufbereitung des Stands der Technik und Wissenschaft und der Praxiserfahrung bei
  - Anwendungsfällen (Szenarienbuch) [HMS93]
  - Sicherheitsmaßnahmen und -mechanismen („Mechanismenbuch") [FFKK93]
  - Sicherheitsmodellen [KeMu93]
  - Attacken aus der Praxis als Erfahrungspotential [FrAm92]
  - Literatur (Literaturdatenbank in REMO)
- Ermittlung, Darstellung und Evaluation von Sicherheits-Anforderungen [Metz92]
- Anpassung, (Weiter-)Entwicklung und Anwendung von Sicherheitsmodellen [GrSt93] [Stra93] und Sicherheitsmechanismen [StLa93] [Klei93]
- Sicherheitsarchitekturen für variable Sicherheitspolitiken (Einsatz eines neuartigen Trägersystems mit Kern/Server Paradigma) [HKL91]
- Auswahl und Einsatzbewertung formaler Spezifikationstechniken [Kurt91]
- Entwurfsanleitung für sichere IT-Systeme (methodischer Leitfaden) [EKMM93].

REMO-E befaßt sich mit der Problematik, wie bestehende, breit eingesetzte IT-Systeme gesichert werden können. Als Maßstab müssen die Risiken wachsender Vernetzung von IT-Systemen dienen und der für den jeweiligen Einsatzzweck angemessene Sicherungsaufwand betrachtet werden. Themenbereiche sind:

- Beispielhafte Vorgehensweise bei der Sicherung existenter IT-Systeme [Schi90]
- Schutz der Kommunikation zwischen IT-Systemen (Sicherheitsschale)
- Entwicklung und Einsatz von Sicherheitsmoduln z.B.
  - Chipkarteneinsatz [HiLa92]
  - Modul zur Analyse von Protokolldaten (Auditanalyse) [FrKa91]
  - Netzsicherheitsmodul [ERKW91]
- Weiterführende Konzeptionen für Sicherheitsmoduln [GeKö93] [Wall93]
- Erste Demonstrationsobjekte für Wirkungsnachweis und Erfahrungssammlung

Im folgenden werden ausgewählte REMO-Ergebnisse etwas vertieft und die wesentlichen Veröffentlichungen aus dem Vorhaben kurz vorgestellt.

2 Sicherheits-Anforderungen – Der Grundstein

Sicherheits-Anforderungen legen den Grundstein bei der Entwicklung sicherer IT-Systeme. Zum einen spiegeln sie den anwendungsspezifischen Sicherheitsbedarf wider, zum anderen bilden sie die Ausgangsbasis für die Gestaltung eines dazu passenden Sicherheitsmodells und die Suche nach Sicherheits-Maßnahmen und -Mechanismen. Sicherheits-Anforderungen zählen ebenso zu den System-Anforderungen wie funktionale Anforderungen, die den Leistungsumfang des Systems beschreiben. Es können verschiedene, zueinander ergänzende Sichten eingenommen werden:

- Aus „bedrohungsorientierter" Sicht fordern Sicherheits-Anforderungen die Vermeidung von Bedrohungen [HMS93].
- Aus „funktionsorientierter" Sicht verlangen sie die Durchsetzung bestimmter funktionaler Anforderungen [PeSt91].

Die Ermittlung von Sicherheits-Anforderungen ist selbst keine REMO-spezifische Aufgabe. Hier kann auf vorhandene Verfahren der Bedrohungs- und Risikoanalyse z.B. [ITSH92] zurückgegriffen werden. Dabei werden die schützenswerten Güter einer Anwendung und die Bedrohungen, die auf diese wirken, aus Anwendersicht identifiziert.

Die neuen Ansätze in REMO konzentrieren sich auf zwei Schwerpunkte:

1. Wie kann die Ermittlung von Sicherheits-Anforderungen systematisch in den Konstruktionsprozeß für sichere IT-Systeme einbezogen werden? (→ Methodik)
2. Welche Formen der (informellen und formalen) Darstellung eignen sich besonders für Sicherheits-Anforderungen (gegenüber Anwendern, für weitere Entwicklung) ?

Es wurde eine Methode zur semi-formalen Darstellung von System- und somit auch von Sicherheits-Anforderungen vorgestellt, die auf einer strukturierten Umgangssprache beruht [PeSt91]. Diese Darstellungsform eignet sich aufgrund ihrer Verständlichkeit gut zur Kommunikation mit dem Aufgabensteller.

Der Übergang von einer informellen Darstellung zu einer formalen Formulierung ist kein einfacher, nach festen Regeln durchführbarer Übersetzungsprozeß [Metz92] [NiCa93]. Der Zwang zur Abstraktion, zur Konzentration auf die „wichtigen" Sicherheits-Anforderungen steht im Vordergrund. Diese können auf zusätzlichen Verfeinerungsstufen ergänzt und erweitert werden. Verschiedene Ansätze (z.B. Zustandsübergangsmodelle, Prädikate und Bedingungen) wurden untersucht und anhand eines Fallbeispiels erprobt. Ziel der Formalisierungsansätze waren anwendungsspezifische Darstellungen (Sicherheitsmodelle), wie sie etwa in [ITSK89] gefordert werden. Als formale Sprache wurde nach einem Auswahlprozeß RAISE/RSL eingesetzt [RLG91].

Die in REMO-I gewonnenen Erkenntnisse bieten dem Anwender eine Hilfestellung zur Ermittlung und formalen Darstellung **seiner eigenen** Sicherheits-Anforderungen.

3 Sicherheits-Architektur – Der Bauplan

Grundlage der Arbeiten in REMO zu Architekturen sicherer verteilter IT-Systeme ist die Erkenntnis:

- daß Nachbesserungen an der Sicherheitsfunktionalität vorhandener Computersysteme in der Vergangenheit zu wenig zufriedenstellenden Lösungen geführt haben [REMO92] und bestenfalls eine kurzzeitige Wirkung erzielen konnten;

- daß die Sicherung von Anwendungssystemen die Anwendungs-Besonderheiten berücksichtigen muß [HMS93];
- daß Anwendungen heute bereits über Systeme ohne gemeinsame zentrale Administration verteilt sind, eine solche also nicht gefordert werden kann.

In den letzten Jahren wurden aber auch neue Architekturkonzepte auf der Basis von Client/Server-Systemen entwickelt und eingesetzt, die eine Erfüllung der oben genannten Forderungen wesentlich wahrscheinlicher erscheinen lassen als es die heute eingesetzten monolithischen Systemstrukturen erlauben.

Der im Rahmen des REMO-Projekts entwickelte Szenarienkatalog [HMS 93] stellt durch die Fülle von Beispielen ein geeignetes Mittel für die Generierung von Anforderungen an eine Sicherheitsarchitektur dar. REMO hat auf der Basis einer solchen modernen Systemarchitektur eine Sicherheits-Architektur konzipiert, die den gestellten Anforderungen gerecht wird.

Ausgehend von BirliX, einem datentyporientierten Betriebssystem, entstand im Rahmen des Verbundprojekts die BirliX-Sicherheits-Architektur (BSA) [BSA92, BSA93]. Sie vermeidet den kritisierten anwendungsunabhängigen Ansatz. Eckdaten dieser Sicherheits-Architektur sind:

- *keine zentrale Administration*
- *sicheres Booten als Grundlage* [Gros 91]
- *dynamische Integration von Sicherheitsmechanismen.* Diese Eigenschaft bildet die Grundlage für die Evolutionsfähigkeit und damit die Zukunftssicherheit der Architektur. Neu entstehende Sicherheits-Anforderungen können mit Hilfe neu entwickelter Sicherheitsmodelle in der Architektur realisiert werden. Notwendige Voraussetzung ist dabei, auch neu entwickelte Basismechanismen integrieren zu können, falls diese dazu erforderlich sind.
- *Realisierung individueller anwendungsgerechter Sicherheitsmodelle.* Das steht im Gegensatz zu einem einzigen, statisch durch das Basissystem vorgegebenen Modell, wie es sonst anzutreffen ist.
- *dynamische Ankopplung von verschiedenen Sicherheits-Anforderungen (Politiken) an Anwendungssysteme.* Diese Eigenschaft liefert die Voraussetzung, eine Anwendung unter verschiedenen Einsatzbedingungen auch mit entsprechenden individuellen Sicherheits-Anforderungen zu betreiben oder aber Änderungen von Sicherheits-Anforderungen einzubringen.

Eine Sicherheitsarchitektur beeinflußt den Entwurfsprozeß sicherer Anwendungssysteme. Sie liefert den Orientierungsrahmen, in dem Anwendungssystem und Sicherheitspolitik realisiert werden. Die dynamische Anbindbarkeit verschiedener Sicherheitspolitiken an Anwendungssysteme und die Realisierbarkeit neuer Sicherheits-Anforderungen in der Architektur erlauben den Einsatz von Anwendungen in einem breiten Feld von Szenarien. Sie garantieren damit auch deren Zukunftssicherheit.

Der Schritt von einer Sicherheitspolitik über ein formales Sicherheitsmodell hin zu einer konkreten Realisierung wurde mit Hilfe der formalen Spezifikationssprache *RAISE* /RSL [RLG91] für eine Beispiel-Sicherheitspolitik bereits vollzogen. Ausgangspunkt der RSL-Spezifikation war die Sicherheitspolitik eines vereinfachten 4-Augenprinzips. Aufsatzpunkt der Spezifikation waren die Paradigmen der BirliX-Sicherheits-Architektur (BSA) und die hierin bereits enthaltenen Standard-Sicherheitsmechanismen.
Im Rahmen eines Workshops mit internationaler Beteiligung [REMO92] wurde die BSA vorgestellt und mit anderen neueren Entwicklungen auf dem Gebiet Sicherheits-Architektur verglichen.

4 Sicherheits-Mechanismen – Die Bausteine

Die Situation bei Sicherheits-Mechanismen ist dadurch gekennzeichnet, daß es zwar viele gibt, aber der Überblick häufig fehlt. Im Einzelfall fällt es daher meist schwer, die angemessenen Mechanismen zu finden und die Gewähr zu bieten, daß sie nicht nur einzeln wirksam sind, sondern auch in Kombination den nötigen Schutz liefern.

4.1 Mechanismenkatalog

Für Entwickler sicherer IT-Systeme wurde in REMO eine Vielzahl von Sicherheits-Mechanismen zusammengetragen [FFKK93]. Sie wurden nach einem einheitlichen Schema erfaßt, um sie besser gegenüberstellen und vergleichen zu können. Das verwendete Schema beinhaltet u.a. Abschnitte zur Funktionalität des Mechanismus, zu Bedrohungen, die bei seiner Nutzung relevant werden können, und zu seiner Effizienz. Außerdem wird auf über- und untergeordnete Mechanismen verwiesen, d.h. in welchen anderen Mechanismen der gerade betrachtete Mechanismus zum Einsatz kommt bzw. welche anderen er seinerseits benutzt.

Neben Einträgen zu Einzelmechanismen gibt es auch Mechanismeneinträge zu abstrakten Konzepten wie beispielsweise zu „Digitale Signatur“. Diese sind übergeordnet zu spezielleren Einträgen wie etwa der „ElGamal Signatur“. Die Funktionalität, die relevanten Bedrohungen etc. vererben sich von den über- auf die untergeordneten Mechanismen. Diese Klassifizierung der Mechanismen unterstützt Entwickler bei der Auswahl und Beurteilung von Sicherheitsmechanismen.

Sind die Sicherheits-Anforderungen bereits ermittelt und werden Mechanismen gesucht, die diese Anforderungen erfüllen, kann ein Entwickler an Hand der vorgegebenen grundlegenden Konzepte eine erste Auswahl treffen. Er muß beispielsweise prüfen, ob die notwendigen Voraussetzungen, die im entsprechenden Abschnitt des Eintrags aufgeführt sind, erfüllt werden können. Diese Voraussetzungen vererben sich, so daß schon auf dieser Ebene feststeht, welche untergeordneten Mechanismen überhaupt in Frage kommen, ohne diese einzeln betrachten zu müssen.

Die im jeweiligen Mechanismeneintrag aufgeführten Voraussetzungen umfassen u.U. den Einsatz weiterer Mechanismen, die in dem gerade beschriebenen zur Anwendung kommen, so daß ein Abhängigkeitsgeflecht entsteht. Auf Probleme, die bei solchen Kombinationen auftreten können, wird in jedem Eintrag besonders hingewiesen.

Der Katalog ist nicht auf Vollständigkeit ausgelegt. Er deckt aber die wichtigsten Bereiche ab (Identifikation/Authentifikation, Integrität, Vertraulichkeit, Zugriffskontrolle, Beweissicherung, Schlüsselverteilung). Vertiefte Aufmerksamkeit wurde den Kategorien Authentifikation und Zugriffskontrolle gewidmet.

4.2 Authentifikationsdienste und ihre verwendeten Mechanismen

Die Kategorie „Authentifikation" ist für sichere IT-Systeme angesichts der Vernetzung besonders wichtig [BuAN89]. Deshalb hat REMO dieses Thema verstärkt untersucht. In dem komplexen Basismechanismus „Authentifikation" wurden zunächst die erforderlichen Komponenten identifiziert [KlDa93, Fumy93]. Anhand des Katalogs [FFKK93] wurden spezielle Mechanismen zusammengestellt.

In REMO wurden eine formale Darstellung von Vertrauensbeziehungen unter den Instanzen eines Authentifikationsdienstes entwickelt und erste Vergleiche der Dienste vorgenommen [YaKB93]. Die Untersuchungen sind dann wesentlich, wenn reale Vertrauensbeziehungen berücksichtigt werden sollen. Im Gegensatz zu den üblichen Voraussetzungen bekannter Dienste sind diese im allgemeinen nicht hierarchisch. Die notwendigen Erweiterungen eines Authentifikationsprotokolls für diese nicht hierarchisch strukturierten Instanzen wurden vorgesehen.

4.3 Zugriffskontrolle

In vertrauenswürdigen IT-Systemen ist eine enge Kooperation der Basisdienste Authentifikation und Zugriffskontrolle notwendig. In offenen und verteilten Systemen ist der Inter-Domain-Bereich zwischen autonomen Systemen von essentieller Bedeutung. Hier kann insbesondere unter dem Druck gesellschaftlicher Forderungen nach verbindlicher IT-Sicherheit und nach entsprechender Evaluierung bzw. Zertifizierung nicht mehr davon ausgegangen werden, daß Dienstleistungssysteme ausschließlich in der Verfügungsgewalt des Service-Anbieters stehen (bzgl. Installation, Änderung, Administration und Konfiguration). Die Software ist hier zumindest Handlungsgegenstand der Institutionen: Hersteller, Evaluierer/Zertifizierer, Service-Anbieter, Service-Nutzer und anderer Parteien.

Der Service-Nutzer hat z.B. ein berechtigtes Interesse daran, daß die im IT-System eingesetzte Software und seine Konfiguration identisch bleibt mit einer zertifizierten Software-Version einer bestimmten Funktionalitäts/-Qualitäts-Einstufung. Allgemeiner können verschiedene Zertifizierungsabläufe verschiedener Parteien relevant werden. Dieses Zertifizierungs-Interesse des Service-Konsumenten kann sich auf andere statische oder dynamische, sicherheitsrelevante Qualifizierungs-, Anwendungs- und Kontroll-/ Steuerungs-Attribute der Software beziehen. Diese Thematik wird auch in innovativen

Vorschlägen wie [ECMA88/89], [GGKL89], [Park91] bisher nicht behandelt. Eine Einbeziehung dieser Attribute in die Systemkonfigurierung und Zugriffskontrolle ist notwendig.

Zur Lösung wird in REMO z. B. ein einfaches und integrierbares IT-Systemmodell (Preskriptoren-Deskriptoren-Modell) vorgeschlagen, das es gestattet, explizit Mehrparteien-, Evaluierungs-, Zusicherungs- und Vertrauenswürdigkeitsaspekte in die Zugriffskontrolle als Kontexte einzubeziehen. Gleichzeitig wird damit ein formalisierbares Ausdrucksmittel für die Bewertung vertrauenswürdiger IT-Systeme angeboten.

Mechanismen zum neuen IT-Systemmodell erlauben es, multiple Zugriffskontexte auch vertragsbasiert zwischen Parteien in verschiedenen Szenarien durchzusetzen (Policy-Server, Snapshot-Lock-Server, geteilte Konfigurationskontrolle mit Delegation). Es wurde gezeigt, wie unter Benutzung bekannter Basistechniken wie „Secure-Booting“ (vgl. [GGKL89], [Gros91]) die Durchsetzung oben genannter Anforderungen in verteilten Systemen mittels dieser neuen Mechanismenkonzepte für Zugriffskontrolle und organisationsgerechte Systemkonfiguration erfolgen kann [Stra93], [StLa93].

Methodisch wurde gleichzeitig die konstruktive Ankopplung der Mechanismen-Ebene an die Modell-Ebene untersucht (inkl. Mehr-Ebenen-Modellierung [Stra92]) und in diesem Zusammenhang Vorschläge in die Begutachtung des Drafts der Europäischen ITSEM-Richtlinie (ITSEM: Information Technology Security Evaluation Manual) eingebracht [StBD92].

5 Methodik – Der Weg zu sicheren IT-Systemen

Analysiert man die umfangreiche Literatur auf dem Gebiet der IT-Sicherheit, fallen zwei Grundprobleme auf:

1. Es gibt viele Arbeiten zu einzelnen Themengebieten (z.B. Sicherheitsmodelle, Sicherheits-Mechanismen und Sicherheits-Architektur), die Einzelvorschläge isoliert behandeln. Es existieren aber kaum Arbeiten zu folgenden Kernfragen:
   - Wie ermittelt man die Sicherheits-Anforderungen?
   - Wie erstellt man ein zu individuellen Sicherheits-Anforderungen passendes Sicherheitsmodell?
   - Wie soll die Sicherheits-Architektur gestaltet sein, damit sie den Sicherheits-Anforderungen gerecht wird?
   - Wie wählt man die geeigneten, zueinander passenden Sicherheits-Maßnahmen/ -Mechanismen aus?
2. Die für den Erhalt der Sicherheit während der System-Entwicklung notwendigen Schritte, wie z.B. die Auswahl der Sicherheits-Mechanismen oder die Erstellung des Sicherheitsmodells, werden nahezu immer losgelöst vom sonstigen Konstruktionsprozeß betrachtet. Für den Entwickler gibt es wenig Anleitung, wie er sicherheitsspezifische Konstruktionsschritte integriert im Entwicklungsprozeß durchführen kann.

Die Arbeiten zur Methodik innerhalb von REMO sind diesen beiden Problemfeldern gewidmet. Ihr Ziel ist, einen roten Faden für die Integration von Sicherheit in den Entwicklungsgang vorzugeben.

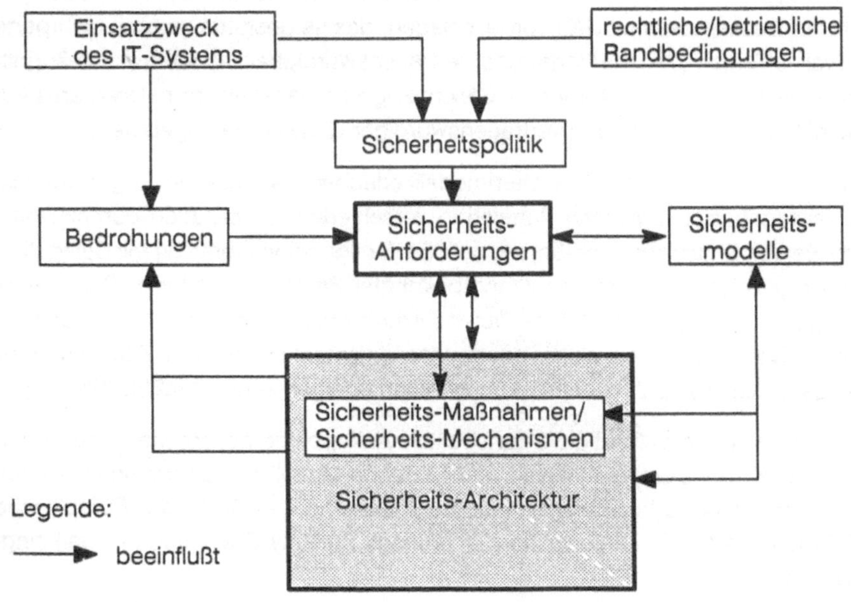

Abhängigkeiten im Konstruktionsprozeß

5.1 Erarbeitung von Konstruktionsschritten

Die Abbildung zeigt die zwischen den einzelnen Themengebieten relevanten Schnittstellen. Jede hat Auswirkungen auf die Beantwortung der vorher genannten Fragen. Die REMO-Ergebnisse zu diesen Fragen sind:

- *Sicherheits-Anforderungen:* (vgl. Kap. 2) Der Entwickler braucht Hilfe bei der Ermittlung und Formulierung seiner aufgrund der Bedrohungen und der geforderten Sicherheitspolitik nötigen Sicherheits-Anforderungen. Der Vorschlag in REMO [EKMM93] skizziert ein Vorgehen auf der Basis der Szenarien [HMS93], der Arbeiten zu den Sicherheits-Anforderungen und des IT-Sicherheitshandbuchs [ITSH92].

- *Sicherheitsmodelle* [AmKe93] werden als unverzichtbare Komponenten auf dem Entwicklungsweg betrachtet. Sie, im Einzelfall passend zu den Sicherheits-Anforderungen zu gestalten, ist schwierig, zumal sich auch die Sicherheits-Architektur und die Sicherheits-Maßnahmen/ -Mechanismen auf die Modellbildung auswirken.

  In REMO wurden aus der Literatur bekannte Modelle bzgl. ihrer Anwendbarkeit untersucht und wo nötig ergänzt [Klei93] [KeMu93]. Darüber hinaus wurden neue Sicherheitsmodelle (Gleichgewichtsmodell, Telekooperationsmodell, Preskriptoren-

Deskriptoren-Modell) für weitere Anwendungsbereiche entwickelt und deren Einsatzmöglichkeiten beschrieben [GrSt93] [Stra93].

- *Sicherheits-Maßnahmen/-Mechanismen:* (vgl. Kap. 4) Für die Erfüllung der Sicherheits-Anforderungen sind Sicherheits-Maßnahmen/ -Mechanismen zu bestimmen. Sicherheits-Architektur und Sicherheitsmodelle bilden dafür Rahmenbedingungen. Als Teil der Methodik wurde ein erstes Verfahren [EKMM93] entwickelt, das auf dem Katalog von Sicherheits-Mechanismen [FFKK93], den Kriterien für die Auswahl von Sicherheits-Mechanismen [BlPf93], deren Klassifikation und einer Zuordnung von Sicherheits-Maßnahmen zu Sicherheits-Anforderungen [Mund93] basiert.

5.2 Integration in den Konstruktionsprozeß

Ziel von REMO war es, in bestehende Entwicklungs-Verfahren die notwendigen sicherheitsrelevanten Konstruktionsschritte zu integrieren. Deswegen wurde zunächst einmal von einem konkreten Software-Engineering Modell abstrahiert und ein verallgemeinertes drei Phasen-Modell bestehend aus Anforderung, Spezifikation und Realisierung zugrunde gelegt. Je nach konkretem Modell sind die Abhängigkeiten zwischen diesen Phasen und die Arbeitsschritte in den Phasen unterschiedlich ausgeprägt.

In [EKMM93] wird gezeigt, wie die von REMO bereitgestellten Hilfsmittel innerhalb des „normalen" Konstruktionsprozesses eingesetzt werden können. So unterstützt z.B. der Katalog von Sicherheits-Mechanismen [FFKK93] die Konstruktion, in dem er beschreibt, in welche Teilkomponenten die Sicherheits-Mechanismen zerlegt bzw. wie diese aus einzelnen Teilkomponenten zusammengesetzt werden können. Darüberhinaus hilft der Katalog bei der Bedrohungs- und Risikoanalyse des Gesamtsystems, indem er die Schwächen der einzelnen Sicherheits-Mechanismen darstellt.

Werden die für den Erhalt der Sicherheit notwendigen Schritte in den allgemeinen Konstruktionsprozeß mit einbezogen, so ändert sich dieser in gewissem Umfang. Es müssen an einzelnen Stellen Ergänzungen vorgenommen werden, z.B. in der Anforderungsphase in Bezug auf die Ermittlung der Sicherheits-Anforderungen oder in der Konstruktionsphase in Bezug auf die Einbindung der Sicherheits-Mechanismen.

Insgesamt zeigte sich in REMO, daß sowohl Fragen der grundsätzlichen Vorgehensweise bei der Konstruktion sicherer Systeme als auch die Integration konkreter sicherheitsspezifischer Tätigkeiten in den Konstruktionsprozeß bislang viel zu wenig untersucht wurden. REMO hat damit begonnen. Das Thema Methodik wird weiter bearbeitet werden müssen.

6 Werkzeuge zur Aufwertung existenter IT-Systeme

Nicht jedes IT-System ist von vornherein mit einem Sicherheitsanspruch konzipiert worden. Viele erprobte, aber nicht mit Sicherheit ausgestattete Systeme werden breit angewendet. Die Verwendung dieser herkömmlichen Systeme wird durch steigende Sicherheitsbedrohungen immer problematischer und langfristig sogar unmöglich.

Zur Lösung dieser Problematik wird in REMO-E eine Erweiterung der herkömmlichen IT-Systeme um ausgewählte Sicherheits-Mechanismen vorgenommen, die deren Komponenten mit einer Sicherheitsschale umgeben. Damit können kurzfristig wesentliche Sicherheitsbedrohungen abgewehrt werden. Durch die hohe Flexibilität dieses Ansatzes können die jeweils akuten Bedrohungen berücksichtigt werden. Der Ansatz ist wichtig, da in Zukunft die Forderung nach sicheren Programmpaketen, aufgrund der steigenden Sensibilität der Anwender in Sicherheitsfragen, Standard werden wird.

In REMO-E wurden Werkzeuge zur Analyse des Sicherheitsbedarfs und zur Modellierung einer Lösung sowie zur Integration [Schi90] von Sicherheitstechnik entwickelt. Diese verwenden eine Sicherheitsbibliothek, in der unterschiedliche Sicherheits-Mechanismen [Gey93], [Witt93], [Mant93] zur Verfügung gestellt werden. Die Werkzeuge unterstützen eine Absicherung sowohl im lokalen Bereich (z.B. eine lokale Zugriffssicherung an einer Workstation), als auch eine Sicherung von verteilten Systemen, wie es z.B. ein Videokonferenzsystem [Schu93] darstellt.

Die Funktionsfähigkeit der entwickelten Werkzeuge und -Mechanismen wird durch den Einsatz in unterschiedlichen Demonstrationsobjekten nachgewiesen. Dabei wurden bisher folgende, wichtigen Anwendungsbereichen entsprechende Szenarien realisiert:

- Nutzungsrechteverwaltung und -durchsetzung in einem Dokumentenverwaltungssystem [Gey93] *(Eine sehr große medizinische Datenbank (Adonis) wird weltweit von Medizinern/Wissenschaftlern/Autoren/Verlegern/.. interaktiv benutzt.)*
- Authentifikation und Vertraulichkeitsgewährleistung in einem PC-integrierten Videokonferenzsystem [Schu93] *(Kooperation von mehreren Teilnehmern per Ton-/Bewegtbild-/Datenübertragung (über Mehrpunktverbindung auf LANs oder WANs) auf der Grundlage beliebiger Anwendungssysteme ihrer PCs.)*

7 Neue Module zur Ergänzung

Die nachträgliche Forderung nach Sicherheit tritt beim Einsatz existenter IT-Systeme immer häufiger auf. Um dieser entsprechen zu können, wurden innerhalb von REMO-E verschiedene neue Module konzipiert und realisiert. Diese ergänzen bestehende Systeme und schützen sie vor bestimmten Grundbedrohungen und Risiken. Den Moduln gemeinsam ist, daß sie auf verfügbare Hard- und Software aufsetzen und damit eine relativ kostengünstige Möglichkeit bieten, bestehende Systeme um Sicherheitsfunktionalität zu ergänzen.

7.1 Chipkartenmodul

Realisiert wurde ein SW-Modul, das auf Anforderung durch eine Anwendung eine digitale Unterschrift erzeugt bzw. überprüft [Laun91]. Diese wird auf der Basis des MD4-Hashverfahrens (MD = Message Digest) und des ElGamal-Protokolls für elliptische Kurven berechnet bzw. verifiziert. Die Chipkarte dient dabei als sicherer Schlüsselspeicher. Die Kommunikation zwischen Modul und Chipkarte ist über eine symmetrische Verschlüsselung abgesichert.

Das Chipkartenmodul bietet vielfältige Einsatzmöglichkeiten, u.a. bei der Software-Versiegelung [HiLa92], E-Mail, dem elektronischen Zahlungsverkehr und der Zugangskontrolle. In all diesen Bereichen kann es der Erkennung unbefugter Zugriffe bei signierten Dokumenten (Dateien, Programmen) und zur Realisierung integrer und authentischer Kommunikation dienen.

7.2 Netzsicherheitsmodul

Das Modul stellt eine universelle Kryptoschnittstelle zwischen Systemkomponenten und verbindendem Netz, aber auch für lokale Zwecke bereit. Es verfügt über die folgenden Grundfunktionen: Ver- und Entschlüsselung, Berechnung und Prüfung eines Message Authentification Codes (MAC) und Schlüsselmanagementfunktionen. Ferner ist es in der Lage, Audit-Daten zu generieren und auf einem gesicherten Kanal an eine zentrale Instanz zu übermitteln [EKRW91].

Das Netzsicherheitsmodul kann einerseits für eine vertrauliche und integre Kommunikation (Netzsicherheit) benutzt werden, andererseits kann es dafür eingesetzt werden, Dateien vertraulich und integer zu speichern (lokale Sicherheitsdienste). Die Protokollierung sicherheitsrelevanter Ereignisse trägt zusätzlich noch zur Beweissicherung bei.

7.3 Audit-Analyse-Tool

Dieses Modul erlaubt sowohl eine satzweise Analyse von Daten als auch eine Analyse von komplexen Verhaltensmustern [FrKa91]. Dazu verfügt es über eine flexible Regelsprache, die eine Formulierung der auszuwertenden Verhaltensmuster ermöglicht. Die Analyse kann dabei je nach Einsatz des Tools online oder offline vorgenommen werden.

Das Audit-Analyse-Tool ist vielseitig einsetzbar, z.B. können Anwendungen wie Transaktionen in Datenbanken überwacht werden, ebenso ist der Einsatz zur Fehlererkennung und Diagnose möglich. In Kombination mit dem Netzsicherheitsmodul lassen sich Sicherheitsüberwachungen in Netzen durchführen.

7.4 Neue Konzepte und Technologien

Viele Sicherheits-Mechanismen, so wie sie in den hier beschriebenen Moduln zum Einsatz kommen, basieren auf kryptographischen Mechanismen. Um diese effizient ausführen und sicher betreiben zu können, bedarf es einer adäquaten Hardware-Unterstützung. Im Rahmen der Weiterentwicklung der Konzepte für die Sicherheitsmoduln und der Prüfung, inwieweit neue Technologien für diese Moduln eingesetzt werden können, war es eine Aufgabe, die entsprechende Hardware-Unterstützung zu ermöglichen. Dazu wurden die Bildung einer flexiblen Modulbibliothek für anwendungsspezifische Kryptobausteine [GeKö93] vorangetrieben und das Thema „modulare Architektur" für Sicherheitsboards [Wall93] untersucht.

Das Audit-Analyse-Tool ist ebenfalls eine gute Basis für weitere Konzepte. Eine Möglichkeit ist die Überwachung und Risikoanalyse eines laufenden Systems

(Sicherheitsleitstand) [FHLPS93]. Dieser soll die Durchsetzung einer definierten Sicherheitspolitik in einem IT-System ermöglichen. Hierfür wurde ein erstes Konzept entwikkelt, dessen Weiterentwicklung und prototypische Realisierung eine Aufgabe für die Zukunft sein wird.

8 Ausblick

Trotz aller vielversprechenden Ansätze und Ergebnisse im Bereich Sicherheit bei IT-Systemen fehlt derzeit eine geschlossene Vorgehensweise, die zielstrebig und zuverlässig zu sicheren Systemen führt. Ergänzend zu methodischen Anleitungen ist natürlich die Erforschung, (Weiter-) Entwicklung und Erprobung grundlegender Konzepte nötig.

In der weiteren Arbeit werden folgende wichtige Ergebnisse angestrebt:

a) Eine *lückenlose Methodik* für die Konstruktion sicherer IT-Systeme in Form einer Anweisung für den Entwickler (*„Entwicklungshandbuch")*. Dieses Handbuch soll an ausgewählten Stellen durch geeignete Entwurfswerkzeuge (*„Entwicklungswerkzeuge"*) ergänzt und unterstützt werden.

b) Der *Nachweis der Praktikabilität*. An einem Demonstrator wird die Durchführung der Entwicklungsschritte erprobt. Aus dem *Einsatz der Methodik* werden wertvolle Erkenntnisse zur Verbesserung und Ergänzung des Entwicklungshandbuchs bzw. der Entwicklungswerkzeuge erwartet.

c) Eine *Sicherheits-Architektur*, die als *„kanonische" Struktur* für sichere IT-Systeme gelten kann. Ähnlich wie in der Vergangenheit beim Compilerbau eine Basisstruktur gefunden wurde, mit der Compiler für verschiedene Sprachen einheitlich, zuverlässig und effizient erstellt werden können, soll die vorgeschlagene Sicherheits-Architektur als „Bauplan" für sichere IT-Systeme evaluiert werden.

d) *Konzepte und Lösungen* für zentrale Basisdienste und den Einsatz. Lücken konzeptioneller Art blockieren die Akzeptanz. Z.B. müssen die diversen Verantwortlichkeiten für IT-Systeme präzise abgebildet werden (*Mehr-Parteien-Verantwortung*) oder das Vertrauen in die Sicherheit von IT-gestützter *Kooperation* zwischen verschiedenen autonomen Bereichen fundiert werden (Zugriffskontrolle und Authentifikation). Hindernisse für den breiten Einsatz liegen auch auf technischer Seite. Es fehlen standardisierte oder *standardisierbare Schnittstellenvorgaben* zwischen Anwender und Anwendung (Bedienung) sowie zwischen Anwendung und verfügbaren Sicherheitsmechanismen.
   Trotz aller Vorkehrungen muß die Sicherheit permanent durch Früherkennung von Risikosituationen und schnelle Reaktionen im operativen Einsatz gewährleistet werden. Der schon genannte *„Sicherheitsleitstand"* ist ein geeignetes Mittel dafür.

9 Literatur

[AmAt92] E. Amann, H. Atzmüller, IT-Sicherheit - was ist das?, DuD 6/92 Vieweg 1992.

[AmKe93] E. Amann, V. Kessler, Sicherheitsmodelle in Theorie und Praxis, Euro-Arch '93

[BlPf93] U. Blöcher, A. Pfau: Auswahlstrategien für Sicherheits-Mechanismen zur Erfüllung von Sicherheitsanforderungen, REMO-Arbeitsbericht Siemens.REMO.0100.

[BSA92] W. E. Kühnhauser, H. Härtig und O. Kowalski, Die BirliX Sicherheitsarchitektur, DuD 11/92, Vieweg 1992.

[BSA93] H. Härtig, W.E. Kühnhauser und O. Kowalski, The BirliX Security Architecture, erscheint in Journal of Computer Security, IOS Press, 1993 (ist auch als GMD Arbeitsbericht 657 und als REMO-Arbeitsbericht GMD.REMO.0054) erhältlich.

[BuAN89] M. Burrows, M. Abadi, R. Needham: A Logic of Authentication, Proceedings of the 12th ACM Symposium on Operating Systems Principles, Litchfield Park, Arizona, December 1989.

[ECMA88/89] ECMA-European Computer Manufactures Association, Security in Open Systems - A Security Framework, ECMA TR/46, Genf, July 1988, Data Elements and Service Definitions, Standard ECMA 138, 1989.

[EKMM93] G. Eisen, H. Kurth, H. Metz, S. Mund: Konstruktion sicherer IT-Systeme: Prinzipien, Hilfsmittel, Techniken, REMO-Arbeitsbericht IABG.REMO.0158.

[EKRW91] A. Eichhorn, P. Kob, H-P. Rieß, D. Walter, Sicherheitsmodule in Netzen, REMO-Arbeitsbericht SIEMENS.REMO.0023.

[FFKK93] O. Fries, A. Fritsch, V. Kessler, B. Klein: Sicherheits-Mechanismen: Bausteine zur Entwicklung sicherer Systeme, Oldenbourg Verlag, Reihe: Sicherheit in der Informationstechnik, erscheint 1993.

[FHLPS93] J. Fichtner, A. Hentschel, J. Lindmeyer, C. Persy, F. Schalkowski, Riskmanagement für IT-Systeme, Anforderungskatalog für einen Sicherheitsleitstand (in Arbeit).

[FrAm92] A. Fritsch, E. Amann, Attackensammlung, REMO-Arbeitsbericht IABG.REMO.0107.

[FrKa91] O. Fries, H. Kramer, Wissensbasierte Auswertung von Protokolldaten, REMO-Arbeitsbericht SIEMENS.REMO.0029.

[Fumy93] W. Fumy: Designprinzipien für Authentifikations-Mechanismen, Tagungsband der VIS 1993, Vieweg Verlag (erscheint 1993).

[GeKö93] J. Geßner, S. Kösters, Architekturkonzept für flexible Kryptomodule (in Arbeit).

[Gey93] M. Gey: Die Nutzungsrechteverwaltung, REMO-Arbeitsbericht TELES.REMO.0028.

[GGHI89] W. Gleißner, R. Grimm, S. Herda, H. Isselhorst, Manipulation in Rechnern und Netzen, Addison-Wesley 1989.

[GGKL89] M. Gasser, A. Goldstein, C. Kaufmann and B. Lampson, The Digital Distributed System Security Architecture, Proceedings of the 1989 National Computer Security Conference, USA, 1989.

[Gros91] M. Gross, Vertrauenswürdiges Booten als Grundlage authentischer Basissysteme, Informatik-Fachberichte 271, Tagungsband VIS'91, Verläßliche Informationssysteme, Springer-Verlag 1991.

[GrSt93] R. Grimm, A. Steinacker, Das Kooperations- und Gleichgewichtsmodell - Theorie und Praxis, Tagungsband der VIS 1993, Springer (erscheint 1993).

[HiLa92] H.-J. Hitz, R. Laun, Softwareversiegelung bei der Entwicklung von Software auf kryptographischer Basis, DuD 1/92, Vieweg 1992.

[HKL91] H. Härtig, W. E. Kühnhauser und J. Liedtke, Issues in Security and Fault Tolerance, in Operating Systems for the Nineties and Beyond, Lecture Notes in Computer Science, No. 563, Springer Verlag, 1991.

[HMS93] S. Herda, S. Mund, A. Steinacker: Szenarien zur Sicherheit informationstechnischer Systeme, Oldenbourg Verlag, Reihe: Sicherheit in der Informationstechnik.

[ITSH92] BSI-Bundesamt für Sicherheit in der Informationstechnik (Hrsg.) IT-Sicherheitshandbuch: Handbuch für die sichere Anwendung der Informationstechnik, BSI 7105, Bonn, März 1992.

[ITSK89] ZSI (Zentralstelle für Sicherheit in der Informationstechnik, jetzt BSI) (Hrsg.), IT-Sicherheitskriterien: Kriterien für die Bewertung der Sicherheit von Systemen der Informationstechnik, Bundesanzeiger 1989.

[KeMu93] U. Kessler, S. Mund, Studie Sicherheits-Modelle, REMO-Arbeitsbericht Siemens.REMO.0118.

[KlDa93] B. Klein, F. Damm: Komponenten informationstechnischer Authentifikationsdienste, Tagungsband der VIS 1993, Vieweg Verlag.

[Klei93] B. Klein (Hrsg), Abschlußbericht Sicherheitsmodelle, REMO-Arbeitsbericht EISS.REMO.0109.

[KoHa90] O. Kowalski und H. Härtig, Protection in the BirliX Operating System, in Proceedings of the 10th International IEEE Conference on Distributed Computing Systems, Paris, Mai 1990.

[Kurt91] H. Kurth, Formale Spezifikation und Verifikation – Ein Überblick, Tagungsband der VIS'91.

[Mant93] H. Manthey, Der Einsatz von Sicherheits-Technik in Videokonferenzsystemen (in Arbeit).

[Metz92] H. Metz, Ermittlung, Darstellung und Evaluation von Sicherheits-Anforderungen. IABG.REMO.0135.

[Mund93] S. Mund: Sicherheitsanforderungen - Sicherheitsmaßnahmen, Tagungsband der VIS 1993, Vieweg Verlag.

[NiCa93] H. Nieters, N. Cacutalua, RSL-Spezifikation der ADT-Schnittstelle der BirliX Sicherheitsarchitektur, GMD.REMO.0068, (wird veröffentlicht).

[Park91] T. Parker, A Secure System for Applications in a multi-vendor Environment, (the SESAME Project), National Computer Security Conference 1991, USA.

[PeSt91] B. Pertzsch, A. Steinacker, Sicherheitsanforderungen - Der Schlüssel zur Sicherheit, Datasafe 1991, Vde-Verlag, 1991.

[REMO92] H-P. Rieß, Bericht über den REMO-Workshop Sicherheits-Architekturen, DuD 10/92, Vieweg 1992.

[RLG91] The RAISE Language Group, The RAISE Specification Language CRI/RAISE/DOK/1, 1991.

[Schi90] S. Schindler, Vortrag: The EDISAM-Toolkit, Safecom 11/90, London.

[Schu93] J. Schulze, Das TELES.VISION-System – Sicherheitsanforderungen und Sicherheitsmodule, Euro-Arch '93.

[StBD92] H. Strack, Th. Beth. Y. Desmedt, Constructive Approaches to overcome Limitations in Modeling, Specifying and Architectures for IT-Security - Comments and Suggestions for ITSEM, Commission of the European Communities, ITSEM Review Workshop, Brüssel, Sept. 1992, auch als E.I.S.S.-Report 92/10.

[StLa93] H. Strack, K.-Y. Lam, Context-Dependent Access Control in Distributed Systems, IFIP/SEC'93 - 9th International Computer Security Symposium and Exhibition, Toronto, Mai 1993 (erscheint im Tagungsband).

[Stra91] H. Strack, Formale Modellierung + Spezifikation + Verifikation = Sicherheit?, Tagungsband Datasafe'91, VDE Verlag, Berlin 1991.

[Stra92] H. Strack, Constructive Methods for IT-Security - the necessary completion of "formal" Approaches, Proceedings of the 7th European Conference on Information Systems Security, Control & Audit (Brüssel, Nov.1992), Elsevier Publishers, Brüssel, 1992.

[Stra93] H. Strack, Mehr-Parteien-Zertifizierung für kontextorientierte Zugriffskontrollen in verteilten IT-Systemen, 3. Deutscher IT-Sicherheitskongreß der BSI, Bonn April 1993, (erscheint im Tagungsband).

[Wall93] S. Wallstab, Modulares Architekturkonzept für die HW-/SW-Implementierung von Sicherheits-Subsystemen, (in Arbeit).

[Witt93] H. Witt: Ein Dienst zur Verteilung von Sitzungsschlüsseln, REMO-Arbeitsbericht REMO.TELES.0031.

[YaKB93] R. Yahalom, B. Klein, Th. Beth: Trust Relationships in Secure Systems - A Distributed Authentication Perspektive, Proceedings IEEE Symposium on Research in Security and Privacy 1993.

Sicherheitsmodelle in Theorie und Praxis

Esther Amann
IABG Abt. ITE
Postfach 1212
D-85503 Ottobrunn
amann@ite.iabg.de

Volker Kessler
Siemens AG
ZFE ST SN 5
D-81730 München
kessler@ztivax.zfe.siemens.de

2. Juli 1993

Zusammenfassung

Die Untersuchung des Begriffs „Sicherheitsmodell“ führt zu dem Ergebnis, daß ein Sicherheitsmodell ein Modell im traditionellen Sinne der Wissenschaft ist, nämlich eine Beschreibung mit Abstraktion auf das Wesentliche. Eine (formale) Modellierung der Sicherheitsanforderungen ist eine wichtige Voraussetzung, um einerseits hohe Sicherheit zu erreichen und andererseits diese Sicherheit nachzuweisen. Die aus der Literatur bekannten Sicherheitsmodelle greifen jeweils einzelne Sicherheitsaspekte heraus, die sie eingehend analysieren. Der Sicherheitsbedarf eines realen Systems umfaßt jedoch typischerweise eine individuelle Kombination verschiedener Sicherheitsaspekte. Deshalb existiert zu einem vorgegebenen System nur in Ausnahmefällen bereits ein für seine Bedürfnisse genau passendes Sicherheitsmodell. Dies wird an einem Beispiel erläutert.

1 Was ist ein Sicherheitsmodell?

Grob gesprochen ist ein Sicherheitsmodell eine abstrakte Beschreibung eines (IT-)Systems, um die Sicherheitseigenschaften analysieren zu können. Bekannte Sicherheitsmodelle sind:

Sicherheitsmodell	Datum	Besonderer Aspekt
Bell-LaPadula [2]	1973-76	Vertraulichkeit (hierarch.)
Denning [8]	1976	Vertraulichkeit (Informationsfluß)
Biba [4]	1977	Integrität (hierarch.)
Goguen-Meseguer [11]	1982	Nichtbeeinflussung
Clark-Wilson [7]	1987	Integrität: wohlgeformte Transaktionen & Aufgabenteilung
Chines. Mauer [5]	1989	Kombination von wahlfreier und festgelegter Zugriffskontrolle
Terry-Wiseman [26]	1989	Vertraulichkeit & Integrität

Tabelle 1: Bekannte Sicherheitsmodelle

Das Bell-LaPadula-Modell ist eines der ersten Sicherheitsmodell und wohl das bekannteste. Die Spalte *Besonderer Aspekt* in Tabelle 1 gibt jeweils stichwortartig die wesentliche

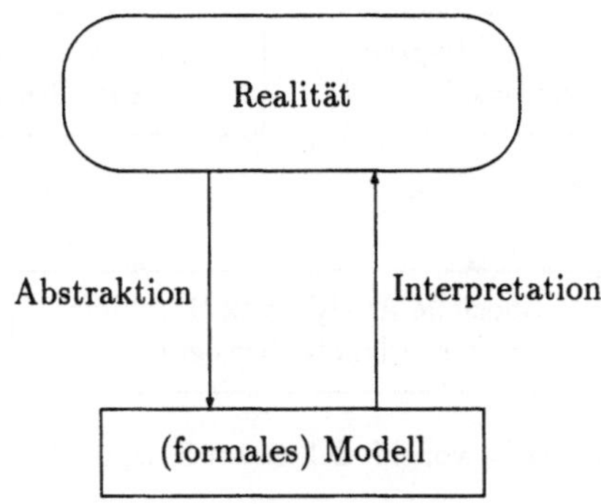

Abbildung 1: Modell als Abbild

Neuerung bei dem Sicherheitsmodell gegenüber seinen Vorgängern an. Eine detaillierte Beschreibung der Modelle findet man u.a. in [14].

Obwohl viele Sicherheitsmodelle präsentiert werden, existiert anscheinend keine einheitliche Meinung darüber, was ein Sicherheitsmodell genau ist. Dieses unterschiedliche Verständnis scheint der (bewußte oder unbewußte) Knackpunkt für manche Auseinandersetzung zu sein, vgl. etwa die Diskussion zwischen Bell und McLean [3, 15, 16].

Dies ist nun ein weiterer Versuch, „endlich ein für allemal zu klären, was ein Sicherheitsmodell ist".

1.1 Modelle

Der Begriff „Modell" wird allgemein in vielfältiger Weise benutzt. In der Wissenschaft gibt es zwei wesentlich verschiedene Verwendungsarten, vgl. [6]:

Modell als Abbild ist ein Abbild der Realität[1] unter Hervorhebung für wesentlich erachteter Eigenschaften und Außerachtlassen als nebensächlich angesehener Aspekte.

In diesem Sinne ist ein Modell eine Abstraktion, siehe Abb. 1. (Dies ist der traditionelle Modellbegriff in der Wissenschaft.)

Modell in der mathematischen Logik (Modelltheorie) ist eine mathematische Struktur, die die Axiome eines vorgegebenen Axiomensystems erfüllt. Insbesondere folgt aus der Existenz eines Modells, daß das Axiomensystem widerspruchsfrei ist (vorausgesetzt, das Modell ist widerspruchsfrei).

Ein solches Modell ist eine Konkretisierung.

Natürlich kann ein Modell im Sinne der mathematischen Modelltheorie gleichzeitig auch ein Abbild der Realität sein. Beispielsweise ist der reelle dreidimensionale Raum einerseits ein Abbild für die uns lokal umgebende Wirklichkeit, andererseits erfüllt er die Axiome der euklidischen Geometrie, ist also unter diesem Aspekt ein Modell der mathematischen Modelltheorie.

[1] z.B. Natur, Wirtschaftsgeschehen,...

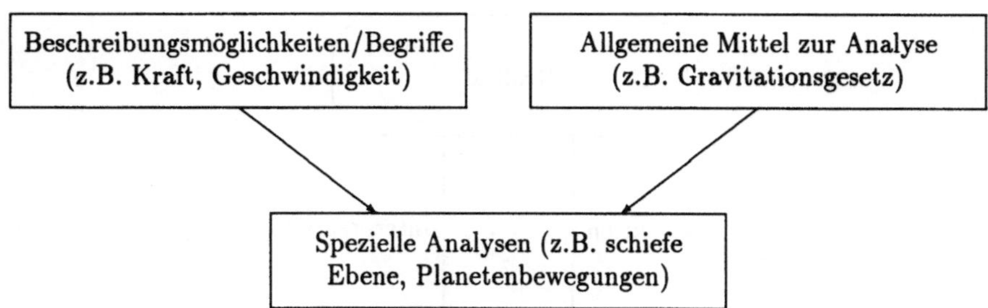

Abbildung 2: Charakteristika von Modellen am Beispiel der klassischen Mechanik

Obwohl Sicherheitsmodelle meistens in mathematisch-logischer Sprache formuliert sind, sind sie in erster Linie Abbilder und keine Modelle im Sinne der mathematischen Logik.[2]

Ein **Modell als Abbild** ist ein Mittel zur Beschreibung der Realität und umfaßt als solches drei Funktionen:

1. **Bildung von Begriffen** der Wirklichkeit
2. Grundlage zur **Erklärung** von bereits beobachteten Phänomenen
3. Grundlage zur **Voraussage** von zukünftigen Phänomenen

Um die genannten Funktionen zu erfüllen, haben Modelle drei charakteristische Eigenschaften, vgl. Abb. 2 und [3]

- **Beschreibungsmöglichkeiten/Begriffe:** Man kann mit Hilfe des Modells die den Beobachter interessierenden Phänomene der Realität präzise beschreiben.
- Es stellt **allgemeine Mittel** zur Analyse der Phänomene zur Verfügung.
- Es enthält **spezielle Analysen** sowohl von bekannten Resultaten wie auch zur Vorhersage zukünftiger Resultate.

Als Beispiel betrachten wir die klassische Mechanik: Durch die Einführung der Begriffe Kraft, Bewegung etc. hat man Beschreibungsmöglichkeiten. Das Gravitationsgesetz ist ein allgemeines Mittel, um die beobachteten Phänomene zu analysieren. Spezielle Analysen erhält man, wenn man diese fundamentalen Gesetze für konkrete Situationen anwendet, z.B. Planetenbewegung, schiefe Ebene etc.

1.2 Sicherheitsmodelle

Bell betont in [3], daß er und LaPadula genau dieses „Modell-als-Abbild"-Verständnis und die oben genannten Kriterien auf Sicherheitsmodelle angewandt haben (S. 9):

> ...the Bell-LaPadula model was undertaken to provide a before-the-fact analysis tool for the consideration of the general design problem of conceiving and constructing "secure computer systems". It was held that such modeling

[2]Ein solcher Hinweis ist erfahrungsgemäß zur Vermeidung von Mißverständnissen notwendig, da sich viele mathematisch Vorgebildete mit dem Thema Sicherheit beschäftigen und evtl. das falsche Vorverständnis von Modell mitbringen.

of computer security required that a resulting "model" satisfies the following characteristics:

- descriptive capability — the ability to describe the situation of interest;
- general mechanisms — analytical tools to aid in the analysis of "secure computer systems"; and
- specific solutions — direct synthesis and analysis aid in the consideration of specific computer systems.

Als Einwand gegen dieses Verständnis von Sicherheitsmodellen könnte man auf einen scheinbar fundamentalen Unterschied zu Modellen im traditionellen Sinne der Wissenschaft verweisen: In den Naturwissenschaften ist die reale Welt vorgegeben und unabhängig von der Modellbildung, wogegen Sicherheitsmodelle dazu dienen, IT-Systeme zu entwickeln, d.h. etwas in der realen Welt zu schaffen (vgl. obiges Zitat von Bell: Sicherheitsmodell als ein „*before-the-fact* analysis tool").

Zum Teil ist aber auch bei bisherigen wissenschaftlichen Modellen eine Rückkopplung möglich, ja teilweise sogar beabsichtigt. So stellt man beispielsweise in der Ökologie und in der Volkswirtschaft Modelle auf, um korrigierend in den ökologischen bzw. wirtschaftlichen Kreislauf eingreifen zu können.

Somit ist diese Eigenschaft des Sicherheitsmodells nicht im Gegensatz zu anderen Modellen als Abbilder, sondern mehr oder weniger auch in diesen vorhanden. Deswegen unterstützen wir die Position von Bell, wonach Sicherheitsmodelle durchaus Modelle im traditionellen wissenschaftlichen Sinne sind. Dies führt zu folgender Definition:

> Ein **Sicherheitsmodell** ist eine abstrakte Beschreibung der nach der zugrundeliegenden Sicherheitsanforderungen für wesentlich gehaltenen Aspekte der Sicherheit eines IT-Systems, wobei die als nicht sicherheitsrelevant geltenden Aspekte unterdrückt werden.

1.3 Formale Sicherheitsmodelle

Ist ein Sicherheitsmodell in mathematischer Formelsprache mit eventuell verbindenden Texten geschrieben, so wird es *formal* genannt. Ein Sicherheitsmodell ist je nach Intention und Thema mehr oder weniger formal. Extremfälle sind einerseits das stark formalisierte Bell-LaPadula-Modell und andererseits das in Prosa gehaltene Clark-Wilson-Modell[3]. Allerdings reicht für eine abstrahierende Beschreibung der formale Anteil nicht aus, es kommen immer noch informelle Bestandteile hinzu, die z.B. in den zugrundeliegenden Annahmen stecken.

Die Vorteile einer Formalisierung sind:

- Präzision und Eindeutigkeit der formalen Sprache
- Möglichkeit, Beweise zu führen
- Unterstützung der formalen Spezifikation und Implementierung

Ein formales Sicherheitsmodell mit zugehörigen Konsistenzbeweisen ist eine notwendige Voraussetzung, um bei der Evaluierung eine hohe Qualitätsstufe zu erreichen, siehe Abschnitt 2.2.

[3]Bei dem letzteren ist eine vollständige Formalisierung gar nicht möglich, da es sich bei der dort angesprochenen Überprüfung der externen Konsistenz (Übereinstimmung der Daten im IT-System mit der realen Welt) um einen semantischen Aspekt handelt, siehe Abschnitt 4.3.

2 Wozu dienen Sicherheitsmodelle?

Abgesehen davon, daß Sicherheitsmodelle grundsätzlich eine Verstehenshilfe sind, wollen wir ihre Rolle für die Konstruktion sicherer Systeme erörtern. Goguen und Meseguer bringen sie als Idealvorstellung auf folgende Kurzform [11, S. 12]

> The purpose of the so-called "security model" is to provide a basis for determining whether or not a system is secure, and if not, for detecting its flaws.

Da IT-Systeme letztendlich verkauft werden sollen, ist der Überzeugungsaspekt wichtig, was im folgenden Zitat von Wiseman auf dem REMO-Workshop [27] zum Ausdruck kommt:

> The purpose of a security model is to convince the buyer of a system that the system is secure.

2.1 Sicherheitsmodelle als Überzeugungsmittel

Sicherheitsmodelle sind deshalb so wichtig, weil *Sicherheit* eine Eigenschaft ist, die im Gegensatz zu anderen Eigenschaften *empirisch nicht verifizierbar* ist. Will man z.B. nachweisen, daß ein Auto 200 km/h fahren kann, so testet man dies einfach. Will man dagegen nachweisen, daß man im Auto geschützt ist, so kann man lediglich gewisse Unfallarten simulieren, um zu demonstrieren, daß bei diesen Unfällen keine Personen zu Schaden kommen. Dies heißt aber noch nicht, daß das Auto wirklich sicher ist, weil es Unfälle geben könnte, die man nicht getestet hat.

Analoges gilt für IT-Systeme: Die Schnelligkeit eines IT-Systems kann man testen. Bei Sicherheitseigenschaften wie z.B. Vertraulichkeit kann man lediglich demonstrieren, daß das IT-System gegen gewisse Angriffe geschützt ist. Aber es könnte ja noch weitere Angriffe geben, gegen die das System nicht geschützt ist.

Die Unmöglichkeit, Sicherheit empirisch zu verifizieren, ist darin begründet, daß Sicherheit im allgemeinen als *negierter Existenzsatz* formuliert wird, etwa „Es soll keine Möglichkeit geben, die Personen im Auto zu verletzen" bzw. „Ein Nichtbefugter darf keine Möglichkeit haben, die vertraulichen Daten zu erfahren". Negierte Existenzsätze sind aber in ihrer logischen Form Allsätze und Allsätze können nicht empirisch verifiziert, sondern höchstens *falsifiziert* werden, vgl. [21, Kap. 3, Abs. 15] [4]. Man kann nicht *alle* Angriffe testen. Dagegen ist die Aussage über die Geschwindigkeit eines Autos oder eines Computers als (positiver) singulärer Satz empirisch verifizierbar.

Wegen der Unmöglichkeit, Sicherheitseigenschaften empirisch zu verifizieren, möchte man Sicherheitseigenschaften so weit wie möglich *formal beweisen.*

Ausgangspunkt sind dabei die anwendungsbezogenen Sicherheitsanforderungen. Diese sind zunächst einmal nur verbal (in Worten) gegeben. Zum Beispiel könnte eine Sicherheitsanforderung lauten: „Wichtige Informationen dürfen nicht nach außen gelangen." Diese Anforderung kann nun noch weiter konkretisiert werden, indem man Klassifikationen (vertraulich, geheim, streng geheim) für die Daten und Personen einführt und fordert, daß eine Person keine Daten oberhalb ihrer Klassifikation erfährt. Würde man nun ein solches System implementieren, so müßte man bei der Argumentation, daß dieses System die Sicherheitsanforderungen erfüllt, eine große Brücke von den Anforderungen zu der Implementierung schlagen. Sinnvoller ist es, auf diesem Weg von oben nach unten mehrere Verfeinerungsschritte einzurichten, so daß man nur auf kleinen Etappen argumentieren

[4] Die Aussage „Alles Kupfer leitet" läßt sich eben empirisch nicht verifizieren, da man nicht jedes Stück Kupfer untersuchen kann.

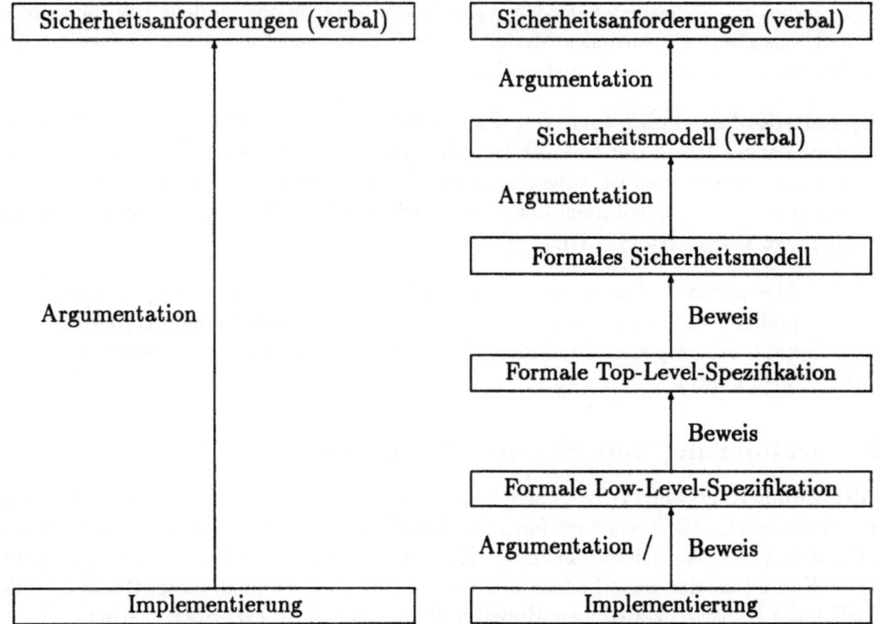

Abbildung 3: Verfeinerungsprozeß für die Entwicklung sicherer IT-Systeme

muß, warum das nachfolgende das vorhergehende impliziert, vgl. Abb. 3. Innerhalb formaler Verfeinerungsschritte kann man diese Übereinstimmung eventuell beweisen, doch selbst wenn man dies nicht kann oder aus Kostengründen nicht macht, ist die Anwendung der formalen Sprache vorteilhaft wegen ihrer Präzision und dem Zwang, das Problem systematisch und detailliert zu durchdenken.

Die Abbildung 3 drückt aus, daß man durch den Wechsel zwischen verbaler und formaler Ausdruckweise keinen vollständigen Sicherheitsbeweis erbringen kann. Insbesondere ist die Lücke zwischen formalem Modell und Implementierung eine Frage der Softwarekorrektheit, vgl. [10, S. 133]:

> The state of the art in verification today does not permit us to eliminate the informal argument between the implementation level and the lowest level of formal specification, and this informal step remains the weakest link in the overall model-to-implementation correspondence argument.

Durch die Einführung der Zwischenstufen kann man das Vertrauen in die Sicherheit des Systems erhöhen. Je nach Komplexität des Systems und beabsichtigtem Sicherheitsniveau kann man entweder manche Stufen auslassen (z.B. das verbale Sicherheitsmodell) oder weitere Stufen einfügen.

Zur Verdeutlichung der Rolle des Sicherheitsmodells grenzen wir es gegenüber der nächsthöheren bzw. nächsttieferen Ebene im Verfeinerungsprozeß ab:

Sicherheitsmodell versus Sicherheitsanforderungen Die Sicherheitsanforderungen seien für den Entwickler vorgegeben. Er modelliert das (geplante) IT-System und integriert die Sicherheitsanforderungen (in der Sprache des Modells!) in dieses Modell. Existiert ein formales Modell, so verifiziert man formal die Konsistenz der Sicherheitsanforderungen zueinander.

Sicherheitsmodell versus formaler Spezifikation Ein wesentlicher Unterschied besteht darin, daß in der Spezifikation das *gesamte Verhalten* der betrachteten Systemteile beschrieben ist, wogegen das Sicherheitsmodell eine Verkürzung darstellt. Insofern ist ein Modell auch deutlich kürzer als eine vollständige Systemspezifikation, vgl. Gasser [10, S. 137]:

> The primary characteristic of a good model is that it is easy to comprehend. It should be possible to describe, in natural language, all the important aspects of the model in a very few pages, or to explain it in a few minutes.[5]

2.2 Evaluierung und Sicherheitsmodelle

Bei der Evaluierung von IT-Systemen verlangen die Sicherheitskriterien für das Erreichen einer hohen Qualitätsstufe ein formales Sicherheitsmodell einschließlich der zugehörigen Konsistenzbeweise. Hierbei bedeutet Konsistenz bis zu einer bestimmten Qualitätsstufe die Konsistenz der Sicherheitsanforderungen zueinander und ab dieser Qualitätsstufe zusätzlich die Konsistenz zwischen Modell und formaler Top-Level-Spezifikation.

- US-Kriterien (Orange Book [9]): verbales Sicherheitsmodell ab Stufe B1 und formales Sicherheitsmodell ab Stufe B2
- Deutsche IT-Sicherheitskriterien (Grünes Buch [28]): Formales Sicherheitsmodell ab Stufe Q5
- Harmonisierte Kriterien (ITSEC, [20]): Formales Sicherheitsmodell (inkl. der informellen Interpretation) ab Stufe E4

3 Über den Mißbrauch von Sicherheitsmodellen

Sicherheitsmodelle wurden (und werden) in zweierlei Hinsicht falsch bewertet.

3.1 Überbetonung eines bestimmten Modells

Im amerikanischen Orange Book [9] wird sehr stark das Bell-LaPadula-Modell [2] und das Denning-Modell[8] betont , die beide nur auf die Vertraulichkeit eingehen. Es entstand dadurch in der Öffentlichkeit der falsche Eindruck, daß ein IT-System genau dann sicher ist, wenn es dem Bell-LaPadula-Modell entspricht. Dabei wurden andere sicherheitsrelevante Aspekte wie z.B. Integrität von Daten nicht berücksichtigt.

Bell und LaPadula war die Beschränktheit ihres Modells durchaus bewußt [3, S.11] :

> A model such as the Bell-LaPadula model that was constructed as an abstraction to allow analysis free of irrelevant detail never claimed ... to capture all facets of intuitive-security.

[5] "Of course, the precise mathematical version of the model might be difficult for a nonmathematician to follow, but any person trained in the notation should be able to understand it easily."

Es kann kein „universelles" Sicherheitsmodell für sämtliche existenten Sicherheitsanforderungen geben, so daß ein gemäß diesem Modell konstruiertes System universell sicher wäre. Dies scheitert schon daran, daß es in manchen Anwendungen Sicherheitsanforderungen gibt, die nicht vereinbar mit Sicherheitsanforderungen aus anderen Szenarien sind, etwa Anonymität im einen Fall und Nachvollziehbarkeit im anderen Fall.

3.2 Formale Methoden = Sicher ?

Durch die starke Betonung der formalen Methoden in den Sicherheitskriterien und der Hoffnung, Verifikation auf allen Stufen hin bis zum Code-Level zu erreichen, ist der Eindruck entstanden, daß Sicherheit vollständig beweisbar wäre. Die Erfahrung zeigt jedoch, daß die Entwicklung noch nicht so weit ist und selbst innerhalb dieser formalen Methoden vielleicht gar nicht so weit kommen kann (siehe oben und [25]). Bisher kann man wegen mangelhafter Toolunterstützung aus Kostengründen sowieso nur für hoch sensitive Systeme formale Verifikation durchführen.

Aber bereits aus prinzipiellen Gründen ist die obige Gleichung nicht erfüllbar. Ein System besitzt Schnittstellen zur Umwelt, die nicht vollständig formal spezifizierbar sind. Ein fundamentaler Sicherheitsmechanismus ist z.B. die Aufgabenteilung (siehe [7, 26, 27]). Das System kann diesen Mechanismus zwar unterstützen, aber es kann nicht verhindern, daß dies von einer bösartigen Koalition der beteiligten Personen unterlaufen wird oder daß die bereitgestellten Mechanismen vom Systembetreiber gar nicht genutzt werden.

Trotzdem ist eine formale Analyse sinnvoll, weil man dabei gut herausarbeitet, wo genau man Vertrauen in die beteiligten Personen haben muß und wo man andererseits Teilbeweise erbringen kann.

4 Praktischer Einsatz von Sicherheitsmodellen

Sicherheitsmodelle gehen in den Entwicklungsprozeß sicherer IT-Systeme unter zweierlei Zielrichtungen ein.

4.1 Anwendungsunabhängige und anwendungsspezifische Sicherheitsmodelle

Es ist zu unterscheiden zwischen allgemeinen Sicherheitsmodellen, die in der Forschung erstellt werden (z.B. die Sicherheitsmodelle aus Tabelle 1), und solchen, die bei einer konkreten Systementwicklung entstehen. Sicherheitsmodelle aus der Forschung beschreiben grundlegende Sicherheitsprinzipien. Insbesondere abstrahieren sie von einem konkreten System und sind somit *anwendungsunabhängig.*

Sicherheitsmodelle für konkrete Systeme hingegen dienen dazu, die Qualität der Sicherheitsfunktionen des Systems zu verbessern und beschreiben jeweils ein bestimmtes System. Sie stellen, je nach Art ihrer Formulierung, eine (semi-)formale oder informelle Beschreibung der Sicherheitsanforderungen an ein konkretes System und deren Umsetzung in Sicherheitsmechanismen dar. Alle sicherheitsspezifischen Modellierungsansätze zielen letztendlich darauf ab, die Entwicklung solcher *anwendungsspezifischer* Sicherheitsmodelle zu unterstützen und damit konstruktiv in den Entwicklungsprozeß sicherer IT-Systeme einzugehen. Die deutschen und europäischen IT-Evaluationskriterien verlangen anwendungsspezifische Sicherheitsmodelle, vgl. Abschnitt 2.2.

4.2 Der Nutzen bekannter Sicherheitsmodelle für die Erstellung anwendungsspezifischer Sicherheitsmodelle

Zur Klärung, inwieweit die existierenden anwendungsunabhängigen Sicherheitsmodelle aus der Literatur die Entwicklung anwendungsspezifischer Sicherheitsmodelle unterstützen, werden zunächst ihre charakteristischen Merkmale herausgestellt.

Jedes der bekannten Sicherheitsmodelle ist — abhängig von seinem jeweiligen Entstehungskontext — auf bestimmte Klassen von Sicherheitsanforderungen ausgerichtet und widmet sich einem oder einigen wenigen fundamentalen Sicherheitsprinzipien[6]. Sie beschreiben typischerweise Sicherheitsmechanismen, mit denen genau „ihre“ Sicherheitsanforderungsklassen durchgesetzt werden können. Durch die Beschränkung auf einzelne Aspekte der Sicherheit wird erreicht, daß die oft recht umfassenden Sicherheitsanalysen innerhalb eines Modells noch relativ überschaubar bleiben.

Es werden fortwährend neue bzw. verbesserte Sicherheitsmodelle vorgestellt. Oftmals modellieren sie Sicherheitsanforderungen, die mit den bisherigen Modellen nicht darstellbar sind. Dies führt hin und wieder zu heftigen fachlichen Auseinandersetzungen zwischen Sicherheitsexperten zur Frage, inwieweit ein „neues“ Sicherheitsmodell die Sicherheitsprinzipien anderer Sicherheitsmodelle mit einschließt und inwieweit es neue Aspekte enthält. Exemplarisch sei hingewiesen auf die Diskussion darüber, ob die Chinesische-Mauer-Politik durch das Bell-LaPadula-Modell ausgedrückt werden kann (vgl. [5, 23]). Es ist zu erwarten, daß auch weiterhin immer wieder Sicherheitsanforderungen auftreten, für die bislang kein geeignetes Sicherheitsmodell existiert.

Terry und Wiseman behaupten allerdings von ihrem Modell, vgl. [26, S. 218]:

> ...(it) is sufficiently powerful to describe any computer system.

Das Terry-Wiseman-Modell nimmt tatsächlich eine Sonderrolle unter den existierenden Sicherheitsmodellen ein. Es stellt im Gegensatz zu anderen kein Modell mit einer festgelegten Sicherheitspolitik dar, sondern bietet vielmehr einen Rahmen an, in den anwendungsspezifische Sicherheitspolitiken integriert werden können und in den bereits einzelne Politiken (Bell-LaPadula, Aufgabenteilung im Sinne von Clark-Wilson) eingebettet sind. Im REMO-Projekt wurde beispielsweise demonstriert, wie zusätzlich das Konzept der Chinesischen Mauer in das Terry-Wiseman-Modell aufgenommen werden kann. Des weiteren ist es möglich, die Idee der wohlgeformten Transaktionen von Clark-Wilson auf das Terry-Wiseman-Modell abzubilden. Offensichtlich ist das Terry-Wiseman-Modell ein ausgesprochen flexibler Rahmen, innerhalb dessen man verschiedene bislang erforschte Sicherheitsprinzipien zu einem Modell integrieren kann.

Für ein zu entwickelndes System existiert aber höchstens in Ausnahmefällen ein geeignetes und zugleich ausreichendes Sicherheitsmodell, das die erforderlichen Sicherheitsmechanismen bereits vollständig enthält. Denn, um anwendungsspezifische Sicherheitsanforderungen adäquat und vollständig umsetzen zu können, benötigt man für jedes konkrete System eine individuelle Kombination mehrerer Sicherheitsprinzipien. Natürlich gibt es Modelle, deren Prinzipien in relativ vielen Systemen Verwendung finden, zum Beispiel geht das Bell-LaPadula-Modell in sehr viele militärische Anwendungen ein. Ein einziges Modell allein reicht in den meisten Fällen jedoch nicht aus. So spielt selbst in militärischen Systemen neben der Vertraulichkeit auch die Integrität von Informationen eine wesentliche Rolle. Nicht zuletzt ist die Durchsetzung der Bell-LaPadula-Politik u.a. von

[6] Z.B. Bell-LaPadula: Einstufungen zur Durchsetzung von multi-level-security-policies, Clark-Wilson: wohlgeformte Transaktionen und Aufgabenteilung zur Gewährleistung von interner und externer Konsistenz, Chinesische Mauer: Konfliktrelation zur Vermeidung von direkten und indirekten Informationsflüssen zwischen konkurrierenden Firmen.

der Integrität der Rechteverwaltungsdaten (z.B. Zugriffsrechtematrix, Sicherheitslevel von Subjekten und Objekten) abhängig. Auch die im Terry-Wiseman-Modell enthaltenen Vertraulichkeits- und Integritätsmechanismen allein sind für ein konkretes System gegebenenfalls nicht ausreichend oder ungeeignet.

Bei jeder Systementwicklung muß deshalb ein individuelles Sicherheitsmodell erstellt werden. Die in der Literatur existierenden Sicherheitsmodelle helfen dabei insofern, als sie beispielhaft demonstrieren, wie einige Sicherheitsanforderungen abgebildet und in Sicherheitsmechanismen umgesetzt werden können.

Dabei dienen die Sicherheitsmechanismen der verschiedenen Modelle als Anregungen bzw. als Realisierungshinweise, nicht aber als verbindliche Vorgaben. Für die Erläuterung grundlegender Sicherheitsprinzipien genügt oftmals eine informelle Darstellung (z.B. Clark-Wilson). Werden diese Sicherheitsprinzipien aber in ein anwendungsspezifisches formales Sicherheitsmodell integriert, müssen sie konkretisiert und mittels eines einheitlichen und ausreichend mächtigen Beschreibungsmittels (z.B. einer formalen Spezifikationssprache) geeignet formalisiert werden.

Die Beweise, die in einem (allgemeinen) formalen Modell der Literatur geführt werden, gelten für ein anwendungsspezifisches formales Sicherheitsmodell nur, sofern es dem allgemeinen Modell (abgesehen von eigenschaftserhaltenden Konkretisierungen) exakt entspricht. Sobald aber das allgemeine Modell — auch nur geringfügig — verändert wird, oder sich die Mechanismen des anwendungsspezifischen Sicherheitsmodells aus Mechanismen verschiedener Sicherheitsmodelle zusammensetzen, ist zu überprüfen, inwieweit die für die ursprünglichen Modelle gültigen Beweise bezüglich dem, was sie jeweils unter Sicherheit verstehen, übertragbar sind. In der Regel muß man für ein anwendungsspezifisches Sicherheitsmodell Sicherheit (z.B. durch sichere Zustände und sichere Zustandsübergänge) neu definieren. Dementsprechend sind auch die Beweise neu durchzuführen. Allerdings können Beweisstrategien teilweise übernommen werden.

4.3 Beispiel

Im folgenden wird exemplarisch die Übertragung der Sicherheitsprinzipien des Clark-Wilson-Modells auf die Umsetzung der Sicherheitsanforderungen eines Beispielsystems demonstriert und skizziert, warum auf der Basis dieses einen Modells unter Umständen nur eine Teillösung erzielt werden kann.

Das Clark-Wilson-Modell [7] beschreibt zwei Sicherheitsprinzipien zur Gewährleistung der Integrität:

Wohlgeformte Transaktionen (wellformed transactions)
: Jede Datenmenge darf nur von einer ausgewählten Menge von Programmen (den wohlgeformten Transaktionen) bearbeitet werden.

Aufgabenteilung (separation of duty)
: Jeder Benutzer darf nur eine bestimmte Menge von Programmen (wohlgeformte Transaktionen) benutzen.

Hat dabei ein Benutzer ein Zugriffsrecht für ein Objekt, dann berechtigt ihn das nicht zu beliebigen Operationen auf diesem Objekt. Er darf das Objekt nur nach festgelegten Regeln, die durch das Zugriffsrecht bestimmt sind, bearbeiten[7]. Diese Bearbeitungsregeln (Vorschriften) werden in sogenannten wohlgeformten Transaktionen zusammengefaßt und

[7]Hat dagegen im Bell-LaPadula-Modell oder Biba-Modell ein Subjekt Schreibzugriff auf ein Objekt, so kann es das Objekt *beliebig* verändern.

die Systembenutzer werden jeweils berechtigt, bestimmte wohlgeformte Transaktionen durchzuführen. Dieser Mechanismus kann aber nur die *interne Konsistenz*[8] der Daten sichern.

Zur Erhaltung der *externen Konsistenz*[9] der Daten dient das Prinzip der Aufgabenteilung. Dazu werden komplexe Operationen in mehrere Teiloperationen zerlegt, die jeweils von verschiedenen Personen auszuführen sind. Insbesondere darf keine Person dazu berechtigt sein, *alle* Teiloperationen einer komplexen Operation auszuführen. Damit definiert das Clark-Wilson-Modell Zugriffsrechte auf der Basis wohlgeformter Transaktionen. Ferner fordern Clark und Wilson regelmäßige Prüfungen (im Sinne einer Revision), ob die Daten intern und extern konsistent sind.

Die Integritätsmechanismen von Clark-Wilson sind nicht in jedem System einsetzbar. Zum Beispiel kann man in einem Weitverkehrsnetz, wo die Leitungen über nicht kontrollierbares Gebiet führen, Integritätsverletzungen a priori gar nicht verhindern. Der Empfänger kann nur bei Einsatz kryptographischer Mechanismen (Digitale Signatur, Message Authentication Code) a posteriori überprüfen, ob eine Integritätsverletzung stattgefunden hat, und die Nachricht dann gegebenenfalls als nicht authentisch ablehnen.

In REMO [1] wurde am Beispiel des Bestellsystems in einer Firma untersucht, inwieweit die Sicherheitsprinzipien des Clark-Wilson-Modells dazu geeignet sind, die Sicherheitsanforderungen des Systems umzusetzen. An das Verfahren werden u.a. folgende Sicherheitsanforderungen gestellt:

1. Es sollen nur solche Bestellungen tatsächlich durchgeführt werden, die nach noch festzulegenden Kriterien sinnvoll sind und die vom Budget gedeckt werden.

2. Sind verschiedene Personen an dem Vorgang beteiligt, soll sichergestellt sein, daß jede Person nur die Bearbeitungsschritte an einer Bestellung vornehmen kann, die ihr entsprechend ihrer Rolle in diesem Verfahren zugeordnet sind.

3. Die interne Konsistenz einer Bestellung soll gewährleistet sein.

Die Sicherheitsanforderung 1 kann durch Aufgabenteilung umgesetzt werden. Eine mögliche Lösung könnte folgendermaßen aussehen. Man führt z.B. die Rollen eines Fachabteilungsleiters, eines Verwaltungsleiters und eines Geschäftsleiters ein. Der Fachabteilungsleiter, in dessen Abteilung ein Bedarf besteht, prüft nach bestimmten Kriterien die Sinnhaftigkeit einer entsprechenden Bestellung und gibt gegebenenfalls die Bestellung auf. Der Verwaltungsleiter übernimmt eine Kontrollfunktion im Sinne des Vieraugenprinzips, indem er überwacht, daß keine Bestellung durchgeführt wird, die nicht vom Budget gedeckt ist. Tritt ein Konflikt zwischen dem Fachabteilungsleiter und dem Verwaltungsleiter auf, weil der Fachabteilungsleiter auf eine Bestellung besteht, die laut Prüfung des Verwaltungsleiters nicht gedeckt ist, schaltet sich der Geschäftsleiter als „Schiedsrichter" in den Vorgang ein. Er trifft letztendlich die verbindliche Entscheidung, ob die Bestellung abgelehnt wird, oder ob er aus anderen Mitteln den fehlenden Geldbetrag zur Verfügung stellt, damit die Bestellung durchgeführt werden kann. Dies sind organisatorische Maßnahmen, deren Durchsetzung vom IT-System durch die Definition unterschiedlicher Rollen mit jeweils spezifischen (Teil-)Aufgaben und Rechten unterstützt wird.

Die Sicherheitsanforderungen 2 und 3 können mittels wohlgeformter Transaktionen erfüllt werden. Es wird dazu ein Zugriffskontrollmechanismus eingesetzt, der den Handelnden jeweils die Ausführung genau derjenigen wohlgeformten Transaktionen gewährt,

---

[8] Logischer Zusammenhang der Daten, z.B. bei doppelter Buchführung.

[9] Übereinstimmung der systeminternen Daten mit der systemexternen Wirklichkeit, wird z.B. bei der Revision geprüft. Integrität setzt sich aus interner und externer Konsistenz zusammen.

die sie für ihre Bearbeitungsschritte benötigen. Einerseits ist dadurch sichergestellt, daß keine Person Veränderungen an einer Bestellung vornimmt, die nicht in ihren Kompetenzbereich fallen. So kann aufgrund der rollenbezogenen Rechteprüfung z.B. kein anderer als der Verwaltungsleiter Ergebnisse aus Überprüfungen der Deckung in elektronische Bestellformulare eintragen. Andererseits sind die wohlgeformten Transaktionen so gestaltet, daß jede Person die Bearbeitungsschritte, die in ihrem Kompetenzbereich liegen, nur nach bestimmten, die interne Konsistenz erhaltenden Vorschriften vornehmen kann.

Das Clark-Wilson-Modell gibt nicht an, wie Integrität in einem konkreten Szenarium zu verstehen ist. Vielmehr ist es die Aufgabe des Systementwicklers im konkreten Fall, z.B. für das genannte Bestellsystem, festzulegen, wann die Daten als integer anzusehen sind. Entsprechend müssen dann die wohlgeformten Transaktionen konstruiert werden.

Für die Integration in einem anwendungsspezifischen Sicherheitsmodell sind die genannten Sicherheitsanforderungen und ihre Umsetzung mittels der Sicherheitsprinzipien von Clark und Wilson weiter zu konkretisieren und gegebenenfalls zu formalisieren.

Zusätzlich zu den drei exemplarisch genannten Sicherheitsanforderungen sind weitere sicherheitsrelevante Forderungen an ein Bestellsystem denkbar, z.B. die Vertraulichkeit oder Verbindlichkeit einer Bestellung betreffend, die von Clark und Wilson nicht abgedeckt werden. Deshalb sind gegebenenfalls weitere Sicherheitsmodelle zu betrachten, deren Sicherheitsprinzipien im Clark-Wilson-Modell nicht enthalten sind. Will man beispielsweise für das Bestellsystem die exakte Einhaltung einer bestimmten Ablaufbeschreibung durchsetzen, so kann das durch eine Kombination der Rechte (Clark-Wilson) einerseits und der Pflichten (Gleichgewichtsmodell für verbindliche Telekooperation [12]) andererseits unterstützt werden.

Der Modellentwickler hat also die Aufgabe, für sein konkretes System Sicherheitsprinzipien, insbesondere Sicherheitsmechanismen aus (möglicherweise verschiedenen) existierenden Sicherheitsmodellen sowie aus seiner Erfahrung bzw. Phantasie zusammenzustellen und aufeinander abzustimmen, so daß sie in ihrer Gesamtheit die Sicherheitsanforderungen angemessen und vollständig umsetzen.

Literatur

[1] E. Amann, *Anwendung des Clark-Wilson-Modells — Ergebnis und Erfahrungen,* IABG.REMO.0166.01 (REMO-Arbeitspapier)

[2] D.E. Bell, L. LaPadula, *Secure Computer Systems: Unified Exposition and Multics Interpretation,* NTIS AD-A023 588, MTR 2997, ESD-TR-75-306, MITRE Corporation, Bedford MA, 3/1976

[3] D.E. Bell, *Concerning "Modelling" of Computer Security,* Proc. of the IEEE Symp. on Security and Privacy 1988, 8-13

[4] K.J. Biba, *Integrity Considerations for Secure Computer Systems,* NTIS AD-A039 324, MTR 3153, ESD-TR-76-372, MITRE Corporation, Bedford MA, April 1977

[5] D.F.C. Brewer, M.J. Nash, *The Chinese Wall Security Policy,* Proc. of the IEEE Sympos. on Security and Privacy 1989, 206-214

[6] *Brockhaus Enzyklopädie,* Brockhaus-Verlag Mannheim, 19. Auflage 1991

[7] D.C. Clark, D.R. Wilson, *A Comparison of Commercial and Military Computer Security Policies,* Proc. of the IEEE Symp. on Security and Privacy 1987, 184-194

[8] D.E. Denning, *A Lattice Model of Secure Information Flow,* Comm. ACM Vol.19, No.5 (1976), 236-243

[9] Department of Defense Standard, *Department of Defense Trusted Computer System Evaluation Criteria,* DOD 5200.28 STD USA, Dec. 1985

[10] M. Gasser, *Building a Secure Computer System,* van Nostrand Reinhold, New York 1988

[11] J.A. Goguen, J. Meseguer, *Security Policies and Security Models,* Proc. of the IEEE Symp. on Security and Privacy 1982, 21-37

[12] R. Grimm, A. Steinacker, *Das Kooperations- und das Gleichgewichtsmodell — Theorie und Praxis,* Proc. Verläßliche Informationssysteme 93, DuD-Fachbeiträge 16, Vieweg-Verlag, 85-106

[13] V. Kessler, *Über Sinn und Unsinn von Sicherheitsmodellen,* Datenschutz und Datensicherung 9/1992, Vieweg-Verlag, 462-466

[14] V. Kessler, S. Mund *Sicherheitsmodelle — Studie,* SIEMENS.REMO.0118.01 (REMO-Arbeitspapier)

[15] J. McLean, *Reasoning about Security Models,* Proc. of the IEEE Symp. on Security and Privacy 1987, 123-131

[16] J. McLean, *The Specification and Modeling of Computer Security,* IEEE Computer Vol. 23, No.1, (1990) 9-16

[17] J.K. Millen, C.M. Cerniglia, *Computer Security Models,* MTR-9531 AD A 166 920, The MITRE Corporation, Bedford, MA, 1984

[18] J.K. Millen, *Models of Multilevel Computer Security,* Advances in Computers, Vol. 29, Academic Press 1989

[19] National Computer Security Center, *A Guide to understand modeling in trusted systems,* NCSC-TG-010, Library No. S-239,669, Version 1, 1992

[20] Office for Official Publications of the European Communities, *Information Technology Security Evaluation Criteria (ITSEC),* Catalogue number CD-71-91-502-EN-C, Luxembourg 1991

[21] K. Popper, *Logik der Forschung,* Verlag Mohr, Tübingen, 9. Aufl. 1989

[22] J. Rushby, *Foundations for Computer Security: A Position Paper,* ACM SIGSAC Meeting on Requirements for Foundation for Computer Security, 1987, 1-6

[23] R. Sandhu, *Lattice-Based Enforcement of Chinese Wall,* Computer & Security 11 (1992), 753-763

[24] D. Sterne, *On the Buzzword "Security Policy",* Proc. of the IEEE Symp. on Research in Security and Privacy 1991, 219-230

[25] H. Strack, *Formale Modellierung + Spezifikation + Verifikation = Sicher ?,* Tagungsband Datasafe 1991, Karlsuhe

[26] P. Terry, S. Wiseman, *A "New" Security Policy Model,* Proc. of the IEEE Sympos. on Security and Privacy 1989, 215-228

[27] S. Wiseman, *Computer Security Research at the Defence Research Agency,* REMO-Workshop Ottobrunn, März 1992

[28] Zentralstelle für Sicherheit in der Informationstechnik (ZSI, Hrsg.) *IT-Sicherheitskriterien,* 1. Fassung vom 11.1.1989, Bundesanzeiger Köln

Das TELES.VISION System

Sicherheitsanforderungen und Sicherheitsmoduln

Dr. J. Schulze
TELES GmbH
Kurfürstendamm 207-208, 10719 Berlin
E-mail: jus@tub.cs.tu-berlin.de

Abstract:

Sicherheitsanforderungen existieren in allen IT-Systemen. Sie werden speziell in modernen, auf Multi- Media- Technik und Mehrpunkt - Kooperationstechnik basierenden Systemen, als nahezu ebenso relevant angesehen wie die eigentliche Funktionalität dieser Systeme. In modernen Videokonferenzen werden die ansonsten getrennten Kommunikationskanäle für Audio- , Video-, Text-, Grafik-, Tabellen-, ... - Informationen analog einem physischem Treffen integriert. Die drängenden, speziell in Videokonferenz-systemen auftretenden Sicherheitsanforderungen und die zu ihrer Erfüllung einzusetzenden Sicherheitsmoduln werden vorgestellt. Ein kurzes Szenario veranschaulicht den Einsatz von Sicherheitsmoduln gegen die zu erwartenden Sicherheitsangriffe aus Sicht eines Videokonferenzteilnehmers. Angriffe auf die Sicherheit werden sich auf den lokalen Arbeitsplatz und allen damit verbundenen Betriebsmitteln, auf die Videokonferenz - Zentralen und auf die Kommunikationsmedien konzentrieren. Mit Hilfe von Sicherheits - Guards werden die Benutzerforderungen nach Vertraulichkeit, Integrität und Authentizität der schutzbedürftigen Informationen, die Nichtabstreitbarkeit ausgeführter Operationen und die eindeutige Identifikation der kooperierenden Benutzer erfüllt.

Einleitung

Sicherheitsanforderungen existieren in allen IT- Systemen. Bisher zugunsten der Anwendungsfunktionalität vernachlässigt, stellt sich die Durchsetzung von Sicherheitsanforderungen mehr und mehr als ökonomische und marktöffnende Notwendigkeit im Bereich der IT-Systeme dar. Sicherheitsanforderungen werden daher speziell in modernen, auf Multi- Media- Technik und Mehr-Punkt-Kooperationstechnik basierenden Systemen, als nahezu ebenso relevant angesehen wie die eigentliche Funktionalität dieser Systeme. Zielsetzung der Integration von Sicherheitsfunktionalität in IT-Systeme ist es vordringlich, mögliche Schäden durch potentielle Angriffe resp. Fehlfunktionen von vornherein weitgehend auszuschließen.

Sicherheitsbedrohungen nehmen speziell im Videokonferenzbereich [1] gegenüber herkömmlichen Anwendungssystemen eine besondere Stellung ein. Dies ist zum einen in der Verknüpfung unterschiedlichster Informationskanäle zu einem qualitativ angereicherten "Hyperkanal" und zum anderen in der - durch die neugewonnene Flexibilität und Leistungsfähigkeit hervorgerufenen - zunehmenden (halb-) privaten, freizügigen Kooperation begründet.[1]

In modernen Videokonferenzen werden die ansonsten getrennten Kommunikationskanäle für Audio-, Video-, Text-, Grafik-, Tabellen-, ...-Informationen analog einem physischen Treffen integriert. Diese, untereinander in Beziehung stehenden, Informationen können mit zunehmender Einfachheit zwischen beliebigen Kooperationsvorgängen (Sessions, Sitzungen) hin- und hergeschaltet werden.

Die Nachteile physischer Treffen, z.B. die reduzierte Erreichbarkeit, der Mangel an schnellen Zugriffen auf lokal verfügbare Informationen und nicht zuletzt die anfallenden Kosten sind durch den Einsatz von Videokonferenzen mühelos zu beseitigen, wohingegen die sonst gar nicht als Schwachpunkte erkannten, fehlenden Möglichkeiten für eine On- Line-Protokollerstellung oder eine Nutzung ansonsten nicht verfügbarer Betriebsmittel, Auswertungs-/Bearbeitungs-/Konvertierungsprogramme problemlos realisierbar sind.

Dieser kurze Bericht soll die drängenden, speziell in Videokonferenzsystemen auftretenden Sicherheitsanforderungen und die zu ihrer Erfüllung einzusetzenden Sicherheitsmoduln auf knappe und sachliche Art darstellen. Der folgende Abschnitt befaßt sich daher kurz mit einigen zu erwartenden Sicherheitsangriffen und den daraus resultierenden Sicherheitsanforderungen. Im anschließenden Abschnitt werden die einzusetzenden Sicherheitsmoduln funktional beschrieben. Den Abschluß dieses Berichtes bildet ein kurzes Szenario, welches den Einsatz der Sicherheitsmoduln aus der Sicht eines Videokonferenzteilnehmers veranschaulicht.

---

[1]In einer Videokonferenz sind mehrere Teilnehmer über öffentliche Netze miteinander verbunden und können von ihrem Arbeitsplatz aus mit allen anderen Konferenzteilnehmern sprechen, diese sehen, Standbildinformationen austauschen und ihre gewohnten Arbeitsplatzaktivitäten auf ihrem - oder bei Bedarf auf einem entfernten- Rechner durchführen.

1. Sicherheitsangriffe und Sicherheitsanforderungen

Unter Sicherheitsangriffen sind hier gewollte Aktivitäten zu verstehen, mittels denen ein Subjekt nicht erlaubten Zugriff auf Objekte (Informationen, Betriebsmittel) erlangen oder den regulären Zugriff hierauf verhindern möchte. Solche Angriffe können sowohl direkt durch Manipulations- und Lauschangriffe erfolgen, als auch indirekt durch Beobachtung (unter Ausnutzung verdeckter Kanäle) durchgeführt werden.
Videokonferenzsysteme zeichnen sich durch heterogene Systeme aus, die über beliebige Netze miteinander verbunden sind. Hierbei sollten letzendlich auch einfache videotelefoniefähige Endgeräte an einer Konferenz teilnehmen können. Der erforderliche Grad der Sicherheit wird jeweils durch die aktuelle Anwendung bestimmt. Innerhalb einer Videokonferenz können die eingesetzten Anwendungssysteme und der jeweilige Anwendungskontext wechseln. Demzufolge wird auch der gewünschte bzw. erforderliche Grad der Sicherheit variieren.

1.1 Sicherheitsangriffe

Durch Sicherheitsangriffe möchte sich ein Subjekt unerlaubterweise lesenden oder schreibenden Zugang zu Informationen verschaffen oder einen berechtigten Zugang auf diese Informationen verhindern. In diesem Bericht soll primär der erste Aspekt betrachtet werden. Schützenswerte Informationen innerhalb von Videokonferenzen sind zunächst die lokal vorhandenen Informationen, die in einem Videokontext ausgetauschten Ton-, Bild- und Nutzdaten sowie Konferfenz-Kontroll/Steuerdaten (Benutzerprofile, Zugangsberechtigungen, Statistische Informationen oder Konferenzkonfigurationen).

Aufgrund der oben beschriebenen Infrastruktur von Vidoekonferenzsystemen ergeben sich eine Vielzahl von Ansatzpunkten für direkte SI- Angriffe. Zunächst ist hierbei das Arbeitsplatzsystem selbst zu nennen. Eine der wesentlichen funktional- technischen Anforderungen an ein zu einem Videokonferenzsystem aufgerüstetes System besagt, daß die Funktionsweise / Kapazität / Verfügbarkeit / Effizienz des ursprünglichen Systems (weitgehend) unbeeinträchtigt bleiben soll. Ein unkontrollierter Zugang zu einem Arbeitsplatzsystem eröffnet dem möglichen Mißbrauch aber Tür und Tor.

Konsequenterweise wird ein Schwerpunkt beim Einsatz von SI-Mechanismen / SI-Moduln daher lokal am Arbeitsplatzsystem und allen damit verbundenen (lokalen) Betriebsmitteln (Maus, Tastatur, Bewegtbildkamera, Dokumentenkamera, Mikrofon, Drucker, Plotter, Scanner, Floppy-LW, Streamer, Festplatte) liegen. Das Arbeitsplatzsystem wird hierzu mit einem "Sicherheits-Guard" ausgestattet. Siehe dazu Bild 1.

Ein weiterer zentraler Angriffspunkt ist in Videokonferenzzentralen und anderen Dienste anbietenden Systemen (Directory- Server, Dokumenten- Verteilungs- Server, Datenbank-Server, IP- Router, ...Informationsquellen) zu sehen. Häufig wird in solchen Systemen ein Angriff auf deren Verfügbarkeit erfolgen. Dies wird hier jedoch nicht primär betrachtet. Statt dessen stehen hier Angriffe im Vordergrund, die eine nichtgerechtfertigte Inanspruchnahme dieser Dienstleistungen zum Ziel haben. Mittel zur Verhinderung solcher Angriffe bestehen häufig in speziellen Moduln, die den Zugang zu diesen Systemen überwachen und die Konsistenz der vorliegenden Datenbestände garantieren. Ein wichtiges Hilfsmittel zur Wahrnehmung / Verhinderung von Angriffen auf die (Dienst-) Verfügbarkeit ist die kontinuierliche (und unabhängige) Messung und Analyse. Auch hierzu werden Sicherheits-Guards eingesetzt.

Der dritte zentrale Angriffspunkt ist in den zwischen den Videokonferenzteilnehmern untereinander und den zwischen Videokonferenzteilnehmern und Diensteanbietern etablierten Verbindungen zu sehen. Die möglichen Angriffe richten sich hierbei natürlich (technisch) nach den jeweiligen, spezifischen Gegebenheiten der gewählten Art des Informationstransportes. Hierbei sind die Übertragungsmöglichkeiten in ISDN- Netzen, X.25-Netzen, Satelliten- Netzen genauso zu betrachten, wie der physikalische Transfer mittels CD, Tape, Post- oder Kurierdiensten. Neben den zu erwartenden Lauschangriffen sind auch hier Verfügbarkeits- und Modifikationsangriffe als mögliche Schwachstellen zu sehen.

1.2 Sicherheitsanforderungen

Grundsätzlich ließe sich nun eine ganze Reihe (spezifischer) Sicherheitsanforderungen anführen. Es ist aber nicht primäres Ziel dieses Berichtes (und der SI-Technik generell) die größtenteils funktional-/anwendungstechnischen Anforderungen (Gewährleistung der Betriebsmittel-Verfügbarkeit, geringe Anzahl von Übertragungsfehlern, hohe Fehlertoleranz, große Ausfallwahrscheinlichkeit,...) zu beschreiben. Statt dessen sollte sich die Betrachtung auf die o.g. expliziten Angriffe konzentrieren. SI-Anforderungen sind immer Benutzer- und damit Anwendungs-abhängig. Daher sind die SI-Anforderungen, die in diesem Bericht im wesentlichen betrachtet werden, als exemplarische, speziell für Kooperationsvorgänge in Videokonferenzsystemen ausgerichtete, SI-Anforderungen zu sehen. Die wichtigsten SI-Anforderungen - hier also der Schutz ausgetauschter Informationen vor Ausspähung, bzw Lauschangriffen jedweder Art, die kontrollierte Teilnahme / Verwaltung / Anwendungs-Nutzung, die Gewährleistung eines lokal sicheren und damit kontrollierbar zugänglichen

Videokonferenz-Arbeitsplatz-Systems oder die Erstellung / Verwaltung / Zugreifbarkeit von Protokollen über Konferenzaktivitäten - lassen sich durch die Realisierung der folgenden vier SI-Attribute (vergl. hierzu auch [2],[3]) erfüllen: Vertraulichkeit, Integrität, Authentizität und Nicht-Abstreitbarkeit. Die Realisierung dieser SI-Attribute basiert letztendlich auf speziellen SI-Maßnahmen / Mechanismen / -Moduln deren Ausprägung vom jeweiligen Einsatz /System abhängig ist.

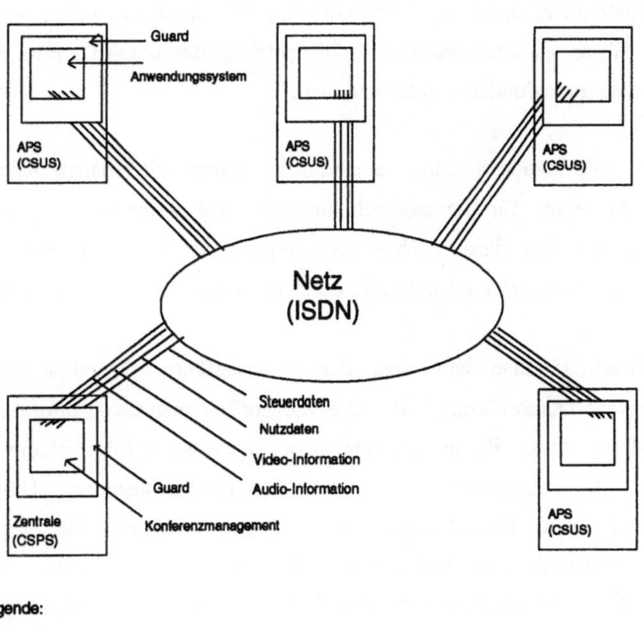

Bild 1: Sicherheits-Guards

Die SI-Attribute sollen kurz charakterisiert werden. Zur Darstellung werden hier die konkreten Begriffe Inhalt, Nachricht und Benutzer anstelle der abstrakten Begriffe Objekt, Prozeß oder Entity verwendet.

Vertraulichkeit: Der Inhalt vertraulicher Nachrichten ist nur den Personen zugänglich, für die er bestimmt ist. Zur Realisierung der Vertraulichkeit werden i.d.R. Verschlüsselungs-Mechnismen eingesetzt.

Integrität: Der Inhalt einer Nachricht ist integer (und integer übertragen/aufbewahrt/bearbeitet/behandelt worden), wenn die Nachricht denselben Informationsgehalt aufweist, wie bei ihrer Erstellung, d.h., wenn die Nachricht nicht in unautorisierter Weise geändert wurde. Die Überprüfung der Integrität erfolgt i.d.R. durch die Verwendung redundanter Informationen.

Authentizität: Informationen sind authentisch, wenn sie nachweislich die Informationen darstellen, für die sie sich ausgeben und wenn bei Angabe eines Erzeugers der Information, dieser nachweislich derjenige ist, für den er sich ausgibt. Der Nachweis der Authentizität erfolgt i.d.R. durch die Verwendung von Zertifikaten.

Nicht-Abstreitbarkeit: Eine von einer Person ausgeführte Operation ist nicht abstreitbar, wenn die Durchführung (z.B. das Erzeugen/Empfangen von Informationen) nachweislich durch diese Person erfolgte. Der Nachweis erfolgt häufig durch Verwendung von Signaturen und Bestätigungsmechanismen. Um der Wiedereinspielung von Informationen zu begegnen werden die signierten Informationen zusätzlich mit Zeitstempeln versehen. Dies bedeutet, daß die kooperierenden Konferenzteilnehmer synchronisiert sein müssen. Verfälchungen der eigentlichen Informationen werden mithilfe der verwendeten Signaturen sowie der Mechanismen zur Realisierung der Authentizität und der Integrietät abgewehrt.

2. Sicherheits-Moduln

Der Einsatz von SI-Moduln orientiert sich an den aufgeführten SI-Angriffen und SI-Anforderungen. Die Auswahl der SI-Moduln richtet sich also nach den aktuellen Benutzerbedürfnissen. Die SI-Moduln müssen hierbei die Realisierung der vier betrachteten SI-Attribute unterstützen. Zur Durchsetzung der SI-Anforderungen wird ein Satz von SI-Mechanismen[4] zur Verfügung gestellt, mit denen - der jeweiligen SI-Politik entsprechend - eine auf die Anwendung zugeschnittene Maßnahme gegen SI-Angriffe erzielt wird.

Einige hierfür eingesetzten Maßnahmen/Mechanismen/Betriebsmittel sind:

Chip-/Smart-Cards zur Verwahrung von Geheimnissen,

Kryptverfahren zur Ver- und Entschlüsselung von Informationen,

Verfahren zur Verifikation von Benutzerzertifikaten,

HW-/SW-Mechanismen zum Einfügen/Entfernen von Redundanz,

Dienste zur Bereitstellung von Schlüsseln /Zertifikaten /Notariats-Urkunden,

Protokolle zur Schlüsselverteilung/Synchronisation und

lokale Mechanismen zur Gewährleistung und Überwachung der Konsistenz des Arbeitsplatzes.

Insgesamt wird das gesamte Anwendungssystem - hier also jeweils das Videokonferenzsystem auf dem Arbeitsplatzsystem (APS,CSUS) oder auf der Zentrale (CSPS) sowie das für den aktuellen Dienst/Kooperationsaspekt eingesetzte Programmsystem - mit einer Sicherheitsschale, dem SI-Guard, umgeben. Der SI-Guard sorgt unter Verwendung der SI-Moduln, die ihrerseits auf SI-Mechanismen basieren, für die Durchsetzung der aktuellen SI-Anforderungen. Hierzu werden zusätzlich eine Reihe - nicht sicherheitsrelevanter - lokaler SW-Moduln eingesetzt, die im Rahmen dieses Berichtes aber nicht weiter betrachtet werden.

Im Gegensatz zu einer völlig neuen Erstellung eines von vornherein gesicherten Anwendungssystems [5] werden Werkzeugsätze entwickelt und genutzt, mit denen ein bereits bestehendes (ungesichertes) Anwendungssystem analysiert und modelliert wird. In diese modellierte Beschreibung werden die SI-Mechanismen / -Moduln aus einer SI-Bibliothek integriert und nach einer iterativen Modellierung / Validierung wird ein gesichertes System erstellt.
Es wird hierbei davon ausgegangen, daß sich die anschließend gesicherte Anwendung nach wie vor in einer ungesicherten und nicht vertrauenswürdigen Umgebung befinden kann. Für eine angemessene Sicherheit wird zunächst jedoch gefordert, daß sich das Arbeitsplatzsystem in einer für den Anwender vertrauenswürdigen Umgebung befindet.

Die wesentlichen SI- Moduln, die durch die SI-Bibliothek zur Verfügung gestellt werden, sind:

CC- Modul:

Die Treibersoftware für das CC-Modul gestattet die Initialisierung, die Modifikation und das Auslesen von auf der ChipCard gespeicherten Informationen.
Weiterhin wird die Ausführung der auf der ChipCard befindlichen Anwendungen zur Signierung, Ver-/Entschlüsselung und lokalen Authentifizierung (PIN- Check) unterstützt. Das Entfernen der ChipCard aus dem Leser führt zum sofortigen Unterbrechen der aktiven Videokonferenz. Die Einbindung dieses Moduls erfolgt über eine ChipCard- API.

Krypt- Modul:

Um Informationen (d.h. Steuerdaten, Nutzdaten, Videoinformationen und Audioinformationen) sowohl lokal als auch während der Übermittlung über öffentliche Netze vertraulich halten zu können, werden unterschiedliche Kryptverfahren angeboten. Die in der SI- Bibliothek enthaltenen Mechanismen werden über eine Krypt- API in das zu sichernde System eingebunden. Hierbei werden die benötigten/verwendeten symmetrichen Schlüssel mittels asymmetrischer Verschlüsselungen ausgetauscht. Auf der Smartcard befindliche Programme erlauben die Überprüfung von Zertifikaten und ermöglichen somit die Aufdeckung von Fälchungen öffentlicher Schlüssel. Wiedereinspielungsversuche lassen sich durch Verwendung von Zeitmarken entdecken.

Schlüssel- Verteil- Modul:

Neben der Generierung und Anwendung kurzlebiger symmetrischer Schlüssel müssen diese auch verteilt werden. In Mehr-Punkt-Anwendungen mit unterschiedlichen Informationskanälen -wie Videokonferenzsysteme sie vorstellen- ist dies eine aufwendige und sehr komplexe Aufgabe. Der

Schlüssel- Verteil- Modul sorgt hierbei nicht nur für den garantierten Austausch der Schlüssel, sondern auch für den synchronisierten Wechsel auf den aktuell gültigen Schlüssel [6].

Nutzungsrechte- Modul:

Die Aktivitäten der Teilnehmer einer Videokonferenz lassen sich grundlegend in zwei Gruppen einteilen. Zum einen in die funktionalen/kooperativen Aktivitäten in der aktuellen Konferenz und zum anderen in die organisatorischen Verwaltungsaktivitäten. Die funktionalen/kooperativen Aktivitäten müssen dahingehend kontrollierbar sein, daß nur ausgewählte (autorisierte) Teilnehmer auf Anwendungen/Dokumente/Betriebsmittel Zugriff haben und auch die in der Konferenz verfügbaren Sprach- und Bildkanäle nur in geordneter Form angefordert/genutzt/abgegeben werden können. Die organisatorischen Aktivitäten, etwa das Einrichten/Aktivieren/Entfernen von Schlüsseln/Zertifikaten/ Nutzungsrechten, haben extrem sensitiven Einfluß auf den Ablauf der Videokonferenzen und sind daher besonders schutzwürdig. Alle diese Aktivitäten oder Operationen werden unter Einbeziehung der betroffenen Informationen durch die Nutzungsrechte-Verwaltung nur den jeweils autorisierten Konferenzteilnehmern gestattet [7].

Die Verwaltung neuer bzw. ausgeschiedener Konferenzteilnehmer erfolgt zunächst im Konferenzkontext auf der Zentrale. Für die Konferenzbenutzer existieren hier Teilnehmerprofile und Zuordnungen von Teilnehmern zu Konferenzen und Anwendungssystemen. Die Teilnahme an Konferenzen wie auch das Verlassen von Konferenzen führen jeweils zu neuen Schlüsselwechseln. Neu aufgenommene Benutzer werden nicht nachträglich zur Teilnahme an aktiven Konferenzen zugelassen. Diese neuen Konferenzteilnehmer werden bei Aufstellung des Systems mit einer persönlichen Smartcard, die über eine persönliche PIN aktiviert wird, versorgt.

3. Ein Szenario

Anhand des folgenden sehr kurz gehaltenen Szenarios soll einerseits der Einsatz der SI-Moduln exemplarisch dargestellt werden und andererseits die sich für den Konferenzteilnehmer ergebenden geänderten Funktionsabläufe kurz diskutiert werden. Die zugrundegelegte Konfiguration sieht vier Konferenzteilnehmer A, B, C, D vor, sowie eine

Zentrale, in der alle nicht an den Arbeitsplatzsystemen vorgenommenen Operationen (Konferenzverwaltung, Schlüssel/Zertifikate/ Nutzungsrechte, Bewegtbild-/Ton- Mischung, Dienste- Angebot, Abrechnung, Überwachung, ...) realisiert werden. Eine Konferenz bestehe hierbei aus den Vorgängen Konferenzteilnahme, Nutzung des entfernten Arbeitsplatzes, Handhabung von Bewegtbild und Ton sowie Verlassen der Konferenz.

Teilnehmer A,B,C und D authentifizieren sich lokal an ihrem Arbeitsplatz durch Eingabe einer PIN gegenüber ihrer Chipkarte bevor sie an der Konferenz aktiv teilnehmen. Jeder Teilnehmer wird durch ein entsprechendes (SI-)Eingabefenster aufgefordert seine (geheime) PIN einzugeben.

Eine Änderung der PIN ist in diesem Szenario nicht vorgesehen. Eine solche Änderung müßte ebenso wie der Verlust der Smartcard durch persönliche Kommunikation mit dem Sicherheitsexperten des Konferenzsystems durchgeführt werden. Hierbei wird also die Vertrauenswürdigkeit des Sicherheitsexperten implizit vorausgesetzt.

Diese wird geprüft, und bei Übereinstimmung wird die eigentliche Benutzeroberfläche des Videokonferenzsystems aktiviert (sensibilisiert). Entsprechend der verfolgten Sicherheitspolitik werden den Teilnehmern bei diesem Vorgang weitergehende Informationen (Initialisierung der ChipCard, Lesen von Benutzerdaten, RSA- Entschlüsselung, ..., Fehlergründe) angezeigt. Die Detailebene ist hierbei einstellbar, ebenso wie die Einflußmöglichkeiten des Benutzers auf die Ausführung spezifischer Sicherheitsfunktionen (Verschlüsselung von Dateien vor dem Speichern).

Nachdem die Konferenzteilnehmer lokal authentifiziert sind und an der Konferenz aktiv teilnehmen wollen, werden sie entsprechend dem X.509- Standard authentifiziert (d.h. ihr öffentlicher Schlüssel und das zugehörige Zertifikat werden überprüft). Auch die Zentrale authentifiziert sich gegenüber den Benutzern. Nun wird ein Sitzungsschlüssel erzeugt und verteilt. Neue Sitzungsschlüssel werden entweder automatisch oder aber durch die Konferenzteilnehmer gesteuert in Intervallen ausgetauscht.

Für die entfernte Benutzung der Arbeitsplätze der kooperierenden Konferenzteilnehmer, wie auch für die Vergabe von Schreib- und Rederechten und die Kontrolle der Bewegtbild- und Tondaten, werden Nutzungsrechte festgelegt, deren Einhaltung überwacht wird. Die hierbei ausgetauschten (Bewegtbild-/Ton- und Nutz-) Daten werden durch den Einsatz des Krypt-Moduls und des ausgetauschten (symmetrischen) Schlüssels verschlüsselt.

An der Konferenz des Szenarios sind die vier Teilnehmer A bis D beteiligt. Diese können nun gemeinsam auf ihren eigenen, lokalen Arbeitsplätzen oder auf den Arbeitsplätzen der anderen Konferenzteilnehmer arbeiten. Jeder Teilnehmer kann hierzu das Recht, einen anderen Teilnehmer auf seinem System arbeiten zu lassen gestatten oder verweigern.

Weiterhin ist einer der vier Teilnehmer der Konferenzleiter dieser Konferenz. Der Konferenzleiter hat die Möglichkeit, anderen Teilnehmern das Rederecht zuzuordnen, es ihnen wieder zu entziehen, potentielle Teilnehmer dieser Konferenz einzuladen oder Teilnehmer auch auszuschließen. Der Konferenzleiter ist also mit weitergehenden Rechten ausgestattet als die anderen Konferenzteilnehmer. Daher hat er auch die Möglichkeit jederzeit einen erneuten Schlüsselaustausch zu veranlassen.

Die einzelnen Konferenzteilnehmer können jederzeit einen neuen gemeinsamen Kontext in einer Unterkonferenz eröffnen. Diese Unterkonferenzen werden beim Einrichten der Konferenz bereits mit eingerichtet. Somit haben die Teilnehmer die Möglichkeit separate Konferenzen zu führen, ohne daß die anderen Teilnehmer Zugang zu den vertraulichen Informationen haben.

Das Verlassen der Konferenz bewirkt einen erneuten Schlüsselaustausch bei den verbleibenden Teilnehmern. Teilnehmer die die Konferenz verlassen haben werden naturgemäß mit den neuen Schlüssseln nicht mehr versorgt. Daher ist es diesen in dem dargestellten Szenario auch nicht möglich sich unerlaubt vertrauliche Informationen zu verschaffen, solche Informationen (unerkannt) zu verfälschen oder solche Informationen unentdeckt wiedereinzuspielen.

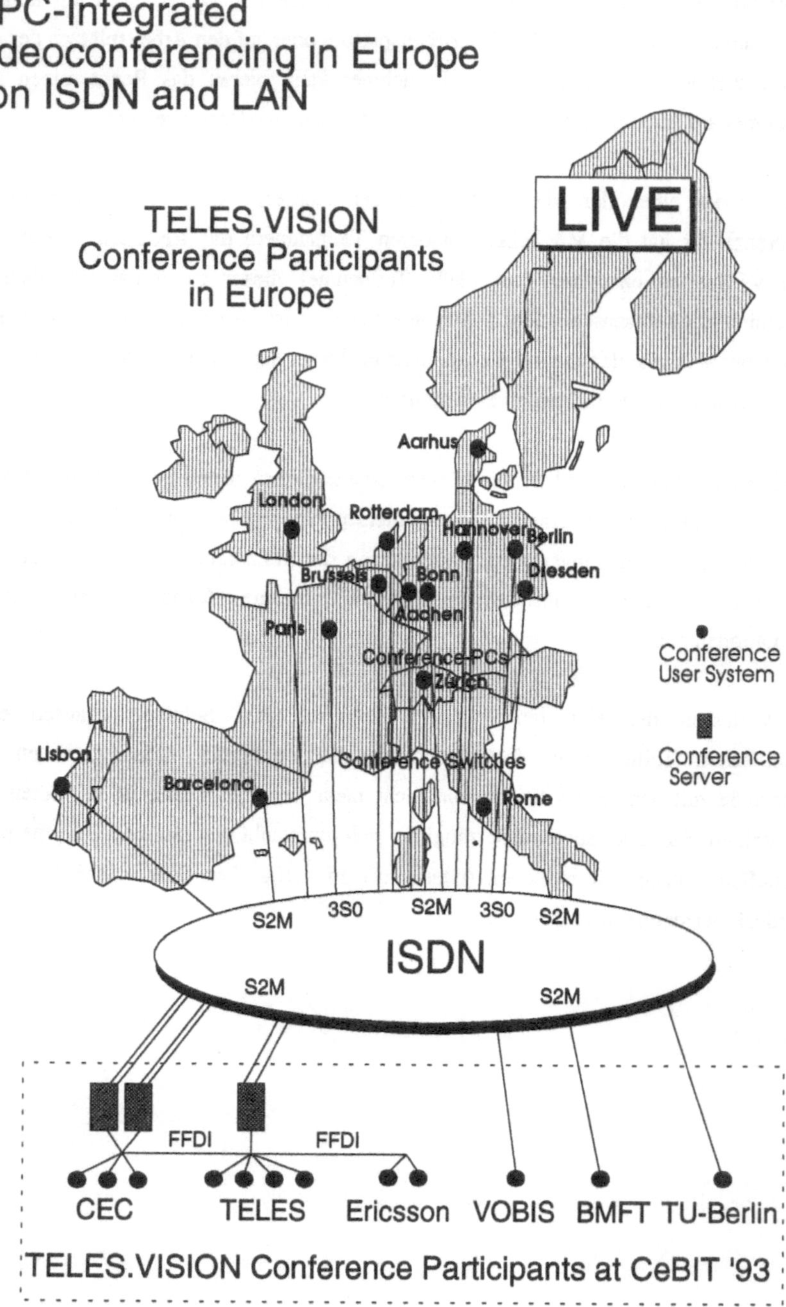
PC-Integrated
Videoconferencing in Europe
on ISDN and LAN
TELES.VISION
Conference Participants
in Europe
LIVE
Aarhus
London
Rotterdam
Hannover
Berlin
Brussels
Bonn
Dresden
Aachen
Paris
Conference-PCs
Zürich
Conference
User System
Conference
Server
Lisbon
Barcelona
Conference Switches
Rome
S2M
3S0
S2M
3S0
S2M
ISDN
S2M
S2M
FFDI
FFDI
CEC
TELES
Ericsson
VOBIS
BMFT
TU-Berlin
TELES.VISION Conference Participants at CeBIT '93

Referenzen

[1] Schindler S. , Das TELES.VISION System -Philosophie und Technologie- Teles GmbH 1991

[2] Schindler S. : Open Security Technology and Electronic Data Interchange The EDI Security Applications Model EDISAM

[3] Aman E : Glossar der Basisbegriffe, REMO 1993

[4] Fries,Fritsch, Kessler, Klein : Katalog von Sicherheitsmechanismen, REMO 1993

[5] Atzmüller H : REMO-Referenzmodell für sichere IT-Systeme; Überblick Remo 1993

[7] Witt H: Ein Dienst zur Verteilung von Sitzungsschlüsseln, 1992

[8] Gey M: Nutzungsrechte-Verwaltung, 1992

Summary: The FIDE ESPRIT Project on Fully Integrated Data Environments

In the FIDE Basic Research project, groups in Glasgow, Hamburg, Paris, Pisa and St. Andrews are working together towards a uniform programming environment for long-lived, data-intensive applications in open environments. FIDE has, collectively, a very strong background in databases, programming languages, type theory, object stores, compiler construction, distribution and commununication as well as systems implementation in general.

FIDE's approach can be viewed as generalizing traditional approaches into three dimensions:

- from conventional databases to polymorhically typed persistent object systems;
- from traditional languages to programming environments with orthogonal persistence;
- from closed systems to open architectures based on typed persistent libraries.

The first presentation summarizes FIDE results in extending databases and providing the integrated technology considered necessary for the construction and maintenance of persistent application systems. As a consequence of FIDE's integrated view, formerly disjoint concepts such as databases, program and module libraries, files or repositories can now be treated uniformly as persistent object systems differentiated essentially by the types of objects they contain and by the operational abstractions they provide. Since FIDE's main goal is to improve substantially a system's capability of persisting successfully over time in changing environments, particular emphasis will be placed on systems scalability and its consequences for interoperability of persistent object systems.

The potential of persistent programming languages is outlined in the second FIDE presentation. Such languages differ from traditional ones in that data of arbitrary lifetimes is fully governed by the type system leading to radically different programming paradigms and methodologies for two important reasons. First of all, the high-level type system may be relied upon as a protection mechanism even for long-term data. Secondly, data of any type, including first-class procedures and abstract data types, may be kept for arbitrary lifetimes. The combination of these means that the kind of sophisticated typing commonly used in programs which operate over short-term data may be extended to all data manipulated by a long-lived system.

The third FIDE contribution presents the basic concepts and the system architecture of Tycoon (Typed Communicating Objects in Open eNvironments). Tycoon is a consistently integrated environment for the construction of persistent object systems intended to be available on multiple software and hardware platforms. Tycoon's contribution to system portability and scalability is achieved by strictly separating concerns of data modelling, data manipulation, and data storage into three distinct system layers.each of which is based on state-of-the-art system technology (polymorphic programmming languages, portable code representations, persistent object stores). Much emphasis is being placed on supporting interoperability between Tycoon applications and off–the–shelf tools and systems, such as database systems, user interface managers, and optimizing code generators.

In summary, research and development in FIDE is leading to uniform linguistic interfaces and highly integrated yet architecturally open environments for data modelling, computation and communication. FIDE extends and integrates the core technology from databases, programming and communication and enables a novel paradigm for application development which is based on interoperating persistent object systems.

Building Persistent Application Systems in Fully Integrated Data Environments: Modularization, Abstraction and Interoperability*

Joachim W. Schmidt Florian Matthes
Universität Hamburg, DBIS
Vogt-Kölln Straße 30
D-22527 Hamburg, Germany

Patrick Valduriez
INRIA
Roquencourt, B.P. 105
F-78153 Le Chesnay Cedex, France

Abstract

Research and development in the FIDE project on Fully Integrated Data Environments has led to the concept of Persistent Object Systems (POS) which generalize database systems by re-interpreting schemas as type definitions and databases as typed variables in addition to treating lifetime as a type-independent property. Furthermore, FIDE develops uniform linguistic interfaces for data modelling, computation and communication, and extends database, programming and communication technology to enable integrated application development based on interoperating POSs.

As a consequence of such an integrated view, formerly disjoint concepts such as databases, program and module libraries, files or repositories can now be treated uniformly as POSs differentiated essentially by the types of objects they contain and by the operational abstractions they provide.

Based on state-of-the-art database technology, this paper outlines FIDE results in extending databases and providing the integrated technology considered necessary for the construction and maintenance of Persistent Application Systems. Since our main goal is to improve substantially a system's capability of persisting successfully over time in changing environments, particular emphasis will be placed on systems scalability and its consequences for POS interoperability.

1 Introduction: Application Development in Fully Integrated Data Environments

Successful application development nowadays is rarely based on extensive *coding* of application programs. Instead, there is a strong tendency to application systems *modelling* by exploiting the services provided through open and modular environments already populated with prefabricated and packaged functionality and information. Examples of such environments are databases, function libraries and module repositories.

This shift in application development has motivated *service suppliers* to improve their market by providing safer and functionally extended servers, in addition to allowing *service consumers* to conveniently buy functionality and information by simply specifying their needs (— and paying for it). However, since such services are developed independently

*This research is supported by ESPRIT Basic Research, Project FIDE, #6309.

of each other with widely varying conventions on naming, typing, binding and whatever else may describe their interfaces, application developers who wish to exploit multiple services within a single application find themselves working in quite complex and finally unfriendly and unsafe environments. Examples are interfaces between C programs and SQL databases, window system or RPC packages.

In the ESPRIT Basic Research project FIDE our response to the situation sketched above is the development of a technology for Fully Integrated Data Environments. Central to the FIDE Research and Development is the concept of Persistent Object Systems (POS) which can be seen as a generalization of database systems along the following lines:

- re-interpreting database schemas as type definitions and databases as typed variables,
- treating lifetime as a property of computational objects which is independent of their type,
- developing uniform linguistic interfaces for data modelling, computation and communication,
- extending database, programming and communication technology to enable integrated application development based on interoperating POSs.

As a result of such a generalized view, formerly disjoint concepts such as databases, program and module libraries, files or repositories can now be treated uniformly as POSs differentiated essentially by the types of objects they contain and by the operational abstractions they provide.

Persistent Object Systems are required to provide the basis for characteristic interoperation needs such as:

- Persistent Object Management: Objects which outlive program executions or exist independently of any application impose specific requirements on their naming, scoping and binding mechanisms. Such mechanisms have to cope not only with the fact that object creation and object use may happen at different times but also on different platforms using diifferent tools.
- Data and Function Control: Within a single language, important classes of constraints on data and functions can be expressed by various type systems and for many of them there exist efficient algorithms to prove constraint satisfaction. Similarly, language-independent mechanisms have to be provided for persistent objects shared across platforms.
- Generic Interfaces and Functionality: The degree of re-usability of Persistent Object Systems is strongly correlated with the genericity of the services offered by the POS. Querying, report generation, form management, sorting and searching are examples of services accomplished best by instantiating generic algorithms with type-specific arguments. On the system level, substantial portions of interoperation protocols, e.g. link functions or marshalling procedures, can be obtained by providing generators with object signatures and platform specific information.

This presentation outlines FIDE results in providing the integrated technology considered necessary for the construction and maintenance of Persistent Application Systems as interoperating POSs. Section 2 reports briefly on the state-of-the-art of the integration and distribution technology developed in the context of Database Management Systems. The scope of the discussion is widened in section 3 by outlining a framework for interoperability across a variety of services represented by Persistent Object Systems. A specific environment for database programming with particular emphasis on interoperability across sites, languages and platforms is discussed in section 4. The paper concludes with a short reference on requirements for open communicating environments[1].

2 Overview: Distribution and Integration of Database Functionality

The success of Database Management Systems (DBMS) as commercial software products lies principally in their well-packaged functionality required by many bulk data processing applications: controlled persistent storage and optimized concurrent iteration. Although the concentration on a particular, well-chosen functionality is a major cornerstone of the DBMS success, it also contains the roots for its limitations. Marketed as closed, sealed servers, DBMSs contribute little to the interoperability *across* services. DBMSs interoperate with other systems only through their built-in interfaces which are either limited in functionality (e.g. SQL) or low in technology (e.g. cursor interfaces). Therefore, applications which require a variety of services, e.g. for objects on disk, on the screen, in memory or on wire, usually end up in low-level interface coding on the basis of strings, addresses and error codes.

On the other hand, in recognition of this shortcoming the database community is further improving interoperability *between* databases. This work can be classified roughly as covering two dimensions: the vertical dimension addresses interoperability issues between components of one logically related database transparently managed by a DBMS distributed over the sites of a network, while the horizontal dimension researches interoperability in the setting of multiple independent databases.

In this section we provide a short overview of the state-of-the-art of both dimensions in addition to reporting on research in the combined areas of distributed multidatabases. In the subsequent sections we open the discussion and outline a framework for interoperability across a variety of services, present a particular system for interoperable database programming and conclude with requirements for open communicating environments.

2.1 Databases as Distributed Systems

A distributed database (DDB) is a collection of multiple, logically interrelated databases distributed over a computer network [ÖV91, ÖV93]. A distributed database management system (DDBMS) is then defined as the software system that manages a DDB transparently according to the following assumptions:

- Data are stored at a number of sites. Each site is assumed to consist logically of a single processor.
- The processors at individual sites are interconnected by a computer network thereby realizing a loose interconnection between independently operating processors.

[1] Earlier versions of the material presented in this paper can be found in [SM93, ÖV91, MS91]

- Data in a DDB are logically connected by relationships defined according to some structural formalism and accessed at a high level via some common interface (e.g. the relational model and its query languages).
- The system has the full DBMS functionality. It is neither a distributed file system nor a transaction processing system [Ber90].

These assumptions are valid for today's technology. Most of the existing distributed systems are built on top of local area networks with sites consisting of a single computer. However, next generation DDBMS environments will include multiprocessor database servers connected to high speed networks linking them and other data repositories to client machines that run application code as well as participating in the execution of database requests [Tay87, KL89, ZM89].

A distributed DBMS as defined above is only one way of providing database management support for a distributed computing environment. In [ÖV91] a working classification of possible design alternatives was presented distinguishing three dimensions: autonomy, distribution, and heterogeneity.

- Autonomy refers to the distribution of control indicating the degree to which individual DBMSs can operate independently. It involves factors such as information exchange between component systems, independent transaction execution, and the degree of individual DBMSs modification.
- Distribution deals with data. Usually two cases are considered: physical data distribution over multiple communicating sites or data concentration at only one site.
- Heterogeneity in distributed systems ranges from hardware heterogeneity and differences in networking protocols to variations in data managers. DBMS heterogeneity relates to data models, query languages, interfaces, and transaction management protocols.

Distribution is identified as one of the major characteristics of next-generation database systems, which will be ushered in by the penetration of database technology into new application areas with different requirements than traditional business data processing and the technological developments in computer architecture and networking. The nature of distribution in next generation DBMSs is a controversial issue. There are a number of documents that attempt to define alternative positions [SSU90, ABW+90, SRL+90, Sto90] all sharing at least the following two characteristics:

- Data model extension: Future data models need to be more powerful than the relational one, yet without compromising its advantages (data independence and high-level query languages). When applied to more complex applications such as CAD/CAM or software design the relational model exhibits severe limitations in terms of complex object support, type system and rule management. To address these issues, three important technologies, persistent polymorphic languages, object-oriented databases and knowledge base management are currently undergoing heavy research.
- Improved interoperability support: An expected consequence of applying database technology to an extended range of application domains is the proliferation of different, yet complementary, DBMSs and other generalized information services. Thus,

interoperability of such systems within a computer network becomes increasingly important. Fully integrated data environments require significant improvements in interoperability. In the following subsections, interoperability is addressed in more detail showing that it is receiving increasing attention in the joint community of databases and programming languages.

2.2 Integrated Views on Multiple Databases

As already indicated above, a *multidatabase* organization is an alternative to logically integrated distributed databases. The fundamental difference between the two is the degree of autonomy afforded to the component data managers at each site. While the independent DBMSs may have, for example, facilities to execute transactions, they have no notion of executing distributed transactions that span multiple components (i.e., they do not have global concurrency control mechanisms or distributed commit protocol implementation). The integration issue of multiple databases definitely deserves more space than available in this paper. In this subsection, we concentrate on issues of global database schema management and highlight some of the potential of object-oriented software for systems with high autonomy .

2.2.1 Global Schema Definition and Management Issues

The arguments against full transparency gain more weight in multidatabase environments. The additional autonomy of individual components and their potential heterogeneity make it more difficult (some claim impossible) to support full transparency. A major difficulty relates to the definition of a global conceptual schema (GCS) as a specification of the structure and constraints of the global database. The definition and role of the GCS is well understood in the case of integrated distributed database systems: it defines a logical single image over physically distributed data. The same clear understanding does not exist in the case of multi-DBMSs with autonomy [SY90]. One way the integration issue can be tackled is to treat the global conceptual schema as a generalization defined over local conceptual schemas. Studies along this line have been conducted before [MB81, DW84] and their practical implications with respect to transparency need to be reconsidered.

Finally, there are arguments that the absence of a GCS may be a significant advantage of multi-DBMSs over DDBMSs [LA87]. A language sufficiently powerful to access multiple databases without defining a GCS is presented in [LA87]. A significant research problem is the nature of such multi-DBMS languages. Problems with languages that are as powerful as the union of the component ones arise, as discussed in [SY90], with non-standard query operators of component DBMSs or with component DBMSs providing different interfaces to general-purpose programming languages. A solution may lie in extensible languages.

2.2.2 Object-Orientation and Multidatabase Interoperability

A central issue is the development of software technology that can deal inherently with autonomous system components. A prime candidate technology is object-orientation. Here we only comment on its role in addressing the interoperability issues. Object-oriented systems treat the entities in their domain typically as instances of some abstract type. In the case of database systems these entities are usually data objects. However, it is quite common for object-oriented models to treat every entity uniformly as objects. Thus, for example, interface definitions, user queries, or programs are considered objects in certain object models and the technology is primarily concerned with providing the necessary tools and methodology for the consistent management of such entities.

Applying object-orientation to interoperability leads to the systematic and abstract treatment of autonomous DBMS components as software objects which can interoperate only through well-defined interfaces. There has been some initial work on the requirements of such interoperation interfaces [Man90, SY90, HZ90], an issue which clearly needs and deserves further investigation.

2.3 Database Interoperability: Multiple Databases in Distributed Environments

Finally, since multiple databases are expected to be available in distributed environments, the two problem spaces sketched above cannot be treated independently. This subsection outlines some of the issues raised when queries and transactions are run against multiple databases in distributed environments and concludes with a short reference to standards and their relevance for interacting autonomous systems.

2.3.1 Query Processing

The autonomy and potential heterogeneity of component systems create problems in query processing and optimization. A fundamental difficulty is global optimization when local cost functions are not known and local cost values cannot be communicated. Proposals have been made to concentrate on semantic optimization based only on qualitative information [SY90], however, semantic query processing is not fully understood either. There seems to be a great potential for hierarchical query optimizers which perform some global query optimization and leave it to each local system to perform further optimization on the localized subquery. Although this partitioning may not lead to optimal solutions, it will improve the tractability of the optimization problem. The emerging standards may also make it easier to define global cost models as well as share cost information.

2.3.2 Transaction Processing

For transaction processing in autonomous multi-DBMSs, the following consensus on a global transaction execution model seems to emerge: Each component DBMS has its own transaction processing services (i.e., transaction manager, scheduler, recovery manager) and is capable of accepting local transactions and running them to completion. In addition, the multi-DBMS layer has its own transaction processing components (global transaction manager, global scheduler) in charge of accepting global transactions accessing multiple databases and coordinating their execution.

Autonomy requires that global transaction management be performed on top of the existing local transaction execution functions. Heterogeneity has the additional implication that the transaction processing components involved may employ different concurrency control, commit, and recovery protocols and the coexistence of local and global transaction further complicates scheduling [BS88]. If serializability is used as the correctness criterion, it has to be ensured that the serialization order of global transactions at each site are the same. Some solutions use global serializability of transactions as their correctness criteria (see, e.g., [Geo91, BS88]) while others relax serializability (e.g., [DE89, Bar90]).

A further difficulty is the development of reliability and recovery protocols for multi-DBMSs and their integration with concurrency control mechanisms. Even though the topic has been discussed in some recent works [BO91, Geo90, WV90], these approaches are initial engineering solutions.

2.3.3 Autonomy and Standards

Probably one of the fundamental impediments to further development of distributed multidatabase systems is the lack of understanding of the nature of autonomy. An initial characterization that has been made identifies three different forms of autonomy: design autonomy, communication autonomy, and execution autonomy. Other characterizations have also been proposed [GMK88]. Furthermore, most researchers treat autonomy as if it were an all-or-nothing criterion and not as a range of possibilities. It seems essential to precisely

- isolate a range of autonomy levels
- identify, on each level, the appropriate degrees of database consistency
- define transaction models appropriate for different levels of autonomy.

This might lead to a layered interoperability architecture for autonomous and possibly heterogeneous DBMSs, similar to ISO Open System Interconnection. Some work along this line is already under way within the Remote Data Access (RDA) standard, possibly improving substantially the development of practical solutions to DB interoperability.

3 Towards Fully Integrated Data Environments

Generalizing from database applications leads to the conclusion that application development benefits greatly from an integrated technology which supports modularized persistent systems and generalized module definition and management. In this section we present a higher-order core language which, essentially by modularizing name and binding spaces, supports module definition and interaction in the presence of module persistence. Reference is made to Modula-2 [Wir85], to DBPL [SM91, MRSS92a], a modular Database Programming Language with persistence, and to Tycoon [MS92, Mat93], which is used as a conceptual basis for our core language.

3.1 Modularity: The Basis for Interoperability

Based on the experience with Modula-2, the Database Programming Language DBPL exploits the power of modular programming and module management for data-intensive and long-lived applications. DBPL programs are structured into modules with well-defined import/export relationships. Definition modules provide signatures for type, value and location[2] bindings defined in implementation modules. Program modules export a single, parameterless function value, the main program.

An interface and a skeleton DBPL module exporting basic data types and values to handle telephone numbers would look as follows:

[2]Locations are the conceptual basis for sharing and updates. In this paper, however, we do not discuss the subtle type issues related to location bindings. The interested reader is referred to [SM93].

```
definition module Phone;
type Number = array [0..20] of char;
var localPrefix, myNr :Number;
procedure operator(prefix:Number):Number;
end Phone.
```

```
implementation module Phone;
procedure operator(prefix :Number) :Number;
begin ... return ... end operator;
begin (* module initialization: *)
   localPrefix:="4940";
   myNr:=concat(localPrefix, "85312");
end Phone.
```

During type checking of these compilation units, the DBPL compiler extracts type and value signatures from the definition module and verifies that the bindings defined in the implementation module match their corresponding signatures. In the next section we introduce a conceptual model that allows us to explain this process and the compilation of client modules against a compiled interface in more detail. This level of detail is required to generalize the simple Modula-2 module mechanism to distributed, multi-language database environments (see Sec. 4).

3.2 A Core Language for Fully Integrated Data Environments

In this section we introduce (informally) a model to describe the naming, typing and binding concepts involved in Persistent Object System interoperability. The model itself (subsequently referred to as the *Tycoon POS model*) is based on concepts of higher-order type systems and is sufficiently expressive to serve as a language-independent framework for program translation, generation and binding. The presentation of the actual DBPL system and its gateways in the following sections makes use of a limited subset of the Tycoon POS model. The potential of the full model is discussed in [MS93].

The Tycoon POS model is based on the notion of *types*, *signatures*, *values* and *bindings*. Types are understood as (partial) specifications of values. Values and types can be named in bindings for identification purposes and to introduce shared or recursive structures at the value and the type level. Signatures act as (partial) specifications of static and dynamic bindings. Bindings are embedded into the syntax of values, i.e. they can be named, passed as parameters, etc.

The syntax for *types* includes a set of base types B_i (**Int**, **Real**, **String**, ...), a type constant **Any** (the trivial type), user-defined type variables, function types, aggregated signatures, parameterized type expressions (type operator definitions) and type operator applications:

Type::= B_i | **Any** | *TypeName* | **Fun***(Signatures) Type* | **Sig***(Signatures)* |
Oper*(Signatures) Type* | *Type(Bindings)*

Function types are used to describe the signatures of parameterized objects like functions, procedures, methods, generators or relational queries. Aggregated signatures are used to describe the signatures of language entities like records, tuples, structures, modules, object definitions, database definitions, or object files.

Type operators denote parameterized type expressions that map types or type operators to types or type operators. Many programming languages have built-in type operators that map types to types (*Array*, *List*, *File*, *Pointer*, ...).

Signatures are sequences of value, location or type signatures. A value signature associates a value name with a type (*peter :Student*). A type signature associates a type name with a supertype specification (*Student <:Person*).

Signatures::= {*TypeSig* | *ValueSig* | *LocationSig*}
TypeSig::= Name <:*Type ValueSig::= Name :Type LocationSig::=* **var** *Name :Type*

Aggregated signatures are used to describe named *declarations* as they occur in function headings, module signatures, **external** declarations in C programs or in database schema definitions.

Signatures specify invariants on bindings and allow the verification of the correctness of (value or type) expressions depending on names without having access to the actual binding in which the name is defined. For example, based on the signature *age :Int*, the type-correctness of the expression *age + 1* can be verified without having access to the actual value bound to age. Signatures therefore play a central role in type-safe module systems.

The syntax for *values* includes base values $b_{ij} : B_i$, like 0, 3.4, "xyz", **true**, a canonical value of the type **Any**, function values including built-in functions like +, –, * of type **Fun**(x :**Int** *y:* **Int**) **Int** and user-defined functions and aggregated bindings:

Value::= b_{ij} | **any** | **fun***(Signatures)Expr* | **bnd***(Bindings)*

The syntax **bnd**(Bindings) defines that aggregated value and type bindings are first-class values, generalizing classical concepts like value, function and type aggregation in records, structures, abstract data types or modules. The syntax of *expressions* in functions is deliberately not specified here in order to be able to describe POS involving multiple languages.

Bindings are sequences of type, value and location bindings. A type binding *Age*≡**Int** defines a name for a type. A value binding *pi=3.1415* defines a name for a value.

Bindings::= {*TypeBnd* | *ValueBnd* | *LocBnd*}
*TypeBnd::= Name≡Type ValueBnd::= Name=Value LocBnd::= Name=***var**(α_i) *Value*

Bindings model type, constant, variable and function declarations in programming languages and instances of database schemas in database systems.

As usual, types are intended to classify values, and signatures are to classify bindings. Moreover, it is possible to define *generic* functions (functions that take type bindings as arguments), value-dependent type operators, abstract data types (bindings that contain partially-specified type components and operations on that type). The formal type rules for this model (defining well-formed types, the types of values, the subtype relationship between types and the signatures of bindings) become therefore quite subtle.

In traditional systems, types and signatures are handled exclusively at compile-time, while values and bindings only appear at run-time. In persistent systems, the distinction between compile-time and run-time blurs, and it becomes possible, for example, to inspect value and type bindings at compile-time, giving rise to powerful reflective algorithms [SSS+92].

We now return to the DBPL example presented in section 3.1 and demonstrate how its modules are modelled in the Tycoon POS model:

CompileEnv ≡ **Sig***(Phone* <:**Sig***(Number* <:**array**...
var *localPrefix :Number* **var** *myNr :Number operator :***Fun***(prefix :Number) Number)*
*linkPhone :***Fun***(imports :***Sig***()) Phone)*

The definition module is represented as a type signature which associates the interface name *Phone* (understood as a type variable) with a supertype that is an aggregate of all types and values signatures exported by the interface. The implementation module is represented as a single function, *linkPhone*, that takes an aggregated binding of all imported module values (in this case an empty binding) and returns a binding that conforms to the interface signature *Phone*.[3]

The signatures of *Phone* and *linkPhone* are both elements of a flat name space modelled by a signature bound to the type variable *CompileEnv*. In a typical DBPL system implementation, this name space is managed implicitly via search paths to look up compiled interfaces, called "symbol files".

The code generated for the implementation module *Phone* is stored as a named binding in a flat name space that collects all compiled modules. This name space is represented in the Tycoon POS model as a named value *linkEnv* whose type matches the signatures specified by *CompileEnv*:

linkEnv = **bnd***(linkPhone=***fun***(imports* :**Sig***()) ...)*

This name space is also utilized by the DBPL linker to compose all module initialization functions that make up an executable application program. The main module

module *Main* **import** *Phone; ...* **end** *Main.*

is represented by the following link function:

linkMain :**Fun***(imports* :**Sig***(phone :Phone)) Main*

It leads to the following module initialization sequence:

initEnv=**bnd***()*
phoneE=initEnv∪{*phone=linkEnv.linkPhone(initEnv)*}
mainE=phoneEnv∪{*main=linkEnv.linkMain(phoneE)*}

3.3 The Potential of Persistent Objects

This section demonstrates how the concept of ***orthogonal persistence*** [AB87] as found in DBPL extends the potential for interoperability along two new dimensions: sharing over time and sharing between multiple users.

DBPL introduces the notion of a ***persistent module*** (database module) to define persistent location bindings in a strongly-typed programming environment. For example, the following local changes marked by underscores are sufficient to turn *localPrefix* and *myNr* into persistent variables (compare Sec. 3.1).

```
database definition module Phone;
   ... (* see Sec. 3.1 *)
end Phone.
```

```
implementation module Phone;
   ... (* see Sec. 3.1 *)
database definition begin
   localPrefix:="4940";
   myNr:=concat(localPrefix, "85312");
end Phone.
```

[3]As we will see later, we would lose some modelling precision if we were to treat the implementation module as a simple binding of type *Phone*.

The compilation of these modules defines a collection of signatures that is identical to the non-persistent environment *CompileEnv* defined in Sec. 3.2. The import semantics of persistent modules differ from volatile modules: the link-time execution of the module initialization code *linkPhone* of a persistent module does not return a new set of bindings to newly created process-local locations (copy semantics), but returns bindings to locations that are *shared* between all programs importing the persistent module (reference semantics). Therefore, side effects created by one application on persistent variables are visible to other applications importing the same persistent module:

module *Main1* **import** *Phone;*
begin *Phone.localPrefix:= "004940"* **end** *Main1.*

module *Main2;* **import** *Phone;*
begin *Phone.localPrefix:=concat(Phone.localPrefix,"-")* **end** *Main2.*

The sequential execution of *Main1* and *Main2* would lead to the following location bindings:

bnd(*localPrefix*=**var**(α_1)*"004940-"* *myNr*=**var**(α_2)*"494085312"*
operator=**fun**(*prefix :Number*)...)

The statement sequence marked by the keywords **database definition begin** is executed only once during the lifetime of the database module *Phone*, namely before it is imported for the first time into a DBPL application program.

The main advantages of persistent modules lie in overcoming the naming, typing and genericity problems associated with file-based solutions [SM93] without introducing additional linguistic complexity in the programming environment. Since the name space populated by database modules is not only persistent but also *shared* between several programs, it is necessary to ensure that destructive updates of persistent data structures performed by concurrent applications are performed *atomically* to handle system and program failures graciously. Therefore, DBPL supports user-defined (parameterized) *transactions* to handle the concurrency-control, recovery and integrity issues based on standard database transaction models.

4 DBPL: An Interoperable Database Programming Environment

A modular environment with persistence and sharing is particularly suited to support long-lived applications which need large collections of data. Since, over time, such applications have a strong tendency to extend functionality and to proliferate information, they also require scalability into open and distributed environments. In this section we outline FIDE results in functionality extension and in interoperability support. We present interoperability examples across database servers, programming languages and system platforms.

4.1 Service Extension: Bulk Types in DBPL

In the process of building a POS, it is often necessary to handle large, dynamic homogeneous collections of objects (e.g., class extents). Furthermore, it is necessary to represent relationships between object collections and to perform efficient, set-oriented update and retrieval operations. Database systems have been designed to provide specific modelling and system support for these tasks. Expanding on our running example, let us assume that there is a need to register variable amounts of telephone entries composed of person names and telephone numbers. This kind of information is adequately described by the following relational database definition:

createdb *SQLPhoneDB* ...
create table *register (name* **char***(50), num* **char***(21))*

The language SQL provides simple, efficient, declarative read and write access to the information held in the database (**insert into table, delete from table, select** ... **from** ... **where** ...). However, it turns out to be surprisingly difficult to access SQL databases from application programs, e.g., to use the *Fax* service to send a message to every person named "Smith". We do not want to go into the detailed problems of SQL host language embedding, but there arise numerous difficulties due to the differences in naming, typing and binding between SQL and host languages such as C, Cobol or Ada (see [SM93] for details).

DBPL overcomes these difficulties by using the persistence and modularization concepts described in Sec. 3.1 in addition to extending the language by a generic bulk types operator **relation** and predefined polymorphic operations on values of type relation. Due to the orthogonality of the DBPL type system, it is possible to define a richer set of data structures than it is possible in the classical relational model, however, this flexibility is not required here [SM91]. The SQL database schema is represented by the following persistent DBPL module:

database definition module *PhoneDB;* **import** *Phone;*
type *Entry* = **record** *name :String num :Phone.Number* **end***;*
type *Register* = **relation** *name* **of** *Entry;*
var *register :Register;*
end *PhoneDB.*

Names have been assigned to all types to be re-usable in application programs importing *PhoneDB*. It is worth noting that, of course, more than one database module can be defined in a DBPL application, thus realizing the concept of multi-databases discussed in Sec. 2.2. DBPL also provides a rich set of set-oriented update operators and an extended relational calculus including recursion based on fixed-point semantics to express bulk operations [ERMS91]:

register:+ Register{{*"John", "249"*}};
print(Register{**each** *n* **in** *register:n.num> "240"*}*);*

DBPL has special (generic) type rules for the built-in relation operators, e.g., to capture the fact that the set-oriented insertion operator ":+" can be applied to relations of arbitrary element type, as long as the right-hand side expression is also a relation of the same element type. In [SM93] it is demonstrated how type operators of the Tycoon POS can be used to capture accurately these built-in type rules for relation types. This formalization is a only a first step towards a generalized type-safe handling of user-defined bulk data types [MS91, MS93].

4.2 The DBPL/SQL Gateway

The DBPL language and system supports bindings to external persistent objects in addition to internal persistent DBPL objects [MRSS92b]. For example, the following modification of the header of module *PhoneDB* binds the location variable *register* to an *external* SQL relation *register* defined in an Ingres database named *SQLPhoneDB*:

database definition <u>**for** *Ingres*</u> **module** *PhoneDB;*
import *Phone; ...* **var** <u>*register*</u> *:Register;* **end** *PhoneDB.*

All DBPL statements and expressions referring to external relation variables are translated fully transparently into SQL update and selection expressions submitted to the Ingres SQL database management system. These SQL expressions typically take DBPL program variables (value and location bindings) as arguments and return (set) values that are converted appropriately for further processing within DBPL. For example, the query

if all *n* **in** *register n.phone* > *x* **then** ... **end**

is translated into a **select from where** SQL expression that uses the actual value stored in the DBPL location *x* of type **String**. Depending on the cardinality of the set-valued result, a boolean value is then returned to the compiled DBPL code.

It should be noted that DBPL can handle arbitrarily nested (possibly recursive) query expressions that mix volatile relations, persistent DBPL relations residing in local or remote databases and SQL database relations. Therefore, much care has been devoted to develop evaluation heuristics that minimize data transfer and make best use of index information available for individual relations. Evaluation strategies are not determined at compile-time but depend on cardinality and index information available at run-time.

Again, a conceptually simple generalization of an existing programming language concept suffices to overcome the interoperability deficiencies of todays database programming interfaces that have developed in a system-driven, bottom-up fashion.

Although the system details of the DBPL/SQL gateway are quite delicate and often require ad-hoc case analysis to achieve good system performance, this specific gateway implementation follows a more general pattern that directly reflects the model of typed programming languages in terms of types, signatures, values and bindings presented in Sec. 3.2. Our general experience in extending a language L_{int} by generic gateways to an external language L_{ext} (i.e., to embed L_{ext} as a sublanguage of L_{int}) is described in more detail in [SM93]. Specific requirements can be stated on the type and expression syntax of L_{int} and L_{ext} as well as on the tools for mapping signatures and bindings between L_{int} and L_{ext}. In the DBPL/SQL scenario this is achieved by using *DynamicSQL*, a set of library routines shipped with the Ingres DBMS to create cursors and communication buffers to convert Ingres values (element-by-element, attribute-by-attribute according to their type structure) to DBPL values and to pass arguments (of scalar types) to SQL query strings.

Our work on gateway construction can be summarized by the experience that the task is simplified considerably if the external functionality is provided through well-structured libraries with abstract and "minimal" signatures, and not through extensive, "verbose" (SQL-like) and informally described interfaces.

4.3 Cross-Language Interoperability

The most primitive (but also most common) form of cross-language interoperability is achieved by having a standardized, language-independent link format (e.g., COFF of Unix

System V) that allows static bindings in a language L_{imp} to bind to values or locations defined in another language L_{exp}. In this setting, L_{imp} is able to import from L_{exp}. The next step is to define standardized, language-independent parameters passing conventions that allow argument values or argument locations defined in L_{imp} to be bound dynamically to function parameters defined in L_{exp}. If the roles of L_{imp} and L_{exp} can be interchanged, full cross-language interoperability (including "call-back" mechanisms) is supported.

Since this interoperability takes place at the value, location and binding level only, all naming and typing consistency control enforced by the use of type names, types and signatures in compilers is effectively lost in this scenario.

The DBPL compilers for VAX, Sparc and Motorola architectures attack this problem by providing the DBPL programmer with a mechanism to recover type and signature information for external bindings via so-called *foreign definition modules*. For example, the interface of the *Fax* module defined in Section 4.4 could be revised as follows to define a FAX service implemented in the programming language C:

```
definition for C module Fax;
import Phone;
type Status = (error, busy, done); ...
end Fax.
```

The compiler will enforce the consistent use of the bindings exported by the external *Fax* package in all importing DBPL programs. For example, it would catch the following type error in the application of the function *Fax.dial* that attempts to pass an integer value as a string argument:

```
module SendFax; import Phone, Fax;
begin Fax.dial(853228);Fax.send("Sample fax.");Fax.hangup(); end SendFax;
```

The skeleton of a C-program to provide value bindings matching the signatures *Fax* looks as follows.

```
typedef char* Phone_Number
typedef int Status
#define error ((Status) 0)
#define busy ((Status) 1) ...
Status Fax_dial(char* number){ ... }
Status Fax_send(char* text) { ... return done; ... }
void Fax_hangup() { ... }
```

Since relation types and relation operations are fully integrated into the DBPL language, they can be freely combined with the cross-language binding mechanisms:

```
for each b in register :contains(n.name, "Smith") do Fax.dial(n.num); end
```

It is also possible to call DBPL transactions on bulk objects from C.

4.4 Cross-Platform Interoperability

The distributed version of DBPL [JGL+88, JLRS88] exploits the basic module concepts to add an additional layer of type-safety to standard remote procedure call mechanisms (RPC) in federated client-server programming models.

To give access to a local fax service at a site called "CentralOffice", this site would compile the following *remote definition module* and then *export* the compiled description (typically together with its source text for documentation purposes) only to those clients on the network who are to be authorized to use the service.

remote definition module *Fax* **for** *"CentralOffice";*
import *Phone;*
type *Status = (error, busy, done);*
procedure *dial(number :Phone.Number) :Status;*
procedure *send(text* **:array of char**) *:Status;*
procedure *hangup();*
end *Fax.*

In this scenario, signatures of compiled definition modules accumulated in the compilation environment serve as protocol specifications. Frequently clients require distribution transparency. In this case it is of considerable advantage if a main program

module *SendFax;* **import** *Phone, Fax;*
begin *Fax.dial("853228");Fax.send("Sample fax.");Fax.hangup();* **end** *SendFax;*

stays textually unchanged whether it uses a local definition module *Fax* or the above remote definition module *Fax* for "Central Office" offered by a server somewhere in the network. This distribution transparency is achieved as usual by a client stub and a server stub that marshal and unmarshal the arguments and results supplied to functions defined in the remote definition module.

In terms of the Tycoon POS model, RPC-based communication mechanisms are an implementation technology that enables the creation of function value bindings between names in a client program and function values in a server program. Using plain RPC mechanisms it is not possible to directly define location bindings spanning machine boundaries. In particular, we would have to revise the module interface *Phone* not to directly export the locations *localPrefix* and *myNr*. However, using the concept of persistent variables introduced in section 3.3 these restrictions are lifted in DBPL by the provision of truly distributed persistent variables.

The crucial feature of DBPL is to retain (static) type safety across machine boundaries by maintaining a distributed compilation environment that allows local and remote modules to *share* signatures for type checking purposes and to share module bindings for transparent connection establishment.

5 Concluding Remarks

After seven years of development, the DBPL system has now reached a level of maturity and interoperability that makes its linguistic abstractions readily available for implementors of non-trivial Persistent Object Systems on several hardware-platforms.[4]

From a research point of view, an interesting side-effect of this DBPL implementation effort is an insight into repeating patterns of language and system extension requirements, some of which are outlined in Sec. 4. Consequently, our current work in the Tycoon project [Mat93, MS91, MS92] investigates languages and architectures that facilitate such incremental, problem-specific extensions in a type-safe environment.

[4]The DBPL system is distributed by Hamburg University.

In contrast to DBPL, Tycoon takes a rather radical approach by not maintaining upward compatibility with existing programming languages (Modula-2) and data models (extended relational models). Also its internal protocols for store access, program representation and linkage do not adhere to pre-existing standards. The rationale behind the design of Tycoon is to provide a lean language and system environment that provides just the kernel services and abstractions needed to define higher-level, problem-oriented "languages" and "data models" and provide an "ideal" basis for systems extensibility and interoperability.

References

[AB87] M.P. Atkinson and P. Bunemann. Types and Persistence in Database Programming Languages. *ACM Computing Surveys*, 19(2), June 1987.

[ABW+90] M. Atkinson, F. Bançilhon, D. De Witt, K. Dittrich, D. Maier, and S. Zdonik. The Object-Oriented Database System Manifesto. In *Deductive and Object-oriented Databases*. Elsevier Science Publishers, Amsterdam, Netherlands, 1990.

[Bar90] K. Barker. *Transaction Management on Multidatabase Systems*. PhD thesis, Department of Computing Science, University of Alberta, Edmonton, Alberta, Canada, 1990. available as Technical Report TR90-23.

[Ber90] P.A. Bernstein. Transaction Processing Monitors. *Communications of the ACM*, 3(11):75–86, 1990.

[BO91] K. Barker and M.T. Özsu. Reliable Transaction Execution in Multidatabase Systems. In *Proc. 1st Int. Workshop on Interoperability in Multidatabase Systems*, Kyoto, Japan, 1991.

[BS88] Y. Breibart and A. Silberschatz. Multidatabase Update Issues. In *Proceedings of the ACM-SIGMOD International Conference on Management of Data, Chicago, Illinois*, June 1988.

[DE89] W. Du and A. Elmagarmid. Quasi-Serializability: A Correctness Criterion for Global Concurrency Control in InterBase. In *Proceedings of the Fifteenth International Conference on Very Large Databases*, August 1989.

[DW84] U. Dayal and H.Y. Wang. View Definition and Generalization for Database System Integration in a Multidatabase System. *IEEE Transactions on Software Engineering*, SE-10(6):628–645, November 1984.

[ERMS91] J. Eder, A. Rudloff, F. Matthes, and J.W. Schmidt. Data Construction with Recursive Set Expressions in DBPL. In *Proceedings of the Kiev East/West Workshop on Next Generation Database Technology*, volume 504 of *Lecture Notes in Computer Science*, April 1991.

[Geo90] D. Georgakopoulos. *Transaction Management on Multidatabase Systems*. PhD thesis, Department of Computer Science, University of Houston, TX, 1990.

[Geo91] D. Georgakopoulos. Multidatabase Recoverability and Recovery. In *Proc. 1st Int. Workshop on Interoperability in Multidatabase Systems*, Kyoto, Japan, 1991.

[GMK88] H. Garcia-Molina and B. Kogan. Node Autonomy in Distributed System. In *Proc. Int. Symp. on Databases in Parallel and Distributed Systems*, Austin, TX, December 1988.

[HZ90] S. Heiler and S. Zdonik. Object Views: Extending the Vision. In *Proceedings of the IEEE Sixth International Conference on Data Engineering*, 1990.

[JGL+88] W. Johannsen, L. Ge, W. Lamersdorf, K. Reinhard, and J.W. Schmidt. Database Application Support in Open Systems: Language Support and Implementation. In *Proc. IEEE 4th Int. Conf. on Data Engineering*, Los Angeles, USA, February 1988.

[JLRS88] W. Johannsen, W. Lamersdorf, K. Reinhard, and J.W. Schmidt. The DURESS Project: Extending Databases into an Open Systems Architecture. In *Advances in Database Technology, EDBT '88*, volume 303 of *Lecture Notes in Computer Science*, pages 616–620. Springer-Verlag, 1988.

[KL89] W. Kim and F.H. Lochowsky. *Object-Oriented Concepts, Databases and Applications.* ACM Press Books, 1989.

[LA87] W. Litwin and A. Abdellatif. An Overview of the Multidatabase Manipulation Language MDL. *Proc. IEEE*, 75(5):621–631, May 1987.

[Man90] F. Manola. Object-Oriented Knowledge Bases – Parts I and II. *AI Exepert*, pages 26–36, 46–57, March and April 1990.

[Mat93] F. Matthes. *Persistente Objektsysteme: Integrierte Datenbankentwicklung und Programmerstellung.* Springer-Verlag, 1993. (In German).

[MB81] A. Motro and P. Buneman. Constructing Superviews. In *Proceedings of the ACM-SIGMOD International Conference on Management of Data*, pages 56–64, 1981.

[MRSS92a] F. Matthes, A. Rudloff, J.W. Schmidt, and K. Subieta. The Database Programming Language DBPL: User and System Manual. FIDE Technical Report FIDE/92/47, Fachbereich Informatik, Universität Hamburg, Germany, July 1992.

[MRSS92b] F. Matthes, A. Rudloff, J.W. Schmidt, and K. Subieta. A Gateweay from DBPL to Ingres. FIDE Technical Report Series FIDE/92/54, Fachbereich Informatik, Universität Hamburg, Germany, November 1992.

[MS91] F. Matthes and J.W. Schmidt. Bulk Types: Built-In or Add-On? In *Proceedings of the Third International Workshop on Database Programming Languages*, Nafplion, Greece, September 1991. Morgan Kaufmann Publishers. (Also appeared as TR FIDE/91/27).

[MS92] F. Matthes and J.W. Schmidt. Definition of the Tycoon Language TL – A Preliminary Report. Informatik Fachbericht FBI-HH-B-160/92, Fachbereich Informatik, Universität Hamburg, Germany, November 1992.

[MS93] F. Matthes and J.W. Schmidt. System Construction in the Tycoon Environment: Architectures, Interfaces and Gateways. In P.P. Spies, editor, *Proceedings Euro-Arch'93*, 1993.

[ÖV91] M.T. Özsu and P. Valduriez. *Principles of Distributed Database Systems.* Prentice Hall, Englewood Cliffs, NJ, 1991.

[ÖV93] M.T. Özsu and P. Valduriez. Distributed Data Management: unsolved problems and new issuses. In T. Casavant and M. Singhal, editors, *Readings in Distributed Computing.* IEEE Computer Society Press, 1993.

[SM91] J.W. Schmidt and F. Matthes. Modular and Rule-Based Database Programming in DBPL. FIDE Technical Report Series FIDE/91/15, Fachbereich Informatik, Universität Hamburg, Germany, February 1991.

[SM93] J.W. Schmidt and F. Matthes. Lean Languages and Models: Towards an Interoperable Kernel for Persistent Object Systems. In *Proceedings of the IEEE International Workshop on Research Issues in Data Engineering, Interoperability in Multidatabase Systems*, pages 2–16, Vienna, Austria, April 1993.

[SRL+90] M. Stonebraker, L.A. Rowe, B. Lindsay, J. Gray, M. Carey, M. Brodie, and P. Bernstein. Third-Generation Data Base System Manifesto. *ACM SIGMOD Record*, 19(3):31–44, September 1990.

[SSS+92] D. Stemple, R.B. Stanton, T. Sheard, P. Philbrow, R. Morrison, G.N.C. Kirby, L. Fegaras, R.L. Cooper, R.C.H. Connor, M.P. Atkinson, and S. Alagic. Type-Safe Linguistic Reflection: A Generator Technology. Research Report CS/92/6, Univ. of St. Andrews, Dept. of Comp. Science, July 1992.

[SSU90] A. Silberschatz, M. Stonebraker, and J.D. Ullman. Database Systems: Achievements and Opportunities, Report of the NSF Invitational Workshop on the Future of Database Systems Research. Technical Report TR-90-22, Department of Computer Science, The University of Texas at Austin, TX, 1990.

[Sto90] M. Stonebraker. Architecture of Future Data Base Systems. *IEEE Quarterly Bulletin Database Engineering*, 13(4):18–23, December 1990.

[SY90] P. Scheuermann and C. Yu. Report of the Workshop on Heterogeneous Database Systems. *IEEE Quarterly Bulletin Database Engineering*, 13(4):3–11, December 1990.

[Tay87] R.W. Taylor. Data Server Architectures: Experiences and Lessons. In *Proc. CIPS (Canadian Information Processing Society) Edmonton '87 Conf.*, pages 334–342, 1987.

[Wir85] N. Wirth. Report on the Programming Language Modula-2. In *Programming in Modula-2*. Springer-Verlag, 3rd edition, 1985.

[WV90] A. Wolski and J. Veijalainen. 2PC Agent Method: Achieving Serializability in Presence of Failures in a Heterogeneous Multidatabase. In *Proc. Int. Conf. on Databases, Parallel Architectures and their Applications*, pages 321–330, Miami Beach, FL, 1990.

[ZM89] S.B. Zdonik and D. Maier. *Readings in Object Oriented Database Management Systems*. Morgan Kaufmann Publishers, 1989.

Programming in Persistent Higher-Order Languages

Connor R.C.H., Morrison R., Atkinson M.P.*, Matthes F.+, Schmidt J.W.+

Department of Mathematical and Computational Science,
University of St Andrews, St Andrews, Fife, Scotland.

*Department of Computer Science, University of Glasgow,
Glasgow G12 8QQ, Scotland.

+Fachbereich Informatik, Universität Hamburg, Vogt-Kölln Straße 30,
D-22527 Hamburg, Germany.

{richard, ron}@dcs.st-and.ac.uk
mpa@dcs.glasgow.ac.uk
{matthes, J_Schmidt}@dbis1.informatik.uni-hamburg.de

Abstract

Persistent programming languages differ from traditional languages in that data of arbitrary lifetimes is fully governed by the type system. Such languages lead to radically different programming paradigms and methodologies for two important reasons:

- the high-level type system may be relied upon as a protection mechanism even for long-term data
- data of any type, including first-class procedures and abstract data types, may be kept for arbitrary lifetimes.

The combination of these means that the kind of sophisticated typing commonly used in programs which operate over short-term data may be extended to all data manipulated by a long-lived system. This paper exposes some of the ways in which well-known type system features may be powerfully used in contexts normally associated with operating systems and database management systems.

1. Introduction

Information systems frequently have to deal with longevity and scale in the data that they support. Data is required with lifetimes which match the real-world processes they represent, which can range from microseconds to years. Data is also commonly required to support the work of large organisations, with time scales of up to hundreds of years.

In an orthogonally persistent programming system, the manner in which data is manipulated is independent of its persistence. The same mechanisms operate on both short-term and long-term data, avoiding the traditional need for separate systems to control access to data of different degrees of longevity. Thus data may remain under the control of a single persistent programming system for its entire lifetime. The benefits of orthogonal persistence have been described extensively in the literature and can be summarised as:

- improving programming productivity from simpler semantics;
- removing ad hoc arrangements for data translation and long term data storage; and
- providing protection mechanisms over the whole environment.

Considerable research has been devoted to the investigation of the concept of persistence and its application in the integration of database systems and programming languages [Atk78, ABC+83]. As a result a number of persistent systems have been developed including Pascal/R [Sch77], PS-algol [PS88], Napier88 [MBC+89], DBPL [MS89], Galileo [ACO85], TI Persistent Memory System [Tha86], Amber [Car85], Trellis/Owl [SCW85] and Tycoon [MS92]. The persistence abstraction is widely recognised as the appropriate underlying technology for long lived, concurrently accessed and potentially large bodies of data and programs. Typical examples of such systems are CAD/CAM systems, office automation, CASE tools and software engineering environments. Object-Oriented Database Systems such as GemStone [BOP+89] and O_2 [BBB+88] have at their core a persistent object store. Process modelling systems use a persistent base to preserve their modelling activities over execution sessions [BPR91]. The goal of persistence research is to allow these socially and economically important persistent application systems to be more sophisticated and more economically viable.

This paper surveys some programming methodologies and styles that have been developed after the extensive use of persistent languages in the construction of medium scale software systems. Section 2 introduces the main point of underlying technology which makes the techniques possible: that of an enforced, persistent type system. Section 3 shows how the sophisticated protection offered by many modern type systems can be used to great effect when extended to cover long-term data. Section 4 surveys hyper-programming, a new style of programming in which the program source itself contains bindings to typed values in the persistent object store. The advantages of hyper-programming are not limited to persistent systems; however, the persistent technology is a requirement for the safe implementation of a hyper-programming system.

2. Type systems and persistence

Type systems are historically viewed as mechanisms which impose static safety constraints upon a program. Within a persistent environment, however, the type system takes on a wider role.

Data manipulated by a programming language is governed by that language's type system. In non-persistent languages, however, data which persists for longer than the invocation of a program may only be achieved by the use of an operating system interface which is shared by all applications. As a consequence of this, such data passes beyond the jurisdiction of the type system of any one language.

Mechanisms which govern long term data, such as protection and module binding, must be dealt with at the level of this interface. Historically this has the consequence that the type system may not be enforced, and knowledge of the typed structure of data may not be taken advantage of. This is shown diagramatically in Figure 2.1.

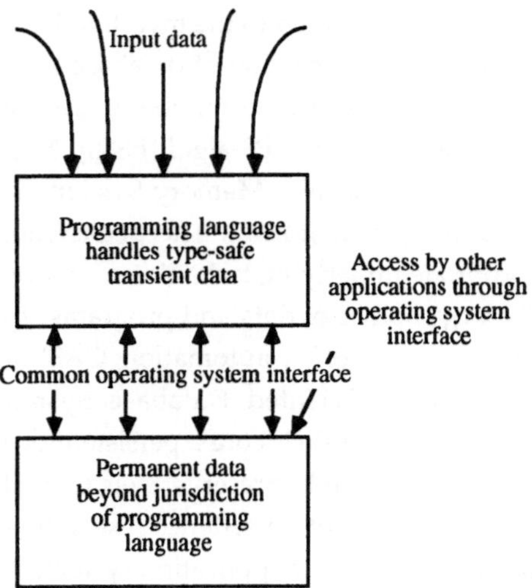

Figure 2.1 Traditional strategy for permanent and shared data

In a persistent system, the storage of data beyond a single program invocation is handled by programming language mechanisms, and no common operating system interface is necessary. The only route by which data may be accessed is through the programming language, and so the type system of a single language may be used to enforce protection upon both transient and permanent data. High-level modelling may be relied upon for the entire lifetime of the data, as it never passes outside the language system. Figure 2.2 gives a diagrammatic view of such a system.

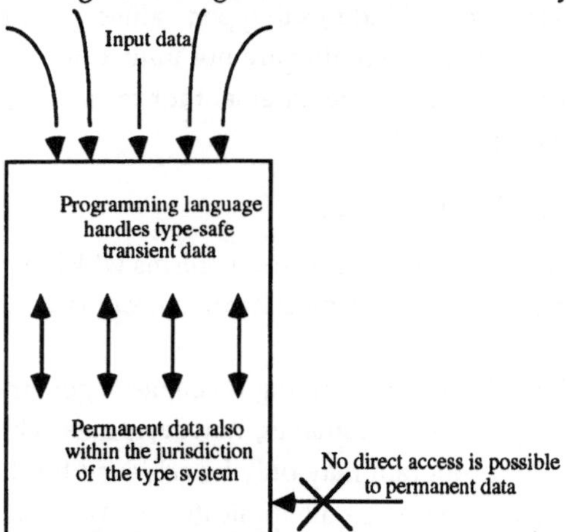

Figure 2.2 The persistent strategy

The universality of the persistent type system has consequences in terms of both the modelling and protection provided by the type system. With respect to modelling, the persistent type system must be sufficiently flexible to allow the modelling of activities normally provided by untyped support systems. Such activities include, for example, the linking of separately prepared program units, and file system access protection. With respect to protection, the increased role of a type system means that any protection mechanisms programmed at a high level may be fully relied upon to protect the data for its lifetime, as access from outside the constraints of the type system is not possible. In particular, various high level information hiding techniques may be used to restrict data access, instead of relying upon the normally coarse grain and typeless control provided by outside technologies.

3. Programming with persistent type systems

Traditionally, computer systems rely upon the type systems of individual programming languages as the only protection mechanism for transient data, and provide a number of different mechanisms, such as file system protection or database constraints, for permanent data. This is because transient and persistent data exist in two separate universes, with different operations available upon them. In persistent programming systems, however, there is no clear difference between transient and permanent data, and this two-level protection scheme is not an appropriate model.

The provision of type-safe permanent data provides one kind of control that is not available in a non-persistent model. Type systems by themselves, however, lack two important categories of integrity protection. These are access protection, to prevent data from being accessed by programs which do not require it, and integrity constraints, which are normally finer-grained than those which may be modelled by type systems.

Both of these categories of protection may be explicitly programmed in many programming languages. However, in a non-persistent system, such programmed protection may not be extended to data exported from a program. In a persistent system, however, data storage is performed entirely within a programming language, and there is no problem with the storage and sharing of any kind of data. Access protection and integrity constraints may therefore be flexibly programmed according to the needs of the individual data.

Access protection may be programmed in a persistent system by the use of constructs which allow information hiding. These include inclusion polymorphism, abstract data types, and higher-order procedures. What these have in common is that they may hide part of the state of a program by introducing state which is not directly denotable. This makes it impossible to specify another program which will access the hidden state.

There are three well-known mechanisms which allow the programming of information hiding within a strong type system. These are subtyping, procedural encapsulation (1st-order information hiding) and existential data types (2nd-order information hiding). Subtyping achieves protection by removing type information, causing the static failure of programs which may try to perform undesirable accesses. 1st-order information hiding prevents the protected data from being named by an untrusted program, allowing access only through a procedural interface. 2nd-order hiding is somewhere between these two, allowing access mainly through procedures, but also allowing the protected data to be named. This data is, however, viewed through a mechanism which causes type information loss, and therefore allows only a limited set of operations to be performed on it.

3.1. Subtyping

In general, systems which allow subtyping allow any data value to be used in place of one typed with less functionality. One type is a subtype of another if all operations allowed on the second type are also allowed on the first. In the most general form of subtyping, often referred to as inclusion polymorphism, it is type correct for the use of any value to be replaced by the use of any of its subtypes.

A number of different semantics are possible for the definition of a subtype rule. Here the semantics of Cardelli [Car84] are adopted, using structural type equivalence and an implicit subtyping rule.

Subtype inheritance is usually regarded as a general modelling technique. In particular it allows the declaration of procedures which operate over any type with at least a set of required properties. However, using an object as one of its supertypes is also equivalent to hiding some of the functionality which the object possesses. For example, the following introduces the names *employee* and *person* as record types:

```
type employee is record( name , address : string ; salary : int )
type person is record( name , address : string )
```

Type *employee* is a subtype of type *person*, and an object of type *employee* may be substituted in any context where an object of type *person* is expected. This would have the effect of hiding the salary field by the loss of type information. If another user is only to be allowed this restricted access to employee objects, this view of the object may be exported, for example by use of an explicit type coercion:

```
let joe = employee( "Joe Doe" , "1 Assignment Boulevard" , 100000 )
let exportJoe : person = joe
```

In this *joe* is declared to be an object of type *employee* with the given field values. *exportJoe* is of type *person*, denoted by the type after the ":" symbol, but has the value *joe*. This means that a user of the value *exportJoe* will now have the value of the original record. However, it is not possible to express an operation to access the salary field of this value due to the restrictions of the static type system. That is, the *salary* field cannot be used with the object *exportJoe* since such a program would fail during static analysis.

In a non-persistent system such protection appears to be of little use. The point of this mechanism applied to persistence, however, is that arbitrary typed values may be made to persist, and the type system strictly enforces any future access to them by other programs. In the above program segment the identifiers *joe* and *exportJoe* denote the same value, but are of different types. It is then possible to set up two different contexts in which these differently typed denotations of the same value are made persistent. Programs which subsequently bind to the *exportJoe* context will be able to use the value only as a type *person*. Subtying of persistent data therefore provides the essence of a database viewing mechanism when applied to persistent data.

3.2. 1st-order information hiding

Access to data can also be restricted by only allowing access to procedures which are defined over the data, and not allowing the data itself to be visible. This is a common model for abstract data types, and is known as 1st-order information hiding [CW85]. It may be achieved in a number of ways but it will be described here in terms of a language which has first-class procedure values and block-style scoping. Access to the original data may then be removed simply by its identifier becoming unavailable. For example, the following type defines a *Person* as a record containing procedures which define three operations:

```
type Person is record
(
        getName,
        getAddress      : proc( → string ) ;
        putAddress      : proc( string )
)
```

This allows a finer grain of restriction than that achieved by subtype inheritance, in that the name and address may be read, but only the address may be changed. Access to the data may be removed by placing its declaration in a block so that its identifier is lost from scope after the *Person* object has been constructed. This is shown in Figure 3.1. The exported procedures, which have the data encapsulated within their closures, are then the only way in which the original value may be accessed. Again, this relies upon the static properties of the system to prevent the access since a program which attempts direct access to *joe* will fail statically by the scoping rules of the language.

```
let exportJoe =
begin
        let joe = employee( "Joe Doe", "1 Assignment Boulevard", 100000 )
        Person(   proc( → string ) ; joe.name ,
                  proc( → string ) ; joe.address ,
                  proc( new : string ) ; joe.address := new   )
end
```

Figure 3.1 Hiding the Data Representation

In Figure 3.1, *exportJoe* is declared to have the value obtained by executing the block. This is a structure of type *Person* with three procedure fields. Each procedure uses the object *joe* which is inaccessible by any other means after exit from the block.

Further flexibility is possible using encapsulation in that dynamic properties may be specified, and access may be denied dynamically if required. For example, perhaps there exists an integrity constraint that an address may not be more than 100 characters long. This can be programmed in the procedural encapsulation, as shown in Figure 3.2. The only difference here is that the *putAddress* procedure checks the dynamic constraint, and raises an exception if it is not met.

```
let exportJoe =
begin
        let joe = employee( "Joe Doe" , "1 Assignment Boulevard" , 100000 )
        Person(  proc( → string) ; joe.name,
                 proc( → string) ; joe.address,
                 proc( new : string ) ;
                      if length( new ) ≤ 100
                           then joe.address := new
                           else raise longAddress( new )          )
end
```

Figure 3.2 Refining the Interface

A particular example of a dynamic constraint allows access to the original data to be protected by password. A procedure can be provided in the interface which will return direct access to a user with sufficient privilege. Figure 3.3 shows the extended definition required, with an extra procedure in type *extraPerson* which returns the representation of the data only if it is supplied with a string equal to the password used to create it. In this situation, the programmer responsible for constructing the view of the data will have enough information to extract the representation. Alternatively, it would be possible to arrange system-wide passwords which would decide whether access is allowed or not.

```
type extraPerson is record
(
        getEmployee    : proc( string → employee ) ;
        getName,
        getAddress     : proc( → string ) ;
        putAddress     : proc( string )
)

let exportJoe = proc( password : string → extraPerson )
begin
        let joe = employee( "Joe Doe" , "1 Assignment Boulevard" , 100000 )
        extraPerson(   proc( attempt : string → employee )
                              if attempt = password
                                   then joe
                                   else failValue,
                       proc( → string ) ; joe.name,
                       proc( → string ) ; joe.address,
                       proc( new : string ) ; joe.address := new)
end
```

Figure 3.3 Protection by Password

This technique gives a result not dissimilar from the kind of module provided by Pebble [BL84] and a high level language analogy of capabilities [DvH66].

Instead of a string password, an unforgeable "software capability" may be used. It is a consequence of orthogonal persistence that, for any type over which identity is defined, the identity of any value is unique for the lifetime of the system. Therefore the identity of such a value is unforgeable. If such a value is bound to the closure of a procedure as its password, then to use the procedure a programmer must somehow have access to the same value.

3.3. 2nd-order information hiding

2nd-order information hiding does not restrict access to the protected values, but instead abstracts over the type of the protected value to restrict operations allowed on it. Thus the protected values may be manipulated for some basic operations, such as assignment and perhaps equality, but their normal operations are not allowed due to the type view. This allows the representation objects themselves to be safely placed in the interface along with the procedures which manipulate them.

One mechanism which allows 2nd-order information hiding is the existential data type as described in [MP88]. This allows the definition of interface types which are abstracted over. As names for these types are declared before the existential type definition, different parts of the definition may be bound to the same type. As before, only the basic operations defined on all types are allowed over the abstracted types, but values which are abstracted by the same name are statically known to be compatible. *Person* as above may be redefined as:

```
type Person is absType[ absPersonType ]
(
        absPerson,mum,dad,favourite  : absPersonType ;
        getName,getAddress           : proc( → string ) ;
        putAddress                   : proc( string )
)
```

The identifier in square brackets before the body of the type declaration declares a name for a type which is abstracted over. This allows a tighter definition of such types, as it can now be seen where the same type appears in the interface. Components of the same instance of an interface may be bound together by a **use** clause. For example,

```
use exportJoe as joe in
        joe.favourite := joe.mum
```

may be statically determined to be type correct, as the *favourite* and *mum* fields must be type compatible to allow the object to be created.

This static binding of equivalent types may also be used to allow the interface procedures to be defined over the type of the hidden representation. A more flexible definition which allows the name and address operations to be performed on any of the people in the interface would be:

```
type Person is abstype[ absPersonType ]
(
        absPerson,mum,
        dad,favourite         : absPersonType ;
        getName,getAddress: proc( absPersonType → string ) ;
        putAddress            : proc( absPersonType,string )
)
```

This allows the definition of n-ary operations over the hidden representation type. For example, a procedure may be placed in the interface which tests if two people have the same address:

```
type Person is absType[ absPersonType ]
(
        absPerson,mum,
        dad,favourite    : absPersonType ;
        getName,
        getAddress       : proc( absPersonType → string ) ;
        putAddress       : proc( absPersonType,string ) ;
        sameAddress      : proc( absPersonType,absPersonType → bool )
)
```

This example illustrates a major difference in power between 1st-order and 2nd-order information hiding. With 2nd-order, a type is abstracted over, and procedures may be defined over this type. With 1st-order hiding, it is the object itself which is hidden within its procedural interface. Procedures which operate over more than one such object may not be defined sensibly within this interface. Therefore any operations defined over two instances must be written at a higher level, using the interface. At best this creates syntactic noise and is inefficient at execution time. It also means that such operations are defined in the module which uses the abstract objects, rather than the module which creates them. Some examples are not possible to write without changing the original interface.

Once again it should be stressed that the type constructs introduced here are well understood and found in many programming languages. The use of these mechanisms in persistent languages relies upon the ability of values of these types to be kept for arbitrary lifetimes, and the binding of new programs to them to be strongly typed. Therefore the protection provided by the mechanism can be used in a much wider context.

4. Hyper-programming

The presence of persistent data in the software construction environment allows the introduction of new binding paradigms, in particular the ability to bind persistent values directly into both source and executable code. This allows programs which contain links to persistent values within their source code, instead of textual denotations of these links which must be evaluated and bound to the program code during or immediately before its execution. This structured form of a program bears a similar relationship to purely textual programs as hyper-text does to ordinary text, and so the new style of program is known as a hyper-program [KCC+92, Kir92, Cut92].

The traditional representation of a program as a linear sequence of text forces a particular style of program construction to ensure good programming practice. Persistent systems have the ability to allow the persistent environment to participate in the program construction process. This raises the possibility of allowing the representations of source programs to include direct links to values that already exist in the environment, giving hyper-programs.

The primary motivation for providing a hyper-programming system is to allow the programmer to compose programs interactively, navigating the persistent store and selecting data items to be incorporated into the programs. The programmer has the option of linking existing data items into a program by pointing to graphical representations. This removes the need to write access specifications for persistent data items that are accessed by a program. The ability to link to data items at run-time is still required in the cases where data becomes available only after a program is written.

Figure 4.1 shows an example representation of a hyper-program. The hyper-program contains both text and links that denotes data items in the persistent store. The first link is to a procedure to write out a string; this is called to write a prompt to the user. The program then calls another procedure to read in a name, and then finds an address corresponding to the name. This is done by calling a lookup procedure which is one of the components of a table package linked into the hyper-program. The address is then written out.

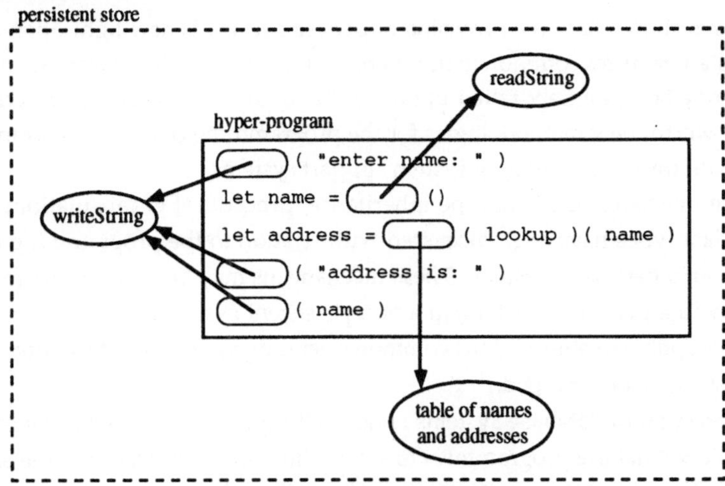

Figure 4.1 A hyper-program

Many programs may share links and the graph of program components can become highly interconnected. Other benefits of hyper-programming include:

- increased ease of program composition;
- being able to perform program checking early;

- being able to enforce associations from executable programs to source programs;
- availability of an increased range of linking times;
- reduced program verbosity; and
- support for source representations of procedure closures.

The principal requirement for supporting a hyper-programming system is a persistent store to contain the program representations and the data items denoted by the links in the programs. The persistent store must be stable, and support referential integrity. Hence when a reference to a data item in the store has been established, the data item will remain accessible for as long as the reference exists. An incremental binding mechanism is also required, to allow newly constructed programs to be bound back into the system within which they were constructed.

Hyper-programming is not possible unless the source and executable forms of programs reside in the same persistent space as the rest of the application data. Thus an implementation requires to be based not only upon a persistent programming language, but one in which full support is available for the entire software lifecycle. This includes for example a program editor, an object browser, a compiler and a window manager, all written in the persistent language itself.

A prototype hyper-programming system is available in the Napier88 release system [KCC+92]. It is important to note that hyper-programming is not an intrinsic part of the Napier88 language, and could be provided in any persistent language given the appropriate support technology.

5. Conclusions

It has been shown how the provision of persistence sheds new light upon the use of type system features common in non-persistent languages. The fact that attributes of a type may be absolutely relied upon for the lifetime of the data it describes gives some powerful new methodologies for the programming of activities normally associated with untyped, operating system support systems.

The mechanisms of subtype inheritance, procedural encapsulation, and existential data types have been discussed with relation to the programming of protection within a persistent system. These mechanisms may be used to program protection only in a persistent system; in a non-persistent system the protected data is always susceptible to abuse by the common operating system interface through which its storage must be arranged.

Protection in database systems is normally provided by viewing mechanisms. These allow database programmers to set up different interfaces over the same data, so that users with different privileges may perform different operations. It is clear that the information hiding techniques presented above may be used to program flexible viewing mechanisms within a persistent programming system.

The last consequence of strongly typed persistent data presented is the ability to safely allow the style of programming known as hyper-programming. The concept of hyper-programming is straightforward: programs may contain direct links to values, rather than textual denotations which are bound to at or after compilation. The only way this programming style can be supported with any reasonable degree of safety is by the system being contained in a strongly-typed persistent environment, so that the types of the direct bindings can be enforced.

6. Acknowledgements

Much of this work was supported by ESPRIT II Basic Research Action 3070 – FIDE, and SERC grant GR/F 02953. Richard Connor is supported by SERC Postdoctoral Fellowship B/91/RFH/9078. The hyper-programming system was partly conceived and wholly implemented by Quintin Cutts and Graham Kirby of St Andrews University.

7. References

[ABC83] Atkinson, M.P., Bailey, P.J., Chisholm, K.J., Cockshott, W.P. & Morrison, R. "An Approach to Persistent Programming." The Computer Journal, 26, 4, (1983), 360-365.

[ACO85] Albano, A., Cardelli, L. & Orsini, R. "Galileo: a Strongly Typed, Interactive Conceptual Language" ACM TODS 10, 2 (1985) pp 230 - 260.

[Atk78] Atkinson, M.P. "Programming Languages and Databases" Proc. 4th International Conference on Very Large Data Bases, Berlin In S.P. Yao (editor), IEEE (September 1978) pp 408 - 419.

[BBB+88] Bancilhon, F., Barbedette, G., Benzaken, B., Delobel, C., Gamerman, S., Lecluse, C., Pfeffer, P., Richard, P. & Valez, F. "The Design and Implementation of O2, an Object-Oriented Database System". In Lecture Notes in Computer Science 334, Springer-Verlag (1988) pp 1-22.

[BL84] Burstall, R. & Lampson, B. "A Kernel Language for Abstract Data Types and Modules" Proc. International Symposium on the Semantics of Data Types LNCS Vol. 173, Springer-Verlag (1984).

[BOP+89] Bretl, B., Otis, A., Penney, J., Schuchardt, B., Stein, J., Williams, E.H., Williams, M. & Maier, D. "The GemStone Data Management System". In Object-Oriented Concepts, Applications, and Databases, Kim, W. & Lochovsky, F. (ed), Morgan-Kaufman (1989).

[BPR91] Bruynooghe, R.F., Parker, J.M. & Rowles, J.S. "PSS: A System for Process Enactment". In Proc. 1st International Conference on the Software Process: Manufacturing Complex Systems (1991).

[Car84] Cardelli, L. "A Semantics of Multiple Inheritance" Proc. International Symposium on the Semantics of Data Types LNCS Vol. 173, Springer-Verlag (1984) pp 51 - 67.

[Car85] Cardelli, L. "Amber". Tech. Report AT7T. Bell Labs. Murray Hill, U.S.A. (1985).

[CW85] Cardelli, L. & Wegner, P. "On Understanding Types, Data Abstraction and Polymorphism" ACM Computing Surveys 17, 4 (Dec. 1985) pp. 471 - 523.

[Cut92] Kirby, G.N.C "Delivering the Benefits of Persistence to System Construction and Execution" Ph.D. Thesis, University of St Andrews (1992).

[DvH66] Dennis, J.B. & van Horn, E.C. "Programming Semantics for Multiprogrammed Computations" CACM 9, 3 (1966) pp 143 - 145.

[KCC92] Kirby, G.N.C., Connor, R.C.H., Cutts, Q.I., Dearle, A., Farkas, A.M. & Morrison, R. "Persistent Hyper-Programs". 5th International Conference on Persistent Object Systems, Italy (1992).

[KCC+92] Kirby, G.N.C., Cutts, Q.I., Connor, R.C.H., Dearle, A. & Morrison, R. "Programmers' Guide to the Napier88 Standard Library, Edition 2.1". University of St Andrews (1992).

[Kir92] Kirby, G.N.C "Reflection and Hyper-Programming in Persistent Programming Systems" Ph.D. Thesis, University of St Andrews (1992).

[MBC89 Morrison, R., Brown, A.L., Connor, R. & Dearle, A. "The Napier88 Reference Manual". Universities of Glasgow & St Andrews Persistent Programming Research Report 77-89 (1989).

[MP88] Mitchell J.C. & Plotkin, G.D. "Abstract Types have Existential Type" ACM TOPLAS 10, 3 (July 1988) pp. 470 - 502.

[MS89] Matthes, F. & Schmidt, J.W. "The Type System of DBPL" In R. Hull, R. Morrison and D. Stemple (editors) Proc. 2nd International Workshop on Database Programming Languages Morgan - Kaufmann (1989) pp 219 - 225.

[MS92] Matthes, F. & Schmidt, J.W. "Definition of the Tycoon Language TL - A Preliminary Report". University of Hamburg Technical Report 062-92 (1992).

[PS88] "PS-algol Reference Manual". Universities of St Andrews and Glasgow PPRR39 (1988).

[Sch77] Schmidt, J.W. "Some High-Level Language Constructs for Data of Type Relation" ACM ToDS 2, 3 (1977) pp 247 - 261.

[SCW85] Schaffert, C., Cooper, T. & Wilpot, C. "Trellis Object-Based Environment Language Reference Manual". DEC Technical Report 372 (1985).

[Tha86] Thatte, S.M. "Persistent Memory: A Storage Architecture for Object Oriented Database Systems". In Proc. ACM/IEEE International Workshop on Object-Oriented Database Systems, Pacific Grove, California (1986) pp 148-159.

System Construction in the Tycoon[1] Environment: Architectures, Interfaces and Gateways

Florian Matthes Joachim W. Schmidt

Universität Hamburg
Vogt-Kölln Straße 30
D-22527 Hamburg, Germany
{matthes,J_Schmidt}@dbis1.informatik.uni-hamburg.de

Abstract

This paper outlines the basic concepts and the system architecture of the Tycoon[1] environment. Tycoon is designed for the construction of persistent object systems intended to be available on multiple software and hardware platforms.

Tycoon's contribution to system portability and scalability is achieved by strictly separating concerns of data modelling, data manipulation, and data storage into three distinct system layers each of which is based on state-of-the-art system technology (polymorphic programmming languages, portable code representations, persistent object stores). Much emphasis is being placed on supporting interoperability between Tycoon applications and off-the-shelf tools and systems, such as database systems, user interface managers, and optimizing code generators.

We illustrate how higher-order functions, polymorphic typing and transparent persistence management reduce the amount of repetitive and type-unsafe programming in typical persistent object systems.

1 Introduction and Overview

In this paper we present the concept of *application frameworks in persistent higher-order languages* as a systematic approach to carry forward the conceptual and technological achievements of fourth-generation languages (4GLs) into open, heterogeneous environments.

In a fist step (section 2), we summarize the relative merits of third-generation languages and fourth-generation languages for the development of information systems. Based on this analysis we explain how persistent higher-order languages equipped with well-designed polymorphic libraries make it possible to blend the advantages of 3GLs and 4GLs in a conceptually simple and linguistically integrated system environment.

In the following sections we present Tycoon, a particular example of a persistent higher-order language that has been developed at the University of Hamburg [MS92, Mat93]. The Tycoon project draws heavily from practical experience gained in implementing successive generations of relational database programming languages [Sch77,

[1]Tycoon: Typed Communicating Objects in Open Environments.

This research is supported by ESPRIT Basic Research, Project FIDE, #6309.

KMP+83, SM92a, SMV93] and from recent research results of the Esprit Basic Research Project FIDE (Fully Integrated Data Environments).

Section 3 sketches Tycoon's characteristic language concepts that are required for the definition of type-safe, high-level application frameworks. Tycoon drastically reduces the amount of repetitive and type-unsafe programming in typical information systems by factoring-out much of the application's functionality into generic, extensible server libraries.

Section 4 outlines the overall Tycoon system architecture that achieves a high degree of portability and scalability by strictly separating concerns of data modelling, data manipulation, and data storage into three distinct system layers each of which is based on state-of-the-art system technology (polymorphic programmming languages, portable code representations, persistent object stores).

Finally, section 5 gives an idea of the organization and functionality of the Tycoon libraries for bulk data management. We distinguish between internal library implementations (written entirely in Tycoon) and external library implementations (imported from external servers like SQL databases, graphical user interfaces, or operating system libraries). Due to the richness of Tycoon's type system it is possible to provide application programmers with a uniform view on both kinds of libraries.

2 Approaches to Persistent Object System Construction

We use the term *persistent object systems* (POS) to denote a class of software systems that give their users a flexible, problem-oriented and safe access to large sets of long-lived objects of various types [SM93, Mat93].

Due to technological and commercial developments there is an ever-increasing demand for persistent object systems that handle new object types like texts (electronic mail, text retrieval, "intelligent" text manipulation), two- and three-dimensional graphics (CAD and geographic information systems), digitized raster images (picture and font finder, fax manager, character recognition software), voice data, or even short, compressed image sequences (presentation software, scene analysis). Furthermore, persistent object systems have to be implemented in substantially different (PC-based, interactive, networked, distributed, semi-autonomous) system environments [Bla90, Cat91, BM91].

In addition to the classical problems of large-scale application development, developers of a POS are faced with the following characteristic tasks (see, e.g., [ZM89, ABW+90, SRL+90]):

Persistent Storage: The primary task in a persistent object system is the manipulation of the state of long-lived data objects shared by multiple, possibly concurrently executing applications. In many persistent object systems it is advantageous to be able to store, share and modify also program objects ("methods", "scripts") as first-class data objects.

Generic Programming: Persistent object systems are characterized by highly repetitive algorithmic and structural patterns (set-oriented queries, integrity constraints, generic data structures, etc.). Therefore, many commercial tools utilize generator techniques to derive automatically stereotyped program fragments (form definitions, format conversions, sorting routines, iterators, etc.) from parameterized, high-level descriptions.

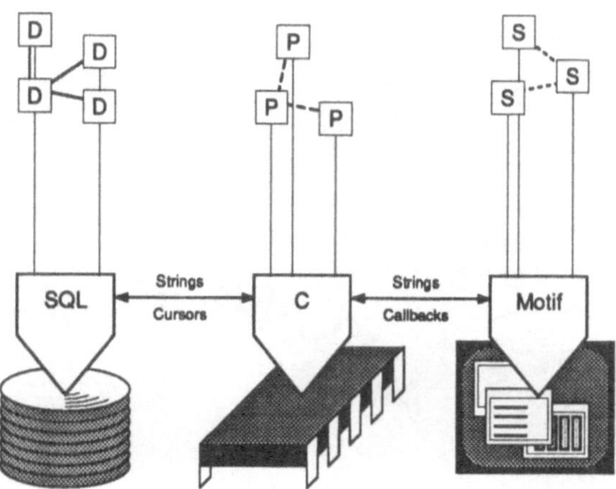

Figure 1: Narrow server interfaces in 3GLs

External Server Integration: The buzzword "open architectures" is of particular relevance for persistent object systems since it is often necessary to interact with external devices (screns, printers, keyboards, pointing devices, scanners, CD-ROMS, modems, fax machines, etc.) and external servers (window libraries, RPC libraries, directory services, etc.) for data acquisition, data presentation and data transfer.

In the following, we first sketch how these requirements are met partially by third- and fourth-generation languages, respectively, and we then develop the idea of application frameworks in persistent higher-order languages which can be understood as a synthesis of the 3GL and 4GL approach.

2.1 Low-Level Server Access from 3GLs

The majority of today's information systems is implemented in third-generation languages (COBOL, FORTRAN, C, Pascal). A severe limitation of these languages is their inability to capture correctly the generity inherent even in simple persistent object models. For example, the relational data model supports the definition of unary, binary, ternary, ... relations over various domains and it includes generic operations over relation variables. These operations cannot be captured adequately by any of the commercial programming languages mentioned above [BHR82].

As a consequence of this conceptual limitation, developers of database programming interfaces like Embedded SQL [Ing90] restrict themselves to the least common denominator of all 3GLs and handle any information interchange via strings, addresses and untyped byte arrays that are transferred at the smallest possible granularity (attribute-wise) between application programs and the database systems. A similar situation can be observed at the interface between programming languages and (graphical) user interfaces.

The resulting POS scenario using 3GLs is depicted in Fig. 1: The overall functionality of a particular POS is provided by a coordinated manipulation of numerous heterogeneous objects on different media (D: database objects, P: program objects, S: screen objects, etc.). Objects on different servers are subject to server-specific naming, typing,

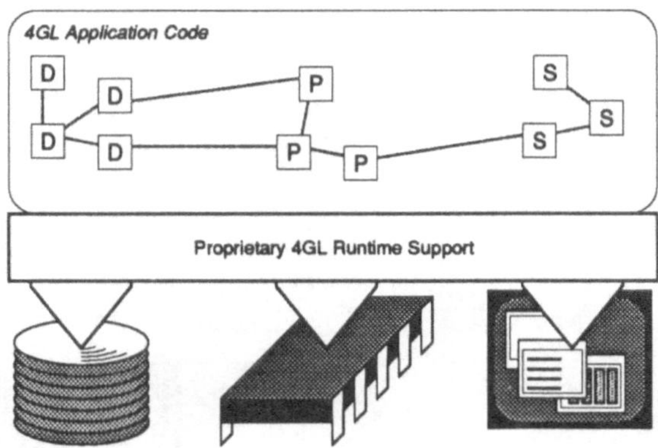

Figure 2: Server integration in proprietary 4GLs

lifetime, and binding rules (indicated by different line styles in Fig. 1) while inter-server communication takes place at a low level of abstraction using simple, machine-oriented protocols.

A crucial advantage of such a loose server coupling is the *openess* of the application development environment. If required, new servers can be integrated freely as libraries into existing persistent object systems. Furthermore, call interfaces provide a minimal common ground for data exchange between independependently developed services and they also constitute a starting point for data abstraction and component exchangeability.

2.2 Server Integration in 4GLs

Fourth-generation languages recognize the need for a uniform, safe and application-oriented development environment across a variety of servers and above the minimal interoperation level of strings and cursors. As depicted in Fig. 2, a well-designed 4GL provides high-level naming, typing and binding mechanisms for objects on different media (on disk, in memory, and on screen) and thereby eliminates a substantial amount of the low-level, repetetive data conversion and data transfer code found in 3GL applications. 4GLs are tailored to the specific requirements of traditional, commercial database applications:

Functional requirements: record- and set-oriented data modelling, data manipulation, data storage and data display; generic operations (search, iterate, insert, delete, update, format, display, validate, ...) applicable uniformly to record and set objects of different component structure.

Operational requirements: persistent storage of data, application code, integrity constraints and user interface definitions; efficient manipulation of data on secondary storage; integration into transactional multi-user systems.

Modal requirements: interactive user-interfaces, access to precompiled queries and update transactions; support for incremental system evolution (e.g. schema changes); provision for *ad-hoc* queries.

Examples of relational 4GLs include Ingres-4GL [Ing89], PL-SQL [Ora91], and Informix-4GL [Inf86]. Furthermore, several object-oriented database systems are shipped with 4GL languages to simplify application development (e.g., O_2SQL and CO_2 for O_2 [BDK92]). Practical experience shows that 4GL constitute a significant advance towards achieving faster software development, improved long-term software maintainability, better software portability, and even enhanced execution efficiency for specialized applications (e.g., queries) when compared with hand-coded third-generation languge solutions like C or COBOL [MJ89].

There are, however, some severe limitations to current 4GL languages that hamper their success in today's open, continually evolving system environments:

- 4GLs are deeply integrated into proprietary DBMSs and it is therefore impossible to move 4GL applications from one DBMS to another. This situation is in sharp contrast to 3GL applications using standardized programming and database languages (e.g., C and OpenSQL).
- It is typically very difficult to interface 4GLs with external servers (window systems, statistical packages, text-retrieval tools) that do not come bundled with the DBMS.
- Applications developed in 4GLs do not scale well due to a lack of appropriate typing and modularization support as found, for example, in Ada, C++, Modula-2 or Eiffel.
- On the system level, 4GL often incur an unnecessary system overhead since it is impossible to "downscale" the extensive 4GL runtime support (form management, event management, query support, report generation, transaction management, ...) to just the functionaliy needed by a particular application.
- The linguistic quality of 4GLs does not compare well with modern (object-oriented, modular, or functional) programming languages.

2.3 Scalable Application Frameworks in Persistent Higher-Order Languages

Most of the above 4GL limitations reflect the deficiencies of the implementation technology that is being used to construct 4GL interfaces. This technology simply does not support the abstractions required for a more flexible, systematic 4GL service integration. To overcome these limitations and to achieve 4GL openess and extensibility, we propose an architecture based on interacting POSs using well-organized safe libraries and an implementation which exploits higher-order language technology. According to our understanding, an ideal POS development environment involves the following components:

1. A persistent higher-order programming language that provides just the core functional, operational and modal primitives required by persistent object systems (see Sec. 3);
2. A lean system architecture that unbundles and repackages the services found in traditional programming languages, database systems, and operating systems to allow scalable system implementations ranging from simple, PC-based, single-user systems to networked, multi-user, client-server architectures (see Sec. 4).

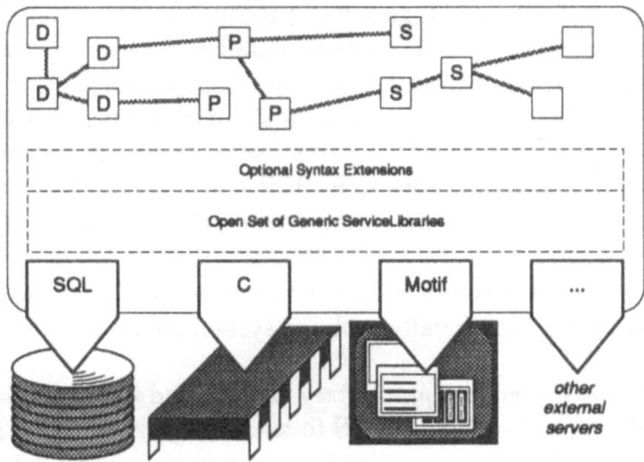

Figure 3: Scalable application frameworks in persistent higher-order languages

3. A systematically designed application framework that consists of a rich and extensible set of libraries. The framework supplies application builders with predefined, composable, high-level services like bulk data structures (relations, sets, lists, graphs, etc.), iteration abstractions (queries, views, traversal patterns for recursive data structures, etc.), and declarative integrity checking mechanisms (see Sec. 5);

The sucess of such a development environment crucially depends (1) on the expressiveness and orthogonality of the base language, (2) on the degree of interoperability with pre-existing services and tools that can be achieved by the system architecture, and (3) on the quality of the initial set of libraries provided by the application framework.

Fig. 3 sketches the architecture of a POS implemented in an application framework provided by a persistent higher-order language. Similar to a 4GL, the relevant application objects (persistent database objects, volatile program objects, virtual screen objects, etc.) are subject to uniform naming, typing and binding rules, indicated by uniform line styles connecting the corresponding symbols in Fig. 3. In contrast to a 4GL, most of these object types are not built into the base language but are provided by an open set of libraries that are an integral part of the programming environment. Some of the libraries are simply interfaces to external services (database systems, language compilers, GUI toolkits), others libraries provide functionality that is implemented in the persistent higher-order language itself. Furthermore, Fig. 3 indicates that access to some of the libraries may be supported by syntax extensions to the persistent core language. The technology for such flexible, problem-oriented syntax extensions using extensible grammars is described in [CMA93].

In the rest of this paper we present the contributions of the Tycoon system, a particular example of a persistent higher-order application framework, to the three areas outlined above.

3 Language Concepts for High-Quality Information Systems

In this section we highlight some of Tycoon's higher-order language concepts. By treating functions and types as first-class language objects, it becomes possible to write generic libraries and generators without leaving Tycoon's language framework. This fact is exploited extensively in the Tycoon libraries and tools (see Sec. 5) to provide 4GL functionality without resorting to inflexible, monolithic built-in solutions.

3.1 Values, Types, Bindings and Signatures

The semantic model of Tycoon is based on higher-order type theories [ML75, CH85, Car88]. The core semantic entities of Tycoon are values, types, bindings and signatures [BL84, Car89]. Values and types can be named in bindings for identification purposes and to introduce shared or recursive structures at the value and the type level. Signatures act as (partial) specifications of static and dynamic bindings. Bindings are embedded into the syntax of values, i.e. they can be named, passed as parameters, etc. Accordingly, signatures appear in the syntax of types to describe these aggregated bindings. The mutual dependencies are illustrated best by the following excerpt from Tycoon's recursive language syntax. Further examples and explanations are given below.

Type::= *Ide* | **Ok** | **Nok** | **Fun***(Signatures):Type* | **Tuple** *Signatures* **end**
    | *Type(Bindings)* | **Oper***(Signatures)Type*
Signatures::= {*TypeSignature* | *ValueSignature* | *LocationSignature*}
TypeSignature::= Ide <:Type
ValueSignature::= Ide :Type
LocationSignature::= **var** *Name :Type*
Value::= Literal | *Ide* | **ok** | **fun***(Signatures)Value* | **tuple** *Bindings* **end** | *Value(Bindings)*
Bindings::= {*TypeBinding* | *ValueBinding* | *LocationBinding*}
TypeBinding::= **Let** *Ide=Type* | *:Type*
ValueBinding::= **let** *Ide=Value* | *Value*
LocationBinding::= **let var** *Ide=Value* | **var** *Value*

Types are partial specifications of values. Here are some examples of types (compare with the type syntax above):

Int, Real, String	library-defined type names
Age, IntPair	user-defined type names
Ok, Nok	top type and bottom type
Fun*(x :Int) :Int*	function type
Tuple *fst :Int snd :Int* **end**	aggregate type

There is no syntactic distinction between library-defined base type names and user-defined type names. The predefined type **Ok** represents the weakest type specification. The predefined type **Nok** represents the strongest (non-satisfiable) type specification. In Tycoon there is a partial order on types based on their degree of precision: *A <:B* ("A is subtype of B") iff type *A* is more precise than type *B*. The order *<:* is defined inductively and Tycoon's type system contains the subsumption rule: if a value a has type *A* and *A<:B* then a has also the weaker supertype *B*. For any type *A*, **Nok** *<:A <:***Ok** holds.

Function types are used to describe the signatures of parameterized objects like functions, procedures, methods, generators or relational queries. Aggregate types are used to describe the signatures of language entities like records, tuples, structures, modules, object definitions, or database definitions,.

For each type constructor there exist corresponding value constructors, for example:

3, 3.4, "XY"	literal values
ok, **raise** *abort*	top value and exception generator
true, false, pi	library-defined value identifiers
*+, -, *, sin, abs*	library-defined function identifiers
fun(*x :Int) x+1*	user-defined function value
tuple let *fst=3* **let** *snd=4* **end**	aggregate value

The builtin value **ok** has type **Ok**. This value is returned by expressions that are not intended to produce a useful value and that only perform side-effects like assignments. There is no value that has type **Nok**. Type **Nok** is assigned by the compiler to expressions whose evaluation does not terminate, like statement sequences that raise an exception.

Bindings are ordered sequences of value, type and location bindings, for example:

let *pi = 3.1415*	value binding
let *succ =* **fun**(*x:Int) x+1*	function value binding
Let *IntPair=***Tuple** *fst:Int snd:Int* **end**	type binding
let var *age = 20*	location binding

A type binding defines a name for a type. A value binding defines a name for a (constant) value. A location binding defines a name for an anonymous location that in turn contains a value. Value, type and location bindings in Tycoon are immutable, i.e., it is not possible to destructively update bindings once they are established. Assignments can be performed only on the contents of locations (*age:=age+1*).

It is sometimes desirable to omit identifiers from bindings and to write *anonymous* bindings, like *succ(3)* or **tuple** *3 4* **end** instead of *succ(***let** *x=3)* and **tuple let** *fst=3* **let** *snd=4* **end**, respectively. There are type rules that govern the compatibility between anonymous bindings and named signatures in Tycoon.

Signatures classify bindings like types classify values. Signatures are ordered sequences of value, location or type signatures, for example:

pi :Real	value signature
*succ :***Fun**(*x:Int) :Int*	function value signature
*IntPair <:***Tuple** *fst:Int snd :Int* **end**	type signature
var *age :Int*	location signature

Signatures specify invariants on bindings and allow the verification of the correctness of (value or type) expressions depending on names without having access to the actual binding in which the name is defined. For example, based on the signature **var** *age :Int*, the type correctness of the expression *age:=age+1* can be verified without having access to the actual value bound to age. Signatures therefore play a central role in type-safe application frameworks that require separate compilation.

3.2 Higher-Order Functions

In Tycoon, functions are first-class typed values. The following examples illustrate three powerful proramming patterns that are based on the use of first-class functions. It should be noted that today's 3GLs and 4GLs impose restrictions on the use of functions that essentially rule out these programming patterns for all "interesting" cases, e.g., if functions contain references to non-local variables, if functions are to be stored persistently, or if functions are to be passed between programs running on different hardware architectures.

Function aggregation allows programmers to build complex data structures ("objects") that contain function values. A particular form of function aggregation underlies the modular and object-oriented programming style where aggregated functions are used to perform operations on encapsulated state variables:

let *object* = **tuple let** *print* = **fun**() **begin...end let** *copy* = **fun**() **begin...end end**

The selection of function components in aggregates is achieved via the usual dot notation (*object.print(), object.copy()*).

Function parameterization allows programmers to pass functions dynamically as arguments to other functions. For example, the higher-order function *twice* takes a function argument and an integer argument and applies its fist argument twice to its second argument:

let *twice* = **fun**(*f* :**Fun**(*x:Int*):*Int a:Int*) *f(f(a))*
twice(succ 3) ⇒ *5*

The capability to pass functions as arguments to other functions is exploited heavily in the Tycoon framework to factor-out application-dependent functionality from otherwise re-usable library code.

Finally, *function generation* allows programmers to return functions as the result of other functions. For example, the function *makeInc* returns a function that adds a fixed value to its argument. The increment step is determined by an argument to the function *makeInc*:

let *makeInc* = **fun**(*step :Int*) **fun**(*x :Int*) *x + step*
let *inc1* = *makeInc(1)* **let** *inc10* = *makeInc(10)*
inc1(3) ⇒ *4*   *inc10(3)* ⇒ *13*

Technically speaking, each invokation of *makeInc* returns a fixed piece of code (*x+step*) with a different static environment that assigns values, types and locations to the global variables (*step* in this example).

3.3 Higher-Order Type Operators

Type operators denote parameterized type expressions that map types or type operators to types or type operators. For example, the type operator *Pair* takes any type *X* that is a subtype of the trivial type **Ok** and returns a tuple type with two fields of type *X*:

Let *Pair*=**Oper**(*X* <:**Ok**) **Tuple** *fst:X snd:X* **end**	type operator binding
Pair(Int), Pair(String), Pair(Pair(Int))	type operator applications

Many programming languages have built-in type operators that map types to types (*Array, List, File, Pointer, ...*); some languages have support for user-defined type operators that map types to types (e.g., type definitions in ML [MTH90] and Haskell [HW86]); very few languages support higher-order type operators (Quest [Car89], Tycoon [MS92]).

The ability to introduce new type operators is required to supply generic data structures like relations, indices, stacks in the application framework. These generic types can later be instantiated with type parameters to construct application-specific types like "supplier relations", "student indices" or "integer stacks".

The syntax for type operator definitions and type operator applications in Tycoon emphasizes the analogy between the concept of (higher-order) functions, mapping (function) values to (function) values, and the concept of (higher-order) type operators. In particular, it is possible to perform type operator aggregation, type operator parameterization, and type operator generation in analogy to the functional concepts outlined in the previous section.

An example of a higher-order type operator is *Twice* which takes a type operator *F* and returns the result of applying *F* twice to a given type *A*:

```
Let Twice=Oper(F <:Oper(X<:Ok)<:Ok A<:Ok) F(F(A))
Twice(Pair Int)
```

For example, *Twice(Pair Int)* is equivalent to *Pair(Pair(Int))*. More useful examples of higher-order type operators require substantially more complex type expressions as they appear in interface specifications of large libraries.

3.4 Type Quantification in Signatures

The parameterization concepts on the value and type level outlined in the previous two secions are complemented in Tycoon by the concept of type quantification in signatures. Type identifiers introduced in a type signature can appear in subsequent type, value and location signatures. This makes it possible to express two kinds of dependencies on type variables[1]:

Existential Quantification: Type components embedded in the signature of an aggregate type allow to model type abstraction as found in modular programming languages:

```
Let ADT = Tuple T <:Ok  zero :T  succ(:T):T  end
let nat =tuple Let T=Int  let zero=0  let succ=fun(x :Int) x+1 end
let one = nat.succ(nat.zero)
```

Intuitively, the existential quantification inside of an aggregate type gives extra flexibility to the service provider, in this case the implementor of the value *nat* of type *ADT*, since he can choose the representation type for *T* freely, as long as the constraints of the other signatures are met:

```
let nat =tuple Let T=String  let zero="" let succ=fun(x :String) concat(x "1") end
```

Universal Quantification: Type components embedded in the signature of a function type lead to the well-known concept of (bounded) parametric polymorphism [CW85]:

```
Let Sort = Fun(X <:Ok  x :Array(X)  {<}:Fun(a:X b:X):Ok):Ok
let quickSort = fun(X <:Ok  x :Array(X)  {<}:Fun(a:X b:X):Ok) begin...end
quickSort(:Int  IntArray  {<})
quickSort(:Person  PersonArray  fun(a,b:Person) string.<(a.name b.name))
```

[1]To a limited extent it is also possible to define type dependencies on value identifiers (*dependent types* [Mac86]).

Sort describes the type of generic sort functions that work uniformly for all types X and that take an array x with elements of type X and a function $<$ to compare two elements of type X.

Intuitively, the universal quantification inherent in generic function types gives extra flexibility to the service consumer, in this case the caller of the function *quickSort*, since he can apply the function to a wider range of arguments.

Another example of a universally quantified type expression is the type of the assignment function ":=":

Let *Assign* = **Fun**(*X* <:**Ok** **var** *lhs* :*X* *rhs* :*X*):**Ok**

This signature expresses the fact that the assignment operation works uniformly over all subtypes X of **Ok** and takes a location of type X and a value of type X as its left-hand-side and right-hand-side argument. Since the type of ":=" is fully representable in the Tycoon type system, it is also possible to export alternative implementations of the assignment function in the Tycoon libraries, e.g. to perform concurency control, integrity checking or recovery operations in addition to the plain assignment operation.

4 The Scalable Tycoon System Architecture

It should be clear from the language overview in the previous section that Tycoon does not attempt to achieve expressiveness by an extensive list of featuers but by generalization and orthogonal combination of relatively few basic concepts. This minimalistic approach also simplifies the implementation of the supporting Tycoon system architecture that is sketched in this section.

The complexity of relational database systems (and recent OODBMS) results essentially from the fact that they are monolithic servers that bundle a large number of tightly coupled services like memory management, concurrency control, recovery, data structuring, access control, etc. Moreover, access to these services is only granted via a narrow database language interface that severely restricts access to individual services.

The Tycoon system attempts to unbundle the above DBMS and 4GL services by strictly separating data modelling, data manipulation and data storage issues. Horizontal bars in Fig. 4 indicate the three central Tycoon system abstractions: TL, TML and TSP.

TL (Tycoon Language) is the strongly-typed higher-order polymorphic programming language presented in Sec. 3 [MS92]. TL serves as a uniform application and system programming language and therefore has to support both, programming using high-level problem-specific data models (like entities and relationships) as well as the implementation of these data models in terms of system-oriented data structures (like hash tables, B-trees, or linear lists).

Large TL programs are typically divided into modules, interfaces and hierachically nested libraries. The Tycoon language processors support separate compilation and dynamic linking. Furthermore, it is possible to evaluate TL expressions interactively, e.g., to perform *ad-hoc* queries. Scanning, parsing, type checking, code generation, linking and execution is then performed immediately, giving the user the illusion of interpretative execution. Since expressions entered interactively may refer to precompiled TL modules, this interactive interface constitutes also a convenient programming development environment.

TML (Tycoon Machine Language) is a minimal intermediate language based on an untyped lambda calculus extended with imperative constructs that serves as a low-level, portable TL program representation in distributed heterogeneous environments. TML

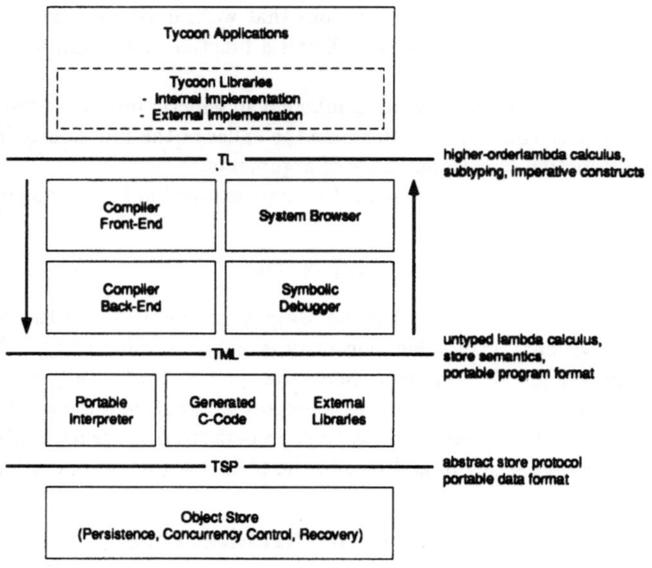

Figure 4: The Tycoon system architecture

was designed to support efficient host-specific target code generation as well as dynamic optimizations analogous to query and transaction rewriting in database systems.

The ability to inspect abstract program representations at run-time, to generate new executable code from program representations, and to link newly created code to "live" systems is a key technology for generic system construction. This functionality has to be emulated in third- and fourth-generation languages either by resorting to interpretation techniques or to non-portable, ad-hoc binding mechanisms.

Currently, there exist two different TML evaluators: a compact, portable interpreter, immediately executable on a wide range of hardware-platforms and an optimizing code generator. The latter uses proprietary C compilers as portable target machine code generators. The current version of the Tycoon system runs on Sun Sparc, DEC Mips, and IBM Power architectures. We intend to make Tycoon also available on IBM PC and Apple Macintosh systems.

TSP (Tycoon Store Protocol) is a data-model-independent object store protocol based on the notion of a *persistent heap* that shields TML evaluators (and TL programmers) from operational aspects of the underlying persistent store like access optimization, storage reclamation, concurrency or recovery. By forcing all higher levels of the system to use the TSP (software) protocol, it provides an ideal starting point to add system functionality at the store-level (e.g. distribution transparency or access-control).

A key contribution of the TSP to the overall Tycoon system functionality is support for *orthogonal persistence* [AB87]: data of any type (including functions) can exist as long or as short as required by the application. Programmers do not need to write explicit code to move data between persistent and volatile store.

Currently, there exist three different TSP implementations that can be combined freely

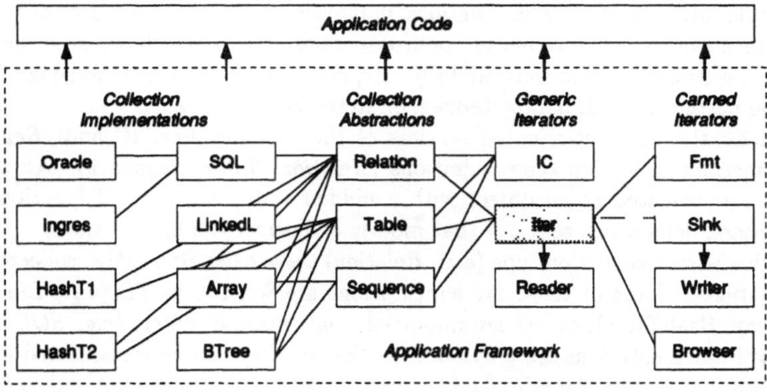

Figure 5: Components of the Tycoon Collection Type Library

with the existing TML evaluators: a compact, paged main memory store implementation with a simple file-based persistence mechanism [MMS92]; an interface to the Napier persistent object store [BMM+91] that provides an efficient single-user stable store with recovery mechanisms based on shadow copying exploiting low-level memory managemement hardware support; and a gateway to the object-oriented database system ObjectStore [LLOW92] supporting recoverable multi-user access to shared databases in client-server architectures. All store implementations feature automatic garbage collection and portable data import and export to files.

To summarize, this layered protocol-oriented architecture aims at system *scalability* and *portability* by de-emphasizing operational aspects of the protocol implementations and focussing on the core requirements of persistent object systems.

5 An Application Framework for Bulk Data Management

As explained in Sec. 2.3, application programmers do not use the bare Tycoon language TL but implement substantial parts of the overall application functionality by instantiating generic library code supplied by an application framework. In this section we give a brief overview of an application framework that is being developed at the University of Hamburg to meet the specific demands of data-intensive applications. One should note that there may be multiple application frameworks supported by the same core language and system architecture. For example, [SM92b] describes a Tycoon application framework for the construction of language processors, exporting scanner, parser and unparser generators as well as utility modules for source code, error log and cross-reference management.

Fig. 5 gives an idea of the organization of the main components of the Tycoon application framework for bulk data management which provides services at several levels of abstraction. For simple applications that only need to print, display and possibly edit (persistent) bulk data, the modules *Browser, Fmt, Sink* and *Writer* provide pre-packaged program patterns that bundle the necessary data retrieval and data formatting code.

Other modules (*Iter, IC, Reader*) export query constructs (like select, project, join, aggregate, sort, or group by), loop statements and predicative integrity control mechanisms.

These modules utilize higher-order functions, polymorphic functions and user-defined type operators to make their functionality applicable uniformly to a wide range of bulk data structures. These query constructs are fully integrated into the Tycoon language TL, i.e., they can be nested, named, parameterized, or stored persistently.

The declarative and set-oriented services of the modules *Iter*, *IC* and *rReader* are based on abstract collection type definitions (*Relation, Table, Sequence*). An abstract collection is represented as an object with a hidden state and a set of functions (size, member, insert, delete, get, set, ...) that modify or inspect the hidden state.

For each abstract collection type (e.g., *Relation*) there exist alternative collection type implementations. Some of these implementations are written in TL (e.g., *LinkedList, BTree, Array, HashTable*), others are imported from external servers (e.g. *SQL* Tables). All of these implementations are polymorphic, that is, they can be instantiated with different element types. For example, the following (simplified) interface *SQL* taken from the current Tycoon libraries describes the signatures of the polymorphic functions exported by the a SQL server:

```
interface SQL export
  Table <:Oper(E<:Tuple end)<:Ok
  openTable:Fun(Dyn E<:Ok name:String):Table(E)
  insert:Fun(E<:Ok table:Table(E) tuple:E):Ok
  insertAll:Fun(E<:Ok table:Table(E) tuples:Table(E)):Ok
  delete:Fun(E<:Ok table:Table(E) where:Fun(e:E):Bool):Ok
  ...
end
```

This interface exports an abstract type operator *Table* that maps a tuple type *E* (any subtype of the empty tuple type) to a hidden type (an arbitrary subtype of the type **Ok**). This parameterized hidden type describes the type of SQL tables with elements of type *E*. The type operator *Table* is used in subsequent function signatures of this interface, capturing the fact that the only way to manipulate SQL tables is via these generic functions. There may be several modules implementing this interface, i.e. defining type, value and location bindings that match the specified signatures. Currently, there exist a Tycoon/Ingres and a Tycoon/Oracle gateway that both have the interface *SQL*.

The following interface imports the type operator *Table* from the module *ingres* with interface *SQL* to define a application-specific database schema that declares two relation variables (*register, fees*).

```
interface PhoneDB import ingres export
  Let Entry=Tuple name:String num:String end
  Let Fee = Tuple prefix :String cost :Int end
  var register :ingres.Table(Entry)
  var fees :ingres.Table(Fee)
  end
```

The binding to the external Ingres relation variables is established in the corresponding implementation module:

```
module phoneDB import ingres export
  let var register=ingres.openTable("register")
  let var fees=ingres.openTable("fees")
end
```

A main program may use the bindings provided by the phone database as arguments to the SQL interface functions:

module *main* **import** *ingres phoneDB* **export**
ingres.insert(phoneDB.register **tuple** *"Peter" "249"* **end***)*
ingres.delete(phoneDB.fees **fun***(f:Fee) f.prefix>="800")*
end

This example illustrates how higher-order type systems contribute to lean languages and open system architectures. All the code necessary to implement the SQL gateway is encapsulated in a library that has to be imported only by those applications that actually need this service. Furthermore, the "type rules" which ensure that clients make proper use of this service are also encapsulated by the library interface signatures and do not need to be hard-wired into the language or its runtime system.

6 Concluding Remarks

Application frameworks in persistent higher-order languages provide the functionality of 4GLs for a much broader class of object types than the classical set- and record-oriented data structures. By a strict separation of data modelling, data manipulation and data storage issues into three distinct system layers, this generalization on the language level can be achieved in a relatively small, scalable and portable system environment with substantially imporoved interoperability.

Our current work in the Tycoon project aims at integrating further relevant generic servers (e.g., authentication, directory and RPC servers) into the Tycoon POS environment and to lift their services using state-of-the-art language technology.

References

[AB87] M.P. Atkinson and P. Bunemann. Types and Persistence in Database Programming Languages. *ACM Computing Surveys*, 19(2), June 1987.

[ABW+90] M. Atkinson, F. Bançilhon, D. De Witt, K. Dittrich, D. Maier, and S. Zdonik. The Object-Oriented Database System Manifesto. In *Deductive and Object-oriented Databases*. Elsevier Science Publishers, Amsterdam, Netherlands, 1990.

[BDK92] F. Bancilhon, C. Delobel, and P. Kanellakis. *Building an Object-Oriented Database System: The Story of O_2*. Morgan Kaufmann Publishers, 1992.

[BHR82] P. Bunemann, J. Hirschberg, and D. Root. A Codasyl Interface to Pascal and Ada. In *Proc. 2nd British National Conference on Databases (BNCOD 2)*. Cambridge University Press, 1982.

[BL84] R. Burstall and B. Lampson. A kernel language for abstract data types and modules. In *Semantics of Data Types*, volume 173 of *Lecture Notes in Computer Science*. Springer-Verlag, 1984.

[Bla90] A. Blaser, editor. *Database Systems of the 90s*, volume 466 of *Lecture Notes in Computer Science*, November 1990.

[BM91] R. Balzer and J. Mylopoulos. International Workshop on the Develpment of Intelligent Information Systems. Technical report, University of Southern California and University of Toronto, April 1991.

[BMM+91] A.L. Brown, G. Mainetto, F. Matthes, R. Müller, and D.J. McNally. An Open System Architecture for a Persistent Object Store. Persistent Programming Research Report CS/91/9, Univ. of St. Andrews, Dept. of Comp. Science, September 1991.

[Car88] L. Cardelli. Structural Subtyping and the Notion of Power Type. In *Proceedings of the Fifteenth ACM Symposium on Principles of Programming Languages*, 1988.

[Car89] L. Cardelli. Typeful Programming. Report 45, DEC Systems Research Center, 130 Lytton Avenue, Palo Alto, 94301 CA, May 1989.

[Cat91] R.G.G. Cattell. Next-Generation Database Systems. *Communications of the ACM*, 34(10), October 1991.

[CH85] T. Coquand and G. Huet. Constructions: a higher order proof system for mechanizing mathematics. Technical Report 401, INRIA, Domaine de Voluceau Rocquencourt 78153 Le Chesnay Cedex - France, May 1985.

[CMA93] L. Cardelli, F. Matthes, and M. Abadi. Extensible Grammars for Language Specialization. In *Proceedings of the Fourth Workshop on Database Programming Languages*, Manhatten, NY, 1993. Springer-Verlag. To appear.

[CW85] L. Cardelli and P. Wegner. On Understanding Types, Data Abstraction, and Polymorphism. *ACM Computing Surveys*, 17(4):471–522, December 1985.

[HW86] P. Hudak and P. Wadler. Report on the Programming Language Haskell Version 1.2. *SCM SIGPLAN Notices*, 21(7):219–233, July 1986.

[Inf86] Informix Software Corp. Informix-4GL Reference Manual. Technical report, Informix Software Corp., 1986.

[Ing89] Ingres Corporation. INGRES ABF/4GL Reference Manual for the UNIX and VMS Operating Systems. Technical Report INGRES Release 6.3, Ingres Corporation, 1080 Marina Village Parkway, Almeda, CA 94501, November 1989.

[Ing90] Ingres Corporation. INGRES Embedded SQL Companion Guide for C. Technical Report INGRES UNIX Release 6.3, Ingres Corporation, 1080 Marina Village Parkway, Almeda, CA 94501, December 1990.

[KMP+83] J. Koch, M. Mall, P. Putfarken, M. Reimer, J.W. Schmidt, and C.A. Zehnder. Modula/R Report, Lilith Version. Technical report, Department Informatik, ETH Zürich, Switzerland, February 1983.

[LLOW92] C. Lamb, G. Landis, J. Orenstein, and D. Weinreb. The ObjectStore Database System. *Communications of the ACM*, 34(10):50–64, 1992.

[Mac86] D.B. MacQueen. Using dependent types to express modular structure. In *Conf. Record 13th Ann. Symp. Principles of Programming Languages*, pages 277–26. ACM, January 1986.

[Mat93] F. Matthes. *Persistente Objektsysteme: Integrierte Datenbankentwicklung und Programmerstellung*. Springer-Verlag, 1993. (In German).

[MJ89] V.M. Matos and P.J. Jalics. An Experimental Analysis of the Performance of 4GL Tools on PCs. *Communications of the ACM*, 32(11):1340–1352, 1989.

[ML75] P. Martin-Löf. An intuitionistic theory of types: predicative part. In H.E. Rose and J.C. Sheperdson, editors, *Logic Colloquium 1973*, pages 73–118, Amsterdam, 1975. North Holland Publishing Company.

[MMS92] F. Matthes, R. Müller, and J.W. Schmidt. Object Stores as Servers in Persistent Programming Environments – The P-Quest Experience. FIDE Technical Report Series TR/92/48, Fachbereich Informatik, Universität Hamburg, Germany, July 1992.

[MS92] F. Matthes and J.W. Schmidt. Definition of the Tycoon Language - A Preliminary Report. Informatik Fachbericht FBI-HH-B-160/92, Fachbereich Informatik, Universität Hamburg, Germany, November 1992.

[MTH90] R. Milner, M. Tofte, and R. Harper. *The Definition of Standard ML.* MIT Press, Cambridge, MA, 1990.

[Ora91] Oracle Corporation. PL/SQL User's Guide and Reference, Version 1.0. Technical Report Part No. 800-V1.0, Oracle Corporation, June 1991.

[Sch77] J.W. Schmidt. Some High Level Language Constructs for Data of Type Relation. In *Proceedings of the ACM-SIGMOD International Conference on Management of Data, Toronto, Canada*, August 1977.

[SM92a] J.W. Schmidt and F. Matthes. The Database Programming Language DBPL: Rationale and Report. FIDE Technical Report Series FIDE/92/46, Fachbereich Informatik, Universität Hamburg, Germany, July 1992.

[SM92b] G. Schröder and F. Matthes. Using the Tycoon Compiler Toolkit. DBIS Tycoon Report 061-92, Fachbereich Informatik, Universität Hamburg, Germany, May 1992.

[SM93] J.W. Schmidt and F. Matthes. Lean Languages and Models: Towards an Interoperable Kernel for Persistent Object Systems. In *Proceedings of the IEEE International Workshop on Research Issues in Data Engineering, Interoperability in Multidatabase Systems*, pages 2–16, Vienna, Austria, April 1993.

[SMV93] J.W. Schmidt, F. Matthes, and P. Valduriez. Building Persistent Application Systems in Fully Integrated Data Environments: Modularization, Abstraction and Interoperability. In P.P. Spies, editor, *Proceedings Euro-Arch'93*, 1993.

[SRL+90] M. Stonebraker, L.A. Rowe, B. Lindsay, J. Gray, M. Carey, M. Brodie, and P. Bernstein. Third-Generation Data Base System Manifesto. *ACM SIGMOD Record*, 19(3):31–44, September 1990.

[ZM89] S.B. Zdonik and D. Maier. *Readings in Object Oriented Database Management Systems.* Morgan Kaufmann Publishers, 1989.

Fehlertolerantes Koordinieren verteilter autonomer Dienste*

eva Kühn

Technische Unversität Wien, Institut für Computersprachen
Argentinierstraße 8, 1040 Wien, Österreich
E-mail: eva@mips.complang.tuwien.ac.at

Abstract

Die Vernetzung von Rechnern führt zu neuen Einsatzbereichen und daher zu neuen Anforderungen an Programmiersprachen. Programmierung war bisher meist mit Erstellung von Softwarepaketen für einen Rechner gleichzusetzen. Sequentielle Programmiersprachen werden verwendet, die weder die Kommunikation zwischen parallelen Prozessen noch deren Synchronisation unterstützen. Neue, verteilte Programmiersprachen sind mit der Koordinierung von in einem im Netz angebotenen autonomen Diensten konfrontiert. Ähnliche Aufgaben entstehen bei der Verwaltung von Teilaufgaben in einem Projekt. Fehler und Ausfälle einzelner Komponenten sollten die Erfolgschance der Gesamtaufgabe nicht verhindern.

Wir beschreiben Techniken zur Koordination solcher Aufgaben. Die vorgeschlagenen Konzepte können in herkömmliche Programmiersprachen eingebaut werden. Wir zeigen, warum das logische Programmierparadigma besonders gut geeignet ist.

Schlüsselworte: Verteilte Sprachen, Koordination, Parallelität,
logische Programmierung, Fehlertoleranz.

1 Einleitung

Netzwerke verbinden Rechner innerhalb von Institutionen oder können weltweit öffentlich zugänglich sein. Die Programmierung verteilter Rechner umfasst neben einer optimaleren Ressourcenausnutzung die Verwendung von autonomen Dienstleistungen und die Unterstützung kooperativen Arbeitens in Gruppen.

1.1 Verwendung von autonomen Dienstleistungen

In öffentlichen Netzen werden Dienste autonomer Institutionen angeboten. Dabei handelt es sich beispielsweise um den Zugriff auf Literaturdatenbanken oder „Mailboxen“, die Zurverfügungstellung hoher Rechenleistung auf Supercomputern, die Ver-

*Diese Arbeit wird vom FWF (Fonds zur Förderung der wissenschaftlichen Forschung), Projekt P9020-PHY „Multidatabase Transaction Processing“ als Kooperationsprojekt mit dem NSF (National Science Foundation) gefördert.

wendung spezialisierter Softwarepakete wie Gleichungslösern oder die Ausführung von Buchungstransaktionen bei Flugliniendatenbanken.

Man kann davon ausgehen, daß es für die meisten Problemstellungen bereits Softwarepakete gibt, deren Ankauf in vielen Fällen - etwa bei einmaliger Verwendung - nicht rentabel ist. Gewisse Dienste, wie etwa eine Geldüberweisung, müssen vom Anbieter ausgeführt werden. Dienstleistungen im Netz werden gegen Gebühren angeboten werden. Die Beschreibung und Verfügbarkeit angebotener Dienste werden von weiteren Dienstleistungsprogrammen verwaltet (Namensverwaltung). Die Koordinierung solcher Dienste unter Berücksichtigung von Kosten- und Zeitoptimierung ist ein neue Anforderung an verteilte Systeme.

Eine Aufgabe wird sich aus mehreren Diensten zusammensetzen, die bereits im Netz existieren. Existierende Systeme sind autonom und können nicht dahingehend verändert werden, daß sie nun mit anderen Systemen zusammenarbeiten - das wäre eine radikale Änderung, die ihrer ursprünglichen (sequentiellen) Entwurfsphilosophie widerspräche. Daher werden neue Werkzeuge zur Koordinierung verteilter Dienste benötigt, deren wesentliche Aufgabe die Kontrolle parallel existierender Abläufe (Prozesse) ist.

Unter der Annahme, daß Dienste autonom verwaltet werden, muß mit dem individuellen Ausfall einzelner Systeme gerechnet werden. Das sollte aber nicht zum Abbruch der gesamten Aufgabe und somit zum Verzicht auf bereits geleistete Dienste führen: Erstellte Teilaufgaben haben bereits Kosten verursacht und andere Wege müssen gefunden werden, um unter Berücksichtigung von Fehlern doch noch eine Lösung zu finden.

Heute kommerziell verwendete Betriebssystemsoftware unterstützt zwar den Zugriff auf Daten sowie den Aufruf von Programmen auf anderen Rechnern, aber es handelt sich hier nur um sehr einfache Protokolle, die die genannten semantischen und applikationsspezifischen Probleme nicht berücksichtigen. Auch herkömmliche Datenbanktransaktionen sind viel zu eingeschränkt. Deren „Alles oder Nichts" Semantik führt unweigerlich zum Abbruch der Gesamtaufgabe (globalen Transaktion), sobald ein Teil fehlschlägt. Es wäre vielmehr wünschenswert, alternative Lösungswege für Teilaufgaben definieren zu können, denn viele äquivalente Dienste werden von verschiedenen Institutionen angeboten. Die Verwendung alternativer Dienste erhöht die Erfolgschance der globalen Transaktion. Die Spezifikation, welche Dienste bevorzugt zu verwenden sind, sollte möglich sein.

1.2 Kooperatives Arbeiten in Teams

Die Organisationsstruktur großer Projekte wird durch die technisch möglich gewordenen Kommunikationsstrukturen beeinflußt werden. Die Bearbeitung gemeinsamer Daten über gemeinsam beschreibbare „Black-Boards", die von mehreren Mitarbeitern gleichzeitig verwendet werden, erfordert neue Formen der Koordination. Jeder Mitarbeiter muß sich auf Mitteilungen auf dem gemeinsamen Kommunikationsmedium verlassen können. Nachrichten dürfen weder verlorengehen noch zerstört werden. Das gleichzeitige Schreiben auf ein Objekt muß ausgeschlossen werden. Bei Entwurfsprojekten müssen beschlossene Planungsschritte festgehalten und ältere Versionen verwaltet werden.

Ein vom Projekt abhängiges Protokoll legt fest, ob Nachrichten von Einzelnen oder in Gruppen erarbeitet werden, bevor sie öffentlich dargestellt werden. Innerhalb von

Gruppen kann dann eine andere, persönlichere Kommunikationsform als das Black-Board gewählt werden. Daten auf dem Black-Board sind öffentlich (global) und generell ist nicht bestimmbar, welche Mitarbeiter bereits die Daten gesehen haben und ihre Arbeit darauf aufbauen, da Sender nicht alle anderen Mitarbeiter kennen müssen. Daher ist im Fall einer nachträglich gewünschten Änderung oder Verbesserung von bereits übermittelten Nachrichten das Löschen der ursprünglichen Nachricht nicht erlaubt. Allerdings ist Korrektur durch Vermitteln weiterer Information möglich. Die Qualität der Daten wird bestimmt, indem spezifiziert wird, innerhalb welcher Zeit korrigierende Zusatzinformationen erlaubt sind, die berücksichtigt werden müssen.

Das Black-Board muß höchst zuverlässig sein. Fehler führen zu Inkonsistenzen und Planungsfehlern, die auf falschen Daten gründen. Ein Projekt kann als langandauernde Transaktion betrachtet werden, die niemals abgebrochen wird [Elm91].

1.3 Anforderungen an Koordination

Verteiltes Programmieren wird zunehmend mit der Koordination von autonomen Daten und Diensten beschäftigt sein [Pan91] und muß auf Fehler, die in der heterogenen Umgebung auftreten, reagieren können. Fehler können Ausfälle von Rechnern, Programmsystemen und Teilen des Netzwerks sein. Auch Ergebnisse, die zwar richtig übermittelt wurden, aber nicht den gestellten Anforderungen entsprechen, sind als „Fehler" einzustufen. Es sollte möglich sein, schlecht erfüllte Teilaufgaben wiederholen zu können, indem man einen anderen Auftrag vergibt und den ersten storniert – falls das mit vertretbaren zusätzlichen Kosten möglich ist.

Ausfallsicheres, verteiltes Programmieren ist komplexer als sequentielles Programmieren. Das Gesamtproblem muß in Unteraufgaben zerteilt werden, die autonom lösbar sind. Ergebnisse von Teilberechnungen sollen andere, eventuell parallel laufende, Berechnungen beeinflussen können. Damit sind Koordinationsaufgaben „reaktiv". Im Gegensatz zu traditionellen, transformationalen Programmen, die eine Menge von Eingabedaten in eine Menge von Ausgabedaten transformieren und während ihrer Laufzeit nicht mit der Umwelt interagieren, kommunizieren reaktive Programme mit anderen Prozessen. Bei Teamwork müssen Teilergebnisse frühzeitig sichtbar gemacht werden, die von anderen Mitarbeitern benötigt werden. Damit muß die isolierte Ausführung von Einzelergebnissen, die von klassischen Datenbanktransaktionen verlangt wird, zumindest teilweise aufgegeben werden. Ist Kommunikation gewünscht, kann nicht gewartet werden, bis die globale Aufgabe fertig ist und erst dann alle Ergebnisse auf einmal sichtbar macht. Die Probleme, die durch ein frühzeitiges Sichtbarwerden von Zwischenergebnissen entstehen, sind lösbar, wenn die Teilergebnisse wieder kompensiert werden können. Damit meinen wir ein „inhaltliches" Zurücknehmen – ein tatsächliches Ungeschehenmachen, so als ob nie jemand diese Teilergebnisse gesehen hätte, ist nicht mehr möglich.

Neben „Koordinationssprache" [GC92] werden in der Literatur die neueren Begriffe „Mega-Programmierung" [WWC92] und „reflektive Programmierung" [LHHK92] verwendet. Mega-Programme koordinieren Mega-Module, die weitgehend autonom Teilaufgaben lösen.

Die verteilte Programmiersprache muß den Aufruf von Diensten bewerkstelligen können. Um Dienste in Anspruch zu nehmen, müssen sie benannt werden können. Dazu kann etwa der Internet-Namensmechanismus verwendet werden kann. Eingabeparameter werden an das andere System weitergegeben und die Ausführung dort veranlaßt. Der Abbruch eines gestarteten Dienstes muß möglich sein. Das kann eintreten, wenn die Gesamtaufgabe fehlschlägt oder wenn eine gleichzeitig ausgeführte, parallel gelaufene Alternative früher fertig wurde. Zum Beipiel wird die Flugbuchung nicht benötigt, wenn der Kunde kein Hotelzimmer mehr bekommt. Ein anderes Beispiel: es wird versucht, bei zwei Fluglinien gleichzeitig den Flug zu buchen, eine Buchung wird abgeschlossen und die andere – noch laufende – wird abgebrochen. Das zweite Beispiel illustriert die Verwendung von Alternativen. Es kann auch der Fall eintreten, daß die nicht benötigte Flugbuchung bereits abgeschlossen wird oder beide Buchungen gleichzeitig fertig werden. Dafür muß eine Kompensation, die einen Flug storniert, spezifizierbar sein, die durchgeführt wird, bevor die globale Transaktion endet.

Idealerweise bieten lokale Datenbanksysteme ein „two-phase-commit" Protokoll [BHG87] an, d.h., das lokale System meldet, daß es die Aufgabe sicher erfüllen kann und wartet dann, bis von der globalen Transaktion die Bestätigung („Commit") geschickt wird. Da wir aber den Einsatzbereich von verteilten Programmiersprachen nicht auf die Domäne von Datenbanken einschränken, sondern beliebige Softwaresysteme und Dienstleistungsprozesse koordinieren wollen, setzen wir das two-phase-commit Protokoll nur in solchen Fällen voraus, wo die Auswirkungen eines Dienstes nicht rückgängig gemacht werden können. Ansonsten wäre die Inanspruchnahme eines solchen Services innerhalb einer globalen Transaktion, die vom Erfolg mehrerer Teilaufgaben abhängig ist, nicht möglich. Die um Kompensation erweiterte „Alles oder Nichts" Semantik der globalen Transaktion wäre sonst nicht zu erfüllen.

Der Zustand der Ausführung einer Teilaufgabe (Untertransaktion) kann durch laufende Nachfrage kontrolliert werden beziehungsweise es wird gewartet, bis das andere System selbständig eine Nachricht über den (nicht) erfolgreichen Abschluß schickt. Auf Systemausfälle kann mit Hilfe von Zeitlimits reagiert werden.

Weder die Meldungen über den lokalen Berechnungszustand noch Ergebnisdaten dürfen verlorengehen. Sowohl das verteilte Programmsystem als auch das übermittelnde System, das die Unteraufgabe durchgeführt hat, müssen kommunizierte Daten wiederherstellen können. Das heißt, daß sich sowohl der Sender als auch der Empfänger von Nachrichten verläßlich darauf berufen kann, daß das „Gespräch" in ebendieser Form stattgefunden hat. Mit „Gespräch" ist nicht notwendigerweise eine Interaktion zwischen zwei Parteien gemeint; sämtliche Kommunikationsformen (1:1, 1:n, m:n) sind denkbar. Ein Übermittler von Nachrichten muß nicht immer alle Empfänger kennen und umgekehrt. Das bedeutet, daß auch anonyme und asynchrone Kommunikationsformen unterstützt werden sollten.

Die Reihenfolge, in der Ergebnisse für andere Prozesse sichtbar werden, muß konsistent sein. Wenn beispielsweise A an B und C eine Frage stellt und dann B an C die passende Antwort schickt, sollte C zuerst die Frage von A und dann die Antwort von B erhalten. Dieses Problem wurde schon in Datenbanken erkannt und wird dort durch die Forderung nach Serialisierbarkeit von Teilaufgaben gelöst [BHG87]. In einem Netzwerk, das sich aus verschieden zuverlässigen Verbindungswegen zusammensetzt, ist die Gewährleistung dieser Eigenschaft recht schwierig.

In Kapitel 2 zeigen wir, wie ein neues Transaktionsmodell, das speziell für Multi-Datenbanksysteme entwickelt wurde, für die Koordination von Diensten eingesetzt werden kann. In Kapitel 3 vergleichen wir einige Programiersprachen und -modelle, die Sprachkonstrukte für die Vervielfältigung von Diensten und die Darstellung parallel ablaufender Prozesse bieten. Für den Fehlerfall bieten die wenigsten Sprachen eine saubere Lösung. In Kapitel 4 diskutieren wir, wie die genannten Techniken besonders gut in einer auf Logik basierenden Sprache realisierbar sind. Wir motivieren auch die Bedeutung von Kommunikation zwischen Transaktionen und zeigen, wie „Kommunikationsobjekte", die nur genau einmal geschrieben werden können, diesen Zweck erfüllen. Ein Kommunikationsprotokoll wird vorgestellt, das den Austausch von Nachrichten über gemeinsam zugreifbare Kommunikationsobjekte erlaubt. Das Verhalten und Wiederanstarten von Transaktionen nach Fehlern wird erklärt.

2 Koordinationseigenschaften eines neuen Transaktionsmodells

Das Flex-Transaktionsmodell [ELLR90, KPE92] wurde ursprünglich für den Zugriff auf verteilte, autonome Datenbanksysteme vorgeschlagen. Die Konzepte sind generell anwendbar und können auch in Programmiersprachen integriert werden. Die Idee, Programmiersprachen um Transaktionen zu erweitern, ist nicht neu [LS87, Lis88]. Im Gegensatz zum traditionellen Transaktionsmodell bietet die Verwendung des Flex-Transaktionsmodells nicht nur die Vorteile persistenter Objekte, sondern erlaubt eine wesentlich flexiblere Koordination paralleler Prozesse.

Flex-Transaktionen bestehen aus einer Ansammlung von Transaktionen, die entweder lokale Dienste sind oder andere Flex-Transaktionen. Transaktionen können kompensierbar sein (vergleiche mit [GMS87]), wodurch sie frühzeitig abgeschlossen („commit") und ihre Ergebnisse sichtbar gemacht werden können. Nicht kompensierbare Transaktionen müssen auf das Ende der globalen Transaktion warten. Die globale Transaktion informiert die kompensierbaren Transaktionen darüber, ob sie benötigt werden oder nicht. Daher wird die Unterstützung des two-phase-commit Protokolls für solche Transaktionen vorausgesetzt. Nicht kompensierbare Transaktionen sind teuer und reduzieren den Gesamtdurchsatz eines verteilten Systems, da sie lokale Systeme wesentlich länger blockieren als nicht kompensierbare Transaktionen.

Die parallele oder sequentielle Ausführung von Transaktionen wird durch die Spezifikation von Abhängigkeiten zum Ausdruck gebracht. Dabei kann angegeben werden, ob die Ausführung einer Transaktion vom Erfolg oder Fehlschlag einer anderen Transaktion abhängig ist. Auch externe Bedingungen, wie zum Beispiel zeitliche Einschränkungen können spezifiziert werden.

2.1 Vervielfältigung von Diensten

Im Flex-Transaktionsmodell kann eine Aufgabe redundant spezifiziert werden. Eine Reihe von Transaktionen werden definiert und verschiedene Mengen von Transaktionen angegeben. Wenn alle Transaktionen einer Menge ihre Teilaufgaben erfüllt haben, ist die gesamte Aufgabe gelöst, das heißt, die Spezifikation akzeptiert verschiedene Ergebnisse. Bei der Ausführung wird dann nicht-deterministisch und abhängig von den Ergebnissen der einzelnen Transaktionen, eine mögliche Ergebnismenge gewählt. Wird dieselbe Flex-Transaktion mehrfach gestartet, liefert sie möglicherweise andere Ergebnisse, da die einzelnen Transaktionen in einer anderen Reihenfolge fertig werden (zu gewissen Tageszeiten ist z.B. das Netzwerk stärker belastet, die Flugbuchungsdatenbank überlastet, etc.) oder (andere) Fehler auftreten können.

Die Lösungen sind zwar unterschiedlich, erfüllen aber alle den gewünschten Zweck. Beispielsweise kann eine Reisebuchung entweder durch die Buchung einer Zugfahrt oder eines Fluges erfüllt werden. Der Zug und das Flugzeug sind Varianten, die alternativ verwendet werden können. Flüge anderer Fluglinien könnten als weitere Alternativen angegeben werden. Eine Flugstrecke kann aus einer oder mehreren Teilstrecken bestehen, die bei verschiedenen Fluglinien gebucht werden können, womit dieselbe Aufgabe durch eine unterschiedliche Anzahl von Diensten lösbar ist. D.h., die Mengen akzeptabler Lösungen müssen nicht die gleiche Anzahl von Transaktionen enthalten und können teilweise aus den gleichen Transaktionen bestehen.

Bei der Ausführung der Gesamtaufgabe ist darauf zu achten, daß keine Transaktion, die in zwei akzeptablen Mengen vorkommt, doppelt ausgeführt wird. Aufgrund der redundanten Spezifikation kann eine beliebige Lösungsmenge gewählt werden, wobei keine Menge von vornherein bevorzugt werden darf. Unter der Annahme, daß es keine Abhängigkeiten zwischen den Transaktionen gibt (diese werden in Kapitel 2.3 behandelt), können alle Transaktionen gestartet werden (Ausnutzung maximaler Parallelität). Wenn eine Transaktion fehlschlägt, fallen alle akzeptablen Mengen weg, in denen sie enthalten ist. Somit fallen entweder sukkzessive alle Mengen weg, was einem Fehlschlagen der Gesamtaufgabe entspricht, oder eine Menge kann gefunden werden, deren Transaktionen erfolgreich waren. Diese Menge stellt die erste Lösung der Flex-Transaktion dar. Entspricht diese Lösung den Wunschvorstellungen des Aufrufers der Flex-Transaktion, dann müssen alle anderen Transaktionen, die nicht der Lösungsmenge angehören, entweder abgebrochen werden, wenn sie noch laufen, oder kompensiert werden, wenn sie bereits abgeschlossen sind. Letzteres ist der Fall bei kompensierbaren Transaktionen.

2.2 Semantische Kompensation

Die Kompensationsaktion einer Transaktion nimmt deren Effekte „semantisch" zurück und ist wiederum eine (Flex) Transaktion. Eine Geldeinzahlung kann durch Abbuchen wieder rückgängig gemacht werden. Allerdings muß in Kauf genommen werden, daß, da ja die Einzahlungstransaktion bereits die Überweisung abgeschlossen hat, andere Transaktionen diese gesehen haben könnten. Der Kunde hat vielleicht bereits Aktien um diesen Geldbetrag gekauft und eine Abbuchung würde in diesem Fall einen negativen Kontostand verursachen. Ist dieses Verhalten akzeptabel, dann kann die Kompensationsaktion in dieser Form spezifiziert werden. Die Kompensationsaktion könnte auch komplexer sein: wenn nicht genügend Geld auf dem Konto ist, muß zuerst der Transfer eines entsprechenden Geldbetrages von einem Sparbuch des Kunden auf das Konto veranlaßt werden.

Ein semantisches Kompensieren kann jedenfalls nicht mit einem tatsächlichen Ungeschehenmachen gleichgesetzt werden. In manchen Fällen kann es dieselbe Bedeutung haben oder sogar automatisch generiert werden; generell muß jedoch die Kompensationsaktion einer Transaktion bei deren Definition mitspezifiziert werden.

Die Kompensationsaktion kompensiert alle Effekte, die durch die Transaktion entstanden sind und somit auch alle Effekte von aufgerufenen (kompensierbaren oder nicht kompensierbaren) Untertransaktionen. Diese Semantik wurde von uns so gewählt, um eine Anhäufung von Kompensationsaktionen zu vermeiden. Weiters glauben wir, daß eine Transaktion, die eine wohldefinierte Schnittstelle darstellt und alle von ihr ausgeführten Unterschritte nach außen versteckt, nicht beim Kompensieren alle Unterschritte aufrollen und durch deren Kompensation sichtbar machen sollte. Eine Transaktion stellt ein gewisses Abstraktionsniveau einer Aufgabe dar. Wenn etwa eine Rundreise, die sich aus diversen Flugstrecken, Hotelzimmerbuchungen, Mietautoreservierungen, Opernkartenreservierungen und anderen Ereignissen zusammensetzt, die bereits alle gebucht wurden, zurückgegeben wird, wird es vorteilhafter sein, diese Reise als Paket anzubieten, als alle Einzelbuchungen rückgängig zu machen – was überhaupt nur möglich wäre, wenn alle Einzelbuchungen kompensierbare Transaktionen sind. Damit kann eine Transaktion kompensiert werden, die auch nicht kompensierbare Transaktionen aufgerufen hat.

Die Ausführung von Kompensationsaktionen kann parallel zu anderen Berechnungen der Flex-Transaktion erfolgen, ist aber Teil der Flex-Transaktion. Diese kann erst als abgeschlossen betrachtet werden, wenn alle notwendig gewordenen Kompensationsaktionen abgeschlossen sind. Dies gilt sowohl für den Fall, daß sie erfolgreich war, als auch für den, daß sie keine Lösung produzierte.

2.3 Parallelität in Flex-Transaktionen

Die Abhängigkeit einer Transaktion T1 von der Ausführung einer anderen Transaktion T2 wird im Flex-Transaktionsmodell durch sogenannte positive (T2 muß gutgegangen sein) und negative (T2 muß fehlgeschlagen haben) Abhängigkeiten dargestellt. Abhängigkeiten zwischen Transaktionen reduzieren die Parallelität: T2 muß vor T1 gelaufen sein und abhängig von dem Ergebnis der Ausführung von T2 darf dann T1 gestartet werden oder nicht.

Eine negative Abhängigkeit entspricht der Spezifikation von Präferenzen und wird zumeist zwischen gleichwertigen Alternativen verwendet. Die Flugbuchung bei der Lufthansa soll erst dann probiert werden, wenn es bei den Austrian Airlines keinen Platz mehr gibt. Positive Abhängigkeiten müssen angegeben werden, wenn eine Transaktion von den Ergebnissen einer anderen abhängig ist. Ansonst hat eine positive Abhängigkeit keine Auswirkung auf mögliche Lösungen der Flex-Transaktion und dient ausschließlich der Optimierung. Der Aufruf sehr kostenintensiver Dienste kann vermieden werden, wenn sowieso klar ist, daß andere Teilaufgaben nicht erfüllt werden können, ohne die eine Gesamtlösung nicht produziert werden kann.

Eine Transaktion T1 darf gestartet werden, wenn für alle noch möglichen, akzeptablen Mengen M_i in denen T1 enthalten ist gilt: jede andere Transaktion T2 aus M_i, von der T1 positiv anhängig ist, muß bereits gutgegangen sein, und alle Transaktionen T3, von denen T1 negativ anhängig ist, müssen bereits fehlgeschlagen haben.

Mit diesem Algorithmus, der in [KPE92] genauer beschrieben ist, kann die maximal mögliche Parallelität bei der Ausführung einer Flex-Transaktion erreicht werden, wobei keine akzeptable Menge bevorzugt und keine Transaktion doppelt gestartet wird.

3 Vergleichbare Programmiersprachenkonzepte

Wir analysieren Programiersprachenkonzepte, die Ähnlichkeiten mit den beschriebenen Eigenschaften des Flex-Transaktionsmodells aufweisen.

3.1 Alternative Berechnungen

„Guarded-Commands“ [Dij75] erlauben die Spezifikation von alternativen Berechnungen. Wir wollen schon als Vorgriff auf unseren auf Logik basierenden Vorschlag, eine Alternative als Klause bezeichnen. Eine Klause besteht aus einem „Guard“, der einer Bedingung entspricht unter der die Klause überhaupt selektiert werden darf. Alle Klausen sind gleichwertig und können parallel gestartet werden. Alle Klausen, deren Guard erfüllt ist, sind Kandidaten. Je nach Sprache, die „Guarded-Commands“ verwendet, besteht der Guard aus Tests, Aufrufen von Prozeduren oder auch synchronen Kommunikationsschritten. Eine Alternative, deren Guard erfüllt ist, wird nichtdeterministisch ausgewählt und alle anderen Alternativen werden verworfen.

Prozedurale Sprachen, die „Guarded-Commands“ unterstützen, sind zum Beispiel occam, Concurrent C, Ada und Orca. Vertreter des logischen Paradigmas sind CL (Concurrent Logic) Programmiersprachen [Sha87, Sha89], zum Beispiel Parlog [Gre87]. Dort entspricht die Darstellung von Alternativen der ODER-parallelen Spezifikation von Klausen für eine Prozedur. Anders ausgedrückt: das Ziel einer Prozedur kann durch jede ihrer Klausen erfüllt werden. Keine dieser Sprachen erlaubt jedoch ein Verwerfen einer bereits gefundenen Lösung und das Probieren anderer Lösungswege. Diesen Mechanismus („Backtracking“) finden wir in Prolog [SS86], das aber nicht Parallelismus und damit auch nicht die Kommunikation zwischen parallelen Prozessen unterstützt und somit auch keine den „Guarded-Commands“ analoge Notation aufweist. CL-Sprachen unterbinden Backtracking.

Diese beiden Welten von Backtracking und parallelen, kommunizierenden Prozessen sind jedoch mit Hilfe des Flex-Transaktionsmodell integrierbar (siehe Kapitel 4, wo wir kurz unseren Vorschlag einer Erweiterung von Prolog um die Konzepte von Flex-Transaktionen erklären): Kommunizierte Werte werden beim Backtracking semantisch kompensiert.

3.2 Synchronisation paralleler Prozesse

Explizite Parallelität in Programmiersprachen, d.h. Sprachkonstrukte mit denen der Programmierer Parallelität spezifizieren und kontrollieren kann, wird in [BST89] untersucht. Dieser Artikel ist ein umfassender Überblick über verteilte Sprachen, der diese nach Art der Synchronisation in nachrichtensendende respektive über gemeinsame Datenstrukturen kommunizierende Sprachen gliedert.

Wir fassen hier nur kurz die wesentlichsten Mechanismen zusammen, um sequentielle beziehungsweise parallele Ausführung zu spezifizieren und erklären, ob und in welcher Form Kommunikation zwischen parallelen Prozessen unterstützt wird.

Explizite Parallelität. In prozeduralen Sprachen kann Parallelität durch „PARBEGIN ... PAREND“ und ähnliche Blockkonstrukte spezifiziert werden, wobei alle Prozesse dieses Blocks parallel ausgeführt werden und nachdem alle erfolgreich fertig wurden, fortgesetzt wird (vergleiche auch mit „SEQ“ und „PAR“ in occam). In funktionalen Sprachen können parallel evaluierbare Ausdrücke durch sogenannte „futures“ gekennzeichnetet werden. Spätestens wenn das Ergebnis benötigt wird, muß die Berechnung erfolgen. In objekt-orientierten Sprachen können Nachrichten zwischen parallel laufenden Objekten ausgetauscht werden. Guardians in der Sprache Argus sind Module, die den Zugriff auf Objekte kapseln und parallel zueinander laufen. Die Größe eines solchen Guardians bestimmt den Grad der Parallelität des

Programms. In logischen Sprachen finden wir UND/ODER Parallelität [Sha89] (siehe Kapitel 4.1).

Kommunikation. Konstrukte wie Semaphore, Monitor, Rendezvous und Remote Procedure Call sind nicht mächtig genug für unsere Ansprüche an Kommunikation in Koordinatiossprachen. Diese Konstrukte können nie den Anschein vermitteln, daß alle Teilnehmer immer alle Nachrichten in derselben Reihenfolge sehen.

Das CSP-Modell unterstützt synchrone Kommunikation. Erst wenn ein Paar, bestehend aus Sender und Empfänger, die einander kennen müssen, gefunden wird, kann der Austausch der Nachricht erfolgen. Es handelt sich hier um 1:1 Kommunikation und es ist sichergestellt, daß beide Partner immer eine konsistente Vorstellung der Reihenfolge aller zwischen ihnen kommunizierten Nachrichten haben. Das Linda Modell [GC92] unterstützt anonyme und asynchrone Kommunikation über einen „Tuple-Space", in den Tupel hineingeschrieben, aus dem Tupel gelesen sowie herausgenommen werden können. Jede einzelne Schreib-, Lese- oder Herausnahmeaktion ist atomar und alle teilnehmenden Prozesse haben immer dieselbe Vorstellung vom aktuellen Zustand des Tupel-Bereichs. Beliebige Kommunikationsformen sind möglich. Ein weiteres Beispiel für Kommunikation über gemeinsame Variablen (Objekte) sind CL-Sprachen, die die logische Variable als Kommunikationsmedium verwenden. Die mächtigsten Sprachen dieser Klasse (z.B. FCP(:) [Sha89]) unterstützen sogar das Gruppieren mehrerer Nachrichten, die atomar (entweder alle oder keine) geschickt werden. In der Sprache Orca [BT91] findet Kommunikation über gemeinsame Objekte statt, auf die in atomaren Aktionen zugegriffen wird. Parallele Prozesse können asynchron Objekte lesen und überschreiben. Die Sprache Argus schreibt Objekte in Transaktionen und garantiert die Ausfallsicherheit von Objekten, die als permanent definiert werden müssen [Bal92]. Wenn ein Modul nach einem Fehler wieder gestartet wird, werden alle Objekte bis hin zur letzten abgeschlossenen Transaktion wiederhergestellt und eine sogenannte „Recovery-Section" ausgeführt, die jedoch vom Benutzer programmiert werden muß und alle möglichen Fehlerursachen behandeln sollte.

4 Logische Programmierung und Koordination

Die von uns vorgeschlagene Erweiterung von Prolog ($\mathcal{V}$PL Vienna Parallel Logic [KPP93]) ist ein Beispiel, wie Nutztung alternativer Dienste, Kompensation und Parallelität in eine Programmiersprache eingebettet werden können. $\mathcal{V}$PL unterstützt alternative Berechnungen, explizite Parallelität (UND/ODER Parallelismus), Backtracking mit semantischer Kompensation sowie Kommunikation über gemeinsame Kommunikationsobjekte, die in Transaktionen geschrieben werden. Wir zeigen im folgenden, warum sich gerade das logische Paradigma besonders gut dafür eignet. Die zusätzlichen Eigenschaften, die nicht direkt durch das Flex Modell motiviert sind, sind die Kommunikation mittels persistenter Kommunikationsobjekte und die Fehlertoleranz von $\mathcal{V}$PL-Programmen.

4.1 Realisierung der Eigenschaften von Flex-Transaktionen

Alternativen werden durch die Angabe verschiedener Klausen für eine Aufgabe (Prozedur) realisiert. Dabei kann in $\mathcal{V}$PL-spezifiziert werden, ob alle alternativen

Klausen ODER-parallel respektive ODER-sequentiell auszuführen sind. Der ODER-Konstruktor führt zu Nicht-Determinismus. Sowohl beim sequentiellen als auch parallelen ODER ist Backtracking erlaubt.

Im Gegensatz zu der restriktiven „Guarded-Commands"-Notation, bei der nach Auswahl einer Alternative andere Lösungen unterbunden werden, kann die Granularität des Commits beliebig variieren. Sie ist nicht an eine Klause gebunden. Die Aufrufe mehrere Klausen können zu Transaktionen zusammengefaßt werden.

Backtracking über Transaktionen löst die Ausführung der Kompensationsaktion aus, die mit Hilfe von VPL-Klausen dynamisch für eine Transaktion definiert wird.

Das Testen des Ausgangs von Transaktionen ist bei logischer Programmierung durch den Erfolg respektive Fehlschlag von Aufgaben (Zielen) implizit gegeben. Logisches UND verlangt, daß alle durch UND verknüpften Ziele erfüllt (bewiesen) sein müssen. Sequentielles UND führt alle Ziele der Reihe nach aus (Vorwärtsausführung). Ist ein Ziel nicht beweisbar, wird Backtracking (Rückwärtsausführung) eingeleitet. Gibt es eine alternative Lösungsmöglichkeit für ein bereits bewiesenes Ziel, so wird die alte Lösung verworfen und mit Vorwärtsausführung der neuen fortgesetzt. Paralleles UND startet die Beweise aller Ziele parallel. Ist nur eines nicht erfüllbar, schlägt die gesamte UND Verknüpfung fehlt, Backtracking wird ausgelöst und alle anderen noch laufenden oder schon fertigen UND-Ziele werden abgebrochen. Sollte eines dieser abzubrechenden UND-Ziele eine Transaktion gewesen sein, wird diese kompensiert.

Positive Abhängigkeiten zwischen Transaktionen werden durch sequentielle UND-Verknüpfung von Zielen repräsentiert. Negative Abhängigkeiten zwischen Transaktionen werden durch sequentielles ODER repräsentiert. Alle relevanten Flex Spezifikationen sind als deklarative VPL-Programme (UND/ODER Baum) darstellbar. Eine spezielle, kleine Menge ist nur mit extra Kommunikation oder durch Verzicht auf etwas Parallelität darstellbar [KPE92].

Eine VPL-Spezifikation einer Flex-Transaktion ist direkt vom VPL-System ausführbar. Der Algorithmus ist äquivalent zu dem in den Kapiteln 2.1 und 2.3 beschriebenen: Abhängigkeiten werden durch Sequentialisierung spezifiziert und Alternativen durch ODER. Die Darstellung aller akzeptablen Mengen ist nicht explizit notwendig, sondern implizit in der UND/ODER-Struktur des VPL-Programms und dem impliziten Testen des Ausgangs von Transaktionen, das die Vorwärts/Rückwärtsausführung steuert, enthalten. Das sukkzessive Aufgeben von möglichen Lösungen (akzeptablen Mengen) – inklusive Abbruch/Kompensation nicht mehr benötigter Transaktionen – und das Durchprobieren alternativer Lösungswege entsprechen dem Backtracking über UND-Verknüpfungen, das automatisch den Abbruch der anderen UND-Ziele verursacht. Backtracking über abgeschlossenen Transaktionen oder deren Abbruch startet automatisch ihre Kompensation.

4.2 Zuverlässige Kommunikation zwischen Transaktionen und Neustart nach Fehlern

Transaktion ist die Sprachabstraktion für die Ausführung von Diensten. Zwischen rufender und aufgerufener Transaktion findet Kommunikation statt (siehe Kapitel 1.3). Der Ausfall von Nachrichten ist kritisch und kann zu Inkonsistenzen des verwendeten Transaktionsprotokolls führen.

Wir verwenden für die Kommunikation „Kommunikationsobjekte", die in VPL Kommunikationsvariablen genannt werden. Auf allen Rechnern, auf die mit dem verteilten Programm zugegriffen wird, d.h., die Dienste anbietete, muß es ein Programm geben (Koordinations-Server, z.B. ein VPL-System), das Kommunikationsobjekte richtig interpretiert und das unten beschriebene Protokoll fährt. Dieses Programm hat eine Schnittstelle zu dem autonomen Softwarepaket und wird zum Beispiel in Multi-Datenbanken durch sogenannte MDIs (Multi-Datenbanken Interfaces) oder auch Gateways realisiert [BKP92]. Dabei werden Anfragen und Ergebnisse an/von Datenbanken mittels Files geschickt.

Kommunikationsobjekte können, wie logische Variablen in CL-Sprachen, nur genau einmal beschrieben werden. Sie sind dann konstant und dürfen nie wieder verändert oder gelöscht werden, solange sie von irgendeinem Prozess benötigt werden. Damit bleibt jede gesandte Nachricht sichtbar und Prozesse können sich auf empfangene Daten verlassen. Würden beim Ausprobieren alternativer Lösungen geschriebene Werte von Kommunikationsobjekten zurückgenommen werden (wie in Prolog, wo Variablenbindungen beim Backtracking aufgehoben werden), das entspräche z.B. einem Löschen der Information vom Black-Board (das Black-Board ist eine Menge von Kommunikationsobjekten), dann müßten alle Prozesse, die die Kommunikationsobjekte bereits gesehen haben, informiert werden. Die Realisierung einer solchen Semantik ist jedoch mit einem sehr großen Aufwand verbunden. Daher kann nur eine weitere Nachricht, daß das vorige Ergebnis nicht mehr aktuell ist, mittels eines neuen Kommunikationsobjekts geschickt werden (in Form einer Kompensationsaktion).

Kommunikationsobjekte werden innerhalb von Transaktionen geschrieben und erst beim Abschluß der Transaktion (Commit) werden alle Werte (in VPL: Variablenbindungen) auf einmal sichtbar. Sollte beim Commit festgestellt werden, daß Bindungen nicht ausgeführt werden können, weil ein Objekt bereits von einer anderen Transaktion, die früher abgeschlossen wurde, gebunden wurde, kann die Transaktion nicht abgeschlossen werden. Es wird dann keine Bindung durchgeführt sondern Backtracking eingeleitet. Damit können mehrere Nachrichten auf einmal (atomar) übermittelt werden. Alle Teilnehmer haben immer eine konsistente Vorstellung aller kommunizierten Werte.

Neben Kommunikationsobjekten gibt es noch lokale Daten, die nicht persistent sind und bei Fehlern verloren gehen können. Nur Kommunikationsobjekte dürfen zur Kommunikation zwischen parallelen Prozessen verwendet werden. Diese brauchen nicht benannt werden (im Gegensatz zu Tupel im Linda Modell oder zu Kanälen in occam), sondern werden als Parameter an Prozesse übergeben. Beliebige Kommunikationsformen sind denkbar, indem Kommunikationsobjekten zusammengesetzte Datenstrukturen zugewiesen werden, die wiederum neue Kommunikationsobjekte enthalten. In VPL, wie auch in CL-Sprachen, werden „Streams“, das sind unendliche Listen, dafür verwendet.

In unserer Implementierung von Kommunikationsobjekten in VPL wird für jeden Prozeß, der auf ein Kommunikationsobjekt Zugriff besitzt, eine Kopie des Kommunikationsobjekts angelegt. Damit entsteht für jedes Kommunikationsobjekt ein (über mehrere Rechner) verteilter Baum. Ein neuer Kommunikationspartner bekommt einen Knoten im Baum, der—entsprechend den physischen Kommunikationsverbindungen—mit dem Prozeß, von dem er das Kommunikationsobjekt übergeben bekam, verbunden ist.

Genau eine Kopie ist als primäre Kopie gekennzeichnet. Der Prozeß, der diese primäre Kopie besitzt, darf schreibend und lesend auf das Kommunikationsobjekt zugreifen. Beim Committen muß ein Prozeß die primären Kopien aller Kommunikationsobjekte besitzen, auf die in dieser Transaktion zugegriffen wurde. Ein ausfallsicheres Protokoll wird in [KP92] beschrieben, das eine Migration der primären Kopie zwischen Prozessen auf verschiedenen Architekturen erlaubt. Dabei muß, wenn die Verbindungswege nicht zuverlässig sind, jedesmal, bevor die Baumstruktur verändert wird, der Zustand des Baums auf einen Festspeicher gesichert werden. Zeitmarken von Transaktionen garantieren, daß keine „Deadlocks" entstehen.

Das Protokoll für Kommunikationsobjekte ist ausfallsicher unter der Annahme, daß die lokalen Festspeicher entsprechende Ausfallsicherheit aufweisen und daß ein lokales System nach einem Fehler nach endlicher Zeit wieder kommunikationsfähig ist. Unter der Annahme, daß lokale Systeme auch VPL-Systeme sind, kann garantiert werden, daß alle Berechnungen bis zum letzten Committment erhalten bleiben, da bei jedem Transaktionsabschluß automatisch der Zustand der Transaktion gespeichert wird sowie der Zustand aller Transaktionen, von denen sie aufgerufen wurde. Zusätzlich werden alle Kompensationsaktionen, die während der Laufzeit des VPL-Systems entstanden und noch nicht abgeschlossen sind oder noch gar nicht gestartet worden sind, gesichert. Beim Wiederaufsetzen müssen diese dann wieder aktiviert (d.h.,in die Liste der lauffähigen Prozesse des VPL-Systems eingereiht) werden, da ein Nicht-Ausführen einer Kompensationsaktion die Semantik des VPL-Programms (vergleiche mit Semantik von Flex-Transaktionen) zerstören würde.

Ganz allgemein muß vom lokalen Koordinations-Server nur gefordert werden, daß die Werte aller von Transaktionen geschriebenen Kommunikationsobjekte (d.h., die Baumstruktur der Kopien aller Kommunikationsobjekte) wiederhergestellt werden. Lokale Berechnungen können notfalls verlorengehen. Auch ein Wiederaufsetzen an genau der Stelle, wo das Programm unterbrochen wurde, ist aus der Sicht der Semantik von Flex-Transaktionen nicht unbedingt notwendig. Allerdings dürfen Anforderungen, Kompensationsaktionen auszuführen, die an das lokale System gesandt wurden und deren Empfang (über das Medium Kommunikationsobjekt) bereits bestätigt wurde, nicht verlorengehen.

Zu langen Wartezeiten kommt es dann, wenn der Besitzer einer primären Kopie ausfällt. Ist das Kommunikationsobjekt jedoch bereits gebunden und wurden, bevor der Fehler eintrat, noch an alle direkten Söhne des Prozesses, der die primäre Kopie besitzt, Nachrichten über den geschriebenen Wert gesandt, tritt keine Verzögerung ein. Auch Ausfälle von Prozessen, die in der Baumstruktur unterhalb aller Prozesse liegen, die jemals die primäre Kopie besitzen wollen, sind für das Protokoll irrelevant.

Neue Kommunikationsobjekte können als Konstante gesehen werden, deren Werte noch nicht bekannt sind. Beim Lesezugriff muß gewartet werden, bis ein anderer Prozeß einen Wert in das Kommunikationsobjekt schreibt (implizite Synchronisation wie in CL-Sprachen). Wenn der Wert einmal global sichtbar ist, wird die verteilte Baumstruktur, die die Kopien des Kommunikationsobjekts verwaltet, nicht mehr benötigt und kann durch entsprechendes Weiterpropagieren des Wertes schrittweise wieder aufgelöst werden.

Die meist verwendete Kommunikationsform hat einen Schreiber und ein oder mehrere Leser. In diesem Fall reduziert sich das Protokoll auf das Schicken des Wertes des Kommunikationsobjekts an alle Leser. Die Migration der primären Kopie ist nicht notwendig, wenn die Baumstruktur von vornherein so angelegt wird, daß der Prozeß, von dem bekannt ist, daß er schreiben wird, die primäre Kopie besitzt.

Bei Koordinationsproblemen ist meist klar, welcher Prozeß schreibend und welcher lesend auf ein Kommunikationsobjekt zugreifen wird: Für die Meldung des Ausgangs einer Transaktion wird ein Kommunikationsobjekt verwendet, das dem Rufer der Transaktion und der Transaktion bekannt ist [BKP92]. Der Rufer wartet (implizit), bis die Transaktion das Kommunikationsobjekt an einen der Werte PREPARED, SUCCEEDED oder FAILED bindet. Im ersten Fall (mehr-Phasen-Commit) muß ein weiteres Kommunikationsobjekt verwendet werden, das dann der Transaktion signalisiert, ob sie abgeschlossen werden darf. Diese Kommunikationsformen werden bei der Koordination autonomer Dienste am häufigsten verwendet und sind, da die Schreiber der Kommunikationsobjekte bekannt sind, mit sehr geringem Aufwand implementierbar.

5 Zusammenfassung

Wir haben in diesem Artikel erläutert, was die neuen Einsatzgebiete verteilter Rechnerarchitekturen sein werden. Dazu gehören das kooperative Arbeiten an großen Projekten sowie das Koordinieren autonomer Dienste, die in einem (öffentlichen) Netzwerk angeboten werden. Notwendige Eigenschaften, die sich daher für verteilte Programmiersprachen ergeben, sind die Spezifikation von alternativen, parallel laufenden Diensten für den Fall, daß eine Teilaufgabe nicht erfüllt werden kann. Ein Mehrfachangebot von Diensten erhöht bei Ausfällen von Systemkomponenten die Wahrscheinlichkeit, daß die Gesamtaufgabe erfüllt werden kann. Zwischenergebnisse müssen sichtbar gemacht werden, mit denen andere Prozesse weiterrechnen können. Damit wird die semantische Kompensation motiviert.

Diese Eigenschaften, die an Hand eines neuen Transaktionsmodells erläutert wurden, sind sehr generell und können in Programmiersprachen eingebettet werden. Wir haben ähnliche Konzepte, die bereits für Programmiersprachen vorgeschlagen wurden, analysiert und gezeigt, wie eine Prolog-Erweiterung um die Eigenschaften von Flex-Transaktionen aussieht. Generell fordern wir aber kein Paradigma für eine Programmiersprache: die vorgeschlagenen Mechanismen können auf jede beliebige Programmiersprache aufgesetzt werden.

Ein Vorteil der Verwendung des logischen Paradigmas ist jedoch eine besonders einfache Darstellung des Kontrollflusses. Eine Spezifikation ist zugleich ein ausführbares Programm. Die von uns vorgestelle Koordinationssprache bietet zusätzlich ausfallsichere Kommunikation über gemeinsame Kommunikationsobjekte. Diese werden innerhalb von Transaktionen atomar geschrieben und können nur einmal einen Wert erhalten. Damit kann sich jeder Prozeß auf kommunizierte Daten verlassen. Da diese nie wieder verändert werden und Systemausfälle überleben, wird dadurch automatisch der gesamte Ablauf der Transaktion inklusive aller Teilergebnisse protokolliert.

Danksagung

Ich möchte mich an dieser Stelle bei Manfred Brockhaus, dem Vorstand des Instituts für Computersprachen, für seine Unterstützung und Alexander Forst, Christian Kühn, Herbert Pohlai und Konrad Schwarz für ihre Anmerkungen zu diesem Text bedanken.

References

[Bal92] H. Bal. Fault-tolerant parallel programming in Argus. *Concurrency: Practice and Experience*, 4(1):37–55, February 1992.

[BHG87] Ph. Bernstein, V. Hadzilacos, and N. Goodman. *Concurrency Control and Recovery in Database Systems.* Addison-Wesley, 1987.

[BKP92] O. Bukhres, e. Kühn, and F. Puntigam. A language multidatabase system communication protocol. In *Proceedings of the 9th International Conference on Data Engineering.* IEEE Computer Society Press, April 1992. (to appear).

[BST89] H. Bal, J. Steiner, and A. Tanenbaum. Programming languages for distributed computing systems. *ACM Computing Surveys*, 21(3), September 1989.

[BT91] H. Bal and S. Tanenbaum. Distributed programming with shared data. *Computer Languages Journal*, 16(2):129–146, 1991.

[Dij75] E. Dijkstra. Guarded commands, nondeterminacy, and formal derivation of programs. *Communications of the ACM*, 18(8), August 1975.

[ELLR90] A. K. Elmagarmid, Y. Leu, W. Litwin, and M. Rusinkiewicz. A multidatabase transaction model for InterBase. In *Proceedings of the 16th International Conference on Very Large Data Bases*, Australia, 1990.

[Elm91] A. K. Elmagarmid, editor. *Database Transaction Models for Advanced Applications.* Morgan Kaufmann Publishers, 1991.

[GC92] D. Gelernter and N. Carriero. Coordination languages and their significance. *Communications of the ACM*, 35(2), February 1992.

[GMS87] H. Garcia-Molina and K. Salem. Sagas. In *Proceedings of the ACM SIGMOD Annual Conference*, San Francisco, May 1987.

[Gre87] S. Gregory. *Parallel Logic Programming in PARLOG. The Language and its Implementation.* Addison-Wesley, England, 1987.

[KP92] e. Kühn and F. Puntigam. Reliable communication in VPL. In *Proceedings of the Parallel Architectures and Languages Europe (PARLE-92)*, Paris, June 15–18 1992. Springer Verlag, LNCS.

[KPE92] e. Kühn, F. Puntigam, and A. K. Elmagarmid. An execution model for distributed database transactions and its implementation in VPL. In *Proceedings of the International Conference on Extending Database Technology, EDBT'92*, Vienna, March 1992. Springer Verlag, LNCS.

[KPP93] e. Kühn, H. Pohlai, and F. Puntigam. Concurrency and backtracking in $V^{ienna}P^{arallel}L_{ogic}$. *Computer Languages Journal*, 1993. to appear.

[LHHK92] J. Lee, Wenwey H., E. Hilsdale, and G. E. Kaiser. Dynamic orthogonal composition in meldc. In *Proceedings of the 2nd Workshop on Objects in Large Distributed Applications*, Vancouver BC, Canada, October 1992.

[Lis88] B. Liskov. Distributed programming in Argus. *Communications of the ACM*, 31(3):300–312, March 1988.

[LS87] B. Liskov and R. Scheifer. Guardians and actions: Linguistic support for robust, distributed programs. In B. Bhargava, editor, *Concurrency Control and Reliability in Database Systems.* Van Nostrand Reinhold, 1987.

[Pan91] C. Pancake. Software support for parallel computing: Where are we headed? *Communications of the ACM*, 34(11), November 1991.

[Sha87] E. Shapiro. *Concurrent Prolog, Collected Papers*, volume 1–2. The MIT Press, 1987.

[Sha89] E. Shapiro. The family of concurrent logic programming languages. *ACM Computing Surveys*, 21(3):412–510, September 1989.

[SS86] L. Sterling and E. Shapiro. *The Art of Prolog.* The MIT Press, 1986.

[WWC92] G. Wiederhold, P. Wegner, and S. Ceri. Toward megaprogramming. *Communications of the ACM*, 35(11), November 1992.

An Intrusion Detection Architecture for System Security

Lucas Hui, Siu-Leung Chung and **Kwok-Yan Lam**
Department of Information Systems and Computer Science
National University of Singapore
Singapore 0511
Email: lhui@iscs.nus.sg

Abstract
Intrusion detection aims to detect security violations from abnormal pattern of system usage. It is required that user activities be monitored by the system and that monitoring information be analysed to recognize behavior pattern of users. While basic monitoring capability is supported by most computer systems, analysis of monitoring data remains a problem of active research in system security. This paper presents a new software architecture for intrusion detection which makes use of a combination of data analysis and classification technologies including: artificial neural network, unconstrainted optimization, noise reduction, clusters recognition and high-dimensional data visualization. By carefully combining different data processing techniques, our scheme makes full use of their respective merits to solve the intrusion detection problem.

1 Introduction

Intrusion detection [3] aims to detect a wide range of security violations ranging from attempted break-ins by outsiders to system penetrations and abuses by insiders. It is based on the hypothesis that users are typically involved in specific types of activity and the programs they use will normally reflect that activity. Hence, security violations could be detected from abnormal patterns of system usage in that exploitation of a system's vulnerabilities involves abnormal use of the system.

Approaches to intrusion detection typically involves, firstly, monitoring of user activities and, secondly, analysis of audit records. General auditing mechanisms often monitor every aspect of the underlying system, and each of the monitored aspect constitutes a component (also called an intrusion detection measure) of the monitoring data set. Almost invariably, general auditing mechanisms tend to create a massive volume of monitoring data. It is therefore essential to process audit records in such a way that user behavior patterns can be recognized efficiently.

In this discussion, we concentrate on the recognition of behavior pattern of user login sessions. A general intrusion detection model [3] recognizes the behavior pattern of subjects, initiators of actions in the target system, on objects, receptors of actions. Subjects and objects may be grouped into classes by role and by type respectively. Audit records represent actions performed by subjects on objects. The behavior of a given subject on a given object is characterized by an activity profile which serves as a description of normal activity for its respective subject and object. Profiles can be defined for individual subject-object pairs, or for aggregates of subjects and objects. As for illustration purposes, our discussion is restricted to the use of the data reduction method to analysis behavior pattern of users in each login session. Hence, in this case, each user is a subject and the set of all programs executed in a login session constitutes the object class.

Our goal is to build an intrusion detection system which gathers user behavior information from the audit trail, and then uses these information to monitor newly created user sessions. In other words, we would like to answer the following question:

> After gathering user behavior information from the past audit trail, suppose the user U_1 has a new user session S_i , does S_i really belong to U_1, or belong to the other people (which is the intruder)?

We call this the intrusion detection problem.

The new scheme is based on the following approach: Periodically, say once a week, the intrusion detection system collects user behavior information from the audit trail of the past week. Thereafter, in the following week, the intrusion detection system will check all user session created in that week, and decides whether the behavior pattern underlying this user session deviated from the norm. If so, we call such sessions, in this discussion, **suspicious** sessions. New user sessions found to be suspicious will be inspected by a more detailed analysis. Hence, suspicious user sessions are analysed by an security official.

The system architecture for intrusion detection therefore consists of a component which efficiently and effectively extracts all suspicious sessions for close inspection by another component. Our system uses a neural network to perform the extraction. Performance of the neural network is improved by means of a noise reduction component which is based on a data analysis technique. In case human intervention is needed for practical reasons, a high-dimensional data visualization subsystem has been designed to faithfully display the multi-variate monitoring data on a 2-dimensional or 3-dimensional plane for visual inspection [7].

This paper starts in the next section with a review of recent work in intrusion detection. Section 3 describes the neural network component of our system which is followed by a discussion of the new optimization technique for training our neural network. Section 4 and Section 5 describe our noise reduction technique for improving the efficiency of the recognition process. The high-dimensional data visualization subsystem is presented in Section 6.

2 Related Work

In [3], Denning described an intrusion-detection model which based on the hypothesis that exploitation of a system's vulnerabilities involves abnormal use of the system; therefore, security violations could be detected from abnormal patterns of system usage. Since then, plenty of work on intrusion-detection have been carried out [7, 8].

Initially, rule-based expert systems and statistical models were used [6, 8]. The statistical component analyzes the audit trail, and signals a warning if a change of user behaviour pattern is believed to have occurred. Since such a warning, which is a probabilistic event, cannot be regarded as a proof of intrusion, so an expert system is used for further analysis. This approach has proven to be successful, and enhancements to the model were made in order to reduce the rate of false alarms.

One of the most difficult problem involved was to fix the threshold of alarm on a statistical variable. Too low a threshold makes false alarm rate to rise to an unacceptable levels while too high a threshold increases the risk of missing real intruder's session. This problem comes from the fact that user behaviour patterns, which we can be treated as high-dimensional random variables, contain noise. To take advantage of the correlation existing between the different measures related to the behaviour of a user, the statistical model has to approximate each of the measures with a gaussian law [6], thus increases the complexity of the statistical model which in turn makes further improvement more difficult.

Debar et al. [2], therefore, suggested the use of a neural network to replace the statistical model. Their work, like ours, concentrated on session level intrusion detection. The network neural component was used to inspect session data. Suspicious sessions, once found, were sent to an expert system component for further investigation. The network topology they used was of the recurrent type [12, 13]. They did not use the classic feed-forward back propagation layered network defined by Rumelhart and McClelland [10] due to the following reasons:

1. Back propagation networks require a priori determination of their input dimension;
2. correlations in the input patterns are not taken into account; and

3. although back propagation networks are fast in testing patterns, they are very slow to converge during training.

However, recurrent neural networks require plenty of memory space when compared to their back propagation counterparts. Moreover, recurrent neural networks are retroactive systems. There are values that the network never learns, even with an increased number of neurons and a long and careful training phase.

The new intrusion detection scheme presented in this paper employs a neural network component which is of the back propagation type. As will be shown in later sections, by carefully combining it with other advanced data analysis technologies, an efficient back propagation network can be used which has the advantages that it uses less memory, is fast in checking the audit data and has more predictable behavior.

3 Neural network for intrusion detection

3.1 The monitoring data

The neural network operates on monitoring data collected by the system auditing mechanism. The audit trail contains session data which are taken as a multivariate data set. The neural network recognizes user behavior pattern in each login session.

Monitoring of a user's activity in a login session includes different measures on each of the set of programs executed by that user within that login session. A measure can be the number of time that a particular program was executed in the session, or the total amount of CPU time consumed by that program, etc. [3]. The actual types of measure will depend on the monitoring mechanism supported by the underlying system. Determining what activities and statistical measures provide the best discriminating power is another area of current research. In fact our proposed intrusion detection software system can be used as a prototyping tool to determine the best set of measures.

The audit trail can be viewed as a two-dimensional matrix, where each row stores the different measures of a past user session, and each column stores a particular measure of all past user sessions.

Following is an example of the audit trail matrix M of p different measures from n different user login sessions.

$$
\begin{array}{cc|ccccc|}
 & & \multicolumn{5}{c}{\text{Measures}} \\
 & & 1 \; 2 & \cdots & j & \cdots & p \\
\hline
 & 1 & & & \cdot & & \\
 & 2 & & & \cdot & & \\
 & \vdots & & & \cdot & & \\
\text{Sessions} & i & & \cdots & x_{ij} & & \\
 & \vdots & & & & & \\
 & n & & & & & \\
\hline
\end{array}
$$

where x_{ij} is a real number stands for the value of measure j ($j = 1, \cdots, p$) in session i ($i = 1, \cdots, n$).

There are two ways to view M geometrically :

- n row vectors of M, $\vec{S}_1, \cdots, \vec{S}_n$, in a p-D Euclidean space, each corresponds to one user session;
- p column vectors of M, $\vec{Y}_1, \cdots, \vec{Y}_p$, in a n-D Euclidean space, each corresponds to one measure.

3.2 The back propagation neural network

The classic feed-forward back propagation neural network [10] is a suitable tool for pattern classification. Intrusion detection is an instance of pattern classification problem. The background of this kind of neural network is given briefly below, interested readers should consult the reference ([10]) for details.

Input of the neural network is a session S_j, and output is a binary variable which indicates whether S_j is a session belonging to monitored user, say U_1. The neural network has a set of internal variables called the **weights**. The weights are initialized to some random values. The output of the neural network is a function of the input values and the internal weights.

A neural network needs to be **trained** before it can be used. This is achieved by presenting to the neural network past user sessions (from the audit trail) that belongs to U_1 (called **positive** training patterns), and user session that does not belong to U_1 (called **negative** training patterns). When a training pattern S_i is presented to the neural network, the output is computed, and is compared to the expected output of S_i. The neural network will modify the weights in some pre-specified way, in order to minimize the difference of the computed output and expected output. Ideally, the training process stops when for every training pattern, the expected output is the same as the real network output. This means the network can correctly classify all given user sessions. At this time, the neural network is said to be trained, and its weights has implicitly store the user behavior pattern of U_1.

Later, when a new user session S_i is to be classified, the neural network, using the stored weights, determines whether S_i is consistent with the previous user behavior of U_1, and thus decide whether S_i is a session of U_1. If the output of the neural network shows that S_i is not a session of U_1, S_i is treated as a suspicious session. In this case the system signals an alarm and presents the details of S_i for further analysis. This is called the testing phase.

There are several reasons supporting the use of neural networks in the intrusion detection problem.

1. Neural networks use the concept of programming by example and repetition. In the case of intrusion detection, the audit trail contains session records, which are examples of user behaviour patterns.

2. Neural networks can determine whether a new session record in the audit trail belongs to a user efficiently after being trained. This is necessary for the massive volume of data involved, and necessary for early detection of intrusion.

3. Neural networks are adaptive to the changing user behaviour pattern.

4. Neural networks can tolerate, to a small extent, noisy input data.

5. Neural networks are easy to implement. This allows quick prototyping, and can shorten system development time.

However, as mentioned in the previous section, there are several drawbacks when feed-forward back propagation neural networks are used directly.

1. The back propagation training algorithm converges very slowly.

2. The trained network will recognize the noise as well as the user behavior pattern if its input data are heavily distorted by noise. This severely degrades the performance of the system.

3. Among the p measures, only strongly correlated measures are discriminative. However, when a neural network operates, all p measures are processed.

Fortunately, a combination of advanced neural network and data analysis technologies, as will be described, can help to surmount these drawbacks.

3.3 Applying optimization techniques to neural networks

The process of training a neural network is to teach the network to recognize patterns by modifying its set of weights. This is equivalent to changing the weights to produce the desired output (i.e. the target output), for input patterns of known classes, with a minimized error.

This process can be treated as an unconstrained optimization. The training process can be formulated as an optimization problem where the weights are adjusted so that, for a given input, the difference between the neural network output and the target result, i.e. the error term, is minimized.

The back propagation learning algorithm corresponds to the gradient method in optimization, which has proven to be slow to converge to a minimum.

Recently, research results of applying advanced optimization techniques, such as the quasi-Newton method, to neural network training are obtained [11]. By using faster learning algorithm (from advanced optimization technique) in the feed-forward neural network, slow convergence is no longer a problem.

4 Reducing input noise by data analysis

The intrusion-detection model is based on the hypothesis that every user will develop his own behavior pattern. The objective of this model is to extract from the audit trail, the behavior pattern that can distinguish every particular user from the others.

However, within a login session of any particular user, the amount of data captured by the auditing mechanism will be huge, and, among them, only strongly correlated data are needed to establish a reliable behavior pattern. The remaining portion of the data set will be considered noise by the model. It has been pointed out that the performance of feed-forward back propagation neural networks will be severely degraded when operating on noisy input data.

In this respect, some tools have to be developed to filter out the noise in the data set prior to input to the neural network. One popular approach for extracting strongly correlated components, and hence filtering out noise from a data set is available in multivariate data analysis.

To this end, we present a data reduction method which helps to improve the recognition process. The method is called **Standardized Principal Components Analysis** (SPCA) [5, 4]. SPCA eliminates noise from the original data set by extracting only discriminating components that best characterize user behavior. It is assumed that users are typically involved in specific types of assignment, and hence their activities exhibit some behavior pattern. When a user is being monitored, audit data from different measures of that user's activity may be strongly correlated in that they are governed by the same behavior pattern. Based on this assumption, such strongly correlated components of the data set are those that most effectively discriminate one user from another. Therefore, the original data set can be reduced by extracting only those components. This, however, means that comparisons of audit data from different measures are needed in order to compute the correlation of various components. Consequently, the original data set, which is inevitably heterogeneous, needs be normalized in order to enable such comparisons. To summarize, this step firstly normalizes the data set and, secondly, identifies the strongly correlated components.

Consider the audit trail matrix M shown in the previous section, the objective of SPCA is to extract those vectors that are strongly correlated among the p column vectors $\vec{Y}_1, \cdots, \vec{Y}_p$. This is equivalent to reducing the column (measures) space in the audit trail matrix M where those measures considered to be noises are filtered out. The procedures for noise filtering by SPCA can be briefly given as follow:

1. The original data matrix M is modified to a standardized data matrix $\tilde{M}$ where each element x_{ij} is replaced by $\tilde{x}_{ij}$ given by

$$\tilde{x}_{ij} = \frac{(x_{ij} - \bar{x}_j)}{\sigma_j \sqrt{n}} \tag{1}$$

where $\bar{x}_j$ is the mean and σ_j is the standard deviation of the elements in column j. The normalization of the data is necessary because much of the measures in the audit-log involves variables in which the means and scale units are arbitrary, such as command counts and CPU time of programs.

2. Now the p standardized column vectors can be treated as p points on the surface of a n-D unit hypersphere. The next step is the rotation of the initial configuration of the p points to a new orientation, of the same dimensionality, that exhibits the characteristic of mutually orthogonal dimensions with sequentially maximal variance. That is, the first dimension displays the largest variance of point projections. The second dimension displays the next largest variance, subject to being orthogonal to the first, and so on. This can be achieved by projecting the points on the eigenvectors $\vec{v}_1, \cdots, \vec{v}_n$ of the symmetric matrix $\tilde{M}\tilde{M}^T$ with corresponding eigenvalues $\mu_1, \cdots, \mu_n$ in descending order of magnitudes. It is assumed that, for most of the time, the rank of the matrix $\tilde{M}\tilde{M}^T$ will equal to the dimensions of the column vectors of $\tilde{M}$.

3. The components that are strongly correlated in the original data set correspond to points that are clustered together on the n-D unit hypersphere. It is, however, very difficult to identify cluster in a n-D hyperspace with n usually greater than 3. This problem can be solved by reducing the dimensionality of the transformed space mentioned in the previous step. The reduction in dimensionality can be done by discarding those higher dimensions that exhibit the smaller variance of point projection, i.e. the projects to the first two or three eigenvectors are retained.

4. Now the cluster of points in the reduced dimension space can be identified by either graphical display or an automated system making use of minimum spanning tree.

5 Automating noise reduction by a graph theoretic technique

In combining the SPCA with neural network, we still have to solve one important problem. Since the output of SPCA is a set of points (each corresponds to one measure) in a 2-D or 3-D space, it is necessary to extract those points which are clustered together, and to ignore other scattered points. One way to extract the clustered points is by human observation. But this is not acceptable for the intrusion detection system since an automated system is preferred.

In this case, techniques from clustering analysis is employed [9]. One method that is applicable in this case is the use of minimum spanning tree to recognize clusters [14].

The following example illustrates the idea: Given a set of points in a 2-D (or 3-D) space. The minimum spanning tree of the points is first built. The points that are grouped together are connected by short edges of the minimum spanning tree. The points that are scattered are connected by long edges of the minimum spanning tree. So by analyzing the length of each edge in the minimum spanning tree, we can extract the points that grouped together. Finding the minimum spanning tree is a standard problem in graph theoretical study [1]. Implementation of this algorithm is straight-forward.

6 High-dimension data visualization

Obviously, the most direct way of recognizing pattern or structure of an objects is by inspecting the graphical display of the object itself. Even though intrusion detection relies on the recognition of user behavior pattern, so far there is no attempt to display the established user pattern for visual inspection in any of the existing model. In fact, it would be helpful if there is a way to display the reduced data set (with noises being filtered out) of the audit trail graphically. This is particularly useful after a user session has been identified to be suspicious by the neural network module where visual inspection will further confirm whether abnormality has really occurred.

For graphical display of multivariate data, the problem of high dimension gets in the way as shown in the last section. Similarly, this problem can be solved by the corresponding dimensional reduction method. This technique, generally known as **Factor Analysis** [5], is an important tool in multivariate data analysis.

Consider the audit trail matrix M. Assume, after the noise reduction process, q strongly correlated measures have been extracted. That is to say, M is now composed of q column vectors $\vec{Y}_1, \cdots, \vec{Y}_q$. In this case, the n row vectors $\vec{S}_1, \cdots, \vec{S}_n$ of M are in a q-D Euclidean space. If these n vectors are displayed graphically in the q-D Euclidean space, the points representing these n vectors will form the desired behavior pattern. If q is greater than 3, it is not possible to visualize the display. The dimensions of these n vectors can be reduced by factor analysis which proceed as follow:

1. The eigenstructure of the symmetric matrix $M^T M$ is computed. Let $\vec{u}_1, \cdots, \vec{u}_q$ be the eigenvectors with the corresponding eigenvalues $\lambda_1, \cdots, \lambda_q$ in descending order of magnitudes.

2. For two dimensional display, choose the first two eigenvectors as coordinate axes. Any point denoted by vector $\vec{S}_i$ will be approximated by the projection of the point upon the 2-D space with coordinates $(\vec{S}_i^T \vec{u}_1, \vec{S}_i^T \vec{u}_2)$.

3. For three dimensional display, the first three eigenvectors will be chosen instead and the same procedure follows.

7 Conclusion

In this paper we described a new scheme for detecting intrusion aiming at providing extra security to existing computer systems. The scheme combines the above mentioned different computing technologies.

The proposed intrusion detector has three major architectural components. The first component applies the standardized principal components analysis to past session data (represented as $S_1, ..., S_n$), and uses the minimum spanning tree clustering algorithm to identify strongly correlated measures. After that the past session data $(S_1, ..., S_n)$ is processed by a measure selection filter. Output of this filter (represented as $S'_1, ..., S'_n$)

contains only strongly correlated measures. Therefore, this algorithm can be regarded as a noise reduction processor.

The second architectural component uses $S'_1, ..., S'_n$ to train the neural network, using training algorithms based on advanced optimization technique. The trained network is the output of this component.

The third architectural component uses the trained neural network to monitor new user sessions. If a session is suspicious, an alarm signal is raised, and detailed information of this session is presented to a security officer for manual investigation. Currently, a 2-D (or 3-D) graphical display tool for showing relationship of all user sessions, which is built upon graphic packages "GNUPLOT" and "XTANGO", is used.

References

[1] A. Aho, J. Hopcroft, and J. Ullman, *Data Structures and Algorithms*, Addison-Wesley, Reading, Massachusetts, 1987.

[2] H. Debar, M. Becker, and D. Siboni. *A Neural Network Component for an Intrusion Detection System,* IEEE Proceedings of Symposium on Security and Privacy, 1992.

[3] D.E. Denning. *An Intrusion-Detection Model,* IEEE Trans. on Software Engineering, SE-13 (1987) 222–232.

[4] P.E. Green.*Analysis Multivariate Data*, The Dryden Press, Hinsdale, Illinois, 1978.

[5] Michel Jambu. *Exploratory and Multivariate Data Analysis*, Academic Press, Inc. (1991).

[6] H.S. Javitz and A. Valdes. *The SRI IDES Statistical Anomaly Detector*, IEEE Proceedings of Symposium on Security and Privacy, Oakland, 1991.

[7] K.Y. Lam and S.L. Chung. *A Data Reduction Method to Abstract User Behavior Pattern for Intrusion Detection,* (submitted).

[8] T. Lunt, R. Jagannathan, R. Lee, S. Listgarten, D. Edwards, P. Neumann, H. Javitz, and A. Valdes. *IDES: The Enhanced Prototype, a Real-time Intrusion-detection Expert System,* SRI report SRI-CSL-88-12, October 1988.

[9] P. Moharir, *Pattern-Recognition Transforms,* John Wiley and Sons, New York, 1992.

[10] D.E. Rumelhart and J.L. McClelland, *Parallel Distributed Processing*, MIT Press, Cambridge, Massachusetts, 1990.

[11] R. Setiono and L. Hui, *Faster Neural Network Training via Quasi-Newton Methods*, (submitted), 1993.

[12] R. Williams and D. Zipser. *A Learning Algorithm for Continually Running Fully Recurrent Neural Networks,* Neural Computation, 1:270–280, 1989.

[13] R. Williams and D. Zipser. *Experimental Analysis of the Real-Time Recurrent Learning Algorithm*, Connection Science, Volume 1 Number 1, 1989.

[14] C. Zahn. *Graph-Theoretical Methods for Detecting and Describing Gestalt Clusters,* IEEE Tran. on Computers, c-20:68–86, 1971.

Entwurf sicherer verteilter Systeme: Formalisierte Sicherheitspolitiken und abstrakte Implementierung

Claudia Eckert
TU München, Fakultät für Informatik
D-80290 München,
e-mail : eckertc@informatik.tu-muenchen.de

Zusammenfassung

Das Papier stellt einen Ansatz zum Entwurf und zur Konstruktion sicherer verteilter Systeme gemäß einer Top–down Vorgehensweise vor. Dabei werden die Stufen der formale Spezifikation von Sicherheitsanforderungen und der abstrakten Implementierung erläutert. Zur Erfassung der gewünschten Sicherheitseigenschaften werden Systemmodelle sowie flexible Konzepte zur Formalisierung von Sicherheitspolitiken benötigt. Entsprechende Modelle und Konzepte werden vorgestellt. Der Einsatz der Konzepte zur Spezifikation von Politiken wird anhand von Beispielszenarien aufgezeigt. Der Übergang zu einer abstrakten Implementierung erfordert wiederum geeignete Konzepte und Methoden, um die spezifizierten Sicherheitseigenschaften durchzusetzen. Einige Konzepte werden exemplarisch beschrieben und deren Einsatz wird erläutert.

1 Einleitung

Das Papier stellt einen Ansatz zum Entwurf und zur Konstruktion sicherer verteilter Systeme gemäß einer Top–down Vorgehensweise vor. Ausgehend von einer formalen Spezifikation, die die Solleigenschaften des zu konstruierenden Systems festlegt, werden Systeme über mehrere Konkretisierungsstufen hinweg realisiert, wobei die spezifizierten Eigenschaften durchzusetzen sind. Im Kontext dieses Papiers steht das Qualitätsattribut der Sicherheit im Vordergrund. Zur Spezifikation der Sicherheits-Solleigenschaften eines Systems wird eine Prädikatensprache eingeführt, deren Semantik formal festgelegt ist. Als Basis für die formale Definition der Semantik dient ein Modell für sichere abstrakt verteilte Systeme, das kurz vorgestellt wird. Der Einsatz der Prädikate zur Spezifikation von Sicherheitspolitiken, die der jeweiligen Problemstellung einer Anwendung angepaßt sind, wird anhand von Beispielszenarien aufgezeigt.
Die Spezifikation wird in einem ersten Realisierungsschritt in eine abstrakte Implementierung transformiert. Für diesen Übergang wurde eine objektbasierte Programmiersprache um geeignete Konzepte erweitert. Einige Konzepte werden exemplarisch beschrieben und deren Einsatz wird erläutert. Der Ansatz stellt damit insgesamt das Instrumentarium zur systematischen Konstruktion sicherer abstrakt verteilter Systeme zur Verfügung.
Die Sicherheits-Solleigenschaften eines Systems legen fest, welche Subjekte, welche Zugriffsrechte an welchen Objekten besitzen und welche Informationen einem Subjekt zugänglich sein dürfen. Die durchzusetzenden Sicherheitseigenschaften werden durch Sicherheitspolitiken beschrieben. Die Sicherheit eines

Systems kann als ein Maß für seine Fähigkeit definiert werden, eine festgelegte Sicherheitspolitik zu realisieren und damit Bedrohungen, denen das System u.a. durch nicht autorisierte Informationsmodifikationen (Verlust der Integrität), durch nicht autorisierte Informationsweitergabe (Verlust der Vertraulichkeit), durch den Verlust der Verfügbarkeit oder durch die Maskierung von Subjekten ausgesetzt ist, zu begegnen. Zur Abwehr dieser Bedrohungen steht ein breites Repertoire an unterschiedliche Mechanismen und Verfahren zur Verfügung.
Zur Formulierung von Sicherheitseigenschaften und zur Analyse von Systemen werden Sicherheitsmodelle benötigt. In der Literatur ist ein weites Spektrum entsprechender Modelle zu finden. Die Klasse der Zugriffskontroll-Modelle (u.a. [Lam71]) deckt den Aspekt der Integrität ab. Die Klasse der Informationsfluß-Modelle (u.a.[Fol87]) erfaßt und kontrolliert die zulässigen Informationskanäle zwischen den Objekten des Systems (Vertraulichkeitsaspekt), während die Klasse der Non-Interference Modelle (u.a. [GM82]) das Ein/Ausgabeverhalten von Systemen modelliert. Die Modelle weisen eine Vielzahl von Mängeln auf. Die zu schützenden Einheiten sind überwiegend von grober Granularität, wie z.B. Dateien, und die Zugriffsrechte beziehen sich auf Operationen mit einfacher Semantik, wie z.B. lesen und schreiben, die keine differenzierte Rechtevergabe ermöglichen. Die Zugriffskontroll-Modelle beschränken sich zumeist auf die Kontrolle der Weitergabe von Zugriffsrechten; der Informationsflußaspekt bleibt entweder unberücksichtigt oder die Modellierung ist zu restriktiv und unflexibel, wie im Fall des Bell LaPadula-Modells [BL75]. In den Informationsflußansätzen und Non-Interference Ansätzen wird demgegenüber der Integritätsaspekt vernachlässigt.
Es wird demnach ein Modell benötigt, das es erlaubt, fein granulare Zugriffsbeschränkungen unter Berücksichtigung von Zugriffskontexten festzulegen, sowie eine systematische Beschränkung von Informationskanälen zwischen Benutzern unter Berücksichtigung der Funktionalität des Systems zu modellieren. Diese Anforderungen werden von dem vorzustellenden Ansatz erfüllt, der eine Verallgemeinerung des Non-Interference Ansatzes darstellt und sich in die Klasse der Informationsfluß-Modelle einordnen läßt, wobei der Integritätsaspekt geeignet berücksichtigt wird. Objekte werden mit beliebiger Granularität mit wohldefinierten Zugriffsoperationen modelliert [CW87], so daß Zugriffsrechte differenziert festgelegt werden können. Verdeckte Kanäle sind ebenfalls modellierbar. Der Aspekt der Verfügbarkeit wird nicht behandelt.
Bedrohungen eines Systems durch die Maskierung von Subjekten sind u.a. durch korrekte Authentifizierungsprotokolle abzuwehren. Eine Logik zur Analyse und Spezifikation derartiger Protokolle wird u.a. in [LABW92] vorgestellt. Auf diesen Bereich wird im folgenden nicht weiter eingegangen.

Für die Stufen der Realisierung werden zusätzlich Konzepte und Methoden benötigt, die zum einen eine zielorientierte abstrakte Implementierung unterstützen und es zum anderen ermöglichen, Aussagen über die Verträglichkeit der Implementierung mit der spezifizierten Politik zu gewinnen.

2 Modellierung sicherer verteilter Systeme

Im folgenden wird ein Modell für sichere abstrakt verteilte Systeme eingeführt, das die Basis für die formale Semantik der Prädikate zur Spezifikation von Sicherheitseigenschaften liefert.
Ein sprachbasierter Ansatz zur Konstruktion von verteilten Systemen liefert die Basis für die Modellierung sicherer Systeme. Eine geeignete Konzeptebasis stellen objektorientierte Ansätze (vgl. u.a. [BHJ+87]) zur Verfügung.
Ein System ist eine Einheit, die mit ihrer Umwelt über Operationen interagiert. Diese Operationen definieren die Schnittstelle des Systems ($\mathcal{E}$). Ein System ist seinerseits aus einer endlichen Menge von Komponenten ($\mathcal{K}$) zusammengesetzt. Die Komponenten können aktiv (Prozeß) oder passiv (Monitor, Modul) sein. Die abstrakte Verteiltheit der Systeme wird durch die aktiven Komponenten definiert. Die Komponenten des Systems interagieren über Operationsaufrufe (Operationsinkarnationen), die von den aktiven Komponenten ausgeführt werden. Jede Komponente k definiert eine Menge von Operationen ($\mathcal{O}(k)$), die an andere Komponenten exportiert oder als Komponenten-lokale Operationen festgelegt werden können. Die Aktionen der Umwelt eines Systems werden von den Systembenutzern ($\mathcal{B}$) initiiert. Der Begriff des Benutzers ist hier abstrakt zu verstehen. Es kann sich dabei sowohl um menschliche Benutzer als auch um Knotenrechner in einer vernetzten Hardware-Umgebung handeln.[1] Die Aktionen der Benutzer werden innerhalb des Systems durch ausgezeichnete aktive Komponenten, die Benutzerrepräsentanten, die die Benutzeraufträge ausführen, nodelliert. Die Benutzer sowie die aktiven Komponenten sind die Subjekte des Systems; für sie sind die Sicherheitsanforderungen festzulegen. Da die Komponenten über ihre Operationen genutzt werden können, sind die Komponenten die zu schützenden Objekte des Systems.
Die Komponenten ($\mathcal{K}$), die Operationen ($\mathcal{O}$), die Schnittstelle ($\mathcal{E}$) und die Benutzer ($\mathcal{B}$) modellieren die **Komponenten-basierte Sicht** des Systems.
Das dynamische Verhalten eines Systems wird durch ein **Transitionssystem** (vgl. u.a. [Pnu86]) modelliert. Ein Transitionssystem definiert eine endliche Menge von Zustandsobjekten V, eine Menge von Systemzuständen Σ, wobei jeder Systemzustand eine Interpretation der Zustandsobjekte liefert, eine endliche Menge atomarer Aktionen $\mathcal{A}$, deren Ausführungen Zustandsübergänge bewirken, und die Zustandsübergangsrelation $\Gamma \subseteq \Sigma \times \mathcal{A} \times \Sigma$.
Der **Effekt** einer Aktion beschreibt die Beziehung zwischen einem Zustand und seinem Nachfolgezustand nach Ausführung der Aktion. Für jede Aktion können Vorbedingungen festgelegt sein, die vor der Ausführung der Aktion erfüllt sein müssen. Eine Aktion ist **zulässig** in einem Zustand des Systems, wenn ihre Vorbedingung in dem Zustand erfüllt ist.
Die Komponenten-basierte Sicht eines Systems wird verfeinert zu einer **Aktionen-basierten Sicht**, indem jede Operationsinkarnation bezüglich einer Operation der Menge $\mathcal{O}$ durch eine sequentielle Folge von Aktionen modelliert wird. Dazu wird jeder Operation aus $\mathcal{O}$ eine Folge von aktionengenerierender Funktionen

[1] Die korrekte Benutzer-Authentifikation wird vorausgesetzt.

zugeordnet. Die atomaren Aktionen der Aktionen-basierten Sicht sind Operationsinkarnierungs- und Operationsterminierungs-Aktionen, wobei für einfache Operationen, wie Schreib- oder Lesezugriffe auf einfache Zustandsobjekte, gilt, daß Inkarnierungs- und Terminierungsaktion zusammenfallen. Der **Effekt einer Operationsausführung** ist bestimmt durch die Effekte der Aktionen, die die Verfeinerung der Operationsinkarnation definieren.

Das Verhalten eines abstrakt verteilten Systems wird über die Menge der **Berechnungen** des Systems definiert. Eine Berechnung ist eine Folge von Zuständen, die einer Aktionenfolge assoziiert ist. Jede Eingabefolge des Systems ist damit eine Aktionenfolge, in der die Aktionen unterschiedlicher aktiver Komponenten vermischt (engl. interleaved) auftreten können. Durch die Zustandsübergangsrelation des Transitionssystems wird nicht-deterministisch in jedem Zustand eine der zulässigen Aktionen ausgewählt und ausgeführt.

Um zugriffskontrollierte Komponenten und die Vergabe von Zugriffsrechten zu modellieren, werden als spezielle Zustandsobjekte abstrakte Capabilities (vgl. u.a. [ABL83]), sowie Capability-Listen und Zugriffskontrollisten eingeführt. Eine abstrakte Capability ist ein qualifiziertes Objekt, das Zugriffsrechte für die Komponente, auf die sie verweist, festlegt. Die Menge der Komponenten des Systems wird um Manager-Komponenten erweitert, die die rechteändernden Operationen des Systems definieren. Die Zugriffsrechte entsprechen den Operationen, die auf den Komponenten des Systems definiert sind. Entsprechend dem semantischen Niveau der Operationen lassen sich damit differenzierte Zugriffsrechte festlegen und vergeben.

Die getroffenen Festlegungen sind in Definition 1 zusammengefaßt. Die Definition besteht aus zwei Teilen. Im ersten Teil wird das Modell für ein abstrakt verteiltes System eingeführt und im zweiten Teil wird dieses Modell um Komponenten zur Modellierung von Sicherheitseigenschaften erweitert.

Definition 1 :

1. Ein abstrakt verteiltes System $\mathcal{VS}$ wird durch ein Tupel $\mathcal{VS} = (KV, AV)$ modelliert. Dabei modelliert $KV = (\mathcal{K}, \mathcal{O}, \mathcal{E}, \mathcal{B})$ die Komponenten-basierte Sicht und $AV = (\mathcal{TS}, \mathcal{FA}, \rho)$ die Aktionen-basierte Sicht des Systems.
   Für $AV = (\mathcal{TS}, \mathcal{FA}, \rho)$ gilt:
   (a) $\mathcal{TS}$ ist ein Transitionssystem.
   (b) $\mathcal{FA}$ ist eine Menge aktionengenerierender Funktionen:
   $\forall f \in \mathcal{FA} : f : WB(v_1) \times \ldots \times WB(v_n) \longrightarrow \mathcal{A}$.
   (c) $\rho : \mathcal{O} \longrightarrow \mathcal{FA}^+$ definiert die Verfeinerung von Operationen durch eine Folge aktionengenerierender Funktionen.
   ρ induziert für jede Operationsinkarnation o' bezüglich $op \in \mathcal{O}$ eine Funktion $\rho'(o')$, die Aktionenverfeinerung von o'.
2. Ein sicheres abstrakt verteiltes System wird durch ein Tupel $\mathcal{MS} = (KV, AV)$ mit folgenden Erweiterungen modelliert:
   (a) Die Menge $CAP \subseteq V$ beschreibt eine Menge von Capability-Objekten, für die gilt[2]:

[2] $\mathcal{P}$ bezeichnet die Potenzmenge.

$\forall k \in \mathcal{K}\ \forall cap_k\ \in CAP:\ WB(cap_k) = \mathcal{P}(\mathcal{O}(k))$.
Die Menge von Objekten $CL = \{cl_k | k \in \mathcal{K} \cup \mathcal{O} \cup \mathcal{B}\} \subseteq V$ modelliert die Capability-Listen. Es gilt:
$\forall cl_k\ \in CL:\ WB(cl_k) = \mathcal{P}(CAP)$.
Die Menge von Objekten $ACL = \{acl_k | k \in \mathcal{K}\}$ modelliert für jede Komponente des Systems eine Zugriffskontrolliste. Der Wertebereich einer Zugriffskontrolliste acl_k ist gegeben durch die Menge von Paaren (k', OP), wobei $k' \in \mathcal{K} \cup \mathcal{O} \cup \mathcal{B}$ und $OP \subseteq \mathcal{O}(k)$.

(b) Die Menge $\mathcal{CO} \subseteq \mathcal{O}$ ist die Menge der rechteändernden Operationen.

(c) Die Menge $\mathcal{KM} \subseteq \mathcal{K}$ ist die Menge der Managerkomponenten, die die rechteändernden Operationen exportieren.

□

Durch das Modell für ein sicheres abstrakt verteiltes System werden die Zugriffsrechte eines Subjekts an Objekten des Systems durch eine subjektbezogene Capability-Liste und durch die objektbezogenen Zugriffskontrollisten beschrieben. Systeme, die gemäß des Modells $\mathcal{MS}$ modelliert sind, werden im folgenden mit $\mathcal{S}$ bezeichnet.
Das eingeführte Modell liefert die Basis zur Definition der formalen Semantik von Prädikaten, die Eigenschaften bezüglich Wechselwirkungen zwischen Komponenten solcher Systeme beschreiben. Die Eigenschaften betreffen den möglichen Informationsfluß zwischen den Benutzern des Systems, der aus der gemeinsamen Nutzung von Komponenten resultiert. In Definition 2 und 3 wird eine informale Semantik einiger Basis-Prädikate angegeben. Die Basis-Prädikate sind Prädikate über der Basis BV, die die Menge V der Zustandsobjekte sowie eine Menge ID von nullstelligen Funktionssymbolen umfaßt. Die Menge ID beschreibt die Menge aller Identifikatoren für Komponenten, Aktionen und Operationen.

Definition 2 :
Gegeben seien ein System $\mathcal{S}$ und eine Folge $< A >$ von Aktionen.

1. Gegeben seien zwei Aktionen $a, b \in < A >$ und ein Objekt $d \in V$ derart, daß die Aktion a in der Folge $< A >$ vor der Aktion b ausgeführt und durch die Ausführung von a das Objekt d modifiziert worden ist. Gegeben sei weiterhin die Aktionenfolge $< A' >$, die sich aus der Folge $< A >$ durch das Entfernen der Aktion a aus $< A >$ ergibt.
   Die Aktion a **beeinflußt** die Aktion b über das Objekt d, genau dann, wenn (i) die Aktion b in der Folge $< A' >$ nicht zulässig ist, oder (ii) wenn die Ausführung der Aktion b in $< A' >$ einen anderen Effekt besitzt als die Ausführung von b in der ursprünglichen Folge $< A >$ und die Veränderung auf den Wert des Objekts d zurückzuführen ist.
2. Eine Komponente **beeinflußt** durch die Ausführung einer Operationsinkarnation o' eine andere Komponente bei der Ausführung einer Operationsinkarnation o'', wenn es eine Aktion a in der Aktionsverfeinerung $\rho'(o')$, eine Aktion b in der Aktionsverfeinerung $\rho'(o'')$ und ein Zustandsobjekt $d \in V$ gibt, so daß a die Aktion b über d beeinflußt. □

Eine Beeinflussung einer Aktion liegt dann vor, wenn (i) die Zulässigkeit der Ausführung der beeinflußten Aktion von der Ausführung der beeinflussenden Aktion abhängig ist, oder wenn (ii) die beeinflußte Aktion in $< A' >$ ausgeführt werden kann, wobei jedoch ein unterschiedlicher Effekt bei der Aktionsausführung in $< A' >$ gegenüber dem Effekt bei der Ausführung in $< A >$ auftritt, der auf die Ausführung der beeinflussenden Aktion zurückzuführen ist. Eine Beeinflussung kann sowohl direkt als auch indirekt über andere Aktionen auftreten.
Der zweite Teil von Definition 2 legt die Beeinflussungseigenschaften auf der Basis der Komponenten-basierten Sicht für einzelne Komponenten fest.
Die Beeinflussungseigenschaft von Komponenten eines Systems ist eine Verallgemeinerung der Non-Interference Eigenschaft von Goguen und Meseguer [GM82], da durch die angegebene Modellierung auch nebenläufige Systeme erfaßt werden, und darüberhinaus durch die Aktionsverfeinerung auch die internen Aktionen des Systems modelliert und Beeinflussungseigenschaften für diese festgelegt werden können.

Definition 3 :
Gegeben sei ein System $\mathcal{S}$.
Für eine Operationsinkarnation o' bezüglich $op \in \mathcal{O}$ ist die Menge der **Ausgabeobjekte** definiert durch die Menge der Ausgabeparameter von op und der Menge der Parameter von Ausgabeoperationen $Out \subseteq \mathcal{E}$ bezüglich Ausgabegeräten des Systems.
Eine Komponente **beobachtet** durch die Ausführung einer Operationsinkarnation o' die Aktivität einer anderen Komponente, wenn (i) diese andere Komponente eine Operationsinkarnation o'' ausgeführt hat, es eine Aktion a in der Aktionsverfeinerung $\rho'(o'')$, eine Aktion b in der Aktionsverfeinerung $\rho'(o')$ und ein Zustandsobjekt $d \in V$ gibt, so daß a die Aktion b über d beeinflußt und wenn (ii) d ein Ausgabeobjekt von o'' ist. □

Die Aktivität einer Komponente ist beobachtbar, falls das Ausgabeverhalten der beobachtenden Operation von dieser Aktivität abhängig ist.
Zwischen zwei Komponenten kommt es potentiell zu einer Interaktion, falls es einen Informationsfluß zwischen ihnen gibt, der aus einer Beeinflussung oder einer Beobachtung resultiert.

3 Formalisierung von Sicherheitspolitiken

Durch eine Sicherheitspolitik sind die Zugriffsrestriktionen für Benutzer und die unzulässigen Informationsflüsse, also die unzulässigen Beobachtungen und Beeinflussungen zwischen Benutzern festzulegen. Dazu werden im folgenden die Prädikate $cninf, cnobs, acc$ eingeführt. Die formale Semantik der Prädikate läßt sich auf der Basis des Systemmodells über die Basis-Prädikate angeben.
Die Prädikate können ihrerseits Restriktionen beinhalten, die n-stellige Prädikate über der Basis BV der Zustandsobjekte und der nullstelligen Funktionssymbole der Identifikatoren sind und die in Abhängigkeit der Systemzustände ausgewertet werden.

Definition 4 :
Gegeben sei ein System $\mathcal{S}$, eine Berechnung σ, zwei Komponenten $k, k' \in \mathcal{K}$, zwei Operationen $op, op' \in \mathcal{O}$ und eine Restriktion R.

1. Die Komponente k heißt **bedingt beeinflussend** bezüglich der Komponente k' unter der Restriktion R über die Operationen op, op' in der Berechnung σ, genau dann, wenn in jedem Zustand der Berechnung σ gilt : $cninf(k, k', op, op', R) = true$.
   Dabei gilt, daß das Prädikat $cninf(k, k', op, op', R)$ im Zustand s erfüllt ist, wenn eine Beeinflussung von k' durch k über op, op' höchstens auftreten kann, wenn das Prädikat R im Zustand s nicht erfüllt ist.
2. Die Komponente k heißt **bedingt beobachtend** bezüglich der Komponente k' unter der Restriktion R über die Operationen op, op' in der Berechnung σ, genau dann, wenn in jedem Zustand der Berechnung σ gilt : $cnobs(k, k', op, op', R) = true$.
   Dabei gilt, daß das Prädikat $cnobs(k, k', op, op', R)$ im Zustand s erfüllt ist, wenn eine Beobachtung der Aktivität von k' durch k über op, op' höchstens auftreten kann, wenn das Prädikat R im Zustand s nicht erfüllt ist.
3. Gegeben sei eine Menge von Operationen $\mathcal{O}(k)$ einer Komponente k und eine Menge $OP \subseteq \mathcal{O}(k)$. Die Komponente k' heißt **zugriffsbeschränkt** in bezug auf k in der Berechnung σ, genau dann, wenn in jedem Zustand der Berechnung σ gilt: $acc(k', OP, k, R) = true$.
   Dabei gilt, daß das Prädikat $acc(k', OP, k, R)$ im Zustand s erfüllt ist, falls für jede Operation $op \in OP$ gilt, daß eine Operationsausführung durch k' im Zustand s höchstens dann zulässig ist, wenn das Prädikat R im Zustand s erfüllt ist. □

Die Restriktionen in Zugriffsbeschränkungsprädikaten können z.B. Attribute beliebiger Zustandsobjekte betreffen (z.B. Tageszeit) und insbesondere die Objekte der Menge CL und ACL. Darüberhinaus können durch die Einführung von Kontrollvariablen als abstrakte Befehlszähler Kontextabhängigkeiten spezifiziert werden (z.B. ein Zugriff ist nur im Kontext der Ausführung einer spezifischen Operation erlaubt). Restriktionen für die Beobachtungs- bzw. Beeinflussungsprädikate können z.B. die Attributierung von Zustandsobjekten mit Sensitivitätsmarken betreffen.
Über die Spezifikation von Prädikaten für Benutzerrepräsentanten lassen sich Sicherheitsanforderungen für Benutzer spezifizieren. Im weiteren werden in den entsprechenden Prädikaten jedoch aus Vereinfachungsgründen direkt die Benutzer angegeben.

Definition 5 :
Gegeben sei ein System $\mathcal{S}$. Eine **Sicherheitspolitik** P für $\mathcal{S}$ ist ein Prädikat, das durch eine Konjunktion aus Zugriffsbeschränkungs-, bedingten Beeinflussungs- und bedingten Beobachtungsprädikaten definiert wird. □

Die Verträglichkeit eines Systems $\mathcal{S}$ mit einer Politik P wird als ein Maß zur Bewertung der Sicherheit des Systems relativ zur spezifizierten Politik benutzt.

Eine Berechnung von $\mathcal{S}$ heißt **P-verträglich**, wenn in jedem Zustand der Berechnung die Politik P erfüllt ist. Das System $\mathcal{S}$ heißt **P-verträglich**, wenn alle Berechnungen von $\mathcal{S}$ P-verträglich sind, und $\mathcal{S}$ heißt **P-unverträglich**, wenn es keine P-verträgliche Berechnung von $\mathcal{S}$ gibt.

Die Formalisierung von Sicherheitspolitiken mittels der eingeführten Prädikate ermöglicht es u.a., die **Konsistenz** einer Politik formal nachzuweisen. Durch Konsistenzbedingungen für z.B. Zugriffskontrollprädikate werden Zusammenhänge, die zwischen den Restriktionen R der Prädikate gelten müssen, erfaßt. Mittels dieser Restriktionen in den Zugriffskontrollprädikate *acc* ist bei einer konsistenten Politik zu spezifizieren, daß einem Benutzer höchstens dann der Zugriff auf eine Operation *op* einer Komponente gewährt werden darf, wenn der Benutzer gemäß der Politik auch das Recht zur Nutzung aller Operationen, die von *op* importiert werden, besitzt.
Betrachtet man z.B. die Zugriffspolitik in einem UNIX-System, dann ist es wegen der einfachen Zugriffsoperationen möglich, eine inkonsistente Politik festzulegen, in der z.B. den Mitgliedern der Gruppe des Owners eines Directories *dir* das Schreib-Recht auf das Directory *dir* gewährt wird, in dem sich eine Datei f befindet, für die ein entsprechendes Schreib-Recht für die Gruppe nicht vergeben worden ist. Über den Directory-Zugriff ist es jedoch für Gruppenmitglieder möglich, auf die Datei f implizit schreibend zuzugreifen.
Modelliert man das Directory als eine passive Komponente, die zugeschnittene Operationen als Schnittstellenoperationen anbietet, wie z.B. *loesche_datei(f)*, bei deren Ausführung schreibend auf die Datei f zugegriffen wird, so lassen sich sowohl für *dir* als auch f Zugriffskontrollprädikate festlegen, für die die Gültigkeit der Konsistenzbedingung nachgewiesen werden kann. Inkonsistente Politikfestlegungen lassen sich erkennen bzw. verhindern, da das Schreib-Recht für f für die *loesche_datei(f)*-Ausführung vorhanden sein muß.

3.1 Beispielpolitiken

Es werden beispielhaft zwei Klassen von Sicherheitspolitiken formalisiert. Zunächst wird die Multi-level Security-Politik von Bell und LaPadula spezifiziert.
Die Multi-level Security-Politik:
Aus Vereinfachungsgründen werden die Zugriffsbeschränkungen nicht angegeben. Gegeben seien eine linear geordnete Menge von Sicherheitsmarken L, mit $L = \{$ *unclassified, confidential, secret, top secret* $\}$, die Menge der Subjekte $S = \mathcal{K} \cup \mathcal{B}$ und die Markierungsfunktion $l : S \longrightarrow L$.
Die Multi-level Politik wird festgelegt durch:

$$MLS = ZP' \wedge \bigwedge_{k \in S} \bigwedge_{k' \in S} \bigwedge_{op, op' \in \mathcal{O}} cninf(k, k', op, op', (l(k) > l(k'))$$

Die Politik zerfällt in einen benutzerbestimmbaren Teil, ZP', auf den nicht näher eingegangen wird, und in einen systembestimmten Teil. Für alle Subjekte k und k' ist ein bedingtes Nichtbeeinflussungsprädikat festgelegt, das beschreibt, daß

es keine Beeinflussung von k bezüglich k' geben darf, falls die Markierung von k größer ist, als die Markierung von k'. Damit wird die Forderung, daß in den Multi-level sicheren Systemen ein Informationsfluß höchstens von 'unten' nach 'oben' stattfinden darf, spezifiziert.
Im Kontext des Bell LaPadula Modells sind schreibende Zugriffe von hoch eingestuften Subjekten auf niedriger eingestufte Objekte generell unzulässig, unabhängig davon, ob gemäß der festgelegten Nutzungsmöglichkeiten des Systems ein niedriger eingestuftes Subjekt überhaupt die Möglichkeit besitzt, lesend auf dieses Objekt zuzugreifen. Durch die Nichtbeeinflussungsprädikate werden die unzulässigen Interferenzen spezifiziert, jedoch die Ausführung von Operationen nicht a priori verboten. Damit läßt sich durch das Instrumentarium der Interferenz-Prädikate die Eigenschaften der MLS-Politik flexibler erfassen.

Klasse von problembezogenen Politiken:
Es wird eine Rahmenpolitik RP für eine Klasse von Anwendungen vorgegeben. In Abhängigkeit von der spezifischen Problemstellung ist diese Politik durch weitere Restriktionen und durch die Festlegung der Restriktionen R in den Prädikaten zu präzisieren.
Gegeben seien ein System $\mathcal{S}$ und disjunkte Benutzergruppen (Benutzerrollen) z.B. $B1$, $B2$ und $B3$. Für die Benutzer der jeweiligen Gruppen werden durch die Rahmenpolitik RP Zugriffsrechte bezüglich jeweils einer Menge $OP_i, i \in \{1, \ldots, 3\}$, von Schnittstellenoperationen des Systems vergeben.
Für jede Menge OP_i gilt, daß es eine Menge von Komponenten $K_i = \{k_i^1, \ldots k_i^l\}$ gibt, mit: $OP_i = \bigcup_{j=1}^{l} OP_i^j$ mit $OP_i^j \subseteq \mathcal{O}(k_i^j)$.
Für jede Komponente $k_i^j \in K_i$ wird durch das Prädikat P_0 die Rechtevergabe an die entsprechende Benutzergruppe in den Anfangszuständen des Systems festgelegt. Darüberhinaus werden durch die **Zugriffskontrollprädikate** die erlaubten Zugriffe spezifiziert.

$$P_0 = \bigwedge b_i \in B_i \ \bigwedge k_i^j \in K_i : \ (b_i, OP_i^j) \in acl_{k_i^j}$$

und

$$\bigwedge b_i \in \mathcal{B} \ \bigwedge k_i^j \in \mathcal{K} : \ acc(b_i, OP_i^j, k_i^j, (b_i, OP_i^j) \in acl_{k_i^j})$$

Mit den acc-Prädikaten wird sichergestellt, daß ein Zugriff auf eine geschützte Komponente k_i^j höchstens dann zulässig ist, wenn das Subjekt b_i in der Zugriffskontrolliste der Komponente mit den entsprechenden Rechten OP_i^j enthalten ist.

Beobachtungs- und Beeinflussungsprädikate seien u.a. wie folgt gegeben:
(1) Benutzer der Gruppe $B1$ dürfen gegenseitig ihre Aktivität nicht beobachten:

$$\bigwedge b, b' \in B1 \ \bigwedge op, op' \in OP_1 : cnobs(b, b', op, op', true)$$

Für die Benutzer der Gruppe $B2$ gelte entsprechendes.
Gruppenübergreifend wird u.a. festgelegt:
(2) Die Benutzer der Gruppe $B2$ dürfen die Aktivität der Benutzer $B1$ nur bedingt beobachten:

$$\bigwedge b \in B2 \ \bigwedge b' \in B1 \ \bigwedge op \in OP_2 \ \bigwedge op' \in OP_1 : \ cnobs(b, b', op, op', R).$$

(3) Die Benutzer der Gruppe $B3$ dürfen keine anderen Benutzer beeinflussen und eine Beobachtung ist nur bedingt zulässig:

$$\bigwedge b \in B3 \bigwedge b' \in B2 \cup B1 \bigwedge op \in OP_3 \bigwedge op' \in OP_2 \cup OP_1 :$$
$$cninf(b, b', op, op', true) \wedge cnobs(b, b', op, op', R).$$

Die Festlegung der Rahmenpolitik erfolgt auf der Basis der durch die jeweiligen Benutzergruppen durchzuführenden Aufgaben. Festlegungen, wie sie u.a. in der Bedingung (1) auftreten, lassen sich z.B. mit der Multi-level Politik nicht erfassen, da dort keine Informationsflußbeschränkung für Benutzer der gleichen Sicherheitsstufe möglich ist.

Anwendungsklassen für die Rahmenpolitik:
I. Betrachtet man z.B. eine Anwendung, die eine Dienstleistung zur Verfügung stellt, die gebührenpflichtig ist. Dann erfaßt $B1$ die Menge der Klienten (z.B. Bankkunden, die rechnerunterstützt Ein- und Auszahlungen vornehmen) und $B2$ ist die Menge der Angestellten, die die Gebührenabrechnung (z.B. monatliche Gebühren) vornehmen können.
Die Bedingung (1) der Rahmenpolitik ist dahingehend zu verschärfen, daß zwischen den Klienten keine Beeinflussung erlaubt sein darf, d.h. das *cnobs*-Prädikat wird ersetzt durch ein entsprechendes *cninf*-Prädikat. Die Restriktion von Bedingung (2) ist z.B. dahingehend festzulegen, daß der Angestellte nur die Aktivität des Kundenstammes, der von ihm betreut wird, beobachten darf.
II. Ein weiteres Beispiel ist ein Szenario aus dem medizinischen Bereich, in dem eine medizinische Datenbank zur Verfügung steht, die Dienste unterschiedlicher Funktionalität anbietet. Die Patienten (Gruppe $B1$) haben z.B. die Möglichkeit, sich bei der Anmeldung zu registrieren. Ärzte (Gruppe $B2$) haben die Möglichkeit, ein Expertensystem zur Diagnoseunterstützung zu nutzen und Auskünfte über ihre Patienten zu erfragen. Für statistische Zwecke wird eine weitere Schnittstelle definiert, die von Benutzern der Gruppe $B3$ genutzt werden darf. Die Restriktionen der Rahmenpolitik sind wiederum zu präzisieren.
III. Die Verwaltung kryptographischer Schlüssel ist ein Szenario aus dem Bereich der Ressourcenverwaltung. Alle Klienten des Schlüsselverteilungsservers lassen sich als Benutzer der Gruppe $B1$ modellieren, für die gefordert wird, daß die gemeinsame Nutzung des Servers gegenseitig weder beobachtbar noch beeinflußbar ist, d.h. die Rahmenpolitik ist zu verschärfen (vgl I.). Damit wird gefordert, daß auf diesem Weg, also über die Nutzung der Schlüsselerzeugungsoperation des Servers, keine Information zwischen den Klienten fließen darf, insbesondere keine Information über den von dem Server erzeugten Schlüssel. Ist ein entsprechender Schlüssel zwischen Klienten auszutauschen, so ist eine entsprechende Operation zu spezifizieren, über die eine Beeinflusung und Beobachtung in bezug auf den Schlüssel zulässig ist.

Bei dem Übergang zu einer abstrakten Implementierung der Systeme besteht nun die Aufgabe, die Top-level Spezifikation des Systems so zu transformieren, daß das abstrakt implementierte System bezüglich der spezifizierten Politik P verträglich ist, das entspricht z.B. dem Vorgehen der Deadlock-Vermeidung im Kontext der Ressourcenverwaltung von Betriebssystemen.

4 Abstrakte Implementierung

Als Basis für die Implementierung dient eine objektbasierte Programmiersprache [Spi92], die Konzepte zur Definition von aktiven Komponenten (task), zur Definition passiver Komponenten (depot) sowie Konzepte zur Definition von Operationen (procedure, entry) zur Verfügung stellt. Eine Kommunikationsoperation (entry) wird durch einen Auftraggeber aufgerufen (entry-call) und von der anbietenden aktiven Komponente angenommen und ausgeführt (accept). Alle Komponenten sind Inkarnationen bezüglich entsprechender Typen (type). Die Sprachkonzepte erlauben die Konstruktion konzeptionell strukturierter Systeme, in denen die unterschiedlichen Beziehungen und Abhängigkeiten zwischen Komponenten durch differenzierte Strukturen beschrieben werden.
Die Konstruktion strukturierter Systeme ermöglicht es, die potentiell auftretenden Wechselwirkungen zwischen Komponenten zu begrenzen. Durch die gezielte Nutzung von Schachtelungsstrukturen (Lokalitätsbeziehung) sowie durch die konzeptionelle Beschränkung der Sichtbarkeitsbereiche (Definitionsbeziehung) lassen sich diese Ziele erreichen. Durch eine konzeptionell festgelegte Lebenszeit von Komponenten läßt sich sicherstellen, daß eine Komponente mindestens solange existiert, wie eine andere Komponente ein Recht zur Nutzung dieser Komponente besitzt.
Um die dynamische Rechtevergabe, wie sie durch den Zugriffskontrollteil der Sicherheitspolitik festgelegt wird, durchzusetzen, wird das Sprachrepertoire um ein Capability-Konzept erweitert. Capability-Typen sind qualifiziert mit der Komponente, die zu schützen ist. Der Rechteteil eines Capability-Typs beschreibt die Menge der Operationen, die auf der zu schützenden Komponente ausführbar sind. Capabilities können über Parameter beim Aufruf von Operationen übergeben werden. Für jeden zugriffskontrollierten Komponententyp ist ein zugehöriger Capability-Manager zu konstruieren, der Capabilities für die Komponenteninkarnationen bezüglich des Typs in Übereinstimmung mit den festgelegten *acc*-Prädikaten vergibt, und im Auftrag der aktiven Komponente, die die zu schützende Komponente erzeugt hat und damit das Ownerrecht darauf besitzt, die Rechte verwaltet. Um die global spezifizierte Zugriffspolitik für ein System dezentral durchzusetzen, kooperieren die Manager miteinander gemäß eines festgelegten Konzepts.
Bei der Konstruktion sicherer verteilter Systeme sind für Subsysteme bzw. Komponenten Rahmeneigenschaften in Form von Invarianten bezüglich der Beobachtungs- und Beeinflussungseigenschaften des Subsystems festzulegen. Entsprechende Eigenschaften werden durch Erweiterungen der Sprache durch Annotationen ausgedrückt. Zusammen mit den Strukturierungsmöglichkeiten stehen damit die Bausteine zur zielgerichteten Konstruktion eines Systems zur Verfügung. Die Rahmen (annotierte Komponenten) sind mit Funktionalität anzureichern und die Gültigkeit der Invarianten ist unter Einsatz bekannter Datenflußanalysemethoden nachzuweisen.

Der Einsatz annotierter Konzepte soll anhand eines Ausschnitts aus einem Beispiel erläutert werden. Gegeben sei ein Ausschnitt des medizinischen Anwendungsszenarios mit der oben angegebenen Klasse von problembezogener Rahmenpolitik. Die Benutzer der Gruppe $B1$ und $B2$ greifen gemeinsam auf eine Komponente *ClientMan* zu, die für die Verwaltung der Information über die Benutzergruppe $B1$ ein lokales Subsystem *PDataMan* definiert.

```
UNI CHANNEL  task type  ClientManType           -- Type declaration
  export  PRODUCING ClRegister,                 -- Register new patient data
          CONSUMING Info;                       -- Lookup informations
  FROM ClRegister TO Info;
    local  UNI CHANNEL depot type PdatManType(MaxCount: IN integer)
                export  PRODUCING  put,            -- local management type
                        CONSUMING Lookup;
                FROM put TO lookup;
    local depot  PDataMan: PdatManType(100); -- local object declaration
begin  loop
         select     accept ClRegister;
                or  accept Info;
        end select;
       end loop;
end ClientManType ;

UNI CHANNEL task ClientMan : ClientManType; -- object declaration
```

Durch die Annotation *uni channel* wird für die Komponente *ClientMan* als Invariante gefordert, daß keine Nutzung einer Operation des *to*-Teils eine Operationsnutzung des *from*-Teils beeinflussen kann, und damit auch nicht durch diese beobachtbar ist. Die Operationsannotation *producing* bzw. *consuming* fordert an Invarianzeigenschaft für jede entsprechende Inkarnation, daß durch die Operationsausführung keine Beobachtung anderer Aktivitäten stattfinden, bzw. daß keine Beeinflussung auftreten darf. Voraussetzung für den Nachweis der Gültigkeit der Invarianten ist, daß für jedes Anweisungskonstrukt der Programmiersprache festgelegt wird, welche Informationsflüsse auftreten können.

Sind die annotierten Eigenschaften für die obige Applikation erfüllt und besitzen die Benutzer der Gruppe $B1$ das Recht zur Ausführung der Operation *clregister*, so ist die Forderung (1) der Rahmenpolitik nach nicht Beobachtbarkeit erfüllt. Sei eine weitere Komponente (*MedMan*) spezifiziert, die sowohl eine Operation *diagnose* zur Unterstützung der Ärzte, als auch eine Operation *statistic* für die Statistiker, anbietet. Der Datenbestand wird wiederum in einem lokalen Subsystem verwaltet. Die potentiellen Informationsflüsse zwischen den drei Benutzergruppen auf Grund der gemeinsamen Komponentennutzungen ist in Abbildung 1 skizziert. Die Benutzer der Gruppe $B2$ besitzen das Recht an der Operation *diagnose*, während die Benutzer der Gruppe $B3$ das Recht zur Nutzung von *statistic* erhalten. Durch die Transitivität des Informationsflusses wird also durch die $B2$-Benutzer ein potentieller Informationskanal von den $B3$-Nutzern zu den $B1$-Nutzern etabliert, der gemäß der Rahmenpolitik jedoch nicht zulässig ist. Das konstruierte System ist also in bezug auf die Politikverträglichkeit zu analysieren.

Für den Nachweis der Verträglichkeit eines Systems mit einer spezifizierten Politik werden die potentiellen Informationsflüsse auf der Basis der invarianten

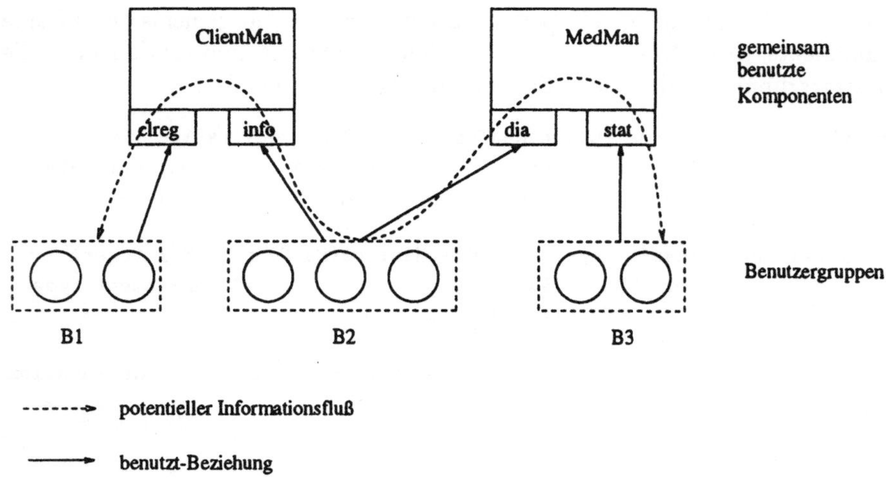

Abb. 1. Potentielle Informationsflüsse zwischen Benutzergruppen

Subsystemeigenschaften, die durch die Annotationen festgelegt sind, analysiert. Wird eine P-Unverträglichkeit des Systems festgestellt, so liefert die Analyse Informationen über die Ursache.
Für das Beispiel gilt, daß sich aus der Gültigkeit der *consuming*-Eigenschaft der von den $B1$-Nutzern aufrufbaren Operationen unmittelbar ergibt, daß durch diese Nutzung keine Beeinflussung auftreten kann und die entsprechenden Prädikate für alle Berechnungen erfüllt sind.
Durch die Schachtelung von Komponenten, d.h. durch die lokale Definition des Depots *PDataMan* innerhalb der aktiven Komponente *ClientMan*, lassen sich die potentiell über die gemeinsame Nutzung von *PDataMan* auftretenden Wechselwirkungen auf die Nutzer von *ClientMan* begrenzen. Durch die Rahmeneigenschaften der annotierten Komponenten wird es zusätzlich möglich, bei der Konstruktion den Informationsfluß zwischen Komponenten systematisch zu begrenzen, so daß insgesamt die potentiellen Wechselwirkungen beherrschbarer werden.

5 Zusammenfassung und Ausblick

Ausgehend von einem allgemeinen Modell für sichere abstrakt verteilte Systeme wurden Prädikate mit ihrer informellen Semantik vorgestellt, mit denen problembezogene Sicherheitspolitiken formalisiert werden können. Eine formale Spezifikation der Sicherheits-Solleigenschaften ist die Voraussetzung für den formalen Nachweis der Konsistenz und Vollständigkeit der Spezifikation, deren korrekte Implementierung dann zu qualitativ hochwertigen Systemen führt.
Die eingeführten Konzepte erlauben es, die Sicherheitsanforderungen für Systeme an der Funktionalität der Systeme orientiert zu spezifizieren und liefern damit die formale Basis für die Anforderungen des BDSG, das fordert, daß jeder Benutzer nur Zugang zu den Informationen erhalten darf, die für seine Aufga-

benerfüllung notwendig sind. Der Einsatz der Konzepte wurde anhand einfacher Politikklassen verdeutlicht.
Für die abstrakte Implementierung werden neben Konzepten zur dezentralen Rechteverwaltung annotierte Sprachkonzepte eingesetzt, die zusammen mit den Strukturierungsmöglichkeiten der benutzten Implementierungssprache die zielgerichtete Konstruktion von Subsystemen mit spezifischen Beeinflussungs- bzw. Beobachtungseigenschaften ermöglichen und darüberhinaus eine Analyse unterstützen, die Aussagen über die Verträglichkeit des konstruierten Systems mit der spezifizierten Politik erlauben. Damit wird eine Brücke von der formalen Spezifikation und Modellierung zu der abstrakten Implementierung geschlagen.
Die weiterführenden Arbeiten beschäftigen sich zum einen mit weiteren Konkretisierungsstufen, in denen eine Sicherheitsarchitektur (vgl. [GGKL89]) als Ausführungsplattform für die konstruierten Systeme zu entwickeln und zur Verfügung zu stellen ist. Zum anderen sind die Spracherweiterungen und Analysemethoden in existierende Entwicklungswerkzeuge zu integrieren, um den Konstruktionsprozeß zu unterstützen.

Literaturverzeichnis

[ABL83] P. Ancilotti, M. Bowi, and N. Lejmaer. Language Features for Access Control. *IEEE Transactions on Software Engineering*, SE-9(1):16, 1983.

[BHJ+87] Andrew Black, Norman Hutchinson, Eric Jul, Henry Levy, and Larry Carter. Distribution and Abstract Types in Emerald. *IEEE Transactions on Software Engineering*, SE–13(1):65–76, January 1987.

[BL75] D. E. Bell and LaPadula. Secure Computer Systems: Unified exposition and MULTICS interpretation . Technical Report MTR - 2997, MITRE Corp, Bedford, July 1975.

[CW87] D.D. Clark and D.R. Wilson. A Comparison of Commercial and Military Computer Security Policies. In *Proceedings of the 1987 IEEE Symposium on Security and Privacy*, pages 184 - 194, 1987.

[Fol87] S.N. Foley. A Universal Theory of Information Flow. In *Proceedings 1987 IEEE Symposium on Security and Privacy*, pages 116 - 122, 1987.

[GGKL89] M. Gasser, A. Goldstein, Ch. Kaufman, and B. Lampson. The Digital Distributed System Security Architecture. In *Proceedings of the 12 th1989 National Computer Security Conference*, pages 305 - 314, 1989.

[GM82] J.A. Goguen and J. Meseguer. Security Policies and Security Models. In *Proceedings of the 1982 IEEE Symposium on Security and Privacy*, pages 11 - 20, 1982.

[LABW92] B. Lampson, M. Abadi, M. Burrows, and T. Wobber. Authentication in Distributed Systems: Theory and Practice. *ACM Transactions on Computer Systems*, 10(4):265–310, Nov. 1992.

[Lam71] B.W. Lampson. Protection. In *Proceedings of the Fifth Annual Princeton Conference on Information Science and Systems*, page 437, 1971.

[Pnu86] A. Pnueli. Applications of Temporal Logic to the Specification and Verification of Reactive Systems: A Survey of Current Trends. *LNCS 224, Current Trends in Concurrency, (ed. de Bakker)*, page 510, 1986.

[Spi92] P.P. Spies. Parallelverarbeitung mit INSEL. In *GI ITG PARS Workshop*, 1992.

Summary
The OLCHFA Project

Industrial Needs For Time-Critical Wireless Communication & Wireless Data Transmission And Application Layer Support For Time-Critical Communication

Authors: Ivan Izikowitz, BSC (Eng.) MSC (Eng.), Dipl.-Inf. Michael Solvie

The OLCHFA project, partly funded by the CEC under the European Strategic Program for Research and Development in Information Technology (ESPRIT), synthesises leading edge technologies to address the communication requirements at the fieldbus level of the manufacturing integration hierarchy. State-of-the-art technology in the areas of wireless communications, fieldbus and time-critical distributed systems is being used to develop a low cost, wireless, time-critical communication architecture. This communication system is targeted at the interconnection of low level devices such as sensors and actuators with their controllers as well as more intelligent distributed computer control systems. The objectives of the project include inherent time-critical support for applications within the message and variable services, robust microwave wireless broadcast with low power emission, high accuracy distributed synchronised time-reference to facilitate meaningful time-stamping, based on existing or forthcoming international standards, and software tools to aid the configuration and management of the OLCHFA system.

The French standard fieldbus, FIP, was chosen as the base platform for the hardware and software developments within OLCHFA. The reasons for this are the close compatibility of FIP with the proposed IEC standards at the physical and data link layers and its fundamental support for time-critical message and variable services. The OLCHFA hardware prototype makes use of commercial FIP integrated circuits as well as a custom clock chip providing a synchronisable microsecond time reference.

The OLCHFA project consortium includes two industrial partners to ensure that the system specification meets real user requirements and to provide demonstration sites incorporating test scenarios for the evaluation of the OLCHFA time-critical communication system. These two industrial partners are both steel manufacturers offering vastly different Beta test applications. The harsh environments of the steel plants and planned applications will exercise the reliability of the wireless transmission system as well as the time-critical support for applications.

After a statement of the objectives and technology employed, the paper charts the developments through the evaluation phase, development of hardware and software prototype modules, and the planned deployment of the system in both Alpha and Beta test environments. The paper concludes with a discussion of the current status of the project and the prognosis for the future.

The OLCHFA Project

Industrial Needs For Time-Critical Wireless Communication
&
Wireless Data Transmission And Application Layer Support For Time-Critical Communication

Ivan Izikowitz, BSC (Eng.) MSC (Eng.)
Institute for Industrial Information Technology Ltd.
Innovation Centre
UK Swansea SA2 8PP
e-mail: iiitih@pyr.swan.ac.uk

Dipl.-Inf. Michael Solvie
Lehrstuhl für Fertigungsautomatisierung und Produktionssystematik
Egerlandstraße 7-9, Postfach 3429
D - 91058 Erlangen
e-mail: solvie@faps.uni-erlangen.de

Abstract

The OLCHFA project synthesises leading-edge technologies in the areas of fieldbus, wireless communication and time-critical systems to address the data communications requirements at the low level of the manufacturing integration hierarchy. It aims at extending an existing fieldbus solution to provide these facilities. The OLCHFA project consortium, which is partly funded by the CEC, includes two industrial demonstration sites to ensure that the system specification meets the real user requirements as well as providing test scenarios for evaluation of the OLCHFA time-critical communication system. For reasons of technical suitability and compatibility with proposed international standards, the French FIP fieldbus is being used as the base platform for the hardware and software development. The software development includes extending the application layer services and creating tools to facilitate easy configuration and management of an OLCHFA communication network. The hardware development includes the production of prototype hardware modules incorporating a custom clock chip and FIP communications processor.

1. INTRODUCTION

The OLCHFA[1] project, funded by the CEC under the European Strategic Program for Research and Development in Information Technology (ESPRIT), synthesizes leading-edge technologies to address industrial needs at the fieldbus level of the manufacturing integration hierarchy. In general, OLCHFA addresses three industrial needs - wireless data communication, time-critical communication and easy network configuration and management. The combination of state-of-the-art techniques for distributed clock synchronisation and microwave wireless transmission is the foundation for the development which is based upon open fieldbus standards.

The OLCHFA development includes the design and manufacture of prototype fieldbus nodes which incorporate custom hardware to assist clock synchronisation and communication protocol processing. The project software component incorporates modules to support time-critical variable and message services, an application programmer's interface and configuration tools, and clock management functions.

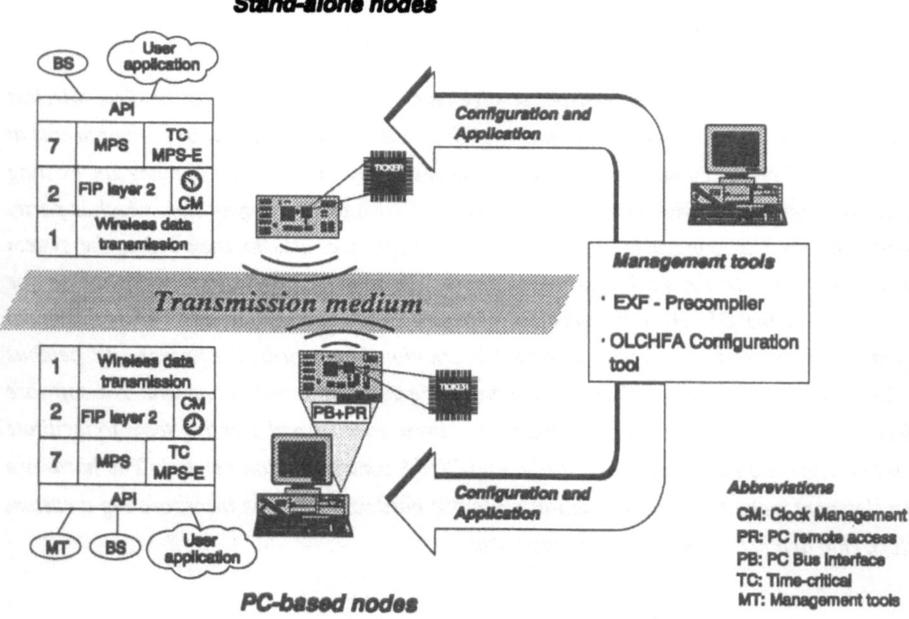

Figure 1: Overview of the OLCHFA system architecture

[1]An Open Low-Cost, Time-Critical Wireless Fieldbus Architecture

The project is managed as a collaborative venture, where the four main partners with state-of-the-art technology in each of the relevant areas are responsible for different aspects of the development, and two associated industrial partners provide pilot sites for the prototype fieldbus system.

This paper is structured in such a way that the background and need for the system is established prior to a definition of the objectives of the project. The main body of the paper then deals with the development of the prototype system and the planned pilot application scenarios. It should be noted that although the hardware issues are discussed, the emphasis of the paper is on the design and architecture of the OLCHFA software.

2. Background to the Project - The Need

Time-critical solutions are most often very specialised bespoke systems which tend to be very costly and inflexible. The amalgamation of distributed clock synchronisation techniques [Kop*87] and proven time-critical methodologies, with the low-cost simplicity of a wireless fieldbus aims to facilitate the rapid deployment of devices such as sensors, actuators and controllers in a time-critical application area.

Time-critical communications is an area in which there has been a large amount of research. The fundamental requirement is that data is transmitted, not merely as "fast as possible", but in a *deterministic* manner. One particular solution is the use of *state-based* messages [Mac84] where data is sampled and transmitted at regular pre-defined intervals. This data contains an inherent *time-stamp* and *currency limit period* after which time the data ceases to be valid. Advantages of this approach include fault detection at the receiving station, events indicated by a change of state, and that the steady-state loading of the communication channel is very similar to the loading under alarm conditions.

In order that consumers of data on the fieldbus may interpret time-based state data in a consistent fashion, it is imperative that all stations have a synchronised time reference - the granularity dependent on the periodicity of the sampled data.

In generic terms, the current fieldbus systems provide time-critical communications but only as far as specifying deterministic data transfer. At this point in time, although their is no unified international fieldbus standard, work on the Physical and Data Link Layers of the 3 layer model has nearly been finished. The Physical Layer will be assigned the status of an international standard this year and the Data Link layer is unlikely to be changed significantly. Of the national European standardised fieldbus systems available (PROFIBUS and FIP), the French FIP standard is most closely aligned with the international standard being developed under the auspices of the International Electrotechnical Commission (IEC).

FIP was chosen as the development platform for the project both for this reason and the fact that it provides good support for the time-critical concepts of OLCHFA.

The advantages of wireless communications in the fieldbus scenario are numerous. Apart from the obvious cost savings related to cabling, wireless nodes may be used in harsh environments which contain corrosive materials or extreme heat. The mobility of the nodes provide the facility for both flexible and rapid deployment of the fieldbus, as well as the potential for use on unfixed carriers - for example AGVs. One clear disadvantage of the wireless medium is the inability to supply power "down the line".

The complexity of network installation tends to be caused by the "soft" configuration and not the physical connection the nodes. Effective tools are therefore required to aid the user during the set-up process of the network. A high-level application programming interface (API) is especially required to support the application integrator by facilitating rapid application development.

3. OBJECTIVES OF OLCHFA

In order to address the requirements described above, the OLCHFA fieldbus architecture has been designed throughout with inherent support for the time-critical distributed systems. This includes a high degree of coupling between the communication processor and the clock synchronisation circuitry, as well as fundamental support for state-based communication at the Application Layer. The OLCHFA fieldbus is also designed to operate over both wired and wireless media in order that they may be interconnected with existing standardised equipment. This implies inherent flexibility where a number of scenarios may be addressed, and the application environment is not constrained to using a wireless medium in a proprietary system.

Owing to the fact that the market for communications products at the fieldbus level contains many proprietary systems - often tying the customer into one particular vendor - a major objective of the OLCHFA project is to maintain compatibility with existing and proposed standards in order that yet another proprietary system is not imposed on the market..

3.1. INHERENT TIME-CRITICAL SUPPORT

Over the last decade various efforts have been made at dealing with the evaluation of requirements, concepts and implementations of time-critical communication. Most of these activities deal in particular with local area networks, for example those described in [Arv*91], [EMUG89], [Kop*91], [Rzeh91], [TCCA92].

Communication in fieldbus systems, although with some support for time-critical communication, is outside the scope of a true time-critical system for several reasons: Communication at the process level of the automated factory today is on the edge of the breakthrough of digital communication replacing old-style analog links. Many of the digital fieldbus systems offer some time-critical functionality, mostly based on the state-based approach. With the increase of processing power and the simultaneous decrease in component costs, it has become possible to introduce more powerful time-critical services and mechanisms even in low-cost fieldbus systems. Such true time-critical fieldbus systems must address the following requirements[2]:

- Meeting application time constraints
- Support for synchronization of applications
- Offer a certain degree of autonomy
  - for the system as a whole
  - for each single fieldbus node
- Time-stamping of data
- Mixture of state and event-based communication
- Support for user assigned priorities
- Support of data consistency attributes
- Support for MMS-like services in a timely fashion

With respect to the implementation of a time-critical fieldbus, the user requirements are well specified. Indeed, some fieldbus solutions have so-called "time-critical support" at the application layer (for example FIP). In most cases, however, this time-critical functionality is limited within one or two lower layers of the ISO model [ISO84] and the support does not permeate the entire system. OLCHFA aims to provide a time-critical fieldbus solution with the required time-critical support in the fundamental system design. A major part of these provisions is the facility to synchronise the local clocks of every node to the required synchronisation granularity.

The overall objective of the OLCHFA consortium is to extend an existing fieldbus system which, apart from other criteria, should meet as many of the above-mentioned requirements as possible. With the FIP fieldbus, a system has been chosen that conceptually meets applications requirements for a deterministic, periodic exchange of variable values and is therefore able to guarantee related application time constraints. FIP also supports synchronization of applications and a certain degree of the required data consistency attributes - although not all of the available FIP ASICs support the entire entire set of FIP functions. Over and above the deterministic state-based communication, FIP also allows aperiodic *event-based* communication. For this type of service there is a two-level, user accessible priority mechanism influencing the order in which aperiodic communication requests are fulfilled. The periodic communications is configured during set-up, and

---

[2]In order to be *time-critical*, a fieldbus system does not have to meet all these requirements.

consequently no dynamic priority mechanism is accessible to the user. Nevertheless, it is up to the user to determine some kind of implicit priority for periodic data exchanges during network configuration by means of assigning the frequency at which periodic variables are transmitted.

The extensions to the FIP system made by the OLCHFA project promise to enrich the time-critical functionality of the system significantly. Based on the availability of a synchronized time reference, time-stamping of data is performed and mechanisms are implemented to elaborate the validity of data in terms of timeliness.

These functions are independent of the choice of FIP ASIC.[3] Additionally, a very efficient event mechanism is implemented to support autonomous operation of individual fieldbus nodes during the occurrence of user-defined event situations. The concept of synchronized clocks provides the foundation for the possible implementation of time-based synchronization and scheduling algorithms within distributed applications.

3.2. Wireless Fieldbus Communication

With respect to wireless communication, the aim of OLCHFA is to provide a wireless medium which is transparent from the point of view of the OLCHFA nodes and the fieldbus applications. This implies that the communications protocols should perceive a similar quality of service to that associated with the wired medium. Obviously the constraints for unlicensed power emmission and frequency bands imposed by the regulatory authorities are a limiting factor for this wireless communication channel. Of the two frequency bands assigned for this type of local area network, the regulation of the band between 2.4GHz and 2.5GHz is not expected to be prescriptive at the protocol level. Consequently, spread-spectrum technology at microwave frequencies was chosen for the wireless implementation. This technology maximises the resilience of the "low-power" medium by making use of greater bandwidth and compensates for the effects of multipath fading.

The OLCHFA fieldbus development aims to produce a fieldbus communications processor prototype which is able to operate over either a wired or a wireless medium with the simple configuration of jumpers on the board. The wireless medium aims to conform to the 1 MBit/s fieldbus standard.

---

[3]There are currently three different ASIC implementations of FIP available - each offering slightly different features and operating characteristics. The FIPIU-based implementation does not offer support for the use of the refreshement attributes.

3.3. User Application and Configuration Tools

Apart from the purely technical aspects of a fieldbus system, aspects of user-friendliness become more and more important and play one of the key roles in the market acceptance and adoption of a fieldbus system. For this reason, the OLCHFA project aims to produce software modules, which are collectively called *System Software*, for the host computer (PC), the OLCHFA PC board, and for standalone nodes. This software fulfils three primary user needs:

- To allow programmers to easily develop distributed applications;
- To provide high-level tools for initialization, configuration, management, and evaluation;
- To adhere to standards as closely as possible.

4. Areas of Major Technical Development

Based on the requirements outlined above, the OLCHFA consortium has specified a solution which is detailed in the following paragraphs.

4.1. Hardware Prototypes

The hardware prototypes consist of a set of three PCBs - one board providing a standalone wired fieldbus communications processor and the two other boards constituting a microwave wireless transmitter/receiver. Standalone nodes will be mounted within an IP 65 conformant box with an external antenna. PC-based nodes will contain an internal communications processor with an external microwave wireless module.

4.1.1. Architecture of the OLCHFA Communications Processor

In order to minimise the hardware development, the Communications Processor has been designed to operate either as a standalone fieldbus node or as a plug-in card for the IBM PC AT Bus.

The main components of the Communications Processor include a microprocessor, the TICKER ASIC providing a microsecond synchronisable time reference, and the FIPIU ASIC which implements the physical and data link protocols and manages the local FIP variable database.[OL1-92] The microprocessor shares a multiplexed address and data bus with the FIPIU and accesses a local variable database and the peripheral devices - including the TICKER - through the memory address map. These peripheral devices incorporate 4 channel

A/D, 2 serial ports, 256K ROM and up to 512K RAM. The interface between the field node and the PC AT Bus is implemented with a 2K Dual Port RAM. [OL2-92]

4.1.2. Wireless Communication using Spread Spectrum Techniques

Of the two commonly used techniques - Frequency Hopping and Direct Sequence - the latter was chosen for its higher degree of determinism. Frequency hopping incurs frequency switching times typically of the order of 100 microseconds where the transmission channel is unavailable.

Direct sequence techniques would typically make use of a priori knowledge which implies the passing of information through higher protocol layers. In order to maintain the transparency of the physical medium, however, matched filter techniques are used to avoid circulating the spread spectrum codes in time.

The actual hardware implementation incorporates one board each for the analogue and digital sections of the transmitter/receiver.

4.2. Clock Synchronisation for Fieldbus Systems

The area of clock synchronisation is not a new one, yet no single globally accepted solution to the problem exists. In fact, the methods reviewed vary diversely in both complexity and efficiency.

Time-critical fieldbus application environments specify reaction times between 1ms and 10ms [FICIM91]. The literature and case studies reviewed indicate that there are very few common fieldbus-type applications which demand synchronisation greater than 1ms. This FICIM reference also specifies a cyclic scan rate as low as 10ms. This is ratified by both [CENE90] and [EMUG89] where the scan or sampling rate is typically between 10ms and 20ms. The Cockerill-Sambre application specified for the beta test has requirements for sampling as frequently as every 0.1ms. The implications are that the synchronisation granularity between stations should be less than 0.1ms in order that time-stamped messages and data maintain their intended meaning in the time domain.

4.2.1. Appropriate synchronisation Mechanisms for Fieldbus

A master-based clock synchronisation approach was found to be most appropriate for the fieldbus scenario because of its simplicity and low communication overhead. Additionally, one objective of autonomous synchronisation is the elimination of the single point of failure in the master clock, which contradicts the fieldbus philosophy where failure of the bus arbitrator renders the network useless. Master based clock synchronisation is based on the assumption that a single node on the network (not necessarily the bus arbitrator) maintains the system time reference and periodically broadcasts this time on the medium. Every receiver of this message then adjusts its local time to the "new" system clock time. A further advantage of this master-based approach is that the problem of tracking an external time reference (such as UTC) becomes trivial.

The synchronisation mechanism and indeed the time-critical messaging concepts demand that the time taken to transfer messages is deterministic within an upper (known) bound. It is therefore crucial that the fieldbus software supports these deterministic requirements. This necessitates a small real-time operating system kernel for scheduling and maintaining a system where time-critical messages have priority over non-time-critical messages.

It is proposed that the concept of clock synchronisation be hidden from the application processes which are just able to make use of a library of services providing facilities for time-stamping, comparison and event generation. The Network Management Agent, in conjunction with the Layer Management Entities [IEC92] are responsible for the management, configuration and maintenance of the synchronisation system.

A degree of fault tolerance [Lam*85] may be achieved by using a second node on the fieldbus which acts as an active standby master clock and begins broadcasting time when it detects an absence of synchronisation messages. This is, however, only successful for a limited number of failure modes.

4.2.2. FUNCTIONS USING THE SYNCHRONISED CLOCK

The TICKER chip incorporating the synchronised time reference is used to provide four separate time-stamp registers which may be stamped using either hardware or software interrupts. Additionally, the TICKER contains four time-bomb registers which are able to generate events at pre-defined times via hardware or software interrupts. Time-stamping is mainly used for synchronisation messages, support of the time-critical application layer extensions, and as basis for potential time-based scheduling mechanisms.

An example of the use of the time-bomb registers within OLCHFA is the control of the A/D convertors where a preset number of samples are assigned to a buffer with a start and end time-stamp. When the time-bomb generates an interrupt signifying the end of the block, a new buffer is used and the old block is processed.

4.3. APPLICATION LAYER PROTOCOL IN SUPPORT OF TIME-CRITICAL COMMUNICATION

An Application Layer protocol supporting time-critical communication is a system which - based on subordinated time-critical communication protocols - manages the temporal integrity of communication requests made by applications. The OLCHFA project addresses this problem with the use of the extended FIP application layer protocol MPS, hereafter referred to as *MPS-E*, which provides the user with time-critical communication services.

MPS-E offers protocol mechanisms together with related services including:

- The ability to handle time-critical data - time and data as an atomic unit;
- Management of timeliness and validity information associated with exchanged data; and
- An efficient event-management mechanism.

4.3.1. TIME-CRITICAL DATA IN MPS-E

The variable model defined by FIP protocol standard [UTE90] is extended for two new types of variables - the *time-critical variable* and the *event variable*. These extensions apply to the class attributes as well as to the instance attributes of the generic variable class.

4.3.1.1. Time-critical variables

Time-critical data in the MPS-E protocol consists of a data content and a time content. The value of time-critical data is held in instances of the time-critical variable. The correctness of time-critical data depends both upon whether its value corresponds with the intention of the user and it is available within the intended period of real time. The time-critical data may be of any type; nevertheless for practical reasons, the variety of types is restricted.

The time content of the time-critical data contains

- A *time stamp*, indicating the creation time of the particular value
- A *validity period*, indicating the length of the period during which the value will be valid relative to the creation time of the variable;
- A *remote validity* flag to enable more intelligent stations to indicate a malfunction which has been detected locally.

Time stamping is a means whereby variables which are produced and consumed by the distributed applications and the corresponding application layer protocols are associated with an accurate creation time and a validity period.

4.3.1.2. Event variables

Event variables are used for the indication of the occurrence of events where events are time-stamped in order to determine the exact time of occurrence. What differentiates event variables from regular time-critical variables is the way in which they are treated in the system. Event variables are transmitted only aperiodically. Their value does not directly represent a process value, e.g. a temperature value, but it carries the identifier of the event situation fulfilled, e.g. "temperature exceeds given threshold".

4.3.1.3. Data consistency attributes

Data consistency is an important issue in distributed systems. Of special interest is the temporal consistency of data, expressed in terms of *local* and *remote timeliness*, where *remote timeliness* expresses timely production of data and *local timeliness* stands for a timely update of the value via the network. To indicate its consistency state, data is assigned corresponding attributes.

As outlined earlier, FIP supports elaboration of data consistency information and the OLCHFA extensions use the available mechanism for evaluatation of *local timeliness*[4]. Indeed, the mechanism available for evaluation of *remote timeliness* is not able to cope with the requirements of time-critical data because it is bound to a fixed period of time. The philosophy in OLCHFA is that a variable remains valid and must not be updated until its validity period expires. Thus, *remote timeliness* must be evaluated relative to this validity period which, although assigned a default value, is accessible by the user.

Besides the time-related consistency information, time-critical variables are assigend the attribute *remote validity*. This attribute is set by the producing application of the variable and allows a locally detected failure to be indicated, for example inconsistent states in either hardware or software.

4.3.1.4. Time-critical application layer services

The FIP application layer protocol MPS primarily provides user services to write and read variables. Both services are available with access to the local database (ReadLocal and WriteLocal) and with access to remote databases (ReadFar and WriteFar).

These services are extended to satisfy the requirements for handling time-critical data where special care is taken with respect to data validity which depends on the given validity period. Thus, if the validity period of a time-critical variable-to-be-read has expired, the particular

---

[4]These attributes are known respectively as *promptness* and *refreshment* in the FIP terminology.

value of the variable is declared invalid and a relevant notification is delivered to the user. The local and remote time-critical write services have been extended for checking the consistency of the time-stamp. Furthermore, on a time-critical write request, the event conditions assigned to the specified variable are checked. If one or more of these conditions are fulfilled, the associated event notification is sent automatically.

For the purpose of easy design of non-cyclic applications, the *Invalid* service is added to the set of services. It tracks the validity period of marked variables and informs the application about expiry in the producing stations. This enables the user to design asynchronous applications.

4.3.2. Event Management

In support of event-based communication, OLCHFA introduces an event management system. This mechanim allows specification and elaboration of event situations, for example the violation of boundary conditions. In the case of such events, often indicating alarm situations in a technical process, remedial measures are normally taken. The relevant notification and invocation of actions are performed autonomously by the distributed event mechanism which is transparent to the user during run-time.

4.3.2.1. Event model

An *Event* in MPS-E is defined by an *Event Condition* and by one or possibly more *Event Actions*. *Event Conditions* specify the conditions that must be fulfilled for specific event-situations to be recognised. *Event Actions* specify actions to be invoked upon occurrence of an event. Notification of the occurrence of a specific event is arranged by the aperiodic exchange (time-critical WriteFar) of the assigned *Event Notification Variable*. With respect to the Producer-Consumer principle of FIP, each station is assigned a specific *Event Notification Variable* and an event mask to delineate the possible events. *Event Actions* are defined in consuming stations and are invoked autonomously upon receipt of an *Event Notification Variable*. Stations are enrolled in the event management for the various events likely to occur in the specific technical process during configuration of the network.

Three different types of events are defined in the OLCHFA system[5] (refer to Fig.2):

- *Descending Threshold*: The current value of the *Monitored Variable* is lower than a reference value and its previous value was higher.

---

[5]These types of events are defined according to the committee draft version 2.0 of the application layer of the IEC-fieldbus.

- *Ascending Threshold*: The current value of the *Monitored Variable* is higher than a reference value and its previous value was lower.
- *Deadband*: The current value of the *Monitored Variable* varies from the reference value in either direction by more than a threshold value.

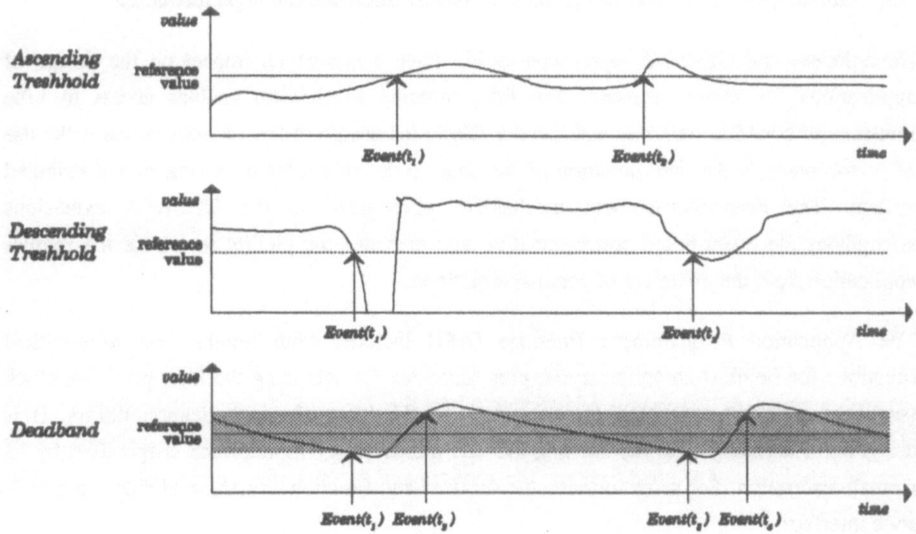

Figure 2: Types of events defined in the OLCHFA MPS-E protocol

4.4. THE APPLICATION INTERFACE AND MANAGEMENT TOOLS

Software tools to provide user support for both the generation of applications for the distributed fieldbus environment, and the configuration and setting-up of the network are incorporated in the OLCHFA development. Nevertheless, some modules provide operational services hidden from the user. These include:

- Node initialization and software download;
- Clock management for the clock synchronisation and diagnostics;
- A management agent to monitor correct functioning;
- Optional functions (for host PC nodes) to manage communication between the PC applications and the communication card.

The remaining parts of the software are roughly divided into two categories: application-oriented modules and end-user tools.

4.4.1. Application design and User interface

The OLCHFA system in general adopts those concepts of the FIP fieldbus which have proven suitable in the past. For example, the new and extended services are defined in a consistent way with the generic FIP services in both the specification and the implementation.

Nevertheless, the OLCHFA extensions to FIP have a non-trivial impact on the design of applications for several reasons. The time-stamping mechanism enables access to time information bound to variables and thereby allows the design of applications which make use of it, for example the determination of the exact order of events occurring in a distributed system. The event-management mechanism introduced by the OLCHFA extensions strengthens the event-based communication and provides the facility to isolate the regular application from the treatment of peculiar situations.

The Application Programmer's Interface (API) includes both regular and time-critical functions for fieldbus communication, plus functions for accessing the high-precision clock (snapshot registers, timebomb registers, etc.) in the form of an application library. It is designed in harmony with the existing FIPLIB philosophy. The interface is specified by its formal description. For programmers, the services and functionality are available via a "C"-style interface.

4.4.2. End-User (Configuration) tools

End-user tools perform functions such as: network initialization, configuration, management, error reporting, diagnostics, and performance measurement. These tools may be used not only by the programmer, but also by technical personnel with non-programming backgrounds and must therefore be intuitive and user-friendly.

Owing to the characteristics of the FIP fieldbus, the configuration of the network and the design of applications should be closely coupled. A set of tools - the FIP Toolbox - already available allows off-line configuration of FIP systems and provides the user with elementary skeleton applications for each station including initialization functions and bus arbitration tables. Central to this set of tools is a configuration language - the FCL (FIP configuration language) - which is used to described the network characteristics as well as the communication behaviour of the fieldbus nodes.

Although quite powerful, this configuraton tool system cannot fulfil the new requirements arising from the OLCHFA project - especially the ability to configure time-critical variables and the event-management system. Consequently, the existing configuration tools must be adapted to meet these requirements. Thus an extended configuration language - EXF (*Extended* FCL) - has been defined to provide expressions that allow the user to describe both time-critical variables and event management. With a new front-end configuration tool incorporating an efficient graphical user interface, the required intuitiveness and user-friendliness is achieved. This tool is designed and implemented is such a way that is is applicable to both the OLCHFA and FIP systems.

This tool allows graphic-oriented configuration of the system simply by placing icons on the workspace and filling in relevant forms. It supports the user by providing cross-reference lists of variables, consistency checking, document generation, etc. The resulting application and network description is then evaluated by an EXF-parser to generate a common FIP-network description file for further processing, time-critical base-main programs for each station, and the necessary information for the new part of the network management dealing with time-critical communication.

5. PROTOTYPE TESTING AND PILOT APPLICATIONS

The implementation of three pilot applications is envisaged in the course of the project. The first application - the *Alpha test application and pilot* - is primarilly a test-bed for the integration of the product's components in order to achieve stability before any disruption of a real production process. The real production processes are the subject of the two *Beta pilot applications.*

5.1. ALPHA TESTING

Various types of OLCHFA applications are planned for the integration phase. The spectrum covers simple operational testing and synthetic applications which are designed to stress the system in particular ways, as well as applications designed for performance measurement.

Apart from these short-term test cases, establishment of two applications is envisaged. The first application stresses the system with respect to its maximum throughput. It incorporates three OLCHFA modules for the measurement of the height of workpieces by a laser-triangulation sensor. Captured values are time-stamped and transferred to the controlling system in blocks. The foreseen digital resolution is 10 bits, at a sampling rate of 1 kHz. An additional sensor will be used to measure the velocity of the moving robot arm. With the aid of the time-stamps of both the height value and the position value, and their coherence, the exact profile of the workpiece can be determined by the system - even if the robot moves at a varying speed.

The second application, involving the observation of the oscillatory characteristics of a moving robot arm, incorporates two OLCHFA modules. One, as in the first application, will be placed in the monitoring system, while the other will be mounted on an industrial robot. Preceeding analysis has shown that the natural frequency of robots of the type being used is about 100 Hz. A single module is therefore sufficient to transmit the data of the three incorporated acceleration sensors. The results obtained may then be analysed, leading to an improved control mechanism for robot control.

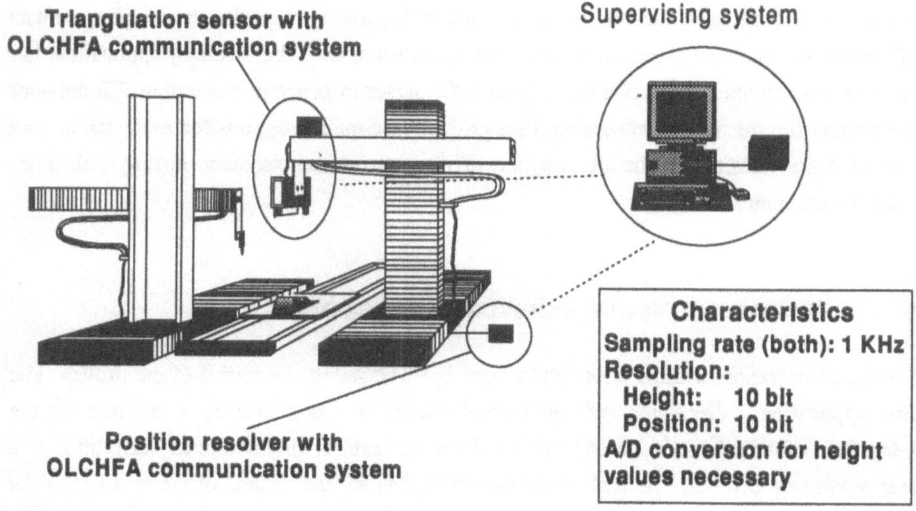

Figure 3: Schematic of the duplex-robot cell

5.2. PILOT APPLICATION A - ALARM MONITORING

The application of OLCHFA is situated within an existing Hot Strip Mill automation system. The steel mill incorporates an alarms system where a central controller collects and processes alarms from numerous PLCs on the site. The current alarms network is based on PLCs communicating events (which are often buffered) over serial links and therefore lacks the necessary time-critical functionality. Current alarm messages are only accurate to within 2 or 3 seconds. Additionally, there are certain alarms PLCs which are not connected to the central controller.

It is envisaged that the OLCHFA fieldbus will run alongside the present system to provide the necessary enhancements. In this deployment, time-stamping will be done when alarm events are initially detected and not at the central controller, where a significant delay has already been incurred. In the case of the majority of the PLCs, the alarms will be detected using spare digital outputs of the PLCs connected to the digital I/O on the OLCHFA node. One of the PLCs will be accessed via a serial link, where the PLC status blocks will be transferred to the fieldbus node and masked to detect alarm conditions.

Logically the whole application may be split into four parts - the three sources for alarms (i.e. the *screw-down PLC*, the *roll-lubrication PLC* and the *roughing mill PLC)*, and the *alarms controller*. In the existing solution, this *alarms controller* periodically samples all possible alarm states from the *screw-down* and the *roughing mill PLCs* - a cumbersome method which may be improved with the use of the OLCHFA system.

OLCHFA will provide the *alarms controller* with time-stamped alarm notifications incorporating the detection time of the alarm. The OLCHFA system will additionally offer the possibilities of expanding the network dimensions, using a higher time-resolution and using a cheap and flexible PC as an *alarms controller* instead of an expensive, dedicated PLC.

This application will stress the OLCHFA system in different ways. Besides the excessive test of the event functionality, it is a hard test for the physical data transmission. Not only does the environment produce electromagnetic interference (motors, thrysistors,...), but also the required communication distance is a real challenge for the wireless data transmission of the OLCHFA system. For example, the *roughing mill PLC* as well as the *roll lubrication PLC* are 300m away from the alarms controller, with four partitions and two brick walls between them, and the latter PLC is only 10m away from the main mill motors. This application is also therefore a severe test of reliability in a harsh industrial environment.

5.3. Pilot Application B - Chatter Analysis

The wireless fieldbus will be used for the real-time monitoring of the vibration level of a cold rolling mill which is subject to the so-called problem of "chatter". "Chatter" is the situation in a steel mill in which an instability arises which makes the vibration of the mill chains increase to a level which badly affects the quality of the steel sheet.

The aim of the pilot application in this environment is to provide high-speed data capture which will enable the analysis of the problem with a view to applying corrective action at a later stage of development. It is therefore necessary to continuously monitor the vibration level on all four stands of the mill simultaneously. This vibration on each of the stands will be measured using accelerometers, each connected to an A/D converter on an OLCHFA fieldbus node fixed on top of an individual stand within the mill. Each of the communication modules serves two separate accelerometers measuring the vibration levels of the individual cages.

Preceeding analyses have shown, that the vibration level is about 1kHz. A sampling frequency of at least 2 kHz is therefore necessary. The A/D converter used has a resolution of 10 bits. This leads to an amount of pure user data of approximately 8 x 10 bits x 2000 per second = 160 kbits/sec. These sampled data will be stored in blocks for transmission to the central host PC for later analysis.

The Beta-testing at this site will verify the time-critical aspects of the OLCHFA fieldbus, as well as the reliability of the wireless communication module in a hostile environment.

6. CONCLUSION

The low-cost, time-critical distributed computer control system described in this document incorporates a number of features which have up until now only been found in expensive bespoke systems. It is hoped that the market will recognise the benefits of such an Open System and adopt the technology for appropriate applications.

In order that the project does not develop a system contrary to the aims of the IEC Fieldbus Standardisation effort, members of the consortium are actively involved in the national standardization bodies in this area. These representations aim to track the advances made in the development of the standards, and to serve as a lobby for the OLCHFA developments in areas not yet covered in the scope of the IEC standard. Examples of such innovations are clock synchronisation and high-speed wireless transmission.

In general, the distributed processing platform provided by the OLCHFA fieldbus opens up a number of avenues for research in the areas of time-based algorithms and truly distributed processes, among others. Unfortunately, owing to the time constraints imposed by the project schedule, investigations in these areas during the scope of this project are limited.

At the time of writing this document, the OLCHFA project is in an advanced stage of development and preparations are being made for the integration of the software components with the hardware prototype (and each other). Although a number of unforeseen technological problems had to be resolved in the earlier stages, the project schedule has not incurred significant delay, and the consortium is looking forward to the field tests and the results of performance measurement.

7. REFERENCES

[Arv*91] K. Arvid, K. Ramamrithan, J.A. Stankovic. *A local area network Architecture for communication in distributed real-time systems*. Journal of Real-Time Systems Vol.3 No.2 May 1991

[FICIM91] FICIM User Requirements Study - First Release, FICIM 91.026/D05/RC, September 1991

[CENE90] Fieldbus Functional Requirements Summary, CENELEC BT/WG 62-6, November 1990.

[EMUG89] European MAP Users Group. *User Requirements for Communications in Time Critical Applications*. EMUG Technical Note, February 1989.

[IEC92] Digital Data Communications for measurement and control - Field bus for use in industrial control systems - Part 1 : Introductory Guide, IEC 1158-1. Draft version 1992.

[ISO84] International Organization for Standardization: 8. Information Processing Systems Open Systems Interconnection - Basic Reference Model, ISO 7498, 1984.

[Kop*87] H. Kopetz, W. Ochsenreiter. *Clock Synchronisation in Distributed Real-Time Systems*, IEEE Transactions on Computers, Vol. C-36, No. 8, August 1987.

[Kop*91] H. Kopetz, W. Ochsenreiter. *A reliable multicast protocol for distributed real-time systems*. 8th IEEE Workshop on Real-Time Operating Systems, Atlanta, USA, May 1987.

[Lam*85] L. Lamport, PM Melliar-Smith. *Synchronising Clocks in the Presence of Faults*, Journal of the ACM, Vol. 32, No. 1, Jan 1985.

[Mac84] I. M. MacLeod, *Using real-time to achive co-ordination in distributed computer control systems*. Proceedings of the IFAC World Congress, Budapest, July 1984.

[OL1-92] OLCHFA project (i^2it) Ticker ASIC Preliminary Specification - Revision F, i^2it, July 1992.

[OL2-92] *Deliverable I.1 : Harmonised Fieldbus User Requirements and Phase I Summary*, OLCHFA Consortium, October 1992.

[Rzeh91] H. Rzehak. *Echtzeitkommunikationssysteme - eine Einführung in die Problembereiche und Lösungsansätze*. Informatik Fachberichte Band 293. Springer Verlag, 1991

[TCCA92] ISO/TC184/SC5/WG2/T.C.C.A. Technical report of the TCCA rapporteurs' group identifying user requirements for systems supporting time-critical communications. Doc. No. 73, 1992

[UTE90] Union technique de l' Électricité, FIP application layer services. C46-602. 1992

Ein Konzept zum rechnergestützten Entwurf von Steuerungssoftware

H. Wolf
Universität Karlsruhe
Institut für Betriebs- und Dialogsysteme
Am Fasanengarten 5, Geb. 50.34
Postfach 6980, 76128 Karlsruhe
Tel.: +49 721 608 4054
E-mail: wolf@ira.uka.de

Zusammenfassung

Es wird eine Methodik vorgestellt, welche speziell die Entwurfs- und Implementierungsphase bei der Erstellung von Software für technische Steuerungen unterstützt. Hierzu wurde eine grafische Beschreibungssprache zur Darstellung nebenläufiger, miteinander agierender Aktivitäten entwickelt. Alle Interaktionsbeziehungen sind in der grafischen Beschreibung enthalten und werden von einem Transformationswerkzeug in den Quellcode der Aktivitätsrümpfe eingefügt. Zusammen mit einer für das Zielsystem angepaßten Bibliothek zur Realisierung von Prozeßverwaltung und -interaktion wird in einem weiteren Transformationsschritt ein ausführbares Steuerprogramm generiert. Eine klare Kapselung der vom Zielsystem abhängigen Teile gewährleistet leichte Portierbarkeit. Zur Unterstützung der Testphase besteht die Möglichkeit, den Steuerungsablauf während des Betriebs grafisch zu visualisieren oder ein Steuerungsprotokoll in Form eines „Filmes" noch einmal ablaufen zu lassen. Das Konzept ist offen für Erweiterungen, von denen als wichtigste die automatische Analyse von Steuerungsentwürfen zu nennen ist.

1 Einführung und Motivation

Im Zuge des fortwährenden technologischen Fortschritts erschließen sich immer mehr Bereiche der Automatisierungstechnik. Zur Steuerung eines zu automatisierenden Systems werden meist Informationsverarbeitungssysteme eingesetzt. Das Spektrum reicht hier von einfachen, speicherprogrammierbaren Steuerungen bis hin zu großen Prozeßrechnern oder gar Prozeßrechnerverbundsystemen.

Charakteristisch für die Umgebung, in der Steuerungssoftware eingesetzt wird, ist das Auftreten einer großen Anzahl asynchroner Ereignisse, welche jeweils in einer maximalen Bearbeitungszeit behandelt werden müssen. Die häufigste Fehlerursache liegt typischerweise nicht in der Realisierung der eigentlichen Steuerungsberechnungen, sondern im Zusammenspiel vieler asynchron ausgeführter Tätigkeiten.

Das hier vorgestellte Konzept unterstützt Entwurfs- und Implementierungsphase durch den Einsatz geeigneter Softwarewerkzeuge. Ausgangspunkt war dabei die Entwicklung einer Beschreibungssprache für Steuerungsentwürfe.

Betrachtet man sich den Vorgang der Programmentwicklung für ein zu automatisierendes System näher, so gliedert er sich in folgende Teile:

- Modularisierung der Problemlösung.
- Spezifikation von Aufrufbeziehungen und Datenaustausch zwischen den Modulen.
- Implementierung der Module.

Die Grundidee des hier vorgestellten Konzepts besteht nun darin, daß der Entwerfer der Steuerungssoftware nur noch ein Modell des Steuerungsteils in einer abstrakten, der Welt des zu automatisierenden Systems angepaßten Form spezifiziert und die Rümpfe der sich daraus ergebenden Module in Form von „herkömmlichen" Programmstücken implementiert. Die Modularisierung und die Spezifikation von Aufrufbeziehungen und Datenaustausch ergeben sich dann aus der Modellbildung. Die Module selbst sind in sich abgeschlossen und können unabhängig voneinander realisiert werden. Die Beziehungen zwischen den Modulen sind nicht mehr zu programmieren, sondern werden anhand der abstrakten Modellbeschreibung automatisch hinzugeneriert. Typische Vertreter für solche Module sind Eingabeformer, z.B. zur Glättung von Eingangswerten oder Berechner zur Berechnung von Ausgabewerten aus Eingangsgrößen ([Wet89]).
Da in der realen Welt viele Aktivitäten unabhängig voneinander ablaufen, soll auch im Softwaremodell Nebenläufigkeit realisiert werden. Die Module werden hierzu als Softwareprozesse gestaltet. Damit ergibt sich eine weitere Entkopplung der Module: aus Aufrufbeziehungen werden Auftragsbeziehungen und Datenaustausch geschieht über Kommunikation oder Kooperation (arbeiten auf gemeinsamen Daten).

2 Die Entwurfsbeschreibungssprache

Da die entwickelte Beschreibungssprache für Steuerungsentwürfe den Grundstein für das gesamte Konzept darstellt, folgt hier eine Kurzbeschreibung derselben.

2.1 Zielsetzungen für die Sprache

Da am hiesigen Institut schon seit langer Zeit die Methoden zur wohlstrukturierten Beschreibung von Systemarchitekturen untersucht werden (siehe [Wet90]), sollten die hierbei gewonnenen Erkenntnisse beim Entwurf der Beschreibungssprache berücksichtigt werden. Alle aus der Systemarchitektur bekannten Grundformen von Interaktion sollten in allen möglichen Ausprägungen spezifizierbar sein. Eine weitere Zielsetzung war die leichte Erlernbarkeit und eine unmittelbar erfaßbare Darstellungsform. Hierzu wurde eine grafische Darstellung gewählt und die Darstellungsobjekte auf das Notwendigste beschränkt.

2.2 Klassifizierung

Die darzustellenden Objekte lassen sich in drei große Klassen aufteilen:

- Objekte zur Beschreibung des statischen Systemanteils.
- Objekte zur Beschreibung der Systemdynamik.
- Objekte zur Kopplung der statischen und dynamischen Teile.

Der statische Anteil manifestiert sich in Modulen als Träger von Aktivität, Datenobjekten zur Kooperation und Nachrichtenkanälen zur Kommunikation. Der dynamische Anteil dient zur Beschreibung von Ablaufbeziehungen und zur Darstellung des Datenflusses zwischen den Modulen. Zur grafischen Repräsentation wird ein gerichteter Graph verwendet, wobei die statischen Komponenten durch Netzknoten und die dynamischen durch Netzkanten dargestellt werden.
Ein Steuerungsprogramm wird als eine Menge miteinander interagierender Aktivitäten angesehen. Zur Interaktion sind die aus der Systemarchitektur her bekannten Grundformen Koordination, Kommunikation und Kooperation einsetzbar (siehe auch [Wet87] oder [Wet90]).

2.3 Sprachbeschreibung

Die Grundkomponenten der grafischen Entwurfsbeschreibungssprache:

- Netzknoten
  - Aktivitätsknoten
  - Koordinationsknoten (&) (if) (sw)
  - Kommunikationsknoten (&)
  - Kooperationsknoten
  - Auftragsknoten
  - Schnittstellenknoten
  - Subnetzknoten
  - Vereinigungsknoten
- Netzkanten
  - Koordinationskanten
  - Kommunikationskanten
  - Auftragskanten
  - Kooperationskanten
- Knotenzusätze
  - Externe Koordinationsobjekte
  - Externe Kooperationsobjekte
  - Initialisierungsobjekte

Die Konstruktionsregeln für Netze sind im wesentlichen durch die Regeln zur Verbindung von Knoten mittels Kanten gegeben.

2.3.1 Koordination

Mit Hilfe der Koordinationskanten werden Ablaufreihenfolgen unter den Aktivitäten hergestellt, sie repräsentieren damit also den Steuerfluß des Programms. Abb. 1 zeigt die einfachste Form der Koordination, die serielle Ausführung. Aktion **B** wird nach Aktion **A** ausgeführt.
Um auch kompliziertere Ablaufreihenfolgen zu ermöglichen, existieren logische Verknüpfungsobjekte und bedingte Verzweigungsobjekte. Die Bedeutung dieser Objekte beschreibt folgende Tabelle:

Eingänge (ankommende Koordinationskanten) werden ODER-verknüpft und unter den Ausgängen wird ein beliebiger ausgewählt (der erste Interessent).

Alle Eingänge werden UND-verknüpft und wenn die UND-Bedingung erfüllt ist, wird die Koordination an alle Ausgänge weitergeleitet.

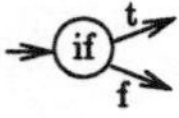

Bedingungsobjekte leiten eine ankommende Koordination nur an die Ausgänge weiter, bei denen zu diesem Zeitpunkt die Bedingung erfüllt ist.

Koordinationsobjekte können mittels Koordinationskanten auch untereinander verknüpft werden, so daß auch komplizierte Koordinationsbeziehungen dargestellt werden können. Abb. 2 zeigt ein Beispiel hierfür.

Abb. 1: Serielle Ausführung

Abb. 2: Kompliziertes Koordinationsnetz

Aktivität **D** wird erst ausgeführt, wenn entweder **A** und **B** schon beendet sind oder **C** fertig ist und zum Zeitpunkt der Beendigung von **C** die Bedingung $x > 0$ wahr war.

Um initiale Koordinationen beim Start des Steuerprogramms auszulösen, gibt es sog. Initialisierungsobjekte (●), welche in Koordinationsknoten abgelegt werden können.

2.3.2 Kommunikation

Kommunikationskanten dienen zur Darstellung von Nachrichtentransport zwischen Aktivitätsknoten. Der Nachrichtentransport läuft dabei stets über einen Kommunikationsknoten, welcher als Nachrichtenkanal aufgefaßt werden kann. Der Nachrichtentransport beinhaltet i.a. implizit eine Koordination in dem Sinne, daß sich Sender und Empfänger zeitlich abstimmen. Im vorgestellten Konzept können unterschiedliche Abstimmungsvarianten eingesetzt werden. Die Auswahl einer konkreten Variante wird durch Angabe eines Attributs bei der sender- bzw. empfängerseitigen Kommunikationskante bestimmt. Die möglichen Attributwerte sind:

synchron — Die zugehörige Aktivität wartet bis der Nachrichtentransport vollständig vollzogen ist.

asynchron — Der Transportauftrag (senden bzw. empfangen) wird erteilt und die Aktivität setzt ihre Ausführung fort. Der eigentliche Nachrichtentransport kann zeitlich versetzt erfolgen, falls der Kommunikationspartner noch nicht an seiner Kommunikationsstelle angelangt ist.

versuchend — Der Nachrichtentransport wird durchgeführt, falls der Kommunikationspartner seine Kommunikationsstelle schon erreicht hat, ansonsten wird fortgesetzt, ohne einen Auftrag zu hinterlassen.

umlenkend — Solange der Kommunikationspartner seine Kommunikationsstelle noch nicht erreicht hat, verhält sich diese Variante wie die asynchrone. Nach dem Nachrichtentransport wird die Aktivität jedoch auf eine angegebene Prozedur umgelenkt.

Abb. 3 zeigt als Anwendungsbeispiel das Rendezvous zweier Aktivitäten.
Durch die Verwendung von Nachrichtenkanalobjekten können auch mehrere Sender mit mehreren Empfängern kommunizieren. Als Operatoren stehen die logische ODER- und UND-Verknüpfung zur Verfügung, welche jeweils auf Sender- und Empfängerseite anzugeben sind. Die Semantik der Verknüpfungsoperatoren ist folgender Tabelle zu entnehmen:

	Senderseite	Empfängerseite
ODER	Jeder sendet eine vollständige Nachricht.	Der erste Empfänger bekommt als einziger die Nachricht. Alle Empfänger sind gleichberechtigt.
UND	Jeder trägt einen Teil zur Gesamtnachricht bei. Erst wenn alle Sender gesendet haben, wird die Gesamtnachricht verschickt.	Alle Empfänger erhalten eine Kopie der Nachricht (Rundruf).

Die Darstellung der vier möglichen Verknüpfungskombinationen ist wie folgt:

	ODER	UND
ODER	( )	( ) ⊢--> (&)
UND	(&) ⊢--> ( )	(&)

Ein typisches Anwendungsbeispiel solcher Verknüpfungstypen zeigt Abb. 4. Dabei schickt **A** per Rundruf eine Nachricht an **B**, **C** und **D**.

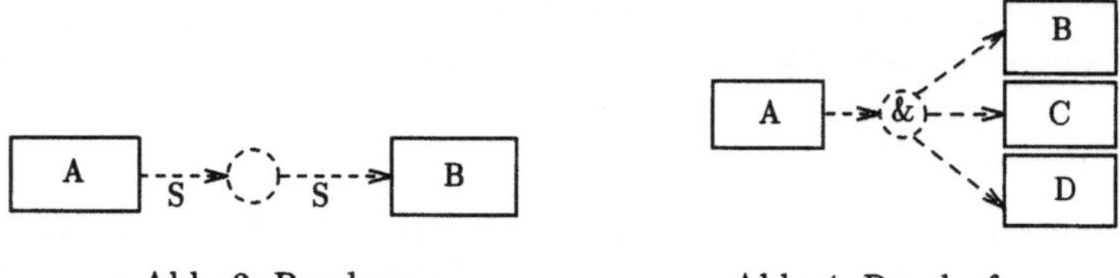

Abb. 3: Rendezvous   Abb. 4: Rundruf

2.3.3 Auftragsbeziehung

Häufig wird man einen Aktivitätsträger als Dienstgeber realisieren, welcher Aufträge annehmen kann und Ergebnisse an die Auftraggeber zurückliefert. Für diese spezielle Kommunikationsform wurde die Auftragsbeziehung in die Beschreibungssprache aufgenommen. Die Kanalobjekte werden dabei ersetzt durch Beauftragungsobjekte (▶) auf der Auftraggeberseite und Auftragsverwaltungsobjekte (▷) auf der Auftragnehmerseite. Abb. 5 zeigt ein Beispiel für eine Auftragsbeziehung.

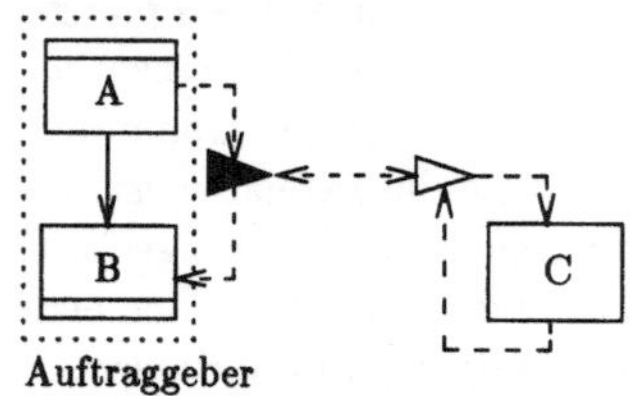

Abb. 5: Auftragsbeziehung

Dabei wird der Auftrag in **A** zusammengestellt und an **C** erteilt. **C** schickt das Ergebnis an **B**, wo es weiterverarbeitet werden kann. Die Abschnitte **A** und **B** sind dabei Teilaktivitäten der Gesamtaktivität des Auftraggebers. Die Ausführungsreihenfolge der Teilaktivitäten wird durch gerichtete Kanten festgelegt. Durch die Verwendung von (if) und (sw) Objekten sind auch Verzweigungen möglich. Es werden hierzu dieselben grafischen Beschreibungsformen wie für Aktivitäten, Koordinationsknoten und -kanten verwendet. Die Zusammengehörigkeit wird durch einen punktierten Vereinigungsrahmen (⋮⋯⋮) angezeigt. Zur Festlegung von Start und Ende der Gesamtaktivität werden Teilaktivitäten speziell gekennzeichnet (Start: ▭, Ende: ▭). Durch die Vereinigung können somit interne Interaktionsstellen dargestellt werden.

2.3.4 Kooperation

Eine losere Kopplung zwischen Aktivitäten entsteht durch die Zusammenarbeit auf gemeinsamen Daten in der Form der Kooperation. Hierbei wird keine Festlegung der Reihenfolge von Operationen auf einem Datum gemacht, es muß jedoch die Exklusivität der einzelnen Datenoperationen gewährleistet sein, damit keine inkonsistenten Datenzustände weitergegeben werden können. Dazu verfügt jedes Kooperationsobjekt über einen Monitor (siehe [Hoa74]) für das zugehörige globale Datum. Auf ein globales Datum kann nur über Monitoroperationen zugegriffen werden. Die Kooperationskanten geben an, welche Aktivität auf welches Datum zugreift. Die Kantenrichtung gibt an, ob der Zugriff verändernd oder nur lesend ist. Der exakte Ort der Kooperationsoperation innerhalb der Aktivität wird damit nicht festgelegt. Er muß durch Benutzung der Operation im Quelltext der Aktivität bestimmt werden. Abb. 6 zeigt ein Beispiel zur Kooperation, wo Aktivität **A** ein Datum **x** verändert, während **B** das Datum **x** liest.

Mit der bisher beschriebenen Kooperationsbeziehung wird der Datenfluß zwischen Aktivitäten dargestellt. Es gibt jedoch noch eine weitere Form des Datenflusses, den Steuerdatenfluß, welcher die Bedingungen in den Verzweigungsobjekten der Koordination steuert. Dieser wird mit denselben Mitteln dargestellt. Abb. 7 zeigt ein Beispiel für einen Steuerdatenfluß. Aktivität **A** setzt eine Größe x, die eine Weiche für die nachfolgende Aktivität darstellt.

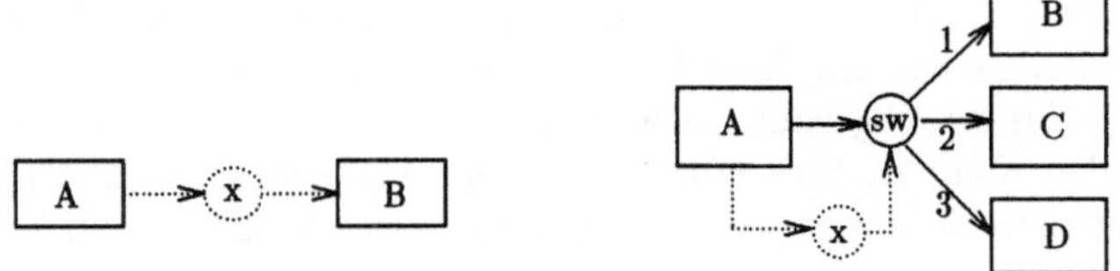

Abb. 6: Kooperationsbeziehung

Abb. 7: Steuerdatenfluß

2.4 Anbindung an den technischen Prozeß

Zur Darstellung der Interaktion mit dem technischen Prozeß gibt es externe Koordinationsobjekte für impulsartige Ein-/Ausgaben und externe Kooperationsobjekte für die Ein-/Ausgabe von Daten. Auf der Eingabeseite können diese Objekte an Koordinations- bzw. Kooperationsobjekte angeknüpft werden. Auf der Ausgabeseite werden sie an Aktivitätsknoten angehängt. Abb. 8 zeigt ein Beispiel hierzu.
Aktivität **A** wird durch das technische Signal **Signal 1** angestoßen und gibt den Steuerwert s an den technischen Prozeß aus.

2.5 Hierarchisierung

Für die praktische Anwendbarkeit ist es notwendig, daß ein Entwurf hierarchisch gegliedert werden kann. Dieser Forderung wird durch die Möglichkeit der Subnetzbildung Rechnung getragen. Jedes Netz kann als Subnetz in einem anderen Netz benutzt werden. Dieses Konzept läßt sich hierarchisch beliebig schachteln, solange keine Rekursion ensteht (wird von den Werkzeugen erkannt). Die Einbindung von Subnetzen geschieht über Schnittstellenobjekte (▷).
Eine weitere Einsatzmöglichkeit für Subnetze ist die Bereitstellung von Bibliotheken mit vorgefertigten Subnetzen oder Subnetzschablonen. Abb. 9 zeigt ein Beispiel für die Integration eines Subnetzes.

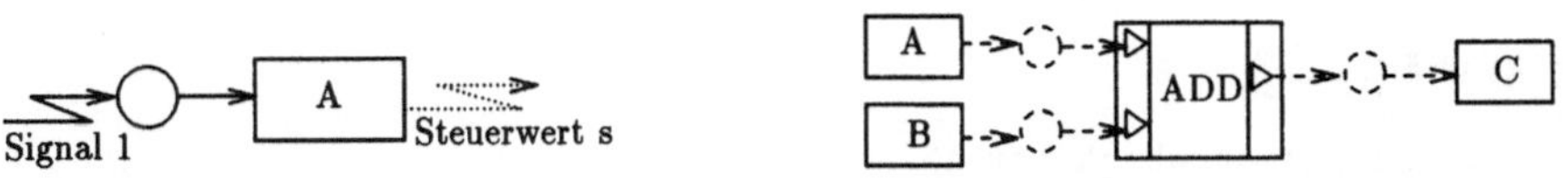

Abb. 8: Technische Ein-/Ausgabe

Abb. 9: Integration eines Subnetzes

3 Die Transformation von Steuerungsentwürfen

Durch einen Transformationsvorgang können Steuerungsentwürfe, die in der oben beschriebenen grafischen Sprache formuliert sind, in ablauffähige Steuerprogramme übersetzt werden. Die wesentliche Aufgabe besteht dabei darin, die für die Aktivitätsknoten vorhandenen Quellcodestücke um die im Beschreibungsnetz formulierten Interaktionsbeziehungen anzureichern und eine Ablaufumgebung bereitzustellen.

3.1 Aktivitätsknoten

Wie schon früher erwähnt, soll das Konzept Nebenläufigkeit unterstützen. Aus diesem Grund werden die Aktivitäten in Form von Softwareprozessen realisiert. Bei mehreren Teilaktivitäten, die durch einen Vereinigungsrahmen zu einer Gesamtaktivität zusammengefaßt sind, wird der Gesamtaktivität ein Softwareprozeß zugeordnet. Diese Softwareprozesse führen den für den zugehörigen Aktivitätsknoten angegebenen Quellcode zyklisch aus. Zu Beginn und am Ende des Zyklusses werden jeweils Kommunkations- und Koordinationsabschnitte eingebaut, deren Inhalte entsprechend der im Beschreibungsnetz anknüpfenden Kommunikationskanten bzw. der vorangehenden und nachfolgenden Koordinationssubnetze generiert werden. Die allgemeine Gestalt des für eine Aktivität erzeugten Codes sieht somit folgendermaßen aus:

```
<Initialisierungsabschnitt>
WHILE (true)
{
  <Koordinationsabschnitt A>
  <Koomunikationsabschnitt A>
  <Quellcode der Aktivitaet>
  <Kommunikationsabschnitt B>
  <Koordinationsabschnitt B>
}
```

3.1.1 Teilaktivitätsknoten

Für die Teilaktivitäten innerhalb einer Gesamtaktivität gelten folgende Umsetzungsregeln:

Startaktivität (□)

```
<Initialisierungsabschnitt>
WHILE (true)
{
  <Koordinationsabschnitt A>
  <Kommunikationsabschnitt A>
  <Quellcode der Teilaktivitaet>
  <Kommunikationsabschnitt B>
  <Koordinationsabschnitt B>
  <Konkatenationsabschnitt>
```

Innere Aktivität (□)

```
<Koordinationsabschnitt A>
<Kommunikationsabschnitt A>
<Quellcode der Teilaktivitaet>
<Kommunikationsabschnitt B>
<Koordinationsabschnitt B>
<Konkatenationsabschnitt>
```

Endeaktivität (□)

```
  <Koordinationsabschnitt A>
  <Kommunikationsabschnitt A>
  <Quellcode der Teilaktivitaet>
  <Kommunikationsabschnitt B>
  <Koordinationsabschnitt B>
} /* end of WHILE */
```

Jede Teilaktivität besitzt eine Sprungmarke T_i am Anfang. Der Konkatenationscode besteht aus einer Sprunganweisung zur Marke der Nachfolgeraktivität, welche durch die ausgehende Ablaufkante bestimmt wird. Gegebenenfalls wird noch Verzweigungscode für nachfolgende Verzweigungsknoten eingefügt. Besitzt eine Teilaktivität keinen Nachfolger, so wird im Konkatenationsabschnitt Code zur Prozeßbeendigung eingefügt.

3.2 Koordinationsknoten

Die logischen Verknüpfungsknoten (○ und (&)) werden durch Signalobjekte realisiert. Die Bedingungsknoten ((if) und (sw)) werden umgesetzt in entsprechenden Quelltext in den Koordinationsabschnitten am Ende der vorangehenden Aktivitätsknoten.
In einem mehrstufigen Koordinationssubnetz können Sende- und Empfangsoperationen mehrere Signalobjekte involvieren. Es muß sichergestellt sein, daß solche komplexen Koordinationsoperationen für jedes Koordinationssubnetz sequentialisiert werden. Hierzu wird für jedes Koordinationssubnetz ein Sperrobjekt erzeugt und zur Realisierung des gegenseitigen Ausschlusses benutzt.

3.3 Kommunikationsknoten

Kommunikationsknoten (◌ , (&)) werden durch Kommunikationskanäle realisiert. Entsprechend der in Abschnitt 2.3.2 beschriebenen Verknüpfungskombinationen wird die Ausprägung ODER–ODER, ODER–UND, UND–ODER bzw. UND–UND gewählt. Zu jeder Kanalausprägung existieren dann jeweils Sende- und Empfangsoperationen für die Kopplungsgrade synchron, asynchron, versuchend und umlenkend. Falls sowohl Koordination als auch Kommunikation an einem Aktivitätsknoten anliegt, wird die Kommunikation stets weiter „innen" liegend realisiert.

3.4 Kooperationsknoten

Für Kooperationsknoten ist vom Entwerfer des Steuerungsnetzes jeweils eine Liste von Monitoroperationen und deren Implementierungen anzugeben. Nur durch diese Operationen kann das Kooperationsdatum manipuliert werden. Das Transformationswerkzeug erzeugt für jedes Kooperationsdatum ein Sperrobjekt. Zu jeder Monitoroperation wird eine Schattenoperation folgender Gestalt erzeugt:

```
Resultattyp Schatten_Monitoroperation(...)
{
  Resultattyp Resultat;
  BelegenSperre(Sperrobjekt);
  Monitoroperation(...);
  FreigebenSperre(Sperrobjekt);
  rueckgeben Resultat;
}
```

Die Aufrufe der Monitoroperationen innerhalb der Aktivitäten werden durch Aufrufe der entsprechenden Schattenoperationen ersetzt.

3.5 Externe Koordinationsknoten

Für jede externe Eingangskoordination (Signal vom technischen Prozeß an die Steuerung) wird eine Unterbrechungsbehandlungsprozedur generiert. Der Code dieser Prozedur wird nach denselben Regeln erzeugt wie der Koordinationsabschnitt B am Ende eines Aktivitätsknotens. Schematisch ensteht folgende Gestalt:

```
Unterbrechungsprozedur_fuer_Signal_i()
{
  <Koordinationsabschnitt>
}
```

Die Anbindung der Unterbrechungsprozedur an das technische Signal wird von der Ablaufumgebung vorgenommen.

4 Generierung einer Ablaufumgebung

Durch den im vorigen Abschnitt beschriebenen Transformationsschritt werden Aufrufe von Interaktionsoperationen in den Quellcode der Steuerungssoftware eingebracht. Um ein so erzeugtes Steuerprogramm tatsächlich ablauffähig zu machen, wird es mit einer sog. Ablaufumgebung ausgestattet. Diese Ablaufumgebung besitzt folgende Aufgaben:

- Bereitstellung des Programmcodes für die benötigten Interaktionsoperationen.
- Bereitstellung und Initialisierung der benötigten Interaktionsobjekte (Sperren, Signale, Kanäle).
- Anbindung der technischen Eingabesignale an Unterbrechungsprozeduren.
- Bereitstellung eines Prozeßumschalters für die erzeugten Softwareprozesse.

Der Programmcode für Interaktionsoperationen und der Prozeßumschalter sind von der Steuerung unabhängig und werden in einer Bibliothek zur Verfügung gestellt. Für jede gewünschte Zielumgebung muß einmal eine solche Bibliothek erstellt werden.
Der Initialisierungscode für die benutzten Interaktionsobjekte und Unterbrechungsprozeduren muß für jeden Steuerungsentwurf neu erzeugt werden. Hierfür erzeugt das Netztransformationswerkzeug eine Liste der benötigten Objekte, welche von einem sog. Ablaufumgebungsgenerator abgearbeitet wird.
Aus dem Initialisierungscode, der Bibliothek für Interaktion und Prozeßumschaltung und den durch die geschilderten Transformationen erweiterten Quellen kann mittels eines herkömmlichen Übersetzers und Binders ein ablauffähiges Steuerprogramm erstellt werden.

5 Werkzeugkonzept

Abb. 10 zeigt den Erstellungsweg für ein ausführbares Steuerprogramm unter Einsatz der vorgestellten Werkzeuge. Neben den schon erwähnten Werkzeugen zur Transformation von Steuerungsentwürfen und zur Generierung einer Ablaufumgebung existiert ein sog. Netzeditor, welcher die Eingabe der grafischen Steuerungsbeschreibung ermöglicht.

6 Visualisierung

Die automatische Umsetzung einer grafischen Beschreibung in ein ablauffähiges Steuerprogramm ermöglicht eine direkte Zuordnung der grafischen Objekte in reale Steuerungskomponenten. Dadurch ist es möglich, den realen Ablauf der Steuerung visuell auf das grafische Netz abzubilden. Der Transformator wurde hierfür um die Fähigkeit erweitert, sog. Visualisierungsaufrufe in den Code der Aktivitäten zu integrieren. Diese Visualisierungsaufrufe haben folgende Gestalt:

```
vis(<Operationskennung>[,<Operationsargumente>][,<Objektkennungen>])
```

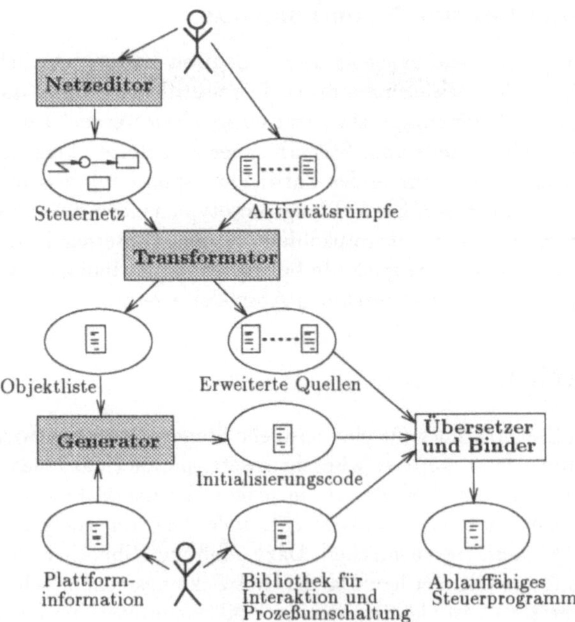

Abb. 10: Werkzeugkonzept

Die Operationskennung bestimmt dabei, welche Art von Ereignis visualisiert werden soll, und die Liste der Objektkennungen identifiziert die beteiligten grafischen Objekte. Visualisiert werden grundsätzlich Prozeßzustandswechsel und Interaktionen.

Die Visualisierungsoperation (`vis(...)`) muß für die Umgebung, auf der das Steuerprogramm abläuft, implementiert sein. Diese ist oft nicht identisch mit der Umgebung, auf der die Entwicklungswerkzeuge laufen. Es ist also der Steuerungsrechner, auf dem das Steuerprogramm abläuft vom Entwicklungsrechner, auf dem es entwickelt wird, zu unterscheiden.

Die Visualisierung selbst läuft auf dem Entwicklungsrechner. Zur Darstellung auf dem Bildschirm werden sog. Darsteller verwendet, die im wesentlichen aus Programmteilen des Netzeditors bestehen. Für die Visualisierung muß es somit eine Möglichkeit der Datenübertragung vom Steuerungsrechner zum Entwicklungsrechner geben (z.B. eine serielle Schnittstelle). Auf dem Entwicklungsrechner läuft ein Verteiler, welcher vom Steuerrechner Visualisierungsanforderungen entgegennimmt und in Aufträge an die involvierten Darsteller umsetzt (siehe Abb. 11). Die Darsteller bewirken dann eine Veränderung in der Darstellung der grafischen Objekte auf dem Bildschirm. Die Art dieser Veränderungen ist konfigurierbar. Die änderbaren Gestaltparameter sind dabei Farbe, Linienstärke und Füllmuster. Weitere Visualisierungsmöglichkeiten sind Blinken, Animation von Netzpfaden und Ausgabe von Texten.

Durch die Visualisierung kann die Entstehung von Fehlersituationen leichter verstanden werden. Auch Prüfer oder potentielle Käufer können von der korrekten Funktionalität schneller überzeugt werden.

6.1 Probleme bei der Visualisierung

Eine Visualisierung des Steuerungsablaufs zur Laufzeit kostet natürlich zusätzliche Bearbeitungszeit für die Visualisierungsaufrufe. In zeitkritischen Situationen kann dadurch evtl. eine wichtige Zeitbedingung nicht mehr eingehalten werden. Ein weiteres Problem ist die notwendige Schnittstelle vom Steuerrechner zum Entwicklungsrechner. In vielen Fällen ist eine Visualisierung nur in der Entwicklungsphase interessant, dann genügt es, diese Schnittstelle nur an einem Entwicklungsprototyp anzubringen. Alle Visualisierungsaufrufe können vom Verteiler mitprotokolliert werden. Hinterher kann der visualisierte Ablauf dann durch einen sog. Abspieler in beliebiger Geschwindigkeit wiederholt werden. Dabei wird das Steuerprogramm durch den Abspieler ersetzt.

7 Simulation

Oftmals muß ein Steuerrechner für eine spezielle Steuerung erst entwickelt werden (eingebettete Systeme). Dann wäre es wünschenswert, parallel dazu das Steuerprogramm entwickeln und austesten zu können. Da in jedem Fall das Entwicklungssystem bereits zur Verfügung stehen muß, ist es angebracht, auch das Steuerprogramm auf dem Entwicklungsrechner ablauffähig zu machen. Dazu muß die Bibliothek für Interaktion und Prozeßumschaltung erstellt werden. Da der Entwicklungsrechner schon mit einem Betriebssystem ausgestattet ist, können dessen Funktionalitäten diesbezüglich ausgenutzt werden. Für UNIX-basierte Systeme wurde eine solche Bibliothek angefertigt. Da auf dem Entwicklungsrechner andererseits i.d.R. nicht dieselben Schnittstellen zum technischen Prozeß existieren, muß ein Ein-/Ausgabeumsetzer erstellt werden (für serielle Schnittstelle erfolgt). An den Umsetzer kann optional ein E/A-Protokollierer angeknüpft werden, welcher alle E/A-Ereignisse in einer E/A-Protokolldatei ablegt (siehe auch Abb. 12).

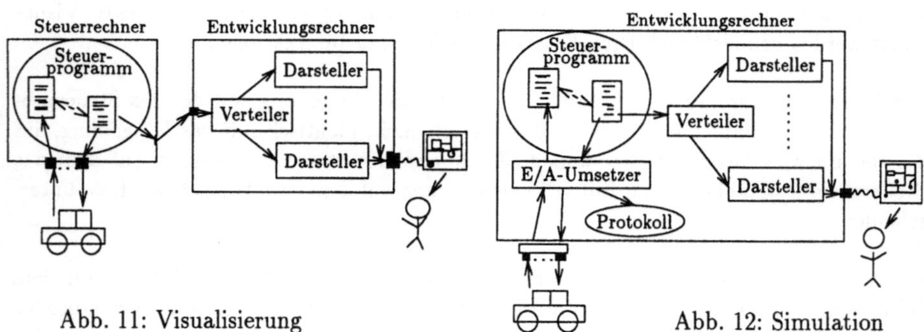

Abb. 11: Visualisierung

Abb. 12: Simulation

Möglicherweise existiert zum Erstellungszeitpunkt der Steuerungssoftware noch nicht einmal ein Prototyp des realen technischen Prozesses. Dann gibt es zwei Varianten, das Steuerprogramm trotzdem ablauffähig zu machen:

- Softwaresimulation: der technische Prozeß wird durch ein Programm simuliert, welches mit dem E/A-Umsetzer kommuniziert (Abb. 13).
- Manuelle Simulation: ein Mensch simuliert den technischen Prozeß und erzeugt die Eingabesignale für die Steuerung. Dazu wurde der Darsteller so erweitert, daß er beim Anklicken eines externen Eingabesignals mit der Maus eine Eingabenachricht an den E/A-Umsetzer schickt. Die Ausgaben an den technischen Prozeß werden nur protokolliert (Abb. 14). Diese Variante beinhaltet die Möglichkeit, Eingabefolgen

zu erzeugen, welche der technische Prozeß nur durch Fehlsituationen oder äußerst selten erzeugen könnte.

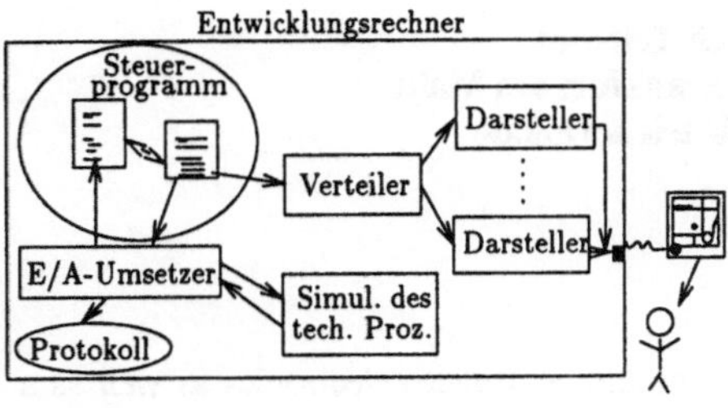

Abb. 13: Softwaresimulation

Entwicklungsrechner
Steuer-
programm
Darsteller
Verteiler
Darsteller
E/A-Umsetzer
Protokoll

Abb. 14: Manuelle Simulation

8 Ausblick

Das hier vorgestellte Konzept eignet sich zur Erstellung und zum Test von Steuerungssoftware. Durch Simulation kann die Korrektheit der Steuerung nicht nachgewiesen werden. Es wäre wünschenswert, wenn durch Analyse des Steuerungsentwurfs Aussagen über die Erfüllung von Zeitbedingungen und dergleichen gemacht werden könnten. Die für eine Analyse notwendigen Informationen (Koordinationsbeziehungen und Laufzeiten) sind im Steuerungsbeschreibungsnetz angegeben. Es wären also noch geeignete Verfahren und ggf. ein Analysewerkzeug zu entwickeln. In einer Voruntersuchung wurde festgestellt, daß sich einige Ideen aus der Analyse von Petri–Netzen übernehmen lassen ([Rei82],[Bau92]). Die in Petri–Netzen analysierbaren Eigenschaften ließen sich dann folgendermaßen interpretieren:

Beschränktheit ⟶ Obergrenze für Nachrichtenwarteschlangenlängen angebbar.
Sicherheit ⟶ Keine Engpässe im System.
Lebendigkeit ⟶ Keine Verklemmungen möglich.

Literatur

[Bal90] Helmut Balzert. *CASE Systeme und Werkzeuge.* Wissenschaftsverlag, 2. Auflage, 1990.

[Bau92] Falko Bause. *Funktionale Analyse zeitbehafteter Petri-Netze.* Deutscher Universitätsverlag Vieweg, 1992. Dissertation an der Universität Dormund 1991.

[Hoa74] C.A.R. Hoare. Monitors: An operating system structuring concept. *Comm. ACM,* 17:666–677, 1974.

[Rei82] W. Reisig. *Petrinetze: Eine Einführung.* Springer Verlag, 1982.

[Wet87] H. Wettstein. *Architektur von Betriebssystemen.* Carl Hanser Verlag, 3. Auflage, 1987.

[Wet89] H. Wettstein. Adaptierbare Betriebssysteme für Steuergeräterechner. Institutsbericht, Juni 1989.

[Wet90] H. Wettstein. Systemarchitektur. Vorlesungsskriptum, November 1990.

Architectural Aspects of Future Private Communication Systems

Dieter Wybranietz

Telenorma Bosch Telecom
Kleyerstraße 94, 60326 Frankfurt am Main
E-mail: wybranie @ telenorma.de

Abstract

The latest achievements in optical fibre, VLSI technology and micro-electronics as well as a growing demand for telecommunications promote the development of high-speed communication networks, preparing the broadband ISDN and the integrated broadband communication network. New services are requested including distribution of TV programmes, full-motion video phones and multimedia services handling simultaneously voice, video and data information. Todays separate worlds of data and telephony communication will close up and merge. Value-Added Network Services and Intelligent Networks will lead to new network applications, which are not fully described yet or even unknown. Facing this background, industry is challenged to develop highly flexible systems, which can accommodate future needs allowing a cost-effective integration of existing equipment by evolution strategies. In this paper, requirements for future private communication systems are stated, aspects of their hardware and software architecture are discussed and prospects of further developments are given.

1. Introduction

The latest achievements in VLSI technology, micro-electronics, and optical fibre provide the basis for new applications that require high computing performance and high-speed communication networks. New services are emerging including distribution of TV programmes, full-motion video phones and multimedia services handling simultaneously voice, video and data information. Todays separate worlds of telecommunications, computing and video technologies are converging and will merge in the near future. This trend is pushed by the way of how information is created, moved and used: as Figure 1 illustrates, the intelligence and performance of firstly more or less isolated equipment and applications increases with time and demands an ever improving connectivity [CHY92].

In the public area, the current trends show that telecommunication users expect a larger diversity of services and features, high transmission bandwidths, accessibility of services from various locations and mobility of equipment. In a medium term range, narrow-band ISDN (64 kbit/s) will meet most of the requirements, but already today there is a demand for broadband communication with bit rates from 2 to 140 Mbit/s. Applications include video conferences, video phones, CAD/CIM, high-resolution/high-quality transmissions for remote printing of newspapers and journals, provision of x-ray photographs in hospitals etc. Access times can be significantly reduced by higher transmission bandwidths. For example, a newspaper of 60 pages occupies more than 618 Mbit. For transmission, 2.7 hours are needed at 64 kbit/s, 5 min at 2 Mbit/s and 4.4 sec at 140 Mbit/s. Especially for CAD/CIM and medical applications it has to be taken into account that users are searching in data bases. In these cases, only response times lower than 2 and 3 seconds are acceptable. Although further achievements in data compression techniques are to be expected, the demand for much higher bandwidth than 64 kbit/s will grow. All signs point toward broadband communication: broadband networks form the backbone of envisioned national (Japan, US), regional (Europe) and global information infrastructures, the performance trends point up, the cost trends point down and a market pull is beginning to be felt.

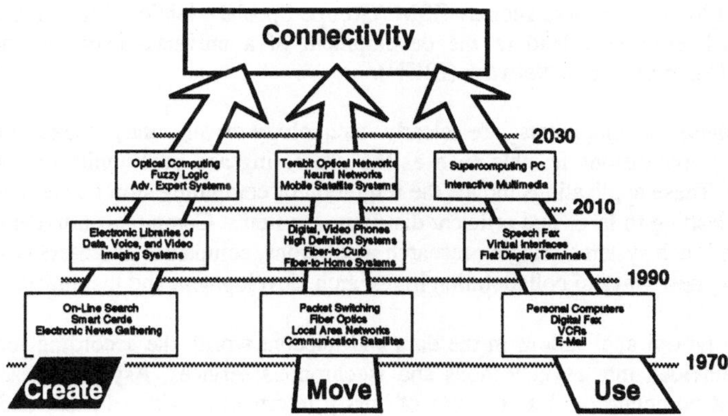

Fig 1: Technology push trends

The evolutionary character of developments in telecommunications requires a close cooperation between users, network operators and communication equipment manufactures. In the past, a satisfactory precise knowledge about the capacity requirements for specific customers had been available. Statistical data had been gathered and evaluated, mathematical models for traffic analyses and prediction had been worked out, which guided the design and dimensioning of switching equipment for traditional telephony services. By the closing up of the data and telecom worlds, network operators as well as service and equipment providers will face major strategic challenges: market forecasts are very difficult due to uncertainties about demand growth, the costs for development of new concepts and the application of new technologies are very high, and the diversity of current situations and strategies in different countries raises problems of evolution and interworking with existing networks. Technical solutions have to be found, which are cost-effective, support different evolution scenarios and are robust to different patterns of demand.

Based on an assessment of the current situation an appropriate sequence of steps towards the introduction of new services and equipment has to be found in order to allow a smooth evolution, so that old equipment can be gradually replaced by new equipment. Investments made in the past have to be preserved.

This paper focuses on architectural aspects of communication systems for the customer premises market. Developments and new services evolving in the public-switched telephone networks (PSTN) as well as requirements of new applications are considered in Section 2. Then various technologies for communication networks are discussed. Architectures and configurations of future private communication systems as well as aspects of their hardware and software structure will be presented in Section 5 and prospects of further developments will be given.

2. Requirements for Future Communication Systems

Communication networks form the basis for the interconnection of distributed computing systems, workstations and terminal equipment. A large spectrum of new services is evolving including - beyond high speed-transmission rates up to several 100 Mbit/s - features such as isochronous and asynchronous services, efficient and reliable protocols, interworking of networks with different architectures and physical implementation, and network management functions. At present, various solutions are being developed such as Metropolitan Area Networks (MAN), the Broadband ISDN based on the Asynchronous Transfer Mode (ATM), and Digital Mobile Networks such as GSM (Groupe Special Mobile). The integration of these networks will eventually lead to the development of a universal network, the Integrated Broadband Communication Network (IBCN).

Although these developments are clearly technology-driven, they make advanced and sophisticated applications feasible such as the processing and communication of multimedia information. These applications induce the migration of computing storage and communication equipment, leading to large and efficient distributed systems. Communication networks are the backbones of such systems bringing research institutions, companies and users closer together, thus allowing new ways of collaboration in research, development and manufacturing.

Considering typical applications in the data and telecom world, the according services can be roughly subdivided into asynchronous and isochronous services. Asynchronous services are characterised by connectionless transfer of bursty information with arbitrary and variable bit rates. Here connectionless transfer is seen at the transmission level, at higher levels connection-oriented transport can be achieved by appropriate software protocols. Current application examples of these services are X25-like services with low delay and bitrate requirements such as low-rate interactive data, electronic mail, software down-load, data base browsing etc. as they are found in the LAN environment.

Isochronous services are characterised by the connection-oriented transfer of stream-like information with constant bit rates for delay- and loss-sensitive applications with guaranteed Quality of Service (QoS). Application examples are digital telephony, video phone, video conference and multimedia communications.

Multimedia Communications comprising the exchange of audio, video and data information will play an increasingly important role in the communications market. These new applications set up new requirements for the communication infrastructure ranging from physical interconnection to the management and control of new services [CWV91]. For example, new features are negotiation of communication contexts with suitable QoS, in-call bandwidth modification, integration of servers providing cascaded connections with end-to-end control etc. A multimedia session or call will consist of several connections, which can be dynamically established, modified and released. Since multimedia applications and communications integrate most of the existing service requirements, the degree of support of multimedia communication will be an important measure for the value of communications systems.

The commercial success of private (and public) communication systems will depend on the provision of services, which go beyond the connection and transport capabilities of the network [REA89]. A so-called Value Added Network (VAN) among others consists of the following components: Basic Network, Generic Services, Information Data Bases, and Network Management. These tasks require computer capacity within the network. Typical examples for VAN Services (VANS) are electronic messaging, electronic information services, free-phone, limited communication charge, free-of-charge service (0800 in US), and services with additional charge.

The Intelligent Network (IN) is a concept allowing multiple points of intelligence to be introduced wherever needed in the network. More specifically, an Intelligent Network can be defined as a network allowing functionality to be distributed flexibly at a variety of nodes on and off the network and allowing service provisioning via a service control architecture. New services can be easily added somewhere in the network and made accessible to every subscriber.

Examples for IN capabilities are Virtual Private Networks (VPN, see below), televoting, retrieval of multimedia documents, multi-connection calls, information services, speaker-independent voice recognition etc.

For large companies it is desirable to view the different systems at various local premises as a single network where the interconnections across public and possibly other private networks are invisible to the users. Such an approach is called a Virtual Private Network (VPN). VPNs require intelligence in the public network in order to employ resources within it to build individual VPNs, a management system and a method enabling the user and network operator to select, specify, set up, monitor and change the system. For example, finding the cheapest paths through the network (e.g. different tariffs at different times in different countries) or alternative paths in the case of an overload situation are typical functions of VPNs.

Although INs and VPNs will have their bases in the public area, private communication systems have to interface to these new services and make use of them. The interfaces have to conform to service and system management standards such as the Telecommunication Management Network (TMN). For example, customers will expect least-cost-routing PABXs, which select the cheapest path through a network. In order to gain product advantages over competitors communication companies will have to create new services, which can be introduced into the public network and made available at additional charge. Since for the installation, operation and maintenance as well as for the efficient usage of the existing services, comprehensive and profound know-how is necessary. The out-sourcing of these communication infrastructure problems to external companies can be seen as a great market potential.

From the users' point of view, the main requirements which have to be taken into account for customer premises networks can be summarised as follows:

- **Integration of services:** In future systems for business communications the integration of existing and new isochronous and asynchronous services with connectionless or connection-oriented transfer and constant or variable bit rate is important. Customers will require a single communication infrastructure as opposed to the separate worlds of voice and data communication co-existing today.

- **Flexible and efficient use of bandwidth:** The variety of supported services requires dynamic allocation of bandwidth to provide an effective means of efficient usage of bandwidth and hence to increase system performance. Here also variable bit rates have to be taken into account as they may be generated by new services such as multimedia terminals. Bandwidth efficiency translates directly into cost savings. A communication system should minimize the amount of bandwidth needed for local access and long distance communications across public networks.

- **Scalability and adaptability to changing user demands:** The introduction of new services should be feasible after the installation of a system. The removal of services and the reconfiguration of a system according to new customer profiles has to be possible. Customers are not willing to pay at installation time for what they might possibly need 3 or 5 years later, but they want to have the option to upgrade the system. Dramatic increases of capacity requirements might occur, for instance, if a number of high-quality video phones operating at 1 Mbit/s is connected to the system, which have not been considered at the time of system configuration. In this case, the communication system must be expandable without trashing the old equipment and replacing it with the next larger version.

- **Increased reliability and availability:** Since the dependency on telecommunication and computing services will further grow, high availability and reliability are key issues. System and network management have to ensure continuing operation of the system in the presence of specific faults and failures, according to the graceful degradation principle. Since the provision of fault tolerance causes overhead in terms of execution time and processor performance, memory usage or additional redundant hardware devices, it is desirable that the degree of fault tolerance can be selected by customers.

- **Openness:** In the current situation a whole bunch of services, protocols, interface standards and physical transmission technologies coexist. The current situation originates from various conditions such as parallel developments in telephone and data networks, the lack of adequate technologies, little or no cooperation of standardisation bodies and so on. Interoperation between different networks is only possible through expensive interworking equipment, and this situation will remain so for some time. Nevertheless, to preserve investments made and to avoid dependability on a single vendor, the communication system should offer a representative set of important standards. On this basis, a system can coexist and interconnect with other standard equipment.

Leaving these more user-related requirements, we will briefly come back to technical aspects. At the network level, these overall requirements can be broken down into transmission, switching, performance and network management requirements [KÜH92]. For transmission, the appropriate technology has to be selected depending on application requirements: Coaxial cable, wire, twisted pair or fibre. Interworking between transmission technologies and switching principles has to be achieved. Switching principles have to support the various service types such as connectionless and connection-oriented packet and circuit switching. The according switching functions can be implemented in a centralized or distributed manner, as sequential or highly parallel single or multi-stage structures. Since the network operator and the user is interested in a high utilisation of network resources, the networks have to meet performance criteria such as through-put, utilisation, connection and call-blocking, cell or packet loss, connection set-up delay and information transfer delay.

In order to operate, control and maintain communication systems, an effective management is a prerequisite. Two basic management areas can be distinguished. System management controls internal resources of the system, which cannot be directly influenced by the operator. For example, automatic load distribution among various processors, check-pointing policies for the recovery from failures etc. are handled by the system management, which can be seen as an extension (or sometimes even part) of the operating system. Network management maintains all components of the network. Main tasks consist in economic usage of transport paths, assuring quality of service requirements, assembly and presentation of accounting information, recording and evaluation of disturbances, maintaining and updating network status etc.

A basic management architecture has been defined in OSI where five major objectives have been identified: configuration, fault, performance, accounting and security management. The standardisation employs the object-oriented approach where managed objects have to be determined which represent a system resource. The manipulation and information exchange between these objects is accomplished by a set of primitives. For example, error detection and reporting as well as overload detection and avoidance are typical network management functions, which cannot be handled manually anymore. Conformance of the different system components to management standards, the possibility of integrating them into an overall management system and the exchange of information between management systems are important requirements for communication systems.

For the software development, a software creation environment is needed, which supports the fast implementation and introduction of new services, online replacement and modification of software modules and remote maintenance functions. Although the user is not directly interested in how the software is produced, he or she wants to participate in new developments and have access to new services and features. In this context, a fast and efficient software production capability is a crucial factor for system suppliers to stay in business and an important evaluation criteria for customers when selecting their communication support and their supplier.

3. Transfer Modes

In this section we give an overview of different transfer modes, present the major existing standards, where and how they are currently applied and which future developments can be expected.

Multiplexing defines the way how different logical information streams are carried across one medium [KÜH92]. For simplification only two basic time division multiplexing schemes are considered here. In synchronous time division (SDT) time is divided into frames and each frame is subdivided into numbered slots. Equally numbered slots of consecutive frames form an STD channel. A physical channel is identified by the position of the slot within the frame. A typical frame clock rate is 8 kHz, which provides frames of 125 sec length.

In Asynchronous Time Division (ATD) time is subdivided again into slots. Each slot carries an information unit of variable length (also called a frame or a packet) or of constant length (called a cell). Packets or cells may occur completely asynchronously. Their headers comprise a label called Virtual Channel Identifier (VCI), a virtual channel is formed by units with identical VCIs.

Switching defines how a transmission path is found through the network from the source to the destination and how channels of intermediate links are associated with each other to form a connection between origin and destination. Circuit Switching (CS) and Packet Switching (PS) are the two basic switching principles. In CS, an exclusive physical connection is established between source and destination. It appears to the users as if they were connected to each other directly by a dedicated cable. A specified bandwidth is guaranteed at the cost that this bandwidth is also reserved when no information is transferred and that in these cases the bandwidth cannot be used by others.

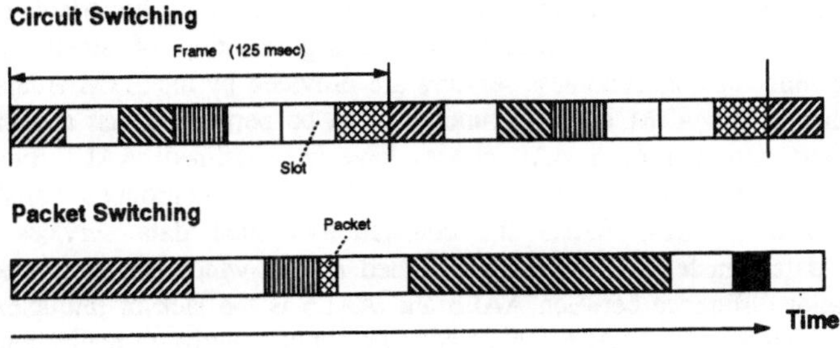

Fig. 2: Packet and Circuit Switching

In PS, an information stream is packetized at the source and transferred to the network in a store-and-forward manner and the packets are assembled again into the original information stream at the destination. Two basic principles can be distinguished: the virtual connection mode and the datagram mode. A virtual connection is established by special protocols between source and destination across intermediate links and a virtual channel identifier is assigned to this connection. A packet sent across a virtual connection uses the VCI as address. During the connection set-up phase the intermediate nodes get the information how to associate the intermediate links. So each incoming packet can be forwarded to the correct link thus eventually reaching the destination. Routing is only necessary during connection set-up, and during the release of a connection, the information about link associations at the intermediate nodes is purged.

In the datagram mode, individual packets are routed through the network on the basis of full destination addresses. The datagram mode is also called connectionless packet transfer, while the virtual connection mechanism supports the connection-oriented connection mode.

Although both connection modes can be emulated on top of the other in principle, the implementation of a connectionless mode on top of a connection-oriented mode causes difficulties, as we will see below in the case of Asynchronous Transfer Mode (ATM).

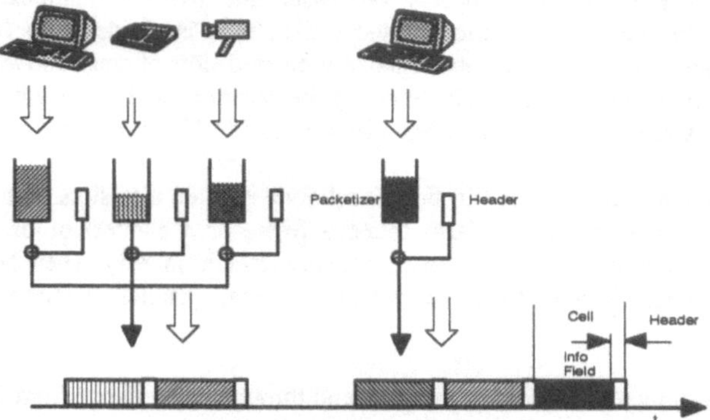

Fig. 3: ATM Principle

The Asynchronous Transfer Mode (ATM) is a virtual-connection-based fast packet switching technique using small fixed sized packets, called cells. Cells are consisting of 53 bytes subdivided into 5 bytes header information and 48 bytes user information. As address information, each header contains Virtual Channel and Virtual Path Identifiers (VCI and VPI), thus providing a hardware-implemented connection-oriented packet-switched communication mode. The ATM barer service integrates any connection-oriented service such as circuit-switched services with constant bit rates as well as services with highly variable bit rates. The functions needed for end-to-end synchronisation, segmentation of stream-type data or connection handling for connectionless services are provided by the ATM Adaptation Layer (AAL) such that at the ATM layer all functions can be performed fast and effectively by hardware support. Up to now 5 AAL classes have been defined: AAL1 for isochronous constant bit rate connection-oriented services, AAL2 for isochronous variable bit rate connection-oriented services, AAL3 for connection-oriented data services, AAL4 for connectionless data transfer and the recently added AAL5, which is a simplified version of AAL3. The major difference between AAL3 and AAL5 is the lack of multiplexing support within a virtual connection in AAL5. This leads to a simpler hardware realisation and thus to cost savings. The basic ATM principle is shown in Fig. 3.

There are still some problems associated with ATM with respect to modelling, traffic engineering and operation. Examples are switching network analyses, source policing, transmission delays, connection acceptance control, and an adequate basis for charging.

4. Transport and Switching Systems

Ethernet and Token Ring

Ethernet and Token Ring are well-recognised LAN standards, which operate in the 10 Mbit and 16 Mbit range. They are widely used and this will remain so for quite a time, even if the network capacity and the access protocols are not suited to high and bursty traffic requirements. Coinciding with increasing bandwidth demand the number of attached stations will decrease and instances of these network types will be interconnected by special equipment with higher capacity.

Fibre Distributed Data Interface (FDDI)

The FDDI standard defines a resilient 100 Mbit/s fibre optic data network based on a token ring protocol. The network topology, a dual ring of trees, is capable of supporting up to 500 stations over a total fibre path length of up to 100 km. Adjacent ring stations can be up to 2 km apart with optical links operating at 1300 nm wave length. FDDI supports two basic traffic classes: synchronous and asynchronous, where in the asynchronous class two different token modes can be distinguished.

FDDI is a well-established standard with products available from a large number of suppliers and a growing number of user applications. Already at the Interop '90 some 100 FDDI products from 30 vendors where assembled into a successful demonstration of interoperability. Typical products available today include bridges, routers, concentrators as well as single and dual attachment workstation controllers from major suppliers. FDDI is becoming the preferred high-speed LAN standard for systems in the 90's.

FDDI-II

FDDI-II is an enhancement to the basic standard catering for the additional provision of variable bandwidth isochronous data transport. The FDDI-II standard is based on FDDI with which it is backward compatible. It is designed to address the need for a high-speed communications network, capable of support for multi-service applications such as voice, video and data. It provides both circuit switching and packet switching. The bit rate, transmission codes, optics, topology etc. for FDDI-II are identical with FDDI.

Expressed simply, FDDI-II can be seen as an extension of FDDI to allow the optical fibre ring to carry isochronous as well as packet data. In order achieve this an 8 kHz cyclic frame structure is defined for data transmission on the ring, each 8 kHz frame corresponding to a PCM sampling interval. A cycle master station produces this frame cycle format. The FDDI-II ring bandwidth may be dynamically allocated between packet and isochronous data in units of 6.144 Mbit/s known as wideband channels [HIL91].

Dual Queue Distributed Bus (DQDB)

The above-mentioned network types use a bus or ring topology with Carrier Sense Multiple Access with Collision Detection (CSMA/CD) or token-passing access control protocols (MAC - Medium Access Control). These access control schemes reach physical boundaries with respect to possible bandwidth and geographical extension. If more than 100 Mbit/s and several tens of kilometres are required, new MAC schemes are needed for these application areas.

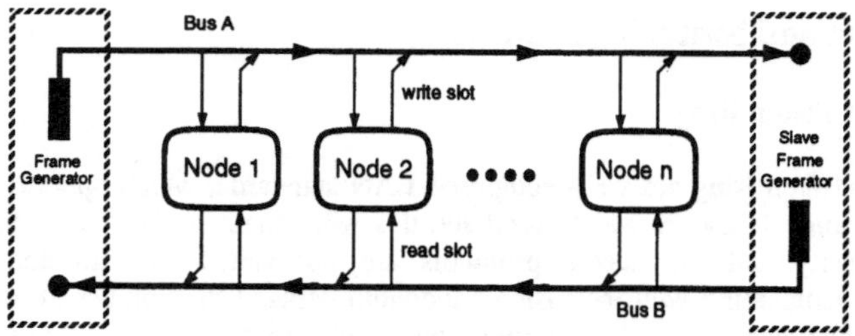

Fig. 4: DQDB Architecture

A network structure proposed as the IEEE 802.6 Metropolitan Area Network (MAN) standard is based on a slotted bus topology. This topology was first proposed by Telecom Australia and is originally called Queue Packet and Synchronous Circuit Exchange (QPSX). Up to now, several modifications and protocol enhancements have been made and the 802.6 proposal is now called Distributed Queue Dual Bus (DQDB). A pair of contra-flowing unidirectional buses form the bases for the architecture of the DQDB network (see Fig. 4).

Each node can handle full duplex communications with each other node by sending information on one bus and receiving it on the opposite bus. Head stations generate frames using an 8 kHz clock, every frame is subdivided into slots. The end station terminating each bus remove all incoming slots and generate the same slot patterns on the opposite bus. DQDB provides isochronous services, connectionless asynchronous services as well as connection-oriented packet-switched services. In 1989, the DQDB slot format was adapted to the CCITT ATM cell sizes, containing a 5 byte header and a 48 byte segment payload. DQDB operates at 155 and 622 Mbit/s [SAS90].

FDDI Follow-On LAN (FFOL)

The FFOL work was initiated in February 1990 by Task Groupe X3T9.5 of ASC X3 to establish requirements and formal projects for a next generation LAN. New developments aim at transmission rates of several 100 Mbit/s up to the Gbit/s range. For FFOL to succeed as the next generation LAN/MAN of choice it will have to satisfy some ambitious requirements. It must improve on the asynchronous data service offer by current LANs and MANs, it must cater for the increasingly important real-time, stream-oriented, types of traffic such as sound and video, it must provide improved resilience and manageability, and it must do this in the most cost-effective way possible [FIR92].

The requirement to provide efficiency for asynchronous traffic while at the same time providing deterministic delay for isochronous traffic, was addressed by adopting a hybrid architecture, which keeps the two service classes separate. This means that asynchronous service can be optimised for bursty data traffic, while separate, very low delay isochronous circuits are available for time-sensitive traffic such as sound and video.

In terms of nodal architecture, the model adopted for FFOL has a strong superficial resemblance than that defined for FDDI-II, however, the functionality of constituent parts will be very different. Although the adaption of a hybrid approach simplifies the requirements for the individual service it does, unfortunately, have the disadvantage of introducing extra complexity envolved in handling the extra layer and its interactions with the other layers. Here a compromise could be envisaged. To support all service types with one MAC protocol is available approach for the gain in architectural elegance. This view has so far not prevailed in the FFOL committee, which has favoured the hybrid approach. However, no proposal for a standard has been made so far.

ATM LANs

An ATM LAN is based on a network of ATM switches and dedicated links to each host, so the aggregate bandwidth of an ATM network increases as hosts are added. Data transfers by any number of hosts can occur in parallel over an ATM LAN. In contrast, LANs that are based on a shared medium, such as FDDI, can be saturated by a small number of hosts. The routing of information over an ATM LAN is based on ATM virtual connections and paths. In the case of a multiple-switch ATM LAN, control software on the switches must cooperate to route the connection through the network, but again only at the time the connection is established. An ATM LAN should be used as a high performance replacement for any existing LAN. Application programs continue to work as before because the same protocols are supported [BCS96].

Broadband ISDN (B-ISDN)

For Broadband ISDN, the narrowband ISDN reference configuration is complemented by broadband capabilities, based on ATM, which also include packet-switching services (see Fig. 5). The B-ISDN is based on a fully optical fibre transmission network operating at about 150 Mbit/s and 600 Mbit/s at the User Network Interface (UNI) and internally in the network, respectively. It provides a very fast and efficient connection-oriented bearer service, i.e. set-up/clearing of virtual connections and packet (cell) transfer between the terminal service access points of the ATM bearer service.

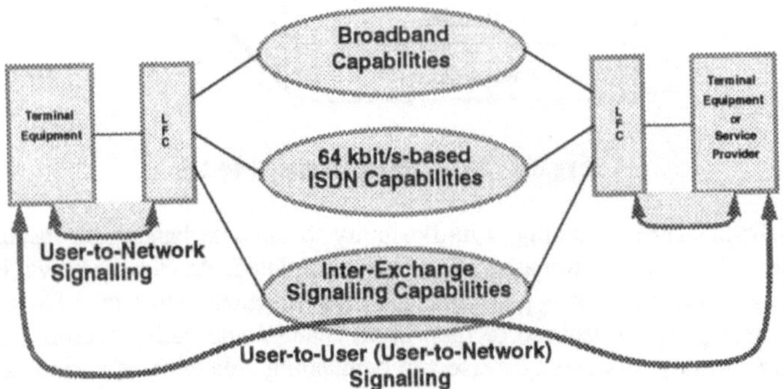

Fig. 5: B-ISDN Reference Configuration

The B-ISDN is the premise to a universal integrated broadband communication network and will provide the public communication infrastructure for high bandwidth communication requirements [POP89].

Brief discussion

As already mentioned before, Ethernet, Token Ring and FDDI are well-established standards and widely used. The main application area for FDDI is as backbone network for the interconnection of LANs, powerful main frames and workstations, file servers or interworking units with the public network. Since FDDI does not offer an isochronous service, the support of, for instance, high-resolution full-motion video, is limited. Quality of service requirements can only be satisfied under special conditions based on worst case assessments depending on the number of attached stations. FDDI-II, DQDB and possibly FFOLs would offer a better choice, since they introduce an isochronous traffic class by which isochronous connections with specific quality of service requirements can be more easily accomplished. Although this is true from the technical point of view, the market success has to be seen quite differently. Since DQDB has been chosen as the IEEE 802.6 MAN standard it has become a serious competitor to FDDI-II. Furthermore, the ATM standardisation activities have proceeded much faster than foreseen, so that ATM can be seen as a serious competitor for DQDB. Since the development and standardisation of communication technologies requires immense efforts and investments, it is very unlikely that several of these network technologies will be developed as products at the same time. There are no FDDI-II field trials known to the author, while the existing DQDB field trials seem not to be continued. Focus is put on national [WAC93] and international ATM field trials starting in '93 in some countries and continuing until 1996 with the participation of more and more countries ending up in an international global field trial. So, FDDI-II will certainly have no commercial success and most probably, the same is true for DQDB: the market window for DQDB is getting smaller and smaller.

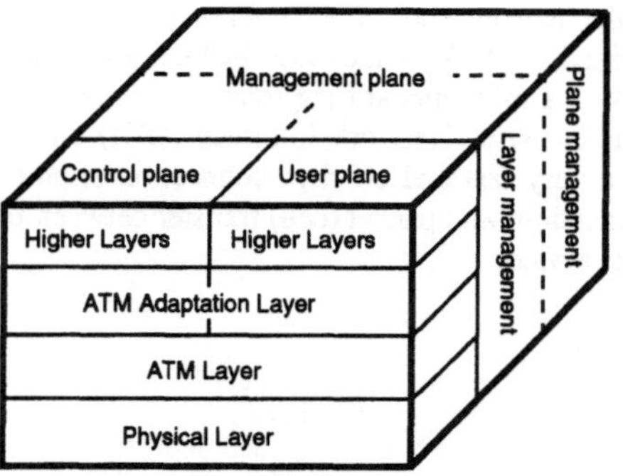

Fig. 6: B-ISDN Reference Model

A major benefit of ATM switching is its flexibility to allocate bandwidth instantaneously on demand, once call set-up preliminaries have been completed. As Fig. 7 shows, in STM-based B-ISDN the overall bandwidth is partitioned in fixed channels while in ATM-based B-ISDN any partitioning is possible because of the virtual channel and path structure. This combined flexibility and capability to serve a diverse and demanding collection of various kinds of traffic contributes to the success of ATM and B-ISDN. With ATM a transmission technology is now available, which makes feasible the integration of delay-sensitive circuit-switched bit streams and packet-oriented data.

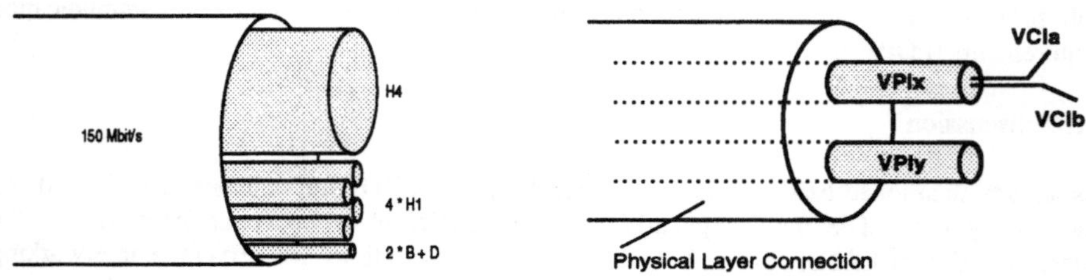

Fig. 7: Flexibility of ATM

The first broad applications of ATM will be found in data communications. The standardisation activities for this application area are pushed forward by the newly formed ATM Forum in which more than 100 major data and telecom suppliers have joined. The ATM Forum proceeds very fast and it can be seen as competitive to the ongoing CCITT activities. This can be demonstrated very well by quoting two consecutive sentences from the latest ATM Forum UNI specification, Release 2.1, May 1993. For the implementor, the first sentence sounds good: *The signalling specified in this implementation agreement is based on CCITT draft recommendation Q.93B*. But then: *However, there are numerous differences, including removal of options, setting of numeric values, removal of messages, information elements and procedures, and enhancements which add new messages, informations elements and procedures.* This second sentence simply means that this protocol is completely different from the CCITT version, that it is a new protocol in fact.

5. Private Network Architectures and Configurations

In this section, some examples of already existing advanced architectures of private networks and possible scenarios for future applications are presented.

Since the introduction of LANs there has been a need to interconnect LANs of same and different types. The internetworking equipment that has been developed over the past years includes bridges, routers, gateways and hubs. Bridges and gateways provide connectivity at the ISO layers 2 and 3, respectively, routers have to find paths through interconnected networks for dedicated communications to avoid internetwork-wide broadcasts. When reduced to essentials, a hub consist of a chassis (backplane) that accepts add-in cards or modules. The simplest add-in cards are those equipped with LAN ports. In this rudimentary configuration - which was originally called a hub - cables run from terminals to a LAN port, which means that the hub structures Ethernet and Token Rings as a physical star. Typically, all of the users connected to one add-in card a considered to be on the same logical LAN segment. More than one card can be linked through the backplane to establish larger segments.

LAN modules were only the beginning: add-in cards also can carry bridges, routers and single board computers executing network management tasks. This advanced configuration is often referred to as a smart hub.

In contrast with conventional backbones, where, for example, departmental LANs are connected to an FDDI network via bridges, hubs can also provide the backbone functionality. The architecture of a so-called collapsed backbone design [ZEI92] is shown in Figure 8.

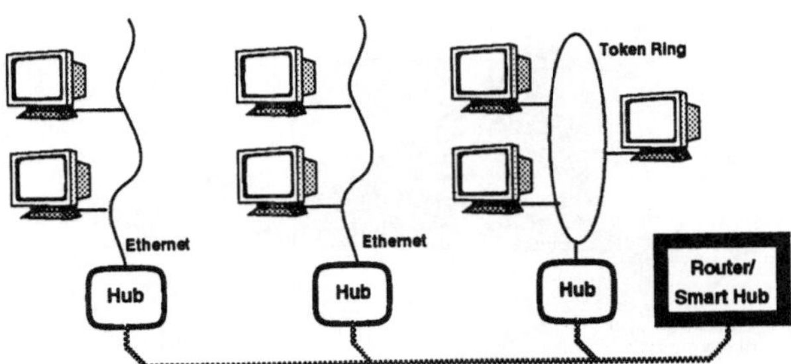

Fig. 8: Collapsed Backbone Design

This centralized solution offers advantages such as simplified network monitoring, maintenance and troubled shooting and could also make it easier to plan future growth. The conventional more distributed backbone architectures might reduce the cabling complexity and achieve higher fault tolerance and network segmentation.

Adding ATM capabilities to the hub - as all major hub vendors are planning - this is first step into the direction of ATM cross connects and ATM LANS (see above). The virtual path principle of ATM allows a very high throughput of the network, since the routing within the ATM switches is done by hardware. Combining this architecture with an ATM architecture in the public area, wide area data communications could be enabled in a similar way as phone calls are handled today.

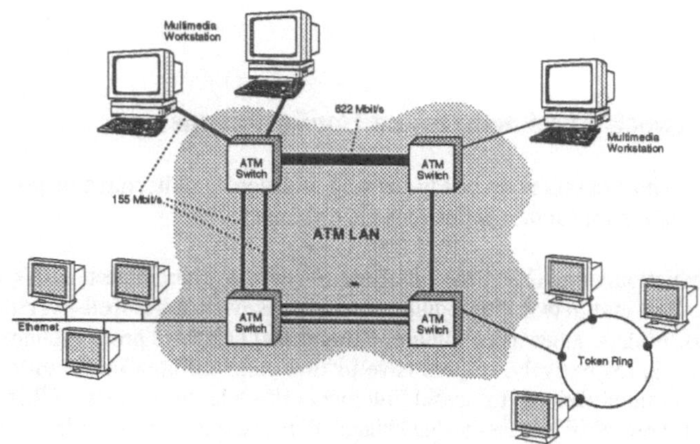

Fig. 9: ATM LAN Structure

The examples presented so far only addressed the needs of data communications. In order to also support the traditional telecom services with one communication infrastructure, hybrid technologies such as FDDI-II, DQDB and FFOL are a good choice from a technical point of view. A DQDB-based network infrastructure is being installed at the Frankfurt Rhein-Main Airport. For the Frankfurt Airport Network (FRANET) a so-called core system solution has been planned which integrates voice and non-voice services and also allows the integration of existing telecommunication and data equipment [BOE92]. DQDB will be used as a first technical implementation of the core system. In a test operation, criteria such as stability, performance, configurability and the adequacy of the ATM technology will be evaluated. Based on these results, the technology for the final implementation of the core system will be determined.

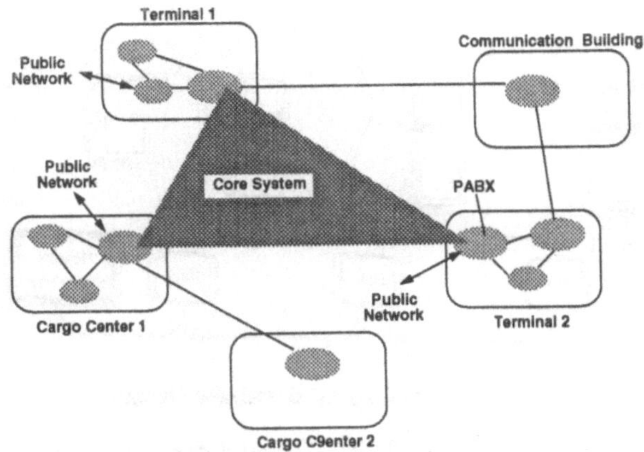

Fig. 10: Network Support at Rhein-Main Airport

In Fig.11 a distributed communication system is shown that can be regarded as a distributed PABX: the nodes have local switching capacity and offer interfaces to different terminal types. The nodes are interconnected by a high-speed backbone network. In Figure 11, a possible scenario is depicted as it has been conceived and evaluated in the course of the ESPRIT Project DAMS (Dynamically Adaptable Multiservice System) [POW93, SAW92, WYS91].

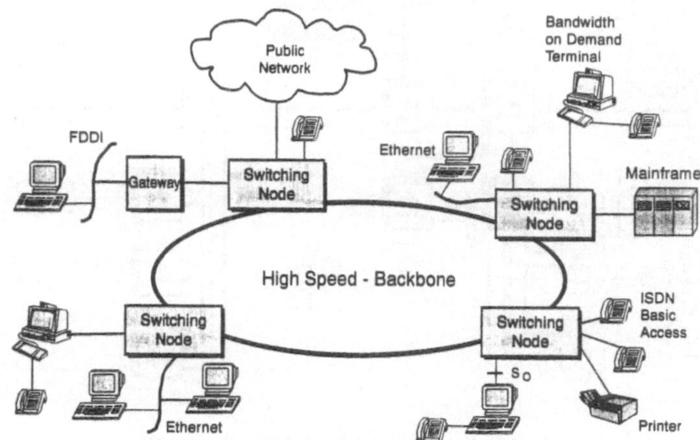

Fig. 11: DAMS Overall Architecture

The nodes can be configured as to the needs of the environment: interfaces to analogue phones (POTS - Plain Old Telephones), ISDN phones, workstations, servers, mainframes, the public network and existing LAN infrastructures are considered. Instead of a ring, any other topology can be envisaged. A DAMS system consists of autonomous nodes, which can operate in a stand-alone mode or can be connected by a backbone system to build large networks or to extend a system to greater geographical distances. As, for example, in [PDO92, SYN92] a hybrid switching principle was chosen, which allows the integration of isochronous and nonisochronous data switching in an easy and cost-efficient way. The boundary between packet-switched and circuit-switched bandwidth can be controlled by software during operation. Furthermore, the nodes support ATM. Depending on application requirements or specific traffic profiles, a DAMS node can cover the range from a full STM up to a full ATM switch.

The access to the internode network is provided by a backbone unit. In principle, more than one backbone unit can be linked to one node thus achieving various interconnection topologies. The backbone unit of the DAMS demonstrator was based on the FDDI-II standard. Since FDDI also provides both circuit and packet switching thus being a hybrid protocol, it fits very well to the node-internal hybrid switching principle. Currently, the backbone capabilities of the demonstrator, which was completed in 1992, are enhanced with a DQDB system, and ATM LANs and cross connects are planned.

One DAMS node can offer up to 1 Gbit internal switching capacity, which is achieved by a passive bus architecture [KSS90]. The hybrid switching principle is a cost-effective approach, since existing narrowband ISDN and isochronous services can be directly connected, without segmenting the bit stream into ATM cells at the source and reassembling the cells to the original bit stream at the destination. The STM/ATM bandwidth allocation can be adjusted to the actual needs: when in the first step the existing narrowband applications predominate, most of the bandwidth will be allocated to STM services and only a small fraction will be used for ATM, as for example the interconnection of LANs. As broadband traffic increases and ATM terminals are getting available, the ATM share in bandwidth will be increased. Again, all this is software-controlled and can be done dynamically at run time.

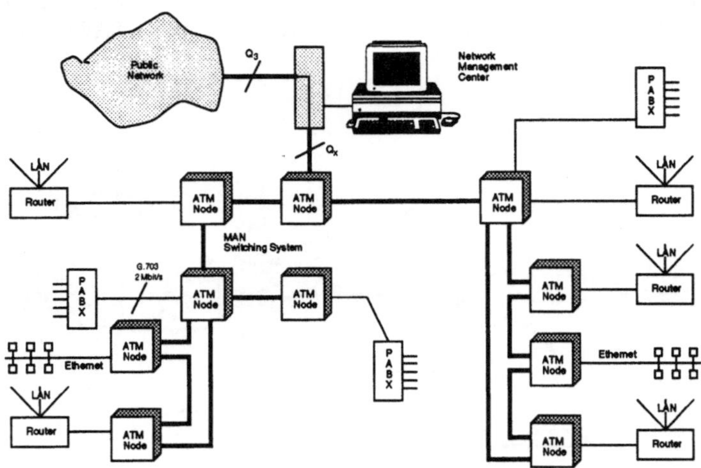

Fig. 12: Interconnection of MANs (MSS)

Looking at the scenarios presented, a hierarchy of networks can be clearly identified. Starting from the top, the public ATM-based B-ISDN provides global wide area connectivity offering the standardised T_B interface at the user network interface (UNI). Metropolitan Area Networks (MANs) serve as gathering or backbone systems for LANs and PABXs. Depending on capacity requirements, several MANs can be connected by a so-called MAN Switching System (MSS). Access from MANs to a wide range of customers premises equipment and LANs is possible via multi-protocol routers or data service units, currently available from several majors suppliers of LAN equipment. PABXs can also be attached. Figure 12 shows such a scenario [NKT93].

In order to offer users a set of adequate interfaces, the 155 Mbit/s of B-ISDN, MANs and ATM LANs have to be broken down into various lower bit rate interfaces such as S_0, S_{2M}, DXI for the connection of routers, hubs etc. In this context, the role of PABXs to a service switch, which concentrates these interfaces and provides a local switching capacity. Whether MANs and MSS are part of the public or private network depends on the communication capacity requirements of the application. MANs and MSS can be preliminary seen in the public area, large customer premises as, for example, Rhein-Main Airport, also need MAN infrastructures. For the end user the main point is that he only wants to have one non-technical interface to an organisation or company that handles all the technical, organisational, administration and maintenance aspects for him.

The examples presented in this section showed that ATM has the potential to integrate different traffic types. Nevertheless, as long as some of the problems associated with ATM, especially end-to-end delay (jitter) and optimal bandwidth allocation in bursty traffic scenarios, have not been completely solved, hybrid approaches offering asynchronous and isochronous services in parallel should not be abandoned for the time being.

6. Conclusion

In the paper, an overview of the current network technologies and possible application scenarios was given. It was shown that in B-ISDN and ATM the standardisation activities are not complete yet and - although the major technological problems seem to be solved - some details are still open and experiences in operating and using these networks still have to be gained. The sometimes completely different architectures and technologies of the different network types will cause serious interworking problems and effort. Nevertheless, users will benefit from these developments since a communication infrastructure will be provided that allows an improved connectivity and thus processing of information, which will eventually lead to an improved collaboration in research, development and manufacturing.

Efficient communication infrastructures will play the key role for the success of enterprises. Fast access to all kinds of data within and outside a company will be the crucial factor along with effective and user-friendly representations and high reliability and availability. The commercial success of communication companies will heavily depend on how they can accommodate the changing customer demands. From developing and marketing proprietary equipment, the value will shift to the successful integration of existing equipment and to the provision of services. Profits will no longer be made by the sale of equipment where due to high competition the prices will dramatically fall, but will be gained by the provision of services and know-how in network configuration, installation, operation and maintenance.

7. Acknowledgements

The author wishes to thank the participants of the DAMS and MOPS ESPRIT-Projects and K. Krautkrämer, R. Cordes, and K. Sauer for contributions and many fruitful discussions. Thanks also to G. Zäh for editorial assistance.

References

ALI92 M. Irfan Ali; Frame Relay in Public Networks; IEEE Communications Magazine, pp. 72-78; March 1992

BCS96 E. Biagioni, E. Cooper, R. Sansoni; Designing a Practical ATM LAN; IEEE Network, pp. 32-39; March 1993

BEP93 R. L. Bennett, G. E. Policello II; Switching Systems in the 21st Centrury; IEEE Communications Magazine; March 1993

BOE92 H. P. Boell; Stille Revolution am Flughafen Frankfurt; online, pp. 51-54; Nov. 1992

CHY92 A. G. Chynoweth; Going Broadband; RACE TG(92) 4/x Concertation Technical Workshop; Conference Handouts; Brussels; Sept. 1992

CWV91 R. Cordes, D. Wybranietz, R. Vautz; Managing Multimedia Sessions on a Private Broadband Communication System; Proc. 2nd Workshop on Operating System and Network Support for Digital Audio and Video; Heidelberg; Nov. 1991

FIR92 R. L. Fink, F. E. Ross; Following the Fiber Distributed Data Interface; IEEE Network; March 1992

GFB91 M. Gerla, L. Fratta, J. Bannister; Evolution of LANs and MANs Towards High Speeds: Gigabits per Second and Beyond; ETT Vol. II, No 1; Jan./Feb. 1991

GHS93 N. Gerner, H.-G. Hegering, J. Swoboda (Eds.); Proc. Kommunikation in verteilten Systemen; Munich, March 1993

HEI91 J. Heinänen; Review of Backbone Technologies; Computer Networks and ISDN Systems, pp. 239-245; 1991

HIL91 A. R. Hills; FDDI-II - An Implementor's Perspective; Proc. 9th Annual European Fibre Optic Communication and Local Area Network Conference; London; June 1991

ISS92 Proc. XIV International Switching Symposium; Yokohama; Oct. 1992

KSS90 W. Krautkrämer, K. Sauer, D. Schlichthärle, R. Knobling; Flexibles Systemkonzept zur Einführung von Breitbanddiensten im privaten Netzbereich; ntz Bd 43/12; 1990

KÜH92 P. J. Kühn; Future Networking; PIK 15, pp. 3-10; 1992

MÜL92 H. R. Müller et al.; Net Access Schemes for Gbit/s-LANs and MANs; Proc. High-Capacity Local and Metropolitan Area Networks; Springer Verlag; Berlin; 1990

NKT93 NKT Elektronik A/S; NKT Public Broadband Data Networks; Technical Brochure; Brondby; March 1993

PDO92 B. Panwels, E. Desmet, H. Orlamünder; Application of the Multipath Self-Routing Switch in a Combined STM/ATM Cross-Connect System; in [ISS92]

POP89 R. Popescu-Zeletin; From Broadband ISDN to Multimedia Computer Networks; Computer Networks and ISDN Systems 18, pp. 47-54; 1989/90

POW93 R. Pohlit, D. Wybranietz; Dynamically Adaptable Multi-Service-System - DAMS; ESPRIT 2146 Project Report; Feb. 1993

REA89 R. Reardon (Ed.); Future Networks; Blenheim Online; London; 1989

SAS90 K. Sauer, W. Schödl; Performance Aspects of the DQDB Protocol; Computer Networks and ISDN Systems 20, pp. 253-260; 1990

SAW92 K. Sauer, A. Weber; A Flexible Customer Premises Network for Introducing ATM-BASED Broadband Communication; in [ISS92]

SYN92 H. Shimizu et al.; Integrated Corporate Communication Platform for Multimedia Networking; in [ISS92]

WAC93 G. Wachholz; The German Broadband Pilot Trial; Proc. Net '93 Telecom Trends, Munich; May 1993

WYS91 D. Wybranietz, F.-J. Stamen; Ein zukünftiges Kommunikationssystem für den privaten Netzbereich - Eine Übersicht über das DAMS-Projekt (ESPRIT 2146); Proc. 21. GI-Jahrestagung "Telekommunikation und multimediale Anwendungen der Informatik"; Darmstadt; Oct. 1991

ZEI92 M. Zeile; Expanding the Enterprise by Collapsing the Backbone; Data Communications, pp. 71-80; Nov. 1992

Design and Assessment of a Parallel High Performance Transport System

Georg Carle [1] and Martin Siegel [2]
Institute for Communication Switching and Data Technics (IND)
University of Stuttgart
Seidenstrasse 36, D-70174 Stuttgart, Germany

Abstract

Applications are not able to make full use of bandwiths offered by high speed networks due to a lack of performance in current communication systems. This paper presents a parallel architecture for a front end processor (FEP) between host and high speed LAN or MAN to overcome the transport system bottleneck. The focus of the project was to demonstrate that implementation issues are of highest importance and that high performance can be achieved based on standard protocols. The FEP is designed for an OSI TP4/CLNP/LLC1 protocol stack, with an architecture general enough to be adapted to other protocols. The architecture is based on three RISC processors which are supported by special-purpose hardware for process synchronisation and for time-critical functions like checksum evaluation, buffer management and timer administration. The paper summarises design steps and features of the system. It also describes modelling and simulation and discusses main results.

1 Introduction

Recent developments in networking technology promise to push the available data rates into the gigabits per second, both in local and wide area networks. At the same time, modern computing equipment is capable of processing and producing data at ever-increasing rates. One of the results of these advances in transmission and processing technology is that the networking hardware and software above the medium access layer is facing increasing difficulty in keeping up with the data rates. (Typically achievable performances are shown in Figure 1, where the measurement packets per second is used above the technology dependent layers 1 and 2b, because the per packet effort largely exceeds the per byte effort in most higher layers.)

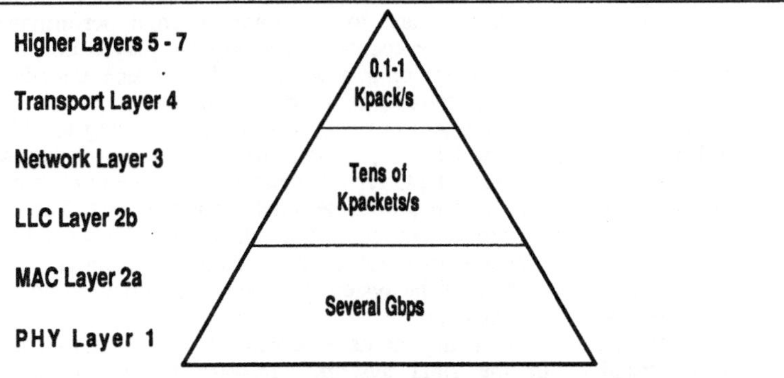

Figure 1: Typical performances of current OSI systems

1 now with Institute of Telematics, University of Karlsruhe, Zirkel 2, P.O. Box 6980, D-76128 Karlsruhe, E-mail carle@ira.uka.de, Tel. ++49 721 608-4027, Fax ++49 721 388097

2 now with Alcatel SEL AG, P.O. Box 40 07 49, D-70435 Stuttgart

In this project, investigations have been performed to evaluate the effects of increasing data rates on protocol performance, location of protocol processing, possible hardware components, remaining software processing effort, and the interfaces between the protocol processing units and the host system on which the application resides. By concentration on the so-called transmission layer (which is defined as a combination of the ISO OSI transport, network and logical link layers), a possible solution for some of these problems is proposed. All components which serve to provide a transport connection except the physical connection to the transmission medium and the MAC layer have been considered. Own and published experiences and measurements show that the protocol itself is not the major performance determiner in communication systems [1]. The surrounding system architecture and operating facilities and the protocol implementation have a far greater influence.
The paper presents general goals and restrictions, introduces the finally chosen architecture, and summarises the characteristics of the transport system. The basic concept of this system has been published in [2], where also an overview on alternative ways to speed up protocol processing as protocol parameter tuning and the development of new (lightweight) protocols is given. This paper focuses on the principal design steps and the verification methods which were applied, presenting modelling and simulation results. The paper is finalized with a conclusion and an overview on the current state of the project.

2 Design Parameters for the Transport System

The first step in the project was to fix the goals for the intended system and to generate a list of assumptions and restrictions. The main goals and their consequences are shortly summarised below:

1. The design should be flexible enough to allow an easy adaptation to different protocol parameters and versions, and even to different (non-OSI) protocol stacks. Therefore, pure hardware solutions are excluded. We intended to obtain flexibility using a general-purpose processor as a controller in combination with dedicated hardware elements. In [3] and [4], this method was investigated, and promising results were obtained.
2. The dependency on a specific environment should be minimized. This implies that the influence of the host architecture and operating system on the overall performance should be as small as possible. The only way to satisfy this requirement is to develop an independent front end processor system, where protocol processing can be performed without interference of an operating system. (Even with special constructs like Clark's up-calls [5] the context switching overhead plays a dominant role when several processes share the same processor).
3. OSI compatibility was chosen to demonstrate the importance of implementation issues for the system performance and to determine inherent performance limits of OSI protocols. Investigations of protocol-oriented aspects played only a minor role. This implies that no development of a new protocol has been intended. In [6], a good overview of already existing lightweight protocol is given.
5. A LAN or MAN environment has been assumed. According to different government OSI profiles (e.g. for the US see [7]) and international groups like MAP or TOP, the protocol class combination LLC type 1, connectionless network protocol (CLNP) and the transport protocol TP4 has been selected for the project. The concentration on a LAN or MAN environment had another effect: the well-known problems due to huge bandwidth-delay products had not to be considered extensively. Nevertheless, an appropriate dimensioning of the system parameters should allow to use the system in a high-speed WAN environment.
5. Hardware support - including the development of own ASICs - should be integrated, where feasible. In the final system, hardware support is provided for buffer management, DMA, checksumming, timers, process synchronisation and on-the-fly separation of packet header and data part.
6. In protocol processing, various kinds of parallelism occur and can be exploited, as shown in [8]. Our goal was to exploit parallelism where it can be done at moderate costs.
7. Any data movements within the system should be avoided as much as possible. This covers not only the user data which crosses the system, but also internal exchange of

information, e.g. for control or synchronisation purposes. A common memory concept for user data has been introduced. To enable an efficient header processing, the headers are separated from the data in real-time during regular data transfer from MAC into the FEP. In send direction, a part of the header is generated during data transfer from host memory into the FEP. As far as possible, information is held decentralized at locations where it is mainly used. The three areas only exchange commands and memory references.

8. The overall system costs should be reasonable. Some examples: the buswidths are restricted to 32 bit, for data memory cheap but rather slow DRAMs is used, the ASICs are based on a conservative semi-custom sea-of-gates technology, and where possible standard elements were used instead of custom designs.

To reduce the complexity of our implementation, some restrictions had to be made. For a separation of header and data part with reasonable effort, the number of positions and formats must be limited. We decided that one MAC-frame shall contain only one header for each layer. The mechanisms to concatenate or separate PDUs are not allowed. In addition, not all combinations of options are possible. However, most of the restrictions are compatible to the standards, and are either totally hidden from the user or can be fixed during connection set-up. The few non-conformant restrictions should not cause problems in the real word either, because they deal mostly with mechanisms to overcome problems in very special situations which should not occur in the intended environments. Even if they occur, the entrance circuit of the FEP is able to by-pass non-FEP conformant messages directly to the host.

Figure 2 shows a block diagram of the resulting architecture of the front end processor, while the design steps are explained in the following section.

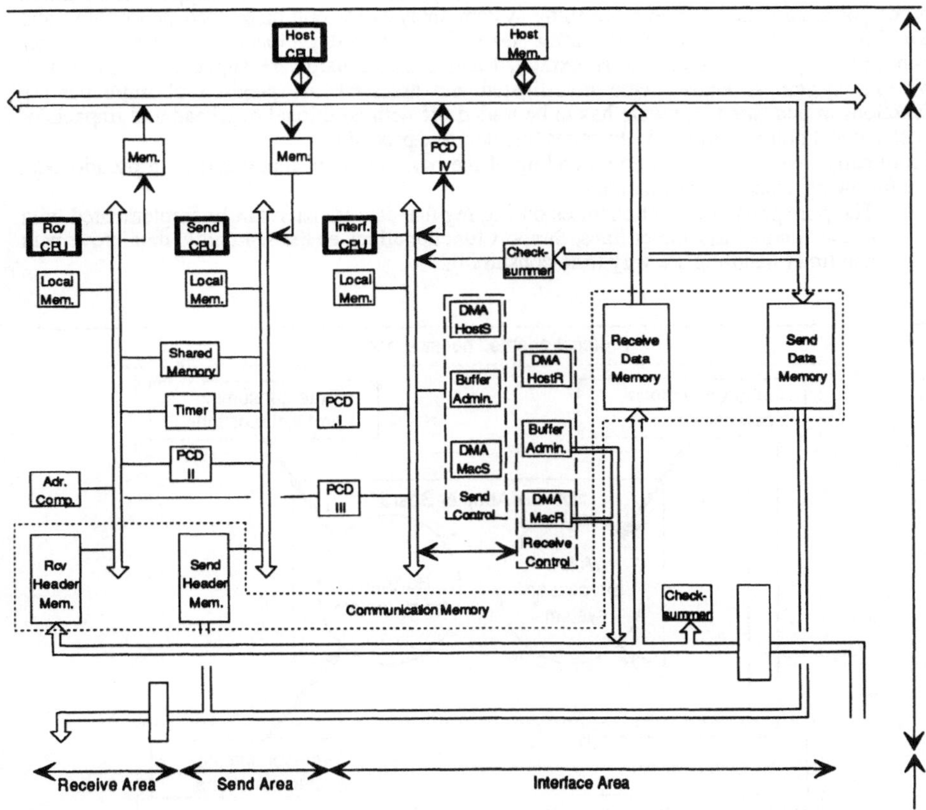

Figure 2: Transport system architecture

3 Design and Verification Methods

A system design with an early concentration on modelling is characteristic for a true top-to-down approach. We went a different way. While closely looking on implementation details from the beginning, we got many good ideas how to improve the system architecture. This combined Top-down and Bottom-up approach was continued in system modelling for verification and performance evaluation. A high-level system design without precise knowledge of implementation details in certain critical areas cannot result in a realistic simulation.

As we did not follow a strategy 'design for modelling', modelling of our system leads to a complex structure with numerous queues, complicating system simulation. Having available precise timing information for the different execution paths, our simulation results can be expected to present a realistic view of the true system behaviour.

After the global system architecture and resulting fundamental architectural decisions had been fixed, refinement procedures for hardware and software design and for verification were performed independently. As a last step, a simulation of the complete system was performed, as a combination of a system level behavioural hardware simulation and a statistical simulation based on a queuing model of the software functions and interactions. Section 4 will provide details of the overall simulation.

3.1 Requirements and Environmental Conditions

In the initial design phase, the exploitation of the inherent parallelism of the OSI TP4 protocol was the main goal. To achieve this goal, protocol function blocks were mapped on a parallel processor architecture, while performing system analysis for optimised load partitioning and avoidance of bottle-necks at the same time. Time-critical protocol functions and time-consuming system functions were extracted and possible hardware support was evaluated. Various system structures were investigated and assessed, as speed-up of implementing functions in dedicated hardware has to be traded off with additional overhead and impacts of cost and technology. Figure 3 illustrates this iterative procedure.

From early investigations based on coding of the basic protocol functionality in pseudocode, the following aspects were obtained:

- The pure *protocol* functionalities during regular data transfer can be implemented with a few hundred assembler lines. Support functionalities as list searching, data movement and timer handling are very time-consuming.

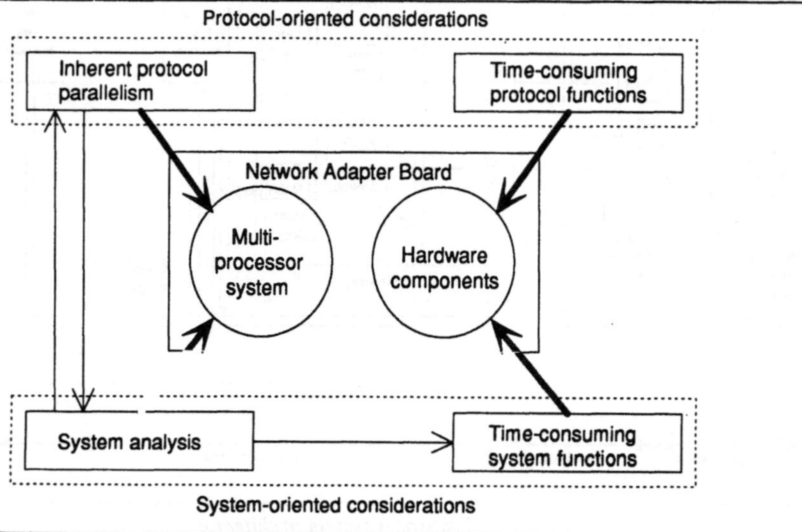

Figure 3: Initial design phase

- TP4 processing dominates processing of LLC1 and CLNP.
- Send and receive areas are nearly independent from each other. The effort for synchronisation of send and receive functions is small in comparison with the potential gain by exploitation of the parallelism.

If protocols of layers 2b to 4 are executed by the host processor, the influence of the operating system limits the achievable performance enormously, as shown in [1]. In a typical VAX/VMS environment, every context switch causes an overhead of approximately 0,5 ms. With only one context switch per packet, this sets an upper limit of some 1000 packets per second. Available solutions for systems of this type achieve a throughput of only several hundred packets per second. Using operating systems optimised for communication applications results in a certain improvement, but the remaining overhead is still large in relation to the time required for protocol processing. A true performance improvement can be found by implementation of the functionality of layers 2b to 4 on a separate front end processor (FEP) where no operating system needs to be involved in protocol processing.
As a result of the *protocol-oriented consideration*, parallel processing in send and receive direction leads to separate send and receive areas with separate processors. Further parallelism could be exploited by pipelined processing of the different layers. For the chosen connectionless protocol classes at layers 2b and 3, the processor load for layer 4 is largely dominating. In [9], potential parallelization of TP4 processing can be found. The resulting subprocesses are characterised by a relatively high coherence and interdependence. We concluded that a cost-effective solution will map protocol processing onto one processor for the send direction and one processor for the receive direction, together with dedicated hardware for timer management, checksumming and on-the-fly-separation of the TPDUs into packet header and data part.
In the *system-oriented considerations*, we put our emphasis both on high performance and on moderate costs. This can be achieved by an equally distributed processor and bus load and by minimizing the synchronisation overhead. The analysis of the system functions led to a set of tasks, which are advantageously executed by a single, third processor (the interface processor), and to the introduction of additional hardware components. These elements support process coupling, buffer and list management, DMA and caching facilities. A generic element, the process coupling device (PCD), supports synchronization of the involved processes with minimal overhead and allows an operation during data transfer with polling instead of interrupts.

3.2 Functionality implemented by Software

3.2.1 Implementation on RISC processors

For protocol processing and FEP system administration, there is no need for optimised arithmetic. In particular, no floating point operations occur. Our assembler programs show that basic instructions for data transfer, simple comparisons, boolean functions and branching are sufficient. The instruction set of a typical RISC processor meets our requirements. We decided to use three KB-class processors of the Intel 80960 family, which are very well suited for communications applications and which have a good prize/perfomance ratio.

3.2.2 Program structure

Following the aspects of modern software engineering, high level languages became more and more widespread, even in time-critical domains like operating systems and signal processing. Functionalities are often distributed on several processes which are executed on the same processor, and programs are highly modular and use numerous procedure calls. In confrontation with performance limits, the conflict modularity versus efficiency can be observed.
RISC processors achieve their performance based on a relatively simple, but highly efficient implementation of the essential processor components. We followed with our software implementation a similar approach. We achieve high performance in keeping our software structure simple, and in using assembly language instead of a high level language. The programs of the three processors are optimised for data transfer. In this case each processor executes a loop with a list of independent program modules. In this main loop polling is used for synchronisation and for dealing with packet arrivals and timers. Interrupts may occur for exception handling, supervisory functions and initialisation. Inside the program modules, the

processors are polling the queues of the various process coupling devices for commands. Depending on the content of these queues, different paths are executed inside the modules, and different execution times occur.
The main task of the *send processor* is the composition of headers, and (together with the *receive processor* which mainly processes the received headers), timer and connection management. The send processor maintains a table of transmit connection areas, where the necessary elementary buffers and additional resources are managed. For each connection, a table with unacknowledged packets is maintained. The receive processor maintains its table of receive connection areas, together with a destination reference table, which helps to speed up data transfer. The *interface processor* maintains its own table of connection areas, and a table with memory areas of the host memory, containing TSDUs which are ready for transmission. The interface processor executes program modules which perform buffer management and provide the interface to the host.

3.2.3 Memory Organisation

Logical organisation and physical distribution of data are key issues in system design. Bottlenecks can be avoided by hardware supported memory management and by table lookup techniques with indexed addressing. The separation of packet header and data part permits the use of fast, but small memory for headers and larger, but slower memory for data. For the header memory, static CMOS RAMs with cycle times below 30 ns are used, whereas much cheaper and larger DRAMs with cycle times around 100 ns are used for receive and send data memories. (*Cycle* times are significantly larger than *access* times.)
Both header and data memory are logically dual ported, with hardware providing semaphore administration. The data memory is organized into elementary buffers of 1 Kbyte size. Memory access control, buffer allocation and garbage collection is performed by special hardware, providing addresses and control signals.
The local memories of the processors contain data and executable code. The data area is partitioned into a system area with pointers on resources (which are all mapped into the address space) and on tables, where each processor maintains the necessary information of connections and packets. As an example, Figure 4 shows the memory structures which are involved in data transfer from the host meomory into the Send Data Memory of the FEP.

3.3 Hardware Design

The necessary steps for hardware development follow common rules. From the global architectural specification, a high-level block diagram was obtained. This diagram is similar to Figure 2, but contains more details as bus widths, control signals and subcomponents. The design steps within each component and module can be summarised as following:

- A first step is the partitioning of control tasks and operational functionalities.
- The control part can be transformed in one or several finite state machines (FSMs). A gate level design of the FSMs can be synthesized automatically using appropriate tools. However, the CAE-program we used (LOG/IC from ISDATA, Karlsruhe, FRG) forced us to introduce many internal partitions. Although a two level boolean optimisation for programmable logic devices (PLDs) can be performed, it produced gate designs far from optimum. Finally, most FSMs have been re-designed manually.
- The operational parts were designed based on the brain-paper-pencil method.
- The modules and FSMs were formally described and verified with a tool for digital gate-based simulations (System HILO from GenRad, Munich, FRG). Blocks are simulated separately and then combined step-by-step with their neighbours. Then the modules of one component are simulated together. For logic simulation, the gates are no longer modelled as physical gates, but as boolean equations with a mean delay.
- Simulation time increases non-linearily with the increasing number of gates, and component internal behaviour is no longer of interest at the next level of abstraction. Using a high level functional description makes an overall simulation of the hardware feasable.

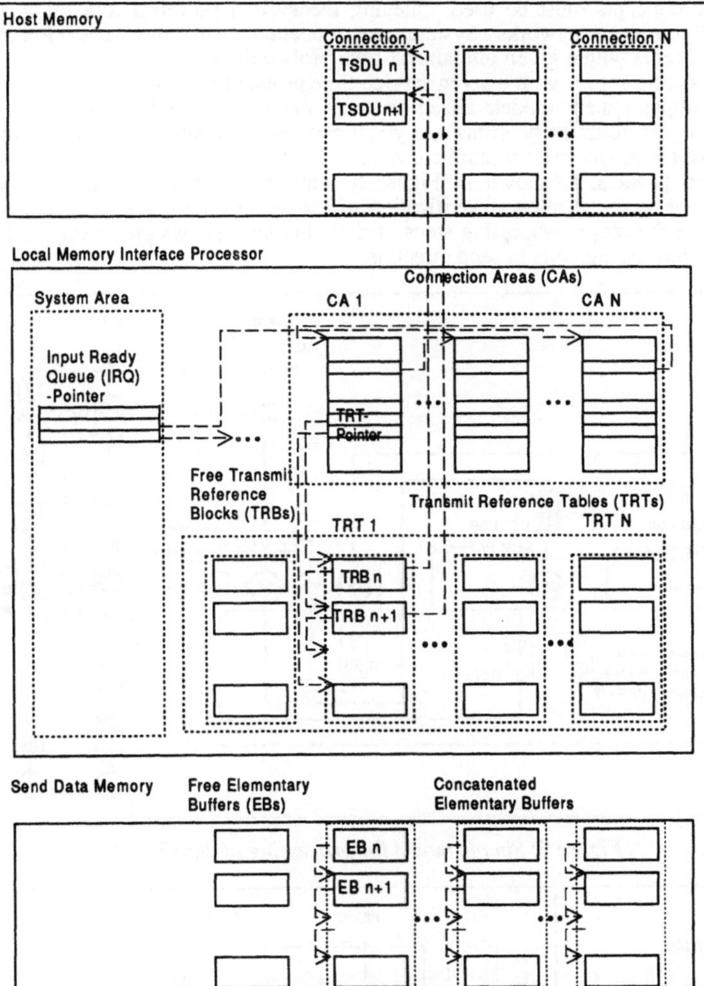

Figure 4: Buffer control structures for send direction

4 Modelling and Simulation

Hardware simulation is important for verification of component design, but it will not localise bottle-necks which may occur at diffenent traffic patterns, and it cannot be used for dimensioning of system parts. The interaction of hardware and software needs a different simulation method. On the other hand, classic traffic engineering methods for performance evaluation of communication systems will not take details of the implementation into account. A prominent example is the missing of accurate models for resource conflicts and resource administration as well as for other operating system functions. To overcome these insufficiencies, a combined simulation method has been set up which is presented in this section. This simulation is used for validation of design assumptions and for dimensioning of many system parameters. The number and length of packets entering the system at any time varies statistically. In order to come up with quantitative measures of performance, probabilistic concepts must be used. Queuing theory is a powerful tool for a quantitative analysis of computer networks. Systems are modelled, using the basic elements Source (generating events with a given interarrival-time probability density function), Queue, Server (processing queue entries with a given service-time probability density function), Phases, and Sink. For simple system models based on these elements, analytical solutions exist. For systems of higher complexity, either analytical methods with subsequent approximation or a simulation of the model must be applied. A simple model of the system, considering only the flow of data packets, is shown in Figure 5. This model can be used for performance estimation, but does not allow a verification of the system design. This model can also be used to derive the major processing steps of data. Figure 6 shows processing and waiting in the different processing units in send direction.

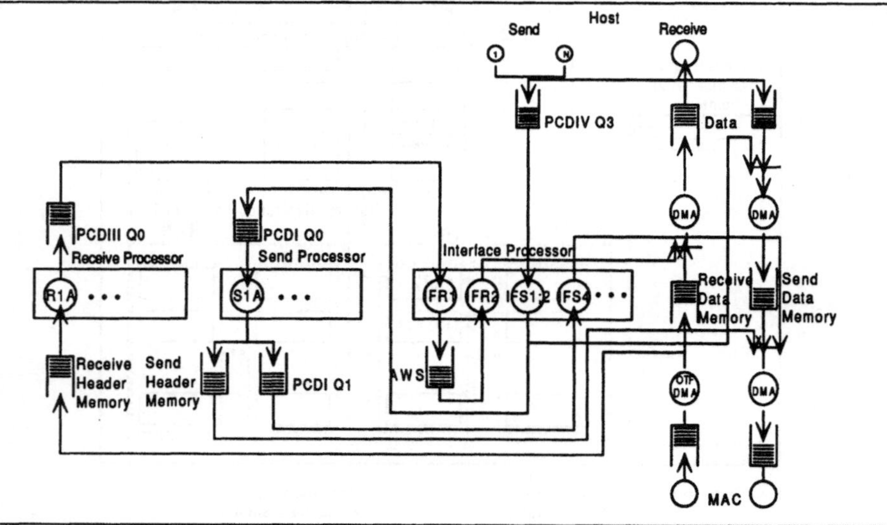

Figure 5: Simple model for processing of data TPDUs

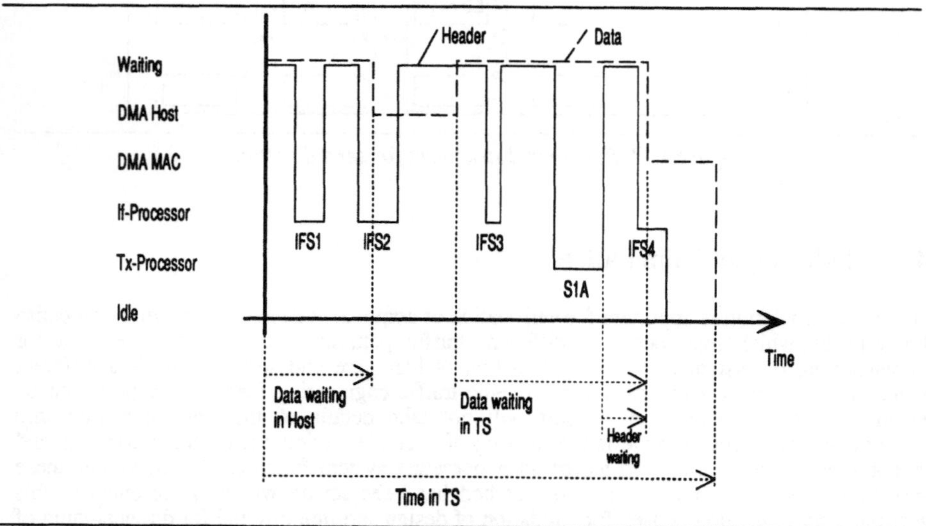

Figure 6: Processing steps of data TPDU in send direction

4.1 Combined Simulation for Performance Evaluation, Dimensioning and Verification

For a sufficiently accurate performance prediction and for verification, we applied a simulation method which combines elements of queuing theory with a functional simulation of the communication software and key performance parameters of the hardware. A detailed model (shown in Figure 7) was developed, where three different types of queues occur:

- Primary queues, where protocol units (data and acknowledgement packets) are waiting for their processing;
- Command queues, where the processors are exchanging information for memory references and for synchronization;
- Secondary queues, where currently blocked connections are waiting that the termination of the blocking condition permits further data transmission.

In this model, not only mechanisms which obviously influence performance are included, but also relevant information exchange mechanisms of the system.

In order to describe the interaction of the processors during the processing of a packet, a modification of Gantt Diagrams was used. In Figure 9, the regular processing sequence of a data packet in send direction is shown. The horizontal direction of the diagram represents the time scale, where the number of instruction cycles for the major program modules is given. Vertical arrows indicate the dependence of a program module on system resources and queues. Equivalent diagrams exist for the processing sequences of data packets in case of retransmission, for sending of acknowledgements and for the reception of data and acknowledgement packets.

In the simulation, system parameters and environmental parameters can be varied. The environmental parameters, originating from host and from the network, are packet type and probability density functions of packet length and arrival times. Scenarios originating from file transfer, scenarios with data strams and scenarios with frequent short packets are used. The following dimensioning of the system parameters avoids bottle-necks and provides high performance for various traffic patterns with moderate costs:

- Processor Speed 25 MHz;

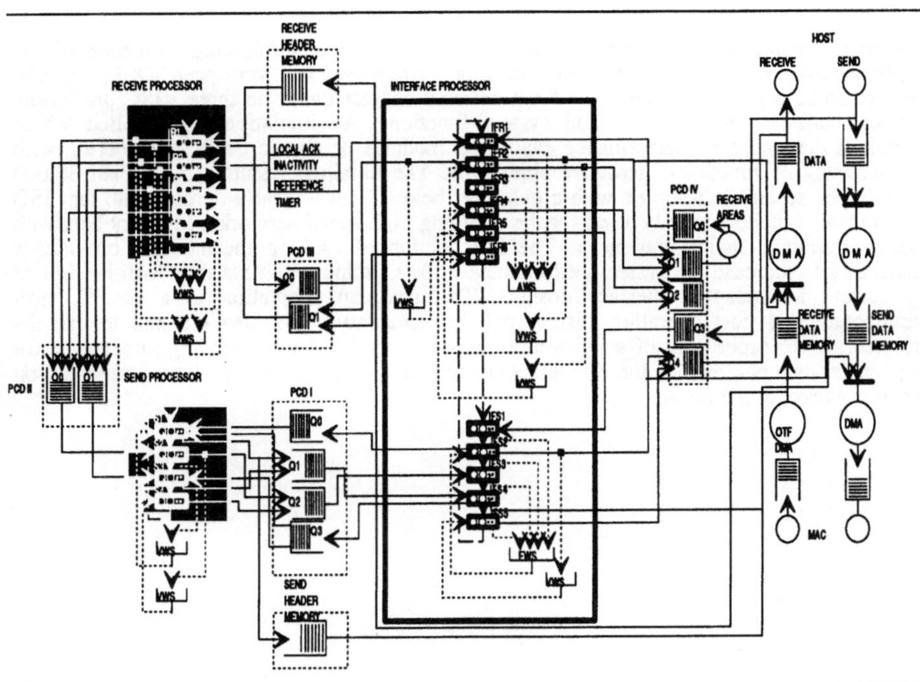

Figure 7: Enhanced System Model

- Size of Send Data Memory 4 Mbyte (dynamic sharing mechanism for all Connections);
- Size of Receive Data Memory 4 Mbyte (assignment of a fix amount of memory for each connection);
- Size of Header Memory 256 Kbyte;
- Process Coupling Device Memory 256 Kbyte;
- Size of table for unacknowledged packets 4000 packets (suitable for a high speed wide area connection with 500 Mbit/s and 60 ms round trip time);
- Maximum number of active connections: 512.

4.2 Results of Performance Evaluation

For processors with 25 MHz, a throughput of 32000 packets/s could be achieved simultaneous in send and in receive direction. If the maximum packet length is 1 KB, the throughput would reach 260 Mbit/s. As the processor load does not increase for larger packets, a maximal throughput of more than 2 Gbit/s could be obtained for packets with a length of 8 KB. However, this throughput requires a very high memory bandwith, which can be achieved only by large bus widths and a large amount of static memory, increasing the system costs significantly. A dimensioning of the memory bandwith suitable for FDDI networks will limit the maximum throughput to 100 Mbit/s, but maintains the capability to process large numbers of short packets (a scenario with higher importance).
The system provides very high packet rates in combination with very low delay. For a system load of 50%, a mean delay of 63 microseconds in send direction and of 67 μs in receive direction was evaluated. Figure 9 shows delay times for different system loads. The low delay is achieved by very short mean program cycle times, which are 12 μs for the send processor, 14 μs for the interface processor and 22 μs for the receive processor for a load of 50%. The differences in program cycle times indicate that the initial goal of a well balanced system is no exactly achieved. A modified scheduling and task distribution will allow further performance enhancement.

5 Conclusions and Outlook

The main intention of this project was to demonstrate the dominating influence of the implementation on the performance of a transport system even for "low-speed" OSI protocols. We presented a parallel architecture for a network adapter based on three RISC processors and on hardware for protocol and system functions. A simulation was applied which combines the statistical performance evaluation methods of classic traffic engineering with the accuracy of functional hardware simulation. The obtained results - more than 30.000 TPDUs per second full-duplex with a delay far below 1 ms - clearly demonstrate that ISO conformant protocols may be used for the evolving high speed networks. Memory bandwith still represents a major bottleneck. The introduction of caching mechanisms provides a possibility to increase the system performance further. Achievable data rates will be limited by current host/adapter interface designs. Therefore, an adaptation to a specific host architecture and host operating system will be necessary. It is also planned to use the architecture for processing of a lighweight protocol. As ATM gets growing importance for high-speed data communications, an adaptation of the architecture to cell-based transmission remains a task for the future.

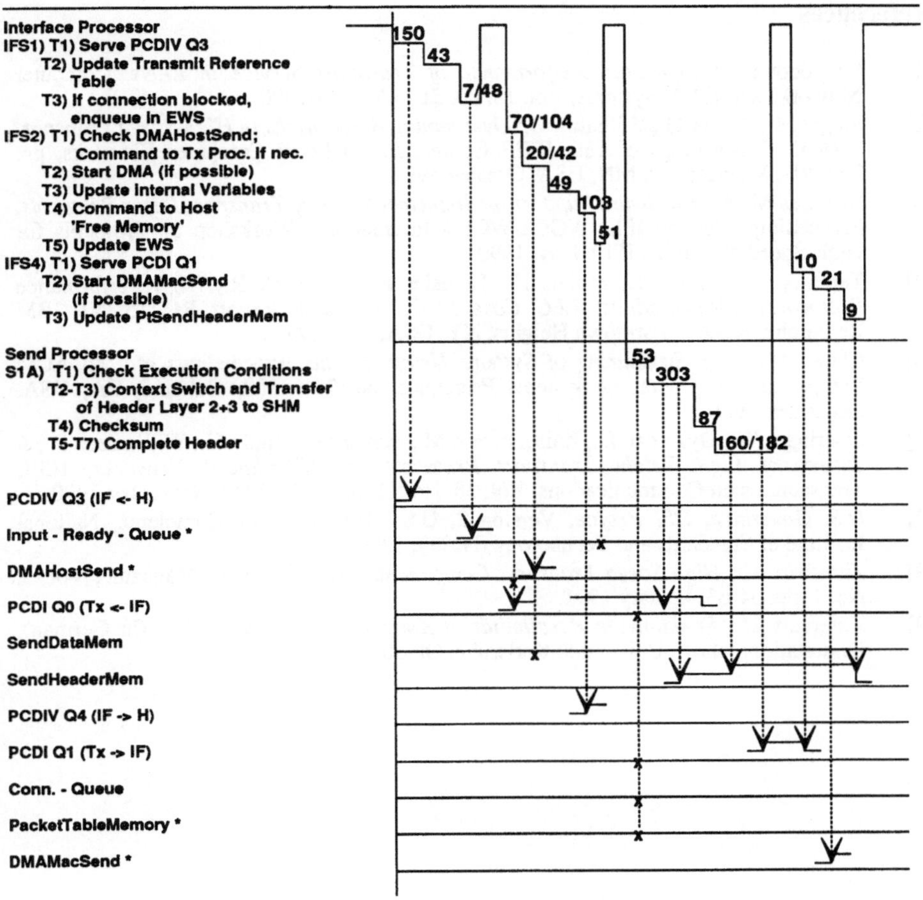

Interface Processor
IFS1) T1) Serve PCDIV Q3
T2) Update Transmit Reference Table
T3) If connection blocked, enqueue in EWS
IFS2) T1) Check DMAHostSend; Command to Tx Proc. if nec.
T2) Start DMA (if possible)
T3) Update Internal Variables
T4) Command to Host 'Free Memory'
T5) Update EWS
IFS4) T1) Serve PCDI Q1
T2) Start DMAMacSend (if possible)
T3) Update PtSendHeaderMem

Send Processor
S1A) T1) Check Execution Conditions
T2-T3) Context Switch and Transfer of Header Layer 2+3 to SHM
T4) Checksum
T5-T7) Complete Header

PCDIV Q3 (IF <- H)
Input - Ready - Queue *
DMAHostSend *
PCDI Q0 (Tx <- IF)
SendDataMem
SendHeaderMem
PCDIV Q4 (IF -> H)
PCDI Q1 (Tx -> IF)
Conn. - Queue
PacketTableMemory *
DMAMacSend *

150 43 7/48 70/104 20/42 49 103 51 53 303 87 160/182 10 21 9

Figure 8: Processing sequence for transmission of a data packet

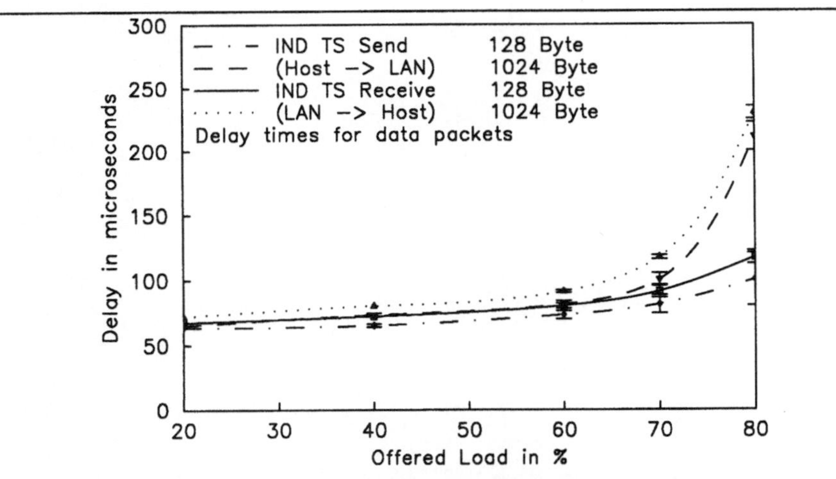

Figure 9: Delay for varying system load

References

[1] Svobodova L.; *Measured Performance of Transport Service in LANs,* Computer Networks and ISDN Systems, Vol. 18, pp. 31 - 45, 1989/1990.

[2] Siegel M., Rößler G., Williams M.; *Overcoming Bottle-necks in High-Speed Transport Systems*, Proceedings of 16th IEEE Conference on Local Computer Networks, pp. 399-407, Minneapolis, MN, USA, October 1991.

[3] Sidenius M. A.; *Hardware Support for Implementaiton of Transport Layer Protocols,* Proceedings, Second IFIP WG6.1/WG6.4 International Workshop on Protocols for High-Speed Networks, IFIP, Nov. 1990.

[4] Tantawy A., Schütt T., Meleis H., Lamaire R., Auerback R.; *High Performance Protocol Implementations: LLC Case Study,* Research Report RC 15.850, IBM Research Division, Yorktown Heights, NY, USA, June 1990,.

[5] Clark D.D.; *The Structuring of Systems Using Upcalls*, Proceedings of 10th ACM Symposium on Operating Systems Principles, pp.171 - 180, Oakland, CA, USA, December 1985.

[6] Doeringer W., Dykeman D., Kaiserswerth M., Meister B., Rudin H., Williamson R.; *A Survey of Light-Weight Transport Protocols for High-Speed Networks*, IEEE Transactions on Communications, Vol. 38, No. 11, pp. 2025-2039, November 1990.

[7] *U.S. Goverment OSI Profile*, Version 2, U.S. Department of Commerce, National Institute of Standards and Technology (NIST), 1989.

[8] Zitterbart M.; *High Speed Transport Components*, IEEE Network Magazine, Vol. 5, No. 1, pp. 54-63, January 1991.

[9] Zitterbart M.; *Funktionelle Parallelität in Kommunikationsprotokollen* (in German), Dissertationsschrift, Universität Karlsruhe, Oktober 1990.

Design Optimisation in Multichannel Lightwave Networks With Grouping Property

S.Z.Guo, B.Quatember
Institut für Informatik
University of Innsbruck
A-6020, Innsbruck, Austria.
E-mail: shanzeng.guo@uibk.ac.at

Abstract

A multichannel lightwave network with grouping property is proposed and studied as a possible architecture for realizing the vast capacity of multiuser lightwave networks subject to electro-optic speed constraints imposed at each access station. It consists of *m* station groups, in each group stations are connected by dual unidirectional WDM channels. Two specific unidirectional WDM channels are assigned to each station in a manner that allows any pair of stations in different groups to communicate directly, which forms an intergroup. A traffic flow control model is developed, and an optimal station grouping algorithm is presented based on this mathematical model which is used to formulate a traffic flow control optimization problem. The performance of this network is studied by discrete event computer simulation. The results clearly indicate that the proposed multichannel lightwave network exhibits a significant throughput performance improvement over the original (single channel) lightwave network.

1. Introduction

Photonic technology is now finding applications not only for point-to-point transport, but also in distributed, packet-oriented communication networks. Here, not only does photonics provide the bandwidth needed to handle high-speed packets, but it also provides the potential for distributed networks that offer an aggregate capacity orders of magnitude higher than any alternative technologies. Although optical fiber waveguides can transport information at the rate of several terabits per second (Tbps), this raw bandwidth can not be easily harnessed, because of the lower transmission and receiving rate of the digital electronic circuits. The Wavelength Division Multiplexing (WDM) technique was proposed to more efficiently utilize the large bandwidth of optical fibre by providing a number of parallel WDM channels whose individual transmission rates are governed by the electronic-optic components. This technology makes it possible for parallel communication in one optical fibre. Therefore, the development of high speed multichannel local and metropolitan lightwave networks is being motivated by new applications such as voice and video services, distributed databases and distributed computation. Adopting a multichannel architecture on an optical fibre LAN/MAN provides a double benefit. First, in considering the implementation of a high capacity LAN/MAN, single channel networks can be limited in their maximum throughput by the speed of the electronic components at the network nodes. The WDM approach, however, overcomes this problem because nodes are only required to operate at the individual channel transmission rate rather than the total network data rate. Secondly, such multichannel optical fibre LANs/MANs exhibit improved efficiency at high speeds.

Chlamtac and Gantz[1] presented an analysis of the performance of the multichannel network architecture. They have shown that for a given system bandwidth, the total system capacity will be increased by bandwidth division and parallel communications. A number of multiple access protocols for multichannel local area networks have been presented [2,3,4,5,6]. The early work concentrated on multichannel contention-based protocols which exhibited traffic throughput performance improvements over the single channel equivalents, but suffered the performance degradation under heavy traffic loading[2]. Later work on token passing protocols adopted a multichannel architecture using wavelength-division-multiplexing[3,4]. Again this approach shows a significant performance improvement over the single channel case under symmetric traffic loading. More recent work has focused on demand assignment protocols to provide efficient operation for mixed service traffic[5,6]. However, all these have two serious drawbacks. First, they require wavelength-agile transmitters or receivers; second, pretransmission co-ordination between two users wishing communication is required, thus the resulting system control introduces a significant pretransmission time penalty and involves a relatively complicated hardware(wavelength-agile interface). To avoid these two problems, multichannel multihop lightwave networks using a shuffle connectivity were recently proposed and studied in [9,10,11,12]. Although the concurrency increases in their network as the number of network interface units increases, it is also true that the channel efficiency decreases and propagation delay increases since the connected number of hops between two randomly selected nodes increases. We propose a new multichannel one hop lightwave network with grouping property, which exhibits better channel efficiency and a remarkable network throughput performance improvement, especially when the network traffic pattern is nonuniform. As a matter of fact, the metropolitan area network always has the nonuniform traffic pattern.

This paper is organized as follows. The basic multichannel lightwave network architecture is presented in section 2. In section 3, an optimal stations grouping strategy is presented. An optimal stations grouping algorithm is developed in section 4, and the performance of the new multichannel lightwave network with grouping property is studied in section 5. Section 6 concludes this paper.

2. Network Architecture Overview

Consider a metropolitan lightwave network which connects several organizations, such as corporations, universities, and government agencies, each of which would most likely be equipped with several computer systems(LANs or workstations), we call them the **stations.** Thus, if a given station in an organization wants to transmit a message on the network, this message would be most likely destined to one station in the same organization, and it is less likely to be destined to a station in another organization. That is, the network traffic is more likely within organizations, and less likely between organizations. Therefore, the network traffic is nonuniform traffic. In the view of these facts, it is reasonable to partition these stations into several groups, in each group stations are communicating through dedicated WDM channels. Among groups each station is connected to other dedicated WDM channels which are different from those in each group. Thus, the network traffic can be efficiently balanced among groups, so that the overall network performance can be improved. These motivate us to propose the new multichannel metropolitan lightwave network with grouping property using WDM channels.

Although the physical topology for the proposed multichannel lightwave network can take a variety of forms(tree, star, etc.), for the simplicity we consider a dual bus topology(though it is not at all practical in optical networks, busses can only support a few 10s of stations due to the power losses). Now let us consider a lightwave dual bus network with a number of stations N, labelled s_1 to s_N, and a limited number of unidirectional WDM channels λ_1, λ_3,..., λ_{2m+1} on one optical fiber(for example, bus A), and λ_2, λ_4,...,λ_{2m+2} on another optical fiber(for example, bus B). The two buses support unidirectional communication in opposite directions. The covered area of the network is metropolitan area that the standard DQDB[7] network covers. As mentioned above, the traffic in the network will be nonuniform distribution. According to these practical assumptions, we can partition N stations into m groups in terms of traffic flow control mechanism, each group may have different number of stations which may or may not be adjacent to each other at geographical locations. Figure 1 shows a configuration example with 4 groups and N stations. In each group, the stations are connected by dual unidirectional WDM channels which support unidirectional communication in opposite directions. Each station in the ***m*** groups is also directly connected to contra-flowing unidirectional WDM channels λ_{2m+1} and λ_{2m+2}, which forms the so called intergroup. Communication in each group and intergroup can obey the DQDB protocol as the configuration of each group and the intergroup can be the same as the configuration of DQDB network. Alternatively, CRMA[8] protocol can also be adopted in each group and intergroup. In group k, all stations are connected by dual unidirectional WDM channels λ_{2k} and λ_{2k-1}. The traffic among stations in group k is restricted to transmit only on WDM channel λ_{2k} and/or λ_{2k-1}. The communication traffic among groups is restricted to transmit on WDM channels λ_{2m+1} and/or λ_{2m+2}. Each station, therefore, requires access to four fixed WDM channels, so that four transmitters and receivers tuned to particular wavelengths are needed at each station.

In the designing of this type network to serve a specific metropolitan area, the network architect is immediately faced with one important design decision to be made, that is, given stations′ locations, how should the station groups be formed ? Next section gives an answer to this question. We will also see that the main advantage of using WDM here is that the stations grouping proposed can be changed easily by retuning transmitters and receivers if the traffic matrix changes.

3. Optimal stations grouping strategy

Our interest in studying networks of this type stems from the potential to balance the network traffic among groups. Thus, the next problem that we will consider in this paper is how N stations can be grouped in order to maximize the network performance ? Given the configuration of the multichannel metropolitan lightwave network and corresponding physical topology, the performance of the network is strongly dependent on the offered traffic and traffic patterns. The previous problem is then to become how to improve its overall performance by balancing the traffic over the entire networks. This can be done by optimal stations grouping in the multichannel metropolitan lightwave networks. The purpose of optimal stations grouping is to balance the traffic in each group in order to maximize the network performance.

A mathematical model based on these assumptions is developed in this paper. It is used to formulate a traffic flow control optimization problem to which a simple and efficient solution algorithm is developed.

3.1. Model Description

We consider a multichannel metropolitan lightwave network which consists of N stations (denoted as s_i, i=1,2,...,N) located at M ($M \geq 2$) physical clusters, each physical cluster may have different number (x_j) of stations with different percentage (p_i>50) intratraffic. Intratraffic is defined as the total traffic goes within the same physical cluster. Here we simplify the problem for the moment by assuming that each physical cluster has x_j number of stations with p (p>50) percent intratraffic. We denote each physical cluster as C_j (j=1,2,...,M): a set of stations in a physical cluster. An NxN traffic matrix $(\gamma_{ij})_{(i,j)\in NxN}$, specifying the rate (packets per second) at which traffic flows from source station s_i to destination station s_j, is given.

Our goal is to partition N stations into m ($N/2 > m \geq 2$) logical groups, such that the total traffic of the network is balanced among these ***m*** logical groups and the intergroup. We denote that G ={s_1, s_2,..., s_N} is the set of all stations in the network; G_k (k=1,2,...,m) is the set of stations in logical group k. It is obvious that $G_m \cup G_{m-1} \cup ... \cup G_1 = G$ and $G_m \cap G_{m-1} \cap ... \cap G_1 = \Phi$, where Φ is an empty set. The total amount of traffic offered to this network is then defined to be $\gamma = \sum_{S_i,S_j \in G} \gamma_{ij}$, where $\gamma_{ii}=0$.

γ_k and γ' are defined as the offered traffic to group k (k=1,2,...,m) and the offered traffic to the intergroup, respectively. Therefore

$$\gamma_k = \sum_{S_i,S_j \in G_k} \gamma_{ij}, \quad \text{where } k=1,2,3,\ldots, m. \tag{1}$$

$$\gamma' = \gamma - \sum_{k=1}^{m} \gamma_k = \gamma - \sum_{k=1}^{m} \sum_{S_i,S_j \in G_k} \gamma_{ij}, \quad \text{where } k=1,2,3,\ldots, m. \tag{2}$$

The equation (1) expresses the traffic flowing only in the group k. The equation (2) means that the total traffic between different stations in different groups is equal to the offered traffic to the intergroup.

3.2. Optimization problem

Our goal is to balance the traffic among groups and the intergroup in order to maximize the network performance. In the case of ideal, γ_k and γ' should be close to γ_{ideal} as possible as they can. γ_{ideal} is defined to be the average value of traffic in each group. That is,

$$\gamma_{ideal} = \frac{1}{m+1}\gamma = \frac{1}{m+1} \sum_{S_i,S_j \in G} \gamma_{ij} \tag{3}$$

Here, we define that $\varepsilon_k = | \gamma_k - \gamma_{ideal} |$ which is the deviation from the average traffic for k^{th} group, and $\varepsilon' = | \gamma' - \gamma_{ideal} |$ which is the deviation from the average traffic for the intergroup, The optimization problem can then be given as follows:

$$\text{minimize} \quad \varepsilon = \max\{ \varepsilon_1, \varepsilon_2, \varepsilon_3, \ldots, \varepsilon_{m-1}, \varepsilon_m, \varepsilon' \},$$

$$\text{subject to} \quad \gamma' = \gamma - \sum_{k=1}^{m} \gamma_k$$

$$G_m \cap G_{m-1} \cap \ldots \cap G_1 = \Phi,$$

$$\gamma_k > 0, \quad \text{where } k=1,2,3,\ldots,m.$$

The first constraint assures the equality between the total offered traffic in the intergroup and the total traffic flowing out of each groups, it also guarantees that $G=G_m \cup G_{m-1} \cup \ldots \cup G_1$. The second constraint assures that there is no common station among groups. The last constraint is traffic flow constraint, it guarantees that every group is not empty. Note that m may or may not be the optimum number of groups. The optimum number of groups for a given traffic matrix is discussed in section 5.

However, it is not intuitive to find a solution for above optimization problem, but we find that it is equivalent to the following optimization problem:

$$\text{minimize} \quad Tr = \max\{ \gamma_1, \gamma_2, \gamma_3, \ldots, \gamma_{m-1}, \gamma_m, \gamma' \},$$

$$\text{subject to} \quad \gamma' = \gamma - \sum_{k=1}^{m} \gamma_k$$

$$G_m \cap G_{m-1} \cap \ldots \cap G_1 = \Phi,$$

$$\gamma_k > 0, \quad \text{where } k=1,2,3,\ldots,m. \tag{4}$$

It is clear that this is a combinatorial optimization problem and intuitively difficult to solve. The solution space consists of all possible partitions of N stations into m groups. Therefore, we must consider approximation algorithm to solve it. Up to now, there exist several general approximation algorithms to be used in combinatorial optimization, such as simulated annealing and local search, but these algorithms are either time-consuming or of low quality. The following section presents an approximation grouping algorithm using problem-specific information, from which we will know how $\gamma_1, \gamma_2, \gamma_3, \ldots, \gamma_m$, and γ' are minimized and how optimal $G_1, G_2, G_3, \ldots, G_{m-1}$ and G_m are determined. We call this algorithm the genetic algorithm.

4. The Genetic Algorithm

First of all, we define that "$C_i \Rightarrow G_i$ " means that all stations in cluster C_i become the elements of group G_i. The genetic algorithm is described and discussed below.

1. *Initialization*: partitioning N stations into m groups according to the following approach, which guarantees that γ' has a minimum value.
   If $m < M$, then $C_i \Rightarrow G_i$ (i=1,2,...,m), and the rest clusters joint the logical group whose γ_k is smaller than γ_{ideal}.
   If $m > M$, then $C_i \Rightarrow G_i$ (i=1,2,...,M), and other groups are empty at the moment.
   If $m = M$, then $C_i \Rightarrow G_i$ (i=1,2,...,m).
   Note that one of our assumptions is that most part of traffic generated by stations in a same physical cluster goes within this physical cluster.
2. *Epoch Initiation*: $Tr = \max\{\gamma_1, \gamma_2, \gamma_3, \ldots, \gamma_{m-1}, \gamma_m, \gamma'\}$,
   If one of the groups is empty, do as following first :
   Two stations in a group that has the maximum traffic value (γ_i) move into the group that is empty (γ_j=0). Re-calculate these quantities γ_i, γ_j, γ'.
   Then goto step 2.
3. *Move/Exchange*:
   a. If ($Tr = \gamma'$) or ($Tr = \gamma_{ideal}$) goto step 4.
   b. If ($Tr \neq \gamma'$) or ($Tr \neq \gamma_{ideal}$) do as following:
      (1).*Move*: One station in a group that has a maximum traffic value (γ_i) moves into the group that has a minimum traffic value (γ_j). Re-calculate these quantities γ_i, γ_j, γ'. If new(Tr) – old(Tr) <0 , then acceptance and goto step 2; else rejection and goto step (2).
      (2).*Exchange*: One station in a group that has a maximum traffic value (γ_i) exchanges with another station in a group that has greater traffic value (γ_j). Re-calculate these quantities γ_i, γ_j, γ'. If new(Tr) – old(Tr) <0 , then acceptance and goto step 2; else rejection and goto step 4.
4. *Convergence Test*: If one of stopping conditions is satisfied, then HALT; else goto step 2.

The first step of the algorithm gives one approach to initialize the partitioning of N stations into m groups, which guarantees that γ' has minimum value. We prove this corollary as following.

Proof: We denote the different quantities corresponding to γ_i, γ_j, γ' as $\underline{\gamma}_i$, $\underline{\gamma}_j$, $\underline{\gamma}'$ after move/exchange operation. Assume that the traffic generated by every station is γ_{st}.

For $\boldsymbol{m \geq M}$, we have

(1). Following the initialization, if we move one station from G_i to G_j, then

$$\underline{\gamma}_i = \gamma_i - \gamma_{st} p, \qquad \underline{\gamma}_j = \gamma_j + (100-p)\Delta\gamma_{st}, \text{ where } 1 \geq \Delta \geq 0.$$

$$\underline{\gamma}' = \gamma - [(\sum_{k=1}^{m} \gamma_k - \gamma_i - \gamma_j) + \underline{\gamma}_i + \underline{\gamma}_j]$$

$$= \gamma - \sum_{k=1}^{m} \gamma_k + \gamma_i + \gamma_j - (\gamma_i - \gamma_{st}p) - (\gamma_j + (100-p)\Delta\gamma_{st})$$

$$= \gamma' + \gamma_{st}p - (100-p)\Delta\gamma_{st}$$

It is clear that $\underline{\gamma}' > \gamma'$. (note that when m=2, Δ=1; when $G_j=\Phi$, Δ=0)

(2). Following the initialisation, if we exchange two stations in groups G_i and G_j, then

$\underline{\gamma}_i = \gamma_i - \gamma_{st}p + (100-p)\Delta\gamma_{st}$. where $1 \geq \Delta > 0$.

$\underline{\gamma}_j = \gamma_j - \gamma_{st}p + (100-p)\Delta\gamma_{st}$

$$\underline{\gamma}' = \gamma - [(\sum_{k=1}^{m} \gamma_k - \gamma_i - \gamma_j) + \underline{\gamma}_i + \underline{\gamma}_j]$$

$$= \gamma - \sum_{k=1}^{m} \gamma_k + \gamma_i + \gamma_j - (\gamma_i - \gamma_{st}p + (100-p)\Delta\gamma_{st}) - (\gamma_j - \gamma_{st}p + (100-p)\Delta\gamma_{st})$$

$$= \gamma' + 2[\gamma_{st}p - (100-p)\Delta\gamma_{st}]$$

It is clear that $\underline{\gamma}' > \gamma'$ (note that when m=2, Δ=1)

For $\boldsymbol{m < M}$, we have

(3). Following the initialisation, if we move one station from G_i to G_j , then

$\underline{\gamma}_i = \gamma_i - \gamma_{st}p - (100-p)\gamma_{st}\theta$, where $1 > \theta \geq 0$

$\underline{\gamma}_j = \gamma_j + (100-p)\Delta\gamma_{st}$, where $1 \geq \Delta \geq 0$.

$$\underline{\gamma}' = \gamma - [(\sum_{k=1}^{m} \gamma_k - \gamma_i - \gamma_j) + \underline{\gamma}_i + \underline{\gamma}_j]$$

$$= \gamma - \sum_{k=1}^{m} \gamma_k + \gamma_i + \gamma_j - (\gamma_i - \gamma_{st}p - (100-p)\gamma_{st}\theta) - (\gamma_j + (100-p)\Delta\gamma_{st})$$

$$= \gamma' + \gamma_{st}p - (100-p)\Delta\gamma_{st} + (100-p)\gamma_{st}\theta$$

It is obvious that $\underline{\gamma}' > \gamma'$. (note that θ=0 if and only if G_i includes only one cluster)

(4). Following the initialisation, if we exchange two stations in groups G_i and G_j, then

$\underline{\gamma}_i = \gamma_i - \gamma_{st}p - (100-p)\beta_1\gamma_{st} + (100-p)\alpha_1\gamma_{st}$, where $1 \geq \alpha_1 > 0$, $1 > \beta_1 \geq 0$,

$\underline{\gamma}_j = \gamma_j - \gamma_{st}p - (100-p)\beta_2\gamma_{st} + (100-p)\alpha_2\gamma_{st}$, where $1 \geq \alpha_2 > 0$, $1 > \beta_2 \geq 0$,

$$\underline{\gamma}' = \gamma - [(\sum_{k=1}^{m} \gamma_k - \gamma_i - \gamma_j) + \underline{\gamma}_i + \underline{\gamma}_j] = \gamma - \sum_{k=1}^{m} \gamma_k + \gamma_i + \gamma_j - [\gamma_i - \gamma_{st}p - (100-p)\beta_1\gamma_{st}$$

$$+ (100-p)\alpha_1\gamma_{st}] - [\gamma_j - \gamma_{st}p - (100-p)\beta_2\gamma_{st} + (100-p)\alpha_2\gamma_{st}]$$

$$= \gamma' + 2\gamma_{st}p - (100-p)(\alpha_1+\alpha_2)\gamma_{st} + (100-p)(\beta_2+\beta_1)\gamma_{st}$$

It is clear that $\underline{\gamma}' > \gamma'$.

Thus, we can say that γ' has the minimum value at the initialisation. ♦

The second step of the algorithm gives a new "epoch" to generate new offspring from the existing partitioning. Note that these moving actions in second step guarantee that $\gamma_k > 0$, We call the new accepted partition the offspring of the former partition. The third step of the algorithm generates a new offspring through move/exchange mechanism which reduces the higher traffic value γ_i and increases the lower traffic value γ_j. γ' changes either higher or lower, which depends upon a specific *move/exchange* operation. This is the reason that initialisation of the algorithm should guarantee that γ' has the minimum value. Each offspring inherits the groups in which the traffic value is not great and not small. The fourth step of the algorithm indicates the convergence requirements. The stopping conditions are a): Tr = γ', b): Tr = γ_{ideal}

and c): new(Tr) – old(Tr) ≥ 0. If any one of them is satisfied, the convergence occurs. It is obvious that each "offspring" is asymptotic to the convergence.

It is clear now that the optimal station grouping strategy is easily determined by solving traffic flow balancing problem according to this algorithm. It is noticed that each station performs the move/exchange operation just for once at most, we can then estimate the computation time of the algorithm at O(N). Again, note that this algorithm is used to determine the optimal station grouping for a given number of groups, it can not determine the optimum number of groups, which is discussed in the following section.

5. Performance

The performance of the multichannel metropolitan lightwave network based on DQDB protocol was investigated by discrete event computer simulation. The network we simulate consists of 24 stations, where adjacent stations are separated by 500 meters. The total length of the end-to-end physical bus is 12 km. Although this separation may seem to be small for a metropolitan area network, the purpose of this study is to show the throughput performance merits of the proposed multichannel metropolitan lightwave dual bus network over the conventional (single channel) dual bus network. And, since it is expected that as the number of stations increases and the separation becomes large, the difference between the proposed multichannel lightwave dual bus network and the conventional (single channel) dual bus network will increase, then it suffices to show that at such a small network the proposed multichannel metropolitan lightwave dual bus network performs much better than the conventional (single channel) dual bus network. Thus, for the comparison purposes, this small network is enough to establish our conclusions.

Stations are assumed to be equipped with finite buffers(only ten buffers are available in our simulation), and the message generation process at each station is Possion. The given traffic matrix indicates that $p(50<p<100)$ percent traffic generated by each station is uniformly destined to $x(1<x<24)$ stations, and $(100-p)$ percent traffic is uniformly destined to other stations. Another characteristic of the given traffic matrix is $\gamma_{ij}=\gamma_{ji}$. That is to say, the amount of traffic from station s_i to station s_j is equal to that from station s_j to station s_i. The system is assumed to be symmetric in all aspects including the message generation rate and the probability of being a destination to a message. The performance measures we use here are the average message delay and network throughput. The average message delay is defined as average queuing delay at source station, and the network throughput is defined as the number of messages transmitted per slot interval. The message length is assumed to be equal to the size of a slot. For the comparison purposes, it is quite enough to establish our conclusions about the network throughput and average message delay under different number of groups m. "m=1" here represents the conventional (single channel) dual bus network.

In the first example in Figure 2, the delay-throughput characteristics with p=75 and x=5 is displayed. Two things can be noticed from Figure 2. First, the network throughput of the proposed multichannel lightwave dual bus network is always larger than that of the conventional dual bus network. When m increases until four, the network throughput increases fast while maintaining lower average message delay; as m increases from 4 to 6, the network throughput decreases. Therefore, the optimal number of groups is four, which provides much better network throughput performance. Second, as compared with "m=1", "m=4" exhibits a remarkable network throughput performance improvement while maintaining the lower average message delay. That is, for the given traffic matrix with p=75 and x=5, the proposed multichannel lightwave dual bus network with 4 groups outperforms the conventional (single channel) dual bus network.

Figure 3 illustrates the average message delay versus the total arrival rate with p=75 and x=5. Note that the total message arrival rate refers to user requests, not to successful transmissions, and hence can not be called network throughput. The two quantities differ because of the rejection of the message transmission requests when the buffers are full. This figure shows that when the total arrival rate increases, the average message delay is becoming lower and lower when m increases from 1 to 4; From m=4 to 6, this performance suffers degradation, especially under heavy traffic loading. Again, the best number of groups is four, which provides much better average message delay performance as the total arrival rate increases.

Figure 4 and Figure 5 display the simulation results in the case of p=75 and x=7. Again, Two things can be noticed from Figure 4. First, the network throughput of the proposed multichannel lightwave dual bus network is always larger than that of the conventional dual bus network. When G increases until three, the network throughput increase fast while maintaining lower average message delay; When m increases from 3 to 6, network throughput decreases. Therefore, the optimum number of groups is three, which provides much better network throughput performance. Second, as compared with "m=1", "m=3" exhibits a remarkable network throughput performance improvement while maintaining the lower average message delay. Figure 5 shows the similar result as Figure 3.

It can also be observed from figure 2 and figure 4 that although the efficiency of the multichannel lightwave dual bus network is higher than that of the conventional dual bus network, a point is reached where the multichannel lightwave dual bus network exhibits the best performance. This point determines the optimum number of groups for a given traffic matrix. The optimum number of groups is dependent on the specific network conditions, i.e. the given traffic matrix. For example, the optimum number of groups is four for the given traffic matrix with p=75 and x=5; and the optimum number of groups is three for the given traffic matrix with p=75 and x=7.

All these observations are attributed to three factors:

1). First, the traffic-handling capacity is increased in the proposed multichannel network, such that the aggregated throughput performance is improved.

2). Second, the heavy traffic loading in the dual bus network is decomposed into light traffic loading in multichannel lightwave dual bus network, such that the average message delay performance of the multichannel lightwave dual bus network is better than that of the conventional dual bus network.

3). Finally, for a given traffic matrix, we are able to find one optimal stations grouping with the optimum number of groups.

6. Conclusion

This paper has presented a new multichannel metropolitan lightwave network with grouping property. A traffic flow control model is developed, and an optimal station grouping algorithm is presented based on this mathematical model which is used to formulate a traffic flow control optimization problem. Based on this algorithm, for a given number of groups and the given traffic matrix, the optimal stations grouping can be found. And also, for a given traffic matrix, the optimum number of groups can be found based on the network performance. The main advantage of using WDM here is that the stations grouping proposed can be changed easily by retuning transmitters and receivers if the traffic matrix changes.

The performance of this network is studied by discrete event computer simulation. The results clearly indicate that the proposed multichannel metropolitan lightwave network with optimum number of groups exhibits a remarkable traffic throughput performance improvement over the conventional (single channel) lightwave network. Our results also show that for a given traffic matrix the optimal station grouping with the optimum number of groups can also provide significant reduction in average message delay over the conventional (single channel) lightwave network.

Acknowledgements

We are indebted to Prof.Dr.R.Albrecht for many helps. Guo gratefully acknowledges the Austria academic exchange service for the financial support.

REFERENCES

1. I.Chlamtac and A. Gantz "Design and analysis of very high speed network architectures" *IEEE Trans. on Comm.* vol.36, No.3, 1988. pp252-262.
2. Marsan,M.A., and Raffinella,D. " Multichannel Local Area Network Protocols " *IEEE Journal on selected areas in Communications*. SAC-1, 5, 1983, pp885-897
3. Senior,J.M., et al "Performance investigation of a token passing access protocol for a multichannel optical fibre LAN" *Computer Communications*, vol.11. 1988. pp304-312.
4. Cusworth,S.D., et al " Wavelenght division multiple access on a high-speed optical fibre LAN" *Computer Networks and ISDN systems*, vol 18. 1990, pp323-333.
5. H.W.Lee. "Protocols for multichannel optical fibre LAN using passive star topology" *Electronics Letter*, vol. 27. 1991, pp1506-1507.
6. Senior J.M, Mcveigh J.M. et al "Multichannel slot reservation protocol for use on WDM optical fibre LAN" *Electronics Letter*, vol. 27. 1991, pp1875-1876.
7. IEEE Standard p802.6: Distributed Queue Dual Bus(DQDB) Metropolitan Area Network(MAN), December 1990.
8. M.Mehdi Nassehi " CRMA: An access scheme for high-speed LANs and MANs " *IEEE ICC'90.*
9. A.S.Acampora and Mark J. Karol "An overview of lightwave packet networks" *IEEE Network*, vol.03, pp29-41, 1989.
10. Labourdette, J,F.P, Acampora,A.S. "Logically rearangable multihop lightwave networks" *IEEE Trans. on Communications,* vol.39, pp1223-30, 1991.
11. J.A.Bannister, L.Fratta, and M.Gerla "Designing Metropolitan Area Network for High Performance Applications" *Computer networks and ISDN systems*, vol.20,pp223-230,1990.
12. J.A.Bannister "The Wavelength-Division Optical Network: Architectures,Topologoes and Protocols" Ph.D theis, Dept. of computer science, University of California, Los Angeles.

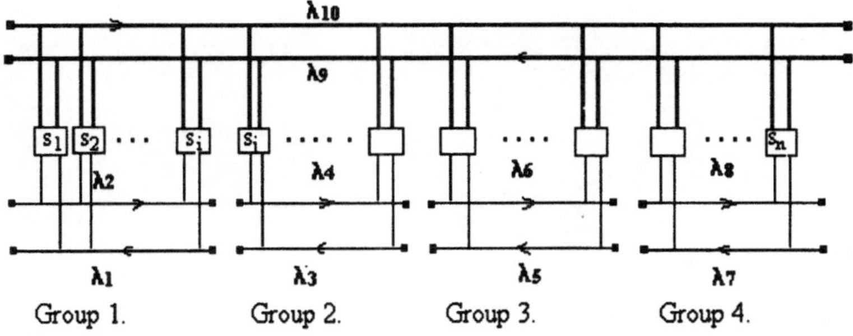

Figure 1. Multichannel Lightwave Network Configuration
With 4 groups and N stations

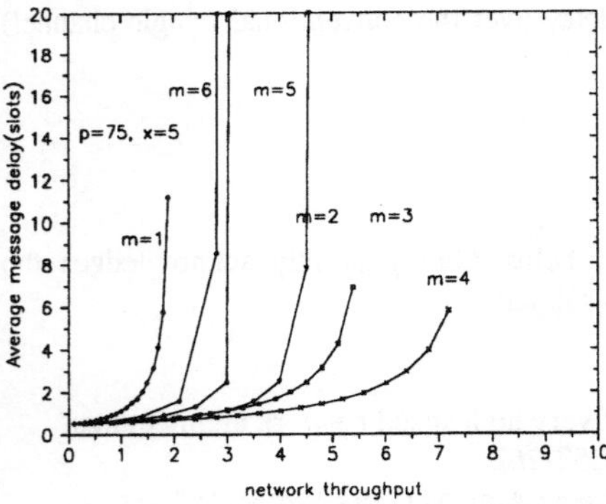

Fig.2. The delay–throughput characteristics

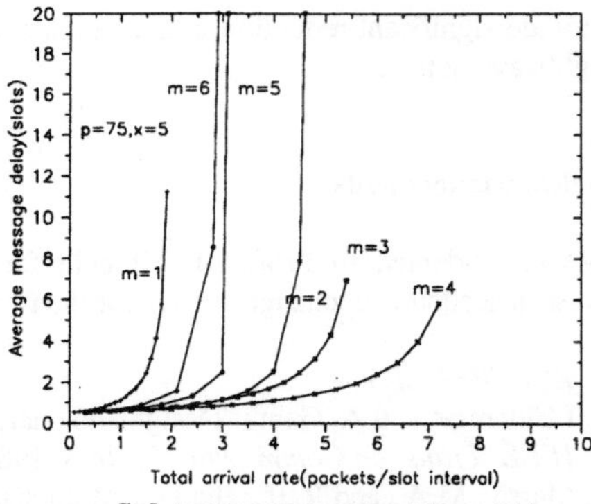

Fig.3. Average message access delay v.s total arrival rate

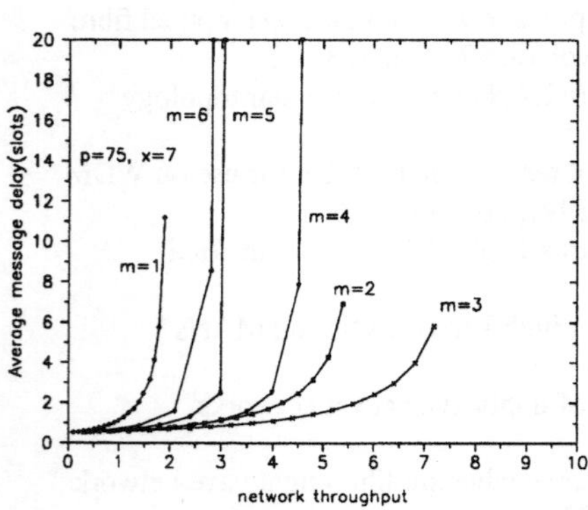

Fig.4. The delay–throughput characteristics

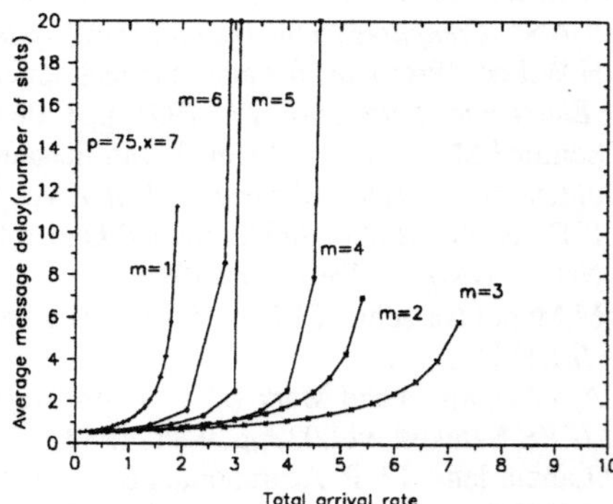

Fig.5. Average message access delay v.s total arrival rate

The RACE II Project *EuroBridge*: An Overview

Bernd Heinrichs, Kai Jakobs, Klaus Lenssen, Wilko Reinhardt
Technical University of Aachen (RWTH Aachen)
Computer Science Dept., Informatik IV
Ahornstr. 55, 52056 Aachen, Germany,
Tel.: +49 241 80-21437, FAX: -21429
email: heibe|jakobs|klaus|wilko@informatik.rwth-aachen.de

Throughout the last years, communication requirements of distributed applications have changed dramatically. Multimedia applications, for instance, impose a variety of different, maybe even conflicting demands: On the one hand, real-time data like audio or video have to be transmitted. These reveal high bandwidth requirements, but may accept a small number of transmission errors. On the other hand, transmission of possibly extreme large files may well tolerate some delay but requires an error free transmission.

Currently, broadband networks like FDDI, DQDB, ATM etc. are or will soon be available off the shelf, providing (almost) sufficient bandwidth (100 - 600 MBit/s), at the same time offering extremely low error rates.

By now it is widely accepted that transport and network layer are the major bottleneck of both, performance and functionality. Furthermore, deficiencies with respect to functionality may be identified for application, presentation and session layer.

The main objective of the RACE II project EuroBridge (R2008) is to accelerate development of multimedia and multipoint applications by providing application developers with the EuroBridge Service Platform. This platform will provide a uniform interface to a number of communication services (including file transfer, database access and electronic mail as well as video conferencing). It will thus enable applications to run on a variety of broadband networks. All services provided are based on international standards, e.g. FTAM, RDA or MHS.

Application layer services make use of the EuroBridge presentation platform. This platform provides implementations of a variety of both, commonly used and new protocols, including the ISODE implementation of the OSI protocols, TCP/IP, ST II, HSTP and a dedicated stack for interactive real time transmissions. Ethernet, FDDI, ISDN, DQDB and ATM are the available test networks.

An application using the EuroBridge platforms has to specify its communication requirements. In accordance with these requirements the presentation platform selects a suitable combination of protocols and network(s).

Efficient protocol implementation is another issue. Using a petri net based description technique we are able to identify protocol inherent parallelism. The method is also used to create a modular specification and implementation. It is demonstrated with a flexible and modular HSTP implementation.

To test the EuroBridge service platform the project major efforts go into building and enhancing multimedia applications. These applications are a video conference system, a sign language training system and a tourist information system. The latter two can be considered as distributed multimedia database systems. These applications will demonstrate the efficiency of the EuroBridge service platform.

EuroBridge started in January 1992 and will run until December 1994, with a total effort of 937 man-months. Ten organisations, based in five countries, participate in the project: Ericsson Eurolab Deutschand (prime contractor, Germany), DeTeBerkom (Germany), Technical University of Aachen (Germany), Broadcom Eireann Research (Ireland), Circuits Test & Systems (CTS, Ireland), Systems and Software Engineering (SSE, Ireland), Intracom (Greece), Technical Research Centre of Finland (VTT, Finland) and CET (Portugal).

Adaptive QOS driven Communication Architecture

Bernd Heinrichs, Wilko Reinhardt

Technical University of Aachen (RWTH Aachen), Dept. of Computer Science (Informatik IV)
52056 Aachen, Germany, Tel.: +49 241 80-21437, FAX: -21429
email: heibelwilko@informatik.rwth-aachen.de

Abstract

The RACE II project EuroBridge has introduced a concept for a flexible and adaptive Quality of Service (QOS) driven communication architecture. This paper will give an overview on the protocol structures within EuroBridge and will highlight the protocol selection mechanism which identifies suitable combinations of protocols in accordance to the requested QOS from the application. The main area will be the mapping from the demands onto the protocols that are available in the EuroBridge project. Furthermore we describe the integration of XTP into the platform and recommend a new distributed jitter control mechanism. The EuroBridge XTP implementation provides a modular design of the various protocol features. In accordance to the demands specified by the selector, only those parts are activated that are needed to fulfil the desired functionality.

1. Introduction

Multimedia applications have raised new demands in computer environments - especially in the communication sector - due to the complexity and diversity of the handled data. Different and even contrary requirements have to be fulfilled. On the one hand isochronous data streams from live video and audio signals request high bandwidth (approximately up to 150 MBit/s), in-time delivery of the data and a low delay variation (jitter). Isochronous media can accept a small amount of bit errors or packet loss depending on the used compression scheme. On the other hand asynchronous streams resulting from the transfer of still images or textual documents need a reliable transmission but can accept small delays. Beside the evolution in the application area high performance networks with increasing transmission capacities and decreasing error rates have come up in parallel (e.g. ATM, FDDI, DQDB, etc.).

The development in these two areas leads to a performance gap within the common protocol structure. Reasons for the gap are insufficient protocol functionality for multimedia data streams, inflexible protocol architectures and inefficient implementations of protocols. Within today's protocols func-

Work described in this paper has been partly funded by the RACE II project EuroBridge. The EuroBridge Consortium consists of the following members: Ericsson EUROLAB, D; RWTH Aachen, D; Teles, D; De-Te-Bercom, D; Broadcom, IRL; CTS, IRL; CET, P; Intracom, GR; VTT, FIN; SSE, IRL.

tional characteristics such as bandwidth reservation, synchronization of multiple related data streams, sufficient multicast mechanisms and flexible error handling routines are missing. Protocols from the ISO and Internet communities are not designed to provide an universal support of Quality of Service (QOS) throughout all layers. They are designed for unreliable low bandwidth networks. E.g. if the transmission media is very reliable (fibre optic media provide an error rate lower than 10^{-12}) error correction mechanisms can be switched off or at least the effort could be reduced. It is well understood that not a single static protocol stack is able to support the adaptation from the application to the network efficiently, because a static stack is very inflexible in handling data streams with opposite demands and much protocol overhead is needed to support the different functions.

This paper introduces the EuroBridge approach to bridge the gap between the various demands of multimedia applications and the features provided by broadband networks. In chapter 2 a brief introduction to various works on QOS semantics is given. Chapter 3 provides describes the EuroBridge QOS driven architecture and within chapter 4 we explain necessary enhancements of XTP which is an evident part of our communication structure.

2. Quality of Service Semantics

With respect to the various demands from multimedia data streams a sufficient support of QOS becomes more and more evident. New QOS concepts have to be invoked since the best effort concept defined by OSI is not suitable to support the new demands. The weakest points of this concept are:

- The service user has no guarantees that the requested QOS parameters will be respected and maintained by the service provider. The service provider is able to reduce the requested value during the connection establishment phase.
- Changes of the requested values are not reported to the service user, neither during the connection establishment phase nor during the data transfer phase.
- The service provider does not monitor the accepted QOS values, neither whether itself supports the negotiated values nor whether the service user keep to it.
- The service user has no possibility to specify a limit value that it could accept.
- The ISO connection oriented transport service allows only the specification of QOS parameters in the connection establishment phase. The agreed values are applied for the whole lifetime of the connection. That implies that during the data transfer phase a re-negotiation of the QOS parameters is impossible.
- A general concept is missing that allows a unique handling of user defined QOS throughout all layers. Each layer and each protocol has its own QOS semantics and syntax.

Several proposals have been made to provide more sufficient concepts of providing QOS [Dant 92, Ferr 90, ZST 93, TFH 93, HeRe 93]. To solve the problems the Esprit project OSI 95 [Dant 92] introduces three different semantic types of QOS parameters: compulsory, threshold and maximal quality QOS values. Compulsory values will be monitored during the data transfer phase of a connection and the service provider will abort the connection immediately if the negotiated value can not be provided any more. The service provider is not allowed to reduce the parameter within the QOS negotiation phase but it is allowed to increase the value up to a bound that is specified by the calling service user. With the definition of a threshold QOS the service provider informs the service user that the negotiated value can not be achieved any more, but it will not abort the connection. When a maximal quality value has been agreed, the service provider will monitor this parameter and avoid occurence of interactions with the service users that would give rise to a violation of the selected value. Both compulsory or the threshold QOS oblige the service provider to monitor the performance values during the data transfer phase. In comparison with the OSI best effort concept the service user can rely on the negotiated values and must not monitor them. If the agreed values are not supported any more the service user will be informed (threshold QOS) or the connection will be aborted (compulsory).

Ferrari [Ferr 90] introduced an additional guaranteed QOS semantic which has a rather strong legal flavor. When a service provider guarantees a performance value to the service user, it commits itself to providing that performance and to paying a penalty if the negotiated value can not be achieved. On the other hand the service user is obliged not to exceed the negotiated value.

3. The EuroBridge Communication Platform

3.1 Protocol Architecture

It is a common view that not only one static protocol stack is able to fulfil all the different requirements from multimedia applications. Solutions are several protocol stacks in parallel, each fulfilling a limited set of QOS requirements or one protocol stack using highly flexible and adaptive protocols. The latter solution provides configurable protocols which are able to fulfil one or a few special QOS parameters. EuroBridge introduces a flexible QOS driven architecture, called the **channel provider** (Fig. 3.1) which is based on both strategies; various pre-configured protocol stacks and highly flexible and adaptive protocols. On one hand several protocol stacks are available each providing different performance and functional characteristics. On the other hand we are using programmable protocols like XTP (Xpress Transfer Protocol) [XTP 92]. Within the channel provider the EuroBridge architecture allows the transparent access to several network types. This includes ATM, DQDB, Ethernet, FDDI, and N-ISDN. At the network and transport level TCP/IP, XTP, OSI TP0 and STII are supported. At the upper layers ISODE and a dedicated multimedia presentation and session providing synchronization facilities are integrated. In addition a real time stack provides the direct access to FDDI and ISDN. Fig. 3.2 depicts the available protocol combinations.

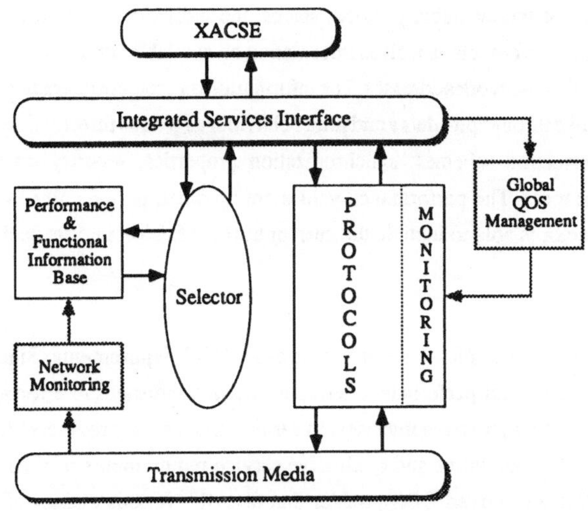

Fig. 3.1: Channel Provider Architecture

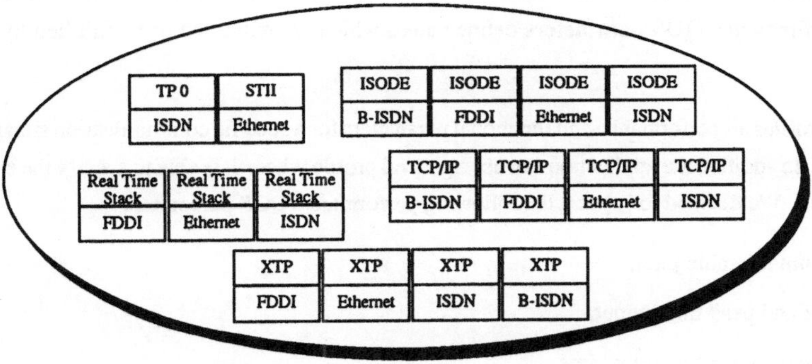

Fig. 3.2: Protocol stacks supported by the EuroBridge Channel Provider

The application layer protocols access the underlying protocols via the **integrated service interface** (ISI). This interface hides the diversity of service calls of the different stacks. Thus the application has a general view of the underlying communication system. At the connection establishment phase the user has to specify the exact QOS demands. The ISI is called with the required QOS and other parameters. After the activation of the ISI it calls the **selector entity** which is responsible for the selection of a suitable stack in accordance to the requirements defined by the applications. The selector entity retrieves all necessary information for the selection process from the **performance and functional information base** (PFIB). This data base stores all information about the performance and functional characteristics of the available protocol stacks, the individual structure of the service primitives from the different protocols as well as information on available protocol elements on most frequented receivers and their network addresses. The information on protocol characteristics includes performance properties like throughput, delay and jitter behaviour as well as information on functional properties e.g. error correction schemes, synchronization properties, security mechanisms and conference management tools. The performance values are up-dated periodically from a network monitor. By this the selector is able to include the current traffic situation into its decision.

3.2 QOS in EuroBridge

Most existing applications are not able to specify their exact QOS requirements. Since the precise information on the functional and performance requirements are indispensable for a flexible and adaptive communication system, we have interviewed various application providers, developers and projects to provide us with quantitative and qualitative service requirements of their applications. From the results [ReTi93] we derived QOS profiles that describe various classes of related QOS requirements. The user selects a profile that fits best the actual requirements. Generally we distinguish between two types of QOS, functional and performance types. **Functional QOS parameters** are concerned with features that provide services to support usefull mechanisms for the data flow throughout the various layers. These mechanisms help to handle the data streams in an efficient manner. **Performance QOS parameters** define values which are requested to be fulfilled by the system.

Within the profiles all performance and functional parameters for a specific communication situation are specified. In addition the application can use a general profile where it is able to specify the exact QOS demands. We decided to support the following performance QOS parameters:

- maximum tolerable jitter,
- average and peak throughput,
- maximum connection setup time,
- transmission delay and
- acceptable error rate (considering the tolerable number of consecutive paket losses).

The functional parameters we are supporting are:

- the selection of different error correction and flow control schemes,
- the selection of different priority values to dicriminate among user data of different importance,
- the support of multipeer communications with different level of reliability and
- intra as well as inter data stream synchronisation.

EuroBridge provides a practical solution for a more sopisticated QOS support. The diversity of protocols leads to different QOS semantics. EuroBridge's XTP and OSI TP0 implementations support the threshold QOS. The protocols have been enhanced to provide an internal monitoring of the QOS parameters. Monitored parameters are throughput, transmission delay and jitter within XTP and throughput and delay within TP0/ISDN. The service user will be informed if a certain QOS value can not be achieved any more. In this case the service user must decide whether it will keep the connection with a reduced quality or if the connection should be aborted. The real time stack as well as TCP do not allow any QOS negotiation. Within the real time stack only the number of ISDN B-channels can be fixed at connection set-up time and may be changed during the data transfer phase.

An important item within future QOS concepts is the re-negotiation of QOS parameters. The service user may wish to in- or decrease the quality of an existing connection. If e.g. the transmission quality of a colour video during a video conference is not sufficient, the user likes to switch to a black and white transmission or totally switch off the video information. In this case the parameters of the connection can be decreased. If however the user requests for colour video instead of an agreed black and white transmission the QOS values of the underlying connection have to be increased. To provide the user with the flexibility to change the demands during a session and not to request values in advance that fits under all circumstances a mechanism is needed that allows to re-negotiate the parameters of a connection. The EuroBridge channel provider offers the 'modify'-function for a re-negotiation. First it tries to re-negotiate the existing connection. If this is not accepted it consults the selector entity to find a more suitable protocol stack. In the case that this procedure is successful the new connection will be established and the user data streams are switched to it, otherwise the user will be informed that a modification of the connection is not possible. In this case the user has to decide to abort the old connection or to keep with the original quality.

3.3 Mapping the QOS demands onto a suitable protocol stack

The selector follows a flexible strategy in its decision. On the first view it might be easy to find a suitable stack since we are using QOS profiles. In this case just a static mapping from the profile onto a fixed stack might be sufficient. But if the parameters are free defined from the application an algorithm is needed, that provides the decision process. In the following this algorithm will be introduced.

The selector entity needs a data storage where all functional and performance characteristics of the installed protocol stacks are stored. The performance and functional information base (PFIB) contains information on the throughput, jitter and delay behaviour, error control and recovery mechanisms, residual error rate, synchronization, priority, resource reservation etc. The performance values are based on measurements performed by the monitor and are updated at fixed time intervals. These measurements take the complete protocol stack into consideration. Therefore the selector considers values which are more realistic than the nominal values defined by the network standards.

In the case that the requested QOS parameters can not be supported, the user or the application requires detailed information on the reasons, so that within the next connection setup request the requirements could be decreased. In our opinion only the user is able to decide whether reduced QOS are accepted. Therefore the selector returns a complete description of the services and values that are not fulfilled.

The first step of the selection process is to identify which protocol stacks are able to support the requested performance parameters. The analysis of the EuroBridge QOS profiles [McGl 93] leads to the conclusion that throughput is the most important parameter. The values of the throughput varies extremely from 56 KBit/s (Audio transmission with telephone quality) up to nearly 150 MBit/s for the transmission of full sized video with 30 Frames/s. Therefore the selector first checks which of the available pre-defined protocol stacks provides the desired bandwidth. The second decision is whether the desired acceptable error rate and transmission delay is supported. If none of the protocol stacks is able to support all values the selector returns the error message '*unable to support performance parameter(s): <list of not supported parameters>*' and stops the selection process.

The first decision phase has decided which of the available protocol stacks is able to support the performance requirements. The next step is to select which of the pre-selected stacks supports the functional requirements. The selector checks step by step in the listed order, if multicast, synchronization, QOS types (best effort, threshold, guaranteed), security or priority is requested. If not all functional QOS are supported by any of the pre-selected protocol stacks, the selector returns the message '*performance parameters suitable, but unable to support the functional parameter(s): <list of not supported parameters>.*'

A more detailed decision is requested, if more than one protocol is suitable. In this case a ranking of the stacks supports the final decision. The ranking values should take into consideration the various stream types. A video stream has a different ranking than an audio or data stream. The selector chose from the pre-selected stacks, that one with the highest ranking number.

4 XTP - A configurable protocol for versatile QOS support

Besides a flexible architecture configurable protocols should be used to achieve high flexibility and performance for the applications. These protocol capabilities are mainly dependent on the following two factors: syntax and semantics. The protocol syntax influences the complexity of parsing and generating of messages. It has an effect on the feasibility and cost of hardware implementations. Protocol designers should omit reverse parsing, backpatching of headers and variable length formats. The protocol semantics controls the effectiveness of a protocol in various environments, especially in interconnected scenarios. Adequate sequence numbers are very crucial as well as the number of end-to-end handshakes for data transfers.

One main disadvantage of most protocols is their static behavior. After setting up a connection the protocols are rather inflexible in adapting to changed network or application conditions. We think more adaptive protocols should be configured which are able to recognize suggestions from users to change the quality of service or to accomodate altered network situations. One possible candidate is XTP.

4.1 Brief Survey of XTP

XTP is a high performance protocol with the primary goal of hardware realization as a VLSI chip set. It is targeted at high performance distributed systems having real-time characteristics based on high speed LANs. One of the main advantages of XTP is that it covers the functionality of network and transport layer protocols. Thereby XTP is able, in contrast to standard transport protocols, to recognize and influence the phenomenon of congestion in high speed interconnected networks. Congestion is usually defined as a condition in the network where an increase in traffic load causes a decrease in throughput; other consequences are long transfer delays, packet losses, blocking of the whole network or breaking down of end user connections. The experience from years of running ARPA Internet shows that congestion has been the major source of vulnerability in network service. The best point at which to operate the network is to the left of the vertical line in fig. 4.1.

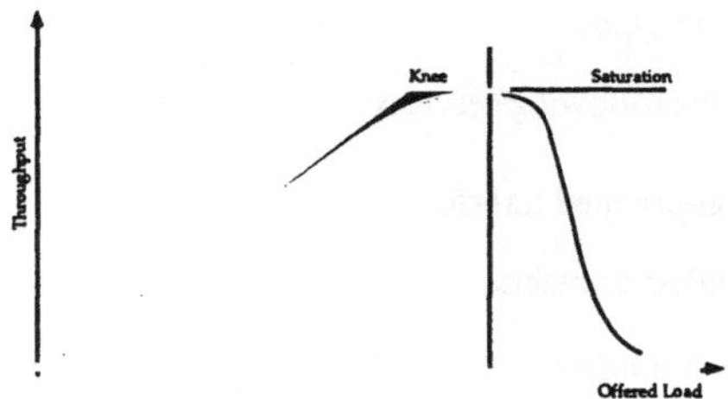

Fig. 4.1: Network Congestion

The problems in the handling of congestion arise from the dynamic variation of throughput requirements and relatively long reaction times. Especially in high speed packet switching networks, data from all sources are statistically multiplexed on shared network resources; therefore the moment-to-moment throughput requirement often varies extremely. Mechanisms for handling congestion may be divided into congestion recovery and congestion avoidance. Congestion avoidance is preventive in nature whereas congestion recovery tries to restore an operating state, when demand has already exceeded capacity. In Internet hosts and gateways only a few mechanisms currently exist to avoid or control congestion: window flow control and Slow Start in TCP or source quench in ICMP (Internet Control Message Protocol used as error reporting mechanism between two Internet Protocol entities). In XTP a distributed rate control mechanism is used.

XTP mechanisms beyond the functionality of existing transport protocols (e.g. concatenation/separation, splitting, segmentation/reassembling, data sequencing, alignment and padding, inactivity control) include:

- connection setup with immediate data transfer,
- multicast data transfers,
- selectable error control (go-back-n, selective retransmission, fast negative acknowledgement, no control)
- rate control (max. rate and burst size),
- out of band signalling (separating control functionality from data handling),
- QOS support (max. throughput, static and dynamic priorities.

XTP mechanisms to enhance the efficiency of transport protocol implementations include:

- fixed format PDUs,
- data field alignment on 4-byte boundaries,
- 32-bit sequence numbers,
- checksum positioning (avoiding header backpatching, also switching off the data checksum)
- limited protocol data unit types.

Furthermore, XTP supports the following services:

- peer-to-peer connection-oriented transfers,
- peer-to-peer connectionless transfers,
- multipeer connectionless transfers,
- multipeer stream transfers,
- peer-to-peer transactions.

Although XTP looks like a rather configurable protocol it lacks of a complete service specification especially covering the support of a requested QOS. There is no support foreseen for jitter and delay control. In order to provide XTP with such services we have designed the following algorithm. In addition to that multicast enhancements are going on [HJC 93].

4.2 XTP Delay/Jitter Control

One of the properties of isochronous applications like voice and video data streams is that their users may be sensitive to the variation in interarrival times between data delivered to the final output device. This interarrival time is called jitter for very small variances.

The idea of providing jitter control in a transport protocol is to find a method whereby frames transmitted into an internet at a constant frame rate are delivered to the destination at the same constant rate. The term "frame" is defined by the application as audio sample, video frame, or whatever. In existing transport protocols there are no explicit mechanism foreseen to achieve this goal. But our XTP implementation is able to provide the applications with this useful and essential mechanism.

This statement of the problem can be transformed into an equivalent statement: find a method for ensuring that the end-to-end propagation delay for each "frame" is constant. If the delays are constant then the frame delivery rate must be equivalent to the frame generation rate (ignoring lost or dropped frames).

The Berkeley proposal for obtaining constant delay jitter [VZF 92] requires synchronized clocks plus timestamps in the packets. It appears "easy" to duplicate the performance of the Berkeley algorithm with a simpler scheme if you have a protocol with the following features:

1. The connection setup packet informs both the intermediate nodes and the destination end node of the required data rate and frame size. This lets all concerned parties do internal bandwidth allocation for the new connection.

2. All packets in the protocol contain a time-to-live field (TTL) which is calibrated in units of time (not hop count). The protocol requires intermediate nodes to decrement the TTL field by the holding time at that node plus an estimate of propagation delay to the next node.

If one imagines each frame with a steadily decreasing TTL value, then the overall problem is solved if:

1. The destination end node delivers each packet just as TTL would decrease to zero (or some other value).

2. The measurements made along the way for decrementing TTL are reasonably accurate.

What a router must do is timestamp each packet as it arrives with its local time and use that to update TTL as the packet is forwarded.

At connection setup time each router, if it decides to make the bandwidth allocation, then forwards the packet but adds an extra amount, call it W, to the TTL decrement. That is, it decrements TTL by more than the strict decrement. The value of W is the scheduling precision in that router which it "knows" it can maintain: a real-time systems deadline concept.

Each node including the destination "remembers" this outgoing value for TTL. This procedure sets up a nominal TTL window at each node. That is, if each router forwards a packet within W time ticks then packets (frames) arrive at the destination within the window which is between original delivered TTL and the sum of all the W's. So end-to-end delay jitter is bounded by this sum.

Note: We ignore the other side of the delay window - when packets arrive "too fast". Probably doesn't happen. But if it did, an intermediate node would hold them up and forward them within the nominal time window or buffering at receiver.

4.3 XTP Performance Monitoring:

The level of QOS has to be monitored in order to control the contract with the user. To achieve this we use the Network Monitoring and Protocol Monitoring Entities. The Application Service can request a fixed value (desired) or flexible range (desired, minimum). The Network Monitoring Entity provides information about the actual traffic prior to call setup. Thus, there is one more parameter influencing the selection of the appropriate protocol stack. Additionally this parameter offers information if a compulsory QOS is achievable or not. The Protocol Monitoring Entities are designed to control the QOS values of specific protocols. These entities are used to collect information about the actual quality of service and to initiate certain protocol operations if the QOS is below desired values. It is also foreseen to inform the protocol user about problems detected by the monitor. The XTP implementation has been enhanced in order to provide the monitoring entity with the requested throughput and delay values the monitoring entity needs for its comparison.

Conclusion

The work described in this paper has confirmed the need of a flexible, requirements driven protocol architecture. In addition programmable protocols like XTP are useful in order to achieve a QOS which exactly meets the applications or user demands. But the current XTP specification has some weak points: None of the agreed QOS parameters are monitored by the service provider and there are no mechanisms for jitter and transmission delay control. This paper introduced a proposal for an efficient jitter and delay control algorithm which is not based on synchronized clocks.

References

[Dant 92] A. Danthine, *A new Transport Protocol for the Broadband Environment*, in A. Casaca, ed., Broadband Communications, Estoril, Jan. 1992, C-4, Elsevier Science Publisher (North-Holland), Amsterdam, 1992.

[Ferr 90] D. Ferrari, *Client Requirements for Real-Time Communication Services*, RFC 1193, Nov. 1990.

[HeRe 93] B. Heinrichs, W. Reinhardt, *The DyCE Concept - Architecture and Implementation Strategies*, in Proceedings of IFIP/ICCC conference on Integrated Broadband Communication Networks and Services, Copenhagen April 1993.

[HJC 93] B. Heinrichs, K. Jakobs, A. Carone: *High Performance Transfer Systems to Support Multimedia Group Communications*, Computer Communications Special Issue on Group Communications, September 1993.

[HJM 93] B. Heinrichs, K. Jakobs, T. Meuser: *DyCAT - A Modular Approach to Specification and Implementation of High Speed Transfer Systems*, Proc. 2nd International Conference on 'Broadband Services Systems and Networks', Brighton, UK, 3-5 November 1993.

[McGl 93] D. Mc Glinchey, *Specification of the XACSE*, EuroBridge CEC Deliverable R2008/BRI/CT3/DS/I/039, 1993.

[ReTi 93] W. Reinhardt, M. Tierney: *Requirements Analysis for the Protocol Selector*, RACE II Project EuroBridge, Deliverable 26, 1993.

[TFH 93] W. Tawbi, L. Fédaoui, E. Horlait, *Dynamic QOS Issues in Distributed Multimedia Systems*, in Proceedings of the Second International Conference on Broadband Island, Athens June 1993.

[VZF 92] D.C. Verma, H. Zhang, D. Ferrari, *Delay Jitter Control for Real-Time Communication in a Packet Switching Network*, Technical Report, University of California at Berkeley, 1992.

[XTP 92] *XTP Protocol Definition Revision 3.6*, 11 January 1992.

[ZST 93] M. Zitterbart, B. Stiller, A. Tantawy, *Application-Driven Flexible Protocol Configuration*, in Proceedings of ITG/GI-Fachtagung Kommunikation in Verteilten Systemen, Munich March 1993.

The EuroBridge Platform - Support Of An EnhancedMultimedia Mail Service

Kai Jakobs, Klaus Lenßen
Technical University of Aachen
Informatik IV, Computer Science Department
Ahornstr. 55, D-51 Aachen, FRG
Tel.: +49-241-80-21405; Fax: +49-241-80-21429
e-mail: {klaus I jakobs}@informatik.rwth-aachen.de

Abstract

This paper discusses the design of the multimedia mail user agent, currently being developed within the framework of the RACE II project EuroBridge. This user agent will be able to interwork with both, MIME and X.420. A brief summary of the overall application layer structure is followed by a top-down description of the internal architecture of the user agent, including the graphical user interface, the information system, and the message management. Finally, some open questions concerning mail transfer are touched on.

1. Background and Motivation

EuroBridge (EB) aims to provide (multimedia) applications with a uniform communication platform, thus relieving the application programmer from virtually all communication oriented tasks. A compilation of communication requirements has subsequently led to the definition of the EuroBridge Service Platform. This platform will provide integrated access to both, store-and-forward data services and interactive video conferencing services. Data services to be supported include file transfer (FTAM [13]), database access (RDA [19]), the directory service (DS [20[) and, most important, electronic mail (MHS [7,8]). According to user demands, those are the most urgently required services. These OSI application layer services will be enhanced in a way enabling them to appropriately support multi-media applications.

To attract a large number of potential users, EB has decided to make use of as many standard components as possible. The communication platform is developed on SUNs and on IBM compatible unix workstations. We support the ISODE implementation of the full OSI stack as well as the TCP/IP protocols. These stacks are required for the sake of backward compatibility. To fully support multimedia applications, newly designed dedicated protocols, covering the functionality of the OSI presentation, session and transport layers will be incorporated as well. Furthermore, we will support a broad range of underlying networks, including Ethernet, FDDI and 2 Mbps links.

The technical aims of EuroBridge are threefold:

- To enhance existing application layer services towards multimedia.
- To enhance implementation and functionality of the underlying layers to adequately support the application layer's requirements.
- To provide the user with an integrated true multimedia service, comprising both, data and conversational services.

This paper focusses on the core of EB's store and forward application services - electronic mail. E-mail may well be considered as the far most popular communication service, and has thus been on the leading edge of developments towards multimedia, take for instance MIME [1], [2-6], and the various developments within RACE [] as examples.

Work described in this papers focusses on design and implementation of a multimedia MHS user agent. The problem of accurately displaying, storing, retrieving and managing the differnt body parts of multimedia messages appears far more important than the mere transport (although some problems remain in this area as well.

The remainder of the paper is organized as follows; section 2 briefly outlines the overall architecture of the EuroBridge application layer. Section 3 focusses on introducing multimedia mail issues. The details of the single components of EMMA, the EuroBridge multimedia mail application, are described throughout section 4. Finally, some open issues are addressed and some concluding remarks are given in section 5.

2. Application Layer Services

Fig. 1 shows the application layer part of the overall communication architecture.

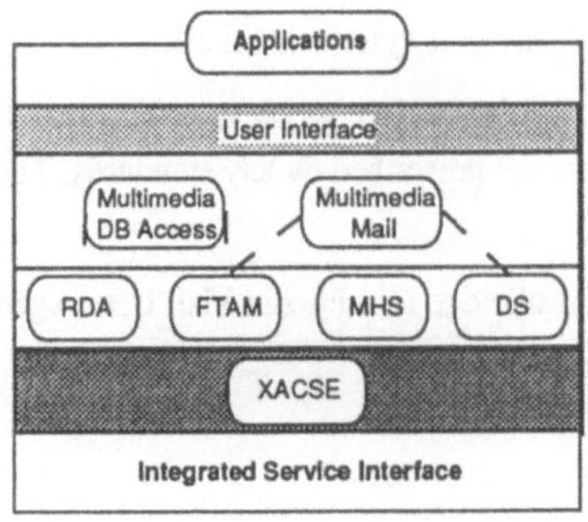

Fig. 1: The EuroBridge Application Layer

One of the basic ideas of EuroBridge is to exploit existing services as much as possible. Hence, basic functionality is provided by the standard OSI services. We use the ISODE implementations of FTAM, X.400 and X.500. RDA is a proprietary implementation provided by one of the partners. Enhancements focus on provision of multimedia and multipoint capabilities, and a guaranteed Quality of Service. These enhancements impose strong requirements on the underlying layers. Those interested in how we will meet these requirements should refer to [10] and [12,14].

FTAM, RDA, X.400 and X.500 will be used by higher-layer systems like the multimedia mail system or the multimedia database access service. It is obvious that at this point compatibility to existing standards is a sine qua non.

3. Multimedia Mail

As of today, most problems related to MHS stem from poor implementation rather than from the standard as such. Although, for instance, the standard explicitly supports multimedia documents, no implementations of a multimedia MHS service are available yet.

Electronic mail is, and will continue to be, the dominant application service. Unfortunately, very little efforts towards multimedia mail services within ISO or CCITT are discernible. Practical problems concerning the Message Transfer System (MTS) include [9]:

- Large message sizes

Storage problems may occur if messages comprise eg. "video" body parts. It has to be decided if such messages/body parts are actually transmitted or if references are transmitted instead.

- Cost and efficiency issues

This may for instance include priorization of messages and accounting problems.

Despite these open questions, EuroBridge for the moment focusses on the user agent rather than the transfer system for the following reasons:

- The transfer system is provided by PTTS or equivalent organizations and the Internet, respectively. Even if we came up with sophisticated enhancements, it would take considerable time to have them incorporated into the providers systems, if at all.

- The user agent is the human user's interface to the system. It is independent from the respective transfer system, and it's design is not prescribed by any standards. Thus, fast solutions can be achieved.

The major components of the EuroBridge Multimedia Mail User Agent (EMMA) is shown in Fig.2

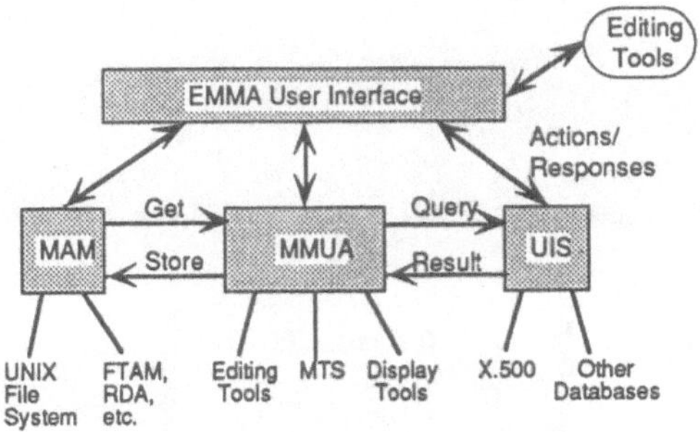

Fig. 2: Components of the EuroBridge Multimedia Mail

EMMA	EuroBridge Multimedia Mail Application
MAM	Message Management and Storage
MMUA	Multimedia Mail User Agent
UIS	User Information System

Within this architecture, the tasks of the single components are as follows:

- Graphical User Interface (GUI)

This will provide a common gloss to the above three components.

- User Information System (UIS)

The UIS is a very generic service, to be used not only by the mail service. It will basically include an interface to the X.500 directory service. Required functionality includes look-up of e-mail addresses and of end-system profiles.

- Message Management and Storage (MAM)

The MMS will store and retrieve messages. It will provide the appropriate functions independent of the local file system.

- Multimedia Mail User Agent (MMUA)

This component is responsible for coordinating the system and for interfacing with the MTS. It will also be responsible for interacting with multimedia tools and utilities for document composing and viewing.

4. The EMMA Components

EuroBridge is going to put the intelligence inside the user agent (UA) rather than the message transfer system. This facilitates the development of a useful tool which does not have to wait for the widespread deployment of advanced messaging protocols. EMMA is designed to overcome the problems of multinetwork addressing, message sizes, terminal heterogeneity and personal mobility in a flexible, integrated manner (see Fig. 3).

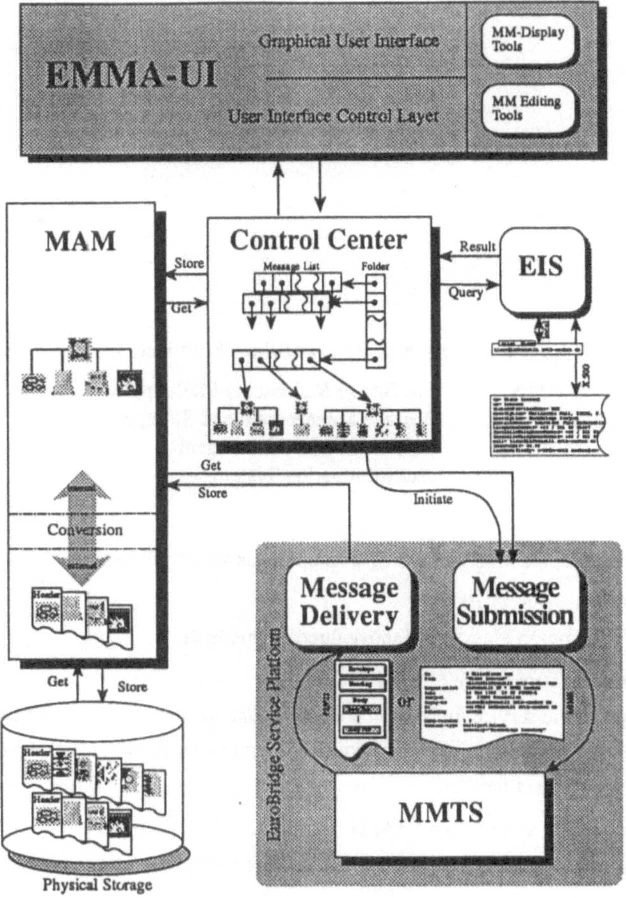

Fig. 3: Architecture of the EuroBridge Multimedia Mail Application (EMMA)

4.1. Day-to-Day Work - The User-Interface

The major goal for the development of the graphical user interface (GUI) was to design a flexible and easy to handle tool, usable for simple day-to-day work as well as for more complex tasks. Based on some general scenarios, e.g. daily reading of messages, replying to a message, maintaining messages, creating or manipulating simple text or complex multimedia messages, printing and so on, user requirements have been identified. Increasing the granularity lead to the identification of single functions. These functions were grouped according to their respective frequency of use. Accordingly, the EMMA GUI [17] offers frequently used functions in a way, that they can be used intuitively. Almost all functions can be accessed via keyboard and mouse, special function keys may be assigned to functions, thus providing shortcuts for the more experienced user.

To avoid overloading the users desktop was another design goal. Logical grouping of functions enables the user to perform most operations with only one or two windows open. However, the number of open windows is in no way restricted and is absolutely at the user's discretion.

Reading, printing and maintaining messages for example are bound to the main window of the application. This includes navigation through the users message folders, incoming messages, message templates, and so on. A *quickview* function provides a means to read simple text messages directly and to browse through the structure of multimedia documents, which are displayed as a structure tree within the quickview window.

4.1.1. Mail Reading and Composition Tool

More complex tasks, e.g.. composition of multimedia messages, are performed by separate modules, as the *mail reading and composition tool* (MRCT, [17]). To compose a message, a second window is opened, with three separated sections: for header information, for the mail body and for some menu functions and status information, respectively. Like the main window, the body part editor has two different operation modes, *overview* (or structured) and *normal*. The EuroBridge widget set allows to display even complex multimedia messages in WYSIWYG manner. TIFF, JPEG, MPEG, H.261, G.711, G.721, SUN-audio are currently supported by the EB widget set [18].

As of today, the MRCT does not offer sophisticated editing or manipulation features for images, audio or video. If the type of a specific body part (a multimedia object) is known to the system, and the UA configuration offers information about this object type, the MRCT calls the appropriate external tool, to manipulate the object (cf.sect. 4.4).

4.1.2. User Interface Control Layer

To achieve a strict functional separation of the GUI and the UA, we introduce a separate *user interface control layer* (UICL). This enables adaptation to different user interfaces, depending on the respective hardware on which the user agent is to be installed. For some future extensions, like for instance mobile services, the graphical interface will not be necessary at all.

The UICL provides a uniform view of a virtual user interface for the underlying UA modules. The translation of the UA operations into equivalent actions the user interface has to perform is the major task of the UICL. Currently EMMA has one GUI, which is MOTIF based. For further extensions like the adaptation to mobile systems, we have to think about new interfaces, which have to provide for speech recognition, to grant phone access to the users mailbox.

4.2. Do you remember? - The User Information System

X.400(84) unfortunately used the misleading term O/R-Name for its addressing concept. The set of attributes was not clearly specified in these recommendations. Attribute types were chosen in a way, that O/R-Names referred to the physical structure of the MHS, e.g. the relation of a UA to the MTA. That is, they were addresses rather than names. The meaning of O/R-Names has changed in the 1988 recommendations. What used to be an O/R-Name is now an O/R-Address, and the O/R-Name has been re-specified. The interworking between X.500 (Directory Service) and X.400 [7,8] has become significant, the O/R-Name of an object is defined as either its directory name or its O/R-Address or both. The recommendations also fixed interworking of MHS and directory and which type of information has to be stored.

To achieve the desired degree of user friendliness, directory support is also integrated in the EMMA concept. The X.500 directory, based on the QUIPU implementation which is delivered with the ISODE package, is used. EMMA uses the directory to maintain profiles of mail users or organisations, that is, the multimedia capabilities of the respective recipient user agents are kept in the database, thus better supporting enhanced multimedia capabilities.

The EIS (EMMA Information Service, [15]) provides normal directory lookup functions for e.g.. e-mail addresses. In addition, information obtained from the directory may be cached locally. Local nicknaming and distribution lists are also provided, but are only available at UA level, they are not accessible form the MTA.

To store information using the directory service, each entry created for an EIS user must include EisObject as an object class:

```
EisObject:      EisObjectClass.1: Person: : \
                rfc822Mailbox, telephoneNumber, \
                facsimileTelephoneNumber, UserEnvironment
```

These entries have to be added to the oidtables (Object Identifier tables) to facilitate the usage of a new object class for information on an EIS user. While most of the attributes in this object class already exist in other object classes, it would be difficult and impractical to have to use all these classes to store the information. Using a dedicated object class is a much more convenient solution.

4.3. Where do I put ...? - Message Management and Storage

The goal to be independent from the underlying transfer syntax (which may be either MIME or X.420 [7]) drove the development of an internal representation structure, which should overcome this problem. The need to deal with various multimedia data types, which were coded in differently in both transfer syntax's, underlines the necessity of the internal structure.

To store and manage multimedia mail messages (with their different body parts) within a UNIX environment is the task of the *message management and storage* (MAM, [16]). This task can be seen as a very specialised application build on top of a more generic multimedia file manager (MFM), which itself is realised on the unix file system. This can be considered as a generic service for any type of multimedia application. All stored data structures will invisible for normal unix users as much as possible. Multimedia applications like EMMA need to store the data using the standard unix file system, which can distinguish only three types of data: data, directory and executable. Currently, each application uses some private conventions to determine the format of a given file. Applications that need to import or export information either assume that the user is specifying the correct file or attempt to use some heuristic methods to guess the file type. To support multimedia applications, the MFM provides a centralised method to deduce the type from the filename via global and local or private rules (cf. Fig. 4). The MFM does not actually know anything about the real contents of a file, it only maintains the relation between the content and type.

```
# global rules

*.tif:image/tiff
*.jpg/image/jpeg
*.fdr/eurobridge/folder
...
```

```
# privat rules

*.wp:application/WordPerfect
*.ODA/application/oda
...
```

Fig. 4: MFM Rules (example)

It has already been mentioned that the MAM is an application of top of the MFM, which provides a multimedia message archive and management for different types of multimedia mail applications. This operates on logical concepts like folders, messages, headers and different type of body parts. Two high level file types are defined by the MAM, the eurobridge/message and the eurobridge/folder as an ordered collection of messages.

Multimedia messages consist of body parts, each of which is of some specific content type. MAM stores every body part in a separate file. The minimum set of recognised content types is given in table 1. The MAM interface provides some generic functions, like load and store, which automati-

Content Type String	Description
eurobridge/folder	recognised by mail application
eurobridge/message	refers to a multimedia mail message
image/jpeg	raster image (JFIF)
image/tiff	raster image (TIFF 6.0)
image/gif	raster image (GIF)
image/cgm	geometric image (CGM)
text/plain	simple text
audio/basic	G.711 8kHz µlaw
video/mpeg	video stream (MPEG)
video/h261	video stream (H.261)
video/x-jpegvideo	video stream (Parallax hardware specific)
application/postscript	postscript code
application/oda	ODA/ODIF interchange format
application/xfig	geometric graphics format (xfig)
application/x-dcs	EuroBridge DCS structure

Table 1: List of minimum set of known content types

cally convert the message data into the internal representation, on which all other EMMA building blocks operate.

4.4. Everything's ok? - The Control Centre

The integration of the different building blocks of the EMMA UA is one of the functions of the control centre. Other functions include memory management, configuration facilities for both, user agent and user interface, and control of message submission and delivery.

Supporting the UICL/GUI, the CC provides a memory management, which deals with single messages, all converted into the EMMA internal representation. The higher level modules access these internal structures via node identifiers. Logical structures like lists, which might represent a folder (of messages) or a directory (containing multimedia objects), are available. List identifiers provide access to those structures.

The concept of virtual lists allows the implementation of functions like e.g.. „list of all messages from sender A“ without overhead, since only a list of different node identifiers has to be created, which is much easier than re-scanning the physical storage to select all message matching the filter.

Another important task is the configuration of the different modules. Two different methods of configuration are used, on-line via the GUI and passive on start-up via profiles. Two different types of profiles are supported, a global system-wide profile, which keeps information about available tools and the mail transport system, and user specific profiles. These local profiles can be used to override or enhance the global settings. User specific information, like signatures, default header settings, auto-forward address, etc., are stored here.

4.5. Hello Mr. Postman! - Submission and Delivery

Within the EuroBridge project the mail transport is based on the PP implementation [11]. Submission and delivery are coded as separate modules within the current implementation of EMMA. The submission process consists of to two different message builders for MIME and for X.420, respectively. After being invoced by the CC, the submission process starts reading the message via the MAM interface, converting it into the internal representation format.

The MMUA will interface to both, MIME and X.420 IPM as transport systems. Although this idea appears to be straightforward, it results in some major problems, most of which could be settled easily if the gateways between the different transport systems worked properly. Unfortunately, as of today this is not the case, even for simple IA5 messages, to say nothing about potential problems if multimedia messages are to be forwarded. Issues to be addressed include:

- How to select the correct transport system?

With user agents being connected to both transport systems, some entity has to decide via which system a message is to be delivered.

- How to handle distribution lists?

Members of one (local) list may well be connected to only one transport system (i.e.. Internet or OSI).

- How to prevail the semantics of a message?

The semantics must not depend on the respective transport system.

Depending on some calling parameters, the message builder produces a MIME- or a X.420 message. Messages for SMTP transport are submitted via the sendmail interface, whereas the PP io_interface is used for IPMs.

Message delivery is handled by a separate daemon program, which is automatically started when the UA is invoked. The current implementation of the X.400/SMTP MTA PP does not offer a P3 nor a P7 protocol. A file based interface is used for delivery. Furthermore, no message store (MS) implementation which would make use of P3/P7 protocols is available. A message parser module provides some basic functionality to access the file system interface of either the standard unix sendmail or the one of PP.

4.6. ... for further studies - The Document Control Structure

As already mentioned, the IPMS structure allows to transmit several body parts, each of a different type, within one message. The structuring capabilities offered by the IPMS specification lacks flexibility in two different ways. First, the variety of available body types is not sufficient to speak about multimedia in this context. The second point is, that only linear structured documents are possible at the moment. The specification offers nothing to declare relations between the different objects (body parts) within a message.

What do we need to overcome these problems. Description languages or multimedia document architectures are one solution. They allow to describe any multimedia object type, and to declare *spatial* and *temporal* relations between this objects. The Open Document Architecture, in combination with the HyperOda Extensions, Coded Representation of Multimedia and Hypermedia Information Objects (MHEG), the Standard Generalised Markup Language (SGML), and HyTime are possible solutions. Currently nobody can really estimate which of these description languages will be used in the future.

Further studies within the EuroBridge Multimedia Mail working group will focus on the work of new and appropriate document control structures to enhance the capabilities of the EuroBridge Multimedia Mail Application.

5. Summary and Some Concluding Remarks

The implementation of a multimedia user agent is one of the major tasks of the EuroBridge project. We have outlined the general ideas of our design of EMMA, the EuroBridge multimedia mail user agent, and we have discussed some of the implementation issues. The modular approach should provide for sufficient flexibility and adaptability.

One of the key issues of the design is the support of two distinct mail transfer systems, MIME and X.420. Although some open questions are still left, the solution to this problem is very likely to be based on an internal intermediate syntax, which will be mapped on the appropriate transfer syntax.

As of today, we are very confident that a first implementation of EMMA will be available early next year at the latest

6. References

[1] RFC 1341 Borenstein, N.; Freed, N.
MIME (Multipurpose Internet Mail Extensions)
Mechanisms for Specifying and Describing the Format of Internet Message Bodies. 1992 June

[2] RFC 821 Postel, J.
Simple Mail Transfer Protocol. 1982 August

[3] RFC 1425 Rose, M.; Stefferud, E.; Crocker, D.
SMTP Service Extensions. 1993 February

[4] RFC 1426 Rose, M.; Stefferud, E.; Crocker, D.
SMTP Service Extension for 8bit-MIMEtransport. 1993 February

[5] RFC 1427 Moore, K.
SMTP Service Extension for Message Size Declaration. 1993 February

[6] RFC 1428 Vaudreuil, G.
Transition of Internet Mail from Just-Send-8 to 8bit-SMTP/MIME., 1993 February

[7] X.419 / ISO 10021-6
Message Handling, Protocol Specifications

[8] X.400 / ISO 10021-1
Message Oriented Text Interchange System (MOTIS)
Part 1: System and Service Overview

[9] Denise Puech, Steven Hand, Seamus Kearney
Requirements Analysis for the EuroBridge Multimedia Mail Service,
EuroBridge Internal Report, March 1993

[10] B. Heinrichs, K. Jakobs, K. Lenssen, W. Reinhardt, A. Spinner

EuroBridge: communications services for multimedia applications, Electronics & Communication Engineering Journal, February 1993

[11] J. Onions, P. Cowen
PP: Volume 1-3, Installation and Operation, Version 6.0, Dec. 1991

[12] Proposed Working Draft to ISO/IEC JTC1/SC6 on High Speed Transport Protocol (HSTP), US-contribution, February 1992

[13] International Organisation for Standardisation: File Transfer, Access and Management, part1 - part4, ISO 8571-1/4:1988(E)

[14] M.T.Rose, J.P. Onions, C.J. Robbins: The ISO Development Environment: User's Manual Volume 3: Applications, July 18, 1991

[15] Architecture and Design of the EMMA Information System (EIS), EB/CT2/SSE/063/E, Denise Puech, Mar 1993, EuroBridge Internal Report

[16] Architecture and Design of Message Archive and Management (MAM), Markku Savela, EB/IREP/VTT/025/A, Mar 1993, Eurobridge Internal Report

[17] User Interface Design, EB/IREP/EED/xxx/Prel, Arno Spinner, Michael Rupprecht, Klaus Lenßen, Atte Kortekangas, April 28, 1993, EuroBridge Internal Report

[18] The EuroBridge Widget Set, EB/IREP/VTT/010/D, Markku Savela, Dec 1992, EuroBridge Report

[19] Remote Database Access, Part 1 and 2, ISO DIS 9579-1/2

[20] The Directory: Part 1, Overview of Concepts, Models, and Services, CCITT X.500

Efficient and Order-Preserving Shifting of Data Streams

Rainer Oechsle
IBM European Networking Center
Vangerowstraße 18
D - 69115 Heidelberg
Germany

Hong Linh Truong
IBM Research Division
Zurich Research Laboratory
Säumerstraße 4
CH - 8803 Rüschlikon
Switzerland

Abstract. In order to exploit the capacity of parallel links we propose a traffic distribution scheme where each data stream is routed over one of the parallel links at a time. In cases of link overload or breakdown the network management entity should be able to shift selected data streams dynamically from one link to another according to some policy. Given that the source and sink of a data stream are able to deal with lost packets, but not with packets arriving out of order, the shifting has to be done in such a way that in-sequence delivery is guaranteed. In this paper we present two approaches that solve this task. The first method uses numbered shift commands that first have to be exchanged between the nodes before the actual shifting can take place. In the second method the shifting is only prepared by exchanging special commands. The actual shifting is done simply by using a prepared link. The methods are useful for remote bridges connecting remote LAN sites over several wide area networks, or for ATM switching nodes being connected by multiple links.

1. Exploiting Parallel Links

Connecting two communicating entities by more than a single communications link is an effective way to increase the communications capacity and reliability between the two entities. Such a set of parallel links can be found in many different environments. For example, in a joint IBM-Ericsson project investigating network management for remote LAN interconnectivity, several remote LAN sites were bridged [IEEE88] by different kinds of wide area networks, namely leased lines and switched public networks. Another example is a configuration with two switching nodes in a network being connected by multiple links. The network we are considering here is the newly emerging Broadband-ISDN [CCIT90a] using ATM (Asynchronous Transfer Mode, [dePr91], [Haen91], [LeBo92]) as transfer mode.

We will use the following model as an abstraction of these concrete examples: Two communicating entities are connected by a set of links, where each link might have different characteristics in terms of speed, cost, reliability, security, and so on. The traffic to be exchanged over the link set can be divided into data streams, with the data belonging to one data stream being totally independent from the data of another data stream. The units to be forwarded are called packets. This notion also comprises frames and cells. Each packet contains a data stream identifier in its header. We assume that data streams are directed. For two-way communication two independent data streams are used (one in each direction). Payload data transmission is therefore considered only for one direction, from a sender to a receiver entity. The links themselves are, however, bidirectional and the reverse direction will be used for control data, as will be seen later. Returning to our examples given above, all the traffic being sent from one LAN-attached workstation to another workstation identified by the source and destination MAC addresses can be defined as a data stream in the remote LAN interconnection example. In the ATM switching nodes example, a virtual connection described by the VPI/VCI field in the ATM header could be seen as a typical data stream. The notion of a data stream is obviously applicable to connection-oriented as well as to connectionless environments.

The model described is summarized in Figure 1: Here we see a sender and a receiver entity being connected by three links. The data of three data streams has to be carried from the sender to the receiver. Currently all the data belonging to the data streams A1-B1, A2-B2 is forwarded over link 1, whereas the data stream A3-B3 is routed over link 3.

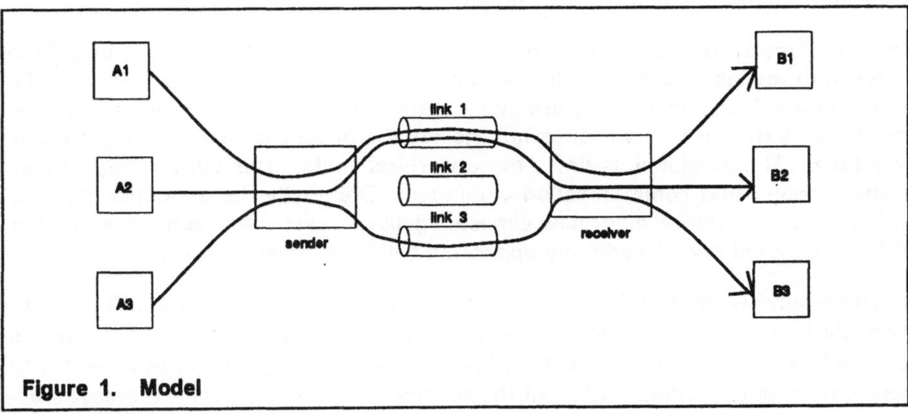

Figure 1. Model

In order to exploit parallel links a method has to be defined to distribute the traffic onto the links. Basically there are two approaches to do this:

- **traffic distribution on a stream-by-stream basis:**

This approach dates back to the early days of telephony. Switching nodes connected by parallel links carry several connections. Whenever a new connection has to be made, a link with sufficient sparse capacity is selected to carry the data for the new connection.

Obviously, because of the long-term decision to map a certain data stream to a certain link, this kind of static traffic distribution is not very flexible. It is thus not appropriate for balancing the traffic load among the parallel links, especially if the bandwidth requirements of the streams vary during their lifetime. In our examples at hand, especially in the ATM example, it is very likely that some of the data streams will carry multi-media traffic. Whenever a user changes from still pictures to video applications, the link that actually carries the data stream may become overloaded and may not be able to continue to provide the requested quality of service.

- **traffic distribution on a packet-by-packet basis:**

Much better suited for load balancing is a packet-by-packet traffic distribution method. A packet to be sent to the peer entity may be sent on the link with the least load, i.e. the link whose service time is supposed to be the shortest of all the parallel links leading to the peer entity. The decision will take into account parameters like queue length, link speed, and so on. The decision is independent from the decision made for previous packets belonging to the same data stream. As a consequence, packets may arrive out of order at the other side. This may or may not lead to problems:

With Autonet [Schr91], reordering is possible. The assumption is that the end-to-end protocols are able to handle the reordering. This is usually true for most of the transport protocols (TCP [Post81] and OSI TP4, e.g.). However, handling out-of-order packets increases the complexity of a protocol considerably (see [Tane89]). If order preservation is guaranteed, the construction of light-weight protocols needed for higher speeds is much simpler.

Some protocols like the classical sliding-window protocols (for example LLC Type 2 [IEEE89]) are able to deal with lost packets, but not with out-of-order packets. To understand why this is so, assume a packet with sequence number 1 is delayed. Because the receiver does not receive the packet, no acknowledgement is sent back. The sender thus times out and retransmits. This copy finally arrives at the receiver and communication continues. Eventually the sequence number wraps around. If the receiver now expects again a packet with a sequence number of 1, the delayed packet suddenly appearing will be erroneously accepted.

In IBM's networking architecture SNA [Mart87], [Meij87] or in the CCITT Recommendation X.75 for the interconnection of public packet-switched networks [CCIT88], for example, the problem is handled by attaching a sequence number to each packet at the sender side. At the receiver side the packets are ordered according to the sequence numbers. If a packet is missing, it is retransmitted on another link until it is successfully received. The overhead of each packet carrying an additional sequence number, and the procedures of packet resequencing, retransmission on different links and of the sequence number wrap-around are considerable.

Order preservation is required for the data streams in both of our examples, namely for the data being exchanged between two LAN stations using the LLC Type 2 protocol end-to-end in the remote bridging example, as has been shown above, and for the ATM virtual path / virtual channel connections, as is described in [CCIT90b]. The sequence number approach is not feasible in the ATM case, because there is no space available for coding the additional sequence number into the fixed-size ATM cells. In addition, the method would be too clumsy for the fast ATM switching nodes. Nor is the approach very well suited for our remote bridging project where network management should have complete control over the data flowing between the LAN sites. For example, certain links should be used only by a selected subset of conversations going on between stations attached to different LAN sites.

We just showed that none of the traffic distribution methods is appropriate for our examples. We thus propose a hybrid traffic distribution method, namely

- **traffic distribution on a stream-by-stream basis combined with mechanisms to shift a stream dynamically from one link to another:**

The idea is illustrated by Figure 2. Here the data stream A2-B2 has been shifted from link 1 to link 2 without affecting any of the other data streams. In addition the shifting shall be non-disruptive for the entities A2 and B2, i.e. A2 and B2 shall not be aware of the shifting.

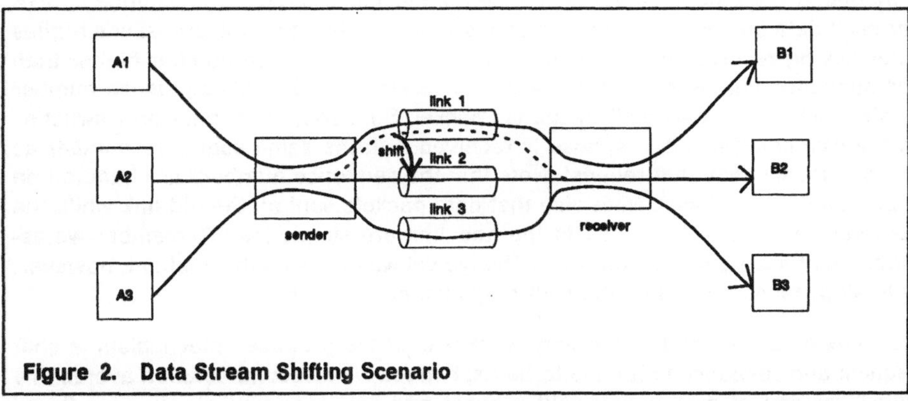

Figure 2. Data Stream Shifting Scenario

If in-sequence delivery for data streams is not required, then there is no problem in shifting a data stream from one link to another. However, although packet loss is tolerable, order preservation is required in our examples, as has been pointed out above. This paper thus proposes methods for order-preserving data stream shifting. The outline of the paper is as follows: In the following section two such methods are introduced in an informal way. In the next two sections each method is described in more detail and verified by a proof. As usual, a summary concludes the paper.

2. Informal Description

In the following we assume that data stream shifting is triggered by a management entity according to some policy. In both methods the sender and the receiver store for each data stream the currently used link, called the active link, and a sequence number that counts the number of shifts for this data stream. The sender transmits the payload data for a given data stream only on the currently active link and the receiver accepts packets for a given data stream only from the currently active link. Thus packets arriving too late on a non-active link are discarded by the receiver. What is needed is a protocol between the sender and the receiver for changing the active link.

In the first solution explicit shift request packets are sent from the sender to the receiver in order to inform the receiver that the active link shall be changed. Shift request packets are always sent over the link to which the data stream shall be shifted, i.e. they are sent over the new link. On receiving such a shift request packet, the receiver changes the active link to that link on which the request packet arrived for the data stream as indicated in the request. In addition the receiver replies to such shift requests by sending shift responses back over the new link. The sender then also changes its active link and thereafter starts to forward packets for the corresponding data stream on the new link. Because such shift request and response packets may be lost or significantly delayed, it may be decided to resend them. The loss or delay of shift packets may be taken as an indication that switching to this particular link is not a good idea. So another link may be selected. This means that shift request packets are resent, possibly over different links. In order to decide at the receiver side which request packet is the most recent one, a sequence number is attached to each shift packet (as it is done in SNA for each data packet). The receiver only switches to the new link and sends replies after having received a shift request packet with a sequence number higher than the sequence numbers of all previously received packets. This sequence number is also included in each shift response packet. Similarly, the sender only switches to the new link if a shift response is received with the same sequence number as the previously sent shift request. Note that the sequence numbers are handled on a per data stream basis. Note also that data packets sent on the old link while the receiver has already switched to the new link are simply lost. Remember we assumed that such a loss is tolerable. The typical way of using this method, however, is to stop transmitting until the shift response has arrived.

Now this delay constitutes the very weakness of the proposed mechanism; a shift request and response first have to be exchanged. The second solution avoids this delay: instead of exchanging shift request and response packets, the candidate links are swept by exchanging sweep request and response packets. These sweep packets, however, do not trigger the change of the active link for a given data stream, but the reception of such a sweep request and response packet is merely taken as an indication by the receiver and the sender, respectively, that the given link is clean and a switching to this link is now possible. The actual shifting takes place by simply using from now on a clean link at the sender side. The receiver switches to a new link upon receiving the first packet over a clean link. After the shifting has been done, all links including the active one are considered to be dirty again. This is done in the same way at the sender and at the receiver side. As in the previous proposal, sweep requests and responses carry sequence numbers to distinguish old and new sweep packets. The sender's sequence number is increased for each shifting action done at the sender side, but not for each sweeping packet sent! The receiver accepts a sweeping packet arriving over a still dirty link and carrying the current sequence number, i.e. the link is added to the set of clean links at the receiver side. Similarly, the sender adds a link to the set of clean links if a sweep response arrives carrying the current sequence number. This allows more than one link to be swept and considered clean. There are thus several links ready to take over the data stream which is very important in a critical situation.

Like the sender, the receiver increases its sequence number with each shifting action. If the receiver gets a sweep request packet with a sequence number larger than the current one, it notices that one shifting is missed. Consequently this case is handled like a shifting action, i.e. all links are considered dirty except the one for which the sweep arrived. The active link is not changed in this case. Note that the active link is usually dirty. Remember that a link being clean is simply an indication that a data stream may be shifted to that link. Now if the active link is swept successfully and thus becomes clean, a packet subsequently arriving on the active link is handled like a shift. That means the sequence number is increased and the new active link is the one from which the packet was received. The old and the new link are identical in this case.

As a variant of the second method the links may be considered clean again after a certain period of time. To this end the maximum lifetime of packets on a link has to be known. This variant will not be investigated further in this paper.

As the reader might have noticed, there is no method for the wrap-around of the sequence numbers. It is not needed because

- the sequence number only counts the shifts per data stream and not globally all individual packets, thus its growth is much smaller and because
- a sequence number is transmitted only in shift or sweep packets, so it is feasible to use as many bits as needed.

In the following two sections a detailed description of both methods is presented.

3. Method I

The algorithms are described by two processes, a sender and a receiver process. They interact with their local system environment by sending and receiving to and from operating systems channels as depicted in Figure 3. The sender process receives messages from the upper layer through the from_upper channel. The messages contain the data stream (ds) and the payload to be transmitted. In addition, the sender process sends and receives messages to and from the lower layer through the channels to_lower and from_lower, respectively. These messages contain a link and a packet. The meaning of such a message is that the packet is to be sent or was received over the given link. The packet itself carries a type field indicating whether it is a pure data packet or a shift request / response packet, the data stream identification and an information field which is interpreted as payload for pure data packets and as a sequence number for shift packets. A management process may send shift request messages to the sender process through the channel from_mngmnt. The messages simply contain the data stream and the new link. Whenever a shifting has been done successfully, this is reported to the management through the channel to_mngmnt. The interaction of the receiver with its environment is very similar to the sender process with the exception that the receiver sends to the upper layer instead of receiving from it and that he only reports shifting actions to the management process, but does not accept any commands from it.

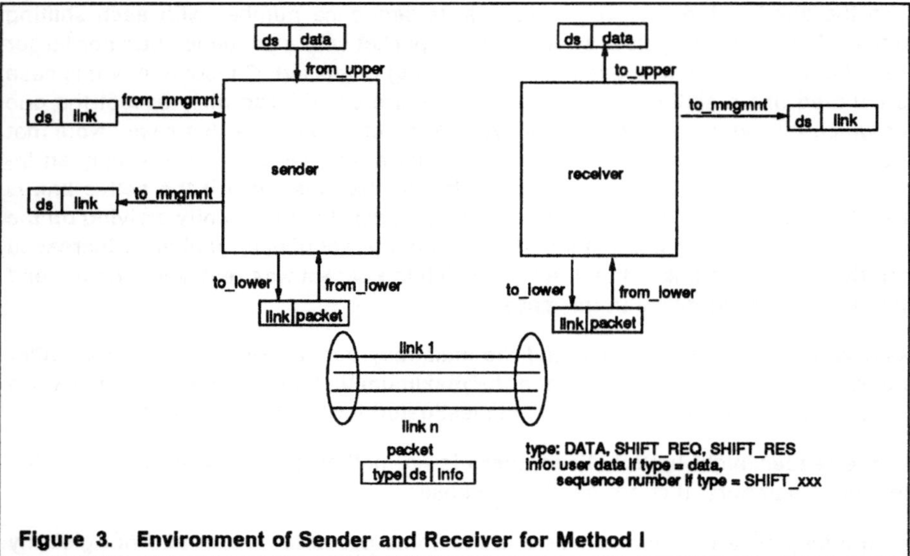

Figure 3. Environment of Sender and Receiver for Method I

In the following the relevant control information held at the sender and at the receiver side together with its initialization is shown in C syntax. For each data stream the sender and the receiver each store the currently active link and the sequence number.

```
typedef struct {LINK active_link; NUMBER seqno} cntrl;

cntrl sendcntrl[MAX_DS];      /* sender's local data   */
cntrl receivecntrl[MAX_DS];   /* receiver's local data */
```

All data streams are initially mapped to some link and the sequence number is set to 0.

```
init()
{
   for(i = 0; i < MAX_DS; i++) {
      sendcntrl[i].active_link = initial_link; sendcntrl[i].seqno = 0;
      receivecntrl[i].active_link = initial_link; receivecntrl[i].seqno = 0;
   }
}
```

The sender and receiver processes are also written in C with the following extensions:

- send() and receive() calls are used for sending and receiving to and from the operating systems channels. In order to wait for the arrival of a message on more than one channel, the notation

  ```
  ch = receive(ch1 or ch2 or ... chn, msg);
  ```

  is used where ch gives the channel on which the message was ultimately received.

- Depending on which channel a message was received from, the components may be accessed through the component names as introduced in Figure 3. E.g., if the message msg was received from channel from_upper, its components are msg.ds and msg.data, whereas the components of a message msg received from from_lower are msg.link and msg.packet.
- A message to be sent is simply indicated by given its components enclosed in <...>.

Note also that there is no timeout and retry built into the code of the sender process in order to protect against lost shift request or response packets. This timeout supervision and triggering of retries has to be all done by the management process. This simplifies the sender code in a significant way:

In an endless loop the sender receives messages. If a message arrives from the upper layer the sender just forwards the message on the active link of the corresponding data stream. If a management request is received, a shift request is sent to the other side on the new link carrying an increased sequence number. If a shift response with the correct sequence number arrives from the lower layer, the data stream is actually shifted and network management is informed.

```
process sender()
{
   forever {
      received = receive(from_mngmnt or from_upper or from_lower,msg);
      if(received == from_upper) { // just send the data on the active link
         ds = msg.ds;
         info = msg.data;
         packet = <DATA,ds,info>;
         link = sendcntrl[ds].active_link;
         send(to_lower,<link,packet>);
      }
      else if(received == from_mngmnt) { // initiate outgoing data stream shifting
         ds = msg.ds;
         sendcntrl[ds].seqno++;
         seqno = sendcntrl[ds].seqno;
         packet = <SHIFT_REQ,ds,seqno>;
         new_link = msg.link;
         send(to_lower,<new_link,packet>);
      }
      else if(received == from_lower) { // outgoing data stream shifting has been done
         new_link = msg.link;
         packet = msg.packet;
         ds = packet.ds;
         if((packet.type == SHIFT_RES)
            && (packet.info == sendcntrl[ds].seqno)) { // correct type and sequence no.
            sendcntrl[ds].active_link = new_link;
            send(to_mngmnt,<ds,new_link>);
         }
      }
   }
}
```

Like the sender, the receiver sits in an endless loop receiving messages. If a data packet arrives over the currently active link, the packet is forwarded to the upper layer. If a shift request arrives with a higher sequence number, the data stream is shifted, a response is sent back, and network management is informed.

```
process receiver()
{
   forever {
      receive(from_lower,msg);
      link = msg.link;
      packet_in = msg.packet;
      ds = packet_in.ds;
      if(packet_in.type == DATA) { // data has been received -> pass to user if active link
         if(link == receivecntrl[ds].active_link)
            send(to_upper,<ds,packet_in.info>);
      }
      else if(packet_in.type == SHIFT_REQ) { // switch incoming active link if correct seqno
         if(packet_in.info > receivecntrl[ds].seqno) {
            receivecntrl[ds].seqno = packet_in.info;
            receivecntrl[ds].active_link = link;
            packet_out = <SHIFT_RES,ds,packet_in.info>;
            send(to_lower,<link,packet_out>);
            send(to_mngmnt,<ds,link>);
         }
      }
   }
}
```

Proof by contradiction: We now show that the proposed protocol indeed preserves the ordering for each data stream. Assume a sender S first sends packet 1 and then packet 2 which are received by a receiver R in the opposite order (see Figure 4(a)). According to R's behavior this is only possible if in the meantime R has received a shift request with some sequence number a on link 1. Because a single link does not reorder packets, this shift request must have been sent by S before sending packet 1 (see Figure 4(b)). On the other hand, according to S's behavior, S only starts sending on link 2 if there was a successful exchange of a shift request and response with some sequence number b on link 2. Again, because there is no reordering on link 2, R must receive this shift request b before packet 2 (see Figure 4(c)). Now looking at the sender we conclude $a < b$. Looking at the receiver, the shift request with number a is only accepted if $a > b$. Thus our initial assumption on packet reordering leads to a contradiction. □

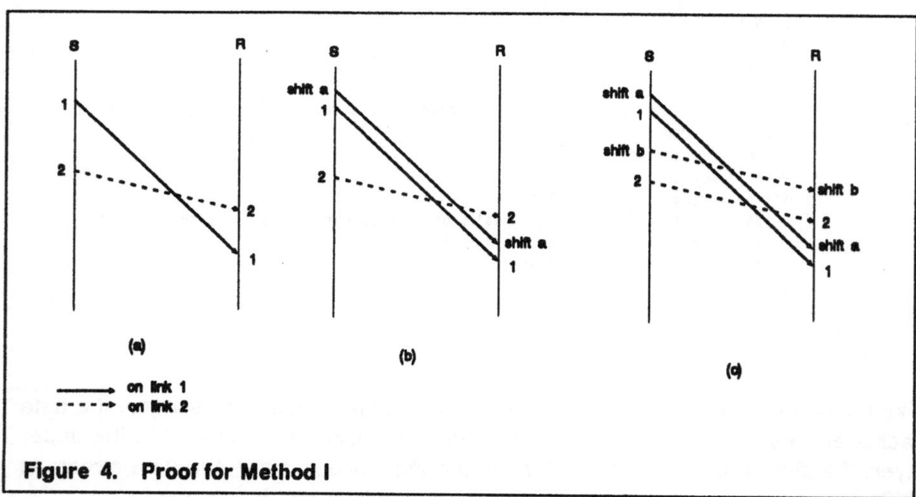

Figure 4. Proof for Method I

4. Method II

In this section the second solution is presented (see Figure 5). The only difference with respect to the interaction of the processes with their local system environment is that the messages exchanged with the management process now have an additional component (cmd / event) indicating whether it has to be interpreted as a sweep or shift message. In addition, the types of the packets transmitted over the links are now either data packets or sweep request / response packets instead of shift packets.

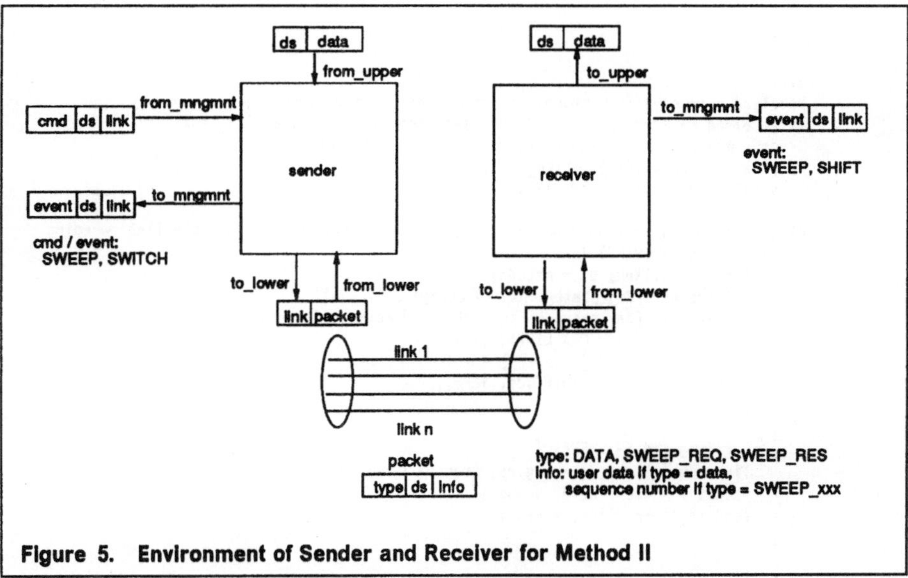

Figure 5. Environment of Sender and Receiver for Method II

The control information stored at each side now also contains the state of the links (clean or dirty) for each data stream. This information is shown below.

```
typedef struct {
   LINK active_link;
   NUMBER seqno
   enum {DIRTY,CLEAN} state[MAX_LINKS];
} cntrl;

cntrl sendcntrl[MAX_DS];    /* sender's local data   */
cntrl receivecntrl[MAX_DS]; /* receiver's local data */
```

During initialization all links are set to be clean.

```
init()
{
   for(i = 0; i < MAX_DS; i++) {
      sendcntrl[i].active_link = initial_link; sendcntrl[i].seqno = 0;
      receivecntrl[i].active_link = initial_link; receivecntrl[i].seqno = 0;
      for(j = 0; j < MAX_LINKS; j++) {
         sendcntrl[i].state[j] = CLEAN; receivecntrl[i].state[j] = CLEAN;
      }
   }
}
```

Finally the sender and receiver processes are as follows: Like in the previous section the sender forwards a packet over the currently active link on receiving a send request from its upper layer. If the sender receives a shift request from network management, the active link is changed given it is clean. The sequence number is increased and all links are considered dirty again. An acknowledgement is returned to network management on success. On receiving a sweep request from network management a sweep request packet is sent over the new link carrying the current sequence number. If a sweep response arrives with the correct sequence number, the link is considered clean and network management is informed.

```
process sender()
{
   forever {
      received = receive(from_mngmnt or from_upper or from_lower,msg);
      if(received == from_upper) { // just send the data on the active link
         ds = msg.ds; info = msg.data; packet = <DATA,ds,info>;
         link = sendcntrl[ds].active_link;
         send(to_lower,<link,packet>);
      }
      else if(received == from_mngmnt) { // switch to clean link or initiate link sweeping
         if(msg.cmd == SHIFT) {
            link = msg.link; ds = msg.ds;
            if(sendcntrl[ds].state[link] == CLEAN) {
               sendcntrl[ds].seqno++; sendcntrl[ds].active_link = link;
               for(j = 0; j < MAX_LINKS; j++)
                  sendcntrl[ds].state[j] = DIRTY;
               send(to_mngmnt,<SHIFT,ds,link>);
            }
         }
         else if(msg.cmd == SWEEP) {
            link = msg.link; ds = msg.ds; seqno = sendcntrl[ds].seqno;
            packet = <SWEEP_REQ,ds,seqno>;
            send(to_lower,<link,packet>);
         }
      }
      else if(received == from_lower) { // outgoing link sweeping has been done
         link = msg.link; packet = msg.packet; ds = packet.ds;
         if((packet.type == SWEEP_RES)
            && (packet.info == sendcntrl[ds].seqno)) { // correct type and sequence no.
            sendcntrl[ds].state[link] = CLEAN;
            send(to_mngmnt,<SWEEP,ds,link>);
         }
      }
   }
}
```

The arrival of a data packet on a clean link at the receiver triggers a shift to this new link which comprises the actions of changing the active link, increasing the shift number, and considering all links to be dirty again. In addition, network management is informed and the packet is passed to the upper layer. If a data packet arrives on the active but dirty link, it is also passed to the upper layer. Otherwise it is discarded. On receiving a sweep request with the current sequence number, the link is considered clean, a response is sent back and a notification is issued to the network management. If the sequence number is higher, in addition all links are considered dirty again except the one from which the sweep request was received.

```
process receiver()
{
   forever {
      receive(from_lower,msg);
      link = msg.link;
      packet = msg.packet;
      ds = packet = ds;
      if(packet.type == DATA) { // data has been received
         if(receivecntrl[ds].state[link] == CLEAN) { // shift if it arrived on a clean link
            receivecntrl[ds].seqno++;
            receivecntrl[ds].active_link = link;
            for(j = 0; j < MAX_LINKS; j++)
               receivecntrl[ds].state[j] = DIRTY;
            send(to_mngmnt,<SHIFT,ds,link>);
         }
         else if(link == receivecntrl[ds].active_link) // else pass to user if active link
            send(to_upper,<ds,packet.info>);
      }
      else if(packet.type == SWEEP_REQ) { // incoming link considered clean if correct seqno
         if(packet.info >= receivecntrl[ds].seqno) {
            if(packet.info > receivecntrl[ds].seqno)
            {
               receivecntrl[ds].seqno = packet.info;
               for(j = 0; j < MAX_LINKS; j++)
                  receivecntrl[ds].state[j] = DIRTY;
            }
            receivecntrl[ds].state[link] = CLEAN;
            packet = <SWEEP_RES,ds,packet.info>;
            send(to_lower,<link,packet>);
            send(to_mngmnt,<ds,link>);
         }
      }
   }
}
```

Proof by contradiction:

As in the previous proof, we assume a reordering scenario as depicted in Figure 6(a). R accepts packet 1 on link 1 only if link 1 is clean at that point in time. So R must have received a sweep request with some sequence number a on link 1. This sweep request may have arrived at R either after or before packet 2 (case 1 and 2, see Figure 6(b) and (c)).

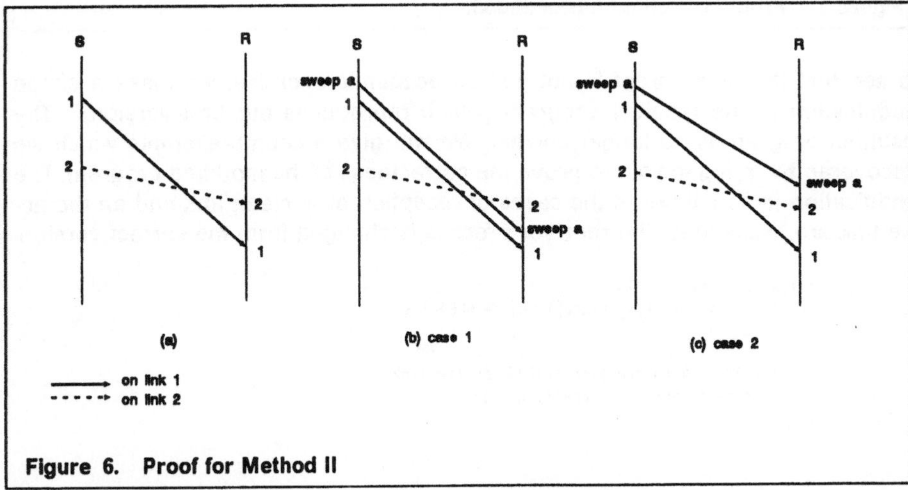

Figure 6. Proof for Method II

Case 1: S only can switch to link 2 if link 2 is clean. Thus there must have been an exchange of sweep request and response packets over link 2 carrying some sequence number b. Because link 2 is order preserving, the sweep request b is received by R before packet 2. Now that link 2 is clean on reception of packet 2, a shifting takes place, thereby increasing the sequence number. Consequently, the sweep request a will be accepted later by R only if $a > b$. Looking at the sender, $a > b$ means that the sweep request b must have been sent before sweep request a and, in addition, that there must have been a shift at the sender's side in the meantime (see Figure 7(a)). But this shift renders link 2 dirty again. Thus S could not have been able to switch to link 2 afterwards. We found a contradiction.

Case 2: With similar reasoning as in case 1, we conclude that R must have received a sweep request b before packet 2. Thus both sweep requests are received before packet 2 (in unknown order, see Figure 7(b)). On reception of packet 2 on the clean link 2, a shifting action is being performed by R thus rendering all links dirty. Packet 1 therefore would not be accepted, because link 1 is dirty at that point in time. Again we found a contradiction. □

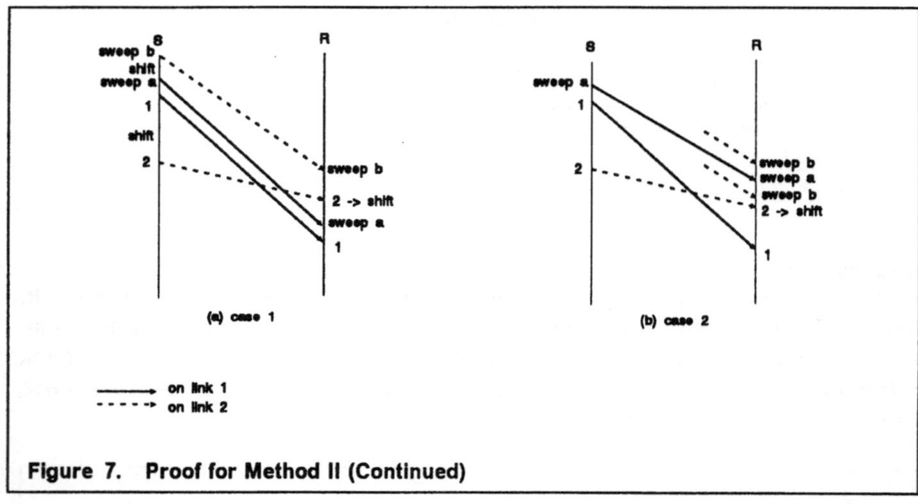

Figure 7. Proof for Method II (Continued)

To see that the given proof is not just an academic exercise, we make a subtle modification to the receiver program (which reproduces our first version). The resulting program is no longer correct. We will give a counterexample which we discovered by trying in vain to prove the correctness of the modified program. The modification is as follows: if the cases of reception on a clean link and on the active link are exchanged, the receiver process is changed from the correct version

```
if(packet.type == DATA) {
   if(receivecntrl[ds].state[link] == CLEAN) {
      ...
   }
   else if(link == receivecntrl[ds].active_link)
      send(to_upper,<ds,packet.info>);
}
```

to the incorrect version

```
if(packet.type == DATA) {
   if(link == receivecntrl[ds].active_link)
      send(to_upper,<ds,packet.info>);
   else if(receivecntrl[ds].state[link] == CLEAN) {
      ...
   }
}
```

The programs behave differently when a packet is received on the active link being clean! This case is shown in the message flow diagram depicted in Figure 8. At the beginning the sender and the receiver are communicating over link 2 which both consider tp be the active link. The sender sweeps link 1 successfully (the response is not shown) and switches to link 1. It now sweeps link 1 again (although this does not make much sense), but because of the shift this time the sweep is done with an increased sequence number. This message is delayed. But because link 1 is already active, the sender does not have to wait for a reply to be able to send data on link 1. The subsequently sent packet 1 is also delayed. Now link 2 is swept successfully (again the response is not shown). The sender switches to link 2 and sends packet 2. This is where the trouble emerges. The receiver does not shift, because link 2 is the active link. Thus the receiver's sequence number is unchanged and the delayed sweep request on link 1 is accepted. The delayed packet 1 is accepted, too, and triggers a shift, because link 1 is erroneously taken to be clean. Note that in the correct version the receiver would switch from link 2 to link 2 on reception of packet 2, because the link is clean. The sequence number would be increased and the delayed sweep on link 1 would thus be rejected. Packet 1 would then also be discarded.

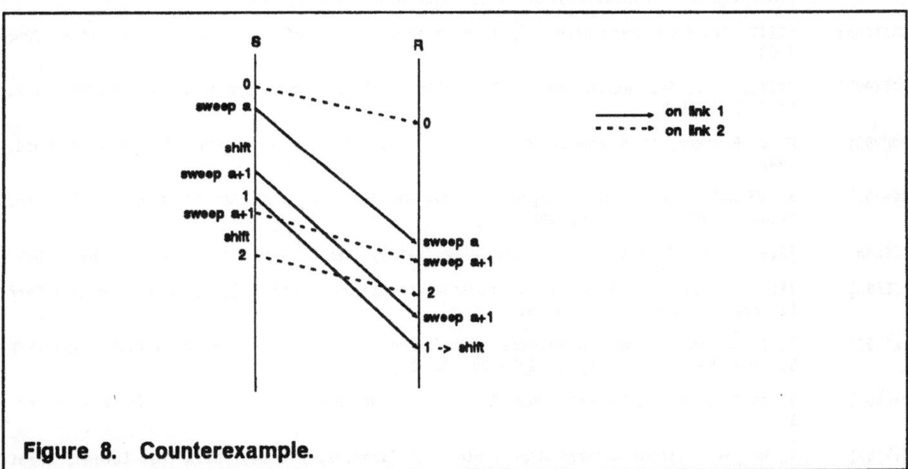

Figure 8. Counterexample.

5. Summary

The topic of this paper is the shift of a data stream flowing from a sender to a receiver entity on one link to a parallel link connecting the same entities. The source and sink of a data stream are able to deal with lost packets, but not with packets arriving out of order. Thus the shift has to be done in such a way that in-sequence delivery is guaranteed. In this paper we presented two approaches that solve this task: the first method uses numbered shift packets that first have to be exchanged between the nodes before the actual data stream shift can take place. In the second method the shift is only prepared by exchanging special packets. The actual shift takes place simply by using an already prepared link.

Obviously, in the second solution a shift can be done immediately if there are clean links available. This advantage, however, has to be paid by storing the information of which link is dirty and which is clean for each data stream. But note that the amount of state information to be remembered can be reduced by grouping several data streams together into one new data stream, i.e. by making the data stream granularity more coarse. In our ATM example this is easily achieved by considering virtual path connections (identified by the VPI value only) instead of virtual connections (identified by the combined VPI/VCI value) as data streams.

Both solutions presented are efficient. The overhead carried in each data packet is very low. The data stream identifier is assumed to be there anyhow, so one just needs the information to distinguish between data and control packets. For this purpose one may use some predefined data stream identifier for the control packets, thus completely avoiding overhead in the data packets. Moreover, the protocols for data stream shifting are simple and require only a very limited amount of extra control packets to be exchanged.

References

[CCIT88] **CCITT**, *Recommendation X.75: Packet-Switched Signalling System between Public Networks Providing Data Transmission Services*, Blue Book, Geneva, 1988.

[CCIT90a] **CCITT**, *Draft Recommendation I.121: Broadband Aspects of ISDN*, COM XVIII-R, 34-E, June 1990.

[CCIT90b] **CCITT**, *Draft Recommendation I.150: B-ISDN ATM Functional Characteristics*, COM XVIII-R, 34-E, June 1990.

[dePr91] **M. de Prycker**, *Asynchronous Transfer Mode - Solution for Broadband ISDN*, Ellis Horwood, 1991.

[Haen91] **R. Händel, M.N. Huber**, *Integrated Broadband Networks - An Introduction to ATM-Based Networks*, Addison-Wesley, 1991.

[IEEE88] **IEEE Network**, *Special Issue on LAN Connectivity*, IEEE Network, Vol.2, No.1, January 1988.

[IEEE89] **IEEE Std. 802.2 / ISO 8802-2**, *Information Processing Systems - Local Area Networks - Part 2: Logical Link Control*, 1989.

[LeBo92] **J.-Y. Le Boudec**, *The Asynchronous Transfer Mode: A Tutorial*, Computer Networks and ISDN Systems, Vol. 24, No. 4, pp. 279-309, May 15, 1992.

[Mart87] **J. Martin**, *SNA: IBM's Networking Solution*, Prentice-Hall, Englewood Cliffs, New Jersey, 1987.

[Meij87] **A. Meijer**, *Systems Network Architecture: A Tutorial*, Pitman Publishing, London, Great Britain, 1987.

[Post81] **J. Postel**, *Transmission Control Protocol - DARPA Internet Program Protocol Specification*, RFC 793, DARPA, September 1981.

[Schr91] **M.D. Schroeder et al.**, *Autonet: A High-Speed, Self-Configuring Local Area Network Using Point-to-Point Links*, IEEE Journal on Selected Areas in Communications, Vol.9, No.8, pp. 1318-1335, October 1991.

[Tane89] **A. Tanenbaum**, *Computer Networks*, Prentice-Hall, 1989.

Design and Implementation of Distributed C++

Markus U. Mock and Alexander B. Schill
Institut für Telematik, Postfach 6980
Universität Karlsruhe, 76128 Karlsruhe
E-Mail: mock@ira.uka.de

Abstract

This paper describes the design and the implementation of a distributed C++ prototype. The system enables distributed placement of objects on a set of cooperating, loosely-coupled workstations, location-transparent object invocations, and dynamic object migration. Applications benefit from this approach due to the high level of abstraction concerning inter object communication. Nevertheless, object placement can be explicitly controlled, e.g. to co-locate communicating objects. The prototype has been implemented as a system service on top of Unix and TCP/IP, and in a follow-up version also on top of the OSF Distributed Computing Environment. As opposed to other approaches, it is offered purely as a class library without a need for C++ language extensions or compiler modifications.

Recent performance numbers, various experiences gathered with our prototype, and relationships with ongoing projects in the distributed systems department of our institute are discussed, too.

Keywords: distributed systems, object-oriented programming, object mobility, C++, system services

1 Introduction

Distributed object-oriented approaches are already common in the research and advanced development area. Such systems have been built as extensions of Smalltalk, Trellis, Eiffel, and C++, for example. They provide facilities for distributed object placement, location independent object invocation, and, in some instances, for object mobility at runtime. These features enable a high level of abstraction during distributed application development. Nevertheless, the developer still can influence static and dynamic object placement

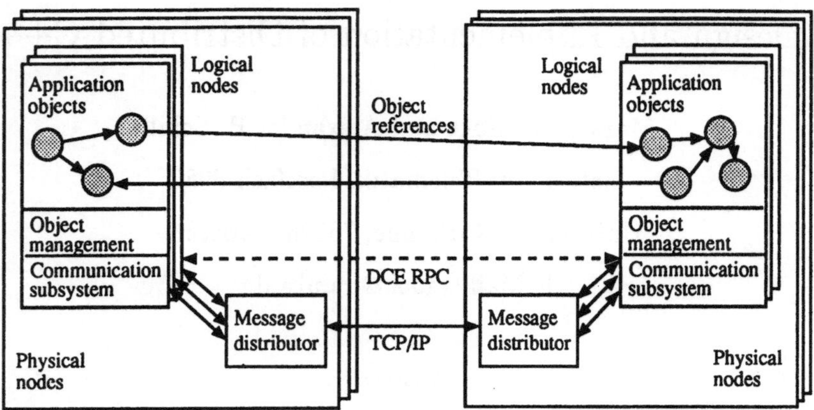

Figure 1: System archictecture

using placement directives and explicit object migration. This way, communicating objects can be co-located, for example.

However, most existing approaches require significant kernel support, and typically also language or at least compiler modifications, and rather complex runtime systems. Therefore, such implementations have been limited to relatively large project efforts in the past. Moreover, implementation details are rarely reported in the accessible literature — leading to various redundant designs of similar features in different systems.

Within our distributed C++ project, we implemented a user-level facility for distributed object management. As opposed to most other approaches, it does not require kernel support or language/compiler modifications. The price for that is a somewhat reduced level of transparency regarding call marshalling. The current communication platform is based on the RPC of the OSF Distributed Computing Environment (DCE) [OSF92]. We also discuss experiences with a former implementation on top of a less suitable TCP/IP communication architecture with a much worse performance — this lead to our redesign.

2 System and Application Architecture

The system architecture of our approach is shown in fig. 1. A distributed C++ environment for distributed applications consists of a number of loosely interconnected physical nodes, in our case DECStations 5000 under Ultrix. On each physical node, several logical nodes can be installed that eventually host the distributed C++ objects. A logical node is implemented by a Unix process. Within each logical node, a communication subsystem implements basic message passing or RPC communication, onto which remote object interactions and migrations are mapped. Within our first implementation, the subsystem

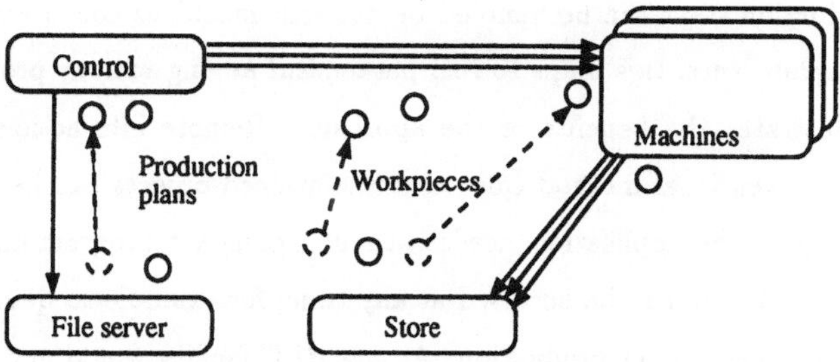

Figure 2: Application structure

accesses local Unix sockets for message exchange with an intermediate message distributor, another Unix process. Messages between logical nodes on the same physical node go through this distributor process; it forwards them to the peer logical node where a receiver thread is waiting to get signalled and handles the received message thereafter. Messages between physical nodes are transferred via TCP/IP connections and are forwarded to the receiver via a peer message distributor. The alternative implementation directly uses DCE RPC interactions between application processes. That is, the communication subsystem both acts as a RPC client and server and contacts the peer subsystem by direct RPCs. RPC addresses are given by DCE "binding handles" and are yielded by our algorithm to locate objects. At the upper interface of the communication subsystem, there is no difference between the two alternative communication mechanisms: A uniform message-based interaction facility is offered to the object management layer in both cases.

As an application of our approach, we implemented a distributed CIM emulation; its structure is shown in fig. 2. A control object with a human interface initiates manufacturing requests. To handle such a request, it fetches an appropriate production plan from a file server, and delegates various production steps defined by that plan to appropriate machines. Machines are somewhat "intelligent"; they are able to fetch the required workpieces from a store server, manipulate them, and finally move the resulting end products or intermediate workpieces back to the store server. All entities are implemented by C++ objects and can be placed at different logical or even physical nodes. They interact via location independent method calls; an example is a request to manufacture a workpiece: it is mapped to a method of the machines to be invoked by the control component. Object mobility is exploited for the more fine grained objects, i.e. for the production plans and the workpieces. They are usually moved to the location where they are accessed, i.e. from the file server to the control component or from the store to a machine and vice versa, respectively. Within the application, significant concurrency exists: multiple production requests can be issued concurrently to the control component. Moreover, within one request, multiple production steps can be handled by different machines concurrently. Due to the distributed architecture, this maps to real parallelism among various processors.

The example illustrates the benefits of the approach: Remote interactions can be easily mapped onto conventional method calls, and fine-grained objects can be relocated dynamically according to the application needs without significant programming effort. Moreover, even mobile objects can be accessed at any time, for example to query for the current status of a workpiece under production. A pure RPC facility would not allow the latter two mechanisms.

3 Distributed C++ Object Management

In this section we discuss how Distributed C++ objects are managed. We show how to identify them, how we keep track of where they are, how object methods can be invoked and how objects are migrated.

3.1 Global Object Identification

Global object IDs To identify objects they need a globally unique object identifier. The global object ID consists of two parts:

1. the node identifier which itself consists of two subparts, the host identifier (the Internet address of the host on which the logical node resides) and the node number which is the number of the logical node on that host.

2. the object number which is the number of the object local to that logical node.

Uniqueness of this ID is guaranteed because either the host part (if the objects are created on different hosts), the node part (for objects that are created on the same host but on different logical nodes) or the object number will be different since the distributor assigns a unique number to each node that is started on its host. Likewise, by calling a static member function of the common root class `Base` which maintains a counter of created objects, uniqueness of the object number is guaranteed.

Class Hierarchy for Objects and Proxies In the previous paragraph we had already mentioned that all classes to be used in the application must be derived from the root class `Base`. This owes to the fact that we need to manage the objects that the application uses and also to empower them to be migrated or called remotely. To better understand

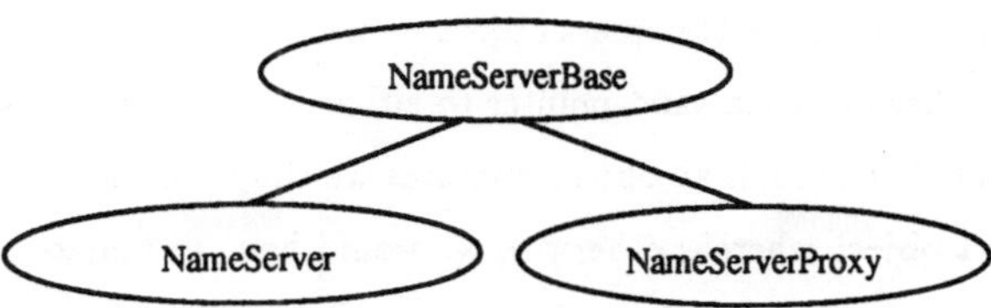

Figure 3: Class structure for application objects

where the user[1] defined objects fit into the whole system we will review the class hierarchy into which user defined objects fall. We will illustrate the class hierarchy by looking at a user defined class which comes with the system, the class `NameServer`. As the name suggests, objects of this type do offer a primitive kind of name service. The root class of the system is class `Base`.

This class must be inherited by all used defined classes. By inheriting from this class objects become migrate-able and are also automatically assigned their object ID upon creation.

The next class in the class hierarchy is the user defined class `NameServerBase` (see figure 3). For each object class the user must define three component classes:

- an abstract base class which must inherit from `Base` (in our example `NameServerBase`)
- the object class itself which must inherit from its base class (in our example `NameServer`)
- a proxy class which must inherit from the user defined base class too (in our case `NameServerProxy`)

Both the object class and the proxy class will have the same methods, however, in the proxy implementation there won't be any code that actually performs the operations, rather the proxy implementation will be the interface for calling the object remotely on another node.

Smart Pointers One of the centerpieces of Distributed C++ is the use of *smart pointers*. Smart pointers are C++ objects that serve as an additional level of indirection when accessing objects. Using direct pointers to objects would create an analogon to the *dangling pointer* problem when the object migrates to another node. Therefore a programmer always uses smart pointers to access objects (their methods, data). The smart pointer is

[1]We use the term *user* interchangeably with the term *application programmer*, seeing an application programmer as a *user* of Distributed C++.

a pointer to a C++ object — the smart object — which maintains the current address of the object, i.e. it has always a valid pointer to either a real object or a proxy in case the object has migrated. Hence, if an object migrates we simply have to update the information in the smart object whereas otherwise we would have to update a whole number of pointers to the object itself which would be less efficient since it would require keeping track of all the pointers to the object.

Since smart pointers are necessary for every user defined class their implementation requires the use of *templates*. In newer versions of C++ compilers these are already available, however, Distributed C++ was built using AT&T's translator 2.1.0. Hence, we had to emulate them by using `#define`-Macros.

3.2 Location Independent Object Invocation

The main purpose of Distributed C++ was to make programming of distributed applications only insignificantly more difficult than the programming of a comparable application running on just one host. To that end it is necessary to hide from the programmer the complexity that is necessary to invoke methods of an object remotely[2]. For that purpose we use the concept of *proxies*, i.e. entities that act on behalf of a remote object. We will now look at the details of object invocation more closely.

When an object is to be called we need a smart pointer to that object. To obtain a smart pointer we first consult the object table using the ID of the object that is to be called as a key. `ObjectTable[oid]` will then return a Base pointer to that object (or its proxy) that will be used to obtain a smart pointer. Then we will call the method as usual being unaware whether we are calling the object locally or not. If the object is local then the smart pointer redirects simply to the C++ object on our local node and the call proceeds as usual. If the smart pointer, however, points to a proxy, the proxy packs the parameter data which are then sent to the expected location of the object. For illustration, look at the following code fragment:

```
WorkpiecePtr LagerProxy::GetWorkpiece( char *name )
{
        active;
        Buffer buf;
        WorkpiecePtr Workpiece;

        buf << name;
```

[2]Of course, this is not the only complexity involved. Other issues such as failure semantics or problems created by concurrency still have to be dealt with by the user.

```
        buf = BufRmCall( 1, buf );
        Workpiece = (Workpiece*)::UnpackObject( buf );
        return Workpiece;
    }
```

In this case, (Workpiece*)::UnpackObject(buf); is called to unpack the data in the returned buffer. The unpack method has to be implemented by the user (just as its analogon the pack method). However, this is simplified by providing overloading of the << and >> operator for many standard data types. For instance, in the current example it is as simple as that:

```
    void Workpiece::UnpackData( Buffer &buf )
    {
        buf >> str >> w;
    }
```

where str is the string representing the workpiece and w an integer used in the modeling of the CIM example.

Its argument is the workpiece that is to be stored which is represented by putting it on a list. The corresponding proxy class has to pack the parameter into a buffer (done by workpiece->PackObject(buf)) and then send this data to the correct place. For that purpose there is a method BufRmCall(2, buf) . As argument it simply gets the number of the method (methods within a class are enumerated from 1 to the number of methods present) and the buffer itself. BufRmCall(int funNo, Buffer buf) is a method of the root class base and actually carries out the remote call by sending the data in the buffer to the appropriate node.

Call forwarding When a node receives a call for an object that no longer resides on that node it simply forwards the call to the suspected location of the object. This is guaranteed to work since a migrating object always leaves behind a proxy knowing where the object migrated to. By following this chain of forwarding addresses we will eventually arrive at the object's true location. This method is also used in the well-known Emerald system[BHJ87]. For efficiency, the answer is not returned via the forwarding chain, rather we send it back directly to the calling node. That's why we prepend the caller's node ID to the message. Every time a proxy receives an answer it updates its suspectedLocation accordingly, which is possible because the answer message does also contain the node ID of the sender of the answer. This is done automatically by the handler thread each time it processes an incoming answer message.

Object References as arguments Another point we have glossed over so far is what is to be done with references to objects that are arguments of method calls. This creates some additional complexity, however, forbidding object references as parameters would in our opinion seriously degrade the usability and performance of the system.

Sending the reference itself in the message does obviously not make any sense. In a different address space this pointer would be completely meaningless. For that reason, when the application programmer uses the >> or << operator to pack an object reference the system will do the following:

- when the object reference is passed it is translated into the object ID of the referenced object.
- when an object reference is unpacked the transmitted object ID is used to to consult the local object table. If the object is known a reference to the object (or proxy) is created. If the object is completely unknown, the name server is consulted and a proxy is created for the referenced object. A reference to that proxy will be used then.[3]

Processing incoming calls Another important design decision was to allow several threads of activity on one node at the same time. Therefore we are using a thread package as previously mentioned. When a message from a different node arrives a handler thread is created that takes care of processing the incoming messages.

3.3 Invocation Marshalling

The term *invocation marshalling* is commonly used to refer to the way a stub in a RPC system encodes the parameters into a message which is sent over the net. Usually these stubs are generated automatically from an interface description that describes the procedures that are called remotely (e.g. in OSF's DCE system). Since we neither made any changes to the C++ compiler nor wrote a special preprocessor it remains the user's responsibility to achieve correct encoding/decoding of parameters in calls. However, this task is greatly simplified because

1. it is limited to the implementation of the proxies
2. and supported by providing packing/unpacking routines for standard data types.

[3]This requires that the implementation code for all classes is available at all nodes which is actually the case. Hence only object data is migrated, not the code that implements the objects' methods.

To see how this looks in the actual implementation, please refer to the previous coding example in section 3.2.

3.4 Object Mobility

In Distributed C++ objects are mobile. Each object can request to be migrated to a different node by calling the Base method **migrate** which takes as parameter the destination node. Likewise, migration can be requested through a proxy such that it is possible to 'summon' an object to a specific site (logical node). When an object requests migration — either directly or through a proxy — its data part is packed into a message and sent to the destination node. There, a new object of the same class is created, its data part is initialized and its ID set to the ID of the original object. Moreover, the object on the originating site is deleted and replaced by a proxy.

Since there can be many different classes and we don't know their data part beforehand it is obvious that the user must write her own code to pack the data part into a message. As for the encoding of method calls, the basic data types are already supported by the system. Hence, it should be fairly easy to write a **PackData** function that encodes the objects' data. To be able to distinguish between objects of different classes each class must be enumerated in an enumeration type thus receiving a unique identifier. This identifier will then be returned by a class specific method (called **GetClassId**) based on which the **PackData** method will pack the data into a message. To be able on the receiving side to install an object of the correct class, the class ID is included in the migration message. When such a message is received the handler thread will find that it received a migration message, it will then create an object of the requested class and unpack the data into that object's data part. Again, since there is no compiler support, the unpack data function has to be written by the user. Provided that the data types are standard types this is a trivial if unpleasant task. Once an object has been received correctly, a notification message is sent to the originator which can then return from the execution of the migration method. Before it does so it changes the existing object to a proxy, which in fact means that the original (C++-) object is destroyed, a new (C++-) object is created and installed as a proxy which expects its corresponding object on the logical node to which the (Distributed C++-) object migrated.

Synchronization issues Synchronization issues are out of the scope of this paper. We will only briefly discuss the associated problems.

Two related problems arise when objects become migrate-able. First, if an object is currently migrating to a different node, incoming calls must be blocked until the migration is completed. Once the object has reached its destination, the blocked calls can be rerouted. Second, if a thread is executing a method of an object we cannot migrate the object until the execution completes. Hence, we have to keep track of *activations* of the objects, that is methods that are still executing on the object and on the other hand we have to mark an object that wants to migrate such that we can block incoming calls.

This is done by maintaining an activation counter that is protected through semaphores. Only when the activation count falls to zero – indicating that no method is currently active on the object – the object will be migrated.

4 Experiences and Related Work

4.1 Performance

We measured the time for remote object invocations and for migrations based on both implementations (using TCP/IP with a distributor process and using DCE RPC directly between application processes, respectively). For performing the measurements, we ran the example application and evaluated the mean remote invocation times. This way, a relatively realistic scenario serves as a base for our measurements. We also did evaluations based on "dummy" calls, leading to slightly improved numbers, but these are much less realistic. All performance tests were run on lightly loaded DECStations 5000 connected by an Ethernet.

Performance of a DCE-based implementation Testing the sample application in this scenario showed the following results:[4]

Migration

Buffer size [bytes]	Min	Max	Average
53	7.8	11.7	8.8
61	7.8	11.7	8.8
66	7.8	11.8	9.8

[4]All times are reported in milli-seconds. Buffer size refers to the size of the byte string that is actually sent between the nodes. The objects in the application were all of moderate size as can be seen in the first table.

Calls via 1 proxy

Buffer size [bytes]	Min	Max	Average
0	15.6	50.8	19.2
1000	27.3	210.9	62.3
10000	113.3	619.3	375.4

The times for remote calls in the order of tens of milli-seconds are competitive with other comparable systems and will allow practical application of the system for the development of distributed object oriented systems.

Performance of the TCP/IP Implementation The performance figures of the earlier prototype based on TCP/IP using a distributor on each host to handle communication were quite disappointing. This was one of the reasons of our redesign. Due to the existence of the distributor, the numbers also depend much more on the allocation of logical to physical nodes. Therefore, the TCP/IP implementation was tested in two scenarios:

- Host A: distributor, control node and machine node, Host B: distributor, store node and machine node
- Host A: distributor and control node, Host B: distributor, store node and machine node.

In the first scenario the average call time was 110.5 ms, in the second scenario 651.4 ms! Especially the second scenario reveals the problem: the store node and the machine node communicate heavily with one another. Being on the same host, each time they communicate a context switch has to take place from the node to the distributor on to the other node. Therefore context switches account for the major part of the call time. This performance penalty is even exacerbated by the fact that the distributor listens on a single Unix socket and has to do an `accept` system call each time a local node wants to contact it. `Accept`, however, is also quite expensive. All this lead to the seemingly paradox observation that running the application on 3 different hosts where communication occurs over the net and not locally on the same host showed a better performance than the second scenario with mostly local communication.

4.2 Experiences and Extensions

We learned some important lessons from our performance measurements:

1. Using a separate process to handle communication between logical nodes is a bad idea. Context switches are likely to occur frequently and carry a heavy performance

penalty rendering the distributor architecture impractical for real distributed application development.

2. Integration of existing RPC mechanisms into the object-oriented paradigm is possible and seems to be promising, especially since we believe that DCE-RPC is going to be a widely available standard in the future.

3. Closer integration of RPC with our architecture is desirable. In the measured DCE implementation packing and unpacking is basically duplicated, once done in the pack/unpack routines and then again in the RPC stub marshalling the byte string. *Moving up* the marshalling would both obviate the need for writing pack/unpack routines and also yield even better performance. This is the goal of ongoing research. First measurements of a recently finished implementation [SCP93] that avoids marshalling at two levels ranked at about 10ms for an empty remote call only barely surpassing the time for a plain (empty) RPC call for which we measured about 6ms in our environment.

Some more general observations are:

- The distributed object model is a very appropriate base for building distributed applications. It provides all major abstractions required for high-level application programming.
- The model can be implemented as a user-level runtime library without kernel or compiler modifications. Based on a well-engineered communication architecture, a sufficient level of efficiency can be reached.
- The use of standards, especially of the emerging DCE, is increasingly important: Heterogeneity of data formats and of communication protocols can only be handled by standards.

4.3 Related Work

Early implementations of distributed object-oriented systems are *Emerald* [BHJ87], *Distributed Smalltalk* [BEN87], and *LII* [BLA89]. They have introduced the major concepts and have shown that they can be implemented efficiently. A survey is also found in [CHC91] However, due to the specialized languages, these and other systems have been limited to a dedicated domain of users.

More recently, extensions of the more general and widely used C++ language have been emerging. Examples are *Amadeus* [HOC91], *Amber* [CAL89], *Arjuna* [SDP91], *Electra* [MAF92], *Peace* [SCP92], and *Panda* [BRE92]. Amadeus offers a general distributed C++ implementation but required many compiler modifications as reported by the authors. The Amber system integrates local multiprocessor parallelism with distributed programming. These facilities are achieved by the use of a dedicated kernel named Topaz. The Arjuna approach focuses on distributed transaction support for objects but does not provide object mobility. The Peace system is based on the specialized operating system kernel with the same name. It is among the most far-reaching approaches with full stub compiler support, mobility, and alternative implementations on a multiprocessor and on a distributed system. The Panda system implements distributed object management based on distributed shared memory at the object level; remote objects are fetched for invocations based on a kernel-level access fault. This makes excellent performance possible but requires kernel modifications.

5 Conclusion

The paper has described the design and implementation of distributed C++ as a user-level library. We have shown the feasibility of such an approach in terms of implementation effort, usability, and performance. The emerging need for standards and the availability of DCE for more than one year at our institute lead us to the idea of a full integration of distributed object management with an underlying RPC facility. The enhancement of this integration, the technical evaluation and application, and the move to OSF/1 on Alpha workstations as well as to a high performance Gigaswitch transport environment available soon (based on FDDI and later on ATM) are our near-term goals.

References

[BEN87] Bennett, J.K.: The Design and Implementation of Distributed Smalltalk; *ACM OOPSLA Conf., Orlando 1987, pp. 318-330*

[BHJ87] Black, A., Hitchinson, N., Jul, E., Levy, H., Carter, L.: Distribution and Abstract Types in Emerald; *IEEE Transactions on Software Engineering, Vol. 13, Nr. 1, Jan. 1987, pp. 65-75*

[BLA89] Black, A., Artsy, Y.: Implementing Location Independent Invocation; *9th Int. Conf. on Distributed Computing Systems, Newport Beach 1989, pp. 550-559*

[BRE92] Breitbach, T.: Panda — eine Basis für verteiltes Programmieren unter C++; *Arbeitskreis Betriebssysteme, Dresden, Okt. 1992*

[CAL89] Chase, J.S., Amador, F.G., Lazowska, E.D., Levy, H.M., Littlefield, R.J.: The Amber System: Parallel Programming on a Network of Multiprocessors; *Internal Report, Univ. of Washington, Seattle, 1989*

[CHC91] Chin, R.S., Chanson, S.T.: Distributed Object-Based Programming Systems; *ACM Computing Surveys, Vol. 23, No. 1, March 1991, pp. 91-124*

[HOC91] Horn, C., Cahill, V.: Supporting Distributed Applications in the Amadeus Environment; *Computer Communications, Vol. 14, No. 6, July/Aug. 1991, pp. 358-365*

[MAF92] Maffeis, S.: The Electra Approach to Object Oriented Programming; *Institut für Informatik der Universität Zürich, IFI TR 92.23, November 1992*

[OSF92] Introduction to OSF DCE; *Open Software Foundation, Cambridge, USA, 1992*

[SCP92] Schroeder-Preikschat, W.: PEACE — The Evolution of a Parallel Operating System; *Arbeitspapiere der GMD Nr. 646, Mai 1992*

[SCP93] Schill, A., Person, M.: Verteilte objektorientierte Erweiterung des OSF Distributed Computing Environments; *erscheint in Offene Systeme, Sommer 1993*

[SDP91] Shrivastava, S.K., Dixon, G.N., Parrington, G.D.: An Overview of the Arjuna Distributed Programming System; *IEEE Software, Jan. 1991, pp. 66-73*

Managing Failures in Distributed Systems

Kwok-Yan Lam and **Siu Leung Chung**
Department of Information Systems and Computer Science
National University of Singapore
Singapore 0511
E-mail: lamky@iscs.nus.sg

Abstract

This paper discusses the problems we experienced with the use of a general purpose distributed operating system. It describes the problems with our approach to system availability, and identifies the major problem that makes the task of improving the availability of a distributed operating system hard to achieve. It then describes a new system service that was developed as a solution to satisfy our needs.

1 Introduction

The scalability feature of distributed operating systems has a negative effect on their availability. Their distributed nature allows incremental growth in processing power and data storage capacity of the system. As a distributed system grows, it becomes less and less consistently available when most of its vital services run on different machines. Since system services are now provided by sets of server machines, the execution of an application can be interrupted if any one of these machines fails.

In order to improve the availability of the system, services which are vital to the normal operations of the system should be implemented in a fault-tolerant way. Fault tolerance is usually achieved through replications; which, however, introduces complications of its own, and is difficult to achieve. The design of a fault-tolerant component of a distributed system involves a compromise between the availability, the resources requirements and the performance overhead of the system.

On the other hand, there are system problems that make the job of achieving high availability debilitating. In a distributed system, one component can make use of services exported by another and hence, failures in one component can bring down other components which import services from it. This closely interdependent nature of various system components suggests the provision of some kind of failure handling service that treats the environment as a coherent entity.

In the Cambridge Distributed Computing System (CDCS) [1], the approach taken to system availability is to reboot a new server instance as soon as possible after a crash. System services are designed to run unattended and to restart automatically after loss of power or any transient failure. Owing to our availability requirement, reboot of a crashed server must be triggered with minimal dalay. This was previously accomplished by means of a special server called the Boot Server. As we shall see, this alone was not an entirely satisfactory solution to meet our availability requirement.

A new system service - the System Monitoring Service - has been designed and implemented as a part of the system infrastructure. This service is aimed at improving system availability and allows components failures to be handled in a coherent manner.

2 System Model

A distributed system is a computer system with many computing nodes and storage devices connected together by a network, where each node is a computer with one or more processors. In general, it is assumed that physical nodes are connected by one or more local area networks which are interconnected within a local environment. The important characteristics of a local internet of current technology include high bandwidth, low latency, and high reliability – it has a very low error rate in the absence of congestion at the receiving machine, and has sufficient redundant links that the probability of partitioning is low enough that the issue can be dismissed.

The type of distributed system that is considered in this paper consists of a collection of **processes** possessing local states and communicating by messages. Each process runs on a computing node, and is regarded as the **fundamental element** of the system.

The distributed operating system is considered a set of **functional components**, called **system services**, provided to users. Examples of system services include name service, file service, time service, and authentication service. Each of these services may be implemented by more than one distributed processes for fault-tolerance or performance reasons.

A service is a set of operations provided to users to allow them to perform a particular function, and is exported by the underlying system elements. A process is called a **server** if it is involved in the implementation of some service, while the process that calls upon a server to perform some operation is called a **client**. A service may make use of operations exported by other components and hence, a server can be the client of some other servers.

3 Availability Requirement

In the CDCS, system services are not usually replicated for economic reason, the approach to system availability is to reboot a new server instance as soon as failure is detected. This decision was based on the assumption that machines do not fail very frequently, and we would not like to sacrifice system performance nor extra computing resource for a higher guarantee of system availability.

This scheme works well as far as **stateless services** are concerned. A stateless server either stores state information in stable object or does not maintain any indispensable state information at all. Since a stateless server does not lose any information about client requests in the case of a server crash, clients will simply sleep until the server comes back and their operations can complete.

With this approach to availability, the process of recovering a **stateful service** from a crash is necessarily more complex since it loses its state when it recovers. Nevertheless, stateful services is not uncommon in distributed systems. There are system services such as network lock manager [2] or resource manager [4] which inherently need to remember essential state information about client requests. If such state information cannot be maintained as stable object, for example, for performance reasons, the state information will be lost in a crash. The service is therefore a **stateful service**.

Therefore some mechanism is required to allow the recovering server to re-establish a consistent state before normal service is resumed. Such a mechanism usually involves the cooperation of its clients which send to the server necessary information needed to reconstruct its state.

In order to clarify the point, let us consider the network lock manager as an example. A network lock manager supports file or record level locking in a network environment. Locking prevents multiple processes from modifying the same file or record at the same time, and allows cooperating processes to synchronize access to shared data. A client is allowed to access the shared data only if it holds a lock that is granted to it by the lock manager. All the locks for a process are released when it finishes. The lock manager has to maintain certain state information describing the status of each locked data. Such information may not be stored as stable objects for performance reasons. The lock manager can solve this problem by cooperating with its clients to ensure that, when a lock manager recovers from a crash, all lock requests previously granted by the crashed server are retransmitted to the recovering lock manager. This retransmitted information is used to reconstruct its locking state. Therefore some kind of mechanism is required to **notify** its clients when a new lock manager recovers from crashes.

Whereas, it is also desirable to **monitor** the status of the clients. If a client terminates abnormally, due to a crash for instance, the locks it claimed can be held forever. This problem can be solved by requiring that the network lock manager is notified of all relevant process crashes. If the failure of a client is detected, the lock manager releases the failed client's locks, on the assumption that the client application will request locks again as needed.

As a consequence of our availability requirement, we have designed a new system service which provides a **failure detection** and an **event notification** mechanism for general use. These mechanisms are provided at the process level. They are made available to ordinary user processes in addition to vital system server processes.

4 Problems of Distributed Systems

A distributed system is considered a set of services provided to users. Many activities in a distributed system are modelled by the **client-server** model, in which a client process wanting some service sends a message to the server and then waits for a reply message. Behaviour of each service is described by the specification of its interface.

Each service makes certain assumptions about its environment, and its normal functioning relies on how realistic these assumptions are. A service manages some kind of computing resources being allocated to it by the system, and provides the specified service. The service may fail to perform its functions properly due to the lack of or insufficiency of resources. System resources that a service may manage usually include persistent storage, network bandwidth, and CPU cycles. For example, in order for a mail service to meet its specified behaviour, the service should be carried out by one or more processes with sufficient CPU cycles, disk storage and network bandwidth. The group of processes that implements the mail service uses the disk for spooling messages, which are delivered through the network. Mail service will not be available if any of these resources are not available or insufficient.

Unfortunately, there are system problems that make the behaviour of a distributed environment difficult to predict. The failure of one system component may have some unpredictably adverse effect on other parts of the system due to the closely interdependent nature of a distributed system. Therefore, in a distributed system, it is possible that two components, each with reasonable behaviour when viewed in isolation, may exhibit undesirable behaviour when combined. Even worse, the failure of a single component may bring the whole system to a grinding halt. Such problems are called **interference** and **propagation of effect**.

As an illustration, consider the Sun's Network File System [8] which was designed to make sharing of filesystem resources between a number of machines. The NFS server exports certain subdirectories of its directory tree to selected clients, and clients can mount some of those exported subtrees remotely if they have the appropriate privileges. Although the server and its clients fail independently, failure of the server may hang client processes until it comes back. Client machines will be unable to create any new process and hence become inaccessible if the file service is not resumed early enough, since they will have too many processes waiting in the kernel for the recovery of the server. The increase in number of processes being suspended in the kernel will eventually exhaust the process table of that kernel.

The closely interdependent nature of various system components suggests that it is necessary to have some kind of system management functions which treat the environment as a coherent entity. Since it is very difficult and expensive, if not impossible, to build a functional component that always operates correctly in spite of hardware failures by using only a finite amount of computing resources, the goal of implementing completely fault-tolerant software is untenable. An analysis of the failure statistics of the Tandem computers [5] [6] has shown that although fault-tolerant systems have better availability than conventional systems, they do fail occasionally. Because of the environmental and operations faults, even the most carefully designed fault-tolerant system is still subject to failure. Therefore, in order to improve the predictability of a distributed system, it is not enough to simply improve the fault tolerance of individual components of the system. Distributed systems should be managed so as to maintain a working environment for various services.

5 The System Monitoring Service

The System Monitoring Service being described here aims at improving system availability. It provides a failure detection mechanism and a notification mechanism as general services for various system components. With the monitoring information it maintains, this service also provides its users with knowledge of the availability of each system component and hence, an overall picture of the availability of the whole system.

5.1 Failure Detection and Notification

Our approach to achieve improved availability is to reboot a new server instance as soon as possible after a crash. This is assisted by the provision of a failure detection and notification mechanism. The monitor server (MS) that implements this functions monitors the status of other system services, and notifies interested parties when failure is detected. Those parties may be a boot server, a recovery manager, the members of a fault-tolerant process group, or the clients of a stateful server.

A process that is required to have a high availability can **register** itself to the system monitoring service. MS provides an interface such that other processes can send requests to it for registration. A registration request specifies a **time-out** period, within which the registering process will contact MS for indicating its aliveness, and a set of processes that MS should notify when it fails. MS keeps track of the availability of all registered processes. If a process is deduced to be unavailable, it notifies all interested parties which in turn may execute some specific protocol so as to allow the service to be resumed as fast as possible and in a consistent state.

Each registered process must periodically send an **aliveness** message to MS within a specified period of time to indicate that it is still alive. MS maintains a timer value for each registered process, and resets the timer associated with a registered process on receiving an aliveness message from that process. It scans through the list of timer values checking for items in which the timer has expired, and hence marks the corresponding service as unavailable. In order to reduce the work load of the server, instead of polling each registered process, it expects to receive an **aliveness** message from each registered process periodically. The failure detection is organized this way since moving as much work as possible from the service to the clients enhances the scalability of the design.

5.2 User-Specified Notification List

The Monitoring Service allows the greatest flexibility that a system can respond to a process failure by the use of a **user-specified notification list**. Associated with each registered process is a notification list such that each item in the list specifies a process which is interested in any change in status of the registered process. When a registered process is declared dead, the monitor server notifies those parties which are specified in the notification list associated with this process.

The notification list associated with each registered process is initialized by the process during registration, and can be changed by the registered process itself or by other privileged processes which are interested in the availability status of that process.

When a process registers to MS, it specifies the set of processes that should be notified when it dies. This set of processes is very likely to be responsible for handling the failure and hence, for maintaining the constant availability of the registering process. Since the notification list is initialized during registration, the process that makes the registration can decide among the ways that its failure should be handled. In the simplest case, this list may just specify the failure handler of the registering process, e.g. the Boot Server or the Resource Manager or even a distributed program debugger [3]. This list is vital for the availability of the registering process since it is used by MS to trigger actions in respond to process failure.

The use of the notification list is generalized so that ordinary user processes can also send requests to MS specifying their interest of any change in status of other registered processes. A process which is interested in the availability of some other processes can register its interest to MS, which then records in its monitoring database the set of processes that it will notify when the registered process dies. A process does this, for example, when it requests service from a registered server process so that it can take appropriate actions when server failure occurs.

Therefore, the notification list can be partitioned to two kinds of list items: those that is vital to the constant availability of the registered process; and those whose normal functioning depends on the availability of the registered process. It is interesting to note that the latter reflects the server-client relationship between running processes and is useful for resource management purposes.

5.3 Dynamic Yellow Pages Service

Another service being exported by MS is the dynamic yellow pages service. It is a kind of yellow pages service because it provides users with information on what services are registered within the distributed system. The yellow pages service is dynamic since the kind of information it provides reflects the current availability of those registered services and is changed dynamically.

The dynamic yellow pages service is essential as a system-wide failure-handling tool. It provides its users with knowledge of the availability of each system components and hence, an overall picture of the availability of the whole system. This information is valuable in that it facilitates the job of locating failures in a distributed environment, and hence eases the task of failure management.

The monitoring database maintained by MS contains up-to-date information on the availability of all registered processes. MS keeps track of the availability of all registered processes and updates its monitoring database if the status of any registered processes changes. Therefore the monitoring information reflects the current availability of all registered processes.

MS exports an interface that allows users to **browse** through its monitoring database to find out the availability status of any registered process or any set of registered processes that are functionally related. It allows several kinds of querying requests with respect to the dynamic yellow pages service to cater for the different requirements of users with different privileges to access the monitoring information.

Therefore sufficiently privileged users are allowed to acquire knowledge of the current availability of each system component by making yellow pages requests to the monitor server. This up-to-date monitoring information allows its users to obtain a comprehensive view of the current availability of the whole system.

In addition, MS provides an extra interface which is not directly related to the dynamic yellow pages service. This interface allows users to inquire the notification list associated with any registered processes. Since the notification lists reflect the server-client relationships between running processes, this interface is useful for resource management purposes.

6 Human-MS Interface

In order to achieve the goal of the system monitoring service, an interface program was developed in addition to the monitor server. The interface program provides interactive facilities for privileged human users to browse through monitoring information, to trigger events manually, and/or to broadcast warning messages to interested parties when certain events are expected to occur.

The potential advantages of the monitoring service for improving system availability can be realized with the help of an human interface. Although component failures are usually handled automatically by software, the possibility of occasional human intervention should not be ruled out. There are situations in which human intervention should be exerted on the system, and this kind of business should be supported by management tools that allow a human user to carry out the job promptly. An human interface to the monitor server is one of such management tools.

6.1 Browsing Monitoring Information

The interface to the monitor server allows its users to retrieve and interpret the monitoring information. Through this interface, a user is able to enquire what is currently available in the system, to list the availability status of some or all of the registered processes, to find out the set of registered processes that are currently unavailable, or to list the set of processes that are interested in the availability of some named processes.

We require that a user can list the availability status of processes that are registered in the monitor server. This is useful for system management purposes for a user can now check interactively the current availability of various system components so that failures, if there are any, can be located easily. Because of the closely interdependent nature of system components, it is possible that the failure of one machine can make the whole system inaccessible. An overall picture of the availability of the whole system that can be built from this interface will help to locate the source of the problem.

6.2 Triggering Events Manually

It is necessary that events can be triggered manually through an human interface to the monitor server. It may be the case that the behaviour of a server is not consistent with its service specification, but is not detected by the monitor server. For example, if we have a printer which is running out of ink, then it is unlikely that the printer can carry out its job properly; however, the print server controlling this printer is unable to detect this fault and will keep sending aliveness messages to the monitor server. Consequently, people still send their document to the spooler of this print server but are unable to collect a hard copy as they expect. Obviously, we would like to have an interface which allows the person who first noticed this fault to inform the monitor server so that other processes in the system that are interested in the status of the printer, e.g. the login shell of an interactive user, will be notified of this event. Hence, appropriate actions can be taken to cope with this problem.

Ideally, the monitor server should be able to detect the failure of any process that it monitors, and hence interested parties are guaranteed to be notified of any change in status of registered processes. However, this will be true only if the way that registered processes fail conforms to that described by the assumed failure model. Deviation from the assumed behaviour may happen, for example, due to the existence of bugs in software. It is possible that an ill-implemented application does not perform its specified behaviour but send out aliveness messages regularly. Therefore, the failure detection mechanism can be fooled by software which crashes in part but continues to refresh. Provision of methods for dealing with situations as this is necessary. The use of an human interface is one such method.

6.3 Advance Warnings of Expected Events

It is desirable to give advance warnings of certain expected events to relevant parties before such events occur. There are events that their occurrence can be expected. For example a machine will be unavailable due for reasons such as that maintenance work is scheduled to be performed, the hardware or software is going to be upgraded, new device drivers are being installed, or new peripheral devices are being added to the machine, etc. It may be desirable to have interested parties warned of such events before they occur. If a server runs on a machine that is expected to be unavailable soon, then it may be necessary to give advance warnings to its dependent clients so that they can take appropriate actions to cope with the forthcoming event.

To illustrate, consider the situation that an additional memory module is to be added to a file server. It is expected that the file server will be down soon. Before the machine can be switched off safely, it is necessary to warn every client of the file server so that they can flush all buffers for files that are being modified before the file server is down. In some other systems, this is usually done by broadcasting warning messages to every interactive user whose progress is likely to be affected.

A combination of this facility and the fact that event notification is at process level gives us an extra benefit that was impossible to achieve before. The point is that if a process is running without the attention of its owner, and its computation is dependent on the availability of some other services, then it is necessary to have ways of warning this process of any change in status of those servers that it depends on. This allows the process to make suitable arrangements before the event occurs. Consider the situation that a person starts a computation, for example, for theoretical modelling, which runs for tens of hours and writes intermediate results to disk, and expects to collect the results in the following evening. This process will be running without its owner's attention. The progress of this computation will be affected if it cannot access the file server for writing intermediate outputs. If that file server is expected to be unavailable soon, it is desirable to give advance warning directly to this process so that it can use an alternative file server and can continue its computation when its original file server is down.

6.4 Notifying Users

In order to handle component failures promptly, the interface should notify the responsible person immediately when certain failures are detected. This can be achieved by writing messages to that person's screen, sending to him messages through the electronic mail system, triggering an alarm signal to draw his attention, or even making a phone call giving him a synthesised message [9]. The human interface to the monitor server should allow the responsible person to specify the ways that he should be notified. Therefore, whenever failures of vital components are detected to have occurred, a message will be generated automatically which will then be sent to the responsible person through the way that he specified.

This facility is necessary since it is not rare to have situations in which component failures occur such that human intervention is required. It is due to the fact that predefined automatic procedures are not always intelligent enough to deal with problems that may arise in real situations, the provision of a facility that is able to draw the immediate attention of human users is essential. It allows human intervention to be exerted on the system as soon as possible.

6.5 Placement

An interface that supports all of the foregoing features will run on the machine that the monitor server runs on. This interface facilitates system management and is used by the person who is responsible for maintaining the constant availability of the whole system. While the design of the monitor server allows a variety of user interface to be built to match different user requirements, the interface program that provides this management facility should run together with the monitor server.

The ultimate vision is to have a machine which does not depend on anything in the system for being able to run. Its responsibility is to check for the availability of various system components from time to time, and to notify the responsible person immediately if there are components that are detected to be crashed. The responsible person can then inspect on the problem by obtaining an overall picture of the availability of the whole system through this machine so that it is possible to have the source of the problem located easily.

Ideally, such a machine should be connected through a modem to the public telephone network so that it is possible to have communications between this machine and remote users. This feature is a desirable one since it allows the responsible person to inspect the system from home, and allows the monitor server to phone to that person telling him about the detected event by means of a synthesised message.

7 Conclusion

A new system service - the System Monitoring Service - for improving the availability of a distributed system has been presented. This service provides a failure detection and notification mechanisms as general services for various system components, and functions as a system-wide failure-handling tool. A design for the System Monitoring Service has been developed and a prototype implementation has been constructed [7]. A prototype of the monitoring service has been built for experimenting ideas and for the study of design features of the new service. The Monitoring Service has been implemented in Cambridge CLU (CCLU). All of the functions provided are available as CLU Remote Procedures. It occupies approximately 5000 lines of CCLU.

References

[1] J.M. Bacon, I.M. Leslie and R.M. Needham. *Distributed Computing with a Processor Bank,* Technical Report 168, Computer Laboratory, University of Cambridge, 1989.

[2] M. Burrows. *Efficient Data Sharing,* PhD Thesis 153, Computer Laboratory, University of Cambridge, 1988.

[3] R.C.B. Cooper. *Debugging Distributed and Concurrent Programs,* PhD Thesis 128, Computer Laboratory, University of Cambridge, 1988.

[4] D.H. Craft. *Resource Management in a Decentralized System,* PhD Thesis 73, Computer Laboratory, University of Cambridge, 1985.

[5] J. Gray. *Why Do Computers Stops and What Can Be Done About It?,* Tandem Computers, TR 85.7, 1985.

[6] J. Gray. *A Census of Tandem System Availability Between 1985 and 1990,* Tandem Computers, TR 90.1, 1990.

[7] K.Y. Lam. *A New Approach for Improving System Availability,* PhD Thesis, Computer Laboratory, University of Cambridge, 1991.

[8] SUN MicroSystems, Inc. *Networking Programming,* May, 1988.

[9] R. Want. *Reliable Management of Voice in a Decentralized System,* PhD Thesis 141, Computer Laboratory, University of Cambridge, 1988.

Konzeptionell strukturierte Verteilte Systeme

P.P. Spies, C. Eckert, D. Marek, H.-M. Windisch
TU München, Fakultät für Informatik
D-80290 München
e-mail: {spies, eckertc, marek, windisch}@informatik.tu-muenchen.de

Zusammenfassung

Verteilte Systeme sind komplexe, technische Systeme, die mit geeigneten Konzepten und Methoden auf Leistungsfähigkeit und Beherrschbarkeit ausgerichtet konstruiert werden müssen. Wesentliche Voraussetzungen zum Erreichen dieses Ziels sind die Möglichkeiten zur Beschreibung von Systemen auf unterschiedlichen Abstraktionsstufen und zur Strukturierung der Systeme. Zunächst wird die Konstruktion verteilter Systeme mittels Sprach-basierter Ansätze motiviert; die Vor- und Nachteile der wichtigsten Klassen solcher Ansätze werden skizziert. Dann wird eine Programmiersprache vorgestellt, mit der konzeptionell strukturierte Systeme konstruiert werden können. Die Bedeutung des Ansatzes als Bindeglied in der Abstraktionshierarchie für Systemkonstruktionen von den Anwendungsanforderungen bis zur Realisierung auf Hardware-Konfigurationen wird erklärt. Die Nutzung der Strukturierungskonzepte der Sprache zur effizienten Ressourcenverwaltung wird am Beispiel der Speicherverwaltung erläutert.

1 Einleitung

Verteilte Systeme bieten gute Chancen, das gesamte Repertoire der heute zur Verfügung stehenden hardware- und softwaretechnischen Möglichkeiten für Anwendungen nutzbar zu machen. Während diese Attraktivität unbestritten ist, gibt es nach wie vor keinen allgemeinen Konsens über die definierenden Eigenschaften verteilter Systeme. Konsens besteht darüber, daß sie Benutzern ihre Dienste als integrierte Bestandteile eines homogenen Gesamtsystems und insbesondere Hilfsmittel für kooperative Problemlösungen mit (echter) Parallelität anbieten sollen sowie auf vernetzten Multiprozessor- und Multicomputer-Konfigurationen realisiert werden. Darüber hinaus entsprechen die Eigenschaften, die als wesentlich genannt werden, den unterschiedlichen Sichten, unter denen Rechensysteme allgemein gesehen werden. Dabei stehen häufig die benutzten Hardware-Konfigurationen oder Eigenschaften der Systeme, die zu verteilten Systemen weiterentwickelt werden, im Vordergrund.
Alternativen zu diesen bottom-up-Sichten von verteilten Systemen erhält man, wenn man -wie in der Softwaretechnik üblich- von Anwendungen und den Anforderungen, die sie an die zu entwickelnden Systeme stellen, ausgeht. Es ergeben sich zunächst abstrakte, verteilte Systeme, die dann zu realisieren sind; bei den hierzu erforderlichen Konstruktionsprozessen sind die zur Verfügung stehenden hardware- und softwaretechnischen Möglichkeiten auszuschöpfen.

Für Durchführungen der skizzierten top-down-Konstruktionen verteilter Systeme sind Sprach-basierte Einprogramm-Ansätze geeignet. Sie gehen -wie für Anwendungen üblich und bewährt- vom Konzeptevorrat einer Programmiersprache aus, der vor allem zwei wesentliche Anforderungen erfüllen muß: dem geforderten homogenen Gesamtsystem entsprechend muß ein Programmkonzept festgelegt sein; damit beherrschbare, große Systeme konstruiert werden können, müssen Konzepte für Systemkomponenten und Konzepte zur Strukturierung der Komponentenmengen eines Systems festgelegt sein.
Ein abstraktes System wird dann durch ein Programm definiert; seine Eigenschaften sind die der Ausführungen des Programms.
Bei geeigneter Wahl des Konzeptevorrats der benutzten Sprache haben die genannten Ansätze den Vorteil, daß die Eigenschaften eines Systems auf dem (hohen) Abstraktionsniveau der Sprache vollständig festgelegt werden; diese Vollständigkeit ist zum Nachweis korrekten Verhaltens insbesondere für kooperative, parallele Systeme unerläßlich. Sie haben zudem den Vorteil, daß sie als Bindeglied zwischen den beiden wesentlichen Teilbereichen der gesamten Abstraktionshierarchie für Systemkonstruktionen von den Anwendungsanforderungen bis zu den von der Hardware ausführbaren Programmen genutzt werden können: dem Teilbereich, in dem von Anforderungsspezifikationen ausgehend algorithmische Problemlösungen zu entwickeln sind, und dem Teilbereich der Betriebssysteme, in dem diese algorithmischen Problemlösungen auf Hardware-Konfigurationen zu realisieren sind.
Mit dieser Thematik befaßt sich der vorliegende Beitrag; er ist im weiteren wie folgt gegliedert:
In Kapitel 2 werden zunächst Sprach-basierte Ansätze zur Konstruktion verteilter Systeme motiviert; für imperative Sprachen werden drei grobe Klassen angegeben und bzgl. ihrer in dem hier interessierenden Zusammenhang wesentlichen Eigenschaften charakterisiert. Anschließend wird die experimentelle Sprache INSEL mit ihren Konzepten für Systemkomponenten und mit ihren Konzepten zur Strukturierung von Systemen eingeführt; die Eigenschaften der entsprechenden Systeme und Möglichkeiten zur Beschreibung ihres dynamischen Verhaltens werden erklärt.
In Kapitel 3 werden einige der für verteilte Systeme wichtigen Einsatzmöglichkeiten der Sprachkonzepte genauer betrachtet. Zudem wird erklärt, wie mit INSEL konstruierte Systeme auf der Grundlage ihrer Strukturen als Bindeglied zwischen den oberen, anwendungsnahen und unteren, hardwarenahen Schichten der Abstraktionshierarchie für Systemkonstruktionen genutzt werden können.
In Kapitel 4 werden die konzeptionellen Eigenschaften und insbesondere die Strukturen von INSEL-Systemen dazu genutzt, Verfahren zur Realisierung der Systeme auf Hardware-Konfigurationen abzuleiten. Dazu werden Kellerbäume als geeignete Realisierungsstrukturen eingeführt; sie liefern die Randbedingungen für die Verfahren zur verteilten Ressourcenverwaltung, die für effiziente Realisierungen benötigt werden.
Der Beitrag wird mit einer Zusammenfassung und einigen Hinweisen auf weitere Arbeiten abgeschlossen.

2 Sprach-basierte Systeme

Verteilte Systeme sollen konstruiert werden, indem eine Folge von systematisch ausgewählten Konkretisierungs- und Problemlösungsmaßnahmen so durchgeführt werden, daß sich Systeme mit Abstraktionshierarchien ergeben. Als Ausgangsbasen für diese Vorgehensweise werden hier imperative Programmiersprachen gewählt; die entsprechend konstruierten Systeme werden Sprach-basiert genannt. Die Vorgehensweise ermöglicht es, die Eigenschaften eines Systems zunächst mit den Konzepten der benutzten Sprache festzulegen und dann das so definierte abstrakte System mit den Konzepten und Verfahren von Betriebssystemen auf einer geeignet gewählten Hardware-Konfiguration zu realisieren. Wesentlich für eine erfolgreiche Durchführung entsprechender Konstruktionen ist das Konzepterepertoire der benutzten Sprache, das es ermöglichen muß, die wesentlichen Eigenschaften verteilter Systeme auf hohem Abstraktionsniveau festzulegen.
Ihren charakteristischen Eigenschaften entsprechend sind verteilte Systeme zu konstruieren, indem kooperierende Teilsysteme definiert werden, die Gesamtprobleme gemeinsam lösen. Dafür ist es notwendig, daß die Teilsysteme einerseits so weit wie nötig über eine gemeinsame Kooperationsbasis verfügen (Integration), und andererseits unabhängige und nebenläufige Beiträge zur Gesamtlösung (Separation) erbringen können. Aus der Sicht eines Systementwicklers ergeben sich damit als Anforderungen an die Programmiersprache, daß neben einem Konzepterepertoire zur Konstruktion von aktiven und passiven Einheiten mit geeigneten Kooperationskonzepten, Strukturierungskonzepte zur Festlegung von Abhängigkeiten zwischen den Einheiten zur Verfügung stehen müssen. Um die gewünschte Funktionalität in Kooperation mit anderen aktiven Einheiten zu erbringen, müssen die Einheiten gemeinsame 'Wissensbasen' besitzen, die analog zu dem aus dem Schutzkontext bekannten 'need-to-know' Prinzip minimal (Intergrationsforderung) sein sollte. Differenzierungsmöglichkeiten zur Festlegung der 'Wissensbasen' durch systematische Strukturierung und die Konzepte zur Kooperation sind wesentliche Kriterien, nach denen sich Sprach-basierte Systeme klassifizieren lassen.

2.1 Systemklassen

Im folgenden werden zunächst drei Klassen Sprach-basierter Systeme kurz charakterisiert.
CSP-artige Systeme: Als CSP-artig (vgl. [Hoa85], [Ltd84]) werden Systeme bezeichnet, die aus einer konstanten Basis und einer statischen Menge sequentieller Prozesse, die mittels Nachrichtenkommunikation kooperieren, bestehen. Die Prozesse haben disjunkte, lokale Zustandsräume; sie können die Komponenten der Basis, zu denen insbesondere die Nachrichtentypen gehören, gemeinsam benutzen. CSP-artige Systeme sind theoretisch fundiert; man kann ihr kooperatives Verhalten spezifizieren und nachweisen; sie sind zudem einfach zu realisieren. Charakteristisch für die Systeme sind ihre einfachen, flachen Strukturen (vgl.

Abbildung 1(a)), die zusammen mit der fehlenden Dynamik die Defizite des Ansatzes sind.

Systeme mit virtuellen Knoten: Virtuelle Knoten sind eine Abstraktion der realen Knoten einer vernetzten Hardware-Konfiguration. Virtuelle Knoten definieren Einheiten mit einer wohldefinierten Schnittstelle, über die mittels Nachrichtenkommunikation kooperiert werden kann. Analog zu den CSP-artigen Systemen wird ihre gemeinsame Basis durch eine Menge von Konstanten festgelegt. Ein verteiltes Programm besteht aus einer statischen Menge virtueller Knoten, die ihrerseits Prozesse dynamisch erzeugen und auflösen können. Die knotenlokalen Prozesse kommunizieren sowohl über gemeinsame Objekte des virtuellen Knotens als auch über knotenlokale Kooperationskonzepte (procedure call, entry call etc.). Die gemeinsame Kommunikationsbasis für diese Prozesse wird durch den jeweiligen virtuellen Knoten differenziert festgelegt, so daß sich die in Abbildung 1(b) angegebene zweistufige Struktur für diese Systeme ergibt. In die Klasse der Ansätze mit virtuellen Knoten fallen u. a. Argus [Lis85], SR [And88], sowie Ansätze aus dem Bereich des verteilten Ada [G+87].

Objektorientierte Systeme: Zu den wesentlichen Charakteristika von objektorientierten Systemen zählen die Klassenbildung einschließlich Vererbung, die Kooperation der Objekte über Methodenaufrufe sowie die flache Objektstruktur. Objekte sind primär passive Einheiten, die lokale Aktivität besitzen können. Im Gegensatz zu dem nachrichtenorientierten Kommunikationskonzept von CSP-artigen Systemen, wird eine operationenorientierte Kommunikation angeboten, d. h. eine Kommunikation über die Schnittstellenoperationen von Objekten mit wohldefinierter Funktionalität. Die Typen der formalen Parameter der Schnittstellenoperationen der Objekte bilden die gemeinsame Kommunikationsbasis der objektorientierten Systeme.
Jedes Objekt ist eine Instanz einer Klasse; die Klassen eines Systems können dem Vererbungskonzept entsprechend hierarchisch strukturiert sein, was jedoch keine Struktur auf der Menge der Objekte induziert. Beispiele für Objekt-orientierte Systeme mit einer flachen Objektstruktur sind Eden [Bla85], sowie Emerald [JLHB88] und Heron [Lö92].

2.2 INSEL-Systeme

Eine Weiterführung des Ansatzes objektorientierter Systeme mit feiner Körnung der Objekte, in dem die Objektmengen systematisch strukturiert werden, und der damit die Möglichkeiten zur Differenzierung der gemeinsamen Basen aktiver Objekte bietet, liefert die Programmiersprache INSEL.

Konzeptevorrat
Die Sprache INSEL (INtegration and SEparation supporting Language) ist eine experimentelle, imperative Programmiersprache [Spi92], die Konzepte zur Definition von aktiven (Akteure) und passiven Komponenten (Depots) zur Verfügung

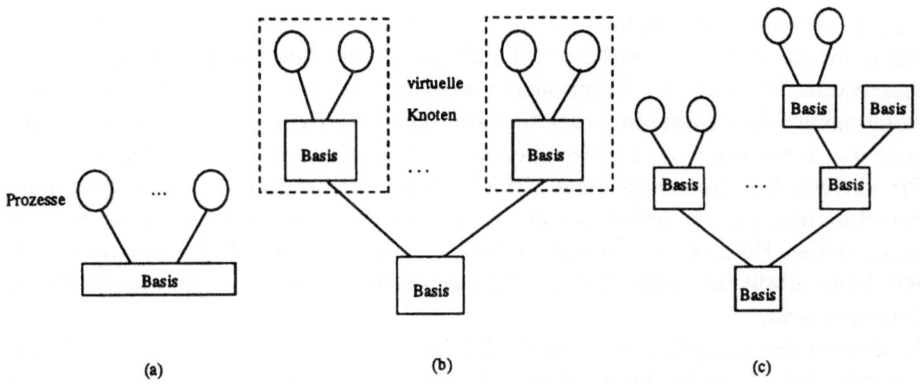

Abb. 1. Strukturcharakteristika der CSP-, virtuellen Knoten- und INSEL-Systeme

stellt. Die Komponenten werden über wohldefinierte Schnittstellenoperationen (Order) genutzt und können mit beliebiger Granularität definiert werden. Akteure, Depots und Order sind die wesentlichen Komponenten von INSEL-Systemen; sie bestehen ihrerseits aus einfachen Komponenten (Daten, Zeiger und Generatoren), die hier jedoch nicht genauer betrachtet werden. Akteure kooperieren sowohl über gemeinsame Datenobjekte als auch über ein operationenorientiertes Rendezvous, indem der Auftraggeber eine Kommunikationsoperation aufruft (entry-call) und der Auftragnehmer die Operation ausführt (accept).

Jede INSEL-Komponente ist ein Element einer Klasse (definiert durch einen Generator), welche die Eigenschaften ihrer Elemente festlegt. INSEL ist eine objektbasierte Sprache ohne Vererbung.

Charakteristisch für INSEL-Systeme ist, daß Akteure und Depots dynamisch erzeugt werden können. Komponenten können sowohl als benannte als auch als anonyme Komponenten, die über Zeigerobjekte identifiziert werden, erzeugt werden. Ein weiteres Charakteristikum besteht darin, daß INSEL-Programme gemäß dem Schachtelungsprinzip konstruiert werden. Aktive und passive Komponenten können beliebig geschachtelt definiert werden. Das Schachtelungsprinzip ermöglicht die gewünschte Differenzierung der gemeinsamen Basen der aktiven Komponenten (vgl. Abbildung 1 (c)), da durch Schachtelung die Wirkungsbereiche von Komponenten beschränkt bzw. erweitert werden können.

Systemstrukturen und - konfigurationen

Die Menge der Komponenten eines INSEL-Systems ist konzeptionell strukturiert, wobei die Systemstrukturen unterschiedliche Abhängigkeiten zwischen den Komponenten differenziert beschreiben.

Die **Definitionsstruktur** erfaßt die definitorischen Abhängigkeiten zwischen den Komponenten, die die Basis für die Festlegung der Ausführungsumgebung einer Komponente sind. Die Ausführungsumgebungen von Komponenten können durch Schachtelung von Komponenten beschränkt werden, indem durch Kapselung Komponenten vor direktem Zugriff geschützt werden. Die Kapselung von Komponenten als lokale Komponenten wird über die **Lokalitätsstruktur** er-

faßt. Eine weitere wesentliche Struktur ist die **Lebenszeitstruktur**. Für jede Komponente in INSEL ist konzeptionell die Lebensdauer so festgelegt, daß sichergestellt ist, daß die Komponente existiert solange potentielle Nutzer der Komponente existieren. Insbesondere sind auch die dynamisch erzeugten Komponenten konzeptionell mit ihrer Lebenszeit in das Gesamtsystem eingebunden. Die aktiven Komponenten eines INSEL-Programms führen primär sequentielle Berechnungen aus; sie liefern parallel zu den anderen aktiven Komponenten einen funktionalen Beitrag zur Gesamtberechnung des Systems. Die **Ausführungsstruktur** erfaßt die sequentiellen und parallelen Beiträge von Komponenten zu Berechnungen.
Zu Beginn der Ausführung eines INSEL-Programms existiert genau eine Komponente, der **Hauptakteur**. Dieser Akteur führt eine Berechnung aus, wobei weitere Komponenten – aktive und passive – dynamisch erzeugt und wieder aufgelöst werden. Das dynamische Verhalten eines INSEL-Systems wird durch Konfigurationen beschrieben. Jede **Konfiguration** beschreibt einen Systemschnappschuß, in dem die Menge der existierenden Komponenten sowie ihre strukturellen Abhängigkeiten erfaßt werden. Die Dynamik eines INSEL-Systems besteht in Veränderungen der Komponentenmenge, der Systemstrukturen und der Eigenschaften der Komponenten.
Auf die Nutzungsmöglichkeiten der Strukturierungskonzepte für den Konstruktionsprozeß wird im nächsten Kapitel näher eingegangen, während in Kapitel 4 die Nutzung der Strukturen für die Realisierung von INSEL-Systemen am Beispiel der Speicherverwaltung erläutert wird.

3 Nutzung der Sprachkonzepte

Die Komponenten- und Strukturierungskonzepte von INSEL sind so gewählt, daß die Eigenschaften eines entsprechenden Systems einschließlich seiner Dynamik über der gesamten Lebenszeit systematisch auf unterschiedlichen Abstraktionsniveaus beschrieben werden können. Hiermit können die Systeme als Bindeglied zwischen den beiden wesentlichen Teilbereichen der gesamten Abstraktionshierarchie für Systemkonstruktionen von den Anwendungsanforderungen bis zu den von der Hardware auszuführenden Programmen genutzt werden. Im folgenden werden zunächst einige der in diesem Zusammenhang wesentlichen Eigenschaften und anschließend die genannte Bindegliedfunktion erklärt.

Abstraktionsebenen für Systembeschreibungen

Wenn man das Verhalten eines Systems verstehen und erklären möchte, muß man alle Eigenschaften, die dieses Verhalten beeinflussen können, erfassen. Wenn das betrachtete System groß ist und aus vielen Komponenten besteht, kann dies nur dann gelingen, wenn man das System mit geeigneten Granularitäten auf unterschiedlichen Abstraktionsniveaus beschreiben kann.
Für Beschreibungen der Eigenschaften eines INSEL-Systems stehen zunächst zwei einander ergänzende, kanonische Abstraktionsebenen zur Verfügung: die Ebene der einfachen Komponenten -EK-Ebene- und die Ebene der wesentlichen

Komponenten –WK–Ebene–. Die EK–Ebene ermöglicht detaillierte Beschreibungen auf dem für Programmiersprachen üblichen Niveau; sie erfaßt die durch ein Programm festgelegten und seinen Ausführungen entsprechenden Eigenschaften vollständig. Die WK–Ebene ergibt sich aus der EK–Ebene durch systematische Abstraktion von der Zusammensetzung der wesentlichen Komponenten; sie ermöglicht es, ein System während seiner Lebenszeit durch Konfigurations–Familien der WK–Ebene zu beschreiben. Eine Konfiguration der WK–Ebene erfaßt die jeweilige Menge der existierenden wesentlichen Komponenten und durch Strukturrelationen über dieser Menge die Abhängigkeiten zwischen diesen Komponenten als vergröbernden Schnappschuß.
Die Vorgehensweise, die von der EK– zur WK–Ebene führt, läßt sich fortsetzen. Die Konfigurationen der WK–Ebene enthalten in der Regel für Übersichten über Gesamtsysteme noch zu viele Komponenten, so daß weitere Vergröberungen notwendig sind. Von den Möglichkeiten hierfür soll noch eine erklärt werden; sie führt von der WK– zur AS–Ebene, der Ebene der Akteur–Sphären. Die AS–Ebene ergibt sich, indem man jede passive, wesentliche Komponente dem Akteur zuordnet, dessen Lebenszeit die der passiven Komponente minimal umfaßt; diese Zuordnung ist nach den festgelegten Konzepten eindeutig. Der Übergang von der WK– zur AS–Ebene erfolgt durch systematische Abstraktion von der Zusammensetzung der Akteur–Sphären; man erhält Beschreibungen für ein System während seiner Lebenszeit durch Konfigurations–Familien der AS–Ebene. Die Konfigurations–Familien der AS–Ebene eines Systems werden in Kapitel 4 für verteiltes Ressourcenmanagement genutzt. Die Vergröberungen des Übergangs zur AS–Ebene sind beispielhaft für weitere nützliche Vergröberungen.

Strukturierte Zustandsräume und kooperative Subsysteme

Der Zustandsraum ist die Basis für die Berechnungen, die ein System ausführt. Für ein verteiltes System, das wesentlich aus kooperativen Subsystemen bestehen und zu Parallelverarbeitung fähig sein soll, kommt der Konstruktion des Zustandsraums entscheidende Bedeutung zu: einerseits sollen die für Berechnungen unbedingt notwendigen gemeinsamen Objekte zur Verfügung stehen (minimale Integration) und andererseits sollen Berechnungen möglichst weitgehend nebenläufig und interferenzfrei ausführbar sein (maximale Separation).
Mit den INSEL–Konzepten lassen sich strukturierte Zustandsräume konstruieren, die dynamisch erweitert und reduziert werden können; dabei werden primär das Schachtelungs– und das Klassenbildungsprinzip ausgenutzt, so daß sich als Grundstrukturen Bäume ergeben. Auf diese Weise kann man insbesondere kooperative Subsysteme mit festgelegter Schnittstellenfunktionalität zum Rest des Systems und eingekapselten Komponenten zur Ausführung der erforderlichen Berechnungen konstruieren. Die eingekapselten Komponenten können Akteure sein, so daß parallele Berechnungen möglich sind; sie können Akteure, die nebenläufig Teilberechnungen ausführen, oder Akteure, die ihre Berechnungen kooperierend ausführen, sein.
Die skizzierten Subsysteme können zur Ausführung von Berechnungen für ihre Umgebungen erzeugt werden; ihre Lebenszeiten enden dann, wenn die ent-

sprechenden Berechnungen ausgeführt sind. Es können jedoch auch Subsysteme erzeugt werden, deren Wurzelkomponenten Akteure mit für die erzeugenden Umgebungen trivialer Funktionalität sind; sie dienen zur Erweiterung der Basis des Systems für Parallelität.

Bindeglied in der Abstraktionshierarchie für Systemkonstruktionen
Ein System soll konstruiert werden, indem man von Anwendungen und ihren Anforderungsspezifikationen ausgehend eine Folge von systematisch ausgewählten Konkretisierungs– und Problemlösungsmaßnahmen durchführt bis schließlich das von den Komponenten der benutzten Hardware–Konfiguration ausführbare Programm (einschließlich Daten) erreicht ist. Die Folge dieser Schritte entspricht einer Abstraktionshierarchie für Systemkonstruktionen; jeder Ebene der Hierarchie entspricht ein System mit den für sie charakteristischen Eigenschaften. Mit jedem Konkretisierungsschritt werden Anforderungen, die an das zu konstruierende System gestellt werden, erfüllt; gleichzeitig wird der Freiraum für Fortsetzungen der Konstruktion eingeschränkt.
Durchführungen des skizzierten Konstruktionsprozesses erfordern einerseits Konkretisierungen, mit denen die gestellten Anforderungen erfüllt werden sollen; sie erfordern andererseits Abstraktionen als Grundlage für Soll–Ist–Vergleiche, mit denen nachzuweisen ist, ob und wie weit gestellte Anforderungen erfüllt werden; gegebenenfalls sind Konkretisierungen zu revidieren. Im Rahmen dieses Konstruktionsprozesses erhalten die Ebenen der Abstraktionshierarchie Bedeutung in zweifacher Hinsicht: sie ermöglichen Soll–Ist–Vergleiche auf dem jeweiligen Abstraktionsniveau und bilden gegebenenfalls die Ausgangsbasis für alternative Systemkonstruktionen. Die zweite dieser Maßnahmen ist immer dann wichtig, wenn die durchgeführten Konkretisierungen und damit die konstruierten Systeme nicht perfekt sind.
In der Abstraktionshierarchie für Systemkonstruktionen gibt es zwei Teilbereiche mit wesentlich verschiedenen Aufgaben: den Teilbereich, in dem von den Anforderungsspezifikationen der Anwendungen ausgehend algorithmische Problemlösungen zu entwickeln sind, und den Teilbereich der Betriebssysteme, in dem diese algorithmischen Problemlösungen auf Hardware–Konfigurationen zu realisieren sind. Die imperativen Programmiersprachen, die hier für Sprachbasierte Ansätze zur Konstruktion verteilter Systeme betrachtet werden, sind an der Schnittstelle zwischen diesen beiden Bereichen einzuordnen. Sie sollen die für Anwendungen relevante Funktionalität eines Systems sowie die Randbedingungen und Freiräume für die noch zu lösenden Ressourcenmanagementprobleme festlegen. Dazu sind Sprachen mit einem bezogen auf die gesamte Hierarchie mittleren Abstraktionsniveau erforderlich. Die Konzepte von INSEL sind diesen Anforderungen entsprechend gewählt. Von INSEL–Systemen ausgehend sind zudem Abstraktionen möglich, die zu Ebenen des ersten der genannten Teilbereiche führen; sie dienen als Grundlage für Soll–Ist–Vergleiche und daraus zu ziehende Konsequenzen im oben erklärten Sinn. Abbildung 2 veranschaulicht diese Bindegliedfunktion von INSEL–Systemen.

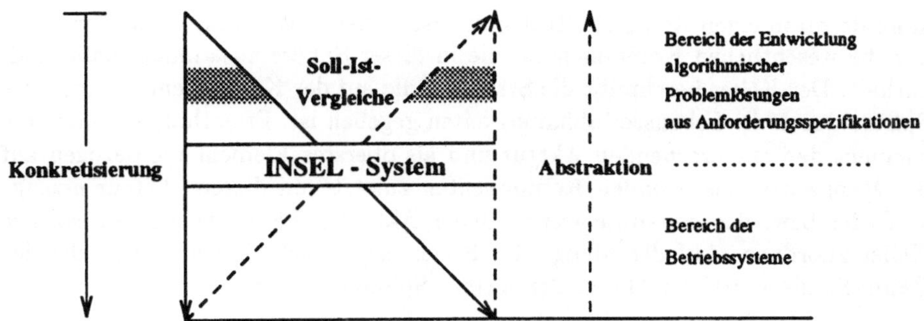

Abb. 2. INSEL-Systeme als Bindeglied in der Abstraktionshierarchie

4 Realisierung konzeptionell strukturierter Systeme

Dieses Kapitel beschäftigt sich mit Aspekten der Realisierung des durch ein INSEL-Programm definierten abstrakt verteilten Systems. Es soll aufgezeigt werden, wie die konzeptionelle Strukturierung der Systeme für die Lösung der Ressourcenverwaltungsprobleme genutzt werden kann. Die Ressourcenverwaltung soll verteilt über kooperierende Verwalter realisiert werden, wobei jeder Verwalter in die Lage versetzt werden muß, die ihm zugeteilten Ressourcen so weit wie möglich autonom und so weit wie nötig in Kooperation mit den anderen Verwalter zu verwalten.
Der Lösungsweg besteht darin, zunächst die INSEL-Strukturen in geeignete Realisierungsdatenstrukturen zu transformieren, die als Ausgangspunkt für die Entwicklung von Ressourcenverwaltungskonzepten dienen. Damit wird ein erster Realisierungsschritt getan; es bleibt die Aufgabe, in weiteren Schritten diese Datenstrukturen auf der jeweils benutzten Hardware-Konfiguration im Hinblick auf die Verwaltung der tatsächlich zur Verfügung stehenden Ressourcen zu realisieren. Das Vorgehen wird in diesem Kapitel beispielhaft für den Bereich der Speicherverwaltung erläutert.

4.1 Kellerbäume als Realisierungsdatenstrukturen

Im Hinblick auf die Ressourcenverwaltung sind vorrangig die Akteure von Interesse, da sie die Komponenten sind, die die Dynamik eines Systems durch die Erzeugung und Auflösung von Komponenten bestimmen und die damit Ressourcen anfordern bzw. freigeben. Eine geeignete Ausgangsbasis für die Entwicklung einer Ressourcenverwaltung ist die Abstraktionsebene der Akteur-Sphären. Die Akteur-Sphäre eines Akteurs enthält zum einen Order (Unterprogramme), die von dem Akteur erzeugt wurden und sequentiell ausgeführt werden und zum anderen benannte Depots als lokale Komponenten des Akteurs bzw. der Order. Die Lebenszeitschachtelung der Order entspricht der Unterprogrammaufrufstruktur herkömmlicher Programmiersprachen. Die benannten Depots ordnen sich als lokale Komponenten systematisch in diese Schachtelung ein. Jede Akteur-Sphäre kann damit in einen Keller als Realisierungsdatenstruktur transformiert werden, der die wesentlichen Komponenten, die in dieser Sphäre zusammengefaßt sind, enthält. Der Keller beschreibt die Struktur, die auf der Komponentenmenge der Sphäre durch die Lebenszeitabhängigkeiten gegeben ist. Er enthält als unterstes Element den entsprechenden Akteur und als oberstes Element die bezogen auf die Menge der existierenden Komponenten zuletzt von diesem Akteur erzeugte Order bzw. das benannte Depot. Jeder Akteur-Sphäre läßt sich ein solcher Keller zuordnen. Auf der Menge der Keller ergibt sich eine Struktur, die der Baum-Struktur auf der Menge der Akteur-Sphären entspricht.

Das für einen Keller durch die Semantik der Einfüge- und Entnehme-Operation gegebene charakteristische 'auf' und 'ab' ergibt sich durch das Erzeugen und Auflösen von INSEL-Komponenten zusammen mit den konzeptionellen Lebenszeitfestlegungen für diese. Dabei ist zwischen der Erzeugung bzw. Auflösung von aktiven und passiven Komponenten zu unterscheiden. Wird ein Akteur erzeugt, so bedeutet dies, daß ein neuer Keller erzeugt wird, der zunächst allein diesen Akteur enthält. Auf dem Keller des Akteurs, von dem der neu erzeugte Akteur lebenszeitmäßig abhängig ist, wird ein Verweis auf den Keller des neuen Akteurs angelegt. Der Keller eines Akteurs enthält somit Verweise auf die Keller aller Akteure, die von ihm lebenszeitmäßig abhängig sind. Durch diese Verweise wird die Baum-Struktur auf der Menge der Keller repräsentiert. Kann ein Akteur gemäß den konzeptionellen Festlegungen aufgelöst werden, so ist zum einen der Verweis auf diesen Akteur im Keller des Akteurs, von dem er lebenszeitmäßig abhängig ist, das oberste Element, und zum anderen enthält der Keller des aufzulösenden Akteurs keine weiteren Elemente. Mit Auflösung des Akteurs wird dann auch der ihm entsprechende Keller aufgelöst.

Bei der Erzeugung von passiven Objekten ist zwischen der Erzeugung von Order bzw. der Erarbeitung benannter Depots und der Erzeugung von anonymen Depots zu unterscheiden. Die Order und benannten Depots lassen sich unmittelbar auf dem Keller des Akteurs 'ablegen', von dem sie erzeugt werden. Die anonymen Depots bzw. generell alle dynamischen Datenstrukturen können wegen ihrer Lebenszeiten nicht unmittelbar auf dem Keller des sie erzeugenden Akteurs 'abgelegt' werden; sie lassen sich jedoch aufgrund der konzeptionellen Lebenszeitfestlegungen systematisch in das 'auf' und 'ab' der Keller einordnen. Für diese Einordnung werden Erweiterungen der Keller um zusätzliche Datenstrukturen, in denen anonyme Depots und die von ihnen lebenszeitmäßig abhängigen passiven Komponenten repräsentiert werden können, notwendig. Die Anker für Verweise auf diese Datenstrukturen ordnen sich systematisch in die Keller der Akteure ein. Mit jeder Komponente eines Kellers, zu dem es im Laufe der Entwicklung des Systems lebenszeitabhängige anonyme Depots geben kann, wird ein Anker für Verweise auf Zusatzdatenstrukturen angelegt. Die Erzeugung und Auflösung der Anker für Verweise auf die Zusatzdatenstrukturen und damit auf die anonymen Depots ordnen sich damit in das 'auf' und 'ab' der Keller ein. Wird aus dem Keller gemäß der Kellersemantik ein entsprechender Anker entfernt und enthält dieser einen Verweis, so werden alle in der damit referenzierten Zusatzdatenstruktur repräsentierten Komponenten aufgelöst.

Durch die Transformation erhält man einen Baum von Kellern mit dem Keller des Hauptakteurs als Wurzel. Die so gegebene Realisierungsdatenstruktur wird im weiteren als **Kellerbaum** bezeichnet. Die Dynamik eines Systems spiegelt sich einerseits in dem 'auf' und 'ab' der Keller des Kellerbaums mit seinen Erweiterungen (Zusatz-Datenstrukturen), das durch die Erzeugung und Auflösung passiver Komponenten verursacht wird, und andererseits in dem 'wachsen' und 'schrumpfen' des gesamten Kellerbaums, das sich aus dem Erzeugen und Auflösen von Akteuren ergibt, wider. Die Regel, daß stets das oberste Kellerelement bzw. falls dieses ein Verweis ist, zusätzlich alle damit referenzierten Komponenten aufgelöst werden, stimmt mit den konzeptionell festgelegten Auflösungsregeln für die Komponenten überein.
Mit dem Kellerbaum ist die Realisierungsdatenstruktur angegeben, die als Ausgangspunkt für die Entwicklung von Ressourcenverwaltungs-Konzepten dient. Im folgenden wird dies für den Bereich der Speicherverwaltung konkretisiert.

4.2 Speicherverwaltung für INSEL-Systeme

Die Speicherverwaltung für INSEL-Systeme muß zwei Hauptaufgaben erfüllen. Zum einen muß zur Zeit der Erzeugung einer INSEL-Komponente Speicherplatz für deren Repräsentation zur Verfügung gestellt werden. Zum anderen muß der belegte Speicherplatz bei der Auflösung einer INSEL-Komponente wieder freigegeben werden. Die Lösung dieser Aufgaben erfordert eine Konkretisierung des ausschließlich an der Lebenszeitstruktur eines INSEL-Systems orientierten Kellerbaumes in Richtung auf eine 'hardwarenähere' Stufe. Diese Stufe sei für das weitere gegeben durch einen linearen Speicher sowie eine Menge abstrakter Prozessoren, die auf den Speicher zugreifen können. Das damit zugrundegelegte Modell der Hardware-Konfiguration vereinfacht die Konkretisierung der Datenstruktur Kellerbaum dadurch, daß zunächst Aspekte der abstrakten, jedoch nicht der physikalischen Verteilung betrachtet werden müssen.
Die geforderte Abbildung der Datenstruktur Kellerbaum auf den gegebenen linearen Speicher ist nun so durchzuführen, daß einerseits die Eigenschaften des linearen Speichers zur schnellen (einstufigen) Adressierung von Komponenten und andererseits die Strukturen des Kellerbaumes erhalten bleiben, da diese zur Auflösung von INSEL-Komponenten und der damit verbundenen Freigabe von Speicherplatz genutzt werden können. Zudem ist darauf zu achten, daß die durch die Knoten des Kellerbaumes zum Ausdruck kommende abstrakte Parallelität (jeder Knoten enthält genau einen Akteur) auch auf der hardwarenahen Stufe erhalten bleibt, also die den Knoten zugeordneten Keller in disjunkten Speicherbereichen realisiert werden.
Zur Lösung der gestellten Aufgabe wird ein Konzept mit verteilten kooperierenden Speicherverwaltern entwickelt. Jeder Akteur-Sphäre wird ein Verwalter zugeordnet, der mit einem Speicherbereich ausgestattet wird, den er so weit wie möglich autonom verwaltet. Die Speicherressource wird als ein Keller verwaltet. Durch die Zuordnung eines Verwalters zu jedem Knoten des Kellerbaumes wird die Baumstruktur auch auf die Menge der Verwalter übertragen. Dies hat zum einen zur Folge, daß jeder Verwalter die Speicheranforderungen der ihm

assoziierten Komponenten lokal mit dem ihm zur Verfügung gestellten Speicher erfüllen kann. Zum anderen kann die globale Verwaltungsaufgabe, nämlich die Repräsentation der Komponenten des Systems in dem gegebenen Speicher, durch Kooperation der Verwalter mit ihren jeweiligen unmittelbaren Vorgängern bzw. unmittelbaren Nachfolgern in dem Baum der Verwalter gelöst werden.

Die Elemente des Kellers eines Verwalters sind im wesentlichen die Repräsentationen des in einer Sphäre zusammengefaßten Akteurs und der diesem assoziierten Komponenten. Die Repräsentation einer Komponente enthält Segmente für Code, Daten etc. Zusätzlich enthält der Keller Verweise auf anonyme Depots, die in den bereits erklärten Hilfsdatenstrukturen repräsentiert werden. Zur Realisierung dieser Hilfsdatenstrukturen wird der einer Sphäre zugeordnete Speicherbereich in einen **Keller** (mit entsprechender Semantik) und eine **Halde** aufgeteilt. Anonyme Depots können damit in der Halde der Sphäre des Akteurs, dem sie lebenszeitmäßig zugeordnet sind, repräsentiert werden. Die zu deren Auflösung nötigen Lebenszeitverweise werden in der Repräsentation dieses Akteurs auf dem Keller gespeichert. Ausgehend von der Wurzel des Kellerbaumes wird ein Sohnknoten in einem für diesen reservierten Teil des Haldenspeichers des Vaterknotens repräsentiert. Auf diese Weise ergibt sich eine Schachtelungsstruktur auf dem linearen Speicher, die der Baumstruktur des Kellerbaumes entspricht (siehe Abbildung 3).

Das Erzeugen einer INSEL-Komponente durch einen Akteur bewirkt eine entsprechende Operation auf dem Verwalter des Knotens, dem die zu erzeugende Komponente assoziiert wird. Handelt es sich bei der zu erzeugenden Komponente um eine Order oder um ein benanntes Depot, so legt der Verwalter eine entsprechende Repräsentation auf dem zugeordneten Keller an. Soll ein anonymes Depot erzeugt werden, so wird die Repräsentation des Depots im Haldenbereich angelegt und ein Verweis auf die erzeugte Repräsentation an entsprechender Stelle im Keller gespeichert. Soll ein Akteur erzeugt werden, so wird zunächst ein Verwalter für den neuen Akteur erzeugt und ein Verweis auf den erzeugten Verwalter gekellert. Der neue Verwalter erhält bei seiner Erzeugung einen Verweis auf den ihn erzeugenden Verwalter (Vorgänger-Verwalter). Dieser Verweis ermöglicht die Kooperation des Verwalters mit seinem Vorgänger-Verwalter zur Nachforderung von Speicher bzw. zur Erzeugung von Repräsentationen von Komponenten, die lebenszeitmäßig nicht von dem dem neuen Verwalter zugeordneten Akteur abhängig sind. Der neue Verwalter nimmt die Aufteilung des ihm zugeteilten Speichers vor und erzeugt dann auf seinem Keller die Repräsentation des zu erzeugenden Akteurs.

Nach der Erzeugung der Repräsentation eines Akteurs bzw. einer Order können die Anweisungen des Codesegments ausgeführt werden. Sind alle Anweisungen ausgeführt und alle ggf. weiteren Voraussetzungen für die Auflösung von Komponenten gemäß den Festlegungen auf der programmiersprachlichen Ebene erfüllt, so kann die Komponente aufgelöst werden. Zu diesem Zeitpunkt befindet sich die Repräsentation der Komponente als oberste auf dem Keller. Die Komponente wird aufgelöst, indem der von der Repräsentation der Komponente belegte Speicherplatz vom entsprechenden Verwalter freigegeben wird. Zuvor muß jedoch gewährleistet sein, daß sämtliche von der aufzulösenden Komponente lebenszeitmäßig abhängigen Komponenten aufgelöst sind. Dazu werden alle lebenszeitmäßig abhängigen Akteure durch entsprechende Operationsaufrufe auf den zugeordneten Verwaltern aufgelöst. Neben der Auflösung der aktiven Komponenten müssen die passiven Komponenten, d. h. die Depots aufgelöst werden. In rekursiver Anwendung des eben beschriebenen Verfahrens werden daher zunächst die entsprechenden Lebenszeitabhängigkeiten der Depots behandelt und schließlich deren Repräsentation entweder auf dem Keller oder bei anonymen Depots auf der Halde aufgelöst.

Charakteristisch für die oben beschriebenen Vorgehensweise ist, daß sich die Reihenfolge, in der die Repräsentationen von Komponenten aufgelöst werden, aus der Keller-Semantik ergibt: Es wird jeweils die Komponente aufgelöst, deren Repräsentation als oberste gekellert ist. Weiter gilt, daß diese Reihenfolge im Einklang mit den Lebenszeitabhängigkeiten der INSEL-Komponenten steht, d.h. keine Komponente vor den von ihr lebenszeitmäßig abhängigen Komponenten aufgelöst wird.

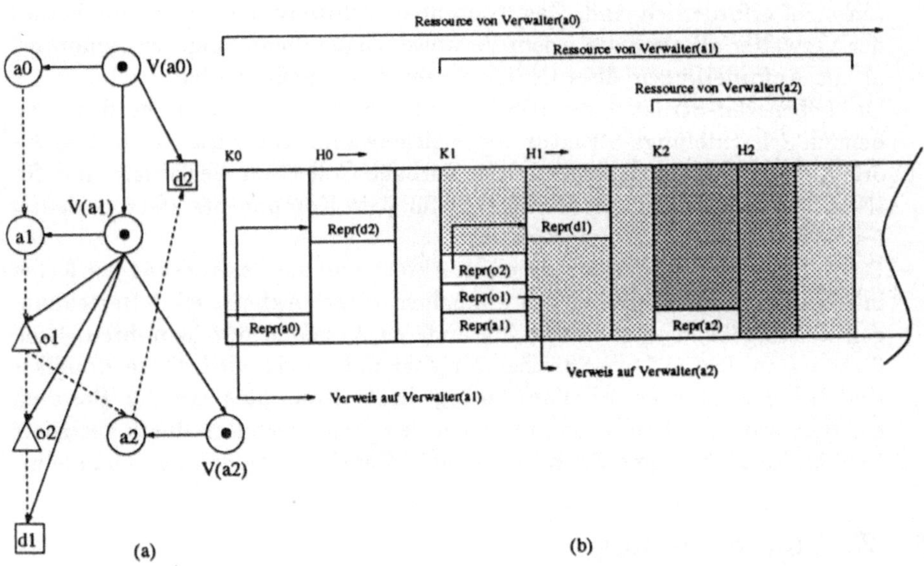

Abb. 3. Speicherbild und Beziehungen zwischen Komponenten und Verwaltern

Abbildung 3 zeigt einen Schnappschuß des Speichers wie er sich nach Durchführung entsprechender Komponentenerzeugungen ergibt. Der in (a) abgebildete Graph stellt den Zusammenhang zwischen der Komponentenerzeugung auf

Sprachebene und der daraus resultierenden Verwaltungsoperation des entsprechenden Verwalters dar. Zu beachten ist hierbei, daß das Depot d2 von Akteur a2 erzeugt, der Speicher zur Repräsentation des Depots jedoch von dem Verwalter des Akteurs a0 bereitgestellt wird, da das Depot d2 lebenszeitmäßig von dem Akteur a0 abhängig ist.
Damit ist das Grundkonzept für die Speicherverwaltung für INSEL-Systeme skizziert. Grundlage für die Verwaltung der Ressourcen eines INSEL-Systems sind die Lebenszeitabhängigkeiten, die in der Struktur über den Akteur-Sphären eines Systems zum Ausdruck kommen. Die wesentlichen Eigenschaften dieses Konzepts sind folgende:

- Das vorgestellte Verwaltungskonzept ist **dezentral**. Die Verwalter können **parallel** und weitgehend unabhängig – Abhängigkeiten ergeben sich bei der Nachforderung bzw. Freigabe von Speicher – auf dem Kellerbaum arbeiten, da sie die ihnen zugeordneten Speicherbereiche unabhängig verwalten. Zur Erfüllung der globalen Verwaltungsaufgabe kooperieren die Verwalter gemäß der Baumstruktur über der Menge der Verwalter miteinander, so daß Broadcast- bzw. Multicast-Nachrichten zur Ermittlung freier Ressourcen nicht erforderlich sind. Das Konzept ist **adaptiv**, da sowohl die Anzahl der Verwalter als auch der jedem Verwalter zugeordnete Speicher dynamisch an die Anforderungen eines INSEL-Systems angepaßt werden.
- Die Lebenszeit-Struktur der INSEL-Komponenten kommt in der sich ergebenden Schachtelungs-Struktur des Speichers zum Ausdruck. Die in Objektorientierten Systemen eingesetzten Garbage-Collection Verfahren sind für INSEL-Systeme nicht erforderlich, da für jede Komponente stets eindeutig festgelegt ist, wann sie aufgelöst wird.
- Die Zuordnung eines Kellers zu jedem Akteur und die Realisierung der Keller in disjunkten Speicherbereichen ermöglicht einem Akteur, seine Berechnungen weitestgehend unabhängig von anderen Akteuren durchzuführen. Konflikte treten dort auf, wo Speicher gemeinsam benutzt wird. Diese Konflikte sind bei der weiteren Konkretisierung dieses Konzeptes auf der Basis einer Hardware-Konfiguration mit vernetzten Stellenrechnern durch geeignete Replikations-Strategien für Komponenten-Repräsentationen zu behandeln.

5 Zusammenfassung

In dem Beitrag wurde die Bedeutung von Sprach-basierten Ansätzen für die Konstruktion verteilter Systeme diskutiert. Sprach-basierte Systeme sind geeignete Bindeglieder in der Abstraktionshierarchie für Systemkonstruktionen, die dazu beitragen, Übergänge zwischen den beiden wesentlichen Teilbereichen dieser Hierarchie zu vereinfachen.
Für den Aufgabenbereich der Ressourcenverwaltung wurde deutlich gemacht, daß unter der systematischen Nutzung von Strukturinformationen neuartige Strategien zur verteilten Verwaltung entwickelt werden können. Die Realisierung entsprechender Verwaltungskonzepte und Strategien ist Gegenstand laufender Arbeiten, die zum Ziel haben, das in Kapitel 4 vorgestellte Konzept für

eine Speicherverwaltung auf eine Hardware-Konfiguration ohne gemeinsamen Speicher abzubilden, sowie Strategien zu entwickeln, die zusätzliche Information aus der programmiersprachlichen Ebene zur Verwaltung des Speichers miteinbeziehen. Das so erweiterte Konzept ist schließlich auf einer entsprechenden Hardware-Basis zu implementieren und dessen Effizienz durch geeignete Messungen zu bewerten.

Literaturverzeichnis

[And88] Gregory R. Andrews. An Overview of the SR Language and Implementation. *ACM Transactions on Programming Languages and Systems*, 10(1):51–86, January 1988.

[Bla85] Andrew P. Black. Supporting Distributed Applications: Experience with Eden. In *Symposium on Operating Systems Principles*, pages 181–193, Washington U.S.A., December 1-4 1985. ACM.

[G+87] S.J. Goldsack et al. ADA for distributed systems – a library of virtual nodes. In *ADA Components: Libraries and Tools*, pages 266–279, Stockholm, May 26–28 1987.

[Hoa85] C.A.R. Hoare. *Communicating Sequential Processes*. Prentice-Hall International, London, 1985.

[JLHB88] Eric Jul, Henry Levy, Norman Hutchinson, and Andrew Black. Fine-Grained Mobility in the Emerald System. *ACM Transactions on Computer Systems*, 6(1):109–133, Feb 1988.

[Lis85] Barbara Liskov. *The Argus Language and System*, volume 190 of *Lecture Notes in Computer Science*, chapter 7, pages 343–430. Springer–Verlag, 85.

[Lö92] K.P. Löhr. Concurrency annotations. In *Proceedings 7. OOPSLA '92, Vancouver* , ACM, 1992.

[Ltd84] Inmos Ltd. *Occam Programming Manual*. Prentice Hall, Englewood Cliffs, 1984.

[Spi92] P.P. Spies. Parallelverarbeitung mit INSEL. In *GI ITG PARS Workshop*, 1992.

Schwerpunktprogramm Informatikforschung des Schweizer Nationalfonds: Massive parallele Systeme

Helmar Burkhart
Universität Basel
Modulsprecher

1. Aufgaben und Ziele

Im November 1992 begannen die Forschungsarbeiten im Schwerpunktprogramm Informatikforschung (SPP IF) des Schweizerischen Nationalfonds zur Förderung der wissenschaftlichen Forschung. Gemäss Ausführungsplan erfolgt die Forschung in drei Modulen (prioritäre Teilbereiche): sichere komplexe Systeme, wissensbasierte Systeme, massiv parallele Systeme. Die Forschung wird an mehreren schweizerischen Hochschulen und teilweise in der Privatwirtschaft ausgeführt. In diesem Kurzbeitrag wird über das letzt genannte Modul 3 berichtet.

Die technologischen Grenzen von Rechnern mit einigen wenigen sehr schnellen Prozessoren sind seit einiger Zeit absehbar. Andererseits ist die Nachfrage nach grösserer Rechenleistung in wichtigen Anwendungsbereichen beschleunigt gestiegen. Dieser Herausforderung begegnen bekannte Architekturen paralleler Rechner. Parallele Systeme sind zwar heute schon hardwaremässig verfügbar, problematisch ist aber nach wie vor die einfache und effiziente Programmierung zur Umsetzung des grossen Architekturpotentials bei rechenintensiven Anwendungen. Der Weg hin zu massiv parallelen Systemen wird heute ergänzt durch Architektur- und Sprachansätze, die auf eine grundsätzliche Abkehr von bekannten Organisationsprinzipien hinzielen. Dieser Ausgangssituation entsprechend können die im Modul 3 angelaufenen Forschungsprojekte in zwei Kompetenzkreise eingeteilt werden:

- Software für Parallelrechner (Theorie, Methoden und Werkzeuge, Algorithmen und Anwendungen)
- Spezialarchitekturen, neue Rechenprinzipien

Neben den Resultaten, die im Modul 3 in den einzelnen Forschungsvorhaben erarbeitet werden, sind gebietsübergreifende Antworten zu erwarten. Insgesamt soll in den nächsten Jahren eine viel stärker verflochtene Forschergemeinschaft auf dem Gebiet paralleler Systeme entstehen.

2. Projekte des Modulprogramms

Das Modulprogramm umfasst 14 Projekte mit einer Kreditsumme von knapp 4 Mill. SFr für eine Laufzeit von 2 Jahren. Verlängerungen ausgewählter Projekte, sowie neue Projekte sind für eine anschliessende zweijährige Forschungsphase geplant.

Die folgende Übersicht zeigt die gegenwärtig bearbeiteten Projekte.

Projektleiter	Projekttitel
B. Sanders, ETH Zürich	Formal methods for parallel programs: foundations and tools
J. Rolim, Université de Genève	Methodology for producing parallel probabilistic algorithm from specification
M. Gengler, EPF Lausanne	Parallélisation d'algorithmes combinatoires
W. F. van Gunsteren, ETH Zürich	Parallel algorithms for exhaustive and heuristic search, with applications to molecular modelling
W. Gander, ETH Zürich	Divide and conquer algorithms in numerical linear algebra
W. Hett, HTL Biel	Mathematische Algorithmenbibiliothek für Transputer-Netzwerke
B. Hirsbrunner, Université de Fribourg	Cola: un langage de coordination pour la programmation heuristique parallèle
H. Burkhart, Universität Basel	Skeleton-oriented programming
K. Decker, CSCS Manno	A tool environment for parallel programming of distributed systems
R.D. Hersch, EPF Lausanne	Parallel hierarchical image storage and retrieval
P. Kropf, Universität Bern	SPINET: Computer Simulation der mechanischen Zusammenhänge der menschlichen Wirbelsäule
W. Guggenbühl, ETH Zürich	Paralleler Mikro-Supercomputer
F. Eggimann, ETH Zürich	Neuronale Netzwerke und deren Anwendung in der Signalverarbeitung und Handschrifterkennung
N.-D. Nicoud, EPF Lausanne	MANTRA: Un centre de compétence en applications et machines neuronales

3. Referenzen

Nähere Einzelheiten zum Schwerpunktprogramm allgemein bzw. zu den einzelnen Projekten des Moduls 3 erteilen die Programmleitung bzw. das Sekretariat.

Programmleitung: Dr. J.-M. Grossenbacher, La Closerie, CH-1787 Mur, Tel. + 37/73 13 07, Fax + 37/73 19 85

Sekretariat: Herr Stefan Bachmann, Sekretariat Schwerpunktprogramme, Schweizerischer Nationalfonds, Wildhainweg 20, CH-3001 Bern, Tel. + 31/27 22 22, Fax + 31/23 30 09

Tupelorientiertes Programmieren am Beispiel von YAPPE *

Jean-Daniel Pouget Helmar Burkhart

Institut für Informatik
Universität Basel
CH-4056 Basel

Zusammenfassung

In diesem Beitrag stellen wir eine tupelorientierte Programmierumgebung für Parallelrechner vor. YAPPE ist eine Umgebung, welche auf dem virtuellen Maschinenmodell Linda basiert. Wir präsentieren neben der Motivation für unseren Ansatz auch die Architektur von YAPPE, sowie den theoretischen Hintergrund dieser Arbeit, welcher sich auf BAKS, das Basler Algorithmen Klassifikations Schema stützt. Den Schluß bilden zwei Beispielprogramme, welche einen Einblick in die Programmierung mit YAPPE vermitteln sollen.

1 Die Software-Krise in der Parallelverarbeitung

Hardware-Entwicklungen sind der Software immer ein paar Jahre voraus. Die Software-Ingenieure haben Mühe bzw. es gelingt ihnen gar nicht, die vorhandenen Hardware-Betriebsmittel richtig auszuschöpfen. Man sprach deshalb schon in den 70-er Jahren von einer eigentlichen Software-Krise. Wenn auch heute noch in der Einprozessor-Welt vieles im argen liegt, so hat doch das Software-Engineering mitgeholfen, diese Krise zu lindern. Die Hilfestellung, die dabei zu Beginn angeboten wurde, bestand weniger aus Werkzeugen (Tools), sondern vielmehr aus der Einführung neuartiger Konzepte wie der Modularisierung, der Verkapselung und in letzter Zeit auch der objektorientierten Programmierung. Wie es scheint, wiederholt sich diese Entwicklung auch im Bereich der Parallelverarbeitung: der Bau leistungsfähiger Parallelrechner und die Entwicklung neuartiger Rechnerarchitekturen sind im Vergleich zur Entwicklung paralleler Software weit voraus und stellen nicht mehr die ganz große Herausforderung dar. Obwohl die Konzepte des Software-Engineerings bekannt sind, nützen sie uns in dieser Situation nicht besonders viel, da sich die Software-Krise in der Parallelverarbeitung differenzierter darstellt. Das Software-Dilemma nach [BBDK91] besteht nämlich aus unterschiedlichen Teilaspekten:

1. Die Einarbeitungszeit in eine parallele Programmierumgebung ist groß. Meist müssen immer wieder neue Betriebssystemschnittstellen erlernt werden. Leider existieren in diesem Bereich keine Standards, so daß für einen Programmierer, der die parallele Programmierumgebung eines bestimmten Parallelrechners kennt, bei einem Wechsel auf einen anderen Parallelrechner, die Einarbeitung wieder von neuem beginnt. Die Produktivität leidet darunter erheblich.

*Dieses Projekt wurde aus Mitteln des Schweizerischen Nationalfonds gefördert.

2. In den meisten Fällen setzt die Programmierumgebung umfangreiche Kenntnisse über die eingesetzte Systemsoftware und der verwendeten Hardware voraus. Sind diese nicht vorhanden, was bei den meisten Anwendungsprogrammierern der Fall ist, so resultieren ineffiziente parallele Programme.

3. Je größer und komplexer die Programme werden, desto mehr Fehler schleichen sich ein. Diese Tatsache stammt noch aus der Einprozessor-Welt. Im parallelen Fall verschärft sich diese Situation nochmals, da hier zusätzliche Fehler möglich sind, wie z.B. Synchronisationsprobleme, Deadlock, Livelock etc.

4. Wenn zum Schluß trotz aller Widrigkeiten ein paralleles Programm läuft, ist es wenig portabel und muß deshalb auf einem anderen Parallelrechner entscheidend verändert werden.

Da die vier Teilaspekte untereinander abhängig sind und jedem die gleiche Bedeutung zukommt, darf ein Lösungsansatz nicht nur in eine Richtung vorstoßen, sondern muß gleichzeitig in jedem Bereich eine Verbesserung bringen. Was die vier Aspekte auch noch offenlegen ist, daß wir offenbar mit unserer Software die Probleme, die uns die Parallelrechner stellen, nicht beherrschen. In solchen Fällen hat die Informatik bis jetzt immer gut daran getan, für die Problemlösung ein Schichtenmodell zu entwickeln. Auf unsere Problemstellung übertragen bedeutet dies, daß versucht werden muß, eine parallele Programmierumgebung als Schichtenmodell eines Parallelrechners (virtuelle Maschine) zu realisieren, wobei der Programmierer nur noch Dienste der "höchsten" Schicht direkt aufrufen sollte.
Genau dieses Ziel verfolgt die Arbeit, welche wir hier vorstellen. Grundlage unserer Bemühungen ist das Klassifikations-Schema BAKS, welches uns helfen wird, die mit YAPPE erstellten Algorithmen einzuordnen und zu bewerten. Das BAKS-Schema wird deshalb auch zuerst eingeführt. Danach werden anhand des BAKS-Tupels Schritt für Schritt die Konzepte, welche YAPPE bereitstellt, vorgestellt und anhand einiger Programme demonstriert.

2 Das Basler Algorithmen Klassifikations-Schema

Die Forderung nach der Skalierbarkeit paralleler Algorithmen bedingt den Einsatz regulärer Ablauf- und Koordinationsstrukturen, weil kein Programmierer Hunderte oder gar Tausende individuell programmierte Prozessoren mehr überblicken kann. Die Koordinationsteile werden in der Literatur oft als Skelette, Program-Templates oder Harnesses bezeichnet und stellen einen vielversprechenden Ansatz zur Bewältigung des beschriebenen Software-Dilemmas dar. Die Grundidee ist, dem Programmierer einen Satz vordefinierter Programmgerüste anzubieten, aus dem er das für seine Problemstellung am ehesten geeignete auswählt und weiter verfeinert. Diese Vorgehensweise wird als "skelettorientiertes Programmieren" (SOP) bezeichnet. Die Identifikation und Klassifizierung der regulären Koordinationsstrukturen stellt deshalb ein zentrales Problem dar. Da die bisherigen Klassifikations-Schemata entweder zu allgemein gehalten oder nur auf spezielle Architekturen anwendbar sind, erschien es angebracht, ein neues Klassifikations-Schema zu entwickeln. Das Resultat dieser Bemühungen ist BAKS [BFKG+92]. Zentrales Element bei der Klassifikation eines parallelen Algorithmus mittels BAKS ist das Tupel (nicht zu verwechseln mit einem "Linda-Tupel") aus Abb. 1.
Die einzelnen Komponenten enthalten dabei folgende Informationen:

Prozeßeigenschaften				Datenattribute	
Struktur	Topologie	Ablaufstruktur	Interaktion	Aufteilung	Verteilung

Abbildung 1: Klassifikationstupel eines parallelen Algorithmus

Struktur: Die Prozeßstruktur kann statisch oder dynamisch sein.

Topologie: Möglichkeiten hierfür sind: Pipeline, Gitter, Baum, Hypercube, Master-Slave und Worker (alles gleichartige Prozesse), wobei die einzelnen Topologien teilweise noch stärker untergliedert werden können.

Ablaufstruktur: Es handelt sich immer um reguläre Ereignissequenzen, also um Schleifen. Dabei sind fixe Schleifen (**FOR**-Loop) oder bedingte Schleifen (**WHILE**-Loop) möglich.

Interaktion: Es existieren drei verschiedene Interaktionsgruppen: globale gekoppelte Interaktionen (z.B. Barrier, Broadcast), globale entkoppelte Interaktionen (z.B. Lock/Unlock, Semaphor, Tupel-Operationen) und direkte Interaktionen (z.B. Send/Receive).

Aufteilung und Verteilung (der Daten): Hierbei wird spezifiziert "WAS" verteilt wird und "WIE" es verteilt werden soll. Die Frage "WAS" verteilt wird, ist relativ leicht zu beantworten: es muß sich um homogene Datenstrukturen wie bspw. Felder handeln. Der eindimensionale Fall (Vektor) ist dabei der einfachste. Wie Abb. 2 zeigt, existieren hierbei zwei Arten der Aufteilung: eine elementweise und eine blockweise.

[a] □□□□□□□□□□□□□□□ [b] □□□□□□□□□□□□□□□

Abbildung 2: Aufteilung eines Vektors in [a] einzelne Elemente [b] Blöcke von Elementen

Der nächstkompliziertere Fall betrifft die Aufteilung einer Matrix. Hier existieren bereits sechs Möglichkeiten, welche in Abb. 3 zusammengefaßt sind.

Diese Art der Aufteilung von Feldern in Elemente und in Blöcke von Elementen, läßt sich für beliebige Dimensionen verallgemeinern. Inhomogene Datenstrukturen wie bspw. Verbund-Strukturen (Records) lassen sich, ebenso wie Skalare, jedoch nicht aufteilen.

Bei der Frage "WIE" Daten auf Prozesse verteilt werden, muß berücksichtigt werden, daß nicht alle Arten von Daten verteilt werden können, da diese teilweise unterschiedliche Eigenschaften aufweisen:

1. Lokale Daten: Sie werden nur prozeßintern verwendet und haben keinerlei Bedeutung für andere Prozesse.
2. Globale Daten: Sie bilden eine unteilbare, logisch gesehen globale Einheit und können nur der Gesamtheit aller Prozesse zugeordnet werden.

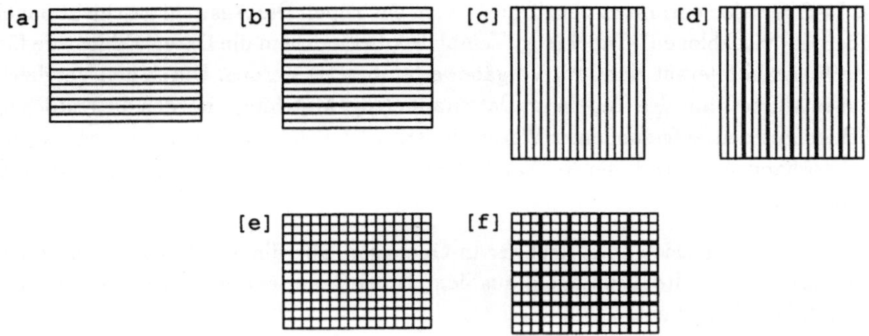

Abbildung 3: Aufteilung einer Matrix in [a] Zeilen [b] Blöcke von Zeilen [c] Spalten [d] Blöcke von Spalten [e] Elemente [f] Blöcke von Elementen

3. Verteilte Daten: Ihre Struktur entspricht jenen Feldern, welche nach den obigen Gesetzmäßigkeiten aufgeteilt werden können. Es existieren folgende Bindungsmöglichkeiten:
   - kopierte Bindung: Jeder Prozeß erhält eine Kopie des Feldes.
   - blockartige Bindung: Jeder Prozeß erhält einen Block von zusammenhängenden Datenelementen.
   - zyklische Bindung: Jeder Prozeß erhält diejenigen Datenelemente, deren Teilungsrest bei der Division ihrer laufenden Nummer durch die Anzahl Prozesse seiner Prozeßnummer entspricht.

   Man überlegt sich leicht, daß damit im zweidimensionalen Fall die gängigen Verteilungsarten wie zeilenweise, spaltenweise oder gitterartig realisiert werden können.

Wir stellen uns vor, daß, ausgehend von den BAKS-Klassifikationstupeln, entsprechende Koordinationsskelette definiert werden können, welche in Skelettbibliotheken verwaltet werden und, integriert in eine parallele Programmierumgebung zusammen mit unterstützenden Werkzeugen, wie etwa Skelettgeneratoren [Gut93], einem Programmierer in Zukunft zur Verfügung stehen werden.

3 YAPPE — eine tupelorientierte parallele Programmierumgebung

Die parallele Programmierumgebung YAPPE (Yet Another Parallel Programming Environment) [Pou93] basiert auf dem virtuellen Maschinenmodell von Linda [ACG86, BCGL87] mit einigen Erweiterungen [PB93], welche vor allem die Effizienz von Linda [PB92] verbessern. Ganz kurz zusammengefaßt, bietet das Linda-Paradigma einem Programmierer drei Operationen an, welche auf einem gemeinsamen Objektspeicher (sog. Tupel-Raum) operieren und in eine Wirtsprogrammiersprache eingebettet sind. Bei den Operationen handelt es sich um

Out: Die Out-Operation fügt ein Tupel in den Tupel-Raum ein. Es können mehrere gleiche Tupel im Tupel-Raum existieren. Das Einfügen eines Tupels führt nie zu einer Prozeßblockierung.

In: Die In-Operation entnimmt dem Tupel-Raum ein Tupel. Die Auswahl geschieht dabei über ein "Schablonen"-Tupel (sog. Template), bei welchem die Daten-Felder, die für die Auswahl relevant sind, mit Vorgabewerten besetzt werden. Durch den Vergleich dieses Musters mit den Tupeln im Datenraum (sog. Matching), werden die restlichen Felder mit den aufgefundenen Werten besetzt. Ist jedoch kein entsprechendes Tupel vorhanden, welches die Auswahlkriterien erfüllt, so wird der aufrufende Prozeß blockiert.

Read: Die Read-Operation entspricht der In-Operation, allerdings mit dem Unterschied, daß das ausgewählte Tupel nicht aus dem Tupel-Raum entfernt wird, sondern nur dem "Matching" dient.

In der vorliegenden Implementation wurde Linda in die Programmiersprache MODULA-2 integriert. Zusätzlich wurde das strenge Typenkonzept auch auf Tupel-Operationen ausgedehnt, weshalb Tupel vor ihrer ersten Verwendung in einer Tupel-Deklaration definiert werden müssen. Man spricht dabei von der Definition einer Tupel-Klasse.

Abb. 4 zeigt in einem Überblick die wichtigsten Komponenten von YAPPE:

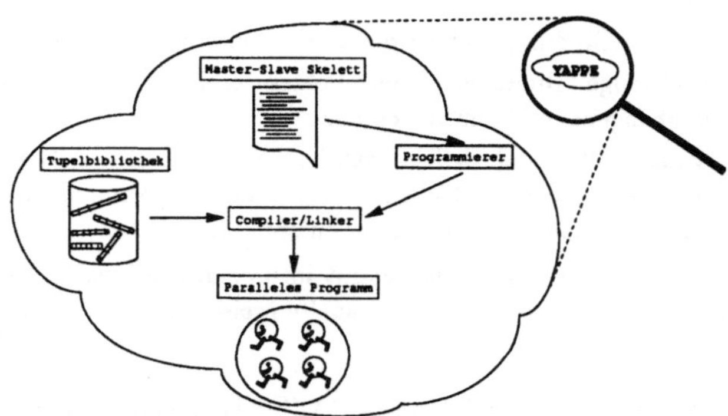

Abbildung 4: Grobübersicht von YAPPE

Jedes YAPPE-Programm besteht zu Beginn aus einem Master-Slave Skelett, welches dem Programmierer zur Verfeinerung und zur Vervollständigung angeboten wird. Das Compiler/Linker-System übersetzt dann den resultierenden Quelltext mit Hilfe von Tupelbibliotheken (enthalten Tupel-Deklarationen) in ein ausführbares paralleles Programm. Während der Ausführung eines parallelen Programms übernimmt ein Laufzeitsystem die Realisierung der eigentlichen Funktionalität, welche zwei Hauptaufgaben erfüllen muß:

1. Verwaltung des Tupel-Raums (Funktionalität der virtuellen Maschine Linda) und
2. Aufbau und Unterhalt einer Client-Server Architektur, welche eine portable Betriebssystemschnittstelle darstellt.

Diese Client-Server Architektur ist in Abb. 5 dargestellt. Man erkennt drei Dämon-Prozesse (Prozeßverwaltung, Speicherverwaltung und Ein/Ausgabe), welche auf Auftrags-Tupel (sog. Requests) warten, die gewünschte Betriebssystemfunktion ausführen und schließlich Antwort-Tupel (sog. Replies) an ihre Klienten (YAPPE-Programme) zurückschicken.

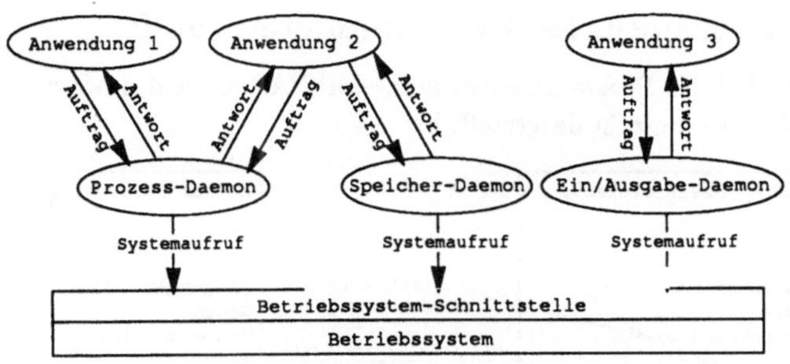

Abbildung 5: Die Client-Server Architektur von YAPPE

Mit dieser Architektur wird eine vollständige Betriebssystemunabhängigkeit der parallelen Programme erreicht, was deren Portabilität zusätzlich erhöht. Dadurch daß YAPPE einerseits nur auf den wohldefinierten Tupel-Operationen basiert und andererseits die in den Dämon-Prozessen notwendigen Betriebssystemaufrufe in einer Zwischenschicht gekapselt werden, ist die eigene Portabilität ebenfalls gewährleistet.

Die Klasse derjenigen Algorithmen, welche mittels YAPPE formuliert werden können (sog. "YAPPE-Algorithmen"), wird durch das BAKS-Tupel aus Abb. 6 zusammenfassend charakterisiert. Die Algorithmen weisen alle eine statische Master-Slave Prozeßtopologie auf, wohingegen die Ablaufstruktur algorithmusabhängig ist und nicht näher spezifiziert werden kann. Die Basis aller Interaktionen bilden die bekannten Tupel-Operationen, auf welchen Operationen höherer Abstraktionsstufe aufgebaut werden. Bei der Datenverteilung können zwei Arten von Daten unterschieden werden: globale Daten, welche im Tupel-Raum verwaltet werden und verteilte Daten, welche mit speziellen Manipulationsoperationen bearbeitet werden.

Struktur	Topologie	Ablaufstruktur	Interaktion	Auf-/Verteilung
Statisch	Master-Slave	*algorithmus-abhängig*	1. Globale entkoppelte Operationen (in, read, out) 2. Globale gekoppelte Operationen (bspw. Barrier, FanIn, Broadcast, CombineSend, CombineRecv)	<u>Globale Daten:</u> im Tupel-Raum <u>Verteilte Daten:</u> Datenverteilungsoperationen (Distribute/Receive)

Abbildung 6: Klassifikation von YAPPE-Algorithmen mittels BAKS

Der Grad an Unterstützung, welche eine Umgebung einem Programmierer bei der Programmentwicklung bietet, ist neben der Effizienz der dabei entstehenden Programme, das wichtigste Maß an welchem jede Programmierumgebung gemessen wird. Wir wollen nun anhand des beschriebenen BAKS-Tupels die Programmierer-Schnittstelle, welche YAPPE zur Verfügung stellt, genauer untersuchen.

3.1 Skelett-orientiertes Programmieren (SOP)

Ausgangspunkt bei der Programmentwicklung mit YAPPE ist das Master-Slave Skelett, welches in Abb. 7 vereinfacht dargestellt ist.

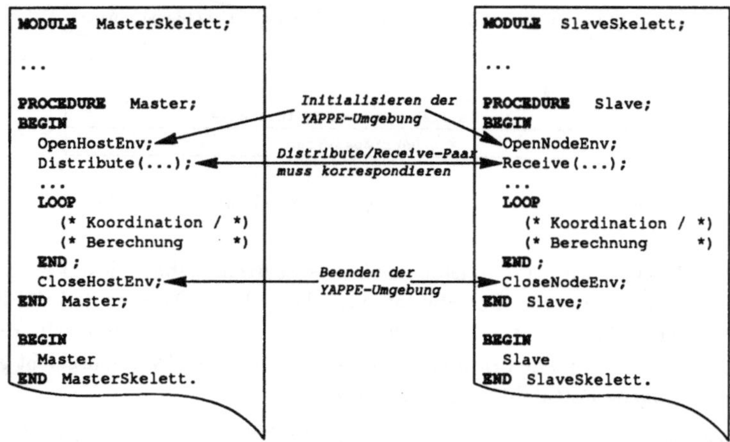

Abbildung 7: Das Master-Slave Skelett

Dieses Skelett wird dem Programmierer als zwei Quelltext-Dateien angeboten - eine für den Master und eine für den Slave, welche er seinen Bedürfnissen entsprechend anpassen und vervollständigen muß. Auf den ersten Blick unterscheidet sich der Master-Teil des Skeletts fast nicht vom Slave-Teil. Erst bei genauerem Betrachten erkennt man einen Unterschied bei der Initialisierung und beim Beenden der Umgebung. Der Master übernimmt bei der Initialisierung die Erzeugung der Prozeßtopologie mittels der Prozedur "OpenHostEnv", welche in einem Benutzerdialog alle wichtigen Parameter (Anzahl und Namen der Slave-Prozesse, Priorität etc.) für die Kreierung der Slaves ermittelt. Die Prozedur "OpenNodeEnv" im Slave-Teil des Skeletts dient nur dazu, relevante Programm-Parameter (Anzahl Slave-Prozesse und die eigene Prozeßnummer) zu erfragen. Das Beenden der Umgebung wird im Master durch "CloseHostEnv" veranlaßt, welches die erzeugte Prozeßtopologie wieder löscht. Die Slaves hingegen warten am Ende darauf vom Master gelöscht zu werden, indem sie sich durch die Ausführung von "CloseNodeEnv" selbst blockieren. Wie man sieht, ist die Prozeßstruktur statisch, denn die Slaves werden zu Beginn kreiert und erst am Schluß wieder gelöscht. Da die allermeisten Master-Slave Algorithmen eine statische Prozeßstrukur aufweisen, stellt dies unserer Meinung nach keine wesentliche Einschränkung dar. Die letzte Prozeßeigenschaft unseres Tupels betrifft die Ablaufstruktur. Wie bereits in Abschnitt 2 erwähnt, betrachten wir nur reguläre Strukturen (Schleifen). Im Skelett haben wir uns für eine allgemeine Schleife (LOOP) entschieden, da mit diesem Konstrukt sowohl fixe als auch bedingte Schleifen realisiert werden können. Da jedoch in einem Skelett keine weiteren Annahmen zur Ablaufstruktur gemacht werden können, ist die Verfeinerung Sache des Programmierers. Ebenfalls in die Kompetenz des Programmierers fällt, da algorithmusabhängig, die Spezifikation eines Koordinations- und eines Berechnungsteils sowie des Wechsels zwischen diesen Phasen. Im Skelett ist hierfür nur ein Kommentar vorgesehen, welcher den Platz markiert, wo diese Spezifikation hingehört. Wir werden weiter unten sehen, wie weit YAPPE den Programmierer beim Einfüllen des Koordinations- und Berechnungsteils unterstützen kann.

3.2 Interaktionsmechanismen

Da das virtuelle Maschinenmodell von YAPPE auf dem Linda-Paradigma basiert, werden die üblichen Tupel-Operationen als globale entkoppelte Interaktionen unterstützt. Zusätzlich bietet YAPPE noch globale gekoppelte Interaktionen wie bspw. Barrier (Warten auf den letzten Prozeß), FanIn (Master berechnet aus den Teilergebnissen der Slaves ein globales Ergebnis und teilt dieses den Slaves mit) und Broadcast (verschicken einer Nachricht an alle beteiligten Prozesse) als Bibliotheksroutinen an, welche mit den bekannten Tupel-Operationen realisiert werden. Diese Art der Implementation besitzt den Vorteil der Portabilität, bedingt aber die Verwaltung von Tupel-Klassen innerhalb von YAPPE-Programmen. Ansätze zur Lösung dieser Verwaltungsaufgabe gehen in Richtung "intelligenter" Editoren [ACG91], welche die verwendeten Tupel-Klassen *eines* Programms intern verwalten und sie auf Wunsch einem Programmierer zur Verwendung in Tupel-Operationen anbieten. Der Weg, den wir gewählt haben, geht hingegen in eine etwas andere Richtung. Anstatt Tupel-Klassen nur eines Programms in einem Editor zu verwalten, bietet YAPPE dem Programmierer sog. Tupelbibliotheken an, welche bereits vordefinierte Tupel-Klassen enthalten. Da die Operationen Barrier und FanIn mit Hilfe dieser Tupel-Klassen definiert sind, werden sie sozusagen als Zugriffsoperationen (im Sinne eines abstrakten Datentyps) ebenfalls in diese Tupelbibliothek integriert. Abb. 8 zeigt beispielhaft die Implementation einer Barrier mittels Tupel-Operationen.

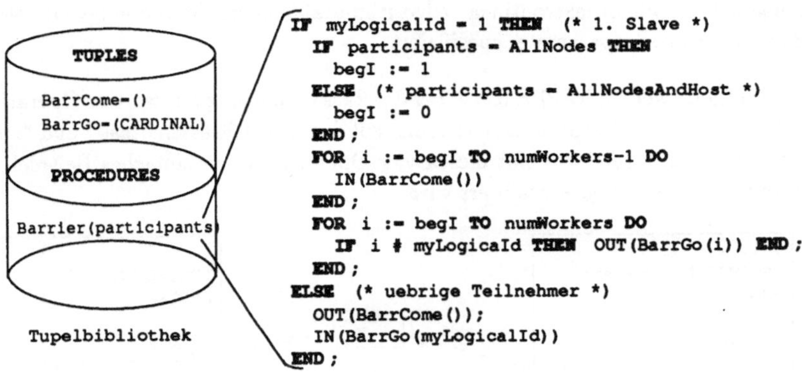

Abbildung 8: Die Realisierung einer Barrier mittels Tupel-Operationen

Der Parameter "participants" dient zur Spezifikation, ob an der Barrier entweder nur alle Slave-Prozesse (AllNodes) oder alle Slave-Prozesse zusammen mit dem Master (AllNodesAndHost) teilnehmen. Weiter findet innerhalb der Routine eine Fallunterscheidung zwischen dem die Barrier verwaltenden Prozeß (1. Slave-Prozeß) und den übrigen beteiligten Prozessen statt. Dies geschieht mittels einer Abfrage der logischen Prozeßidentifikation (myLogicalId). Der verwaltende Prozeß wartet zuerst bis alle Teilnehmer bei der Barrier angekommen sind (1. **FOR**-Schleife) und schickt diesen dann das Zeichen zum Weiterfahren (2. **FOR**-Schleife). Die Teilnehmer ihrerseits melden dem Verwalter zuerst ihre Ankunft und warten dann auf das Signal zum Weiterarbeiten. In ähnlicher Art und Weise wurden auch die FanIn- und die Broadcast-Operation realisiert. Im Fall von Broadcast muß jedoch mit einem zusätzlichen Parameter (send/receive) noch spezifiziert werden, ob der aufrufende Prozeß als Sender oder Empfänger arbeitet.

3.3 Interaktionsklassen

Die Taskverwaltung (Task-Bag, Task-List etc. [CG90]) ist ein zentrales Konzept in der tupelorientierten Programmierung. Dabei legt der Master zu Beginn des Programms einen oder gar mehrere Aufträge (Tasks) in den Tupel-Raum und wartet dann auf deren Erledigung. Die Slaves entnehmen diese Aufträge dem Tupel-Raum, arbeiten sie ab und schicken dann eine Meldung, welche die Erledigung des betreffenden Auftrags charakterisiert, an den Master zurück. Der einzige Unterschied, der zwischen der Taskverwaltung mittels Task-Bag und derjenigen mittels einer Task-List besteht, ist, daß bei ersterer die Reihenfolge in welcher die Aufträge bearbeitet werden irrelevant ist, wohingegen bei der letzteren eine strikte Reihenfolge (FIFO oder LIFO) eingehalten werden muß. Diese Art von Koordinations- und Berechnungs-Muster tritt sehr häufig auf. Ihre Verwendung sollte deshalb von einer Programmierumgebung in irgendwelcher Form unterstützt werden. Wir sprechen in diesem Zusammmenhang von der Bildung sog. Interaktionsklassen, welche diese Koordinations- und Berechnungs-Muster in geeigneter Art und Weise beschreiben. YAPPE selbst verwendet zwei Methoden zur Implementation von Interaktionsklassen:

1. Die Definition von Zugriffsoperationen auf Tupel-Klassen (wieder im Sinne eines abstrakten Datentyps).
2. Die Integration ganzer Ablaufstrukturen inklusive Koordinationsskelett und Berechnungsteil in Bibliotheksroutinen. Algorithmusabhängige Berechnungsteile werden dabei als Prozedurparameter spezifiziert.

Die erste Methode wendet YAPPE bspw. bei der Taskverwaltung an, wo vier Operationen (PutTask, GetTask, PutResult und GetResult) auf den Tupel-Klassen "task" und "result" definiert sind. Abb. 9 zeigt wie mit diesen vier Operationen ein einfaches Beispiel - die Verwaltung eines Task-Bags - realisiert wird.

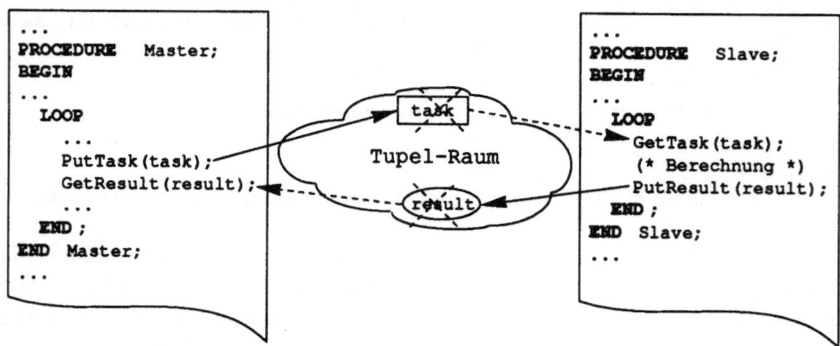

Abbildung 9: Die Verwaltung eines Task-Bags

Mit Hilfe der zweiten Methode wurde eine DIBL [KBT89] nachempfundene Version von DIB[1] (Distributed Implementation of Backtracking) [FM85] in eine Interaktionsklasse integriert.

[1]ein Algorithmenpaket, welches verschiedene Suchverfahren in einer Umgebung mit verteiltem Speicher implementiert

3.4 Datenverteilung

Wie aus dem BAKS-Klassifikations-Schema hervorgeht, nimmt die Aufteilung und Verteilung der Daten eines parallelen Algorithmus eine zentrale Rolle ein. Eine parallele Programmierumgebung muß deshalb vor allem in diesem Bereich eine starke Unterstützung anbieten. Im Gegensatz zu High Performance Fortran (HPF) [For92], wo die Aufteilung und die Verteilung der Daten auf die Prozesse in zwei Schritten erfolgt, werden die Daten eines parallelen Programms von YAPPE in einem einzigen Abbildungsschritt auf die Prozesse verteilt. Ein weiterer Unterschied besteht im Abbildungsablauf: während bei HPF nur eine Angabe zur Methode der Auf- resp. Verteilung bei der Datendeklaration erfolgen muß und die eigentliche Auf- resp. Verteilung dann implizit erfolgt, verlangt YAPPE den expliziten Aufruf einer Datenverteilungsfunktion (Distribute/Receive), wobei die Bindungsart für jede Dimension über Parameter spezifiziert wird. Als Möglichkeiten für den Bindungstyp sind zyklisch (cyclic), blockweise (block) und kopiert (copy) vorgesehen. Abb. 10 zeigt wie eine Matrix in Blöcke von Zeilen auf vier Slave-Prozesse verteilt wird.

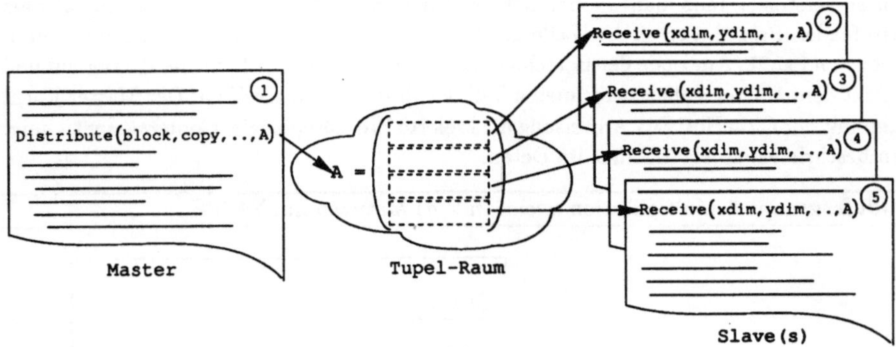

Abbildung 10: Die Verteilung einer Matrix

Der Master ruft dabei eine Distribute-Operation auf, welche die Zeilenblöcke im Tupel-Raum ablegt. Die Slaves ihrerseits müssen an der entsprechenden Stelle eine korrespondierende Receive-Operation ausführen, welche den ihnen zustehenden Zeilenblock aus dem Tupel-Raum abholt. YAPPE unterstützt alle Möglichkeiten zur Aufteilung von ein- und zweidimensionalen Datenstrukturen ([a] - [f]), welche bereits im Abschnitt 2 erläutert wurden.

Das Gegenstück zur Datenverteilung bildet die Datenkombination. Diese wird praktisch immer am Schluß eines parallelen Programms durchgeführt, um die bei den Slaves vorliegenden Teilergebnisse zu einem Gesamtergebnis zusammenzufassen. YAPPE bietet hierfür das Datenkombinationspaar CombineSend/CombineRecv an, wobei der Master die Operation CombineRecv und die Slave-Prozesse die Operation CombineSend ausführen. Kombiniert werden können all jene Datenstrukturen, welche durch die Datenverteilung bereits in der entsprechenden Teilstruktur ([a] - [f]) bei den Slaves vorliegen.

4 Anwendungen

Um die Praxistauglichkeit von YAPPE zu demonstrieren, haben wir mehrere parallele Master-Slave Algorithmen programmiert. Uns scheint, daß die Entwicklungszeit im Vergleich zu früher zurückgegangen ist. Es handelt sich hierbei jedoch um einen subjektiven

Eindruck, da bis jetzt nur die Autoren mit YAPPE gearbeitet haben. Wir wollen an dieser Stelle auch weniger eine vorhandene Produktivitätssteigerung quantifizieren, sondern vielmehr die Eleganz dieses Ansatzes an zwei Beispielprogrammen zeigen.

4.1 Matrix-Multiplikation

Einer der einfachsten Beispielalgorithmen, welchen man immer wieder antrifft, ist die Matrix-Multiplikation. Im vorliegenden Fall sollen zwei $(n \times n)$ Matrizen miteinander multipliziert werden. Matrix A wird in Zeilenblöcke aufgeteilt und an die Slave-Prozesse verschickt (1. Distribute Anweisung). Matrix B wird nicht aufgeteilt, damit jeder Slave eine Kopie erhält (2. Distribute Anweisung). Zum Schluß wartet der Master an einer Barrier auf das Ende der Slaves, um danach deren Teilresultatsmatrizen zur Gesamtresultatsmatrix C zu kombinieren. Die Slaves erhalten zuerst den ihnen zustehenden Teil von Matrix A (1. Receive Anweisung) und dann die ganze Matrix B als Kopie (2. Receive Anweisung). Die eigentliche Berechnung findet in der anschließenden **FOR**-Schleife statt. Um den Ablauf zu verstehen, muß man wissen, daß die Funktion `OwnI(i,nrAparts,myAchunk)` dem aufrufenden Prozeß, der die i.te Zeile der Matrix A besitzt, den Wert `TRUE` zurückliefert, ansonsten `FALSE`. Am Ende der Berechnungsphase ruft jeder der Slaves die Barrier auf und schickt dem Master seinen berechneten Teil der Resultatsmatrix C zu. Der Master löscht dann mit der CloseHostEnv Anweisung die kreierte Prozeßtopologie. Codefragment 1 zeigt den beschriebenen Algorithmus im Detail.

Codefragment 1 Multiplikation zweier $(n \times n)$ Matrizen mit YAPPE

Master ↔ Slave(s)

```
Master
...
VAR A, B, C : Matrix;
...
OpenHostEnv;
Distribute(block,copy,
           n,n,mat,ADR(A));
Distribute(copy,copy,
           n,n,mat,ADR(B));
CombineRecv(n,n,ADR(C));
CloseHostEnv
```

```
Slave(s)
...
VAR A, B, C : Matrix;
...
OpenNodeEnv;
Receive(n,n,myAchunk,nrAparts,ADR(A));
Receive(n,n,myBchunk,nrBparts,ADR(B));
FOR i := 1 TO n DO
 IF OwnI(i,nrAparts,myAchunk) THEN
  FOR j := 1 TO n DO
   C[i,j] := 0.0;
   FOR k := 1 TO n DO
    C[i,j] := C[i,j]+A[i,k]*B[k,j]
   END;
  END;
 END;
END;
CombineSend(block,copy,n,n,mat,ADR(C));
CloseNodeEnv
```

4.2 Warshallalgorithmus

Ein häufig zu lösendes Problem in der Graphentheorie ist das Auffinden der transitiven Hülle eines gerichteten Graphen. Diese gibt für jeden Knoten des Graphen an, welche anderen Knoten von ihm aus erreichbar sind. Üblicherweise wird die Problemstellung über eine

Adjazenzmatrix A spezifiziert, welche für jeden Knoten des Graphen die direkte Erreichbarkeit seiner unmittelbaren Nachbarknoten definiert. Der Warshallalgorithmus [War62] führt nun die Adjazenzmatrix A in die Matrix T über, in welcher zum Schluß die transitive Hülle gespeichert ist. Abb. 11 zeigt anhand eines kleinen Beispiels das Prinzip. Dabei bedeutet eine 1 in der j-ten Spalte der i-ten Zeile in A, daß Knoten j von Knoten i aus direkt erreichbar ist, während in T dadurch nur die Erreichbarkeit, nicht aber die direkte Erreichbarkeit, angegeben wird.

$$A = \begin{pmatrix} 0 & 0 & 0 & 1 \\ 1 & 0 & 0 & 0 \\ 0 & 0 & 0 & 1 \\ 0 & 0 & 1 & 0 \end{pmatrix} \xrightarrow{\text{Warshallalgorithmus}} \begin{pmatrix} 0 & 0 & 1 & 1 \\ 1 & 0 & 1 & 1 \\ 0 & 0 & 1 & 1 \\ 0 & 0 & 1 & 1 \end{pmatrix} = T$$

Abbildung 11: Abbildung $A \rightarrow T$

Codefragment 2 Der Warshallalgorithmus mit YAPPE

Master

```
...
VAR A, T : Matrix;
...
OpenHostEnv;
Distribute(block,copy,
           n,n,mat,ADR(A));
CombineRecv(n,n,ADR(T));
CloseHostEnv
```

↔

Slave(s)

```
...
VAR A : Matrix;
...
OpenNodeEnv;
Receive(n,n,myAchunk,nrAparts,A);
FOR i := 1 TO n DO
 IF OwnI(i,nrAparts,myAchunk) THEN
  Broadcast(AllNodes,send,vect,ADR(A[i]))
 ELSE
  Broadcast(AllNodes,receive,vect,ADR(A[i]))
 END;
 FOR j := 1 TO n DO
  IF OwnI(j,nrAparts,myAchunk) THEN
   IF A[j,i] THEN
    FOR k := 1 TO n DO
     A[j,k] := A[j,k] OR A[i,k]
    END;
   END;
  END;
 END;
END;
CombineSend(block,copy,n,n,mat,ADR(A));
CloseNodeEnv
```

Die Philosophie des Warshallalgorithmus ist nun folgende: Wenn ein Knoten j einen Knoten i erreicht, dann erreicht j auch alle Knoten, welche von i aus erreichbar sind. Wird nun diese Überlegung auf alle Kombinationen von i und j ausgeführt, erhält man den Warshallalgorithmus. Für die Parallelisierung wird die Adjazenzmatrix A in Zeilenblöcke aufgeteilt und an die Slave-Prozesse verschickt (Distribute Anweisung). Abschließend wartet der Master an einer Barrier auf das Ende und kombiniert dann die Teilresultate der Slaves zur transitiven Hülle T (CombineRecv Anweisung). Die Slave-Prozesse erhalten zuerst den ihnen zustehenden Teil der Matrix A (Receive Anweisung). Dann durchlaufen alle Slaves die Matrix zeilenweise, wobei der Prozeß, welcher die jeweilige Zeile besitzt, diese an alle anderen sendet (Broadcast Anweisung). Erst in der nachfolgenden **FOR**-Schleife findet die eigentliche Aktualisierung der eigenen Zeilen eines jeden Slaves statt. Zum Schluß ruft jeder Slave-Prozeß noch die Barrier auf und schickt sein Teilresultat an den Master (CombineSend Anweisung), womit dieser das Zeichen zur Beendigung des Programms erhält. Codefragment 2 zeigt das beschriebene Verfahren.

5 Schlußbemerkungen

Die vorliegende Implementation von YAPPE hat gezeigt, daß die Wahl eines Tupel-Konzepts als Basis einer parallelen Programmierumgebung einige Vorteile aufweist:

Portabilität: Viele der existierenden parallelen Programmierumgebungen sind weder portabel noch erlauben sie es, über Betriebssystemgrenzen hinweg portable Programme zu erstellen. YAPPE versucht gerade in diesem Bereich einen Beitrag zu leisten, indem YAPPE-Programme keine Betriebssystemfunktionen mehr direkt aufrufen, sondern diese über Tupel-Operationen anstoßen. Damit wird einerseits eine Betriebssystemunabhängigkeit erreicht und andererseits wird, da das Linda-Paradigma auf verschiedenen Parallelrechner-Architekturen (Workstation-Netzwerk, Hypercube, VAX SMP) implementiert ist, auch eine Portabilität der resultierenden Programme zwischen diesen Rechnern erzielt. Die Portierung von YAPPE selbst wird durch den Umstand erleichtert, daß alle Betriebssystemabhängigkeiten in der Interface-Schicht zwischen dem Betriebssystem und den Dämon-Prozessen gekapselt sind. YAPPE kann auch gänzlich unabhängig vom Linda-Paradigma implementiert werden, falls man auf anderen Basissynchronisationen aufbaut.

Wiederverwendbarkeit: Die Einführung des Konzepts von Tupelbibliotheken, welche bereits vordefinierte Tupel-Klassen und Zugriffsoperationen enthalten, ist nicht nur zur Definition neuer Interaktionsoperationen geeignet. Ebenso gut können damit oft benötigte parallele Algorithmen als Bibliotheksroutinen beschrieben werden, um in anderen Programmen als Bausteine wiederverwendet zu werden.

Skalierbarkeit: YAPPE-Programme sind bezüglich der Anzahl Prozesse vollständig transparent. Die YAPPE-Umgebung selbst trifft keinerlei Annahmen zur maximalen Anzahl Prozesse. Intern wird immer nur mit der gerade aktuellen Anzahl Prozesse (numWorkers) gearbeitet. Die Skalierbarkeit ist deshalb ohne Einschränkungen gewährleistet.

Effizienz: Die Einführung einer zusätzlichen Abstraktionsebene ist nie gratis. Bereits das Linda-Paradigma birgt eine Quelle der Ineffizienz in sich. Genauere Untersuchungen hierzu haben wir bereits in [PB92] veröffentlicht. Da die Interaktions- sowie die Datenverteilungs- und -kombinationsmechanismen ausschließlich auf Tupel-Operationen basieren, weisen YAPPE-Programme auf keinen Fall eine höhere Effizienz als Linda-Programme auf. Hingegen bietet YAPPE, wie aus den zwei Beispielprogrammen ersichtlich ist, eine größere Bequemlichkeit beim Programmieren. Gerade die Funktion `OwnI` ermöglicht es, parallele Programme in ähnlicher Art und Weise wie sequentielle Programme hinzuschreiben, indem jedem Prozeß das Gesamtproblem vorgelegt wird, dieser aber nur das ihn betreffende Teilproblem bearbeitet. Dieser erhöhte Komfort kostet natürlich wieder etwas Effizienz, wobei es aber möglich ist, die Beispielprogramme so umzuformulieren, daß jeder Prozeß nur noch mit denjenigen Schleifenindizes arbeitet, welche den Datenstrukturen seines Teilproblems entsprechen.

Korrektheit: Mit der Korrektheit ist an dieser Stelle nicht die formale Beweisbarkeit eines Algorithmus gemeint, vielmehr verstehen wir darunter eine erhöhte Sicherheit in der Anwendung von Interprozeß-Synchronisation und -Kommunikation. Dadurch daß YAPPE für diese beiden wichtigen Aspekte des parallelen Programmierens bereits ausgetestete Bibliotheksroutinen anbietet, nimmt die Wahrscheinlichkeit eines Interaktions- oder Synchronisationsproblems in einem Algorithmus ab. Die Programme werden übersichtlicher und der Programmierer kann sich auf das Wesentliche – die Beschreibung seines Problems – konzentrieren.

Literatur

[ACG86] S. Ahuja, N. Carriero und D. Gelernter. Linda and Friends. *IEEE Computer*, 19(8):26–34, August 1986.

[ACG91] S. Ahmed, N. Carriero und D. Gelernter. The Linda Program Builder. In *Proc. Third Workshop Languages and Compilers for Parallelism (Irvine, 1990) (invited paper)*. Languages and Compilers for Parallel Computing II, MIT Press, 1991.

[BBDK91] J.E. Boillat, H. Burkhart, K.M. Decker und P.G. Kropf. Parallel Computing in the 1990's: Attacking the Software Problem. *Physics Reports (Review Section of Physics Letters)*, 207(3–5):141–165, 1991.

[BCGL87] R. Bjornson, N. Carriero, D. Gelernter und J. Leichter. Linda, the Portable Parallel. Research Report YALE/DCS/RR-520, YALE University; Department of Computer Science, New Haven, Connecticut. USA, Februar 1987.

[BFKG+92] H. Burkhart, C. Falcó Korn, S. Gutzwiller, P. Ohnacker und S. Waser. BAKS: Basler Algorithmen Klassifikations-Schema. Technischer Bericht 92-1, Universitätsrechenzentrum und Institut für Informatik; Universität Basel, Oktober 1992.

[CG90] N. Carriero und D. Gelernter. *How to Write Parallel Programs: A First Course*. The MIT Press, Cambridge, Mass., 1990.

[FM85] R. Finkel und U. Manber. DIB – A Distributed Implementation of Backtracking. In *Proceedings of the Fifth International Conference on Distributed Computer Systems*, Seiten 446–458, Mai 1985.

[For92] High Performance Fortran Forum. *DRAFT* High Performance Fortran Language Specification. Technical report, Rice University, Houston Texas, August 1992.

[Gut93] S.E. Gutzwiller. *Werkzeuge und Methoden des Skelettorientierten Programmierens*. Dissertation, Universität Basel, 1993. In Vorbereitung.

[KBT89] M.F. Kaashoek, H.E. Bal und A.S. Tanenbaum. Experience with the Distributed Datastructure Paradigm in Linda. In *Distributed & Multiprocessor Systems Workshop*, Seiten 175–191. USENIX Association, 1989.

[PB92] J-D. Pouget und H. Burkhart. Portabilität zu welchem Preis ? — Experimentelle Untersuchungen an einer Linda-Implementierung. In A. Jammel, Editor, *Architektur von Rechensystemen*, Seiten 250–261. Springer Verlag, März 1992.

[PB93] J-D. Pouget und H. Burkhart. Von Linda zu Linda^{+}. Technischer Bericht 93-1, Universitätsrechenzentrum und Institut für Informatik; Universität Basel, Januar 1993. (eingereicht).

[Pou93] J-D. Pouget. YAPPE - *Eine tupelorientierte Programmierumgebung für Parallelrechner*. Dissertation, Universität Basel, 1993.

[War62] S. Warshall. A theorem on boolean matrices. *Journal of the ACM*, 9(1):11–12, 1962.

High Performance Computing Applications for Industrial Embedded Systems

Joachim K. Irion
AEG Electrocom GmbH
Max-Stromeyer-Str. 160
78467 Konstanz

representing the HAMLET[1] consortium

Abstract:

The prime objective of the ESPRIT Project 6290 HAMLET is to provide the technology required to enable European industry to develop innovative products required by their markets using High Performance Computing in the fields of pattern recognition, image generation, and in other real-time/time-critical applications. These products will significantly increase the competitiveness in the global market. The HAMLET project brings together major industrial product suppliers with major technology suppliers to work together on technology and application development.

The project is driven by the industrial applications. They formulate the detailed application development system and hardware architecture requirements. By building on existing developments the technology providers initially deliver an appropriate application development system. It is then upgraded by a series of incremental developments. This report describes the progress midway through the project.

[1] The work in the HAMLET project is done within the framework of the ESPRIT programme and partly funded by the Commission of the European Communities. The following companies form the consortium: AEG(D), CAP Gemini(F), CASA(E), DLR(D), HITEC(GR), INESC(P), INMOS(GB), Parsytec(D), Gabriel(GR), TNO-FEL(NL), TNO-TPD(NL), TUM(D).

1. Introduction

This project entitled HAMLET (High Performance Computing for Industrial Applications) provides the technology required to enable European industries to develop innovative products in the fields of pattern recognition and image generation as well as real-time and time-critical applications that will prove competitive in the global market. The project unites major industrial product suppliers with major technology suppliers to work together on technology and application development.

The industrial applications drive the project. The technology suppliers assist the industrial partners in the formulation of their detailed application development system and hardware architecture requirements. The first version of the application development system builds on already existing development work and is delivered midway through the project, followed by a series of gradual improvements. This process allows the industrial partners to assess the accomplished development tasks early in the project and to set the priorities for the subsequent incremental developments. A professional management and software quality organisation co-ordinates these activities. The above process thus fully meets the needs of the industrial application developers.

The major results of the project are

- Product prototypes to demonstrate the advantages using the new hardware architecture and application development system in the construction of competitive industrial products.
- An application development system which integrates the early algorithm and timing simulations required with the final activities of debugging and monitoring the target system.
- A scalable hardware architecture which supports the high levels of computational power and the high bandwidth data delivery requirements of the applications.

These results provide the basis for commercial products for both industrial applications and the underlying technology. The consortium members have both the commitment and the market access needed to subsequently introduce and exploit these products on a world-wide basis.

2. The raison d'être of HAMLET

Europe still leads technologically in certain areas of High Performance Computing (HPC). Hardware as well as software (development environments) have improved over the years. Unfortunately, until today there is a lack of ability for application providing industries to use the technology in their products. The two main reasons for this are software development tools that are not yet on the level of normal programming aids, and current hardware technology without the required real time and interactive characteristics. While European industries are still struggling with the use of HPC in their products, it appears that the US and Japan are also developing HPC technology for industrial applications and are catching up to today's European advantage. In many global industrial markets the competitiveness of European products decreases as a result.

HAMLET overcomes this potential problem and makes European HPC technology available and usable for European companies to innovate their products. To achieve this ambitious goal, a number of representative applications have been selected, which will benefit from HPC because they will become more competitive with respect to non-European products. Typically, the applications are boosted in performance in such a way as to either make new applications possible or to become more cost efficient through HPC technology. Hardware and software technology providers are selected to develop HPC technology for industrial applications on the basis of existing technology. The development of this technology is completely controlled and specified by the application providers, in order to make sure that the technology products will be usable in the application products. This combination of technology providers and application providers makes HAMLET not only unique but also guarantees that the technology will be used.

3. Project description

There are five main workpackages in HAMLET. Three workpackages deal with the development of representative applications respectively. The fourth workpackage contains the hardware technology developments, and the fifth deals with the development of the software technology, i.e. the development environment.

As representative examples of the use of HPC in real products for real markets there are three applications, provided by AEG (pattern recognition for postal automation), by CASA, TNO-FEL and DLR (real time system simulation, especially visual simulation), and by HITEC together with Gabriel (quality control for the production of textiles).

The hardware technology will be provided by Parsytec and INMOS, and the software technology by CAP Gemini, TNO-TPD, Technical University of Munich, INMOS and INESC.

4. Representative examples from HPC technology in industrial products

Pattern recognition in postal automation

In the frame work of postal automation services the automatic reading and understanding of the mail piece address is presumably one of the most computational intensive tasks. Hence, HPC offers the natural choice to meet the demands. The address reading machine exhibits an overall pipelined data flow structure which consists of three main building blocks through which the data is passed during the recognition process: image processing, character processing and finally address interpretation. The amount of data passed through these blocks decreases rapidly as the process continues. While at the input about 6 MBytes per mail piece (scanned colour image) at a rate of 10-20 mail pieces per second have to be processed, there are only about several hundreds of KBytes per mail piece leaving the image processing. The character processing reduces the amount of data further down to some KBytes per mail piece ending up after the address interpretation with only about 10 - 20 Bytes per mail piece.

A special implementation of the address reader is a machine for remote processing of address images, the so called Remote Computer Reader. The Remote Computer Reader gets the images from a data base, and not from the scanning device. Also, the reading results are given back to a data base, instead of controlling the sorting device of the on-line Reader. The Remote Computer Reader itself can contain one to several Remote Reading Electronic Units which basically feature a complete address reading unit, as outlined above.

Within the HAMLET Project, both software and hardware modules of the Remote Reading Electronic Units are developed. For the software, the main emphasis is on the development of the Process Control, and on the Diagnostics Software. For the hardware, the development of special co-processors and their respective driver software is undertaken.

Real time system simulation

The application area of real time system simulation is very demanding as far as the required computational power is concerned. Careful analysis indicates that there is a requirement for 2 GFLOPS in processing and more than 300 MByte/s for the final communication. Also the intermediate communication sets requirements for the communication architecture in a parallel solution for this type of problem. In situations with 'hardware-in-the-loop' or 'human-in-the-loop' the real time constraints can be very strict. In general this means that HPC offers solutions to many problems in this field.

A specific simulation system has been chosen to be developed within HAMLET. It aims at the simulation of visual environments in areas like training simulators, virtual reality and other visualisation systems.

At the moment most commercially available systems are built with special hardware to perform the most time consuming functions. This gives overall systems a life cycle of some 5 years, which is relatively short compared to the high cost. HPC technology is not widely used yet in commercial systems. There are only a few exceptions. These, however, are of low performance and functionality because unfortunately the HPC technology of today is not very well suited for the application types. This is the main reason to use the application for the development of a new generation of real time oriented HPC systems.

Quality control for the production of textiles

The Textile Quality Control system will serve as a functional front-end system in the production process of the textile industry. It enables a fast and reliable computer vision based quality inspection process which is efficiently integrated in the actual manufacturing of the textile.

The Textile Quality Control system is able to detect and accurately discriminate fabric production faults in all three textile manufacturing steps, i.e.

- warping,
- weaving,
- finishing.

In the context of HAMLET, a quality control system detects the defects after each production phase. At present visual inspection is accomplished by humans inspectors operating off-line. No direct feedback to the complete process is possible. Only a local decision can be taken e.g. to stop a machine when the fabric is too defective. The automatic system that will be developed will allow on-line verification of the entire product and fast tuning of the operation parameters depending on the detected defects.

5. Architecture for real time HPC for industry

Generalised requirements from the applications

The detailed analysis of the requirements analysis of the applications is summarised in the following table:

	AEG	HITEC	CASA/DLR/TNO
cycle time [ms]	25	40	33
latency [ms]	few 100	100	< 80
input [MB/cycle]	6	-	5
input [MB/s]	160 - 240	n x 20	> 300
output [MB/cycle]	0.0001	-	5
output [MB/s]	0.004	0.001	> 300
ratio input/output	60,000 : 1	>2,000 : 1	1 : 1
computing performance	2 GOPS	2 GOPS	2 GFLOPS
operations per byte I/O	8 - 12	100	4 - 8
on-line RAM store [GB]	0.5 - 1	-	0.1 - 0.5

From this table it follows that the applications have a very similar profile in bandwidth and processing:

- high bandwidth I/O at one end — > 300 MByte/s
- scalable processing in the centre — up to 2 GFLOPS
- low bandwidth I/O at the other end (most cases) — 1 kByte/s to 1 MByte/s
- cycle time — 25 ms
- on-line RAM store — up to 1 GByte

The basic software requirements for the run-time system are:

process control: creation and deletion of threads, scheduling, dynamic loading and binding;

communication: synchronous and asynchronous communication, broadcast, time stamps, queues;

process synchronisation: semaphores, event handlers, input selection;

clock, timers: global time, local timers;

data pool: virtual global memory, local memory pools;

support of tools: debug and trace support;

Description of the system

The system is communication oriented. It is designed to be highly modular in order to scale with growing requirements. Most components consist of three functional units:

communication backbone, synchronisation mechanism and processing. The elements with communication backbone are a general purpose processor, video I/O, and filter elements. For post processing a simplified processing node is specified. The low level system software consists of a real time communication kernel, device driver for the communication backbone and for the distributed global memory.

There are two different types of communication: Bulk transfer for data distribution or gathereing and local inter-processor communication. For the first a communication backbone is used to handle the I/O at high speed (100-400 MByte/s). The second is using the communication method based on the transputer concept.

The backbone is a 128-bit 400 MByte/s bi-directional data transfer system. Like in a shift register, data is clocked from one board to the next. Data can be sent to any individual board, to a group of boards or broadcast to all. More than one data transfer at a time is possible as long as the communication uses different segments of the backbone. For frame assembly a gathering function in hardware is available to collect data from many sources. On each board data is shifted into the serial port of video rams. The local processor has access through the random port.

The control network is used for basic system functions, like the set-up and booting of individual processors, the transfer of error messages to the system manager or the remote control of processors. This control network is separated from the data communication network to avoid interference of systems activities with application activities.

The system software is based on concepts dealing with parallel and distributed processing under real-time constrains. The conceptual base of the Hamlet real time system software comes from RTSM, TIPSET and UTOPIA. The real time kernel is needed for the applications to do the low level work of communication, task control and I/O interconnects. It provides a library of building blocks and enables topology independent programming. It is based on RTSM and the INMOS parallel libraries.

6. Development environment for real time HPC for industry

Generalised requirements from the applications

The analysis of the applications and extensive discussions between the application developers and the technology providers revealed four consistent themes in their requirements, namely

- Ease of use

  It must be possible for engineers who are new to parallel processing to be able to get started rapidly. The style of user interface must be consistent across tools which span the development life cycle; engineers developing industrial systems are frequently involved in all stages of development from initial design through to implementation. All developers want the means to construct graphical representations of their systems and to access the functionality of the development system through these graphical representations.

- Scope of functionality

  It is important to enable the application developers to

  - enter the design graphically;
  - perform some analysis of the eventual behaviour of the system before a detailed implementation was available;
  - have a high level of debugging support for the application executing on the target machine;
  - have support for optimising the final system through monitoring and profiling techniques.

- Real time programming model

  A multiprocessing and multiprocessor system with a range of inter-process communication and synchronisation capabilities is mandatory. The programming model must support the access to real time clocks and external events.

- Quality

  The majority of the application developers want of tools commercial quality and the tools to be supported commercially in the long run. If the tools are not of a sufficiently high quality, their development engineers would refuse to use them. As the application development activity within HAMLET relates to products that need to be supported and developed further over a long time period, it is also essential that the tools are supported commercially.

Description of the system

The development environment is built on the solid technology baseline available in the HAMLET consortium. This will allow an early delivery of the initial system, and for the application developers to use some baseline tools immediately. The overall architecture of the development environment is shown in the diagram below.

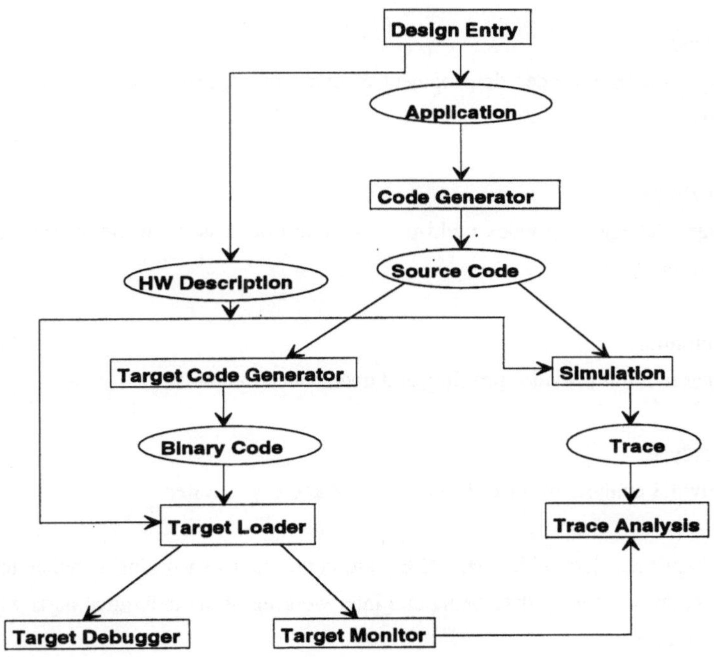

Functional architecture of the HAMLET development environment

The different parts of this architecture are:

- Design entry system
  The design entry system supports the graphical entry and manipulation of both software and hardware designs, and a window for assessing the functionality of other tools.

- Code generator
  Code will be generated from the graphical design descriptions. This will be used both to drive the simulator and to provide input to the target code generation tools.

- Simulation tool, application simulator
  The simulation tool provides application on host machine allowing some debugging activity and the generation of simulation trace files.

- Target code generator
  The target code generator generates binary images for execution on the target machine.

- Target loader
  The target loader provides development resource management and programme loading facilities.

- Target debugger
  The target debugger provides multi-process, multi-processor, symbolic debugging with graphical interface.

- Target monitor
  The target monitor provides profiling and trace collection tools.

- Trace analysis
  This provides analysis of traces from simulator and target system.

The technology providers within HAMLET are committed to working together to develop these modules fully realising that the natural inter working of the individual parts will greatly enhance the total result.

7. Conclusion

By bringing together applications providers and technology providers the HAMLET consortium arrived at a detailed analysis of the applications yielding clear requirements for both the application architecture and the application development system.

Based on the requirements of the application builders a logical and efficient architecture has been defined. On the software side a set of tools available from the technology providers has been identified. From this set of tools an integrated, complete toolset is built within the project. A continuous feedback from the application builders steers the technology providers during the integration and extension of this toolset.

The hardware development progresses very well. A first version will be available January 1994. Also the work on the development environment is on schedule. First versions of each tool are already delivered to the application builders. More mature and integrated tools will be delivered in October 1993 and January 1994. These in turn are used for the development of the applications.

Finally, the approach for the common work between application providers and technology providers allows constant feedback and interaction between the two groups. This will lead to a successful implementation of the applications. Furthermore, the newly developed software environment is immediately integrated into the above applications as well as into many other similar ones.

Automatic Parallelization for Distributed-Memory Systems: Experiences and Current Research *

Hans P. Zima, Peter Brezany, Barbara M. Chapman, and Jan Hulman

Institute for Software Technology and Parallel Systems
University of Vienna, Brünner Strasse 72,
A-1210 VIENNA, AUSTRIA
E-Mail: zima@par.univie.ac.at

Abstract

Distributed-memory systems (DMMPs) are powerful tools for solving large-scale scientific and engineering problems. However, these machines are difficult to program since the data must be distributed across the processors and message-passing operations must be inserted for communicating non-local data. In this paper, we discuss the automatic parallelization of Fortran programs for DMMPs, based on the programming paradigms associated with Vienna Fortran and High Performance Fortran. After introducing the state of the art, as represented by currently implemented systems, we will identify a number of limitations of this technology. In addition to insufficient functionality for handling many real applications, a major deficiency of current systems is the lack of intelligence in selecting good transformation strategies. We argue that a knowledge-based approach to compiling will contribute to more powerful and intelligent automatic parallelization systems in the future.

Keywords: distributed-memory multiprocessor systems, numerical computation, data parallel algorithms, program analysis, optimization, knowledge-based compilation.

1 Introduction

Distributed-memory multiprocessing systems (DMMPs), such as Intel's hypercubes, the Paragon, the nCUBE, Thinking Machine's CM-5, and the Meiko Computing Surface, have rapidly gained user acceptance during the past few years. DMMPs are relatively inexpensive to build, and are potentially scalable to large numbers of processors. However, these machines are difficult to program: the non-uniformity of memory accesses implies that the locality of algorithms must be exploited in order to achieve high performance. The management of data, with the twin goals of both spreading the computational workload and minimizing the delays caused when a processor has to wait for non-local data, becomes of paramount importance.

*The work described in this paper was carried out as part of the ESPRIT projects GENESIS and PREPARE funded by the Austrian Research Foundation (FWF) and the Austrian Ministry for Science and Research (BMWF)

In this paper, we discuss the automatic parallelization of numerical Fortran programs for DMMPs. In order to parallelize a code, the program's work and data must be distributed to the processors which will execute it. One of the common approaches to do so makes use of the regularity of most numerical computations. This is the so-called **Single Program Multiple Data (SPMD)** or **data parallel** model of computation. With this method, the data arrays in the original program are each partitioned and mapped to the processors according to a user-defined annotation. This is known as **distributing** the arrays. A processor is then thought of as **owning** the data assigned to it; these data elements are stored in its local memory. The compiler implements the data distribution in two steps: First, the work is partitioned following the **owner-computes** paradigm: each processor executes exactly those assignments which define data elements owned by it. The processors then execute essentially the same code in parallel, each on the data stored locally. Secondly, accesses to non-local data must be explicitly handled by inserting communication constructs to send and receive data at the appropriate positions in the code. Communication can be avoided by **replicating** data, i.e., allocating a copy in each processor. Replication is usually applied to scalar variables and small arrays. Each processor executes the same operations on replicated data.

During the past years, much research activity has been concentrated on developing an optimizing general parallelization strategy for DMMPs; moreover, a number of proposals for language extensions for data distribution annotations were specified. Important developments in this area include Vienna Fortran [50, 10], Fortran D [16] and High Performance Fortran (HPF) [25].

This paper gives an overview of currently implemented parallelization strategies, discusses their limitations, and outlines new research directions.

In Section 2 we describe the current state of the art in compiling Fortran programs that are annotated by a data distribution specification. The *basic parallelization strategy*, dealing with the optimizing transformation of programs characterized by regular accesses to regularly structured data, will be shortly outlined in Section 2.2; this topic has been extensively discussed in the literature (see [52] and the references given there). Algorithms for sparse matrices or Finite Element problems cannot be adequately handled in this way because too little information is available at compile time. In Section 2.3 we describe a method that can be applied to these classes of problems by combining compile time and run time analysis strategies.

In Section 3, we discuss the limitations of the current compiler technology and give an overview of current research directions. One of these areas, to which little attention has been paid until now, is that of knowledge-based compiling. This is treated in Section 4. The paper closes with an overview of related work (Section 5).

2 First Generation Compilation Systems: General Parallelization Strategy

2.1 Compilation Framework

We discuss automatic parallelization in the framework of a **source-to-source translation** from Fortran, extended by a language for data distribution specification, to message passing Fortran. Without loss of generality, we will use a subset of Vienna Fortran for the syntax of the input language.

Vienna Fortran programs are executed by a DMMP according to the SPMD programming model. Central concepts of the language are processors and distributions: **Processor arrays** may be explicitly specified to define the set of *abstract* processors used to execute a program. **Distributions** map arrays to non-empty sets of processors; they can be specified by declaration annotations.

We illustrate the basic features of the annotation language by means of a simple example (Figure 1). The **PROCESSORS** declaration introduces $R1$ as a one-dimensional processor array with four elements. The annotations attached to the declarations specify

- a regular *block distribution* for A: *BLOCK* distributes an array dimension to a processor dimension in evenly sized portions: array A is partitioned into 4 blocks of length 3.
- (total) *replication* for array B. Every processor owns a copy of the whole array.
- a *general block distribution* for C: *GENERAL_BLOCK* distributes an array dimension to a processor dimension in arbitrarily sized portions. Array C is partitioned into 4 blocks of lengths 1,5,5, and 1. General block distributions were introduced to deal with situations in which regular block distributions may lead to an unbalanced load, for example, if the boundary region of a data domain needs considerably more work than the interior.
- a block distribution of the columns of D. (The *elision symbol* ":" indicates that an array dimension is not distributed.)

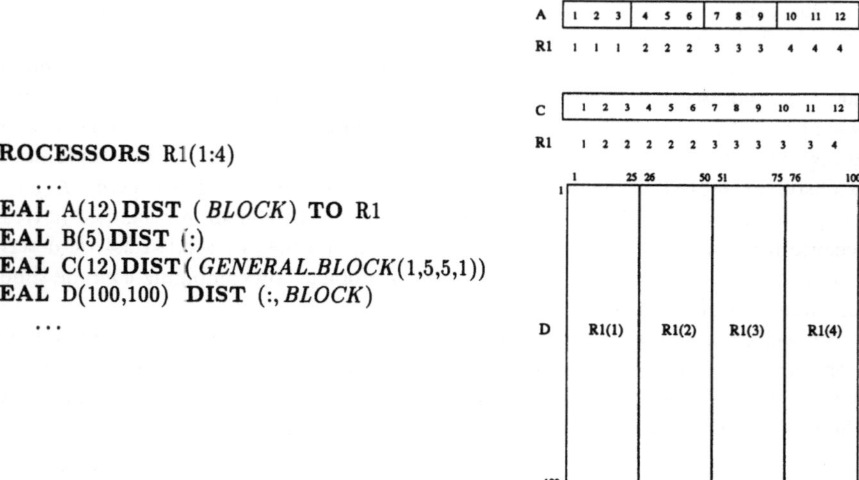

Figure 1: Basic Distributions

In the rest of this section, we restrict the annotation language to *BLOCK* and *GENERAL_BLOCK* distributions as well as replication, and assume that the number of processors and all distribution parameters are compile-time constants. For each processor p, the set of local variables associated with an array A can then be represented as a rectilinear section of A. This will be called the *distribution segment* of A with respect to p.

2.2 Basic Parallelization and Optimization

The translation from Vienna Fortran to message passing Fortran can be described as a sequence of four **phases**:

- Phase 1, the **Front End** performs the following three tasks: it transforms the source code into an *internal representation* suitable for further compiler manipulation, it performs the *initial analysis* of the program, and it *normalizes* the code.

  Thus Phase 1 includes syntactic and semantic analysis, control flow analysis, data flow analysis, data dependence analysis and the construction of the call graph. Further, some standard transformations such as constant propagation and dead code elimination may be applied at this stage. Normalizations have the purpose of simplifying subsequent compiler operations; they include loop normalization, if conversion and subscript standardization [51]. The resulting program is called the **normalized program**.

- In Phase 2, **splitting**, the normalized program is split into a **host program** and a **node program**. The host program will, after compilation, be executed on the host computer or a specially designated host node of the target system, as the **host process**. It performs global management tasks, such as requesting resources, loading code, and terminating program execution; it also handles all input/output.

  The node program is still sequential and contains the actual computation; input/output is represented by communication with the host program. All I/O statements are removed from the node program: reads require a SEND statement in the host and a RECEIVE in the node program; writes require a RECEIVE in the host and a SEND in the node program.

  The host and node programs resulting from this phase are loosely coupled; all synchronization necessary between them at run time will be achieved through message passing.

- Phase 3, **initial parallelization**, maps the node program to the **defining parallel program**. This transformation is performed by processing the data distribution in two steps, which are referred to as masking and communication insertion:

  - **Masking** enforces the owner computes paradigm by associating a boolean guard, called the **mask**, with each statement, in accordance with the ownership implied by the distributions.
  - For all potentially non-local data accesses, **communication insertion** generates communication statements which copy non-local data items to private variables of the processor.

  According to the SPMD execution model, each processor will execute the same program, receiving its parameters and initial data from the host program.

- The final Phase 4, **optimization and target code generation** creates an optimized target program.

  The defining parallel program – as produced by Phase 3 – specifies exactly the work distribution and communication required by the input program. However, it would be very inefficient to actually compile and execute such a program on a parallel computer since communication involves only single data items and in general each processor has to evaluate the mask of a statement for all instances of that statement.

In Phase 4, the defining parallel program is transformed into an optimized parallel message passing Fortran target program. Communication and masking are improved: communication statements are moved out of loops and combined to perform aggregate communication where possible; the *strip mining* of loops [51] across the processors can be achieved in many cases by propagating the information in masks to the loop bounds [19]. A prerequisite for many optimizations is precise flow and data dependence information, as gathered in Phase 1, and **overlap analysis**, which detects certain simple regular communication patterns and re-organizes communication based upon this information. Overlap analysis also helps determine the minimum amount of storage which must be reserved for each partitioned data array in the memory of a node processor.

The overlap concept is not an appropriate approach if there is any form of indirection in the code, or the communication structure is irregular. In such a case, alternative methods as discussed in the next subsection, are required. A more general strategy for the optimization of communication has been proposed by Li and Chen [34].

We conclude with a remark on the compilation of procedures, based on the assumption that the distributions of formal parameters are **inherited** from the corresponding argument distributions. This strategy is described in detail in [52].

The SPMD paradigm is applied to procedures in an obvious way: a procedure call in the node program is executed by all processors allocated to the program; masking and communication is performed as described above. Different incarnations of the same procedure may associate the same formal parameter with arrays that have different distribution characteristics. The code implementing the accesses to a formal array parameter has to take into account all possible cases for the corresponding argument. The quality of the code generated for procedures then depends critically on how much information is available at compile time about the distributions of formal parameters in different incarnations of the procedure, and on how efficiently run-time information can be organized. An interprocedural optimization strategy can be based on the *call graph* of the program. For each incarnation of a procedure, a *distribution vector* is computed that establishes a binding between the formal parameters of the procedure and the distributions of the associated arguments. Conflicts can be resolved by **cloning**: if the same formal parameter is bound to replicated as well as partitioned arguments in different iterations, copies of the procedure are automatically generated.

The same interprocedural analysis can be used to optimize communication in the case where the distribution of a formal parameter is not inherited at procedure entry but enforced by an explicit specification.

2.3 Runtime Analysis for Loops with Irregular Accesses

A compiler cannot efficiently handle loops with irregular accesses, as they arise in sparse or unstructured problems, where subscript functions often depend on data available at runtime only. In such a situation, the compiler cannot recognize the absence of loop-carried dependences [51], and, as a consequence, has to make worst case assumptions.

For example, in the code segment shown below an index array X, is used to assign values to another array A.

```
DO I = 1, N
    A(X(I)) = ...
END DO
```

Here, if the values of the array X are unique, then the execution of the iterations will not create a loop-carried output dependence, but this fact cannot in general be verified by a compiler.

In order to deal with situations like this, Vienna Fortran provides the FORALL loop, which by definition asserts that the iterations are in fact independent – there are no loop-carried dependences – and may be logically executed in parallel.[1] The above loop can then be written in the form

```
FORALL I = 1, N ON ...
    A(X(I)) = ...
END FORALL
```

where the optional ON clause specifies an explicit association of iterations with processors (see below).

FORALL loops are processed using an integration of compile-time and runtime techniques. The compiler generates code which analyzes such a loop and adapts it to the target architecture at runtime. Advanced compile-time analysis can be utilized to minimize the runtime overhead by reusing the results of runtime analysis. The strategy discussed here generates two code phases for such loops, known as the **inspector** and the **executor**. The inspector analyzes the communication patterns of the loop, while the executor performs the actual communication and executes the loop iterations. Hence, in this context the term **inspector-executor paradigm** is frequently used. We first introduce the general inspector-executor model and then we discuss an approach which is based on the Parti runtime library.

In the following, we denote by *SENDS(p,q)* the set of elements that must be sent from processor p to processor q as a consequence of non-local uses in q. We let *RECEIVES(p,q)* be the set of elements that must be received by p from q as a consequence of non-local uses in p. Clearly, *SENDS(p,q)=RECEIVES(q,p)* for each pair of processors. We will use the code in Figure 2 as a running example.

```
PROCESSORS R(M)
  ...
REAL A(N), B(N) DIST (...)
INTEGER X(N), Y(N)
        ...
  ... initialization of X and Y ...
        ...
FORALL I = 1,N ON OWNER(A(X(I)))
       A(X(I)) = B(Y(I))
       ...
END FORALL
```

Figure 2: FORALL statement specifying irregular computations.

[1] The corresponding HPF construct is called *independent* loop.

The Inspector

The **inspector** implements the first phase in the execution of a FORALL loop by analyzing the loop and computing the communication and iteration sets. The inspector consists of three steps.

Step 1 implements the **work distribution** by computing for each processor p the set of all iterations of the loop, $exec(p)$, which are to be executed by p.

The work distribution can be explicitly specified in the ON clause. For example, the work distribution for the loop below is determined by including iteration I of the loop in $exec(p)$ iff $A(X(I))$ is owned by p.

```
FORALL I = 1, N ON OWNER(A(X(I))
    A(X(I)) = ...
END FORALL
```

If, in this case, *OWNER(A(X(I))* is processor *R(I)* for all values of I, the same effect would be achieved by writing ON*R(I)*.

If an ON clause is not specified explicitly, the work distribution is determined by the compiler. One possible method is to select an array reference $A(\ldots)$ in the loop body according to certain criteria, and then implicitly inserting ON $A(\ldots)$ in the FORALL head.

Step 2 performs a dynamic loop analysis: a simplified version of the loop is executed, in which only those components are analyzed that are relevant for the generation of communication. For each iteration in *exec(p)*, it is determined whether or not it is a *local iteration* in the sense that it only accesses local variables of p. For each non-local iteration, the non-local uses and their associated processors are determined: this yields the sets *RECEIVES(p,q)* for all processors q.

Step 3 uses the relationship *SENDS(p,q)=RECEIVES(q,p)* to compute, as a result of a global communication phase, the sets of values which must be transmitted prior to execution of the loop.

Although it is far superior to individual communication of values, the inspector phase nevertheless represents a significant run time overhead. It is therefore important to recognize situations in which one execution of the inspector suffices to organize the communication for multiple executions of the executor. This may happen when the same work distribution is used for several different loops. If arrays are not redistributed, then repeated executions of the same loop (at each time step, for example) will use the same iteration sets and the same communication structure; hence, the inspector phase need only be executed once.

The Executor

The **executor** is the second phase in the execution of the forall statement; it performs the actual computation. When the executor commences, all communication and iteration sets have been computed in the inspector. The executor consists of four steps (see Figure 3). The first of these sends all local data that are required by other processes. Then all local iterations are executed.

Non-local data required in p are received from other processes in parallel (if the target machine permits this), and stored in a temporary buffer. Finally, the executor performs all iterations with at least one non-local use, accessing the corresponding buffer elements.

Step 1: Send
Whenever SENDS(p,q)$\neq$ ϕ: **SEND** SENDS(p,q) **TO** q

Step 2: Execute Local Iterations

Step 3: Receive
For each $q \in P$ such that RECEIVES(p,q)$\neq$ ϕ: **RECEIVE** temps **FROM** q

Step 4: Execute Non-local Iterations

Figure 3: Executor code for processor p.

Library Support for Runtime Analysis

The implementation of the inspector-executor parallelization strategy in the Vienna Fortran Compilation System [46] is based on the **Parti** library [43], developed by Joel Saltz and coworkers at ICASE and at the University of Maryland. These routines represent a concrete system that addresses the specific problems related to the fact that either distributions of data or data dependence patterns are determined by program data not known until run time. Parti routines support the sending and receiving of irregularly distributed non-local data, and the implementation of reduction operations. The strategy described below generalizes the *inspector-executor paradigm* discussed above.

Construction of Local Iteration Sets The computation of the set *exec(p)* in a processor p is determined by the *iteration set* of the FORALL loop and the work distribution specification strategy. In our example, each processor p executes:

```
exec(p) = φ
DO i = 1, N
    IF OWNED(A(X(i)) THEN
        exec(p) = exec(p) ∪ {i}
    END IF
END DO
```

If the index array X is itself partitioned, or if there are more levels of indirection in the left hand side subscript function, the application of the above basic algorithm for the construction of execution sets would require each processor to broadcast the local segment of this array to each processor; this would cause extreme runtime inefficiency and large storage requirements.
Hence in this case, local iteration sets are computed in parallel. The corresponding algorithm is introduced in [7].

Generation of Schedules for Nonlocal Accesses The PARTI primitives (gathering and scattering procedures) that are called in the executor phase move data between processors. The work of each subroutine is controlled by a data structure called a **schedule** whose contents specifies the locations in distributed memory from which data is to be acquired. On each processor, schedules for distributed arrays which occur in a FORALL loop body are generated by a call to a Parti procedure (for details see [12]). The schedule produced is essentially a pattern of communication for gathering and/or scattering data.

In order to avoid duplicate data accesses, a list of nonlocal data references is stored locally (for each processor) in a hash table. The primitives thus only fetch a single copy of each unique nonlocal reference.

Executor Based on the Parti Library

The purpose of the executor is to perform the communication specified by schedules, and perform the actual computation prescribed by the FORALL loop body.

The semantics of the FORALL loop guarantees that all communication for non-local reads can be performed *before*, and all communication required for non-local writes and reductions can be done *after* the loop. This communication is supported by special Parti routines (*gather* and *scatter exchangers*).

Gather exchangers place copies of data values obtained from distribution segments of other processors in a local buffer. Before a call of a scatter exchanger, copies of data values to be scattered to other processors are placed in the buffer. Local and buffer data are referenced using local reference lists.

3 Limitations of First Generation Compilation Systems and Current Research Directions

The compilation strategy as described in the previous section represents the state of the art as far as existing implementations are concerned. It can be successfully applied to programs with statically distributed data structures, and produces good speedups if either the problem structure is simple or interactive tuning of the restructuring process is possible. But there are still many challenges left: much improvement is needed with regard to functionality, the efficiency of the generated code, and the quality of the interaction with the user.

First, we note that existing techniques do not fully cover the spectrum of features in languages such as Vienna Fortran [50, 10] and High Performance Fortran [25], and furthermore, the complexities posed by "real" codes have not been solved completely. In particular, the **functionality of systems must be improved** to

- derive data distributions automatically from the sequential program,
- deal efficiently with dynamic data and work distributions,
- generate efficient code for the use of library routines which may be called with partitioned data,
- refine the application of source level transformations to facilitate the generation of high-quality code,
- handle parallel I/O, and
- deal with multiple levels of parallelism.

One inherent problem with the transformation systems discussed above lies in the fact that the user is required to explicitly specify the data distribution. This is the intellectually most demanding task of the whole porting process, and severely influences the quality of the resulting programs. While it may be relatively easy to select a good data distribution manually for small programs whose behavior is well known, it may be an extremely difficult task for larger codes in which the information determining the quality of a data distribution may be spread across the whole program. Therefore, **automatic data distribution**, i.e., the development of automatic support for the user in the crucial task of selecting a data distribution, is a major research topic. The techniques employed depend on the kind of program under consideration and require extensive support from performance analysis tools. Li and Chen have developed a strategy for aligning data in regular codes within the Crystal compiler [33]; several other researchers have made substantial contributions to the problem [40, 26, 21, 28, 9]. A useful extension of this work would be a tool which determines the distribution of data (thus generating Vienna Fortran or HPF annotations, at least in part), displays the results and permits graphical user modification of them.

Irregular codes will require a different approach, using *general distribution routines* provided by the programmer or the system. At run-time, these routines must compute data and work distributions based on the data access pattern for a particular loop.

Furthermore, there exists a variety of complex application areas – ranging from signal processing to multidisciplinary problems – for which an adequate load balance cannot be achieved on the basis of the SPMD model alone. Language features are needed for the explicit creation and manipulation of asynchronous tasks. Current proposals in that direction include [45, 17].

Another weakness of current systems is the **lack of explicit, structured knowledge**. While there is a significant body of knowledge in these systems, it is mostly "hardwired" and unstructured, scattered across many thousands lines of code, and thus not explicitly accessible to user or system alike. Explicit knowledge is present only at a relatively low level, as exemplified by control flow and data dependence graphs or procedure interface information. Furthermore, key areas of analysis, in particular performance analysis and prediction, are usually missing. One consequence of this is that the system relies on the user to determine the transformation strategy; another that modification and adaptation to new hardware or software environments is difficult.

Finally, a compiler in the conventional sense does not, of its own, suffice to support the highly complex and challenging task of producing efficient programs for parallel systems. We believe that advanced compilation systems will be part of sophisticated **integrated programming environments** including an extensive set of **programming support tools**. These will be needed to provide guidance in a number of forms; they must satisfy the needs of a broad spectrum of users, some of whom will require an integrated system to work as automatically as possible, whereas others will expect to be provided with detailed and precise information and transformation tools, enabling them to make the major strategic decisions for parallelization themselves. Since one of the primary motivations for using parallel systems is to attain high performance, appropriate tools for **performance prediction and selective measurement** must be integrated [13, 14]. Performance tools will not only identify the most important areas of existing code. They will also support the selection of appropriate algorithms, and help determine appropriate transformation strategies. This may involve invoking a performance prediction tool, running selected areas of the corresponding code with sample input values, or accessing performance information stored within the database of information on the program.

Additional tools include *debuggers* which will need to relate programming errors to the source program in a comprehensible manner, and *visualization tools* that will help the user monitor a program's behavior and utilization of the machine's resources.

The following section will be devoted to a more detailed discussion of knowledge-based compilation, a new approach that promises to solve many of the inherent problems of current systems.

4 Knowledge-Based Compilation

4.1 The Problem

The knowledge of a few useful *transformation sequences* has enabled an automatic approach to certain tasks in current compilation systems: these include applying transformations to simplify program analysis, and some simple methods for distributing loop iterations. Evolving systems will be expected to perform many tasks which require a **global program transformation strategy**. Performance tools will provide a means to obtain knowledge about the performance characteristics of the program and the way performance is affected by the application of transformation sequences. There are different, and sometimes conflicting, goals to be attained (e.g., load balancing vs. minimization of communication), and non-trivial trade-offs to be considered. The results of analysis, combined with a set of heuristics, may be used to select predetermined transformation strategies. More advanced transformation strategies might include the detection of certain patterns in code and their replacement by highly optimized routines for the target machine.

The hardware and software architectures of parallel computing systems are currently undergoing rapid evolution. These modifications affect the parallelization strategy for a machine: whereas the basic strategy may remain unchanged, the details of optimization could be radically different. The representation and use of *explicit knowledge* on both architectures and their software systems (including the compilers), and the identification of *rules for the application of optimization strategies* in terms of this knowledge, may enable parallelizing systems to keep up with the pace of change, and permit them to be retargeted in response to system developments without a major reprogramming effort.

There are significant advantages in organizing an advanced programming environment as a collection of *knowledge-based subsystems* with different levels of expertise: 1) The possibility of rapid prototyping, 2) relatively easy modification of the programming environment if the underlying system changes, and 3) the availability of an explanation facility. So far, only few attempts have been made to develop restructuring systems using these techniques ([4, 47, 48]). This method has been explicitly applied to the problem of generating code for DMMPs by Ko-Yang Wang at Purdue University. He has constructed a prototype system which has a description of a target machine, a set of program transformations, and rules for applying the transformations which are written in terms of the machine parameters. This approach permits code to be transformed for a variety of different machines by a single compilation system [48].

Parallelizing compilers cannot always perform well without assistance from the user. One of the main reasons for this is the undecidability or intractability of many relevant problems and the lack of adequate heuristics for handling them; furthermore, a static analyzer will have no information at all on variables whose value is input during program execution. The user may play an important role, informing the system via *assertions* of global relationships (some of which may be due to high-level properties of the algorithm) which an automatic state-of-the-art tool cannot detect.

4.2 The Knowledge Base

The knowledge-based approach to program parallelization aims to see the parallelization process as a whole. As a consequence, a *uniform representation* for different components of knowledge is required, whose sources may include user input as well as the results of automatic analysis.

The system may contain knowledge about

- **Languages**
  Features of the *source*, *target*, and *machine* languages, including knowledge about their semantics and performance characteristics.
- **Target Machine Configuration**
- **Application Domains**
  This can simplify the reasoning process by taking into account heuristics about successful transformation strategies in that domain.
- **Restructurer and Target Machine Compiler**
  Knowledge about transformations, transformation sequences, their applicability and effect on the performance of the program.
- **Transformation Strategy**
  This knowledge must be in general expressed as a function, depending on parameters such as target machine configuration, problem size, performance parameters, and the application domain. Incorporating such knowledge may drastically decrease the search space of the solution.
- **Source Programs**
- **State of the Parallelization Process**

Knowledge components can be classified as **static** if they specify inherent features of the underlying system which do not change during the parallelization of a program; and as **dynamic** otherwise.

Sources of knowledge may be the results yielded by automatic analysis tools, or human experience, encoded by a knowledge engineer. The creation of the knowledge base comprises obtaining, grouping and structuring of the relevant information; this process is known as **knowledge acquisition**. Such preprocessed knowledge is then represented by **facts** and **rules** of an expert system.

4.3 The Expert Adviser

The knowledge-based component of an advanced parallelization tool is designed as a separate system, the **Expert Adviser (XPA)**, with precisely specified connections to other components such as the transformation or analysis modules (see Figure 4). The components of XPA include **knowledge base management**, **the inference engine**, and support for the **interfaces** to the end user and the knowledge engineer.

We expect that the development of XPA will be guided by an *evolutionary approach*, beginning with a strongly interactive paradigm and proceeding to largely automatic system operation. In the interactive mode, XPA generates **queries** and **recommendations** for program improvement, which are addressed to the user. This mode is important for the development and refinement of the knowledge base in situations where several or the most of the relevant aspects of parallelization are not yet known, or are only vaguely specified. This permits easier experimentation with the system and the acquisition of the relevant knowledge. As soon as the experimentation leads to stable procedures for solving particular situations, these procedures are incorporated into the knowledge base in the form of rules, and the superfluous interface to the user is replaced by the corresponding interface routines, which realize the necessary information and control flow to the other part of the parallelization system without user assistance.

The **inference engine** performs reasoning over the information stored in the knowledge base. Its strength and flexibility determines the efficiency, quality and the outcome of the search process. We consider the following features of the inference engine as important in the context of our discussion:

- **forward, backward chaining and backtracking**
- **approximate reasoning**
  The knowledge about the transformation process is often inexact in its nature. Major sources of such uncertainty are the inaccuracies of performance analysis and prediction.
- **Planning**
  In addition to the standard inference strategies, generative planning methods are required to formulate user advice and automate the development of transformation strategies.
- **Procedural Knowledge**
  The rule based paradigm is sometimes too awkward to solve problems for which a procedural solution is already known or is more natural. For such cases, an interface between the rule language and a procedural implementation language (such as C or C++) is required.

5 Related Work

SUPERB is an interactive restructuring tool which was developed at the University of Bonn by H.P.Zima and co-workers ([49]). It translates Fortran 77 programs into message-passing Fortran in accordance with the general strategy described in Section 2.2. It was completed in 1989 and thus was the first system which compiled code for DMMPs from Fortran 77 code and a description of the distribution of data. SUPERB provides special support for handling work arrays, as are commonly used in Fortran codes, for example to store several grids in one array. This strategy is described in [52], based on Gerndt's Ph.D.Thesis [18]. The description of SUPERB in [49] is the first journal publication in the area of compiling Fortran for DMMPs. Callahan and Kennedy propose a similar compilation approach in [8].

A commercially available system is the **MIMDizer** ([37]) which may be used to parallelize sequential Fortran programs according to the SPMD model. The MIMDizer takes a similar approach to SUPERB; it deals with a number of specific Fortran issues, including a very flexible handling of common blocks.

The programming language **Fortran D** [16] proposes a Fortran language extension in which the programmer specifies the distribution of data by aligning each array to a *decomposition*, and then specifying a distribution of the decomposition to a virtual machine. These are executable statements, and array distributions are dynamic only. A subset of Fortran D – roughly corresponding to SUPERB – has been implemented for the iPSC/860 [24].

The concept of defining processor arrays and distributing data to them was first introduced in the programming language **BLAZE** [30] in the context of shared memory systems with non-uniform access times. This research was continued in the **Kali** programming language [35, 29] for distributed memory machines, which requires that the user specify data distributions in much the same way that Vienna Fortran does.

The **Parti** routines and the **ARF compiler** ([43, 44]), developed by Saltz and coworkers at ICASE, represent techniques to handle the kind of codes written for sparse and unstructured problems, as described in Section 2.3. They are designed to handle the general case of arbitrary data mappings, and efficient techniques were developed for a number of subproblems.

The source language for the **Crystal** compiler built by Li and Chen at Yale University ([32]) is the functional language Crystal, which includes constructs for specifying data parallelism. Thus there is a certain amount of parallelism explicit in the original code. Experimental compilers have been constructed for the iPSC hypercube and the nCUBE; they place particular emphasis on an analysis of the communication requirements to generate efficient communication.

Cray Research Inc. is implementing **MPP Fortran** [39], a set of language extensions to Cray Fortran which enable the user to specify the distribution of data and work. They provide intrinsics for data distribution and permit redistribution at subroutine boundaries. Further, they permit the user to structure the executing processors by giving them a shape and weighting the dimensions. Several methods for distributing iterations of loops are provided. In the Cray programming model, many of the features of shared memory parallel languages have been retained: these include critical sections, events and locks. New instructions for node I/O are provided.

Other systems include **Pandore**, a C-based system [2], **Id Nouveau**, a compiler for a functional language [41], **Oxygen** [42], **ASPAR** [27], **Adapt**, developed at the University of Southampton [36], and the **Yale Extensions** [11]. In a few systems, dynamic data distributions have been implemented within narrow constraints [3, 2].

The systems described above are not the only efforts to provide either suitable language constructs for mapping code onto DMMPs or to generate message passing programs from higher–level code. Other important approaches include **Linda** [1], **Strand** [15], and **Booster** [38].

Knowledge-based techniques have been applied in a few systems which restructure code for different machines. The expert adviser **EAVE** was developed to assist in the transformation of program for input to the IBM 3090 VF; it identifies patterns within the code and contains rules specifying how code can be transformed to obtain an equivalent form that can be efficiently vectorized [4].

Wang and Gannon [47, 48] developed concepts for the hierarchical parallelization of programs to run on different multi-processors architectures. The project concentrates on formal representation and specification of knowledge about the transformation process. An advanced knowledge acquisition tool has been built in Prolog for collecting the knowledge about various target machines architectures.

PAT is a knowledge-based system being developed at the University of Illinois [22] that matches syntactic patterns (with semantic predicates) to derive a program's underlying meaning.

The rule based transformation system **ParTool** [5] for semiautomatic SPMD code generation is being developed at the Delft University of Technology.

The strategy described in Section 4 is currently being implemented at the University of Vienna in the framework of the Vienna Fortran Compilation System [46].

6 Conclusion

In this paper, we discussed the automatic parallelization of Fortran programs for DMMPs. After introducing the state of the art, as represented by currently implemented systems, we identified a number of limitations of this technology. In addition to insufficient functionality for handling many real applications, a major deficiency of current systems is the lack of intelligence in selecting good transformation strategies, leading to a situation in which the user frequently has to take the responsibility for strategic decisions. We argue that a knowledge-based approach to compiling, combined with more advanced analysis and transformation techniques, will contribute to more powerful and intelligent automatic parallelization systems in the future.

References

[1] S. Ahuja, N. Carriero, and D. Gelernter. Linda and friends. *IEEE Computer*, 19:26–34, August 1986.

[2] F. André, J.-L. Pazat, and H. Thomas. PANDORE: A system to manage data distribution. In *International Conference on Supercomputing*, pages 380–388, June 1990.

[3] Marc Baber. Hypertasking support for dynamically redistributable and resizeable arrays on the iPSC. In *Proceedings of the Fifth Distributed Memory Computing Conference*, 59-66, 1990.

[4] P. Bose Interactive Program Improvement via EAVE: an Expert Adviser for Vectorization. In: Proc.Int.Conf.on Supercomputing,St. Malo,pp.119-130(July 1988).

[5] L.C.Breebaart,E.M.Paalvast,H.J.Sips. A Rule Based Transformation System for Parallel Languages. In: Proc.Third Workshop on Compilers for Parallel Computers,Vienna,Austria. Technical Report ACPC/TR 93-8, Austrian Center of Parallel Computation,pp. 13-21 (July 1992).

[6] P. Brezany, H.M. Gerndt, V. Sipkova and H. Zima. SUPERB support for irregular scientific computations. In *Proceedings of the Scalable High Performance Computing Conference*, 1992.

[7] P.Brezany, V.Sipkova, R.Das, J.Saltz. Compilation of Vienna Fortran Forall Loops. Paper submitted to the Conference SUPERCOMPUTING'93, Portland, Oregon, November 1993.

[8] D.Callahan and K.Kennedy. Compiling programs for distributed-memory multiprocessors. Journal of Supercomputing, 2(2), 151-69 (October 1988).

[9] B.M.Chapman,T.Fahringer, and H.P.Zima. *Automatic Support for Data Distribution on Distributed Memory Multiprocessor Systems.* In: Proc.Sixth Annual Workshop on Compilers for Parallelism, Portland,OR (August 1993) (to appear).

[10] B.M. Chapman, P. Mehrotra, and H.P. Zima. Programming in Vienna Fortran. *Scientific Programming* 1,1

[11] M. Chen and J. Li. Optimizing Fortran 90 programs for data motion on massively parallel systems. Technical Report YALE/DCS/TR-882, Yale University, January 1992.

[12] R. Das, J. Saltz. A manual for Parti runtime primitives - revision 2. *Internal Research Report*, University of Maryland, 1992.

[13] T.Fahringer,R.Blasko, and H.P.Zima. *Automatic Performance Prediction to Support Parallelization of Fortran Programs for Massively Parallel Systems.* Proc.6th ACM Int.Conf.on Supercomputing,Washington D.C.,July 1992.

[14] T.Fahringer and H.P.Zima. *A Static Parameter Based Performance Prediction Tool for Parallel Programs.* Proc.7th ACM Int.Conf.on Supercomputing,Tokyo,July 1993.

[15] I. Foster and S. Taylor. *Strand: New Concepts in Parallel Programming.* Prentice-Hall, Englewood Cliffs, NJ, 1990.

[16] G. Fox, S. Hiranandani, K. Kennedy, C. Koelbel, U. Kremer, C. Tseng, and M. Wu. Fortran D language specification. Department of Computer Science Rice COMP TR90079, Rice University, March 1991.

[17] I.T.Foster and M.Chandy. Fortran M: A Language for Modular Parallel Programming. Technical Report, Department of Computer Science, California Institute of Technology (June 1992).

[18] H. M. Gerndt. *Automatic Parallelization for Distributed-Memory Multiprocessing Systems.* Ph.D. thesis, University of Bonn, December 1989.

[19] H.M. Gerndt. Work Distribution in Parallel Programs for Distributed Memory Multiprocessors. In *Proceedings of the International Conference on Supercomputing*, 1991.

[20] A.Gupta and B.E.Prasad.(Eds.). Principles of Expert Systems, IEEE Press, 1988.

[21] M. Gupta, and P. Banerjee. Automatic Data Partitioning on Distributed Memory Multiprocessors. In *Proceedings of the Sixth Distributed Memory Computing Conference*, 1991.

[22] M.T.Harandi and J.Q.Ning. Knowledge-Based Program Analysis. IEEE Software, January 1990, pp. 74-81.

[23] P.J.Hatcher and M.J.Quinn. *Data-Parallel Programming on MIMD Computers.* MIT Press Scientific and Engineering Computation Series, 1991.

[24] S.Hiranandani, K.Kennedy and C.-W.Tseng. Compiling Fortran D for MIMD Distributed–Memory Machines. Comm.ACM Vol.35,No.8, pages 66–80, August 1992.

[25] High Performance Fortran Forum. *High Performance Fortran Language Specification. Version 1.0*, May 3, 1993.

[26] David E. Hudak and Santosh G. Abraham. Compiler Techniques for Data Partitioning of Sequentially Iterated Parallel Loops. In *Proceedings of the ACM International Conference on Supercomputing*, 187-200 (1990)

[27] K. Ikudome, G. Fox, A. Kolawa, and J. Flower. An automatic and symbolic parallelization system for distributed memory parallel computers. In *Proceedings of the The Fifth Distributed Memory Computing Conference*, pages 1105–1114, Charleston, SC, April 1990.

[28] Kathleen Knobe, Joan D. Lukas, and Guy L. Steele. Data Optimization: Allocation of Arrays to Reduce Communication on SIMD Machines. Journal of Parallel and Distributed Computing 8, 102-118 (1990)

[29] C. Koelbel. *Compiling programs for nonshared memory machines.* Ph.D. Thesis, Purdue University, August 1990.

[30] C. Koelbel, P. Mehrotra, and J.Van Rosendale. Semi-automatic Process Partitioning for Parallel Computation. *International Journal of Parallel Programming*, 16(5),pp.365-382, 1987.

[31] J.Liebowitz,D.A.De Salvo (Eds.). Structuring Expert Systems, Prentice-Hall Inc. (1989).

[32] J.Li. *Compiling Crystal for Distributed–Memory Machines.* Ph.D. Thesis, Yale University, Technical Report DCS/RR-876, October 1991.

[33] J. Li and M. Chen. Index Domain Alignment: Minimizing Cost of Cross reference between Distributed Arrays. In: *Frontiers'90: The Third Symposium on the Frontiers of Massively Parallel Computation*, October 1990.

[34] J. Li and M. Chen. Compiling Communication-Efficient Programs for Massively Parallel Machines. *IEEE Transactions on Parallel and Distributed Systems* Vol.2(3), 361-376, July 1991.

[35] P. Mehrotra and J. Van Rosendale. Programming distributed memory architectures using Kali. In A. Nicolau, D. Gelernter, T. Gross, and D. Padua, editors, *Advances in Languages and Compilers for Parallel Processing*, pages 364–384. Pitman/MIT-Press, 1991.

[36] J. H.Merlin. ADAPTing Fortran 90 Array Programs for Distributed Memory Architectures. In H.P.Zima, editor,*Parallel Computation. Proc.First International ACPC Conference, Salzburg, Austria*, pages 184–200. Lecture Notes in Computer Science 591, Springer Verlag, 1991

[37] *MIMDizer User's Guide, Version 8.0.* Applied Parallel Research Inc., Placerville, CA., 1992.

[38] E. Paalvast and H. Sips. A high-level language for the description of parallel algorithms. In *Proceedings of Parallel Computing 89*, Leyden, Netherlands, August 1989.

[39] D. Pase. MPP Fortran programming model. In *High Performance Fortran Forum,* Houston, TX, January 1992.

[40] J.Ramanujam, and P.Sadayappan. Compile-Time Techniques for Data Distribution in Distributed Memory Machines. TR-90-09-03, Dept. Electrical and Comp. Engineering, Louisiana State University (Sept. 1990).

[41] A. Rogers and K. Pingali. Process decomposition through locality of reference. In *Conference on Programming Language Design and Implementation*, pages 69–80. ACM SIGPLAN, June 1989.

[42] R. Rühl and M. Annaratone. Parallelization of Fortran code on distributed-memory parallel processors. In *Proceedings of the ACM International Conference on Supercomputing*, June 1990.

[43] J. Saltz, H. Berryman, and J. Wu. Multiprocessors and Run-Time Compilation: Concurrency, Practice and Experience, Vol.3(6), 573-592 (December 1991).

[44] J. Saltz, K. Crowley, R. Mirchandaney, and H. Berryman. Run-time scheduling and execution of loops on message passing machines. *Journal of Parallel and Distributed Computing*, 8(2):303–312, 1990.

[45] J.Subhlok,J.M.Stichnoth,D.R.O'Hallaron, and T.Gross. Exploiting Task and Data Parallelism on a Multicomputer. Proc.Forth ACM SIGPLAN Symposium on Principles and Practice of Parallel Programming (PPoPP'93),pp.13-22.

[46] Vienna Fortran Compilation System Version 1.0 User's Guide. Department of Statistics and Computer Science, University of Vienna, Austria (January 1993).

[47] K.Y.Wang,D.Gannon. Applying AI Techniques to Program Optimization for Parallel Computers. In: *K.Hwang,D.DeGroot(Eds.): Parallel Processing for Supercomputers and Artificial Intelligence.* McGraw-Hill Pub. Company, Chap.12., pp.441-485 (1989).

[48] K.Y.Wang. Intelligent Program Optimization and Parallelization for Parallel Computers. Tech. Rept. No. CSD-TR-91-030, Department of Computer Science, Purdue University (April 1991).

[49] H.P. Zima, H. Bast, and H.M. Gerndt. Superb: A tool for semi-automatic MIMD/SIMD parallelization. *Parallel Computing*, 6:1–18, (January 1988).

[50] H.P. Zima, P. Brezany, B.M. Chapman, P. Mehrotra, and A. Schwald. Vienna Fortran – a language specification. ICASE Internal Report 21, ICASE, Hampton, VA, 1992.

[51] H.P. Zima and B.M. Chapman. *Supercompilers for Parallel and Vector Computers.* ACM Press Frontier Series, Addison-Wesley, 1990.

[52] H.P. Zima and B.M.Chapman. Compiling for Distributed-Memory Systems. Invited Paper, Proceedings of the IEEE, Special Section on Languages and Compilers for Parallel Machines. To appear (February 1993). Also: Technical Report ACPC/TR 92-16, Austrian Center for Parallel Computation (November 1992).

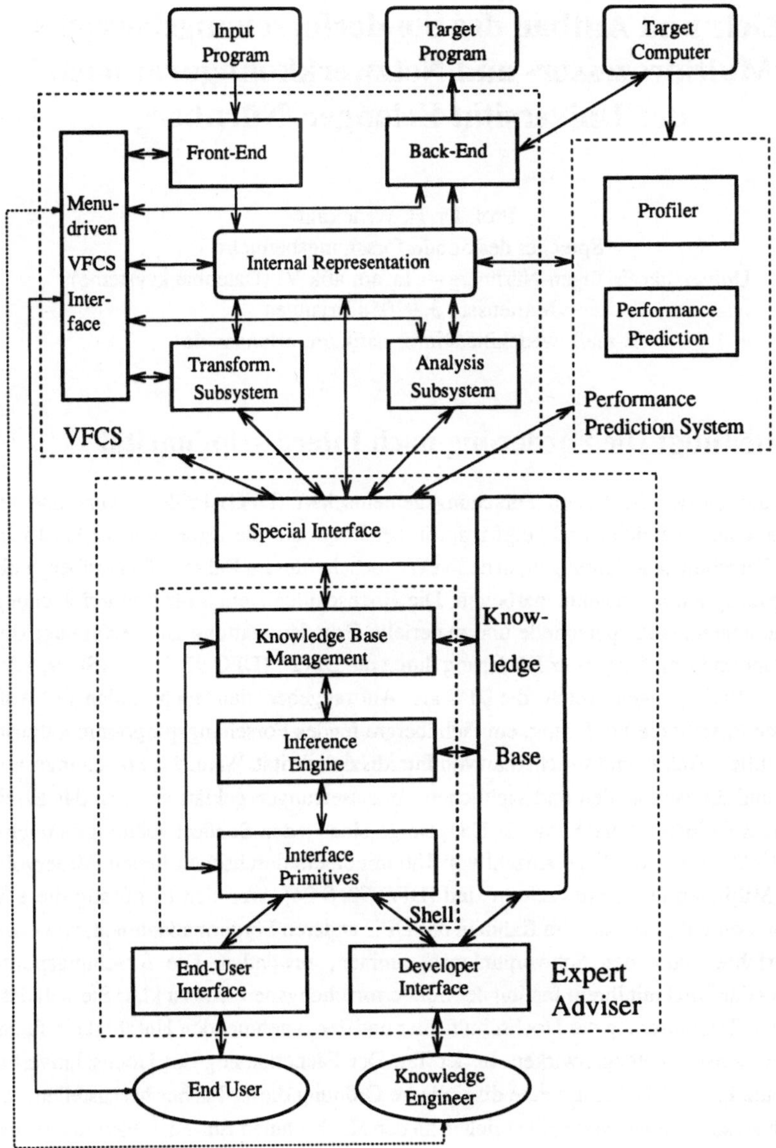

Figure 4: Knowledge-Based Parallelization Environment

Ziele und Aufbau des Sonderforschungsbereichs "Multiprozessor- und Netzwerkkonfigurationen" der Universität Erlangen-Nürnberg

Prof. Dr. H. Wedekind
Sprecher des Sonderforschungsbereichs
Universität Erlangen-Nürnberg — Informatik VI (Datenbanksysteme)
Martensstr. 3, 91058 Erlangen
E-mail: wedekind@informatik.uni-erlangen.de

1 Einleitung: Die Forderung nach Interdisziplinarität

In Publikationen der Deutschen Forschungsgemeinschaft (DFG) heißt es kurz und knapp: "Sonderforschungsbereiche sind langfristig, in der Regel auf die Dauer von 12 bis 15 Jahren angelegte Forschungseinrichtungen, in denen Wissenschaftler im Rahmen fächerübergreifender Forschungsprogramme zusammenarbeiten. Die Hochschulen stellen für Sonderforschungsbereiche eine angemessene personelle und materielle Grundausstattung zur Verfügung; sie sind Antragsteller und Empfänger der Förderung durch die DFG". [DFG 92, S.22], [St 89, S.V]. Im Zentrum der Bedingungen, welche die DFG als "Auftraggeber" den Hochschulen als "Auftragnehmer" stellt, steht die Forderung, ein fachübergreifendes Forschungsprogramm aufzustellen und auszufüllen. Abkürzend spricht man von Interdisziplinarität. Wenn das Forschungsziel festgelegt ist und die personellen und sächlichen Voraussetzungen geklärt sind, ist das Erreichen einer interdisziplinären Forschung die Hauptsorge eines jeden Sonderforschungsbereichs, die im Jahre 1992 auf die stattliche Anzahl von 180 mit einem durchschnittlichen Fördervolumen von zwei Millionen DM angewachsen sind [DFG 92, S.24]. Wer sich langfristig diese Sorge nicht aufbürden will, mag sich im Rahmen der DFG anderen Fördermaßnahmen, wie etwa den Normalverfahren oder den Schwerpunktprogrammen, zuwenden. Die forschungspolitische Zielsetzung der DFG mit ihrem Institut der Sonderforschungsbereiche ist klar: Sie will der fortschreitenden Zersplitterung der Hochschulfächer und der zunehmenden Unfähigkeit, fachübergreifend zu denken, entgegenwirken. In der Tat: Der Fächerkatalog des Hochschulverbandes umfaßt heute über 4000 Fächer; eine disziplinäre Ordnung dieser Fächer herzustellen, scheint unmöglich zu sein. Organisatorisch sprießen an den Hochschulen Ein-Fach Fakultäten aus dem Boden. "Ein-Fach-Fakultäten (mit und ohne Bindestrich) sind die McDonald's der neuen Hochschulstruktur, Fächer wie Hymnologie, Brasilianische Sprachwissenschaften, Szientometrie, Gerontopsychologie oder Didaktik der Astronomie sind ihre Unübersichtlichkeitsmacher" meint Mittelstraß ironisch [Mi 89, S.70]. Um die Atomisierung der Fächer zu beklagen, ist es nicht erforderlich, auf die Weite des universitären Fächerkanons einzugehen. In der Informatik sollten wir uns an die eigene Brust klopfen, wenn wir vornehmlich zu den Anwendungen hin diverse Bindestrichinformatiken, von der Bau-Informatik bis zur Wirtschafts-Informatik, alphabetisch geordnet betrachten und nur Fächerzusammenstellungen, bloße Aggregationen sehen, die sich z.B. um ein Fortran- oder Cobolprogrammieren aufgetan haben. Informatik scheint beliebig paarbar zu sein, und Archäologie sowie Zoologie gehören schon zum Nebenfächerkanon in einigen Informatik-Fakultäten. Multidisziplinarität ist aber keine Interdisziplinarität. Diese ist schwer, jene leicht zu haben. Interdisziplinarität ist mit einer Mannschaftssportart, etwa Fußball zu vergleichen. Multidisziplinarität ist in diesem Bilde dem Olympischen Mehrkampf in der Leichtathletik verwandt. Über den mühsamen Weg des Erlanger Sonderforschungsbereichs, der nunmehr fast schon sieben Jahre begangen wird, ist zu berichten.

2 Der Erlanger Versuch einer interdisziplinären Forschung

Ich möchte in diesem Abschnitt nicht in die Details der Forschungsprogramme der 14 Teilprojekte gehen, die im Anhang aufgezählt werden. Ziel dieses Abschnitts ist es, die großen Schwierigkeiten aufzuzeigen, denen wir Anfang 1987 nach der Bewilligung durch die DFG gegenüberstanden. Der SFB wurde in einer vertikalen Struktur mit der Absicht konzipiert, die Erfahrungen der Erlanger Informatiker mit Multiprozessoren und Verteilten Systemen zu bündeln, um die rasante Hardwareentwicklung über eine systematische Softwarekonstruktur in exemplarisch ausgesuchten Anwendungen schnellstmöglich nutzbar zu machen. "Die rasche und erfolgreiche Nutzung des Leistungspotentials von Parallelrechnern hängt nicht zuletzt davon ab, wie gründlich die Anwendungsprogrammierer aus den unterschiedlichen Bereichen an die neue Technologie herangeführt werden" vermerkt Prof. Reuter (Stuttgart) zutreffend [Re93]. Wegen seiner Anwendungsorientierung, die im Hardwarebereich beginnt, ist der SFB vertikal und deshalb im Verhältnis zu anderen Sonderforschungsbereichen, die in die Breite gehen, außerordentlich heterogen. Neben den klassischen Informatik-Fächern sind die Physik, Fertigungstechnik, Strömungsmechanik, Industriebetriebslehre und die Theoretische Chemie vertreten. Wir stellten sehr bald fest, daß unser Ansinnen, in unserem SFB die Differenzierung der Fachwissenschaften wieder rückgängig zu machen, voller Romantik war. Die Fächer haben sich eben gegeneinander verhärtet und verkrustet, und in der Tat "als Kruste diente uns das Gehäuse der Terminologie und Nomenklaturen", die wie Prof. Weinrich vom Bielefelder ZiF (Zentrum für interdisziplinäre Forschung) einmal feststellte, "mit großer Befriedigung rezipiert und reproduziert werden, weil sie so schön leicht lehrbar und lernbar sind". Man braucht nur so schillernde Begriffe wie "Datei", "Prozeß", "Objekt", "Abstraktion", "Verteiltes System" usw. in eine Diskussion zu bringen und schon gibt es bei n Fachvertretern n Begriffsfestlegungen. Dateien der Betriebssysteme sind nunmal etwas ganz anderes als Dateien der Anwendung. Man mag dieses Faktum beklagen, die terminologische Kruste verändert sich dadurch nicht. Uns wurde klar, daß eine gemeinsame terminologische Basis vonnöten ist, um unser genehmigtes, fachübergreifend fomuliertes Forschungsprogramm zum Erfolg zu führen. Interdisziplinäre Forschung setzt infradisziplinäre Grundlagen in Form eines gemeinsamen terminologischen Wissens voraus [Lo74]. Es entstand der Gedanke, gemeinsam ein Lexikon über Verteilte Systeme herauszubringen, um so eine Art "Gesetzbuch" zu schaffen, mit dem eine gewisse Verbindlichkeit hergestellt werden sollte. Über 200 Termini wurden aufgelistet und in die Kategorien Kurz-, Mittel- und Langbeiträge gegliedert. Organisatorische Vorbereitungen wurden getroffen. Der Versuch scheiterte kläglich. Die Gründe sind vielfältig und sollen hier nicht en detail erläutert werden. Wissenschaftler wollen Ergebnisse erarbeiten und publizieren und nicht Stichworte eines Fachlexikons bearbeiten. Über Umwege wurde der Mißerfolg doch noch zu einem Teilerfolg, bescheiden gesprochen. Entscheidend war die Idee, aus der laufenden Forschungsarbeit heraus gemeinsam ein Buch, ein ca. 550 Seiten umfassendes Kompendium mit dem Titel "Verteilte

Systeme - Grundlagen und zukünftige Entwicklungen aus der Sicht des Sonderforschungsbereichs 182 (Multiprozessor- und Netzwerkkonfigurationen)" zu verfassen [We93]. Es handelt sich nicht wie bei Tagungsbänden um eine Ansammlung isolierter Arbeiten, sondern um "verkettete" Beiträge, die durch gegenseitige Bezüge charakterisiert sind. Das Buch, an dem 46 Autoren beteiligt waren, besteht aus sieben Kapiteln:

1. Umgrenzung des Begriffs "Verteiltes System",
2. Grundprobleme und Basismechanismen,
3. Verteilte Hardware- und Software-Architekturen,
4. Grundlagen und Anwendungen objektorienter Konzepte,
5. Anwendungen,
6. Bewertung verteilter Echtzeitsysteme,
7. Spezifikation und Verifikation.

Es kommt mir nicht darauf an, das umfangreiche Stichwortverzeichnis hervorzuheben, das in jedem guten Buch zu finden ist. Eine Besonderheit ist das Glossar mit ca. 400 Einträgen am Ende, ein "Lexikon-Ersatz", das als Nebenprodukt anfiel. Es hat viele Verständigungsschwierigkeiten bei seiner Erstellung gegeben, die aber in kollegialer Zusammenarbeit überwunden werden konnten. Die Frühjahrs- und Herbsttagungen auf Schloß Pommersfelden waren häufig der Rahmen, um in Rede und Gegenrede zum Konsens zu gelangen. Auch die gemeinsamen Tagungen mit den verwandten Sonderforschungsbereichen in Kaiserslautern/Saarbrücken (SFB 124) und München (SFB 342) haben zur Klärung wichtiger interdisziplinärer Fragen erheblich beigetragen [HWZ90], [BD93].

Im Laufe der noch am Anfang isoliert ablaufenden Arbeiten wurde deutlich, daß zur Überwindung der Verkrustung nicht nur ein infradisziplinäres Wissen in Form einer gemeinsamen Terminoligie "unterstellt" werden mußte. Ohne eine "Überstellung", ein supradisziplinäres Ziel ist eine produktive Interdisziplinarität nicht zu erreichen. Gemeint ist die Projektforschung, in der viele Disziplinen in einem definierten Zeitrahmen spezifizierte Projektaufgaben zu erledigen haben. Mit dem Begriff "Projekt" werden nach DIN zeitlich befristete außergewöhnliche Vorhaben gekennzeichnet, die relativ komplex und neuartig, oft auch einmalig sind und funktionsübergreifendes Wissen erfordern [DIN87]. Hochschulprojekte im Rahmen eines SFB sind etwas anderes als Industrieprojekte. Wenn eine Produktforschung - wie in unserem Fall im Projekt MEMSY - zur Debatte steht, können im Hochschulbereich nur Prototypen angestrebt werden. Man muß zeigen können, "daß es geht". Prototypen enthalten in der Regel viele Programmierfehler, diverse Spezifikationsunebenheiten und sind schlecht dokumentiert. Im Gegensatz zu professionell durchführbaren Industrieprojekten sind Projekte in SFB'en auch unter dem Aspekt der Ausbildung zu sehen. "Sonderforschungsbereiche ermöglichen die Bearbeitung anspruchsvoller, aufwendiger und langfristig konzipierter Forschungsvorhaben. Die Förderung des wissenschaftlichen Nachwuchses gehört zu ihren besonderen Aufgaben" [DFG92, S.22]. Studenten, Diplomierte, Promovierte und Professoren sind Mitarbeiter in Hochschulprojekten, die wegen der Ausbildungsverpflichung auch persönliche Fragestellungen zu klären haben. Demgegenüber meint Plessner zur industriellen Forschung: "Der moderne Forscher arbeitet zwar unter Einsatz aller Kräfte, aber unter Ausschaltung seiner Persönlichkeit und ist im Sinne dieser Ausschaltung in der Zucht einer unpersönlichen Fragestellung im einzelnen Falle vielleicht als genialer Kopf unschätzbar, als Indiviudalität jedoch prinzipiell ersetzbar. Die Logik der Problementwicklung hält seine Wissenschaft in Gang wie der Produktionsplan in einem Betrieb" [Pl66, S.132].

3. Die Projekte des Sonderforschungsbereichs

Der SFB besteht aus 14 Teilprojekten und zwei interdisziplinären Projekten, die Querschnittsprojekte MEMSY (Modulares Erweiterbares MultiprozessorSystem) und HEDAS (HEterogene Durchgängige AnwendungsSysteme). Ein drittes Querschnittsprojekt MULTIMEDIA - Speicherung, Übertragung und Präsentation großer Datenobjekte in Rechnernetzen - ist im Aufbau. Teil- und Querschnittsprojekte mit ihren Verknüpfungen lassen sich am besten in einer Matrixform darstellen:

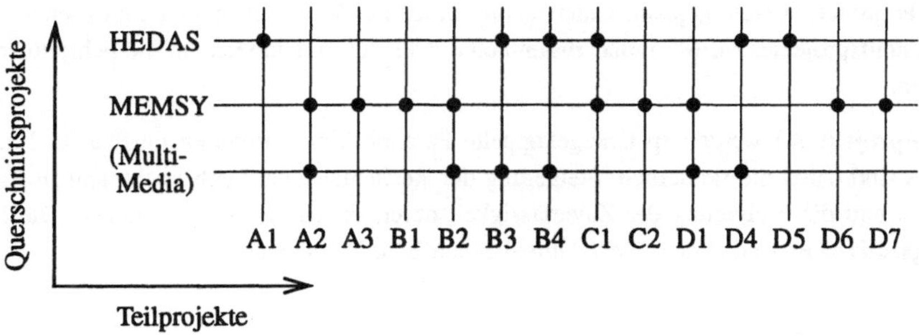

Das MEMSY-Projekt umfaßt ein breites Spektrum von Gesichtspunkten der Multiprozessortechnik. Einige seien aufgezählt: Zerlegung von Anwenderaufgaben in parallel ausführbare Teile, Programmierung praktischer Lösungen der Kommunikations- und Synchronisationsabwicklung, Betriebssysteme für verschiedene Topologien, Messung und Analyse des Ablaufgeschehens, Zusammenhang von Aufgaben bzw. Algorithmenstruktur und erforderlicher Multiprozessorstruktur, Fehlertoleranzaspekte etc. Der Schwerpunkt der Arbeiten im Querschnittsprojekt HEDAS liegt auf der softwaretechnischen Verbindung netzgekoppelter verteilter Rechensysteme. Es werden Methoden und Forschungsergebnisse über lose gekoppelte Systeme vorgestellt, um komplexe Anwendungen zu realisieren. Der Bereich des "Computer Integrated Manufacturing" (CIM) dient als exemplarisches Anwendungsgebiet. Das Projekt konzentriert sich auf gemischt technisch/planerische Aufgabenstellungen und ihre praktischen Verknüpfungen mit den Problemen verschiedener Rechensysteme auf den einzelnen CIM-Ebenen. Beide Querschnittsprojekte werden in gesonderten Beiträgen genauer dargestellt, so daß wir uns unmittelbar den Teilprojekten mit den vier Projektbereichen A, B, C und D zuwenden können.

Projektbereich A:

Im Projektbereich A werden Hardewarekomponenten und Verbindungsstrukturen für eng gekoppelte Multiprozessoren und lose gekoppelte Rechnersysteme untersucht. Die Aktivitäten beinhalten grundlegende Untersuchungen (z.B. geeignete Topologien der Verbindungsstrukturen und Kommunikationsstrategien), Konzeption der verschiedenen Systemteile unter Verwendung sowohl von käuflichen Hardwarekomponenten als auch von eigens entwickelten Teilen sowie Aufbau und Erprobung von Prototypen.

Das **Teilprojekt A1** widmet sich innerhalb des Querschnittsthemas Q2 ("HEDAS") dem Anwendungsschwerpunkt CIM. Akzentuiert werden die Kommunikationsaspekte. Für die "Durchgängigkeit" wird dabei gefordert, daß sie von der Anwenderschnittstelle bis in unmittelbare Nähe zum technischen Prozeß zu gelten habe. In diesem Zusammenhang sind die A1-Themen zu sehen, die die Untersuchung von Kommunikationskonzepten für Feldbusse und die Schaffung leistungsfähiger ISO-OSI-"Kommunikationswerke" zum Gegenstand haben.

Ziel des **Teilprojektes A2** ist es, Prototypen optischer Kommunikationsnetze für Parallelrechner aufzubauen. Neben der hierzu notwendigen Fortschreibung der Aktivitäten bei mikrooptischen Bauelementen ist der Aufbau eines optischen Kommunikationsbusses und einer optischen Permutationsstufe geplant. Untersuchungen an diesen Systemen sollen im Rahmen der Querschnittsprojektes MEMSY und zusammen mit TP A3 im Hinblick auf die Fehlertoleranz erfolgen.

Im **Teilprojekt A3** werden speichergekoppelte Parallelrechnerstrukturen untersucht. Hauptaspekte sind dabei die skalierbare Steigerung der Rechenleistung durch hochgradigen Parallelismus und die Steigerung der Zuverlässigkeit durch Fehlertoleranzmaßnahmen. Die Forschungsaktivitäten sind in das Querschnittsthema MEMSY eingebettet.

Projektbereich B:

Zentrales Thema innerhalb des Projektbereichs B sind Methoden zum Entwurf von Software-Strukturen für verteilte Systeme. Dabei stehen Fragen der Behandlung von Nebenläufigkeit und Verteilung, der Anpassung von Softwarekomponenten an konkrete Aufgabenstellungen und verteilte Problemlösungsstrategien teilprojektübergreifend im Vordergrund. Nachdem sich das objektorientierte Paradigma zur Programmierung verteilter Systeme weitgehend durchgesetzt hat, dient es auch innerhalb des Projektbereichs als gemeinsame Basis. Darauf aufbauend werden in den einzelnen Teilprojekten Fragen der Spezifikation von Softwarekomponenten und deren Abbildung auf eine gegebene Hardware-Struktur, der Konstruktion eines Ablaufsystems und Kommunikationsdienstes, die Funktions- und Datenverteilung und die Erstellung von Plänen vertieft.

Ziel des **Teilprojekts B1** ist die Entwicklung einer Programmierumgebung für Multiprozessor- und Netzwerkkonfigurationen, deren Methoden und Werkzeuge alle Phasen der Softwareentwicklung unterstützen, ausgehend von der Anforderungsspezifikation, über die Implementierung bis zum Systemtest.

Schwerpunkt des **Teilprojektes B2** ist die Entwicklung von Strukturierungs- und Programmiermethoden für komplexe nebenläufige und verteilte Systeme sowie deren Anwendung beim Entwurf von wiederverwendbaren Betriebssystemkomponenten, die sich an verschiedene Aufgabenklassen adaptieren lassen. Es ist vorgesehen, die hardwareabhängige Schicht des Ablaufsystems als Basis eines Monitorsystems zur Verwaltung des Parallelrechners MEMSY zu verwenden.

Ziele der Forschungsarbeiten des **Teilprojekts B3** sind der Entwurf, die Implementierung und die Bewertung von Kommunikationsdiensten, die für ausgewählte verteilte Systeme eine transparente, effiziente und zuverlässige Kommunikation garantieren. Unabhängig von der Anwendung und der Konfiguration wird dabei eine Methodik verfolgt, die aus drei Phasen besteht: Last-/Maschinenmodellierung, Mapping von Last- auf Maschinenkomponenten und Bewertung des Gesamtsystems unter Berücksichtigung der geforderten Leistungs- und Gütermerkmale. Die Abbildungs- und Bewertungsphase wird dabei häufig mehrmals durchlaufen, insbesondere bei dynamischen Rekonfigurationsvorgängen in Zusammenhang mit Netzmanagementaufgaben im Querschnittsprojekt HEDAS.

Aufgabe des **Teilprojekts B4** ist die Entwicklung von Mechanismen zur Funktions- und Datenverteilung in Rechnernetzen unter besonderer Berücksichtigung der Anforderungen des Anwendungsbereichs der rechnerintegrierten Fertigung (CIM). Aufbauend auf den entwickelten Möglichkeiten der anwendungsorientierten Datenverteilung mit dem DDMS-Ansatz (Distributed Data Management System) bildet im Rahmen von HEDAS die Erforschung und Entwicklung von Mechanismen für den Entwurf und Betrieb verteilter kooperativer Datenbankanwendungen den Schwerpunkt der Arbeiten. Die STEP-Norm (Standard for the Exchange of Product Model Data) ist dabei eine wichtige Grundlage.

Projektbereich C:

Im Projektbereich C werden Forschungsaktivitäten mit einer gegenstandsübergreifenden wie auch anwendungsübergreifenden Zielsetzung zusammengefaßt. Gemeinsames Anliegen im Projektbereich ist es, sowohl die Funktionssicherheit als auch die Leistungsfähigkeit eines verteilt ablaufenden Systems zu gewährleisten bzw. zu bewerten. Dazu werden Methoden in den Gebieten Spezifikation, Verifikation, Modellbildung, Leistungsmessung und -bewertung entwickelt und untersucht.

Im **Teilprojekt C1** werden Methoden entwickelt, um das Ablaufverhalten in Multiprozessor- und verteilten Systemen zu bewerten. Erfolgversprechende Meß- und Modellierungsmethoden werden als praktisch einsetzbare Werkzeuge implementiert. Dabei geht es über eine konstatierende Leistungsbewertung zur Bestimmung der Leistungsfähigkeit (performance evaluation) hinaus: Die Gewinnung von Einsichten steht im Vordergrund, um so eventuelle Fehler oder Engpässe in parallel ablaufenden Programmes zu finden (debugging, tuning). Es werden grundlegende Themen zur Leistungsbewertung wie "Bewertung von Modellierungsmethoden", "Wissensbasiertes Messen und Auswerten" und "Beobachtung hochparalleler Systeme" mit dem Anspruch auf praktische Anwendbarkeit ohne Vernachlässigung der realen Bewertungsprobleme untersucht.

Bei der Entwicklung verteilt ablaufender Systeme ist es wichtig, neben ihrer Leistungsfähigkeit auch die Korrektheit ihres Verhaltens sicherzustellen. Dazu werden im **Teilprojekt C2** Methoden entwickelt, wie man bereits beim Entwurf eines verteilten Systems dessen Korrektheit gewährleisten kann. Ziel des Projekts ist der Entwurf einer Breitbrandsprache für verteilte Systeme. Darunter versteht man eine Sprache, die es gestattet, ein verteiltes System ausgehend von einer abstrakten, globalen Spezifikation über mehrere überschaubare Zwischenschritte bis hin zu einer korrekten, verteilten Implementierung in einem einheitlichen Formalismus zu entwickeln.

Projektbereich D

Damit einerseits die im Rahmen des SFB entstehenden Hardware- und Software-Bausteine an praxisnahen Anwendungen getestet werden können und andererseits die Basisentwicklung die Anforderungen der Nutzer kennenlernt, wurde der Projektbereich D geschaffen. Bei der Organisation dieses Bereiches hat man sehr bewußt darauf geachtet, daß Anwendungsgebiete darin vorkommen, die der Praktischen Informatik ebenso zuzurechnen sind wie den Ingenieurwissenschaften, den Naturwissenschaften und der Betriebswirtschaft. Die Teilprojekte sollen ihrerseits wieder einen gewissen interdisziplinären Charakter besitzen. Beispielsweise wurden sie an Grenzgebieten zwischen betriebswirtschaftlicher Produktionssteuerung und Fertigungsautomation angeordnet.

Untersuchungen, die zu einem praktisch einsetzbaren "Rechnersehen" führen sollten, sind Gegenstand der Arbeiten im **Teilprojekt D1**, das sich mit der wissensbasierten Bildanalyse beschäftigt. Gesamtziel des Teilprojektes ist die Entwicklung und Realisierung eines modularen Systems zur automatischen Generierung einer symbolischen Beschreibung dreidimensionaler Szenen, wie sie z.B. in industriellen Arbeitsumgebungen vorgefunden werden können. Neben der Untersuchung und Realisierung wichtiger Verarbeitungsmodule eines Bildanalysesystems können daher die im Querschnittsprojekt MEMSY und den Teilprojekten zur Erarbeitung von Hard- und Softwarearchitekturen erzielten Ergebnisse unter verschiedenen Gesichtspunkten validiert werden.

Zentraler Forschungsgegenstand des **Teilprojekts D4** innerhalb einer hierarchischen Produktionsstruktur ist die flexible Montagezelle. Sie umfaßt nicht nur die Handhabungsgeräte an sich, sondern auch die Teilebereitstellung, Meß- und Prüfsysteme sowie das interne Transportsystem. D4 ist ein Projekt der Fertigungstechnik und ein zentraler Bestandteil von HEDAS.

Im Zusammenhang mit dem anhaltenden Trend zur Hierarchisierung bzw. Verteilung in der Produktionsplanung und -steuerung befaßt sich das **Teilprojekt D5** mit der Unterstützung der Produktions-Feinplanung durch Verteilte Wissensbasierte Systeme. Die folgenden Schwerpunkt stehen zur Debatte: Verteilte Leitstände, Nutzung von Wissensbasierten Komponenten bei der Feinplanung, Anwendung von marktähnlichen Koordinationsmechanismen sowie Anwendungen von Multi-Agenten-Systemen.

Ziel des **Teilprojekts D6** ist die Entwicklung, Realisierung und Erweiterung von parallelen Algorithmen zur Lösung der strömungsmechanischen Grundgleichungen. Die Berechnung dreidimensionaler Strömungsfelder praktisch interessierender Probleme erfordert Speicher- und Rechenleistungen, welche die Kapazitäten heutiger Großrechner bei weitem übersteigen. Es können heute wissenschaftliche Erkenntnisse gewonnen werden, die ohne Nutzung des Hochleistungsrechnens nicht denkbar wären. Als ein Beispiel sei die direkte numerische Simulation in der Turbulenz genannt. Ein wichtiger Arbeitsschwerpunkt ist die Optimierung der Programme zum Einsatz auf der MEMSY-Architektur.

Das **Teilprojekt D7** "Quantenmechanische Berechnungen an chemischen Systemen" beschäftigt sich mit der Parallelisierung von Programmen aus der Quantenchemie. Ein wesentliches Ziel ist die Bestimmung der elektronischen Eigenschaften von Polymeren unter Ausnutzung ihrer eindimensional-periodischen Struktur. Der Schwerpunkt der Aktivitäten des Teilprojektes liegt in der Nutzung der im Querschnittsprojekt MEMSY entwickelten Hardwarekonfigurationen.

Der Sonderforschungsbereich ist bis Ende 1995 finanziert. Die nächste Begehung durch die Gutachter der DFG findet im Frühjahr 1995 statt. Damit eine Förderung bis Ende 1998 gelingen kann, sind außergewöhnliche Anstrengungen erforderlich, um die erreichten Forschungsergebnisse zu stabilisieren und um neue Forschungsperspektiven zu erschließen.

Anhang

Gliederung des SFB 182 "Multiprozessor- und Netzwerkkonfigurationen"

Projektbereich A — *Architektur der speichernden, verarbeitenden und transportierenden Hardwarekomponenten*

- A1 Kommunikationsmittel für Multiprozessor- und Netzwerkkonfigurationen (D. Seitzer)
- A2 Optoelektronische Feldverbindungen für Multiprozessorsysteme (J.Schwider, N. Streibl)
- A3 Architektur von speichergekoppelten Multiprozessoren mit Fehlertoleranz-Eigenschaften (M. Dal Cin)

Projektbereich B — *Architektur der speichernden, verarbeitenden und transportierenden Softwarekomponenten*

- B1 Programmierumgebung (für Multiprozessor- und Netzwerkkonfigurationen) (H.J. Schneider)
- B2 Entwurf und Implementierung eines an Hardwarearchitektur und Aufgabenklassen adaptierbaren Multiprozessorbetriebssystems (F. Hofmann)
- B3 Entwurf, Implementierung und Bewertung von Kommunikationsdiensten (W. Dulz, U. Herzog)
- B4 Funktions- und Datenverteilung in Rechnernetzen (H. Wedekind)

Projektbereich C — *Theorie und Werkzeuge zur Beschreibung und Bewertung von Multiprozessoren und verteilten Systemen*

- C1 Messung, Modellierung und Bewertung von Multiprozessoren und Rechnernetzen (R. Klar)
- C2 Spezifikation und Verifikation verteilter Systeme (H. Müller)

Projektbereich D *Überprüfung der Konzepte an ausgewählten Pilotanwendungen*

D1 Wissensbasierte Bildanalyse (H. Niemann)

D4 Anwendungen von Multiprozessor- und Netzwerkkonfigurationen im Bereich der Fertigungsautomatisierung (K. Feldmann)

D5 Unterstützung der Produktions-Feinplanung durch Verteilte Wissensbasierte Systeme (P. Mertens)

D6 Parallelisierung von Berechnungsverfahren für Probleme der Strömungsmechanik (F. Durst)

D7 Quantenmechanische Berechnungen an chemischen Systemen (P. Otto)

Literatur

[BD 93] Bode, A., Dal Cin, M.: Parallel Computer Architectures - Theory, Hardware, Software and Applications, Fachtagung der Sonderforschungsbereiche 342 und 182, München 1992, Springer-Verlag LNCS, 1993.

[DFG 92] Deutsche Forschungsgemeinschaft: Perspektiven der Forschung und ihrer Förderung, VCH Verlag, Weinheim, 1992.

[HWZ 90] Härder, T., Wedekind, H., Zimmermann, G.: Entwurf und Betrieb verteilter Systeme, Fachtagung der Sonderforschungsbereiche 124 und 182,Dagstuhl, September 1990, Informatik-Fachberichte 264, Springer-Verlag

[Lo 74] Lorenzen, P.: Interdisziplinäre Forschung und infradisziplinäres Wissen, In: Derselbe: Konstruktive Wissenschaftstheorie, Suhrkamp Taschenbuch Wissenschaft, Frankfurt, 1974, S. 133-146.

[Mi 89] Mittelstraß, J.: Wohin geht die Wissenschaft? Über Disziplinarität, Transdisziplinarität und das Wissen in einer Leibniz-Welt, in: Derselbe: Der Flug der Eule, Suhrkamp Taschenbuch Wissenschaft, Frankfurt, 1989.

[Mi 92] Mittelstraß, J.: Die Stunde der Interdisziplinarität? In: Derselbe: Leonardo-Welt, Suhrkamp Taschenbuch Wissenschaft, Frankfurt, 1992, S. 96-102.

[Pl 66] Plessner, H.: Zur Soziologie der modernen Forschung und ihre Organisation in der deutschen Universität - Tradition und Ideologie, In: Derselbe: Diesseits der Utopie, Ausgewählte Beiträge zur Kultursoziologie, Düsseldorf/Köln, 1966.

[Re 93] Reuter, A.: Vorwort zu: Bräunl: Parallele Programmierung. Eine Einführung, Vieweg Verlag, Braunschweig, 1993.

[St 89] Streiter, A. (Hrsg.): 20 Jahre Sonderforschungsbereiche, VCH Verlag, Weinheim, 1989. Wissenschaft, Frankfurt, 1989, S. 60-88.

[We 93] Wedekind, H. (Hrsg): Verteilte Systeme - Grundlagen und zukünftige Entwicklungen aus der Sicht des Sonderforschungsbereichs 182 “Multiprozessor- und Netzwerkkonfigurationen”, Bibliographisches Institut, Mannheim, 1993.

Das Querschnittsprojekt "MEMSY"
Ein Modulares Erweiterbares Multiprozessor SYstem

Prof. Dr. F. Hofmann
Universität Erlangen-Nürnberg — Informatik IV (Betriebssysteme)
Martensstr. 1, 91058 Erlangen
E-mail: fhofmann@informatik.uni-erlangen.de

Überblick

Die Erfahrung der Erlanger Informatiker mit Multiprozessoren und Verteilten Systemen umfaßt ein breites Spektrum von Gesichtspunkten, wie Verarbeitungs- und Speichereinheiten, Verbindungsstrukturen, Zerlegung von Anwenderaufgaben in parallel ausführbare Teile, Programmierung praktischer Lösungen der Kommunikations- und Synchronisationsabwicklung, Betriebssysteme für verschiedene Topologien, Messung und Analyse des Ablaufgeschehens, Zusammenhang von Aufgaben bzw. Algorithmenstruktur und erforderlicher Multiprozessorstruktur und Fehlertoleranzaspekte. In diesen umfassenden Rahmen ist die Architektur einer Familie von modular erweiterbaren und konfigurierbaren Multiprozessorsystemen mit breitem Leistungsspektrum realisiert worden. Es sind grundlegende Untersuchungen der "Parallelität" in der Systemstruktur, der Kommunikation, der Berechnungsalgorithmen der Anwenderaufgaben, sowie der Leistungsmessung und -bewertung durchgeführt worden.

1 Motivation

Der starke Entwicklungstrend zu Parallelrechnern in den letzten Jahren hat seine Ursachen u.a. in

- der erkennbaren Annäherung an die technisch mögliche Grenzleistung konventioneller Computer und Vektorrechner
- dem steigenden Rechenleistungs- und Speicherbedarf auf der Anwenderseite
- dem erreichten technologischen Stand sehr leistungsfähiger und preisgünstiger, hochintegrierter Rechnerkomponenten, welche die wirtschaftliche Realisierung parallelverarbeitender Systeme möglich machen
- der Erkenntnis, daß ein weites Spektrum von Anwendungsproblemen nur unzulänglich vektorisierbar ist
- dem extrem besseren Preis/Leistungsverhältnis heutiger Riscarchitekturen in der Floating-Point-Skalarleistung gegenüber konventionellen Vektorprozessoren

Von den Parallelrechnern sind Systeme der MIMD-Klasse (*multiple instruction - multiple data*) besonders vielseitig einsetzbar, da sie wegen ihrer unabhängigen Befehlswerke gleiche oder verschiedene Datenströme gleich oder unterschiedlich bearbeiten können.

Die Größe solcher Systeme wird im allgemeinen beschränkt durch die Anzahl der Prozessoren, die auf einen Speicher zugreifen, oder durch die Komplexität des Verbindungsnetzwerkes. Diese Beschränkungen können weitgehend aufgehoben werden durch den Einsatz verteilter Speicher (distributed shared memory) und durch die Verwendung von Verbindungsstrukturen mit (größenunabhängiger) konstanter lokaler Komplexität. Mit solchen speichergekoppelten Multiprozessoren können, wie Untersuchungen gezeigt haben, insbesondere Aufgaben mit überwiegend lokalem Datenaustausch mit hoher Effizienz bearbeitet werden. Dazu gehört u.a. die numerische Simulation physikalischer und chemischer Vorgänge, die heute in Forschung und Industrie eine große Rolle spielt.

Bei der Durchsetzbarkeit von Parallelrechnern stellt die Notwendigkeit für die Anwender

- in asynchronen parallelen Abläufen "zu denken" und
- extrem architekturabhängig zu programmieren

das Haupthindernis dar.

Allen Anstrengungen, die Anwender durch geeignete Hilfsmittel bzw. durch Einziehen geeigneter Abstraktionsebenen von diesen Notwendigkeiten zu entbinden, ist bisher nur in Ansätzen gelungen und in der Regel mit erheblichen Leistungsverlusten verbunden. Gegenläufig zu diesen Bemühungen ist nicht zuletzt auch die Tatsache, daß die kommerziellen Anbieter - wohl zu Recht - zunächst den klassischen "Fortran-Naturwissenschaftler" als potentiellen Kunden sehen, dessen Bedürfnisse in erster Linie zu befriedigen sind.

Für Beiträge zur Lösung der o.g. Fragestellungen sollte ein interdisziplinärer Sonderforschungsbereich besonders prädestiniert sein. Insbesondere dann, wenn durchgängig über alle klassischen Ebenen eines Parallelrechensystems hinweg das notwendige "know how" an einem Ort konzentriert ist. Diesen Zusammenhalt weiter zu fördern, dient das Querschnittsthema MEMSY.

1.1 Zielsetzung

Die Erfahrung der Erlanger Informatiker mit Multiprozessoren und verteilten Systemen an verschiedenen Lehrstühlen erstreckt sich auf ein breites Spektrum von Gesichtspunkten, wie Verbindungsstrukturen, Zerlegung von Anwenderaufgaben in parallel ausführbare Teile, Programmierung praktischer Lösungen der Kommunikations- und Synchronisationsabwicklung, Betriebssysteme für verschiedene Topologien, Messung und Analyse des Ablaufgeschehens, Zusammenhang von Aufgaben- bzw. Algorithmenstruktur und erforderliche Multiprozessorstruktur für den Fall der Fehlertoleranz.

Die bisher geleisteten Forschungsarbeiten mit den enggekoppelten Multiprozessorsystemen EGPA, SYMPOS, DIRMU, MUPSY und SUPRENUM haben bewiesen, daß grundsätzlich Parallelisierung erfolgreich zur Leistungssteigerung eingesetzt werden kann. Es hat sich gezeigt, daß offene Probleme des E/A- und des Verbindungssystems, der Adaptierbarkeit von Betriebssystemen auf verschiedene Rechnerarchitekturen, der Programmier- und Ablaufumgebung, der Aufgabenverteilung, der Integration von Leistungsmessung und -bewertung, sowie der Einführung von Standardschnittstellen und -komponenten weiter erforscht werden sollten. Dabei kommt der Speicherkopplung als Schnittstelle besondere Bedeutung zu. Die bisherige

Forschung ergab aber auch, daß nur die Verbindung von wohlüberlegter Planung mit tatsächlicher Erprobung der Konzepte zu relevanten Aussagen über die Tragfähigkeit von Ideen führen kann.

2 Einführung in den Hardware-Aufbau von MEMSY

Das hier vorgestellte Multiprozessor-Familienkonzept "MEMSY" basiert auf gemeinsamen grundlegenden Architektureigenschaften:

- Interprozessorkommunikation durch Speicherkopplung zwischen benachbarten Prozessoren: Konstante lokale Komplexität bei beliebiger Ausbaubarkeit.
- Die Prozessor-Speicher-Knoten haben denselben Aufbau. Eine Anpassung an die Zielanwendung kann u.a. durch geeignete Spezial-Prozessoren (z.B. für schnelle Gleitkommaverarbeitung) erfolgen.

Es werden Universalprozessoren eines Typs (oder weniger Typen) verwendet. Unterschiedliche Spezialprozessoren können hinzugefügt werden. Jeder Universalprozessor hat Zugriff zu mehreren (i.a. aber nicht zu allen) Speichermoduln. Es gibt Speicher, auf die mehrere Prozessoren zugreifen. Diese verhalten sich logisch wie Multiport-Speicher. Es gibt Speicher mit nur einem Prozessor als Zugreifer (Privatspeicher).

2.1 Topologie

MEMSY hat eine pyramidenförmige Struktur und kann in zwei Ebenen unterteilt werden (A- und B-Ebene). Der schematische Aufbau eines Systems mit 20 Knoten, das als Experimentalsystem aufgebaut wurde, ist in Abb. 2.1 dargestellt. Die Knoten der beiden Ebenen sind

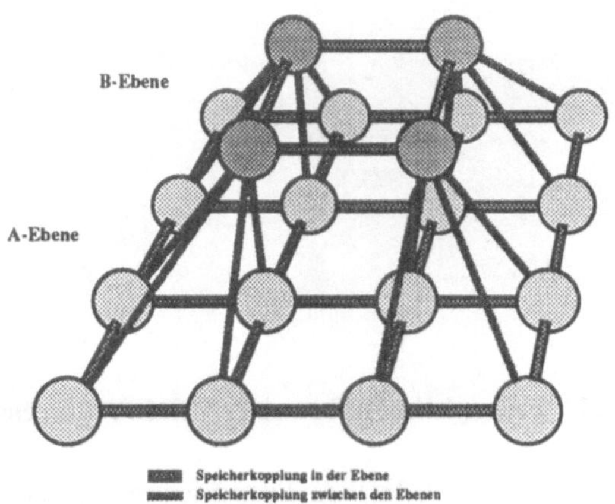

Abb. 2.1 20er MEMSY System (ohne Torusverbindungen)

jeweils in einem Gitter angeordnet, das zum Torus geschlossen ist. Jedem Knoten der B-Ebene sind genau vier Knoten aus der untersten Ebene, der A-Ebene, zugeordnet. Diese fünf Knoten bilden eine *Elementarpyramide*. Die Kopplung zwischen den Knoten innerhalb einer Ebene erfolgt über gemeinsame Speichermoduln. Dazu ist jedem Knoten ein zusätzlicher Speicher, der Kommunikationsspeicher, zugeordnet. Ein Knoten kann dann auf den Kommunikationsspeicher seiner vier direkten Nachbarn zugreifen (Nearest-Neighbour-Prinzip). Dadurch ergibt sich eine konstante lokale Verbindungskomplexität. Die Verbindung zwischen den Ebenen erfolgt ebenfalls über gemeinsame Speicher, wobei sie nicht, wie innerhalb einer Ebene, symmetrisch ist. Das heißt, die Knoten der B-Ebene können zwar auf den Kommunikationsspeicher der zugeordneten vier Knoten der A-Ebene zugreifen, nicht aber umgekehrt. Die Knoten der B-Ebene sind über einen Bus mit einem Front-End-Rechner verbunden. Eine ausführliche Beschreibung des Aufbaus und des Verbindungsnetzwerks kann in [Hil92] gefunden werden.

2.2 Aufbau eines MEMSY-Knotens

Ein Knoten der A- oder B-Ebene setzt sich aus dem Prozessormodul mit integriertem Cache, dem lokalen Hauptspeicher und spezieller Zusatzbaugruppen zusammen, von denen einige im Rahmen des MEMSY-Projekts entwickelt wurden. Diese dienen im wesentlichen zur Ansteuerung der Kommunikationsspeicher und zur Erzeugung von Unterbrechungen bei Nachbarknoten über dedizierte Verbindungen. Darüberhinaus ist pro Knoten ein privater Plattenspeicher und ein FDDI-Anschluß vorhanden. Der prinzipielle Aufbau eines Knotens ist in Abb. 2.2 dargestellt.

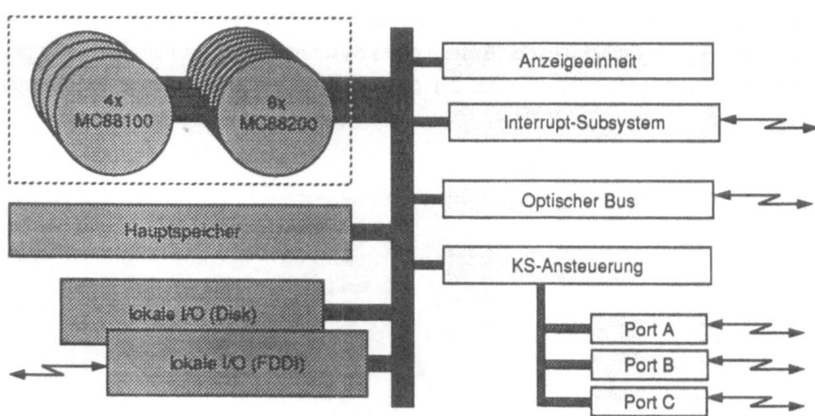

Abb. 2.2 Prinzipieller Aufbau eines MEMSY-Knotens

Das Konzept von MEMSY sieht vor, daß sich das System soweit möglich aus käuflichen Komponenten zusammensetzen soll. Als Prozessormodul wurde daher eine Multiprozessor-Baugruppe von Motorola gewählt, die vier RISC-Prozessoren und insgesamt acht Cache-Einheiten der 88k-Familie trägt und über einen lokalen Hochgeschwindigkeitsbus und einen VME-Bus verfügt. An den lokalen Bus ist die Ansteuerschaltung für die Kommunikationsspeicher angeschlossen. Die Kommunikationsspeicher werden grundsätzlich wie normaler Hauptspeicher behandelt. Im gekoppelten System entscheidet lediglich die Adressierung auf welchen der verfügbaren Speicher (Hauptspeicher, eigener Kommunikationsspeicher oder Nachbar-Kommunikationsspeicher) zugegriffen wird. Das Interrupt-Subsystem ermöglicht es Unterbrechungen bei anderen Knoten auszulösen. Dazu müssen eigene Knoten-zu-Knoten Verbindungen hergestellt werden. In MEMSY laufen diese Verbindungen parallel zur Speicherkopplung, das heißt ein Knoten hat zu genau dem Nachbarn eine Interrupt-Verbindung, mit dem er einen gemeinsamen Kommunikationsspeicher hat.

2.3 Leistungsdaten

Für das Experimentalsystem aus 20 Knoten mit insgesamt 80 Prozessoren ergeben sich folgende Leistungsdaten:

- 2000 MIPS (peak) ca. 1440 MIPS Dauerleistung
- 1000 MFLOPS (peak) ca. 800 MFLOPS Dauerleistung
- 10 MByte physikalischen Cache
- 640 MByte lokaler Hauptspeicher (auf 3840 MByte ausbaubar)
- 80 MByte Kommunikationsspeicher (auf 320 MByte ausbaubar)
- 10 GByte lokale Plattenkapazität (nahezu beliebig ausbaubar)
- 100 MByte/s IO-Bandbreite zu den Festplatten (auf 300 MByte/s ausbaubar)
- 100 MBit/s Bandbreite (FDDI) zum Datentransport von und zu dem System
- Vervielfachung der Bandbreite durch den Einsatz mehrerer FDDI-Ringe
- optisches Experimental-Bussystem (z.Zt. voraussichtlich 5 MBit)
- 400 MByte/s Bandbreite zu den lokalen Hauptspeichern
- 177 MByte/s Bandbreite zu den Kommunikationsspeichern

3 Programmiermodell

Wichtig für den Erfolg oder Mißerfolg eines Multiprozessorsystems sind nicht allein seine technischen Leistungsdaten, sondern auch die Programmierumgebung und das Programmiermodell, das den Anwendern zur Verfügung gestellt wird.

Für das MEMSY-System wurde der Ansatz gewählt, ein neues Programmiermodell zu entwerfen und sich nicht an bestehende Systeme anzulehnen, da die Hardware von MEMSY einige Eigenheiten aufweist, die sich in anderen Systemen nicht oder nur in abgewandelter Form finden lassen (mehrere gemeinsame Speicher mit Zugriff einer Teilmenge der Prozessoren und mehrere unterschiedliche Kommunikationsmedien).

Das im folgenden beschriebene Programmiermodell soll dem Anwender einen einfachen Zugriff auf die Fähigkeiten des MEMSY-Systems bieten und ihn bei der Entwicklung und Effizienzsteigerung seiner Anwendungsprogramme unterstützen.

3.1 Architektur von MEMSY aus der Sicht des Anwenders

Die Sicht des Anwenders auf die Architektur entspricht im wesentlichen der tatsächlichen Architektur, wie sie in Abschnitt 2.1 beschrieben wurde. Unsichtbar für den Anwender sind lediglich einige Besonderheiten der Hardware-Implementierung, wie die teilweise diagonale Kopplung der Knoten und die durch das Verbindungsnetzwerk möglichen Mehrfachzugriffe auf die Kommunikationsspeicher [Hil92].

3.1.1 Speicher

Jeder Prozessor hat einen oder mehrere Kommunikationsspeicher, auf den seine Nachbarprozessoren oder eine Teilmenge davon ebenfalls Zugriff haben. Als Nachbarprozessoren gelten die vier in der Ebene direkt anschließenden Prozessoren, der in der Pyramide übergeordnete Prozessor (für die untere Ebene) und die vier unterhalb eines Prozessors angeordneten Prozessoren (für die obere Ebene).

3.1.2 Knoten

Jeder Knoten des MEMSY-Systems ist wieder ein Mehrfachprozessorsystem, das aus vier Prozessoren aufgebaut ist. Die Anwendung hat die Möglichkeit, mehrere Prozesse auf einem Knoten zu erzeugen, um die volle Parallelität der Knoten nutzen zu können. Die Adressierung der Knoten erfolgt in der Regel durch Angabe der relativen Position, dadurch sind Verbindungen zu den Nachbarknoten uniform für alle Knoten programmierbar. Eine absolute Adressierung ist ebenfalls möglich. Die Position im Feld ist durch das Koordinaten Tripel (x,y,z) definiert, wobei ein Prozessor der oberen Ebene als (0,0,1) definiert ist. Der in der unteren Ebene direkt südwestlich von ihm angeordnete Prozessor definiert den Nullpunkt dieser Ebene (0,0,2).

3.2 Applikationen

Alle Prozesse, die zu einer Anwendung gehören, werden zu einer Applikation zusammengefaßt. Mehrere Applikationen können gleichzeitig im System ablaufen. Wenn sie auf unterschiedlichen Teilmengen der Knoten ablaufen, so beeinflussen sie sich nicht, ansonsten konkurrieren sie um die Betriebsmittel (Rechenzeit, Speicher, etc.).

Jede Applikation hat ihren eigenen Namensraum bei der Benutzung der Mechanismen, die im folgenden erläutert werden. Eine gegenseitige Beeinflussung ist damit ausgeschlossen.

Das System überwacht den Ablauf der zu einer Applikation gehörenden Prozesse. Bei Abbruch eines Prozesses kann die gesamte Applikation terminiert werden und die von ihr belegten Betriebsmittel können freigegeben werden, so daß Fehler in einer Anwendung eine begrenzte Auswirkung auf das Gesamtsystem haben.

3.3 Funktionen

Das MEMSY-Programmiermodell bietet im einzelnen folgende Funktionen an, deren genaue Beschreibung den Rahmen dieses Artikels sprengen würde, und für die deshalb auf [Kar91] verwiesen wird.

3.3.1 Gemeinsamer Speicher

Der Zugriff auf die Kommunikationsspeicher erfolgt durch ein, dem shared-memory Mechanismus von System V ähnliches System. Wie dort werden Abschnitte (Segmente) des gemeinsamen Speichers von einem Prozeß alloziert (*create*) und können dann von anderen Prozessen in ihren Adreßraum eingeblendet werden (*attach*).

Ein Nachteil der MEMSY-Architektur ist, das im allgemeinen die Caches beim Zugriff auf die Kommunikationsspeicher ausgeschaltet werden müssen, da sonst die Konsistenz der Daten zwischen den einzelnen Knoten nicht gesichert wäre. Wenn eine Anwendung sicher ist, daß es bei Zugriff auf ein bestimmtes Segment für eine gewisse Zeit nicht zu Konsistenzproblemen kommen kann (weil z.B. nur lesend oder nur von einem Knoten aus darauf zugegriffen wird), so kann sie für dieses Zeit den Cache für dieses Segment aktivieren.

3.3.2 Messages

Messages sind kurze Nachrichten, die ein Prozeß an Prozesse derselben Applikation auf einem Nachbarknoten senden kann. Die Nachrichten werden beim Empfänger gepuffert. Ein Empfang der Nachrichten kann entweder blockierend oder nicht blockierend erfolgen. Dem Empfänger wird neben dem Inhalt der Nachricht auch die Identität des Absenders mitgeteilt.

3.3.3 Semaphore

Als weitere Koordinierungsmöglichkeit bietet das System globale Semaphore an, welche die üblichen P- und V-Operationen unterstützen. Vor ihrer Benutzung müssen die Semaphore kreiert werden. Es können auf jedem Knoten Semaphore angelegt werden.

3.3.4 Signale

Es ist möglich, einem Prozeß auf einem Nachbarknoten ein Signal zustellen zu lassen, worauf dann dessen normaler Ablauf unterbrochen wird und eine vorher definierte Signalbehandlungsroutine aufgerufen wird. Auf diese Weise kann schnell auf asynchrone oder außergewöhnliche Ereignisse reagiert werden. Es können zwei verschiedene Signale verschickt werden.

3.3.5 Spinlocks

Für die Koordination kurzer kritischer Abschnitte gibt es die Spinlocks. Dies sind gemeinsame Variablen im Kommunikationsspeicher, welche die Zustände „frei" und „belegt" annehmen können.

3.3.6 Transport

Zum Transport größerer Datenmengen ist ein weiterer Nachrichtenmechanismus vorgesehen, den wir zur Unterscheidung von den Messages „Transport" genannt haben. Im Unterschied zu den Messages ist ein Transport auch zu weiter entfernten Knoten möglich. Das Betriebssystem wählt dabei den günstigsten Weg aus (Kommunikationsspeicher, FDDI-Netz oder optisches Bussystem), wobei es auch die aktuelle Lastsituation und Ausfälle von Teilsystemen berücksichtigen kann.

3.3.7 Informationsfunktionen

Zu den Informationsroutinen gehören Routinen, mit denen zwischen absoluten Knotenidentifikation, relativer Knotenidentifikation und Position im Gesamtsystem (x,y,z-Koordinaten) umgerechnet werden kann.

3.3.8 Ein-/Ausgabe

Für jeden Knoten gibt es einen knotenlokalen Plattenbereich und für das Gesamtsystem einen globalen Plattenbereich, auf die mit Varianten der UNIX-Bibliotheksfunktionen für gepufferte Ein-/Ausgabe zugegriffen werden kann.

Jeder Knoten im Experimentalsystem ist mit einer lokalen Platte ausgestattet, so daß die Zugriffe auf die knotenlokalen Datenbereiche schnell und unabhängig von anderen Knoten abgewickelt werden können.

4 Betriebssystemarchitektur

Es sind verschiedene Überlegungen angestellt worden, welches Betriebssystem für MEMSY eingesetzt werden soll. Grundsätzlich gibt es zwei Möglichkeiten. Zum einen kann man ein komplett neues Betriebssystem entwickeln. Dies bietet den Vorteil, daß das System genau an die vorliegende Hardware angepaßt werden kann. Allerdings besteht ein großer, nicht zu unterschätzender Nachteil darin, daß dies mit sehr viel Zeit- und Arbeitsaufwand verbunden ist. Die zweite Möglichkeit, die sich bietet, besteht darin, auf ein bereits verfügbares Betriebssystem zurückzugreifen. In diesem Fall müßten nur noch die notwendigen Anpassungen an selbstentwickelte Hardware erfolgen. Im Fall von MEMSY wurde zugunsten der zweiten Alternative entschieden. Als Basis für MEMSOS, dem Betriebssystem von MEMSY, wird das UNIX

SYSTEM V/88 Release 3 von Motorola auf jedem Knoten eingesetzt. Diese Unix-Implementierung ist bereits speziell an die knotenlokale Multiprozessorarchitektur der verwendeten Hardware angepaßt.

4.1 Modifikationen und Erweiterungen am eingesetzten Betriebssystem

Vielfältige Änderungen sind am Betriebssystem vorgenommen worden. Einerseits waren Erweiterungen notwendig, um die zusätzliche Hardware in das Betriebssystem zu integrieren. Dies betrifft insbesondere die Ansteuerung der Kommunikationsspeicher und des Interrupt-Subsystems. Obwohl die gängigen Multiprozessorkonzepte bereits integriert waren, konnten sie nicht für den knotenübergreifenden Einsatz verwendet werden, da diesen Konzepten die Annahme zugrunde liegt, daß alle Prozessoren Zugriff auf einen gemeinsamen globalen Speicher haben. Dies trifft in besonderem Maße für die Interprozeßkommunikation zu, die sich mit Hilfe eines globalen gemeinsamen Speichers und simpler Lock-Techniken einfacher durchführen läßt, als in einem System mit verteiltem gemeinsamen Speicher. Innerhalb eines Knotens kann jedoch auf die vorhanden Mechanismen zurückgegriffen werden. Für knotenübergreifende Aktionen sind neue Basismechanismen eingesetzt worden, die auf den bereits erwähnten Erweiterungen aufbauen. Hier sind unter anderem die Kommunikationsspeicherverwaltung, der Unterbrechungsmechanismus und ein einfacher Nachrichtenmechanismus zu nennen. Damit MEMSY den verschiedensten Anforderungen der Anwender gerecht werden kann ist zudem das Applikationskonzept eingeführt worden. Zur Integration der meisten erwähnten Erweiterungen mußten nur wenige Modifikationen am ursprünglichen Kern vorgenommen werden, so daß Standard-Unix Anwendung weiterhin ohne Einschränkungen einsetzbar sind.

4.1.1 Anwendungsunterstützung - Applikationen

Von Seiten der Anwender werden an ein Hochleistungsrechensystem verschiedene Anforderungen gestellt. Hier sind unter anderem hohe Verfügbarkeit des Systems (Ausfallsicherheit und einfaches Aufsetzen nach einem Knotenausfall), einfache Handhabbarkeit, kurze Aufsetzphasen von Anwendungen, gewohnter oder gar erweiterter Funktionalitätsumfang und die Möglichkeit zu interaktivem Testen von Anwendungen, ohne den Produktionsbetrieb zu stark zu stören, zu nennen.

Damit der Großteil der oben angeführten Anforderungen erfüllt werden kann, ist in MEMSOS das *Applikationskonzept* eingeführt worden. Die Gesamtheit aller Prozesse, die durch eine einzige Anwendung auf dem System erzeugt werden, wird als eine Einheit gesehen. Diese Einheit wird als *Applikation* bezeichnet (vergleiche auch Abschnitt 3.2). Eine Applikation ist somit ein knotenübergreifendes Prozessystem. Um mehrere parallele Applikationen realisieren zu können, muß jede Applikation global eindeutig identifizierbar sein. Dies wird durch eine Applikationsnummer erreicht. Die Prozesse einer Applikation werden *Tasks* genannt. Sie erben die Applikationsnummer und erhalten eine knotenlokal eindeutige Tasknummer. Tasks können somit eindeutig durch ihre Applikations-, Task- und Knotennummer identifiziert werden.

Durch dieses einfache Applikationskonzept ist es möglich eine Applikation, also alle zu einer Anwendung gehörenden Prozesse, eindeutig zu identifizieren und in ihrer Gesamtheit zu überwachen und zu steuern. Dadurch ist es möglich auch mehrere Applikationen zu einer Zeit auf dem System zu erlauben, da diese nun einzeln erfaßt und differenziert behandelt werden können.

5 Zusammenfassung und Ausblick

In Zusammenarbeit zwischen mehreren Lehrstühlen des IMMD und anderen Instituten der Universität Erlangen-Nürnberg wurde mit "MEMSY" ein umfassendes Konzept für ein Multiprozessor-Projekt erarbeitet und ein funktionsfähiges System aufgebaut. Die gewonnenen Ergebnisse werden möglicherweise bei entsprechender Industriebeteiligung in die Entwicklung eines Hochleistungsprototyps einfließen. In diesem umfassenden Rahmen (einschließlich der SFB-Forschungsarbeiten) sollen nicht nur die genannten Multiprozessorkonzepte weiterentwickelt werden, es soll auch eine verbesserte SW- und HW-Architektur entstehen, mit der eine Familie von modular erweiterbaren und konfigurierbaren Multiprozessorsystemen mit breitem Leistungsspektrum realisiert werden kann.

Es sollen grundlegende Untersuchungen der "Parallelität" in der Systemstruktur, der Kommunikation, den Berechnungsalgorithmen der Anwenderaufgaben, sowie der Leistungsmessung und -bewertung durchgeführt werden. In dem gegebenen günstigen Umfeld ist zu erwarten, daß die flexible und effiziente Zusammenarbeit der Gruppen umfassende konzeptionelle und praktische Erkenntnisse über Strukturen und dynamisches Verhalten von Multiprozessorsystemen erbringen wird.

Das MEMSY Experimentalsystem wird bereits jetzt von verschiedenen Anwendungen aus den Bereichen Strömungsmechanik, Theoretische Chemie und Bildverarbeitung genutzt. Es ist zu erwarten, daß sich die Anzahl an Anwendungen noch erhöht und damit auch die Praxistauglichkeit des Systems demonstriert werden kann.

6 Literaturverzeichnis

[Dal92] M. Dal Cin, „Rechnerbaukasten für funktionsorientierte Multiprozessoren mit Fehlertoleranzeigenschaften"; in: *Arbeits- und Ergebnisbericht des SFB 182 Multiprozessor- und Netzwerkkonfigurationen 1990 - 1992*, Seite 114 ff.

[Hil92] U. Hildebrand, *Konzeption, Bewertung und Realisierung einer dynamischen Netzwerkkomponente für speichergekoppelte Multiprozessoren*; Dissertation, Arbeitsberichte des IMMD, Univ. Erlangen-Nürnberg, Band 25, No. 5, 1992

[Hof92] F. Hofmann, „Entwurf und Implementierung eines an Hardwarearchitektur und Aufgabenklassen adaptierbaren Multiprozessorbetriebssystems"; in: *Finanzierungsantrag Multiprozessor- und Netzwerkkonfigurationen 93-95 des SFB182*, Seite 179ff

[Kar91] F. Kardel, W. Stukenbrock, T. Thiel, S. Turowski, *Anleitung zur Benutzung des MEMSY-Programmiermodells für Anwender*; interner Bericht, IMMD 4, Univ. Erlangen-Nürnberg, Oktober 1991

[Rus90] K. Rusnock, P. Raynoha, „Adapting the Unix operating system to run on a tightly coupled multiprocessor system"; *VMEbus Systems*, Oct. 1990, Vol. 6, No. 5, pp. 8-28

Das Querschnittsprojekt "HEDAS"
Heterogene, durchgängige Anwendungssysteme

Dr. Thomas Ruf
Universität Erlangen-Nürnberg — Informatik VI (Datenbanksysteme)
Martensstr. 3, 91058 Erlangen
E-mail: ruf@informatik.uni-erlangen.de

Überblick

Im Querschnittsthema "Heterogene, durchgängige Anwendungssysteme (HEDAS)" werden die Forschungsrichtungen von Teilprojekten zusammengefaßt, die vornehmlich Netzwerkarchitekturen als Grundlage haben. Es werden zum einen grundlegende Methoden und Forschungsergebnisse über lose gekoppelte Systeme bereitgestellt, zum anderen komplexe Anwendungen exemplarisch realisiert. Derzeit hat sich der CIM-Bereich als Anwendungsschwerpunkt herauskristallisiert. Die dort laufenden Kooperationen erweisen sich in Hinsicht auf die gemischt technisch/planerischen Aufgabenstellungen und ihre praktische Verknüpfung mit den Problemen verschiedener Rechnersysteme auf den einzelnen CIM-Ebenen als besonders reizvoll.

1 Motivation

Netzgekoppelte verteilte Systeme stellen im Unterschied zu den Möglichkeiten bei der Realisierung speichergekoppelter Multiprozessorsysteme, wie sie im Querschnittsthema MEMSY untersucht werden, grundsätzlich andere Anforderungen, die sich hauptsächlich aus dem Zwang der Weiternutzung bestehender, oft heterogener Hardware- und Softwarekomponenten ergeben. Im Hardwarebereich gilt es, eine leistungsfähige Verbindung der oftmals unabhängig voneinander entwickelten und unabänderlichen Bausteine zu realisieren, was vor allem zu Anforderungen im Kommunikationsbereich führt. Im Bereich der Software ist zwischen Systemsoftware und Anwendungssoftware zu unterscheiden. Anforderungen an die zu entwickelnde Systemsoftware resultieren wie auch im Hardwarebereich wesentlich aus der Heterogenität der zu verwendenden Komponenten. Zur Integration der Anwendungssoftware sind in der Regel zunächst konzeptionelle Grundlagen zu erarbeiten, damit das resultierende Gesamtsystem über das bloße 'Zusammenschalten' seiner Teilkomponenten hinausgehende Merkmale aufweist.

Die obigen Ausführungen machen deutlich, daß für das Querschnittsprojekt statt einer Unterteilung der Arbeiten nach Hardware- und Softwarebereich eine Untergliederung in einen Teilbereich 'Systemdienste und Methodenaustausch' einerseits und in einen Teilbereich 'Anwendungen' andererseits vorzuziehen ist. Durch eine enge Abstimmung beider Bereiche wird gewährleistet, daß die entwickelten Systemdienste und Methoden auch unmittelbaren Nutzen in einer konkreten Anwendungssituation erbringen. Als gemeinsamer Anwendungsbereich ist das Gebiet der rechnerintegrierten Fertigung besonders reizvoll, da hier vielfältige Aufgaben der Heterogenität und Durchgängigkeit in den Bereichen Hardware, System- und Anwendungssoftware bestehen.

2 Gliederung des Querschnittsprojekts

Die Vorstellung von HEDAS folgt der im obigen Kapitel motivierten Untergliederung des Themenkomplexes in einen Teilbereich 'Systemdienste und Methodenaustausch' sowie einen Teilbereich 'Anwendungen', die auch in der organisatorischen und inhaltlichen Struktur des Querschnittsprojekts reflektiert ist (siehe Abbildung 2.1).

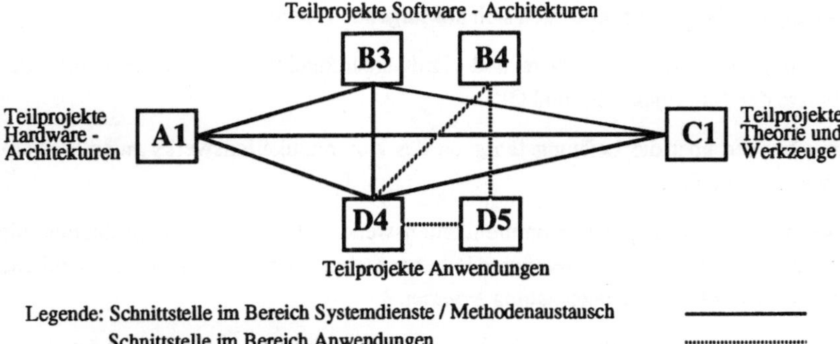

Abb. 2.1 Schnittstellen der am Querschnittsprojekt HEDAS beteiligten Teilprojekte

Im Bereich 'Systemdienste und Methodenaustausch' werden grundsätzliche Fragestellungen der Kommunikations- und Datenbanktechnologie mit einer Hinwendung zum Umfeld der rechnerintegrierten Produktion untersucht. Der Teilbereich 'Anwendungen' befaßt sich mit der exemplarischen Realisierung eines von der Leitebene über die Zellenebene bis hin zur Prozeßebene durchgängigen Anwendungssystems zur Produktionsplanung und -steuerung. Hervorzuheben ist die in Abbildung 1 erkennbare enge Verzahnung der Teilbereiche und die Beteiligung aller im Sonderforschungsbereich etablierten Projektbereiche. Nachfolgend werden die für ein Querschnittsthema besonders wichtigen Schnittstellen zwischen mehreren Teilprojekten sowie von allen Teilprojekten gemeinsam benutzbare Basisdienste überblicksartig beschrieben. Die in den Kapitelüberschriften angegebenen Bezeichnungen der beteiligten Teilprojekte beziehen sich auf die im Beitrag von Wedekind zu findende Gliederung des SFB 182.

2.1 Teilbereich 'Systemdienste und Methodenaustausch'

2.1.1 Transportorientierte Kommunikationsdienste (TP A1-B3)

Ziel der Zusammenarbeit ist es, geeignete Hard- und Softwarearchitekturen für die Behandlung der transportorientierten Schichten des ISO-OSI-Referenzmodells zu entwerfen. Im Teilprojekt A1 wird geeignete Multiprozessorhardware (HYTRA, **Hy**brid gekoppelte **Tra**nsputer) entworfen und aufgebaut. Eine Auswahl exemplarischer Teilprotokolle wird implementiert. Aus den dabei gewonnenen Erfahrungen und Meßergebnissen können im Teilprojekt B3 Vorhersagen über die Auswirkung bestimmter Entwurfsentscheidungen gemacht werden. In einem weiteren Schritt kann die Implementierung eines Protokollstacks durch Variation von freien Parametern (Zahl der Prozessoren, Abbildung von Prozessoren auf Prozessoren usw.) automatisch optimiert werden.

Das HYTRA-Konzept wurde durch mehrere Veröffentlichungen und Vorträge auf internationalen Konferenzen dargestellt. Im Teilprojekt B3 wird versucht, die bisher aus Erfahrung gewonnenen Abbildungsvorschriften von Prozessoren auf Transputer durch geeignete Verfahren automatisch zu generieren. Dabei entstand das Konzept von DSPL (**D**ata **S**tream **P**rocessing **L**anguage), einer integrierten Entwicklungsumgebung für Entwurf und Realisierung von anwenderspezifischen Transputersystemen.

Die gegenwärtigen Arbeiten konzentrieren sich auf folgende Bereiche:

- Optimierung von Protokollsoftware und Hardwarearchitektur unter Einbeziehung der Ergebnisse der Teilprojekte B3 und C1.
- Untersuchungen über die Leistungsfähigkeit des Kommunikationswerks unter Verwendung von anderen Protokollen.
- Realisierung eines Transputer-"Kommunikationswerks", das alle Protokollschichten bis einschließlich Ebene 7 des Referenzmodells bearbeitet. Dadurch wird eine erhebliche Verbesserung der Übertragungsleistung erwartet.
- Vergleich zwischen handoptimierter Software und der mit DSPL generierten Lösung.

2.1.2 Kommunikationsvorgänge in Transputersystemen (TP A1-C1)

In den bereits durchgeführten Arbeiten wurde im Teilprojekt A1 das Transputer-Kommunikationssystem TRACOS entwickelt, das die Parallelisierung von Anwenderprogrammen auf Transputern stark vereinfacht. Entgegen den üblicherweise in Transputernetzwerken eingesetzten synchronen Kommunikationsmechanismen realisiert TRACOS eine asynchrone und gepufferte Kommunikation zwischen beliebigen Transputern in einem Transputer-Netzwerk. Erreicht wird diese Systemeigenschaft mittels spezieller Kommunikationsprozesse, welche die Transputer-Kommunikationskanäle und verschiedene Warteschlangen zur Pufferung der Datenströme verwalten. Im Rahmen der Kooperationen der Teilprojekte A1 und C1 wird meßtechnisch erfaßt, welche Kommunikationsleistung von TRACOS erbracht wird, wo die Systemengpässe liegen und wie sie beseitigt werden können. Alle Messungen und Auswertungen werden mit dem vom Teilprojekt C1 entwickelten Zählmonitor ZM4 und der zugehörigen Auswertungsumgebung SIMPLE durchgeführt. Die erzielten Ergebnisse sind nicht nur für die Optimierung von TRACOS von Interesse, sondern konnten wegen ihrer Allgemeingültigkeit auch erfolgreich auf internationalen Konferenzen präsentiert werden.

Die an dem Kommunikationssystem TRACOS durchgeführten Messungen zeigen, daß die Transputerlinks für Anwendungen, die eine hohe Kommunikationsleistung benötigen, zu langsam sind. Diese Einsicht führte zur Konzipierung des PADI-Rechensystems (Parallel Processor with Distributed Image Memory) auf Transputerbasis. Hier findet Interprozessor-Kommunikation nicht mehr über die Transputerlinks, sondern über ein synchrones Hochleistungsbussystem zwischen lokalen Zweitor-Arbeitsspeichern der einzelnen Transputer statt. Die Messung dieses neuen Systems mit ZM4 bildet die Grundlage zur Bewertung und Optimierung des PADI-Systems und zur Erprobung von hybridem Knotenmonitoring in Kombination mit Hardware-Verbindungsmonitoring. Zugleich werden verallgemeinerte Darstellungsmöglichkeiten von Kommunikationsabläufen untersucht.

2.1.3 MAP-konforme Kommunikation (TP A1-D4)

MAP-konforme Kommunikation ist bisher den höheren Ebenen der CIM-Hierarchie vorbehalten gewesen, weil "Full-MAP"-Architekturen für den Einsatz innerhalb flexibler Fertigungszellen in unmittelbarer Nähe zum technischen Prozeß mit seinen Echtzeitanforderungen nicht taugen. Aus der Forderung nach durchgängiger MAP-konformer Kommunikation in der gesamten CIM-Hierarchie folgt, daß die fertigungsspezifischen MAP-Anwendungsdienste (MMS) in sinnvollen Teilmengen auch auf unteren Ebenen verfügbar sein müssen.

Das Kommunikationskonzept LABORINTH liegt abgeschlossen in portierbarer Form vor; eine Pilotimplementierung über einem Mehrprozeßbetriebssystem für Mikrorechner wurde durchgeführt. Zur Erprobung in repräsentativen Anwendungsumgebungen wurden eine Reihe von LABORINTH-Unterstationen geschaffen, so z.B. RC-Stationen mit und ohne MMS-Funktionalität und Sensor/Aktor-Einfachstationen.

Für die innerhalb von Flexiblen Fertigungszellen auftretenden und hinsichtlich der Kommunikation recht unterschiedlich ausgestatteten Geräte wurden repräsentative Kommunikationsarchitekturen konzipiert und z.T. auch implementiert. Zur Festlegung der Funktionalität wurde ein Klassifikationsschema erarbeitet, das maßgebliche Eigenschaften für die zelleninterne Kommunikation angibt und Grundlage für den Vergleich der Kommunikationsfähigkeit verschiedener Automatisierungsgeräte bzw. prozeßnaher Kommunikationssysteme sein kann. Vertieft wurde die Thematik der Einfachgeräte bearbeitet.

2.1.4 VLSI-unterstützte Feldbus-Konzepte sowie MMS-Dienste (TP A1-B3-D4)

In dieser relativ neuen Kooperation werden aktuelle VLSI-unterstützte Feldbus-Konzepte, die Anwartschaft auf internationale Verbreitung bzw. Standardisierung erheben, klassifiziert und bewertet. In einer ersten Stufe, in der die physische Modellierung als Grundlage dient (TP A1), werden die ausgewählten Vertreter zunächst an der Medienzugangsschnittstelle beobachtet. In der zweiten Stufe erfolgt die kontrollierte Einbindung in eine fertigungstechnische Anwendungsumgebung ("Modellfabrik", TP D4). Bei der Untersuchung von "Standard-Kommunikationssituationen" zwischen MMS-Client- und MMS-Server-Partnern (TP D4) kommen auf Basis exemplarischer Realisierungen (TP A1) neue Methoden der Lastcharakterisierung zum Einsatz. Damit wird das Teilprojekt B3 in die bereits bestehende A1/D4-Kooperation eingebunden. Schließlich ist geplant, eine bereits existierende Zusammenarbeit der Teilprojekte A1 und D4 um die Vermessung verschiedener Feldbus-Systeme zu erweitern und die Methodik der Lastcharakterisierung mittels attributierter Grammatiken für das Netzbenchmarking von Feldbussystemen in der "Modellfabrik" der Fertigungstechnik zu erproben. Außerdem wird hiermit die Verbindung zum A1-Thema "ISO-OSI-Kommunikationswerke für MAP-Netze und HSLANs" hergestellt. Auf der im Rahmen des Projekts HYTRA (s.o.) entstandenen hybrid gekoppelten Transputer-Architektur, die (als sog. "Kommunikationswerk") den gesamten ISO-OSI-Protokollstack abdecken kann, sollen repräsentative MMS-Dienste realisiert und evaluiert werden. Ziel der Bestrebungen ist es, die vom jeweiligen Medium zugelassenen Übertragungsraten zukünftiger Hochgeschwindigkeitsnetze mit so wenig Einbußen wie möglich an der Anwenderschnittstelle von ISO-OSI-Kommunikationssystemen verfügbar zu machen.

2.1.5 Lastbedingungen bei der Maschinensteuerung (TP B3-C1-D4)

Im Rahmen der Leistungsbewertung von Lastverbundalgorithmen in Rechnernetzen (TP B3) und einer Anforderungsanalyse für Kommunikationssysteme im Anwendungsbereich Fertigungsautomatisierung (TP D4) werden am Beispiel einer konkreten Fertigungszelle auftretende Lastbedingungen bei der Maschinensteuerung genau untersucht. Für die dafür erforderlichen Messungen werden der in Teilprojekt C1 entwickelte Hybridmonitor und die Auswertewerkzeuge eingesetzt. Um die gewünschten Lastdaten zu erhalten, müssen zusätzlich zu den Software-Ereignissen auf Steuerungsebene auch Hardware-Ereignisse auf Maschinenebene erfaßt und miteinander in Beziehung gesetzt werden. Der Meßadapter für das Objektsystem wurde von Teilprojekt C1 entwickelt. Die Testphase konnte an einer am Lehrstuhl für Fertigungsautomatisierung zu diesem Zweck zur Verfügung gestellten Maschine durchgeführt werden. Die eigentlichen Messungen fanden im Testlabor des Maschinenherstellers, der Firma Siemens in München, statt.

Die Meßdaten dienen der Validierung eines zuvor erstellten Lastmodells der untersuchten Anwendung und der Ermittlung quantitativer Lastparameter. Die dabei festgestellten Rechenlasteigenschaften (bzgl. Gruppenanknüpfverhalten, Termineigenschaften, Bedienzeitverteilung, Datenabhängigkeiten) werden hinsichtlich ihres Einflusses auf die Effizienz von Lastverteilverfahren untersucht. Dabei erfolgt eine enge Zusammenarbeit mit Teilprojekt D4 in Hinblick auf die Festlegung weiterer Modellparameter und Untersuchungen zu deren Repräsentativität.

In Teilprojekt D4 fließen die Erkenntnisse über die Eigenschaften der Kommunikationslast in den Leistungsvergleich von Feldbussystemen im Zellbereich ein. Von besonderem Interesse ist hier auch die Ermittlung von Kenngrößen zur Leistungsbewertung für Fertigungszellen mit verteilter Struktur.

2.1.6 Untersuchung von Realzeitproblemen in Robotersteuerungen sowie Validierung des Fertigungszellenkonzeptes (TP C1-D4)

Zur Messung zeitkritischer Abläufe in einer Multiprozessor-Robotersteuerung wird der im Teilprojekt C1 entwickelte Hardwaremonitor ZM4 eingesetzt. Interessierende Ereignisse werden per Software instrumentiert und damit eine Hybridmessung ermöglicht. Besonders interessierende Ereignisse sind dabei jene, die den Synchronbetrieb zweier Industrieroboter zu charakterisieren gestatten und z.B. die Dauer von Interpretation, Interpolation und Koordinatenübergabe für verschiedene Prozessorvergabestrategien ermitteln. Aus den gemessenen Ereignisspuren werden mit dem Meßdatenanalysepaket SIMPLE Aussagen über Laufzeitverteilungen, Laufzeitmaxima, etc. von Robotersteuermodulen, aber auch über Laufzeitverzögerungen zwischen den kooperierenden Modulen abgeleitet. Diese Resultate dienen der ablauforientierten Bewertung des Konzeptes. So können mit den Ergebnissen Angaben darüber gemacht werden, inwieweit aufwendigere Anwendungsfunktionen (z.B. Spline-Interpolation) von der Robotersteuerung zu bewältigen sind.

Die Möglichkeit, mit ereignisgesteuerten ZM4-Messungen Einsicht in Abläufe auf mehreren kooperierenden Systemen, insbesondere in Kommunikationsabläufe, gewinnen zu können, wird gegenwärtig in zwei Bereichen eingesetzt:

(1) Validierung des Fertigungszellenkonzeptes
Im Zuge dieser Untersuchungen wird das Konzept der Fertigungszelle, das sich heute dediziert eingesetzter Knoten bedient, dahingehend generalisiert, daß Prinzipien, die sich bei verteilten Systemen bewährt haben, Eingang finden. Von der Thematik der Fertigungsautomatisierung her kommen die Realzeitbedingungen hinzu. Damit ergibt sich auch eine interessante Beziehung zur Spezifikation, denn bei Realzeitsoftware sind Zeitbedingungen eine Vorgabe, die den Charakter einer verbindlichen Spezifikation haben. Die Zusammenarbeit der Teilprojekte C1 und D4 bietet einmal die Möglichkeit, Realzeitspezifikationen als Instrumentierungsparameter in die Meßvorbereitung einzubringen; zum anderen dienen die daraus abgeleiteten Messungen der Validierung. Die gemessenen Ereignisspuren werden so ausgewertet, daß implizit enthaltene Leistungsaussagen mit den Vorgaben verglichen werden, also eine Validierung des implementierten Konzeptes erfolgt.

(2) Realzeitprobleme in Robotersteuerungen
Das Teilprojekt D4 befaßt sich mit Realzeitproblemen in Robotersteuerungen, die sich auf verteilte Komponenten stützen. Die Umsetzung von Vorgaben aus der HEDAS-Funktionshierarchie stellt auf Geräteebene zeitliche und räumliche Anforderungen an die Steuerungskomponenten. Es wird das Ziel verfolgt, die Funktionalität auf die räumlich getrennten Komponenten so zu verteilen, daß bei einem hohen Maße an Echtzeitfähigkeit möglichst einfache Funktionsmodule entstehen. Dabei muß geklärt werden, wie weit eine Aufteilung der Aufgaben auf die einzelnen verteilten Komponenten unter Beachtung der Gesichtspunkte Zeitanforderungen, Busauslastung und benötigter Rechenleistung sinnvoll erscheint. Das Zusammenwirken der verteilten und über Busse gekoppelten Komponenten wird durch Messungen mit dem Monitorsystem ZM4 (TP C1) beobachtet und bewertet.

Im Rahmen des Querschnittsprojekts HEDAS ist das Fernziel die Konzeption eines transparenten Systems von Gerätesteuerung und verteilten Komponenten. Zu diesem Zweck wird eine Schnittstelle konzipiert, mit deren Hilfe die Gerätesteuerung und die verteilten Komponenten als geschloßene Einheit betrachtet werden können.

2.1.7 Bereitstellung flexibler, anwendungsspezifisch konfigurierbarer Datenverwaltungskonzepte (TP B4)

Die in diesem Bereich vorgenommenen Untersuchungen unterstützen die für das Querschnittsthema HEDAS typischen Aufgabenstellungen aus Datenverwaltungs- und -verteilungssicht. Klassische Ansätze zur Datenverwaltung, die vornehmlich für den Bereich der kaufmännischen Datenverarbeitung entwickelt worden sind (z.B. verteilte Dateisysteme, DB-Server-Architekturen und verteilte Datenbanksysteme), greifen in heterogen strukturierten

Anwendungsgebieten wie CIM mit den typischen spezifischen Anforderungen eines Knotens hinsichtlich Datenverfügbarkeit und Datenaktualität nicht oder nur unter Inkaufnahme erheblicher Performanceeinbußen.

Zur Unterstützung der Anforderungen im Bereich der Datenverwaltung in technischen Anwendungen wurde das verteilte Datenverwaltungssystem DDMS (**D**istributed **D**ata **M**anagement **S**ystem) als Basisdienst für die verschiedenen HEDAS-Anwendergruppen konzipiert und implementiert. Grundlegend im DDMS ist die Unterscheidung der Teilbereiche Datenhaltung und Datenverteilung zur Realsierung der Gesamtaufgabe 'verteilte Datenverwaltung'. Für die lokale Datenhaltung in den verschiedenen Rechnerknoten lassen sich sowohl einfache Dateien (z.B. RMS-Filesystem) als auch relationale Datenbanksysteme (z.B. VAX/Rdb, Ingres) einsetzen. Dies ermöglicht es den Anwendern insbesondere, vorhandene Datenbestände leicht unter dem Dach des DDMS zu integrieren. Knotenübergreifende Verarbeitungen und die Aktualisierung replizierter Teildatenbestände werden mittels eines anwendungsspezifisch konfigurierbaren Datenverteilmechanismus durchgeführt, der die Verteiltheit und Replikation von Daten im Rechnernetz für den Endbenutzer transparent hält.

Der DDMS-Ansatz wurde bei einem Hersteller von Turboladern in einer praxisnahen Anwendungssituation validiert. Die Erfahrungen zeigen, daß die ereignisgesteuerte verteilte Datenverwaltung nach dem DDMS-Konzept dem Anwendungsentwickler unmittelbaren Nutzen bei seinen Datenverwaltungsaufgaben bringt.

2.1.8 Unterstützung geregelter und ungeregelter arbeitsteiliger Anwendungen (TP B4)

Die Zielsetzung in diesem Bereich ist die Realisierung einer integrierten Produktdatenbank mit Schwerpunkt auf der Unterstützung geregelter und ungeregelter arbeitsteiliger Anwendungen. In einem ersten Schritt wird untersucht, wie die beim Entwicklungsprozeß entstehenden Produktdaten in einer logisch zentralen Datenbank abgelegt und den nachfolgenden Komponenten im Fertigungsprozeß zur Weiterverarbeitung effizient verfügbar gemacht werden können. Um eine breite Nutzbarkeit und Portabilität der gemeinsamen Produktdatenbank zu gewährleisten, wird sie auf Grundlage des aktuellen Produktdatenmodellstandards STEP (*St*andard for the *E*xchange of *P*roduct Definition Data) realisiert. Der Schwerpunkt der Untersuchungen liegt auf dem in der STEP-Normierung offengelassenen Übergang von der konzeptionellen Ebene zur internen Ebene. Die Abbildung der Produktdaten auf ein geeignetes Datenverwaltungssystem soll an begrenzten vertikalen Ausschnitten aus dem STEP-Modell (z.B. am Form Feature Information Model, FFIM) validiert werden.

Der Betrieb der STEP-Produktdatenbank vollzieht sich in dem verteilten Rechnersystem der HEDAS-Anwendungsumgebung unter Zuhilfenahme des verteilten Datenverwaltungsdienstes DDMS. Die Notwendigkeit des Datenaustausches im verteilten Rechnersystem ergibt sich aus der Ausführungsreihenfolge der HEDAS-Anwendungen entsprechend einer definierten Ablaufstruktur. Die Ablaufstruktur entsteht aufgrund inhaltlicher Abhängigkeiten der Anwendungen, da die produzierten Ergebnisse von Vorgänger-Anwendungen notwendige Arbeitsgrundlage für Nachfolger-Anwendungen sind. Diese kooperative Beziehung zwischen den Anwendungen wird a priori in der Anwendungsdefinition festgelegt, so daß geregelte arbeitsteilige Abläufe entstehen. Mit dem System ActMan (Activity Management) steht ein Dienst bereit, der den Kontroll- und Datenfluß in geregelten arbeitsteiligen Abläufen unterstützt. Dieser Dienst umfaßt das automatische Auslösen von Anwendungen entsprechend einer definierten Ablaufstruktur und das Bereitstellen der zur Ausführung der Anwendungen notwendigen Daten. Die DDMS-Mechanismen zur asynchronen Verwaltung replizierter Daten, erweitert um den spezifischen Aspekt des Ablaufs bzw. des Datenflusses zwischen Anwendungen, bilden die Basis für die Datenbereitstellung.

Neben geregelten arbeitsteiligen Abläufen, deren Ausführung und Kontrolle mit dem Workflow-Management-System ActMan erfolgt, treten in der HEDAS-Anwendungsumgebung auch ungeregelte arbeitsteilige Abläufe auf, die es systemseitig geeignet zu unterstützen gilt. Während geregelte arbeitsteilige Abläufe eine Kooperation auf funktionaler Ebene in Form einer Aufrufreihenfolge von Anwendungen ermöglichen, muß bei ungeregelten Abläufen eine 'Regelung' der verschiedenen Anwendungsinstanzen auf Datenebene vorgenommen werden. Bekannte Mechanismen aus dem Bereich Datenbanksysteme, etwa das Serialisierungskonzept für konkurrierende Transaktionen, sind hierfür im allgemeinen zu restriktiv, da beispielsweise unangemessene Wartezeiten durch exklusive Belegung von Daten mit Sperren (Stichwort: langandauernde Transaktionen) entstehen können. Weiterhin unterstützen Datenbanksysteme mit dem 'Commit' am Ende einer Transaktion nur einen einzigen Freigabemechanismus, der einer endgültigen Freigabe eines Datums gleichkommt. Eine Transaktion hat nach dem Commit keinerlei Kontrolle mehr über ein Datum. Bei einer vorzeitigen Freigabe eines Datums mit einem 'unsicheren' Wert entstehen jedoch Abhängigkeiten zwischen den kooperierenden Anwendungen, die systemseitig verwaltet werden können. Einen Ausweg verspricht hier eine Nuancierung des endgültigen Commits am Ende einer Transaktion durch die Freigabe von Daten mit Prädikaten, die Einschränkungen hinsichtlich der Verwendung oder der Gültigkeit der Daten in kooperierenden Anwendungen machen. Konventionelle Datenbanksysteme bieten für diese Modalitäten keine geeigneten Beschreibungsmöglichkeiten. Im prototypischen System PSA (*P*roblem *S*olving *A*ctivities) werden deshalb Systemdienste bereitgestellt, die eine Verwaltung von Datenprädikaten und Freigabemodalitäten in Einheit mit den Objektdaten selbst ermöglichen. Derzeit werden Untersuchungen über Benachrichtigungen und Verhandlungen zwischen kooperierenden Anwendungen durchgeführt, um im Falle der nachträglichen Änderung tentativ freigegebener Daten systemseitig geeignete Aktualisierungs- und Kompensationsmaßnahmen durchführen zu können.

2.2 Teilbereich 'Anwendungen'

Gemeinsames Ziel der am HEDAS-Bereich 'Anwendungen' beteiligten Teilprojekte ist die Realisierung eines von der Leitebene über die Zellenebene bis hin zur Prozeßebene durchgängigen Anwendungssystems zur Produktionsplanung und -steuerung (siehe Abbildung 2.2).

Der Grundidee eines hierarchischen Planungsansatzes folgend, wird zunächst eine zellenorientierte Produktionsplanung (TP B4) über einen weiten Planungshorizont vorgenommen. Die komponentenorientierte Zellensteuerung (TP D4) hat im folgenden die Aufgabe, aus dem ihr zugewiesenen Auftragspool unter Berücksichtigung der aktuellen technischen Restriktionen real umsetzbare Maschinenbelegungspläne für jeweils einen Fertigungstag zu entwickeln.

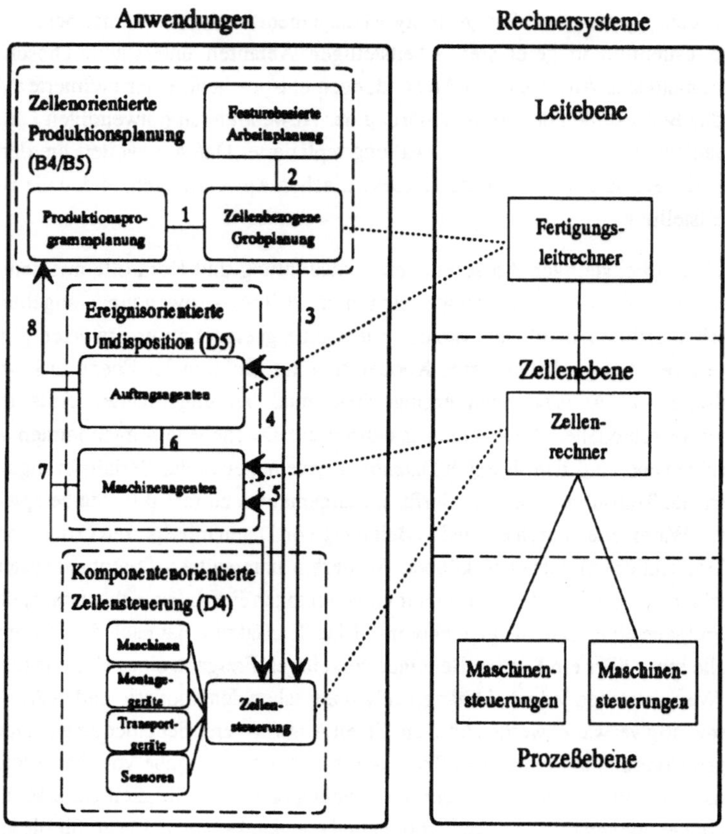

1 Fertigungsaufträge
2 Arbeitspläne
3 Zellenspezifischer Arbeitsgangpool
4 Geplante Maschinenbelegungspläne (periodisch)
5 Störungsmeldung
6 Verhandlungen über Umdispositionsmaßnahmen
7 Aktualisierte Maschinenbelegungspläne
8 Anregung zu Neuaufwurf

Abb. 2.2 Kooperation des Teilbereichs Anwendungen innerhalb von HEDAS

Infolge der Nähe zum Fertigungsprozeß ist hier diese Einschränkung des zeitlichen und räumlichen Planungshorizontes angebracht. Für kurzfristig erforderliche Umplanungen ist die ereignisorientierte Umdisposition (TP D5) zuständig. Reichen zelleninterne Maßnahmen zur Störungsbekämpfung nicht aus, werden auch zellenübergreifende Maßnahmen analysiert. Nur bei extremen Turbulenzen in der Fertigung wird ein kompletter Neuaufwurf der Planung angeregt. Dank der verschiedenen Rückkopplungen zwischen der Grob- und der Feinplanung sowie der

Werkstattsteuerung über die Umplanung beschreibt diese Konzeption ein äußerst flexibles Produktionsplanungs- und -steuerungssystem mit teils zentralen/teils dezentralen Komponenten (vgl. Abbildung 2.3). Gerade diese Regelungsmechanismen werden von konventionellen PPS-Paketen meist vergeblich gefordert.

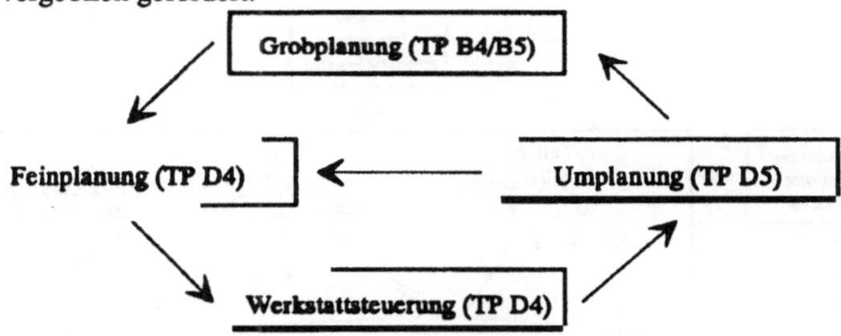

Abb. 2.3 Rückkopplungen innerhalb des Gesamtsystems

2.2.1 Funktionsweise und Schnittstellen der zellenorientierten Produktionsplanung (TP B4)

Der Schwerpunkt in diesem Bereich liegt auf der zellenorientierten Produktionsplanung der in einer Planungsperiode abzuarbeitenden Kundenaufträge. Als Planungsgrundlagen dienen zum einen featurebasierte Arbeitspläne, die mit Hilfe des im FIPS-Projekts realisierten Featureerkenners und Ressourcenplaners automatisiert aus einer geometrisch/topologischen Teilebeschreibung abgeleitet werden können. Zum anderen bilden die für die betrachtete Planungsperiode von der Produktionsprogrammplanung freigegebenen Fertigungsaufträge die Grundlage der zellenorientierten Grobplanung.

Da die hochflexible Einzel- und Kleinserienfertigung mechanischer Bauteile den Anwendungsbereich für HEDAS darstellt, können die klassischen kapazitätsbezogenen Planungsphasen der Produktionsprogrammplanung weitgehend entfallen; bei Fertigung mit "Losgröße 1" entspricht ein extern eingehender Kundenauftrag unmittelbar einem Fertigungsauftrag. Die PPS-Funktion wird deshalb durch eine dialogorientierte Systemschnittstelle simuliert. Die im FIPS-Projekt entstandenen Komponenten FREDOS und SSM liefern für jedes herzustellende Teil aus der im CAD-System erzeugten geometrischen Teilebeschreibung einen halbgeordneten Graphen mit den zur Teileherstellung abzuarbeitenden exakten Arbeitsgängen; die Halbordnung gibt die konstitutiven Reihenfolgebeziehungen zwischen den verschiedenen Arbeitsgängen wieder. Aufgabe der zellenbezogenen Grobplanung ist es somit, die in einer Planungsperiode anfallenden Arbeitsgänge günstig auf die verschiedenen Fertigungszellen zu verteilen. In Abbildung 2.4 ist das zugrundeliegende Planungsmodell im Überblick dargestellt.

Die für die verschiedenen herzustellenden Teile unmittelbar ausführbaren Arbeitsgänge bzw. Features werden in einen zentralen Arbeitsgangpool eingestellt. Aus diesem Pool werden die Arbeitsgänge durch eine heuristische Planungskomponente mit begrenztem Vorausschauhorizont auf Basis des A*-Algorithmus sukzessive auf die Zellen verteilt. Durch die Verplanung eines Arbeitsgangs aus dem Pool werden in der Regel weitere Arbeitsgänge für das betreffende Teil zugänglich und können ihrerseits in den Planungspool aufgenommen werden. Die Planung terminiert, wenn für alle Arbeitsgänge eine Zellzuordnung vorgenommen wurde.

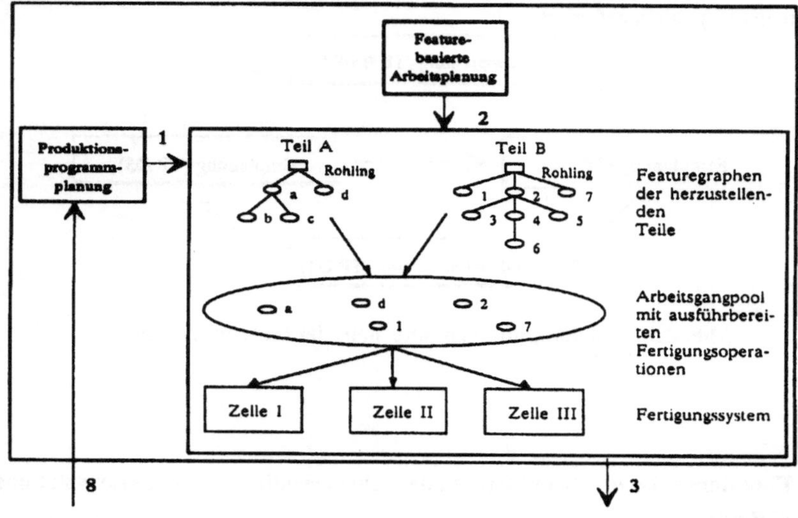

Abb. 2.4 HEDAS-Baustein des TP B4: Zellenorientierte Produktionsplanung

Zur Realisierung des beschriebenen Planungsmodells wurde ein Simulationsbasissystem geschaffen und auf die spezifischen Aufgaben im HEDAS-Anwendungsbereich angepasst. Als Planungsergebnis wird für jede Zelle eine Liste der abzuarbeitenden Arbeitsgänge einschließlich der zu beachtenden Reihenfolgebeziehungen gemäß den Featuregraphen aufgestellt (Pfeil 3 in Abbildung 2.2 bzw. 2.4). Mit Hilfe des Simulationssystems können auch verschiedene Planungsheuristiken untersucht und miteinander verglichen werden.

2.2.2 Funktionsweise und Schnittstellen der komponentenorientierten Zellensteuerung (TP D4)

Das Zellensteuerungskonzept als Schwerpunkt der Beteiligung des Teilprojekts D4 innerhalb des HEDAS-Anwendungsbereichs kann, basierend auf dem Rahmenwerk zur Zellenrechner-software, mit bekannten Softwaretools als asynchrones Prozeßsystem konfiguriert werden. Im Zellenrechner ergeben sich dann aus funktionaler, organisatorischer und ressourcenbezogener Sicht unterschiedliche Module zur:

- Verwaltung des Arbeitsgangpools,
- Materialdisposition,
- Material- und Werkzeugflußorganisation,
- Stationsverwaltung und zur
- Zellenablaufsteuerung.

Diese Module können direkt als abstrakte synchronisierte Prozeßdatentypen dargestellt werden. Zur Ausführung der Aktionen können zusätzliche Objekte definiert werden, auf denen Operationen (z.B. bestellen, Bedarf_ermitteln) ausgeführt werden.

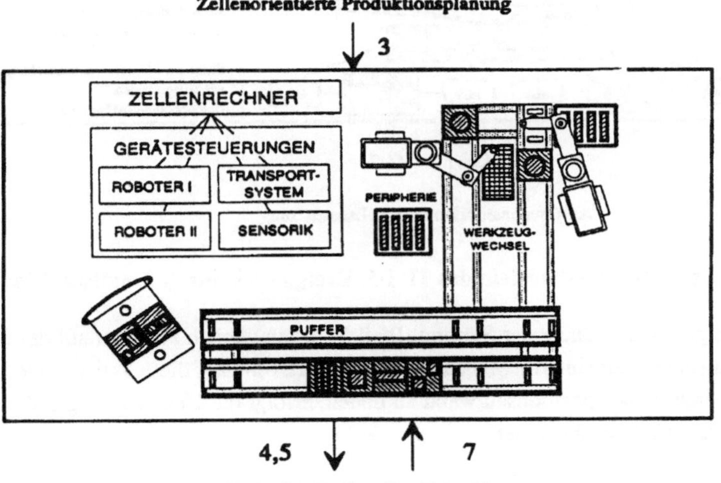

Abb. 2.5 HEDAS-Baustein des TP D4: Komponentenorientierte Zellensteuerung

Von der zellenorientierten Produktionsplanung wird dabei ein zellenspezifischer Arbeitsgangpool bereitgestellt (Pfeil 3 in Abbildung 2.5), den es für die jeweilige Zelle zu disponieren gilt. Die zu ermittelnden Belegungspläne werden periodisch an die ereignisorientierte Umdisposition weitergeleitet (Pfeil 4). Treten bei der Abarbeitung dieses Plans Störungen auf, so müssen sie von den Gerätesteuerungen an den Zellenrechner weitergeleitet werden. Dieser entscheidet auf Grundlage der Störungsursachen, ob eine unmittelbare Behebung möglich ist. Falls nicht, werden die Störungen mit voraussichtlicher Störungsdauer an die Umdisposition gemeldet (Pfeil 5). Die aktualisierten Maschinenbelegungspläne werden nach vollzogener Störungsbewältigung wieder entgegengenommen (Pfeil 7).

2.2.3 Funktionsweise und Schnittstellen der ereignisorientierten Umdisposition (TP D5)

Der Schwerpunkt der Beteiligung des Teilprojekts D5 innerhalb des HEDAS-Anwendungsbereichs liegt auf der ereignisorientierten Umdisposition für das in Abbildung 2.2 dargestellte Gesamtsystem. Als Grundlage und Basismechanismus dient dabei ein achtstufiges Phasenschema zur kurzfristigen Störungsbewältigung in der Produktion. Die ereignisorientierte Umdisposition selbst erfolgt in einer zweistufig-hierarchischen Blackboardarchitektur mit Auftrags- und Maschinenagenten gemäß Abbildung 2.6.

Grundsätzlich erfolgt eine periodische (z.B. tägliche) Meldung der gegenwärtigen Maschinenbelegungspläne von der komponentenorientierten Zellensteuerung (Pfeil 4). Den Anstoß zu einer aktiven Störungsbewältigung bildet eine Störungsmeldung über die betroffenen Maschi-

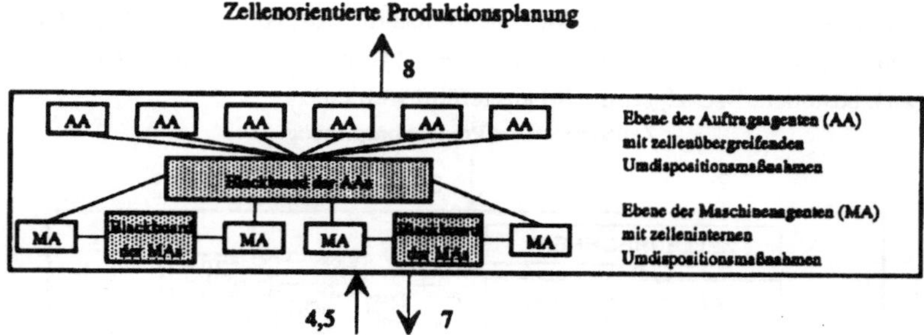

Abb. 2.6 HEDAS-Baustein des TP D5: Ereignisorientierte Umdisposition

nen und die geschätzte Dauer der Störung (Pfeil 5). Dann werden zunächst auf der Ebene der Maschinenagenten zelleninterne Maßnahmen analysiert. Sind auf diese Weise keine Lösungen mit vertretbarem Umdispositionsaufwand zu finden, erfolgt die Untersuchung zellenübergreifender Umdispositionsmaßnahmen.

Bei der Analyse der betriebswirtschaftlichen Konsequenzen der verschiedenen Alternativen muß der Anwender stets im Dialog einbezogen werden, um undurchsichtige Automatismen bei der Lösungsfindung zu vermeiden. Nach der Analyse werden die aktualisierten und an den realen Fertigungszustand angepaßten Maschinenbelegungspläne an die komponentenorientierte Zellensteuerung zurückgemeldet (Pfeil 7). Ist infolge extremer Störungen keine kurzfristige Problemlösung mehr möglich,wird ein Neuaufwurf bei der zellenorientierten Produktionsplanung angeregt (Pfeil 8). Somit kann mit Hilfe der Umplanung sowohl eine Rückkopplung zur Fein- als auch zur Grobplanung geschaffen werden (vgl. auch Abbildung 2.3).

3 Zusammenfassung und Ausblick

Die im Querschnittsprojekt HEDAS untersuchten Fragestellungen bezüglich Aufbau und Betrieb netzgekoppelter Rechensysteme decken ein weites Spektrum der in realen lose gekoppelten Systemen auftretenden Forschungsgebiete ab. Neben harwarenahen Untersuchungen im Kommunikationsbereich werden aus Sicht der Systemsoftware vorrangig die Problembereiche Kommunikationsdienste und Datenverwaltungsarchitekturen bearbeitet. Die dort entwickelten Bausteine können anhand der gemeinsamen Anwendungsarchitektur unmittelbar validiert werden. Bereits begonnene Untersuchungen der Einsetzbarkeit der entwickelten Verfahren in anderen Anwendungsbereichen (Bildverarbeitung, Strömungsmechanik) zeigen den universellen Charakter der eingeschlagenen Forschungsrichtungen auf. Mit der Einrichtung eines weiteren Querschnittsprojekts, MultiMedia, ergibt sich eine weitere Möglichkeit der interdisziplinären Zusammenarbeit der am Sonderforschungsbereich 182 beteiligten Wissenschaftler und Institutionen.

A Formalization of a Hierarchical Model for RISC Processors

Sofiène Tahar
University of Karlsruhe,
Institute of Computer Design (Prof. D. Schmid),
Geb. 20.20, 76128 Karlsruhe, Germany
E-mail: tahar@ira.uka.de

Ramayya Kumar
Forschungszentrum Informatik,
Department of Automation in Circuit Design,
Haid-und-Neu Straße 10-14, 76131 Karlsruhe, Germany
E-mail: kumar@fzi.de

Abstract. Since microprocessors are used in many areas of real-time control, the use of *formal methods* provides an alternative approach for achieving high reliability. In this paper, a methodology based on a hierarchical model of interpreters is presented for formalizing RISCs in general. The abstraction levels used by a designer in the implementation of RISCs, namely the instruction set level, the pipeline stage level, the phase level and the hardware implementation, are mirrored by this hierarchical model. Hence the informal specifications given by the user, at each level of abstraction, can be easily converted into a formal specification, in higher order logic. Such a model is of great use in formal verification and also synthesis using transformational reasoning.

1 Introduction

As computer systems are becoming increasingly complex, the trustworthiness of their design is questionable. Conventional approaches such as simulation and testing have a very high cost to confidence-gain ratio and furthermore, the correctness of the design cannot be guaranteed due to the combinatorial explosion of test vectors. This situation is particularly unsatisfactory in the case of embedded computers for safety-critical systems, such as aircraft, spacecraft and nuclear reactor control etc., where design errors could lead to loss of life and expensive property. Hence, there is a need to produce high-integrity processors that are correct in *all* situations. Although completely reliable systems cannot be guaranteed, the use of *formal methods* is an alternative approach that systematically analyses all cases in a design and specification [Cohn89].

In the recent past several successful microprocessor specification and verification efforts have been performed using formal methods; some using high order logic [Cohn88,Joyc89, Wind90] and others based on functional calculi [Hunt87,SeSr89,SrBi90]. These efforts handle very simplified processors, so-called toy machines, when compared with today's commercially available microprocessors. Furthermore, except the work of Windley [Wind90], these efforts were concerned with a specific microprocessor.

With the aim of advancing the state of technology in microprocessor specification, we set up the following goals:

- To develop a model for specifying classes of microprocessor cores in general
- To formally reason about new aspects in microprocessor design which were not sufficiently addressed by previous efforts (e.g. pipelining)
- To use this model as a framework for verifying and synthesizing large, realistic processors that are not designed just for the purpose of verification or synthesis.

In this paper, we concentrate on the first two goals, the use of the model for verification is reported in [TaKu93b] and its use in synthesis is a subject for future research.

A look at the microprocessor market shows that there are two kinds of design philosophies: CISCs (Complex Instruction Set Computers) and RISCs (Reduced Instruction Set Computers). Our studies of real CISC microprocessors have shown that they have a very unstructured and dirty design including a large control part (approx. 70% of the chip area) encoded in an intricate way. The available CISC processors are therefore not suited for a reasonable use of formal methods. This complexity is also the reason why conventional validation methods such as logic simulation or breadboarding are the major bottleneck in CISC microprocessor design projects [Tred88]. The RISC philosophy is based on the idea of pushing the complexity from the hardware to the software. This characteristic leads to a much simpler design with a higher throughput. In contrast to CISCs, RISC designs are better structured and so more tractable for using formal methods [Bode90]. However, additional problems such as pipelining have to be tackled since they form the core of RISCs.

The purpose of this work is the development of a generic methodology for the hierarchical specification of a large number of cores of realistic RISC processors. Furthermore, we are integrating this specific microprocessor specification tool into a general verification framework [KuSK93]. The methodology is illustrated by means of a RISC example: DLX[1] [HePa90].

The organization of this paper is as follows. Section 2 first shows an existent specification and verification model for CISCs and then describes infomally a novel hierarchical model for RISC cores. Section 3 gives a formalization of the specification of this model. Section 4 presents the formalization of the implementation. Section 5 explores ways of using this model for formal verification and section 6 concludes the paper.

2 The Hierarchical Specification Model

2.1 Related Work

Most related work in microprocessor specification and verification were concerned with microprogrammed processors [Gord83,Hunt87,Joyc89,Wind90]. Some recent work has shown that the specification and verification of microprogrammed processors can be simplified through the insertion of intermediate abstraction levels, so-called Interpreters, (figure 1) between the specification as an instruction set and the implementation EBM (Electronic Block Model) [Joyc89,Wind90,Aror90].

---

1. DLX is an hypothetical RISC core which includes the most common features of many existing RISCs (Intel i860, Motorola M88000, SPARC, MIPS R3000).

An interpreter is a state transition system built up of states and state transition functions as predicates on the corresponding abstract state. The state components of an interpreter is the set of the visible memory elements at a level, e.g. register file, PC and memory at the instruction level. The overall approach of abstraction reflects the way complex microprocessor designs are carried out and designed [Ance86]. The macro level reflects the programmer's view of instruction execution. At the micro level, an instruction is interpreted by executing a sequence of microinstructions. The phase level description decomposes the interpretation of a single microinstruction into the execution of a set of elementary operations. Using the interpreter model for formal verification, it is sufficient to prove that each level correctly implements the next abstraction level instead of verifying that each instruction is correctly implemented by the EBM at the RT-level. Through these appropriate intermediate levels, long and complex proofs are replaced by many more routine proofs, since the gap between the neighbouring levels is small. For example, one has only to prove that the EBM implements 4 to 6 phases instead of directly implying the whole instruction set. As mentioned earlier, this model is also restricted to very simplified processors and is not usable for real CISC processors.

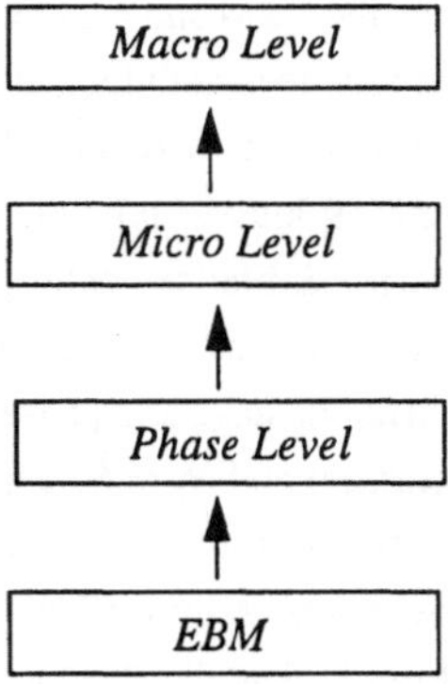

Figure 1: CISC Interpreter Model

The way RISC designs are carried out and structured is different from that of CISCs, e.g. because of the hardwired control the micro level does not exist more. The mentioned structuring of the specification using this interpreter model is hence unsuitable and we have to look for another specification model for RISC cores.

2.2 A Specification Model for RISC Cores

A RISC processor executes every instruction in a number of physical steps, so-called pipeline stages (e.g. IF, ID, EX, WB) [HePa90]. The duration of a pipeline stage instruction corresponds to one machine clock period. A stage instruction is the set of transfers, which occur during the corresponding pipeline segment. Using a multiple phase non-overlapping clock, each stage instruction is partitioned into a number of clock phase instructions. A phase instruction of a specific stage is a part of the transfer that occurs during that clock phase.

The instructions of the RISC cores are simple, elementary and less encoded. Their complexity can be compared to that of CISC microinstructions. The pipeline stages are also comparable to CISC phases, since their number is limited by the pipeline depth, and is constant for almost all instructions. The RISC phases can be compared to CISC instances [Ance86]. Using this analogy, a naive model for RISCs, similar to that of CISCs, could be given. However, the RISC phase instructions are stage dependent and the stage instructions differ from one instruction to another. If such a model is used for verification, the number of verification steps between the EBM and the phase level is $N_i * n_s * n_p$, where N_i, n_s, n_p are the number of instructions, pipeline stages and phases, respectively. Since the complexity of the proof between the EBM and the next abstraction level is the largest [Cohn89], the use of a naive interpreter model does not yield any advantages.

As a first solution to reduce this number, we exploit the notion of instruction classes [Moto88,SunM89,Inte89,HePa90]. An instruction class intuitively corresponds to the set of instructions with similar semantics, e.g. ALU, FLP, LOAD, CONTROL. The stage and phase instructions can now be parameterized in accordance to the class abstraction. Thus the total number of different stage and phase level instructions can be reduced to $N_s = N_c * n_s$ (N_c is the number of classes) and $N_p = N_c * n_s * n_p$, respectively. The class level is therefore introduced as the top level of our interpreter model.

Real RISC cores show further regularities which can be incorporated into our interpreter model. A closer look at the stage level shows that some stage instructions are common to more than one class (e.g. the IF-stage instruction is shared by all classes), and additionally some classes do not require the full pipeline depth (e.g. only 2 stages for CONTROL). This implies that the number of different possible stage instructions N_s is much less then $N_c * n_s$. Furthermore, examining the phase level of realistic RISCs, it can be seen that not all stage operations are broken down into phases. Such phase level instructions can be modelled by letting the state of the interpreter at the phase level unchanged. Incorporating this observation into our model yields N_p (the number of different possible phase instructions) as $N_p \ll N_s * n_p$.

Table 1 shows the pipeline structure of DLX. "$\leftarrow$" represents that the stage transfer is not broken down into phase transfers. "$\xleftarrow[\phi_1]{}$", "$\xleftarrow[\phi_2]{}$" represent that the transfers take place in phase 1, 2, respectively. Using this DLX architecture ($N_i = 51$, $n_s = 5$, $n_p = 2$), a naive calculation would have yielded $51 * 5 * 2 = 510$ different phase operations instead of 16.

	ALU	LOAD	STORE	CONTROL
IF	IR $\leftarrow$ Mem[PC] PC $\leftarrow$ PC+4	IR $\leftarrow$ Mem[PC] PC $\leftarrow$ PC+4	IR $\leftarrow$ Mem[PC] PC $\leftarrow$ PC+4	IR $\leftarrow$ Mem[PC] PC $\leftarrow$ PC+4
ID	A $\xleftarrow[\phi_2]{}$ RF[rs1] B $\xleftarrow[\phi_2]{}$ RF[rs2] IR1 $\leftarrow$ IR	A $\xleftarrow[\phi_2]{}$ RF[rs1] B $\xleftarrow[\phi_2]{}$ RF[rs2] IR1 $\leftarrow$ IR	A $\xleftarrow[\phi_2]{}$ RF[rs1] B $\xleftarrow[\phi_2]{}$ RF[rs2] IR1 $\leftarrow$ IR	BTA $\xleftarrow[\phi_1]{}$ f (PC) PC $\xleftarrow[\phi_2]{}$ BTA
EX	ALUout $\leftarrow$ A op B or ALUout $\leftarrow$ A op (IR1)	MAR $\leftarrow$ A+(IR1)	MAR $\leftarrow$ A+(IR1) SMDR $\leftarrow$ B	
MEM	ALUout1 $\leftarrow$ ALUout	LMDR $\leftarrow$ Mem[MAR]	Mem[MAR] $\leftarrow$ SMDR	
WB	RF[rd] $\xleftarrow[\phi_1]{}$ ALUout1	RF[rd] $\xleftarrow[\phi_1]{}$ LMDR		

Table 1: DLX Pipeline Structure

The overall hierarchical model yielded is given in figure 2, where the arrow between the levels means that the upper level specification is an abstraction of the next lower one. Through this hierarchical structuring of the specification steps, we have closed the big gap between the EBM and the architecture top level. Each abstraction level can be specified independently and helps the designer in successively refining the design.

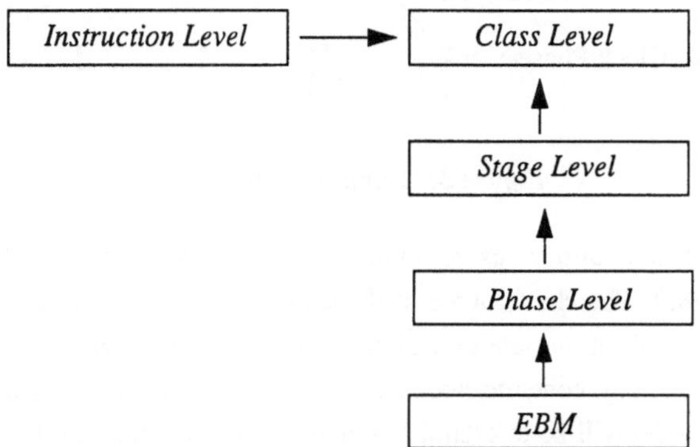

Figure 2: RISC Interpreter Model

Summarizing the overall specification of the different abstraction levels, we have to specify:

- the instruction level from the instruction set of the RISC core,
- the class level from the instruction set of the RISC core,
- the stage level from the pipeline architecture,
- the phase level from the pipeline architecture and
- a formal implementation of EBM.

3 Formal Specification

Before we formally specify the interpreters at each level of abstraction, we shall briefly explain the concept of temporal abstraction [Melh88].

3.1 Temporal Abstraction

Formal specifications that describe the behaviours of two interpreters, which use different notions of discrete time, are related by temporal abstraction. This type of abstraction is used when the implementation gives more detail about how a device behaves over time, than its abstract specification does. The class and the instruction level have the same time granularity, which corresponds to the execution of each individual RISC instruction. The stage level granularity is that of a clock cycle and the phase level granularity corresponds to the phases of the clock (figure 3).

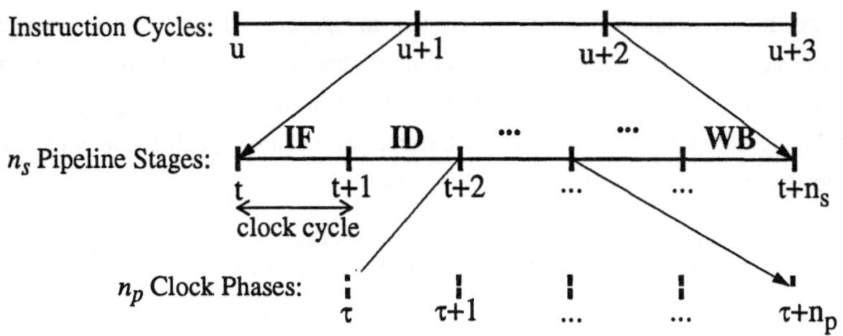

Figure 3: Temporal Abstraction

Temporal abstraction allows us to hide the unnecessary details at higher levels of abstractions [Melh88]. The chief source of difficulty in the formal definition of this timing relationship is that a unit of discrete time at the abstract level time scales does not correspond to discrete time points at the concrete clock time scales. A fundamental step in the formalization of the interpreter model will be to establish a mathematical relationship between the abstract time scales and the next concrete time scale. In a pipelined execution this mapping function is not linear, since the state changes at the abstract level can take place at some time between the two discrete end-points of its time interval. For example specifying an ADD-instruction at the instruction level as follows:

$$ADD\_Pred\,(...) := \forall \mathbf{u}: Inst\_cycle.$$
$$RF(\mathbf{u}+1)[rd(\mathbf{u})] = RF(\mathbf{u})[rs1(\mathbf{u})] + RF(\mathbf{u})[rs2(\mathbf{u})]$$ [2]

is not accurate, since reading the register file *RF* is done at the ID-stage and the addresses are computed during the IF-stage. These stages occur at some time between u and $u+1$, which depends upon the implementation. Referring to table 1, the exact specification of the ADD-instruction, using the more concrete time granularity, is given below:

$$ADD\_Pred\,(...) := \forall \mathbf{t}: Clk\_cycle.$$
$$RF\,(\mathbf{t}+5)[rd(\mathbf{t})] = RF(\mathbf{t}+1)[rs1(\mathbf{t})] + RF(\mathbf{t}+1)[rs2(\mathbf{t})]$$

This motivates us to define a time abstraction function which takes an implementation dependent context and converts the abstract time to a more concrete one. For example, reading during the IF-stage yields -"$f\,([IF, read], u) = t$"- and reading during the ID-stage yields -"$f\,([ID, read], u) = t+1$"-. The context parameter is a tuple comprising of the corresponding stage identifier and a read/write information. Hence, the formal specification of the ADD-instruction at the instruction level (using instruction cycle time units) should take the context parameters also into consideration. The insertion of the time abstraction function and context parameters allows the specifications to be abstract and implementation independent. A detailed

2. RF is the register file and rd, rs1, rs2 are the destination and source addresses of some registers. These addresses correspond to fields of the actual instruction word, which is addressed by the PC

description of the definition of this time abstraction function, as well as a possible implementation of it can be found in [TaKu93a].

At a lower level, i.e. between the stage and the phase levels, we have the same problem since state transitions can occur at time points within the clock cycle interval at some specific phases. Hence, a time abstraction function can be defined in a similar manner between the stage and the phase levels and corresponding context parameters will be included in the formal specification of the stage level.

3.2 Instruction Level Specification

The instruction semantics given in the instruction set manual of a specific processor implicitly involve time. For example the semantic of an ADD-instruction defined as a state transition occurring in an instruction cycle is:

$$ADD := RF[rd] \leftarrow RF[rs1] + RF[rs2]$$

Given that u is a unit for an instruction cycle, f the time abstraction function and $c1$-$c3$ are contexts, the semantic of the ADD-instruction involving time can be described formally by means of a predicate as follows:

$$\begin{aligned}&ADD\_Pred\,(PC, I\text{-}MEM, RF, D\text{-}MEM) :=\\&\forall u{:}\ Inst\_cycle.\\&\exists\, c1, c2, c3{:}Context.\\&let\ (rs1 = [I\text{-}MEM(PC)]_{25..21} \wedge rs2 = [I\text{-}MEM(PC)]_{22..16} \wedge rd = [I\text{-}MEM(PC)]_{15..11})\ in\\&RF(f(c1,u+1))\,[rd(f(c2,u))] = (RF(f(c3,u))\,[rs1(f(c2,u))]) + (RF(f(c3,u))\,[rs2(f(c2,u))])\end{aligned}$$

Depending on the implemented pipeline architecture, the context parameters used in the formal specification are directly derived from the pipeline structure (table 1), e.g. since the register file is *read* at the *ID-stage* the time abstraction function f is applied using the context parameter $c3 = [ID;read]$.

3.3 Class Level Specification

The class level is only an abstraction of the semantics of the architectural instructions. The same state components, the same time granularity and the same context parameters are used for the description of the state transitions at the instruction and class levels. The formal specification is almost the same as that of the instruction level except that a generalized class parameter instead of a specific operator or function is introduced. For example, *op* represents all ALU-operators. Using the results of the discussion given above, the semantics for the ALU-class can be specified by the following predicate:

$$\begin{aligned}&ALU\_Pred\,(PC, I\text{-}MEM, RF, D\text{-}MEM) :=\\&\forall u{:}\ Inst\_cycle.\\&\exists\, c1, c2, c3{:}Context.\\&let\ (rs1 = [I\text{-}MEM(PC)]_{25..21} \wedge rs2 = [I\text{-}MEM(PC)]_{22..16} \wedge rd = [I\text{-}MEM(PC)]_{15..11})\ in\\&RF(f(c1,u+1))\,[rd(f(c2,u))] = (RF(f(c3,u))\,[rs1(f(c2,u))])\ \mathbf{op}\ (RF(f(c3,u))\,[rs2(f(c2,u))])\end{aligned}$$

3.4 Stage Level Specification

Individual stage instructions are specified as predicates on the visible states at this level. The stage predicates are built up of conjunctions of elementary state transitions, that implement the corresponding semantic. These state transitions can be directly read from the pipeline architecture (table 1) and encoded formally to build the specification predicate of the corresponding stage instruction. For example, from the ID-row and the class columns ALU, LOAD and STORE, a common ID-stage instruction can be directly specified by the following predicate, where g is the time abstraction function between the stage and the phase levels and $c1$-$c5$ are register related context variables:

$$
\begin{aligned}
&ID_A\_Pred\,(A, B, RF, IR, IR1) := \\
&\quad \forall t{:}Clk\_cycle. \\
&\quad\quad \exists\, c1, c2, c3, c4, c5{:}Context. \\
&\quad\quad\quad let\ (rs1 = [IR]_{25..21} \wedge rs2 = [IR]_{22..16})\ in \\
&\quad\quad\quad\quad A(g(c1,t+1)) = RF(g(c2,t))\,[rs1(g(c3,t))] \wedge \\
&\quad\quad\quad\quad B(g(c4,t+1)) = RF(g(c2,t))\,[rs2(g(c3,t))] \wedge \\
&\quad\quad\quad\quad IR1(g(c5,t+1)) = IR(g(c3,t))
\end{aligned}
$$

The context parameters used here are again directly derived from the implemented pipeline architecture (table 1), e.g. the B-register is *written* in *phase* 2, and hence the time abstraction function g is applied using the context parameter $c4 = [Ph2;write]$.

3.5 Phase Level Specification

Using a multiphase non-overlapping clock, we associate each phase of the clock with an operation on the phase interpreter. The phase instructions define the state transition that occurs during each phase of the clock which corresponds to the finest time granularity. Hence no time abstraction function is required for phase level specifications. Individual phase instructions are specified using predicates on the visible states at this level. In a manner similar to stage instructions, the state transitions can be directly read from the pipeline architecture (table 1) and encoded formally. For phase transitions which are not explicitly marked in the pipeline architecture, e.g. between IR and IR1-register in the ID-stage, we simply let the state values, which are read, unchanged until the last phase. From the ID-row and the class columns ALU, LOAD and STORE, the two ID-phase instructions can be directly specified with the following predicates:

$$
\begin{aligned}
&\phi_1 ID_A\_Pred\,(A, B, RF, IR, IR1) := \\
&\quad \forall \tau{:}Clk\_phase. \\
&\quad\quad IR(\tau+1) = IR(\tau)
\end{aligned}
$$

$$
\begin{aligned}
&\phi_2 ID_A\_Pred\,(A, B, RF, IR, IR1) := \\
&\quad \forall \tau{:}Clk\_phase. \\
&\quad\quad let\ (rs1 = [IR]_{25..21} \wedge rs2 = [IR]_{22..16})\ in \\
&\quad\quad\quad A(\tau+1) = RF(\tau)[rs1(\tau)] \wedge \\
&\quad\quad\quad B(\tau+1) = RF(\tau)[rs2(\tau)] \wedge \\
&\quad\quad\quad IR1(\tau+1) = IR(\tau)
\end{aligned}
$$

4 Implementation

The EBM does not correspond to an interpreter, but is the structure of the circuit. We use a predicate to describe each of the components of the EBM and compose their behaviour using conjunctions [HaDa86]. The input/output lines are universally quantified and the internal lines of the circuit are modelled using existential quantification. The EBM is in general structured hierarchically at the RT-level. At the top most level of this hierarchy, the EBM is specified formally by a conjunction of predicates for the datapath, the control unit, the instruction and data memory (see figure 4). The datapath and the control unit are themselves compositions of simpler blocks, e.g. register file, ALU, multiplexers, pipeline latches, etc., which may again be conjunctions of lower building blocks.

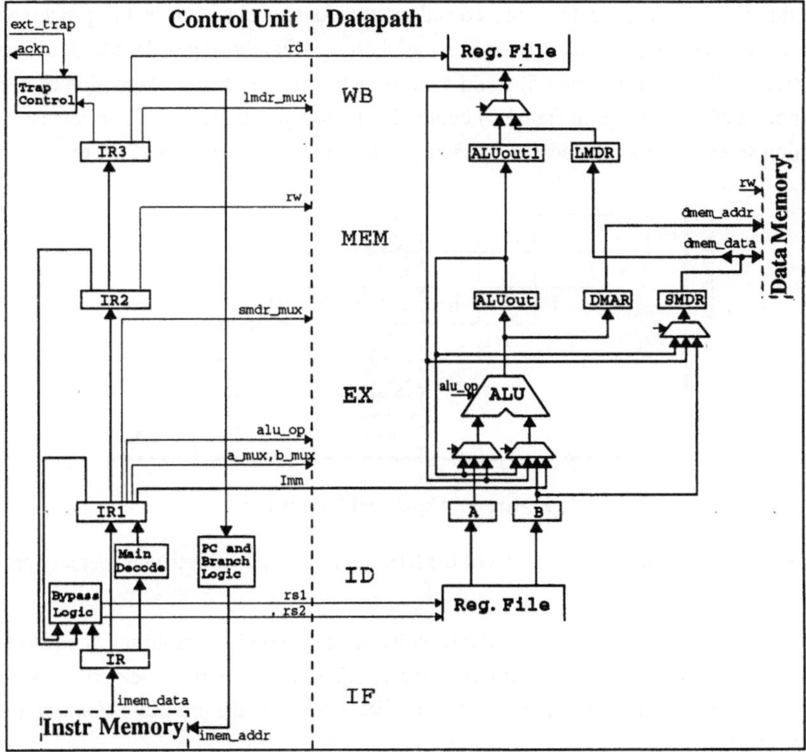

Figure 4: Electronic Block Model of DLX (simplified)

The formal implementation of the EBM looks as follows:

EBM *(PC, I_MEM, RF, D_MEM, A, B, ALUout, ALUout1, DMAR, SMDR, LMDR, IR, IR1, IR2, IR3, BTA, IAR, ext_trap, ackn, clk1, clk2) :=*

$\exists$ *rs1, rs2, rd, Imm, a_mux, b_mux, alu_op, smdr_mux, lmdr_mux, imem_addr, imem_data, dmem_addr, dmem_data, rw.*

DataPath *(RF, A, B, ALUout, ALUout1, DMAR, SMDR, LMDR, dmem_addr, dmem_data, rs1, rs2, rd, Imm, a_mux, b_mux, alu_op, smdr_mux, lmdr_mux, clk1, clk2)* $\wedge$

Control_Unit (*PC, IR, IR1, IR2, IR3, BTA, IAR, ext_trap, ackn, rw, imem_addr, imem_data, rs1, rs2, rd, Imm, a_mux, b_mux, alu_op, smdr_mux, lmdr_mux, clk1, clk2*) ∧

Instr_Memory (*I_MEM, imem_addr, imem_data, clk2*) ∧

Data_Memory (*D_MEM, dmem_addr, dmem_data, rw, clk2*)

5 Use of the Model for Formal Verification

Verification is the process of formally proving the equivalence between two mathematical models of a system or proving some of its properties [Gupta92]. The aim of the formal verification of RISC cores is to show that the instruction set is executed correctly by the EBM, taking the pipelined architecture into consideration. At any clock cycle the processor can potentially be executing n_s instructions in parallel, in n_s different stages. Due to this, these n_s stages (see hatched box in figure 5) could disturb each other, so that the execution of a single instruction (see shaded box in figure 5) could also be hampered. Thus the correctness of the instruction semantics should necessarily incorporate the temporal aspects of the execution.

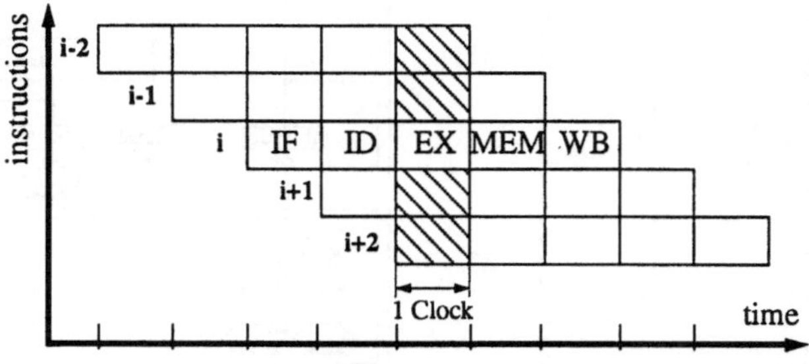

Figure 5: Pipelined Execution

A possible approach for verification of the RISC core is to perform the correctness proof in two steps as follows:

1. given the implementation, which includes some conflict resolution hardware, and assuming some software conditions of the actual architecture (represented by *SW_Ass*), we can prove that none of the possible conflicts occur, i.e. the predicate *Conflict_Pred* is never true:

$$SW\_Ass,\ EBM \quad \vdash \neg Conflict\_Pred$$

2. assuming that no conflicts occur during the execution of any instruction and given the implementation and the specification of the interpreter levels, the EBM implements each single instruction correctly:

$$\neg Conflict\_Pred \vdash EBM \Rightarrow Instruction\ Level$$

Step1 consists mainly in the formal specification of the different conflicts, also called hazards. There are three kinds of hazards, namely structural, data and control hazards. The specification of these hazards is closely related to our hierarchical model since each hazard is relevant only at a specific abstraction level of our model.

In proving step2 we can consider a sequential execution of the instruction. Using our interpreter model (figure 2), it can be partitioned hierarchically as follows:

EBM $\Rightarrow$ *Phase Level* (N_p)	(2.1): Implying all N_p phase instructions from EBM.
Phase Level (N_p) $\Rightarrow$ *Stage Level* (N_s)	(2.2): Implying all N_s stage instructions from the phase instructions.
Stage Level (N_s) $\Rightarrow$ *Class Level* (N_c)	(2.3): Implying all N_c class instructions from the stage instructions.

The steps (2.1), (2.2) and (2.3) prove the correctness of all instruction classes. Through this hierarchical structuring of the verification steps, we have closed the big gap between the EBM and the architecture top level. Step (2.1) is the hardest one, since the EBM is a complex structural description and the phase instructions are behavioural ones. However, the proofs are quite similar in nature and a strategy can therefore be evolved. Steps (2.2) and (2.3) are relatively straightforward. The correctness of the architectural instructions can then be shown by simple instantiation of the previous steps (2.1, 2.2 and 2.3) for each particular instruction.

For completeness, we can prove furthermore the statement that the instruction classes abstract all N_i instructions of the architecture:

Instruction Level (N_i) $\Rightarrow$ *Class Level* (N_c) (2.4)

A detailed description of the verification tasks of step1 and step2 is reported in [TaKu93b]. An implementation of step2 can be found in [TaKu93a].

6 Conclusions and Future Work

In this paper we have described a hierarchical interpreter model which is applicable for RISCs in general. This model is a modification of the one given by Anceau [Ance86] for designing microprogrammed processors and closely reflects the design hierarchy which is used for designing RISCs. Because of the parallelism in the execution of each instruction, resulting from the pipelined architecture of the RISC, a concept of temporal abstraction has been adopted. The insertion of temporal abstraction and context parameters into the formal specifications makes them abstract and implementation independent. Hence, the hierarchical model can be used by computer architecture designers for successively refining and specifying the design. Further, the hierarchy present in the model can be exploited, to split the overall verification task into a number of manageable subtasks, that help the designers formally verifying their designs during the design phase itself.

We have implemented the given model in a higher order theorem proving environment and we are currently using it for formal verification purposes [TaKu93a]. We have also implemented the hardware for the DLX in a commercial VLSI design environment and are using it as one of the benchmarks for our methodology. In our future work, we shall investigate the use of this model for formal synthesis.

7 References

Ance86 Anceau, F.: The Architecture of Microprocessors; Addison-Wesley Publishing Company, 1986

Aror90 Arora, T.: The Formal Verification of the VIPER Microprocessor: EBM to Phase, Phase to Microcode Level; Master's thesis, University of California, Davis, 1990.

Bode 90 Bode, A.: RISC-Architekturen; BI-Wiss.-Verlag; Mannheim; 1990.

Cohn88 Cohn, A.: A Proof of the Viper Microprocessor: The First Level; In: VLSI Specification, Verification and Synthesis, Eds. G. Birtwistle and P.A. Subrahmanyam, Kluwer, 1988.

Cohn89 Cohn, A.: The Notion of Proof in Hardware Verification; Journal of Automated Reasoning, Vol. 5, pp. 127-139, 1989.

Gord83 Gordon, M.: Proving a Computer Correct; Technical Report No. 42, Computer Laboratory, University of Cambridge, 1983.

Gupt92 Gupta, A.: Formal Hardware Verification Methods: A Survey; Journal of Formal Methods in System Design, No. 1, pp. 151-238, 1992.

HaDa86 Hanna, K., Daeche, N.: Specification and Verification of Digital Systems Using Higher-Order Predicate Logic; IEE Proc. Pt. E, Vol. 133, No. 3, September 1986, pp. 242-254.

HePa90 Hennessy, J.L., Patterson, D.A.: Computer Architecture A Quantitative Approach; Morgan Kaufmann Publishers, Inc. San Mateo, California, 1990.

Hunt87 Hunt, W.: The Mechanical Verification of a Microprocessor Design; In: From HDL Description to Guaranteed Correct Circuit Designs, Ed. D. Borrione, North-Holland, 1987.

Inte89 INTEL: i860 64-Bit Microprocessor Programmer's Reference Manual; 1989.

Joyc89 Joyce, J.: Multi-Level Verification of Microprocessor-Based Systems; PhD thesis, Cambridge University, December 1989.

KuSK93 Kumar, R., Schneider, K., Kropf, Th.: Structuring and Automating Hardware Proofs in a Higher-Order Theorem-Proving Environment; Journal of Formal Methods in System Design, Vol. 2, pp. 165-230, 1993.

Melh88 Melham, Th.: Abstraction Mechanisms for Hardware Verification; In: VLSI Specification, Verification and Synthesis, Eds. G. Birtwistle and P. A. Subrahmanyam, Kluwer, 1988.

Moto88 MOTOROLA: MC88100 RISC Microprocessor User's Manual; 1988.

SeSr89 Sekar, R., Srivas, M.: Formal Verification of a Microprocessor Using Equational Techniques; In: Current Trends in Hardware Verification and Automated Theorem Proving, Eds. G. Birtwistle and P.A. Subrahmanyam, Springer, 1989.

SrBi90 Srivas, M., Bickford, M.: Verification of a Pipelined Microprocessor Using Clio; In: Hardware Specification, Verification and Synthesis: Mathematical Aspects, Eds. M. Leeser and G. Brown, Springer, 1990.

SunM89 Sun Microsystems, Inc., USA: The SPARC Architecture Manual; Version 8, Part No. 800-1399-09, August 1989.

TaKu93a Tahar, S., Kumar, R.: Implementing a Methodology for Formally Verifying RISC Processors in HOL; to appear in Proc. of the 1993 International Meeting on Higher Order Logic Theorem Proving and its Applications, Vancouver, Canada, August, 1993.

TaKu93b Tahar, S., Kumar, R.: Towards a Methodology for the Formal Hierarchical Verification of RISC Processors; to appear in Proc. of the 1993 International Conference on Computer Design, Cambridge, Massachusetts, October, 1993.

Tred88 Tredemick, N.: Experiences in Commercial VLSI Microprocessor Design; Microprocessors and Microsystems, Vol. 12, no. 8, October 1988.

Wind90 Windley, P.: The Formal Verification of Generic Interpreters; PhD thesis, University of California, Davis, Division of Computer Science, July 1990. Research Report CSE-90-22.

Ein neuer Ansatz für den integrierten Entwurf komplexer heterogener Systeme

Stefan Kahlert, Dieter Monjau
TU Chemnitz-Zwickau, Fachbereich Informatik
Straße der Nationen 62, 09111 Chemnitz
Email: Stefan.Kahlert@informatik.tu-chemnitz.de

Abstract. Heute verbreitete Hardwarebeschreibungs- oder Programmiersprachen wie VHDL oder C sind als alleinige Beschreibungsmittel für den Entwurfsprozeß, ausgehend von einer Spezifikation auf der Systemebene, der höchsten Abstraktionsebene im Y-Diagramm, ungeeignet. Die Komplexität und Heterogenität moderner rechnerbasierter Systeme, die aus Hardware in unterschiedlichen Technologien sowie Software bzw. Firmware bestehen, erfordern neue Vorgehensweisen bei der Spezifikation, dem Entwurf und der Analyse solcher Systeme als Ganzes bzw. ihrer Teilsysteme. Dafür wird eine Methodik vorgestellt. Auf der Basis eines Modells für die Systembeschreibung in den verschiedenen Entwurfsphasen erfolgt die Nutzung bzw. Integration geeigneter CASE- und EDA-Werkzeuge. Dabei werden vorrangig grafische Beschreibungsmittel sowie die Sprachen SDL, VHDL und C verwendet. Die Methodik wird an einem Beispiel illustriert.

1 Einleitung

Moderne rechnerbasierte Systeme sind komplexe und häufig in Echtzeit arbeitende Systeme. Sie bestehen aus miteinander verbundenen individuellen Teilsystemen.

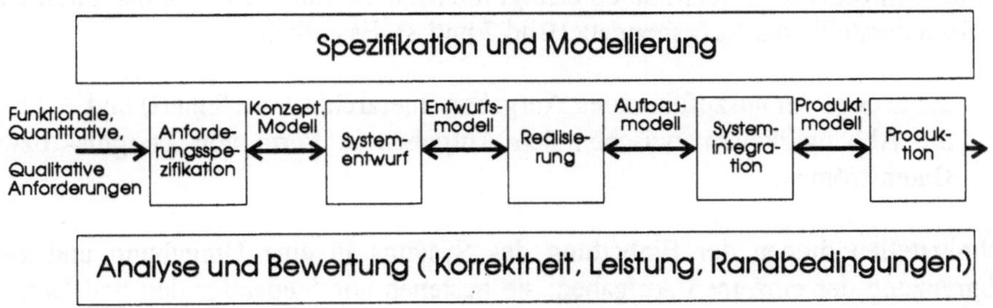

Bild 1: Funktionsmodell des Systementwurfs

Ihre Bausteine sind heterogen; sie umfassen Hardware mit unterschiedlichen Technologien wie Elektronik, Mechanik, Elektromechanik bzw. Optoelektronik und Software bzw. Firmware. Realisierungsformen elektronischer Bausteine können Standardkomponenten, programmierbare Bausteine, ASICs oder PCBs sein. Einige typische Einsatzgebiete sind Telekommunikationssysteme, Prozeßsteuerungen und Automatisierungssysteme. Die Komplexität bzw. Heterogenität erfordert neue

Methoden für die Spezifikation, den Entwurf und die Analyse solcher Systeme als Ganzes und ihrer Teilsysteme. Für spezielle Teilsysteme, die entweder aus hochintegrierten elektronischen Bausteinen oder aus Software bestehen, existiert bereits eine große Anzahl adäquater Methoden und Werkzeuge. Das Funktionsmodell des Systementwurfs (Bild 1) beinhaltet die Durchgängigkeit aller Phasen von der Anforderungsspezifikation bis zur Produktion [JaLa92]. Es schließt die Integration der für die einzelnen Phasen zur Verfügung stehenden Methoden und Werkzeuge ein. Für gemischte Hardware/Software-Systeme bedeutet das die Integration von CASE- und EDA-Werkzeugen. Dafür wird in diesem Beitrag eine Methodik vorgestellt.

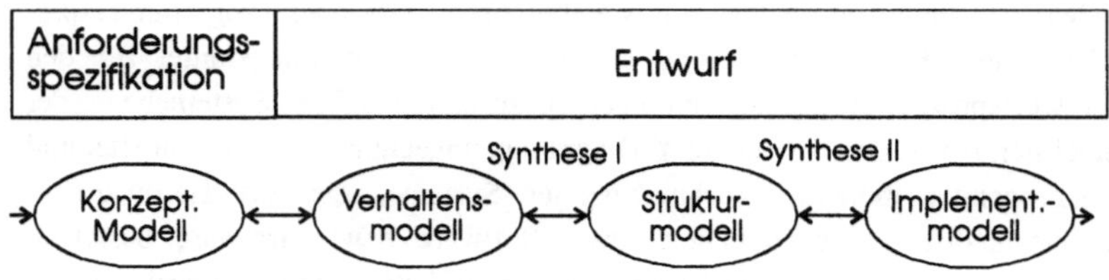

Bild 2: Modelle im Systementwurf

Wir beginnen mit der Beschreibung des Modells, das einem System in den Phasen der Anforderungsspezifikation und des Systementwurfs zugrunde gelegt wird. Es folgt eine Übersicht zu den verwendeten Werkzeugen und zur methodischen Vorgehensweise. Danach wird der Entwurf einer Vergasersteuerung als Beispiel für die Anwendung dieser Methodik dargestellt.

2 Systemmodellierung

Es werden die Phasen Anforderungsspezifikation und Entwurf betrachtet (Bild 2). Bei der Anforderungsspezifikation erfolgt die Modellierung des Systems durch ein grafisch darstellbares Aufgabennetz (Bild 7 und 8). Es enthält

- die Menge der auszuführenden Aufgaben (hierarchisch verfeinert) und
- die Abhängigkeiten zwischen den Aufgaben in Form von Ereignis- bzw. Datenströmen.

Schnittstellen dienen der Einbettung des Systems in eine Umgebung und zur Abgrenzung der einzelnen Aufgaben; sie bestehen aus Steuersignalen und Daten. Die Steuersignale triggern die Ausführung der Aufgaben.

Das Modell für die Systembeschreibung in der Entwurfsphase basiert auf nebenläufigen kommunizierenden Prozessen. Die Kommunikation erfolgt über Nachrichten. Nachrichten synchronisieren Prozesse, übertragen Daten und lösen Operationen aus. Prozesse sind erweiterte FSMs (Finite State Machines). Diese erweiterten endlichen Automaten besitzen jeweils einen lokalen Speicher und Queues zu Pufferung eingehender Signale, sie nehmen verschiedene Zustände ein, empfangen bzw. senden Nachrichten und führen Operationen aus.

Die Modellierung erfolgt in drei Sichten, denen jeweils ein Modell zugeordnet ist, die beim Entwurf nacheinander durchlaufen werden; dabei erfolgt eine Verringerung der Abstraktion (Bild2). Der Übergang von dem bei der Anforderungsspezifikation erzeugten konzeptuellen Modell zu dem Verhaltensmodell erfolgt dadurch, daß für jede Aufgabe ein Prozeß eingeführt wird und die Steuersignale bzw. Daten, die in Aufgaben eingehen bzw. von ihnen ausgehen, durch Nachrichten zwischen Prozessen modelliert werden. Jedem Prozeß wird eine Queue zugeordnet, in der die eingehenden Nachrichten gepuffert werden. Beim Entwurf erfolgt im Verhaltensmodell die Einführung von Zuständen und die Formulierung zustands- bzw. nachrichtenabhängiger Aktionsfolgen.

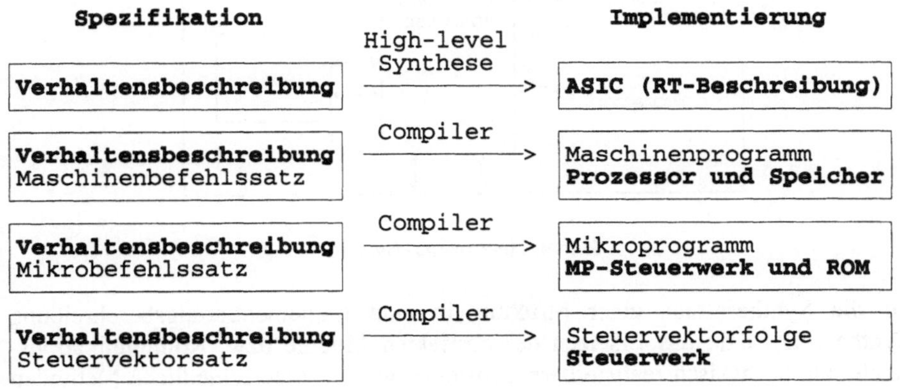

Bild 3: Arten der Implementierung der Module

Das Strukturmodell beschreibt eine Systemstruktur. Es besteht aus abstrakten Modulen, in denen Prozesse zusammengefaßt sind, und abstrakten Kommunikationskanälen für den Nachrichtenaustausch zwischen den Modulen. Das Strukturmodell beschreibt eine Systemarchitektur durch die Strukturierung in Module (Teilsysteme) und Kommunikationskanäle. Letztere führen notwendige Datenkonvertierungen beim Austausch aus. Die Module stellen Entwurfseinheiten mit einem spezifizierten Verhalten dar. Ihre Beschreibung ist ausführbar. Zu ihrer Implementierung (z.B. als Hardware oder Software) gibt es jedoch noch keine Festlegungen. Die Verhaltensbeschreibungen der Module können in unterschiedlichen Formen vorliegen. Um eine Austauschbarkeit von Modulen bei der Untersuchung von Entwurfsalternativen bzw. bei der Wiederverwendung vorhandener Module zu ermöglichen, müssen die Module gut spezifizierte Schnittstellen besitzen.

Das Implementierungsmodell (= Entwurfsmodell) enthält für die Module und ihre Schnittstellen sowie für die Kommunikationspfade eine Beschreibung der physischen Realisierung. Sie ist in jedem Fall Hardware, gegebenenfalls mit einer in einen Speicher "eingebetteten" Software in Form eines Maschinen- oder Mikroprogrammes bei einer Software- oder Firmwareimplementierung. Für die Kommunikationspfade kommen prinzipiell alle seriell oder parallel bzw. gepuffert oder ungepuffert arbeitenden Verbindungsstrukturen infrage. Die Beschreibung der Module bzw. Kommunikationspfade kann relativ abstrakt sein, z.B. eine Strukturbeschreibung auf der RT-Ebene. Aus ihr muß aber die Realisierung bis zum Layout (bei elektronischen Schaltungen) ableitbar sein. Während des Entwurfsvorganges erfolgt der Übergang von der Verhaltens- zu einer Strukturbeschreibung durch einen Syntheseschritt (Synthese I), bei dem die Prozesse nach einer entsprechenden Analyse und Bewertung des Systems zu Entwurfseinheiten zusammengefaßt werden (schon mit dem Blick auf eine spätere Implementierung) bzw. Module zur Realisierung von Prozessen aus einer Komponentenbibliothek entnommen werden.

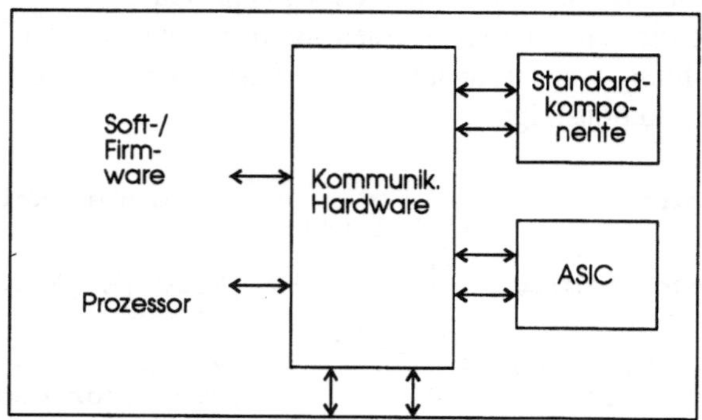

Bild 4: Heterogenes System

Für die Synthese aus einer Struktur- in eine Implementierungsbeschreibung (Synthese II), d.h., das Ersetzen der abstrakten Module bzw. Kommunikationskanäle durch physisch realisierbare Bausteine, werden unterschiedliche Methoden angewandt (Bild 3 bzw. [GlKr]). Sie hängen von der Entwurfsentscheidung ab, ob die Implementierung durch Hardware, Software oder Firmware bzw. bezüglich der Hardware durch Standardkomponenten oder durch ASICs (nach einer High-level Synthese) erfolgen soll (Bild 4).

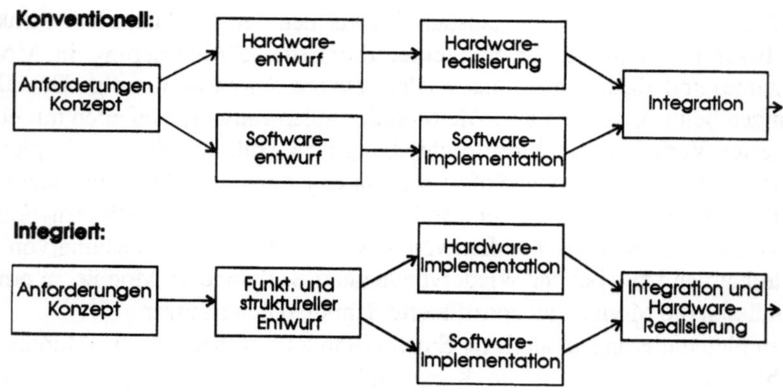

Bild 5: Entwurfsmethodiken

Ohne auf Details einzugehen, soll darauf hingewiesen werden, daß in allen Phasen des Entwurfs eine Analyse erfolgen muß (Bild 1). In den auf das Struktur- bzw. Implementierungsmodell bezogenen Entwurfsphasen bezieht sich die Analyse auf die funktionale bzw. zeitbezogene Korrektheit, die Leistungsfähigkeit sowie auf die

Kosten bzw. die Einhaltung von vorgegebenen Randbedingungen. Korrektheit und Leistungsfähigkeit werden durch Simulation ermittelt. Zeitabhängigkeiten werden im Strukturmodell als Ausführungszeiten der Operationen in einem Modul bzw. als Reaktionszeiten auf empfangene Nachrichten eingebracht (diskrete Realzeit), im Implementierungsmodell sind es an Grundbausteine gebundene Ausführungszeiten bzw. Taktzyklen. Damit sind bereits bei der Simulation des Strukturmodells eine frühe Bewertung des Systems, die Untersuchung von Entwurfsalternativen sowie Schlußfolgerungen für die physische Realisierung möglich. Durch Simulation des Implementierungsmodells kann die Bewertung präzisiert werden.

Auf der Grundlage des vorgestellten Konzeptes wird eine integrierte - im Gegensatz zur konventionellen - Vorgehensweise für die Anforderungsanalyse und den Entwurf ermöglicht (Bild 5). Sie ist charakterisiert durch die einheitliche Spezifikation, Modellierung und Simulation heterogener Komponenten, frühe Integration der Komponenten, späte Entscheidungen bezüglich der Implementierung sowie die frühe Analyse der Korrektheit und Leistungsfähigkeit.

3 Werkzeuge und Methoden

Zuerst werden die Methoden und verfügbaren Werkzeuge, die beim Entwurf verwendet werden sollen, charakterisiert. AKL ("Aufgabenklärung") ist eine Methode zur Anforderungsspezifikation und zum Entwurf von Systemen, die von der Siemens AG entwickelt wurde. Graphisch-orientierte Werkzeuge für diese Methode stehen mit SET-KLAR (in SIGRAPH-SET [KLAR]) zur Verfügung. Die von dem System zu lösenden Aufgaben bzw. Teilaufgaben werden in abstrakter Form durch Begriffe (Text) eingeführt und als hierarchischer Aufgabenbaum dargestellt (Bild 7). Die Darstellung der Datenbeziehungen zwischen den Aufgaben erfolgt in Blockdiagrammen (Bild 8). Jede Aufgabe bzw. Teilaufgabe (bei hierarchischer Verfeinerung) wird durch einen Block, die Daten- bzw. Ereignisströme zwischen den Aufgaben (Schnittstellen) werden durch Verbindungen beschrieben. Das Transformationswerkzeug DAX-PD [DAX] wandelt die einzelnen Aufgaben bzw. Teilaufgaben, die als Prozesse spezifiziert werden, in Prozeßdiagrammrahmen um (unter Verwendung von graphischen INPUT-, OUTPUT- und TASK-Symbolen der Sprache SDL).

Die Methode AKL bietet darüber hinaus die Möglichkeit, Komponenten, die die Aufgaben ausführen, zu definieren und in Komponentenbäumen zusammenzufassen. Mit Hilfe des Werkzeugs DAX-SC können ausgehend von der AKL-Beschreibung die "Nachrichten"-Sequenzen zwischen ausgewählten Komponenten als Sequence Charts graphisch dargestellt.

Als Sprache für den Entwurf des Verhaltensmodells wird die durch den CCITT standardisierte Specification and Description Language SDL [CCIT89] in Verbindung mit den durch SET-SDL zur Verfügung stehenden Werkzeugen [SDL] benutzt. Mit SDL werden Systeme als nebenläufige Prozesse beschrieben, die durch Nachrichten, d.h. OUTPUT- bzw. INPUT-Signale, asynchron miteinander kommunizieren. Nachrichten lösen Ereignisse aus bzw. übertragen Daten. Jedem Prozeß ist eine Queue für die eingehenden INPUT-Signale zugeordnet. Das Verhalten von SDL-Prozessen wird in Form erweiterter FSMs beschrieben; der Prozeß wartet in einem bestimmten Zustand, bis ein akzeptierbares Signal in seiner INPUT-Queue erscheint, danach führt er als Aufgabe Operationen über seinen lokalen bzw. durch das Signal übermittelten Daten aus. Für SDL-Beschreibungen werden grafische Symbole verwendet, die durch Text angereichert werden.

Wesentliche grafische Darstellungsmittel für SDL-Beschreibungen sind Prozeßdiagramme (Bild 9) und Sequence-Charts. Sequence-Charts beschreiben für jeden Prozeß den Ablauf über der Zeit (OUTPUTS, INPUTS, Aktionen) in linearer Form sowie die kausalen Abhängigkeiten zwischen den Prozessen (INPUTS, OUTPUTS). Ausgehend von den durch DAX-PD erzeugten Prozeßdiagrammrahmen kann als Entwurfsschritt das Verhalten jedes Prozesses entsprechend der auszuführenden Aufgabe durch die Einführung von Zuständen, Entscheidungen, Tasks bzw. Prozeduraufrufen unter Verwendung graphischer Symbole bzw. eines Subsets von VHDL oder C zur Beschreibung von Aktionen und der Deklaration von Datenobjekten beschrieben werden. Eine Visualisierung des zeitlichen Ablaufs des Signalaustauschs zwischen Prozessen bzw. der Beziehungen zwischen Aktionen in unterschiedlichen Prozessen kann durch die Erzeugung von Sequence Charts erfolgen.

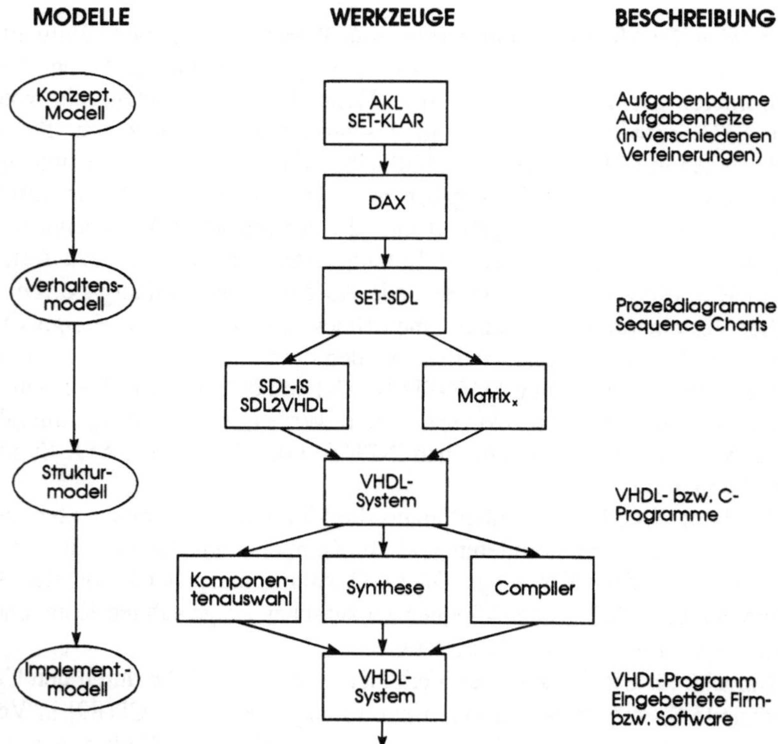

Bild 6: Vorgehensweise beim Entwurf

Ein weiteres Werkzeug, das ausgehend von dem Prozeßdiagrammrahmen zum Entwurf der Verhaltensbeschreibungen von Prozessen verwendet werden kann, ist

$Matrix_X$. $Matrix_X$ [MAT] ist ein Werkzeug zur Beschreibung und Simulation von Streckenmodellen und Regelkreisen. Die Systembeschreibung erfolgt mit einem grafischen Editor; dazu können über 90 verschiedene Blöcke (regelungstechnische Symbole) frei positioniert werden, parametrisiert und gegebenenfalls hierarchisch strukturiert miteinander verbunden werden. Nach der Analyse, Simulation bzw. Parameterabstimmung kann eine ausführbare Verhaltensbeschreibung des Systems in Form von C-, Ada- oder FORTRAN-Code generiert werden.

Als Basissprache für die Beschreibung des Strukturmodells bzw. das Implementierungsmodell wird die Hardwarebeschreibungssprache VHDL gewählt [LiSU90]. Aus den Prozeßdiagrammen können sowohl C-Code als auch unter Verwendung des Werkzeuges SDL2VHDL [LuGl92] simulierbarer VHDL-Code generiert werden. Funktionale bzw. zeitbezogene Korrektheit sowie die Leistungsfähigkeit des Entwurfs werden durch Simulation ermittelt. Obwohl das Verhalten der Module im Strukturmodell grundsätzlich mit VHDL beschrieben wird, ist es aus verschiedenen Gründen zweckmäßig, weitere ausführbare Formen wie zum Beispiel C-Code zuzulassen. Der VHDL-Simulator soll deshalb auch C-Code verarbeiten können; das ist beispielsweise bei dem SYNOPSYS-Simulator [SYN] für Unterprogramme bzw. Architekturkörper möglich.

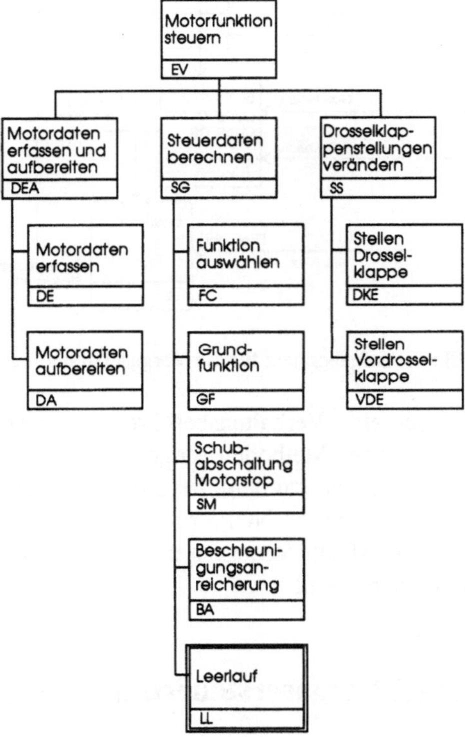

Bild 7: Aufgabenbaum für die Vergasersteuerung

Bezüglich der Transformation einer SDL-Beschreibung des Verhaltensmodells in eine Beschreibung der abstrakten Module und Kommunikationskanäle des Strukturmodells mit VHDL wird auf [LuGl92] verwiesen. Eine Methode zur Erzeugung physisch realisierbarer Kommunikationspfade in der Implementierungsbeschreibung aus SDL- bzw. VHDL-Spezifikationen ist in [GlKr92] dargestellt. Sie basiert auf einer Beschreibung der Kommunikationshardware (Standardkomponenten oder synthetisierbar) und den Protokollen für den Informationsaustausch zwischen dem Sender-Modul und der Kommunikationshardware bzw. dem Empfänger-Modul und der Kommunikationshardware. In der Implementierungsbeschreibung wird jedem SDL-Signal ein spezifisches Protokoll aus der Protokollbibliothek zugeordnet.

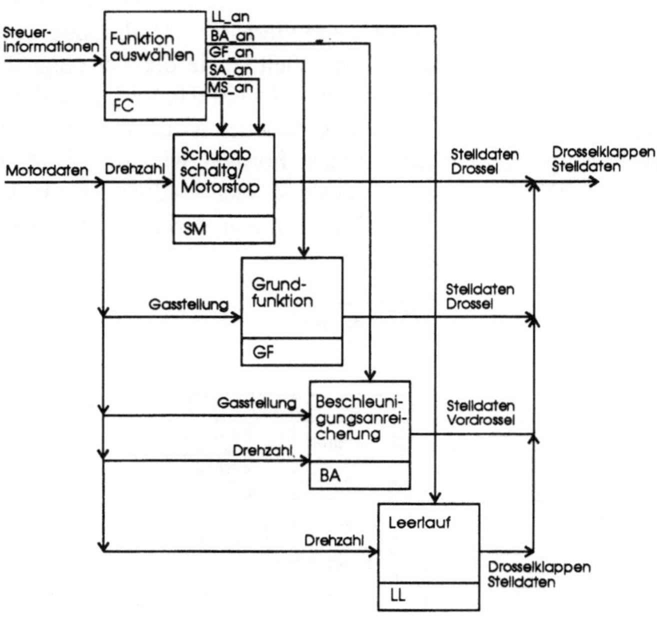

Bild 8: Aufgabennetz für die Vergasersteuerung

Für das Ersetzen der durch eine Verhaltensbeschreibung spezifizierten abstrakten Module werden verschiedene Methoden angewandt (Bild 3). Sofern nicht Standardkomponenten verwendet werden, ist eine High-level Synthese mittels CALLAS [DuKr89] oder mit dem SYNOPSYS-Synthesetool [SYN] möglich. Die Vorgehensweise beim Entwurf und die verwendeten Werkzeuge bzw. Beschreibungsmittel sind in Bild 6 dargestellt.

4 Entwurfsbeispiel Vergasersteuerung

Für einen elektronisch gesteuerten Vergaser soll die Steuerung entworfen werden. Die Steuerung hat die Aufgabe, aus aufbereiteten Motordaten (Temperatur, Drehzahl, Pedalstellungen, eingelegter Gang, Zündung, Stellung der Vordrossel- bzw. Drosselklappe) Daten für die Neueinstellung der Drosselklappen zu berechnen. Dabei wird zwischen den Betriebszuständen normaler Fahrbetrieb (Grundfunktion),

Beschleunigung, Leerlauf (normaler Leerlauf und Start- bzw. Warmlauf) und Schubabschaltung/Motorstop unterschieden. Für jede Betriebsart ist ein eigenes Steuerteilsystem als Komponente vorzusehen. Ausgehend von einer umgangssprachlichen Beschreibung werden in der Phase der Anforderungsspezifikation mit Hilfe des Werkzeugs SET-KLAR AKL-Beschreibungen des Systems erstellt. Aus den Ergebnissen der Anforderungsspezifikation mit AKL sind der Aufgabenbaum für die Vergasersteuerung einschließlich ihrer Umgebung (Motordatenaufbereitung, Stellsystem) (Bild 7) und das Aufgabennetz mit den fünf Aufgaben, die von der Steuerung zu bearbeiten sind (Bild 8) dargestellt. Auf der Grundlage der AKL-Blockdiagramme wird für jede Aufgabe, die Blatt im Aufgabenbaum ist, unter Verwendung des Werkzeuges DAX-PD ein SDL-Prozeßdiagramm erzeugt. In den Prozessen werden durch den Entwerfer manuell Zustände eingeführt und die Aktivitäten innerhalb der Tasks spezifiziert (Werkzeug SET-SDL). Eine (noch nicht verfeinerte) Beschreibung des Prozesses "Schubabschaltung/Motorstop" mit SDL zeigt Bild 9. Aus der SDL-Beschreibung der Entwurfseinheiten kann nun mit dem Werkzeug SDL2VHDL VHDL-Code erzeugt werden.

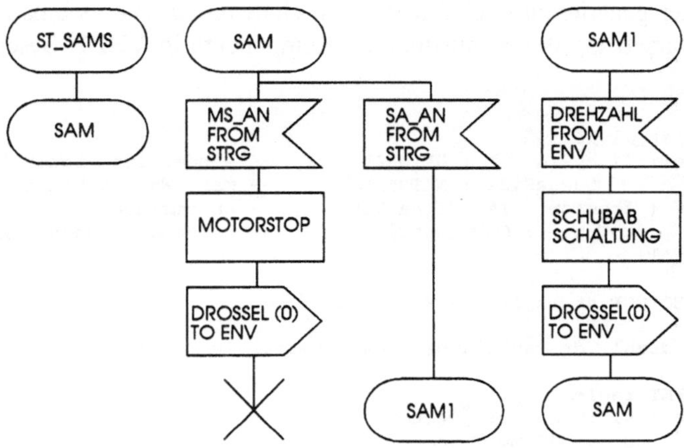

Bild 9: Prozeßdiagramm für Schubabschaltung/Motorstop

Voraussetzung dafür ist, daß die Tasks der entstehenden Entwurfseinheiten durch VHDL-Code (SDL) bzw. C-Code ($Matrix_X$) beschrieben werden. Auf der Grundlage einer Simulation mit dem VHDL Simulation System (VSS) der Firma SYNOPSYS kann das Modell nun analysiert und bewertet werden. Mit Hilfe dieses Werkzeugs ist es möglich, Beschreibungen von Aktivitäten in der Sprache C über sogenannte bmod's (behavioral models) in die VHDL Simulation einzubinden.

```
%BMOD_INFO
   name regler
   library synopsys
   use types arithmetic
   port input  s1 event 2 32
   port output s    -   - 32
%%
%BMOD_NOTE
%%
```

```
%BMOD_CODE
   #include "bmod.h"
   #include "regler.h"
   #include "matrixx.c"   /* C-Funktion für den Leerlaufregler */

   sbmod_regler_event() {
      int help;
      leerlaufregler_diskret_1 = (double) sbmod_iGetPinArray(s1);
      task1();
      help = (int) (leerlaufregler_diskret_15_1[1] * 500);
      sbmod_SetPinArray(s, help);
   }

   sbmod_regler_open(){}
   sbmod_regler_restart(){}
   sbmod_regler_error(){}
   sbmod_regler_close(){}
%%
```

Bild 10: SYNOPSYS-bmod zur Einbindung des $Matrix_X$ C-Codes in die Simulation

Bild 10 zeigt die Schnittstellendefinition zur Einbindung des von $Matrix_X$ für den Leerlaufregler generierten C-Codes in Form eines bmod. Dieses bmod wird nach einer Neuübersetzung des Simulators als Komponente in VHDL-Beschreibungen verwendet.

```
ENTITY st_ll IS
   generic ( MyPid     : NATURAL;       -- eindeutige Prozeß-ID
             QueueSize : NATURAL);      -- max. Warteschlangenlänge
   port ( fromTop : IN  SignalTop;      -- ankommende Signale
          toTop   : OUT sentSignal);    -- versendete Nachrichten
END st_ll;

ARCHITECTURE st_ll_arc OF st_ll IS
   ...
SIGNAL dzahl, drosselklappe : mvl7_vector (0 to 31);
   ...
COMPONENT regler
   port ( s1 : IN  mvl7_vector;
          s  : OUT mvl7_vector);
END COMPONENT;

BEGIN
   ...
   matrixx_comp : regler PORT MAP (dzahl, drosselklappe);

   SDL_behavior: PROCESS
   ...
   BEGIN
      ...
      drz := fromTop.value.t_REAL;
      ...
      dzahl <= mvl7_vector(conv_unsigned(integer(drz),32));
      WAIT FOR 50 ns;
      dro := real(conv_integer(signed(drosselklappe))) / 500.0;
      WAIT FOR 50 ns;
      ...
      toTop.value.t_REAL <= dro;
      ...
   END PROCESS;
END;
```

Bild 11: Ausschnitt aus dem mit SDL2VHDL generierten VHDL-Code

Bild 11 zeigt die Einbindung des Reglers in den durch das Werkzeug SDL2VHDL generierten VHDL-Code (Entity st_ll) für den Prozeß "Leerlauf".

Eine zweite Möglichkeit der Verifikation des Gesamtsystems ist die Generierung von C-Code mit Hilfe des Implementationssystems SDL-IS und die nachfolgende Simulation auf der Grundlage dieses C-Codes. Dabei muß jedoch beachtet werden, daß die Beschreibung der Tasks ausschließlich in der Sprache C vorgenommen werden muß.

Vorteil dieser Vorgehensweise ist allerdings die mögliche Visualisierung des Simulationsablaufes mit Hilfe von Sequence Charts. Wurde das System mit Hilfe von Sequence Charts spezifiziert und entworfen, ist ein einfacher Vergleich des tatsächlichen und spezifizierten Systemverhaltens möglich.In Abhängigkeit von den zu treffenden Entwurfsentscheidungen erfolgt die Implementierung der Entwurfseinheiten unter Verwendung von entweder Standardkomponenten, synthetisierten ASICs (z.B. mit SYNOPSYS-Synthesetool), Software (auf einem Standardprozessor plus Speicher) oder Firmware (auf einem mikroprogrammierten Steuerwerk).

5 Schlußbemerkungen

In diesem Beitrag haben wir gezeigt, wie die Anforderungsspezifikation und der Entwurf von heterogenen Systemen auf einem hohen Abstraktionsniveau implementierungsunabhängig und durchgängig bis zur Realisierungsphase unter Verwendung bekannter Werkzeuge durchgeführt werden kann. Weitere Untersuchungen sind erforderlich bezüglich der Integration der einzelnen Werkzeuge zu einem Gesamtwerkzeug, der Ergänzung um weitere Werkzeuge sowie zu den Subsets der Sprachen, die zur Beschreibung der Eingangs- bzw. Ausgangscodes von Werkzeugen dienen.

Literatur

[CCIT89] CCITT. Functional Specification and Description Language (SDL), Recommendation Z.100-Z.104, Blue Book, 1989

[DAX] DAX - User Manual, Siemens AG, 1991

[DuKr89] Duzy, P.; Krämer, H.; et al.: "CALLAS - Conversion of Algorithms to Library Adaptable Structures", In Proceedings of the IFIP VLSI Conference Munich, Seiten 197-208, 1989

[BuKa92a] Buchenrieder, K.; Kahlert, S.; Monjau, D.: "Methodik und Werkzeuge für den Entwurf komplexer heterogener Systeme", in ITG-Fachbericht 122 "Rechnergestützter Entwurf und Architektur mikroelektronischer Systeme", vde-verlag GmbH, Berlin-Offenbach, 1992

[BuKa92b] Buchenrieder, K.; Kahlert, S.; Monjau, D.: Methoden und Werkzeuge für das Hardware/Soft-ware-CoDesign", CADS - Fachzeitschrift für Design Automation in der Elektronik (7) 1992

[BuKa93] Buchenrieder, K.; Kahlert, S.; Monjau, D.; Veith, C.: "A new model-based approach to the CoDesign of heterogeneous Systems", In Proceedings of the EUROCAST'93, Las Palmas, Gran Canaria, Spanien, Februar 1993

[GlKr92] Glunz, W.; Kruse, T.; Monjau, D.: "Hardware-Entwurf mit SDL", in ITG-Fachbericht 122 "Rechnergestützter Entwurf und Architektur mikroelektronischer Systeme", vde-verlag GmbH, Berlin-Offenbach, 1992

[GlKr93] Glunz, W.; Kruse, T.; Monjau, D.; Rössel, T.: "Integrating SDL and VHDL for System-Level Hardware Design", in Proceedings of the CHDL, Ottawa, Canada, April 1993

[JaLa92] Jackson, K.; Lavi, J. Z.; et al.: "Standards for conceptual and design models of computer-based systems", CBS standards, März 1992

[Kahl92] Kahlert, S.: "Systementwurf mit einheitlichen Beschreibungsmitteln für Hard- und Software", Diplomarbeit, TU Chemnitz/Siemens AG München, September 1992

[KLAR] SIGRAPH-SET-KLAR - Ein Werkzeug zur Aufgabenklärung, Benutzeranleitung, Siemens AG, Juni 1990

[LiSU90] Lipsett, R.; Schaefer, C.; Ussery, C. : VHDL - Hardware Description and Design, Kluwer Academic Publishers, 1990

[LuGl92] Lutter, B.; Glunz, W.; Rammig, F.:"VHDL Based Simulation of SDL Specifications", erscheint in: Proceedings of the EURO-VHDL '92

[MAT] Matrix_X/Systembuild - Version Description Document for Version 2.4, Integrated Systems Incorporation, Santa Clara, Californien, 1991

[SDL] SIGRAPH-SET-SDL - Werkzeuge für Systementwurf und Implementierung, Benutzeranleitung, Siemens AG, Mai 1988

[SYN] SYNOPSYS - User's Manual, Synopsys Incorporation, November 1990

Software-Roboter
Aufzeichnen und Wiedergeben von Benutzereingaben bei interaktiven Programmen

Bernd Waldbauer

Universität Ulm,
Mathematik/SAI

ABSTRACT

Die Realität zeigt: Software unterliegt Änderungen. Jede Veränderung kann Fehler in bisher korrekten Teilen verursachen. Mit den Ansprüchen an die Software-Qualität steigt der Aufwand für den Test von Software-Produkten. Tests nach Veränderungen dürfen sich nicht nur eng auf die modifizierten Stellen beschränken, sie müssen auch die "Umgebung" berücksichtigen und frühere Testfälle miteinbeziehen.

Einfach zu erreichende — mechanisierte/automatisierte — Reproduzierbarkeit bei Testläufen bewirkt Produktivitätssteigerungen in der Debug- und Testphase. Neben einer Kostenreduktion bei Regressionstests können Software-Hersteller oder Prüfinstitutionen mit reproduzierbaren Testläufen Nachweis führen über Art und Umfang ihrer Testprozeduren.

Der Software-Roboter führt "mechanisch" fixierte Testläufe durch. Diese entstehen durch Aufzeichnen der Eingabesequenz und der Programm-Reaktionen bei einer Beispielsitzung mit dem zu testenden Programm. Dabei darf die Aufzeichung den Dialog nicht beeinflussen. Bei der Testwiederholung erhält das Kandidaten-Programm die mitgeschnittene Eingabesequenz identisch (inklusive aller Tippfehler) zugespielt. Der Software-Roboter ermöglicht es Software-Testern, die Reihenfolge der gedrückten Tasten beliebig oft in verschiedenen Testläufen identisch zu wiederholen.

Besonderes Design-Ziel beim Entwurf des Software-Roboters für reproduzierbare Testläufe in einer UNIX-Umgebung war es, alle Aktionen auf einem einzelnen Host, ohne zusätzliche Hardware und möglichst an einer Terminal-Schnittstelle durchführen zu können. Speziell Programme, die interaktiv und bildschirmorientiert arbeiten, stellen hierbei erhöhte Anforderungen an den Kommunikations-Mechanismus.

Neben technischen Details beim Implementieren des Software-Roboters, soll eine Kommandosprache, die über den schlichten Eingabedaten definiert ist, zur Diskussion stehen.

Schlüsselworte:
Software-Roboter, reproduzierbares Testen, interaktive Software.

Datum:
1993/06/27.

Universität Ulm, Mathematik/SAI, Bernd Waldbauer, Helmholtzstr. 18, 89081 Ulm.
Tel.: 0731/502-3573. Fax: 0731/502-3579. E-mail: wald@mathematik.uni-ulm.de

1. Motivation für Reproduzierbarkeit

Alltägliches Ärgernis

Der "Chef" testet die neue, beim Entwickler stabile Version eines Programms. Innerhalb kürzester Zeit stürzt das Programm ab:

```
$ brandnewtoy
        ...einige Benutzeraktionen
bus error - core dumped
```

Der Absturz läßt sich nicht zuverlässig reproduzieren. Der Testbenutzer kann seine Eingabesequenz leider nicht exakt wiederholen. Hilfestellung bietet hier ein Werkzeug, das Benutzereingaben mitprotokolliert und reproduzieren kann.

Präsentationen

Vorführungen unterliegen grundsätzlich den bekannten Gesetzen von Murphy. Verlangt eine Demonstration die Eingabe noch so weniger Zeichen über eine Tastatur, so schleicht sich mit Sicherheit ein verheerender Tippfehler ein. Ein Werkzeug, das einen "mechanischen" und programmierbaren Benutzer simuliert, trägt hier zu einer wesentlich besser kalkulierbaren Präsentation bei. Der gewünschte Ablauf läßt sich in Ruhe vorbereiten, überprüfen, iterativ verbessern und für beliebig viele Präsentationen in gleichbleibender Qualität wiederholen. Anwendungen hierzu finden sich sowohl im Schulungs- als auch im Marketingsektor.

Aspekte der Software Qualitätssicherung

Reklamiert interaktive Software ein hohes Maß an Qualität für sich, muß auch der Software-Produktionsprozeß speziellen Anforderungen genügen. International erfahren einige Normen und Standards in diesem Zusammenhang eine wachsende Bedeutung: ISO 9000 Part 3, IEEE 823.

Neben strukturiertem, diszipliniertem und dokumentiertem Vorgehen aller Entwickler muß sich vor allem das Testteam Nachvollziehbarkeit der Tests als wesentliches Ziel vorgeben. Exakte Reproduzierbarkeit von Benutzereingaben verbessert dabei nicht nur die Effizienz der Kommunikation zwischen Entwicklungs- und Testteam, sie ermöglicht auch die Archivierung von wiederholbaren Testfällen. Der Software-Produzent dokumentiert damit Umfang und Sorgfalt seiner QS-Maßnahmen.

Produkthaftung

In seinen Publikationen unterstreicht der Jurist F.A. Koch [Koch 1991] klar den Grundsatz:

Software unterliegt der Produkthaftung.

Laut Koch gesteht der Gesetzgeber dem Software-Produzenten zwar gewisse Einschränkungsmöglichkeiten bei der Produkthaftung zu, doch verlangt er dafür eine fachgerecht durchgeführte Qualitätssicherung bei der Entwicklung.

Gemäß den Sicherheitserwartungen an ein Software-Produkt müsse der Software-Produzent mit einem bestimmten Produkt*fehl*gebrauch rechnen und angemessene Absicherungsmaßnahmen treffen. Die in der Praxis bestätigte These der *unerreichbaren Fehlerfreiheit* bei Software führe auf keinen Fall zur Haftungsentlastung des Software-Produzenten. Sie könne ihn sogar umgekehrt wegen des erhöhten Gefährdungspotentials zu einer Intensivierung seiner QS-Maßnahmen verpflichten.

Im Streitfall habe der Produzent *einzelfallbezogen* nachzuweisen, daß ein "Ausreißer" vorliegt, und daß er bei der Software-Erstellung alle möglichen Anstrengungen unternommen hat, genau diesen "Ausreißer" zu verhindern. Häufig scheitere dieser Nachweis an der unzureichenden und deshalb nicht beweisfähigen Dokumentation zu QS-Maßnahmen [Koch 1992].

Dokumentiert und archiviert ein Software-Produzent jedoch sämtliche Testfälle in einer Art, daß er sie jederzeit reproduzieren kann, erfüllt er damit nachvollziehbar einen Teil seiner Sorgfaltspflicht.

2. Problemstellung und Lösungsansatz

Aus den Motivationsgedanken leitet sich der Bedarf nach einer Testumgebung mit einem Software-Roboter ab, der reproduzierbare Aktionen ermöglicht. Die Testumgebung soll einem Benutzer einen ungestörten (Beispiel-) Dialog mit dem zu testenden *Kandidaten-Programm* ermöglichen, diese Sitzung mitschneiden und später beliebig oft, mechanisch und identisch wiederholen können.

Anforderungen

Im Einzelnen muß die Testumgebung folgenden Anforderungen genügen:

(1) Aufzeichnen eines Dialogs zwischen Benutzer und Kandidaten-Programm.

(2) Wiedergabe der Benutzereingaben ohne den Benutzer.

(3) Bearbeiten des aufgezeichneten Dialogs und Programmieren von Testfällen.

Zu (1): Bei der Aufzeichnung arbeitet der Benutzer völlig ungestört mit dem Kandidaten-Programm. Aufgabe des Software-Roboters ist es, Daten zu sammeln, die den Dialog beschreiben, ohne daß dies die Kommunikation zwischen Benutzer und Kandidat beeinträchtigt. Im Idealfall bemerkt weder der Testbenutzer noch das Kandidaten-Programm die Aufzeichnung. Der Software-Roboter "merkt" sich die Aktionen und Reaktionen von Benutzer und Programm.

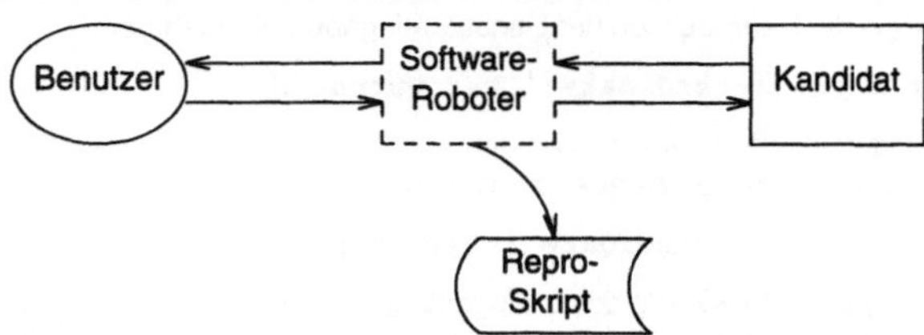

Zu (2): Bei der Wiedergabe simuliert der Software-Roboter den Benutzer. Der Roboter verhält sich wie der Benutzer in dem aufgezeichneten Dialog. Mit dem Roboter läßt sich der Dialog beliebig oft identisch reproduzieren. Das Kandidaten-Programm "sieht" einen Benutzer, der immer wieder exakt die gleichen Eingaben tätigt.

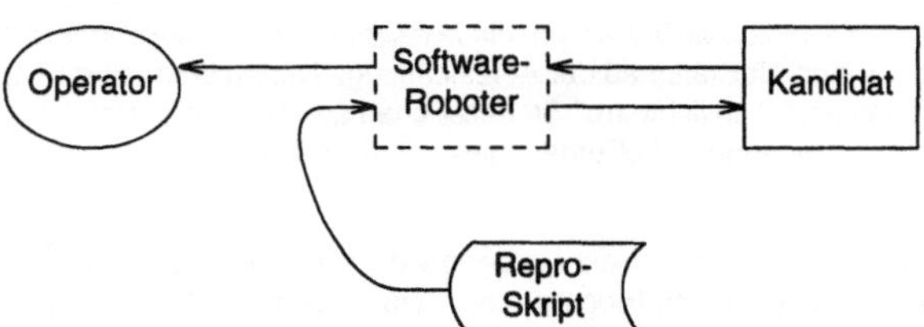

Zu (3): Der aufgezeichnete Dialog liegt in einer Form vor, die eine Nachbearbeitung ermöglicht. Die Philosophie von UNIX empfiehlt eine "lesbare" Textform für die Speicherung der Datenströme. Dadurch eröffnet sich eine große Flexibilität für die Manipulation der Aufzeichnung mit Texteditoren und anderen Tools aus dem UNIX Werkzeugkasten [K&P 1984]. Zusätzlich vereinfacht die Textform die Definition und Implementierung einer Metasprache über den bloßen Datenströmen. Damit lassen sich auf Basis einer oder mehrerer Aufzeichnungen neue Testfälle konstruieren und programmieren.

Lösungsansatz für Dialogprogramme mit einfacher Benutzer-Schnittstelle

Für die Klasse der zeilenorientierten Dialogprogramme enthält der UNIX Werkzeugkasten bereits die notwendigen Programme und Mechanismen. Eine simple Lösung [Faison 1986] benutzt den Pipe-Mechanismus und das Dienstprogramm *tee*(1) für die Aufzeichnung eines Dialogs:

```
tee master_input | candidate | tee master_output
```

Sollen Ein- und Ausgaben gemeinsam in einer Protokolldatei erscheinen, sorgt die **-a** Option bei *tee* für das korrekte Anhängen und Vermischen der aufzuzeichnenden Datenströme

```
tee -a logfile | candidate | tee -a logfile
```

Enthält diese Pipeline die Shell als Kandidaten-Programm

```
tee -a ses.log | 2>&1 sh -i | tee -a ses.log
```

so umfaßt die Aufzeichnung auch die Interaktion mit allen von dieser Shell aus gestarteten Programmen. Bedingung dafür ist, daß die gestarteten Programme nur die von der Shell für sie geöffneten I/O-Verbindungen verwenden. Die Aufzeichnung enthält anschließend ein komplettes Sitzungsprotokoll.

Bei der Wiedergabe der aufgezeichneten Eingabedaten kann im einfachsten Fall das Dienstprogramm *cat*(1) die Reproduktion der Benutzereingaben übernehmen:

```
cat master_input | candidate | tee output_N
```

Aufgrund der Puffereigenschaften der Pipe und den Annahmen verschiedener Programme über ihre Interaktion mit dem Benutzer, bedarf es aber oft eines modifizierten *cat*-Programms:

```
feed master_input | candidate | tee output_N
```

Das Programm *feed*(1) schreibt wie *cat* seine Eingabedaten in die Standardausgabe, die jedoch eine Pipe sein sollte. Jeder *write*(2) System Call transferiert nämlich genau eine Zeile und danach wartet *feed*, mit Hilfe des *fstat*(2) System Calls, bis das Kandidaten-Programm diese Zeile aus der Pipe gelesen hat. *feed* versucht, den Kommando**zeilen**-Stil eines Benutzers nachzubilden.

Lösungsansatz für bildschirm-/maskenorientierte Dialogprogramme

Handelt es sich bei dem Kandidaten jedoch um ein *bildschirm*- oder *maskenorientiertes* Dialog-Programm, erhöht sich der Komplexitätsgrad der Aufzeichnung. Neben dem reinen Text, der ein- und ausgegeben wird, fallen noch "unsichtbare" Steuerzeichen an, die zum Beispiel den Cursor frei über den gesamten Bildschirm bewegen. Außerdem gewinnt die Zeitkomponente bei dieser Interaktionsart an Bedeutung.

Der für ein UNIX System "natürliche" Ansatz mit der oben vorgestellten Ein-/Ausgabe-Umlenkung funktioniert nicht bei allen interaktiven Programmen. Grund dafür ist, daß Programme, wie *vi*(1), nicht von einem zeilenorientierten Datenstrom-Modell (*line*-Mode) ausgehen, sondern ganz spezielle Terminal-Charakteristika erwarten. Derartige Programme akzeptieren deshalb keine Standard-IPC-Kanäle für die Kommunikation mit ihrer Umgebung. Nur mit Hilfe eines *Pseudo-Terminal-Geräts* kann der Software-Roboter diesen Kandidaten-Programmen, die auf der Kommunikation mit einem Terminal-Gerät beharren, per Software einen interaktiven Benutzer vorspiegeln.

Zwei spezialisierte Komponenten des Software-Roboters teilen sich die Aufgabe, Benutzereingaben aufzuzeichnen und wiederzugeben. Eine Komponente schneidet die Eingaben eines echten Benutzers mit, die andere spielt dem Probanden die fixierten Benutzereingaben "mechanisch" und reproduzierbar vor. Beide benutzen ein Pseudo-Terminal als Kommunikations-Kanal zum Kandidaten-Programm und ein festgelegtes Format für die abgespeicherten Benutzereingaben.

Die nächsten Abschnitte beschreiben verschiedene Eigenschaften der beiden Komponenten und des Datenformats sowie einige Implementierungsdetails.

3. Recording Tool — Aufzeichnungskomponente des Software-Roboters

3.1. Aufgabenstellung

In der Aufzeichnungsphase schneidet der Software-Roboter die Kommunikation eines Benutzers mit einem interaktiven Programm mit.

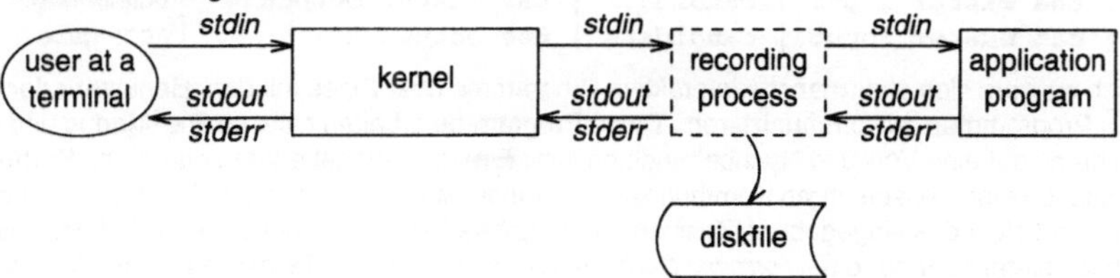

Gemäß der Anforderung muß die Aufzeichnung für Benutzer und Kandidaten-Programm möglichst transparent sein. Das Programm darf die Abhöraktion nicht bemerken. Der Testbenutzer sollte aus Gründen des Persönlichkeitsschutzes von der Aufzeichnung wissen, seinen Dialog aber völlig unbeeinträchtigt abwickeln können.

Wegen der erklärten Absicht, die aufgezeichneten Benutzer*eingaben* für weitere Testläufe ohne den Benutzer zu verwenden, muß die Aufzeichnungskomponente des Software-Roboters die gesammelten Daten markieren. Dazu unterscheidet das Werkzeug die Daten nach ihrer Flußrichtung: Daten, die vom Benutzer zum Kandidaten-Programm (Eingabedaten) und Daten, die umgekehrt (Ausgabedaten) fließen. Außerdem notiert es mit den Daten auch Zeitstempel für die Reproduktion.

Die aufgezeichneten Daten landen in einer oder zwei Dateien. Sie bestehen nur aus "lesbaren" Zeichen und sind sowohl änderbar als auch für die Reproduktion verwendbar.

3.2. Existierende Werkzeuge

Das aus der Berkeley Line bekannte Tool *script*(1) erstellt ein Protokoll einer Sitzung. *script* existiert in verschiedenen Implementierungsvarianten. Eine davon benutzt das oben vorgestellte Verfahren mit dem Kandidaten-Programm zwischen zwei Aufzeichnungsprozessen und Pipes als Kommunikations-Kanal. Eine andere benutzt Pseudo-Terminals für die Kommunikation und besitzt damit genügend Transparenz den Kandidaten gegenüber. Alle Implementierungen zeichnen jedoch die Ein- und Ausgabedaten vermischt und unmarkiert in einer Datei auf. Die Daten lassen sich nicht trivial nach ihrer Art trennen. Die Eingabedaten für eine Reproduktion kann man deshalb aus der Aufzeichnung nicht einfach wiedergewinnen.

Eine andere Möglichkeit, dem Kandidaten-Programm eine Terminal-Schnittstelle mit einem Programm dahinter anzubieten, ist die Verwendung von zwei echten Schnittstellen, die über ein spezielles Kabel miteinander verbunden sind. Varianten ergeben sich aus der Anordnung der beiden Schnittstellen am selben Rechner oder an zwei verschiedenen Rechnern. Kommunikationsprogramme, wie *kermit*(1), verfügen meistens über eine Protokollfunktion, die eine Sitzung aufzeichnet, und eine Skriptfunktion, die Dialogteile aus einer Datei in die Sitzung einspielt. Diese "Hardware-Lösungen" bleiben hier jedoch unberücksichtigt.

3.3. Spezialisierte Komponente des Software-Roboters

Das *recording tool* des Software-Roboters muß, ohne zu stören, Daten abfangen, die vom Benutzer zur Applikation und umgekehrt fließen. Theoretisch müßte auch hier die Lösung mit den Pipes möglich sein.

```
$ tee master_input | candidate | tee master_output     Aufzeichnug
$ cat master_input | candidate | tee output_N          Wiedergabe
```

Praktisch weigern sich aber manche interaktive Programme über Pipes mit dem Benutzer oder mit anderen Programmen zu kommunizieren. Diese Programme arbeiten nicht im *line*-Modus und verzichten damit auf eine Vor- und Nachbehandlung ihrer Ein- und Ausgabedaten durch den Kernel. Sie versuchen statt dessen, ihren Kommunikations-Kanal mit dem System Call *ioctl*(2) so zu konfigurieren, daß sie jedes eingegebene Zeichen sofort, unbearbeitet und ungepuffert erhalten. Diese Möglichkeit bietet aber nur eine *Terminal-Schnittstelle* (*tty*) mit einem Terminal-Treiber hinter sich.

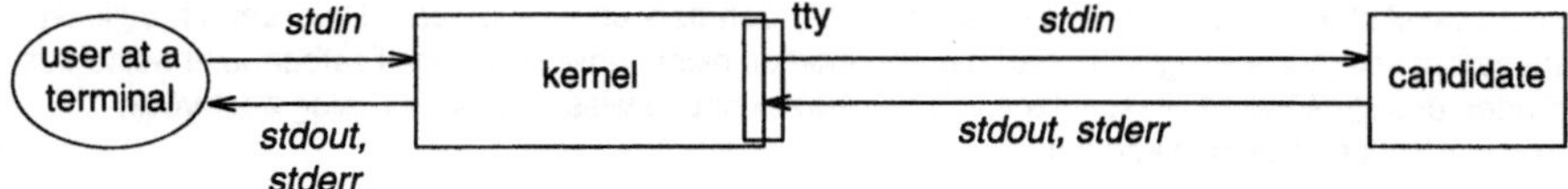

Die Dialog-Programme erwarten eine vom Kernel bereitgestellte Terminal-Schnittstelle für ihre Kommunikation mit einem "realen" Benutzer. Die Aufzeichnungskomponente muß sich deshalb völlig transparent in den Kommunikationskanal einfügen und dem Kandidaten-Programm eine scheinbar echte Terminal-Schnittstelle bieten.

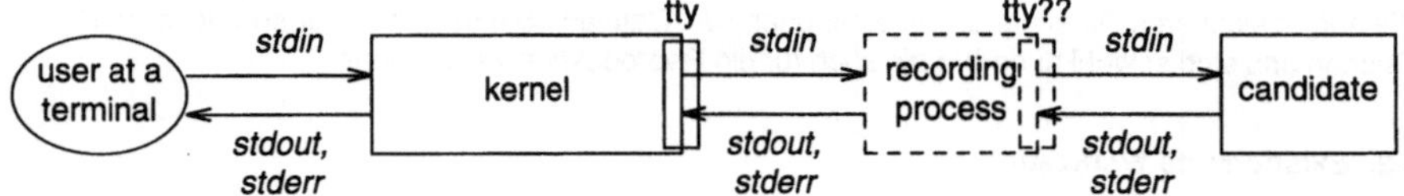

IPC mit Pseudo-Terminals

Pseudo-Terminals sind ein bidirektionaler IPC-Kanal. Sie verfügen am einen Ende, *slave*-Seite, über eine Software-Schnittstelle, genannt *line discipline*, die alle Charakteristika eines "echten" Terminals zeigt. Das andere Ende, *master*-Seite, führt aber nicht zu einem Peripherie-Gerät sondern zu einem Prozeß. Damit genügt diese IPC-Form der Forderung mancher interaktiver Programme, wie *vi*, mit einem scheinbar echten Terminal-Gerät kommunizieren zu können. Außerdem realisiert die Pseudo-Terminal-Schnittstelle das gleiche Protokoll für den Datenaustausch mit dem Kandidaten wie eine echte Terminal-Schnittstelle.

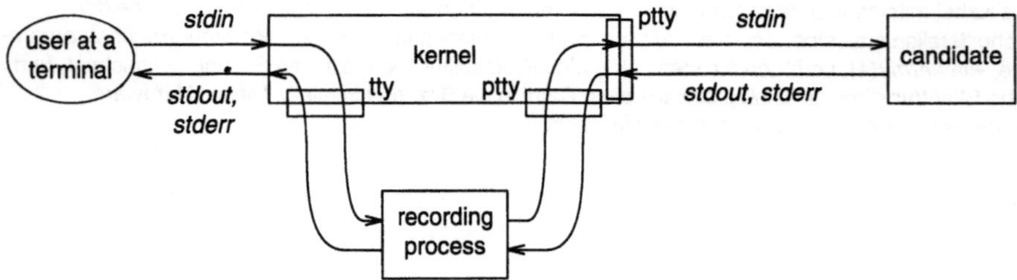

Verbindet ein Pseudo-Terminal den Kandidaten mit der Aufzeichnungskomponente, läßt sich der Aufzeichnungsprozeß transparent zwischen Benutzer und Kandidaten-Programm schieben. Der Kandidat wird durch das Mitschneiden nicht beeinflußt, er wird die Anwesenheit eines Lauschers nicht einmal bemerken.

Probleme

Die Probleme erschienen bei ersten Implementationen der Aufzeichnungskomponente unter UNIX System V Release 3.2 (SVR3.2).

Timer: UNIX SVR3.2 sieht keinen Zeitgeber mit einer Auflösung kleiner als eine Sekunde vor. Dadurch lassen sich nur sehr grobe Zeitstempel mit den Eingabedaten notieren. Versuche bei der ersten Implementierung ergaben, daß für eine zeitidentische Reproduktion des Benutzerverhaltens diese Auflösung zu grob ist. In der zweiten Version bot ein Timer im Millisekunden-Bereich auf Basis des *poll*(2) System Calls eine bessere Auflösung. Diesen Timer beschreibt [Waldbauer 1993]. Die Idee stammt aus einem Artikel in den Network-News [Pizzi 1992].

Simultanes Lesen: Ein Problem für den Software-Roboter besteht in der Notwendigkeit, Daten *simultan* aus zwei I/O-Verbindungen, sowohl vom Benutzer als auch vom Kandidaten-Programm, lesen zu müssen. SVR3.2 erlaubt zwar, I/O-Verbindungen so zu konfigurieren, daß der *read*(2) System Call nicht blockiert, doch aufgrund eines historischen Design-Fehlers verliert das Programm dabei die Möglichkeit, EOF zu erkennen. Zudem erzeugt diese "busy wait" Lösung unnötig viel Systemlast, was zu Verzerrungen beim Laufzeitverhalten führt. Der *poll*(2) System Call kann mehrere I/O-Verbindungen simultan überwachen, jedoch nur bei STREAMS-Geräten. Unter SVR3.2 ist der Terminal-Treiber kein STREAMS-Gerät. Die Standard-Technik zur Lösung dieses Problems benutzt mehrere Prozesse, von denen jeder einen Datenfluß bearbeitet [Stevens 1990].

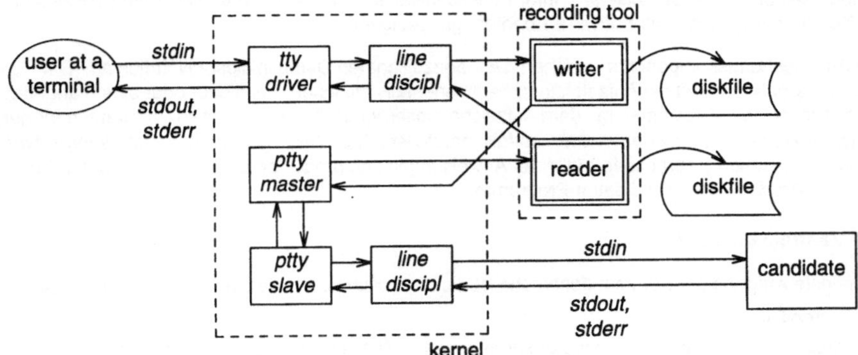

Der Prozeß *writer* protokolliert den Strom vom Benutzer zum Kandidaten-Programm, *reader* den entgegengesetzten Strom. Mit Hilfe des **O_APPEND** Flags beim *open*(2) System Call können die beiden Prozesse auch gemeinsam in eine Datei schreiben.

Terminationsreihenfolge: Wegen des Einsatzes von drei Prozessen (Writer, Reader und Kandidat) und einer nicht notwendig deterministischen Terminationsreihenfolge verlangt die Implementierung hier besondere Sorgfalt [Nathe 1992]. Da Aufräumarbeiten in vorgegebener Reihenfolge zu erledigen sind, bedarf es etwas Aufwand, die Prozesse korrekt zu synchronisieren.

Die Evaluation der Lösung mit drei Prozessen ergab ein verbessertes Modell mit vier Prozessen für die zweite Version [Kleber 1993]. Der vierte Prozeß übernimmt zentral die Vorbereitungs-, Prozeß-überwachungs- und Aufräumaufgaben. Dadurch läßt sich der Code besser strukturieren und vereinfachen. Die Teilaufgaben sind klarer getrennt und besser lokalisiert.

Trennen der Ein- und Ausgabeströme: Das Isolieren des Eingabestroms (Benutzer zur Applikation) bei der Aufzeichnung funktioniert gut, dagegen ist das Isolieren des Ausgabestroms mit dieser Technik nicht möglich. In diesem Aufbau befinden sich zwei Lagen der *line discipline* Software, eine beim realen Terminal-Gerät und eine beim Pseudo-Terminal. Die Aufzeichnungskomponente kontrolliert das reale Terminal und schaltet die line discipline in den "raw" Mode, so daß alle Zeichen unverändert durchfließen. Der Kandidat darf die line discipline des Pseudo-Terminals manipulieren. Er mag das "Echo" für die eingegebenen Zeichen selbst übernehmen oder aber diese Aufgabe seiner line discipline im Kernel überlassen. Der Software-Roboter hat jedoch keine Möglichkeit, zwischen Echo-Zeichen und echten Ausgabezeichen des Kandidaten zu unterscheiden.

4. Kommandosprache für den Software-Roboter

4.1. Idee

Bei der Aufzeichnung notiert der Software-Roboter die Eingabezeichen in der Reihenfolge, wie der Benutzer die Tasten gedrückt hat. Bei der Reproduktion spielt er dem Kandidaten-Programm die Eingabedaten beliebig oft identisch vor.

Die dritte der eingangs formulierten Anforderungen verlangt eine Möglichkeit, die aufgezeichneten Daten nach der Aufzeichnung bearbeiten zu können. Gemäß der UNIX Philosophie empfiehlt sich als Datenformat für die aufgezeichneten Daten eine "lesbare" Textform. Neben der einfachen Behandlung mit jedem Texteditor stehen auch viele weitere Tools aus dem UNIX Werkzeugkasten für Manipulationen zur Verfügung.

Gefordert war ebenfalls die Funktionalität, Testfälle mit aufgezeichneten Daten zu programmieren. Hier kommt eine kleine Kommandosprache [Bentley 1986] zum Einsatz. Sie definiert sich mit einer einfachen Grammatik und ausschließlich aus Textsymbolen:

cmd [*timestamp*] [*options*] [*arguments*]

Die Prefix-Notation ermöglicht den Einsatz eines einfachen Parsers [Kleber 1993]. In der nächsten Version wird die Syntax der *embeddable* Kommandosprache *Tcl* [Ousterhout 1990, 1993] zu Grunde gelegt. Diese Sprache ist in ihrer Funktionalität leicht erweiterbar und deshalb als Basis für die Kommandosprache des Software-Roboters gut geeignet.

Die Aufzeichnungskomponente speichert die aufgezeichneten Daten in dieser Notation ab. Der Testoperator bearbeitet die Aufzeichnung gegebenenfalls mit einem Texteditor oder einem anderen Dienstprogramm. Zusammen mit dem Aufzeichnungsprogramm *generiert* er so Programme für den Software-Roboter, die wiederholbare Testfälle darstellen. Die Wiedergabekomponente *interpretiert* die in der Kommandosprache formulierten Anweisungen und produziert daraus Eingabedaten für einen Testlauf mit dem Kandidaten-Programm.

4.2. Zentrale Elemente

Wichtigste Aufgabe der Kommandosprache ist die Darstellung der aufgezeichneten Datenströme.

`send` *time data*

beschreibt Daten, die der Testbenutzer zur gegebenen Zeit zum Programm geschickt hat.

`receive` *time data*

beschreibt Daten, die zum gegebenen Zeitpunkt vom Kandidaten-Programm angekommen sind. Das Datenfeld besteht nur aus lesbaren Zeichen und lehnt sich bei den Steuerzeichen an die C-Syntax an. Daneben existieren weitere Anweisungen, mit deren Hilfe man *statisch* und *dynamisch* Testfälle programmieren und kontrollieren kann.

Wegen der Textform lassen sich Testfälle *statisch*, vor dem Ablauf, modifizieren und programmieren. Der Testoperator kann bei den Eingabedaten Zeichen verändern, löschen oder hinzufügen, ohne den Aufzeichnungsprozeß erneut durchführen zu müssen. Außerdem enthält die Sprache Anweisungen, durch die der Testoperator im Voraus auf den zeitlichen Ablauf Einfluß nehmen kann:

`wait` *intervall*
`waitfor` *intervall data*
`keywait` *intervall data*

Einige Elemente der Kommandosprache unterstützen den Testoperator bei der präzisen Steuerung des Software-Roboters für einzelne Testläufe. Durch Hinzufügen von Anweisungen ermöglichen sie ihm *dynamisch*, während des Testlaufs, Veränderungen an den Testfall-Eingabedaten vorzunehmen. Mit diesen Anweisungen kann er

- Breakpoints setzen
- "on the fly" zusätzliche Eingaben vom Terminal verlangen
- Teile des Testfalls überspringen

während das Kandidaten-Programm die Eingabedaten zugespielt bekommt.

4.3. Generator und Interpreter

Die Aufzeichnungskomponente des Software-Roboters transformiert die mitgeschnittenen Eingabedaten in die von der Testfall Kommandosprache definierte Repräsentationsform. Sie erzeugt ein *Repro-Skript*, eine Textdatei mit den Testfall-Eingabedaten als **send/receive** Kommandos.

Die Wiedergabekomponente liest ein Repro-Skript und interpretiert die Daten entsprechend der Kommandosprache. Sie führt im Skript enthaltene Anweisungen aus und schickt die so erzeugten Daten über das Pseudo-Terminal zu dem Kandidaten-Programm.

5. Replaying Tool — Wiedergabekomponente des Software-Roboters

5.1. Aufgabenstellung

Interpreter

Neben der offensichtlichen Aufgabe, das Kandidaten-Programm mit Eingabedaten zu versorgen, muß das *replaying tool* des Software-Roboters vor allem die Kommandosprache interpretieren. Dazu liest es die Datei mit den Testfall-Kommandos für den Software-Roboter, interpretiert die Daten und führt darin enthaltene Anweisungen aus. Erst die dadurch erzeugten Daten schickt das Werkzeug über ein Pseudo-Terminal zum Kandidaten.

I/O-Switch

Primär liest die Wiedergabekomponente die Datei mit den Testfall-Eingabedaten und erzeugt daraus die Eingabedaten für das Kandidaten-Programm. Dies entspricht dem statisch programmierten Testlauf. Der Testoperator kann aber zu jedem Zeitpunkt dynamisch in den Testlauf eingreifen. Dazu unterbricht er entweder den Interpreter oder er hat in den Testfall-Eingabedaten einen Breakpoint definiert. In beiden Fällen schaltet der Roboter seinen Eingabefocus auf den Operator am Terminal um. Er kann nun Kommandos an den Interpreter absetzen oder sich direkt zum Kandidaten-Programm durchschalten lassen. Das Werkzeug schaltet die Eingabe des Kandidaten hin und her zwischen dem vorgefertigten Testfall-Programm und dem Testoperator am Terminal.

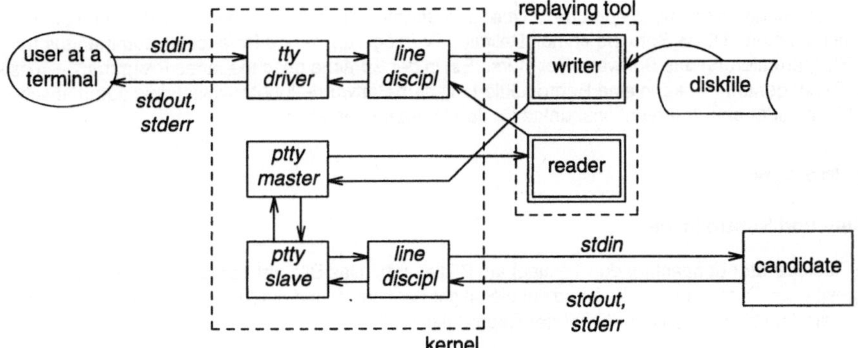

5.2. Synchronisation

Die schwierigste Aufgabe für den Software-Roboter besteht darin, zu entscheiden, wann und wieviel Daten er zum Kandidaten-Programm schicken soll. Im Gegensatz zu Batch-Programmen findet bei interaktiven Kandidaten ein synchronisierter Dialog zwischen Benutzer und Programm statt.

Der Benutzer am Terminal erzeugt wiederholt eine Menge von zusammengehörenden Eingabezeichen als Reaktion auf Programmausgaben. Der Software-Roboter muß diesen synchronisierten Kreislauf aus Aktion und Reaktion bei der Reproduktion nachbilden. Ihm fehlt aber jedes Kontextverständnis. Stattdessen muß er aufgrund der räumlich/zeitlichen Anordnung der Daten in den aufgezeichneten Strömen entscheiden, wann und wieviel Daten er zum Kandidaten-Programm schickt. Für das Analysieren und Erkennen der Synchronisations-Struktur in den Datenströmen existieren verschiedene Methoden.

Methode "*Ausgabe-Kontext*": Bei der Reproduktion sucht der Software-Roboter nach den Zeichenketten im Ausgabestrom des Kandidaten-Programms, die bei der Aufzeichnung den Eingaben vorausgingen. Dabei darf sich der Roboter aber nicht auf "Zeilen" verlassen. Die Kandidaten sind interaktive Programme, die meist keine Kommando**zeilen**-Schnittstelle besitzen.

Methode "*Videorecorder*": Mit jedem Eingabezeichen wird ein Zeitstempel aufgezeichnet. Bei der Wiedergabe fließen die Zeichen exakt zur gleichen Zeit wie bei der Aufzeichnung dem Kandidaten-Programm zu. Der "Videorecorder" kann die Aufzeichnung auch beschleunigt oder verlangsamt wiedergeben. Probleme mit der *zeitidentischen* Wiedergabe können bei verändertem Laufzeitverhalten des Kandidaten-Programms entstehen. Andere Antwortzeiten ergeben sich etwa durch unterschiedlich starke Rechnerbelastung oder unterschiedlich effiziente Programmversionen.

Methode "*Lücke*": Bei der Aufzeichnung versucht der Software-Roboter zusammenhängende Ketten von Eingabezeichen dadurch zu identifizieren, daß er auf zeitliche Lücken in den Datenströmen achtet. Bei der Wiedergabe beobachtet der Roboter ebenfalls die Datenströme und synchronisiert sich auf vergleichbare Lücken.

Methode "*rastloser Benutzer*": Gelte die Annahme, daß die Antwortzeiten des Kandidaten-Programms vernachlässigbar gering sind und der Benutzer ohne Denkpausen ununterbrochen Daten eingibt. Der Software-Roboter bildet diesen Benutzer dadurch nach, daß er bei der Reproduktion pro Zeiteinheit, Bruchteil einer Sekunde, ein aufgezeichnetes Zeichen zum Kandidaten schickt.

Methode "*Kommandosprache*": Über den Strömen der aufgezeichneten Daten wird eine Syntax definiert. Diese Sprache enthält Delimiter, Verzögerungs- und Breakpoint-Kommandos für die Programmierung des Software-Roboters. Ein in der Sprache geschriebenes Programm — Testlauf-Skript genannt — kann eine Reproduktion mit dem Software-Roboter vollständig automatisch ausführen oder aber Interventionspunkte für den Operator vorsehen.

5.3. Probleme

Daten- und Kontrollkanal

Der Testoperator beobachtet den Testlauf am Bildschirm. Das Bild am Terminal zeigt das Echo der eingespielten Daten, sofern der Kandidat dies nicht verhindert, und die Ausgaben des Kandidaten. Das Terminal bildet den *Datenkanal* der Reproduktion ab.

Will der Testoperator jedoch dynamisch in den Testlauf eingreifen, ergibt sich am Bildschirm ein Problem mit der Darstellung der Interaktion zwischen ihm und dem Software-Roboter. Insbesondere bei bildschirm- oder maskenorientierten Kandidaten stört Text, der durch die Interaktion entsteht, den Bildschirmaufbau. Nötig ist hier ein *Kontrollkanal*, über den Testoperator und Wiedergabekomponente kommunizieren können, ohne den Datenkanal des Testlaufs zu beeinflussen.

Die erste Implementierung löst das Problem dadurch, daß die Kommunikation zwischen Operator und Wiedergabekomponente "blind" erfolgen muß. Am Bildschirm erscheint kein Feedback, der Bildaufbau des Testlaufs bleibt ungestört. Für die nächste Version werden Statuszeile und Seitenspeicher in Terminals sowie virtuelle Terminals und andere Window-Techniken untersucht.

Synchronisations-Mechanismen

Die Bedeutung der Synchronisation zeigte sich besonders bei der ersten Implementierung der Wiedergabekomponente unter UNIX SVR3.2. Keine der aufgezeigten Methoden ließ sich in der ersten Version vollständig umsetzen.

Für die Methode "Videorecorder" fehlte wiederum ein Timer mit einer Auflösung kleiner als eine Sekunde. Gleiches gilt auch für den "rastlosen Benutzer" und die Methode "Lücke".

Die Methode "Ausgabe-Kontext" scheitert vorerst am simultanen Lesen mehrerer I/O-Verbindungen unter SVR3.2. Da zwei unabhängige Prozesse, *reader* und *writer*, die beiden Datenströme bearbeiten, kann das Wiedergabeprogramm folgende Aufgabe nicht trivial lösen:

> Schick dem Kandidaten erst dann die nächsten Zeichen,
> wenn von ihm bestimmte Zeichen angekommen sind.

Der *writer* Prozeß muß dem *reader* mitteilen, auf welche Zeichen vom Kandidaten-Programm er wartet und der *reader* muß den *writer* benachrichtigen, wenn er diese Zeichen gesehen hat.

Die erste Implementierung realisiert die Synchronisation mit dem Verzögerungskommando **`wait`** aus der Kommandosprache und nach der Methode "rastloser Benutzer". Da die Zeitauflösung nur mit der Feinheit eine Sekunde möglich war, entstand keine befriedigende Lösung.

In der zweiten Version verbessert der Timer mit Millisekunden-Auflösung deutlich die Reproduktions-Qualität bei den Methoden "rastloser Benutzer" und "Videorecorder". Die Kommandosprache wurde etwas verfeinert und bietet ebenfalls bessere Unterstützung für die Synchronisation.

Zur Unterstützung der am meisten versprechenden Methode "Ausgabe-Kontext" wird in der nächsten Version der Aufbau der Wiedergabekomponente und die tatsächlich zwingende Notwendigkeit einer Mehrprozeß-Konfiguration untersucht. Eine Abkehr von der zur Aufzeichnungskomponente symmetrischen Anordnung bei der Wiedergabekomponente könnte die Realisierung der Methode "Ausgabe-Kontext" möglich machen. Der bisher gefundene Ansatz dient dabei als Prototyp und Basis für die Weiterentwicklung.

6. Zusammenfassung

Wegen des grundlegenden Modells von UNIX (Terminal-Treiber, Terminal-Charakteristiken) stellt es sich als eine sehr subtile Aufgabe dar, Benutzereingaben für ein interaktives Programm aufzuzeichnen und gleichartig, "mechanisch" und reproduzierbar, wieder abzuspielen.

Hauptprobleme bei einer Implementierung unter UNIX System V Release 3.2 sind die Notwendigkeit, simultan von mehreren I/O-Verbindungen lesen zu müssen, und das Fehlen eines Zeitgebers mit einer Auflösung kleiner als eine Sekunde. Obwohl sich beide Probleme mit UNIX System V Release 4 leicht lösen lassen, werden Lösungsmöglichkeiten für das Release 3.2 entwickelt.

Derzeit ist die Aufzeichnungskomponente zufriedenstellend realisiert. Die Wiedergabekomponente dagegen befindet sich noch in einem verbesserungsfähigen Entwicklungszustand. Die prinzipielle Machbarkeit des Konzepts ließ sich aber bereits zeigen.

7. Literatur

Bentley 1986
Jon L. Bentley. »Little Languages.« *Comm ACM* **29** (8): 711-721, Aug 1986.

Faison 1986
George S. Faison. »Script Revisited (Wizard's Grabbag).« *UNIX World* **3** (3): 79-88, Mar 1986.
Shell script, which records a session with pipes and *tee*(1). Early solution, no replay.

Kleber 1993
Hermann Kleber. *Weiterentwicklung eines Tools zur automatischen Reproduktion von interaktiven, bildschirmorientierten UNIX-Applikationen*. Ulm: Universität, Mathematik/SAI; 1993. - Diplomarbeit, Betreuer: Schweiggert/Waldbauer.

Koch 1991
Frank A. Koch. *Software-Recht, Teil 1*.
Berlin: Springer; 1991. ISBN 3-540-52493-2.

Koch 1992
Frank A. Koch. »Produkthaftung für Software — Haftungsentlastung durch Qualitätssicherung.« In: *Qualität in der Informationsverarbeitung*. Wiesbaden: Forkel-Verlag; 1992: 54-61. (HMD; Heft 163, 29. Jahrgang). ISSN 0939-2602.

K&P 1984
Brian W. Kernighan, Rob Pike. *The UNIX Programming Environment*. Englewood Cliffs, NJ: Prentice-Hall; 1984. (Prentice-Hall Software Series). ISBN 0-13-937681-X.

Nathe 1992
Michael Nathe. *Automatische Reproduzierbarkeit von interaktiven, bildschirmorientierten UNIX-Applikationen*. Ulm: Universität, Mathematik/SAI; 1992. - Diplomarbeit, Betreuer: Schweiggert/Waldbauer.

Ousterhout 1990
John K. Ousterhout. »Tcl: An Embeddable Command Language.« In: *Proc of USENIX 1990 Winter Technical Conf*. Berkeley, CA: USENIX Association; Jan 1990: 133-146.
Intro to the *tool command language*. First paper about *Tcl*.

Ousterhout 1993
John K. Ousterhout. *An Introduction To Tcl and Tk*.
Reading, MS: Addison-Wesley; to appear in 1993. Draft on Internet available.
Complete intro to Tcl and Tk with excellent and concise examples.

Pizzi 1992
Riccardo Pizzi. »using *poll*(2) to sleep for X milliseconds on ISC 2.2.« *comp.unix.sysv386*, Jun 1992. Network News, Message-ID: <1992Jun16.212958.8684@nervous.com>, From: pizzi@nervous.com.

Stevens 1990
W. Richard Stevens. *UNIX Network Programming*. Englewood Cliffs, NJ: Prentice-Hall; 1990. (Prentice-Hall Software Series). ISBN 0-13-949876-1.

Waldbauer 1993
Bernd Waldbauer. »Software Timer — Wie genau kann ein Unix System Zeitabstände messen?« *Offene Systeme* **2** (2): 101-107, Jun 1993.

Methods and Tools for the Use of Parallel Computer Architectures

A. Bode

Institut für Informatik
Lehrstuhl für Rechnertechnik und Rechnerorganisation
Sonderforschungsbereich 342
Technische Universität München,
Arcisstr. 21, D–80290 München,
Tel.: +49+89-2105-8240, email: bode@informatik.tu-muenchen.de,

Abstract. Main goal of the research group "Methods and Tools for the Use of Parallel Computer Architectures" is the development of techniques for the efficient use of existing parallel architectures for a number of applications. The research activities are described in the following four papers. This first paper gives an overview on the research goals and the working plan, whereas the three following papers cover particular areas of interest such as a very high level programming language, heuristical methods for parallel computation and low and high level tools for program development. This work is sponsored by the German Science Foundation under contract number SFB342.

1 Virtualization of Parallel Architectures

The German Science Foundation started funding the project "Methods and Tools for the Use of Parallel Computer Architectures" in January 1990 for a period of two years. Currently, the project is in its second funding phase ending December 1994. About 100 researchers are involved in the activities, almost 25 % of them being payed by the German Science Foundation.

The main starting point for the initiative of the research group at Technische Universität München was the observation, that scalable Parallel Computer Architectures based on distributed memory arrangements are available, but that there is no generally applicable theory on the efficient construction and implementation of parallel application algorithms and related systems software. Moreover, no standards for programming such systems are available. Efficient programming of such systems is mainly possible through the use of highly architecture–specific message passing libraries. By this fact, most of the programs developed for such systems are neither scalable nor portable. Other problems are related to the lack of distributed programming tools such as distributed debuggers, performance analyzers, parallel program visualizers etc.

This situation is the main reason for the fact, that even though commercial multi–processor systems based on cheap of-the-shelf multiprocessor and memory hardware offer very good price/performance ratios, industrial applications of such systems remain rather restricted. It was the conviction of the research partners that the industrial application of distributed memory systems highly depends on standardization and at least partly virtualisation of the distributed machine architecture. In this way, not only portability and scalability of programs would be addressed, but also efficiency in developing programs for such systems.

For this reason, the main goal of the research initiative was the development of methods and tools for the efficient use of parallel systems including programming aspects. To evaluate the techniques and strategies developed, a number of representative application areas were chosen.

Today, SFB342 consists of 15 research groups, organized in five project areas (compare table 1). Main contractor for the research grant is the department for informatics at Technische Universität München including 8 research groups, the department for electrical engineering of TU München with one research group, the department of informatics of Ludwig Maximilians Universität München with one research group, two research groups within the department of informatics at Humboldt Universität Berlin as well as two industrial partners (Siemens AG and the European Supercomputer Development Center of Intel Germany).

2 Individual Project Description

The following is a more detailed description of the individual project areas and projects in the order of their appearance in table 1. Projects grouped in project area A: "Fundamentals and tools for virtualizing parallel computer architectures" develop methods and tools for the entire design cycle of parallel and distributed programs starting from specification and ending with the execution. Projects grouped in project area B: "Methods and applications for virtualizing parallel architectures" are the representative users for the methods and tools developed in project area A. Themes in the project areas C, D and EY, which are external partners, fall either in the application or user category.

When the project was started in 1990, the main machine architectures at which the solutions were targeted were multiprocessor systems with distributed memory. Several versions of Intel's iPSC–systems (iPSC, iPSC/2, iPSC/860) and Parsytec (Parsytec SC) were available. In the meantime, a number of different architectures are also considered: Shared memory architectures (Alliant FX 2800, Sequent Symmetry), virtual shared memory machines (KSR–1) and heterogeneous networks of workstations.

2.1 Integration of Tool Environment and Computer Architecture

Main topic of this project is the development of tools for the late phases of the life cycle of distributed and parallel software. Two main classes of tools may be distinguished:

- Elementary tools for the interactive and cyclic development of parallel software such as parallel debuggers, parallel program flow visualizers, parallel mapping instruments, parallel performance analysis tools

Table 1. Organisation of SFB342 "Methods and Tools for the Use of Parallel Computer Architectures" into project areas and projects (names in brackets stand for research project leaders)

A	**Fundamentals and tools for virtualizing parallel computer architectures**
A1	Integration of tool environment and computer architecture (Bode)
A3	Formalisms for specification, design and analysis (Brauer, Kröger, Reisig)
A4	Classification and parallelization by reduction analysis (Brauer, Lange)
A5	Parallelization in inference systems (Fronhöfer, Jessen, Radig)
A6	Design methodology for distributed systems (Broy)
B	**Methods and applications for virtualizing parallel architectures**
B1	Parallelization of CAD algorithms for VLSI (Antreich, Johannes)
B2	Virtualised parallelization of database systems (Bayer, Paul)
B3	Parallelization of hierarchically structured numerical algorithms (Zenger)
B4	Parallel simulation of digital systems with high complexity (Antreich, Johannes, Bauer)
C	**Industrial Partner: Siemens AG (Müller-Stoy)**
C1	Virtualization of local memories in parallel computer architectures (Kober)
C2	Methods for automatic generation of fine grained parallelism for VLIW architectures (Böckle)
C3	Parallelization of CAD algorithms for VLSI (Grüter, Hörbst)
D	**Industrial Partner: Intel GmbH, ESDC - European Supercomputer Development Center (Bemmerl)**
D1	Portable performance analysis system for parallel architectures (Bemmerl)
EY	**Humboldt University Berlin**
EY1	Design and implementation of analysis algorithms for Petri-nets based on structured labels (Starke)
EY2	Object-oriented methods and tools for rapid prototyping of distributed software and hardware systems using the formal specification language OSDL (Fischer)

- High level development tools for application–transparent (automatic) parallelization such as dynamic load balancer and specialized application–oriented tools (visualizers, expert systems for parallel algorithm evaluation)

An elementary tool environment TOPSYS (TOols for Parallel SYStems) was developed covering the following main features:

- Integrated system of debugger, visualizer and performance analyzer
- Use of common graphical user interface based on X Windows
- Evaluation of different monitoring techniques (hardware, software, hybrid)
- Runtime oriented tools
- Hierarchical views of system and application program
- Support of highly dynamic programs (dynamic process creation/deletion)

TOPSYS was developed in conjunction with MMK (Multiprocessor Multitasking Kernel), a message passing library offering location–transparency. This feature was also the prerequisite to the implementation of an application transparent dynamic load balancing system. For a detailed description see companion paper by [Lud93] and [BB91].

All of the tools were developed to be used by all application projects described in the following.

2.2 Formalisms for Specification, Design and Analysis

Until now there is no generally accepted and widely used set of definitions, methods and techniques for the specification, design and analysis of distributed interactive systems. A number of different approaches is known from the literature. In this project, new formalisms based on the concept of Petri–nets are developed. An integration with traditional concepts, stemming from the area of sequential programming is tried and ideas and results from other important approaches such as process algebras, UNITY–based specification and temporal logic are used. Main difference to other approaches is the attempt of not merely adding additional constructs to techniques for sequential programs and systems but to start with concurrency as a basic feature of the systems, which implies different procedures for system construction. The techniques developed have been applied to the specification of real problems of other groups, e.g. the specification of a protocol for virtual shared memory [GK93].

2.3 Classification and Parallelization by Reduction Analysis

The design and analysis of parallel algorithms regarding efficiency, correctness and tractability are important aspects. This project aims at methods and constructions of parallel complexity theory. Parameters, models and features relevant for parallelization are characterized by the use of conventional complexity theory. Pragmatic aspects in the development of parallel algorithms are treated in the framework of the concept of the SyPrAM. Compare [GHLR91] and [Lan93].

2.4 Parallelization in Inference Systems

Inference systems pose new problems for programming and parallelization. Within this project, a number of different parallelization strategies are analyzed with regard to the potential for parallelism in inference systems and their efficient use. A number of sequential inference systems were chosen to be ported into functionally identical parallel systems. Main aim was the virtualization of parallelism in that sense, that the user of such systems must not explicitly control the parallel execution of queries or theorems. Additionally, the stepwise transition to systems with distributed agents and massive parallelism was evaluated. For more details see companion paper [SG93].

2.5 Design Methodology for Distributed Systems

The systematic design and provably correct implementation of robust distributed system architectures needs new methods and techniques. Research in the field of distributed systems today is characterized by a large number of different approaches which are either rather theoretic or not well founded. A design methodology must start with a formal specification of the system and end with an executable program well adopted for the special needs of the target architecture and environment. The design methodology must allow for the description of distributed systems on different abstract levels such that an efficient implementation may be derived from an abstract representation and finally allowing for the prove of correctness. For more detail see companion paper [BDS93].

2.6 Parallelization of CAD Algorithms for VLSI

Existing tools for the design of highly integrated circuits (VLSI) have problems both regarding quality of design and size of the integrated circuits in number of gates or transistors. The development of better design methods than those available on sequential computer architectures is the main aim of the group parallelization of CAD algorithms. It is beyond the scope of this project, to obtain a full and integrated design system. Rather, the following problems were chosen for development: layout synthesis and generation of test patterns. The project proceeded in the following four steps:

- Definition of program parts suitable for parallelization
- Design of new parallel algorithms
- Implementation of the algorithms on different parallel architectures
- Evaluation with examples relevant for the industrial application.

The applications were chosen from the industrial partner, Siemens AG in close cooperation with project C3 [SJ93], [KA93].

2.7 Virtualized Parallelization of Database Systems

Within this project, the problems related to porting an existing database system to parallel achitectures with distributed memory are investigated. The database system chosen is TransBase. When parallelizing database systems, two different goals may be distinguished:

- Increasing the number of transactions per time unit.
- Highly complex transactions.

The following investigations are essential for advances in parallel database systems:

- Query–optimization through vertical and horizontal parallelization of the operator–tree generated by the query.
- Distributed design of a database cache.
  The concept of data base cache is mainly based on a shared–memory–approach. Synchronization, logging, commit–processing and recovery turnout to be a bottleneck already for sequential highspeed transaction systems. Therefore a distributed solution for parallel data base systems is investigated.
- Load balancing within huge operator–trees: communication mechanisms and process boarders should be dynamically configurable and adaptable.

The investigations within this project are highly dependend on powerful performance analysis and program visualization tools. For details refer to [PB93].

2.8 Parallelization of Hierarchically Structured Numerical Algorithms

The design, analysis and implementation of parallel, hierarchically structured, numerical algorithms for applications in the natural sciences and in engineering is an important problem for further performace gains on parallel computer architectures. This project has chosen solvers for elliptical and parabolic differential equations and discrete optimization problems (such as the placement problem in the layout design of integrated circuits as addressed in project B1) as examples for new parallel algorithms. For the solution of differential equations the method of "sparse grids" is chosen. This technique is a member of the group of finite–elemente–methods, which are particularly suitable for differential equations.

A second topic to be addressed is a new programming technique using stream based functional elements. All of the example algorithms to be developed are used as test cases for this new programming technique. Tools for the development of such a new technique are developed in cooperation with the other projects. Compare [GSZ90], [GHSZ93].

2.9 Parallel Simulation of Digital Systems with High Complexity

The design of highly complex technical systems is not feasable without highly performant simulation systems. Most of the simulators follow the event–driven execution principle with a fully sequential timing. To circumvent the limitation of sequential processing, a parallel simulator based on the time–warp–method is developed. Different algorithms for the partitioning of structures are investigated. A static as well as a dynamic partitioning method leading to adaptive load balancing are implemented and tested for different examples.

2.10 Virtualization of Local Memories in Parallel Computer Architectures

The design of suitable memory structures is one of the most difficult problems for parallel computer architectures. Since most of the sequential computer architectures are memory–bounded in their performance, computer architectures with physically shared memory will never allow for massive parallelism. On the other hand, programming of shared memory is the more familiar model. For that reason, the concept of virtual shared memory was proposed. The main aim of this project is to evaluate the different possibilities for implementing virtual shared memory. Especially, the idea of hashing, as proposed by theoretical studies, is compared to the more classical method of cashing.

A simulator was designed, based on realistic assumptions on processor, interconnection network, memory and memory management unit behaviour to evaluate a model of virtual shared memory, derived from the execution model of bulk–synchronous–parallelism. It was shown, that the method is efficient [Hel93].

Another topic addressed in this project is the integration of secondary memory in the abstraction of virtual shared memory.

2.11 Methods for Automatic Generation of Fine Grained Parallelism for VLIW Architectures

Modern microprocessor architectures used as node processors in multiprocessor systems generally use internal fine grain parallelism such as superscalar, superpipelined and VLIW–architectures. This project aims at the development and evaluation of compiling techniques for such architectures. The evaluation is based on a simulator similar to an off–the–shelf RISC microprocessor with parametrizable superscalar architecture. This simulator is coupled with a compiler for the programming language C in which different optimization techniques are tested. Standard software and system software are used as application benchmarks (in contrary to most VLIW–studies, were only numerical algorithms are used because of their inherent parallelisms). Compare [BSW93].

2.12 Portable Performance Analysis System for Parallel Architectures

This project is a contribution by the second industrial partner: Intel's European Supercomputer Development Center, headed by Dr. T. Bemmerl, a former member of project A1. The aim is the development of a performance analysis system with the main emphasis on portability, scalability and configurability. Most of the performance analysis instruments, that have been developed for different multiprocessor systems are highly architecture–specific. The idea is to implement a system with different hierarchical levels, fully separated by a well defined and small interface. In this way, the different system layers such as monitoring, data assembling and evaluation and finally, graphical user interface are clearly separated and may be developed independently. Scalability and configurability mainly address the problem of how to collect data and how to display the huge amount of information in a massively parallel system. The target architecture is a Paragon XP/S system.

2.13 Design and Implementation of Analysis Algorithms for Petri–Nets Based on Structured Labels

This project develops theoretical background and an analysis tool for net-schemes applied to distributed systems. The net-schemes are developed in project A3.

2.14 Object–Oriented Methods and Tools for Rapid Prototyping of Distributed Software and Hardware Systems Using the Formal Specification Language OSDL

Main aim of the project is the developement of tools for rapid prototyping integrating design, specification, analysis and code generation. Object–oriented paradigms (data abstraction, inheritance, polymorphy, late–binding, overloading) will be used by applying object–oriented languages for the different phases of the design. The analysis of automatically generated structural and functional software prototypes is supported.

3 References

[BB91] T. Bemmerl and A. Bode. An Integrated Environment for Programming Distributed Memory Multiprocessors. In. A. Bode, editor, Distributed Memory Computing, Springer, LNCS Vol. 487, pp. 130–142,1991

[BDS93] M. Broy, C. Dendorfer and K. Stølen. HOPSA – a High-level Programming Language for Parallel Computations, in this proceedings

[BSW93] G. Böckle, Störmann and S. Wildgruber. Methods for Fine–Grain Parallelism Exploitation. In. A. Bode and M. Dal Cin, editors: Parallel Computer Architectures, Springer LNCS, to appear, 1993

[GHLR91] D. Gomm, M. Heckner, K.-J. Lange and G. Riedle. On the design of parallel programs for machines with distributed memory, In. A. Bode, editor, Distributed Memory Computing, Springer, LNCS Vol. 487, pp. 381–391,1991

[GHSZ93] M. Griebel, Huber, Störtkuhl and C. Zenger. On the Parallel Solution of 3D PDE's on a Network of Workstations and on Vector Computers. In. A. Bode and M. Dal Cin, editors: Parallel Computer Architectures, Springer LNCS, to appear, 1993

[GK93] D. Gomm and E. Kindler. Causality Based Proof of a Distributed Shared Memory System. In. A. Bode and M. Dal Cin, editors: Parallel Computer Architectures, Springer LNCS, to appear, 1993

[GSZ90] M. Griebel, M. Schneider and C. Zenger. A Combination Technique for the Solution of Sparse Grid Problems. SFB Bericht 342/19/90, TU München, 1990

[Hel93] M. Hellwagner. Randomized Shared Memory – Concept and Efficiency of a Scalable Shared Memory Scheme. In. A. Bode and M. Dal Cin, editors: Parallel Computer Architectures, Springer LNCS, to appear, 1993

[KA93] P. Kraus and K. Antreich. Application of Fault Parallelism to the Automatic Test Pattern Generation for Sequential Circuits. In. A. Bode and M. Dal Cin, editors: Parallel Computer Architectures, Springer LNCS, to appear, 1993

[Lan93] K.-J. Lange. Unambiguity of Circuits, Theoretical Computer Science 107, pp. 77/94, 1993

[Lud93] T. Ludwig. UPAS – Universally Programmable Architecture and Basic Software, in this proceedings

[PB93] M. Pawlowski and Bayer. Parallel Sorting of Large Data Volumes on Distributed Memory Multiprocessors. In. A. Bode and M. Dal Cin, editors: Parallel Computer Architectures, Springer LNCS, to appear, 1993

[SG93] C. Suttner and C. Goller. HEUROPA, Heuristic Optimization of Parallel Computations, in this proceedings

[SJ93] H. Spruth and F. Johannes. Architectures for Parallel Slicing Enumeration in VLSI Layout. In. A. Bode and M. Dal Cin, editors: Parallel Computer Architectures, Springer LNCS, to appear, 1993

HOPSA — a High-level Programming Language for Parallel Computations

Manfred Broy, Claus Dendorfer, Ketil Stølen
SFB342, Technische Universität München
Arcisstraße 21, 80290 München
E-mail: broy,dendorfe,stoelen@informatik.tu-muenchen.de

Abstract

The use of massive parallel computer architectures for the solution of computation intensive tasks requires specific programming concepts and thus makes programming more difficult. This is because the parallel execution and the particular properties of the chosen machine architecture must be taken into consideration. An abstract programming language more closely reflecting the specification notation is therefore desirable. Programs written in this language should allow a translation into efficient code for massive parallel computers. In that connection, one may ask: which aspects of parallel programming should be treated explicitly in the source code, and which aspects (like load balancing, parallelization and process administration) should be generated by a translator with certain analyzing capabilities. Our long term goal is the implementation of such a language based, for example, on the operating system MMK, *Multitasking Multiprocessing Kernel,* which has been developed at the Technische Universität München.

1 Introduction

Because of the very complicated process interactions, parallel programming is much more difficult than programming in traditional sequential languages. Since parallel programs often are expected to work in environments where high reliability is essential (telecommunication, industrial process controlling etc.), some means are needed to develop such programs in a systematic fashion, and to formally verify their critical parts with respect to specifications. As an additional difficulty, in many cases, because of high performance requirements, massive parallel machines have to be used. Therefore the programs must be written in languages which permit translation into efficient code for such architectures. Such languages should offer a suitable model for parallel processing that does not depend upon a particular computer architecture and therefore can be adapted to a variety of machines. Hence there are (at least) four major issues to consider in the development of realistic parallel programs:

- ease of programming and appropriate programming concepts,
- reasonably efficient implementation,

- embedding into a development method which allows for formal verification,
- suitable abstraction from concrete computer architectures.

In this introduction, we will discuss some approaches to parallel programming with respect to these criteria.

Conventional shared-state languages with parallel constructs like some dialects of FORTRAN usually provide very efficient implementations. However, in such programming languages even the behavior of programs consisting of only a few lines of code can be hard to figure out. Moreover, large and complicated proofs are often required to formally verify that such programs satisfy certain properties. For many of these languages there is not even a proper semantics.

An interesting new development are "parallel" languages that have no explicit parallel constructs at all. This is for example the case in Jade [RSL92], where a "parallel" program is basically a sequential program augmented with pragmatic declarations intended to help the compiler find a sensible parallelization. All parallel executions of a Jade program deterministically generate the same result as a sequential execution. Thus nondeterminism and time-dependencies, which normally make parallel programs hard to debug, cannot occur. Standard refinement calculi for sequential programs like [Jon90], [Mor90] can easily be extended to allow for the development of programs in a language like Jade (see for example [Len82]). However, the fact that nondeterminism and time-dependency cannot occur also indicates the weaknesses of this approach: only a restricted amount of parallelization can be gained, and moreover, the language is unsuitable for modeling inherently concurrent systems like communication systems.

Sequential programming languages are often "parallelized" by adding some additional programming constructs for parallel executions. Linda [CG89] is a formalism for conducting such extensions. Linda only deals with process creation and communication. The actual computing must be coded in the sequential language in which Linda is embedded. Linda can be used to model coarse, medium and fine-grained approaches to parallelism. The communication primitives of Linda are quite low-level, which means that the use of formal methods can be difficult.

PCN [FT91] is a procedural language with explicit programming constructs for parallel execution. The individual processes are coded in C, and processes can communicate only over definitional variables. A definitional variable is initially undefined, and what is thereafter assigned to it can never be overwritten. This ensures that there is no nondeterminism due to different interleavings of atomic statements. Since definitional variables for example can be of type stream, stepwise read/write communication is possible. The creators of PCN estimate that only 3% of the total execution time is spent by the parts written in PCN code. Thus, the overhead is low. Moreover, the exclusive use of definitional variables simplifies formal reasoning.

Another well-known concept for procedural parallel languages appears in formalisms like CSP [Hoa86] and languages like Occam [Ltd88]. A CSP process can only send and receive messages by synchronous communication. This means that the processes interact in a much more controlled way than in a shared-state language. A problem is that Occam is not really a high-level language; it is rather designed for low-level system programming.

There are also many approaches to parallel programming in the object-oriented tradition. However, so far there are no fully compositional development methods for this type of languages (some interesting preliminary attempts are described in [Ame89], [Jon92], [Mey93]).

Often it is claimed that declarative languages are easier to use. For example, pure functional languages like Haskell [HW90] seem to be very convenient for programming. Also the efficiency of sequential implementations of these languages has been improved to such a degree that functional and C [KR88] programs reach the same order of magnitude in execution times [AJ89]. Because functional programming is very close to writing equations, it is quite easy to design such programs and reason about them. Theoretically, functional programs can be executed both by sequential and parallel machines without modification [PJ89], [Rep91]. There is, however, currently no efficient distributed implementation of such a programming language. An additional problem is that functional programming languages offer too many constructs that do not fit well into a development method. We think that by suitably restricting the programming languages program engineering becomes easier. Note that there are also approaches which enrich functional programming languages with explicit parallel constructs and communication primitives (see for example [vENPS90]).

There are a number of other languages which claim to be both easy to use and specification close. In some application areas, the use of executable specification languages has become standard, for example in the field of communication systems [Hog89]. For less specialized applications, it can be argued that some sort of logic programming language would be very suitable. However, we do not think that programs written in such a language are more understandable than functional programs, and the implementations of logic programming languages are much less efficient. Constraint programming may be an alternative, but currently it is difficult to use (see [SHW93]).

In this paper we will present a simple, data-flow like, functional language, called HOPSA, currently being designed at the Technische Universität München. In this language, the sequential processes are coded in functional programming notation, while "standard" communication tools are employed to connect the processes in a systematic way. The communication structure is basically characterized by a set of equations.

Programs written in this language are easy to write. A development method for HOPSA programs, called Focus, is also available. HOPSA programs are specification close and therefore well-suited for formal program development.

All the mentioned programming languages have their respective merits. However, they differ from HOPSA in that the latter has been specially designed to meet the four requirements stated above. In this paper, we will devote one section to each of these requirements. In particular, we will comment on

- the programming language HOPSA,
- a possible implementation of HOPSA,
- the development method Focus aimed at writing correct HOPSA programs,
- methods to map HOPSA programs onto different computer architectures using dynamic load balancing techniques.

2 The Programming Language HOPSA

A HOPSA program can be modeled in terms of networks of *agents*. Each agent has a fixed number of input/output ports, which are connected to other agents by directed, asynchronous communication channels. Agents communicate only via these channels. This model is compositional in the sense that whole networks of agents can be viewed as agents again. Hence there are two types of agents:

- *basic* agents, which can be thought of as the sequential processes of our language or the atomic building blocks performing the computations,
- *composite* agents, i.e. agents representing whole networks of agents.

A HOPSA program consists of three disjoint sets of declarations:

- declarations of basic agents,
- declarations of composite agents,
- declarations of channels.

The declaration of a basic agent is nothing else than a functional program defining a continuous function which, given a tuple of complete input histories represented by the streams of messages received on the input channels, yields a tuple of complete output histories represented by the streams of messages sent along the output channels. The syntax for the declaration of basic agents does not differ significantly from the syntax of well-known functional languages like Haskell or ML [HMM86]. An example is given in Figure 2.

The declaration of a composite agent is basically a **let** construct with a set of channel declarations, characterizing a network of agents, in its body.

The declaration of a channel is an equation with free channel variables. It characterizes the way messages are assigned to channels.

The declarations of channels together with the declarations of composite agents constitute what we will refer to as the *network definition.*

The network definition of a simple sorting network is given in Figure 1 and represented graphically in Figure 3. It consists of two channel declarations defining the channels i and o, respectively, and a declaration of the composite agent *sort*, which has two additional channel declarations in its right-hand side. $frontend$ and *cell* are basic agents. $frontend$ basically sends the sequence of messages to be sorted along i and receives the sorted sequence on o.

The functional definition of *cell* is given in Figure 2. The agent *cell* can store one message and has two input channels and two output channels. If the next message received along its first input channel is less than the stored message, the new message is stored, and the old message is sent along its second output channel, otherwise the stored message remains in its store, and the new message is forwarded. When a special end of sequence message **eof** is received, the agent *cell* passes this message on, sends the stored message

$$i = frontend(d)$$

$$o = \textsf{await}\ i\ \textsf{then}\ sort(i)$$

$$\begin{aligned} sort(c) = \textsf{let}\ & \\ & (d, b) = cell(c, a) \\ & a = \textsf{await}\ b\ \textsf{then}\ sort(b) \\ \textsf{in}\ d & \end{aligned}$$

Figure 1: Network Definition of the Sorting Network.

$$\begin{array}{lll} cell & : & StreamData \times StreamData \rightarrow StreamData \times StreamData \\ store & : & Data \times StreamData \times StreamData \rightarrow StreamData \times StreamData \\ copy & : & StreamData \times StreamData \rightarrow StreamData \times StreamData \end{array}$$

$$\begin{array}{lll} cell(\textsf{eof}\ \&\ i, a) & = & [\textsf{eof}, \langle\rangle]\ \&\ cell(i, a) \\ cell(d\ \&\ i, a) & = & store(d, i, a) \end{array}$$

$$\begin{array}{lll} store(s, \textsf{eof}\ \&\ i, a) & = & [s, \textsf{eof}]\ \&\ copy(i, a) \\ store(s, d\ \&\ i, a) & = & [\langle\rangle, max(s, d)]\ \&\ store(min(s, d), i, a) \end{array}$$

$$\begin{array}{lll} copy(i, \textsf{eof}\ \&\ a) & = & [\textsf{eof}, \langle\rangle]\ \&\ cell(i, a) \\ copy(i, d\ \&\ a) & = & [d, \langle\rangle]\ \&\ copy(i, a) \end{array}$$

Figure 2: Functional Definition of a Single Sort Cell.

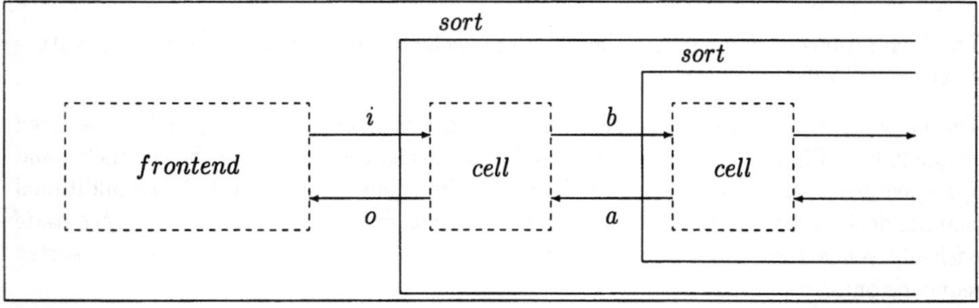

Figure 3: Graphical Representation of the Sorting Network.

along the first output channel, and thereafter forwards the messages it receives on its second input channel along its first output channel until it once more receives the end of sequence message, which has been "reflected" by the first *cell* not storing a message.

Clearly, the unfolding of the potentially infinite network of sort cells must be conducted in line with the progress of the computation, so that there are always "enough" sort cells available, and, at the same time, only the required number of sort cells is created. This is the task of the composite agent *sort*, i.e. it controls the unfolding of the sorting algorithm. Each *sort* call creates a new *cell* agent, and when (if at all) the first message is received on the local channel b, a new *sort* agent is also created. Thus, **await** b **then** $sort(b)$ waits until a message is received on b and then creates a new *sort* agent. As a result we get an unbounded (potentially infinite) list of sorting cells which forward new messages until they "fall" in place and then send them back in sorted order. The algorithm is linear with respect to both time and space.

Observe that in channel declarations global names for channels are introduced, while the channel variables occurring in, say, *sort*, are just formal parameters. If we substitute i and o for respectively c and d in *sort* we get exactly the same network. However, if we substitute c and d for respectively i and o in the second channel declaration only, we get a network with four unconnected channels.

The **await** construct may seem unnecessary at a first glance. An obvious alternative would be "lazy creation", where each process is created as soon as the first input message arrives. However, this would lead to unexpected results for agents declared, for example, by $f(x) = \langle 1, 2, 3 \rangle$. Such an agent would only produce output if at least one input message is received on its input channel, which does not agree with its (seemingly) obvious equational definition. Therefore, we decided to control process creation explicitly in terms of the **await** construct.

A second alternative would be to implement a demand driven process creation mechanism, where new processes are only created if their output is actually needed. However, this would require the use of a request-supply protocol for each of the asynchronous channels, which does not fit very well into the simple framework of asynchronous communication.

3 The Implementation of HOPSA

Some implementation experiments have been carried out based on the core language as defined above. In particular, a compiler has been written that translates network definitions into system calls of MMK [BKMR91]. MMK provides basic process creation mechanisms and supports process communication in terms of so-called mailboxes. These mailboxes can be configured in a number of ways, in particular they can be used to approximate asynchronous, buffered channels (in fact there is a maximum buffer length, which we disregarded in our experiments).

The compiler is a rather small program written in Standard ML, which takes HOPSA programs and produces a variety of files that are further processed by an MMK preprocessor and the standard C compiler.

Up to now, the sequential agents themselves have to be written in pure C extended with some of MMK's communication instructions. A compiler for the translation of sequential agents written in the functional programming notation is of course also planned. However, since the sequential implementation of functional languages is quite well understood, we have so far concentrated on the implementation of the network definitions.

4 The Development Method Focus

Focus is a general framework, in the tradition of [Kah74], [Kel78], for the formal specification and development of distributed systems. A system is modeled by a network of agents communicating asynchronously via unbounded FIFO channels. A large number of different reasoning styles and techniques is supported (see for example [BDD+92], [Bro92c], [Bro92a], [SDW93]).

Focus provides mathematical formalisms which support the formulation of highly abstract, not necessarily executable specifications with a clear semantics. Moreover, Focus offers powerful refinement calculi, which allow distributed systems to be developed in the same style as sequential programs can be developed in VDM [Jon90] and the refinement calculi of [Bac88], [Mor90]. Finally, Focus is modular in the sense that design decisions may be checked at the point where they are taken, that component specifications can be developed in isolation, and that already completed developments can be reused.

A development of a program in Focus can be split into three main phases:

- a requirement phase where the requirement specification is formulated,
- a design phase where the architecture independent system development is carried out,
- an implementation phase where the system specification is mapped onto a particular architecture.

Any Focus specification can be modeled by a set of timed stream processing functions as defined in [Bro92b]. The same type of semantics can be assigned to HOPSA. Because of the close relationship between stream processing functions and the programming notation in HOPSA, Focus is particularly suited for the development of HOPSA programs. HOPSA may be used either as the final implementation language or as an executable prototype language.

5 The Mapping of Agents onto Processors

A network of agents characterized by a HOPSA program must be mapped onto a real processor architecture in some suitable way. As for example in UNITY [CM88], a HOPSA program as defined above only specifies the *maximum* possible parallelism. Considering that communication usually is rather expensive, it is not sensible to map every single agent to a new processor. This is especially obvious in the sorting example above, where a sort cell only stores one data element, and the number of sort cells required equals the length of the input.

Such a mapping from agents (and channels) to processors is a very basic theoretical concept. Nevertheless, it allows us to model and analyze all difficult pragmatic questions of process scheduling and load balancing. The mapping may change dynamically, i.e. during the execution of the program, which mirrors dynamic load balancing and process migration. An interesting question at this point is of course to what degree this mapping should (and can) be expressed explicitly in the HOPSA language, and how efficient heuristic mapping strategies are.

6 Extensions

As already pointed out, the HOPSA language is still at an experimental stage. In fact so far only a core language has been fixed, and a number of extensions are currently being considered.

In particular additional constructs for the manipulation of dynamic networks are needed. Currently, a network can be *expanded* via the **await** construct. However, there is no possibility to shrink a network by deleting agents and channels. Thus, pulsating networks cannot be expressed in the current version of HOPSA. One relatively straightforward extension to handle this problem is to have a construct which kills some part of the network structure when a certain end of computation message is received. For example with respect to the sorting algorithm above, we could employ this construct in the declaration of *sort* to kill the next *cell* and *sort* agents together with the local channels b and a when a certain message is received on the channel a. Here the question arises whether agents should be "killed" or "sent asleep", i.e., whether agents that are repeatedly deleted and created in a pulsating network should each time start from the same initial state, or from the last state of the previous incarnation. This leads also to questions regarding the garbage collection of processes.

We are also considering more general types of agent communications such as broadcasting. The communication of higher-order messages can also be used to express dynamic networks. Higher-order messages are nothing else than agents communicated via channels. Some interesting implementation issues arise when higher-order messages are allowed, for example whether the whole program should be transferred or just a pointer to the (shared) code and some status information.

It is well-known that certain weakly time-dependent agents like fair merge are hard to express in a functional setting [Kel78]. One straightforward way to handle this problem in HOPSA is to incorporate a specific fair merge construct [Bro88]. This construct characterizes an agent performing a fair merge of the messages received on its input channels. This construct can be modeled in the same way as any other HOPSA agent — by a set of timed stream processing functions.

The issue of dynamic network reconfiguration deserves further attention. The FOCUS framework seems to be well-suited for the:

- description of dynamic networks,
- reconfiguration of networks during execution,
- mapping of dynamic process networks onto static networks of processors,
- reconfiguration of processor mappings.

These issues are of high importance for the modeling of distributed systems. We plan to study them in more detail in the future.

7 Conclusions

In this paper we have advocated the use of a high-level, data-flow like, functional programming language called HOPSA. We have outlined a possible implementation, a design methodology, and some thoughts about efficient execution on parallel hardware.

Because

- the individual, sequential agents are conveniently coded in a functional programming notation,
- an efficient implementation is possible since the communication structure is given explicitly,
- the programming language is embedded into a formal development method,
- the concept of agents and channels, which are dynamically mapped onto processors, provides a suitable abstraction level for the writing of parallel programs,

we claim that the concept on which HOPSA is based meets the basic requirements stated in the introduction.

References

[AJ89] L. Augustsson and T. Johnsson. The chalmers lazy-ML compiler. *The Computer Journal*, 32:127–141, 1989.

[Ame89] P. America. Issues in the design of a parallel object-oriented language. *Formal Aspects of Computing*, 1:366–411, 1989.

[Bac88] R. J. R. Back. A calculus of refinments for program derivations. *Acta Informatica*, 25:593–624, 1988.

[BDD+92] M. Broy, F. Dederichs, C. Dendorfer, M. Fuchs, T. F. Gritzner, and R. Weber. The design of distributed systems — an introduction to Focus. Technical Report SFB 342/2/92 A, Technische Universität München, 1992.

[BKMR91] T. Bemmerl, C. Kasperbauer, M. Mairandres, and B. Ries. Programming tools for distributed multiprocessor computing environments. Technical Report SFB 342/31/91 A, Technische Universität München, 1991.

[Bro88] M. Broy. Nondeterministic data flow programs: How to avoid the merge anomaly. *Science of Computer Programming*, 10:65–85, 1988.

[Bro92a] M. Broy. Compositional refinement of interactive systems. Working Material, International Summer School on Program Design Calculi, August 1992.

[Bro92b] M. Broy. Functional specification of time sensitive communicating systems. In M. Broy, editor, *Proc. Programming and Mathematical Method*, pages 325–367. Springer, 1992.

[Bro92c] M. Broy. (Inter-) action refinement: the easy way. Working Material, International Summer School on Program Design Calculi, August 1992.

[CG89] N. Carriero and D. Gelernter. Linda in context. *Communications of the ACM*, 32:444–458, 1989.

[CM88] K. M. Chandy and J. Misra. *Parallel Program Design, A Foundation*. Addison-Wesley, 1988.

[FT91] I. Foster and S. Tuecke. Parallel programming with PCN. Technical Report ANL-91/32, Version 1.2, Argonne National Laboratory, 1991.

[HMM86] R. W. Harper, D. B. MacQueen, and R. G. Milner. Standard ML. Technical Report ECS-LFCS-86-2, University of Edinburgh, 1986.

[Hoa86] C. A. R. Hoare. *Communicating Sequential Processes*. Prentice-Hall, 1986.

[Hog89] D. Hogrefe. *Estelle, LOTOS and SDL, Standard-Spezifikationssprachen für verteilte Systeme*. Springer, 1989.

[HW90] P. Hudak and P. Wadler. Report on the programming language Haskell. Technical Report YALEU/DCS/RR-777, Yale University, 1990.

[Jon90] C. B. Jones. *Systematic Software Development Using VDM, Second Edition*. Prentice-Hall, 1990.

[Jon92] C. B. Jones. An object-based design method for concurrent programs. Technical Report UMCS-92-12-1, University of Manchester, 1992.

[Kah74] G. Kahn. The semantics of a simple language for parallel programming. In J.L. Rosenfeld, editor, *Proc. Information Processing 74*, pages 471–475. North-Holland, 1974.

[Kel78] R. M. Keller. Denotational models for parallel programs with indeterminate operators. In E. J. Neuhold, editor, *Proc. Formal Description of Programming Concepts*, pages 337–366. North-Holland, 1978.

[KR88] B. W. Kernighan and D. M. Ritchie. *The C Programming Language*. Prentice Hall, 1988.

[Len82] C. Lengauer. *A Methodology for Programming with Concurrency*. PhD thesis, University of Toronto, 1982.

[Ltd88] INMOS Ltd., editor. *Occam 2 Reference Manual*. Prentice Hall, 1988.

[Mey93] B. Meyer. Systematic concurrent object-oriented programming. Technical Report TR-EI-37/SC, ISE, Santa Barbara, 1993.

[Mor90] C. Morgan. *Programming from Specification*. Prentice-Hall, 1990.

[PJ89] S. L. Peyton Jones. Parallel implementations of functional programming lanuages. *The Computer Journal*, 32:175–186, 1989.

[Rep91] J. H. Reppy. *Concurrent Programming with Events — The Concurrent ML Manual.* Cornell University, 1991.

[RSL92] M. C. Rinard, D. J. Scales, and M. S. Lam. Heterogeneous parallel programming in Jade. In *Proceedings of Supercomputing'92*, pages 245–256, 1992.

[SDW93] K. Stølen, F. Dederichs, and R. Weber. Assumption/commitment rules for networks of asynchronously communicating agents. Technical Report SFB 342/2/93 A, Technische Universität München, 1993.

[SHW93] G. Smolka, M. Henz, and J. Würtz. Object oriented concurrent constraint programming in OZ. Technical Report RR-93-16, DFKI, 1993.

[vENPS90] M. van Eekelen, E. Nöcker, R. Plasmeijer, and S. Smetsers. *Concurrent Clean (Manual).* University of Nijmegen, 1990.

HEUROPA*
Heuristic Optimization of Parallel Computations

Christian B. Suttner Christoph Goller

SFB342, TU München
Arcisstr. 21, D-80290 München
E-mail: suttner@informatik.tu-muenchen.de

Abstract. The performance of almost all parallel algorithms and systems can be improved by the use of heuristics that affect the parallel execution. However, since optimal guidance usually depends on many different influences, establishing such heuristics is often difficult. Due to the importance of heuristics for optimizing parallel execution, and the similarity of the problems that arise for establishing such heuristics, the HEUROPA activity was founded to attack these problems in a uniform way. To overcome the difficulties of specifying heuristics by hand, machine learning techniques have been employed to obtain heuristics automatically. This paper presents the general approach used for learning heuristics, describes the applications arising in the various subprojects, and provides a detailed case study using the approach for a particular application.

1 Introduction

Parallel algorithms represent complex software, with a large number of parameters that need to be adjusted for optimal performance. However, algorithms which compute such optimal parameter values are usually intractable or unknown. As an example, even when precise data on the run-time of individual tasks is available, computing the parameters for achieving a minimal overall run-time is NP-complete. In the more realistic case where no precise information is available, optimal parameters cannot be established at all; instead, dynamic adjustment of the parameters is necessary as the computation proceeds. As a consequence, most parallel algorithms incorporate implicit or explicit heuristics for optimizing the parallel execution. Typical examples are heuristics for controlling the number of parallel tasks being generated, and the distribution of tasks among the processors.

* The HEUROPA acronym denotes an ongoing collaboration among subprojects of the SFB342 (Tools and Methods for Utilizing Parallel Computers) funded by the DFG (Deutsche Forschungsgemeinschaft). This collaboration currently involves the subprojects A1 (Basic Operating System for Multiprocessor Systems), A4 (Classification and Parallelization by Reduction Analysis), A5 (Parallelization of Inference Systems), B1 (Parallelization of Design Methods for VLSI Circuits), and B2 (Parallelization of Database Systems).

Since the optimization of parallel execution is desirable for all types of parallel algorithms, it has arisen as a natural cross-section among several subprojects of the SFB342. This common activity is termed HEUROPA - for HEURistic Optimization of PArallel executions. The goal of the HEUROPA activity is to study such heuristic optimization, and to develop and apply a methodology which allows appropriate heuristics to be established.

Obviously, the first step for establishing heuristics is to define what is to be optimized. Next, it is necessary to determine relevant information on which heuristics for the desired optimization can be based. This is already a crucial step in the process, since no useful guidance can be based on insufficient or irrelevant information. The question remains how to establish appropriate heuristics once all relevant information has been determined. As indicated above, the problems are that usually the algorithm is complex, with many parameters that may be tuned, and that the relevance of a particular piece of information to the optimization is not known. These problems commonly result in comparatively simple heuristics being constructed by hand. These are tested and improved until their performance seems acceptable. For this process, the information assumed to be most relevant is used and combined according to the intuition of the designer. While this traditional approach already allows improvement of the performance of a parallel algorithm and contributes insight into the system operation, it has several disadvantages. It is quite difficult and time-consuming to build heuristics this way, and the quality fully depends on the ability of the designer. Due to the required effort, usually only a small part of the relevant information is given to the heuristic, and the heuristic itself is limited to comparatively simple computations on that information. It basically is a trial and error approach, and it is not easy to establish a large set of heuristics which can be used selectively according to the current execution context (e.g. different load balancing heuristics for optional operational goals of an operating system).

In order to overcome these problems, the HEUROPA group focusses on the use of machine learning techniques for establishing appropriate heuristics automatically. It is based on evaluation function learning, early approaches to which date back as far as 1959 [Sam59, Sam67].

The paper is organized as follows. In Section 2, our approach to automatic learning of heuristics is described. Then, in Section 3, an overview of the HEUROPA activities, grouped according to the SFB342 subprojects, is presented. Section 4 contains a more detailed case study of the automatic learning as it occurred in one of the subprojects. Finally, a summary of the experiences and results obtained so far is given.

2 Learning Approach

Based on experience in automatic learning of heuristics for guiding the search of an automated theorem prover [SE90], a simple methodology for obtaining heuristics automatically has arisen. It can be separated into the following three phases:

I. Definitional Phase.
Given a parallel system which is to be improved.
1) Define the optimization goal and a set of tuning parameters.
The intended optimization depends on the user intentions, and the set of parameters for influencing the relevant performance depends on the system.
2) Define a set of presumably useful features.
The features encode the computation context that is required as input for a heuristic decision. A list of values for a particular set of features will be called *feature-vector*.

II. Learning Phase.
1) Generate training data from optimal system runs.
The training data consist of pairs of feature-vectors and desired evaluation function outputs (i.e., parameter settings). Such data may be obtained by simulations, empirical data, or theoretical considerations.
2) Learn an evaluation function which provides a generalized mapping from ideal feature-vector/parameter-vector tuples.

III. Working Phase.
Whenever an adjustment of the parameters is desired during a computation:
1) Compute the current feature-vector.
2) Apply the learned evaluation function to adjust the parameter values.

Figure 1 depicts the flow of information in the learning phase and the working phase. While the definitional phase is performed by the user only once at the beginning, the learning phase can be performed automatically with different sets of training data, each time producing a new heuristic evaluation function. In the working phase, a previously learned evaluation function is used for adjusting the system parameters during new system runs.

Since the heuristic decisions will depend on the quality of the information available, a suitable set of features providing enough relevant information is crucial for success. Appropriate learning methods will allow dealing with redundant and useless features, but there is no hope if too little information is conveyed. Thus, in case of doubt, rather too many features than too few should be included. Obviously, the definition of the features is a part within the approach where user knowledge and intuition contribute significantly to the results. Another part which allows user guidance is the selection of the training data. Since the feature-vector/desired parameter value tuples define the heuristic concept that will be learned, such data needs to be selected according to the user's intentions. Furthermore, depending on the number of different cases the data are drawn from and the similarity among these cases, the generality of the learned heuristics can be adjusted. A specific (and therefore hopefully powerful) heuristic is achieved by selecting data from cases similar to the intended application case. On the other hand, mixing many different cases will lead to general (but probably less powerful) heuristics.

Regarding appropriate machine learning techniques, it is desirable to ensure that nonlinear evaluation functions can be learned. Also, since a particular set

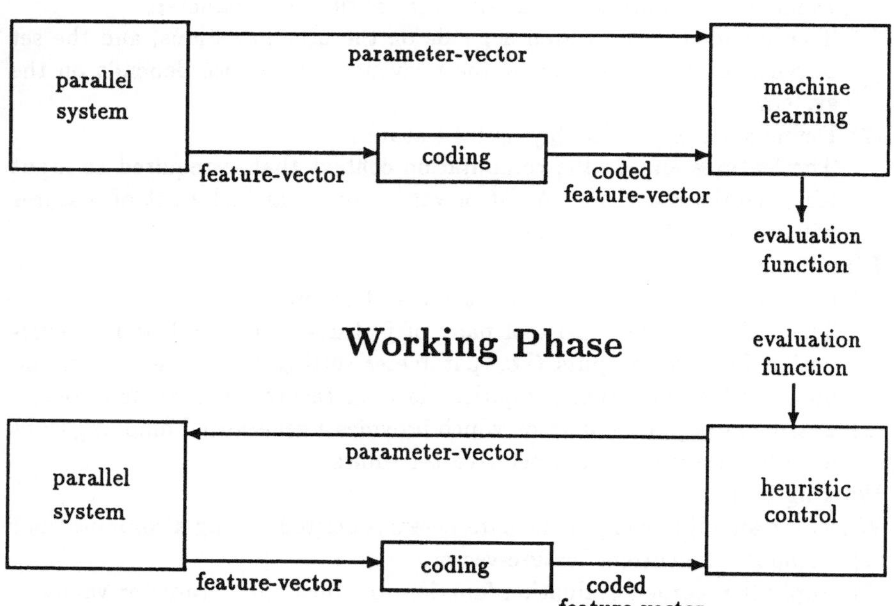

Fig. 1. The flow of information in the learning and the working phase.

of features may be insufficient to properly distinguish different situations in all cases, the method should be able to deal with contradictory evidence in the training data. Finally, irrelevant and redundant features should be handled appropriately. As methods providing such properties we employed back-propagation [SE91] and several other connectionist learning methods [Mic92] and, as a classical alternative, bayes decision theory [Wei91].

The general approach described above is currently used by the HEUROPA participants for establishing heuristics in their respective applications. Since most of them also experiment with hand-derived heuristics, it will be possible to compare the differences that arise through automatic learning. The individual applications are briefly described below, grouped according to the involved SFB subprojects.

3 HEUROPA Activities

3.1 Dynamic Load Balancing (A1)

The aim here is to provide dynamic load balancing by process migration, managed by the operating system. Most load management approaches for multiprocessor systems follow a common scheme (e.g., [SS84]). A measurement component determines the current load of the system resources. Based on these values an evaluation component decides if process migration is necessary, and where it should take place. Depending on this decision, a load movement may be performed by a migration component. Successful load management critically depends on the evaluation component. The operation of this component can be split into detection of imbalance, determination of the most relevant nodes (nodes with high and low load), and determination of the best candidate processes on the respective nodes for movement. Each decision can be treated by a separate heuristic, with a particular feature-vector as input. The basic paradigm used for load management fits our approach well, since the load measurement component already provides a feature-vector as output. The features for load balancing can be grouped into node load measures (e.g., processor idle time, available memory, message handling statistics) and process load measures (e.g., cpu time, memory usage, message handling statistics). As one of the particular problems for heuristic load management is the little knowledge about the significance of specific features for the decision, automatic learning provides a means for detecting and eliminating useless features. This is crucial for successful load management, as it is very important to keep the overhead as small as possible (eliminating irrelevant features both reduces the overhead due to the load measurement component as well as due to the evaluation component). A testbed has been implemented which allows specifying heuristics by hand, and a large number of experiments have been performed using straightforward hand-designed heuristics (see [Lud93]). Training data for automatic learning can be obtained by selecting good decisions from these previous runs.

3.2 Speedup-Phenomena for Boolean Satisfiability (A4)

Superlinear speedup results have been observed when parallelizing Davis-Putnam-like algorithms for the satisfiability problem of Boolean formulae [SMV87]. The sequence in which the variables of a formula are treated is of decisive influence on both the sequential and parallel run-time. Several heuristics for controlling this sequence have been constructed by hand, and compared on different families of formulae. Examples of features that are used for deriving heuristics are the frequency of literals and the pairs of variables inside a formula. It still needs to be clarified how appropriate training data should be generated.

At present, the choice of the probability distribution according to which the input formulae are drawn is not well understood [FP83]. Therefore, an important aspect of these investigations is the close connection between some features that the heuristics are based upon and some quantities of the chosen distribution. The general goal is not only to find efficient heuristics but also to give partial answers to the question of choosing an appropriate probability distribution. The ability to identify the relative significance of individual features for heuristic decisions by inspecting the learned evaluation functions promises further insight into this question.

3.3 Automated Theorem Proving (A5)

In this application the goal is to find a proof for a given theorem automatically, starting out from axioms defining a theory. This is closely related to solving queries in deductive data bases and expert systems. Automated theorem proving as well as human theorem proving can be regarded as a highly combinatorial search problem. Brute force approaches that explore every branch of the search tree, i.e., carrying out every applicable inference step, are usually not practicable for proving interesting theorems. Therefore parallelization by pure splitting of the search tree is of limited promise, as one can expect at most a linear speedup. Superlinear speed-up results reported by nearly all parallel theorem provers are mostly caused by changes in the search strategy. These changes had often not been intended, but were accidental side effects of the parallalization. New search strategies and heuristics for identifying the most promising parts of the search tree are very important, in order to cope with the complexity of the search. In this research, heuristic evaluation functions are used for obtaining a rating for each of the applicable inference steps at a decision point. The input information for such evaluation functions consists of a set of features describing the current state of the inference process and one of the possible inference steps to be rated. Since it is very difficult to develop heuristics by hand, and since it may be necessary to develop heuristics specifically for each problem domain (theory), they are derived automatically using machine learning techniques. Experiments have been performed with different strategies that allow to use such heuristic evaluation functions for guiding the seach process in sequential theorem proving. Strategies for using them to control the generation of search tasks in the parallel case are straightforward, and will be included in the prover currently under development. More details about the approach are provided in the case study in Section 4.

3.4 Automatic Test Pattern Generation (B1)

The aim for automatic test pattern generation is to find test patterns which detect all possible faults in a manufactured circuit. Due to the high complexity involved in such computations, heuristic search methods are commonly used. They are crucial for the success of sequential and parallel test pattern generation. The aim is now to improve the known heuristic methods by searching for common characteristics of the various circuit structures, by comparing the results of different heuristic methods used during the test pattern generation for these circuits, and by analyzing this accumulated data with automatic learning methods.

3.5 Adaptive Task Assignment (B2)

The aim here is to obtain heuristics for task assignment in a distributed multi-user environment. The execution of a parallel program is assumed to consist of the execution of a set of independent tasks of varying, but known, size (an important example where this scenario arises is task-oriented parallel query processing in relational database systems). The parallel execution is controlled by an assignment strategy that determines the mapping between tasks and processors. Initially, one task is given to each processor (the number of tasks is assumed to be larger than the number of available processors). By observing the run-time of previous tasks, the current load of individual processors can be estimated. Based on such estimates, the assignment strategy determines a successor for each terminating task (or decides not to give another task to the respective processor). The goal is now to obtain a heuristic assignment strategy which minimizes the time required to complete all tasks. Whenever a task terminates, the heuristic needs to determine which (if any) of the remaining tasks is sent to which processor. The features that can be used for such a decision are the task sizes, and the previous and current speeds of the processors. As a first step, straightforward choices for possible heuristics have been developed by hand and tested [Tro92]. The results show that intuitively appealing heuristics do not necessarily perform well. Training data for automatic learning can be obtained from the experiments with these strategies, with the goal of establishing a generalization of the strategies, combining the advantages of each and avoiding their disadvantages.

4 Case Study: Automated Theorem Proving

The approach of learning heuristics for automated theorem proving has been realized within SETHEO (for SEquential THEOremprover), which is a Model Elimination (ME) [Lov68] theorem prover, being sound and complete for full first-order logic. The ME calculus is very close to PROLOG's SLD-resolution, and in fact SETHEO can be seen as an extension of PROLOG to full first-order logic. It is implemented in C and utilizes compilation techniques, so that very high inference rates are attained. A detailed description of the prover and performance evaluations can be found in [LSBB92]. We will now give a brief description of the relevant issues in order to provide a better understanding of the way heuristics are derived and used.

Clause normal form is used for expressing formulas (axioms and theorems) in first-order predicate logic. In this format a formula consists of a conjunction of clauses, where each clause is a disjunction of literals. Each literal is a (possibly negated) predicate with zero or more arguments (called terms).

The search for a proof can be described in the following simplified way: A proof is a sequence of inference steps starting with a query, which is a clause resulting from the clausal representation of the theorem. There are two kinds of inference steps, namely *extension steps*[2] and *reduction steps* (although reduction steps are crucial to attain completeness for full first-order logic, they will not be treated here for the sake of simplicity). An *extension step* connects a literal s (called subgoal) in a clause C to a literal h (called head) of a clause D, if $\neg h$ is unifiable with s. The subgoal s is replaced by the subgoals (all literals except

[2] These are basically PROLOG-inference steps.

the head) of clause D. Such a clause D is either a fact (one-literal-clause), which terminates the proof for the current subgoal s, or it contains additional literals (subgoals), each of which in turn needs to be solved in order to complete the proof. Since, for each subgoal s, usually several candidate clauses exist for an extension step, a decision needs to be made which one to use (the decision point mentioned in Section 3.3). In case the decision later turns out not to lead to a proof, the other alternatives need to be tried instead (*backtracking*). Summarizing this, the prover enumerates proof attempts during the searching until a complete proof is constructed.

Since there are possibly infinitely many proof attempts, and since the execution mechanism performs a depth-first search, formulas may lead to non-terminating inference chains[3]. Therefore SETHEO allows the specification of various bounds which restrict the size and/or shape of possible proofs (respectively proof attempts), in order to define a finite part of the search space for exploration. The most important ones are the depth bound (depth of a proof) and the inference bound (number of inferences in a proof). Violation of a given bound during the search leads to backtracking. In practice, usually no proof can be found unless appropriate bounds are supplied. Since these bound values are unknown in advance, *iterative deepening search* is used. This means that the bounds are successively increased until a proof is found.

4.1 Definitional Phase

The heuristics we realized for SETHEO control the selection of inference steps at decision points. Each applicable inference step is rated by an evaluation function that estimates the probability that it will lead to a proof in the current proof context. The input for the evaluation function consists of features for describing the inference step (clause) to be rated, and, in order to get some information about the context, features which describe the state of the inference process. As clauses do not change during the proof search, the features describing them can be calculated statically at compile time. Examples of such features are the numbers of literals, different predicates, variables, and connections through variables from head to subgoals. Features describing the state of the inference process have to be calculated dynamically during the search. Their calculation therefore causes more overhead than static features. There are various measures for the size of the current proof attempt, such as the depth and the number of inferences. Other features describe the current subgoal to be solved (complexity of arguments, number of applicable inference steps) and measure the changes in the current proof attempt which will be caused by choosing the inference step being evaluated.

[3] In PROLOG, the programmer has to prevent this explicitely by carefully choosing the order of clauses and facts. Such orderings usually do not exist in automated theorem proving.

4.2 Learning Phase

Training data about good and bad decisions are produced from successful proof searches. These are obtained by choosing theorems which SETHEO can prove without heuristics. Reasonable bounds are selected (a combination of SETHEO's standard bounds: depth and inferences), so that the proofs which are discovered do not become too big, compared to the shortest possible proof. The search tree defined by these bounds is completely explored. For an example, see Figure 2. The nodes of the tree represent proof attempts and proofs. Each branch emerging from a node represents an applicable inference step. The training data produced during the search consists of pairs of feature-vectors and desired ratings. As these ratings are probabilities (see last section), the desired value is 1 for positive and 0 for negative training data. Machine learning techniques (various neural network paradigms such as backpropagation, delta-bar-delta, learning vector quantization and self-organizing nets, and a Bayes classifier) are used to provide a generalized mapping from feature-vectors to ratings.

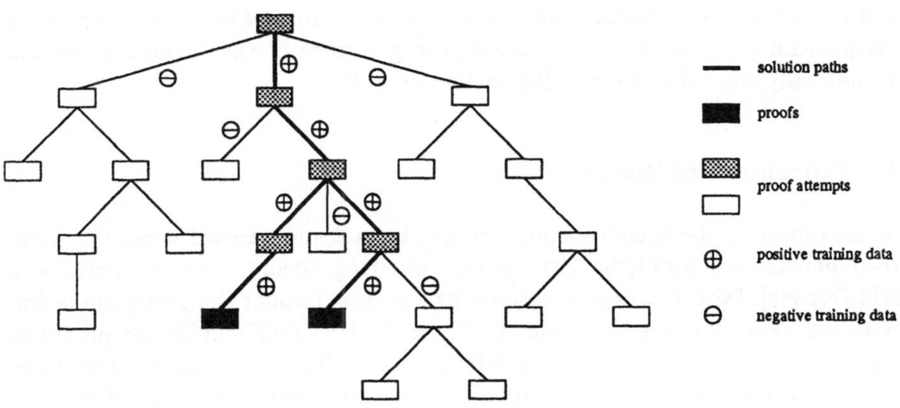

Fig. 2. Search tree and training data.

4.3 Application Phase

We now describe how the search for proofs of new theorems is guided using heuristic evaluation functions. The first idea is to order all applicable inference steps at a decision point according to their rating, so that the step with the highest rating is tried first. Assuming perfect ratings this would already be a sufficient strategy. But our evaluation functions are of a heuristic nature, giving estimations only. Even good heuristics working well on most decision points are not likely to work well on all. Consider the case that an inference step which does not lead to a proof mistakenly gets a high rating. Before applying other inference steps at the current decision point (which may have nearly equally good ratings), the whole part of the search tree lying below that step has to be explored, no matter how bad ratings may become. As a remedy we use the ratings not only to direct the search locally at a decision point, but also to restrict the search. If an applicable inference step has a very bad rating (worse than a given bound set by the user), it will probably not lead to a proof in the current context and therefore its application is forbidden. If the search tree, restricted in this way, does not contain a proof, the bound is decreased and the search starts again (*iterative deepening search*). This search strategy can still be refined. If there are a few nodes on the solution paths, which mistakenly have a very low rating, an equally low bound must be chosen, in order to get all the solution paths explored. However, choosing a higher bound and allowing a few violations can provide a much more effective restriction of the search space.

The heuristics can be used in several ways to optimize parallel execution. Most influential regarding parallelism is the guidance of task generation. The goal here is to ensure that the parallel processing power is spent where solutions are most likely to be. A more detailed proposal for how this can be achieved is found in [Sut92]. Furthermore, since the parallel versions of the prover are based on sequential processing of proof tasks, the guidance of the sequential system automatically supports the parallel system as well.

4.4 Experimental Results

The usefulness of the learning approach has been demonstrated using two well-known benchmark problems from group and ring theory, namely wos15 and wos22 [Wos65]. Wos15 says that subgroups are closed under the group operation and wos22 says that the equation $X * Y = (-X) * (-Y)$ holds for all rings. These are problems that are quite difficult for SETHEO. Training data from 21 simpler theorems (also group and ring theory problems from [Wos65]) were collected, and a 3-layer backpropagation network was used to learn a heuristic, called *21-mixed* in the following.

Since both test problems allow proofs of depth 4, a fixed depth bound of 4 has been applied in all subsequent experiments. The left part of Table 1 shows how the search space (measured in seconds needed to explore it completely) develops for wos15, performing iterative deepening on the inference bound. The same is shown for the heuristic *21-mixed* on the right side. As one is free to change the bound for ratings as well as the number of allowed violations, there are many possibilities for performing iterative deepening with heuristics. A simple, straightforward strategy was applied here.

Figure 3 shows the times required to explore the complete search space at the first deepening level yielding solutions, and the times at which proofs were found. For each of the two problems, this is done for the nonheuristic (i.e., inference bounded) case, for the *21-mixed* heuristic, and for a heuristic which has been trained on the successful proof search for the given problem. The latter

search with inference bound		
inference bound	time[s]	result
11	3.5	failure
12	8.5	failure
13	27.1	failure
14	54.2	failure
15	146.0	failure
16	415.3	8 solutions

search with the heuristic 21-mixed			
heuristic: 21-mixed		time[s]	result
bound for ratings	number of violations		
0.6	0	1.0	failure
0.7	1	0.2	failure
0.8	2	0.05	failure
0.9	3	0.1	failure
0.5	0	23.1	failure
0.6	1	135.5	13 solutions
0.7	2	18.8	2 solutions

Table 1. Iterative deepening search with and without heuristic for wos15.

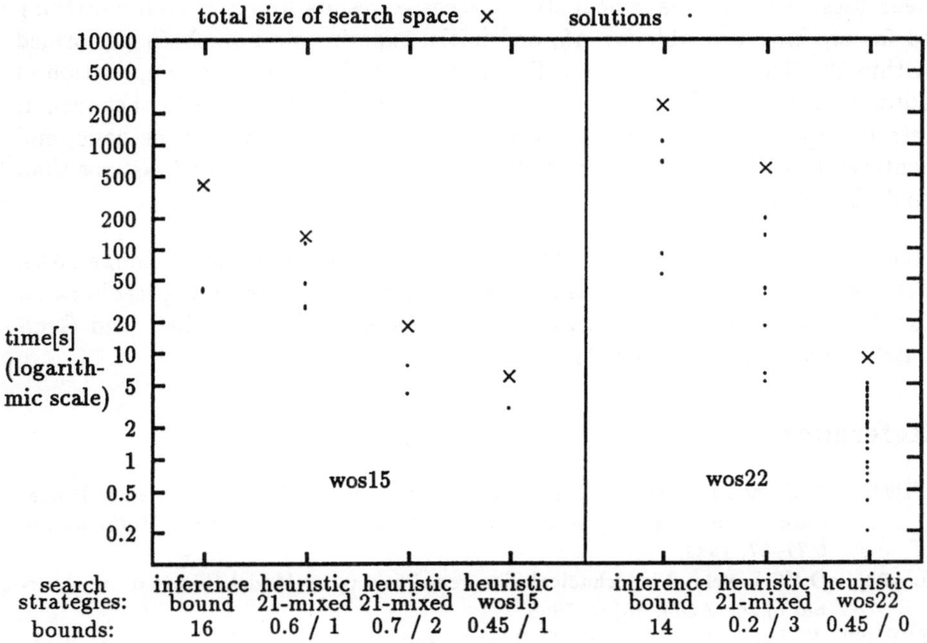

Fig. 3. Search space reductions achieved by heuristics for wos15 and wos22.

case is obviously not realistic in practice, but provides an interesting comparison. Intuitively, it shows the best expectable performance of a heuristic on a problem (based on the available feature vectors). In each column in Figure 3, the lowest dot denotes the time required to find the first proof. In practice, the proof search terminates at that point. Thus, the figure shows that using an adequate control strategy for the heuristic-based iterative deepening, the search time can be reduced by one order of magnitude. Even a less attractive set of bound values (0.6/1 for wos15) reduces the time required to find the first solution by one half, when compared to the unguided case. The figure also reveals that the solution density seems to be higher in the heuristic iterative deepening case than in the nonheuristic case. It should be noted that the runtimes given include the incurred overheads for evaluating the heuristics, and that the figure does not include the benefit achieved through heuristics with respect to the iterative deepening (this effect is shown in Table 1 for wos15).

5 Conclusion

In all participating subprojects, heuristics are crucial for the performance of the system. There already exist good experiences with hand designed heuristics in the subprojects A1, A4, B1, B2. These provide the basis for the informed selection of features for learning and will allow a comparison of automatically learned heuristics with man-made heuristics. Extensive results from automatic learning so far are only available for A5, and initial experiments have been performed within B2. The next step in the HEUROPA activity will be the application of automatic learning for the other applications. This will provide further insight into the appropriate selection of features, training data, learning methods, and control strategies, and hopefully will lead to more powerful parallel systems than could be achieved before.

Acknowledgements. Thanks to Thomas Ludwig (A1), Klaus-Jörn Lange (A4), Peter Krauss (B1) and Thomas Schnekenburger (B2) for providing feedback on the description of their applications. Also, thanks to Reinhold Letz and Geoff Sutcliffe for commenting drafts.

References

[FP83] J. Franco and M. Paul. Probabilistic Analysis of the Davis-Putnam Procedure for Solving the Satisfiability Problem. *Discrete applied Mathematics*, 5:77–87, 1983.

[Lov68] D.W. Loveland. Mechanical Theorem-Proving by Model Elimination. *Journal of the ACM*, 15(2), 1968.

[LSBB92] R. Letz, J. Schumann, S. Bayerl, and W. Bibel. SETHEO: A High-Performance Theorem Prover. *Journal of Automated Reasoning*, 8(2):183–212, 1992.

[Lud93] T. Ludwig. *Automatische Lastverwaltung für Parallelrechner*. BI-Wissenschaftsverlag, Heidelberg, September 1993.

[Mic92] Ilko Michler. Neuronale Netzwerk-Paradigmen zum Erlernen von Heuristiken. SFB-Bericht 342/22/92 A, TU München, 1992.

[Sam59] A.L. Samuel. Some Studies in Machine Learning Using the Game of Checkers. *IBM Journal*, 1(3):210–229, 1959.

[Sam67] A.L. Samuel. Some Studies in Machine Learning Using the Game of Checkers, II. *IBM Journal*, 11(6):601–617, 1967.

[SE90] C.B. Suttner and W. Ertel. Automatic Acquisition of Search Guiding Heuristics. In *Proceedings of the 10. International Conference on Automated Deduction (CADE)*, pages 470–484. Springer LNAI 449, 1990.

[SE91] C.B. Suttner and W. Ertel. Using Back-propagation for Guiding the Search of a Theorem Prover. *Int. Journal of Neural Networks Research & Applications*, 2(1):3–16, 1991.

[SMV87] E. Speckenmeyer, B. Monien, and O. Vornberger. Superlinear Speedup for Parallel Backtracking. In *Proceedings of Supercomputing 1987*, LNCS 297, pages 985–993. Springer Verlag, 1987.

[SS84] J.A. Stankovic and I.S. Sidhu. An Adaptive Bidding Algorithm For Processes, Clusters and Distributed Groups. In *Proceedings of the Fourth International Conference on Distributed Computing Systems*, pages 49–59. IEEE Computer Society Press, 1984.

[Sut92] C.B. Suttner. A Parallel Theorem Prover with Heuristic Work Distribution. In *Parallelization in Inference Systems*, pages 243–252. Springer LNCS 590, 1992.

[Tro92] M. Trost. Untersuchung von Verfahren zur dynamischen Aufgabenverteilung in verteilten Systemen. Diplomarbeit, Institut für Informatik, Technische Universität München, 1992.

[Wei91] D. Weidlich. Lernen von Heuristiken für den Theorembeweiser SETHEO mit stochastischen Methoden. Diplomarbeit, Institut für Informatik, Technische Universität München, 1991.

[Wos65] L. Wos. Unpublished Notes. Argonne National Laboratory, 1965.

UPAS — Universally Programmable Architecture and Basic Software

Thomas Ludwig

SFB342, Technische Universität München
Institut für Informatik
80290 München
E-mail: ludwig@informatik.tu-muenchen.de

Abstract. The aim of UPAS is to provide a common programming model and programming environment for the project partners within the SFB. Based on the MMK message passing library several tools have been developed to support programming parallel computers. Interactive tools for debugging, performance analysis and visualization and an automatic tool for load balancing were implemented and tested. Experiences from users revealed issues of improvement that have to be considered in future research. Additional flexibility and performance is provided by an adaptation of the programming environment to workstation nets.

1 The UPAS Environment

The major goal of the UPAS project is to simplify the usage and programming of parallel systems for widening the range of applications for these types of machines. Massively parallel systems should become as easy to use as todays conventional sequential workstations. Therefore, UPAS concentrates on designing, implementing and evaluating a programming environment for parallel computers.

Considering the phases of the software lifetime cycle several issues have to be covered. First, users would like to have a tool for the specification of parallel programs. This tool should allow to express the inherent parallelism of algorithms. Implementation of specifications should be supported by a programming model that guarantees efficient production runs of the application code as well as an abstraction of hardware specific details. Running programs must be supported by various tools, which work either interactively or automatically. Interactive tools are necessary for debugging, performance analysis and visualization. Our aim was to provide the user with interactive tools, but post-mortem analysis tools should also be available. As an automatic tool a dynamic load balancer was developed, which is able to keep the load of the parallel computer balanced in order to increase its throughput.

Design and implementation of these tools were carried out in the TOPSYS project (TOols for Parallel SYStems)[2]. The more general task of UPAS is their intensive usage and conceptual improvement. For this purpose, all TOPSYS tools were installed at the sites of the SFB project partners.

The rest of this section will give a detailed description of the tools of the programming environment. The next chapter will concentrate on the experiences made and discuss possible improvements and modifications. In the last part a short summary of current activities in the enhancement of the programming environment will be given.

1.1 The MMK Message Passing Library

The message passing library MMK (Multiprocessor Multitasking Kernel) is the basis for all application programming within the project (see [4]). Currently two different approaches exist to program parallel computers with distributed memory: Programming models are either based on parallel extensions of programming languages or based on completely new language constructs, like e.g. LISP or Concurrent PROLOG. MMK is a compromise between the two approaches but is closer to the conventional one for reasons of compatibility. The MMK programming model enriches static language extensions of conventional programming languages with more dynamic constructs and global operations on objects. The result is a transparent programming model which allows the programmer to abstract from the concrete machine architecture during program implementation. The key features and main design concepts of MMK are:

- MMK offers a multitasking process model with a global object space, meaning that programmers can define multiple parallel processes. Neither do they have to keep in mind processor numbers nor locations of processes on processor nodes.
- When using the MMK programming model, the programmer thinks about the parallel program in an object oriented style. MMK offers active objects (tasks), communication objects (mailboxes) and synchronization objects (semaphores) with an appropriate set of manipulation functions. Object management is only possible via these predefined operations.
- All objects of a parallel program based on MMK can be dynamically created and deleted. This dynamic characteristic of the MMK mainly supports the implementation of non-numerical applications based on code (task) partitioning.

When developing programs based on MMK the programmer has to divide an application into parts which can be computed concurrently. These parts form the tasks of the program. If interaction between tasks is necessary, mailboxes and semaphores must be added. As a result, we obtain an object graph describing the static structure of the application. Support for this phase by an appropriate specification tool will be discussed in a latter section.

Having finished the design of the task graph and the implementation of the task bodies the source code can be compiled. The next step is to specify a mapping of the objects of the program onto the nodes of the machine. This mapping information is written into a special file which is evaluated by the loader. Upon startup of an application only those objects will initially be available which are specified in the mapping file.

Most of the parallel applications use either data partitioning or code partitioning as a parallelization paradigm. With data partitioning each processor runs the same code but on a different subset of the data. Usually this leads to a good load balance between the nodes and is the easiest way of parallelizing an algrithm. By using the mapping file we can quickly adapt the task graphs of the application to the available number of processor nodes: task, mailbox and semaphore entries in this file are replicated so that the number of tasks equals the number of processors. Using code partitioning the application is divided into tasks being distinct from each other and each solving specialized problems. This method is mainly used with non-numerical applications being more heterogeneous in their structure. The mapping file allows to arrange the tasks on the nodes such that the efficiency is maximum. The multitasking facility on each node allows grouping tasks to minimize the load imbalance between the nodes. As a conclusion we can say that MMK is suitable for both, application programs with data and code partitioning. In addition, we can also implement any mixture of the two parallelization strategies and use the machine efficiently for a wide spectrum of parallel algorithms.

Three interactive tools were developed to support MMK programs during runtime. All tools offer access to various information and manipulation functions by specifying names of MMK objects. Thus, programmers will stay on the same level of abstraction on which they used during implementation. The next three sections will give a short overview of these tools.

1.2 The Debugging System

The debugging tool DETOP (DEbugging TOol for Parallel systems) provides a global view of the running application. All objects are addressed via their names, node numbers are not necessary. One part of its functionality is identical to every sequential debugger: The user can inspect the program state and even can modify it during runtime; he can specify breakpoints and collect interesting information in trace files. In addition, the program can be controlled with single-step functions to support easy error detection.

All functions work source code oriented, i.e. the user of the debugger manipulates the same programming constructs (variables, procedures, etc.) that he used to write his program. Moreover, machine and compiler dependend information like e.g. node number of an object or memory address of a variable are also listed.

Furthermore, DETOP provides some functionality which is necessary to handle the distribution of programming objects of an application in the parallel computer. The breakpoint function offers local and global mechanisms depending on whether the specified predicates and/or the triggered activities refer to objects on a single node or on several nodes. However, breakpoints that involve several nodes are more difficult to handle and require thorough investigation of the temporal behavior of the program. Figure 1 shows the specification of a complex breakpoint, triggered on a combination of a message exchange and the execution of a certain line of source code.

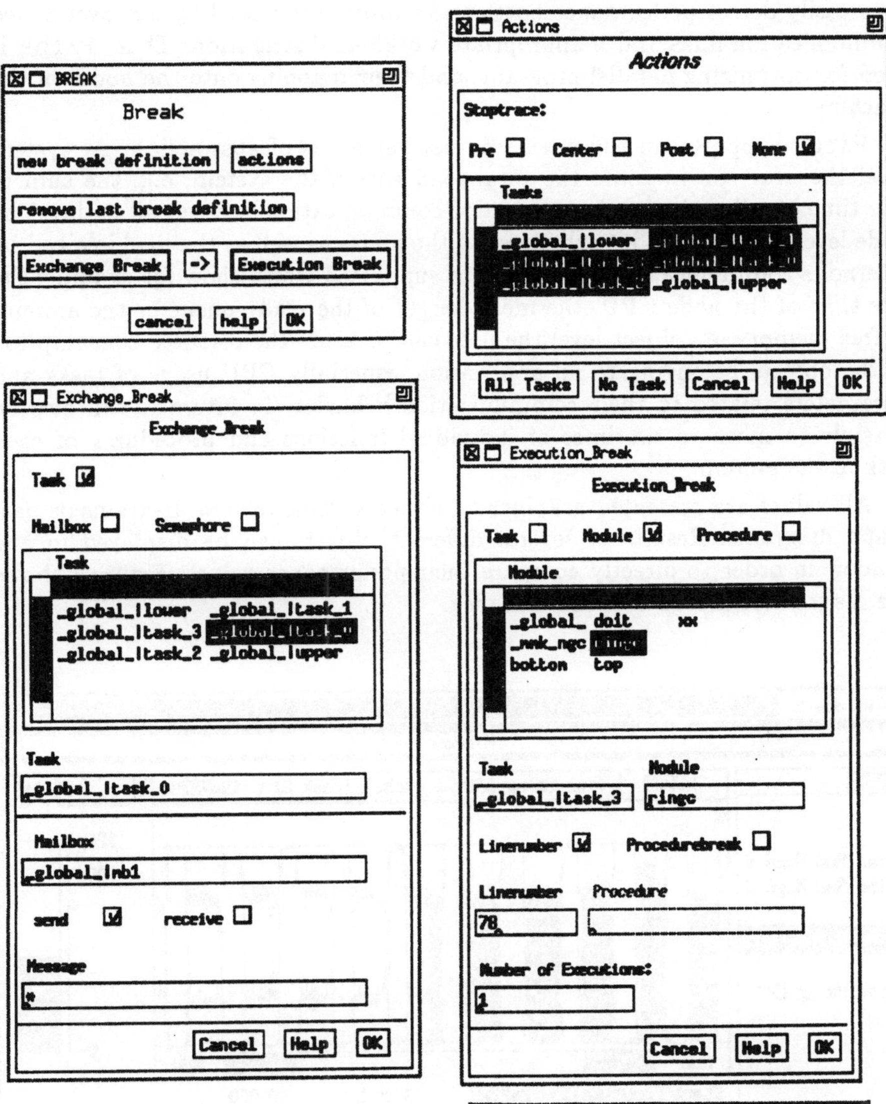

Fig. 1. Specification of a complex breakpoint

1.3 The Performance Analysis System

The performance analysis tool PATOP (Performance Analysis TOol for Parallel Systems) is an online measurement and analysis tool (see [3]). Its main purpose is to easily detect performance bottlenecks which are caused by e.g. overloaded communication links and inappropriate workload distribution. Thus, PATOP is used for optimizing parallel programs and their mapping onto the nodes of the machine.

PATOP supports measurements on several levels of abstraction. At system level the user can measure the total load within the system, e.g. the sum of idle time on all nodes or the amount of communication between all nodes. The node level gives insight into the load on the nodes as well as the load invoked by internode communication. Measures are supported which show for example the idle time of the node CPU, the mean length of the ready queue or the amount of free memory. At object level the user can measure the resource consumption of the objects belonging to an application, especially CPU usage of tasks and parameters related to their communication behavior. In future it will also be possible to measure runtimes of individual functions and procedures of each task in the system.

All values are presented graphically, either as time related diagrams or bargraph diagrams. Results of several different objects can be displayed in one window in order to directly compare their performance values. Figure 2 shows the diagram of the CPU usage of a task.

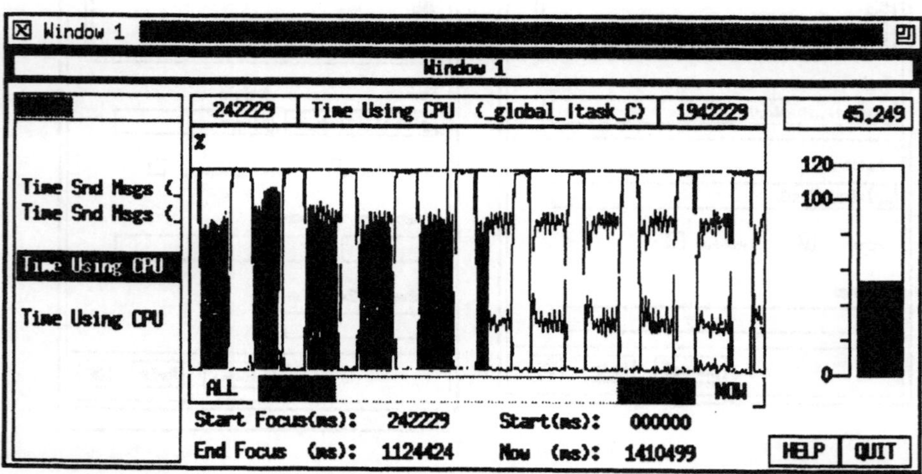

Fig. 2. CPU usage of a specified task of the program

1.4 The Visualization System

The last tool of this environment is the visualizer VISTOP (VISualization TOol for Parallel systems)[6]. It provides an animated view of the behavior of parallel programs by showing the interactions between the MMK objects. Thus, it animates only at the abstraction level ob individual objects, but further informations on their status can also be obtained. VISTOP shows a graph that represents the interrelations between all objects: e.g. waiting queues at mailboxes and semaphores are animated and the father/son relations of dynamically created objects (see for example fig. 3).

VISTOP uses online collection of appearing events but of course animates them at a reduced speed. The user can go through the events and inspect the behavior of the program while event collection is still running.

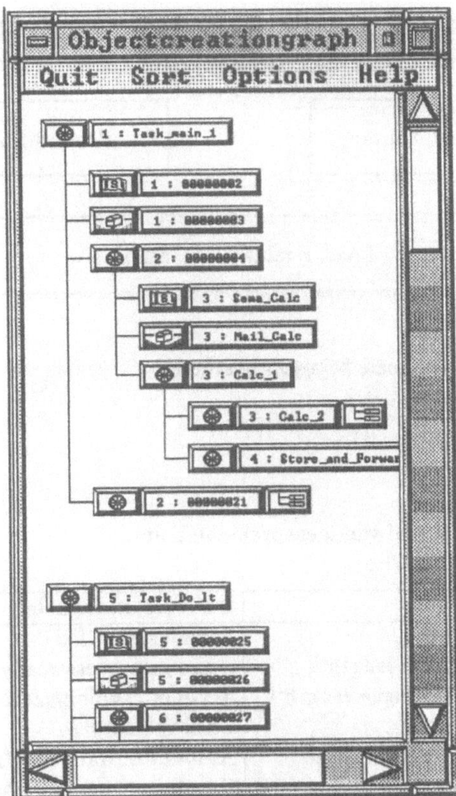

Fig. 3. Father/son relations of dynamically created objects

1.5 The Dynamic Load Balancer

In addition to these interactive tools we developed also an automatic tool which serves for load balancing on a parallel computer with distributed memory. Although load balancing schemes are well known for workstation nets this issue is completely different for our type of computer (see [7, 8]). Most of the programs running on these machines do not create new processes during runtime and there is usually no sharing of a set of nodes between multiple users. This causes load movement by process migration to be indispensable. We implemented a testbed to investigate the feasibility of migrating running processes and to find out which load parameters are significant to decide on whether to rebalance the system or not. The testbed also allows to investigate other important aspects of load management schemes.

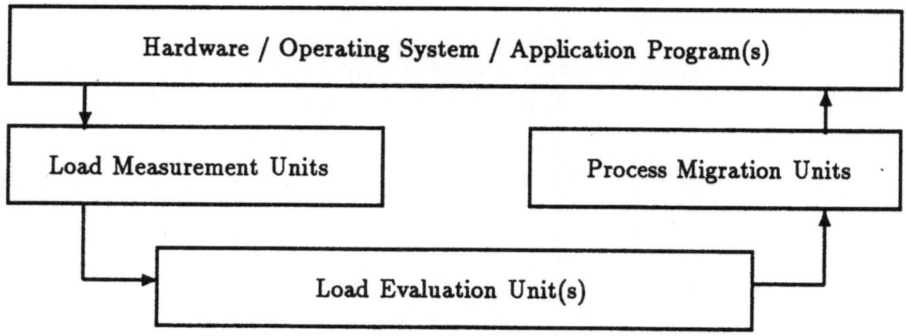

Fig. 4. Control loop of the load balancer testbed

Table 1. Load parameters of the measurement unit

Node measures	**Process measures**
Processor idle time	Time using CPU
Process ready queue length	Time in process ready queue
Sending/receiving queue length	Time in sending/receiving queue
Free memory	Used memory
Amount of data sent/received	Amount of data sent/received
Number of messages sent/received	Number of messages sent/received
	Number of page faults

The load management system follows the principle of a control loop (see fig. 4). The system to be controlled is a multiprocessor system with distributed memory together with its operating system and one or more running application programs of the user. A measurement component examines the current state of the system by monitoring the load of its resources (processor, communication network, memory). A detailed list of available measures is given in table 1. These values are compared by an evaluation component which has to determine whether process migration is necessary. If so, it sends a command to the migration component to start load movement.

The influence of load measures on the migration decisions is of crucial importance for the efficiency of load management. In a description file we can specify parameters that will be considered by the load evaluation component as well as their relative weighting and the way of combining them into single load values. This allows a rapid comparison of different types of heuristics for load evaluation.

In a first experimentation phase we studied programs with different types of behavior. For about 2.500 program runs with various configurations of the load balancer system we evaluated completion times of the programs and the number of process migrations (see [9, 10]). As a conclusion of the results we can say that the load balancer worked efficiently for all test programs. As load heuristics the simple measure 'idle time' yields good results, especially in reducing the number of activated process migrations. However, some program types require more sophisticated load heuristics like e.g. a combination of idle time and mean ready queue length.

2 Experiences with UPAS

The programming model MMK was implemented for the Intel parallel computers iPSC/2 and iPSC/860, both forming the basic computing resources for the research of the SFB. All interactive tools are running on SUN workstations which serve as development machines for parallel programs. The graphical user interface of these tools is based on XWindows and can therefore be used from other remote workstations via local network facilities. All interactive tools have been installed at the users' sites to efficiently support their implementation development. However, there are only two parallel computers for all project partners.

During the last years, the programming environment has been used in several projects of the SFB. Applications of various types have been implemented and tested, e.g. data base systems, numerical algorithms, programming of logical problems, and VLSI design. Experiences were discussed in several meetings and a questionnaire filled in by the users gave additional insight into the programmers' needs. Some of these issues will be discussed in the next paragraphs.

First of all and most important, there is a considerable lack of support during the specification phase of parallel applications[1]. In addition to that, it is also not clear how to handle the parallelization paradigms and issues of replication and mapping. Furthermore, the problem how to describe dynamic aspects like

[1] First experiences with an interactive specification and mapping tool (SAMTOP) showed the difficulties of this topic which can only be tackled in a separate research project (see [5]).

object creation and deletion during runtime is not solved. Several projects of the SFB investigate specification methods for parallel programs, but the results can not yet be used for the design of an interactive tool.

The second problem is, that the tool environment does not support sophisticated trace functions, especially it does not produce meaningful traces in a standardized format. Two important issues are closely related to the availability of traces. First, traces would allow a careful quantitative analysis of programs' performance. PATOP currently offers a mixture of qualitative and quantitative measurements but no data is stored for later analysis. Traces would provide means to work up results from different points of view and to apply mathematical methods like e.g. statistical analysis. Second, with the debugger it may be difficult and sometimes even impossible to exactly reproduce the execution of a program run. However, this is necessary for detecting errors that occur only in particular situations. With the help of traces we could integrate a mechanism for instant replay of parallel programs. The user could rerun the program up to the position where the error is likely to occur.

All tools are working on that level of abstraction which programmers use for application implementation. As already mentioned this implies access to the program via object and variable names instead of their corresponding memory addresses. However, most users take the MMK objects as a a basis for compound objects with new functions and data structures. For example for database systems the concept of transactions becomes important and for numerical applications data structures like layered grids are essential. As this introduces an even higher level of abstraction users want the tools to express program activity in terms of these compound objects. This is not possible with the current version of the tool environment. Furthermore, restructuring the tool functionality together with the graphical interface is not sensible. Instead, it is not too difficult to develop new tools as they can be based on the command/trace-interface of the tool environment (see for example [1]). This interface provides access to all functions of the monitoring system and transfers results back to the tools. In most cases it will be possible to compose new tool functionalities by using the already available set of primitive functions of the monitoring system[2].

In addition to the discussed topics the questionnaire uncovered several other problems referring to the implementation of the tool environment. First of all, speed is a main concern. Insufficient speed of the graphical interface strongly reduces the acceptance of the tools. As a consequence, users prefer simple UNIX tools to the TOPSYS environment. This problem has been almost eliminated with several improvements, especially in the communication layer between tools and the parallel computer. As all tools offer a mostly menu-driven graphical interface users sometimes complain about the depth of the menu system. They would prefer more complex windows to walking through several hierarchies to reach a particular function. For some functions this has already been improved in the new release of the tools.

[2] This method was also chosen for the implementation of the current tool environment.

3 Extension of the Programming Environment

A major problem is the access to the parallel computer. All tools are interactive tools which means that program development permanently requires a subset of the processor nodes. This is different to the situation without any tools where the parallel computer is only occupied during runtime of the program. Thus, the improvement of the programming environment decreased the availability of the parallel system. As a solution to this problem we decided to use the computing power of workstations for program development. First step for achieving this goal was an adaptation of the MMK programming model to coupled SUN workstations. This special programming library, called MMK/X, allows the user to run MMK programs without change of source code on both, a parallel computer and a workstation net (see [11]).

Although both machine architectures are similar from the programmers' point of view, we introduced a new concept with MMK/X to make it even more convenient to use. This concept is called 'virtual node' and is an abstraction of the real node of a parallel computer. In more detail a virtual node manages all objects that have been mapped onto a (real) node number. For the workstation net virtual nodes are the atomic units of distribution (see fig. 5 for an example). Therefore, it is possible to map all virtual nodes onto a single workstation and not to occupy computing power of other sites. For production runs of the code one can either use a set of workstations or a parallel computer. However, for communication intensive programs it is more reasonable to use the parallel computer due to its low message latency time.

To provide full compatibility with the programming environment available for the parallel computer also the tools were adapted to the workstation net. However, performance evaluation with PATOP is of no use as the speed of computation strongly depends on activities of other users logged in on the used workstations. Thus, the workstation net environment will mainly be used for developing and testing parallel applications and for production runs during night hours, where the net can be almost exlusively used by a single user.

4 Future Work

In the future we will concentrate on programming environments for parallel computers as well as for workstation nets. For parallel computers we are especially improving the performance of the analysis tool. Furthermore, we will adapt this tool to other machines with even different architectural characteristics.

The programming environment for workstation nets will be enhanced by a distributed file sysem to improve the efficiency of program I/O. In addition to that, we will also provide other programming models, as for example the Intel Paragon OSF/1 programming model, which is almost identical to that of the iPSC systems.

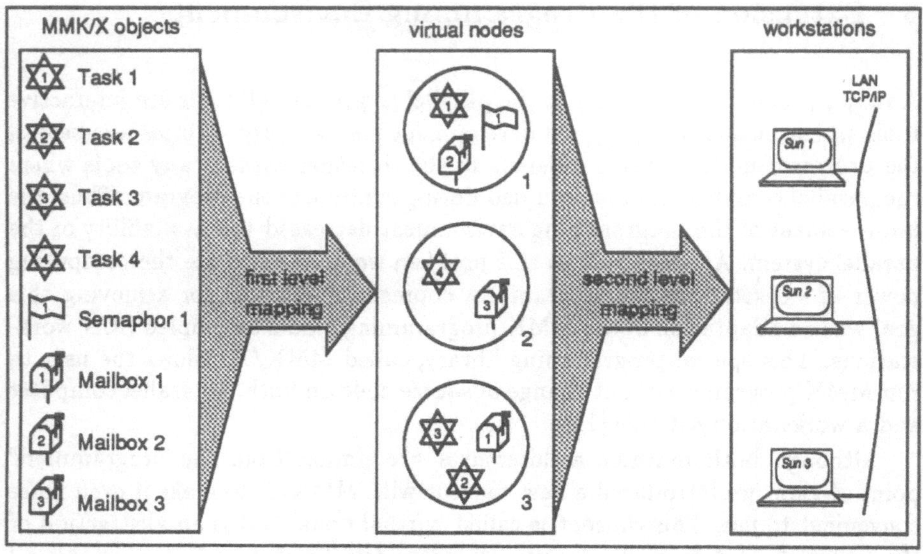

Fig. 5. Mapping of MMK objects onto workstation nets

References

1. Werner Anderschitz. Erweiterung des Concurrency View des VISTOP um dynamisch erzeugte Objekte. Master's thesis, Technische Universität, München, May 1993.
2. T. Bemmerl. The TOPSYS architecture. In H. Burkhart, editor, *Proceedings of the CONPAR 90 - VAPP IV Joint International Conference on Vector and Parallel Processing, Zurich, Switzerland*, pages 732–743, Berlin, 1990. Lecture Notes in Computer Science, Vol. 457, Springer.
3. T. Bemmerl, O. Hansen, and T. Ludwig. PATOP for performance tuning of parallel programs. In H. Burkhart, editor, *Proceedings of the CONPAR 90 - VAPP IV Joint International Conference on Vector and Parallel Processing, Zurich, Switzerland*, pages 840–851, Berlin, 1990. Lecture Notes in Computer Science, Vol. 457, Springer.
4. T. Bemmerl and T. Ludwig. MMK — A distributed operating system kernel with integrated dynamic loadbalancing. In H. Burkhart, editor, *Proceedings of the CONPAR 90 - VAPP IV Joint International Conference on Vector and Parallel Processing, Zurich, Switzerland*, pages 744–755, Berlin, 1990. Lecture Notes in Computer Science, Vol. 457, Springer.
5. T. Bemmerl, T. Ludwig, and B. Ries. A design and specification environment for distributed memory multiprocessors. In N.N. Mirenkov, editor, *Proceedings of the International Conference Parallel Computing Technologies, PaCT-91, Novosibirsk, USSR*, pages 280–291, Singapore, September 1991. World Science.
6. Thomas Bemmerl and Peter Braun. Visualization of message passing parallel programs. In L. Bougé, M.Cosnard, Y. Robert, and D. Trystram, editors, *Parallel*

Processing: CONPAR 92 - VAPP V, pages 79 – 90, Lyon, France, September 1992. Springer-Verlag.

7. T.L. Casavant and J.G. Kuhl. A taxonomy of scheduling in general-purpose distributed computing systems. *IEEE Transactions on Software Engineering*, SE-14(2):141–154, February 1988.
8. A. Goscinski. *Distributed Operating Systems — The Logical Design*. Addison-Wesley, Sydney, 1991.
9. T. Ludwig. Load balancing on the Intel hypercube. In *Proceedings of the Intel 1992 Annual Users' Conference, Dallas, Texas, USA*, pages 199–203, Beaverton, USA, October 1992. Intel Supercomputer Systems Division.
10. T. Ludwig. *Automatische Lastverwaltung für Parallelrechner*. BI–Wissenschaftsverlag, to appear 1993.
11. Georg Stellner. MMK/X — Using a network of workstations as a supercomputer. In *Proceedings of the Euro-ARCH'93, Munich*, 1993.

Proceedings CONPAR 92 [illegible], pages [illegible]–[illegible], Lyon, France, September 1992. Springer-Verlag.

7. T. L. Casavant and J. G. Kuhl. A taxonomy of scheduling in general-purpose distributed computing systems. *IEEE Transactions on Software Engineering*, SE-14(2):141–154, February 1988.

8. A. Goscinski. *Distributed Operating Systems — The Logical Design*. Addison-Wesley, Sydney, 1991.

9. T. Ludwig. Load balancing [illegible] approaches. In *Proceedings of the Intel 1992 Supercomputer Users' Group*, Dallas, Texas, USA, pages [illegible]–203, Beaverton, USA, October 1992. Intel Supercomputer Systems Division.

10. T. Ludwig. *Automatische Lastverwaltung für Parallelrechner*. BI-Wissenschaftsverlag, Mannheim, 1993.

11. Georg Stellner, [illegible] Using [illegible] workstations as a supercomputer. In *Proceedings of the* [illegible], 1993.

Springer-Verlag und Umwelt

Als internationaler wissenschaftlicher Verlag sind wir uns unserer besonderen Verpflichtung der Umwelt gegenüber bewußt und beziehen umweltorientierte Grundsätze in Unternehmensentscheidungen mit ein.

Von unseren Geschäftspartnern (Druckereien, Papierfabriken, Verpackungsherstellern usw.) verlangen wir, daß sie sowohl beim Herstellungsprozeß selbst als auch beim Einsatz der zur Verwendung kommenden Materialien ökologische Gesichtspunkte berücksichtigen.

Das für dieses Buch verwendete Papier ist aus chlorfrei bzw. chlorarm hergestelltem Zellstoff gefertigt und im pH-Wert neutral.